# Introduction to Literature: POEMS

# Introduction to Literature

# POEMS

THIRD EDITION

Edited, with a Handbook
for the Study of Poetry, by

## LYNN ALTENBERND
UNIVERSITY OF ILLINOIS

## LESLIE L. LEWIS
LATE OF UNIVERSITY OF COLORADO

MACMILLAN PUBLISHING CO., INC.
New York

Macmillan Publishing Co., Inc.
866 Third Avenue, New York, New York 10022

Collier-Macmillan Canada, Ltd.

Library of Congress Cataloging in Publication Data

Altenbernd, Lynn, ed.
  Introduction to literature: poems.

1. English poetry.  2. American poetry.  I. Lewis,
Leslie Lisle, (date)    joint ed.  II. Title.
PR1175.A653  1975      821'.008        74–14506
ISBN 0–02–302060–1


Printing: 12345678      Year: 567890

CREDITS AND ACKNOWLEDGMENTS

Copyrighted works, listed in the order of appearance, are reprinted in the United States, its possessions and dependencies, the Philippine Republic, and Canada by permission of the following.

"I Am," "The Swallow," "Secret Love" by John Clare, from THE POEMS OF JOHN CLARE, edited by J. W. Tibble, published by J. M. Dent & Sons Ltd.

Poems 76, 108, 241, 258, 318, 328, 338, 435, 449, 465, 510, 712, 754, 861, 875, 986, 1100, 1129, 1484, 1593, 1624, and 1732 by Emily Dickinson. *Reprinted by permission of the publishers from* Thomas H. Johnson, Editor, THE POEMS OF EMILY DICKINSON. *Cambridge, Mass:* The Belknap Press of *Harvard University Press,* Copyright 1951, '55 by The President and Fellows of Harvard College.

"Heaven-Haven," "The Habit of Perfection," "God's Grandeur," "The Starlight Night," "Spring," "The Windhover," "Pied Beauty," "Hurrahing in Harvest," "The Caged Skylark," "Binsey Poplars," "The Candle In-

doors," "Felix Randal," "Spring and Fall," "The Leaden Echo and the Golden Echo," "(Carrion Comfort)," "I Wake and Feel the Fell of Dark," "Thou Art Indeed Just, Lord," by Gerard Manley Hopkins. From Gerard Manley Hopkins, POEMS OF GERARD MANLEY HOPKINS, copyright 1931 by Oxford University Press (London), publisher.

"Neutral Tones," "Drummer Hodge," "The Darkling Thrush," "The Man He Killed," "The Woman in the Rye," "Shut Out That Moon," "The Year's Awakening," "The Convergence of the Twain," "I Found Her Out There," "Ah, Are You Digging on My Grave?" "Channel Firing," "In Time of the 'Breaking of Nations,'" "Near Lanivet, 1872," "During Wind and Rain," "Snow in the Suburbs," by Thomas Hardy. Reprinted with permission of Macmillan Publishing Co., Inc., from COLLECTED POEMS by Thomas Hardy. Copyright 1925 by Macmillan Publishing Co., Inc.

Reprinted from COLLECTED POEMS by Thomas Hardy, by permission of The Trustees

# Preface

Each revision of *Introduction to Literature: Poems* faces a narrower scope for improvement than its predecessor. Some new works emerge between editions, but the process of reselecting from seven hundred years' poetry verges on a game of substitution for substitution's sake, unless the limitations of the anthology itself are redefined. We have revised those limitations for this third edition and present a more inclusive anthology in which the goal is no longer a sufficient but a generous representation.

Few selections have been dropped, whereas a good many have been added in the third edition. The new material includes additional selections by authors represented in the earlier editions, work by older authors not previously represented, and a wide sampling of the variety of new writing that has come into prominence during the past few years. Once again, we have tried in making selections to reconcile several needs that are not always harmonious. We have included a number of works that we know will provide excellent bases for discussion, but since teachers, students, and the goals of courses are so various, we have taken a broad view of what selections will be useful in the classroom. This broad view also serves our desire to represent a very wide range of themes, types, modes, and strategies.

The handbook has been revised in the interest of greater clarity and better example; its basic plan has not been changed. As in earlier editions, it sets forth its principles briefly, without elaboration, and with modest illustration. The editors have concentrated on preliminary and elementary suggestions for reading poetry. The aim of the handbook is what we suppose to be the aim of introductory poetry courses: to get things started, to encourage and enable the reader to go ahead on his own in increasingly sophisticated and enjoyable reading of poetry throughout his lifetime.

Of the many persons who gave invaluable advice and help during the preparation of this book, the following must be given my special thanks: Professor Charles L. Andersen, University of Maine; Professor Peter S. Bracher, Wright State University; Professor Arthur C. Buck, West Virginia University; Professor Donald Crawford, Hofstra University; Professor Oliver Evans, California State University, Northridge; Professor Lorna Farrington, University of Pittsburgh; Professor Joseph Langland, University of Massachusetts; Professor Davena M. Kellner, Harcum Junior College; Professor Edward Krickel, Editor, *The Georgia Review*; Professor Joseph Kruppa, The University of Texas; Captain John K. Lyons, United States Military Academy; Professor Lawrence Markert, University of Baltimore; Professor Margot Moran, State College of Massachusetts at Westfield; Professor William C. Pratt, Miami University; Professor Richard Vietti, Merritt College; and Professor Bernice O. Zelditch, Foothill College. Their numerous suggestions for improving the original design have been incorporated to the best of my ability, and any remaining faults must be laid solely to my account. A final word of gratitude is due Mr. D. Anthony English of Macmillan. He has been an unfailing source of encouragement and good counsel.

L. A.

**XV**

# Contents

## THE EIGHTEENTH CENTURY

## THE ROMANTIC PERIOD

## THE VICTORIAN AGE

# Introduction

We include in *Poems* both acknowledged masterpieces and less celebrated works of special merit or usefulness for teaching. The arrangement of poems is chronological within a poet's work, and the poets are arranged by date of birth. Thus the student may view the poem in its historical setting when a sense of its intellectual milieu contributes—as it usually does—to its thorough explication. Yet the teacher may also group poems to suit the requirements of his own course organization.

Because we intend this book primarily for introductory courses, we have at times modernized spelling, capitalization, and punctuation to eliminate irrelevant difficulties. In no case have we made changes that would affect the sound values or substance of the poems. Hence, Middle English and dialect poems have not been normalized, and the texts of such poets as Spenser and Emily Dickinson, whose archaisms and eccentricities are personal rather than the accident of the period, have not been edited.

The annotations of the poems are designed to reduce unproductive drudgery without doing the student's thinking for him. We have therefore glossed words which cannot reasonably be expected to form part of an educated adult's active vocabulary, or which the student could not gloss without extended research even if he recognized the need. We have sometimes supplied information necessary to an interpretation, but we have refrained from suggesting or insisting upon particular readings. In addition, we have restricted the annotations of Biblical, mythological, and historical references to the portions of the events cited that are relevant to the poem.

Our concern throughout has been to assist the teacher in his fundamental task of helping the student to understand and enjoy poetry.

L.A.

# Introduction to Literature: POEMS

# A Handbook
# for the Study
# of Poetry

# I. The Nature of Poetry

Poetry probably appeared earlier in human history than any other literary form; indeed, pure lyric outbursts to express joy, fear, outrage, or contentment may have preceded utilitarian communication. Thus the tradition runs without a break from the earliest cultures we know anything about to this present moment, and though our age may be, as we often hear, prosaic or scientific or material, it is also one of the great eras of poetic creation. One source of poetry's durability is its power to adapt to changing circumstances. Homer sang of the wonders Ulysses found on his long homeward voyage; the poets of the Renaissance celebrated the discovery of the New World; today's poets ponder the meaning of humankind's adventures in space. But poetry is not a news medium; its enduring concern is with the human condition—with adventures in inner space. Hence, whatever new subjects it assimilates or whatever novelties of form it takes on, poetry is unchanged in its essential nature. It not only records and comments on events, but also helps to define our responses to them, for although poetry is thoroughly capable of telling stories or dramatizing ideas, it is especially valuable in expressing emotion. Whatever its diversity, we may still define poetry as *imaginative discourse that gives powerful expression to experience, ideas, and emotion in heightened, patterned language.*

Poetry communicates in many ways at once. The several means of communication interact with each other to produce a net effect that is greater than the impact of the several components taken separately. Hence the poem must be experienced as a whole; it is not merely a theme carted along in a vehicle, but an inseparable fusion—a complete flowing together—of theme and form. Consider this brief poem by Robert Browning:

### Meeting at Night

The grey sea and the long black land;
And the yellow half-moon large and low;
And the startled little waves that leap
In fiery ringlets from their sleep,
As I gain the cove with pushing prow,
And quench its speed i' the slushy sand.

Then a mile of warm sea-scented beach;
Three fields to cross till a farm appears;
A tap at the pane, the quick sharp scratch
And blue spurt of a lighted match,
And a voice less loud, through its joys and fears,
Than the two hearts beating each to each!

10

The narrative content of this poem is slim indeed. The slender story is implied rather than stated, for the poet has used no complete sentence in either stanza. In addition, to say only that the poem embodies the emotions of a lover hastening to a nighttime tryst is to drain it of all the vividly realized experience that can be conveyed only by the whole poem. The images of the opening lines are rather general in order to suggest that only the vague outlines of sea and land are visible in the darkness. The colors are similarly muted. Indeed, because the scene does not provide precise and brilliant visual images, the poet appeals to the several other senses that become more alert when eyesight does not serve. The sixth line with its sequence of *s* sounds (including the variants *ch* and *sh*) suggests the hushed noise of the boat nosing into the beach. In the seventh line the glow of the heat remaining in the sand and the smell of the seashore appeal to other senses. In the ninth line the series of short, rapid syllables in "A tap at the pane" and the slower, longer, accented syllables of "the quick sharp scratch" aptly imitate the sounds named in the phrases. The tenth line contains one final vivid but brief visual image. The effect of the images is to make the reader live through the experience rather than merely hear about it.

Browning has also deftly manipulated rhythms and combined them with the sounds of the words to suggest the tempo of the action and emotional quickening or relaxation. The basic meter is iambic tetrameter; that is, the normal line would have eight syllables alternately unaccented and accented. Few of the lines are perfectly regular and several kinds of variation occur. The normal line is smooth, easy, and moderately slow in movement, but the conversion of one or more normally unaccented syllables to accents slows the pace. Thus in the first line "grey," "sea," "long," "black," and "land" are all accented; the line is slowed down and lengthened so that it suggests prolonged gliding over a calm sea. The second line is regular except for the addition of an unaccented syllable at the beginning; its movement is similarly moderate. The effect of the rhythm is strengthened by the frequent occurrence of *l* sounds which are prolonged in reading. In the third line the *l*'s alternate with *t*'s to produce the choppy effect of wavelets near the shore. In the last two lines the movement is quickened by the addition of unaccented syllables, which, though they add to the total of syllables in the line, must be pronounced rapidly and hence hasten the movement. Thus "And a," "through its," and "Than the" all speed up the lines to suggest quickening of the pulse at the moment of encounter. In the last line "two," "hearts," and "beat-" are all accented (although "hearts" has a light accent) to slow down the pace and prepare for reassurance and repose as the poem concludes on two regular iambic measures like heartbeats.

An additional kind of language patterning appears in the rhyming of the stanzas. In each set of six lines, the first and last, the second and the second last, and the middle two rhyme with each other. The fulfillment of the pattern is delayed and indeed the rhyme scheme is so unobtrusive that it is likely to escape notice. But it does bind the lines of each stanza together and provide an aesthetic satisfaction in the filling out of a regular arrangement.

This prose commentary, already much longer than the poem itself, is certainly no fair substitute for it. Our analysis is far from exhaustive, and it arbitrarily separates elements that in the poem work together to produce the total effect. "Meeting at Night" also illustrates several qualities distinctive to poetry.

Poetry differs from some kinds of prose in usually being more *concrete* and *specific*. That is, it communicates experiences, emotions, attitudes, and ideas by dealing with a particular situation that gives body to abstractions without stating them. Poets do sometimes state the abstract principles demonstrated in their work, but we usually conclude that abstract statement fails when it is not thoroughly incorporated in concrete and specific *dramatic symbols*. Like other literature, poetry uses a *dramatic method* in the sense that it acts out whatever ideas it conveys.

Poetry often uses an imagined *dramatic situation* which can be defined by the answers to some or all of these questions: Who is speaking? To whom? Under what circumstances? What is the speaker's attitude toward the subject of his discourse? Toward his audience? Sometimes quotation marks indicate that the poem consists of the words of a fictional speaker, but their absence does not mean that the poet has not imagined a character who speaks the lines.

Poetry sometimes includes an element of *narrative;* this story, overt or implied, may be the matter of chief interest in the poem, or it may be the means of conveying emotions or attitudes. Narrative occupies much of the space in "Meeting at Night," but it is clearly a vehicle for dramatizing the emotions aroused by the experience as it is recalled in the lover's revery. Poetry is effective in the domain of narrative or ideas, but its special province is emotion.

## II. The Language of Poetry

The choice of words in a poem is called its *diction.* Because poetry is compressed and intense, and because it communicates in many ways at once, each word bears a heavier load of meaning and implication in a poem than it would in even the most carefully written prose. The poet chooses his words with utmost care, and the reader must therefore be alert to the precise sense appropriate to the context. This is not to say that there is a special vocabulary appropriate only to poetry; indeed, the vocabulary of poetry is identical with that of other kinds of writing. The poet uses the words most appropriate to his purpose in a given line. Since the whole range of human activities, ideas, and emotions is within the province of poetry, the entire vocabulary of the language may be sifted for the right words.

### A. DICTION: DENOTATION AND CONNOTATION

Two aspects of a word may usefully be distinguished: *denotation* and *connotation.*

We must be sure, of course, that we understand the sense of each word as it is used in the poem. These lines from "The Starlight Night" by Gerard Manley Hopkins include a number of words that you may not recognize:

> Look at the stars! look, look up at the skies!
> O look at all the fire-folk sitting in the air!
> The bright boroughs, the circle-citadels there!
> Down in dim woods the diamond delves! the elves'-eyes!
> The grey lawns cold where gold, where quickgold lies!
> Wind-beat whitebeam! airy abeles set on a flare!
> Flake-doves sent floating forth at a farmyard scare!—

A first reading of the lines shows that they all contain exclamations over bright and shining objects in a night scene. This context suggests that "fire-folk" refers to the stars, picturing them as people shining in the sky. Then "bright boroughs" and "circle-citadels" would be other characterizations of the stars, presumably in clusters so that they look like gleaming cities and fortresses. So far we have got along without the dictionary, matching Hopkins's ingenuity with our own by figuring out the meanings from their context. We might do the same with the noun "delves," remembering that the verb "to delve" is an old synonym for "to dig." But all the other exclamations are about objects rather than actions, and a quick trip to the dictionary shows that "delve" as a noun means a pit or cave or mine. Hence in the woods something glistens in reflected starlight like diamond mines or like elves' eyes. The dictionary won't help with "quickgold" any more than it would have with "fire-folk," but we should recognize a resemblance to "quicksilver"; Hopkins has imagined a pool of light shining like liquid gold. "Whitebeam" doesn't appear in my desk dictionary, but the unabridged dictionary tells us that it is a small tree with white hairs on the underside of the leaves. The abridged dictionary does show "abele" to be a synonym for white poplar, another tree with white undersides on its leaves. The trees are "wind-beat" and "airy" so that their leaves, turned up by the wind, gleam in the starlight. "Flake-doves" is apparently another coinage comparing white pigeons to snowflakes. By a combination of alertness and patience, then, we have been able to discover that almost all the nouns in the passage contribute to the poem's celebration of starry brightness. This passage was chosen because it provides a number of examples in a few lines; rarely will so many challenges occur in so small a space.

In these instances we have been concerned with the *denotation* of a word—with what it names, describes, or narrates in a neutral, rather than evaluative manner. Similarly we must respond to the emotional associations or the implications of a word. The second line of Edwin Arlington Robinson's "Credo" contains an unexpected word:

> I cannot find my way: there is no star
> In all the *shrouded* heavens anywhere; . . .

The sound values of the line would be nearly the same if the poet had written "clouded," and the statement would be literally accurate. "Shrouded" means wrapped in a shroud, a burial garment. Thus the denotation of the word figuratively pictures the skies as a once living entity that is now dead. But "shrouded" also carries with it associations of death, corpses, mourning, and muteness; it imparts an uneasy sense of horror and loathing. This accumulation of emotional associations that a word has gathered through its history or acquires in a given setting is called its *connotation*. Connotation supplements denotation by indicating attitudes and values, by fleshing out the bare bones of meaning with flavor or wit. Consider the differences of connotation in these pairs of words which are essentially synonymous in denotation: house–home; dog–cur; girl–wench; face–visage; report–rumor; damage–mischief; conciliate–appease; mundane–worldly; enmity–hostility; pride–vanity; tremble–shudder; adventurous–daring; disciple–henchman. In each instance some shift in denotation is involved, but the difference in connotation is much more striking. Usually the poet communicates through widely shared connotations, but sometimes he uses limited or even personal connotations that may be discovered by a study of his times, his life, or his other works. The reader, too, may bring personal connotations to the reading of a poem, as some people have leaned to love snakes and loathe puppies, but these idiosyncratic responses will almost certainly obscure the poem's meaning and tone.

Denotations and connotations may change over the years, to that we usually benefit from knowing the date of the poem. In "To the Memory of . . . Shakespeare," Ben Jonson wrote, about 1623,

> . . . I confess thy writings to be such
> As neither man nor Muse can praise too much.
> 'Tis true, and all men's *suffrage*. . . .

Here "suffrage" appears in a sense not listed in current dictionaries, but the *Oxford English Dictionary* shows, among a number of possibilities, the meaning of *consensus, general opinion*—a definition that makes sense in this context. Literature tends to give connotations wide currency and hence to fix them; nevertheless shifting connotations may also puzzle us. In his ode "To Autumn," Keats refers approvingly to the cells of a honeycomb as "clammy." In current usage this word, especially in the pat phrase, "cold and clammy," suggests something damp, chilly, and repulsive. The dictionary defines the term as "soft, moist, and sticky," so that the denotation of the word is perfectly appropriate in "To Autumn" if we disregard the popular connotations it has acquired.

## B. SENTENCE PATTERNS

Poetry is usually written in normal English sentences—though not always, as the two sentence fragments of "Meeting at Night" show—so that there is no difficulty in understanding the *plain sense* of the lines. Occasionally, though, the compression characteristic of poetry makes a sentence obscure. In such instances we must be guided by the poet's punctuation and our own knowledge of grammar and sentence structure. Three kinds of difficulty occur with some frequency: suspension, inversion, and ellipsis.

Sometimes sentences in poems—or in prose, for that matter—are rather long because many dependent elements intervene between subject and verb or verb and complement:

> Old Eben Flood, climbing alone one night
> Over the hill between the town below
> And the foresaken upland hermitage
> That held as much as he should ever know
> On earth again of home, paused warily.

Even when the suspension is longer and more complicated than this one, a simple device will help: leave out the modifiers to discover the subject-verb skeleton of the sentence: Flood . . . paused. In some instances many dependent elements precede the subject-verb connection and require us to thread our way through a long passage, as in Keats's "When I Have Fears That I May Cease to Be":

> When I have fears that I may cease to be
> Before my pen has gleaned my teeming brain,
> Before high-piléd books, in charactery,
> Hold like rich garners the full-ripened grain;
> When I behold, upon the night's starred face,
> Huge cloudy symbols of a high romance,
> And think that I may never live to trace
> Their shadows, with the magic hand of chance;
> And when I feel, fair creature of an hour,
> That I shall never look upon thee more,                                          *10*
> Never have relish in the faery power
> Of unreflecting love;—then on the shore
> Of the wide world I stand alone, and think
> Till love and fame to nothingness do sink.

Here the structure of the Shakespearean sonnet helps; each of the quatrains is a "when" clause concluded by a semicolon. (Actually the third quatrain is short by half a line.) A dash followed by "then" introduces the main clause as a summary. Thus the sentence, though long and suspended, becomes clear when we recognize how it builds to a climax: "When . . .; when . . .; and when . . .;—then . . . I stand alone, and think. . . ."

A remarkable example of sentence control is Frost's "The Silken Tent," in which the basic parts of the single sentence that composes the sonnet are in the first line: "She is . . . a silken tent." So ingeniously is this metaphor developed that one reads through the following thirteen lines of dependent elements without hesitation, but perhaps also without noticing that the construction of the poem is much like that of the tent thrust heavenward by its central pole and bound lightly to earth. Thus the structure of the sonnet becomes a metaphor for the nature of literature as it mediates between the abstract universal and the concrete specific, as well as for the condition of humanity, existing by virtue of the tension between heavenward aspiration and earthward necessity.

*Inversion,* the arrangement of sentence elements out of their customary order, is much commoner in poetry than in prose; it is one source of the heightened formality, the rhetorical quality, of some verse. While English is a word-order language in the sense that the meaning of the sentence depends to some degree on the arrangement of its parts, word order is not rigidly fixed and can be altered to shift emphasis or to change the level of formality. Clearly "Peter hit Emil" is quite different from "Emil hit Peter," and the order of subject and object cannot be reversed without changing the meaning of the sentence. "After dark he went down town" differs little from "He went down town after dark," but "After dark down town went he" sounds a little odd. Its denotation is still the same as that of the two earlier versions; what has happened is a shift in tone: the sentence now seems rather formal or oratorical, and probably a bit old-fashioned as well. The usual sentence order is subject-verb-complement, with modifiers placed as close as possible to the element modified. Contemplate the difference between a normal-order revision of the first line of Frost's "Stopping by Woods on a Snowy Evening" and the line as Frost actually published it: "I think I know whose woods these are"; Frost wrote, "Whose woods these are I think I know."

*Ellipsis* is the omission of words necessary to complete the grammatical construction, but not essential to clarity. Sometimes the poet records the ellipsis characteristic of casual speech, as Eliot does in the opening lines of "Journey of the Magi":

> "A cold coming we had of it,
> Just the worst time of the year
> For a journey, and such a long journey:
> The ways deep and the weather sharp,
> The very dead of winter."

In other situations ellipsis produces swiftness of expression or strong emphasis by avoiding wordy, though customary, locutions. In "American Letter: For Gerald Murphy" MacLeish writes

> America is alone: many together,
> Many of one mouth, of one breath,
> Dressed as one—and none brothers among them:
> Only the taught speech and the aped tongue.

This compressed passage can be expanded to mean: "America means being isolated: many people are together there who speak the same language, breathe the same air, and dress alike, but do not share a common descent: they are united only by a language and an accent not native to them (presumably because they are immigrants), but borrowed from another country." The experienced reader probably need not spell the meaning out so explicitly. In a somewhat different kind of ellipsis, Pope uses the phrase "giddy heights." Because we know that hilltops do not suffer from dizziness but produce it in human beings, we are not confused by Pope's shorthand phrase.

## C. IMAGERY

Language has the power to create in the mind an effect very nearly the same as that created by stimulation of the sensory organs. When we speak of mental pictures, we mean an effect in the mind much like that produced by our perceiving a visible object through the eye, the optic nerve, and the appropriate regions of the brain. Here are the opening lines of "Apology for Bad Dreams" by Robinson Jeffers:

> In the purple light, heavy with redwood, the slopes drop seaward,
> Headlong convexities of forest, drawn in together to the steep ravine. Below on
>     the sea-cliff,
> A lonely clearing; a little field of corn by the streamside; a roof under spared
>     trees. Then the ocean
> Like a great stone someone has cut to a sharp edge and polished to shining. Beyond
>     it, the fountain
> And furnace of incredible light flowing up from the sunk sun.

The passage presents a sequence of images by naming and describing more or less familiar objects. These mental pictures and the language that presents them are called *imagery*. Once again we must understand the meanings of the words, which in this connection probably also means that we must be able to recall a sense experience of the objects named and described, or imaginatively construct such an experience out of related ones, so that the words will be genuinely meaningful to us. Either from vacation travel or from pictures we have a fairly good idea of what a redwood looks like, as well as slopes, ravines, and the ocean. But because the ocean varies in its appearance with changing conditions, Jeffers shows it at the moment of the action in the poem by comparing it to an enormous polished stone. Similarly the light radiating from the set sun is compared to a fountain and furnace. This comparison not only produces a visual image of the light, but also conveys its vigor and intensity. Hence imagery usually recalls, rather than originates, mental impressions, so that the reader is involved in the creation of the poetic image by contributing from his store of recollections. The reader will be responsive to the extent that his experience has provided him with a rich stock of images. This creative participation of the reader in the poetic process should not lead us to suppose that the able reader weaves his own fancies into the poem, but only that he responds fully to the stimuli actually in the poem.

These illustrations have dealt with *visual imagery*, the most frequent kind. Yet poetry also appeals to other senses. These lines from Keats's "The Eve of St. Agnes" contain images appealing to what we loosely call the sense of touch:

> Soon, trembling in her soft and chilly nest,
> In sort of wakeful swoon, perplexed she lay,
> Until the poppied warmth of sleep oppressed
> Her soothéd limbs, and soul fatigued away; . . .

"Trembling," "soft," "chilly," "wakeful swoon," "poppied" (i.e., like the drowsiness produced by opium), "warmth," "soothéd" all suggest the sensations preceding sleep. Since it is dark, none of the images is visual. In Robert Frost's "Birches," these remarkable tactile images occur:

> . . . life is too much like a pathless wood
> Where your face burns and tickles with the cobwebs
> Broken across it, and one eye is weeping
> From a twig's having lashed across it open.

*Auditory imagery* is also fairly frequent. It may be produced by naming and describing sounds as in this example, again from "The Eve of St. Agnes":

> The boisterous, midnight, festive clarion,
> The kettle-drum and far-heard clarinet,
> Affray his ears, though but in dying tone:—
> The hall door shuts again, and all the noise is gone.

Elsewhere Keats reinforces auditory imagery by imitating natural sounds in the sound of his words:

> The silver, snarling trumpets 'gan to chide: . . .
> . . . . . . . . . . . .
> . . . meantime the frost-wind blows
> Like Love's alarum *pattering the sharp sleet*
> Against the window-panes; . . .

This device, which we shall discuss more fully in a later section, is known as *onomatopoeia*.

The other senses—taste and smell—in the traditional list of five are less frequently involved in imagery, and they almost invariably operate by reminding us of our own sense experiences or by comparing a novel taste or odor to a familiar one. In "Thyrsis" Matthew Arnold writes,

> Soon shall we have . . .
> Sweet-William with his homely cottage small,
> And stocks in fragrant blow, . . .

and later, "And scent of hay new mown." Terms describing flavors and odors are few and imprecise compared with those for shapes and colors.

Imagery, then can be produced by names, descriptions, comparisons, rhythms ("the tolling tolling bells' perpetual clang"), intellectual associations ("The music, yearning like a God in pain"), or several of these devices working together. Finally, imagery is one of the chief means by which literature achieves the concrete, specific, and hence moving and impressive quality we have attributed to it.

## D. FIGURATIVE LANGUAGE

*Figures of speech,* however varied, have one thing in common: they deal with one thing by relating it to another, to produce an astonishing variety of effects.

### 1. METAPHOR

A *metaphor* is an assertion or suggestion that something is, or is equivalent to, another thing (though in literal fact the two things are unlike each other in most

ways). How many such equivalences appear in the following brief poem by Sir
Walter Ralegh?

### What Is Our Life?

> What is our life? a play of passion:
> Our mirth, the music of division;
> Our mothers' wombs the tiring-houses be
> Where we are dressed for this short comedy.
> Heaven the judicious sharp spectator is,
> That sits and marks still who doth act amiss;
> Our graves that hide us from the searching sun
> Are like drawn curtains when the play is done.
> Thus march we playing to our latest rest;
> Only we die in earnest—that's no jest.

Ralegh's assertion that our life is "a play of passion" is a metaphor equating
"life" and "play." Frequently the *principal term*—here life—is abstract, vague,
intangible, or unfamiliar, whereas the *secondary term*—"play" in our example—is
concrete, definite, and familiar. Since the two things are basically unlike, the
metaphor throws great emphasis on the qualities they do share, as when Ralegh
calls attention to the brevity and triviality of stage plays and then attributes these
characteristics to life, "this short comedy." Note that Ralegh has produced an
*extended metaphor* by asserting, with some ingenuity, that the identity he has
perceived between life and a play also holds between parts of each spectacle:
laughter is musical accompaniment; wombs are dressing rooms (both are places
of preparation); Heaven is the spectator who judges; graves are the curtains which
fall at the end of the performance. Finally, the metaphor also frequently passes
judgment on the principal term by comparing it to a secondary term chosen with
a particular attitude in mind. Ralegh's "play of passion" becomes a "short
comedy," to suggest, somewhat sadly perhaps, that life is not so serious as we
might like to think it.

Even though Ralegh refers casually to life as "this short comedy" without
using the full form of the metaphor, "life is a short comedy," none of the meta-
phoric force is lost. Such a figure is called an *implicit metaphor*. In Tennyson's
"Ulysses" the hero says, "I will drink/Life to the lees." Here the implicit meta-
phor that pictures a man thirsty for experience drinking down his life is reinforced
by "lees," the sediment in the bottom of the cup.

Much of our language is metaphoric in origin, though we are inclined to
forget the original comparisons that gave rise—sometimes centuries ago—to new
words. As Emerson says in "Nature," "Every word which is used to express a
moral or intellectual fact, if traced to its root, is found to be borrowed from some
material appearance, 'Right' means 'straight'; 'wrong' means 'twisted.' 'Spirit'
primarily means 'wind'; 'transgression,' the 'crossing of a line'; 'supercilious,'
the 'raising of the eyebrow.'" Slang often begins as witty implicit metaphor but
soon becomes so worn through overuse that we forget its metaphoric origin. The
person who first said, "Don't monkey with that" had a brilliant satiric insight,
but few of us now imagine a meddlesome little animal when we use the tired
phrase. The result, like such standard phrases as "the arm of a chair" or "the
brow of a cliff," is a *dead metaphor*. Similarly, many apparently abstract terms are

dead implicit metaphors. With a little effort we are able to remember that the phrase "grasp an idea" (or slang "catch on") suggests that the mental operation is much like taking hold of a solid object with the hand. We may, however, be unaware that "comprehension" embodies the same metaphor until we remember what "prehension" is and that elephants have prehensile trunks.

Some writers, incidentally, use *metaphor* as a generic term synonymous with *figurative language* to include the following figures as varieties.

A figure of speech closely related to metaphor is *simile,* in which similarity, rather than identity, is asserted. The figure includes one of several words such as "like," "as," or "than." Thus "Our graves . . . are *like* drawn curtains" is a simile. In the following example the poet is interested in a single quality— swiftness—which identifies the two terms of the simile, and a point-by-point comparison like that in "What Is Our Life?" would be fruitless:

> Swift as the weaver's shuttle fleet our years.

A formal variety of the simile is the *epic simile,* so named from its frequent occurrence in the Homeric epics. It is developed at some length according to a fairly strict formula: *as* a person in mythology, history, or the Bible once did something (or as a thing in nature does), *so* now a character in the epic does something similar. Milton uses the device in *Paradise Lost,* the great Christian epic:

> . . . As when the potent rod
> Of Amram's son in Egypt's evil day
> Waved round the coast, up called a pitchy cloud
> Of locusts, warping on the eastern wind,
> That o'er the realm of impious Pharaoh hung
> Like night, and darkened all the land of Nile;
> So numberless were those bad Angels seen
> Hovering on wing under the cope of Hell
> 'Twixt upper, nether, and surrounding fires, . . .

The secondary term refers to Moses' calling down the plague of locusts upon Egypt. Milton was able to rely upon his readers' knowledge of the Bible, classic myth, and ancient history; these sources of allusion were available to explain or describe the new matter of the principal term following "So." Sometimes only the secondary term of an epic simile is expanded.

An elaborately ingenious metaphor or simile in which the things compared are more than usually unlike each other is called a *conceit.* "What Is Our Life?" may be considered a conceit because of its ingenuity. The work of the seventeenth-century metaphysical school is characterized by the *metaphysical conceit,* an often strained association of almost wholly dissimilar things. The last four stanzas of John Donne's "A Valediction: Forbidding Mourning" contain a famous example in which the poet compares the souls of two lovers to the legs of a draftsman's compass.

## 2. METONYMY AND SYNECDOCHE

Two other important figures related to metaphor are *metonymy* and *synecdoche,* both occasionally very striking, but far less frequent than metaphor or simile. *Metonymy* is the use of an attribute of an object or of something closely associated

with it to represent that object. The following stanza by James Shirley illustrates
this figure:

> The glories of our blood and state
>     Are shadows, not substantial things;
> There is no armour against Fate;
>     Death lays his icy hand on kings:
>         Sceptre and crown
>         Must tumble down,
> And in the dust be equal made
> With the poor crooked scythe and spade.

Here "sceptre and crown" stand for rulers, while "scythe and spade" stand for
peasants. The choice of these emblems and implements has a twofold effect:
First, the concrete terms are more vivid—that is, they produce more clearly
realized images—than the more general terms we have substituted for them.
Second, the contrasting of these implements emphasizes the disparity of social
status between royalty and commoners. The objects are in the one case actual,
and in the other appropriate, though not actual, badges of rank.

*Synecdoche* substitutes a significant part for a whole thing, as when Shirley
uses "blood" to stand for lineage or race. Similarly, Dunbar refers in his "Four
Epitaphs" to John Keats as "sweet lyric throat."

### 3. PERSONIFICATION

*Personification* endows abstraction with the qualities of a human being in such
a way as to render a normally disembodied idea dramatically effective. Shirley's
"Death lays his icy hand on kings" uses one of the commonest personifications
but rescues it from banality by precise and appropriate imagery. Less obvious is
the personification in the preceding line: "There is no armour against Fate," but
the capital letter calls attention to the device. Personification often appears in
*allegory,* which we shall encounter in another connection.

Personification is also involved in *apostrophe,* a rhetorical device in which
the poet speaks to a personified abstraction or to an absent person:

> Eternal Spirit of the chainless mind!
> Brightest in Dungeons, Liberty! thou art,
> For there thy habitation is the heart—. . .
> .   .   .   .   .   .   .   .   .   .
> Milton, thou shouldst be living at this hour;
> England hath need of thee; . . .

## E. RHETORICAL DEVICES

*Rhetorical devices* are intellectual stratagems, rather than image-making
figures. They convey attitudes and sometimes imply underlying assumptions of a
kind not associated with figurative language.

### 1. IRONY

In a very general way, *irony* is the quality that arises from a discrepancy between
just expectations and actualities. Thus we may speak of circumstances as ironic
if we feel that we have a right to expect some kind of success and are denied that

success in a perversely appropriate way. In Shelley's "Ozymandias" the contrast between the pride of the ambitious "king of kings" and the "decay of that colossal wreck" amid its "lone and level sands" is an example of the *irony of circumstance*. In this instance the effect of the irony is to deride human vanity. Hardy's "The Convergence of the Twain" also shows the defeat of human vanity by natural processes, thus again depicting the irony of circumstance, but here there is more emphasis on an indifferent or even malevolent force, personified as "The Immanent Will" and the "Spinner of the Years."

Language that on the surface appears to mean something innocent but that has a different import for the person sufficiently informed is called *verbal irony*. "Look on my works ye mighty, and despair!" meant to Ozymandias, "Despair of matching my achievements," but to the reader, who sees the end to which all human vanity must come, the message is, "Despair of defying time's destruction."

## 2. HYPERBOLE AND UNDERSTATEMENT

*Hyperbole* is deliberate, and often outrageous, exaggeration. It may be used to magnify a fact or an emotion in such a way as to attribute great importance to it:

> Hark, how my Celia, with the choice
> Music of her hand and voice
> Stills the loud wind; and makes the wild
> Incensèd boar and panther mild;
> Mark how these statues like men move,
> Whilst men with wonder, statues prove!
> This stiff rock bends to worship her,
> That idol turns idolator.

In other uses, hyperbole may be ironic and have the final effect of deflating the significance of the matter treated:

> Then flashed the living lightning from her eyes,
> And screams of horror rend th'affrighted skies.
> Not louder shrieks to pitying heaven are cast,
> When husbands, or when lapdogs breathe their last; . . .

The juxtaposing of husbands and lapdogs makes clear that we are not to take the "living lightning" very seriously.

The opposite device is known as *understatement*. Here the effect is almost always to magnify the matter discussed, by implying that the means of expression is inadequate to the task:

> We know, too, they are very fond of war,
> A pleasure—like all pleasures—rather dear; . . .

Calling war "rather dear" is understatement; calling it a pleasure is irony—an irony in which the discrepancy is that between men's professed horror of war and their real fascination with it.

*Litotes* is a negative statement that usually has the magnifying effect of understatement. In E. A. Robinson's "How Annandale Went Out," the narrator says coolly of his dying friend, "And the sight was not so fair/As one or two that I had seen elsewhere"—an effective way of expressing his horror.

*Anticlimax* also results in ironic understatement. Normally the most important or climactic element of an utterance comes at the end—of a sentence, stanza, or poem. When an important item is followed by a trivial one, we exprience an intellectual and emotional deflation. If such anticlimax is deliberate and controlled, it produces comic or satiric effects. Pope uses this device brilliantly in his mock epic, "The Rape of the Lock": "Or stain her honor or her new brocade; . . ." Punning on "stain," Pope suggests the moral shallowness of a society that fails to distinguish between a significant and a trivial calamity.

### 3. AMBIGUITY

A number of devices involve *ambiguity,* or what we commonly call double meaning. In scientific prose, ambiguity is a fault, but in literature ambiguity may produce humor, or enrich meaning, or reflect the writer's perception of the complexity of life. In "How Annandale Went Out" the narrator says, "Now view yourself as I was, on the spot." By "on the spot" he means that he was at the scene, but he implies also the slang sense of the phrase—that he was forced to make a decision. The ambiguity of the phrase reflects the opposition between the demands of his professional code and the appeal to his human sympathies.

The *pun* is a familiar kind of ambiguity—that is, the use of words with more than one possible meaning—usually for comic effect. Puns are of many sorts, ranging from those exploiting vague similarities in sound, through plays on distinctly separate meanings of the same word in various settings, to the use of such etymological and metaphorical relationships as we discovered in "stain." Ben Jonson, in "To the Memory of . . . Shakespeare" puns on the name of his subject:

> . . . his well-turnéd and true-filéd lines;
> In each of which he seems to *shake a lance,* . . .

This example is little more than good fun, but a pun can also contribute to the idea of a poem. In a poem written during the Great Depression of the 1930s, a modern version of a Renaissance poem, C. Day Lewis puns on two senses (not etymologically or metaphorically related) of the word "tire." An archaic sense of the verb is "to attire," to clothe (recall "tiring houses" in "What Is Our Life?"):

> . . . not silken dress
> But toil shall *tire* thy loveliness.

In this instance the pun adds to the poem's bitter comedy.

George Herbert's "The Windows" pictures man as a window in God's temple:

> Lord, how can man preach thy eternal word?
> He is a brittle *crazy* glass. . . .

As applied to glass, "crazy" (our modern form is "crazed") means covered with a network of tiny cracks. Here the pun is part of a metaphor; indeed, the two senses of the word arose originally by a metaphoric transfer of meaning from physical objects to an intangible mental condition. In the metaphor the word applies to both glass and man; as applied to man it means insane or at least deficient in divine wisdom. The same pun appears in the slang term "cracked." In each of these examples a shift in our understanding of the key word changes the sense of the whole sentence.

A *paradox* is a statement which is either apparently self-contradictory or at odds with ordinary exprience, and yet reveals a truth normally hidden:

> Stone walls do not a prison make,
>   Nor iron bars a cage; . . .

Usually some unexpressed condition explains the paradox. In this quotation the reader understands, even though he does not articulate the point, that the spirit is free even though the body is confined. In Donne's "Batter My Heart," paradox expresses the inexplicable mystery of man's relationship to God, while in McKay's "The White City" paradox shows the bittersweet relationship of the Black man to white society. *Oxymoron,* the associating of opposite terms in a single expression, usually reflects a mixture of attitudes toward an event, as in Shakespeare's "Parting is such *sweet sorrow.*"

## III. The Form of Poetry

Literature is distinguished from nonliterary writing by its closely relating—indeed, actually fusing—form and idea. We shall sometimes pretend that we can detach the meaning from the form of a work, but we had better remember that this maneuver is preliminary to apprehending the whole piece and that the extracted "meaning"—by which we probably designate a prose paraphrase—is far less than the total work of literature. Drama and fiction both have *significant form,* for the arrangement of events, the prose style—its diction, figures, and rhythms—and the selection of detail are all part of the meaning of the work. But in poetry the union of form and content is so intimate that, although the extraction of a theme is unsatisfactory for the other genres, it is impossible in a successful poem. A poem is not an idea carried in a basket woven of sentences; it is an organism whose substance does not exist apart from the shape that it has.

### A. SOUND VALUES

In language the sounds of speech blend with the sense of the words to produce a meaningful whole. The poet often organizes speech sounds more intricately and formally than the prose writer does. All of the sound values interact, but we can momentarily isolate elements of the fusion so that we can respond more fully to the poem in its integrated form.

### 1. RHYME

Lines of verse are said to *rhyme*—or to have a *rhyme scheme*—when the ends of their final words have identical sounds. By the end of a word we mean here the vowel of the last accented syllable and any sounds that may follow it:

> Come with bows bent and with emptying of quivers,
>   Maiden most perfect, lady of light,
> With a noise of winds and many rivers,
>   With a clamour of waters, and with might;

> Bind on thy sandals, O thou most fleet,
> Over the splendour and speed of thy feet;
> For the faint east quickens, the wan west shivers,
> Round the feet of the day and the feet of the night.

Here "quivers," "rivers," "shivers"; "light," "might," "night"; and "fleet," "feet" are rhyming groups. In each of these clusters both pronunciation and spelling coincide. Since rhyming is a matter of sound, though, a difference in spelling is of no consequence so long as the various spellings represent the same sound:

> There be none of Beauty's daughters
>   With a magic like thee;
> And the music on the waters
>   Is thy sweet voice to me: . . .
>
> . . . . . . . . . . .
>
> With a full but soft emotion
> Like the swell of Summer's ocean.

A number of effects are possible by the use of rhyme. One of these is simply the pleasure that we experience in the chiming of like sounds. In addition, a pattern of rhymes established early in a poem arouses expectation as each successive rhyming word of a new set occurs, so that the arrival of the second rhyming word of the group fulfills that expectation. One kind of aesthetic enjoyment lies in discerning a pattern.

We have described so far the usual—what might be regarded as the normal—condition of rhyme; there are, though, a number of interesting variations. When the accented vowel is in the final syllable of the line—and again, this is the usual situation—the rhymes are said to be *masculine*. The effect is sometimes thought to be stronger, the utterance more positive, than in the other arrangement. When one or two unaccented syllables follow the accented syllable in the rhyming words, the rhyme is *feminine*. The movement of the lines is then graceful and continuous, without the firm close produced by a masculine rhyme. The more frequent kind of feminine rhyme, that of two syllables, is called *double rhyme*. *Triple rhyme* is the variety of feminine rhyme in which two unaccented syllables follow the accented syllable and all three rhyme with a similar arrangement in a nearby line. More often than not triple rhyme is used for humorous verse; we delight in the poet's display of an ingenuity that often serves a flippant or satiric attitude. The effect is especially ludicrous if the challenge of a trisyllabic word can be met only by putting together two or three words to produce a synthetic rhyming word or if the rhyming contract can be filled only by warping the pronunciation or stress of a phrase. The following stanza from Byron's *Don Juan* shows masculine rhyme in lines 1, 3, and 5; double feminine rhyme in lines 2, 4, and 6; and triple feminine rhyme in lines 7 and 8:

> 'Tis pity learnéd virgins ever wed
>   With persons of no sort of education,
> Or gentlemen, who, though well born and bred,
>   Grow tired of scientific conversation;
> I don't choose to say much upon this head,
>   I'm a plain man, and in a single station,
> But—Oh! ye lords of ladies intellectual,
> Inform us truly, have they not hen-pecked you all?

A special variety of rhyme is the *inexact* or *near* or *slant rhyme.* Here the sounds of the rhyming words are not identical but only similar, and they may be more similar or less in one instance or another. In "Arms and the Boy," for example, Wilfred Owen rhymes "blade-blood," "flash-flesh." "heads-lads," "teeth-death," "apple-supple," "heels-curls." Inexact rhymes retain the general suggestion of pattern produced by the regular recurrence of like sounds, but they do not insist on it. Slant rhyme is especially useful to link very brief lines like Emily Dickinson's, for it binds them together without producing the jingling effect that results when a precise (and perhaps even predictable) rhyming word comes around too soon. In addition, inexact rhymes have something of the effect of slight dissonances in music; they support moods of tartness, doubt, or melancholy rather than of sweetness, assurance, or joy. Emily Dickinson used them liberally, and twentieth-century poets have sometimes found them expressive of the uncertainty and disharmony of the modern world.

We usually expect to find rhymes in the final position of lines of verse. This customary use is called *end rhyme.* Some poets enrich their verbal melody by placing a word within the line (usually at or near the middle) to rhyme with the final word. Such *internal rhyme* enhances the binding effect of rhymes; it may also give great stress to certain lines if most lines in the poem do not share this quality:

> The fair breeze blew, the white foam flew,
> The furrow followed free;
> We were the first that ever burst
> Into that silent sea.
>
> Down dropped the breeze, the sails dropped down,
> 'Twas sad as sad could be;
> And we did speak only to break
> The silence of the sea!

In the first of these stanzas the first and third lines contain exact internal rhymes; "blew-flew"; "first-burst"; the device supports the tone of confidence in the sense of the lines. In the second stanza the reader expects the final word of the first line to rhyme with "breeze," but he is disappointed. In the third line "speak-break" looks like a rhyme (this peculiarity is sometimes called an *eye rhyme*), but it too is a disappointment, harmonious with the slackening of the ship's headway.

We should note at this point that the usual practice in marking rhyme schemes is to label the first rhyming line and each successive line that rhymes with it with a small *a.* The next line that ends with a different rhyme is marked *b,* as are all successive lines that rhyme with it. This system may be extended indefinitely, although letters beyond *g* are rarely needed. Lines without rhyming companions are labeled *x.*

## 2. ALLITERATION AND ASSONANCE

A sound effect closely related to rhyme is *alliteration,* or the repetition of a sound, usually a consonant, in the initial position of various words, or of a consonant sound within the words.

In the first of the stanzas just quoted from "The Rime of the Ancient

Mariner," note the intertwining of several alliterative sequences involving *f, b, w,* and *s:*

> The *f*air *b*reeze *b*lew, the white *f*oam *f*lew,
> The *f*urrow *f*ollowed *f*ree;
> *We we*re the *f*irst that ever *b*urst
> Into that *s*ilent *s*ea.

This heavy use of alliteration coincides with the use of internal rhyme to impart great intensity to the lines. In the second of the stanzas the alliterative sequences of *d* and *s* are somewhat less intense in keeping with the emotional slackening of the lines. In addition, a relationship may be asserted between words beginning with the same sound, as in "sad," "silence," and "sea." Similarly A. E. Housman uses alliteration to link beer and a bard, thus belittling the importance of the poet:

> Oh, many a peer of England brews
> Livelier liquor than the Muse,
> And *malt* does more than *Milton* can
> To justify God's ways to man.

Finally, certain emotions may be echoed by the repetition of appropriate consonants:

> Li*k*e *t*o the Pon*t*ic *s*ea,
> Who*s*e i*c*y *c*urren*t* and *c*ompul*s*ive *c*our*s*e
> Ne'er feel*s* re*t*iring e*bb*, *b*ut *k*eeps *d*ue on
> *T*o the Propon*t*ic and the Helle*sp*ont;
> Even *s*o my *b*loody though*ts*, with violen*t p*ace,
> Shall ne'er loo*k* ba*ck*, ne'er e*bb* to hum*b*le love,
> *T*ill tha*t* a *c*apable and wi*d*e revenge
> *S*wallow them u*p*.

This is Othello, maddened by Iago's insinuations, swearing revenge upon his wife's supposed seducer. His violence expresses itself in a spluttering outburst of explosive consonant sounds (*b, d, k, p, t*), intermixed with hissing *s* sounds.

We usually think of alliteration as involving repetition of the same sounds, but consonants merely similar, rather than identical, may also be alliterative. Thus *n* and *m* sounds may be interlinked to strengthen the alliterative effect:

> The *n*ight shakes the*m* round *m*e i*n* legio*n*s.

When the writer varies the surrounding consonant sounds, but repeats vowel sounds, the device is known as *assonance*. Although assonance is used as frequently as alliteration, its effects are more subtle. Thus the reader is less likely to be immediately aware of this additional means of distributing emphasis or imparting emotional tone:

> Cold *eye*lids that h*i*de l*i*ke a jewel
> Hard *eyes* that grow soft for an hour; . . .

### 3. ONOMATOPOEIA

*Onomatopoeia* is the imitation of natural sounds in the sounds of words. Many common words, such as "hum" or "clatter" or "moo," sound somewhat like the sounds they name. In poetry such words are only one means to suggest natural sounds. Rhythm ("Half a league, half a league, half a league onward" to represent hoofbeats, for example), the sounds of words even though they do not refer to natural sounds, and both alliteration and assonance may contribute an onomatopoetic effect. In the following passage from Tennyson's "Morte d'Arthur" all of these elements combine to imitate the sound of a knight in armor striding over rocky ground:

> Dry clashed his harness in the icy caves
> And barren chasms, and all to left and right
> The bare black cliff clanged round him, as he based
> His feet on juts of slippery crag that rang
> Sharp smitten with the dint of arméd heels—. . .

It should be noted, of course, that this effect, like the others we have discussed, will operate only if the sense of the passage reinforces and is reinforced by the sound devices. Substitution of key words with similar sounds but different meanings will destroy the effect:

> The bear's blunt claws clung round him.

Hence some critics doubt that onomatopoeia really exists.

## B. VERSIFICATION

All of these "sound effects" are related to the structural practices known collectively as *versification,* including rhythm, meter, and stanza form.

### 1. RHYTHM AND METER

An important element in all language is *rhythm.* We may define it as the regular recurrence of *accent* or *stress.*

In any polysyllabic word in English, one of the syllables receives greater stress than the others. Pronounce these words in sequence: "photograph," "photographer," "photographic." Which syllable is most heavily stressed in each word? Precisely what have you done to lend stress to a particular syllable? Note that stress consists of greater than normal volume of sound, elevation in vowel pitch, and a slight increase in the time during which the vowel of the stressed syllable is intoned. (Duration may also be longer or shorter in unstressed syllables.) In addition to the *primary stress* in a polysyllabic word, one or more of the other syllables may receive a secondary stress. Marking a primary stress with a single accent mark and a secondary stress with a double mark, we would indicate

the accenting of the words cited earlier as follows: pho·to·gráph; pho·tóg·ra·pher; pho·to·gráph·ic. In the early stages of our study, we may consider all stressed syllables as equal; later we shall want to distinguish several degrees of stress.

Monosyllabic words may be thought of as stressed when they stand alone, but, when associated with other words in phrases, they are stressed or unstressed according to the meaning of the phrase: "dówn the stréet." In turn, when phrases are grouped into sentences, the stresses in the phrases may shift: "As we walked down the street, we met two of our friends." Again, the stressing of a sentence may be changed, without any change in its wording, to suggest different meanings by different intonation patterns: "[On the way up the street, we saw no one;] but as we walked down the street, we met two of our friends." The alternation of stressed and unstressed syllables, then, is the rhythm of all language, including prose as well as poetry. In prose the distribution of stresses may be very irregular—that is, few or no or many unstressed syllables may fall between the stressed syllables, and there may be no discernible pattern to the recurrence of stresses.

In verse we can usually identify a normal, regular pattern of stressed and unstressed syllables. Reverting for a moment to a single degree of stress, we can mark the opening lines of Coleridge's "Frost at Midnight" to show a pattern of stresses with few complications:

> The frost performs its secret ministry,
>
> Unhelped by any wind. The owlet's cry
>
> Came loud—and hark, again! loud as before.
>
> The inmates of my cottage, all at rest,
>
> Have left me to that solitude, which suits
>
> Abstruser musings; save that at my side
>
> My cradled infant slumbers peacefully.
>
> 'Tis calm indeed! so calm, that it disturbs
>
> And vexes meditation with its strange
>
> And extreme silentness . . .                                        10

In six of the ten lines the pattern is the same: five unstressed and five stressed syllables precisely alternate. In three of the remaining lines this pattern is disturbed at only one point, so that even in these lines the usual alternation is dominant. The normal pattern is called the *meter* of the verse, and we call it normal, rather than fixed, because the actual distribution of stresses rarely conforms to the pattern very long without a momentary deviation. Still, there is a general tendency which may be thought of as the meter—the normal pattern—struggling to confine the logical rhythms of the sentences. We can usually identify the meter without great difficulty and discover the effect of the degree of conformity of the *actual rhythm* to this norm.

It is customary to divide the metric line into units called *feet,* each foot usually containing one stressed syllable and its associated unstressed syllables. (In the *spondee* both syllables are stressed.) The most important foot in English verse is the *iamb,* or *iambic foot,* consisting of an unstressed syllable followed by a stressed one ($\smile$ ´):

> My heart | is like | a sing | ing bird
>
> Whose nest | is in | a wa | tered shoot.

By far the greater bulk of English verse is written in a basically iambic meter. Several other meters, of the number of possible ones, are of sufficient frequency to be identified here. The *trochee* or *trochaic foot* is another two-syllable foot; the accented syllable comes first (´ ˘):

There they | are, my | fifty | men and | women

Naming | me the | fifty | poems | finished!

Two trisyllabic feet appear with some frequency in English verse. The commoner of these is the *anapest* (˘ ˘ ´), which, like the iamb, is called a *rising meter* because the accent occurs at the end of the foot:

For the moon | never beams | without bring | ing me dreams

Of the beau | tiful An | nabel Lee;

And the stars | never rise | but I feel | the bright eyes

Of the beau | tiful An | nabel Lee.

The effect of anapestic lines is often light and swift. The lines also tend to fall into singsong, especially when the verse is thoroughly regular as it is here, or when the regularity is reinforced by internal rhymes, such as "beams," "dreams" in the first of these lines and "rise," "eyes" in the third. In this example the effect is further strengthened by the identity of the second and fourth lines so that the poem can be read acceptably only by varying the intensity of stresses and muting the normal meter through a greater than usual attention to the logical rhythm.

The trisyllabic foot in *falling meter* is called a *dactyl* (´ ˘ ˘). It is the least frequently used of the four major English meters and is more important as a source of substitute feet than as a predominant meter. Note also that since the foot ends in two unaccented syllables, the rhyme must be either feminine triple rhyme, or the unusual and awkward rhyming of unaccented syllables only. Hence, dactylic lines are likely to be unrhymed, as in *Evangeline*, or a substitution is made for the final dactyl. Thomas Hood's "The Bridge of Sighs" shows the triple feminine rhyme in lines 1 and 3 of each stanza and the substitution of a single accent in lines 2 and 4:

One more un | fortunate

Weary of | breath

Rashly im | portunate

Gone to her | death!

Several kinds of variation on these basic meters are possible. Two later lines of Christina Rossetti's "A Birthday," which we have cited as an example of iambic meter, show a frequent kind of variation:

Raise me | a dais | of silk | and down;

Hang it | with vair | and pur | ple dyes; . . .

Here the imperative requires stress on the verb, which is the first syllable of each line, so that the first foot is a trochee. Note also that some diversity of reading is possible here: "dais" may be pronounced as one syllable with a long *a,* in which case the foot is a normal iamb. If, however, the reader chooses to pronounce the word with two syllables ("dá·is"), as is usual, the third foot might be thought of as having two unstressed syllables before the stressed one ("-is of silk"), in which case it would be an anapest. Actually the tendency would be to slur "-is" and "of" together into a single unstressed syllable so that once again we would have an iambic foot.

Other variations appear in the following basically trochaic stanza:

Out u | pon it! | I have | loved

Three whole | days to | gether;

And am | like to | love three | more,

If it | prove fair | weather.

The dropping of an unaccented syllable at the ends of lines 1 and 3 permits the use of a masculine rhyme. The emphasis of the sentences requires an extra stress in lines 2 and 4 so that two accents fall together in one foot to produce a *spondee,* a foot sometimes used as a substitute, and only rarely as the prevailing meter of a line.

The terms used for line lengths are these: a one-foot line is called *monometer* (mo·nom·e·ter); two-foot line, *dimeter* (dim·e·ter); three-foot line, *trimeter* (trim·e·ter); four-foot line, *tetrameter* (te·tram·e·ter); five-foot line, *pentameter* (pen·tam·e·ter); six-foot line, *hexameter* (hex·am·e·ter). Thus the meter of Blake's "The Tyger" is trochaic tetrameter, while the most frequent English line, used in sonnets, heroic couplets, blank verse, and a variety of other stanza forms, is iambic pentameter. Occasionally an iambic pentameter line will be extended by the addition of one extra foot to produce an *Alexandrine.* Spenser regularly uses such lines to conclude his characteristic stanzas, and they occur occasionally elsewhere. In the Spenserian stanza, the Alexandrine brings the stanza to rest, rounds it off, and concludes it.

## 2. LINES OF VERSE

Another element in the rhythm of poetry is the natural pause within some lines known as a *caesura.* In many lines the logic of phrasing produces a brief interruption along with a fall in pitch somewhere near the middle of the line:

A time there was, ‖ ere England's griefs began, . . .

In very long lines, as in the hexameter of *Evangeline,* secondary caesuras appear within the halves; indeed, any line longer than ten syllables tends to break into two parts, and in audible reading it will sound like two lines. The skillful poet finds in the caesura one more tool for shaping verse to his ends: he can increase regularity by a precise placing of the caesura in the same location in each succeeding line, or he can give a loose, flowing, or informally conversational effect to his lines by varying the position of the caesura. Compare the practice of the following examples, assuming the position of the caesura to coincide with the internal mark of punctuation in each line:

> Be judge yourself, I'll bring it to the test,
> Which is the basest creature, man or beast:
> Birds feed on birds, beasts on each other prey;
> But savage man alone, does man betray.
> Pressed by necessity, *they* kill for food;
> Man undoes man, to do himself no good.
>
> . . . . . . . . . . . .
>
> . . . Will share thy destiny. The gay will laugh
> When thou art gone, the solemn brood of care
> Plod on, and each one as before will chase
> His favorite phantom; yet all these shall leave
> Their mirth and their employments, and shall come
> And make their bed with thee. As the long train . . .

The reader can find clues to the significance of the lines or to an effective oral reading of them by observing the caesura position along with the other elements of form.

Lines may further be distinguished as *end stopped* or *run on*. The end-stopped line coincides with a logical unit of thought so that the line is usually ended by a mark of punctuation. The run-on (or *enjambed*) line contains a part of a unit of thought, or parts of two units of thought. Again, the poet can manipulate this feature of verse to produce, for example, an easily flowing discourse produced by run-on lines as against a flatly oracular utterance produced by end-stopped lines.

## 3. STANZA FORMS

Finally, we should examine some of the ways in which lines are grouped to produce larger structural units.

Sometimes lines are irregularly grouped so that the divisions correspond to important stages in the development of the narrative or discussion. Such units vary in length and are not marked by any set scheme of rhymes, if, indeed, the lines are rhymed at all. These groupings are called *verse paragraphs*. They are likely to appear in long poems in *blank verse*—unrhymed iambic pentameter. Wordsworth's "Lines Composed a Few Miles above Tintern Abbey" provides a good example. *Free verse* also usually includes verse paragraphs.

Groups of a definite number of lines, bound together by a *rhyme scheme* that reappears in each successive group, are called *stanzas*. (The term *verse* is sometimes incorrectly substituted for *stanza*. It should be reserved for its popular use in connection with songs, or to designate a single line of poetry.)

Pairs of two successive lines are called *couplets*. They are likely to be rhymed; if they are unrhymed, the second line of the couplet will be end stopped. Rhymed couplets may be open; that is, the second line will be run on so that the movement of the verse is free and continuous from one couplet to the next:

> A thing of beauty is a joy forever;
> Its loveliness increases; it will never
> Pass into nothingness; but still will keep

> A bower of quiet for us, and a sleep
> Full of sweet dreams, and health, and quiet breathing.
> Therefore, on every morrow, are we wreathing . . .

Closed couplets are self-contained. The first line is likely to be end stopped; the second line is sure to be. The effect is more formal and epigrammatic or more oracular than the free movement of open couplets:

> True wit is nature to advantage dressed,
> What oft was thought, but ne'er so well expressed;
> Something, whose truth convinced at sight we find,
> That gives us back the image of our mind.

Three rhyming lines, of whatever length, handled as an independent stanza, form a *tercet*. Usually the three lines have the same rhyme, but other arrangements are possible if only two of the lines rhyme. An old development of the tercet, borrowed from Dante, is *terza rima,* iambic pentameter lines in which the first tercet rhymes *a b a*. The second tercet picks up the rhyme of the middle line in the first tercet so that its rhyme scheme is *b c b*. This pattern is repeated; the whole poem is tightly linked by its rhymes:

> As in that trance of wondrous thought I lay,
> This was the tenour of my waking dream:—
> Methought I sat beside a public way
>
> Thick with summer dust, and a great stream
> Of people there was hurrying to and fro,
> Numerous as gnats upon the evening gleam, . . .

Similar linking appears in the Spenserian stanza and the Spenserian sonnet.

A four-line stanza is known as a *quatrain*. Here some interesting variations are possible, not only because of the different line lengths and meters available, but also because the rhymes can be arranged in several ways. A common form rhymes *a b a b:*

> The curfew tolls the knell of parting day,
> The lowing herd winds slowly o'er the lea,
> The plowman homeward plods his weary way,
> And leaves the world to darkness and to me.

When the lines are of iambic pentameter, as they are here, the stanza is known as the *heroic* or *elegiac stanza,* the latter term from Gray's "Elegy Written in a Country Churchyard," from which we have quoted.

Some quatrains rhyme two lines only, thus: *x a x a*. One such quatrain is the *ballad stanza,* in which tetrameter and trimeter lines alternate:

> There lived a Wife at Usher's Well,
>     And a wealthy wife was she;
> She had three stout and stalwart sons,
>     And she sent them o'er the sea.

Note, by the way, that ballads are not always composed in this stanza form.

Once we have passed four lines, the possible variations in stanza form are too numerous to describe in detail, and we add only the few stanza forms that have been used with some frequency or that show some distinctive features. Of the seven-line stanzas, *rime royal* is interesting because of its effective use by Chaucer and some of his successors:

> Look how a tigress that hath lost her whelp
> Runs fiercely ranging through the woods astray,
> And seeing herself deprived of hope or help,
> Furiously assaults what's in her way,
> To satisfy her wrath, not for a prey;
> So fell she on me in outrageous wise,
> As could disdain and jealousy devise.

These are iambic pentameter lines rhyming *a b a b b c c.*

*Ottava rima* consists of eight iambic pentameter lines rhyming *a b a b a b c c:*

> He knew whose gentle hand was at the latch
> Before the door had given her to his eyes;
> And from her chamber window he would catch
> Her beauty farther than the falcon spies;
> And constant as her vespers would he watch,
> Because her face was turned to the same skies;
> And with sick longing all the night outwear,
> To hear her morning step upon the stair.

This stanza requires a good bit of ingenuity in finding two sets of three successive rhymes for each stanza (to say nothing of the concluding couplet), but it has been used with great success in long poems.

One notable nine-line form is the *Spenserian stanza,* devised by Spenser for *The Faerie Queene,* but also used successfully by such later poets as Keats and Byron:

> Once more upon the waters! yet once more!
> And the waves bound beneath me as a steed
> That knows his rider. Welcome to their roar!
> Swift be their guidance, whereso'er it lead!
> Though the strained mast should quiver as a reed,
> And the rent canvas fluttering strew the gale,
> Still must I on; for I am as a weed,
> Flung from the rock, on Ocean's foam to sail
> Where'er the surge may sweep, the tempest's breath prevail.

The first eight lines are iambic pentameter; the ninth is iambic hexameter, that is, an Alexandrine. The prolongation of the final line combines with its rhyming with the preceding line to bring the stanza to the repose of a definite conclusion. Another Spenserian trait, shown also in Spenser's personal variation on the English sonnet, is the linking of rhymes, in which the second rhyme of the first quatrain becomes the first rhyme of the second quatrain. Thus the rhyme scheme is *a b a b b c b c c.*

## 4. THE SONNET

Perhaps the most esteemed stanza form is the *sonnet*. Its rather rigid rules have seemed a challenge to the poet to show how much range and variety he can create within the confines of its one hundred forty syllables, with the result that some of the most deftly fashioned poems in English, as well as many of the most intense and moving, take this form.

The term "sonnet" normally designates a lyric of fourteen iambic pentameter lines rhyming in one of several ways. Two basic forms, distinguished by their rhyme schemes and by their logical organization, are frequent in English. The *Petrarchan* or *Italian sonnet* rhymes *a b b a, a b b a, c d e, c d e.* (The rhyming of the last six lines may vary; for example, *c d, c d, c d* is possible.) Such a sonnet tends to fall into two stages: the first eight lines form the *octave,* and the last six the *sestet.* This formal division is frequently reflected in the logical progression of the content: The octave will pose a problem, depict a situation, or offer an observation; the sestet will provide a resolution of this opening and bring the matter to a conclusion.

A somewhat more widely used form is the *English* or *Shakespearean sonnet,* which rhymes *a b a b, c d c d, e f e f, g g.* Here the formal and logical divisions fall into three quatrains followed by a couplet. The quatrains will offer three successive images, or experiences, or observations which move by some rationale toward the resolution or conclusion of the couplet, which ends the sonnet much as Shakespeare's rhyming couplet marks the close of a blank-verse scene in the plays ("The play's the thing/Wherein I'll catch the conscience of the king.") Spenser's variation on the English sonnet, the *Spenserian sonnet,* a variation not much used by his successors, is a characteristic enhancing of the musical effect by linking rhymes to produce the scheme *a b a b, b c b c, c d c d, e e.*

While poets, as we have said, have been challenged by the strict form of the sonnet, they have also liked to experiment with it. A few sonneteers of the Renaissance used hexameter lines while observing all the other conventions, as Sidney did in *Astrophel and Stella,* I, whereas more recent poets have varied the number of lines. Thus Gerard Manley Hopkins produced what he called the "curtal" sonnet, curtailed to ten and a fraction lines. The sixteen-line poems of George Meredith's *Modern Love* are sometimes called sonnets because their logical development is much the same as that of the standard sonnet.

## 5. FREE VERSE

Before leaving our consideration of versification, we should note the vigorous unorthodoxy of *free verse.* In this style, brought to full development only during the past century, but now probably the most frequently used verse form, the poet rejects all predetermined meters and stanzaic structures on the grounds that they are molds into which his ideas must be poured. He maintains that the ideas have a form implicit within them which will sprout, branch, and flower as the poem grows. This theory of *organic form* produces poetry which looks on the page quite unlike any regular poetry, for both its lines and its verse paragraphs are of widely varying lengths. In addition, such poetry is unrhymed and does not conform to any regular meter. Yet free verse is not simply prose chopped up into arbitrary line lengths. Its diction, its liberal use of figurative language and of symbols, and its essentially dramatic method all mark it as belonging to the great tradition of poetry. As verse, it is considerably more rhythmic than prose, tending to fall into iambic patterns that coincide with the logical rhythms of the phrases so that as in stanzaic verse there is a pulse in the lines that reinforces the sense of the sentences. Similarly, the contours of the verse paragraphs parallel the development of the thought. In Walt Whitman's poetry, the typical verse paragraph begins with lines of moderate length, proceeds through lines of increasing length to a climax, and concludes with lines of decreasing length:

> Till of a sudden,
> May-be killed, unknown to her mate,
> One forenoon the she-bird crouched not on the nest,
> Nor returned that afternoon, nor the next,
> Nor ever appeared again,

The effect is something like that of a wave gathering strength, cresting, and subsiding. Clearly no rules of scansion or stanza analysis will apply to free verse; we must deal with each example on its own terms to discover how its highly individual metric effects contribute to the whole poem.

## C. FORM AND MEANING

This observation brings us to the most important phase of our discussion of poetic form. An understanding of meters and their relationship to rhythm, of rhyme schemes and sound values, of stanza forms and strategies of organization is essential to the full apprehension and appreciation of poetry, but it is only preliminary to our realization of the total effect of poetic form. From time to time we have suggested that one device or another may have a given effect; actually the effect of any stratagem may be judged only in its total setting, and there the result may be slightly to wholly different from its usual effect. The practice of judging effects may seem subjective or vaguely impressionistic. Actually it is based on a solid knowledge of the techniques that we have been describing, but it also proceeds by the application of this knowledge through sensitivity and imagination.

The analysis of poetic form is not an end in itself. There is not much value in determining that a stanza is an iambic tetrameter quatrain rhyming *a b b a,* or that the poet has used alliteration of certain sounds, or that he has used this or that figure of speech if we do not go on to assemble these separate observations into some kind of comprehensive account of the poem. To do that we must consider certain aspects of the content of poems, so that we may discover the relationship of the form and the meaning.

## IV. The Content of Poetry

### A. NARRATIVE

We said some distance back that poetry sometimes has a *narrative* element, which may be either the main concern in the poem or subordinate to the treatment of an emotion, idea, or character portrait. Only two problems—neither of them very difficult—present themselves here. The first is simply the matter of tracing out the story. In many narrative poems we shall have no difficulty at all. The story will be told in a straightforward manner, with a full array of expository statements to make things just as clear as possible, as it is in many ballads, Scott's long narratives such as "The Lady of the Lake," Longfellow's "The Courtship of Miles Standish," Tennyson's *Idylls of the King,* Jeffers's "The Roan Stallion," and, indeed, most other narrative poems. As a general rule, if the narrative is not immediately clear, we should examine the nature and source of the obscurity to determine its effect. What we are really trying to find out, of course, is why the poet somewhat veiled his story. We cannot interview the poet about his intention nor expect him to give a complete answer if we could, but we can determine the the effect of what he does. It is possible that the story is made more vivid by dramatization and consists only of dialogue. In such a situation the reader becomes an active participant in creating the setting of the poem. Sometimes the reader's imagination is stimulated by unspecified joys or horrors as it could not be by precise detail. Occasionally the poet will tell his story in a roundabout manner so that the poem's significance is more powerful when it occurs to the reader. For an effective example of the powerful effect of deliberately obscured narration, try to reconstruct the story in Edwin Arlington Robinson's "How Annandale Went Out." Indirect narration is uncommon, though, and we need not plague ourselves about "hidden meanings"; generally poets labor to make their meanings clear, and we find difficulties only because there is so much meaning to be found in a brief work.

The second problem is to discover whether the narrative is central or only tributary to another matter. The poems named at the beginning of this section seem to be concerned primarily with telling an exciting or moving story, as we deduce from the prominence given to action for its own sake. Some narratives, though, use action and speech chiefly as means of character revelation, as do the dramatic monologues of Robert Browning or such narratives of Frost as "The Death of the Hired Man." Others use narrative to dramatize ideas. "Ozymandias" is one brief example; a more fully elaborated one is Robinson's "The Man Against the Sky." Autobiographical poems may deal with the growth and nature of the poet's vocation. Two such different poems as Wordsworth's "The Prelude" and Whitman's "Out of the Cradle Endlessly Rocking" develop this theme. Epics such as *Beowulf* and *Paradise Lost* deal by narrative means with such large themes as the heroic past of a people or the vindication of God's ways. Finally, almost all lyrics use an incident, however simple, to provide the occasion for the poet's emotion and the means of expressing it.

If there is any need to determine the relative importance of narrative and other elements, some well-established criteria can be applied. What portion of the space of the poem is given to the story? What devices of emphasis such as vivid wording or climactic position are given to the story as against the meditation or character portrait? Actually, we are only trying to decide where the chief weight of the poem lies, for narrative, emotion, and idea are likely to help each other along and may actually be inseparable. Poems are not often versified philosophy, and in some sense, at least, the ideas they convey are realizable only in the context of the experience related in the poem.

## B. EMOTION

Literature is distinguished from nonliterary writing by its concern with conveying the emotion that accompanies an experience. Of all the literary forms, poetry deals with emotion most ably. The very large body of poetry concerned primarily with expressing emotion is called *lyric poetry.*

Emotion can be conveyed in many ways: the connotations of the diction, the lilt or drag of the rhythms, the associations surrounding the images, the significance of the events narrated—all these elements cooperate to establish the emotion. Hence the reader's experience, learning, and sensitivity are all necessary to help detect the emotional quality of a poem. Sometimes, it is true, a poet will declare his emotion by naming it, by saying that he experiences it. Modern critics are inclined to distrust the efficacy of this method of communicating emotion, and indeed T. S. Eliot, one of the most influential of recent critics as well as a distinguished poet, has insisted that art can convey emotion *only* by presenting what he calls an "objective correlative"—an object, an action, a situation which is the "formula" of that particular emotion and which, when presented to the reader, produces a sense impression that elicits the emotion. This idea implies a widely or universally shared response to particular objects and situations. Presumably the formal aspects of poetry—sound values, diction, and structure, for example—support the effect of objective correlatives.

In Gerard Manley Hopkins's "God's Grandeur" the interplay of emotions is conveyed by several aspects of the poem working in combination:

> The world is charged with the grandeur of God.
> It will flame out, like shining from shook foil;
> It gathers to a greatness, like the ooze of oil
> Crushed. Why do men then now not reck his rod?
> Generations have trod, have trod, have trod;
> And all is seared with trade; bleared, smeared with toil;
> And wears man's smudge and shares man's smell: the soil
> Is bare now, nor can foot feel, being shod.
> And for all this, nature is never spent;
> There lives the dearest freshness deep down things;          10
> And though the last lights off the black West went
> Oh, morning, at the brown brink eastward, springs—
> Because the Holy Ghost over the bent
> World broods with warm breast and with ah! bright wings.

In the first quatrain the diction is intense: "charged," "grandeur" (rather than "greatness," for example), "flame out," "shining from shook foil"; together the phrases create an image of sudden lightning-flashes that manifest the power of God. The same intensity shows itself in the alliterations of the third and fourth lines. Then awe gives way to chiding indignation in the sequence of sharp monosyllables: "Why do men then now not reck his rod?" The images of the second quatrain are not highly specific, but they are effective in evoking the familiar scene of dirt and wear in a crowded world. The sounds of these words are more important than the images in creating a tone of disgust: the repetition of "have trod"; the alliteration of "trod," "trade," and "toil"; the internal rhymes of "seared," "bleared," "smeared" and of "wears," "shares"; and the alliteration combined with the unpleasant connotations of "smeared," "smudge," and "smell" all add to the effect of revulsion at man's profanation of nature. In the sestet the image of light giving way to blackness at sunset and returning in the east at dawn calls up a familiar sight, now invested with broader meaning as a symbol of natural renewal and of resurrection. In the last two lines the traditional figure of the Holy Ghost as a dove is rendered in an image of the sunrise. The joyful assurance of the sestet is reinforced by the easy sweep of the rhythm in these lines;

they are pervaded by a sense of release from the clogged plodding of the quatrains. The last lines show an interweaving of alliteration of *w* and *b* sounds with long open vowels of rising pitch along the line to convey the speaker's hushed awe at God's grandeur. All of these effects interact with the meaning of the sentences to express in turn wonder, indignation, disgust, reassurance, and awe—without naming any of those emotions. The "ah!" is so well supported by the speaker's observation and so deftly placed that we accept it as an involuntary, unaffected outburst, and exempt it from the usual censure of exclamatory expressions in poetry.

A special aspect of emotion is the *tone* of a literary work, which may be defined as the attitude of the author toward his subject matter as it reveals itself in the literary work. Ordinarily the reader will have to draw inferences from the diction, the sound effects, the figures, and the ideas of the poem, as we have done in characterizing "God's Grandeur." Light, jingling rhythms imply one attitude, whereas sonorous stately measures suggest another. Laudatory epithets probably indicate the author's esteem, while grotesque appellations or comparisons may show his contempt for a character. A poet can even control tone by using specific language sounds. Edwin Meade Robinson once suggested that the orotund vowels in the phrase "bold rodents" produced an inappropriately noble tone. He recommended revision to "savage rats."

Two pitfalls need to be avoided here. First, we must be sure whether an attitude is to be attributed to the poet or to a character. In Browning's dramatic monologues, the views of the fictional speaker are overtly expressed, or fairly clearly implied, as in "Soliloquy of the Spanish Cloister"; the attitudes of the poet must be deduced from the gradually revealed portrait of the speaker.

Second, we must be careful not to mistake ironic expressions for literal ones. In Housman's "To an Athlete Dying Young" the speaker praises a young man for being clever enough to die before his honors fade. The wryly humorous lines are a kind of ironic understatement that conveys a sense of loss more effectively than exaggerated lament could do—but we must, of course, not take the speaker's praise as literal.

## C. IDEAS

We have already said that poems are not versified philosophy, and, in repeatedly insisting that the poem is a unified whole that should be dissected only as a means toward realizing its wholeness, we have implied that the idea, or theme, or meaning of a poem is not a separable part that can be better understood after the clutter of versification or metaphor is stripped away. The ideas of poems are important, though, and poets give memorable embodiment to ideas or, better, provide a rich sensuous, emotional, and intellectual realization of a theme which no purely rational process could provide.

### 1. HISTORICAL CONTEXT

One important clue to the pattern of ideas in a poem is its date. In successive periods of history certain dominant climates of belief prevail; in fact, we may define periods of history partly by identifying their dominant outlooks, so that we are able to speak of "the Age of Faith," or "the Age of Reason," or "the

Age of Skepticism." Certainly not everyone will accept the majority view in a given period, but we can usually relate a particular poem to the dominant view of its time.

Suppose we concentrate for the moment on the nature of the Deity. Poets, like all imaginative writers, are concerned ultimately with the human condition; it matters greatly to them, then, whether the world as we know it was created by some intelligent Force or just happened as the result of a series of undesigned unique accidents. If it was created by an intelligent Force, then in turn it matters greatly whether that Force is an eternal fatherly God or a vast impersonal power indifferent to man and perhaps no longer active. Mankind, through its long history, has examined an amazing variety of solutions to these problems, and the poets have given voice to them.

One aspect of the Romanticism that arose late in the eighteenth century and flowered in the early nineteenth century was an image of the Deity as a spirit interfused in all things, as Wordsworth suggests in "Tintern Abbey":

> . . . And I have felt
> A presence that disturbs me with the joy
> Of elevated thoughts; a sense sublime
> Of something far more deeply interfused,
> Whose dwelling is the light of setting suns,
> And the round ocean and the living air,
> And the blue sky, and in the mind of man:
> A motion and a spirit, that impels
> All thinking things, all objects of all thought,
> And rolls through all things.      *10*

In contrast to Wordsworth's living universe is Edwin Arlington Robinson's picture of a dead, meaningless universe that offers no moral guidance. Even here the poet finds hope, but his "Credo" ("I believe") is a testament of faith—of belief, that is, without evidence:

*Credo*

> I cannot find my way: there is no star
> In all the shrouded heavens anywhere;
> And there is not a whisper in the air
> Of any living voice but one so far
> That I can hear it only as a bar
> Of lost, imperial music, played when fair
> And angel fingers wove, and unaware,
> Dead leaves to garlands where no roses are.
> No, there is not a glimmer, nor a call,
> For one that welcomes, welcomes when he fears,      *10*
> The black and awful chaos of the night;
> For through it all—above, beyond it all—
> I know the far-sent message of the years,
> I feel the coming glory of the Light.

The date of Robinson's poem, about 1896, is hardly necessary to tell us that he is echoing the troubled doubt of a modern world struggling to reconcile traditional faith and new skepticism.

## 2. RECURRENT IDEAS

If there are certain ways of perceiving things characteristic of a particular age, there are also ideas that persist or reappear from time to time through history. The Wordsworth passage from "Tintern Abbey," for example, reflects the idea that the Soul of the Universe flows through and encompasses all things, including "the mind of man." In this view all individual souls are parts of one great Oversoul and are either temporarily or incompletely separated from it. While separated they are in a fallen and imperfect condition, and their intensely desired destiny is to be reunited with the Oversoul, and hence with each other. Thus ultimately all mankind would achieve a reunion in which painful individual identities would be merged in the great Soul which is God. This idea is not restricted to any single period of history but has formed part of the world view of various cultures that have borrowed it from older eras and added their own modifications, or perhaps have discovered or invented it anew. It occurs in both Hindu and Neo-Platonic philosophy and reappears in the English metaphysical poets of the seventeenth century and in German, English, and American romantic philosophy in the nineteenth century. Here is a seventeenth-century expression of the idea from "The Waterfall" by Henry Vaughan:

> Dear stream! dear bank, where often I
> Have sat and pleased my pensive eye,
> Why, since each drop of thy quick store
> Runs thither whence it flowed before,
> Should poor souls fear a shade or night,
> Who came, sure, from a sea of light?
> Or since those drops are all sent back
> So sure to thee, that none doth lack,
> Why should frail flesh doubt any more
> That what God takes he'll not restore?                            *10*

The following poem shows a late nineteenth-century version of the idea by an American Romantic, Ralph Waldo Emerson:

> *Pan*
>
> O what are heroes, prophets, men,
> But pipes through which the breath of Pan doth blow
> A momentary music. Being's tide
> Swells hitherward, and myriads of forms
> Live, robed with beauty, painted by the sun;
> Their dust, pervaded by the nerves of God,
> Throbs with an overmastering energy
> Knowing and doing. Ebbs the tide, they lie
> White hollow shells upon the desert shore,
> But not the less the eternal wave rolls on                        *10*
> To animate new millions, and exhale
> Races and planets, its enchanted foam.

In these examples, the Oversoul is pictured as water—a stream, or the sea—a great reservoir of which each individual soul is an inlet, or from which it is separated as a drop, a current, or a tidal pool.

## 3. EXPLICIT STATEMENT VERSUS METAPHOR

How have the ideas in our examples been embodied? The quotation from Wordsworth proceeds largely by explicit statement. In a perfectly direct way the poet makes an essentially expository statement, bringing to his aid little more than the resources of versification. Several of the important nouns are abstract: "Presence," "something," "motion," "spirit," "things"; only the barest hint of personification or metaphor appears in "interfused," "dwelling," "impels," "rolls." In our insistence upon the concrete and dramatic quality of poetry, we may seem to have implied that there is no place in it for explicit, literal, abstract statement. Actually there is, but it is a minor place; the characteristic method of poetic statement is dramatic and figurative. The essence of figurative language is doubleness. Such figures as metaphor, simile, metonymy, synecdoche, and personification, and the rhetorical devices of ambiguity—the pun, paradox, oxymoron, and verbal irony—all involve the linking of two things. Thus the poet attends simultaneously to the concrete and the abstract, the literal and the figurative, the near at hand and the absent or intangible. Our selections from Vaughan and Emerson proceed largely by metaphor; some equivalence is asserted so that the idea stated abstractly by Wordsworth can be dramatized by visible, palpable objects, some of whose qualities are shared by the abstraction. Though by no means superior to the Wordsworth extract as poetry, these passages do use the commoner, more characteristic method of indirection.

## 4. ALLEGORY

When a metaphor is much extended, and especially when the poet develops a narrative out of its parts, we call the story an *allegory*. In an earlier section we examined Ralegh's "What Is Our Life?" as an example of extended metaphor. That ingenious little poem falls short of allegory only by a lack of narrative. Matthew Arnold's "To Marguerite" is clearly also an extended metaphor, which, since it contains a stronger narrative element than the Ralegh poem does, is closer to allegory:

### To Marguerite

Yes! in the sea of life enisled,
With echoing straits between us thrown,
Dotting the shoreless watery wild,
We mortal millions live *alone*.
The islands feel the enclasping flow,
And then their endless bounds they know.

But when the moon their hollows lights,
And they are swept by balms of spring,
And in their glens, on starry nights,
The nightingales divinely sing;
And lovely notes, from shore to shore,
Across the sounds and channels pour—

Oh! then a longing like despair
Is to their farthest caverns sent;
For surely once, they feel, we were
Parts of a single continent!
Now round us spreads the watery plain—
Oh might our marges meet again!

*10*

Who ordered, that their longing's fire
Should be, as soon as kindled, cooled?                    20
Who renders vain their deep desire?—
A God, a God their severance ruled!
And bade betwixt their shores to be
The unplumbed, salt, estranging sea.

The opening lines establish the main metaphor of which all the others are parts:
life is represented by a sea. The human race is represented by islands separated
by the "unplumbed, salt, estranging sea." (Compare this idea with John Donne's
"No man is an island.") Our moments of joy are balmy spring nights. Our inter-
mittent communications are the distant songs of nightingales. In our original
united condition we were an unbroken continent. (Compare with Vaughan's
"The Waterfall" and Christopher Pearse Cranch's "Enosis.")

What qualities of this poem mark it as allegorical? First, it is a fabric of con-
sistently related metaphors connected into a narrative. The secondary terms of
these metaphors—the concrete, literal objects (sea; islands) that stand for
abstract or undepicted things (life; human beings)—are called *allegorical signs*.
Second, the relationship between each allegorical sign and the thing it signifies is
arbitrary: islands bear no very close actual resemblance to people; there is no
natural relationship between them. Third, each of the allegorical signs has but a
single significance, even though a number of them (moon; balms of spring;
nightingales) evoke a cluster of emotions. Allegory, even though highly elaborated
into a very long narrative furnished with many characters and incidents as in
*The Faerie Queene*, still retains these characteristics.

## 5. SYMBOL

Still another way of embodying meaning is the *symbol*. In the broadest sense,
a symbol is any thing that stands for something else. In this very general way any
thing that is of interest chiefly to the extent that it represents some single, un-
complicated idea can be called a symbol, so that the term sometimes is used to
include allegorical signs, all words, red lights that signify "stop," or asterisks
that say "Look at the bottom of the page." Actually such things are more properly
designated *signs*. *Symbol* can then be reserved for an object, an action, a situation,
or a verbal formula that represents the complexity of an abstraction, an unseen
object, an unfamiliar object, or any phenomenon so vast or complex that it
cannot be dealt with directly or literally:

### The Sick Rose

O rose, thou art sick!
The invisible worm
That flies in the night.
In the howling storm,

Has found out thy bed
Of crimson joy,
And his dark secret love
Does thy life destroy.

The symbol will usually evoke emotions appropriate to the symbolized thing, and
it will in various contexts suggest varying aspects of the thing represented, or

even signify different things. In addition, the symbol will have some kind of natural relationship to the thing it stands for. It can be a representative example of a large group so that, for example, a particular soldier might symbolize all fighting men. It can embody many characteristics of what it represents: the rose as a symbol of beauty is itself beautiful, and it is also fragile, transient, and without utility; a circle may symbolize wholeness or unity, for it is itself whole and unified. The symbol can be closely associated with the history of what it stands for: the cross was the object actually used for the crucifixion of Christ, and it has come to symbolize all things related to Christianity—not only the suffering of Christ, but also the history of the religion, the company of believers, and the doctrines of Christianity. (The cross may also be used as a sign to mark a church building, either in actuality or on a map; in the form of a lapel button it may be a sign identifying a Christian. Though thus used as a sign, it may also still operate as a symbol to the extent that it represents the complex, unseen things we have listed.) Finally, the symbol usually stands for several things, which may or may not be related. While we can identify the several referents of the symbol, we cannot wholly elucidate its complex meaning, so that to an extent the symbol is the only way of expressing what it symbolizes.

Clearly the symbol, like the allegorical sign, is a kind of metaphor in associating two things generally unlike each other but sharing a number of important qualities. The symbol, as it appears in literature, usually stands for a thing un-named. The question becomes, then, how we know that an object, an action, a situation, or a verbal formula is a symbol, and how we know what it stands for. There has been a vast amount of quarreling over these questions in recent years among professional critics, so that the student need not grieve if he misses symbolic meanings or if he does not always agree with interpretations that are offered to him. Actually the disagreements of the critics are more spectacular and amusing than their agreements, so that the quarrels obscure the large areas of generally accepted theory and the large body of settled interpretation. One man's guess is not as good as another's, but we are dealing with a complex and difficult matter that in the nature of things can never be reduced to an exact science. There are some guides, though, that we can use to get us started toward the in-quisitive ingenuity of the practiced reader of poetry.

First, many objects have been used for so long and so consistently as symbols that we do well to be alert to symbolic possibilities wherever they occur. Life has been symbolized by roads, streams, and journeys so many times that it takes a really inventive mind to use such a symbol effectively; yet great writers repeatedly manage such a feat. The sea is sometimes used to represent the source of life, or life itself, or death, or the unconscious. The passage of day and night, or the progress of the seasons can represent the transience of human life. William Blake's "The Lamb" not only uses traditional associations of gentleness and innocence but also reminds us that the lamb is a symbol of Christ. All these things may become *public symbols,* for they are the common possession of most literate beings; they have been used by most nations and throughout history. Authors may also use *nonce* or *private symbols,* which occur uniquely in a single literary work, or only in their collected works, as William Butler Yeats uses the city of Byzantium to symbolize an ideal alternative to the actual modern world. Sometimes it is necessary to discover the significance of a symbol from sources outside the work itself, such as autobiography, letters, or prose works like Yeats's *A Vision,* but this necessity is really very rare. The work under examination will ordinarily tell us what we need to know. Sometimes the poet tells us what his symbol means, as Whitman does when he refers to his locomotive as "type of the modern." Even without such help, we recognize that William Blake in "The Tyger" uses a powerful and terrifying animal to represent all the malevolent forces of the universe. Thus the line "Did he who made the Lamb make thee?" asks whether the God who created the goodness of Christ also created evil.

Second, if an object is given great prominence, as by repetition at crucial points, we should suspect that it carries symbolic meaning. This observation is especially true if no other purpose can be attributed to the object. Good writers write less casually than they may seem to do; everything in a work is directed to some end. A difficulty here is that the truly effective literary artist usually accomplishes several ends with each move he makes. A well-assimilated symbol, then, will also advance the literal narrative, or create valuable atmosphere, and will probably not cry out for symbolic interpretation to justify its existence.

The final test of an interpretation of a piece of symbolism is that it legitimately illuminates the work. By "legitimately" we mean that the interpretation is founded solidly on evidence in the work and is not a ramshackle remodeling of the original structure, hanging over the void without a foundation. A sound interpretation carries conviction with it; it comports with good sense; it accounts for everything in the poem and requires nothing that is not either in the poem or clearly relevant to it.

## 6. ALLUSION

Another aspect of the content of poems is *allusion,* which may be defined as reference, without lengthy explanation, to literature, history, or current events. In these few lines of Emerson, we should recognize allusions by means of paraphrase to the proverbial expression "poor but proud," to the Declaration of Independence ("men are endowed by their Creator with certain unalienable rights"), and to "America" ("Long may our land be bright/With freedom's holy light"):

> I am not poor, but I am proud,
>     Of one inalienable right,
> Above the envy of the crowd,—
>     Thought's holy light.

Only when we recognize these allusions can we understand how Emerson is extending and altering the popular American credo. Similarly the last line of Frost's "Once by the Pacific" refers to the destruction of the world by saying, "Until God's last '*Put out the light*' is spoken." The quoted words are a paraphrase of "Let there be light"—the words that announced the creation. In addition, we are reminded that Othello says, "Put out the light, and then put out the light" shortly before he smothers Desdemona. Obviously the author assumes a certain range of knowledge in the reader or a willingness to acquire that knowledge. Usually the sources of allusion are fairly well known, and some are so frequently used that they would deserve study simply as sources even if they had not high interest or merit in themselves. World history, the Bible, classical mythology, and Shakespeare's works are among the most important sources of allusions. The reader can look up items that he recognizes as allusions important to the understanding of the work at hand. He can also remind himself that as he gains experience of both life and literature, he will be more richly rewarded by everything he reads. Alertness and a good memory help.

The effect of allusion is to reinforce and illustrate the writer's point. An allusion may, like a metaphor or simile, clarify the new and unfamiliar by relating it to something already present in the reader's experience. In addition, it may underscore the similarity of man's experience in various periods of history, so that when we speak of a modern gift as a Trojan horse, for example, we are reminded that deceit playing upon curiosity and covetousness has breached defences repeatedly through history. Finally, an allusion may enlarge the implications of a work of literature by annexing to it the significance of the work alluded to. In his "Ode: Inscribed to W. H. Channing" Emerson includes these lines:

> The over-god
> Who marries Right to Might,
> Who peoples, unpeoples,—
> He who exterminates
> Races by stronger races,
> Black by white faces,—
> Knows to bring honey
> Out of the lion;
> Grafts gentlest scion
> On pirate and Turk.                                    *10*

"Knows to bring honey/Out of the lion" alludes to a story in the fourteenth chapter of Judges in which Samson slays a lion and leaves it exposed to the sun. Returning a few days later, he finds that bees have built honeycomb in the rotting carcass. Emerson interprets this story to mean that God can produce nourishing sweetness out of corruption. Hence the evils mentioned in the preceding lines may be understood, in Emerson's optimistic philosophy, to be preludes to good—a point made clear by the Biblical allusion.

### 7. MYTHS AND ARCHETYPES

Finally, we should recognize the modern use of myth as a kind of amplified allusion. A *myth* is a narrative telling of the exploits of gods or heroes, or dramatizing a people's beliefs about such matters as the creation of the world, the nature of the universe, or the origins and destiny of a nation. The myth of Prometheus, for instance, tells us that man was made of earth, like the other animals, but that Prometheus stole fire from heaven and bestowed it upon man so that he could develop the useful arts and maintain his superiority over other creatures. This myth is not merely a fanciful tale, but a commentary on the nature of human beings, who are thus alleged to be compounded of beastlike flesh and a divine spirit—what Shakespeare called "the Promethean fire."

Poets may retell portions of the ancient myths as a basis for a vivid narrative, or they may reinterpret the myth, not so much to reconstruct what it meant to the society from which it arose (as an anthropologist or historian might do), as to embody a meaning for his own readers. Tennyson's "Ulysses" is a dramatic monologue which develops a character portrait of the Homeric hero based not so much on Homer's version of the character as on Tennyson's version of Victorian ideals. Shelley's *Prometheus Unbound* recreates the classic myth but also contains references to contemporary politics, science, and philosophy. The half dozen or more poems on nightingales included in this volume, particularly those by Sidney, Coleridge, and Ransom, show the varied ways in which the Philomela myth has been adapted to the interests of various ages by poets from the sixteenth century to the present. A few poets, including Blake and Yeats, have developed private mythologies, but most poets draw upon the public resources of world literature.

A retrospective view of world literature shows the frequent recurrence from the earliest times to the present of a number of themes, situations, narratives, and character types, usually rendered through dramatic symbols drawn from the author's own time. These repeated motifs are known as *archetypes*. C. G. Jung and his followers have offered the theory that archetypes recur to writers and readers over many generations because they embody ancient experiences of the race which survive in the racial memory or the collective unconscious. Opponents of this concept of an eternal underground oversoul do not deny the recurrence of archetypes or the strong emotional appeal they have to many readers, but they explain the recurrence as part of a consciously transmitted cultural tradition, or as repeatedly similar responses to inherent psychic needs or to enduring conditions in the social or natural environment. Prominent archetypes include, among others, the descent into Hades, the night journey, the search for a father, dying and rebirth, initiation, the Oedipus scenario, woman as earth goddess, the Satan-rebel figure, and the guilty wanderer telling his tale as expiation. Maud Bodkin points out in *Archetypal Patterns in Poetry* that the death-rebirth theme is common to Dante's *Divine Comedy,* Coleridge's "The Rime of the Ancient Mariner," T. S. Eliot's "The Waste Land," and many shorter poems. In "The Rime of the Ancient Mariner" this theme merges with those of the night journey, the guilty wanderer, and the relationship of heaven and hell. Joseph Campbell maintains, in *The Hero with a Thousand Faces,* that all of these themes are subsumed in the perilous quest. In this archetypal narrative a hero sets out to seek a prize (which may take the form of knowledge), undergoes dangers and trials, penetrates a stronghold with the aid of guides and protectors acquired on the journey, is tempted to remain in the other world of his quest, but usually returns to enlighten and serve his fellows.

Identification of an archetype permits the reader to recognize the total pattern of a poem so that many otherwise obscure details become meaningful. The scenic effects in Muir's "The Mythical Journey" begin to come clear when we see in the overall structure of the poem another version of the quest archetype. One caution is needed: In dealing with archetypes, as with myths and allusions, we must not assume that every recurrence of a familiar element will be just like every other, but must recognize the distinctive quality contributed to tradition by each new poet.

What we have said in these pages may look like a systematic formula for reading poetry. We hope, rather, that the suggestions made here will help you get started. Only your own skillful reading will permit you to gain insight, and consequently enjoyment, from poems that might otherwise elude you. No set of hints, no formula, is a substitute for your own experience with poetry. Some poems will speak to you at once with a clear and insistent voice; others will keep silent for a long time. The most important thing you can do is to read and listen. Trust the poet, but trust yourself too.

## For Further Reading

I. A. RICHARDS. *Practical Criticism: A Study of Literary Judgement*. London and New York, 1929, 1962. Harvest Books, HB–16.

DOUGLAS BUSH. *Mythology and the Renaissance Tradition in English Poetry*. London, 1932; New York, 1963. Norton Library, N–187.

F. R. LEAVIS. *New Bearings in English Poetry*. London, 1932; New York, 1950, Ann Arbor Paperbacks, AA–36.

ELIZABETH DREW. *Discovering Poetry*. New York, 1933, 1940. Norton Library, N–110.

MAUD BODKIN. *Archetypal Patterns in Poetry*. London, 1934, 1965. Oxford Paperbacks, No. 66.

DOUGLAS BUSH. *Mythology and the Romantic Tradition in English Poetry*. Cambridge, Mass., 1937, 1969. Norton Library, N–186.

CLEANTH BROOKS and ROBERT PENN WARREN. *Understanding Poetry*. New York, 1938, 1950, 1960.

JOHN CROWE RANSOM. *The World's Body*. New York, 1938, 1968.

CLEANTH BROOKS. *Modern Poetry and the Tradition*. Chapel Hill, N.C., 1939; New York, 1965. Galaxy Books, GB–150.

HORACE GREGORY and MARYA ZATURENSKA, *A History of American Poetry: 1900–1940*. New York, 1946, 1969.

DONALD A. STAUFFER. *The Nature of Poetry*. New York, 1946. Norton Library, N–167.

CLEANTH BROOKS. *The Well-Wrought Urn: Studies in the Structure of Poetry*. New York, 1947, 1964. Harvest Books, HB–11.

JOSEPH CAMPBELL. *The Hero with a Thousand Faces*. New York, 1949, 1968.

RANDALL JARRELL. *Poetry and the Age*. New York, 1953, 1955. Vintage Books, K–12.

JAMES R. KREUZER. *Elements of Poetry*. New York, 1955.

M. L. ROSENTHAL and A. J. M. SMITH. *Exploring Poetry*. New York, 1955, 1973.

MURRAY KRIEGER. *The New Apologists for Poetry*. Minneapolis, 1956. Midland Books, MB–49.

ROY HARVEY PEARCE. *The Continuity of American Poetry*. Princeton, 1961.

JOSEPH M. KUNTZ. *Poetry Explication: A Checklist of Interpretation Since 1925 of British and American Poems Past and Present*. Denver, 1962. Swallow Paperbook.

ALEX PREMINGER, ed. *Princeton Encyclopedia of Poetry and Poetics*. Princeton, 1965.

KARL SHAPIRO and ROBERT BEUM. *A Prosody Handbook*. New York, 1965.

HYATT H. WAGGONER. *American Poets: From the Puritans to the Present*. Boston, 1968.

HARVEY GROSS, ed. *The Structure of Verse: Modern Essays on Prosody*. Greenwich, Conn., 1966.

MORRIS HALLE and SAMUEL JAY KEYSER. *English Stress: Its Form, Its Growth, and Its Rôle in Verse*. New York, 1971.

WILLIAM K. WIMSATT, ed. *Versification: Major Language Types; Sixteen Essays*. New York, 1972.

# Poems

# The Middle Ages

## ANONYMOUS LYRICS

### Sumer Is Icumen In

*Sing cuccu nu!*[1] *Sing cuccu!*
*Sing cuccu! Sing cuccu nu!*

Sumer is icumen in,
  Lhude[2] sing cuccu;
Groweth sed and bloweth med[3]
  And springth the wde[4] nu.
    Sing cuccu!
Awe[5] bleteth after lomb,
  Lhouth[6] after calve cu;
Bulluc sterteth,[7] bucke verteth;[8]    *10*
  Murie[9] sing cuccu.
    Cuccu, cuccu,
  Wel singes thu, cuccu,
  Ne swik[10] thu naver nu.   (*c. 1240*)

### Ubi Sunt Qui Ante Nos Fuerunt?[1]

Were beth they biforen us weren,
Houndes ladden and havekes beren[2]
  And hadden feld and wode?
The riche levedies[3] in hoere bour,
That wereden gold in hoere tressour,[4]
  With hoere brightte rode?[5]

Eten and drounken, and maden hem glad;
Hoere lif was al with gamen ilad;[6]
  Men kneleden hem biforen;
They beren hem wel swithe heye;[7]    *10*

And, in a twincling of an eye,
  Hoere soules were forloren.[8]

Were is that lawing[9] and that song,
That trayling and that proude gong,[10]
  Tho havekes and tho houndes?
Al that joye is went away,
That wele is comen to "Weylaway!"—
  To manie harde stoundes.[11]

Hoere paradis they nomen[12] here,
And nou they lien in helle ifere;[13]
  The fuir hit brennes[14] hevere.[15]    *20*
Long is ay, and long is o,
Long is wy, and long is wo;
  Thennes[16] ne cometh they nevere.
              (*c. 1275*)

### Jesu, Lord, Welcome Thou Be

Jesu, Lord, welcome thou be,
In form of bread as I thee see.
Jesu, for thine Holy Name,
Shield me today from sin and shame.
As thou were of a maide born,
Thou let me never be forlorn.
Ne let me never for no sinne
Lese[1] the joy that thou art inne.
Thou, rightwise King of all thing,
Grant me Shrifte, Housil[2] and good
  ending,           *10*
Right beleve beforn my ded day,
And blisse with thee that leste shall ay.

---

[1] now
[2] loudly. The final *e* here and elsewhere in Middle English is pronounced as an unaccented neutral vowel (approximately *uh*), so that such words as *wde*, *calve*, and *singes* have two syllables.
[3] mead, meadow    [4] wood    [5] ewe    [6] lows
[7] leaps    [8] breaks wind    [9] merrily    [10] cease

[1] Where Are Those Who Were Before Us?
[2] led hounds and bore hawks    [3] ladies
[4] tresses    [5] complexion    [6] led
[7] very high    [8] lost    [9] laughing    [10] going
[11] hours, times    [12] took    [13] together
[14] burns    [15] ever    [16] thence
[1] lose    [2] communion

## I Sing of a Maiden

I sing of a maiden
That is makeles:[1]
King of alle kinges
To her sone she ches.[2]

He cam also stille
There his moder was,
As dew in Aprille
That falleth on the grass.

He cam also stille
To his moderes bowr,                                    10
As dew in Aprille
That falleth on the flowr.

He cam also stille
There his moder lay,
As dew in Aprille
That falleth on the spray.

Moder and maiden
Was never non but she:
Well may swich[3] a lady
Godes moder be.                                         20

## Adam Lay I-bowndyn

Adam lay i-bowndyn,
    Bowndyn in a bond;
Fowre thowsand wynter
    Thowt he not to long;
And al was for an appil,
    An appil that he tok,
As clerkes[1] fyndyn wretyn
    In here[2] book.

Ne hadde the appil take ben,
    The appil taken ben,                                10
Ne hadde never our lady
    A ben hevene qwen.
Blyssid be the tyme
    That appil take was.
Therefore we mown[3] syngyn
    *Deo gracias.*

## I Have a Young Sister

I have a yong suster,
Fer beyonden the se;
Many be the drowryes[1]
That she sente me.

She sente me the cherry
Withouten ony stone;
And so she dede the dove
Withouten ony bone;

She sente me the brer[2]
Withouten ony rind;[3]                                  10
She bad me love my leman[4]
Withoute longing.

How should ony cherry
Be withoute stone?
And how should ony dove
Ben withoute bone?

How should ony brer
Ben withoute rind?
How should I love mine leman
Without longing?                                        20

When the cherry was a flower
Then hadde it non stone;
When the dove was an ey[5]
Then hadde it non bone.

When the brer was unbred[6]
Then hadde it non rind;
When the maiden hath that she loveth
She is without longing.

## Nay! Ivy, Nay!

    Nay! Ivy, nay!
    It shall not be, iwis:[1]
    Let Holly have the mastery,
    As the manner is.

Holly stond in the hall
Faire to behold:
Ivy stond without the dore—
She is full sore a-cold.

---

[1] unequalled; matchless    [2] chose    [3] such
[1] scholars    [2] their    [3] may
[1] tokens of love    [2] briar    [3] bark

[4] mistress    [5] egg    [6] unsprouted
[1] indeed

Holly and his merry men
They daunsen and they sing;                    10
Ivy and her maidenes
They wepen and they wring.[2]

Ivy hath a kibe—[3]
She caught it with the colde.
So mot they all have ay
That with Ivy holde.

Holly hath berries
As red as any rose:
The foster,[4] the hunters
Keep them from the does.                        20

Ivy hath berries
As black as any sloe:
There come the owle
And eat them as she go.

Holly hath birdes,
A full faire flock:
The nightingale, the poppinjay,[5]
The gentle laverock.[6]

Gode Ivy, gode Ivy,
What birdes hast thou?                          30
None but the owlet
That creye, "How! how!"

## Love Saint George

Enforce we us with all our might
To love Saint George, our Lady's knight.

Worship of virtue is the meed,
And seweth[1] him ay of right:
To worship George then have we need,
Which is our sovereign Lady's knight.

## Bring Us in Good Ale

Bring us in good ale, and bring us in good ale,
For our blessed Lady's sake, bring us in good ale.

Bring us in no brown bread, for that is made of brane,
Nor bring us in no white bread, for therein is no game;
But bring us in good ale.

He keped the maid from dragon's dread,
And fraid[2] all France and put to flight.
At Agincourt—the chronicle ye read—
The French him saw foremost in
        fight.                                   10

In his virtue he wol us lede
Against the fiend, the foul wight,[3]
And with his banner us oversprede,
If we him love with all our might.

## An Epitaph

All ye that pass by this holy place,
Both spiritual and temporal of every
        degree,
Remember yourself well during time and
        space:
I was as ye are now, and as I ye shall be.
Wherefore I beseech you, of your
        benignite,
For the love of Jesu and his mother
        Mare,
For my soul to say a Pater Noster and
        an Ave.

## Jesus' Wounds So Wide

Jesus' wounds so wide
Ben wells of life to the goode,
Namely the strond[1] of his side,
That ran full breme[2] on the Rode.[3]

Yif thee list to drinke,
To flee fro the fiends of helle,
Bow thou down to the brinke,
And meekly taste of the welle.

---

2 suffer      3 chilblain
4 forester     5 parrot      6 lark

1 follows      2 frightened    3 creature
1 stream       2 fiercely      3 cross

Bring us in no beef, for there is many bones;
But bring us in good ale, for that goth down at ones,
And bring us in good ale.

Bring us in no bacon, for that is passing fat;
But bring us in good ale, and give us enough of that,
And bring us in good ale.

Bring us in no mutton, for that is often lean,
Nor bring us in no tripes, for they be seldom clean;
But bring us in good ale.

Bring us in no egges, for there are many shelles,
But bring us in good ale, and give us nothing elles;
And bring us in good ale.

Bring us in no butter, for therein are many hairs,
Nor bring us in no pigges flesh, for that will make us boars;
But bring us in good ale.

Bring us in no puddings, for therein is all goats' blood,
Nor bring us in no venison, for that is not for our good;
But bring us in good ale.

Bring us in no capon's flesh, for that is often dear,
Nor bring us in duck's flesh, for they slobber in the meer;[1]
But bring us in good ale.

## Go! Heart, Hurt with Adversity

Go! heart, hurt with adversity,
And let my lady thy woundes see,
And say her this, as I say thee,
"Farewell! my joy, and welcome pain,
Till I see my lady again."

## I Must Go Walk the Wood So Wild

I must go walk the wood so wild
And wander here and there
In dread and deadly fear,

For where I trusted I am beguiled,
And all for one.

Thus am I banished from my bliss
By craft and false pretense,
Faultless, without offense,
As of return no certain[1] is,
And all for fear of one.

My bed shall be under the greenwood tree,
A tuft of brakes[2] under my head,
As one from joy were fled.
Thus from my life day by day I flee,
And all for one.

The running streams shall be my drink,
Acorns shall be my food.
Nothing may do me good,
But when of your beauty I do think,
And all for love of one.

---
[1] pond

---
[1] certainty    [2] ferns

## The Corpus Christi Carol

Lully, lulley, lully, lulley,
The faucon hath borne my make[1] away.
He bare him up, he bare him down,
He bare him into an orchard brown.
In that orchard there was an hall,
That was hanged with purple and pall.
And in that hall there was a bed,
It was hanged with gold so red.
And in that bed there lieth a knight,
His woundes bleeding day and night.     10

By that bedside kneeleth a may,[2]
But she weepeth both night and day.
And by that bedside there standeth a
   stone,
*Corpus Christi* written thereon.

## Western Wind

Western wind, when will thou blow,
The small rain down can rain?
Christ, if my love were in my arms
And I in my bed again!

# GEOFFREY CHAUCER / 1340?–1400

## Proem to Book II of *Troilus and Criseyde*

Owt of thise blake wawes for to saylle,
O wynd, o wynd, the weder gynneth clere;
For in this see the boot hath swych travaylle,
Of my connying,[1] that unneth[2] I it steere.
This see clepe[3] I the tempestous matere
Of disespeir that Troilus was inne;
But now of hope the kalendes[4] bygynne.

O lady myn, that called art Cleo,[5]
Thow be my speed fro this forth, and my Muse,
To ryme wel this book til I have do;[6]                    10
Me nedeth here noon other art to use.
Forwhi[7] to every lovere I me excuse,
That of no sentement I this endite,[8]
But out of Latyn[9] in my tonge it write.

Wherfore I nyl have neither thank ne blame
Of al this werk, but prey yow mekely,
Disblameth me, if any word be lame,
For as myn auctour seyde, so sey I.
Ek though I speeke of love unfeelyngly,
No wondre is, for it nothyng of newe is;                  20
A blynd man kan[10] nat juggen[11] wel in hewis.[12]

---

[1] mate    [2] maid

---

[1] because of my (lack of) skill
[2] with difficulty    [3] call
[4] first of the month; hence, beginning
[5] Clio, the muse of history    [6] done

[7] wherefore    [8] write; here, compose originally
[9] Chaucer appears actually to have followed chiefly Italian sources.    [10] knows how
[11] to judge    [12] colors

Ye knowe ek that in forme of speche is chaunge
Withinne a thousand yeer, and wordes tho
That hadden pris,[13] now wonder nyce[14] and straunge
Us thinketh hem, and yet thei spake hem so,
And spedde[15] as wel in love as men now do;
Ek for to wynnen love in sondry ages,
In sondry londes, sondry ben usages.

And forthi if it happe in any wyse,
That here by any lovere in this place
That herkneth, as the storie wol devise,[16]                    *30*
How Troilus com to his lady[17] grace,
And thenketh, "so nold[18] I nat love purchace,"
Or wondreth on his speche or his doynge,
I noot; but it is me no wonderynge.

For every wight which that to Rome went
Halt nat o[19] path, or alwey o manere;
Ek in some lond were al the game shent,[20]
If that they ferde[21] in love as men don here,
As thus, in opyn doyng or in chere,[22]                         *40*
In visityng, in forme,[23] or seyde hire sawes;[24]
Forthi[25] men seyn, ecch contree hath his lawes.

Ek scarsly ben ther in this place thre
That have in love seid lik, and don, in al;[26]
For to thi[27] purpos this may liken[28] the,
And the right nought;[29] yet al is seid or schal;[30]
Ek som men grave[31] in tree, some in ston wal,
As it bitit;[32] but syn I have bigonne,
Myn auctour shal I folwen, if I konne.   (*c. 1385*)

# To Rosemounde

Madame, ye ben of alle beauté shryne
As fer as cercled is the mapemounde,[1]
For as the cristal glorious ye shyne,
And lyke ruby ben your chekes rounde.
Therewith ye ben so mery and so jocounde
That at a revel what that I see you
　　daunce,
It is an oynement unto my wounde,
Thogh ye to me ne do no daliaunce.[2]

For thogh I wepe of teres ful a tyne[3]
Yet may that wo myn herte nat
　　confounde;                               *10*
Your seemly voys, that ye so smal
　　outtwyne,[4]
Maketh me thoght in joye and blis
　　habounde.
So curtaysly I go, with love bounde,
That to myself I sey, in my penaunce,
"Suffyseth[5] me to love you, Rosemounde,
Thogh ye to me ne do no daliaunce."

---

13 esteem　　14 foolish　　15 succeeded
16 relate　　17 lady's　　18 ne wold, would not
19 one　　20 spoiled　　21 proceeded
22 good humor　　23 formality　　24 sayings
25 therefore
26 spoken alike and done (alike) in everything

27 thy　　28 please, suit　　29 not at all
30 shall (be said)　　31 engrave　　32 betideth
1 world map　　2 flirting, caressing
3 tun, large wine cask　　4 utter
5 (it) suffices

Nas nevere pyk[6] walwed[7] in galauntyne[8]  
As I in love am walwed and ywounde,  
For which ful ofte I of myself devyne  
That I am trewe Tristam the secounde. *20*  
My love may not refreyd[9] be nor  
　affounde;[10]

I brenne ay in an amorous plesaunce.  
Do what you lyst, I wyl your thral be  
　founde,  
Thogh ye to me ne do no daliaunce.  

　　　　　　　　　　　　　　*(c. 1385)*

## Lak of Stedfastnesse

Somtyme this world was so stedfast and stable  
That mannes word was obligacioun;  
And now it is so fals and deceivable  
That word and werk, as in conclusioun,  
Ben nothing lyk, for turned up-so-doun  
Is al this world for mede[1] and wilfulnesse,  
That al is lost for lak of stedfastnesse.  

What maketh this world to be so variable  
But lust[2] that folk have in dissensioun?  
For among us now a man is holde unable,     *10*  
But if he can, by som collusioun,  
Don his neighbour wrong or oppressioun.  
What causeth this but wilful wrecchednesse,  
That al is lost for lak of stedfastnesse?  

Trouthe is put doun, resoun is holden fable;  
Vertu hath now no dominacioun;  
Pitee exyled, no man is merciable;  
Through covetyse is blent[3] discrecioun.  
The world hath mad a permutacioun  
Fro right to wrong, fro trouthe to fikelnesse,     *20*  
That al is lost for lak of stedfastnesse.  

### LENVOY TO KING RICHARD

O prince, desyre for to be honourable,  
Cherish thy folk and hate extorcioun!  
Suffre nothing that may be reprevable[4]  
To thyn estat don in thy regioun.  
Shew forth thy swerd of castigacioun,  
Dred God, do law, love trouthe and worthinesse,  
And wed thy folk agein to stedfastnesse.  

## The Compleint of Chaucer to His Empty Purse

To you, my purse, and to non other wight  
Compleyne I, for ye be my lady dere!  
I am so sorry, now that ye be light;  

For certes, but ye make hevy chere,  
Me were as leef by leyd up-on my bere;  
For whiche un-to your mercy thus I crye:  
Beth hevy ageyn, or elles mot I dye!  
Now voucheth sauf this day, or[1] hit be  
　night,  

---

6 pike, a fish    7 wallowed  
8 a sauce    9 cooled    10 perish  
1 gain    2 desire

3 blinded    4 deserving of reproof, discreditable  
1 ere

That I of you the blisful soun may here,
Or see your colour lyk the sonne
    bright,       10
That of yelownesse hadde never pere.
Ye be my lyf, ye be myn hertes stere,[2]
Quene of comfort and of good companye:
Beth hevy ageyn, or elles mot I dye!

Now purs, that be to me my lyves light,
And saveour, as doun in this worlde here,
Out of this toune help me through your
    might,

Sin that ye wole nat been my tresorere;
For I am shave as ny as any frere.
But yit I pray un-to your curtesye:    20
Beth hevy ageyn, or elles mot I dye!

### LENVOY DE CHAUCER

O conquerour of Brutes Albioun!
Which that by lyne[3] and free eleccioun
Ben verray king, this song to you I sende;
And ye, that mowen al our harm
    amende,
Have minde up-on my supplicacioun!

## *from* The Canterbury Tales

### THE GENERAL PROLOGUE

Whan that Aprille with his shoures soote[1]
The droghte of March hath perced to the rote,
And bathed every veyne in swich licour[2]
Of which vertu[3] engendred is the flour;
Whan Zephirus eek with his swete breeth
Inspired hath in every holt and heeth
The tendre croppes, and the yonge sonne
Hath in the Ram[4] his halve cours yronne,
And smale foweles maken melodye,
That slepen al the nyght with open ye    10
(So priketh[5] hem nature in hir corages):[6]
Than longen folk to goon on pilgrymages,
And palmers for to seken straunge strondes,
To ferne halwes,[7] kouthe[8] in sondry londes;
And specially from every shires ende
Of Engelond to Caunterbury they wende,
The holy blisful martir[9] for to seke,
That hem hath holpen whan that they were seke.

Bifel that, in that seson on a day,
In Southwerk at the Tabard as I lay    20
Redy to wenden on my pilgrimage
To Caunterbury with ful devout corage,
At nyght was come into that hostelrye
Wel nyne and twenty in a companye,
Of sondry folk, by aventure[10] yfalle
In felaweshipe, and pilgrymes were they alle,
That toward Caunterbury wolden ryde.
The chambres and the stables weren wyde,

---

[2] star    [3] line; i.e., by hereditary right
[1] sweet    [2] such moisture    [3] power
[4] Aries, the constellation in the Zodiac through
which the sun travels from March 21 to April 19

[5] influences    [6] feelings
[7] distant hallowed places, shrines    [8] known
[9] St. Thomas à Becket    [10] by chance

And wel we weren esed atte beste.[11]
And shortly, whan the sonne was to reste,                    30
So hadde I spoken with hem everichon,
That I was of hir felaweshipe anon,
And made forward erly for to ryse,
To take our wey there as I yow devyse.[12]

But natheles, whil I have tyme and space,
Er that I ferther in this tale pace,
Me thynketh it acordant to resoun
To telle yow al the condicioun
Of ech of hem, so as it semed me,
And whiche they weren, and of what degree,          40
And eek in what array that they were inne:
And at a knight than wol I first biginne.

A Knight ther was, and that a worthy man,
That fro the tyme that he first bigan
To riden out, he loved chivalrye,
Trouthe and honour, fredom[13] and curteisye.
Ful worthy was he in his lordes werre,
And ther-to hadde he riden, no man ferre,[14]
As wel in Christendom as in hethenesse,
And ever honoured for his worthynesse.               50
At Alisaundre he was whan it was wonne.
Ful ofte tyme he hadde the bord bigonne[15]
Aboven alle nacions in Pruce.[16]
In Lettow[17] hadde he reysed and in Ruce,[18]
No Cristen man so ofte of his degree.
In Gernade at the seege eek hadde he be
Of Algezir, and riden in Belmarye.
At Lyeys was he and at Satalye,
Whan they were wonne; and in the Grete See[19]
At many a noble armee hadde he be.                   60
At mortal batailles hadde he been fiftene,
And foghten for our feith at Tramyssene[20]
In lystes thries, and ay slayn his foo.
This ilke worthy knight hadde been also
Som-tyme with the lord of Palatye,
Agayn another hethen in Turkye.
And evere-moore he hadde a sovereyn prys;[21]
And though that he were worthy, he was wys,
And of his port as meke as is a mayde.
He nevere yet no vileynye ne sayde                   70
In al his lyf un-to no manner wight.
He was a verray[22] parfit gentil knight.

---

[11] entertained in the best possible manner
[12] narrate   [13] liberality   [14] farther
[15] sat at the head of the table   [16] Prussia
[17] Lithuania   [18] Russia   [19] the Mediterranean

[20] Granada, Algeciras, Benmarin, Lyas, Atalia'
Tlemcen; sites of fourteenth-century battles
[21] worth   [22] true

But for to tellen yow of his array,
Hise hors were goode, but he was nat gay.[23]
Of fustian he wered a gypoun[24]
Al bismotered with his habergeoun,[25]
For he was late ycome from his viage,
And wente for to doon his pilgrymage.

With hym ther was his sone, a young Squyer,
A lovere and a lusty bachelor,                            *80*
With lokkes crulle,[26] as they were leyd in presse.
Of twenty yeer of age he was, I gesse.
Of his stature he was of evene lengthe,
And wonderly delyvere,[27] and of greet strengthe.
And he hadde been som-tyme in chivachye[28]
In Flaundres, in Artoys, and Picardye,
And born hym wel, as of so litel space,[29]
In hope to stonden in his lady grace.
Embrouded was he, as it were a meede
Al ful of fresshe floures, white and reede.            *90*
Syngynge he was, or floytynge,[30] al the day;
He was as fressh as is the monthe of May.
Short was his gowne, with sleves longe and wyde.
Wel koude he sitte on hors and faire ryde.
He koude songes make and wel endite,
Juste and eek daunce, and wel purtreye and write,
So hoote he lovede, that by nyghtertale
He slepte namoore than dooth a nyghtyngale.
Curteys he was, lowely, and servysable,
And carf biforn his fader at the table.                *100*

A Yeman hadde he and servants namo
At that tyme, for hym liste ryde so;
And he was clad in coote and hood of grene.
A sheef of pecok arwes bright and kene
Under his belt he bar ful thriftily,
(Wel koude he dresse his takel yemanly:[31]
His arwes drouped noght with fetheres lowe),
And in his hand he bar a myghty bowe.
A not[32] heed had he, with a broun visage.
Of wodecraft wel koude he al the usage.                *110*
Upon his arm he bar a gay bracer,
And by his syde a swerd and a bokeler,
And on that oother syde a gay daggere,
Harneysed[33] wel and sharp as poynt of spere,
A Cristofre[34] on his brest of silver shene.

---

[23] showy    [24] vest
[25] stained from contact with his coat of mail
[26] curled    [27] agile    [28] cavalry attacks
[29] considering his short apprenticeship
[30] playing the flute

[31] prepare his equipment in a yeomanly manner
[32] cropped    [33] sheathed
[34] an image of St. Christopher, patron saint of foresters

An horn he bar, the bawdryk [35] was of grene;
A forster was he, soothly, as I gesse.

Ther was also a nonne, a Prioresse,
That of hir smylyng was ful symple and coy;
Hir gretteste ooth was but by Seint Loy;                        *120*
And she was cleped [36] Madame Eglentyne.
  Ful wel she soong the servyce dyvyne,
Entuned in hir nose ful semely,
And Frensh she spak ful faire and fetisly, [37]
After the scole of Stratford-atte-Bowe, [38]
For Frensch of Parys was to hire unknowe.
  At mete wel ytaught was she with alle:
She let no morsel from hir lippes falle,
Ne wette hir fyngres in hir sauce depe.
Wel koude she carie a morsel and wel kepe                        *130*
That no drope ne fille up-on hir brest.
In curteisie was set ful muche hir lest. [39]
  Hir over lippe wyped she so clene
That in hir coppe ther was no ferthyng [40] sene
Of grece, whan she dronken hadde hir draughte.
Ful semely after hir mete she raughte. [41]
And sikerly [42] she was of greet desport, [43]
And ful plesaunt, and amyable of port,
And peyned hire to countrefete cheere
Of court, [44] and to been estatlich of manere,                  *140*
And to been holden digne of reverence.
  But, for to speken of hir conscience,
She was so charitable and so pitous
She wolde wepe, if that she saw a mous
Caught in a trappe, if it were deed or bledde.
Of smale houndes hadde she, that she fedde
With rosted flessh, or mylk and wastel breed.
But soore wept she if oon of hem were deed,
Or if men [45] smoot it with a yerde [46] smerte; [47]
And al was conscience and tendre herte.                          *150*
  Ful semely hir wympel pynched [48] was;
Hir nose tretys, [49] hir eyen greye as glas,
Hir mouth ful smal, and ther-to softe and reed;
But sikerly she hadde a fair forheed:
It was almoost a spanne brood, I trowe;
For, hardily, she was nat undergrowe.
Ful fetys was hir cloke, as I was war.
Of smal coral aboute hir arm she bar

---

[35] strap by which the horn was slung
[36] called   [37] fastidiously
[38] the inferior French of an English nunnery
[39] she greatly esteemed good deportment
[40] bit   [41] reached   [42] certainly

[43] good humor
[44] took pains to imitate courtly manners
[45] one   [46] stick   [47] smartly   [48] pleated
[49] well-formed

A peyre of bedes, gauded al with grene,
And there-on heng a brooch of gold ful shene,                    *160*
On which ther was first writ a crowned A,
And after *Amor vincit omnia.*[50]
  Another Nonne with hire hadde she,
That was hir chapeleyne, and preestes thre.

  A Monk ther was, a fair for the maistrye,[51]
An outridere,[52] that lovede venerye,[53]
A manly man, to been an abbot able.
Ful many a deyntee hors hadde he in stable,
And whanne he rood, men myghte his brydel heere
Gynglen in a whistlynge wynd as cleere,                          *170*
And eek as loude, as dooth the chapel belle,
Ther-as this lord was kepere of the celle.
  The reule of Seint Maure or of Seint Beneit,
By cause that it was old and somdel streit,[54]—
This ilke Monk leet olde thynges pace,
And heeld after the newe world the space.[55]
He yaf nat of that text a pulled hen,
That seith that hunters been nat holy men,
Ne that a monk whan he is recchelees,
Is likned til a fissh that is waterlees—                         *180*
This is to seyn, a monk out of his cloystre;
But thilke text heeld he nat worth an oystre,
And I seyde his opinion was good.
What sholde he studie and make hym-selven wood,[56]
Upon a book in cloystre alwey to poure,
Or swynken[57] with his handes, and laboure,
As Austin[58] bit? How shal the world be served?
Lat Austyn have his swynk to hym reserved!
Therefore he was a prikasour[59] aright;
Grehoundes he hadde, as swift as fowel in flight;               *190*
Of prikyng[60] and of huntyng for the hare
Was al his lust, for no cost wolde he spare.
  I seigh his sleves purfiled[61] at the hond
With grys,[62] and that the fyneste of a lond;
And, for to festne his hood under his chyn,
He hadde of gold y-wrought a curious pyn;
A love knotte in the gretter ende ther was.
His heed was balled, that shoon as any glas,
And eek his face, as he hadde been enoynt.
He was a lord ful fat and in good poynt;                         *200*
Hise eyen stepe,[63] and rollynge in his heed,
That stemed as a forneys of a leed;[64]

---

[50] love conquers all
[51] extremely; hence, a very good monk
[52] inspector of the monastery's estates
[53] hunting    [54] somewhat strict
[55] meanwhile    [56] mad    [57] toil

[58] St. Augustine    [59] mounted hunter
[60] riding    [61] bordered    [62] costly gray fur
[63] his eyes were prominent
[64] gleamed like the fire under a cauldron

His bootes souple, his hors in greet estat.
    Now certeynly he was a fair prelat;
He was nat pale as a forpyned[65] goost.
A fat swan loved he best of any roost.
His palfrey was as broun as is a berye.

    A Frere ther was, a wantowne[66] and a merye,
A lymytour,[67] a ful solempne man.
In alle the ordres foure is noon that kan[68]                    *210*
So muche of daliaunce and fair langage.
He hadde maad ful many a mariage
Of yonge wommen at his owene cost.
    Un-to his ordre he was a noble post.
Ful wel biloved and famulier was he
With frankeleyns[69] over al in his contree,
And eek with worthy wommen of the toun;
For he hadde power of confessioun,
As seyd hym-self, moore than a curat,
For of his ordre he was licenciat.                              *220*
Ful swetely herde he confessioun,
And plesaunt was his absolucioun;
He was an esy man to yeve[70] penaunce,
Ther-as he wiste[71] to have a good pitaunce.[72]
For un-to a poure ordre for to yive
Is signe that a man is wel yshryve;
For if he yaf, he dorste make avaunt,[73]
He wiste that a man was repentaunt;
For many a man so hard is of his herte,
He may not wepe, al-thogh hym soore smerte.                     *230*
Ther-fore in stede of wepynge and preyeres,
Men moote yeve silver to the poure freres.
    His typet[74] was ay farsed[75] ful of knyves
And pynnes, for to yeven faire wyves.
And certeynly he hadde a murye note;
Wel koude he synge and pleyen on a rote;[76]
Of yeddynges[77] he bar outrely[78] the prys.
His nekke whit was as the flour de lys;
Ther-to he strong was as a champioun.
    He knew the tavernes wel in every toun,                     *240*
And every hostiler and tappestere[79]
Bet than a lazar[80] or a beggestere;[81]
For un-to swich a worthy man as he
Accorded nat, as by his facultee,
To have with sike lazars aqueyntaunce.
It is nat honeste,[82] it may not avaunce[83]

---

[65] wasted away
[66] gay, and perhaps also licentious
[67] a friar privileged to beg in a specified area
[68] knew     [69] rural gentry     [70] give
[71] knew how     [72] gift     [73] boast     [74] cape

[75] always stuffed     [76] a stringed instrument
[77] songs or ballads     [78] utterly     [79] barmaid
[80] leper     [81] female beggar     [82] respectable
[83] be profitable

For to deelen with no swich poraille,[84]
But al with riche and selleres of vitaille.
And over-al, ther as profit shoulde arise,
Curteys he was and lowely of servyse.                                    *250*
Ther was no man no wher so vertuous.
He was the beste beggere in his hous,
For thogh a wydwe hadde noght a sho,[85]
So plesant was his *In principio*,
Yet wolde he have a ferthyng, er he wente.
His purchas[86] was wel bettre than his rente.[87]
And rage he koude, as it were right[88] a whelpe.
    In lovedayes[89] ther koude he muchel helpe:
For ther he was nat lyk a cloysterer
With a tredbare cope, as is a povre scoler,                              *260*
But he was lyk a maister or a pope.
Of double worstede was his semycope,
That rounded as a belle out of the presse.
    Somewhat he lipsed, for his wantownesse,
To make his English sweete up-on his tonge;
And in his harpyng, whan that he hadde songe,
Hise eyen twynkled in his heed aright,
As doon the sterres in the frosty nyght.
This worthy lymytour was cleped Huberd.

    A Marchant was ther with a forked berd,                             *270*
In mottelee, and hye on hors he sat,
Up-on his heed a Flaundrysh bevere hat,
His bootes clasped faire and fetisly.
    Hise resons[90] he spak ful solempnely,
Sownynge[91] alwey th' encrees of his wynnyng.
He wolde the see were kept for any thyng
Bitwixe Middelburgh and Orewelle.[92]
Wel koude he in eschaunge sheeldes[93] selle.
    This worthy man ful wel his wit bisette:
Ther wiste no wight that he was in dette,                                *280*
So estatly was he of his governaunce,
With his bargaynes and with his chevysaunce.[94]
    For sothe he was a worthy man with alle,
But, sooth to seyn, I noot[95] how men hym calle.

    A Clerk ther was of Oxenford also,
That un-to logyk hadde longe ygo.
    As leene was his hors as is a rake,
And he nas nat right fat, I undertake,

---

[84] poor rabble     [85] shoe
[86] graft     [87] legitimate income     [88] as befits
[89] days designated for the general settlement of
disputes     [90] opinions     [91] relating to
[92] a Dutch and an English port on the Channel

important to trade with the Continent
[93] French coins, legally handled for profit only by
Royal money changers
[94] business dealings, probably illicit
[95] ne wot, know not

But looked holwe, and ther-to sobrely.
Ful thredbare was his overest courtepy;[96]                          *290*
For he hadde geten hym yet no benefice,
Ne was so worldly for to have office.
For hym was levere[97] have at his beddes heed
Twenty bookes, clad in blak or reed,
Of Aristotle and his philosophie,
Than robes riche, or fithele, or gay sautrie.[98]
   But al be that he was a philosophre,[99]
Yet hadde he but litel gold in cofre;
But al that he myghte of his frendes hente,[100]
On bookes and on lernynge he it spente,                            *300*
And bisily gan for the soules preye
Of hem that yaf hym wher-with to scoleye.[101]
   Of studie took he moost cure and moost heede,
Noght oo word spak he moore than was neede,
And that was seid in forme and reverence,
And short and quyk and ful of heigh sentence.[102]
Sownynge in moral vertu was his speche,
And gladly wolde he lerne and gladly teche.

   A Sergeant of the Lawe, war and wys,[103]
That often hadde been at the parvys,[104]                           *310*
Ther was also, ful riche of excellence.
Discreet he was and of greet reverence—
He seemed swich, hise wordes weren so wyse.
   Justice he was ful often in assise,
By patente and by pleyn commissioun.
For his science and for his heigh renoun,
Of fees and robes hadde he many oon.
So greet a purchasour was nowher noon;
Al was fee symple to hym in effect,
His purchasyng myghte nat been infect.[105]                        *320*
   Nowher so bisy a man as he ther nas,
And yet he semed bisier than he was.
   In termes hadde he caas and doomes[106] alle,
That from the tyme of Kyng William were falle.
Ther-to he koude endite, and make a thyng,[107]
Ther koude no wight pynche[108] at his writyng;
And every statut koude he pleyn by roote.[109]
   He rood but hoomly in a medlee coote,
Girt with a ceynt[110] of silk, with barres smale;
Of his array telle I no lenger tale.                               *330*

---

[96] outermost jacket    [97] he would rather
[98] fiddling, or gay music of the psaltery, a plucked or strummed stringed instrument
[99] a reference to Aristotle, but also to alchemists popularly called "philosophers," who attempted to turn base metals into gold    [100] get
[101] to turn scholar    [102] significance
[103] wary and wise

[104] the porch of St. Paul's, a meeting place of lawyers and their clients
[105] As a landbuyer, he gained outright title so that his possession could not be questioned.
[106] cases and judgments    [107] legal document
[108] object to
[109] knew clearly by its basic principles
[110] cincture, belt

A Frankeleyn was in his compaignye;
Whit was his berd as is the dayesye;
Of his complexioun he was sangwyn.[111]
Wel loved he by the morwe[112] a sop in wyn.
To lyven in delyt was evere his wone,[113]
For he was Epicurus owene sone,
That heeld opynyoun that pleyn delit
Was verray felicitee parfit.

An housholdere, and that a greet, was he;
Seint Julyan[114] he was in his contree.                                    340
His breed, his ale, was alweys after oon;[115]
A better envyned[116] man was nevere noon.
Without bake mete was nevere his hous,
Of fish and flesh, and that so plentevous,
It snewed in his hous of mete and drynke.
Of alle deyntees that men koude thynke
After the sondry sesons of the yeer,
So chaunged he his mete and his soper.
Ful many a fat partrich hadde he in muwe,[117]
And many a breem and many a luce in stuwe.[118]                              350
Wo was his cook, but if his sauce were
Poynaunt and sharp, and redy al his geere.
His table dormaunt[119] in his halle alway
Stood redy-covered al the longe day.

At sessions ther he was lord and sire;
Ful ofte tyme he was knight of the shire.
An anlaas[120] and a gipser[121] al of silk
Heeng at his girdel, whit as morne mylk.
A shirreve[122] hadde he been, and a contour;[123]
Was nowher swich a worthy vavasour.[124]                                     360

An Haberdassher and a Carpenter,
A Webbe,[125] a Dyere, and a Tapycer—[126]
And they were clothed alle in oo lyveree
Of a solempne and a greet fraternytee.
Ful fressh and newe hir geere apiked[127] was;
Hir knyves were chaped[128] noght with bras,
But al with silver; wrought ful clene and wel
Hir girdles and hir pouches everydel.
Wel semed ech of hem a fair burgeys
To sitten in a yeldehalle[129] on a deys.[130]                              370
Everych for the wisdom that he kan,
Was shaply for to been an alderman.

---

[111] ruddy, and hence of an optimistic temperament   [120] short dagger   [121] purse   [122] sheriff
[112] in the morning   [113] custom   [123] accountant
[114] patron saint of hospitality   [124] land holder below noble rank   [125] weaver
[115] uniformly good   [116] supplied with wine   [126] tapestry weaver   [127] ornamented
[117] mews, coop   [118] fishpond   [128] mounted
[119] fixed table, ready for company   [129] guildhall   [130] dais

For catel hadde they ynogh and rente,
And eek hir wyves wolde it wel assente;
And elles certeyn were they to blame:
It is ful fair to been ycleped madame,
And goon to vigilies al bifore,
And have a mantel royalliche ybore.

A Cook they hadde with hem for the nones,
To boille the chiknes with the marybones,                            *380*
And poudre marchaunt[131] tart, and galyngale.[132]
Wel koude he knowe a draughte of Londoun ale
He koude rooste, and sethe, and broille, and frye,
Maken mortreux,[133] and wel bake a pye.
But greet harm was it, as it thoughte me,
That on his shyne a mormal[134] hadde he,
For blankmanger[135] that made he with the beste.

A Shipman was ther, wonyng[136] fer by weste:
For aught I woot,[137] he was of Dertemouthe.
He rood upon a rouncy,[138] as he kouthe,[139]                       *390*
In a gowne of faldyng[140] to the knee.
A daggere hangynge on a laas[141] hadde he
Aboute his nekke, under his arm adoun.
The hoote somer had maad his hewe al broun.
And certeynly he was a good felawe;
Ful many a draughte of wyn hadde he drawe
Fro Burdeuxward, whil that the chapman sleep.
Of nyce conscience took he no keep.
If that he faught, and had the hyer hond,
By water he sente hem hoom to every lond.[142]                       *400*
But of his craft to rekene wel his tydes,
His stremes and his daungers hym bisydes,
His herberwe,[143] and his moone, his lodemenage,[144]
Ther nas noon swich from Hulle to Cartage.
Hardy he was, and wys to undertake;
With many a tempest hadde his berd been shake.
He knew alle the havenes, as they were,
Fro Gootland to the cape of Fynystere,
And every cryke in Britaigne and in Spayne.
His barge ycleped was the Mawdelayne.                               *410*

With us ther was a Doctour of Phisik;
In al this world ne was ther noon hym lyk,
To speke of phisik and of surgerye,
For he was grounded in astronomye.
He kepte his pacient[145] a ful greet deel
In houres by his magik natureel.

---

131 a flavoring powder     132 a spice
133 thick soup     134 a running sore
135 a creamed meat dish     136 dwelling
137 know     138 carthorse
139 as best he knew how     140 coarse wool

141 cord lace
142 made his victims walk the plank
143 harbors     144 navigation
145 performed treatment at the most propitious
hours, as determined by his science

Wel koude he fortunen the ascendent
Of his ymages for his pacient.
He knew the cause of every maladye,
Were it of hoot, or coold, or moyste, or drye,     *420*
And where engendred, and of what humour.
He was a verray, parfit practisour.
    The cause yknowe, and of his harm the rote,
Anon he yaf the sike man his boote.[146]
Ful redy hadde he hise apothecaries,
To sende hym drogges and his letuaries,[147]
For ech of hem made oother for to wynne:
Hir frendshipe nas nat newe to begynne.
    Wel knew he the olde Esculapius,
And Deïscorides, and eek Rufus,     *430*
Old Ypocras, Haly, and Galyen,
Serapion, Razis, and Avycen,
Averrois, Damascien, and Constantyn,
Bernard, and Gatesden, and Gilbertyn.
    Of his diete mesurable was he,
For it was of no superfluitee,
But of greet norissynge and digestible.
His studie was but litel on the Bible.
    In sangwyn[148] and in pers[149] he clad was al,
Lyned with taffata and with sendal;[150]     *440*
And yet he was but esy of dispence;[151]
He kepte that he wan in pestilence.
For gold in phisik is a cordial,
Therefore he loved gold in special.

    A good Wyf was ther of biside Bathe,
But she was somdel deef, and that was scathe.[152]
    Of clooth makyng she hadde swich an haunt,[153]
She passed hem of Ypres and of Gaunt.
In al the parisshe wyf ne was ther noon
That to the offrynge bifore hire sholde goon;     *450*
And if ther dide, certeyn so wrooth was she,
That she was out of alle charitee.
Hir coverchiefs ful fyne were of ground;[154]
I dorste swere they weyeden ten pound
That on a Sonday weren up-on hir heed.
Hir hosen weren of fyn scarlet reed,
Ful streite yteyd, and shoes ful moyste and newe.
Boold was hir face, and fair, and reed of hewe.
    She was a worthy womman al hir lyve;
Housbondes at chirche dore she hadde fyve,     *460*
With-outen oother[155] compaignye in youthe—
But ther-of nedeth nat to speke as nouthe.[156]

---

[146] help
[147] remedies    [148] blood-red    [149] blue
[150] thin silk    [151] slow to spend    [152] a pity
[153] skill    [154] texture
[155] without counting others    [156] at present

And thries hadde she been at Jerusalem;
She hadde passed many a straunge strem;
At Rome she hadde been, and at Boloyne,
In Galice at Seint Jame, and at Coloyne.
She koude muche of wandrynge by the weye.
Gat tothed[157] was she, soothly for to seye.
    Upon an amblere esily she sat,
Ywympled wel, and on hir heed an hat                            *470*
As brood as is a bokeler or a targe;
A foot mantel aboute hir hipes large,
And on hir feet a peyre of spores sharpe.
In felawshipe wel koude she laughe and carpe.[158]
Of remedies of love she knew par chaunce,
For she koude of that art the olde daunce.

    A good man was ther of religioun,
And was a poure Persoun[159] of a toun,
But rich he was of holy thoght and werk.
He was also a lerned man, a clerk,                              *480*
That Cristes gospel trewely wolde preche;
His parisshens devoutly wolde he teche.
Benygne he was, and wonder diligent,
And in adversitee ful pacient,
And swich he was y-preved ofte sithes.
    Ful looth were hym to cursen[160] for his tithes,
But rather wolde he yeven, out of doute,
Un-to his poure parisshens aboute
Of his offrynge and eek of his substaunce.
He koude in litel thyng have suffisaunce.                       *490*
Wyd was his parisshe, and houses fer asonder,
But he ne lafte nat, for reyn ne thonder,
In siknesse nor in meschief, to visite
The ferreste in his parisshe, muche and lite,[161]
Up-on his feet, and in his hond a staf.
This noble ensample to his sheep he yaf,
That first he wroghte, and afterward he taughte.
Out of the gospel he tho wordes caughte,
And this figure he added eek ther-to,
That if gold ruste, what sholde iren do?                        *500*
For if a preest be foule, on whom we truste,
No wonder is a lewed[162] man to ruste;
And shame it is, if a preest take keep,
A shiten shepherde and a clene sheep.
Wel oughte a preest ensample for to yive,
By his clennesse, how that his sheep sholde lyve.

---

157 with teeth widely spaced; hence supposedly     161 high as well as lowly
amorous      158 talk      159 parson                162 unlearned
160 recommend for excommunication

He sette nat his benefice to hyre,
And leet his sheep encombred in the myre,
And ran to Londoun, un-to Seint Poules,
To seken hym a chaunterie for soules,[163]     *510*
Or with a bretherhede[164] to been withholde;[165]
But dwelte at hoom, and kepte wel his folde,
So that the wolf ne made it nat myscarye;
He was a shepherde and noght a mercenarye.
And thogh he hooly were and vertuous,
He was noght to synful men despitous,
Ne of his speche daungerous ne digne,[166]
But in his techyng discreet and benigne.
To drawen folk to hevene by fairnesse,
By good ensample, this was his bisynesse,     *520*
But it were any persone obstinat,
What so he were, of heigh or lowe estat,
Hym wolde he snybben[167] sharply for the nonys.[168]
A bettre preest I trowe that nowher noon ys.
He wayted after no pompe and reverence,
Ne maked hym a spiced conscience,
But Cristes loore, and his apostles twelve,
He taughte, but first he folwed it hym-selve.

With him ther was a Plowman, was his brother,
That hadde y-lad[169] of dong ful many a fother.[170]     *530*
A trewe swynkere[171] and a good was he,
Lyvynge in pees and parfit charitee.
God loved he best with al his hoole herte
At alle tymes, though hym gamed or smerte,[172]
And thanne his neighebour right as hym-selve.
He wolde thresshe, and ther-to dyke and delve,
For Cristes sake, for every poure wight,
With-outen hire, if it lay in his myght.
His tithes payde he ful faire and wel,
Bothe of his propre swynk and his catel.     *540*
In a tabard he rood upon a mere.

Ther was also a Reve,[173] and a Millere,
A Somnour,[174] and a Pardoner,[175] also,
A Maunciple,[176] and my-self: ther were namo.

The Miller was a stout carl[177] for the nones,
Ful big he was of brawn, and eek of bones;
That proved wel, for over-al ther he cam,
At wrastlynge he wolde have alwey the ram.
He was short sholdred, brood, a thikke knarre;[178]

---

[163] a stipend for singing masses for the dead
[164] guild    [165] retained (as chaplain)
[166] arrogant nor disdainful    [167] rebuke
[168] indeed    [169] drawn    [170] load
[171] worker
[172] whether he was pleased or pained

[173] assistant to the steward of an estate
[174] police agent of an ecclesiastical court
[175] a peddler of Papal indulgences
[176] buyer of supplies for an inn of court
[177] churl, fellow    [178] gnarled fellow

Ther was no dore that he nolde heve of harre,[179]          *550*
Or breke it at a rennyng, with his heed.
His berd as any sowe or fox was reed,
And ther-to brood as though it were a spade.
Upon the cop[180] right of his nose he hade
A werte, and ther-on stood a tuft of herys,
Reed as the bristles of a sowes erys;
His nosethirles[181] blake were and wyde
A swerd and a bokeler bar he by his syde.
His mouth as greet was as a greet fourneys.
He was a jangler[182] and a goliardeys,[183]               *560*
And that was moost of synne and harlotries.
Wel koude he stelen corn and tollen thries;[184]
And yet he hadde a thombe of gold, pardee.
A whit cote and a blew hood wered hee.
A baggepipe wel koude he blowe and sowne,
And therwithal he broghte us out of towne.

A gentil Maunciple was ther of a temple,
Of which achatours[185] myghte take exemple
For to be wys in byynge of vitaille;
For wheither that he payde or took by taille,[186]         *570*
Algate he wayted so in his achaat,[187]
That he was ay biforn and in good staat.
Now is nat that of God a ful fair grace
That swich a lewed mannes wit shal pace
The wisdom of an heep of lerned men?
Of maistres hadde he mo than thries ten,
That weren of lawe expert and curious,[188]
Of whiche ther were a dozeyne in that hous
Worthy to been stywardes of rente and lond
Of any lord that is in Engelond,                          *580*
To make hym lyve by his propre good,
In honour detteles, but he were wood,[189]
Or lyve as scarsly as hym list desire;
And able for to helpen al a shire
In any caas that myghte falle or happe;
And yet this Maunciple sette hir aller cappe.[190]

The Reve was a sclendre, colerik man.
His berd was shave as neigh as ever he kan;
His heer was by his erys ful round yshorn;
His top was dokked lyk a preest byforn.                   *590*
Ful longe were his legges and ful lene,
Ylik a staf ther was no calf ysene.
Wel koude he kepe a gerner[191] and a bynne;
Ther was noon auditour koude on hym wynne.

---

179 off hinge    180 top    181 nostrils       187 in every way he kept watch in his purchasing
182 prattler   183 coarse jokester             188 skillful    189 mad
184 charge three prices for grinding grain     190 made fools of them all
185 buyers    186 on credit                    191 garner, granary

Wel wiste he by the droghte and by the reyn
The yeldynge of his seed and of his greyn.
His lordes sheep, his neet,[192] his dayerye
His swyn, his hors, his stoor,[193] and his pultrye,
Was hoolly in this Reves governynge,
And by his covenant yaf the rekenynge,      *600*
Syn that his lord was twenty yeer of age.
Ther koude no man brynge hym in arrerage.
Ther nas baillif, ne hierde,[194] ne oother hyne,[195]
That he ne knew his sleighte and his covyne:[196]
They were adrad of hym as of the deeth.

His wonyng was ful faire upon an heeth,
With grene trees yshadwed was his place.
He koude bettre than his lord purchace.
Ful riche he was astored pryvely:
His lord wel koude he plesen subtilly,      *610*
To yeve and lene hym of his owene good,
And have a thank, and yet a coote and hood.

In youthe he hadde lerned a good myster:[197]
He was a wel good wrighte, a carpenter.

This Reve sat up-on a full good stot,[198]
That was al pomely[199] grey and highte[200] Scot.
A long surcote of pers up-on he hade,
And by his syde he baar a rusty blade.
Of Northfolk was this Reve of which I telle,
Biside a toun men clepen Baldeswelle.      *620*
Tukked he was as is a frere aboute,
And evere he rood the hyndreste of oure route.

A Somnour was ther with us in that place,
That hadde a fyr-reed cherubynnes face,
For saucefleem[201] he was, with eyen narwe.
As hoot he was and lecherous as a sparwe:
With scaled[202] browes blake, and piled[203] berd;
Of his visage children were aferd.
Ther nas quyk silver, lytarge, ne brymstoon,
Boras, ceruce, ne oille of tarte noon,      *630*
Ne oynement that wolde clense and byte,
That hym myghte helpen of his whelkes[204] white,
Nor of the knobbes sittynge on his chekes.

Wel loved he garlek, oynons, and eek lekes,
And for to drynke strong wyn, reed as blood.
Thanne woulde he speke and crye as he were wood;
And whan that he wel dronken hadde the wyn,
Thanne wolde he speke no word but Latyn.

---

192 cattle
193 store, stock, especially livestock
194 herdsman    195 servant    196 deceit
197 craft    198 stallion    199 dappled

200 was called    201 pimpled    202 scabby
203 thin, with hair falling out in patches
204 pimples

A fewe termes hadde he, two or thre,
That he had lerned out of some decre—  640
No wonder is: he herde it al the day—
And eek ye knowen wel how that a jay
Kan clepen "Watte" as wel as kan the pope.
But who so koude in oother thyng hym grope,[205]
Thanne hadde he spent al his philosophie;
Ay "*Questio quid juris*"[206] wolde he crie.

He was a gentil harlot[207] and a kynde;
A bettre felawe sholde men noght fynde.
He wolde suffre for a quart of wyn
A good felawe to have his concubyn  650
A twelf monthe, and excuse hym atte fulle.
Ful pryvely a fynch eek koude he pulle.[208]
And if he foond owher[209] a good felawe,
He wolde techen hym to have noon awe,
In swich caas, of the ercedekenes[210] curs,
But if a mannes soule were in his purs;
For in his purs he shoulde ypunysshed be.
"Purs is the ercedekenes helle," seyde he.
But wel I woot he lyed right in dede;
Of cursyn oghte ech gilty man hym drede,  660
For curs wol slee right as assoillyng savith,
And also war hym of a *Significavit!*[211]

In daunger[212] hadde he at his owene gyse[213]
The yonge gerles[214] of the diocise,
And knew hir counseil, and was al hir reed.[215]

A gerland hadde he set up-on his heed
As greet as it were for an ale stake;[216]
A bokeler hadde he maad hym of a cake.

With hym ther rood a gentil Pardoner
Of Rouncival, his freend and his comper,[217]  670
That streight was comen fro the court of Rome.
Ful loude he soong, "Com hider, love, to me!"
This Somnour bar to hym a stif burdoun,[218]
Was nevere trompe of half so greet a soun.

This Pardoner hadde heer as yelow as wex,
But smoothe it heeng as dooth a strike[219] of flex;
By ounces[220] henge his lokkes that he hadde,
And ther-with he his shuldres overspradde;
But thynne it lay, by colpons[221] oon and oon;
But hood, for jolitee, ne wered he noon,  680
For it was trussed up in his walet.

---

205 test
206 the question is what part of the law is relevant
207 rascal
208 have his concubine like any other good fellow
209 anywhere    210 archdeacon's
211 beware of a warrant for arrest by the ecclesias-
tical court    212 control    213 manner
214 young people of either sex    215 adviser
216 a pole over the door of an inn on which garlands
were draped for a sign    217 comrade
218 accompanied him with a strong bass note
219 hank    220 bunches    221 shreds

Hym thoughte he rood al of the newe jet;[222]
Dischevelee, save his cappe, he rood al bare.
Swiche glarynge eyen hadde he as an hare.

A vernycle[223] hadde he sowed up-on his cappe.
His walet lay biforn hym in his lappe,
Bret-ful to pardoun, comen from Rome al hoot.

A voys he hadde as smal as hath a goot.
No berd hadde he, ne nevere sholde have,
As smothe it was as it were late yshave:                      690
I trowe he were a geldyng or a mare.

But of his craft, fro Berwyk into Ware,
Ne was ther swich another pardoner.
For his male[224] he hadde a pilwe beer,[225]
Which that he seyde was Our Lady veyl;
He seyde he hadde a gobet[226] of the seyl
That Seint Peter hadde, whan that he wente
Up-on the see, til Jesu Crist hym hente.[227]
He hadde a croys of latoun[228] ful of stones,
And in a glas he hadde pigges bones.                          700
But with thise relikes, whan that he fond
A poure persoun dwellyng up-on lond,
Up-on a day he gat hym moore moneye
Than that the persoun gat in monthes tweye.
And thus, with feyned flaterye and japes,[229]
He made the persoun and the peple his apes.

But trewely to tellen atte laste,
He was in chirche a noble ecclesiaste.
Wel koude he rede a lessoun or a storie,
But alderbest[230] he song an offertorie;                     710
For wel he wiste, whan that song was songe,
He moste preche and wel affile his tonge
To wynne silver, as he ful wel koude;
Ther-fore he song the murierly and loude.

Now have I told yow soothly, in a clause,
Th' estaat, th' array, the nombre, and eek the cause
Why that assembled was this companye
In Southwerk, at this gentil hostelrye
That highte the Tabard, faste by the Belle.
But now is tyme to yow for to telle                           720
How that we baren us that ilke[231] nyght,
Whan we were in that hostelrie alyght;
And after wol I telle of oure viage,
And al the remenant of oure pilgrymage.

But first I pray yow, of your courteisye,

---

222 in the latest style
223 a copy of St. Veronica's handkerchief, bearing the imprint of Christ's face
224 pouch    225 pillow case    226 scrap

227 caught
228 cross of an alloy resembling brass
229 jokes    230 best of all
231 same

That ye narette it nat my vileynye,[232]
Thogh that I pleynly speke in this matere,
To telle yow hir wordes and hir cheere,[233]
Ne thogh I speke hir wordes proprely.
For this ye knowen also wel as I,                                    730
Who-so shal telle a tale after a man,
He moot reherce as neigh as evere he kan
Everich a word, if it be in his charge,
Al[234] speke he nevere so rudeliche and large,
Or ellis he moot telle his tale untrewe,
Or feyne thyng,[235] or fynde wordes newe.
He may nat spare, al-thogh he were his brother,
He moot as wel seye o word as another.
Crist spak hym-self ful brode in holy writ,
And wel ye woot, no vileynye is it.                                  740
Eek Plato seith, who-so that kan hym rede,
The wordes mote by cosyn to the dede.
    Also I pray yow to foryeve it me,
Al have I nat set folk in hir degree
Here in this tale, as that they sholde stonde:
My wit is short, ye may wel understonde.
    Greet cheere made oure Hoost us everichon,
And to the soper sette he us anon.
He served us with vitaille at the beste;
Strong was the wyn, and wel to drynke us leste.                     750
    A semely man oure Hoost was with-alle
For to been a marchal in an halle.
A large mane he was with eyen stepe,
A fairer burgeys was ther noon in Chepe,[236]
Boold of his speche, and wys, and wel ytaught,
And of manhode hym lakkede right naught.
    Eke ther-to he was right a murye man,
And after soper pleyen he bigan,
And spak of myrthe amonges othere thynges,
Whan that we hadde maad oure rekenynges,                            760
And seyde thus, "Now, lordynges, trewely,
Ye been to me right welcome, hertely;
For by my trouthe, if that I shal not lye,
I saugh nat this yeer so murye a compaignye
At ones in this herberwe[237] as is now.
Fayn wolde I doon yow myrthe, wiste I how.
And of a myrthe I am right now bythoght,
To doon yow ese, and it shal coste noght.
    "Ye goon to Caunterbury—God yow spede,
The blisful martir quyte[238] yow youre mede!                       770
And wel I woot, as ye goon by the weye,

---

232 do not attribute it to low breeding          236 Cheapside, a principal street in London
233 behavior    234 although                      237 lodging    238 pay
235 invent something

Ye shapen yow to talen [239] and to pleye;
For trewely, confort ne myrthe is noon
To ryde by the weye domb as a stoon;
And ther-fore wol I maken yow disport,
As I seyde erst, and doon yow som confort.
And if yow liketh alle, by oon assent,
For to stonden at my juggement,
And for to werken as I shal yow seye,
Tomorwe, whan ye riden by the weye,                    *780*
Now, by my fader soule that is deed,
But ye be murye, I wol yeve yow myn heed!
Hoold up youre hondes, with-outen moore speche."
　　Our conseil was nat longe for to seche;
Us thoughte it was nat worth to make it wys, [240]
And graunted hym with-outen moore avys, [241]
And bad hym seye his voirdit [242] as hym leste.
　　"Lordynges," quod he, "now herkneth for the beste;
But tak it not, I pray yow, in desdeyn;
This is the poynt, to speken short and pleyn,          *790*
That ech of yow, to shorte with oure weye,
In this viage shal telle tales tweye
To Caunterburyward, I mene it so,
And homward he shal tellen othere two,
Of aventures that whilom han bifalle.
And which of yow that bereth hym best of alle,
That is to seyn, that telleth in this caas
Tales of best sentence [243] and moost solaas,
Shal have a soper at oure aller cost
Here in this place, sittyng by this post,               *800*
Whan that we come agayn fro Caunterbury.
And for to make yow the moore mury,
I wol my-selven goodly with yow ryde,
Right at myn owene cost, and be your gyde;
And who-so wole my juggement withseye
Shal paye al that we spende by the weye.
And if ye vouche sauf that it be so,
Tel me anoon, with-outen wordes mo,
And I wol erly shape me ther-fore."
　　This thyng was graunted, and oure othes swore        *810*
With ful glad herte, and preyden hym also
That he wolde vouche sauf for to do so,
And that he wolde been oure governour,
And of oure tales juge and reportour, [244]
And sette a soper at a certeyn prys,
And we wol reuled been at his devys [245]
In heigh and lough; [246] and thus by oon assent

---

[239] talk, tell stories
[240] to pretend wisdom　　[241] deliberation
[242] verdict　　[243] significance

[244] commentator　　[245] under his direction
[246] in all matters

Wc been acorded to his juggement.
And ther-upon the wyn was fet[247] anoon;
We dronken, and to reste wente echon,                              *820*
With-outen any lenger taryynge.
      Amorwe, whan that day bigan to sprynge,
Up roos oure Hoost, and was oure aller cok,
And gadred us togidre in a flok,
And forth we riden, a litel moore than pas,[248]
Unto the wateryng of Seint Thomas;
And there oure Hoost bigan his hors areste,
And seyde, "Lordynges, herkneth, if yow leste:
Ye woot youre forward,[249] and I it yow recorde.
If evensong and morwesong acorde,                                 *830*
Lat se now who shal telle the firste tale.
As evere moot I drynke wyn or ale,
Who so be rebel to my juggement
Shal paye for al that by the wey is spent.
Now draweth cut, er that we ferrer twynne;[250]
He which that hath the shortest shal bigynne.
Sir Knyght," quod he, "my master and my lord,
Now draweth cut, for that is myn acord.
Cometh neer," quod he, "my lady Prioresse,
And ye, sire Clerk, lat be youre shamefastnesse.[251]            *840*
Ne studieth noght; ley hond to, every man!"
      Anoon to drawen every wight bigan,
And shortly for to tellen as it was,
Were it by aventure, or sort, or cas,
The sothe is this, the cut fil to the Knight,
Of which ful blithe and glad was every wight,
And telle he moste his tale, as was resoun,
By forward and by composicioun,[252]
As ye han herd; what nedeth wordes mo?
      And whan this goode man saugh that it was so,             *850*
As he that wys was and obedient
To kepe his forward by his free assent,
He seyde, "Syn I shal bigynne the game,
What, welcome be the cut, a Goddes name!
Now lat us ryde, and herkneth what I seye."
And with that word we ryden forth oure weye,
And he bigan with right a murye cheere
His tale anoon, and seyde as ye may heere.   (*c. 1387*)

## THE WIFE OF BATH'S TALE

      In th'olde dayes of the kyng Arthour,
Of which that Britons speken greet honour,
All was this land fulfild of faierye;
The elf queene with hir joly compaignye

---

247 fetched
248 faster than a walk        249 agreement

250 travel farther        251 bashfulness
252 arrangement

Dauncéd ful ofte in many a grene mede.
This was the olde opinion, as I rede[1]—
I speke of manye hundred yeres ago.
But now kan no man se none elves mo;
For now the grete charitee and prayeres
Of lymytours[2] and othere hooly freres,                                10
That serchen every lond and every streem,
As thikke as motes in the sonne beem,
Blessynge halles, chambres, kichenes, boures,
Citees, burghes, castels, hye toures,
Thropes, bernes, shipnes,[3] dayeryes—
This maketh that ther been no faieryes;
For ther as wont to walken was an elf,
Ther walketh now the lymytour hymself
In undermeles[4] and in morwenynges,
And seyth his matyns and his hooly thynges                               20
As he gooth in his lymytacioun.
Wommen may go saufly up and doun:
In every bussh, or under every tree,
Ther is noon oother incubus[5] but he,
And he ne wol doon hem but dishonour.

    And so bifel it that this kyng Arthour
Hadde in his hous a lusty bacheler,
That on a day cam ridynge fro ryver;[6]
And happed that, allone as she was born,
He saugh a mayde walknge hym biforn;                                     30
Of which mayde anon, maugree hir heed,[7]
By verray force birafte hire maydenhed.
For which oppressioun was swich clamour
And swich pursute unto the kyng Arthour,
That dampned was this knyght for to be deed
By cours of lawe, and sholde han lost his heed—
Paraventure swich was the statut tho—
But that the queene, and othere ladyes mo,
So longe preyeden the kyng of grace
Til he his lyf hym graunted in the place,                                40
and yaf hym to the queene, al at hir wille,
To chese[8] wheither she wolde hym save or spille.
    The queene thanketh the kyng with al hir myght,
And after this, thus spak she to the knyght,
Whan that she saugh hir tyme upon a day:
"Thou standest yet," quod she, "in swich array
That of thy lyf yet hastow no suretee.
I grante thee lyf if thou kanst tellen me

---

[1] read   [2] a friar licensed to beg
[3] villages, barns, stables   [4] afternoon
[5] an evil spirit who couples with women as they
sleep. The friar can only dishonor them, not

impregnate them, as a "real" incubus might.
[6] from the hawking-ground by the river
[7] "in spite of her head": despite all she could do
[8] choose

What thyng is it that wommen moost desiren.
Be war, and keepe thy nekke boon from iren.                    *50*
And if thou kanst nat tellen it anon,[9]
Yet shal I yeve thee leve for to gon
A twelfmonth and a day, to seche and leere
An answere suffisant in this mateere;
And suretee wol I han, er that thou pace,
Thy body for to yelden in this place."
     Wo was this knyght and sorwefully he siketh;
But what! he may not do al as hym liketh.
And at the laste he chees hym for to wende,
And come agayn right at the yeres ende                         *60*
With swich answere as God wolde hym purveye;
And taketh his leve and wendeth forth his weye.

     He seketh every hous and every place
Where-as he hopeth for to fynde grace,[10]
To lerne what thyng wommen loven moost;
But he ne koude arryven in no coost
Wher-as he myghte fynde in this mateere
Two creatures accordynge in feere.[11]
Somme seyde wommen loven best richesse,
Somme seyde honour, somme seyde jolynesse,                     *70*
Somme riche array, somme seyden lust abedde
And ofte tyme to be wydwe and wedde.
Somme seyde that oure hertes been moost esed
Whan that we been yflatered and yplesed.
He gooth ful ny the sothe, I wol nat lye;
A man shal wynne us best with flaterye;
And with attendance and with bisynesse,
Been we ylymed,[12] bothe moore and lesse.
And somme seyen that we loven best
For to be free and do right as us lest,                        *80*
And that no man repreve us of oure vice,
But seye that we be wise and nothyng nice;[13]
For trewely ther is noon of us alle,
If any wight wol clawe us on the galle,
That we nel kike for he seith us sooth.[14]
Assay,[15] and he shal fynde it that so dooth;
For be we never so vicious withinne,
We wol been holden wise and clene of synne.
And somme seyn that greet delit han we
For to been holden stable, and eke secree,[16]                 *90*
And in o purpos stedefastly to dwelle,
And nat biwreye[17] thyng that men us telle,

---

[9] at once        [10] favor
[11] agreeing together
[12] caught (Lime is a sticky substance spread on
twigs to catch small birds.)
[13] wanton

[14] If anyone scratches us on a sore spot (by telling
us something unpleasant), there isn't one of us who
wouldn't kick. (Proverbial)        [15] try it
[16] discreet        [17] reveal

But that tale is not worth a rake-stele:[18]
Pardee, we wommen konne no thyng hele;[19]
Witnesse on Myda; wol ye heere the tale?

Ovyde, amonges othere thynges smale,
Seyde Myda hadde, under his longe heres,
Growynge upon his heed, two asses eres;
The which vice he hydde as he best myghte,
Ful subtilly, from every mannes sighte,                    *100*
That save his wyf, ther wiste of it namo.
He loved hire moost and trustede hire also;
He preyede hire that to no creature
She sholde tellen of his disfigure.
She swoor him nay, for al this world to wynne,
She nolde do that vileynye or synne,
To make hir housbonde han so foul a name.
She nolde nat teele it for his owene shame.
But nathelees, hir thoughte that she dyde,[20]
That she so longe sholde a conseil hyde;                   *110*
Hir thoughte it swal so soore about hir herte
That nedely som word hire moste asterte;[21]
And sith she dorste telle it to no man,
Doun to a mareys[22] faste by she ran—
Til she came there, hir herte was a-fyre—
And as a bitore bombleth[23] in the myre,
She leyde hir mouth unto the water doun,
"Biwreye me nat, thou water with thy soun!"
Quod she; "to thee I telle it and namo.
Myn housbonde hath longe asses erys two!                   *120*
Now is myn herte all hool; now is it oute.
I myghte no lenger kepe it, out of doute."
Heere may ye se, thogh we a tyme abyde,
Yet out it moot; we kan no conseil hyde.
The remenant of the tale if ye wol heere.
Redeth Ovyde, and ther ye may it leere.[24]

This knyght of which my tale is specially,
Whan that he saugh he myghte nat come therby,
This is to seye, what wommen love moost,
Withinne his brest ful sorweful was the goost.[25]         *130*
But hoom he gooth, he myghte nat sojourne;
The day was come that homward moste he tourne.
And in his wey it happed hym to ryde,
In al this care, under a forest syde,
Wher-as he saugh upon a daunce go
Of ladyes foure and twenty and yet mo;

---

[18] rake-handle
[19] conceal    [20] would die    [21] escape
[22] marsh    [23] bittern bumbles

[24] Ovid says that Midas's barber, rather than his
wife, tells the secret.    [25] spirit

Toward the whiche dames he drow ful yerne,[26]
In hope that some wysdom sholde he lerne.
But certeinly, er he cam fully there,
Vanysshed was this daunce, he nyste where.                        *140*
No creature saugh he that bar lyf,
Save on the grene he saugh sittynge a wyf—
A fouler wight ther may no man devyse.
Agayn the knyght this olde wyf gan ryse,
And seyde, "Sire knyght, heer forth ne lith no wey.[27]
Tel me what that ye seken, by youre fey.
Paraventure it may the bettre be;
Thise olde folk kan muchel thyng," quod she.[28]
     "My leeve[29] mooder," quod this knyght, "certeyn,
I nam but deed but if that I kan seyn                             *150*
What thyng it is that wommen moost desire.
Koude ye me wisse, I wolde wel quite youre hire."[30]
     "Plight me thy trouthe, heere in myn hand," quod she,
"The nexte thyng that I requere thee,
Thou shalt it do, if it lye in thy myght;
And I wol telle it yow er it by nyght."
     "Have heer my trouthe," quod the knyght, "I grante."
     "Thanne," quod she, "I dar me wel avante[31]
Thy lyf is sauf; for I wol stonde therby,
Upon my lyf, the queene wol seye as I.                            *160*
Lat se which is the proudeste of hem alle,
That wereth on a coverchief or a calle[32]
That dar seye nay of that I shal thee teche!
Lat us go forth, withouten lenger speche."
Tho rowned she a pistel[33] in his ere,
And bad hym to be glad and have no fere.

     Whan they be comen to the court, this knyght
Seyde he had holde his day as he hadde hight,
And redy was his answere, as he sayde.
Ful many a noble wyf and many a mayde,                           *170*
And many a wydwe, for that they been wise,
The queene hirself sittynge as justise,
Assembled been, his answere for to heere;
And afterward this knyght was bode appeere.
To every wight comanded was silence,
And that the knyght sholde telle in audience
What thyng that worldly wommen loven best.
This knyght ne stood nat stille as doth a best,[34]
But to this question anon answerede,
With manly voys, that al the court it herde:                     *180*
     "My lige lady, generally," quod he,

---

26 eagerly     27 There is no roadway here.             effort.     31 boast     32 hair net
28 These old folks know many things. (Proverbial)       33 whispered a message (epistle)
29 dear                                                  34 beast, probably specifically a horse
30 If you could tell me, I would well reward your

"Wommen desiren have sovereynetee
As wel over hir housbond as hir love,
And for to been in maistrie hym above.
This is youre mooste desir, thogh ye me kille;
Dooth as yow list, I am heer at youre wille."
  In al the court ne was ther wyf, ne mayde,
Ne wydwe, that contraried that he sayde,
But seyden he was worthy han his lyf.
  And with that word, up stirte the olde wyf
Which that the knyght saugh sittynge in the grene.
"Mercy," quod she, "my sovereyn lady queene!
Er that youre court departe, do me right.
I taughte this answere unto the knyght;
For which he plighte me his trouthe there,
The first thyng that I wolde him requere,
He wolde it do, if it lay in his myght.
Bifore the court thanne preye I thee, sir knyght,"
Quod she, "that thou me take unto thy wyf;
For wel thou woost that I have kept thy lyf.
If I sey fals, sey nay, upon thy fey."
  This knyght answerde, "Allas, and weylawey!
I woot right wel that swich was my biheste.
For Goddes love, as chees a newe requeste!
Taak al my good and lat my body go."
  "Nay, thanne," quod she, "I shrewe [35] us bothe two!
For though that I be foul, and oold, and poore,
I nolde for al the metal, ne for oore
That under erthe is grave [36] or lith above,
But-if thy wyf I were, and eek thy love."
  "My love?" quod he, "nay, my dampnacioun!
Allas, that any of my nacioun
Sholde evere so foule disparaged be!"
But al for noght; th'ende is this, that he
Constreyned was, he nedes moste hire wedde;
And taketh his olde wyf and gooth to bedde.

  Now wolden som men seye, paraventure,
That for my necligence I do no cure [37]
To tellen yow the joye and all th'array
That at the feeste was that ilke [38] day.
To which thyng shortly answeren I shal:
I seye ther has no joye ne feeste at al.
Ther nas but hevynesse and muche sorwe;
For prively he wedded hire on a morwe,
And al day after hidde hym as an owle,
So wo was hym, his wyf looked so foule.
  Greet was the wo the knyght hadde in his thoght
Whan he was with his wyf a-bedde ybroght;

190

200

210

220

---

[35] curse    [36] buried    [37] I am not careful    [38] same

He walweth,[39] and he turneth to and fro.

His olde wyf lay smylynge everemo,                                    *230*

and seyde, "O deere housbonde, benedicitee!

Fareth every knyght thus with his wyf as ye?

Is this the lawe of kyng Arthures hous?

Is every knyght of his so dangerous?[40]

I am youre owene love, and youre wyf;

I am she which that saved hath youre lyf;

And certes, yet ne dide I yow nevere unright;

Why fare[41] ye thus with me this firste nyght?

Ye faren lyk a man had lost his wit.

What is my gilt? for Goddes love tel it,                              *240*

And it shal been amended, if I may."

     "Amended?" quod this knyght, "allas! nay, nay!

It wol nat been amended nevere mo!

Thou art so loothly, and so oold also,

And thereto comen of so lough a kynde,

That litel wonder is thogh I walwe and wynde.

So wolde God my herte wolde breste!"[42]

     "Is this," quod she, "the cause of youre unreste?"

"Ye, certeinly," quod he, "no wonder is."

     "Now sire," quod she, "I koude amende al this,          *250*

If that me liste, er it were dayes thre,

So wel ye myghte bere yow unto me.

     "But for ye speken of swich gentillesse

As is descended out of old richesse,

That therefore sholden ye be gentilmen,

Swich arrogance is nat worth an hen.

Looke who[43] that is moost vertuous alway,

Pryvee and apert,[44] and moost entendeth ay

To do the gentil dedes that he kan,

Taak hym for the grettest gentilman.                                  *260*

Crist wole we clayme of hym oure gentillesse,

Nat of oure eldres for hire old richesse;

For thogh they yeve us al hir heritage,

For which we clayme to been of heigh parage,[45]

Yet may they nat bequethe for nothyng

To noon of us hir vertuous lyvyng,

That made hem gentilmen ycalled be,

And bad us folwen hem in swich degree.

     "Wel kan the wise poete of Florence

That highte Dant[46] speken in this sentence.[47]                    *270*

Lo, in swich maner rym is Dantes tale:

'Ful selde up riseth by his branches smale

Prowesse of man; for God, of his goodnesse,

Wole that of hym we clayme oure gentillesse;

---

[39] tossed (wallowed)    [40] disdainful         [44] privately as well as publicly    [45] lineage
[41] behave   [42] burst   [43] whoever            [46] called Dante   [47] on this theme

For of oure eldres may we no thyng clayme
But temporel thyng that man may hurte and mayme.'
    "Eek every wight woot this as wel as I:
If gentillesse were planted natureelly
Unto a certeyn lynage doun the lyne,
Pryvee nor apert thanne wolde they nevere fyne                  280
To doon of gentillesse the faire office;
They myghte do no vileynye or vice.
    "Taak fyr and ber it in the derkeste hous
Bitwix this and the mount of Kaukasous,
And lat men shette the dores and go thenne,
Yet whole the fyr as faire lye and brenne[48]
As twenty thousand men myghte it biholde.
His office natureel ay wol it holde,
Up peril of my lyf, til that it dye.
    "Heere may ye se wel how that genterye              290
Is nat annexed to possessioun
Sith folk ne doon hir operacioun
Alwey, as dooth the fyr, lo, in his kynde.[49]
For God it woot,[50] men may wel often fynde
A lordes sone do shame and vileynye;
And he that wole han pris[51] of his gentrye,
For he was boren of a gentil hous
And hadde hise eldres noble and vertuous,
And nel[52] hymselven do no gentil dedis
Ne folwen his gentil auncestre that deed[53] is,              300
He nis nat gentil, be he duc or erl;
For vileyns synful dedes make a cherl.
For gentillesse nys but renomee[54]
Of thyne auncestres for hire heigh bountee,
Which is a strange thyng to thy persone;[55]
Thy gentillesse cometh fro God allone.
Thanne comth oure verray gentillesse of grace;
It was no thyng biquethe us with oure place.
    "Thenketh hou noble, as seith Valerius,
Was thilke Tullius Hostillius,                            310
That out of poverte roos to heigh noblesse.
Reedeth Senek, and redeth eek Boece;
Ther shul ye seen expresse that no drede is
That he is gentil that dooth gentil dedis.
And therefore, leeve housbonde, I thus conclude:
Al were it that myne auncestres weren rude,
Yet may the hye God—and so hope I—
Grante me grace to lyven vertuously.
Thanne am I gentil whan that I bigynne

---

[48] blaze and burn    [49] according to their nature    [55] Gentility is not an inherited aspect of your per-
[50] knows    [51] esteem    [52] will not    [53] dead    son, but a gift of God's grace.
[54] renown

To lyven vertuously and weyve [56] synne.       320
"And theras ye of poverte me repreeve,
The hye God on whom that we bileeve
In wilful poverte chees to lyve his lyf.
And certes every man, mayden, or wyf,
May understonde that Jesus, hevene kyng,
Ne wolde nat chesen vicious lyvyng.
Glad poverte is an honeste thyng certeyn.
This wole Senec and othere clerkes seyn.
Whoso that halt hym payd [57] of his poverte,
I holde hym riche, al hadde he nat a sherte.     330
He that coveiteth is a povere wight;
For he wolde han that is nat in his myght.
But he that noght hath, ne coveiteth have,
Is riche, although ye holde hym but a knave.
"Verray poverte, it syngeth proprely.
Juvenal seith of poverte myrily,
'The poure man, whan he goth by the weye
Bifore the theves, he may synge and pleye.'
Poverte is hateful good, and as I gesse,
A ful greet bryngere out of bisynesse;      340
A greet amendere eek of sapience
To hym that taketh it in pacience.
Poverte is this, although it seme alenge: [58]
Possessioun that no wight wol chalenge.
Poverte ful ofte, whan a man is lowe,
Maketh his God and eek hymself to knowe.
Poverte a spectacle is, as thynketh me,
Thurgh which he may hise verray freendes see.
And therfore, sire, syn that I noght yow greve,
Of my poverte namoore ye me repreve.      350
"Now, sire, of elde ye repreve me.
And certes, sire, thogh noon auctoritee
Were in no book, ye gentils of honour
Seyn that men sholde an oold wight doon favour,
And clepe [59] hym fader, for youre gentillesse.
And auctours shal I fynden as I gesse.
"Now ther ye seye that I am foul and old,
Than drede you noght to been a cokewold. [60]
For filthe and eelde, al so moot I thee, [61]
Been grete wardeyns upon chastitee.      360
But nathelees, syn I knowe youre delit,
I shal fulfille youre worldly appetit.
"Chese now," quod she, "oon of thise thynges tweye:
To han me foul and old til that I deye,

---

[56] waive; put aside    [57] satisfied    [61] so may I prosper
[58] miserable    [59] call    [60] cuckold

And be to yow a trewe, humble wyf,
And nevere yow displese in al my lyf;
Or elles ye wol han me yong and fair,
And take youre aventure of the repair
That shal be to youre hous bycause of me,
Or in some oother place, may wel be.                            *370*
Now chese yourselven wheither that yow liketh."

    This knyght avyseth hym, and sore siketh,
But atte laste, he seyde in this manere:
"My lady and my love, and wyf so deere,
I put me in youre wise governance.
Chescth youreself which may be moost plesance
And moost honour to yow and me also.
I do no fors the wheither of the two;
For as yow liketh it suffiseth me."
    "Thanne have I gete of yow maistrie," quod she,    *380*
"Syn I may chese and governe as me lest."
"Ye, certes, wyf," quod he, "I holde it best."
"Kys me!" quod she; "we be no lenger wrothe;[62]
For by my trouthe, I wol be to yow bothe,
This is to seyn, ye, bothe fair and good.
I prey to God that I moote sterven wood[63]
But I to yow be al so good and trewe
As evere was wyf syn that the world was newe;
And but I be tomorn as fair to seene
As any lady, emperice or queene,                               *390*
That is bitwixe the est and eke the west,
Dooth with my lyf and deth right as yow lest.
Cast up the curtyn; looke how that it is!"
    And whan the knyght saugh verraily all this,
That she so fair was, and so yong therto,
For joye he hente hire in hise armes two,
His herte bathed in a bath of blisse.
A thousand tyme a-rewe[64] he gan hire kisse;
And she obeyed hym in everythyng
That myghte doon hym plesance or likyng.                       *400*

    And thus they lyve unto hir lyves ende
In parfit joye. And Jesu Crist us sende
Housbondes meeke, yonge, fressh a-bedde,
And grace t'overbyde hem that we wedde!
And eek, I praye, Jesu shorte hir lyves
That wol not be governed by hir wyves;
And olde and angry nygardes of dispence,
God sende hem soone verray pestilence!   (*c. 1394*)

---

[62] angry     [63] die insane     [64] in a row

# ANONYMOUS BALLADS

## Riddles Wisely Expounded

There was a knicht riding frae the east,
   *Sing the cather banks, the bonnie brume*[1]
Wha had been wooing at monie a place,
   And ye may beguile a young thing sune.

He came unto a widow's door,
And speird[2] whare her three dochters were.

The auldest one's to the washing gane,
The second's to a baking gane.

The youngest ane's to a wedding gane,
And it will be nicht or she be hame.     *10*

He sat him doun upon a stane,
Till thir three lasses came tripping hame.

The auldest ane's to the bed making,
And the second ane's to the sheet spreading.

The youngest ane was bauld and bricht,
And she was to lye wi' this unco[3] knicht.

"Gin[4] ye will answer me questions ten,
This morn ye sall be made my ain.

"O what is heigher nor the tree?
And what is deeper nor the sea?     *20*

"Or what is heavier nor the lead?
And what is better nor the breid?

"O what is whiter nor the milk?
Or what is safter nor the silk?

"Or what is sharper nor a thorn?
Or what is louder nor a horn?

"Or what is greener nor the grass?
Or what is waur[5] nor a woman was?"

"O heaven is higher nor the tree,
And hell is deeper nor the sea.     *30*

"O sin is heavier nor the lead,
The blessing's better than the bread.

"The snaw is whiter nor the milk,
And the down is safter nor the silk.

---

[1] Cather and broom are wild plants believed to    [3] strange    [4] if    [5] worse
impart prophetic vision.    [2] inquired

"Hunger is sharper nor a thorn,
And shame is louder nor a horn.

"The pies[6] are greener nor the grass,
And Clootie's waur nor a woman was."

As sune as she the fiend did name,
He flew awa in a blazing flame.                40

## The Twa Sisters

There was twa sisters in a bow'r,
  *Edinburgh, Edinburgh*
There was twa sisters in a bow'r,
  *Stirling for ay*
There was twa sisters in a bow'r,
There came a knight to be their wooer.
  *Bonny Saint Johnston stands upon Tay.*

He courted the eldest wi' glove and ring,
But he loved the youngest above a' thing.

He courted the eldest wi' brotch and knife,   10
But loved the youngest as his life.

The eldest she was vexéd sair,
An' much envied her sister fair.

Into her bow'r she could not rest,
Wi' grief an' spite she almos' brast.

Upon a morning fair an' clear,
She cried upon her sister dear:

"O sister, come to yon sea stran',
An' see our father's ships come to lan'."

She's ta'en her by the milk-white han',       20
An' led her down to yon sea stran'.

The Younges' stood upon a stane,
The eldest came and threw her in.

She took her by the middle sma',
An' dashed her bonny back to the jaw.[1]

"O sister, sister, take my middle,
An ye's get my goud[2] and my gouden girdle.

"O sister, sister, save my life,
An' I swear I'se never be nae man's wife."

"Foul fa' the han' that I should take,         30
It twined me an' my wardles make.[3]

---

[6] birds

[1] wave    [2] gold

[3] separated me and my mate of this world

"Your cherry cheeks an' yellow hair
Gars[4] me gae maiden for evermair."

Sometimes she sank, an' sometimes she swam,
Till she came down yon bonny mill-dam.

O out it came the miller's son,
An' saw the fair maid swimmin' in.

"O father, father, draw your dam,
Here's either a mermaid or a swan."

The miller quickly drew the dam,                          *40*
An' there he found a drowned woman.

You cou'dna see her yellow hair
For gold and pearle that were so rare.

You cou'dna see her middle sma'
For gouden girdle that was sae braw.[5]

You cou'dna see her fingers white,
For gouden rings that was sae gryte.[6]

An' by there came a harper fine,
That harpéd to the king at dine.

When he did look that lady upon,                          *50*
He sighed and made a heavy moan.

He's ta'en three locks o her yellow hair,
An' wi' them strung his harp sae fair.

The first tune he did play and sing,
Was, "Farewell to my father the king."

The nextin tune that he played syne,[7]
Was, "Farewell to my mother the queen."

The lasten tune that he played then,
Was, "Wae to my sister, fair Ellen."

## Lord Randal

"O where hae ye been, Lord Randal, my son?
O where hae ye been, my handsome young man?"
"I hae been to the wild wood; mother, make my bed soon,
For I'm weary wi hunting, and fain wald lie down."

"Where gat ye your dinner, Lord Randal, my son?
Where gat ye your dinner, my handsome young man?"
"I dined wi my true-love; mother, make my bed soon,
For I'm weary wi hunting and fain wald lie down."

---

[4] makes    [5] splendid    [6] great    [7] then

"What get ye to your dinner, Lord Randal, my son?
What gat ye to your dinner, my handsome young man?"    *10*
"I gat eels boiled in broo; mother, make my bed soon,
For I'm weary wi hunting, and fain wald lie down."

"What became of your bloodhounds, Lord Randal, my son?
What became of your bloodhounds, my handsome young man?"
"O they swelld and they died; mother, make my bed soon,
For I'm weary wi hunting and fain wald lie down."

"O I fear ye are poisond, Lord Randal, my son!
O I fear ye are poisond, my handsome young man!"
"O yes! I am poisond; mother, make my bed soon,
For I'm sick at the heart, and I fain wald lie down."    *20*

## The Twa Corbies

As I was walking all alane,
I heard twa corbies[1] making a mane:[2]
The tane unto the tither did say
"Whar sall we gang and dine the day?"

"In behint yon auld fail[3] dyke
I wot[4] there lies a new-slain knight;
And naebody kens[5] that he lies there
But his hawk, his hound, and his lady fair.

"His hound is to the hunting gane,
His hawk to fetch the wild-fowl hame,  *10*
His lady's ta'en anither mate,
So we may mak our dinner sweet.

"Ye'll sit on his white hause[6] bane,
And I'll pike out his bonney blue e'en:
Wi' ae lock o' his gowden hair
We'll theek[7] our nest when it grows bare.

"Mony a one for him maks mane,
But nane sall ken whar he is gane:
O'er his white banes, when they are bare,
The wind sall blaw for evermair."  *20*

## Fair Annie

"It's narrow, narrow make your bed,
And learn to lie your lane;[1]
For I'm ga'n oer the sea, Fair Annie,
A braw[2] bride to bring hame.

Wi' her I will get gowd and gear;[3]
Wi' you I ne'er got nane.

"But wha will bake my bridal bread,
Or brew my bridal ale?
And wha will welcome my brisk bride,
That I bring oer the dale?"    *10*

"It's I will bake your bridal bread,
And brew your bridal ale,
And I will welcome your brisk bride,
That you bring oer the dale."

"But she that welcomes my brisk bride
Maun gang[4] like maiden fair;
She maun lace on her robe sae jimp,[5]
And braid her yellow hair."

"But how can I gang maiden-like,
When maiden I am nane?    *20*
Have I not born seven sons to thee,
And am with child again?"

She's ta'en her young son on her arms,
Another in her hand,
And she's up to the highest tower,
To see him come to land.

"Come up, come up, my eldest son,
And look oer yon sea-strand,
And see your father's new-come bride,
Before she come to land,"    *30*

"Come down, come down, my mother
dear,
Come fra the castle wa!

---

[1] ravens    [2] moan    [3] sod    [4] know
[5] knows    [6] neck    [7] thatch

[1] alone    [2] well-dressed; fine
[3] gold and property    [4] must go    [5] slim

I fear, if langer ye stand there,
  Ye'll let yourself down fa."

And she gaed down, and farther down,
  Her love's ship for to see,
And the topmast and the mainmast
  Shone like the silver free.

And she's gane down, and farther down,
  The bride's ship to behold,     40
And the topmast and the mainmast
  They shone just like the gold.

She's ta'en her seven sons in her hand,
  I wot she didna fail;
She met Lord Thomas and his bride,
  As they came oer the dale.

"You're welcome to your house, Lord
    Thomas,
  You're welcome to your land;
You're welcome with your fair ladye,
  That you lead by the hand.     50

"You're welcome to your ha's,[6] ladye,
  You're welcome to your bowers;
You're welcome to your hame, ladye,
  For a'that's here is yours."

"I thank thee, Annie; I thank thee, Annie,
  Sae dearly as I thank thee;
You're the likest to my sister, Annie,
  That ever I did see.

"There came a knight out oer the sea,
  And steald my sister away;     60
The shame scoup[7] in his company,
  And land where'er he gae!"

She hang ae napkin at the door,
  Another in the ha,
And a' to wipe the trickling tears,
  Sae fast as they did fa.

And aye she served the lang tables,
  With white bread and with wine,
And aye she drank the wan water,
  To had her colour fine.     70

And aye she served the lang tables,
  With white bread and with brown;
And ay she turned her round about,
  Sae fast the tears fell down.

And he's ta'en down the silk napkin,
  Hung on a silver pin,
And aye he wipes the tear trickling
  A' down her cheik and chin.

And aye he turned him round about,
  And smiled amang his men;    80
Says, "Like ye best the old ladye,
  Or her that's new come hame?"

When bells were rung, and mass was sung,
  And a' men bound to bed,
Lord Thomas and his new-come bride
  To their chamber they were gaed.

Annie made her bed a little forbye,
  To hear what they might say;
"And ever alas!" Fair Annie cried,
  "That I should see this day!    90

"Gin[8] my seven sons were seven young
    rats,
  Running on the castle wa!,
And I were a grey cat mysell,
  I soon would worry them a'.

"Gin my seven young sons were seven
    young hares,
  Running oer yon lilly lee,
And I were a grey hound mysell,
  Soon worried they a' should be."

And wae and sad Fair Annie sat,
  And drearie was her sang,    100
And ever, as she sobbed and grat,[9]
  "Wae to the man that did the wrang!"

"My gown is on," said the new-come
    bride,
  "My shoes are on my feet,
And I will to Fair Annie's chamber
  And see what gars her greet.[10]

"What ails ye, what ails ye, Fair Annie,
  That ye make sic a moan?
Has your wine barrels cast the girds,
  Or is your white bread gone?    110

"O wha was't was your father, Annie,
  Or wha was't was your mother?
And had ye ony sister, Annie,
  Or had ye ony brother?"

---

6 halls    7 skip    8 if    9 wept        10 makes her weep

"The Earl of Wemyss was my father,
  The Countess of Wemyss my mother;
And a' the folk about the house
  To me were sister and brother."

"If the Earl of Wemyss was your father,
  I wot sae was he mine;    *120*
And it shall not be for lack of gowd
  That ye your love sall tine.

"For I have seven ships o' mine ane,
  A' loaded to the brim,
And I will gie them a' to thee,
  Wi' four to thine eldest son:
But thanks to a' the powers in heaven
  That I gae maiden hame!"

## Clerk Saunders

Clerk Saunders and a gay lady
  Was walking in yonder green,
And heavy, heavy was the love
  That fell this twa lovers between.

"A bed, a bed," Clerk Saunders said,
  "And ay a bed for you and me";
"Never a ane," said the gay lady,
  "Till ance we twa married be.

"O I have seven bold brethren
  And they are all valiant men,    *10*
If they knew a man that would tread my bower
  His life should not go along wi' him."

"Then take me up into your arms,
  And lay me low down on your bed,
That ye may swear, and keep your oath clear,
  That your bower-room I did na tread.

"Tie a handkerchief round your face,
  And you must tie it wondrous keen,
That you may swear, and keep your oath clear,
  Ye saw na me since late yestreen."    *20*

But they were scarsley gone to bed,
  Nor scarse fa'n owre asleep,
Till up and started her seven brethren,
  Just at Lord Saunders' feet.

Out bespoke the first brither,
  "Oh but love be wondrous keen!"
Out bespoke the second brither,
  "It's ill done to kill a sleeping man."

Out bespoke the third brither,
  "We had better gae and let him be";    *30*
Out bespoke the fourth brither,
  "He'll no be killed this night for me";

Out bespoke the fifth brither,
    "This night Lord Saunders he shall die;
Tho there were not a man in all Scotland,
    This night Lord Saunders he shall die."

He took out a rusty rapier,
    And he drew it three times thro the strae;
Between Lord Saunders' short rib and his side
    He gard the rusty rapier gae.        *40*

"Awake, awake, Lord Saunders," she said,
    "Awake, awake, for sin and shame!
For the day is light, and the sun shines bricht,
    And I am afraid we will be ta'en.

"Awake, awake, Lord Saunders," she said,
    "Awake, awake, for sin and shame!
For the sheets they are asweat," she said,
    "And I am afraid we will be ta'en.

"I dreamed a dreary dream last night,
    I wish it may be for our good,        *50*
That I was cutting my yellow hair,
    And dipping it in the wells o' blood."

Aye she waukened[1] at this dead man,
    Aye she put on him to and fro;
Oh aye she waukened at this dead man,
    But of his death she did not know.

"It's I will do for my love's sake
    What many ladies would think lang;
Seven years shall come and go
    Before a glove go on my hand.        *60*

"And I will do for my love's sake
    What many ladies would not do;
Seven years shall come and go
    Before I wear stocking or shoe.

"There'll ne'er a shirt go on my back,
    There'll ne'er a kame go in my hair,
There'll never coal nor candle-light
    Shine in my bower nae mair."

## The Wife of Usher's Well

There lived a wife at Usher's Well,
    And a wealthy wife was she;
She had three stout and stalwart sons,
    And sent them o'er the sea.

They hadna been a week from her,
    A week but barely ane,
Whan word came to the carlin wife[1]
    That her three sons were gane.

They hadna been a week from her,
    A week but barely three,        *10*

---

[1] watched; looked

[1] old woman

Whan word came to the carlin wife
  That her sons she'd never see.

"I wish the wind may never cease,
  Nor fashes[2] in the flood,
Till my three sons come hame to me,
  In earthly flesh and blood."

It fell about the Martinmass,
  When nights are lang and mirk,
The carlin wife's three sons came hame,
  And their hats were o the birk.[3]    20

It neither grew in syke[4] nor ditch,
  Not yet in ony sheugh;[5]
But at the gates o Paradise,
  That birk grew fair eneugh.

"Blow up the fire, my maidens,
  Bring water from the well;
For a' my house shall feast this night,
  Since my three sons are well."

And she has made to them a bed,
  She's made it large and wide,    30

And she's taen her mantle her about,
  Sat down at the bed-side.

Up then crew the red, red cock,
  And up and crew the gray;
The eldest to the youngest said,
  "'Tis time we were away."

The cock he hadna crawd but once,
  And clappd his wings at a',
When the youngest to the eldest said,
  "Brother, we must awa.    40

"The cock doth craw, the day doth daw,
  The channerin[6] worm doth chide;
Gin we be mist out o our place,
  A sair pain we maun bide.

"Fare ye weel, my mother dear!
  Fareweel to barn and byre!
And fare ye weel, the bonny lass
  That kindles my mother's fire!"

# The Sixteenth Century

## SIR THOMAS WYATT / 1503?–1542

### The Long Love

The long love that in my thought doth harbour,
And in mine heart doth keep his residence,
Into my face presseth with bold pretence,
And therein campeth, spreading his banner.
She that me learneth to love and suffer,
And wills that my trust and lust's negligence
Be reined by reason, shame, and reverence,
With his hardiness taketh displeasure.
Wherewithal, unto the heart's forest he fleeth,
Leaving his enterprise with pain and cry;                    *10*
And there him hideth, and not appeareth.
What may I do when my master feareth
But in the field with him to live and die?
For good is the life ending faithfully.

### I Find No Peace

I find no peace and all my war is done,
I fear and hope, I burn and freeze like ice,
I fly above the wind, yet can I not arise,
And naught I have and all the world I seize on;
That looseth nor locketh holdeth me in prison,
And holdeth me not; yet can I 'scape nowise;
Nor letteth me live nor die at my devise,[1]
And yet of death it giveth me occasion.
Without eyen[2] I see; and without tongue I plain;[3]
I desire to perish, and yet I ask health;                    *10*
I love another, and thus I hate myself;
I feed me in sorrow, and laugh in all my pain.
Likewise displeaseth me both death and life,
And my delight is causer of this strife.

### My Galley

My galley, chargéd with forgetfulness,
Thorough sharp seas in winter nights doth pass
'Tween rock and rock; and eke mine enemy, alas!
That is my Lord, steereth with cruelness;

---

[1] desire    [2] eyes    [3] complain

And every oar a thought in readiness,
As though that death were light in such a case.
An endless wind doth tear the sail apace
Of forcéd sighs, and trusty fearfulness;
A rain of tears, a cloud of dark disdain,
Hath done the wearéd cords great hinderance,          10
Wreathéd with error and eke with ignorance.
The stars be hid that led me to this pain.
Drownéd is reason that should me comfort,
And I remain despairing of the port.

## Divers Doth Use

Divers doth use, as I have heard and know,
(When that to change their ladies do begin),
To moan and wail, and never for to lin,[1]
Hoping thereby to pease their painful woe.
And some there be, that when it chanceth so
That women change, and hate where love hath been,
They call them false, and think with words to win
The hearts of them which otherwhere doth go.
But as for me, though that by chance indeed
Change hath outworn the favor that I had,          10
I will not wail, lament, nor yet be sad,
Nor call her false that falsely did me feed;
But let it pass, and think it is of kind,[2]
That often change doth please a woman's mind.

## Whoso List to Hunt

Whoso list to hunt, I know where is an hind,[1]
But as for me—alas, I may no more.
The vain travail hath wearied me so sore,
I am of them that farthest come behind.
Yet may I, by no means, my wearied mind
Draw from the deer; but as she fleeth afore,
Fainting I follow. I leave off therefore,
Since in a net I seek to hold the wind.
Who list her hunt, I put him out of doubt,
As well as I, may spend his time in vain.          10
And graven with diamonds in letters plain
There is written her fair neck round about:
*Noli me tangere*,[2] for Caesar's I am,
And wild for to hold, though I seem tame.

---

[1] cease    [2] natural                                    [2] touch me not
[1] doe; usually supposed to refer to Anne Boleyn

## My Lute, Awake!

My lute, awake! perform the last
Labour that thou and I shall waste,
  And end that I have now begun;
For when this song is sung and past,
  My lute, be still, for I have done.

As to be heard where ear is none,
As lead to grave in marble stone,
  My song may pierce her heart as soon.
Should we then sigh, or sing, or moan?
  No, no, my lute, for I have done.      10

The rocks do not so cruelly
Repulse the waves continually,
  As she my suit and affection;
So that I am past remedy,
  Whereby my lute and I have done.

Proud of the spoil that thou hast got
Of simple hearts thorough love's shot,
  By whom, unkind, thou hast them won,
Think not he hath his bow forgot,
  Although my lute and I have done.   20

Vengeance shall fall on thy disdain,
That makest but game on earnest pain;
  Think not alone under the sun
Unquit[1] to cause thy lovers plain,[2]
  Although my lute and I have done.

Perchance thee lie withered and old,
The winter nights that are so cold,
  Plaining in vain unto the moon;
Thy wishes then dare not be told.
  Care then who list, for I have done.   30

And then may chance thee to repent
The time that thou hast lost and spent
  To cause thy lovers sigh and swoon;
Then shalt thou know beauty but lent,
  And wish and want as I have done.

Now cease, my lute! this is the last
Labour that thou and I shall waste,
  And ended is that we begun;
Now is this song both sung and past.
  My lute, be still, for I have done.   40

## They Flee from Me

They flee from me, that sometime did me seek,
With naked foot, stalking in my chamber:
I have seen them gentle, tame, and meek,
That now are wild, and do not remember
That sometime they put themselves in danger
To take bread at my hand; and now they range,
Busily seeking with a continual change.

Thankéd be fortune, it hath been otherwise
Twenty times better; but once, in special,
In thin array, after a pleasant guise,                    10
When her loose gown from her shoulders did fall,
And she me caught in her arms long and small,
Therewithal sweetly did me kiss,
And softly said, "Dear heart, how like you this?"

It was no dream; I lay broad waking.
But all is turned, thorough my gentleness,
Into a strange fashion of forsaking;
And I have leave to go of her goodness,
And she also to use new-fangleness.
But since that I so kindely am served,                    20
I would fain know what she hath deserved.

---

[1] with impunity                        [2] (to) complain, i.e., give expression to grief

## Tangled I Was

Tangled I was in love's snare,
Oppressed with pain, torment[1] with care,
Of grief right sure, of joy full bare,
Clean in despair by cruelty,—
But ha! ha! ha! full well is me,
For I am now at liberty.

The woeful day so full of pain,
The weary night all spent in vain,
The labor lost for so small gain,
To write them all it will not be.          10
But ha! ha! ha! full well is me,
For I am now at liberty.

Everything that fair doth show,
When proof is made it proveth not so,
But turneth mirth to better woe;
Which in this case full well I see.
But ha! ha! ha! full well is me,
For I am now at liberty.

Too great desire was my guide
And wanton will went by my side;          20
Hope ruléd still, and made me bide
Of love's craft th' extremity.
But ha! ha! ha! full well is me,
For I am now at liberty.

With feignéd words that were but wind
To long delays I was assigned;
Her wily looks my wits did blind;
Thus as she would I did agree.
But ha! ha! ha! full well is me,
For I am now at liberty.          30

Was never bird tangled in lime[2]
That brake away in better time
Than I, that rotten boughs did climb,
And had no hurt, but scapéd free.
Now ha! ha! ha! full well is me,
For I am now at liberty.

# HENRY HOWARD, EARL OF SURREY / 1517?–1547

## Description of Spring

The soote[1] season, that bud and bloom forth brings,
With green hath clad the hill and eke the vale.
The nightingale with feathers new she sings;
The turtle to her make[2] hath told her tale.
Summer is come, for every spray now springs.
The hart hath hung his old head on the pale;
The buck in brake his winter coat he flings;
The fishes float with new repairéd scale;
The adder all her slough away she slings;
The swift swallow pursueth the flies small;          10
The busy bee her honey now she mings;[3]
Winter is worn that was the flower's bale.
And thus I see among these pleasant things
Each care decays; and yet my sorrow springs.

---

[1] tormented
[2] a sticky material spread on branches to catch birds

[1] sweet     [2] mate     [3] mingles; blends

## Love That Doth Reign

Love, that doth reign and live within my thought,
And built his seat within my captive breast,
Clad in the arms wherein with me he fought,
Oft in my face he doth his banner rest.
But she that taught me love and suffer pain,
My doubtful hope and eke my hot desire
With shamefast look to shadow and refrain,
Her smiling grace converteth straight to ire.
And coward Love, then, to the heart apace
Taketh his flight, where he doth lurk and plain,[1]          10
His purpose lost, and dare not show his face.
For my lord's guilt thus faultless bide I pain,
Yet from my lord shall not my foot remove:
Sweet is the death that taketh end by love.

## Set Me Whereas the Sun Doth Parch the Green

Set me whereas the sun doth parch the green,
Or where his beams may not dissolve the ice,
In temperate heat, where he is felt and seen;
With proud people, in presence sad and wise,
Set me in base, or yet in high degree;
In the long night, or in the shortest day;
In clear weather, or where mists thickest be;
In lusty youth, or when my hairs be gray;
Set me in earth, in heaven, or yet in hell;
In hill, in dale, or in the foaming flood;          10
Thrall, or at large—alive whereso I dwell;
Sick or in health, in ill fame or in good;
Yours I will be, and with that only thought
Comfort myself when that my hap is naught.

## Wyatt Resteth Here

Wyatt resteth here, that quick[1] could never rest;
Whose heavenly gifts increaséd by disdain,[2]
And virtue sank the deeper in his breast;
Such profit he of envy could obtain.
A head where wisdom mysteries did frame;
Whose hammers beat still in that lively brain
As on a stithy,[3] where some work of fame
Was daily wrought, to turn to Britain's gain.
A visage stern and mild; where both did grow,

---

[1] complain; express grief

[1] alive     [2] humility     [3] forge

Vice to condemn, in virtues to rejoice;                              *10*
Amid great storms, whom grace assuréd so,
To live upright, and smile at fortune's choice.
A hand that taught what might be said in rhyme;
That reft Chaucer the glory of his wit;
A mark, the which—unperfited,[4] for time—
Some may approach, but never none shall hit.
A tongue that served in foreign realms his king;
Whose courteous talk to virtue did enflame
Each noble heart; a worthy guide to bring
Our English youth, by travail, unto fame.                            *20*
An eye whose judgment no affect[5] could blind,
Friends to allure, and foes to reconcile;
Whose piercing look did represent a mind
With virtue fraught, reposéd, void of guile.
A heart where dread yet never so impressed
To hide the thought that might the truth advance;
In neither fortune lift,[6] nor so repressed,
To swell in wealth, nor yield unto mischance.
A valiant corpse,[7] where force and beauty met,
Happy, alas! too happy, but for foes,                                *30*
Lived, and ran the race that nature set;
Of manhood's shape, where she the mold did lose.
But to the heavens that simple soul is fled;
Which left with such as covet Christ to know
Witness of faith that never shall be dead;
Sent for our health, but not receivéd so.
Thus for our guilt, this jewel have we lost;
The earth his bones, the heavens possess his ghost.

## So Cruel Prison

So cruel prison how could betide, alas,
As proud Windsor, where I in lust and joy
With a king's son my childish years did pass
In greater feast than Priam's sons of Troy?
Where each sweet place returns a taste full sour;
The large green courts where we were wont to hove
With eyes cast up unto the maidens' tower,
And easy sighs, such as folk draw in love;
The stately sales,[1] the ladies bright of hue,
The dances short, long tales of great delight,               *10*
With words and looks that tigers could but rue,
Where each of us did plead the other's right;
The palm-play where, despoiléd for the game,

---

[4] unperfected
[5] emotion    [6] lifted    [7] (living) body

[1] halls

With dazéd eyes oft we by gleams of love
Have missed the ball and got sight of our dame,
To bait her eyes, which kept the leads[2] above;
The gravelled ground, with sleeves tied on the helm,
On foaming horse, with swords and friendly hearts,
With cheer, as though the one should overwhelm,
Where we have fought and chaséd oft with darts;                20
With silver drops the meads yet spread for ruth,
In active games of nimbleness and strength,
Where we did strain, trailed by swarms of youth,
Our tender limbs that yet shot up in length;
The secret groves which oft we made resound
Of pleasant plaint and of our ladies' praise,
Recording soft what grace each one had found,
What hope of speed, what dread of long delays;
The wild forest, the clothéd holts with green,
With reins avaled,[3] and swift ybreathéd horse,             30
With cry of hounds and merry blasts between,
Where we did chase the fearful hart aforce;
The void walls eke that harboured us each night,
Wherewith, alas! revive within my breast
The sweet accord, such sleeps as yet delight,
The pleasant dreams, the quiet bed of rest,
The secret thoughts imparted with such trust,
The wanton talk, the divers change of play,
The friendship sworn, each promise kept so just,
Wherewith we passed the winter nights away.                  40
And with this thought the blood forsakes my face,
The tears berain my cheeks of deadly hue,
The which as soon as sobbing sighs, alas!
Upsuppéd have, thus I my plaint renew:
"O place of bliss, renewer of my woes,
Give me account where is my noble fere,[4]
Whom in thy walls thou didst each night enclose,
To other lief,[5] but unto me most dear."
Echo, alas! that doth my sorrow rue,
Returns thereto a hollow sound of plaint.                    50
Thus I alone, where all my freedom grew,
In prison pine with bondage and restraint;
And with remembrance of the greater grief
To banish the less, I find my chief relief.

---

[2] lead-covered roofs used as platforms    [3] slack    [4] company    [5] dear

## SIR EDWARD DYER / 1540?–1607

### My Mind to Me a Kingdom Is

My mind to me a kingdom is,
  Such present joys therein I find,
That it excels all other bliss
  That world affords or grows by kind.
Though much I want which most would have,
Yet still my mind forbids to crave.

No princely pomp, no wealthy store,
  No force to win the victory,
No wily wit to salve a sore,
  No shape to feed a loving eye;    10
To none of these I yield as thrall,
For why my mind doth serve for all.

I see how plenty suffers oft,
  And hasty climbers soon do fall;
I see that those which are aloft
  Mishap doth threaten most of all;
They get with toil, they keep with fear:
Such cares my mind could never bear.

Content I live, this is my stay,
  I seek no more than may suffice;    20
I press to bear no haughty sway;
  Look, what I lack my mind supplies.
Lo! thus I triumph like a king,
Content with that my mind doth bring.

Some have too much, yet still do crave;
  I little have, and seek no more.
They are but poor, though much they have,
  And I am rich with little store.
They poor, I rich; they beg, I give;
They lack, I leave; they pine, I live.    30

I laugh not at another's loss;
  I grudge not at another's gain;
No worldly waves my mind can toss;
  My state at one doth still remain.
I fear no foe, I fawn no friend;
I loathe not life, nor dread my end.

Some weigh their pleasure by their lust,
  Their wisdom by their rage of will;
Their treasure is their only trust,
  A cloakéd craft their store of skill:    40
But all the pleasure that I find
Is to maintain a quiet mind.

My wealth is health and perfect ease,
  My conscience clear my choice defence;
I neither seek by bribes to please,
  Nor by deceit to breed offence.
Thus do I live; thus will I die;
Would all did so as well as I!   *(1588)*


## WILLIAM STEVENSON / d. 1575

### *from* Gammer Gurton's Needle

Back and side go bare, go bare,
  Both foot and hand go cold;
But, belly, God send thee good ale enough,
  Whether it be new or old.

I cannot eat but little meat,
  My stomach is not good;
But sure I think that I can drink
With him that wears a hood.
Though I go bare, take ye no care,
  I am nothing a-cold;    10
I stuff my skin so full within
  Of jolly good ale and old.
    Back and side go bare, go bare, etc.

I love no roast but a nutbrown toast,
  And a crab laid in the fire;
A little bread shall do me stead,
  Much bread I not desire.

No frost nor snow, no wind, I trow,
  Can hurt me if I would
I am so wrapt, and thoroughly lapt    20
  Of jolly good ale and old.
    Back and side go bare, go bare, etc.

And Tib my wife, that as her life
  Loveth well good ale to seek,
Full oft drinks she, till ye may see
  The tears run down her cheek.
Then doth she troll to me the bowl,
  Even as a maltworm should;
And saith, "Sweetheart, I took my part
  Of this jolly good ale and old."    30
    Back and side go bare, go bare, etc.

Now let them drink, till they nod and
  wink,
  Even as good fellows should do;
They shall not miss to hae the bliss
  Good ale doth bring men to.
And all poor souls that have scouréd
  bowls,
  Or have them lustily trolled,
God save the lives of them and their
  wives,
  Whether they be young or old.
    Back and side go bare, go bare,
     etc. *(1575)*    40

# DR. GILES FLETCHER / 1549?–1611

*from* Licia

### XXVIII

In time the strong and stately turrets fall,
In time the rose and silver lilies die,
In time the monarchs captives are, and thrall,
In time the sea and rivers are made dry;
The hardest flint in time doth melt asunder;
Still-living fame in time doth fade away;
The mountains proud we see in time come under;
The earth, for age, we see in time decay.
The sun in time forgets for to retire
From out the east where he was wont to rise;    10
The basest thoughts we see in time aspire,
And greedy minds in time do wealth despise.
Thus all, sweet fair, in time must have an end,
Except thy beauty, virtues, and thy friend.   *(1593)*

# BARTHOLOMEW GRIFFIN / d. 1602

*from* Fidessa

### XV

Care-charmer sleep, sweet ease in restless misery,
The captive's liberty, and his freedom's song,
Balm of the bruiséd heart, man's chief felicity,
Brother of quiet death, when life is too, too long!
A comedy it is, and now an history.
What is not sleep unto the feeble mind?
It easeth him that toils and him that's sorry,
It makes the deaf to hear, to see the blind.
Ungentle sleep, thou helpest all but me,
For when I sleep my soul is vexéd most.                    *10*
It is Fidessa that doth master thee;
If she approach, alas, thy power is lost.
But here she is. See, how he runs amain!
I fear at night he will not come again.

### XXXV

I have not spent the April of my time,
The sweet of youth, in plotting in the air,
But do at first adventure seek to climb,
Whilst flowers of blooming years are green and fair.
I am no leaving of all-withering age,
I have not suffered many winter lours;
I feel no storm unless my love do rage,
And then in grief I spend both days and hours.
This yet doth comfort, that my flower lasted
Until it did approach my sun too near,                     *10*
And then, alas, untimely was it blasted,
So soon as once thy beauty did appear.
But after all, my comfort rests in this,
That for thy sake my youth decayéd is.    *(1596)*


# EDWARD DE VERE, EARL OF OXFORD / 1550–1604

## If Women Could Be Fair

If women could be fair and yet not fond,
Or that their love were firm, not fickle, still,
I would not marvel that they make men bond,
By service long to purchase their good will.

But when I see how frail those creatures are,
I muse that men forget themselves so far.

To mark the choice they make and how they change,
How oft from Phoebus they do fly to Pan,
Unsettled still, like haggards wild they range,
These gentle birds that fly from man to man;                    10
    Who would not scorn, and shake them from the fist,
    And let them fly, fair fools, which way they list?

Yet for disport we fawn and flatter both,
To pass the time when nothing else can please;
And train them to our lure with subtle oath
Till, weary of their wiles, ourselves we ease;
    And then we say, when we their fancy try,
    To play with fools, oh, what a fool was I!   *(1588)*

# EDMUND SPENSER / 1552–1599

*from* The Shepheardes Calender

## APRILL: ÆGLOGA QUARTA

ARGUMENT: This Æglogue is purposely intended to the honor and prayse of our most gracious sovereigne, Queene Elizabeth. The speakers herein be Hobbinoll[1] and Thenott, two shepheardes: the which Hobbinoll being before mentioned, greatly to have loved Colin, is here set forth more largely, complayning him of that boyes great misadventure in Love, whereby his mynd was alienate and with drawen not onely from him, who moste loved him, but also from all former delightes and studies, as well in pleasaunt pyping, as conning[2] ryming and singing, and other his laudable exercises. Whereby he taketh occasion, for proofe of his more excellencie and skill in poetrie, to recorde a songe, which the sayd Colin sometime made in honor of her majestie, whom abruptely[3] he termeth Elysa.

THENOT        HOBBINOLL

THENOT: Tell me good Hobbinoll, what garres thee greete?[4]
What? hath some Wolfe thy tender Lambes ytorne?
Or is thy Bagpype broke, that soundes so sweete?
Or art thou of thy lovéd lasse forlorne?[5]

Or bene thine eyes attempred to the yeare,
Quenching the gasping furrowes thirst with rayne?
Like April shoure, so stremes the trickling teares
Adowne thy cheeke, to quenche thy thristye payne.

---

[1] Hobbinoll is a conventional pastoral name, which here identifies Gabriel Harvey, a friend of Spenser. Thenott and Rosalind are unidentified. Colin is Spenser. Elisa, Queen Elizabeth; Pan, Henry VIII; Syrinx, Anne Boleyn.   [2] studying   [3] for short   [4] makes you weep   [5] deserted

HOBBINOLL: Nor thys, nor that, so muche doeth make me mourne,
But for the ladde, whome long I lovd so deare, *10*
Nowe loves a lasse, that all his love doth scorne:
He plonged in payne, his tresséd[6] locks dooth teare.

Shepheards delights he dooth them all forsweare,
Hys pleasaunt Pipe, whych made us meriment,
He wylfully hath broke, and doth forbeare
His wonted songs, wherein he all outwent.[7]

THEN: What is he for a Ladde, you so lament?
Ys love such pinching payne to them, that prove?[8]
And hath he skill to make[9] so excellent,
Yet hath so little skill to brydle love? *20*

HOB: *Colin* thou kenst,[10] the Southerne shepheardes boye:
Him Love hath wounded with a deadly darte.
Whilome on him was all my care and joye,
Forcing with gyfts to winne his wanton heart.
But now from me hys madding mynd is starte,
And woes[11] the Widdowes daughter of the glenne:
So nowe fayre *Rosalind* hath bredde hys smart,[12]
So now his frend is chaunged for a frenne.[13]

THEN: But if hys ditties bene so trimly dight,[14]
I pray thee *Hobbinoll*, recorde some one: *30*
The whiles our flockes doe graze about in sight,
And we close shrowded in thys shade alone.

HOB: Contented I: then will I singe his laye
Of fayre *Elisa,* Queene of shepheardes all:
Which once he made, as by a spring he laye,
And tuned it unto the Waters fall.

Ye dayntye Nymphs, that in this blessed Brooke
    doe bathe your brest,
Forsake your watry bowres, and hither looke,
    at my request: *40*
And eke[15] you Virgins[16] that on *Parnasse* dwell,
Whence floweth *Helicon* the learnéd well,
    Helpe me to blaze
    Her worthy praise,
Which in her sexe doth all excell.

Of fayre *Elisa* by your silver song,
    that blessed wight:
The flowre of Virgins, may shee florish long,
    in princely plight.[17]

---

[6] braided    [7] outdid    [8] try it
[9] compose poetry    [10] know    [11] woos
[12] caused his pain    [13] stranger

[14] nicely turned    [15] also
[16] the nine Muses, who often sojourned on
Parnassus    [17] condition

For shee is *Syrinx* daughter without spotte,                                    *50*
Which *Pan* the shepheards God of her begot:
   So sprong her grace
   Of heavenly race,
No mortall blemishe may her blotte.

See, where she sitts upon the grassie greene,
   (O seemely sight)
Yclad in Scarlot like a mayden Queene,
   And Ermines white.
Upon her head a Cremosin[18] coronet,
With Damaske roses and Daffadillies set:                                    *60*
   Bayleaves betweene,
   And Primroses greene
Embellish the sweete Violet.

Tell me, have ye seene her angelick face,
   Like *Phoebe*[19] fayre?
Her heavenly haveour,[20] her princely grace
   can you well compare?
The Redde rose medled with the White yfere,[21]
In either cheeke depeincten lively chere.[22]
   Her modest eye,                                    *70*
   Her majestie,
Where have you seene the like, but here?

I sawe *Phoebus*[23] thrust out his golden hedde,
   upon her to gaze:
But when he sawe, how broade her beames did spredde,
   it did him amaze.
He blusht to see another Sunne belowe,
Ne durst againe his fyrye face out showe:
   Let him, if he dare,
   His brightnesse compare                                    *80*
With hers, to have the overthrowe.

Shewe thy selfe *Cynthia* with thy silver rayes,
   and be not abasht:
When shee the beames of her beauty displayes,
   O how art thou dasht?
But I will not match her with *Latonaes* seede,[24]
Such follie great sorrow to *Niobe* did breede.
   Now she is a stone,
   And makes dayly mone,
Warning all other to take heede.                                    *90*

---

18 crimson
19 identified as Diana or Artemis, the huntress and
goddess of woodlands, and as Cynthia or Selene,
the goddess of the moon   20 demeanor
21 the houses of Lancaster (red rose) and York
(white rose) mingled together

22 displaying a lively disposition
23 god of the sun, identified also as Apollo, god of
the arts
24 The children, fathered by Jove, were Artemis
and Apollo.

*Pan* may be proud, that ever he begot
    such a Bellibone,[25]
And *Syrinx* rejoyse, that ever was her lot
    to beare such an one.
Soone as my younglings cryen for the dam,
To her will I offer a milkwhite Lamb:
    Shee is my goddesse plaine,
    And I her shepherds swayne,
Albee forswonck and forswatt[26] I am.

I see *Calliope*[27] speede her to the place,                    100
    where my Goddesse shines:
And after her the other Muses trace,
    with their Violines.
Bene they not Bay braunches, which they doe beare,
All for *Elisa* in her hand to weare?
    So sweetely they play,
    And sing all the way,
That it a heaven is to heare.

Lo how finely the graces can it foote
    to the Instrument:                    110
They dauncen deffly, and singen soote,[28]
    in their meriment.
Wants not a fourth grace, to make the daunce even?
Let that rowme to my Lady be yeven:
    She shalbe a grace,
    To fyll the fourth place,
And reigne with the rest in heaven.

And whither rennes this bevie of Ladies bright,
    raunged in a rowe?
They bene all Ladyes of the lake behight,[29]                    120
    that unto her goe.
*Chloris*, that is the chiefest Nymph of al,
Of Olive braunches beares a Coronall:
    Olives bene for peace,
    When wars doe surcease:
Such for a Princesse bene principall.

Ye shepheards daughters, that dwell on the greene,
    hye you there apace:
Let none come there, but that Virgins bene,
    to adorne her grace.                    130
And when you come, whereas shee is in place,
See, that your rudenesse doe not you disgrace:
    Binde your fillets faste,

---

[25] fair maid
[26] worn out and sweaty from work

[27] the muse of epic poetry    [28] sweetly
[29] called

And gird in your waste,
For more finesse, with a tawdrie lace.[30]

Bring hether the Pincke and purple Cullambine,
   With Gelliflowres:
Bring Coronations, and Sops in wine,[31]
   worne of Paramoures.
Strowe me the ground with Daffadowndillies,                    140
And Cowslips, and Kingcups, and loved Lillies:
   The pretie Pawnce,[32]
   And the Chevisaunce,[33]
Shall match with the fayre flowre Delice.[34]

Now ryse up *Elisa*, decked as thou art,
   in royall aray:
And now ye daintie Damsells may depart
   echeone her way
I feare, I have troubled your troupes to longe:
Let dame *Elisa* thanke you for her song.                      150
   And if you come hether,
   When Damsines[35] I gether,
I will part them all you among.

THEN: And was thilk[36] same song of *Colins* owne making?
Ah foolish boy, that is with love yblent:[37]
Great pittie is, he be in such taking,
For naught caren, that bene so lewdly[38] bent.

HOB: Sicker[39] I hold him for a greater fon,[40]
That loves the thing he cannot purchase.                       160
But let us homeward: for night draweth on,
And twincling starres the daylight hence chase.

THENOTS EMBLEME: *O quam te memorem virgo?*
HOBBINOLS EMBLEME: *O dea certe.*[41]   (1579)


## *from* Amoretti

### XV

Ye tradefull Merchants, that with weary toyle,
Do seeke most pretious things to make your gain;
And both the Indias of their treasures spoile,
What needeth you to seeke so farre in vaine?
For loe my love doth in her selfe containe
All this worlds riches that may farre be found,

---

[30] from the fair of St. Audrey; not necessarily shoddy   [31] carnations and garden pinks
[32] pansy   [33] wallflower   [34] fleur-de-lys: iris
[35] plums   [36] this   [37] dazzled
[38] foolishly   [39] certainly   [40] fool

[41] Thenot's emblem: "O what are you called, maiden?" Hobbinoll's emblem: "A goddess indeed." The emblems, quoted from *Aeneid*, I, 327–328, identify Queen Elizabeth with Venus.

If Saphyres, loe her eies be Saphyres plaine,
If Rubies, loe hir lips be Rubies sound:
If Pearles, hir teeth be pearles both pure and round;
If Yvorie, her forhead yvory weene;[1]                                   *10*
If Gold, her locks are finest gold on ground;
If silver, her faire hands are silver sheene.[2]
But that which fairest is, but few behold,
Her mind adornd with vertues manifold.

### XIX

The merry Cuckow, messenger of Spring,
His trompet shrill hath thrise already sounded:
That warnes al lovers wayt upon their king,
Who now is comming forth with girland crounéd.
With noyse whereof the quyre of Byrds resounded
Their anthemes sweet, devizéd of Loves prayse,
That all the woods theyr ecchoes back rebounded,
As if they knew the meaning of their layes.
But mongst them all, which did Loves honor rayse,
No word was heard of her that most it ought,                            *10*
But she his precept proudly disobayes,
And doth his ydle message set at nought.
Therefore, O Love, unlesse she turne to thee
Ere Cuckow end, let her a rebell be.

### XXII

This holy season fit to fast and pray,
Men to devotion ought to be inclynd:
Therefore, I lykewise on so holy day,
For my sweet Saynt some service fit will find.
Her temple fayre is built within my mind,
In which her glorious ymage placéd is,
On which my thoughts doo day and night attend
Lyke sacred priests that never thinke amisse.
There I to her as th'author of my blisse.
Will builde an altar to appease her yre:                                *10*
And on the same my hart will sacrifise,
Burning in flames of pure and chast desyre:
The which vouchsafe O goddesse to accept,
Amongst thy deerest relicks to be kept.

### XXVI

Sweet is the Rose, but growes upon a brere;
Sweet is the Junipere, but sharpe his bough;
Sweet is the Eglantine, but pricketh nere;
Sweet is the firbloome, but his braunches rough.
Sweet is the Cypresse, but his rynd is tough,
Sweet is the nut, but bitter is his pill;

---

[1] beautiful      [2] shining

Sweet is the broome-flowre, but yet sowre enough;
And sweet is Moly, but his root is ill.
So every sweet with soure is tempred still,
That maketh it be coveted the more:                    *10*
For easie things that may be got at will,
Most sorts of men doe set but little store.
Why then should I accoumpt of little paine,
That endlesse pleasure shall unto me gaine.

### XXXIV

Lyke as a ship that through the Ocean wyde,
By conduct of some star doth make her way,
Whenas a storme hath dimd her trusty guyde
Out of her course doth wander far astray.
So I whose star, that wont with her bright ray,
Me to direct, with cloudes is overcast,
Doe wander now in darknesse and dismay,
Through hidden perils round about me plast.
Yet hope I well, that when this storme is past
My *Helice* the lodestar of my lyfe                    *10*
Will shine again, and looke on me at last,
With lovely light to clear my cloudy grief.
Till then I wander carefull comfortlesse,
In secret sorrow and sad pensivenesse.

### XLI

Is it her nature or is it her will,
To be so cruell to an humbled foe?
If nature, then she may it mend with skill,
If will, then she at will may will forgoe.
But if her nature and her will be so,
That she will plague the man that loves her most:
And take delight t'encrease a wretches woe,
Then all her natures goodly guifts are lost.
And that same glorious beauties ydle boast,
Is but a bayt such wretches to beguile:                    *10*
As being long in her loves tempest tost,
She meanes at last to make her piteous spoyle.
O fayrest fayre let never it be named,
That so fayre beauty was so fowly shamed.

### LIV

Of this worlds Theatre in which we stay,
My love lyke the Spectator ydly sits
Beholding me that all the pageants play,
Disguysing diversly my troubled wits.
Sometimes I joy when glad occasion fits,
And mask in myrth lyke to a Comedy:
Soone after when my joy to sorrow flits,
I waile and make my woes a Tragedy.

Yet she beholding me with constant eye,
Delights not in my merth nor rues my smart:
But when I laugh she mocks, and when I cry
She laughes, and hardens evermore her hart.
What then can move her? if nor merth nor mone,
She is no woman, but a sencelesse stone.

*10*

### LXVII

Lyke as a huntsman after weary chace,
Seeing the game from him escapt away,
Sits downe to rest him in some shady place,
With panting hounds beguiléd of their pray:
So after long pursuit and vaine assay,
When I all weary had the chace forsooke,
The gentle deare returned the selfe-same way,
Thinking to quench her thirst at the next brooke.
There she beholding me with mylder looke,
Sought not to fly, but fearelesse still did bide:
Till I in hand her yet halfe trembling tooke,
And with her owne goodwill hir fyrmely tyde.
Strange thing me seemd to see a beast so wyld,
So goodly wonne with her owne will beguyld.

*10*

### LXX

Fresh spring the herald of loves mighty king,
In whose cote armour[1] richly are displayd
All sorts of flowers the which on earth do spring
In goodly colours gloriously arrayd.
Goe to my love, where she is carelesse layd,
Yet in her winters bowre not well awake:
Tell her the joyous time wil not be staid
Unlesse she doe him by the forelock take.
Bid her therefore her selfe soone ready make,
To wayt on love amongst his lovely crew:
Where every one that misseth then her make,[2]
Shall be by him amearst[3] with penance dew.
Make hast therefore sweet love, whilest it is prime,
For none can call againe the passéd time.

*10*

### LXXV

One day I wrote her name upon the strand,
But came the waves and washéd it away:
Agayne I wrote it with a second hand,
But came the tyde, and made my paynes his pray.
Vayne man, sayd she, that doest in vaine assay,
A mortell thing so to immortalize,
For I my selve shall lyke to this decay,
And eek my name bee wypéd out lykewize.

---

[1] herald's garb    [2] mate    [3] punished

Not so, (quod I) let baser things devize
To dy in dust, but you shall live by fame:               *10*
My verse your vertues rare shall eternize,
And in the hevens wryte your glorious name.
Where whenas death shall all the world subdew,
Our love shall live, and later life renew.    *(1595)*


# Epithalamion[1]

Ye learnéd sisters, which have oftentimes
Beene to me ayding, others to adorne,
Whom ye thought worthy of your gracefull rymes,
That even the greatest did not greatly scorne
To heare theyr names sung in your simple layes,
     But joyéd in theyr praise;
And when ye list your owne mishaps to mourne,
Which death, or love, or fortunes wreck did rayse,
Your string could soone to sadder tenor turne,
And teach the woods and waters to lament             *10*
     Your dolefull dreriment:
Now lay those sorrowful complaints aside,
And having all your heads with girland crownd,
Helpe me mine owne loves prayses to resound;
Ne let the same of any be envide:
So Orpheus did for his owne bride:
So I unto my selfe alone will sing;
The woods shall to me answer, and my eccho ring.

Early, before the worlds light giving lampe
His golden beame upon the hils doth spred,             *20*
Having disperst the nights unchearefull dampe,
Doe ye awake, and, with fresh lustyhed,
Go to the bowre of my belovéd love,
     My truest turtle dove:
Bid her awake; for Hymen is awake,
And long since ready forth his maske to move,
With his bright tead[2] that flames with many a flake,
And many a bachelor to waite on him,
     In theyr fresh garments trim.
Bid her awake therefore, and soone her dight,        *30*
For lo! the wishéd day is come at last,
That shall, for all the paynes and sorrowes past,
Pay to her usury of long delight:
     And whylest she doth her dight,[3]
Doe ye to her of joy and solace sing,
That all the woods may answer, and your eccho ring.

---

[1] a song in celebration of a wedding      [2] torch      [3] dress (v.)

Bring with you all the nymphes that you can heare,
Both of the rivers and the forrests greene,
And of the sea that neighbours to her neare,
Al with gay girlands goodly wel beseene.
And let them also with them bring in hand
   Another gay girland,
For my fayre love, of lillyes and of roses,
Bound truelove wize with a blew silke riband.
And let them make great store of bridale poses,
And let them eeke bring store of other flowers,
   To deck the bridale bowers.
And let the ground whereas her foot shall tread,
For feare the stones her tender foot should wrong,
Be strewed with fragrant flowers all along,
And diapred⁴ lyke the discolored mead.
Which done, doe at her chamber dore awayt,
   For she will waken strayt;
The whiles doe ye this song unto her sing,
The woods shall to you answer, and your eccho ring.

Ye nymphes of Mulla, which with careful heed
The silver scaly trouts doe tend full well,
And greedy pikes which use therein to feed,
(Those trouts and pikes all others doo excel)
And ye likewise which keepe the rushy lake,
   Where none doo fishes take,
Bynde up the locks the which hang scatterd light,
And in his waters, which your mirror make,
Behold your faces as the christall bright,
That when you come whereas my love doth lie,
   No blemish she may spie.
And eke ye lightfoot mayds which keepe the dere
That on the hoary mountayne use to towre,
And the wylde wolves, which seeke them to devoure,
With your steele darts doo chace from coming neer,
   Be also present heere,
To helpe to decke her, and to help to sing,
That all the woods may answer, and your eccho ring.

Wake now, my love, awake! for it is time:
The rosy Morne long since left Tithones bed,
All ready to her silver coche to clyme,
And Phœbus gins to shew his glorious hed.
Hark how the cheerefull birds do chaunt theyr laies,
   And caroll of loves praise!
The merry larke hir mattins sings aloft,
The thrush replyes, the mavis descant playes,
The ouzell⁵ shrills, the ruddock⁶ warbles soft,

---

⁴ decorated    ⁵ blackbird    ⁶ robin

40

50

60

70

80

So goodly all agree, with sweet consent,
   To this dayes merriment.
Ah! my deere love, why doe ye sleepe thus long,
When meeter were that ye should now awake,
T'awayt the comming of your joyous make,
And hearken to the birds love-learnéd song,
   The deawy leaves among?
For they of joy and pleasance to you sing,                    90
That all the woods them answer, and theyr eccho ring.

My love is now awake out of her dreame,
And her fayre eyes, like stars that dimméd were
With darksome cloud, now shew theyr goodly beams
More bright then Hesperus his head doth rere.
Come now, ye damzels, daughters of delight,
   Helpe quickly her to dight.
But first come ye, fayre Houres, which were begot,
In Joves sweet paradice, of Day and Night,
Which doe the seasons of the year allot,                      100
And al that ever in this world is fayre
   Do make and still repayre.
And ye three handmayds of the Cyprian Queene,
The which doe still adorne her beauties pride,
Helpe to addorne my beautifullest bride:
And as ye her array, still throw betweene
   Some graces to be seene:
And as ye use to Venus, to her sing,
The whiles the woods shal answer, and your eccho ring.

Now is my love all ready forth to come:                       110
Let all the virgins therefore well awayt,
And ye fresh boyes, that tend upon her groome,
Prepare your selves, for he is comming strayt.
Set all your things in seemely good aray,
   Fit for so joyfull day,
The joyfulst day that ever sunne did see.
Faire Sun, shew forth thy favourable ray,
And let thy lifull heat not fervent be,
For feare of burning her sunshyny face,
   Her beauty to disgrace.                                 120
O fayrest Phœbus, father of the Muse,
If ever I did honour thee aright,
Or sing the thing that mote thy mind delight,
Doe not thy servants simple boone refuse,
But let this day, let this one day be myne,
   Let all the rest be thine.
Then I thy soverayne prayses loud wil sing,
That all the woods shal answer, and theyr eccho ring.

Hark how the minstels gin to shrill aloud
Their merry musick that resounds from far,                    130

The pipe, the tabor, and the trembling croud,[7]
That well agree withouten breach or jar.
But most of all the damzels doe delite,
   When they their tymbrels smyte,
And thereunto doe daunce and carrol sweet,
That all the sences they doe ravish quite,
The whyles the boyes run up and downe the street,
Crying aloud with strong confuséd noyce,
   As if it were one voyce.
"Hymen, Iö Hymen, Hymen," they do shout,         *140*
That even to the heavens theyr shouting shrill
Doth reach, and all the firmament doth fill;
To which the people, standing all about,
As in approvance doe thereto applaud,
   And loud advaunce her laud,
And evermore they "Hymen, Hymen" sing,
That al the woods them answer, and theyr eccho ring.

Loe! where she comes along with portly pace,
Lyke Phœbe, from her chamber of the east,
Arysing forth to run her might race,         *150*
Clad all in white, that seemes a virgin best.
So well it her beseemes, that ye would weene
   Some angell she had beene.
Her long loose yellow locks lyke golden wyre,
Sprinckled with perle, and perling flowres atweene,
Doe lyke a golden mantle her attyre,
And being crownéd with a girland greene,
   Seeme lyke some mayden queene.
Her modest eyes, abashéd to behold
So many gazers as on her do stare,         *160*
Upon the lowly ground affixéd are;
Ne dare lift up her countenance too bold,
But blush to heare her prayses sung so loud,
   So farre from being proud.
Nathlesse doe ye still loud her prayses sing,
That all the woods may answer, and your eccho ring.

Tell me, ye merchants daughters, did ye see
So fayre a creature in your towne before,
So sweet, so lovely, and so mild as she,
Adorned with beautyes grace and vertues store?         *170*
Her goodly eyes lyke saphyres shining bright,
Her forehead yvory white,
Her cheekes lyke apples which the sun hath rudded,
Her lips lyke cherryes charming men to byte,
Her breast like to a bowle of creame uncrudded,[8]
   Her paps lyke lyllies budded,

---

[7] an instrument resembling a violin        [8] not curdled

Her snowie necke lyk to a marble towre,
And all her body like a pallace fayre,
Ascending uppe, with many a stately stayre,
To honors seat and chastities sweet bowre.                              *180*
Why stand ye still, ye virgins, in amaze,
   Upon her so to gaze,
Whiles ye forget your former lay to sing,
To which the woods did answer, and your eccho ring.

But if ye saw that which no eyes can see,
The inward beauty of her lively spright,[9]
Garnisht with heavenly guifts of high degree,
Much more then would ye wonder at that sight,
And stand astonisht lyke to those which red [10]
   Medusaes mazeful hed.                                  *190*
There dwels sweet Love and constant Chastity,
Unspotted Fayth, and comely Womanhood,
Regard of Honour, and mild Modesty;
There Vertue raynes as queene in royal throne,
   And giveth lawes alone,
The which the base affections doe obay,
And yeeld theyr services unto her will;
Ne thought of thing uncomely ever may
Thereto approch to tempt her mind to ill.
Had ye once seene these her celestial threasures,                       *200*
   And unrevealéd pleasures,
Then would ye wonder, and her prayses sing,
That al the woods should answer, and your echo ring.

Open the temple gates unto my love,
Open them wide that she may enter in,
And all the postes adorne as doth behove,
And all the pillours deck with girlands trim,
For to receyve this saynt with honour dew,
   That commeth in to you.
With trembling steps and humble reverence,                              *210*
She commeth in before th' Almighties view:
Of her, ye virgins, learne obedience,
When so ye come into those holy places,
   To humble your proud faces.
Bring her up to th' high altar, that she may
The sacred ceremonies there partake,
The which do endlesse matrimony make;
And let the roring organs loudly play
The praises of the Lord in lively notes,
   The whiles with hollow throates                        *220*
The choristers the joyous antheme sing,
That al the woods may answere, and their eccho ring.

---

9 spirit      10 saw

Behold, whiles she before the altar stands,
Hearing the holy priest that to her speakes,
And blesseth her with his two happy hands,
How the red roses flush up in her cheekes,
And the pure snow with goodly vermill[11] stayne,
 Like crimson dyde in grayne:[12]
That even th' angels, which continually
About the sacred altare doe remaine,       *230*
Forget their service and about her fly,
Ofte peeping in her face, that seemes more fayre,
 The more they on it stare.
But her sad eyes, still fastened on the ground,
Are governéd with goodly modesty,
That suffers not one looke to glaunce awry,
Which may let in a little thought unsownd.
Why blush ye, love, to give to me your hand,
 The pledge of all our band?
Sing, ye sweet angels, Alleluya sing,       *240*
That all the woods may answere, and your eccho ring.

Now al is done; bring home the bride againe,
Bring home the triumph of our victory,
Bring home with you the glory of her gaine,
With joyance bring her and with jollity.
Never had man more joyfull day then this,
 Whom heaven would heape with blis.
Make feast therefore now all this live long day;
This day for ever to me holy is;
Poure out the wine without restraint or stay,     *250*
Poure not by cups, but by the belly full,
 Poure out to all that wull,
And sprinkle all the postes and wals with wine,
That they may sweat, and drunken be withall.
Crowne ye God Bacchus with a coronall,
And Hymen also crowne with wreathes of vine;
And let the Graces daunce unto the rest,
 For they can doo it best:
The whiles the maydens doe theyr carroll sing,
The which the woods shal answer, and theyr eccho ring.  *260*

Ring ye the bels, ye yong men of the towne,
And leave your wonted labors for this day:
This day is holy; doe ye write it downe,
That ye for ever it remember may.
This day the sunne is in his chiefest hight,
 With Barnaby[13] the bright,
From whence declining daily by degrees,
He somewhat loseth of his heat and light,

---

11 bright red   12 in a fast color      day of the year in the old style calendar.
13 St. Barnabas's Day was July 11, the longest

When once the Crab behind his back he sees.
But for this time it ill ordainéd was,                                        270
To chose the longest day in all the yeare,
And shortest night, when longest fitter weare:
Yet never day so long, but late would passe.
Ring ye the bels, to make it weare away,
      And bonefires make all day,
And daunce about them, and about them sing:
That all the woods may answer, and your eccho ring.

Ah! when will this long weary day have end,
And lende me leave to come unto my love?
How slowly do the houres theyr numbers spend!                                  280
How slowly does sad Time his feathers move!
Hast thee, O fayrest planet, to thy home
      Within the westerne foame:
Thy tyréd steedes long since have need of rest.
Long though it be, at last I see it gloome,
And the bright evening star with golden creast
      Appeare out of the east.
Fayre childe of beauty, glorious lampe of love,
That all the host of heaven in rankes doost lead,
And guydest lovers through the nightes dread,                                  290
How chearefully thou lookest from above,
And seemst to laugh atweene thy twinkling light,
      As joying in the sight
Of these glad many, which for joy doe sing,
That all the woods them answer, and their echo ring!

Now ceasse, ye damsels, your delights forepast;
Enough is it that all the day was youres:
Now day is doen, and night is nighing fast:
Now bring the bryde into the brydall boures
The night is come, now soone her disaray,                                      300
      And in her bed her lay;
Lay her in lillies and in violets,
And silken courteins over her display,
And odoured sheetes, and Arras coverlets.
Behold how goodly my faire love does ly,
      In proud humility!
Like unto Maia, when as Jove her tooke
In Tempe, lying on the flowry gras,
Twixt sleepe and wake, after she weary was
With bathing in the Acidalian brooke.                                          310
Now it is night, ye damsels may be gon,
      And leave my love alone.
And leave likwise your former lay to sing:
The woods no more shal answere, nor your echo ring.
And all my cares, which cruell Love collected,
Hast sumd in one, and cancelléd for aye:

Spread thy broad wing over my love and me,
   That no man may us see, 320
And in thy sable mantle us enwrap,
From feare of perrill and foule horror free.
Let no false treason seeke us to entrap,
Nor any dread disquiet once annoy
   The safety of our joy:
But let the night be calme and quietsome,
Without tempestuous storms or sad afray:
Lyke as when Jove with fayre Alcmena lay,
When he begot the great Tirynthian groome:
Or lyke as when he with thy selfe did lie, 330
   And begot Majesty.
And let the mayds and yongmen cease to sing:
Ne let the woods them answer, nor theyr eccho ring.

Let no lamenting cryes, nor dolefull teares,
Be heard all night within, nor yet without:
Ne let false whispers, breeding hidden feares,
Breake gentle sleepe with misconceivéd dout.
Let no deluding dreames, nor dreadful sights,
   Make sudden sad affrights;
Ne le house-fyres, nor lightnings helplesse harmes, 340
Ne let the Pouke, nor other evill sprights,
Ne let mischivous witches with theyr charmes,
Ne let hob goblins, names whose sense we see not,
   Fray us with things that be not.
Let not the shriech oule, nor the storke be heard,
Nor the night raven that still deadly yels,
Nor damnéd ghosts cald up with mighty spels,
Nor griesly vultures make us once affeard:
Ne let th' unpleasant quyre of frogs still croking
   Make us to wish theyr choking. 350
Let none of these theyr drery accents sing;
Ne let the woods them answer, nor theyr eccho ring.

But let stil Silence trew night watches keepe,
That sacred Peace may in assurance rayne,
And tymely Sleep, when it is tyme to sleepe,
May poure his limbs forth on your pleasant playne,
The whiles an hundred little wingéd loves,
   Like divers fethered doves,
Shall fly and flutter round about our bed,
And in the secret darke, that none reproves, 360
Their prety stealthes shall worke, and snares shal spread
To filch away sweet snatches of delight,
   Conceald through covert night.
Ye sonnes of Venus, play your sports at will:
For greedy Pleasure, careless of your toyes,
Thinks more upon her paradise of joyes,

Then what ye do, albe it good or ill.
All night therefore attend your merry play,
    For it will soone be day:
Now none doth hinder you, that say or sing,                    370
Ne will the woods now answer, nor your eccho ring.

Who is the same which at my window peepes?
Or whose is that faire face that shines so bright?
Is it not Cinthia, she that never sleepes,
But walkes about high heaven al the night?
O fayrest goddesse, do thou not envy
    My love with me to spy:
For thou likewise didst love, though now unthought,
And for a fleece of woll, which privily
The Latmian shephard once unto thee brought,                  380
    His pleasures with thee wrought.
Therefore to us be favorable now;
And sith of wemens labours thou hast charge,
And generation goodly dost enlarge,
Encline thy will t' effect our wishful vow,
And the chast wombe informe with timely seed,
    That may our comfort breed:
Till which we cease our hopefull hap to sing,
Ne let the woods us answere, nor our eccho ring.

And thou, great Juno, which with awful might                  390
The lawes of wedlock still dost patronize,
And the religion of the faith first plight
With sacred rites hast taught to solemnize,
And eeke for comfort often calléd art
    Of women in their smart,
Eternally bind thou this lovely band,
And all thy blessings unto us impart,
And thou, glad Genius, in whose gentle hand
The bridal bowre and geniall bed remaine,
    Without blemish or staine,                                400
And the sweet pleasures of theyr loves delight
With secret ayde doest succour and supply,
Till they bring forth the fruitfull progeny,
Send us the timely fruit of this same night.
And thou, fayre Hebe, and thou, Hymen free,
    Grant that it may so be.
Til which we cease your further prayse to sing,
Ne any woods shal answer, nor your eccho ring.

And ye high heavens, the temple of the gods,
In which a thousand torches flaming bright                    410
Doe burne, that to us wretched earthly clods
In dreadful darknesse lend desiréd light,
And all ye powers which in the same remayne,
    More then we men can fayne,

Poure out youre blessing on us plentiously,
And happy influence upon us raine,
That we may raise a large posterity,
Which from the earth, which they may long possesse
    With lasting happinesse,
Up to your haughty pallaces may mount,                          *420*
And for the guerdon of theyr glorious merit,
May heavenly tabernacles there inherit,
Of blessed saints for to increase the count.
So let us rest, sweet love, in hope of this,
And cease till then our tymely joyes to sing:
The woods no more us answer, nor our eccho ring.

Song, made in lieu of many ornaments
With which my love should duly have bene dect,
Which cutting off through hasty accidents,
Ye would not stay your dew time to expect,                      *430*
    But promist both to recompens,
Be unto her a goodly ornament,
And for short time an endlesse moniment.   (*1594*)


# SIR WALTER RALEGH / 1552?–1618


## Farewell, False Love

Farewell, false love, the oracle of lics,
A mortal foe and enemy to rest;
An envious boy, from whom all cares arise,
A bastard vile, a beast with rage possessed;
A way of error, a temple full of treason,
In all effects contrary unto reason.

A poisoned serpent covered all with flowers,
Mother of sighs and murderer of repose,
A sea of sorrows from whence are drawn such showers
As moisture lends to every grief that grows;                    10
A school of guile, a net of deep deceit,
A gilded hook that holds a poisoned bait.

A fortress foiled which reason did defend,
A siren song, a fever of the mind,
A maze wherein affection finds no end,
A raging cloud that runs before the wind,
A substance like the shadow of the sun,
A goal of grief for which the wisest run.

A quenchless fire, a nurse of trembling fear,
A path that leads to peril and mishap;                                                                20
A true retreat of sorrow and despair,
An idle boy that sleeps in pleasure's lap,
A deep distrust of that which certain seems,
A hope of that which reason doubtful deems.

Sith then thy trains[1] my younger years betrayed,
And for my faith ingratitude I find,
And sith repentance hath my wrongs bewrayed[2]
Whose course was ever contrary to kind[3]—
False love, desire, and beauty frail, adieu!
Dead is the root whence all these fancies grew.   (*1588*)         30

## Methought I Saw the Grave Where Laura Lay

Methought I saw the grave where Laura lay,
Within that temple where the vestal flame
Was wont to burn; and passing by that way
To see that buried dust of living fame,
Whose tomb fair love and fairer virtue kept,
All suddenly I saw the Fairy Queen;[1]
At whose approach the soul of Petrarch wept,
And from thenceforth those graces were not seen,
For they this Queen attended; in whose stead
Oblivion laid him down on Laura's hearse.                                               10
Hereat the hardest stones were seen to bleed,
And groans of buried ghosts the heavens did pierce;
Where Homer's sprite[2] did tremble all for grief,
And cursed th' access of that celestial thief.   (*1590*)

## The Nymph's Reply to the Shepherd[1]

If all the world and love were young,
And truth in every shepherd's tongue,
These pretty pleasures might me move,
To live with thee, and be thy love.

Time drives the flocks from field to fold,
When rivers rage, and rocks grow cold,
And Philomel becometh dumb,
The rest complains of cares to come.

The flowers do fade, and wanton fields,
To wayward winter reckoning yields,   10

A honey tongue, a heart of gall,
Is fancy's spring, but sorrow's fall.

Thy gowns, thy shoes, thy beds of roses,
Thy cap, thy kirtle, and thy posies,
Soon break, soon wither, soon forgotten:
In folly ripe, in reason rotten.

Thy belt of straw and ivy buds,
Thy coral clasps and amber studs,
All these in me no means can move,
To come to thee, and be thy love.   20

But could youth last, and love still breed,
Had joys no date, nor age no need,
Then these delights my mind might move,
To live with thee and by thy love.   (*1600*)

---

[1] deceits    [2] exposed    [3] nature

[1] This sonnet first appeared as a preface to Spenser's *Faerie Queene*.    [2] spirit

[1] Ralegh's poem is a reply to Marlowe's "The Passionate Shepherd to His Love," page 129. See also Donne's "The Bait," page 145, and C. Day Lewis's "Come Live with Me and Be My Love," page 749.

# The Passionate Man's Pilgrimage

Give me my scallop-shell of quiet,
My staff of faith to walk upon,
My scrip of joy, immortal diet,
My bottle of salvation,
My gown of glory, hope's true gage,
And thus I'll take my pilgrimage.

Blood must be my body's balmer,
No other balm will there be given,
Whilst my soul like a white palmer
Travels to the land of heaven,                  10
Over the silver mountains,
Where spring the nectar fountains;
And there I'll kiss
The bowl of bliss,
And drink my eternal fill
On every milken hill.
My soul will be a-dry before,
But after it will ne'er thirst more.

And by the happy blissful way
More peaceful pilgrims I shall see,             20
That have shook off their gowns of clay
And go apparelled fresh like me.
I'll bring them first
To slake their thirst,
And then to taste those nectar suckets,
At the clear wells
Where sweetness dwells,
Drawn up by saints in crystal buckets.

And when our bottles and all we
Are filled with immortality,                    30
Then the holy paths we'll travel,
Strewed with rubies thick as gravel,
Ceilings of diamonds, sapphire floors,
High walls of coral and pearl bowers.

From thence to heaven's bribeless hall
Where no corrupted voices brawl,
No conscience molten into gold,
Nor forged accusers bought and sold,
No cause deferred, nor vain-spent journey,
For there Christ is the King's
    Attorney,                                    40
Who pleads for all without degrees,
And he hath angels, but no fees.

When the grand twelve million jury
Of our sins and sinful fury
'Gainst our souls black verdicts give,
Christ pleads his death, and then we live.
Be thou my speaker, taintless pleader,
Unblotted lawyer, true proceeder;
Thou movest salvation even for alms,
Not with a bribéd lawyer's palms.               50

And this is my eternal plea
To him that made heaven, earth, and sea:
Seeing my flesh must die so soon,
And want a head to dine next noon,
Just at the stroke when my veins start and
    spread,
Set on my soul an everlasting head.
Then am I ready, like a palmer fit,
To tread those blest paths which before I
    writ.  (*1604*)

# The Lie

Go, soul, the body's guest,
    Upon a thankless arrant:
Fear not to touch the best;
    The truth shall be thy warrant.
        Go, since I needs must die,
        And give the world the lie.

Say to the court, it glows
    And shines like rotten wood;
Say to the church, it shows
    What's good, and doth no good:             10
        If church and court reply,
        Then give them both the lie.

Tell potentates, they live
    Acting by others' action,
Not loved unless they give,
    Not strong but by their faction:
        If potentates reply,
        Give potentates the lie.

Tell men of high condition
    That manage the estate,                     20
Their purpose is ambition,
    Their practice only hate:
        And if they once reply,
        Then give them all the lie.

Tell them that brave it most,
  They beg for more by spending,
Who, in their greatest cost,
  Seek nothing but commending:
    And if they make reply,
    Then give them all the lie.     30

Tell zeal, it wants devotion;
  Tell love, it is but lust;
Tell time, it is but motion;
  Tell flesh, it is but dust:
    And wish them not reply,
    For thou must give the lie.

Tell age, it daily wasteth;
  Tell honour how it alters;
Tell beauty how she blasteth;
  Tell favour how it falters:    40
    And as they shall reply,
    Give every one the lie.

Tell wit how much it wrangles
  In tickle points of niceness;
Tell wisdom, she entangles
  Herself in over-wiseness:
    And when they do reply,
    Straight give them both the lie.

Tell physic of her boldness;
  Tell skill, it is prevention;    50
Tell charity of coldness;
  Tell law, it is contention:
    And as they do reply,
    So give them still the lie.

Tell fortune of her blindness;
  Tell nature of decay;
Tell friendship of unkindness;
  Tell justice of delay:
    And if they will reply,
    Then give them all the lie.    60

Tell arts, they have no soundness,
  But vary by esteeming;
Tell schools, they want profoundness,
  And stand too much on seeming:
    If arts and schools reply,
    Give arts and schools the lie.

Tell faith, it's fled the city;
  Tell how the country erreth;
Tell, manhood shakes off pity;
  Tell, virtue least preferreth:    70
    And if they do reply,
    Spare not to give the lie.

So when thou hast, as I
  Commanded thee, done blabbing,
Although to give the lie
  Deserves no less than stabbing,
    Stab at thee he that will,
    No stab the soul can kill.   (*1608*)

## What Is Our Life?

What is our life? a play of passion;
Our mirth, the music of division;
Our mothers' wombs the tiring-houses be
Where we are dressed for this short
  comedy.
Heaven the judicious sharp spectator is,
That sits and marks still who doth act
  amiss;
Our graves that hide us from the
  searching sun
Are like drawn curtains when the play is
  done.
Thus march we playing to our latest rest;
Only we die in earnest—that's no jest.  10
                       (*1612*)

# SIR PHILIP SIDNEY / 1554–1586

## The Nightingale

The nightingale, as soon as April bringeth
Unto her rested sense a perfect waking,
While late bare earth, proud of new clothing, springeth,
Sings out her woes, a thorn her song-book making,[1]
And mournfully bewailing,
Her throat in tunes expresseth
What grief her breast oppresseth
For Tereus' force on her chaste will prevailing.[2]
O Philomela fair, O take some gladness,
That here is juster cause of plaintful sadness:                    10
Thine earth now springs, mine fadeth;
Thy thorn without, my thorn my heart invadeth.

Alas, she hath no other cause of anguish
But Tereus' love, on her by strong hand wroken,[3]
Wherein she suffering, all her spirits languish;
Full womanlike complains her will was broken.
But I, who daily craving,
Cannot have to content me,
Have more cause to lament me,
Since wanting is more woe than too much having.                    20
O Philomela fair, O take some gladness,
There here is juster cause of plaintful sadness:
Thine earth now springs, mine fadeth;
Thy thorn without, my thorn my heart invadeth.   *(1581)*

## *from* Astrophel and Stella

### I

Loving in truth, and fain in verse my love to show,
That she, dear she, might take some pleasure of my pain,
Pleasure might cause her read, reading might make her know,
Knowledge might pity win, and pity grace obtain,
I sought fit words to paint the blackest face of woe;
Oft turning others' leaves to see if thence would flow
Some fresh and fruitful showers upon my sun-burned brain.
But words came halting forth, wanting Invention's stay;
Invention, Nature's child, fled step-dame Study's blows,           10

---

[1] Classic myth accounts for the plaintive quality of the nightingale's song by depicting the bird as singing with its breast pressed against a thorn. The myth implies that suffering is a source of art, and that all great beauty has an element of sadness.
[2] See note 1 on Matthew Arnold, "Philomela."
[3] imposed

And others' feet still seemed but strangers in my way.
Thus, great with child to speak, and helpless in my throes,
Biting my truant pen, beating myself for spite,
"Fool," said my Muse to me, "look in thy heart and write."

### XV

You that do search for every purling spring
Which from the ribs of old Parnassus flows,
And every flower, not sweet perhaps, which grows
Near thereabout, into your poesy wring;
You that do dictionary's method bring
Into your rhymes, running in rattling rows:
You that poor Petrarch's long deceaséd woes
With newborn sighs and denizened wit do sing:
You take wrong ways; those far-fet[1] helps be such
As do bewray[2] a want of inward touch,                                    10
And sure at length stolen goods do come to light;
But if, both for your love and skill, your name
You seek to nurse at fullest breasts of Fame,
Stella behold, and then begin to indite.

### XXVIII

You that with allegory's curious frame
Of others' children changelings use to make,
With me those pains, for God's sake, do not take;
I list not dig so deep for brazen fame.
When I say Stella, I do mean the same
Princess of beauty, for whose only sake
The reins of Love I love, though never slack,
And joy therein, though nations count it shame.
I beg no subject to use eloquence,
Nor in hid ways do guide philosophy;                                    10
Look at my hands for no such quintessence;
But know that I in pure simplicity
Breathe out the flames which burn within my heart,
Love only reading unto me this art.

### XXXI

With how sad steps, O Moon, thou climb'st the skies!
How silently, and with how wan a face!
What! may it be that even in heavenly place
That busy archer his sharp arrows tries?
Sure, if that long-with-love-acquainted eyes
Can judge of love, thou feel'st a lover's case;
I read it in thy looks; thy languished grace
To me, that feel the like, thy state descries.
Then, even of fellowship, O Moon, tell me,
Is constant love deemed there but want of wit?                                    10

---

[1] farfetched        [2] betray, reveal

Are beauties there as proud as here they be?
Do they above, love to be loved, and yet
Those lovers scorn whom that love doth possess?
Do they call virtue there ungratefulness?

### XXXIX

Come sleep! O sleep, the certain knot of peace,
The baiting place[1] of wit, the balm of woe,
The poor man's wealth, the prisoner's release,
The indifferent judge between the high and low;
With shield of proof[2] shield me from out the prease[3]
Of those fierce darts despair at me doth throw;
O make in me those civil wars to cease;
I will good tribute pay, if thou do so.
Take thou of me smooth pillows, sweetest bed,
A chamber deaf to noise and blind to light,                    *10*
A rosy garland and a weary head;
And if these things, as being thine by right,
Move not thy heavy grace, thou shalt in me,
Livelier than elsewhere, Stella's image see.

### XLI

Having this day my horse, my hand, my lance
Guided so well that I obtained the prize,
Both by the judgment of the English eyes
And of some sent from that sweet enemy, France,
Horsemen my skill in horsemanship advance,
Town-folks my strength; a daintier judge applies
His praise to sleight which from good use doth rise;
Some lucky wits impute it but to chance;
Others, because of both sides I do take
My blood from them who did excel in this,                     *10*
Think nature me a man-at-arms did make.
How far they shoot awry! The true cause is,
Stella looked on, and from her heavenly face
Sent forth the beams which made so fair my race.

### LIX

Dear, why make you more of a dog than me?
If he do love, alas, I burn in love;
If he wait well, I never thence would move;
If he be fair, yet but a dog can be;
Little he is, so little worth is he:
He barks, my songs in one voice oft doth prove;
Bidden, (perhaps) he fetcheth thee a glove;
But I unbid, fetch even my soul to thee.
Yet while I languish, him that bosom clips,[1]

---

[1] a rest and feeding stop on a trip
[2] of tested impenetrability
[3] press; i.e., throng
[1] clutches

That lap doth lap, nay lets in spite of spite                    *10*
This fawning mate taste of those sugared lips;
Alas, if you grant only such delight
To witless things, then love I hope, (since wit
Becomes a clog) will soon ease me of it.

### LXIV

No more, my dear, no more these counsels try;
Oh, give my passions leave to run their race;
Let Fortune lay on me her worst disgrace;
Let folk o'ercharged with brain against me cry;
Let clouds bedim my face, break in mine eye;
Let me no steps but of lost labour trace;
Let all the earth with scorn recount my case;
But do not will me from my love to fly.
I do not envy Aristotle's wit,
Nor do aspire to Caesar's bleeding fame;                    *10*
Nor aught do care though some above me sit;
Nor hope nor wish another course to frame,
But that which once may win thy cruel heart;
Thou art my wit, and thou my virtue art.

### LXXXIV

Highway, since you my chief Parnassus[1] be,
And that my Muse, to some ears not unsweet,
Tempers her words to trampling horses' feet
More oft than to a chamber-melody,
Now, blesséd you, bear onward blesséd me
To her, where I my heart, safe left, shall meet;
My Muse and I must you of duty greet
With thanks and wishes, wishing thankfully.
Be you still fair, honoured by public heed;
By no encroachment wronged, nor time forgot;                    *10*
Nor blamed for blood, nor shamed for sinful deed;
And, that you know I envy you no lot
Of highest wish, I wish you so much bliss,
Hundreds of years you Stella's feet may kiss!   (*1591*)


## Since Nature's Works Be Good

Since nature's works be good, and death doth serve
As nature's work, why should we fear to die?
Since fear is vain, but when it may preserve,
Why should we fear that which we cannot fly?
Fear is more pain, than is the pain it fears,
Disarming human minds of native might:
While each conceit an ugly figure bears,

---

[1] mountain in Greece; home of Apollo and the Muses, and hence a source of poetic inspiration

Which were not evil, well viewed in reason's light.
Our owly eyes, which dimmed with passions be,
And scarce discern the dawn of coming day,     *10*
Let them be cleared, and now begin to see,
Our life is but a step, in dusty way.
Then let us hold the bliss of peaceful mind,
Since this we feel, great loss we cannot find.   (*1593*)

## My True Love Hath My Heart

My true Love hath my heart, and I have his,
By just exchange one for the other given:
I hold his dear, and mine he cannot miss;
There never was a better bargain driven.
His heart in me keeps me and him in one,
My heart in him his thoughts and senses guides:
He loves my heart, for once it was his own;
I cherish his because in me it bides.
His heart his wound receivéd from my sight,
My heart was wounded with his wounded heart;     *10*
For as from me, on him his hurt did light,
So still methought in me his hurt did smart.
Both, equal hurt, in this change sought our bliss:
My true Love hath my heart, and I have his.   (*1593*)

# JOHN LYLY / 1554–1606

## *from* Alexander and Campaspe

Cupid and my Campaspe played
At cards for kisses; Cupid paid.
He stakes his quiver, bow, and arrows,
His mother's doves, and team of sparrows;
Loses them too; then, down he throws
The coral of his lip, the rose
Growing on 's cheek (but none knows how);
With these, the crystal of his brow,
And then the dimple of his chin:
All these did my Campaspe win.     *10*
At last, he set her both his eyes;
She won, and Cupid blind did rise.
O Love! has she done this to thee?
What shall (alas!) become of me?   (*1584?*)

## Pan's Syrinx

Pan's Syrinx[1] was a girl indeed,
Though now she's turned into a reed;
From that dear reed Pan's pipe does
   come,
A pipe that strikes Apollo dumb;
Nor flute, nor lute, nor gittern[2] can
So chant it as the pipe of Pan;
Cross-gartered swains and dairy girls,
With faces smug and round as pearls,
When Pan's shrill pipe begins to play,
With dancing wear out night and day: 10
The bagpipe's drone his hum lays by
When Pan sounds up his minstrelsy;
His minstrelsy! oh, base! this quill—
Which at my mouth with wind I fill—
Puts me in mind, though her I miss,
That still my Syrinx' lips I kiss.

# CHIDIOCK TICHBORNE / 1558?–1586

## Tichborne's Elegy

My prime of youth is but a frost of cares,
   My feast of joy is but a dish of pain,
My crop of corn is but a field of tares,
   And all my good is but vain hope of gain;
      The day is past, and yet I saw no sun,
      And now I live, and now my life is done.

My tale was heard and yet it was not told,
   My fruit is fallen and yet my leaves are green,
My youth is spent and yet I am not old,
   I saw the world and yet I was not seen;          10
      My thread is cut and yet it is not spun,
      And now I live, and now my life is done.

I sought my death and found it in my womb,
   I looked for life and saw it was a shade,
I trod the earth and knew it was my tomb,
   And now I die, and now I was but made;
      My glass is full, and now my glass is run,
      And now I live, and now my life is done.   (1586)

---

[1] Syrinx, an Arcadian nymph, was pursued by the lecherous god Pan. She prayed to the water nymphs for help, and was transformed into a clump of reeds. Pan fastened together reeds cut to varying lengths and thus made the first syrinx, or Pan's pipes.
[2] a sixteenth-century instrument of the guitar family

## THOMAS LODGE / 1558?–1625

### from Phillis

#### XIII

Love guards the roses of thy lips
And flies about them like a bee;
If I approach he forward skips,
And if I kiss he stingeth me.
Love in thine eyes doth build his bower,
And sleeps within their pretty shine;
And if I look the boy will lour,
And from their orbs shoot shafts divine.
Love works thy heart within his fire,
And in my tears doth firm the same;   10
And if I tempt it will retire,
And of my plaints doth make a game.
Love, let me cull her choicest flowers,
And pity me, and calm her eye,
Make soft her heart, dissolve her lours,
Then will I praise thy deity.
But if thou do not, Love, I'll truly serve her
In spite of thee, and by firm faith deserve her.   (*1593*)

## ROBERT GREENE / 1560?–1592

### Sephestia's Song to Her Child

Weep not, my wanton, smile upon my knee;
When thou art old there's grief enough for thee.
    Mother's wag, pretty boy,
    Father's sorrow, father's joy;
    When thy father first did see
    Such a boy by him and me,
    He was glad, I was woe;
    Fortune changéd made him so,
    When he left his pretty boy,
    Last his sorrow, first his joy.   10

Weep not, my wanton, smile upon my knee;
When thou art old there's grief enough for thee.
    Streaming tears that never stint,
    Like pearl-drops from a flint,
    Fell by course from his eyes,
    That one another's place supplies;
    Thus he grieved in every part,
    Tears of blood fell from his heart,
    When he left his pretty boy,
    Father's sorrow, father's joy.   20

Weep not, my wanton, smile upon my knee;
When thou art old there's grief enough for thee.

The wanton smiled, father wept,
Mother cried, baby leapt;
More he crowed, more we cried,
Nature could not sorrow hide:
He must go, he must kiss
Child and mother, baby bliss,
For he left his pretty boy,
Father's sorrow, father's joy.                    30
Weep not, my wanton, smile upon my knee;
When thou art old there's grief enough for thee.  (1589)

## Maesia's Song

Sweet are the thoughts that savor of content;
    The quiet mind is richer than a crown;
Sweet are the nights in careless slumber spent;
    The poor estate scorns Fortune's angry frown.
Such sweet content, such minds, such sleep, such bliss,
Beggars enjoy, when princes oft do miss.

The homely house that harbors quiet rest;
    The cottage that affords no pride nor care;
The mean[1] that 'grees with country music best;
    The sweet consort[2] of mirth and music's fare;        10
Obscuréd life sets down a type of bliss:
A mind content both crown and kingdom is.   (1591)

# ROBERT SOUTHWELL / 1561?–1595

## The Burning Babe

As I in hoary winter's night stood shivering in the snow,
Surprised I was with sudden heat, which made my heart to glow;
And lifting up a fearful eye to view what fire was near,
A pretty Babe all burning bright, did in the air appear,
Who scorchéd with excessive heat, such floods of tears did shed,
As though His floods should quench His flames which with His tears were fed;
Alas! quoth He, but newly born, in fiery heats I fry,
Yet none approach to warm their hearts or feel my fire but I!
My faultless breast the furnace is, the fuel wounding thorns,
Love is the fire, and sighs the smoke, the ashes shame and scorns;    10

---

[1] the intermediate voice in part singing        [2] concord

The fuel Justice layeth on, and Mercy blows the coals,
The metal in this furnace wrought are men's defiléd souls,
For which, as now on fire I am to work them to their good,
So will I melt into a bath to wash them in My blood:
With this He vanished out of sight, and swiftly shrank away,
And straight I calléd unto mind that it was Christmas-day.   (*1595?*)

# HENRY CONSTABLE / 1562–1613

*from* Diana

### VI, ii

To live in hell and heaven to behold;
To welcome life and die a living death;
To sweat with heat, and yet be freezing cold;
To grasp at stars and lie the earth beneath;
To tread a maze that never shall have end;
To burn in sighs and starve in daily tears;
To climb a hill and never to descend;
Giants to kill, and quake at childish fears;
To pine for food, and watch th' Hesperian tree;[1]
To thirst for drink, and nectar still to draw;                    *10*
To live accursed, whom men hold blest to be,
And weep those wrongs which never creature saw:
If this be love, if love in these be founded,
My heart is love, for these in it are grounded.   (*1592*)

# SAMUEL DANIEL / 1562?–1619

*from* Delia

### VI

Fair is my love, and cruel as she's fair:
Her brow shades frowns, although her eyes are sunny,
Her smiles are lightning, though her pride despair,
And her disdains are gall, her favors honey.

---

[1] tree bearing the golden apples received by Juno as a wedding present

A modest maid, decked with a blush of honor,
Whose feet do tread green paths of youth and love;
The wonder of all eyes that look upon her,
Sacred on earth, designed a saint above.
Chastity and Beauty, which were deadly foes,
Live reconciléd friends within her brow;                    *10*
And had she pity to conjoin with those,
Then who had heard the plaints I utter now?
Oh had she not been fair and thus unkind,
My muse had slept, and none had known my mind.

### XXXI

Look, Delia, how we esteem the half-blown rose,
The image of thy blush, and summer's honor!
Whilst yet her tender bud doth undisclose
That full of beauty Time bestows upon her.
No sooner spreads her glory in the air
But straight her wide-blown pomp comes to decline;
She then is scorned that late adorned the fair;
So fade the roses of those cheeks of thine.
No April can revive thy withered flowers,
Whose springing grace adorns thy glory now;                    *10*
Swift, speedy Time, feathered with flying hours,
Dissolves the beauty of the fairest brow.
Then do not thou such treasure waste in vain,
But love now, whilst thou mayst be loved again.

### XLV

Care-charmer Sleep, son of the sable Night,
Brother to Death, in silent darkness born,
Relieve my languish, and restore the light,
With dark forgetting of my cares return.
And let the day be time enough to mourn
The shipwreck of my ill-adventured youth;
Let waking eyes suffice to wail their scorn,
Without the torment of the night's untruth.
Cease, dreams, the images of day-desires,
To model forth the passions of the morrow;                    *10*
Never let rising sun approve you liars,
To add more grief to aggravate my sorrow.
Still let me sleep, embracing clouds in vain;
And never wake to feel the day's disdain.    (*1592*)

# MICHAEL DRAYTON / 1563–1631

## *from* Idea

### XX

An evil spirit, your beauty, haunts me still,
Wherewith, alas, I have been long possessed,
Which ceaseth not to tempt me to each ill,
Nor gives me once but one poor minute's rest;
In me it speaks, whether I sleep or wake,
And when by means to drive it out I try,
With greater torments then it me doth take,
And tortures me in most extremity;
Before my face it lays down my despairs,
And hastes me on unto a sudden death,　　　　　　10
Now tempting me to drown myself in tears,
And then in sighing to give up my breath.
Thus am I still provoked to every evil
By this good wicked spirit, sweet angel devil.　(*1599*)

### XXXVII

Dear, why should you command me to my rest,
When now the night doth summon all to sleep?
Methinks this time becometh lovers best;
Night was ordained together friends to keep.
How happy are all other living things,
Which though the day disjoin by several flight,
The quiet evening yet together brings,
And each returns unto his love at night!
Oh thou that art so courteous else to all,
Why shouldst thou, Night, abuse me only thus,　　10
That every creature to his kind dost call,
And yet 'tis thou dost only sever us?
Well could I wish it would be ever day,
If when night comes you bid me go away.　(*1602*)

### LXI

Since there's no help, come let us kiss and part.
Nay, I have done; you get no more of me,
And I am glad, yea, glad with all my heart,
That thus so cleanly I myself can free;
Shake hands for ever, cancel all our vows,
And when we meet at any time again,
Be it not seen in either of our brows
That we one jot of former love retain.
Now at the last gasp of Love's latest breath,
When, his pulse failing, Passion speechless lies,　　10

127

When Faith is kneeling by his bed of death,
And Innocence is closing up his eyes,
Now if thou wouldst, when all have given him over,
From death to life thou mightst him yet recover.   (*1599*)


## To the Virginian Voyage

You brave heroic minds
Worthy your country's name,
　That honour still pursue,
　Go, and subdue,
Whilst loitering hinds
Lurk here at home, with shame.

Britons, you stay too long;
Quickly aboard bestow you,
　And with a merry gale
　Swell your stretchéd sail,          10
With vows as strong
As the winds that blow you.

Your course securely steer,
West and by south forth keep,
　Rocks, lee-shores, nor shoals,
　When Æolus scowls,
You need not fear
So absolute the deep.

And cheerfully at sea,
Success you still entice,          20
　To get the pearl and gold,
　And ours to hold,
Virginia,
Earth's only paradise,

Where nature hath in store
Fowl, venison, and fish,
　And the fruitful'st soil
　Without your toil
Three harvests more,
All greater than your wish.          30

And the ambitious vine
Crowns with his purple mass,
　The cedar reaching high
　To kiss the sky,
The cypress, pine,
And useful sassafras.

To whom the golden age
Still nature's laws doth give,
　No other cares that tend,
　But to them to defend          40
From winter's age,
That long there doth not live.

Whenas the luscious smell
Of that delicious land,
　Above the seas that flows,
　The clear wind throws,
Your hearts to swell
Approaching the dear strand,

In kenning[1] of the shore,
(Thanks to God first given,)          50
　O you, the happi'st men,
　Be frolic then,
Let cannons roar,
Frighting the wide heaven.

And in regions far
Such heroes bring ye forth
　As those from whom we came,
　And plant our name
Under that star
Not known unto our north          60

And as there plenty grows
Of laurel everywhere,
　Apollo's sacred tree,
　You it may see
A poet's brows
To crown, that may sing there.

Thy voyages attend,
Industrious Hakluyt,[2]
　Whose reading shall enflame
　Men to seek fame,          70
And much commend
To after-times thy wit.   (*1606*)

---

[1] discerning
[2] author of *Principal Navigations, Voyages, and Discoveries of the English Nation* (1589–1600)

## The Crier

Good folk, for gold or hire,
But help me to a crier;
For my poor heart is run astray
After two eyes that passed this way.
    Oyez, oyez, oyez,
    If there be any man
    In town or country can
    Bring me my heart again,
    I'll please him for his pain;
And by these marks I will you show    *10*
That only I this heart do owe.[1]

It is a wounded heart,
Wherein sticks the dart;
Every piece sore hurt throughout it,
Faith and troth writ round about it;
It was a tame heart, and a dear,
    And never used to roam;
But having got this haunt, I fear
    'Twill hardly stay at home.
For God's sake, walking by the way,    *20*
    If you my heart do see,
Either impound it for a stray,
    Or send it back to me.

## CHRISTOPHER MARLOWE / 1564–1593

## The Passionate Shepherd to His Love

Come live with me and be my love,
And we will all the pleasures prove,
That valleys, groves, hills and fields,
Woods, or steepy mountain yields.

And we will sit upon the rocks,
And see the shepherds feed their flocks,
By shallow rivers to whose falls
Melodious birds sing madrigals.

And I will make thee beds of roses
With a thousand fragrant posies,    *10*
A cap of flowers, and a kirtle
Embroidered all with leaves of myrtle;

A gown made of the finest wool
Which from our pretty lambs we pull;
Fair lined slippers for the cold,
With buckles of the purest gold;

A belt of straw and ivy buds,
With coral clasps and amber studs:
And if these pleasures may thee move,
Come live with me and be my love.    *20*

The shepherds' swains shall dance and
    sing
For thy delight each May morning:
If these delights thy mind may move,
Then live with me and be my love.

    *(1600)*

---

[1] own

## Songs from the Plays

### from THE TWO GENTLEMEN OF VERONA

Who is Silvia? what is she,
  That all our swains commend her?
Holy, fair, and wise is she;
  The heaven such grace did lend her,
That she might admiréd be.

Is she kind as she is fair?
  For beauty lives with kindness.
Love doth to her eyes repair,
  To help him of his blindness;
And, being helped, inhabits there.      10

Then to Silvia let us sing,
  That Silvia is excelling;
She excels each mortal thing
  Upon the dull earth dwelling;
To her let us garlands bring.   *(1591)*

### from LOVE'S LABOUR'S LOST

#### SPRING

When daisies pied and violets blue
  And lady-smocks all silver-white
And cuckoo-buds of yellow hue
  Do paint the meadows with delight,
The cuckoo then, on every tree,
Mocks married men; for thus sings he,
      Cuckoo!
Cuckoo, cuckoo! O, word of fear,
Unpleasing to a married ear!

When shepherds pipe on oaten
    straws,      10
  And merry larks are ploughmen's
    clocks,
When turtles tread, and rooks, and daws,
  And maidens bleach their summer
    smocks,
The cuckoo then, on every tree,
Mocks married men; for thus sings he,
      Cuckoo!

Cuckoo, cuckoo! O, word of fear,
Unpleasing to a married ear!

#### WINTER

When icicles hang by the wall,
  And Dick the shepherd blows his nail,
And Tom bears logs into the hall,
  And milk comes frozen home in pail,
When blood is nipped, and ways be foul,
Then nightly sings the staring owl,
      To-whit!
To-who!—a merry note,
While greasy Joan doth keel[1] the pot.

When all aloud the wind doth blow,      10
  And coughing drowns the parson's saw,
And birds sit brooding in the snow,
  And Marian's nose looks red and raw,
When roasted crabs hiss in the bowl,
Then nightly sings the staring owl,
      To-whit!
To-who!—a merry note,
While greasy Joan doth keel the pot.
                          *(1593)*

### from THE MERCHANT OF VENICE

  Tell me where is fancy bred,
    Or in the heart or in the head?
  How begot, how nourishéd?
    Reply, reply.
  It is engendered in the eyes,
    With gazing fed; and fancy dies
  In the cradle where it lies.
    Let us all ring fancy's knell.
    I'll begin it. Ding, dong, bell.
*Chorus.* Ding, dong, bell.   *(1596)*      10

### from AS YOU LIKE IT

  Under the greenwood tree
  Who loves to lie with me,
  And turn his merry note
  Unto the sweet bird's throat,
Come hither, come hither, come hither:
  Here shall he see

---

1 stir, to prevent boiling over

No enemy
But winter and rough weather.

Who doth ambition shun
And loves to live i' the sun,          *10*
Seeking the food he eats,
And pleased with what he gets,
Come hither, come hither, come hither:
Here shall he see
No enemy
But winter and rough weather.

.          .          .

Blow, blow, thou winter wind,
Thou are not so unkind
As man's ingratitude;
Thy tooth is not so keen,
Because thou art not seen,
Although thy breath be rude.
Heigh-ho! sing, heigh-ho! unto the green
holly:
Most friendship is feigning, most loving
mere folly.
Then heigh-ho! the holly!
This life is most jolly.          *10*

Freeze, freeze, thou bitter sky,
That dost not bite so nigh
As benefits forgot:
Though thou the water warp,
Thy sting is not so sharp
As friend remembered not.
Heigh-ho! sing, heigh-ho! unto the green
holly:
Most friendship is feigning, most loving
mere folly.
Then heigh-ho! the holly!
This life is most jolly.          *20*

.          .          .

It was a lover and his lass,
With a hey, and a ho, and a hey
nonino,
That o'er the green corn field did pass
In spring time, the only pretty ring
time,
When birds do sing, hey ding a ding,
ding:
Sweet lovers love the spring.

Between the acres of the rye,
With a hey, and a ho, and a hey
nonino,
These pretty country folks would lie,
In spring time, &c.          *10*

This carol they began that hour,
With a hey, and a ho, and a hey
nonino,
How that a life was but a flower
In spring time, &c.

And therefore take the present time,
With a hey, and a ho, and a hey
nonino;
For love it is crowned with the prime
In spring time &c.          *(1600)*

*from TWELFTH NIGHT*

Oh! mistress mine! where are you
roaming?
Oh! stay and hear; your true love's
coming,
That can sing both high and low.
Trip no further, pretty sweeting;
Journeys end in lovers meeting,
Every wise man's son doth know.

What is love? 'tis not hereafter;
Present mirth hath present laughter;
What's to come is still unsure:
In delay there lies no plenty;          *10*
Then come kiss me, sweet and twenty,
Youth's a stuff will not endure.

.          .          .

Come away, come away, Death!
And in sad cypress[1] let me be laid;
Fly away, fly away, breath;
I am slain by a fair cruel maid.
My shroud of white, stuck all with yew,
O, prepare it!
My part of death, no one so true
Did share it.

Not a flower, not a flower sweet,
On my black coffin let there be
strown;          *10*
Not a friend, not a friend greet

---

[1] cypress lawn, a filmy black fabric used for burial robes

My poor corpse, where my bones shall
          be thrown
A thousand thousand sighs to save
          Lay me, O, where
Sad true lover never find my grave,
          To weep there!   (*1601*)

## from MEASURE FOR MEASURE

Take, O! take those lips away,
    That so sweetly were forsworn,
And those eyes, the break of day,
    Lights that do mislead the morn;
But my kisses bring again,
          Bring again,
Seals of love, but sealed in vain,
          Sealed in vain.   (*1604*)

## from CYMBELINE

Hark, hark! the lark at heaven's gate sings,
    And Phœbus 'gins arise,
His steeds to water at those springs
    On chaliced flowers that lies;
And winking Mary-buds begin
    To ope their golden eyes:
With every thing that pretty is,
    My lady sweet, arise!
          Arise, arise!

Fear no more the heat o' the sun,          *10*
    Nor the furious winter's rages;
Thou thy worldly task hast done,
    Home art gone, and ta'en thy wages;
Golden lads and girls all must,
As chimney-sweepers, come to dust.

Fear no more the frown o' the great,
    Thou art past the tyrant's stroke:
Care no more to clothe and eat;

To thee the reed is as the oak:
The sceptre, learning, physic, must     *20*
All follow this, and come to dust.

Fear no more the lightning-flash,
    Nor the all-dread thunder-stone;
Fear no slander, censure rash;
    Thou hast finished joy and moan;
All lovers young, all lovers must
Consign to thee, and come to dust.

No exorciser harm thee!
    Nor no witchcraft charm thee!
Ghost unlaid forbear thee!               *30*
    Nothing ill come near thee!
Quiet consummation have;
And renownèd be thy grave!   (*1609*)

## from THE TEMPEST

Full fathom five thy father lies;
    Of his bones are coral made;
Those are pearls that were his eyes:
    Nothing of him that doth fade,
But doth suffer a sea-change
Into something rich and strange:
Sea nymphs hourly ring his knell.
          Ding-dong!
    Hark now I hear them,
          Ding-dong, bell!                 *10*

Where the bee sucks, there suck I,
In a cowslip's bell I lie,
There I couch when owls do cry,
On the bat's back I do fly
After summer merrily.
    Merrily, merrily, shall I live now
    Under the blossom that hangs on the
      bough.   (*1611*)

## from The Sonnets

### XVIII

Shall I compare thee to a summer's day?
Thou art more lovely and more temperate:
Rough winds do shake the darling buds of May,
And summer's lease hath all too short a date:
Sometimes too hot the eye of heaven shines,
And often is his gold complexion dimmed;

And every fair from fair sometime declines,
By chance, or nature's changing course untrimmed;
But thy eternal summer shall not fade,
Nor lose possession of that fair thou owest, *10*
Nor shall Death brag thou wander'st in his shade,
When in eternal lines to time thou growest;
So long as men can breathe, or eyes can see,
So long lives this, and this gives life to thee.

### XXVII

Weary with toil, I haste me to my bed,
The dear repose for limbs with travel tired;
But then begins a journey in my head
To work my mind, when body's work's expired:
For then my thoughts, from far where I abide,
Intend a zealous pilgrimage to thee,
And keep my drooping eyelids open wide,
Looking on darkness which the blind do see:
Save that my soul's imaginary sight
Presents thy shadow to my sightless view, *10*
·Which, like a jewel hung in ghastly night,
Makes black night beauteous and her old face new.
Lo! thus, by day my limbs, by night my mind,
For thee and for myself no quiet find.

### XXIX

When in disgrace with fortune and men's eyes
I all alone beweep my outcast state,
And trouble deaf heaven with my bootless cries,
And look upon myself, and curse my fate,
Wishing me like to one more rich in hope,
Featured like him, like him with friends possessed,
Desiring this man's art, and that man's scope,
With what I most enjoy contented least;
Yet in these thoughts myself almost despising,
Haply I think on thee, and then my state, *10*
Like to the lark at break of day arising
From sullen earth, sings hymns at heaven's gate;
For thy sweet love remembered such wealth brings
That then I scorn to change my state with kings.

### XXX

When to the sessions of sweet silent thought
I summon up remembrance of things past,
I sigh the lack of many a thing I sought,
And with old woes new wail my dear time's waste:
Then can I drown an eye, unused to flow,
For precious friends hid in death's dateless night,
And weep afresh love's long since cancelled woe,
And moan the expense of many a vanished sight:

Then can I grieve at grievances foregone,
And heavily from woe to woe tell o'er                              *10*
The sad account of fore-bemoanéd moan,
Which I new pay as if not paid before.
But if the while I think on thee, dear friend,
All losses are restored and sorrows end.

### XXXII

If thou survive my well-contented day,
When that churl Death my bones with dust shall cover,
And shalt by fortune once more resurvey
These poor rude lines of thy deceaséd lover,
Compare them with the bett'ring of the time,
And though they be outstripped by every pen,
Reserve them for my love, not for their rhyme,
Exceeded by the height of happier men.
O, then vouchsafe me but this loving thought:
"Had my friend's Muse grown with this growing age,                *10*
A dearer birth than this his love had brought,
To march in ranks of better equipage;
But since he died and poets better prove,
Theirs for their style I'll read, his for his love."

### XXXIII

Full many a glorious morning have I seen
Flatter the mountain-tops with sovereign eye,
Kissing with golden face the meadows green,
Gilding pale streams with heavenly alchemy;
Anon permit the basest clouds to ride
With ugly rack on his celestial face,
And from the forlorn world his visage hide,
Stealing unseen to west with this disgrace:
Even so my sun one early morn did shine,
With all-triumphant splendour on my brow;                        *10*
But out! alack! he was but one hour mine,
The region cloud hath masked him from me now.
Yet him for this my love no whit disdaineth;
Suns of the world may stain when heaven's sun staineth.

### LV

Not marble, nor the gilded monuments
Of princes, shall outlive this powerful rhyme;
But you shall shine more bright in these contents
Than unswept stone, besmeared with sluttish time.
When wasteful war shall statues overturn,
And broils root out the work of masonry,
Nor Mars his sword nor war's quick fire shall burn
The living record of your memory.
'Gainst death and all oblivious enmity
Shall you pace forth; your praise shall still find room           *10*

Even in the eyes of all posterity
That wear this world out to the ending doom.
So, till the judgment that yourself arise,
You live in this, and dwell in lovers' eyes.

### LX

Like as the waves make towards the pebbled shore,
So do our minutes hasten to their end,
Each changing place with that which goes before,
In sequent toil all forwards do contend.
Nativity, once in the main of light,
Crawls to maturity, wherewith being crowned,
Crookéd eclipses 'gainst his glory fight,
And Time that gave doth now his gift confound.
Time doth transfix the flourish set on youth,
And delves the parallels in beauty's brow,                          *10*
Feeds on the rarities of nature's truth,
And nothing stands but for his scythe to mow.
And yet to times in hope my verse shall stand,
Praising thy worth, despite his cruel hand.

### LXIV

When I have seen by Time's fell hand defaced
The rich proud cost of outworn buried age;
When sometime lofty towers I see down razed,
And brass eternal slave to mortal rage;
When I have seen the hungry ocean gain
Advantage on the kingdom of the shore,
And the firm soil win of the watery main,
Increasing store with loss, and loss with store;
When I have seen such interchange of state,
Or state itself confounded to decay,                                *10*
Ruin hath taught me thus to ruminate,
That Time will come and take my love away.
This thought is as a death, which cannot choose
But weep to have that which it fears to lose.

### LXXI

No longer mourn for me when I am dead,
Than you shall hear the surly sullen bell
Give warning to the world that I am fled
From this vile world, with vilest worms to dwell:
Nay, if you read this line, remember not
The hand that writ it; for I love you so,
That I in your sweet thoughts would be forgot,
If thinking on me then should make you woe.
O! if, I say, you look upon this verse,
When I perhaps compounded am with clay,                             *10*
Do not so much as my poor name rehearse,
But let your love even with my life decay;

Lest the wise world should look into your moan,
And mock you with me after I am gone.

### LXXIII

That time of year thou mayst in me behold
When yellow leaves, or none, or few, do hang
Upon those boughs which shake against the cold,
Bare ruined choirs, where late the sweet birds sang.
In me thou see'st the twilight of such day
As after sunset fadeth in the west,
Which by and by black night doth take away,
Death's second self that seals up all in rest.
In me thou see'st the glowing of such fire,
That on the ashes of his youth doth lie,      *10*
As the death-bed, whereon it must expire
Consumed with that which it was nourished by.
This thou perceiv'st, which makes thy love more strong
To love that well, which thou must leave ere long.

### XCVII

How like a winter hath my absence been
From thee, the pleasure of the fleeting year!
What freezings have I felt, what dark days seen!
What old December's bareness every where!
And yet this time removed was summer's time,
The teeming autumn, big with rich increase,
Bearing the wanton burthen of the prime,[1]
Like widowed wombs after their lords' decease:
Yet this abundant issue seemed to me
But hope of orphans and unfathered fruit;      *10*
For summer and his pleasures wait on thee,
And, thou away, the very birds are mute;
Or, if they sing, 'tis with so dull a cheer
That leaves look pale, dreading the winter's near.

### XCVIII

From you have I been absent in the spring,
When proud-pied April, dressed in all his trim,
Hath put a spirit of youth in everything,
That heavy Saturn laughed and leaped with him.
Yet nor the lays of birds, nor the sweet smell
Of different flowers in odor and in hue,
Could make me any summer's story tell,
Or from their proud lap pluck them where they grew;
Nor did I wonder at the lily's white,
Nor praise the deep vermilion in the rose;      *10*
They were but sweet, but figures of delight,
Drawn after you, you pattern of all those.

---

[1] springtime

Yet seemed it winter still, and, you away,
As with your shadow I with these did play.

### CIX

O, never say that I was false of heart,
Though absence seemed my flame to qualify.[1]
As easy might I from myself depart
As from my soul, which in thy breast doth lie:
That is my home of love: if I have ranged,
Like him that travels I return again,
Just to the time, not with the time exchanged,[2]
So that myself bring water for my stain.
Never believe, though in my nature reigned
All frailties that besiege all kinds of blood,          *10*
That it could so preposterously be stained,
To leave for nothing all thy sum of good;
For nothing this wide universe I call,
Save thou, my rose; in it thou art my all.

### CXVI

Let me not to the marriage of true minds
Admit impediments. Love is not love
Which alters when it alteration finds,
Or bends with the remover to remove:
O, no! it is an ever-fixéd mark
That looks on tempests and is never shaken;
It is the star to every wandering bark,
Whose worth's unknown, although his height be taken.
Love's not Time's fool, though rosy lips and cheeks
Within his bending sickle's compass come;
Love alters not with his brief hours and weeks,          *10*
But bears it out even to the edge of doom.
If this be error and upon me proved,
I never writ, nor no man ever loved.

### CXXVIII

How oft, when thou, my music, music play'st,
Upon that blesséd wood[1] whose motion sounds
With thy sweet fingers, when thou gently sway'st
The wiry concord that mine ear confounds,
Do I envy those jacks[2] that nimble leap
To kiss the tender inward of thy hand,
Whilst my poor lips, which should that harvest reap,
At the wood's boldness by thee blushing stand!
To be so tickled, they would change their state
And situation with those dancing chips,          *10*
O'er whom thy fingers walk with gentle gait,
Making dead wood more blest than living lips.

---

[1] moderate (verb)     [2] altered               [1] probably a spinet     [2] keys

Since saucy jacks so happy are in this,
Give them thy fingers, me thy lips to kiss.

### CXXIX

Th' expense of spirit in a waste of shame
Is lust in action; and till action, lust
Is perjured, murd'rous, bloody, full of blame,
Savage, extreme, rude, cruel, not to trust,
Enjoyed no sooner but despiséd straight,
Past reason hunted, and no sooner had
Past reason hated, as a swallowed bait
On purpose laid to make the taker mad;
Mad in pursuit and in possession so;
Had, having, and in quest to have, extreme;          *10*
A bliss in proof, and proved,[1] a very woe;
Before, a joy proposed; behind, a dream.
All this the world well knows; yet none knows well
To shun the heaven that leads men to this hell.

### CXXX

My mistress' eyes are nothing like the sun;
Coral is far more red than her lips' red;
If snow be white, why then her breasts are dun;
If hairs be wires, black wires grow on her head.
I have seen roses damask'd, red and white,
But no such roses see I in her cheeks,
And in some perfumes there is more delight
Than in the breath that from my mistress reeks.
I love to hear her speak, yet well I know
That music hath a far more pleasing sound.          *10*
I grant I never saw a goddess go;
My mistress, when she walks, treads on the ground:
And yet, by heaven, I think my love as rare
As any she belied with false compare.

### CXXXVIII

When my love swears that she is made of truth,
I do believe her, though I know she lies,
That she might think me some untutored youth,
Unlearnéd in the world's false subtleties.
Thus vainly thinking that she thinks me young,
Although she knows my days are past the best,
Simply[1] I credit her false-speaking tongue:
On both sides thus is simple truth suppressed.
But wherefore says she not she is unjust?
And wherefore say not I that I am old?              *10*
O, love's best habit is in seeming trust,
And age in love loves not to have years told:[2]
Therefore I lie with her and she with me,
And in our faults by lies we flattered be.

---

[1] while being tried, and once tried            [1] foolishly     [2] counted

### CXLIII

Lo, as a careful housewife runs to catch
One of her feathered creatures broke away,
Sets down her babe, and makes all swift dispatch
In pursuit of the thing she would have stay;
Whilst her neglected child holds her in chase,
Cries to catch her whose busy care is bent
To follow that which flies before her face,
Not prizing her poor infant's discontent:
So runn'st thou after that which flies from thee,
Whilst I thy babe chase thee afar behind;                          10
But if thou catch thy hope, turn back to me,
And play the mother's part, kiss me, be kind;
So will I pray that thou mayst have thy "Will,"
If thou turn back and my loud crying still.   (*1609*)


## RICHARD BARNFIELD / 1574–1627


## To His Friend, Master R. L., in Praise of Music and Poetry

If music and sweet poetry agree,
As they must needs (the sister and the brother),
Then must the love be great 'twixt thee and me,
Because thou lov'st the one, and I the other.
Dowland[1] to thee is dear, whose heavenly touch
Upon the lute doth ravish human sense;
Spenser to me, whose deep conceit is such
As, passing all conceit, needs no defense.
Thou lov'st to hear the sweet melodious sound
That Phoebus' lute (the queen of music) makes;          10
And I in deep delight am chiefly drowned
Whenas himself to singing he betakes.
One god is god of both (as poets feign),
One knight loves both, and both in thee remain.   (*1598*)

---

[1] John Dowland (1563–1626), songwriter and lutenist

# The Seventeenth Century

## ANONYMOUS LYRICS

### Crabbed Age and Youth

Crabbed age and youth cannot live together:
Youth is full of pleasance, age is full of care;
Youth like summer morn, age like winter weather;
Youth like summer brave, age like winter bare.
Youth is full of sport, age's breath is short;
    Youth is nimble, age is lame;
Youth is hot and bold, age is weak and cold;
    Youth is wild, and age is tame.
Age, I do abhor thee, youth, I do adore thee;
    Oh! my love, my love is young:      10
Age, I do defy thee: Oh! sweet shepherd, hie thee,
    For methinks thou stay'st too long.  (*1599*)

### Madrigal

My Love in her attire doth shew her wit,
  It doth so well become her;
For every season she hath dressings fit,
For Winter, Spring, and Summer.
No beauty she doth miss
When all her robes are on:
But Beauty's self she is
When all her robes are gone.  (*1602*)

### The Silver Swan

The silver swan, who living had no note,
When death approached unlocked her silent throat;
Leaning her breast against the reedy shore,
Thus sung her first and last, and sung no more:
"Farewell all joys, O death come close mine eyes,
More geese than swans now live, more fools than wise."  (*1612*)

### Shine Out, Fair Sun

Shine out, fair Sun, with all your heat,
  Show all your thousand-colored light!
Black winter freezes to his seat;
  The grey wolf howls, he does so bite;
Crookt Age on three knees creeps the
    street;
The boneless fish close quaking lies
And eats for cold his aching feet;
  The stars in icicles arise:
Shine out, and make this winter night
Our Beauty's Spring, our Prince of
    Light!      10

# THOMAS CAMPION / 1567-1620

## When to Her Lute Corinna Sings

When to her lute Corinna sings,
Her voice revives the leaden strings,
And doth in highest notes appear
As any challenged echo clear;
But when she doth of mourning speak,
Ev'n with her sighs the strings do break.

And as her lute doth live or die,
Led by her passion, so must I:
For when of pleasure she doth sing,
My thoughts enjoy a sudden spring,          10
But if she doth of sorrow speak,
Ev'n from my heart the strings do break.
                                        (*1601*)

## When Thou Must Home

When thou must home to shades of underground
And there arrived, a new-admiréd guest,
The beauteous spirits do ingirt thee round,
White Iope, blithe Helen, and the rest,
To hear the stories of thy finished love
From that smooth tongue whose music hell can move;

Then wilt thou speak of banqueting delights,
Of masks and revels which sweet youth did make,
Of tourneys and great challenges of knights,
And all these trimphs for thy beauty's sake:          10
When thou hast told these honours done to thee,
Then tell, O tell, how thou didst murder me.   (*1601*)

## The Man of Life Upright

The man of life upright,
  Whose guiltless heart is free
From all dishonest deeds,
  Or thought of vanity;

The man whose silent days
  In harmless joys are spent,
Whom hopes cannot delude,
  Nor sorrow discontent;

That man needs neither towers
  Nor armor for defense,          10
Nor secret vaults to fly
  From thunder's violence.

He only can behold
  With unaffrighted eyes
The horrors of the deep
  And terrors of the skies.

Thus scorning all the cares
  That fate or fortune brings,
He makes the heaven his book,
  His wisdom heavenly things,          20

Good thoughts his only friends,
  His wealth a well-spent age,
The earth his sober inn
  And quiet pilgrimage.   (*1601*)

## The Writer to His Book

"Whither thus hastes my little book so fast?"
"To Paul's Churchyard."[1] "What! in those cells to stand,
With one leaf like a rider's cloak put up
To catch a termer?[2] or lie musty there
With rimes a term set out, or two, before?"
"Some will redeem me." "Few." "Yes, read me too."
"Fewer." "Nay, love me." "Now thou dot'st, I see."
"Will not our English Athens art defend?"
"Perhaps." "Will lofty courtly wits not aim
Still at perfection?" "If I grant?" "I fly."
"Whither?" "To Paul's." "Alas, poor book I rue                    10
Thy rash self-love; go, spread thy pap'ry wings:
Thy lightness cannot help or hurt my fame."     (1602)


## What If a Day, or a Month, or a Year

What if a day, or a month, or a year
Crown thy delights with a thousand sweet contentings?
Cannot a chance of a night or an hour
Cross thy desires with as many sad tormentings?
    Fortune, honor, beauty, youth
    Are but blossoms dying;
    Wanton pleasure, doting love
Are but shadows flying.
    All our joys are but toys,
    Idle thoughts deceiving;                                     10
    None have power or an hour
    In their lives' bereaving.

Earth's but a point to the world, and a man
Is but a point to the world's compared centure;[1]
Shall then the point of a point be so vain
As to triumph in a seely[2] point's adventure?
    All is hazard that we have,
    There is nothing biding;
    Days of pleasure are like streams
    Through fair meadows gliding.                               20
    Weal and woe, time doth go,
    Time is never returning;
    Secret fates guide our states,
    Both in mirth and mourning.     (1606)

---

[1] Booksellers' stalls were set up in the vicinity of St. Paul's Cathedral.

[2] a person attending the Law Terms in London

[1] center  [2] trivial

## Jack and Joan

Jack and Joan they think no ill,
But loving live, and merry still;
Do their week-day's work, and pray
Devoutly on the holy day:
Skip and trip it on the green,
And help to choose the Summer
  Queen:
Lash out, at a country feast,
Their silver penny with the best.

Well can they judge of nappy[1] ale,
And tell at large a winter tale;　　*10*
Climb up to the apple loft,
And turn the crabs till they be soft.
Tib is all the father's joy,
And little Tom the mother's boy.
All their pleasure is content;
And care, to pay the yearly rent.

Joan can call by name her cows,
And deck her windows with green boughs;
She can wreaths and tutties[2] make
And trim with plums a bridal cake.　　*20*
Jack knows what brings gain or loss;
And his long flail can stoutly toss:
Make the hedge, which others break,
And ever thinks what he doth speak.

Now, you courtly dames and knights,
That study only strange delights;
Though you scorn the home-spun gray,
And revel in your rich array:
Though your tongues dissemble deep,
And can your heads from danger keep;　*30*
Yet, for all your pomp and train,
Securer lives the silly[3] swain.　(*1613*)

## Never Love Unless You Can

Never love unless you can
Bear with all the faults of man;

---
[1] heady　　[2] bouquets　　[3] innocent

Men sometimes will jealous be,
Though but little cause they see,
And hang the head, as discontent,
And speak what straight they will repent.

Men that but one saint adore
Make a show of love to more;
Beauty must be scorned in none,
Though but truly served in one;　　*10*
For what is courtship but disguise?
True hearts may have dissembling eyes.

Men when their affairs require
Must a while themselves retire,
Sometimes hunt, and sometimes hawk,
And not ever sit and talk.
If these and such like you can bear,
Then like, and love, and never fear.
　　　　　　　　　　　　　(*1617*)

## There Is a Garden in Her Face

There is a garden in her face,
  Where roses and white lilies grow,
A heavenly paradise is that place,
  Wherein all pleasant fruits do flow.
There cherries grow, which none may buy
Till "Cherry-ripe" themselves do cry.

Those cherries fairly do enclose
  Of orient pearl a double row,
Which when her lovely laughter shows,
  They look like rosebuds filled with
    snow.　　　　　　　　　　*10*
Yet them nor peer nor prince can buy,
Till "Cherry-ripe" themselves do cry.

Her eyes like angels watch them still;
  Her brows like bended bows do stand,
Threatening with piercing frowns to kill
  All that attempt with eye or hand
Those sacred cherries to come nigh,
Till "Cherry-ripe" themselves do cry.
　　　　　　　　　　　　　(*1617*)

## THOMAS MIDDLETON / 1570?–1627

### from The Spanish Gipsy

Trip it gipsies, trip it fine,
  Show tricks and lofty capers;
At threading needles[1] we repine,
  And leaping over rapiers.
Pindy-pandy rascal toyes,
  We scorn cutting purses,
Though we live by making noise,
  For cheating none can curse us.

Over high ways, over low,
  And over stones and gravel,      10
Though we trip it on the toe,
  And thus for silver travel;
Though our dances waste our backs,
  At night fat capons mend them;
Eggs well brewed in buttered sack,
  Our wenches say befriend them.

Oh that all the world were mad!
  Then should we have fine dancing,
Hobby-horses would be had,
  And brave girls keep a-prancing.      20
Beggars would on cock-horses ride,
  And boobies fall a-roaring,
And cuckolds, though no horns be
    spied,
  Be one another goring.

Welcome, poet, to our ging,[2]
  Make rimes, we'll give thee reason;
Canary bees thy brain shall sting,
  Mull-sack did ne'er speak treason.
Peter-see-me[3] shall wash thy noll,[4]
  And Malaga glasses fox[5] thee,      30
If, poet, thou toss not bowl for bowl,
  Thou shalt not kiss a doxy.   (*1623*)


## JOHN DONNE / 1572–1631

### Song

Go and catch a falling star,
  Get with child a mandrake root,
Tell me where all past years are,
  Or who cleft the devil's foot,
Teach me to hear mermaids singing,
Or to keep off envy's stinging,
    And find
    What wind
Serves to advance an honest mind.

If thou be'st born to strange sights,      10
  Things invisible to see,
Ride ten thousand days and nights,
  Till age snow white hairs on thee.

Thou, when thou return'st, wilt tell me,
All strange wonders that befell thee,
    And swear,
    No where
Lives a woman true and fair.

If thou find'st one, let me know;
  Such a pilgrimage were sweet.      20
Yet do not, I would not go,
  Though at next door we might meet:
Though she were true when you met her,
And last till you write your letter,
    Yet she
    Will be
False, ere I come, to two or three.
                              (*1633*)

---

[1] dancing   [2] gang   [3] a wine   [4] head   [5] intoxicate

## The Sun Rising

    Busy old fool, unruly Sun,
    Why dost thou thus,
Through windows, and through curtains, call on us?
Must to thy motions lovers' seasons run?
    Saucy pedantic wretch, go chide
    Late school-boys and sour prentices,
Go tell court-huntsmen that the king will ride,
Call country ants to harvest offices;
Love, all alike, no season knows nor clime,
Nor hours, days, months, which are the rags of time.    *10*

    Thy beams so reverend and strong
    Why shouldst thou think?
I could eclipse and cloud them with a wink,
But that I would not lose her sight so long.
    If her eyes have not blinded thine,
    Look, and to-morrow late tell me,
Whether both th' Indias of spice and mine
Be where thou left'st them, or lie here with me.
Ask for those kings whom thou saw'st yesterday,
And thou shalt hear, "All here in one bed lay."    *20*

    She's all states, and all princes I;
    Nothing else is;
Princes do but play us; compared to this,
All honour's mimic, all wealth alchemy.
    Thou, Sun, art half as happy as we,
    In that the world's contracted thus;
Thine age asks ease, and since thy duties be
To warm the world, that's done in warming us.
Shine here to us, and thou art everywhere;
This bed thy centre is, these walls thy sphere.   *(1633)*   *30*

## The Bait

Come live with me, and be my love,
And we will some new pleasures prove,[1]
Of golden sands, and crystal brooks,
With silken lines, and silver hooks.

There will the river whispering run,
Warmed by thy eyes more than the sun.
And there th' enamoured fish will stay,
Begging themselves they may betray.

When thou wilt swim in that live bath,
Each fish, which every channel hath,    *10*

Will amorously to thee swim,
Gladder to catch thee, than thou him.

If thou, to be so seen, beest loath,
By sun or moon, thou dark'nest both;
And if myself have leave to see,
I need not their light, having thee.

Let others freeze with angling reeds,
And cut their legs with shells and weeds,
Or treacherously poor fish beset
With strangling snare, or windowy
    net.    *20*

---

[1] test

Let coarse bold hands from slimy nest
The bedded fish in banks out-wrest,
Or curious traitors, sleave-silk[2] flies,
Bewitch poor fishes' wandering eyes.

For thee, thou need'st no such deceit,
For thou thyself art thine own bait;
That fish that is not catched thereby,
Alas, is wiser far than I.   (*1633*)

## A Valediction: Forbidding Mourning

As virtuous men pass mildly away,
  And whisper to their souls, to go,
Whilst some of their sad friends do say,
  The breath goes now, and some say, no:

So let us melt, and make no noise,
  No tear-floods, nor sigh-tempests move,
T'were profanation of our joys
  To tell the laity our love.

Moving of th' earth brings harms and
    fears,
  Men reckon what it did and meant,   10
But trepidation of the spheres,
  Though greater far, is innocent.

Dull sublunary lovers' love
  (Whose soul is sense) cannot admit
Absence, because it doth remove
  Those things which elemented it.

But we by a love, so much refined
  That our selves know not what it is,
Inter-assuréd of the mind,
  Care less, eyes, lips, and hands to
    miss.                               20

Our two souls therefore, which are one,
  Though I must go, endure not yet
A breach, but an expansion,
  Like gold to airy thinness beat.

If they be two, they are two so
  As stiff twin compasses are two,
Thy soul, the fixt foot, makes no show
  To move, but doth, if th' other do.

And though it in the center sit,
  Yet when the other far doth roam,   30
It leans, and hearkens after it,
  And grows erect, as that comes home.

Such wilt thou be to me, who must
  Like th' other foot, obliquely run;
Thy firmness makes my circle just,
  And makes me end, where I
    begun.   (*1633*)

## Love's Diet

To what a cumbersome unwieldiness
And burdenous corpulence my love had grown,
  But that I did, to make it less,
  And keep it in proportion,
Give it a diet, made it feed upon
That which love worst endures, discretion.

Above one sigh a day I allowed him not,
Of which my fortune, and my faults had part;
  And if sometimes by stealth he got
  A she sigh from my mistress' heart,   10
And thought to feast on that, I let him see
'Twas neither very sound, nor meant to me.

If he wrung from me a tear, I brined it so
With scorn or shame, that him it nourished not;

---

[2] loosely twisted floss

If he sucked hers, I let him know
'Twas not a tear, which he had got;
His drink was counterfeit, as was his meat;
For, eyes which roll towards all, weep not, but sweat.

Whatever he would dictate, I writ that,
But burnt my letters; when she writ to me,                    20
   And that that favour made him fat,
   I said, if any title be
Conveyed by this, Ah, what doth it avail,
To be the fortieth name in an entail?

Thus I reclaimed my buzzard love, to fly
At what, and when, and how, and where I choose;
   Now negligent of sport I lie,
   And now as other falconers use,
I spring a mistress, swear, write, sigh and weep;
And the game killed, or lost, go talk, and sleep.   (*1633*)   30

## Love's Deity

I long to talk with some old lover's ghost,
   Who died before the god of love was born.
I cannot think that he, who then loved most,
   Sunk so low as to love one which did scorn.
But since this god produced a destiny,
And that vice-nature, custom, lets it be,
   I must love her that loves not me.

Sure, they which made him god, meant not so much,
   Nor he in his young godhead practised it:
But when an even flame two hearts did touch,                  10
   His office was indulgently to fit
Actives to passives. Correspondency
Only his subject was; it cannot be
   Love, till I love her, that loves me.

But every modern god will now extend
   His vast prerogative as far as Jove.
To rage, to lust, to write to, to commend,
   All is the purlieu of the god of love.
O! were we wakened by this tyranny
To ungod this child again, it could not be
   I should love her, who loves not me

Rebel and atheist too, why murmur I,
   As though I felt the worst that love could do?
Love might make me leave loving, or might try
   A deeper plague, to make her love me too;
Which, since she loves before, I'm loth to see.
Falsehood is worse than hate; and that must be,
   If she whom I love, should love me.   (*1633*)

## The Relic

When my grave is broke up again
Some second guest to entertain
(For graves have learned that woman-head
To be to more than one a bed),
  And he that digs it, spies
A bracelet of bright hair about the bone,
  Will he not let'us alone,
And think that there a loving couple lies,
Who thought that this device might be some way
To make their souls, at the last busy day,     *10*
Meet at this grave, and make a little stay?

If this fall in a time, or land,
Where mis-devotion doth command,
Then, he that digs us up, will bring
Us to the bishop, and the king,
  To make us relics; then
Thou shalt be a Mary Magdalen, and I
  A something else thereby;
All women shall adore us, and some men;
And since at such time, miracles are sought,    *20*
I would have that age by this paper taught
What miracles we harmless lovers wrought.

First, we loved well and faithfully,
Yet knew not what we loved, nor why,
Difference of sex no more we knew,
Than our Guardian Angels do;
  Coming and going, we
Perchance might kiss, but not between those meals;
  Our hands ne'er touched the seals,
Which nature, injured by late law, sets free:    *30*
These miracles we did; but now alas,
All measure, and all language, I should pass,
Should I tell what a miracle she was.  (*1633*)

## The Dissolution

She is dead; and all which die
To their first elements resolve;
And we were mutual elements to us,
  And made of one another.
My body then doth hers involve,
And those things whereof I consist,
  hereby
In me abundant grow, and burdenous,
And nourish not, but smother.
My fire of passion, sighs of air,
Water of tears, and earthly sad
  despair,    *10*
  Which my materials be,
But near worn out by love's security,
She, to my loss, doth by her death repair,
  And I might live long wretched so
But that my fire doth with my fuel grow.
  Now as those active kings
  Whose foreign conquest treasure brings,

Receive more, and spend more, and
    soonest break,
This (which I am amazed that I can speak)
    This death, hath with my store    *20*
    My use increased.

And so my soul more earnestly released,
Will outstrip hers; as bullets flown before
A latter bullet may o'ertake, the powder
    being more.   (*1633*)

## Holy Sonnets

### I

Thou hast made me, and shall Thy work decay?
Repair me now, for now mine end doth haste;
I run to death, and death meets me as fast,
And all my pleasures are like yesterday.
I dare not move my dim eyes any way,
Despair behind, and death before doth cast
Such terror, and my feeble flesh doth waste
By sin in it, which it towards hell doth weigh.
Only Thou art above, and when towards Thee
By Thy leave I can look, I rise again;    *10*
But our old subtle foe so tempteth me
That not one hour myself I can sustain.
Thy grace may wing me to prevent his art,
And Thou like adamant[1] draw mine iron heart.

### VII

At the round earth's imagined corners blow
Your trumpets, angels, and arise, arise
From death, you numberless infinities
Of souls, and to your scattered bodies go,
All whom the flood did, and fire shall o'erthrow,
All whom war, dearth, age, agues, tyrannies,
Despair, law, chance, hath slain, and you whose eyes
Shall behold God, and never taste death's woe.
But let them sleep, Lord, and me mourn a space;
For, if above all these my sins abound,    *10*
'Tis late to ask abundance of Thy grace,
When we are there. Here on this lowly ground,
Teach me how to repent, for that's as good
As if Thou hadst sealed my pardon with Thy blood.

### IX

If poisonous minerals, and if that tree
Whose fruit threw death on else immortal us,
If lecherous goats, if serpents envious
Cannot be damned, alas! why should I be?
Why should intent or reason, born in me,
Make sins, else equal, in me more heinous?

---

[1] lodestone

And mercy, being easy, and glorious
To God, in his stern wrath why threatens he?
But who am I, that dare dispute with thee,
O God? O! of thine only worthy blood                          *10*
And my tears, make a heavenly Lethean[1] flood,
And drown in it my sin's black memory;
That thou remember them, some claim as debt;
I think it mercy, if thou wilt forget.

### X

Death, be not proud, though some have calléd thee
Mighty and dreadful, for thou art not so,
For those whom thou think'st thou dost overthrow
Die not, poor Death, nor yet canst thou kill me.
From rest and sleep, which but thy pictures be,
Much pleasure, then from thee much more must flow;
And soonest our best men with thee do go—
Rest of their bones and souls' delivery!
Thou'rt slave to fate, kings and desperate men,
And dost with poison, war, and sickness dwell,          *10*
And poppy or charms can make us sleep as well,
And better than thy stroke; why swell'st thou then?
One short sleep past, we wake eternally,
And death shall be no more: Death, thou shalt die!

### XIII

What if this present were the world's last night?
Mark in my heart, O Soul, where thou dost dwell,
The picture of Christ crucified, and tell
Whether that countenance can thee afright:
Tears in his eyes quench the amazing light,
Blood fills his frowns, which from his pierced head fell.
And can that tongue adjudge thee unto hell,
Which prayed forgiveness for his foes' fierce spite?
No, no; but as in my idolatry
I said to all my profane mistresses,                         *10*
Beauty, of pity, foulness only is
A sign of rigour: so I say to thee,
To wicked spirits are horrid shapes assigned,
This beauteous form assures a piteous mind.

### XIV

Batter my heart, three personed God; for you
As yet but knock, breathe, shine, and seek to mend;
That I may rise and stand, o'erthrow me and bend
Your force to break, blow, burn and make me new.
I, like an usurped town, to another due,

---

[1] of Lethe, the river of forgetfulness dividing this world from the next

Labour to admit you, but oh, to no end;
Reason, your viceroy in me, me should defend,
But is captived and proves weak or untrue.
Yet dearly I love you and would be loved fain,
But am betrothed unto your enemy:       *10*
Divorce me, untie or break that knot again,
Take me to you, imprison me, for I
Except you enthrall me, never shall be free,
Nor ever chaste, except you ravish me.

### XVIII

Show me, dear Christ, thy spouse so bright and clear.
What! is it she, which on the other shore
Goes richly painted? or which rob'd and tore
Laments and mourns in Germany and here?
Sleeps she a thousand, then peeps up one year?
Is she self truth and errs? now new, now outwore?
Doth she, and did she, and shall she evermore
On one, on seven, or on no hill appear?
Dwells she with us, or like adventuring knights
First travail we to seek and then make love?   *10*
Betray, kind husband, thy spouse to our sights
And let mine amorous soul court thy mild dove,
Who is most true, and pleasing to thee, then
When she's embraced and open to most men.   (*1633*)

## The Broken Heart

He is stark mad, whoever says
   That he hath been in love an hour;
Yet not that love so soon decays,
   But that it can ten in less space devour.
Who will believe me if I swear
That I have had the plague a year?
   Who would not laugh at me if I should say
   I saw a flask of powder burn a day?

Ah, what a trifle is a heart,
   If once into love's hands it come!   *10*
All other griefs allow a part
   To other griefs, and ask themselves but some;
They come to us, but us love draws,
He swallows us, and never chaws;
   By him, as by chained shot,[1] whole ranks do die,
   He is the tyrant pike, our hearts the fry.[2]

If 'twere not so, what did become
   Of my heart when I first saw thee?

---

[1] two cannonballs joined by a chain, to sweep down ranks of men     [2] young fish

I brought a heart into the room,
   But from the room I carried none with me;     *20*
If it had gone to thee, I know
Mine would have taught thine heart to show
   More pity unto me, but love, alas,
   At one first blow did shiver it as glass.

Yet nothing can to nothing fall,
   Nor any place be empty quite;
Therefore I think my breast hath all
   Those pieces still, though they be not unite;
And now as broken glasses show
A hundred lesser faces, so     *30*
   My rags of heart can like, wish, and adore,
   But after one such love, can love no more.   (*1633*)

## The Ecstasy

Where like a pillow on a bed,
   A pregnant bank swelled up, to rest
The violet's reclining head,
   Sat we two, one another's best.

Our hands were firmly cemented
   With a fast balm, which thence did
      spring;
Our eye-beams twisted, and did thread
   Our eyes upon one double string;

So t' entergraft our hands, as yet
   Was all the means to make us
      one;     *10*
And pictures in our eyes to get
   Was all our propagation.

As, 'twixt two equal armies, Fate
   Suspends uncertain victory,
Our souls (which to advance their state
   Were gone out) hung 'twixt her, and
      me.

And whilst our souls negotiate there,
   We like sepulchral statues lay;
All day, the same our postures were,
   And we said nothing, all the day.     *20*

If any, so by love refined,
   That he soul's language understood,
And by good love were grown all mind,
   Within convenient distance stood,

He (though he knew not which soul
      spake,
   Because both meant, both spake the
      same)
Might thence a new concoction take,
   And part far purer than he came.

This ecstasy doth unperplex
   (We said) and tell us what we
      love;     *30*
We see by this, it was not sex;
   We see, we saw not what did move:

But as all several souls contain
   Mixture of things, they know not what,
Love, these mixed souls, doth mix
      again,
   And makes both one, each this and
      that.

A single violet transplant,
   The strength, the colour, and the size
(All which before was poor and scant)
   Redoubles still, and multiplies.   *40*

When love with one another so
   Interinanimates two souls,
That abler soul, which thence doth flow,
   Defects of loneliness controls.

We then, who are this new soul, know,
   Of what we are composed, and made,
For th'atomies of which we grow,
   Are souls, whom no change can invade.

But, O alas! so long, so far
  Our bodies why do we forbear?   *50*
They are ours, though not we; we are
  Th'intelligences, they the spheres.

We owe them thanks, because they thus
  Did us, to us, at first convey,
Yielded their forces, sense, to us,
  Nor are dross to us, but allay.

On man heaven's influence works not so,
  But that it first imprints the air;
For soul into the soul may flow,
  Though it to body first repair.   *60*

As our blood labours to beget
  Spirits, as like souls as it can,
Because such fingers need to knit
  That subtle knot, which makes us man;

So must pure lovers' souls descend
  T' affections, and to faculties,
Which sense may reach and apprehend,
  Else a great prince in prison lies.

To'our bodies turn we then, that so
  Weak men on love revealed may
    look;   *70*
Love's mysteries in souls do grow,
  But yet the body is his book.

And if some lover, such as we,
  Have heard this dialogue of one,
Let him still mark us, he shall see
  Small change when we're to bodies
    gone.   (*1633*)

## A Hymn to God the Father

Wilt Thou forgive that sin where I begun,
  Which is my sin, though it were done before?
Wilt Thou forgive those sins, through which I run,
  And do run still, though still I do deplore?
    When Thou hast done, Thou hast not done,
    For I have more.

Wilt Thou forgive that sin by which I have won
  Others to sin, and made my sin their door?
Wilt Thou forgive that sin which I did shun
  A year or two, but wallowed in a score?   *10*
    When Thou hast done, Thou hast not done,
    For I have more.

I have a sin of fear, that when I have spun
  My last thread, I shall perish on the shore;
Swear by Thyself, that at my death Thy Son
  Shall shine as he shines now, and heretofore;
    And, having done that, Thou hast done:
    I fear no more.   (*1633*)

## A Valediction: Of Weeping

Let me pour forth
My tears before thy face whilst I stay here,
For thy face coins them, and thy stamp they bear,
And by this mintage they are something worth,
  For thus they be
  Pregnant of thee;

Fruits of much grief they are, emblems of more—
When a tear falls, that Thou falls which it bore,
So thou and I are nothing then, when on a diverse shore.

         On a round ball                         *10*
A workman that hath copies by, can lay
An Europe, Afric, and an Asia,
And quickly make that, which was nothing, all:
         So doth each tear
         Which thee doth wear,
A globe, yea world, by that impression grow,
Till thy tears mixed with mine do overflow
This world; by waters sent from thee, my heaven dissolvéd so.

         O more than moon,
Draw not up seas to drown me in thy sphere;         *20*
Weep me not dead, in thine arms, but forbear
To teach the sea what it may do too soon.
         Let not the wind
         Example find
To do me more harm than it purposeth;
Since thou and I sigh one another's breath,
Whoe'er sighs most is cruelest, and hastes the other's death.   (*1633*)

## The Canonization

     For God's sake hold your tongue, and let me love,
         Or chide my palsy, or my gout,
     My five gray hairs, or ruined fortune, flout,
            With wealth your state, your mind with arts improve
                Take you a course, get you a place,
                Observe His Honor, or His Grace,
     Or the King's real, or his stampéd face
            Contemplate; what you will, approve,[1]
            So you will let me love.

     Alas, alas, who's injured by my love?             *10*
         What merchant's ships have my sighs drowned?
     Who says my tears have overflowed his ground?
            When did my colds a forward spring remove?
                When did the heats which my veins fill
                Add one more to the plaguy bill?[2]
     Soldiers find wars, and lawyers find out still
            Litigious men, which quarrels move,
            Though she and I do love.

     Call us what you will, we are made such by love;
         Call her one, me another fly,             *20*
     We're tapers too, and at our own cost die,

---

[1] try      [2] the list of those dead from the plague

And we in us find the eagle and the dove.
　　The phoenix[3] riddle hath more wit
　　By us: we two being one, are it.
So, to one neutral thing both sexes fit.
　　We die and rise the same, and prove
　　Mysterious by this love.

We can die by it, if not live by love,
　　And if unfit for tombs and hearse
Our legend be, it will be fit for verse;　　　　　　　　　　　　　*30*
　　And if no piece of chronicle we prove,
　　　We'll build in sonnets pretty rooms;
　　　As well as well-wrought urn becomes
The greatest ashes, as half-acre tombs,
　　And by these hymns, all shall approve
　　Us canonized for love:

And thus invoke us: You whom reverend love
　　Made one another's hermitage;
You, to whom love was peace, that now is rage;
　　Who did the whole world's soul contract, and drove　　　*40*
　　　Into the glasses of your eyes
　　　(So made such mirrors, and such spies,
That they did all to you epitomize)
　　Countries, towns, courts: Beg from above
　　A pattern of your love!　(*1633*)

## The Flea

Mark but this flea, and mark in this,
How little that which thou deniest me is;
It sucked me first, and now sucks thee,
And in this flea our two bloods mingled be;
Thou know'st that this cannot be said
A sin, nor shame, nor loss of maidenhead,
　　Yet this enjoys before it woo,
　　And pampered swells with one blood made of two,
　　And this, alas, is more than we would do.

Oh stay, three lives in one flea spare,　　　　　　　　　　　*10*
Where we almost, yea more than married, are.
This flea is you and I, and this
Our marriage bed and marriage temple is;
Though parents grudge, and you, we are met,
And cloistered in these living walls of jet,
　　Though use make you apt to kill me
　　Let not to that, self-murder added be,
　　And sacrilege, three sins in killing three.

---

[3] Only one of these legendary birds exists at one time. It lights its own funeral fire and then rises from the ashes to live for another thousand years before repeating the process.

Cruel and sudden, hast thou since
Purpled thy nail, in blood of innocence?                                  20
Wherein could this flea guilty be,
Except in that drop which it sucked from thee?
Yet thou triumph'st, and say'st that thou
Find'st not thy self nor me the weaker now;
   'Tis true, then learn how false fears be;
   Just so much honor, when thou yield'st to me,
Will waste, as this flea's death took life from thee.   (*1633*)


## The Good-Morrow

I wonder, by my troth, what thou and I
Did, till we loved? Were we not weaned till then,
But sucked on country pleasures, childishly?
Or snorted we in the seven sleepers' den?[1]
'Twas so; But this, all pleasures fancies be.
If ever any beauty I did see,
Which I desired, and got, 'twas but a dream of thee.

And now good morrow to our waking souls,
Which watch not one another out of fear;
For love all love of other sights controls,                              10
And makes one little room an everywhere.
Let sea-discoverers to new worlds have gone,
Let maps to other, worlds on worlds have shown,
Let us possess one world; each hath one, and is one.

My face in thine eye, thine in mine appears,
And true plain hearts do in the faces rest;
Where can we find two better hemispheres
Without sharp North, without declining West?
Whatever dies was not mixed equally;[2]
If our two loves be one, or thou and I                                   20
Love so alike that none do slacken, none can die.   (*1633*)


## The Triple Fool

   I am two fools, I know,
  For loving, and for saying so
    In whining poetry;
But where's that wiseman, that would not be I,
    If she would not deny?
Then as th'earth's inward narrow crooked lanes

---

[1] Seven legendary youths slept in a cave for nearly 200 years to escape persecution.
[2] Alchemists believed that a perfect mixture of elements in a substance guaranteed its immutability.

Do purge sea water's fretful salt away,
   I thought, if I could draw my pains,
Through rime's vexation, I should them allay.
Grief brought to numbers cannot be so fierce,     *10*
For he tames it that fetters it in verse.

   But when I have done so,
Some man, his art and voice to show,
   Doth set[1] and sing my pain,
And, by delighting many, frees again
   Grief, which verse did restrain.
To love and grief tribute of verse belongs,
But not of such as pleases when 'tis read;
   Both are increaséd by such songs,
For both their triumphs so are publishéd,     *20*
And I, which was two fools, do so grow three;
Who are a little, the best fools be.   (*1633*)

## The Curse

Whoever guesses, thinks, or dreams he knows
Who is my mistress, wither by this curse;
   His only, and only his purse
   May some dull heart to love dispose,
And she yield then to all that are his foes;
   May he be scorned by one, whom all else scorn,
   Forswear to others, what to her he hath sworn,
   With fear of missing, shame of getting, torn.

Madness his sorrow, gout his cramp, may he
Make, by but thinking who hath made him such;     *10*
   And may he feel no touch
   Of conscience, but of fame, and be
Anguished, not that 'twas sin, but that 'twas she;
   In early and long scarceness may he rot,
   For land which had been his, if he had not
   Himself incestuously an heir begot.

May he dream treason, and believe that he
Meant to perform it, and confess, and die,
   And no record tell why;
   His sons, which none of his may be,     *20*
Inherit nothing but his infamy;
   Or may he so long parasites have fed,
   That he would fain be theirs, whom he hath bred,
   And at the last be circumcised for bread.

[1] to music

The venoms of all stepdames, gamesters' gall,
What tyrants and their subjects interwish,
What plants, mines, beasts, fowl, fish
Can cóntribute, all ill which all
Prophets or poets spake, and all which shall
Be annexed in schedules unto this by me,                        *30*
Fall on that man; for if it be a she
Nature beforehand hath out-curséd me.   *(1633)*


## Hymn to God My God, in My Sickness

Since I am coming to that holy room
    Where, with Thy choir of saints for evermore,
I shall be made Thy music; as I come
    I tune the instrument here at the door,
    And what I must do then, think here before.

Whilst my physicians by their love are grown
    Cosmographers, and I their map, who lie
Flat on this bed, that by them may be shown
    That this is my southwest discovery
    *Per fretum febris*,[1] by these straits to die,           *10*

I joy, that in these straits, I see my West;
    For, though their currents yield return to none,
What shall my West hurt me? As West and East
    In all flat maps (and I am one) are one,
    So death doth touch the resurrection.

Is the Pacific Sea my home? Or are
    The Eastern riches? Is Jerusalem?
Anyan,[2] and Magellan, and Gibraltar,
    All straits, and none but straits, are ways to them,
    Whether where Japhet dwelt, or Cham, or Shem.[3]           *20*

We think that Paradise and Calvary,
    Christ's cross, and Adam's tree, stood in one place;
Look, Lord, and find both Adams[4] met in me;
    As the first Adam's sweat surrounds my face,
    May the last Adam's blood my soul embrace.

So, in his purple wrapped, receive me, Lord
    By these his thorns give me his other crown;
And, as to others' souls I preached Thy word,
    Be this my text, my sermon to mine own;
    Therefore that he may raise the Lord throws down.   *(1635)*   *30*

---

[1] via the straits of fever      [2] the Bering Straits      respectively, Europe, Africa, and Asia
[3] the sons of Noah, who after the Flood peopled,      [4] In Christian typology, Adam prefigures Christ.

# BEN JONSON / 1572–1637

## *from* Cynthia's Revels

Slow, slow, fresh fount, keep time with my salt tears;
   Yet slow, yet, O, faintly gentle springs:
List to the heavy part the music bears,
   Woe weeps out her division, when she sings.
     Droop herbs, and flowers;
     Fall grief in showers;
     Our beauties are not ours:
      Oh, I could still
(Like melting snow upon some craggy hill)
     Drop, drop, drop, drop,     *10*
Since nature's pride is, now, a withered daffodil.

Queen and huntress, chaste and fair,
Now the sun is laid to sleep,
Seated in thy silver chair,
State in wonted manner keep:
   Hesperus[1] entreats thy light,
   Goddess, excellently bright.

Earth, let not thy envious shade
Dare itself to interpose;
Cynthia's[2] shining orb was made
Heaven to clear, when day did close:     *10*
   Bless us then with wishéd sight,
   Goddess, excellently bright.

Lay thy bow of pearl apart,
And thy crystal-shining quiver;
Give unto the flying hart
Space to breathe, how short soever:
   Thou that mak'st a day of night,
   Goddess, excellently bright.   (*1600*)

## *from* The Silent Woman

Still to be neat, still to be dressed,
As you were going to a feast;
Still to be powdered, still perfumed:
Lady, it is to be presumed,
Though art's hid causes are not found,
All is not sweet, all is not sound.

Give me a look, give me a face
That makes simplicity a grace;
Robes loosely flowing, hair as free:
Such sweet neglect more taketh me     *10*
Than all th' adulteries of art;
They strike mine eyes, but not my heart.
     (*1609*)

---

[1] Venus, the evening star       [2] goddess of the moon

## Song: To Celia

Drink to me only with thine eyes,
  And I will pledge with mine;
Or leave a kiss but in the cup
  And I'll not look for wine.
The thirst that from the soul doth rise
  Doth ask a drink divine;
But might I of Jove's nectar sup,
  I would not change for thine.

I sent thee late a rosy wreath,
  Not so much honoring thee      *10*
As giving it a hope that there
  It could not withered be;
But thou thereon didst only breathe,
  And sent'st it back to me;
Since when it grows, and smells, I swear,
  Not of itself, but thee!  *(1616)*

## from The Poetaster

### HERMOGENES'S SONG

If I freely may discover,[1]
What would please me in my lover:
  I would have her fair and witty,
  Savouring more of court than city;
  A little proud, but full of pity:
  Light and humorous in her toying.
  Oft building hopes and soon destroying,
  Long, but sweet in the enjoying,
Neither too easy, nor too hard:
All extremes I would have barred.  *10*

She should be allowed her passions,
So they were but used as fashions;
  Sometimes froward, and then frowning,
  Sometimes sickish, and then swowning,
  Every fit, with change, still crowning.
  Purely jealous, I would have her,
  Then only constant when I crave her.
  'Tis a virtue should not save her.
Thus, nor her delicates would cloy me,
Neither her peevishness annoy me.  *20*
                *(1616)*

## from Volpone

### SONG: TO CELIA

Come, my Celia, let us prove,[1]
While we may, the sports of love;
Time will not be ours for ever:
He at length our good will sever.
Spend not then his gifts in vain:
Suns that set, may rise again;
But if once we lose this light,
'Tis with us perpetual night.
Why should we defer our joys?
Fame and rumour are but toys.  *10*
Cannot we delude the eyes
Of a few poor household spies?
Or his easier ears beguile,
Thus removéd by our wile?
'Tis no sin love's fruits to steal,
But the sweet theft to reveal:
To be taken, to be seen,
These have crimes accounted been.
                *(1616)*

## To Heaven

Good and great God! can I not think of Thee,
  But it must straight my melancholy be?
Is it interpreted in me disease,
  That, laden with my sins, I seek for ease?
O be Thou witness, that the reins dost know
  And hearts of all, if I be sad for show;
And judge me after, if I dare pretend
  To aught but grace, or aim at other end.

---

[1] reveal           [1] try

As Thou art all, so be Thou all to me,
  First, midst, and last, converted One and Three!      *10*
My faith, my hope, my love; and, in this state,
  My judge, my witness, and my advocate!
Where have I been this while exiled from Thee,
  And whither rapt, now Thou but stoop'st to me?
Dwell, dwell here still! O, being everywhere,
  How can I doubt to find Thee ever here?
I know my state, both full of shame and scorn,
  Conceived in sin, and unto labor born,
Standing with fear, and must with horror fall,
  And destined unto judgment, after all.      *20*
I feel my grief too, and there scarce is ground
  Upon my flesh t'inflict another wound;
Yet dare I not complain or wish for death
  With holy Paul, lest it be thought the breath
Of discontent; or that these prayers be
  For weariness of life, not love of Thee.

## On Lucy, Countess of Bedford

This morning, timely rapt with holy fire,
  I thought to form unto my zealous muse
What kind of creature I could most desire,
  To honor, serve, and love; as poets use.
I meant to make her fair, and free, and wise.
  Of greatest blood, and yet more good than great;
I meant the day star should not brighter rise,
  Nor lend like influence from his lucent seat.
I meant she should be courteous, facile, sweet,
  Hating that solemn vice of greatness, pride;      *10*
I meant each softest virtue there should meet,
  Fit in that softer bosom to reside.
Only a learnéd and a manly soul
  I purposed her; that should, with even powers,
The rock,[1] the spindle, and the shears control
  Of destiny, and spin her own free hours.
Such when I meant to fain, and wished to see,
  My muse bade, Bedford write, and that was she.

## Inviting a Friend to Supper

Tonight, grave sir, both my poor house and I
  Do equally desire your company;
Not that we think us worthy such a guest,
  But that your worth will dignify our feast,

---

[1] distaff

With those that come; whose grace may make that seem
   Something, which else could hope for no esteem.
It is the fair acceptance, Sir, creates
   The entertainment perfect, not the cates.[1]
Yet shall you have, to rectify your palate,
   An olive, capers, or some better salad                10
Ush'ring the mutton; with a short-legg'd hen,
   If we can get her, full of eggs, and then,
Lemons, and wine for sauce: to these a coney[2]
   Is not to be despaired of, for our money;
And, though fowl now be scarce, yet there be clerks,
   The sky not falling, think we may have larks.
I'll tell you of more, and lie, so you will come;
   Of partridge, pheasant, woodcock, of which some
May yet be there; and godwit if we can:
   Knot, rail,[3] and ruff[4] too. How so ere, my man      20
Shall read a piece of Virgil, Tacitus,
   Livy, or of some better book to us,
Of which we'll speak our minds, amidst our meat;
   And I'll profess no verses to repeat;
To this, if aught appear, which I know not of,
   That will the pastry, not my paper, show of.
Digestive cheese and fruit there sure will be;
   But that which most doth take my muse, and me,
Is a pure cup of rich Canary wine,
   Which is the Mermaid's[5] now, but shall be mine;    30
Of which had Horace or Anacreon tasted,
   Their lives, as do their lines, till now had lasted.
Tobacco, nectar, or the Thespian spring
   Are all but Luther's beer to this I sing.
Of this we will sup free, but moderately,
   And we will have no Pooly or Parrot[6] by;
Nor shall our cups make any guilty men:
   But at our parting we will be as when
We innocently met. No simple word
   That shall be uttered at our mirthful board      40
Shall make us sad next morning or affright
   The liberty that we'll enjoy tonight.   (*1616*)

## To the Memory of My Beloved, the Author Master William Shakespeare

To draw no envy, Shakespeare, on thy name,
Am I thus ample to thy book and fame;
While I confess thy writings to be such
As neither man nor Muse can praise too much.

---

[1] viands    [2] rabbit    [3] three more game birds    foregathered at the Mermaid Tavern.
[4] a fish                                         [6] two government informers
[5] Jonson and his cronies (the "Tribe of Ben")

'Tis true, and all men's suffrage. But these ways
Were not the paths I meant unto thy praise;
For silliest ignorance on these may light,
Which, when it sounds at best, but echoes right;
Or blind affection, which doth ne'er advance
The truth, but gropes, and urgeth all by chance;      10
Or crafty malice might pretend this praise,
And think to ruin, where it seemed to raise.
These are, as some infamous bawd or whore
Should praise a matron. What could hurt her more?
But thou art proof against them, and indeed,
Above the ill fortune of them, or the need.
I therefore will begin. Soul of the age!
The applause, delight, the wonder of our stage!
My Shakespeare, rise! I will not lodge thee by
Chaucer, or Spenser, or bid Beaumont lie              20
A little further, to make thee a room;
Thou art a monument without a tomb,
And art alive still while thy book doth live
And we have wits to read and praise to give.
That I not mix thee so, my brain excuses,
I mean with great, but disproportioned Muses;
For if I thought my judgment were of years,
I should commit thee surely with thy peers,
And tell how far thou didst our Lyly outshine,
Or sporting Kyd, or Marlowe's mighty line.            30
And though thou hadst small Latin and less Greek,
From thence to honor thee I would not seek
For names; but call forth thundering Aeschylus,
Euripides, and Sophocles to us;
Pacuvius, Accius,[1] him of Cordova[2] dead,
To life again, to hear thy buskin tread,
And shake a stage; or, when thy socks were on,
Leave thee alone for the comparison
Of all that insolent Greece or haughty Rome
Sent forth, or since did from their ashes come.       40
Triumph, my Britain, thou hast one to show
To whom all scenes of Europe homage owe.
He was not of an age, but for all time!
And all the Muses still were in their prime,
When, like Apollo, he came forth to warm
Our ears, or like a Mercury to charm!
Nature herself was proud of his designs
And joyed to wear the dressing of his lines,
Which were so richly spun, and woven so fit,
As, since, she will vouchsafe no other wit.           50
The merry Greek, tart Aristophanes,
Neat Terence, witty Plautus, now not please,

---

[1] Roman poets of the second century B.C.
[2] Seneca, Roman philosopher, statesman, and tragedian of the first century

But antiquated and deserted lie,
As they were not of Nature's family.
Yet must I not give Nature all; thy art,
My gentle Shakespeare, must enjoy a part.
For though the poet's matter Nature be,
His art doth give the fashion; and, that he
Who casts to write a living line, must sweat
(Such as thine are) and strike the second heat                    60
Upon the Muses' anvil; turn the same
(And himself with it) that he thinks to frame,
Or, for the laurel, he may gain a scorn;
For a good poet's made, as well as born.
And such wert thou! Look how the father's face
Lives in his issue; even so the race
Of Shakespeare's mind and manners brightly shines
In his well-turnéd, and true-filéd lines;
In each of which he seems to shake a lance,
As brandished at the eyes of ignorance.                    70
Sweet Swan of Avon! what a sight it were
To see thee in our waters yet appear,
And make those flights upon the banks of Thames,
That so did take Eliza,[3] and our James!
But stay, I see thee in the hemisphere
Advanced, and made a constellation there!
Shine forth, thou star of poets, and with rage
Or influence, chide or cheer the drooping stage,
Which, since thy flight from hence, hath mourned like night,
And despairs day, but for thy volume's light.   (*1623*)                    80

## *from* The Sad Shepherd

Here she was wont to go, and here! and here!
Just where those daisies, pinks, and violets grow;
The world may find the spring by following her,
For other print her airy steps ne'er left;
Her treading would not bend a blade of grass!
Or shake the downy blow-ball from his stalk!
But like the soft west-wind she shot along,
And where she went the flowers took thickest root,
As she had sowed 'em with her odorous foot.

     .   .   .

Though I am young and cannot tell
  Either what death or love is well,
Yet I have heard they both bear darts,
  And both do aim at human hearts.
And then again I have been told
  Love wounds with heat, as death with cold;

[3] Queen Elizabeth; James: King James I

So that I fear they do but bring
 Extremes to touch, and mean one thing.

As in a ruin we it call
 One thing to be blown up, or fall;                                    *10*
Or to our end, like way may have
 By a flash of lightning or a wave;
So love's infláméd shaft or brand
 May kill as soon as death's cold hand;
Except love's fires the virtue have
 To fright the frost out of the grave.   (*1637?*)


## An Ode to Himself

Where dost thou careless lie,
 Buried in ease and sloth?
Knowledge that sleeps doth die;
And this security,
 It is the common moth
That eats on wits and arts, and destroys them both.

Are all the Aonian springs[1]
 Dried up? Lies Thespia[2] waste?
Doth Clarius'[3] harp want strings,
That not a nymph now sings?                                            *10*
 Or droop they as disgraced,
To see their seats and bowers by chattering pies defaced?

If hence thy silence be,
 As 'tis too just a cause,
Let this thought quicken thee:
Minds that are great and free
 Should not on fortune pause;
'Tis crown enough to virtue still, her own applause.

What though the greedy fry
 Be taken with false baits                                            *20*
Of worded balladry,
And think it poesy?
 They die with their conceits,
And only piteous scorn upon their folly waits.

Then take in hand thy lyre;
 Strike in thy proper strain;
With Japhet's line[4] aspire
Sol's chariot for new fire
 To give the world again;
Who aided him will thee, the issue of Jove's brain.                   *30*

---

[1] a spring at the foot of Mt. Helicon, which was a source of poetic inspiration
[2] a center of the worship of the Muses
[3] an oracle of Apollo
[4] the descendants of one of the sons of Noah, who peopled Europe after the Flood

And, since our dainty age
   Cannot endure reproof,
Make not thyself a page
To that strumpet the stage;
   But sing high and aloof,
Safe from the wolf's black jaw, and the dull ass's hoof.   (*1640*)


## The Triumph of Charis

See the Chariot at hand here of Love,
   Wherein my Lady rideth!
Each that draws is a swan or a dove,
   And well the car Love guideth.
As she goes, all hearts do duty
     Unto her beauty;
And enamoured do wish, so they might
     But enjoy such a sight,
That they still were to run by her side,
Through swords, through seas, whither she would ride.     *10*

Do but look on her eyes, they do light
   All that Love's world compriseth!
Do but look on her hair, it is bright
   As Love's star when it riseth!
Do but mark, her forehead's smoother
     Than words that soothe her;
And from her arched brows such a grace
     Sheds itself through the face,
As alone there triumphs to the life
All the gain, all the good, of the elements' strife.     *20*

Have you seen but a bright lily grow
   Before rude hands have touched it?
Have you marked but the fall of the snow
   Before the soil hath smutched it?
Have you felt the wool of beaver,
     Or swan's down ever?
Or have smelt of the bud of the brier,
     Or the nard[1] in the fire?
Or have tasted the bag[2] of the bee?
O so white, O so soft, O so sweet is she!   (*1640*)     *30*

---

[1] a fragrant ointment derived from spikenard       [2] honey sac (honeybag)

## JOHN FLETCHER / 1579–1625

### *from* The Maid's Tragedy

Lay a garland on my hearse
  Of the dismal yew;
Maidens, willow-branches bear,
  Say I diéd true.

My love was false, but I was firm
  From my hour of birth;
Upon my buried body lie
  Lightly, gentle earth. (*1622*)

### Care-Charming Sleep

Care-charming sleep, thou easer of all woes,
Brother to Death, sweetly thyself dispose
On this afflicted prince; fall like a cloud,
In gentle showers; give nothing that is loud,
Or painful to his slumbers; easy, light,
And as a purling stream, thou son of Night
Pass by his troubled senses; sing his pain,
Like hollow murmuring wind or silver rain;
Into this prince gently, oh, gently slide,
And kiss him into slumbers like a bride.          10

### Hold Back Thy Hours, Dark Night

Hold back thy hours, dark Night, till we have done;
  The Day will come too soon.
Young maids will curse thee, if thou steal'st away
And leav'st their losses open to the day.
  Stay, stay, and hide
  The blushes of the bride.
Stay, gentle Night, and with thy darkness cover
  The kisses of her lover.
Stay, and confound her tears and her shrill cryings,
Her weak denials, vows, and often-dyings;          10
  Stay, and hide all:
  But help not, though she call.

## FRANCIS BEAUMONT / 1584–1616
### *and*
## JOHN FLETCHER / 1579–1625

### Come, Sleep

Come, Sleep, and with thy sweet deceiving
  Lock me in delight awhile!
  Let some passing dreams beguile
  All my fancies; that from thence
  I may feel an influence,
All my powers of care bereaving!

Though but a shadow, but a sliding,
  Let me know some little joy!
  We that suffer long annoy
  Are contented with a thought       *10*
  Through an idle fancy wrought:
Oh, let my joys have some abiding!


## JOHN WEBSTER / 1580?–1634?

### *from* The White Devil

Call for the robin-redbreast and the wren,
Since o'er shady groves they hover,
And with leaves and flowers do cover
The friendless bodies of unburied men.
  Call unto his funeral dole
  The ant, the field-mouse, and the mole,
To rear him hillocks that shall keep him
  warm,
And, when gay tombs are robbed, sustain
  no harm;
But keep the wolf far thence, that's foe
  to men,
For with his nails he'll dig them up
  again.  *(1612)*     *10*

### All the Flowers of the Spring

All the flowers of the spring
Meet to perfume our burying;
These have but their growing prime,
And man doth flourish but his time:
Survey our progress from our birth;
We are set, we grow, we turn to earth.
Courts adieu, and all delights,
All bewitching appetites!
Sweetest breath and clearest eye,
Like perfumes, go out and die;    *10*
And consequently this is done
As shadows wait upon the sun.
Vain the ambition of kings
Who seek by trophies and dead things
To leave a living name behind,
And weave but nets to catch the wind.

## WILLIAM DRUMMOND OF HAWTHORNDEN /
1585–1649

### Madrigal

Like the Idalian queen,
Her hair about her eyne,[1]
With neck and breast's ripe apples to be
    seen,
At first glance of the morn
In Cyprus' gardens gathering those
    fair flowers
Which of her blood were born,
I saw, but fainting saw, my paramours.
The Graces naked danced about the place,
The winds and trees amazed
With silence on her gazed,                    10
The flowers did smile, like those upon
    her face;
And as their aspen stalks those fingers
    band,
That she might read my case,
A hyacinth I wished me in her hand.

### The Ivory, Coral, Gold

The ivory, coral, gold,
Of breasts, of lips, of hair,
So lively Sleep doth show to inward sight,
That, wake, I think I hold
No shadow, but my fair:
Myself so to deceive,
With long-shut eyes I shun the irksome
    light.
Such pleasure thus I have,
Delighting in false gleams,
If Death Sleep's brother be,                    10
And souls relieved of sense have so
    sweet dreams,
That I would wish me thus to dream
    and die.

## WILLIAM BROWNE / 1591?–1643?

### On the Countess Dowager of Pembroke

Underneath this sable hearse
Lies the subject of all verse:
Sidney's sister, Pembroke's mother.
Death, ere thou hast slain another
Fair and learn'd and good as she,
Time shall throw a dart at thee.
Marble piles let no man raise
To her name, for after-days
Some kind woman, born as she,
Reading this, like Niobe                    10
Shall turn marble, and become
Both her mourner and her tomb.    (*1623*)

---

[1] eyes

## ROBERT HERRICK / 1591–1674

### The Argument of His Book

I sing of brooks, of blossoms, birds, and bowers:
Of April, May, of June, and July-flowers.
I sing of May-poles, hock-carts,[1] wassails, wakes,
Of bride-grooms, brides, and of their bridal-cakes.
I write of youth, of love, and have access
By these, to sing of cleanly-wantonness.
I sing of dews, of rains, and piece by piece
Of balm, of oil, of spice, and ambergris.
I sing of time's trans-shifting; and I write
How roses first came red, and lilies white.                    10
I write of groves, of twilights, and I sing
The Court of Mab, and of the Fairy King.
I write of Hell; I sing (and ever shall)
Of Heaven, and hope to have it after all.    (*1648*)

### To the Sour Reader

If thou dislik'st the piece thou light'st on
    first;
Think that, of all that I have writ, the
    worst;
But if thou read'st my book unto the end,
And still dost this and that verse
    reprehend,
O perverse man! if all disgustful be,
The extreme scab take thee and thine,
    for me.    (*1648*)

### His Prayer to Ben Jonson

When I a verse shall make,
    Know I have prayed thee,
For old religion's sake,
    Saint Ben, to aid me.

Make the way smooth for me,
    When I, thy Herrick,
Honouring thee, on my knee
    Offer my lyric.

Candles I'll give thee,
    And a new altar;                    10
And thou, Saint Ben, shalt be
    Writ in my psalter.    (*1648*)

### Delight in Disorder

A sweet disorder in the dress
Kindles in clothes a wantonness:
A lawn about the shoulders thrown
Into a fine distraction,
An erring lace, which here and there
Enthralls the crimson stomacher,
A cuff neglectful, and thereby
Ribbands to flow confusedly,
A winning wave (deserving note)
In the tempestuous petticoat,                    10
A careless shoe-string, in whose tie
I see a wild civility,
Do more bewitch me, than when art
Is too precise in every part.    (*1648*)

---

[1] the last harvest wagons loaded, and hence the occasion for rejoicing

## To the Virgins to Make Much of Time

Gather ye rose-buds while ye may,
  Old Time is still a-flying:
And this same flower that smiles today,
  Tomorrow will be dying.

The glorious lamp of heaven, the Sun,
  The higher he's a-getting
The sooner will his race be run,
  And nearer he's to setting.

That age is best which is the first,
  When youth and blood are warmer; *10*
But being spent, the worse, and worst
  Time, still succeed the former.

Then be not coy, but use your time;
  And while ye may, go marry:
For having lost but once your prime,
  You may for ever tarry. (*1648*)

## The Night-Piece, to Julia

Her eyes the glow-worm lend thee,
The shooting stars attend thee:
  And the elves also,
  Whose little eyes glow
Like the sparks of fire, befriend thee.

No will-o'-th'-wisp mislight thee;
Nor snake, or slow-worm bite thee:
  But on, on thy way,
  Not making a stay,
Since ghost there's none to affright
  thee. *10*

Let not the dark thee cumber;
What though the moon does slumber:
  The stars of the night
  Will lend thee their light,
Like tapers clear without number.

Then, Julia, let me woo thee,
Thus, thus to come unto me:
  And when I shall meet
  Thy silv'ry feet,
My soul I'll pour into thee. (*1648*) *20*

## Upon Julia's Clothes

Whenas in silks my Julia goes
Then, then (methinks) how sweetly flows
That liquefaction of her clothes.

Next, when I cast mine eyes and see
That brave vibration each way free;
O how that glittering taketh me! (*1648*)

## To Perilla

Ah, my Perilla! dost thou grieve to see
Me, day by day, to steal away from thee?
Age calls me hence, and my gray hairs bid come,
And haste away to mine eternal home:
'Twill not be long (Perilla) after this,
That I must give thee the supremest kiss.
Dead when I am, first cast in salt, and bring
Part of the cream from the religious spring,
With which (Perilla) wash my hands and feet;
That done, then wind me in that very sheet *10*
Which wrapt thy smooth limbs (when thou didst implore
The gods' protection, but the night before);
Follow me weeping to my turf, and there
Let fall a primrose, and with it a tear;
Then lastly, let some weekly strewings be
Devoted to the memory of me:
Then shall my ghost not walk about, but keep
Still in the cool and silent shades of sleep. (*1648*)

## Meat Without Mirth

Eaten I have, and though I had good
   cheer
I did not sup, because no friends were
   there.
Where mirth and friends are absent when
   we dine
Or sup, there wants the incense and the
   wine.  (*1648*)

## Ceremonies for Candlemas Eve

Down with the rosemary and bays,
   Down with the mistletoe;
Instead of holly, now upraise
   The greener box (for show.)

The holly hitherto did sway;
   Let box now domineer,
Until the dancing Easter-day,
   Or Easter's eve appear.

Then youthful box which now hath
    grace,
   Your houses to renew,                    10
Grown old, surrender must his place,
   Unto the crispéd yew.

When yew is out, then birch comes in,
   And many flowers beside;
Both of a fresh and fragrant kin
   To honour Whitsuntide.

Green rushes then, and sweetest bents,
   With cooler oaken boughs,
Come in for comely ornaments,
   To re-adorn the house.                    20

Thus times do shift; each thing his turn
    does hold;
New things succeed, as former things
   grow old.  (*1648*)

## The Ceremonies for Candlemas Day

Kindle the Christmas brand and then
   Till sunset, let it burn;
Which quenched, then lay it up again,
   Till Christmas next return.

Part must be kept wherewith to teend[1]
   The Christmas log next year;
And where 'tis safely kept, the fiend,
   Can do no mischief there.  (*1648*)

## Kings and Tyrants

'Twixt kings and tyrants there's this
   difference known,
Kings seek their subjects' good; tyrants
   their own.  (*1648*)

## His Return to London

From the dull confines of the drooping west
To see the day spring from the pregnant east,
Ravished in spirit, I come, nay more, I fly
To thee, blest place of my nativity!
Thus, thus with hallowed feet I touch the ground
With thousand blessings by thy fortune crowned.
O fruitful genius! that bestowest here
An everlasting plenty, year by year.
O place! O people! Manners framed to please
All nations, customs, kindreds, languages!          10
I am a free-born Roman, suffer then
That I amongst you live a citizen.

---

[1] kindle

London my home is, though by hard fate sent
Into a long and irksome banishment;
Yet since called back, henceforward let me be,
O native country, repossessed by thee!
For rather than I'll to the west return,
I'll beg of thee first here to have mine urn.
Weak I am grown, and must in short time fall;
Give thou my sacred relics burial.  (*1648*)                    20

## His Creed

I do believe that die I must,
And be returned from out my dust:
I do believe that when I rise,
Christ I shall see, with these same eyes:
I do believe that I must come,
With others, to the dreadful Doom:
I do believe the bad must go
From thence, to everlasting woe:

I do believe the good, and I,
Shall live with Him eternally:                    10
I do believe I shall inherit
Heaven, by Christ's mercies, not my
  merit:
I do believe the One in Three,
And Three in perfect Unity:
Lastly, that JESUS is a Deed
Of Gift from God: *And here's my Creed.*
                                   (*1648*)

## The Resurrection Possible and Probable

For each one body that i' th' earth is sown
There's an uprising but of one for one,
But for each grain that in the ground is thrown
Three score or fourscore spring up thence for one;
So that the wonder is not half so great
Of ours, as is the rising of the wheat.  (*1648*)

## Dew Sat on Julia's Hair

Dew sat on Julia's hair,
  And spangled too,
Like leaves that laden are
  With trembling dew;
Or glittered to my sight,
  As when the beams
Have their reflected light
  Danced by the streams.  (*1648*)

## To Daisies, Not to Shut So Soon

Shut not so soon; the dull-eyed night
  Has not as yet begun
To make a seizure on the light,
  Or to seal up the sun.

## Discontents in Devon

More discontents I never had
  Since I was born, than here,
Where I have been, and still am sad,
  In this dull Devonshire;

Yet justly too I must confess,
  I ne'er invented such
Ennobled numbers for the press,
  Than where I loathed so much.  (*1648*)

No marigolds yet closéd are;
  No shadows great appear;
Nor doth the early shepherd's star
  Shine like a spangle here.

Stay but till my Julia close
  Her life-begetting eye;                    10
And then let the whole world then dispose
  Itself to live or die.  (*1648*)

## To the Water Nymphs
## Drinking at the Fountain

Reach with your whiter hands to me
  Some crystal of the spring;
And I about the cup shall see
  Fresh lilies flourishing.

Or else, sweet nymphs, do you but this—
  To the glass your lips incline;
And I shall see by that one kiss
  The water turned to wine.   (*1648*)

## Corinna's Going A-Maying

Get up, get up for shame! The blooming morn
Upon her wings presents the god unshorn.
See how Aurora[1] throws her fair
Fresh-quilted colours through the air:
  Get up, sweet slug-a-bed, and see
  The dew bespangling herb and tree!
Each flower has wept and bowed toward the east
Above an hour since, yet you not drest;
  Nay! not so much as out of bed?
  When all the birds have matins[2] said          10
  And sung their thankful hymns: 'tis sin,
  Nay, profanation, to keep in,
Whenas a thousand virgins on this day
Spring sooner than the lark, to fetch in May.

Rise and put on your foliage, and be seen
To come forth, like the spring-time, fresh and green,
  And sweet as Flora. Take no care
  For jewels for your gown or hair:
Fear not; the leaves will strew
  Gems in abundance upon you:                      20
Besides, the childhood of the day has kept,
Against you come,[3] some orient[4] pearls unwept.
  Come, and receive them while the light
  Hangs on the dew-locks of the night:
  And Titan[5] on the eastern hill
  Retires himself, or else stands still
Till you come forth! Wash, dress, be brief in praying:
Few beads are best when once we go a-Maying.

Come, my Corinna, come; and coming, mark
How each field turns a street, each street a park,          30
  Made green and trimmed with trees! see how
  Devotion gives each house a bough
  Or branch! each porch, each door, ere this,
  An ark, a tabernacle[6] is,

---

[1] goddess of the dawn      [2] morning prayers
[3] for your coming      [4] bright and lustrous
[5] Helius, the sun-god
[6] In Jewish history, the Ark was an oblong chest

containing the two tablets of stone bearing the
Ten Commandments. The tabernacle was a cur-
tained framework carried through the wilderness
to serve as a place of worship.

Made up of white-thorn neatly interwove,
As if here were those cooler shades of love.
    Can such delights be in the street
    And open fields, and we not see't?
    Come, we'll abroad: and let's obey
    The proclamation made for May.       *40*
And sin no more, as we have done, by staying;
But, my Corinna, come, let's go a-Maying.

There's not a budding boy or girl this day
But is got up and gone to bring in May.
    A deal of youth ere this is come
    Back, and with white-thorn laden home.
    Some have dispatched their cakes and cream,
    Before that we have left to dream:
And some have wept, and wooed, and plighted troth,
And chose their priest, ere we can cast off sloth:     *50*
    Many a green-gown has been given,
    Many a kiss, both odd and even:
    Many a glance too has been sent
    From out the eye, love's firmament:
Many a jest told of the keys betraying
This night, and locks picked: yet we're not a-Maying!

Come, let us go, while we are in our prime,
And take the harmless folly of the time!
    We shall grow old apace, and die
    Before we know our liberty.       *60*
    Our life is short, and our days run
    As fast away as does the sun.
And, as a vapour or a drop of rain,
Once lost, can ne'er be found again,
    So when or you or I are made
    A fable, song, or fleeting shade,
    All love, all liking, all delight
    Lies drowned with us in endless night.
Then, while time serves, and we are but decaying,
Come, my Corinna, come, let's go a-Maying.   (*1648*)     *70*

# To Anthea, Who May Command Him Any Thing

Bid me to live, and I will live
    Thy Protestant to be;
Or bid me love, and I will give
    A loving heart to thee.

A heart as soft, a heart as kind,
    A heart as sound and free,
As in the whole world thou canst find,
    That heart I'll give to thee.

Bid that heart stay, and it will stay,
    To honour thy decree;     *10*
Or bid it languish quite away,
    And 't shall do so for thee.

Bid me to weep, and I will weep
    While I have eyes to see;
And having none, yet I will keep
    A heart to weep for thee.

Bid me despair, and I'll despair,
  Under that cypress tree;
Or bid me die, and I will dare
  E'en death, to die for thee.     *20*

Thou art my life, my love, my heart,
  The very eyes of me;
And hast command of every part,
  To live and die for thee.   *(1648)*

## The Bad Season Makes the Poet Sad

Dull to myself, and almost dead to these
My many fresh and fragrant mistresses,
Lost to all music now, since every thing
Puts on the semblance here of sorrowing.
Sick is the land to the heart, and doth endure
More dangerous faintings by her desperate cure.
But if that golden age would come again,
And Charles[1] here rule, as he before did reign,
If smooth and unperplexed the seasons were,
As when the sweet Maria livéd here,        *10*
I should delight to have my curls half drowned
In Tyrian dews and head with roses crowned,
And once more yet, ere I am laid out dead,
*Knock at the star with my exalted head.*

## To His Lovely Mistresses

One night in the year, my dearest beauties, come
And bring those dew-drink offerings to my tomb.
When thence ye see my reverend ghost to rise,
And there to lick th' effuséd sacrifice,
Though paleness be the livery that I wear,
Look ye not wan, nor colorless for fear.
Trust me, I will not hurt ye; or once shew
The least grim look, or cast a frown on you;
Nor shall the tapers, when I'm there burn blue.
This I may do, perhaps, as I glide by,      *10*
Cast on my girls a glance, and loving eye;
Or fold mine arms and sigh, because I've lost
The world so soon, and in it, you the most.
Than these, no fears more on your fancies fall,
Though then I smile, and speak no words at all.

---

[1] Charles I, whose queen was Henrietta Maria

# HENRY KING / 1592–1669

## The Exequy

Accept, thou shrine of my dead saint,
Instead of dirges, this complaint;
And for sweet flowers to crown thy
    hearse,
Receive a strew of weeping verse
From thy grieved friend, whom thou
    might'st see
Quite melted into tears for thee.

Dear loss! since thy untimely fate
My task hath been to meditate
On thee, on thee; thou art the book,
The library whereon I look,                    10
Though almost blind. For thee, loved
    clay,
I languish out, not live, the day,
Using no other exercise
But what I practice with mine eyes;
By which wet glasses I find out
How lazily time creeps about
To one that mourns: this, only this,
My exercise and business is.
So I compute the weary hours
With sighs dissolvéd into showers.             20

Nor wonder if my time go thus
Backward and most preposterous;
Thou hast benighted me, thy set
This eve of blackness did beget,
Who wast my day, though overcast
Before thou hadst thy noontide passed;
And I remember must in tears,
Thou scarce hadst seen so many years
As day tells hours. By thy clear sun
My love and fortune first did run;            30
But thou wilt never more appear
Folded within my hemisphere,
Since both thy light and motion
Like a fled star is fallen and gone;
And 'twixt me and my soul's dear wish
An earth now interposéd is,
Which such a strange eclipse doth make
As ne'er was read in almanac.

---

1 reduce to dust by heating

I could allow thee for a time
To darken me and my sad clime;                40
Were it a month, a year, or ten,
I would thy exile live till then,
And all that space my mirth adjourn,
So thou wouldst promise to return;
And putting off thy ashy shroud,
At length disperse this sorrow's cloud.

But woe is me! the longest date
Too narrow is to calculate
These empty hopes; never shall I
Be so much blest as to descry                 50
A glimpse of thee, till that day come
Which shall the earth to cinders doom,
And a fierce fever must calcine[1]
The body of this world—like thine,
My little world! That fit of fire
Once off, our bodies shall aspire
To our souls' bliss; then we shall rise
And view ourselves with clearer eyes
In that calm region where no night
Can hide us from each other's sight.          60
Meantime, thou hast her, earth: much
    good
May my harm do thee. Since it stood
With heaven's will I might not call
Her longer mine, I give thee all
My short-lived right and interest
In her whom living I loved best;
With a most free and bounteous grief
I give thee what I could not keep.
Be kind to her, and prithee look
Thou write into thy doomsday book             70
Each parcel of this rarity
Which in thy casket shrined doth lie.
See that thou make thy reckoning straight,
And yield her back again by weight;
For thou must audit on thy trust
Each grain and atom of this dust,
As thou wilt answer Him that lent,
Not gave thee, my dear monument.

So close the ground, and 'bout her shade
Black curtains draw; my bride is laid.        80

Sleep on, my love, in thy cold bed,
Never to be disquieted!
My last good-night! Thou wilt not wake
Till I thy fate shall overtake;
Till age, or grief, or sickness must
Marry my body to that dust
It so much loves; and fill the room
My heart keeps empty in thy tomb.
Stay for me there; I will not fail
To meet thee in that hollow vale.  90
And think not much of my delay;
I am already on the way,
And follow thee with all the speed
Desire can make, or sorrows breed.
Each minute is a short degree,
And every hour a step towards thee.
At night when I betake to rest,
Next morn I rise nearer my west
Of life, almost by eight hours' sail,
Than when sleep breathed his drowsy
 gale.  100

Thus from the sun my bottom[2] steers,
And my day's compass downward bears;
Nor labor I to stem the tide
Through which to thee I swiftly glide.

'Tis true, with shame and grief I yield,
Thou like the van first took'st the field,
And gotten hast the victory
In thus adventuring to die

Before me, whose more years might crave
A just precedence in the grave.  110
But hark! my pulse like a soft drum
Beats my approach, tells thee I come;
And slow howe'er my marches be,
I shall at last sit down by thee.

The thought of this bids me go on,
And wait my dissolution
With hope and comfort. Dear (forgive
The crime), I am content to live
Divided, with but half a heart,
Till we shall meet and never part.  120
         (c. 1624)

## Sic Vita[1]

Like to the falling of a star;
Or as the flights of eagles are;
Or like the fresh Spring's gaudy hue;
Or silver drops of morning dew;
Or like a wind that chafes the flood;
Or bubbles which on water stood;
Even such is man, whose borrowed light
Is straight called in, and paid to night.

 The wind blows out; the bubble dies;
 The Spring entombed in Autumn
  lies;  10
 The dew dries up; the star is shot;
 The flight is past; and man forgot.

# GEORGE HERBERT / 1593–1633

## The Quip

The merry World did on a day
 With his train-bands and mates agree
To meet together, where I lay,
 And all in sport to jeer at me.

First, Beauty crept into a rose,
 Which when I plucked not, "Sir,"
  said she,

"Tell me, I pray, whose hands are
  those?"—
But Thou shalt answer, Lord for me.

Then Money came and chinking still,
 "What tune is this, poor man?" said
  he:  10

---

[2] ship

[1] Such is life.

"I heard in music you had skill."—
  But Thou shalt answer, Lord, for me.

Then came brave Glory puffing by
  In silks that whistled—who but he?
He scarce allowed me half an eye—
  But Thou shalt answer, Lord, for me.

Then came quick Wit and Conversation,
  And he would needs a comfort be,
And, to be short, make an oration—
  But Thou shalt answer, Lord, for
    me.                                           20

Yet when the hour of Thy design
  To answer these fine things shall come,
Speak not at large, say, I am Thine,
  And then they have their answer
    home.   (*1633*)


## The Collar

I struck the board, and cried, No more.
  I will abroad.
What? shall I ever sigh and pine?
My lines and life are free; free as the road,
  Loose as the wind, as large as store.
    Shall I be still in suit?
Have I no harvest but a thorn
  To let me blood, and not restore
What I have lost with cordial fruit?
  Sure there was wine                            10
Before my sighs did dry it: there was corn
  Before my tears did drown it.
Is the year only lost to me?
  Have I no bays to crown it?
No flowers, no garlands gay? all blasted?
  All wasted?
Not so, my heart: but there is fruit,
  And thou hast hands.
Recover all thy sigh-blown age
On double pleasures: leave thy cold
    dispute                                       20
Of what is fit, and not. Forsake thy cage,
  Thy rope of sands,
Which petty thoughts have made, and
    made to thee

Good cable, to enforce and draw,
  And be thy law,
While thou didst wink and wouldst not
    see.
  Away; take heed:
  I will abroad.
Call in thy death's head there: tie up
  thy fears.
  He that forbears                               30
To suit and serve his need,
  Deserves his load.
But as I raved and grew more fierce and
    wild
  At every word,
Methought I heard one calling, *Child.*
  And I replied, *My Lord.*   (*1633*)


## The Pulley

When God at first made man,
Having a glass of blessings standing by,
  Let us (said He) pour on him all we can.
Let the world's riches, which disperséd lie,
  Contract into a span.

  So strength first made a way,
Then beauty flowed, then wisdom,
    honour, pleasure.
  When almost all was out, God made
    a stay,
Perceiving that alone of all His treasure
  Rest in the bottom lay.                        10

  For if I should (said He)
Bestow this jewel also on My creature,
  He would adore My gifts instead of Me,
And rest in Nature, not the God of
    Nature.
  So both should losers be.

  Yet let him keep the rest,
But keep them with repining restlessness.
  Let him be rich and weary, that at least,
If goodness lead him not, yet weariness
  May toss him to My breast.                     20
                                          (*1633*)

## To His Mother

My God, where is that ancient heat towards thee
Wherewith whole shoals of martyrs once did burn,
Besides their other flames? Doth poetry
Wear Venus' livery, only serve her turn?
Why are not sonnets made of thee, and lays
Upon thine altar burnt? Cannot thy love
Heighten a spirit to sound out thy praise
As well as any she? Cannot thy dove
Outstrip their Cupid easily in flight?
Or, since thy ways are deep and still the same,          10
Will not a verse run smooth that bears thy name?
Why doth that fire, which by thy power and might
Each breast does feel, no braver fuel choose
Than that which one day worms may chance refuse?  (*1633*)

## Jordan: I

Who says that fictions only and false hair
Become a verse? Is there in truth no beauty?
Is all good structure in a winding stair?
May no lines pass except they do their duty
Not to a true, but painted chair?

Is it no verse except enchanted groves
And sudden arbors shadow coarse-spun lines?
Must purling streams refresh a lover's loves?
Must all be veiled, while he that reads, divines,
Catching the sense at two removes?                       10

Shepherds are honest people; let them sing.
Riddle who list for me, and pull for prime;
I envy no man's nightingale or spring,
Nor let them punish me with loss of rhyme,
Who plainly say, *My God, my King.*  (*1633*)

## The Windows

Lord, how can man preach thy eternal
  word?
He is a brittle crazy glass,
Yet in thy temple thou dost him afford
  This glorious and transcendent place
  To be a window, through thy grace.

But when thou dost anneal in glass thy
  story,
  Making thy life to shine within

The holy preacher's, then the light and
  glory
  More reverend grows, and doth more
  win;
  Which else shows wat'rish, bleak, and
  thin.                                                   10

Doctrine and life, colors and light in one,
  When they combine and mingle, bring
A strong regard and awe; but speech alone
  Doth vanish like a flaring thing,
  And in the ear, not conscience, ring.
                                           (*1633*)

## Prayer: I

Prayer, the Church's banquet, Angel's age,
  God's breath in man returning to his birth,
  The soul in paraphrase, heart in pilgrimage,
The Christian plummet sounding heaven and earth;

Engine against th' Almighty, sinner's tower,
  Reversèd thunder, Christ-side-piercing spear,
  The six days' world-transposing in an hour,
A kind of tune, which all things hear and fear;

Softness, and peace, and joy, and love, and bliss,
  Exalted Manna, gladness of the best,        *10*
  Heaven in ordinary, men well drest,
The Milky Way, the bird of Paradise,

  Church-bells beyond the stars heard, the soul's blood,
  The land of spices, something understood.  (*1633*)

## Virtue

Sweet day, so cool, so calm, so bright,
The bridal of the earth and sky,
The dew shall weep thy fall to-night;
    For thou must die.

Sweet rose, whose hue angry and brave
Bids the rash gazer wipe his eye,
Thy root is ever in its grave,
    And thou must die.

Sweet spring, full of sweet days and roses,
A box where sweets compacted lie,    *10*
My music shows ye have your closes,[1]
    And all must die.

Only a sweet and virtuous soul,
Like seasoned timber, never gives;
But though the whole world turn to coal,
    Then chiefly lives.  (*1633*)

## The Altar

A broken ALTAR, Lord, thy servant rears,
Made of a heart, and cemented with tears:
  Whose parts are as thy hand did frame;
  No workman's tool hath touched the same.
      A HEART alone
      Is such a stone,
      As nothing but
      Thy power doth cut.
      Wherefore each part
      Of my hard heart    *10*
      Meets in this frame,
      To praise thy Name:
  That, if I chance to hold my peace,
  These stones to praise thee may not cease.
O let thy blessed SACRIFICE be mine,
And sanctify this ALTAR to be thine.

---

[1] My score shows that your musical phrase comes to an end.

## Church-Monuments

While that my soul repairs to her devotion,
Here I intomb my flesh, that it betimes
May take acquaintance of this heap of dust;
To which the blast of death's incessant motion,
Fed with the exhalation of our crimes,
Drives all at last. Therefore, I gladly trust

My body to this school, that it may learn
To spell his elements, and find his birth
Written in dusty heraldry and lines;
Which dissolution sure doth best discern,                          *10*
Comparing dust with dust, and earth with earth.
These laugh at jet and marble put for signs.

To sever the good fellowship of dust,
And spoil the meeting. What shall point out them,
When they shall bow, and kneel, and fall down flat
To kiss those heaps, which now they have in trust?
Dear flesh, while I do pray, learn here thy stem
And true descent; that when thou shalt grow fat,

And wanton in thy cravings, thou mayst know,
That flesh is but the glass, which holds the dust             *20*
That measures all our time; which also shall
Be crumbled into dust. Mark here below
How tame these ashes are, how free from lust,
That thou mayst fit thy self against thy fall.    (*1633*)

## Ungratefulness

Lord, with what bounty and rare clemency
        Hast thou redeemed us from the grave!
                If thou had'st let us run,
                Gladly had man adored the sun,
                        And thought his god most brave;
Where now we shall be better gods than he.

Thou hast but two rare cabinets full of treasure,
                The *Trinity,* and *Incarnation:*
                Thou hast unlocked them both,
                And made them jewels to betroth               *10*
                        The work of thy creation
Unto thyself in everlasting pleasure.

The statelier cabinet is the *Trinity,*
                Whose sparkling light access denies;
                Therefore, thou dost not show
                This fully to us, till death blow
                        The dust into our eyes:
For by that powder thou wilt make us see.

But all thy sweets are packed up in the other;
  Thy mercies thither flock and flow:     *20*
   That as the first affrights,
  This may allure us with delights;
   Because this box we know:
For we have all of us just such another.

But man is close, reserved, and dark to thee:
  When thou demandest but a heart,
   He cavils instantly.
  In his poor cabinet of bone
   Sins have their box apart,
Defrauding thee, who gavest two for one. (*1633*)  *30*


## Confession

  O what a cunning guest
Is this same grief! within my heart I made
  Closets; and in them many a chest;
  And, like a master in my trade,
In those chests, boxes; in each box, a till:
Yet grief knows all, and enters when he will.

  No screw, no piercer can
Into a piece of timber work and wind,
  As God's afflictions into man,
  When he a torture hath designed    *10*
They are too subtle for the subtlest hearts;
And fall, like rheums, upon the tend'rest parts.

  We are the earth; and they,
Like moles within us, heave, and cast about:
  And till they foot and clutch their prey,
  They never cool, much less give out.
No smith can make such locks but they have keys:
Closets are halls to them; and hearts, high-ways.

  Only an open breast
Doth shut them out, so that they cannot enter;  *20*
  Or, if they enter, cannot rest,
  But quickly seek some new adventure.
Smooth open hearts no fastening have; but fiction
Doth give a hold and handle to affliction.

  Wherefore my faults and sins,
Lord, I acknowledge; take thy plagues away:
  For since confession pardon wins,
  I challenge here the brightest day,
The clearest diamond: let them do their best,
They shall be thick and cloudy to my breast. (*1633*)  *30*

## Death

Death, thou wast once an uncouth hideous thing,
>      Nothing but bones,
>    The sad effect of sadder groans;
Thy mouth was open, but thou couldst not sing.

For we considered thee as at some six
>      Or ten years hence,
>    After the loss of life and sense,
Flesh being turned to dust, and bones to sticks.

We lookt on this side of thee, shooting short;
>      Where we did find                                    10
>    The shells of fledge souls left behind,
Dry dust, which sheds no tears, but may extort.

But since our Saviour's death did put some blood
>      Into thy face,
>    Thou art grown fair and full of grace,
Much in request, much sought for as a good.

For we do now behold thee gay and glad,
>      As at doomsday;
>    When souls shall wear their new array,
And all thy bones with beauty shall be clad.          20

Therefore we can go die as sleep, and trust
>      Half that we have
>    Unto an honest faithful grave,
Making our pillows either down or dust.   (*1633*)

## Denial

When my devotions could not pierce
>      Thy silent ears;
>    Then was my heart broken, as was my verse:
>      My breast was full of fears
>        And disorder:

My bent thoughts, like a brittle bow,
>      Did fly asunder:
>    Each took his way; some would to pleasure go,
>      Some to the wars and thunder
>        Of alarms.                                         10

As good go anywhere, they say,
>      As to benumb
>    Both knees and heart in crying night and day,
>      *Come, come, my God, O come!*
>        But no hearing.

O that thou shouldst give dust a tongue
    To cry to thee,
And then not hear it crying! All day long
    My heart was in my knee,
      But no hearing.         *20*

Therefore my soul lay out of sight,
    Untuned, unstrung:
My feeble spirit, unable to look right,
    Like a nipped blossom, hung
      Discontented.

O cheer and tune my heartless breast;
    Defer no time,
That so thy favors granting my request,
    They and my mind may chime,
      And mend my rhyme.   *(1633)*     *30*

# THOMAS CAREW / 1594?–1639?

## A Song

Ask me no more where Jove bestows,
When June is past, the fading rose:
For in your beauty's orient deep,
These flowers as in their causes sleep.

Ask me no more whither do stray
The golden atoms of the day:
For in pure love heaven did prepare
Those powders to enrich your hair.

Ask me no more whither doth haste
The nightingale, when May is past:     *10*

For in your sweet dividing throat
She winters, and keeps warm her note.

Ask me no more where those stars light,
That downwards fall in dead of night:
For in your eyes they sit, and there,
Fixed, become as in their sphere.

Ask me no more if east or west,
The phoenix builds her spicy nest:
For unto you at last she flies,
And in your fragrant bosom dies.     *20*
                *(1640)*

## The Spring

Now that the winter's gone, the earth hath lost
Her snow-white robes; and now no more the frost
Candies the grass, or casts an icy cream
Upon the silver lake or crystal stream:
But the warm sun thaws the benumbéd earth,
And makes it tender; gives a second birth
To the dead swallow; wakes in hollow tree
The drowsy cuckoo and the humble-bee.
Now do a choir of chirping minstrels sing,
In triumph to the world, the youthful spring:     *10*

The valleys, hills, and woods in rich array
Welcome the coming of the longed-for May.
Now all things smile; only my love doth lower;
Nor hath the scalding noonday sun the power
To melt that marble ice, which still doth hold
Her heart congealed, and makes her pity cold.
The ox, which lately did for shelter fly
Into the stall, doth now securely lie
In open field; and love no more is made
By the fireside, but in the cooler shade.                    20
Amyntas now doth by his Cloris sleep
Under a sycamore, and all things keep
Time with the season: only she doth carry
June in her eyes, in her heart January.   (1640)

## Celia Singing

Hark, how my Celia, with the choice
Music of her hand and voice
Stills the loud wind; and makes the wild
Incensèd boar and panther mild;
Mark how these statues like men move,
Whilst men with wonder, statues prove!
This stiff rock bends to worship her,
That idol turns idolator.

Now see how all the new inspired
Images with love are fired;               10
Hark how the tender marble groans,
And all the late transfor*mèd stones
Court the fair nymph with many a tear,
Which she, more stony than they were,
Beholds with unrelenting mind;
Whilst they, amazed to see combined
Such matchless beauty with disdain,
Are all turned into stones again.   (1640)

## Disdain Returned

He that loves a rosy cheek,
    Or a coral lip admires,
Or from starlike eyes doth seek
    Fuel to maintain his fires;
As old Time makes these decay,
So his flames must waste away.
But a smooth and steadfast mind,
    Gentle thoughts and calm desires,
Hearts with equal love combined,
Kindle never-dying fires.               10
Where these are not, I despise
Lovely cheeks, or lips, or eyes.

No tears, Celia, now shall win
    My resolved heart to return;
I have searched thy soul within,
    And find naught but pride and scorn;
I have learned thy arts, and now
    Can disdain as much as thou.
Some power, in my revenge convey
That love to her I cast away.   (1640)   20

## JAMES SHIRLEY / 1596–1666

### from Contention of Ajax and Ulysses

The glories of our blood and state
  Are shadows, not substantial things;
There is no armour against fate;
  Death lays his icy hand on kings:
    Sceptre and crown
    Must tumble down,
And in the dust be equal made
With the poor crookéd scythe and spade.

Some men with swords may reap the field,
  And plant fresh laurels where they
    kill:          *10*

But their strong nerves at last must yield;
  They tame but one another still:
    Early or late
    They stoop to fate,
And must give up their murmuring breath
When they, pale captives, creep to death.

The garlands wither on your brow;
  Then boast no more your mighty deeds;
Upon Death's purple altar now
  See, where the victor-victim bleeds.   *20*
    Your heads must come
    To the cold tomb:
Only the actions of the just
Smell sweet, and blossom in their dust.
                  *(1659)*

## WILLIAM STRODE / 1602–1645

### In Commendation of Music

When whispering strains do softly steal
With creeping passion through the heart,
And when at every touch we feel
Our pulses beat and bear a part;
    When threads can make
    A heartstring shake,
    Philosophy
    Can scarce deny
The soul consists of harmony.

When unto heavenly joy we feign    *10*
Whate'er the soul affecteth most,
Which only thus we can explain
By music of the wingéd host,
    Whose lays we think
    Make stars to wink,
    Philosophy
    Can scarce deny
Our souls consist of harmony.

O lull me, lull me, charming air,
My senses rock with wonder sweet;   *20*

Like snow on wool thy fallings are,
Soft, like a spirit's, are thy feet:
    Grief who need fear
    That hath an ear?
    Down let him lie
    And slumbering die,
And change his soul for harmony.
                  *(1640)*

### On Chloris Walking in the Snow

I saw fair Chloris walk alone,
Whilst feathered rain came softly down,
And Jove descended from his tower
To court her in a silver shower.
The wanton snow flew on her breast
Like little birds unto their nest;
But overcome with whiteness there,
For grief it thawed into a tear;
Thence falling on her garment's hem,
To deck her, froze into a gem.   *(1640)* *10*

# THOMAS RANDOLPH / 1605–1635

## On the Death of a Nightingale

Go, solitary wood, and henceforth be
Acquainted with no other harmony
Than the pies' chattering, or the shrieking note
Of boding owls, and fatal raven's throat.
Thy sweetest chanter's dead, that warbled forth
Lays that might tempests calm, and still the north
And call down angels from their glorious sphere
To hear her songs, and learn new anthems there.
That soul is fled and to Elysium gone;
Thou a poor desert left; go then and run,         *10*
Beg there to stand a grove, and if she please
To sing again beneath thy shadowy trees,
The souls of happy lovers crowned with blisses
Shall flock about thee, and keep time with kisses.   (*1638*)

# WILLIAM DAVENANT / 1606–1668

## Under the Willow Shades

Under the willow shades they were
   Free from the eye-sight of the sun,
For no intruding beam could there
   Peep through to spy what things were done:
     Thus sheltered, they unseen did lie,
     Surfeiting on each other's eye;
Defended by the willow shades alone,
The sun's heat they defied, and cooled their own.

Whilst they did embrace unspied,
   The conscious willows seemed to smile,        *10*
That they with privacy supplied,
   Holding the door, as 'twere, the while,
     And, when their dalliances were o'er,
     The willows, to oblige 'em more,
Bowing, did seem to say, as they withdrew,
We can supply you with a cradle, too.

## Wake All the Dead!

Wake all the dead! what ho! what ho!
How soundly they sleep whose pillows lie low!
They mind not poor lovers who walk above
On the decks of the world in storms of love.
   No whisper now nor glance can pass
   Through wickets or through panes of glass;
For our windows and doors are shut and barred.
Lie close in the church, and in the churchyard;
   In every grave make room, make room!
   The world's at an end, and we come, we come.    *10*

The state is now Love's foe, Love's foe;
Has seized on his arms, his quiver and bow;
Has pinioned his wings, and fettered his feet,
Because he made way for lovers to meet.
   But, O sad chance, his judge was old;
   Hearts cruel grow when blood grows cold.
No man being young his process would draw.
O heavens, that love should be subject to law!
   Lovers go woo the dead, the dead!
   Lie two in a grave, and to bed, to bed!    *20*

# EDMUND WALLER / 1606–1687

## Song

Stay, Phoebus, stay!
The world to which you fly so fast,
Conveying day
From us to them, can pay your haste
With no such object, nor salute your rise
With no such wonder, as De Mornay's
   eyes.

Well does this prove
The error of those antique books,
Which made you move
About the world; her charming looks  *10*
Would fix your beams, and make it ever
   day,
Did not the rolling earth snatch her
   away.   (*1645*)

## Go, Lovely Rose

   Go lovely Rose,
Tell her that wastes her time and me,
   That now she knows,
When I resemble her to thee,
   How sweet and fair she seems to be.

   Tell her that's young,
And shuns to have her graces spied,
   That hadst thou sprung
In deserts, where no men abide,
   Thou must have uncommended died.  *10*

   Small is the worth
Of beauty from the light retired;
   Bid her come forth,
Suffer herself to be desired,
   And not blush so to be admired.

Then die, that she
The common fate of all things rare
  May read in thee;
How small a part of time they share,
  That are so wondrous sweet and fair. 20
                                    (1645)


## To My Young Lady Lucy Sidney

Why came I so untimely forth
Into a world which, wanting thee,
Could entertain us with no worth
Or shadow of felicity,
    That time should me so far remove
    From that which I was born to love?

Yet, fairest blossom, do not slight
That age which you may know so soon;
The rosy morn resigns her light,
And milder glory to the noon;            10
    And then what wonders shall you do,
    Whose dawning beauty warms us so?

Hope waits upon the flowery prime,
And summer, though it be less gay,
Yet is not looked on as a time
Of declination or decay,

For with a full hand that does bring
All that was promised by the spring.
                                    (1645)


## To Phyllis

Phyllis, why should we delay
Pleasures shorter than the day?
Could we (which we never can)
Stretch our lives beyond their span;
Beauty like a shadow flies,
And our youth before us dies;
Or would youth and beauty stay,
Love hath wings, and will away.
Love hath swifter wings than time;
Change in love to heaven does climb.    10
Gods that never change their state,
Vary oft their love and hate.
Phyllis, to this truth we owe,
All the love betwixt us two:
Let not you and I require,
What has been our past desire;
On what shepherds you have smiled,
Or what nymphs I have beguiled;
Leave it to the planets too,
What we shall hereafter do;              20
For the joys we now may prove,[1]
Take advice of present love.   (1645)

---

## JOHN MILTON / 1608-1674


## O Nightingale, That on Yon Bloomy Spray

O Nightingale, that on yon bloomy spray
Warbl'st at eve, when all the woods are still,
Thou with fresh hope the lover's heart dost fill,
While the jolly hours lead on propitious May.
Thy liquid notes that close the eye of day,
First heard before the shallow cuckoo's bill,
Portend success in love; O if Jove's will
Have linked that amorous power to thy soft lay,

---

[1] test by experience

Now timely sing, ere the rude bird of hate
Foretell my hopeless doom in some grove nigh:        10
As thou from year to year hast sung too late
For my relief, yet hadst no reason why,
Whether the Muse or Love call thee his mate,
Both them I serve and of their train am I.

# On the Morning of Christ's Nativity

### I

This is the month, and this the happy morn,
Wherein the Son of Heaven's eternal King,
Of wedded Maid and Virgin Mother born,
Our great redemption from above did bring;
For so the holy sages once did sing,
    That he our deadly forfeit should release,
And with his Father work us a perpetual peace.

### II

That glorious form, the light unsufferable,
And that far-beaming blaze of majesty,
Wherewith he wont at Heaven's high council-table        10
To sit the midst of Trinal Unity,
He laid aside; and here with us to be,
    Forsook the courts of everlasting day,
And chose with us a darksome house of mortal clay.

### III

Say, Heavenly Muse, shall not thy sacred vein
Afford a present to the infant God?
Hast thou no verse, no hymn, or solemn strain,
To welcome him to this his new abode,
Now while the Heaven, by the sun's team untrod,
    Hath took no print of the approaching light,        20
And all the spangled host keep watch in squadrons bright?

### IV

See how from far upon the eastern road
The star-led wizards haste with odors sweet!
O run, prevent[1] them with thy humble ode,
And lay it lowly at his blessèd feet;
Have thou the honor first thy Lord to greet,
    And join thy voice unto the angel choir,
From out his secret altar touched with hallowed fire.

---

[1] anticipate

*The Hymn*

### I

It was the winter wild
While the Heaven-born child        *30*
   All meanly wrapped in the rude manger lies;
Nature in awe to him
Had doffed her gaudy trim,
   With her great Master so to sympathize;
It was no season then for her
To wanton with the sun, her lusty paramour.

### II

Only with speeches fair
She woos the gentle air
   To hide her guilty front with innocent snow,
And on her naked shame,        *40*
Pollute with sinful blame,
   The saintly veil of maiden white to throw,
Confounded, that her Maker's eyes
Should look so near upon her foul deformities.

### III

But he her fears to cease,
Sent down the meek-eyed Peace;
   She, crowned with olive green, came softly sliding
Down through the turning sphere,
His ready harbinger,
   With turtle wing the amorous clouds dividing,        *50*
And waving wide her myrtle wand,
She strikes a universal peace through sea and land.

### IV

No war or battle's sound
Was heard the world around:
   The idle spear and shield were high uphung;
The hookéd chariot stood
Unstained with hostile blood;
   The trumpet spake not to the arméd throng;
And kings sat still with awful eye,
As if they surely knew their sovran Lord was by.        *60*

### V

But peaceful was the night
Wherein the Prince of Light
   His reign of peace upon the earth began:
The winds with wonder whist,
Smoothly the waters kissed,
   Whispering new joys to the mild ocëan,
Who now hath quite forgot to rave,
While birds of calm sit brooding on the charméd wave.

### VI

The stars with deep amaze
Stand fixed in steadfast gaze, 70
   Bending one way their precious influence,
And will not take their flight
For all the morning light,
   Or Lucifer[2] that often warned them thence;
But in their glimmering orbs did glow,
Until their Lord himself bespake, and bid them go.

### VII

And though the shady gloom
Had given day her room,
   The sun himself withheld his wonted speed,
And hid his head for shame, 80
As his inferior flame
   The new-enlightened world no more should need;
He saw a greater sun appear
Than his bright throne or burning axletree could bear.

### VIII

The shepherds on the lawn,
Or ere the point of dawn,
   Sat simply chatting in a rustic row;
Full little thought they than
That the mighty Pan[3]
   Was kindly come to live with them below; 90
Perhaps their loves, or else their sheep,
Was all that did their silly[4] thoughts so busy keep.

### IX

When such music sweet
Their hearts and ears did greet,
   As never was by mortal finger strook,
Divinely warbled voice
Answering the stringéd noise,
   As all their souls in blissful rapture took;
The air, such pleasure loth to lose,
With thousand echoes still prolongs each heavenly close. 100

### X

Nature that heard such sound
Beneath the hollow round
   Of Cynthia's seat,[5] the airy region thrilling,
Now was almost won

---

[2] the planet Venus, as the morning star            pastures, and flocks     [4] innocent    [5] the moon
[3] the universal pagan god; the god of forests,

To think her part was done,
    And that her reign had here its last fulfilling;
She knew such harmony alone
Could hold all Heaven and Earth in happier union.

### XI

At last surrounds their sight
A glove of circular light,                                    *110*
    That with long beams the shame-faced Night arrayed;
The helméd Cherubim
And swordéd Seraphim[6]
    Are seen in glittering ranks with wings displayed,
Harping in loud and solemn choir,
With unexpressive notes to Heaven's new-born Heir.

### XII

Such music (as 'tis said)
Before was never made,
    But when of old the sons of morning sung,           *120*
While the Creator great
His constellations set,
    And the well-balanced world on hinges hung,
And cast the dark foundations deep,
And bid the weltering waves their oozy channel keep.

### XIII

Ring out, ye crystal spheres,[7]
Once bless our human ears
    (If ye have power to touch our senses so),
And let your silver chime
Move in melodious time,
    And let the bass of Heaven's deep organ blow;        *130*
And with your ninefold harmony
Make up full consort to the angelic symphony.

### XIV

For if such holy song
Enwrap our fancy long,
    Time will run back and fetch the age of gold,
And speckled Vanity
Will sicken soon and die,
    And leprous Sin will melt from earthly mold,
And Hell itself will pass away,
And leave her dolorous mansions to the peering day.      *140*

### XV

Yea, Truth and Justice then
Will down return to men,

---

[6] the highest order of angels, ranked just above the Cherubim
[7] Milton adopts the Ptolemaic conception of the universe as composed of nine concentric crystalline spheres which, in rotating, produce a celestial music.

Orbed in a rainbow; and, like glories wearing,
Mercy will sit between,
Throned in celestial sheen,
   With radiant feet the tissued clouds down steering;
And Heaven, as at some festival,
Will open wide the gates of her high palace hall.

XVI

But wisest Fate says no,
This must not yet be so;                         *150*
   The Babe lies yet in smiling infancy,
That on the bitter cross
Must redeem our loss,
   So both himself and us to glorify;
Yet first to those ychained in sleep,
The wakeful trump of doom must thunder through the deep,

XVII

With such a horrid clang
As on Mount Sinai rang
   While the red fire and smoldering clouds outbrake:[8]
The agéd Earth aghast                        *160*
With terror of that blast,
   Shall from the surface to the center shake,
When at the world's last session
The dreadful Judge in middle air shall spread his throne.

XVIII

And then at last our bliss
Full and perfect is,
   But now begins; for from this happy day
The old Dragon under ground,
In straiter limits bound,
   Not half so far casts his unsurpéd sway,        *170*
And, wroth to see his kingdom fail,
Swinges[9] the scaly horror of his folded tail.

XIX

The oracles are dumb,
No voice or hideous hum
   Runs through the archéd roof in words deceiving.
Apollo from his shrine
Can no more divine,
   With hollow shriek the steep of Delphos[10] leaving.
No nightly trance or breathéd spell
Inspires the pale-eyed priest from the prophetic cell.   *180*

---

[8] "There were thunders and lightnings" on Mt. Sinai when the Lord descended to give the Ten Commandments to Moses. Exodus 19:16–18

[9] lashes

[10] site of a famous oracle in ancient Greece

### XX

The lonely mountains o'er,
And the resounding shore,
   A voice of weeping heard, and loud lament;
From haunted spring and dale,
Edged with poplar pale,
   The parting Genius is with sighing sent;
With flower-inwoven tresses torn
The nymphs in twilight shade of tangled thickets mourn.

### XXI

In consecrated earth,
   And on the holy hearth,                                   *190*
   The Lars and Lemures[11] moan with midnight plaint;
In urns and altars round,
A drear and dying sound
   Affrights the flamens at their service quaint;
And the chill marble seems to sweat,
While each peculiar power forgoes his wonted seat.

### XXII

Peor and Baalim[12]
Forsake their temples dim,
   With that twice-battered god of Palestine;
And moonéd Ashtaroth,                                              *200*
Heaven's queen and mother both,
   Now sits not girt with tapers' holy shine;
The Libyc Hammon shrinks his horn,
In vain the Tyrian maids their wounded Thammuz mourn

### XXIII

And sullen Moloch, fled,
Hath left in shadows dread
   His burning idol all of blackest hue;
In vain with cymbal's ring
They call the grisly king,
   In dismal dance about the furnace blue;                     *210*
The brutish gods of Nile as fast,
Isis and Orus, and the dog Anubis, haste.

### XXIV

Nor is Osiris seen
In Memphian grove or green,
   Trampling the unshowered grass with lowings loud;
Nor can he be at rest
Within his sacred chest,
   Nought but profoundest Hell can be his shroud;
In vain with timbreled anthems dark
The sable-stoléd sorcerers bear his worshiped ark.               *220*

---

11 In Roman myth Lars were minor spirits of certain places; the Lemures were the spirits of the dead.

12 In this and the next two stanzas Milton depicts the abdication of various pagan deities of ancient lands.

### XXV

He feels from Juda's land
The dreaded Infant's hand,
  The rays of Bethlehem blind his dusky eyn;
Nor all the gods beside
Longer dare abide,
  Not Typhon huge ending in snaky twine:
Our Babe, to show his Godhead true,
Can in his swaddling bands control the damnéd crew.

### XXVI

So when the sun in bed,
Curtained with cloudy red,                                                            230
  Pillows his chin upon an orient wave,
The flocking shadows pale
Troop to the infernal jail;
  Each fettered ghost slips to his several grave,
And the yellow-skirted fays
Fly after the night-steeds, leaving their moon-loved maze.

### XXVII

But see, the Virgin blest
Hath laid her Babe to rest.
  Time is our tedious song should here have ending;
Heaven's youngest-teeméd star                                                         240
Hath fixed her polished car,
  Her sleeping Lord with handmaid lamp attending;
And all about the courtly stable
Bright-harnessed angels sit in order serviceable.      (*1629*)

## L'Allegro

Hence, loathéd Melancholy
  Of Cerberus[1] and blackest Midnight
    born,
In Stygian[2] cave forlorn
  'Mongst horrid shapes, and shrieks,
    and sights unholy!
Find out some uncouth cell,
  Where brooding Darkness spreads his
    jealous wings,
And the night-raven sings;
  There under ebon shades, and low-
    browed rocks

As ragged as thy locks,
  In dark Cimmerian[3] desert ever
    dwell.                                                                             10
  But come, thou Goddess fair and
    free,
In heaven yclept[4] Euphrosyne,
And by men, heart-easing Mirth,
Whom lovely Venus at a birth
With two sister Graces[5] more
To ivy-crownéd Bacchus[6] bore;
Or whether (as some sager sing)
The frolic wind that breathes the
    spring
Zephyr,[7] with Aurora[8] playing,

---

[1] the three-headed dog that guarded the gate of hell
[2] of the river Styx in Hades, over which Charon ferried dead souls
[3] The Cimmerians lived in eternal darkness at the outer edge of the world.      [4] called
[5] The Graces, Euphrosyne, Aglaia, and Thalia, were personifications of grace and beauty.
[6] god of wine      [7] god of the west wind
[8] the dawn

As he met her once a-Maying,    20
There on beds of violets blue
And fresh-blown roses washed in
    dew
Filled her with thee, a daughter
    fair,
So buxom, blithe, and debonair.
  Haste thee, Nymph, and bring
    with thee
Jest, and youthful jollity,
Quips, and cranks, and wanton
    wiles,
Nods, and becks, and wreathéd
    smiles,
Such as hang on Hebe's [9] cheek,
And love to live in dimple sleek;    30
Sport that wrinkled Care derides,
And Laughter holding both his sides.
Come, and trip it as you go
On the light fantastic toe;
And in thy right hand lead with thee,
The mountain-nymph, sweet
    Liberty;
And if I give thee honour due,
Mirth, admit me of thy crew,
To live with her, and live with thee,
In unreprovéd pleasures free;
To hear the lark begin his flight,
And singing startle the dull night
From his watch-tower in the skies,
Till the dappled dawn doth rise;
Then to come, in spite of sorrow,
And at my window bid good-morrow
Through the sweetbriar, or the vine,
Or the twisted eglantine:
While the cock with lively din,
Scatters the rear of darkness
    thin,    50
And to the stack, or the barn-door,
Stoutly struts his dames before;
Oft listening how the hounds and
    horn
Cheerly rouse the slumbering morn,
From the side of some hoar hill,
Through the high wood echoing
    shrill.
Sometime walking not unseen,

By hedge-row elms, on hillocks
    green,
Right against the eastern gate,
Where the great Sun begins his
    state    60
Robed in flames and amber light,
The clouds in thousand liveries
    dight;
While the ploughman, near at hand,
Whistles o'er the furrowed land,
And the milkmaid singeth blithe,
And the mower whets his scythe,
And every shepherd tells his tale
Under the hawthorn in the dale.
  Straight mine eye hath caught
    new pleasures
Whilst the landscape round it
    measures;    70
Russet lawns, and fallows gray,
Where the nibbling flocks do stray;
Mountains, on whose barren breast
The labouring clouds do often rest;
Meadows trim with daisies pied,
Shallow brooks, and rivers wide;
Towers and battlements it sees
Bosomed high in tufted trees,
Where perhaps some beauty lies,
The cynosure of neighbouring
    eyes.    80
  Hard by, a cottage chimney
    smokes,
From betwixt two agéd oaks,
Where Corydon and Thyris, met,
Are at their savoury dinner set
Of herbs and other country messes,
Which the neat-handed Phillis
    dresses;
And then in haste her bower she
    leaves,
With Thestylis [10] to bind the sheaves;
Or, if the earlier season lead
To the tanned haycock in the
    mead.    90
  Sometimes with secure delight
The upland hamlets will invite,
When the merry bells ring round,
And the jocund rebecks [11] sound

---

[9] cupbearer to the gods
[10] conventional pastoral names
[11] a small viol

To many a youth and many a maid,
Dancing in the chequered shade;
And young and old come forth to
    play
On a sun-shine holyday,
Till the live-long day-light fail:
Then to the spicy nut-brown ale,   *100*
With stories told of many a feat,
How Faery Mab[12] the junkets eat,
She was pinched, and pulled, she
    said,
And he, by friar's lantern[13] led;
Tells how the drudging goblin sweat
To earn his cream-bowl duly set,
When in one night, ere glimpse of
    morn,
His shadowy flail hath threshed the
    corn
That ten day-labourers could not
    end;
Then lies him down the lubber
    fiend,   *110*
And, stretched out all the chimney's
    length,
Basks at the fire his hairy strength;
And crop-full out of doors he flings,
Ere the first cock his matin rings.
    Thus done the tales, to bed they
        creep,
By whispering winds soon lulled
    asleep.
    Towered cities please us then,
And the busy hum of men,
Where throngs of knights and
    barons bold,
In weeds of peace, high triumphs
    hold,   *120*
With store of ladies, whose bright
    eyes
Rain influence, and judge the prize
Of wit or arms, while both contend
To win her grace, whom all
    commend.

There let Hymen[14] oft appear
In saffron robe, with taper clear,
And pomp, and feast, and revelry,
With mask, and antique pageantry;
Such sighs as youthful poets dream
On summer eves by haunted
    stream.   *130*
Then to the well-trod stage anon,
If Jonson's learned sock be on,
Or sweetest Shakespeare, Fancy's
    child,
Warble his native wood-notes wild.
    And ever against eating cares,
Lap me in soft Lydian[15] airs,
Married to immortal verse
Such as the meeting soul may pierce
In notes with many a winding bout
Of linkéd sweetness long drawn
    out,   *140*
With wanton heed and giddy
    cunning,
The melting voice through mazes
    running,
Untwisting all the chains that
    tie
The hidden soul of harmony;
That Orpheus' self may heave his
    head
From golden slumber, on a bed
Of heaped Elysian flowers and hear
Such strains as would have won the
    ear
Of Pluto, to have quite set free
His half-regained Eurydice.[16]   *150*
These delights, if thou canst give,
Mirth, with thee I mean to
    live.   (*1631?*)

---

12 queen of the fairies
13 will o' the wisp     14 god of marriage
15 an effeminate or voluptuous mode in music
16 Orpheus followed his wife, Eurydice, into
Hades when she died. His music so moved Pluto,
the god of the underworld, that he agreed to
release Eurydice from death if Orpheus would
precede her out of Hades and not look back to see
if she was following. Orpheus complied until the
last moment, but then looked back, only to see
Eurydice snatched back into Hades.

## Il Penseroso

Hence, vain deluding Joys,
   The brood of Folly without father
      bred!
How little you bestead
   Or fill the fixéd mind with all your toys!
Dwell in some idle brain,
   And fancies fond with gaudy shapes
      possess
As thick and numberless
   As the gay motes that people the
      sunbeams,
Or likest hovering dreams,
   The fickle pensioners of Morpheus'
      train.                                    10
    But hail, thou goddess sage and holy,
Hail, divinest Melancholy!
Whose saintly visage is too bright
To hit the sense of human sight;
And therefore to our weaker view,
O'erlaid with black, staid Wisdom's
      hue;
Black, but such as in esteem
Prince Memnon's sister[1] might
      beseem,
Or that starred Ethiop queen[2] that
      strove
To set her beauty's praise above        20
The sea-nymphs, and their powers
      offended.
Yet thou art higher far descended:
Thee bright-haired Vesta,[3] long of yore,
To solitary Saturn[4] bore;
His daughter she (in Saturn's reign
Such mixture was not held a stain).
Oft in glimmering bowers and glades
He met her, and in secret shades
Of woody Ida's[5] inmost grove,
While yet there was no fear of Jove.    30
   Come, pensive Nun, devout and
      pure
Sober, steadfast, and demure,
All in a robe of darkest grain,[6]

Flowing with majestic train,
And sable stole of cypress lawn,[7]
Over thy decent shoulders drawn.
Come, but keep thy wonted state,
With even step, and musing gait,
And looks commercing with the skies,
Thy rapt soul sitting in thine eyes:    40
There, held in holy passion still,
Forget thyself to marble, till
With a sad leaden downward cast,
Thou fix them on the earth as fast.
And join with thee calm Peace, and
      Quiet,
Spare Fast, that oft with gods doth
      diet,
And hears the Muses in a ring
Aye round about Jove's altar sing.
And add to these retired Leisure
That in trim gardens takes his
      pleasure;                                50
But first and chiefest, with thee bring,
Him that yon soars on golden wing
Guiding the fiery-wheeléd throne,
The cherub Contemplation;
And the mute Silence hist along,
'Less Philomel[8] will deign a song
In her sweetest saddest plight,
Smoothing the rugged brow of Night,
While Cynthia[9] checks her dragon
      yoke,
Gently o'er the accustomed oak.         60
—Sweet bird, that shunn'st the noise
      of folly,
Most musical, most melancholy!
Thee, chauntress, oft, the woods
      among,
I woo, to hear thy even-song;
And missing thee, I walk unseen
On the dry smooth-shaven green,
To behold the wandering Moon,
Riding near her highest noon,
Like one that had been led astray
Through the heaven's wide pathless
      way;                                     70

---

[1] Hemera. Prince Memnon, an Ethiopian, fought in the Trojan War.
[2] Cassiopeia, proud of her beauty, was placed among the stars after her death.
[3] goddess of the hearth

[4] mythical king of Italy's golden age
[5] sacred mountain in Crete    [6] dye
[7] a filmy black cloth    [8] the nightingale
[9] goddess of the moon, who drove a team of dragons

And oft, as if her head she bowed,
Stooping through a fleecy cloud.
   Oft, on a plat of rising ground,
I hear the far-off curfew sound,
Over some wide-watered shore,
Swinging slow with sullen roar;
Or, if the air will not permit,
Some still removéd place will fit,
Where glowing embers through the
   room
Teach light to counterfeit a gloom,   *80*
Far from all resort of mirth,
Save the cricket on the hearth,
Or the bellman's drowsy charm
To bless the doors from nightly harm:
   Or let my lamp at midnight hour,
Be seen in some high lonely tower,
Where I may oft out-watch the Bear,[10]
With thrice-great Hermes,[11] or
   unsphere[12]
The spirit of Plato, to unfold
What worlds or what vast regions
   hold   *90*
The immortal mind, that hath forsook
Her mansion in this fleshly nook:
And of those demons that are found
In fire, air, flood, or under ground,
Whose power hath a true consent
With planet, or with element.
Sometime let gorgeous Tragedy
In sceptered pall come sweeping by,
Presenting Thebes,[13] or Pelop's line,
Or the tale of Troy divine;   *100*
Or what (though rare) of later age
Ennobled hath the buskined stage.
   But, O sad Virgin, that thy power
Might raise Musaeus[14] from his
   bower,
Or bid the soul of Orpheus sing
Such notes as, warbled to the string,
Drew iron tears down Pluto's cheek
And made Hell grant what Love did
   seek.
   Or call up him that left half-told

The story of Cambuscan bold,   *110*
Of Camball, and of Algarsife,
And who had Canacé to wife
That owned the virtuous ring and glass;
And of the wondrous horse of brass,
On which the Tartar kind did ride;[15]
And if aught else great bards beside,
In sage and solemn tunes have sung,
Of tourneys, and of trophies hung;
Of forests, and enchantments drear,
Where more is meant than meets the
   ear.   *120*
   Thus, Night, oft see me in thy pale
   career,
Till civil-suited Morn[16] appear,
Not tricked and frounced as she was
   wont
With the Attic Boy[17] to hunt,
But kerchiefed in a comely cloud,
While rocking winds are piping loud,
Or ushered with a shower still,
When the gust hath blown his fill,
Ending on the rustling leaves,
With minute drops from off the
   eaves.   *130*
And when the sun begins to fling
His flaring beams, me, goddess, bring
To archéd walks of twilight groves,
And shadows brown, that Sylvan[18]
   loves,
Of pine, or monumental oak,
Where the rude axe, with heavéd stroke,
Was never heard the nymphs to daunt,
Or fright them from their hallowed
   haunt.
There in close covert by some brook,
Where no profaner eye may look,   *140*
Hide me from day's garish eye,
While the bee with honeyed thigh,
That at her flowery work doth sing,
And the waters murmuring,
With such consort as they keep,
Entice the dewy-feathered Sleep;
And let some strange mysterious dream

---

[10] the Big Dipper, a constellation which never sets at England's latitude
[11] Hermes Trismegistus, allegedly the author of books of secret lore
[12] recall from immortality
[13] legendary capital of Boeotia
[14] sixth-century Greek poet
[15] references to Chaucer's unfinished "Squire's Tale"
[16] Aurora
[17] Cephalus, beloved of Aurora
[18] god of the woods

Wave at his wings in airy stream
Of lively portraiture displayed,
Softly on my eyelids laid.                    150
And, as I wake, sweet music breathe
Above, about, or underneath,
Sent by some Spirit to mortals good,
Or the unseen Genius of the wood.
   But let my due feet never fail
To walk the studious cloister's pale,
And love the high-embowéd roof,
With antique pillars massy proof,
And storied windows richly dight,
Casting a dim religious light.                 160
There let the pealing organ blow
To the full-voiced choir below,
In service high and anthems clear,

As may with sweetness, through mine
   ear,
Dissolve me into ecstasies,
And bring all Heaven before mine eyes.
   And may at last my weary age
Find out the peaceful hermitage,
The hairy gown and mossy cell,
Where I may sit and rightly spell        170
Of every star that heaven doth shew,
And every herb that sips the dew;
Till old experience do attain
To something like prophetic strain.
   These pleasures, Melancholy, give,
And I with thee will choose to
   live.    (*1631?*)

## On Shakespeare

What needs my Shakespeare for his honored bones
The labor of an age in piléd stones,
Or that his hallowed relics should be hid
Under a star-ypointing pyramid?
Dear son of memory, great heir of fame,
What need'st thou such weak witness of thy name?
Thou in our wonder and astonishment
Hast built thyself a livelong monument.
For whilst to the shame of slow-endeavoring art
Thy easy numbers flow, and that each heart                10
Hath from the leaves of thy unvalued book
Those Delphic[1] lines with deep impression took,
Then thou, our fancy of itself bereaving,
Dost make us marble with too much conceiving,
And so sepúlchered in such pomp dost lie,
That kings for such a tomb would wish to die.    (*1632*)

## Lycidas

In this monody the author bewails a learned friend, unfortunately drowned in his passage
from Chester on the Irish Seas, 1637. And by occasion foretells the ruin of our corrupted
clergy, then in their height.

Yet once more, O ye laurels, and once more,
Ye myrtles brown, with ivy never sere,
I come to pluck your berries harsh and crude,
And with forced fingers rude
Shatter your leaves before the mellowing year.
Bitter constraint and sad occasion dear

---

[1] oracular

Compels me to disturb your season due;
For Lycidas is dead, dead ere his prime,
Young Lycidas, and hath not left his peer.
Who would not sing for Lycidas? He knew                              10
Himself to sing, and build the lofty rhyme.
He must not float upon his wat'ry bier
Unwept, and welter to the parching wind,
Without the meed of some melodious tear.
    Begin, then, Sisters of the Sacred Well[1]
That from beneath the seat of Jove doth spring,
Begin, and somewhat loudly sweep the string.
Hence with denial vain and coy excuse:
So may some gentle Muse
With lucky words favor my destined urn,                              20
And, as he passes, turn
And bid fair peace be to my sable shroud!
For we were nursed upon the self-same hill,
Fed the same flocks, by fountain, shade, and rill;
    Together both, ere the high lawns appeared
Under the opening eyelids of the Morn,
We drove a-field, and both together heard
What time the gray-fly winds her sultry horn,
Battening our flocks with the fresh dews of night,
Oft till the star that rose at evening bright                        30
Towards Heaven's descent had sloped his westering wheel.
Meanwhile the rural ditties were not mute,
Tempered to the oaten flute,
Rough Satyrs danced, and Fauns with cloven heel
From the glad sound would not be absent long;
And old Damætas[2] loved to hear our song.
    But, O the heavy change, now thou art gone,
Now thou art gone, and never must return!
Thee, Shepherd, thee the woods and desert caves,
With wild thyme and the gadding vine o'ergrown,
And all their echoes mourn.                                          40
The willows, and the hazel copses green,
Shall now no more be seen
Fanning their joyous leaves to thy soft lays.
As killing as the canker to the rose,
Or taint-worm to the weanling herds that graze,
Or frost to flowers, that their gay wardrobe wear
When first the white thorn blows;
Such, Lycidas, thy loss to shepherd's ear.
    Where were ye, Nymphs, when the remorseless deep                 50
Closed o'er the head of your loved Lycidas?
For neither were ye playing on the steep
Where your old bards, the famous druids, lie,

---

[1] the muses, who dwelt at the Pierian spring        [2] conventional pastoral name for an older man

Nor yet on the shaggy top of Mona[3] high,
Nor yet where Deva[4] spreads her wizard stream.
Ay me! I fondly dream
"Had ye been there" . . . for what could that have done?
What could the Muse herself that Orpheus bore,[5]
The Muse herself, for her enchanting son,
Whom universal Nature did lament,                                    60
When, by the rout that made the hideous roar,
His gory visage down the stream was sent,
Down the swift Hebrus to the Lesbian shore?
    Alas! what boots it with uncessant care
To tend the homely, slighted, shepherd's trade,
And strictly meditate the thankless Muse?
Were it not better done, as others use,
To sport with Amaryllis in the shade,
Or with the tangles of Neæra's[6] hair?
Fame is the spur that the clear spirit doth raise            70
(That last infirmity of noble mind)
To scorn delights and live laborious days;
But the fair guerdon when we hope to find,
And think to burst out into sudden blaze,
Comes the blind Fury with the abhorréd shears,
And slits the thin-spun life. "But not the praise,"
Phœbus replied, and touched my trembling ears:
"Fame is no plant that grows on mortal soil,
Nor in the glistering foil.
Set off to the world, nor in broad rumor lies,            80
But lives and spreads aloft by those pure eyes
And perfect witness of all-judging Jove;
As he pronounces lastly on each deed,
Of so much fame in Heav'n expect thy meed."
    O fountain Arethuse,[7] and thou honored flood,
Smooth-sliding Mincius,[8] crowned with vocal reeds,
That strain I heard was of a higher mood:
But now my oat proceeds,
And listen to the Herald of the Sea,[9]
That came in Neptune's plea.                                    90
He asked the waves, and asked the felon winds,
What hard mishap hath doomed this gentle swain?
And questioned every gust of rugged wings
That blows from off each beakéd promontory:
They knew not of his story;
And sage Hippotadés[10] their answer brings,

---

3 island of Anglesey, off Wales    4 river Dee
5 Calliope could not prevent a mob of Thracian
women from murdering Orpheus. They threw his
head into the river Hebrus, whence it floated out
to the island of Lesbos in the Aegean Sea.
6 conventional pastoral names for shepherdesses

7 a nymph, transformed into a fountain in Sicily
8 river in Lombardy. Like Arethuse, it represents
pastoral poetry.
9 Triton, who here pleads Neptune's innocence
10 Aeolus, god of the winds

That not a blast was from his dungeon strayed:
The air was calm, and on the level brine
Sleek Panopé[11] with all her sisters played.
It was the fatal and perfidious bark,                    *100*
Built in the eclipse, and rigged with curses dark,
That sunk so low that sacred head of thine.
    Next, Camus,[12] reverend sire, went footing slow,
His mantle hairy, and his bonnet sedge,
Inwrought with figures dim, and on the edge
Like to that sanguine flower inscribed with woe,
"Ah! who hath reft," quoth he, "my dearest pledge?"
Last came, and last did go,
The pilot of the Galilean lake;[13]
Two massy keys he bore of metals twain                   *110*
(The golden opes, the iron shuts amain).
He shook his mitered locks, and stern bespake:—
"How well could I have spared for thee, young swain,
Enow of such, as for their bellies' sake,
Creep, and intrude, and climb into the fold!
Of other care they little reckoning make
Than how to scramble at the shearers' feast,
And shove away the worthy bidden guest.
Blind mouths! that scarce themselves know how to hold
A sheep-hook, or have learned aught else the least       *120*
That to the faithful herdsman's art belongs!
What recks it them? What need they? they are sped;
And, when they list, their lean and flashy songs
Grate on their scrannel pipes of wretched straw;
The hungry sheep look up, and are not fed,
But swollen with wind and the rank mist they draw,
Rot inwardly, and foul contagion spread;
Besides what the grim wolf with privy paw
Daily devours apace, and nothing said;
But that two-handed engine at the door                   *130*
Stands ready to smite once, and smite no more."
    Return, Alphéus;[14] the dread voice is past
That shrunk thy streams; return, Sicilian Muse,
And call the vales, and bid them hither cast
Their bells and flowerets of a thousand hues.
Ye valleys low, where the mild whispers use
Of shades, and wanton winds, and gushing brooks,
On whose fresh lap the swart star sparely looks,
Throw hither all your quaint enameled eyes,
That on the green turf suck the honied showers,          *140*
And purple all the ground with vernal flowers.

---

[11] the principal sea nymph
[12] god of the river Cam; hence Cambridge University
[13] St. Peter, to whom Christ gave the keys of Heaven; who, as the first bishop, is pictured here as wearing a miter
[14] god of a river in Arcadia, representing pastoral poetry

Bring the rathe primrose that forsaken dies,
The tufted crow-toe, and pale jessamine,
The white pink, and the pansy freaked with jet,
The glowing violet,
The musk-rose, and the well-attired woodbine,
With cowslips wan that hang the pensive head,
And every flower that sad embroidery wears;
Bid Amaranthus all his beauty shed,
And daffadillies fill their cups with tears,                              *150*
To strew the laureate hearse where Lycid lies.
For so, to interpose a little ease,
Let our frail thoughts dally with false surmise,
Ay me! whilst thee the shores and sounding seas
Wash far away, where'er thy bones are hurled;
Whether beyond the stormy Hebrides,
Where thou, perhaps, under the whelming tide
Visit'st the bottom of the monstrous world;
Or whether thou, to our moist vows denied,
Sleep'st by the fable of Bellerus[15] old,                               *160*
Where the great Vision of the guarded mount
Looks toward Namancos and Bayona's[16] hold:
Look homeward, angel, now, and melt with ruth;
And, O ye Dolphins, waft the hapless youth.
    Weep no more, woeful shepherds, weep no more,
For Lycidas, your sorrow, is not dead,
Sunk though he be beneath the watery floor:
So sinks the day-star in the ocean bed,
And yet anon repairs his drooping head,
And tricks his beams, and with new-spangled ore                          *170*
Flames in the forehead of the morning sky:
So Lycidas sunk low, but mounted high,
Through the dear might of Him that walked the waves,
Where, other groves and other streams along,
With nectar pure his oozy locks he laves,
And hears the unexpressive nuptial song,
In the blest kingdoms meek of Joy and Love.
There entertain him all the Saints above,
In solemn troops, and sweet societies,
That sing, and singing in their glory move,                              *180*
And wipe the tears forever from his eyes.
Now, Lycidas, the shepherds weep no more;
Henceforth thou art the Genius of the shore,
In thy large recompense, and shalt be good
To all that wander in that perilous flood.
    Thus sang the uncouth swain to the oaks and rills,
While the still Morn went out with sandals gray;

---

[15] a giant of fable, said to be buried at Land's End,        [16] Spanish strongholds of Catholic power
Cornwall

He touched the tender stops of various quills,
With eager thought warbling his Doric lay:
And now the sun had stretched out all the hills,                    *190*
And now was dropped into the western bay.
At last he rose, and twitched his mantle blue:
Tomorrow to fresh woods and pastures new.   (*1638*)


## When I Consider How My Light Is Spent

When I consider how my light is spent
Ere half my days in this dark world and wide,
And that one talent which is death to hide
Lodged with me useless, though my soul more bent
To serve therewith my Maker, and present
My true account, lest He returning chide,
"Doth God exact day-labor, light denied?"
I fondly ask. But Patience, to prevent
That murmur, soon replies, "God doth not need
Either man's work or his own gifts. Who best               *10*
Bear His mild yoke, they serve Him best. His state
Is kingly: thousands at His bidding speed,
And post o'er land and ocean without rest;
They also serve who only stand and wait."   (*1652?*)


## On the Late Massacre in Piedmont

Avenge, O Lord, thy slaughtered saints,[1] whose bones
Lie scattered on the Alpine mountains cold;
Ev'n them who kept thy truth so pure of old,
When all our fathers worshipped stocks and stones,
Forget not: in thy book record their groans
Who were thy sheep, and in their ancient fold
Slain by the bloody Piedmontese, that rolled
Mother with infant down the rocks. Their moans
The vales redoubled to the hills, and they
To heav'n. Their martyred blood and ashes sow            *10*
O'er all th' Italian fields, where still doth sway
The triple Tyrant[2] that from these may grow
A hundredfold, who, having learnt thy way,
Early may fly the Babylonian woe.[3]   (*1655*)

---

[1] The Waldenses, an old Protestant sect, were allowed to live in northern Italy until 1655, when they were massacred by order of the Duke of Savoy.

[2] the Pope, in reference to his tiara of three crowns [3] Catholic oppression. The Roman Catholic Church was once called, by polemical Protestants, "the whore of Babylon."

## To Mr. Cyriack Skinner, Upon His Blindness

Cyriak, this three years' day these eyes, though clear
To outward view of blemish or of spot,
Bereft of light, their seeing have forgot;
Nor to their idle orbs doth sight appear
Of sun or moon or star, throughout the year,
Or man or woman. Yet I argue not
Against Heaven's hand or will, nor bate a jot
Of heart or hope, but still bear up and steer
Right onward. What supports me, dost thou ask?
The conscience, friend, to have lost them overplied     *10*
In liberty's defense, my noble task,
Of which all Europe talks from side to side.
This thought might lead me through the world's vain mask,
Content though blind, had I no better guide.   (*1655*)

## Methought I Saw My Late Espoused Saint

Methought I saw my late espoused Saint
Brought to me like Alcestis[1] from the grave,
Whom Jove's great son to her glad husband gave,
Rescued from death by force though pale and faint.
Mine as whom washt from spot of child-bed taint,
Purification in the old Law[2] did save,
And such, as yet once more I trust to have
Full sight of her in Heaven without restraint,
Came vested all in white, pure as her mind:
Her face was veiled; yet to my fancied sight,     *10*
Love, sweetness, goodness, in her person shined
So clear, as in no face with more delight.
But O as to embrace me she enclined
I waked, she fled, and day brought back my night.   (*1658?*)

---

[1] the wife of Admetus, returned from death by Hercules

[2] rules for purification of women after childbirth, set forth in Leviticus, 12

# SIR JOHN SUCKLING / 1609–1642

## Song

Why so pale and wan, fond Lover?
  Prithee why so pale?
Will, when looking well can't move her,
  Looking ill prevail;
  Prithee why so pale?

Why so dull and mute young Sinner?
  Prithee why so mute?
Will, when speaking well can't win her,
  Saying nothing do't:
  Prithee why so mute?          10

Quit, quit for shame, this will not move,
  This cannot take her;
If of herself she will not love,
  Nothing can make her:
  The Devil take her.    (*1646*)

## Sonnet III

Oh! for some honest lover's ghost,
  Some kind unbodied post
  Sent from the shades below!
  I strangely long to know
Whether the nobler chaplets wear,
Those that their mistress' scorn did bear,
  Or those that were used kindly.

For whatso'er they tell us here
  To make those sufferings dear,
  'Twill there, I fear, be found          10
  That to the being crowned
T' have loved alone will not suffice,
Unless we also have been wise
  And have our loves enjoyed.

What posture can we think him in,
  That here unloved again
  Departs, and 's thither gone

Where each sits by his own?
Or how can that Elysium be,
Where I my mistress still must          20
  Circled in others' arms?

For there the judges all are just,
  And Sophonisba must
  Be his whom she held dear,
  Not his who loved her here;
The sweet Philoclea, since she died,
Lies by her Pirocles his side,
  Not by Amphialus.

Some bays, perchance, or myrtle bough,
  For difference crowns the brow          30
  Of those kind souls that were
  The noble martyrs here;
And if that be the only odds,
(As who can tell?) ye kinder gods,
  Give me the woman here.    (*1646*)

## Out Upon It!

Out upon it! I have loved
  Three whole days together;
And am like to love three more,
  If it prove fair weather.

Time shall moult away his wings,
  Ere he shall discover
In the whole wide world again
  Such a constant lover.

But the spite on 't, is, no praise
  Is due at all to me;          10
Love with me had made no stays,
  Had it any been but she.

Had it any been but she,
  And that very face,
There had been at least ere this
  A dozen dozen in her place.    (*1659*)

209

# WILLIAM CARTWRIGHT / 1611–1643

## No Platonic Love

Tell me no more of minds embracing minds,
    And hearts exchanged for hearts;
That spirits spirits meet, as winds do winds,
    And mix their subtlest parts;
That two unbodied essences may kiss,
And then like angels, twist and feel one bliss.

I was that silly thing that once was wrought
    To practise this thin love;
I climbed from sex to soul, from soul to thought;
    But thinking there to move,           10
Headlong I rolled from thought to soul, and then
From soul I lighted at the sex again.

As some strict down-looked men pretend to fast
    Who yet in closets eat,
So lovers who profess they spirits taste,
    Feed yet on grosser meat;
I know they boast they souls to souls convey;
Howe'er they meet, the body is the way.

Come, I will undeceive thee: they that tread
    Those vain aerial ways           20
Are like young heirs and alchemists, misled
    To waste their wealth and days;
For searching thus to be forever rich,
They only find a med'cine for the itch.   *(1651)*

# RICHARD CRASHAW / 1612–1649

## An Epitaph Upon a Young Married Couple Dead and Buried Together

To these, whom death again did wed,
This grave's their second marriage-bed.
For though the hand of fate could force
'Twixt soul and body a divorce,
It could not sunder man and wife,
'Cause they both livéd but one life.
Peace, good reader. Do not weep.
Peace, the lovers are asleep.

They, sweet turtles, folded lie
In the last knot love could tie.       10
And though they lie as they were dead,
Their pillow stone, their sheets of lead,
(Pillow hard, and sheets not warm)
Love made the bed; they'll take no harm;
Let them sleep; let them sleep on.
Till this stormy night be gone,
Till th'eternal morrow dawn;
Then the curtains will be drawn
And they wake into a light,
Whose day shall never die in
    night.  *(1646)*       20

## Upon the Body of Our Bless&eacute;d Lord, Naked and Bloody

They have left thee naked, Lord; O that they had!
This garment too I would they had denied.

Thee with thyself they have too richly clad,
Opening the purple wardrobe in thy side.

O never could there be garment too good
For thee to wear, but this, of thine own blood.   (*1652*)


## On the Bless&eacute;d Virgin's Bashfulness

That on her lap she casts her humble eye,
'Tis the sweet pride of her humility.
The fair star is well fixed, for where, O where
Could she have fixed it on a fairer sphere?
'Tis heaven, 'tis heaven she sees, heaven's God there lies;
She can see heaven, and ne'er lift up her eyes:
This new guest to her eyes new laws hath given,
'Twas once look up, 'tis now look down to heaven.   (*1646*)


## ANNE BRADSTREET / 1612?–1672


## To My Dear and Loving Husband

If ever two were one, then surely we.
If ever man were loved by wife, then thee;
If ever wife was happy in a man,
Compare with me ye women if you can.
I prize thy love more than whole mines
    of gold,
Or all the riches that the East doth hold.
My love is such that rivers cannot quench,
Nor aught but love from thee, give
    recompense.
Thy love is such I can no way repay,
The heavens reward thee manifold I
    pray.                                            10
Then while we live, in love let's so
    perséver,
That when we live no more, we may live
    ever.   (*1678*)


## The Author to Her book

Thou ill-formed offspring of my feeble brain,
Who after birth did'st by my side remain
Till snatched from thence by friends less wise than true
Who thee abroad, exposed to public view,[1]

---

[1] Bradstreet's book, *The Tenth Muse Lately Sprung Up in America*, was published in London without her knowledge.

Made thee in rags, halting to the press to trudge,
Where errors were not lessened (all may judge)—
At thy return my blushing was not small
My rambling brat (in print) should mother call.
I cast thee by as one unfit for light,
Thy visage was so irksome in my sight.                    10
Yet being mine own, at length affection would
Thy blemishes amend, if so I could:
I washed thy face, but more defects I saw,
And rubbing off a spot, still made a flaw.
I stretched thy joints to make thee even feet,
Yet still thou run'st more hobbling than is meet;
In better dress to trim thee was my mind,
But naught save homespun cloth, i'th' house I find.
In this array, 'mongst vulgars mayst thou roam;
In critics' hands beware thou dost not come,              20
And take thy way where yet thou art not known.
If for thy father asked, say, thou hadst none:
And for thy mother, she alas is poor,
Which caused her thus to send thee out of door.   (*1678*)


# RICHARD LOVELACE / 1618–1657?

## To Althea, from Prison

When Love with unconfinéd wings
  Hovers within my gates;
And my divine Althea brings
  To whisper at the grates:
When I lie tangled in her hair,
  And fettered to her eye;
The birds, that wanton in the air,
  Know no such liberty.

When flowing cups run swiftly round
  With no allaying Thames,                    10
Our careless heads with roses bound,
  Our hearts with loyal flames;
When thirsty grief in wine we steep,
  When healths and draughts go free,
Fishes that tipple in the deep,
  Know no such liberty.

When (like committed linnets) I
  With shriller throat shall sing
The sweetness, mercy, majesty,

And glories of my King;                       20
When I shall voice aloud, how good
  He is, how great should be,
Enlargéd winds that curl the flood,
  Know no such liberty.

Stone walls do not a prison make,
  Nor iron bars a cage;
Minds innocent and quiet take
  That for an hermitage;
If I have freedom in my Love,
  And in my soul am free;                     30
Angels alone that soar above,
  Enjoy such liberty.   (*1649*)

## To Lucasta, Going Beyond the Seas

If to be absent were to be
  Away from thee;
Or that when I am gone

You or I were alone;
  Then, my Lucasta, might I crave
Pity from blustering wind, or swallowing
    wave.

But I'll not sigh one blast or gale
    To swell my sail,
  Or pay a tear to 'suage
    The foaming blue-god's rage;   *10*
For whether he will let me pass
Or no, I'm still as happy as I was.

Though seas and land betwixt us
    both,
    Our faith and troth,
    Like separated souls,
  All time and space controls:
Above the highest sphere we meet
Unseen, unknown, and greet as Angels
    greet.

So then we do anticipate
    Our after-fate,     *20*
  And are alive i' the skies,
  If thus our lips and eyes
Can speak like spirits unconfined
In Heaven, their earthly bodies left
    behind.  (*1649*)

## To Lucasta, Going to the Wars

Tell me not, Sweet, I am unkind,
  That from the nunnery
Of thy chaste breast, and quiet mind,
  To war and arms I fly.

True; a new mistress now I chase,
  The first foe in the field;
And with a stronger faith embrace
  A sword, a horse, a shield.

Yet this inconstancy is such,
  As you too shall adore;   *10*
I could not love thee, Dear, so much,
  Loved I not honour more.  (*1649*)

## Why Should You Swear?

Why should you swear I am forsworn,
Since thine I vowed to be?
Lady, it is already morn,
And 'twas last night I swore to thee
That fond impossibility.

Have I not loved thee much and long,
A tedious twelve hours' space?
I must all other beauties wrong,
And rob thee of a new embrace,
Could I still dote upon thy face.   *10*

Not but all joy in thy brown hair
By others may be found:
But I must search the black and fair,
Like skilful mineralists that sound
For treasure in unploughed-up ground.

Then if, when I have loved my round,
Thou prov'st the pleasant she,
With spoils of meaner beauties crowned
I laden will return to thee,
Ev'n sated with variety.   *20*

# ABRAHAM COWLEY / 1618–1667

## The Wish

    Well then; I now do plainly see,
  This busy world and I shall ne'er agree;
  The very honey of all earthly joy
    Does of all meats the soonest cloy;

And they, methinks, deserve my pity
Who for it can endure the stings,
The crowd, and buzz, and murmurings
   Of this great hive, the city.

Ah, yet, ere I descend to the grave
May I a small house and large garden have!          *10*
And a few friends, and many books, both true,
   Both wise, and both delightful too!
   And since love ne'er will from me flee,
A mistress moderately fair,
And good as guardian angels are,
   Only beloved, and loving me!

O fountains, when in you shall I
Myself, eased of unpeaceful thoughts, espy?
O fields! O woods! when, when shall I be made
   The happy tenant of your shade?                  *20*
   Here's the spring-head of pleasure's flood,
Here's wealthy Nature's treasury,
Where all the riches lie that she
   Has coined and stamped for good.

   Pride and ambition here
Only in farfetched metaphors appear;
Here naught but winds can hurtful murmurs scatter,
   And naught but Echo flatter.
   The gods, when they descended, hither
From heavens did always choose their way;          *30*
And therefore we may boldly say
   That 'tis the way, too, thither.

   How happy here should I
And one dear she live and, embracing, die!
She who is all the world, and can exclude
   In deserts, solitude.
   I should have then this only fear,
Lest men, when they my pleasures see,
Should hither throng to live like me,
   And so make a city here.   (*1647*)             *40*


## Of Myself

This only grant me, that my means may lie
Too low for envy, for contempt too high.
   Some honor I would have,
Not from great deeds, but good alone;
The unknown are better than ill known;
   Rumor can ope' the grave.
Acquaintance I would have, but when't depends
Not on the number, but the choice, of friends.

Books should, not business, entertain the light,
And sleep, as undisturbed as death, the night.     *10*
　　My house a cottage more
Than palace, and should fitting be
For all my use, no luxury.
　　My garden painted o'er
With nature's hand, not art's, and pleasures yield,
Horace might envy in his Sabine field.[1]

Thus would I double my life's fading space;
For he, that runs it well, twice runs his race.
　　And in this true delight,
These unbought sports, this happy state,     *20*
I would not fear nor wish my fate;
　　But boldly say each night,
Tomorrow let my sun his beams display,
Or in clouds hide them; I have lived today.     *(1668)*

# ANDREW MARVELL / 1621–1678

## On a Drop of Dew

See how the orient[1] dew,
　　Shed from the bosom of the morn
　　Into the blowing roses,
Yet careless of its mansion new;
For the clear region where 'twas born
　　Round in itself encloses:
　　And in its little globe's extent,
Frames as it can its native element.
　　How it the purple flower does slight,
　　　Scarce touching where it lies,     *10*
　　But gazing back upon the skies,
　　　Shines with a mournful light;
　　　Like its own tear,
Because so long divided from the sphere.
　　Restless it rolls and unsecure,
　　　Trembling lest it grow impure:
　　Till the warm sun pity its pain,
And to the skies exhale it back again.
　　So the soul, that drop, that ray
Of the clear fountain of eternal day,     *20*
Could it within the human flower be seen,
　　Rememb'ring still its former height,

Shuns the sweet leaves and blossoms
　　green;
　　And, recollecting its own light,
Does, in its pure and circling thoughts,
　　express
The greater heaven in a heaven less.
　　In how coy a figure wound,
　　Every way it turns away:
　　So the world excluding round,
　　Yet receiving in the day.     *30*
　　Dark beneath, but bright above:
　　Here disdaining, there in love.
　　How loose and easy hence to go:
　　How girt and ready to ascend.
　　Moving but on a point below,
　　It all about does upwards bend.
Such did the manna's[2] sacred dew distill:
White, and entire, though congealed and
　　chill.
Congealed on earth: but does, dissolving,
　　run
Into the glories of the almighty
　　sun.     *(1681)*     *40*

---

[1] Roman lyric poet of the first century B.C.

[1] bright and lustrous, like a pearl

[2] a food (perhaps a fungus) that appeared by a

miracle to sustain the Israelites in their flight from
Egypt. The manna appeared in the night, and
melted in the sun.

# The Garden

How vainly men themselves amaze
To win the palm, the oak, or bays;
And their incessant labors see
Crowned from some single herb, or
    tree,
Whose short and narrow-vergéd shade
Does prudently their toils upbraid;
While all flowers and all trees do close
To weave the garlands of repose!

Fair Quiet, have I found thee here,
And Innocence, thy sister dear?        *10*
Mistaken long, I sought you then
In busy companies of men.
Your sacred plants, if here below,
Only among the plants will grow;
Society is all but rude
To this delicious solitude.

No white nor red was ever seen
So amorous as this lovely green.
Fond lovers, cruel as their flame,
Cut in these trees their mistress'
    name:        *20*
Little, alas! they know or heed
How far these beauties hers exceed!
Fair trees! wheres'e'er your barks I
    wound
No name shall but your own be
    found.

When we have run our passion's heat,
Love hither makes his best retreat.
The gods, that mortal beauty chase,
Still in a tree did end their race;
Apollo hunted Daphne so,[1]
Only that she might laurel grow;    *30*
And Pan did after Syrinx speed,[2]
Not as a nymph, but for a reed.

What wondrous life is this I lead!
Ripe apples drop about my head;
The luscious clusters of the vine
Upon my mouth do crush their wine;

The nectarine, and curious peach,
Into my hands themselves do reach;
Stumbling on melons, as I pass,
Ensnared with flowers, I fall on
    grass.        *40*

Meanwhile, the mind, from pleasure
    less,
Withdraws into its happiness:
The mind, that ocean where each kind
Does straight its own resemblance find;
Yet it creates, transcending these,
Far other worlds, and other seas;
Annihilating all that's made
To a green thought in a green shade.

Here at the fountain's sliding foot,
Or at some fruit-tree's mossy root,    *50*
Casting the body's vest aside,
My soul into the boughs does glide:
There like a bird it sits, and sings,
Then whets and combs its silver wings;
And, till prepared for longer flight,
Waves in its plumes the various light.

Such was that happy garden-state,
While man there walked without a mate:
After a place so pure and sweet,
What other help could yet be meet?    *60*
But 'twas beyond a mortal's share
To wander solitary there:
Two paradises 'twere in one,
To live in paradise alone.

How well the skillful gardener drew
Of flowers, and herbs, this dial new;
Where, from above, the milder sun
Does through a fragrant zodiac run;
And, as it works, the industrious bee
Computes its time as well as we.    *70*
How could such sweet and wholesome
    hours
Be reckoned but with herbs and
    flowers!   (*1681*)

---

[1] Daphne prayed for help when Apollo had almost overtaken her; she was transformed into a laurel tree.

[2] Under similar circumstances, Syrinx was metamorphosed into a reed, from which Pan then made a flute.

## The Mower's Song

My mind was once the true survey
Of all these meadows fresh and gay,
And in the greenness of the grass
Did see its hopes as in a glass;
When Juliana came, and she,
What I do to the grass, does to my thoughts and me,

But these, while I with sorrow pine,
Grew more luxuriant still and fine,
That not one blade of grass you spied,
But had a flower on either side,                               *10*
When Juliana came, and she,
What I do to the grass, does to my thoughts and me.

Unthankful meadows could you so
A fellowship so true forego,
And in your gaudy May-games meet,
While I lay trodden under feet?
When Juliana came, and she,
What I do to the grass, does to my thoughts and me.

But what you in compassion ought,
Shall now by my revenge be wrought;                            *20*
And flowers, and grass, and I, and all
Will in one common ruin fall;
For Juliana comes, and she,
What I do to the grass, does to my thoughts and me.

And thus, ye meadows, which have been
Companions of my thoughts more green,
Shall now the heraldry become
With which I shall adorn my tomb;
For Juliana comes, and she,
What I do to the grass, does to my thoughts and me.          *30*
                              (*1681*)


## The Mower Against Gardens

Luxurious man, to bring his vice in use,
    Did after him the world seduce,
And from the fields the flowers and plants allure,
    When nature was most plain and pure.
He first enclosed within the garden's square
    A dead and standing pool of air;
And a more luscious earth for them did knead,
    Which stupefied them while it fed.
The pink grew then as double as his mind;
    The nutriment did change the kind.                         *10*

With strange perfumes he did the roses taint;
    And flowers themselves were taught to paint.
The tulip, white, did for complexion seek,
    And learned to interline its cheek;
Its onion root they then so high did hold
    That one was for a meadow sold.[1]
Another world was searched, through oceans new,
    To find the marvel of Peru.[2]
And yet these rarities might be allowed
    To man, that sov'reign thing and proud,                    20
Had he not dealt[3] between the bark and tree,
    Forbidden mixtures there to see.
No plant now knew the stock from which it came;
    He grafts upon the wild the tame,
That the uncertain and adult'rate fruit
    Might put the palate in dispute.
His green seraglio has its eunuchs too,
    Lest any tyrant him outdo;
And in the cherry he does nature vex,
    To procreate without a sex.                                30
'Tis all enforced, the fountain and the grot,
    While the sweet fields do lie forgot,
Where willing nature does to all dispense
    A wild and fragrant innocence;
And fauns and fairies do the meadows till
    More by their presence than their skill.
Their statues, polished by some ancient hand,
    May to adorn the gardens stand;
But howsoe'er the figures do excel,
    The gods themselves with us do dwell.   (*1681*)          40

## The Mower to the Glow-Worms

Ye living lamps, by whose dear light
    The nightingale does sit so late,
And studying all the summer night,
    Her matchless songs does meditate;

Ye country comets, that portend
    No war, nor prince's funeral,
Shining unto no higher end
    Than to presage the grasses' fall;

Ye glow-worms, whose officious flame
    To wandering mowers shows the way,   10
That in the night have lost their aim,
    And after foolish fires do stray;

Your courteous lights in vain you waste,
    Since Juliana here is come;
For she my mind hath so displaced
    That I shall never find my home.
                                   (*1681*)

---

[1] a reference to tulipomania
[2] the common garden four-o'clock

[3] delivered a blow; i.e., made a cleft in which to insert a cion

## Bermudas

Where the remote Bermudas ride
In th' ocean's bosom unespied,
From a small boat, that rowed along,
The list'ning winds received this song.
    What should we do but sing His
      praise
That led us through the wat'ry maze,
Unto an isle so long unknown,
And yet far kinder than our own?
Where He the huge sea-monsters wracks,
That lift the deep upon their backs;    10
He lands us on a grassy stage,
Safe from the storms, and prelate's
      rage.
He gives us this eternal spring,
Which here enamels everything;
And sends the fowls to us in care,
On daily visits through the air.
He hangs in shades the orange bright,
Like golden lamps in a green night,
And does in the pomegranates close
Jewels more rich than Ormus[1] shows.   20
He makes the figs our mouths to meet,
And throws the melons at our feet;
But apples plants of such a price,
No tree could ever bear them twice.
With cedars, chosen by His hand,
From Lebanon, He stores the land;
And makes the hollow seas, that roar,
Proclaim the ambergris on shore.
He cast (of which we rather boast)
The gospel's pearl upon our coast;    30
And in these rocks for us did frame
A temple, where to sound His name.
Oh let our voice His praise exalt,
Till it arrive at Heaven's vault:
Which thence (perhaps) rebounding,
      may
Echo beyond the Mexique Bay.
    Thus sung they, in the English boat,
An holy and a cheerful note,
And all the way, to guide their chime,
With falling oars they kept the time.   40
                  (*1681*)

[1] Ormuz, a Portuguese port in the Middle East, suggestive of great wealth

## To His Coy Mistress

Had we but world enough, and time,
This coyness, lady, were no crime.
We would sit down, and think which
      way
To walk, and pass our long love's day.
Thou by the Indian Ganges' side
Shouldst rubies find: I by the tide
Of Humber[1] would complain. I would
Love you ten years before the Flood:
And you should if you please refuse
Till the conversion of the Jews.    10
My vegetable love should grow
Vaster than empires, and more slow.
An hundred years should go to praise
Thine eyes, and on thy forehead gaze.
Two hundred to adore each breast:
But thirty thousand to the rest.
An age at least to every part,
And the last age should show your heart.
For, lady, you deserve this state;
Nor would I love at lower rate.    20
    But at my back I always hear
Time's wingèd chariot hurrying near:
And yonder all before us lie
Deserts of vast eternity.
Thy beauty shall no more be found,
Nor, in thy marble vault, shall sound
My echoing song; then worms shall try
That long preserved virginity:
And your quaint honour turn to dust;
And into ashes all my lust.    30
The grave's a fine and private place,
But none, I think, do there embrace.
    Now therefore, while the youthful
      hue
Sits on thy skin like morning dew,
And while thy willing soul transpires
At every pore with instant fires,
Now let us sport us while we may;
And now, like am'rous birds of prey,
Rather at once our time devour,
Than languish in his slow-chapped[2]
      pow'r.    40

[1] a rather commonplace English river
[2] slow-jawed

Let us roll all our strength, and all
Our sweetness, up into one ball:
And tear our pleasures with rough strife,
Through the iron gates of life.
Thus, though we cannot make our sun
Stand still, yet we will make him run.

                           (1681)

## The Definition of Love

My love is of a birth as rare
As 'tis for object strange and high:
It was begotten by Despair
Upon Impossibility.

Magnanimous Despair alone
Could show me so divine a thing,
Where feeble Hope could ne'er have
    flown
But vainly flapped its tinsel wing.

And yet I quickly might arrive
Where my extended soul is fixed,         10
But Fate does iron wedges drive,
And always crowds itself betwixt.

For Fate with jealous eye does see
Two perfect loves, nor lets them close:
Their union would her ruin be,
And her tyrannic power depose.

And therefore her decrees of steel
Us as the distant poles have placed,
(Though love's whole world on us doth
    wheel)
Not by themselves to be embraced,      20

Unless the giddy heaven fall,
And earth some new convulsion tear,
And, us to join, the world should all
Be cramped into a planisphere.

As lines, so loves oblique may well
Themselves in every angle greet;
But ours, so truly parallel,
Though infinite, can never meet.

Therefore the love which us doth bind,
But fate so enviously debars,          30
Is the conjunction[1] of the mind,
And opposition[2] of the stars.    (1681)

# HENRY VAUGHAN / 1622–1695

## Quickness

False life! a foil and no more, when
    Wilt thou be gone?
Thou fool deception of all men
That would not have the true come on!
Thou art a moon-like toil, a blind
    Self-posing state,
A dark contest of waves and wind,
A mere tempestuous debate.
Life is a fixed discerning light,
    A knowing joy;                10

No chance or fit, but ever bright
And calm and full, yet doth not cloy.
'Tis such a blissful thing, that still
    Doth vivify
And shine and smile, and hath the skill
To please without eternity.
Thou art a toilsome mole, or less,
    A moving mist;
But life is what none can express,
A quickness which my God hath
    kissed.   (1650)         20

[1] the passing of heavenly bodies in the same house of the Zodiac

[2] the relationship of heavenly bodies separated by 180° of longitude

## The Bird

Hither thou com'st; the busy wind all night
Blew through thy lodging, where thy own warm wing
Thy pillow was. Many a sullen storm,
For which course man seems much the fitter born,
    Rained on thy bed
    And harmless head.

And now as fresh and cheerful as the light,
Thy little heart in early hymns doth sing
Unto that Providence whose unseen arm
Curbed them, and clothed thee well and warm.         *10*
    All things that be praise him, and had
    Their lesson taught them when first made.

So hills and valleys into singing break,
And though poor stones have neither speech nor tongue,
While active winds and streams both run and speak,
Yet stones are deep in admiration.
Thus praise and prayer here beneath the sun
Make lesser mornings, when the great are done.

For each encloséd spirit is a star
    Enlight'ning his own little sphere,         *20*
Whose light, though fetched and borrowéd from far,
    Both mornings makes and evenings there.

But as these birds of light make a land glad,
Chirping their solemn matins on each tree,
So in the shades of night some dark fowls be,
Whose heavy notes make all that hear them sad.

    The turtle then in palm trees mourns,
        While owls and satyrs howl;
    The pleasant land to brimstone turns
        And all her streams grow foul.         *30*

Brightness and mirth, and love and faith, all fly,
Till the day-spring breaks forth again from high.   (*1650*)


## The Waterfall

    With what deep murmurs through time's silent stealth
    Doth thy transparent, cool, and wat'ry wealth
        Here flowing fall,
        And chide, and call,
    As if his liquid, loose retinue stayed
    Ling'ring, and were of this steep place afraid,
        The common pass
        Where, clear as glass,

All must descend—
Not to an end,                                        *10*
But quickened by this deep and rocky grave,
Rise to a longer course more bright and brave.

Dear stream! dear bank, where often I
Have sat and pleased my pensive eye,
Why, since each drop of thy quick store
Runs thither whence it flowed before,
Should poor souls fear a shade or night,
Who came, sure, from a sea of light?
Or since those drops are all sent back
So sure to thee, that none doth lack,                 *20*
Why should frail flesh doubt any more
That what God takes he'll not restore?

O useful element and clear!
My sacred wash and cleanser here,
My first consigner unto those
Fountains of life where the Lamb goes!
What sublime truths and wholesome themes
Lodge in thy mystical deep streams!
Such as dull man can never find
Unless that spirit lead his mind                      *30*
Which first upon thy face did move,
And hatched all with his quick'ning love.
As this loud brook's incessant fall
In streaming rings restagnates all,
Which reach by course the bank, and then
Are no more seen, just so pass men.
O my invisible estate,
My glorious liberty, still late!
Thou art the channel my soul seeks,
Not this with cataracts and creeks.  (*1650*)        *40*


## The World

I saw eternity the other night
Like a great ring of pure and endless light,
    All calm, as it was bright,
And round beneath it, time in hours, days, years
    Driv'n by the spheres
Like a vast shadow moved, in which the world
    And all her train were hurled;
The doting lover in his quaintest strain
    Did there complain,
Near him, his lute, his fancy, and his flights,       *10*
    Wit's sour delights,

With gloves, and knots the silly snares of pleasure;
  Yet his dear treasure
All scattered lay while he his eyes did pour
  Upon a flower.
The darksome statesman, hung with weights and woe,
Like a thick midnight fog moved there so slow
  He did nor stay, nor go;
Condemning thoughts, like sad eclipses, scowl
  Upon his soul,                   20
And clouds of crying witnesses without
  Pursued him with one shout.
Yet digged the mole, and lest his ways be found
  Worked under ground,
Where he did clutch his prey, but one did see
  That policy;
Churches and altars fed him, perjuries
  Were gnats and flies,
It rained about him blood and tears, but he
  Drank them as free.             30
The fearful miser on a heap of rust
Sat pining all his life there, did scarce trust
  His own hands with the dust,
Yet would not place one piece above, but lives
  In fear of thieves.
Thousands there were as frantic as himself
  And hugged each one his pelf;
The downright epicure placed heaven in sense
  And scorned pretense
While others, slipped into a wide excess,       40
  Said little less;
The weaker sort slight, trivial wares enslave
  Who think them brave,
And poor, despiséd truth sat counting by
  Their victory.
Yet some, who all this while did weep and sing,
And sing, and weep, soared up into the ring,
  But most would use no wing.
O fools, said I, thus to prefer dark night
  Before true light,               50
To live in grots, and caves, and hate the day
  Because it shows the way,
The way which from this dead and dark abode
  Leads up to God,
A way where you might tread the sun, and be
  More bright than he.
But as I did their madness so discuss
  One whispered thus,
This ring the Bridegroom did for none provide
  But for his bride.   (*1650*)       60

## Unprofitableness

How rich, O Lord, how fresh thy visits are!
'Twas but just now my bleak leaves hopeless hung,
    Sullied with dust and mud;
Each snarling blast shot through me, and did share
Their youth and beauty; cold showers nipped and wrung
    Their spiciness and blood;
But since thou didst in one sweet glance survey
Their sad decays, I flourish, and once more
    Breathe all perfumes and spice;
I smell a dew like myrrh, and all the day                          *10*
Wear in my bosom a full sun; such store
    Hath one beam from thy eyes.
But ah, my God, what fruit hast thou of this?
What one poor leaf did ever I let fall
    To wait upon thy wreath?
Thus that all day a thankless weed dost dress,
And when th' hast done, a stench or fog is all
    The odor I bequeath.   *(1650)*


## Man

Weighing the steadfastness and state
Of some mean things which here below reside,
Where birds, like watchful clocks, the noiseless date
    And intercourse of times divide.
Where bees at night get home and hive, and flowers,
    Early as well as late,
Rise with the sun and set in the same bowers;

    I would (said I) my God would give
The staidness of these things to man! for these
To His divine appointments ever cleave,                            *10*
    And no new business breaks their peace;
The birds nor sow nor reap, yet sup and dine;
    The flowers without clothes live,
Yet Solomon was never dressed so fine.

    Man hath still either toys or care;
He hath no root, nor to one place is tied,
But ever restless and irregular
    About this earth doth run and ride.
He knows he hath a home, but scarce knows where;
    He says it is so far                                          *20*
That he hath quite forgot how to go there.

    He knocks at all doors, strays and roams,
Nay, hath not so much wit as some stones have,
Which in the darkest nights point to their homes,

By some hid sense their Maker gave;
Man is the shuttle, to whose winding quest
    And passage through these looms
God ordered motion, but ordained no rest.   (*1650*)

## They Are All Gone into the World of Light

They are all gone into the world of light!
    And I alone sit lingering here;
Their very memory is fair and bright,
    And my sad thoughts doth clear.

It glows and glitters in my cloudy breast,
    Like stars upon some gloomy grove,
Or those faint beams in which this hill is dressed,
    After the sun's remove.

I see them walking in an air of glory,
    Whose light doth trample on my days;                    10
My days, which are at best but dull and hoary,
    Mere glimmering and decays.

O holy Hope! and high Humility!
    High as the heavens above!
These are your walks, and you have showed them me,
    To kindle my cold love.

Dear beauteous Death! the jewel of the just,
    Shining nowhere but in the dark;
What mysteries do lie beyond thy dust,
    Could man outlook that mark!                            20

He that hath found some fledged bird's nest may know
    At first sight if the bird be flown;
But what fair well or grove he sings in now,
    That is to him unknown.

And yet, as angels in some brighter dreams
    Call to the soul when man doth sleep,
So some strange thoughts transcend our wonted themes,
    And into glory peep.

If a star were confined into a tomb,
    Her captive flames must needs burn there;               30
But when the hand that locked her up gives room,
    She'll shine through all the sphere.

O Father of eternal life, and all
    Created glories under Thee!
Resume Thy spirit from this world of thrall
    Into true liberty.

Either disperse these mists, which blot and fill
    My perspective still as they pass;
Or else remove me hence unto that hill
    Where I shall need no glass.   (*1655*)                 40

## Unfold! Unfold!

Unfold! unfold! Take in his light,
Who makes thy cares more short than
   night.
The joys which with his day-star rise
He deals to all but drowsy eyes;
And, what the men of this world miss,
Some drops and dews of future bliss.

Hark! how His winds have changed their
   note,
And with warm whispers call thee out!
The frosts are past, the storms are gone,
And backward life at last comes on.     *10*
The lofty groves in express joys
Reply unto the turtle's voice;
And here in dust and dirt, oh, here
The lilies of His love appear!

## JOHN DRYDEN / 1631–1700

### Song from Marriage à la Mode

> Why should a foolish marriage vow,
>    Which long ago was made,
> Oblige us to each other now
>    When passion is decayed?
> We loved, and we loved, as long as we could,
>    Till our love was loved out in us both:
> But our marriage is dead, when the pleasure is fled:
>    'Twas pleasure first made it an oath.
>
> If I have pleasures for a friend,
>    And farther love in store,     *10*
> What wrong has he whose joys did end,
>    And who could give no more?
> 'Tis a madness that he should be jealous of me,
>    Or that I should bar him of another:
> For all we can gain, is to give ourselves pain,
>    When neither can hinder the other.   (*1672*)

### from The Conquest of Granada

#### SONG OF THE ZAMBRA DANCE

> Beneath a myrtle shade
> Which love for none but happy lovers made,
> I slept, and straight my love before me brought
> Phyllis, the object of my waking thought;
> Undressed she came my flames to meet,
> While love strowed flowers beneath her feet;
> Flowers which so pressed by her became more sweet.

From the bright vision's head
A careless veil of lawn was loosely spread:
From her white temples fell her shaded hair,                          *10*
Like cloudy sunshine not too brown nor fair:
Her hands, her lips did love inspire;
Her every grace my heart did fire:
But most her eyes which languished with desire.

Ah, charming fair, said I,
How long can you my bliss and yours deny?
By nature and by love this lonely shade
Was for revenge of suffering lovers made:
Silence and shade with love agree:
Both shelter you and favor me;                                        *20*
You cannot blush because I cannot see.

No, let me die, she said,
Rather than lose the spotless name of maid:
Faintly methought she spoke, for all the while
She bid me not believe her, with a smile.
Then die, said I, she still denied:
And is it thus, thus, thus she cried
You use a harmless maid, and so she died!

I waked, and straight I knew
I loved so well it made my dream prove true:                          *30*
Fancy, the kinder mistress of the two,
Fancy had done what Phyllis would not do!
Ah, cruel nymph, cease your disdain,
While I can dream you scorn in vain;
Asleep or waking you must ease my pain.   (*1672*)

## Prologue to *Aureng-Zebe*

Our author by experience finds it true,
'Tis much more hard to please himself, than you:
And out of no feigned modesty, this day,
Damns his laborious trifle of a play:
Not that it's worse than what before he writ,
But he has now another taste of wit;
And to confess a truth, (though out of time)
Grows weary of his long-loved mistress, rhyme.
Passion's too fierce to be in fetters bound,
And nature flies him like enchanted ground.                           *10*
What verse can do, he has performed in this,
Which he presumes the most correct of his.
But spite of all his pride, a secret shame
Invades his breast at Shakespeare's sacred name:
Awed when he hears his god-like Romans rage,
He, in a just despair, would quit the stage.

And to an age less polished, more unskilled,
Does, with disdain, the foremost honours yield,
As with the greater dead he dares not strive,
He would not match his verse with those who live;                    *20*
Let him retire, betwixt two ages cast,
The first of this, and hindmost of the last.
A losing gamester, let him sneak away;
He bears no ready money from the play.
The fate which governs poets thought it fit,
He should not raise his fortunes by his wit.
The clergy thrive, and the litigious bar;
Dull heroes fatten with the spoils of war;
All southern vices, heaven be praised are here;
But wit's a luxury you think too dear.                    *30*
When you to cultivate the plant are loath,
'Tis a shrewd sign 'twas never of your growth:
And wit in northern climates will not blow,
Except, like orange trees 'tis housed from snow.
There needs no care to put a playhouse down,
'Tis the most desert place of all the town.
Wit and our neighbours, to speak proudly, are
Like monarchs, ruined with expensive war.
While, like wise English, unconcerned, you sit,
And see us play the tragedy of wit.   (*1676*)                    *40*

## *from* Absalom and Achitophel

What shall we think! Can people give away
Both for themselves and sons their native sway?
Then they are left defenseless, to the sword
Of each unbounded, arbitrary lord:
And laws are vain, by which we right enjoy,
If kings unquestioned can those laws destroy.
Yet if the crowd be judge of fit and just,
And kings are only officers in trust,
Then this resuming covenant was declared
When kings were made, or is forever barred.                    *10*
If those who gave the scepter, could not tie
By their own deed their own posterity,
How then could Adam bind his future race?
How could his forfeit on mankind take place?
Or how could heavenly justice damn us all
Who ne'er consented to our father's fall?
Then kings are slaves to those whom they command,
And tenants to their people's pleasure stand.
Add that the power, for property allowed,
Is mischievously seated in the crowd;                    *20*
For who can be secure of private right,
If sovereign sway may be dissolved by might?

Nor is the people's judgment always true:
The most may err as grossly as the few.
And faultless kings run down, by common cry,
For vice, oppression, and for tyranny.
What standard is there in a fickle rout,
Which, flowing to the mark, runs faster out?
Nor only crowds, but Sanhedrins[1] may be
Infected with this public lunacy: *30*
And share the madnesss of rebellious times,
To murder monarchs for imagined crimes.
If they may give and take when e'er they please,
Not kings alone, (the Godhead's images,)
But government itself at length must fall
To nature's state, where all have right to all.
Yet, grant our lords the people, kings can make,
What prudent men a settled throne would shake?
For whatsoe'er their sufferings were before,
That change they covet makes them suffer more. *40*
All other errors but disturb a state;
But innovation is the blow of fate.
If ancient fabrics nod, and threat to fall,
To patch the flaws, and buttress up the wall,
Thus far 'tis duty; but here fix the mark:
For all beyond it is to touch our Ark.[2]
To change foundations, cast the frame anew,
Is work for rebels who base ends pursue:
At once divine and human laws control,
And mend the parts by ruin of the whole. *50*
The tampering world is subject to this curse,
To physic their disease into a worse. (*1681*)

## *from* The Spanish Fryar

### FAREWELL UNGRATEFUL TRAITOR

Farewell ungrateful traitor,
  Farewell my perjured swain,
Let never injured creature
  Believe a man again.
The pleasure of possessing
Surpasses all expressing,
But 'tis too short a blessing,
  And love too long a pain.

'Tis easy to deceive us
  In pity of your pain, *10*

But when we love you leave us
  To rail at you in vain.
Before we have descried it,
There is no bliss beside it,
But she that once has tried it
  Will never love again.

The passion you pretended
  Was only to obtain;
But when the charm is ended
  The charmer you disdain. *20*
Your love by ours we measure
Till we have lost our treasure,
But dying is a pleasure,
  When living is a pain. (*1681*)

---

[1] parliaments; the name of the supreme council of the Jews in ancient Israel

[2] the chest containing the stone tablets bearing the Ten Commandments; hence, the fundamental law

## To the Pious Memory of the Accomplished Young Lady Mrs. Anne Killigrew

*EXCELLENT IN THE TWO SISTER ARTS OF POESY AND PAINTING*

AN ODE

Thou youngest virgin-daughter of the skies,
Made in the last promotion of the blest,
Whose palms, new plucked from paradise,
In spreading branches more sublimely rise,
Rich with immortal green above the rest;
Whether, adopted to some neighboring star,
Thou roll'st above us in thy wandering race,
　　Or in procession fixed and regular,
　　Moved with the heavens' majestic pace,
　　Or called to more superior bliss,                           *10*
Thou tread'st with seraphims the vast abyss:
Whatever happy region is thy place,
Cease thy celestial song a little space;
Thou wilt have time enough for hymns divine,
　　Since heaven's eternal year is thine.
Hear then a mortal Muse thy praise rehearse,
　　　　In no ignoble verse;
But such as thy own voice did practice here,
When thy first fruits of poesy were given,
To make thyself a welcome inmate there,                         *20*
　　　While yet a young probationer,
　　　And candidate of heaven.

If by traduction[1] came thy mind,
　　Our wonder is the less to find
A soul so charming from a stock so good;
Thy father was transfused into thy blood;[2]
So wert thou born into the tuneful strain
(An early, rich, and inexhausted vein).
　　But if thy pre-existing soul
　　Was formed at first with myriads more,                      *30*
It did through all the mighty poets roll
　　Who Greek or Latin laurels wore,
And was that Sappho[3] last, which once it was before.
　　If so, then cease thy flight, O heaven-born mind!
　　Thou hast no dross to purge from thy rich ore;
　　Nor can thy soul a fairer mansion find
　　Than was the beauteous frame she left behind:
Return, to fill or mend the choir of thy celestial kind.

---

[1] inheritance                              [3] female poet of ancient Greece
[2] Anne Killigrew's father was also a poet.

May we presume to say that at thy birth
New joy was sprung in heaven, as well as here on earth? 40
  For sure the milder planets did combine ⎫
On thy auspicious horoscope to shine, ⎬
And even the most malicious were in trine.[4] ⎭
Thy brother-angels at thy birth
  Strung each his lyre, and tuned it high,
  That all the people of the sky
Might know a poetess was born on earth.
  And then, if ever, mortal ears
Had heard the music of the spheres!
And if no clustering swarm of bees 50
On thy sweet mouth distilled their golden dew,
  'Twas that such vulgar miracles
  Heaven had not leisure to renew:
  For all the blest fraternity of love
Solemnized there thy birth, and kept thy holiday above.

  O gracious God! how far have we
Profaned thy heavenly gift of poesy!
Made prostitute and profligate the Muse,
Debased to each obscene and impious use,
Whose harmony was first ordained above 60
For tongues of angels, and for hymns of love!
O wretched we! why were we hurried down
  This lubric and adulterate[5] age
(Nay, added fat pollutions of our own)
  To increase the steaming ordures of the stage?
What can we say to excuse our second fall?
Let this thy vestal,[6] Heaven, atone for all:
Her Arethusan stream[7] remains unsoiled,
Unmixed with foreign filth, and undefiled;
Her wit was more than man, her innocence a child? 70

  Art she had none, yet wanted none,
  For nature did that want supply;
  So rich in treasures of her own,
  She might our boasted stores defy:
Such noble vigor did her verse adorn
That it seemed borrowed where 'twas only born.
  Her morals too were in her bosom bred, ⎫
    By great examples daily fed, ⎬
What in the best of books, her father's life, she read. ⎭
And to be read herself she need not fear; ⎫ 80
Each test and every light her Muse will bear, ⎬
Through Epictetus with his lamp were there.[8] ⎭
  Even love (for love sometimes her Muse expressed)

---

4 an auspicious relationship in the position of the planets     5 lascivious and corrupt    6 virgin attendant upon a shrine     7 a source of pastoral inspiration    8 though judged by the most rigorous standards

Was but a lambent flame, which played about her breast,
Light as the vapors of a morning dream;
So cold herself, whilst she such warmth expressed,
'Twas Cupid bathing in Diana's stream.

Born to the spacious empire of the Nine,[9]
One would have thought she should have been content
To manage well that mighty government;                          *90*
But when can young ambitious souls confine?
   To the next realm she stretched her sway,
   For painture near adjoining lay,
A plenteous province, and alluring prey.
   A chamber of dependences was framed
(As conquerors will never want pretense,
   When armed, to justify the offense)
And the whole fief in right of Poetry she claimed.
The country open lay without defense;
For poets frequent inroads there had made,                      *100*
   And perfectly could represent
   The shape, the face, with every lineament;
And all the large demains which the dumb Sister[10] swayed,
   All bowed beneath her government,
   Received in triumph wheresoe'er she went.
Her pencil drew whate'er her soul designed,
And oft the happy draft surpassed the image in her mind.
   The sylvan scenes of herds and flocks
   And fruitful plains and barren rocks;
   Of shallow brooks that flowed so clear                 *110*
   The bottom did the top appear;
   Of deeper too and ampler floods,
   Which, as in mirrors, showed the woods;
   Of lofty trees, with sacred shades
And pérspectives of pleasant glades,
Where nymphs of brightest form appear,
And shaggy satyrs standing near,
Which them at once admire and fear;
The ruins, too, of some majestic piece,
Boasting the power of ancient Rome or Greece,                   *120*
   Whose statues, friezes, columns broken lie,
   And, though defaced, the wonder of the eye:
   What nature, art, bold fiction e'er durst frame,
   Her forming hand gave feature to the name.
   So strange a concourse ne'er was seen before
But when the peopled ark the whole creation bore.

   The scene then changed; with bold erected look
Our martial king[11] the sight with reverence strook;

---

[9] the Muses
[10] While later tradition assigned specific arts to
Muses, none is identified as in charge of painting.

Perhaps Dryden identifies as the "dumb Sister,"
Erato, who presided over mime.
[11] James II, who had been a soldier

For, not content to express his outward part,
Her hand called out the image of his heart: 130
His warlike mind, his soul devoid of fear,
His high-designing thoughts were figured there,
As when by magic, ghosts are made appear.
    Our phoenix queen[12] was portrayed, too, so bright,
Beauty alone could beauty take so right:
Her dress, her shape, her matchless grace
Were all observed, as well as heavenly face.
With such a peerless majesty she stands
As in that day she took the crown from sacred hands;
Before a train of heroines was seen, 140
In beauty foremost, as in rank the queen.
Thus nothing to her genius was denied,
    But like a ball of fire, the further thrown,
    Still with a greater blaze she shone,
And her bright soul broke out on every side.
What next she had designed, heaven only knows;
To such immoderate growth her conquest rose
That fate alone its progress could oppose.

    Now all those charms, that blooming grace,
The well-proportioned shape, and beauteous face, 150
Shall never more be seen by mortal eyes:
In earth the much-lamented virgin lies!
    Not wit nor piety could fate prevent;
    Nor was the cruel destiny content
    To finish all the murder at a blow,
    To sweep at once her life and beauty too;
But, like a hardened felon, took a pride
    To work more mischievously slow,
And plundered first, and then destroyed.
O double sacrilege on things divine, 160
To rob the relic, and deface the shrine!
    But thus Orinda died:[13]
Heaven, by the same disease, did both translate,
As equal were their souls, so equal was their fate.

    Meantime her warlike brother on the seas
His waving streamers to the winds displays,
And vows for his return with vain devotion pays.
    Ah, generous youth, that wish forbear;
    The winds too soon will waft thee here!
    Slack all thy sails, and fear to come, 170
Alas, thou know'st not thou art wrecked at home!
No more shalt thou behold thy sister's face;
Thou hast already had her last embrace.

---

12 of unique beauty                    Killigrew, also died of smallpox.
13 Katharine Phillips, a contemporary of Anne

But look aloft, and if thou kenn'st from far,
Among the Pleiads,[14] a new-kindled star,
If any sparkles than the rest more bright,
'Tis she that shines in that propitious light.

When in mid-air the golden trump shall sound,
 To raise the nations under ground;
 When in the Valley of Jehosaphat       *180*
The judging God shall close the book of fate,
 And there the last assizes keep
 For those who wake and those who sleep;
 When rattling bones together fly
 From the four corners of the sky;
When sinews o'er the skeletons are spread,
Those clothed with flesh, and life inspires the dead;
The sacred poets first shall hear the sound,
And foremost from the tomb shall bound,
For they are covered with the lightest ground,    *190*
And straight, with inborn vigor, on the wing,
Like mounting larks, to the new morning sing.
There thou, sweet saint, before the choir shalt go,
As harbinger of heaven, the way to show,
The way which thou so well hast learned below.  *(1686)*

---

# A Song for Saint Cecilia's[1] Day, November 22, 1687

From harmony, from heavenly harmony
 This universal frame began;
 When Nature underneath a heap
  Of jarring atoms lay,
  And could not heave her head,
The tuneful voice was heard from high,
  Arise, ye more than dead.
The cold and hot and moist and dry[2]
 In order to their stations leap,
  And Music's power obey.  *10*
From harmony, from heavenly harmony
 This universal frame began;
  From harmony to harmony
Through all the compass of the notes it ran,
The diapason closing full in Man.

What passion cannot Music raise and
  quell?
  When Jubal[3] struck the corded
   shell,[4]
 His listening brethren stood around,
  And, wondering, on their faces fell
To worship that celestial sound. *20*
Less than a god they thought there could
  not dwell
 Within the hollow of that shell,
 That spoke so sweetly, and so well.
What passion cannot Music raise and
  quell?

The trumpet's loud clangor
  Excites us to arms
With shrill notes of anger
  And mortal alarms.
The double, double, double beat
  Of the thundering drum *30*

---

14 a cluster of seven stars; a name applied to a group of illustrious persons
1 patron saint of music, to whom the invention of the organ was attributed
2 the attributes associated with earth, fire, water, and air, the four elements of ancient science
3 said in Genesis to be "the father of all such as handle the harp and organ"
4 The lyre was originally made of tortoise shell.

Cries, "Hark! the foes come;
Charge, charge, 'tis too late to retreat!"

The soft complaining flute
In dying notes discovers
The woes of hopeless lovers,
Whose dirge is whispered by the
warbling lute.

Sharp violins proclaim
Their jealous pangs and desperation,
Fury, frantic indignation,
Depth of pains and height of passion,  40
For the fair, disdainful dame.

But, oh! what art can teach,
What human voice can reach
The sacred organ's praise?
Notes inspiring holy love,
Notes that wing their heavenly ways
To mend the choirs above.

Orpheus[5] could lead the savage race,
And trees unrooted left their place,
Sequacious[6] of the lyre,  50
But bright Cecilia raised the wonder
higher;
When to her organ vocal breath was
given,
An angel heard, and straight appeared,
Mistaking earth for heaven.

As from the power of sacred lays
The spheres began to move,
And sung the great Creator's praise
To all the blest above;
So when the last and dreadful hour
This crumbling pageant shall devour,  60

The trumpet shall be heard on high,
The dead shall live, the living die,
And Music shall untune the sky.  *(1687)*

# Song to a Fair Young Lady Going Out of Town in the Spring

Ask not the cause, why sullen spring
So long delays her flowers to bear;
Why warbling birds forget to sing,
And winter storms invert the year?
Chloris is gone; and fate provides
To make it spring, where she resides.

Chloris is gone, the cruel fair;
She cast not back a pitying eye:
But left her lover in despair;
To sigh, to languish, and to die:  10
Ah, how can those fair eyes endure
To give the wounds they will not cure!

Great god of love, why hast thou made
A face that can all hearts command,
That all religions can invade,
And change the laws of every land?
Where thou hadst placed such power
before,
Thou shou'dst have made her mercy
more.

When Chloris to the temple comes,
Adoring crowds before her fall;  20
She can restore the dead from tombs,
And every life but mine recall.
I only am by love designed
To be the victim for mankind.  *(1693)*

# An Ode: On the Death of Mr. Purcell

Mark how the lark and linnet sing,
With rival notes
They strain their warbling throats
To welcome in the spring.
But in the close of night,
When Philomel begins her heavenly lay,

---

[5] in Greek mythology, the greatest poet and a musician of great power     [6] inclined to follow

They cease their mutual spite,
Drink in her music with delight,
And listening and silent, and silent and listening, and
             listening and silent obey.
So ceased the rival crew when Purcell came,                    10
They sung no more, or only sung his fame.
             Struck dumb, they all admired
                   The godlike man,
             Alas too soon retired,
                   As he too late began.
We beg not Hell our Orpheus to restore;[1]
             Had he been there,
             Their sovereign's fear
Had sent him back before.
The power of harmony too well they knew;                        20
He long e'er this had tuned their jarring sphere,
             And left no Hell below.

The heavenly choir, who heard his notes from high,
Let down the scale of music from the sky:
             They handed him along,
And all the way he taught, and all the way they sung.
Ye brethren of the lyre and tuneful voice,
Lament his lot, but at your own rejoice.
Now live secure and linger out your days,
The gods are pleased alone with Purcell's lays,                30
             Nor know to mend their choice.        (*1696*)

## Alexander's Feast, or the Power of Music

'Twas at the royal feast for
     Persia won
By Philip's warlike son—[1]
Aloft in awful state
The godlike hero sate
On his imperial throne;

His valiant peers were placed
     around,
Their brows with roses and with
     myrtles bound,

(So should desert in arms be
     crowned);
The lovely Thais[2] by his side
Sat like a blooming Eastern
     bride                                                      10
In flower of youth and beauty's
     pride:—
Happy, happy, happy pair!
     None but the brave
     None but the brave
None but the brave deserves the
     fair!
Timotheus[3] placed on high
Amid the tuneful choir

---

[1] Orpheus, a minstrel of Thrace endowed with exceptional musical powers, descended into Hell in an effort to recover his dead wife Eurydice. His playing on the lyre so charmed Hades and Persephone, the king and queen of Hell, that he won permission to return to earth with Eurydice, provided he did not look at her on the way. He turned to see that she was following, and she was snatched back into death.

[1] Alexander the Great (356–323 B.C.), King of Macedonia, defeated the Persians under Darius III in 334 and 331 B.C. After the second of these battles, Alexander occupied Persepolis, the Persian capital.
[2] a courtesan who, according to legend, persuaded Alexander to set fire to the Persian palaces
[3] the court musician

With flying fingers touched the lyre:
The trembling notes ascend the sky
And heavenly joys inspire.                      20
The song began from Jove [4]
Who left his blissful seats above—
Such is the power of mighty love!
A dragon's fiery form belied the god;
Sublime on radiant spires he rode
When he to fair Olympia [5] pressed,
And while he sought her snowy breast,
Then round her slender waist he curled,
And stamped an image of himself, a
        sovereign of the world.
—The listening crowd admire the lofty
        sound;                                  30
A present deity! they shout around:
A present deity! the vaulted roofs
        rebound:
With ravished ears
The monarch hears,
Assumes the god,
Affects to nod
And seems to shake the spheres.

      The praise of Bacchus [6] then the sweet
        musician sung,
Of Bacchus ever fair and ever young:
The jolly god in triumph comes;             40
Sound the trumpets, beat the drums!
Flushed with a purple grace
He shows his honest face:
Now give the hautboys [7] breath; he
        comes, he comes!
Bacchus, ever fair and young,
Drinking joys did first ordain;
Bacchus' blessings are a treasure,
Drinking is the soldier's pleasure:
Rich the treasure,
Sweet the pleasure,                          50
Sweet is pleasure after pain.

      Soothed with the sound, the king grew
        vain;
Fought all his battles o'er again,
And thrice he routed all his foes, and
        thrice he slew the slain!
The master saw the madness rise,

His glowing cheeks, his ardent eyes;
And while he Heaven and Earth defied
Changed his hand and checked his
        pride.
He chose a mournful Muse
Soft pity to infuse:                         60
He sung Darius great and good,
By too severe a fate
Fallen, fallen, fallen, fallen,
Fallen from his high estate.
And weltering in his blood;
Deserted at his utmost need
By those his former bounty fed;
On the bare earth exposed he lies
With not a friend to close his eyes.
—With downcast looks the joyless victor
        sate,                                   70
Revolving in his altered soul
The various turns of chance below;
And now and then a sigh he stole,
And tears began to flow.

      The mighty master smiled to see
That love was in the next degree;
'Twas but a kindred sound to move,
For pity melts the mind to love.
Softly sweet, in Lydian measures [8]
Soon he soothed his soul to pleasures.   80
War, he sung, is toil and trouble,
Honour but an empty bubble;
Never ending, still beginning,
Fighting still, and still destroying;
If the world be worth thy winning,
Think, O think, it worth enjoying:
Lovely Thais sits beside thee,
Take the good the gods provide thee!
—The many rend the skies with loud
        applause;
So Love was crowned, but Music won
        the cause.                              90
The prince, unable to conceal his pain,
Gazed on the fair
Who caused his care,
And sighed and looked, sighed and
        looked,
Sighed and looked, and sighed again:

---

4 Jupiter, king of heaven and of the gods
5 Olympias, Alexander's mother

6 god of wine      7 oboes
8 languid, effeminate music

At length with love and wine at once
    oppressed
The vanquished victor sunk upon her
    breast.

    Now strike the golden lyre again:
A louder yet, and yet a louder strain!
Break his bands of sleep asunder        *100*
And rouse him like a rattling peal of
    thunder.
Hark, hark! the horrid sound
Has raised up his head:
As awaked from the dead
And amazed he stares around.
Revenge, revenge, Timotheus cries,
See the Furies[9] arise!
See the snakes that they rear
How they hiss in their hair,
And the sparkles that flash from their
    eyes!                                *110*
Behold a ghastly band,
Each a torch in his hand!
Those are Grecian ghosts, that in battle
    were slain
And unburied remain
Inglorious on the plain:
Give the vengeance due
To the valiant crew!
Behold how they toss their torches on
    high,

How they point to the Persian abodes
And glittering temples of their hostile
    gods.                               *120*
—The princes applaud with a furious joy:
And the king seized a flambeau with zeal
    to destroy;
Thais led the way
To light him to his prey,
And like another Helen, fired another
    Troy![10]

    —Thus, long ago,
Ere heaving bellows learned to blow,
While organs yet were mute,
Timotheus, to his breathing flute
And sounding lyre                       *130*
Could swell the soul to rage, or kindle
    soft desire.
At last divine Cecilia[11] came,
Inventress of the vocal frame;
The sweet enthusiast from her sacred
    store
Enlarged the former narrow bounds,
And added length to solemn sounds,
With Nature's mother-wit, and arts
    unknown before.
—Let old Timotheus yield the prize
Or both divide the crown;
He raised a mortal to the skies;        *140*
She drew an angel down!   (*1697*)

# THOMAS TRAHERNE / 1636–1674

## Insatiableness

This busy, vast, inquiring soul
    Brooks no control,
    No limits will endure,
    Nor any rest; it will all see,
Not time alone, but ev'n eternity.
    What is it? Endless sure.

'Tis mean ambition to desire
    A single world;
    To many I aspire
    Though one upon another hurled;     *10*
Nor will they all, if they be all confined,
    Delight my mind.

---

[9] the Avenging Deities, three loathsome sisters
who punished many crimes
[10] In Homer's *Iliad*, the abduction of Helen
occasioned the Trojan War.
[11] patron saint of music, reputed inventor of the
organ (the "vocal frame" of l. 133)

This busy, vast, inquiring soul
    Brooks no control;
    'Tis very curious too.
Each one of all those worlds must be
Enriched with infinite variety
    And worth, or 'twill not do.

'Tis nor delight nor perfect pleasure
    To have a purse                    20

That hath a bottom in its treasure,
Since I must thence endless expense
    disburse.
Sure there's a God, for else there's no
    delight,
    One infinite.

## The Salutation

These little limbs,
These eyes and hands which here I find,
This panting heart wherewith my life begins;
    Where have ye been? Behind
What curtain were ye from me hid so long?
Where was, in what abyss, my new made tongue?

When silent I
So many thousand thousand years
Beneath the dust did in a chaos lie,
    How could I smiles, or tears,                    10
Or lips, or hands, or eyes, or ears perceive?
Welcome ye treasures which I new receive.

I that so long
Was nothing from eternity,
Did little think such joys as ear and tongue
    To celebrate or see:
Such sounds to hear, such hands to feel, such feet,
Such eyes and objects on the ground to meet.

New burnisht joys!
Which finest gold and pearl excell!                    20
Such sacred treasures are the limbs of boys
    In which a soul doth dwell:
Their organizéd joints and azure veins
More wealth include than the dead world contains.

From dust I rise
And out of nothing now awake;
These brighter regions which salute mine eyes
    A gift from God I take:
The earth, the stars, the light, the lofty skies,
The sun and stars are mine; if these I prize.                    30

A stranger here
Strange things doth meet, strange glory see;
Strange treasures lodged in this fair world appear,
    Strange all and new to me:
But that they are mine should be who nothing was,
That strangest is of all, yet brought to pass.

## Shadows in the Water

In unexperienced infancy
Many a sweet mistake doth lie:
Mistake though false, intending true;
A seeming somewhat more than view;
    That doth instruct the mind
    In things that lie behind,
And many secrets to us show
Which afterwards we come to know.

Thus did I by the water's brink
Another world beneath me think;          10
And while the lofty spacious skies
Reverséd there, abused mine eyes,
    I fancied other feet
    Came mine to touch or meet;
As by some puddle I did play
Another world within it lay.

Beneath the water people drowned,
Yet with another heaven crowned,
In spacious regions seemed to go
As freely moving to and fro:             20
    In bright and open space
    I saw their very face;
Eyes, hands, and feet they had like mine;
Another sun did with them shine.

'Twas strange that people there should
      walk,
And yet I could not hear them talk:
That through a little watery chink,
Which one dry ox or horse might drink,
    We other worlds should see,
    Yet not admitted be;                 30

And other confines there behold
Of light and darkness, heat and cold.

I called them oft, but called in vain;
No speeches we could entertain:
Yet did I there expect to find
Some other world to please my mind.
    I plainly saw by these
    A new antipodes,
Whom, though they were so plainly seen,
A film kept off that stood between.      40

By walking men's reverséd feet
I chanced another world to meet;
Though it did not to view exceed
A phantom, 'tis a world indeed,
    Where skies beneath us shine,
    And earth by art divine
Another face presents below,
Where people's feet against ours go.

Within the regions of the air,
Compassed about with heavens fair,       50
Great tracts of land there may be found
Enriched with fields and fertile ground;
    Where many numerous hosts
    In those far distant coasts,
For other great and glorious ends
Inhabit, my yet unknown friends.

O ye that stand upon the brink,
Whom I so near me through the chink
With wonder see: what faces there,
Whose feet, whose bodies, do ye wear? 60
    I my companions see
    In you, another me.
They seemed others, but are we;
Our second selves these shadows be.

## SIR CHARLES SEDLEY / 1639?–1701

### Advice to the Old Beaux

Scrape no more your harmless chins,
  Old beaux, in hope to please;
You should repent your former sins,
  Not study their increase;
Young awkward fops, may shock our
    sight,
But you offend by day and night.

In vain the coachman turns about,
  And whips the dappled greys;
When the old ogler looks out,
  We turn away our face.          *10*
True love and youth will ever charm,
But both affected, cannot warm.

Summer fruits we highly prize,
  They kindly cool the blood;
But winter berries we despise,
  And leave 'em in the wood;
On the bush they may look well,
But gathered, lose both taste and smell.

That you languish, that you die,
  Alas, is but too true;          *20*
Yet tax not us with cruelty,
  Who daily pity you.
Nature henceforth alone accuse,
In vain we grant, if she refuse.          (*1693*)

### Get You Gone

Get you gone, you will undo me,
If you love me don't pursue me;
Let that inclination perish
Which I dare no longer cherish.
With harmless thoughts I did begin,
But in the crowd love entered in;
I knew him not, he was so gay,
So innocent and full of play.
At every hour, in every place,
I either saw or formed your face;          *10*
All that in plays was finely writ
Fancy for you and me did fit;
My dreams at night were all of you,
Such as till then I never knew.
I sported thus with young desire,
Never intending to go higher;
But now his teeth and claws are grown,
Let me the fatal lion shun.
You found me harmless; leave me so;
For, were I not, you'd leave me too.          *20*

## EDWARD TAYLOR / 1645?–1729

### The Preface

Infinity, when all things it beheld,
In nothing, and of nothing all did build,
Upon what base was fixed the lathe wherein
He turned this globe and riggaled[1] it so trim?
Who blew the bellows of His furnace vast?
Or held the mould wherein the world was cast?

---

[1] rigged

241

Who laid its corner-stone? On whose command?
Where stand the pillars upon which it stands?
Who laced and filleted the earth so fine
With rivers like green ribbons smaragdine?[2]                    10
Who made the seas its selvedge, and it locks
Like a quilt ball within a silver box?
Who spread its canopy? Or curtains spun?
Who in this bowling alley bowled the sun?
Who made it always when it rises, set:
To go at once both down and up to get?
Who the curtain rods made for this tapestry?
Who hung the twinkling lanthorns in the sky?
Who? who did this? or who is he? Why, know
It's only Might Almighty this did do.                          20
His hand hath made this noble work which stands
His glorious handiwork not made by hands.
Who spake all things from nothing; and with ease
Can speak all things to nothing, if He please.
Whose little finger at His pleasure can
Out mete ten thousand worlds with half a span.
Whose might almighty can by half a look
Root up rocks and rock the hills by th' roost.
Can take this mighty world up in His hand
And shake it like a squitchen[3] or a wand.                    30
Whose single frown will make the heavens shake
Like as an aspen leaf the wind makes quake.
Oh! what a might is this! Whose single frown
Doth shake the world as it would shake it down?
Which all from nothing fet, from nothing all;
Hath all on nothing set, lets nothing fall.
Gave all to nothing man indeed, whereby
Through nothing man all might Him glorify.
In nothing is embossed the brightest gem
More precious than all preciousness in them.                   40
But nothing man did throw down all by sin,
And darkened that lightsome gem in him,
    That now His brightest diamond is grown
    Darker by far than any coal-pit stone.

## The Ebb and Flow

When first Thou on me, Lord, wrought'st Thy sweet print,
    My heart was made Thy tinder box.
My 'ffections were Thy tinder in't:
    Where fell Thy sparks by drops.
Those holy sparks of heavenly fire that came
Did ever catch and often out would flame.

--------

[2] emerald    [3] switch

But now my heart is made Thy censer trim,
    Full of the golden altar's fire,
    To offer up sweet incense in
        Unto Thyself entire:                                  *10*
I find my tinder scarce Thy sparks can feel
That drop out from Thy holy flint and steel.

Hence doubts out-bud for fear Thy fire in me
    'S a mocking Ignis Fatuus,
    Or lest Thine altar's fire out be,
        It's hid in ashes thus.
Yet when the bellows of Thy spirit blow
Away mine ashes, then Thy fire doth glow.

## Meditation 6

### CANTICLES 2:1. I AM THE LILY OF THE VALLEYS

Am I Thy gold? or purse, Lord, for Thy wealth,
    Whether in mine or mint refined for Thee?
I'm counted so, but count me o'er Thyself,
    Lest gold-washed face, and brass in heart I be.
    I fear my touchstone touches when I try
    Me and my counted gold too overly.

Am I new minted by Thy stamp indeed?
    Mine eyes are dim; I cannot clearly see.
Be Thou my spectacles that I may read
        Thine image and inscription stamped on me.      *10*
    If Thy bright image do upon me stand,
    I am a golden angel[1] in Thy hand.

Lord, make my soul Thy plate; Thine image bright
    Within the circle of the same enfoil.
And on its brims in golden letters write
    Thy superscription in an holy style.
    Then I shall be Thy money, Thou my hoard;
    Let my Thy angel be, be Thou my Lord.

## Housewifery

Make me, O Lord, Thy spinning-wheel complete.
    Thy holy Word my distaff[1] make for me;
Make mine affections Thy swift flyers[2] neat;
    And make my soul Thy holy spool to be;
    My conversation make to be Thy reel,
    And reel the yarn thereon spun of Thy wheel.

[1] an English gold coin of the fifteenth to seventeenth centuries

[1] the staff holding the fibers in spinning

[2] the part of the spinning wheel that twists the fibers

Make me Thy loom then; knit therein this twine;
　　And make Thy Holy Spirit, Lord, wind quills;[3]
Then weave the web Thyself. The yarn is fine.
　　Thine ordinances make my fulling[4] mills.                    *10*
　　　　Then dye the same in heavenly colors choice,
　　All pinked[5] with varnished flowers of paradise.

Then clothe therewith mine understanding, will,
　　Affections,[6] judgment, conscience, memory,
My words and actions, that their shine may fill
　　My ways with glory and Thee glorify.
　　Then mine apparel shall display before Ye
　　That I am clothed in holy robes for glory.

---

[3] bobbins to hold the thread in the shuttle of the loom

[4] cleaning and thickening cloth after weaving

[5] decorated　　　[6] emotions

# The Eighteenth Century

## LATER BALLADS AND FOLK SONGS

### Edward

"Why dois your brand sae drap wi bluid,
    Edward, Edward,
Why dois your brand sae drap wi bluid,
    And why sae sad gang¹ yee O?"
"O I hae killed my hauke sae guid,
    Mither, mither,
O I hae killed my hauke sae guid,
    And I had nae mair bot hee O."

"Your haukis bluid was nevir sae reid,
    Edward, Edward,
Your haukis bluid was nevir sae reid,        10
    My deir son I tell thee O."
"O I hae killed my reid-roan steid,
    Mither, mither,
O I hae killed my reid-roan steid,
    That erst was sae fair and frie O."

"Your steid was auld, and ye hae got mair,
    Edward, Edward,
Your steid was auld, and ye hae got mair,
    Sum other dule² ye drie³ O."        20
"O I hae killed my fadir deir,
    Mither, mither,
Oh I hae killed my fadir deir,
    Alas, and wae is mee O!"

"And whatten penance wul ye drie for that,
    Edward, Edward,
And whatten penance will ye drie for that?
    My deir son, now tell me O."
"Ile set my feit in yonder boat,
    Mither, mither,        30
Ile set my feit in yonder boat,
    And Ile fare ovir the sea O."

"And what wul ye doe wi your towirs and your ha,⁴
    Edward, Edward?
And what wul ye doe wi your towirs and your ha,
    That were sae fair to see O?"

---

¹ go    ² woe    ³ suffer    ⁴ hall

"Ile let thame stand tul they doun fa,
    Mither, mither,
Ile let thame stand tul they doun fa,
    For here nevir mair maun I bee O."        *40*

"And what wul ye leive to your bairns and your wife,
    Edward, Edward?
And what wul ye leive to your bairns and your wife,
    Whan ye gang ovir the Sea O?"
"The warldis room, late them beg thrae life,
    Mither, mither,
The warldis room, late them beg thrae life,
    For thame nevir mair wul I see O."

"And what wul ye leive to your ain mither deir,
    Edward, Edward,        *50*
And what wul ye leive to your ain mither deir?
    My deir son, now tell me O."
"The curse of hell frae me sall ye beir,
    Mither, mither,
The curse of hell frae me sall ye beir,
    Sic counseils ye gave to me O."

## Sir Patrick Spens

The king sits in Dumferling toune,
    Drinking the blude-reid wine:
"O whar will I get guid sailor,
    To sail this schip of mine?"

Up and spak an eldern knicht,
    Sat at the kings richt kne:
"Sir Patrick Spens is the best sailor,
    That sails upon the se."

The king has written a braid letter,
    And signd it wi his hand,    *10*
And sent it to Sir Patrick Spens,
    Was walking on the sand.

The first line that Sir Patrick red,
    A loud lauch lauchéd[1] he;
The next line that Sir Patrick red,
    The teir blinded his ee.

"O wha is this has don this deid,
    This ill deid don to me,
To send me out this time o' the yeir,
    To sail upon the se!    *20*

"Mak hast, make hast, my mirry men all
    Our guid schip sails the morne:"
"O say na sae, my master deir,
    For I feir a deadlie storme.

"Late, late yestreen I saw the new moone,
    Wi the auld moone in hir arme,
And I feir, I feir, my deir master,
    That we will cum to harme."

O our Scots nobles wer richt laith[2]
    To weet their cork-heild schoone,[3]    *30*
Bot lang owre[4] a' the play wer playd,
    Their hats they swam aboone.

O lang, lang may their ladies sit,
    Wi thair fans into their hand,
Or eir they se Sir Patrick Spens
    Cum sailing to the land.

O lang, lang may the ladies stand,
    Wi thair gold kems in their hair
Waiting for thar ain deir lords,
    For they'll se thame na mair.    *40*

Half owre,[5] half owre to Aberdour,
    It's fiftie fadom deip,
And thair lies guid Sir Patrick Spens,
    Wi the Scots lords at his feit.

---

[1] laughed    [2] loath    [3] shoes    [4] ere    [5] over

## The Unquiet Grave

Cold blows the wind to my true love,
    And gently drops the rain,
I never had but one sweethcart,
    And in greenwood she lies slain,
    And in greenwood she lies slain.

I'll do as much for my sweetheart
    As any young man may;
I'll sit and mourn all on her grave
    For a twelvemonth and a day.

When the twelvemonth and one day was past,      *10*
    The ghost began to speak;
"Why sittest here all on my grave,
    And will not let me sleep?"

"There's one thing that I want, sweetheart,
    There's one thing that I crave;
And that is a kiss from your lily-white lips—
    Then I'll go from your grave."

"My breast it is as cold as clay,
    My breath smells earthly strong;
And if you kiss my cold clay lips,      *20*
    Your days they won't be long.

"Go fetch me water from the desert,
    And blood from out of a stone;
Go fetch me milk from a fair maid's breast
    That a young man never had known."

"O down in yonger grove, sweetheart,
    Where you and I would walk,
The first flower that ever I saw
    Is withered to a stalk.

"The stalk is withered and dry, sweetheart,      *30*
    And the flower will never return;
And since I lost my own sweetheart,
    What can I do but mourn?

"When shall we meet again, sweetheart?
    When shall we meet again?"
"When the oaken leaves that fall from the trees
    Are green and spring up again,
    Are green and spring up again."

## Helen of Kirconnell

I wish I were where Helen lies,
Night and day on me she cries;
O that I were where Helen lies
    On fair Kirconnell lea!

Curst be the heart that thought the
    thought,
And curst the hand that fired the shot
When in my arms burd[1] Helen dropt,
    And died to succour me!

---
[1] lady

O think na ye my heart was sair,
When my Love dropt down and spake
   nae mair!                       10
I laid her down wi' meikle[2] care
  On fair Kirconnell lea.

As I went down the water-side,
None but my foe to be my guide,
None but my foe to be my guide
  On fair Kirconnell lea;

I lighted down my sword to draw,
I hacked him in pieces sma',
I hacked him in pieces sma',
  For her sake that died for me.    20

O Helen fair, beyond compare!
I'll make a garland o' thy hair
Shall bind my heart for evermair
  Until the day I dee!

O that I were where Helen lies!
Night and day on me she cries;
Out of my bed she bids me rise,
  Says, "Haste, and come to me!"

O Helen fair! O Helen chaste!
If I were with thee, I were blest,    30
Where thou lies low and takes thy rest,
  On fair Kirconnell lea.

I wish my grave were growing green,
A winding-sheet drawn over my een,
And I in Helen's arms lying,
  On fair Kirconnell lea.

I wish I were where Helen lies!
Night and day on me she cries;
And I am weary of the skies,
  Since my Love died for me.    40

## Young Molly Bán

Come all you young fellows that follow the gun,
Beware of goin' a-shootin' by the late setting sun.
It might happen to anyone as it happened to me,
To shoot your own true love in-under a tree.

She was going to her uncle's, when the shower it came on,
She went under a bush, the rain for to shun.
With her apron all around her, I took her for a swan
And I levelled my gun and I shot Molly Bán.

I ran to her uncle's in haste and great fear,
Saying Uncle, dear Uncle, I've shot Molly dear.    10
With her apron all around her I took her for a swan,
But oh and alas! it was my Molly Bán.

I shot my own true love—alas I'm undone,
While she was in the shade by the setting of the sun;
If I thought she was there I'd caress her tenderly,
And soon I'd get married to my own dear Molly.

My curses on you, Toby, that lent me your gun
To go out a-shooting by the late setting sun,
I rubbed her fair temples and found she was dead;
A fountain of tears for my Molly I shed.    20

Up comes my father and his locks they were grey,
Stay in your own country and don't run away,
Stay in your country till your trial comes on,
And I'll see you set free by the laws of the land.

---

[2] much

Oh the maids of this country they will all be very glad
When they hear the sad news that my Molly is dead.
Take them all in their hundreds, set them all in a row,
Molly Bán she shone above them like a mountain of snow.

## The Old Orange Flute

In the County Tyrone, in the town of Dungannon,
Where many a ruction myself had a han' in,
Bob Williamson lived, a weaver by trade,
And all of us thought him a stout Orange blade.
On the Twelfth of July as around it would come
Bob played on the flute to the sound of the drum;
You may talk of your harp, your piano or lute,
But there's nothing compared with the old Orange flute.

But Bob the deceiver he took us all in,
For he married a Papish called Brigid McGinn,　　　　　　　*10*
Turned Papish himself, and forsook the old cause
That gave us our freedom, religion, and laws.
Now the boys of the place made some comment upon it,
And Bob had to fly to the Province of Connacht.
He fled with his wife and his fixings to boot,
And along with the latter his old Orange flute.

At the chapel on Sundays, to atone for past deeds,
He said *Paters* and *Aves* and counted his beads,
Till after some time, at the priest's own desire,
He went with his old flute to play in the choir.　　　　　　　*20*
He went with his old flute to play for the Mass,
And the instrument shivered and sighed: "Oh, alas!"
And blow as he would, though it made a great noise,
The flute would play only "The Protestant Boys."

Bob jumped, and he started, and got in a flutter,
And threw his old flute in the best Holy Water;
He thought that this charm would bring some other sound.
When he blew it again, it played "Croppies[1] Lie Down";
And for all he could whistle, and finger, and blow,
To play Papish music he found it no go;　　　　　　　*30*
"Kick the Pope," "The Boyne[2] Water," it freely would sound,
But one Papish squeak in it couldn't be found.

At a council of priests that was held the next day,
They decided to banish the old flute away,
For they couldn't knock heresy out of its head
And they bought Bob a new one to play in its stead.

---

[1] Irish rebels of 1798 who cropped their hair to show sympathy for the French Revolution
[2] The Battle of the Boyne in 1690, in which William III and the Protestant army defeated the Catholic James II, was fought across the river Boyne.

So the old flute was doomed and its fate was pathetic;
'Twas fastened and burned at the stake as heretic.
While the flames roared around it they heard a strange noise—
'Twas the old flute still whistling "The Protestant Boys."                    *40*

## MATTHEW PRIOR / 1664–1721

### A Simile

Dear Thomas, didst thou never pop
Thy head into a tin-man's shop?
There, Thomas, didst thou never see
('Tis but by way of simile)
A squirrel spend his little rage
In jumping round a rolling cage?
The cage, as either side turned up,
Striking a ring of bells atop—?
   Moved in the orb, pleased with the chimes,
The foolish creature thinks he climbs;                    *10*
But here or there, turn wood or wire,
He never gets two inches higher.
   So fares it with those merry blades,
That frisk it under Pindus' shades.[1]
In noble songs and lofty odes,
They tread on stars and talk with gods;
Still dancing in an airy round,
Still pleased with their own verses' sound—
Brought back, how fast soe'er they go,
Always aspiring, always low.                    *20*

### For My Own Monument

As doctors give physic by way of prevention,
   Matt, alive and in health, of his tombstone took care,
For delays are unsafe, and his pious intention
   May haply be never fulfilled by his heir.

Then take Matt's word for it, the sculptor is paid,
   That the figure is fine, pray believe your own eye,
Yet credit but lightly what more may be said,
   For we flatter ourselves, and teach marble to lie.

---

[1] a ridge of rugged mountains in Greece which Prior may associate with Pindar, a Greek lyric poet of the fifth century B.C., noted for his odes in a grand style

Yet counting as far as to fifty, his years,
　　His virtues and vices were as other men's are,                     *10*
High hopes he conceived, and he smothered great fears,
　　In a life parti-colored, half pleasure, half care.

Nor to business a drudge, nor to faction a slave,
　　He strove to make interest and freedom agree;
In public employments industrious and grave,
　　And alone with his friends, Lord how merry was he.

Now in equipage stately, now humbly on foot,
　　Both fortunes he tried, but to neither would trust,
And whirled in the round, as the wheel turned about
　　He found riches had wings, and knew man was but dust.       *20*

This verse little polished, though mighty sincere
　　Sets neither his titles nor merit to view,
It says that his relics collected lie here,
　　And no mortal yet knows too if this may be true.

Fierce robbers there are that infest the highway
　　So Matt may be killed, and his bones never found,
False witness at court, and fierce tempests at sea,
　　So Matt may yet chance to be hanged, or be drowned.

If his bones lie in earth, roll in sea, fly in air,
　　To Fate we must yield, and the thing is the same,             *30*
And if passing thou giv'st him a smile or a tear,
　　He cares not—yet prithee be kind to his fame.   (*1740*)


# JONATHAN SWIFT / 1667–1745


## To Their Excellencies the Lords Justices of Ireland, the Humble Petition of Frances Harris, Who Must Starve and Die a Maid if It Miscarries

*Humbly Showeth.*
That I went to warm myself in Lady *Betty's* Chamber, because I was cold,
And I had in a Purse, seven Pound, four Shillings and six Pence (besides
　　Farthings) in Money, and Gold;
So because I had been buying things for my *Lady* last Night,
I was resolved to tell[1] my Money, to see if it was right:
Now you must know, because my Trunk has a very bad Lock,
Therefore all the Money I have, which, *God* knows, is a very small Stock,

---
[1] count (cf. bank *teller*)

I keep in a Pocket tied about my Middle, next my Smock.
So when I went to put up my Purse, as *God* would have it, my Smock was
    unripped,
And, instead of putting it into my Pocket, down it slipped;              *10*
Then the Bell rung, and I went down to put my *Lady* to Bed,
And, God knows, I thought my Money was as safe as my Maidenhead.
So when I came up again, I found my Pocket feel very light,
But when I searched, and missed my Purse, *Lord!* I thought I should have sunk
    outright.
*Lord! Madam*, says *Mary*, how d'ye do? Indeed, says I, never worse;
But pray, *Mary*, can you tell what I have done with my Purse!
*Lord* help me, said *Mary*, I never stirred out of this Place!
Nay, said I, I had it in Lady *Betty's* Chamber, that's a plain Case.
So *Mary* got me to Bed, and covered me up warm;
However, she stole away my Garters, that I might do myself no Harm:     *20*
So I tumbled and tossed all Night, as you may very well think,
But hardly ever set my Eyes together, or slept a Wink.
So I was a-dreamed, methought, that we went and searched the Folks round,
And in a Corner of Mrs. *Dukes'* Box, tied in a Rag, the Money was found.
So next morning we told *Whittle*, and he fell a Swearing;
Then my Dame *Wadgar* came, and she, you know, is thick of Hearing;
*Dame*, said I, as loud as I could bawl, do you know what a Loss I have had?
Nay, said she, my Lord *Collway's* Folks are all very sad,
For my Lord *Dromedary* comes a *Tuesday* without fail;
Pugh! said I, but that's not the Business that I ail.             *30*
Says *Cary*, says he, I have been a Servant this Five and Twenty Years, come
    Spring,
And in all the Places I lived, I never heard of such a Thing.
Yes, says the *Steward*, I remember when I was at my Lady *Shrewsbury's*,
Such a thing as this happened, just about the time of *Gooseberries*.
So I went to the Party suspected, and I found her full of Grief;
(Now you must know, of all Things in the World, I hate a Thief.)
However, I was resolved to bring the Discourse slily about,
Mrs. *Dukes*, said I, here's an ugly Accident has happened out;
'Tis not that I value the Money three Skips of a Louse;
But the Thing I stand upon, is the Credit of the House;         *40*
'Tis true, seven Pound, four Shillings, and six Pence, makes a great Hole in my
    Wages,
Besides, as they say, Service is no Inheritance in these Ages.
Now, Mrs. *Dukes*, you know, and every Body understands,
That though 'tis hard to judge, yet Money can't go without Hands.
The *Devil* take me, said she, (blessing herself,) if I ever saw't!
So she roared like a *Bedlam*,[2] as though I had called her all to naught;
So you know, what could I say to her any more,
I e'en left her, and came away as wise as I was before.
Well: But then they would have had me gone to the Cunning Man;
No, said I, 'tis the same Thing, the *Chaplain* will be here anon.     *50*

---

[2] inmate of a lunatic asylum, from the Middle    Mary of Bethlehem Hospital in London
English form of *Bethlehem*, in reference to St.

So the *Chaplain* came in; now the Servants say, he is my Sweet-heart,
Because he's always in my Chamber, and I always take his Part;
So, as the *Devil* would have it, before I was aware, out I blundered,
*Parson*, said I, can you cast a *Nativity*,[3] when a Body's plundered?
(Now you must know, he hates to be called *Parson*, like the *Devil*)
Truly, says he, Mrs. *Nab*, it might become you to be more civil:
If your Money be gone, as a Learned *Divine* said, d'ye see,
You are no *Text* for my Handling, so take that from me:
I was never taken for a Conjurer before, I'd have you to know.
*Lord*, said I, don't be angry, I'm sure I never thought you so;                60
You know, I honour the Cloth, I design to be a *Parson's* Wife,
I never took one in *Your Coat for a Conjurer* in all my Life.
With that, he twisted his Girdle at me like a Rope, as who should say,
Now you may go hang yourself for me, and so went away.
Well; I thought I should have swooned; *Lord*, said I, what shall I do?
I have lost my *Money*, and shall lose my *True-Love* too.
Then my *Lord* called me; *Harry*, said my *Lord*, don't cry,
I'll give something towards thy Loss; and says my *Lady*, so will I.
Oh but, said I, what if after all my Chaplain won't *come to?*
For that, he said (an't please your *Excellencies*) I must Petition You.        70

The Premises tenderly considered, I desire your *Excellencies'* Protection,
And that I may have a Share in next *Sunday's* Collection:
And over and above, that I have your *Excellencies'* Letter,
With an Order for the *Chaplain* aforesaid; or instead of Him, a Better:
And then your poor *Petitioner*, both Night and Day,
Or the *Chaplain* (for 'tis his *Trade*) as in Duty bound, shall ever *Pray*.   (*1709*)


# A Description of the Morning

Now hardly here and there a hackney-coach
Appearing, showed the ruddy morn's approach.
Now Betty from her master's bed had flown,
And softly stole to discompose her own;
The slip-shod 'prentice from his master's door
Had pared the dirt, and sprinkled round the floor.
Now Moll had whirled her mop with dext'rous airs,
Prepared to scrub the entry and the stairs.
The youth with broomy stumps began to trace
The kennel-edge where wheels had worn the place.                10
The small-coal man was heard with cadence deep,
Till drowned in shriller notes of chimney-sweep:
Duns at his lordship's gate began to meet;
And brick-dust Moll had screamed through half the street.
The turnkey now his flock returning sees,
Duly let out a-nights to steal for fees:
The watchful bailiffs take their silent stands,
And schoolboys lag with satchels in their hands.                (*1709*)

---
[3] horoscope

## A Description of a City Shower

Careful observers may foretell the hour  
(By sure prognostics) when to dread a shower:  
While rain depends,[1] the pensive cat gives o'er  
Her frolics, and pursues her tail no more.  
Returning home at night, you'll find the sink  
Strike your offended sense with double stink.  
If you be wise, then go not far to dine;  
You'll spend in coach hire more than save in wine.  
A coming shower your shooting corns presage,  
Old achés throb, your hollow tooth will rage.                    10  
Sauntering in coffeehouse is Dulman seen;  
He damns the climate and complains of spleen.  

    Meanwhile the South, rising with dabbled wings,  
A sable cloud athwart the welkin flings,  
That swilled more liquor than it could contain,  
And, like a drunkard, gives it up again.  
Brisk Susan whips her linen from the rope,  
While the first drizzling shower is borne aslope:  
Such is that sprinkling which some careless quean[2]  
Flirts on you from her mop, but not so clean:                    20  
You fly, invoke the gods; then turning, stop  
To rail; she singing, still whirls on her mop.  
Not yet the dust had shunned the unequal strife,  
But, aided by the wind, fought still for life,  
And wafted with its foe by violent gust,  
'Twas doubtful which was rain and which was dust.  
Ah! where must needy poet seek for aid,  
When dust and rain at once his coat invade?  
Sole coat, where dust cemented by the rain  
Erects the nap, and leaves a mingled stain.                      30  

    Now in contiguous drops the flood comes down,  
Threatening with deluge this devoted town.  
To shops in crowds the daggled females fly,  
Pretend to cheapen[3] goods, but nothing buy.  
The Templar[4] spruce, while every spout's abroach,  
Stays till 'tis fair, yet seems to call a coach.  
The tucked-up sempstress walks with hasty strides,  
While streams run down her oiled umbrella's sides.  
Here various kinds, by various fortunes led,  
Commence acquaintance underneath a shed.                         40  
Triumphant Tories and desponding Whigs  
Forget their feuds, and join to save their wigs.  
Boxed in a chair the beau impatient sits,  
While spouts run clattering o'er the roof by fits,  
And ever and anon with frightful din  

---

[1] impends    [2] wench    [3] haggle for        Middle Temple, two of the Inns of Court  
[4] a law student residing in the Inner Temple or the

The leather[5] sounds; he trembles from within.
So when Troy chairmen bore the wooden steed,
Pregnant with Greeks impatient to be freed
(Those bully Greeks, who, as the moderns do,
Instead of paying chairmen, run them through),                    50
Laocoön struck the outside with his spear,
And each imprisoned hero quaked for fear.
    Now from all parts the swelling kennels[6] flow,
And bear their trophies with them as they go:
Filth of all hues and odors seem to tell
What street they sailed from, by their sight and smell.
They, as each torrent drives with rapid force,
From Smithfield or St.Pulchre's shape their course,
And in huge confluence joined at Snow Hill ridge,
Fall from the conduit prone to Holborn Bridge,                    60
Sweepings from butchers' stalls, dung, guts, and blood,
Drowned puppies, stinking sprats, all drenched in mud,
Dead cats, and turnip tops, come tumbling down the flood.

                                              *(1710)*

## Clever Tom Clinch Going to Be Hanged

As clever Tom Clinch, while the rabble was bawling,
Rode stately through Holborn, to die in his calling;
He stopped at the George for a bottle of sack,
And promised to pay for it when he'd come back.
His waistcoat and stockings and breeches were white,
His cap had a new cherry ribbon to tie't.
The maids to the doors and the balconies ran,
And said, "Lack-a-day! He's a proper young man."
But as from the windows the ladies he spied,
Like a beau in a box, he bowed low on each side;                    10
And when his last speech the loud hawkers did cry,
He swore from his cart, it was all a damned lie.
The hangman for pardon fell down on his knee;
Tom gave him a kick in the guts for his fee.
Then said, "I must speak to the people a little,
But I'll see you all damned before I will whittle.[1]
My honest friend Wild,[2] may he long hold his place,
He lengthened my life with a whole year of grace.
Take courage, dear comrades, and be not afraid,
Nor slip this occasion to follow your trade.                    20
My conscience is clear, and my spirits are calm,
And thus I go off without prayerbook or psalm."
Then follow the practice of clever Tom Clinch,
Who hung like a hero and never would flinch.

---

[5] roof of the sedan chair     [6] gutters         [2] the noted thief-catcher (Swift's notes)
[1] a cant word for confessing at the gallows

## The Day of Judgment

With a whirl of thought oppressed,
I sink from reverie to rest.
An horrid vision seized my head,
I saw the graves give up their dead.
Jove, armed with terrors, burst the skies,
And thunder roars and lightning flies.
Amazed, confused, its fate unknown,
The world stands trembling at his throne.
While each pale sinner hangs his head,
Jove, nodding, shook the heavens and said,                          10
"Offending race of human kind,
By nature, reason, learning, blind;
You who through frailty stepped aside,
And you who never fell—through *pride;*
You who in different sects have shammed,
And come to see each other damned
(So some folks told you, but they knew
No more of Jove's designs than you);
The world's mad business now is o'er,
And I resent these pranks no more.                                  20
I to such blockheads set my wit!
I damn such fools!—Go, go, you're bit."   (c.*1731*)

# ISAAC WATTS / 1674–1748

## The Incomprehensible

Far in the heavens my God retires,
  My God, the mark of my desires,
    And hides His lovely face;
When He descends within my view
He charms my reason to pursue,
But leaves it tired and fainting in th'
    unequal chase.

Or if I reach unusual height
  Till near His presence brought,
There floods of glory check my flight,
Cramp the bold pinions of my wit,   10
  And all untune my thought;
Plunged in a sea of light I roll,
Where wisdom, justice, mercy shines;
Infinite rays in crossing lines
Beat thick confusion on my sight, and
    overwhelm my soul.

Come to my aid, ye fellow minds,
  And help me reach the throne;
(What single strength in vain designs
  United force hath done;
Thus worms may join, and grasp the
    poles,                            20
  Thus atoms fill the sea)
But the whole race of creature-souls
Stretched to their last extent of thought,
  plunge and are lost in Thee.

Great God, behold my reason lies
Adoring; yet my love would rise
  On pinions not her own:
Faith shall direct her humble flight
Through all the trackless seas of light
To thee th' Eternal Fair, the Infinite
  Unknown.   (*1706*)

# The Day of Judgment: An Ode Attempted in English Sapphic

When the fierce north wind with his airy forces
Rears up the Baltic to a foaming fury;
And the red lightning with a storm of hail comes
        Rushing amain down,

How the poor sailors stand amazed and tremble!
While the hoarse thunder like a bloody trumpet
Roars a loud onset to the gaping waters
        Quick to devour them.

Such shall the noise be, and the wild disorder,
(If things eternal may be like these earthly)        *10*
Such the dire terror when the great archangel
        Shakes the creation;

Tears the strong pillars of the vault of Heaven,
Breaks up old marble, the repose of princes;
See the graves open and the bones arising,
        Flames all around 'em.

Hark the shrill outcries of the guilty wretches!
Lively bright horror and amazing anguish
Stare through the eyelids, while the living worm lies
        Gnawing within them.        *20*

Thoughts like old vultures prey upon their heartstrings,
And the smart twinges, when their eye beholds the
Lofty Judge frowning, and a flood of vengeance
        Rolling afore him.

Hopeless immortals! how they scream and shiver
While devils push them to the pit wide yawning
Hideous and gloomy, to receive them headlong
        Down to the center.

Stope here my fancy: (all away ye horrid
Doleful ideas) come arise to Jesus,        *30*
How he sits God-like! and the saints around him
        Throned, yet adoring!

O may I sit there when He comes triumphant
Dooming the nations: then ascend to glory,
While our hosannahs all along the passage
        Shout the Redeemer.   (*1706*)

# JOHN GAY / 1685–1732

## *from* The Shepherd's Week

### FRIDAY: OR, THE DIRGE

#### Bumkinet   Grubbinol

Bumkinet: Why, Grubbinol, dost thou so wistful seem?
There's sorrow in thy look, if right I deem.
'Tis true, yon oaks with yellow tops appear,
And chilly blasts begin to nip the year;
From the tall elm a shower of leaves is borne,
And their lost beauty riven beeches mourn.
Yet even this season pleasance blithe affords,
Now the squeezed press foams with our apple hoards.
Come, let us hie, and quaff a cheery bowl,
Let cider new wash sorrow from thy soul.   *10*

Grubbinol: Ah Bumkinet! since thou from hence wert gone,
From these sad plains all merriment is flown;
Should I reveal my grief 'twould spoil thy cheer,
And make thine eye o'erflow with many a tear.

Bum: Hang sorrow! Let's to yonder hut repair,
And with trim sonnets cast away our care.
"Gilion of Croydon" well thy pipe can play,
Thou sing'st most sweet, "O'er Hills and Far Away."
Of "Patient Grissel" I devise to sing,
And catches quaint shall make the valleys ring.   *20*
Come, Grubbinol, beneath this shelter come,
From hence we view our flocks securely roam.
Grub: Yes, blithesome lad, a tale I mean to sing,
But with my woe shall distant valleys ring.
The tale shall make our kidlings droop their head,
For woe is me!—our *Blouzelind* is dead.

Bum: Is Blouzelinda dead? farewell my glee!
No happiness is now reserved for me.
As the woodpigeon coos without his mate,
So shall my doleful dirge bewail her fate.   *30*
Of Blouzelinda fair I mean to tell,
The peerless maid that did all maids excel.

 Henceforth the morn shall dewy sorrow shed,
And evening tears upon the grass be spread;
The rolling streams with watry grief shall flow,
And winds shall moan aloud—when loud they blow.
Henceforth, as oft as autumn shall return,
The dropping trees, whene'er it rains, shall mourn;
This season quite shall strip the country's pride,
For 'twas in autumn Blouzelinda died.   *40*

258

Where'er I gad, I Blouzelind shall view,
Woods, dairy, barn and mows our passion knew.
When I direct my eyes to yonder wood,
Fresh rising sorrow curdles in my blood.
Thither I've often been the damsel's guide,
When rotten sticks our fuel have supplied;
There I remember how her faggots large,
Were frequently these happy shoulders' charge.
Sometimes this crook drew hazel boughs adown,
And stuffed her apron wide with nuts so brown;     50
Or when her feeding hogs had missed their way,
Or wallowing 'mid a feast of acrons lay;
The untoward creatures to the sty I drove,
And whistled all the way—or told my love.
    If by the dairy's hatch I chance to hie,
I shall her goodly countenance espy,
For there her goodly countenance I've seen,
Set off with kerchief starched and pinners clean.
Sometimes, like wax, she rolls the butter round,
Or with the wooden lily prints the pound.     60
Whilom I've seen her skim the clotted cream,
And press from spongy curds the milky stream.
But now, alas! these ears shall hear no more
The whining swine surround the dairy door,
No more her care shall fill the hollow tray,
To fat the guzzling hogs with floods of whey.
Lament, ye swine, in gruntings spend your grief,
For you, like me, have lost your sole relief.
    When in the barn the sounding flail I ply,
Where from her sieve the chaff was wont to fly,     70
The poultry there will seem around to stand,
Waiting upon her charitable hand.
No succour meet the poultry now can find,
For they, like me, have lost their Blouzelind.
    Whenever by yon barley mow I pass,
Before my eyes will trip the tidy lass.
I pitched the sheaves (oh could I do so now)
Which she in rows piled on the growing mow.
There every deal my heart by love was gained,
There the sweet kiss my courtship has explained.     80
Ah Blouzelind! that mow I ne'er shall see,
But thy memorial will revive in me.
    Lament, ye fields, and rueful symptoms show,
Henceforth let not the smelling primrose grow;
Let weeds instead of butter-flowers appear,
And meads, instead of daisies, hemlock bear;
For cowslips sweet let dandelions spread,
For Blouzelinda, blithesome maid, is dead!
Lament, ye swains, and o'er her grave bemoan,

And spell ye right this verse upon her stone:    *90*
"Here Blouzelinda lies—Alas, alas!
Weep shepherds—and remember flesh is grass."

GRUB: Albeit thy songs are sweeter to mine ear,
Than to the cattle rivers clear;
Or winter porridge to the laboring youth,
Or buns and sugar to the damsel's tooth;
Yet Blouzelinda's name shall tune my lay,
Of her I'll sing for ever and for aye.
    When Blouzelind expired, the wether's bell
Before the drooping flock tolled forth her knell;    *100*
The solemn death-watch clicked the hour she died,
And shrilling crickets in the chimney cried;
The boding raven on her cottage sate,
And with hoarse croaking warned us of her fate;
The lambkin, which her wonted tendance bred,
Dropped on the plains that fatal instant dead;
Swarmed on a rotten stick the bees I spied,
Which erst I saw when goody Dobson died.
    How shall I, void of tears, her death relate,
While on her dearling's bed her mother sate!    *110*
These words the dying Blouzelinda spoke,
And of the dead let none the will revoke.
    "Mother," quoth she, "let not the poultry need,
And give the goose wherewith to raise her breed,
Be these my sister's care—and every morn
Amid the ducklings let her scatter corn:
The sickly calf that's housed, be sure to tend,
Feed him with milk, and from bleak colds defend.
Yet e'er I die—see, Mother, yonder shelf,
There secretly I've hid my worldly pelf.    *120*
Twenty good shillings in a rag I laid,
Be ten the parson's, for my sermon paid.
The rest is yours—my spinning wheel and rake,
Let Susan keep for her dear sister's sake;
My new straw hat that's trimly lined with green,
Let Peggy wear, for she's a damsel clean.
My leathern bottle, long in harvests tried,
Be Grubbinol's—this silver ring beside;
Three silver pennies, and a ninepence bent,
A token kind, to Bumkinet is sent."    *130*
Thus spoke the maiden, while her mother cried,
And peaceful, like the harmless lamb, she died.
    To show their love, the neighbours far and near,
Followed with wistful look the damsel's bier.
Sprigged rosemary the lads and lasses bore,
While dismally the parson walked before.
Upon her grave the rosemary they threw,

The daisy, butter-flower, and endive blue.
   After the good man warned us from his text,
That none could tell whose turn would be the next;   *140*
He said that heaven would take her soul no doubt,
And spoke the hour-glass in her praise—quite out.
   To her sweet memory flowery garlands strung,
O'er her now empty seat aloft were hung.
With wicker rods we fenced her tomb around,
To ward from man and beast the hallowed ground,
Lest her new grave the parson's cattle raze,
For both his horse and cow the churchyard graze.
   Now we trudged homeward to her mother's farm,
To drink new cider mulled with ginger, warm.   *150*
For gaffer Treadwell told us by the by,
Excessive sorrow is exceeding dry.
   While bulls bear horns upon their curled brow,
Or lasses with soft strokings milk the cow;
While paddling ducks the standing lake desire,
Or battening hogs roll in the sinking mire;
While moles the crumbled earth in hillocks raise,
So long shall swains tell Blouzelinda's praise.

   Thus wailed the louts in melancholy strain,
Till bonny Susan sped across the plain;   *160*
They seized the lass in apron clean arrayed,
And to the ale-house forced the willing maid;
In ale and kisses they forget their cares,
And Susan Blouzelinda's loss repairs.   *(1714)*

## *from* The Beggar's Opera

### AIR I

Through all the employments of life
   Each neighbour abuses his brother;
Whore and rogue they call husband and wife:
   All professions be-rogue one another.
The priest calls the lawyer a cheat,
   The lawyer be-knaves the divine;
And the statesman, because he's so great,
   Thinks his trade as honest as mine.

### AIR XVI

MACH:   Were I laid on Greenland's coast,
      And in my arms embraced my lass;
   Warm amidst eternal frost,
      Too soon the half year's night would pass.
POLLY:   Were I sold on Indian soil,
      Soon as the burning day was closed,
   I could mock the sultry toil,
      When on my charmer's **breast** reposed.

MACH:   And I would love you all the day,
POLLY:  Every night would kiss and play,                          *10*
MACH:   If with me you'd fondly stray
POLLY:  Over the hills and far away.

### AIR XXVI

Man may escape from rope and gun;
Nay, some have outlived the doctor's pill;
Who takes a woman must be undone,
That basilisk is sure to kill.
The fly that sips treacle is lost in the sweets,
So he that tastes woman, woman, woman,
He that tastes woman, ruin meets.   (*1728*)

## GEORGE BERKELEY / 1685–1753

### Verses on the Prospect of Planting Arts and Learning in America

The muse, disgusted at an age and clime,
  Barren of every glorious theme,
In distant lands now waits a better time,
  Producing subjects worthy fame:

In happy climes, where from the genial
    sun
And virgin earth such scenes ensue,
The force of art by nature seems outdone,
  And fancied beauties by the true:

In happy climes the seat of innocence,
  Where nature guides and virtue
    rules,                                                        *10*

Where men shall not impose for truth
    and sense,
  The pedantry of courts and schools:

There shall be sung another golden age,
  The rise of empire and of arts,
The good and great inspiring epic rage,
  The wisest heads and noblest hearts.

Not such as Europe breeds in her decay;
  Such as she bred when fresh and young,
When heavenly flame did animate her
    clay,
  By future poets shall be sung.                                 *20*

Westward the course of empire takes its
    way;
  The four first acts already past,
A fifth shall close the drama with the day;
  Time's noblest offspring is the last.
                                                         (*1752*)

# ALEXANDER POPE / 1688–1744

## *from* An Essay on Criticism

### PART II

Of all the causes which conspire to blind
Man's erring judgment, and misguide the mind,
What the weak head with strongest bias rules,
Is *Pride*, the never-failing vice of fools.
Whatever Nature has in worth denied,
She gives in large recruits of needful pride;
For as in bodies, thus in souls, we find
What wants in blood and spirits, swelled with wind:
Pride, where wit fails, steps in to our defence,
And fills up all the might void of sense.                    10
If once right reason drives that cloud away,
Truth breaks upon us with resistless day.
Trust not yourself; but your defects to know,
Make use of ev'ry friend—and ev'ry foe.
  A little learning is a dang'rous thing;
Drink deep, or taste not the Pierian spring:[1]
There shallow draughts intoxicate the brain,
And drinking largely sobers us again.
Fired at first sight with what the Muse imparts,
In fearless youth we tempt the heights of arts,              20
While from the bounded level of our mind,
Short views we take, nor see the lengths behind;
But more advanced, behold with strange surprise
New distant scenes of endless science rise!
So pleased at first the tow'ring Alps we try,
Mount o'er the vales, and seem to tread the sky,
Th' eternal snows appear already past,
And the first clouds and mountains seem the last:
But, those attained, we tremble to survey
The growing labours of the lengthened way,                   30
Th' increasing prospect tires our wand'ring eyes,
Hills peep o'er hills, and Alps on Alps arise!
  A perfect judge will read each work of wit
With the same spirit that its author writ:
Survey the whole, nor seek slight faults to find
Where nature moves, and rapture warms the mind;
Nor lose, for that malignant dull delight,
The gen'rous pleasure to be charmed with wit.
But in such lays as neither ebb, nor flow,
Correctly cold, and regularly low,                           40

---

[1] a spring sacred to the Muses; source of poetic inspiration

That shunning faults, one quiet tenour keep;
We cannot blame indeed—but we may sleep.
In wit, as nature, what affects our hearts
Is not th' exactness of peculiar parts;
'Tis not a lip, or eye, we beauty call,
But the joint force and full result of all.
Thus when we view some well-proportioned dome,
(The world's just wonder, and ev'n thine, O Rome!)
No single parts unequally surprise,
All comes united to th' admiring eyes;                                  *50*
No monstrous height, or breadth, or length appear;
The whole at once is bold, and regular.
    Whoever thinks a faultless piece to see,
Thinks what ne'er was, nor is, nor e'er shall be.
In ev'ry work regard the writer's end,
Since none can compass more than they intend;
And if the means be just, the conduct true,
Applause, in spite of trivial faults, is due.
As men of breeding, sometimes men of wit,
T' avoid great errors, must the less commit:                            *60*
Neglect the rules each verbal critic lays,
For not to know some trifles, is a praise.
Most critics, fond of some subservient art,
Still make the whole depend upon a part:
They talk of principles, but notions prize,
And all to one loved folly sacrifice.
    Once on a time, La Mancha's knight,[2] they say,
A certain bard encount'ring on the way,
Discoursed in terms as just, with looks as sage,
As e'er could Dennis,[3] of the Grecian stage,                          *70*
Concluding all were desp'rate sots and fools,
Who durst depart from Aristotle's rules.
Our author, happy in a judge so nice,[4]
Produced his play, and begged the knight's advice;
Made him observe the subject, and the plot,
The manners, passions, unities; what not?
All which, exact to rule, were brought about,
Were but a combat in the lists left out.
"What! leave the combat out?" exclaims the knight;
"Yes, or we must renounce the Stagirite,"[5]                            *80*
"Not so by Heav'n," he answers in a rage,
"Knights, squires, and steeds, must enter on the stage."
"So vast a throng the stage can ne'er contain."
"Then build a new, or act it in a plain."
    Thus critics, of less judgment than caprice,
Curious, not knowing, not exact but nice,

[2] Don Quixote. The episode is not from Cervantes, but from the spurious second part by Fernandez de Avellaneda.

[3] John Dennis (1657–1734), critic and long-time foe of Pope

[4] precise   [5] Aristotle, born at Stagira

Form short ideas; and offend in arts
(As most in manners) by a love to parts.
　　Some to conceit alone their taste confine,
And glitt'ring thoughts struck out at ev'ry line;     *90*
Pleased with a work where nothing's just or fit;
One glaring chaos and wild heap of wit.
Poets, like painters, thus, unskilled to trace
The naked nature and the living grace,
With gold and jewels cover ev'ry part,
And hide with ornaments their want of art.
True wit is nature to advantage dressed,
What oft was thought, but ne'er so well expressed;
Something, whose truth convinced at sight we find,
That gives us back the image of our mind.     *100*
As shades more sweetly recommend the light,
So modest plainness sets off sprightly wit.
For works may have more wit than does 'em good,
As bodies perish through excess of blood.
　　Others for language all their care express,
And value books, as women men, for dress:
Their praise is still,—the style is excellent;
The sense, they humbly take upon content.
Words are like leaves; and where they most abound,
Much fruit of sense beneath is rarely found:     *110*
False eloquence, like the prismatic glass,
Its gaudy colours spreads on ev'ry place;
The face of nature we no more survey,
All glares alike, without distinction gay:
But true expression, like th' unchanging sun,
Clears and improves whate'er it shines upon,
It gilds all objects, but it alters none.
Expression is the dress of thought, and still
Appears more decent, as more suitable;
A vile conceit in pompous words expressed,     *120*
Is like a clown in regal purple dressed:
For diff'rent styles with diff'rent subjects sort,
As several garbs with country, town, and court.
Some by old words to fame have made pretence,
Ancients in phrase, mere moderns in their sense;
Such laboured nothings, in so strange a style,
Amaze th' unlearned, and make the learned smile.
Unlucky, as Fungoso[6] in the play,
These sparks with awkward vanity display
What the fine gentleman wore yesterday;     *130*
And but so mimic ancient wits at best,
As apes our grandsires, in their doublets dressed.
In words, as fashions, the same rule will hold;

---

[6] inept dandy in Johnson's *Every Man Out of His Humour*

Alike fantastic, if too new, or old:
Be not the first by whom the new are tried,
Nor yet the last to lay the old aside.
　　But most by numbers judge a poet's song;
And smooth or rough, with them, is right or wrong:
In the bright Muse though thousand charms conspire,
Her voice is all these tuneful fools admire;                    *140*
Who haunt Parnassus[7] but to please their ear,
Not mend their minds; as some to church repair,
Not for the doctrine, but the music there.
These equal syllables alone require,
Though oft the ear the open vowels tire;
While expletives their feeble aid do join;
And ten low words oft creep in one dull line:
While they ring round the same unvaried chimes,
With sure returns of still expected rhymes.
Wher-e'er you find "the cooling western breeze,"              *150*
In the next line, it "whispers through the trees;"
If crystal streams "with pleasing murmurs creep."
The reader's threatened (not in vain) with "sleep."
Then, at the last and only couplet fraught
With some unmeaning thing they call a thought,
A needless Alexandrine ends the song,
That, like a wounded snake, drags its slow length along.
Leave such to tune their own dull rhymes, and know
What's roundly smooth, or languishingly slow;
And praise the easy vigour of a line,                          *160*
Where Denham's[8] strength, and Waller's[9] sweetness join.
True ease in writing comes from art, not chance,
As those move easiest who have learned to dance.
'Tis not enough no harshness gives offence,
The sound must seem an echo to the sense:
Soft is the strain when Zephyr[10] gently blows,
And the smooth stream in smoother numbers flows;
But when loud surges lash the sounding shore,
The hoarse, rough verse should like the torrent roar;
When Ajax[11] strives some rock's vast weight to throw,       *170*
The line too labours, and the words move slow;
Not so, when swift Camilla[12] scours the plain,
Flies o'er th' unbending corn, and skims along the main.
Hear how Timotheus'[13] varied lays surprise,
And bid alternate passions fall and rise!
While, at each change, the son of Libyan Jove
Now burns with glory, and then melts with love;

---

[7] mountain in Greece, sacred to Apollo and the Muses
[8] Sir John Denham (1615–1669)
[9] Edmund Waller (1606–1687). Denham and Waller were both forerunners of Dryden and Pope in neo-Classic verse.
[10] god of the west wind
[11] hero in the Trojan War, noted for strength
[12] a servant of Diana, noted for fleetness of foot
[13] court musician to Alexander the Great, the "son of Libyan Jove"; cf. Dryden, "Alexander's Feast"

Now his fierce eyes with sparkling fury glow,
Now sighs steal out, and tears begin to flow:
Persians and Greeks like turns of nature found,     *180*
And the world's victor stood subduced by sound!
The pow'r of music all our hearts allow,
And what Timotheus was, is Dryden now.
   Avoid extremes; and shun the fault of such,
Who still are pleased too little or too much.
At ev'ry trifle scorn to take offence,
That always shows great pride, or little sense;
Those heads, as stomachs, are not sure the best,
Which nauseate all, and nothing can digest.
Yet let not each gay turn thy rapture move;     *190*
For fools admire, but men of sense approve:
As things seem large which we through mists descry,
Dullness is ever apt to magnify.
   Some foreign writers, some our own despise;
The ancients only, or the moderns prize.
Thus wit, like faith, by each man is applied
To one small sect, and all are damned beside.
Meanly they seek the blessing to confine,
And force that sun but on a part to shine,
Which not alone the southern wit sublimes,     *200*
But ripens spirits in cold northern climes;
Which from the first has shone on ages past,
Enlights the present, and shall warm the last;
Though each may feel increases and decays,
And see now clearer and now darker days.
Regard not then if wit be old or new,
But blame the false, and value still the true.
   Some ne'er advance a judgment of their own,
But catch the spreading notion of the town;
They reason and conclude by precedent,     *210*
And own stale nonsense which they ne'er invent.
Some judge of author's names, not works, and then
Nor praise nor blame the writings, but the men.
Of all this servile herd, the worst is he
That in proud dullness joins with quality,
A constant critic at the great man's board,
To fetch and carry nonsense for my lord.
What woeful stuff this madrigal would be,
In some starved hackney sonneteer, or me?
But let a lord once own the happy lines,     *220*
How the wit brightens! how the style refines!
Before his sacred name flies ev'ry fault,
And each exalted stanza teems with thought!
   The vulgar thus through imitation err;
As oft the learn'd by being singular;
So much they scorn the crowd, that if the throng

By chance go right, they purposely go wrong:
So schismatics the plain believers quit,
And are but damned for having too much wit.
Some praise at morning what they blame at night;                    230
But always think the last opinion right.
A Muse by these is like a mistress used,
This hour she's idolized, the next abused;
While their weak heads, like towns unfortified,
'Twixt sense and nonsense daily change their side.
Ask them the cause; they're wiser still, they say;
And still tomorrow's wiser than today.
We think our fathers fools, so wise we grow;
Our wiser sons, no doubt, will think us so.
Once school-divines this zealous isle o'erspread;                    240
Who knew most sentences,[14] was deepest read;
Faith, Gospel, all, seemed made to be disputed,
And none had sense enough to be confuted:
Scotists and Thomists,[15] now, in peace remain,
Amidst their kindred cobwebs in Duck Lane.[16]
If faith itself had diff'rent dresses worn,
What wonder modes in wit should take their turn?
Oft, leaving what is natural and fit,
The current folly proves the ready wit;
And authors think their reputation safe,                            250
Which lives as long as fools are pleased to laugh.
    Some, valuing those of their own side or mind,
Still make themselves the measure of mankind:
Fondly we think we honour merit then,
When we but praise ourselves in other men.
Parties in wit attend on those of state,
And public faction doubles private hate.
Pride, malice, folly, against Dryden rose,
In various shapes of parsons, critics, beaus;
But sense survived, when merry jests were past;                     260
For rising merit will buoy up at last.
Might he return, and bless once more our eyes,
New Blackmores[17] and new Milbourns[18] must arise:
Nay, should great Homer lift his awful head,
Zoilus[19] again would start up from the dead.
Envy will merit, as its shade, pursue;
But like a shadow, proves the substance true;
For envied wit, like Sol eclipsed, makes known
Th' opposing body's grossness, not its own.
When first that sun too pow'rful beams displays,                    270

---

14 maxims or conclusions
15 followers of Duns Scotus (c. 1265–1308) and of
St. Thomas Aquinas (1226–1274). These medieval
theologians are the "school divines" of l. 240.
16 street of second-hand book stores

17 Sir Richard Blackmore, *Satyr Against Wit*
(1700)
18 Rev. Luke Milbourn, *Notes on Dryden's Virgil*
(1698). Both attacked Dryden.
19 ancient critic of Homer

It draws up vapours which obscure its rays;
But ev'n those clouds at last adorn its way,
Reflect new glories, and augment the day.
  Be thou the first true merit to befriend;
His praise is lost, who stays 'till all commend.
Short is the date, alas, of modern rhymes,
And 'tis but just to let 'em live betimes.
No longer now that golden age appears,
When patriarch-wits survived a thousand years:
Now length of fame (our second life) is lost,                    *280*
And bare threescore is all ev'n that can boast;
Our sons their fathers' failing language see,
And such as Chaucer[20] is, shall Dryden be.
So when the faithful pencil has designed
Some bright idea of the master's mind,
Where a new world leaps out at his command,
And ready nature waits upon his hand;
When the ripe colours soften and unite,
And sweetly melt into just shade and light,
When mellowing years their full perfection give,                *290*
And each bold figure just begins to live,
The treach'rous colours the fair art betray,
And all the bright creation fades away!
  Unhappy wit, like most mistaken things,
Atones not for that envy which it brings.
In youth alone its empty praise we boast,
But soon the short-lived vanity is lost:
Like some fair flow'r the early spring supplies,
That gayly blooms, but ev'n in blooming dies.
What is this wit, which must our cares employ?                   *300*
The owner's wife, that other men enjoy;
Then most our trouble still when most admired,
And still the more we give, the more required;
Whose fame with pains we guard, but lose with ease,
Sure some to vex, but never all to please;
'Tis what the vicious fear, the virtuous shun,
By fools 'tis hated, and by knaves undone!
  If Wit so much from ign'rance undergo,
Ah let not learning too commence its foe!
Of old, those met rewards who could excel,                      *310*
And such were praised who but endeavoured well:
Though triumphs were to gen'rals only due,
Crowns were reserved to grace the soldiers too.
Now, they who reach Parnassus' lofty crown
Employ their pains to spurn some others down;
And while self-love each jealous writer rules,
Contending wits become the sport of fools:

---

[20] Chaucer seemed nearly indecipherable to the eighteenth century.

But still the worst with most regret commend,
For each ill author is as bad a friend.
To what base ends, and by what abject ways,                320
Are mortals urged through sacred lust of praise!
Ah, ne'er so dire a thirst of glory boast,
Nor in the critic let the man be lost.
Good nature and good sense must ever join;
To err is human, to forgive, divine.
   But if in noble minds some dregs remain
Not yet purged off, of spleen and sour disdain;
Discharge that rage on more provoking crimes,
Nor fear a dearth in these flagitious [21] times.
No pardon vile obscenity should find,                      330
Though wit and art conspire to move your mind;
But dullness with obscenity must prove
As shameful sure as impotence in love.
In the fat age of pleasure,[22] wealth, and ease,
Sprung the rank weed, and thrived with large increase:
When love was all an easy monarch's care;
Seldom at council, never in a war:
Jilts ruled the state, and statesmen farces writ;
Nay, wits had pensions, and young lords had wit:
The fair sat panting at a courtier's play,                 340
And not a mask went unimprov'd away:
The modest fan was lifted up no more,
And virgins smiled at what they blushed before.
The following license of a foreign reign [23]
Did all the dregs of bold Socinus [24] drain;
Then unbelieving priests reformed the nation,
And taught more pleasant methods of salvation;
Where Heav'n's free subjects might their rights dispute,
Lest God himself should seem too absolute:
Pulpits their sacred satire learned to spare,              350
And vice admired to find a flatt'rer there!
Encouraged thus, wit's Titans braved the skies,
And the press groaned with licensed blasphemies.
These monsters, critics! with your darts engage,
Here point your thunder, and exhaust your rage!
Yet shun their fault, who, scandalously nice,
Will needs mistake an author into vice;
All seemed infected that th' infected spy,
As all looks yellow to the jaundiced eye.   (*1711*)

---

21 scandalous      22 reign of Charles II        24 Italian religious reformer (1539–1604), founder
23 reign of William and Mary              of the heretical sect of Socinians

# The Rape of the Lock

## AN HEROI-COMICAL POEM

*Noluerum, Belinda, tuos violare capillos;*
*Sed juvat, hoc precibus me tribuisse tuis.*
—*Martial, Epigrams XII, 84.*[1]

### CANTO I

What dire offense from am'rous causes springs,
What mighty contests rise from trivial things,
I sing—This verse to *Caryl,*[2] Muse! is due:
This, even Belinda may vouchsafe to view:
Slight is the subject, but not so the praise,
If she inspire, and he approve my lays.
  Say what strange motive, Goddess! could compel
A well-bred lord t' assault a gentle belle?
O say what stranger cause, yet unexplored,
Could make a gentle belle reject a lord?                                    10
In tasks so bold, can little men engage,
And in soft bosoms dwells such mighty rage?
  Sol through white curtains shot a tim'rous ray,
And oped those eyes that must eclipse the day:
Now lap-dogs give themselves the rousing shake,
And sleepless lovers, just at twelve, awake:
Thrice rung the bell, the slipper knocked the ground,
And the pressed watch[3] returned a silver sound.
Belinda still her downy pillow pressed,
Her guardian sylph prolonged the balmy rest:                                20
'Twas he had summoned to her silent bed
The morning-dream that hovered o'er her head;
A youth more glitt'ring than a birth-night beau,[4]
(That even in slumber caused her cheek to glow)
Seemed to her ear his winning lips to lay,
And thus in whispers said, or seemed to say.
  "Fairest of mortals, thou distinguished care
Of thousand bright inhabitants of air!
If e'er one vision touched thy infant thought,
Of all the nurse and all the priest have taught;                           30
Of airy elves by moonlight shadows seen,
The silver token, and the circled green,
Or virgins visited by angel-powers,
With golden crowns and wreaths of heav'nly flowers;
Hear and believe! thy own importance know,
Nor bound thy narrow views to things below.

---

[1] "I did not wish, Belinda, to profane your locks, but I am delighted to yield this to your beseeching."
[2] John Caryll, a close friend, who suggested the subject of the poem to Pope
[3] Pressing the stem makes the watch chime the hour.
[4] young man dressed in brilliant costume for a royal birthday

Some secret truths, from learnéd pride concealed,
To maids alone and children are revealed:
What though no credit doubting wits may give?
The fair and innocent shall still believe.                          *40*
Know, then, unnumbered spirits round thee fly,
The light militia of the lower sky:
These, though unseen, are ever on the wing,
Hang o'er the box,[5] and hover round the Ring.[6]
Think what an equipage thou hast in air,
And view with scorn two pages and a chair.[7]
As now your own our beings were of old,
And once inclosed in woman's beauteous mould;
Thence, by a soft transition, we repair
From earthly vehicles to these of air.                              *50*
Think not, when woman's transient breath is fled,
That all her vanities at once are dead;
Succeeding vanities she still regards,
And though she plays no more, o'erlooks the cards.
Her joy in gilded chariots, when alive,
And love of ombre,[8] after death survive.
For when the fair in all their pride expire,
To their first elements their souls retire:
The sprites of fiery termagants[9] in flame
Mount up, and take a salamander's[10] name.                         *60*
Soft yielding minds to water glide away,
And sip, with nymphs, their elemental tea.
The graver prude sinks downward to a gnome,
In search of mischief still on earth to roam.
The light coquettes in sylphs aloft repair,
And sport and flutter in the fields of air.
    "Know further yet; whoever fair and chaste
Rejects mankind, is by some sylph embraced:
For spirits, freed from mortal laws, with ease
Assume what sexes and what shapes they please.                      *70*
What guards the purity of melting maids,
In courtly balls, and midnight masquerades,
Safe from the treach'rous friend, the daring spark,
The glance by day, the whisper in the dark,
When kind occasion prompts their warm desires,
When music softens, and when dancing fires?
'Tis but their sylph, the wise celestials know,
Though honor is the word with men below.
    "Some nymphs there are, too conscious of their face,
For life predestined to the gnomes' embrace.                        *80*
These swell their prospects and exalt their pride,

---

[5] at the theater
[6] the drive in Hyde Park    [7] sedan chair
[8] the card game that Belinda plays with the Baron
in Canto III

[9] shrewish women
[10] a lizard-like creature, once believed capable of
living in fire

When offers are disdained, and love denied:
Then gay ideas crowd the vacant brain,
While peers, and dukes, and all their sweeping train,
And garters, stars, and coronets appear,
And in soft sounds, 'Your Grace' salutes their ear.
'Tis these that early taint the female soul,
Instruct the eyes of young coquettes to roll,
Teach infant-cheeks a bidden blush to know,
And little hearts to flutter at a beau.                                     90
    "Oft, when the world imagine women stray,
The sylphs through mystic mazes guide their way,
Through all the giddy circle they pursue,
And old impertinence expel by new.
What tender maid but must a victim fall
To one man's treat, but for another's ball?
When Florio what virgin could withstand,
If gentle Damon [11] did not squeeze her hand?
With varying vanities, from every part,
They shift the moving toyshop of their heart;                             100
Where wigs with wigs, with sword-knots sword-knots strive,
Beaux banish beaux, and coaches coaches drive.
This erring mortals levity may call;
Oh blind to truth! the sylphs contrive it all.
    "Of these am I, who thy protection claim,
A watchful sprite, and Ariel is my name.
Late, as I ranged the crystal wilds of air,
In the clear mirror of thy ruling star
I saw, alas! some dread event impend,
Ere to the main this morning sun descend,                                 110
But heaven reveals not what, or how, or where:
Warned by the sylph, oh pious maid, beware!
This to disclose is all thy guardian can:
Beware of all, but most beware of man!"
    He said; when Shock, [12] who thought she slept too long,
Leaped up, and waked his mistress with his tongue.
'Twas then, Belinda, if report say true,
Thy eyes first opened on a billet-doux;
Wounds, charms, and ardors were no sooner read,
But all the vision vanished from thy head.                                120
    And now, unveiled, the toilet stands displayed,
Each silver vase in mystic order laid.
First, robed in white, the nymph intent adores,
With head uncovered, the cosmetic powers.
A heav'nly image in the glass appears,
To that she bends, to that her eyes she rears;
Th' inferior priestess, [13] at her altar's side,
Trembling begins the sacred rites of pride.

---

[11] conventional names in pastoral poetry      [13] Betty, Belinda's lady's maid
[12] Belinda's lap dog

Unnumbered treasures ope at once, and here
The various off'rings of the world appear;                    *130*
From each she nicely culls with curious[14] toil,
And decks the goddess with the glitt'ring spoil.
This casket India's glowing gems unlocks,
And all Arabia breathes from yonder box.
The tortoise here and elephant unite,
Transformed to combs, the speckled, and the white.
Here files of pins extend their shining rows,
Puffs, powders, patches, bibles,[15] billet-doux.
Now awful Beauty puts on all its arms;
The fair each moment rises in her charms,                     *140*
Repairs her smiles, awakens every grace,
And calls forth all the wonders of her face;
Sees by degrees a purer blush arise,
And keener lightnings quicken in her eyes.
The busy sylphs surround their darling care,
These set the head, and those divide the hair,
Some fold the sleeve, whilst others plait the gown;
And Betty's praised for labors not her own.

### CANTO II

Not with more glories, in th' ethereal plain,
The sun first rises o'er the purpled main,
Than, issuing forth, the rival of his beams
Launched on the bosom of the silver Thames.
Fair nymphs, and well-dressed youths around her shone,
But every eye was fixed on her alone.
On her white breast a sparkling cross she wore,
Which Jews might kiss, and infidels adore.
Her lively looks a sprightly mind disclose,
Quick as her eyes, and as unfixed as those:                   *10*
Favors to one, to all she smiles extends;
Oft she rejects, but never once offends.
Bright as the sun, her eyes the gazers strike,
And, like the sun, they shine on all alike.
Yet graceful ease, and sweetness void of pride,
Might hide her faults, if belles had faults to hide:
If to her share some female errors fall,
Look on her face, and you'll forget 'em all.
    This nymph, to the destruction of mankind,
Nourished two locks, which graceful hung behind               *20*
In equal curls, and well conspired to deck
With shining ringlets the smooth iv'ry neck.
Love in these labyrinths his slaves detains,
And mighty hearts are held in slender chains.
With hairy springes we the birds betray,
Slight lines of hair surprise the finny prey,

[14] painstaking                     [15] perhaps curling papers

Fair tresses man's imperial race ensnare,
And beauty draws us with a single hair.
    Th' advent'rous Baron the bright locks admired;
He saw, he wished, and to the prize aspired.     *30*
Resolved to win, he meditates the way,
By force to ravish, or by fraud betray;
For when success a lover's toil attends,
Few ask, if fraud or force attained his ends.
    For this, ere Phœbus rose, he had implored
Propitious heaven, and every power adored,
But chiefly Love—to Love an altar built,
Of twelve vast French romances, neatly gilt.
There lay three garters, half a pair of gloves;
And all the trophies of his former loves;     *40*
With tender billet-doux he lights the pyre,
And breathes three am'rous sighs to raise the fire.
Then prostrate falls, and begs with ardent eyes
Soon to obtain, and long possess the prize:
The powers gave ear, and granted half his prayer,
The rest, the winds dispersed in empty air.
    But now secure the painted vessel glides,
The sun-beams trembling on the floating tides:
While melting music steals upon the sky,
And softened sounds along the waters die;     *50*
Smooth flow the waves, the zephyrs gently play,
Belinda smiled, and all the world was gay.
All but the sylph—with careful thoughts oppressed,
Th' impending woe sat heavy on his breast.
He summons straight his denizens of air;
The lucid squadrons round the sails repair:
Soft o'er the shrouds aërial whispers breathe,
That seemed but zephyrs to the train beneath.
Some to the sun their insect-wings unfold,
Waft on the breeze, or sink in clouds of gold;     *60*
Transparent forms, too fine for mortal sight,
Their fluid bodies half dissolved in light.
Loose to the wind their airy garments flew,
Thin glitt'ring textures of the filmy dew,
Dipped in the richest tincture of the skies,
Where light disports in ever-mingling dyes,
While every beam new transient colors flings,
Colors that change whene'er they wave their wings.
Amid the circle, on the gilded mast,
Superior by the head, was Ariel placed;     *70*
His purple pinions opening to the sun,
He raised his azure wand, and thus begun.
    "Ye sylphs and sylphids, to your chief give ear!
Fays, fairies, genii, elves, and dæmons, hear!
Ye know the spheres and various tasks assigned

By laws eternal th' aëriel kind.
Some in the fields of purest ether play,
And bask and whiten in the blaze of day.
Some guide the course of wand'ring orbs on high,
Or roll the planets through the boundless sky.     *80*
Some less refined, beneath the moon's pale light
Pursue the stars that shoot athwart the night,
Or suck the mists in grosser air below,
Or dip their pinions in the painted bow,
Or brew fierce tempests on the wintry main,
Or o'er the glebe[16] distil the kindly rain.
Others on earth o'er human race preside,
Watch all their ways, and all their actions guide:
Of these the chief the care of nations own,
And guard with arms divine the British throne.     *90*
"Our humbler province is to tend the fair,
Not a less pleasing, though less glorious care;
To save the powder from too rude a gale,
Nor let th' imprisoned essences exhale;
To draw fresh colors from the vernal flowers;
To steal from rainbows ere they drop in showers
A brighter wash; to curl their waving hairs,
Assist their blushes, and inspire their airs;
Nay oft, in dreams, invention we bestow,
To change a flounce, or add a furbelow.     *100*
"This day, black omens threat the brightest fair,
That e'er deserved a watchful spirit's care;
Some dire disaster, or by force, or sleight;
But what, or where, the fates have wrapped in night.
Whether the nymph shall break Diana's law,[17]
Or some frail China jar receive a flaw;
Or stain her honor or her new brocade;
Forget her prayers, or miss a masquerade;
Or lose her heart, or necklace, at a ball;
Or whether Heaven has doomed that Shock must fall.     *110*
Haste, then, ye spirits! to your charge repair:
The flutt'ring fan be Zephyretta's care;
The drops[18] to thee, Brillante, we consign;
And, Momentilla, let the watch be thine;
Do thou, Crispissa, tend her fav'rite lock;
Ariel himself shall be the guard of Shock.
"To fifty chosen sylphs, of special note,
We trust th' important charge, the petticoat:
Oft have we known that seven-fold fence to fail,
Though stiff with hoops, and armed with ribs of whale;     *120*
Form a strong line about the silver bound,
And guard the wide circumference around.

[16] cultivated land      [17] the law of chastity      [18] pendant earrings

"Whatever spirit, careless of his charge,
His post neglects, or leaves the fair at large,
Shall feel sharp vengeance soon o'ertake his sins,
Be stopped in vials, or transfixed with pins;
Or plunged in lakes of bitter washes lie,
Or wedged whole ages in a bodkin's eye:
Gums and pomatums shall his flight restrain,
While clogged he beats his silken wings in vain;    130
Or alum styptics with contracting power
Shrink his thin essence like a riveled flower:
Or, as Ixion[19] fixed, the wretch shall feel
The giddy motion of the whirling mill,
In fumes of burning chocolate shall glow,
And tremble at the sea that froths below!"
    He spoke; the spirits from the sails descend;
Some, orb in orb, around the nymph extend;
Some thrid the mazy ringlets of her hair;
Some hang upon the pendants of her ear:    140
With beating hearts the dire event they wait,
Anxious, and trembling for the birth of Fate.

### CANTO III

Close by those meads, forever crowned with flowers,
Where Thames with pride surveys his rising towers,
There stands a structure[20] of majestic frame,
Which from the neighb'ring Hampton takes its name.
Here Britain's statesmen oft the fall foredoom
Of foreign tyrants and of nymphs at home;
Here thou, great Anna![21] whom three realms obey,
Dost sometimes counsel take—and sometimes tea.
    Hither the heroes and the nymphs resort,
To taste awhile the pleasures of a court;    10
In various talk th' instructive hours they past,
Who gave the ball, or paid the visit last;
One speaks the glory of the British queen,
And one describes a charming Indian screen;
A third interprets motions, looks, and eyes;
At every word a reputation dies.
Snuff, or the fan, supply each pause of chat,
With singing, laughing, ogling, and all that.
    Meanwhile, declining from the noon of day,
The sun obliquely shoots his burning ray;    20
The hungry judges soon the sentence sign,
And wretches hang that jury-men may dine;
The merchant from th' Exchange returns in peace,
And the long labors of the toilet cease.

[19] punished by being chained to a wheel that rolled eternally through the air
[20] Hampton Court, a royal palace
[21] Queen Anne, ruler of "three realms": England, Scotland, and Wales

Belinda now, whom thirst of fame invites,
Burns to encounter two advent'rous knights,
At ombre [22] singly to decide their doom;
And swells her breast with conquests yet to come.
Straight the three bands prepare in arms to join,
Each band the number of the sacred nine. [23]                    *30*
Soon as she spreads her hand, th' aërial guard
Descend, and sit on each important card:
First Ariel perched upon a matadore,
Then each, according to the rank they bore;
For sylphs, yet mindful of their ancient race,
Are, as when women, wondrous fond of place.

Behold, four kings in majesty revered,
With hoary whiskers and a forky beard;
And four fair queens whose hands sustain a flower,
Th' expressive emblem of their softer power;                    *40*
Four knaves in garbs succinct, a trusty band,
Caps on their heads, and halberts in their hand;
And particolored troops, a shining train,
Draw forth to combat on the velvet plain.

The skilful nymph reviews her force with care:
Let spades be trumps! she said, and trumps they were.

Now move to war her sable matadores,
In show like leaders of the swarthy Moors.
Spadillio first, unconquerable lord!
Led off two captive trumps, and swept the board.                    *50*
As many more Manillio forced to yield,
And marched a victor from the verdant field.
Him Basto followed, but his fate more hard
Gained but one trump and one plebeian card.
With his broad sabre next, a chief in years,
The hoary Majesty of Spades appears,
Puts forth one manly leg, to sight revealed,
The rest, his many-colored robe concealed.
The rebel knave, who dares his prince engage,
Proves the just victim of his royal rage.                    *60*
Even mighty Pam, [24] that kings and queens o'erthrew
And mowed down armies in the fights of loo,
Sad chance of war! now destitute of aid,
Falls undistinguished by the victor spade!

Thus far both armies to Belinda yield;
Now to the Baron fate inclines the field.
His warlike Amazon [25] her host invades,
Th' imperial consort of the crown of spades.

---

[22] The card game is played out accurately. The three "matadores" or high cards are called "Spadillio," "Manillio," and "Basto," but the cards which carry these names vary with the trump suit. Belinda's matadores are "sable" (l. 47) because she declares spades trumps.

[23] the Muses. A player's hand consists of nine cards.

[24] in loo, the highest card, the jack (knave) of clubs

[25] in Greek mythology, one of a tribe of female warriors; here, the queen of spades

The club's black tyrant first her victim died,
Spite of his haughty mien, and barb'rous pride:
What boots the regal circle on his head,
His giant limbs, in state unwieldy spread;
That long behind he trails his pompous robe,
And, of all monarchs, only grasps the globe?
   The Baron now his diamonds pours apace;
Th'embroidered king who shows but half his face,
And his refulgent queen, with powers combined
Of broken troops an easy conquest find.
Clubs, diamonds, hearts, in wild disorder seen,
With throngs promiscuous strow the level green.
Thus when dispersed a routed army runs,
Of Asia's troops, and Afric's sable sons,
With like confusion different nations fly,
Of various habit, and of various dye,
The pierced battalions disunited fall,
In heaps on heaps; one fate o'erwhelms them all.
   The knave of diamonds tries his wily arts,
And wins (oh shameful chance!) the queen of hearts.
At this, the blood the virgin's cheek forsook,
A livid paleness spreads o'er all her look;
She sees, and trembles at th' approaching ill,
Just in the jaws of ruin, and codille.[26]
And now (as oft in some distempered state)
On one nice trick depends the general fate.
An ace of hearts steps forth: The king unseen
Lurked in her hand, and mourned his captive queen:
He springs to vengeance with an eager pace,
And falls like thunder on the prostrate ace.
The nymph exulting fills with shouts the sky;
The walls, the woods, and long canals reply.
   Oh thoughtless mortals! ever blind to fate,
Too soon dejected, and too soon elate.
Sudden, these honors shall be snatched away,
And cursed for ever this victorious day.
   For lo! the board with cups and spoons is crowned,
The berries crackle,[27] and the mill turns round;
On shining altars of Japan[28] they raise
The silver lamp; the fiery spirits blaze:
From silver spouts the grateful liquors glide,
While China's earth receives the smoking tide:
At once they gratify their scent and taste,
And frequent cups prolong the rich repast.
Straight hover round the fair her airy band;
Some, as she sipped, the fuming liquor fanned,

70

80

90

100

110

[26] failure to make one's bid
[27] Coffee is ground at the table.

[28] japanned (lacquered) tables

Some o'er her lap their careful plumes displayed,
Trembling, and conscious of the rich brocade.
Coffee (which makes the politician wise,
And see through all things with his half-shut eyes)
Sent up in vapors to the Baron's brain
New stratagems, the radiant lock to gain.                    120
Ah cease, rash youth! desist ere 'tis too late,
Fear the just gods, and think of Scylla's[29] fate!
Changed to a bird, and sent to flit in air,
She dearly pays for Nisis' injured hair!
   But when to mischief mortals bend their will,
How soon they find fit instruments of ill!
Just then, Clarissa drew with tempting grace
A two-edged weapon from her shining case:
So ladies in romance assist their knight,
Present the spear, and arm him for the fight.                    130
He takes the gift with rev'rence, and extends
The little engine on his fingers' ends;
This just behind Belinda's neck he spread,
As o'er the fragrant steams she bends her head.
Swift to the lock a thousand sprites repair,
A thousand wings, by turns, blow back the hair;
And thrice they twitched the diamond in her ear;
Thrice she looked back, and thrice the foe drew near.
Just in that instant, anxious Ariel sought
The close recesses of the virgin's thought;                    140
As on the nosegay in her breast reclined,
He watched th' ideas rising in her mind,
Sudden he viewed, in spite of all her art,
An earthly lover lurking at her heart.
Amazed, confused, he found his power expired,
Resigned to fate, and with a sigh retired.
   The peer now spreads the glitt'ring forfex wide,
T' inclose the lock; now joins it, to divide.
Even then, before the fatal engine closed,
A wretched sylph too fondly interposed;                    150
Fate urged the shears, and cut the sylph in twain,
(But airy substance soon unites again)
The meeting points the sacred hair dissever
From the fair head, forever, and forever!
   Then flashed the living lightning from her eyes,
And screams of horror rend th' affrighted skies.
Not louder shrieks to pitying heaven are cast,
When husbands, or when lap-dogs breathe their last;
Or when rich China vessels fall'n from high,
In glitt'ring dust and painted fragments lie!                    160

---

[29] daughter of King Nisus of Megara. She fell in love with an enemy besieging the city, and pulled out of her father's head the golden hair on which the safety of the city depended. When Nisus, metamorphosed into a sea eagle, pounced upon Scylla, she was changed into a bird.

"Let wreaths of triumph now my temples twine,"
(The victor cried); "the glorious prize is mine!
While fish in streams, or birds delight in air,
Or in a coach and six the British fair,
As long as *Atalantis*[30] shall be read,
Or the small pillow grace a lady's bed,
While visits shall be paid on solemn days,
When num'rous wax-lights in bright order blaze,
While nymphs take treats, or assignations give,
So long my honor, name, and praise shall live!"          *170*
What time would spare, from steel receives its date,
And monuments, like men, submit to fate!
Steel could the labor of the gods destroy,
And strike to dust th' imperial towers of Troy;
Steel could the works of mortal pride confound,
And hew triumphal arches to the ground.
What wonder then, fair nymph! thy hairs should feel,
The conq'ring force of unresisted steel?

### CANTO IV

But anxious cares the pensive nymph oppressed,
And secret passions labored in her breast.
Not youthful kings in battle seized alive,
Not scornful virgins who their charms survive,
Not ardent lovers robbed of all their bliss,
Not ancient ladies when refused a kiss,
Not tyrants fierce that unrepenting die,
Not Cynthia[31] when her manteau's pinned awry,
E'er felt such rage, resentment, and despair,
As thou, sad virgin! for thy ravished hair.          *10*
  For, that sad moment, when the sylphs withdrew
And Ariel weeping from Belinda flew,
Umbriel, a dusky, melancholy sprite,
As ever sullied the fair face of light,
Down to the central earth, his proper scene,
Repaired to search the gloomy Cave of Spleen.[32]
  Swift on his sooty pinions flits the gnome,
And in a vapour reached the dismal dome.
No cheerful breeze this sullen region knows,
The dreaded east is all the wind that blows.          *20*
Here in a grotto, sheltered close from air,
And screened in shades from day's detested glare,
She sighs forever on her pensive bed,
Pain at her side, and Megrim[33] at her head.
  Two handmaids wait the throne: alike in place,
But diff'ring far in figure and in face.
Here stood Ill-nature like an ancient maid,

[30] a contemporary book filled with fashionable gossip   [31] Diana, goddess of chastity   [32] bad temper; malice   [33] low spirits

Her wrinkled form in black and white arrayed;
With store of prayers, for mornings, nights, and noons,
Her hand is filled; her bosom with lampoons.                                    *30*
   There Affectation, with a sickly mien,
Shows in her cheek the roses of eighteen,
Practised to lisp, and hang the head aside,
Faints into airs, and languishes with pride,
On the rich quilt sinks with becoming woe,
Wrapt in a gown, for sickness, and for show.
The fair ones feel such maladies as these,
When each new night-dress gives a new disease.
   A constant vapor o'er the palace flies;
Strange phantoms rising as the mists arise;                                    *40*
Dreadful, as hermit's dreams in haunted shades,
Or bright, as visions of expiring maids.
Now glaring fiends, and snakes on rolling spires,[34]
Pale specters, gaping tombs, and purple fires:
Now lakes of liquid gold, Elysian scenes,
And crystal domes, and angels in machines.
   Unnumbered throngs on every side are seen,
Of bodies changed to various forms by Spleen.
Here living tea-pots stand, one arm held out,
One bent; the handle this, and that the spout:                                 *50*
A pipkin[35] there, like Homer's tripod[36] walks;
Here sighs a jar, and there a goose-pie talks;
Men prove with child, as powerful fancy works,
And maids turned bottles, call aloud for corks.
   Safe past the gnome through this fantastic band,
A branch of healing spleenwort[37] in his hand.
Then thus addressed the power: "Hail, wayward Queen!
Who rule the sex to fifty from fifteen:
Parent of vapors[38] and of female wit,
Who give th' hysteric or poetic fit,                                           *60*
On various tempers act by various ways,
Make some take physic, others scribble plays;
Who cause the proud their visits to delay,
And send the godly in a pet to pray.
A nymph there is, that all thy power disdains,
And thousands more in equal mirth maintains.
But oh! if e'er thy gnome could spoil a grace,
Or raise a pimple on a beauteous face,
Like citron-waters[39] matrons' cheeks inflame,
Or change complexions at a losing game;                                        *70*
If e'er with airy horns[40] I planted heads,

---

[34] coils    [35] earthen jar    [36] three-legged stool
[37] a fern formerly believed effective in relieving
spleen
[38] affected emotional depression
[39] a liquor prepared with citrus rinds, believed
good for the complexion
[40] The man whose wife is unfaithful is traditionally
pictured as growing horns; "airy" here would
mean imaginary.

Or rumpled petticoats, or tumbled beds,
Or caus'd suspicion when no soul was rude,
Or discomposed the head-dress of a prude,
Or e'er to costive lap-dog gave disease,
Which not the tears of brightest eyes could ease:
Hear me, and touch Belinda with chagrin,
That single act gives half the world the spleen."
    The goddess with a discontented air
Seems to reject him though she grants his prayer.       *80*
A wondrous bag with both her hands she binds,
Like that where once Ulysses held the winds;[41]
There she collects the force of female lungs,
Sighs, sobs, and passions, and the war of tongues.
A vial next she fills with fainting fears,
Soft sorrows, melting griefs, and flowing tears.
The gnome rejoicing bears her gifts away,
Spreads his black wings, and slowly mounts to day.
    Sunk in Thalestris'[42] arms the nymph he found,
Her eyes dejected and her hair unbound.      *90*
Full o'er their heads the swelling bag he rent,
And all the furies issued at the vent.
Belinda burns with more than mortal ire,
And fierce Thalestris fans the rising fire.
"Oh wretched maid!" she spread her hands, and cried,
(While Hampton's echoes, "Wretched maid!" replied)
"Was it for this you took such constant care
The bodkin, comb, and essence to prepare?
For this your locks in paper durance bound,
For this with torturing irons wreathed around?      *100*
For this with fillets strained your tender head,
And bravely bore the double loads of lead?
Gods! shall the ravisher display your hair,
While the fops envy, and the ladies stare!
Honor forbid! at whose unrivaled shrine
Ease, pleasure, virtue, all our sex resign.
Methinks already I your tears survey,
Already hear the horrid things they say,
Already see you a degraded toast,
And all your honor in a whisper lost!      *110*
How shall I, then, your helpless fame defend?
'Twill then be infamy to seem your friend!
And shall this prize, th' inestimable prize,
Exposed through crystal to the gazing eyes,
And heightened by the diamond's circling rays,
On that rapacious hand forever blaze?
Sooner shall grass in Hyde Park Circus grow,

---

[41] In the Odyssey, Ulysses visits Aeolus, god of winds, who gives the wanderer a bag containing all the winds that might hinder his sailing.

[42] Pope gives this supporter of Belinda the name of a queen of the warlike Amazons.

And wits take lodgings in the sound of Bow,[43]
Sooner let earth, air, sea, to chaos fall,
Men, monkeys, lap-dogs, parrots, perish all!"                    *120*
    She said; then raging to Sir Plume repairs,
And bids her Beau demand the precious hairs:
(Sir Plume of amber snuff-box justly vain,
And the nice conduct of a clouded cane)
With earnest eyes, and round unthinking face,
He first the snuff-box opened, then the case,
And thus broke out—"My Lord, why, what the devil?
Z—ds! damn the lock! 'fore Gad, you must be civil!
Plague on't! 'tis past a jest—nay prithee, pox!
Give her the hair"—he spoke, and rapped his box.                    *130*
    "It grieves me much" (replied the Peer again)
"Who speaks so well should ever speak in vain.
But by this lock, this sacred lock I swear,
(Which never more shall join its parted hair;
Which never more its honors shall renew,
Clipped from the lovely head where late it grew)
That while my nostrils draw the vital air,
This hand, which won it, shall for ever wear."
He spoke, and speaking, in proud triumph spread
The long-contended honours of her head.                    *140*
    But Umbriel, hateful gnome! forbears not so;
He breaks the vial whence the sorrows flow.
Then see! the nymph in beauteous grief appears,
Her eyes half-languishing, half-drowned in tears;
On her heaved bosom hung her drooping head,
Which, with a sigh, she raised; and thus she said.
    "Forever cursed be this detested day,
Which snatched my best, my fav'rite curl away!
Happy! ah ten times happy had I been,
If Hampton Court these eyes had never seen!                    *150*
Yet am not I the first mistaken maid,
By love of courts to numerous ills betrayed.
Oh had I rather unadmired remained
In some lone isle, or distant northern land;
Where the gilt chariot never marks the way,
Where none learn ombre, none e'er taste bohea![44]
There kept my charms concealed from mortal eye,
Like roses, that in deserts bloom and die.
What moved my mind with youthful lords to roam?
Oh had I stayed, and said my prayers at home!                    *160*
'Twas this, the morning omens seemed to tell,
Thrice from my trembling hand the patch-box[45] fell;

---

[43] "Within sound of Bow bells"—the bells of the church of St. Mary-le-Bow—is the cockney region of London; hence lower class and unfashionable.
[44] a kind of tea

[45] a box for "beauty spots": bits of court plaster (a forerunner of adhesive tape) used to ornament the face

The tott'ring china shook without a wind,
Nay, Poll sat mute, and Shock was most unkind!
A sylph too warned me of the threats of fate,
In mystic visions, now believed too late!
See the poor remnants of these slighted hairs!
My hands shall rend what even thy rapine spares:
These in two sable ringlets taught to break,
Once gave new beauties to the snowy neck; 170
The sister-lock now sits uncouth, alone,
And in its fellow's fate foresees its own;
Uncurled it hangs, the fatal shears demands,
And tempts once more, thy sacrilegious hands.
Oh hadst thou, cruel! been content to seize
Hairs less in sight, or any hairs but these!"

CANTO V

She said: the pitying audience melt in tears.
But Fate and Jove had stopped the Baron's ears.
In vain Thalestris with reproach assails,
For who can move when fair Belinda fails?
Not half so fixed the Trojan could remain,
While Anna begged and Dido [46] raged in vain.
Then grave Clarissa graceful waved her fan;
Silence ensued, and thus the nymph began.
  "Say why are beauties praised and honored most,
The wise man's passion, and the vain man's toast? 10
Why decked with all that land and sea afford,
Why angels called, and angel-like adored?
Why round our coaches crowd the white-gloved beaux,
Why bows the side-box from its inmost rows;
How vain are all these glories, all our pains,
Unless good sense preserve what beauty gains:
That men may say, when we the front-box grace:
'Behold the first in virtue as in face!'
Oh! if to dance all night, and dress all day,
Charmed the small-pox, or chased old age away; 20
Who would not scorn what housewife's cares produce,
Or who would learn one earthly thing of use?
To patch, nay ogle, might become a saint,
Nor could it sure be such a sin to paint.
But since, alas! frail beauty must decay,
Curled or uncurled, since locks will turn to gray;
Since painted, or not painted, all shall fade,
And she who scorns a man, must die a maid;
What then remains but well our power to use,
And keep good-humor still whate'er we lose? 30

[46] Aeneas was unmoved by the reproaches of his wife, Dido, and her sister, Anna, when he proposed to leave Carthage for further wanderings.

And trust me, dear! good-humor can prevail,
When airs, and flights, and screams, and scolding fail.
Beauties in vain their pretty eyes may roll;
Charms strike the sight, but merit wins the soul."
    So spoke the dame, but no applause ensued;
Belinda frowned, Thalestris called her prude.
"To arms, to arms!" the fierce virago cries,
And swift as lightning to the combat flies.
All side in parties, and begin th' attack;
Fans clap, silks rustle, and tough whalebones crack;    *40*
Heroes' and heroines' shouts confus'dly rise,
And bass and treble voices strike the skies.
No common weapons in their hands are found,
Like gods they fight, nor dread a mortal wound.
    So when bold Homer makes the gods engage,
And heavenly breasts with human passions rage;
'Gainst Pallas, Mars; Latona, Hermes arms;[47]
And all Olympus rings with loud alarms:
Jove's thunder roars, heaven trembles all around,
Blue Neptune storms, the bellowing deeps resound:    *50*
Earth shakes her nodding towers, the ground gives way,
And the pale ghosts start at the flash of day!
    Triumphant Umbriel on a sconce's height
Clapped his glad wings, and sat to view the fight:
Propped on their bodkin spears, the sprites survey
The growing combat, or assist the fray.
    While through the press enraged Thalestris flies,
And scatters death around from both her eyes,
A beau and witling perished in the throng,
One died in metaphor, and one in song.    *60*
"O cruel nymph! a living death I bear,"
Cried Dapperwit, and sunk beside his chair.
A mournful glance Sir Fopling upwards cast,
"Those eyes are made so killing"—was his last.
Thus on Meander's[48] flowery margin lies
Th' expiring swan, and as he sings he dies.[49]
    When bold Sir Plume had drawn Clarissa down,
Chloe stepped in, and killed him with a frown;
She smiled to see the doughty hero slain,
But, at her smile, the beau revived again.    *70*
    Now Jove suspends his golden scales in air,
Weighs the men's wits against the lady's hair;
The doubtful beam long nods from side to side;
At length the wits mount up, the hairs subside.
    See, fierce Belinda on the Baron flies,
With more than usual lightning in her eyes:

---

[47] The specific identifications are less important than the comparison of the brawl to a battle of goddesses against gods.

[48] a wandering river in Phrygia
[49] According to legend the swan, normally mute, sings just once before it dies.

Nor feared the chief th' unequal fight to try,
Who sought no more than on his foe to die.
But this bold lord with manly strength endued,
She with one finger and a thumb subdued:                    *80*
Just where the breath of life his nostrils drew,
A charge of snuff the wily virgin threw;
The gnomes direct, to every atom just,
The pungent grains of titillating dust.
Sudden, with starting tears each eye o'erflows,
And the high dome re-echoes to his nose.
  "Now meet thy fate," incensed Belinda cried,
And drew a deadly bodkin from her side.
(The same, his ancient personage to deck,
Her great grandsire wore about his neck,                    *90*
In three seal-rings; which after, melted down,
Formed a vast buckle for his widow's gown:
Her infant grandame's whistle next it grew,
The bells she jingled, and the whistle blew;
Then in a bodkin graced her mother's hairs,
Which long she wore, and now Belinda wears.)
  "Boast not my fall" (he cried) "insulting foe!
Thou by some other shalt be laid as low,
Nor think, to die dejects my lofty mind:
All that I dread is leaving you behind!                     *100*
Rather than so, ah let me still survive,
And burn in Cupid's flames—but burn alive."
  "Restore the lock!" she cries; and all around
"Restore the lock!" the vaulted roofs rebound.
Not fierce Othello in so loud a strain
Roared for the handkerchief that caused his pain.[50]
But see how oft ambitious aims are crossed,
And chiefs contend till all the prize is lost!
The lock, obtained with guilt, and kept with pain,
In every place is sought, but sought in vain:               *110*
With such a prize no mortal must be blest,
So heaven decrees! with heaven who can contest?
  Some thought it mounted to the lunar sphere,
Since all things lost on earth are treasured there.
There heroes' wits are kept in pond'rous vases,
And beaux' in snuff-boxes and tweezer-cases.
There broken vows and death-bed alms are found,
And lovers' hearts with ends of riband bound,
The courtier's promises, and sick man's prayers,
The smiles of harlots, and the tears of heirs,             *120*
Cages for gnats, and chains to yoke a flea,
Dried butterflies, and tomes of casuistry.

---

[50] Othello suspects that his wife, Desdemona, has given a prized handkerchief to her supposed lover and demands that she produce it. (Shakespeare, *Othello*, III, iv.)

But trust the Muse—she saw it upward rise,
Though marked by none but quick, poetic eyes:
(So Rome's great founder to the heavens withdrew,
To Proculus alone confessed in view)[51]
A sudden star, it shot through liquid air,
And drew behind a radiant trail of hair.
Not Berenice's Locks[52] first rose so bright,
The heavens bespangling with disheveled light.                          130
The sylphs behold it kindling as it flies,
And pleased pursue its progress through the skies.
   This the beau monde shall from the Mall[53] survey,
And hail with music its propitious ray.
This the blest lover shall for Venus take,
And send up vows from Rosamonda's lake.[54]
This Partridge[55] soon shall view in cloudless skies,
When next he looks through Galileo's eyes,[56]
And hence th' egregious wizard shall foredoom
The fate of Louis, and the fall of Rome.                                140
   Then cease, bright nymph! to mourn thy ravished hair,
Which adds new glory to the shining sphere!
Not all the tresses that fair head can boast,
Shall draw such envy as the lock you lost.
For, after all the murders of your eye,
When, after millions slain, yourself shall die:
When those fair suns shall set, as set they must,
And all those tresses shall be laid in dust,
This lock, the Muse shall consecrate to fame,
And 'midst the stars inscribe Belinda's name.   (*1714*)                150

## Epitaph

### INTENDED FOR SIR ISAAC NEWTON

Nature, and Nature's laws, lay hid in
   night.
God said, *Let Newton be!* And all was
   light.   (*1730*)

## Ode: The Dying Christian to His Soul

Vital spark of heavenly flame!
Quit, oh quit this mortal frame:
Trembling, hoping, ling'ring, flying,
Oh the pain, the bliss of dying!

Cease, fond nature, cease thy strife,
And let me languish into life.

Hark! they whisper; angels say,
Sister Spirit, come away.
What is this absorbs me quite?
Steals my senses, shuts my sight,                                        10
Drowns my spirits, draws my breath?
Tell me, my soul, can this be death?

The world recedes; it disappears!
Heaven opens on my eyes! my ears
   With sounds seraphic ring:
Lend, lend your wings! I mount! I fly!
O grave! where is thy victory?
   O death, where is they
     sting?   (*1730*)

---

[51] Romulus was translated to heaven in a storm cloud; he later appeared to Proculus, a Senator.
[52] A constellation (*Coma Berenicia*) is said to have been formed from the hair that Berenice, an Egyptian queen, dedicated to the gods in exchange for her husband's return from war.
[53] a fashionable walk in St. James's Park
[54] a pond in St. James's Park
[55] John Partridge (1644–1715), a foolish stargazer and prognosticator, who is also the butt of Swift's "Bickerstaff" joke
[56] a telescope

## The Universal Prayer

Father of all! in every age,
  In every clime adored,
By saint, by savage, and by sage,
  Jehovah, Jove, or Lord!

Thou First Great Cause, least
    understood:
  Who all my sense confined
To know but this, that Thou art good,
  And that myself am blind;

Yet gave me, in this dark estate,
  To see the good from ill;      *10*
And binding nature fast in fate,
  Left free the human will.

What conscience dictates to be done,
  Or warns me not to do,
This, teach me more than hell to shun,
  That, more than heaven pursue.

What blessings thy free bounty gives,
  Let me not cast away;
For God is paid when man receives,
  T' enjoy is to obey.      *20*

Yet not to earth's contracted span,
  Thy goodness let me bound,
Or think Thee lord alone of man,
  When thousand worlds are round:

Let not this weak, unknowing hand
  Presume thy bolts to throw,
And deal damnation round the land,
  On each I judge thy foe.

If I am right, they grace impart,
  Still in the right to stay;      *30*
If I am wrong, oh teach my heart
  To find that better way.

Save me alike from foolish pride,
  Or impious discontent,
At aught thy wisdom has denied,
  Or aught thy goodness lent.

Teach me to feel another's woe,
  To hide the fault I see;
That mercy I to others show,
  That mercy show to me.      *40*

Mean though I am, not wholly so
  Since quickened by thy breath;
Oh lead me wheresoe'er I go,
  Through this day's life or death.

This day, be bread and peace my lot:
  All else beneath the sun,
Thou knowest if best bestowed or not,
  And let thy will be done.

To thee, whose temple is all space,
  Whose alter, earth, sea, skies!      *50*
One chorus let all being raise!
  All nature's incense rise!  (*1738*)

## On a Certain Lady at Court

I know the thing that's most uncommon;
  (Envy be silent, and attend!)
I know a reasonable woman,
  Handsome and witty, yet a friend.

Not warped by passion, awed by rumour,
  Not grave through pride, or gay
    through folly,
An equal mixture of good humour,
  And sensible soft melancholy.

"Has she no faults then (Envy says) sir?"
  Yes, she has one, I must aver;      *10*
When all the world conspires to praise
    her,
  The woman's deaf, and does not
    hear.  (*1751*)

# SAMUEL JOHNSON / 1709–1784

## A Short Song of Congratulation

Long-expected one and twenty
  Lingering year at last is flown,
Pomp and Pleasure, Pride and Plenty,
  Great Sir John, are all your own.

Loosened from the minor's tether,
  Free to mortgage or to sell,
Wild as wind, and light as feather
  Bid the slaves of thrift farewell.

Call the Bettys, Kates, and Jennys
  Every name that laughs at Care,    *10*
Lavish of your grandsire's guineas,
  Show the spirit of an heir.

All that prey on vice and folly
  Joy to see their quarry fly,
Here the gamester light and jolly
  There the lender grave and sly.

Wealth, Sir John, was made to wander,
  Let it wander as it will;
See the jockey, see the pander,
  Bid them come, and take their fill.    *20*

When the bonny blade carouses,
  Pockets full, and spirits high,
What are acres? What are houses?
  Only dirt, or wet or dry.

If the guardian or the mother
  Tell the woes of willful waste,
Scorn their counsel and their pother,
  You can hang or drown at last.

                    (*1780*)

# THOMAS GRAY / 1716–1771

## Ode on a Distant Prospect of Eton College

  Ye distant spires, ye antique towers,
That crown the wat'ry glade,
Where grateful Science still adores
Her Henry's[1] holy shade;
And ye, that from the stately brow
Of Windsor's heights th' expanse below
Of grove, of lawn, of mead survey,
Whose turf, whose shade, whose flowers
    among
Wanders the hoary Thames along
His silver-winding way.    *10*

  Ah happy hills, ah pleasing shade,
Ah fields beloved in vain,
Where once my careless childhood
    strayed,
A stranger yet to pain!
I feel the gales, that from ye blow,
A momentary bliss bestow,
As waving fresh their gladsome wing,
My weary soul they seem to soothe,
And, redolent of joy and youth,
To breathe a second spring.    *20*

  Say, Father Thames, for thou hast seen
Full many a sprightly race
Disporting on thy margent green
The paths of pleasure trace,
Who foremost now delight to cleave
With pliant arm thy glassy wave?
The captive linnet which enthrall?
What idle progeny succeed
To chase the rolling circle's speed,
Or urge the flying ball?    *30*

  While some on earnest business bent
Their murm'ring labours ply
'Gainst graver hours, that bring constraint
To sweeten liberty:
Some bold adventurers disdain
The limits of their little reign,
And unknown regions dare descry:

---

[1] Eton was founded by Henry VI in 1440–1441.

Still as they run they look behind,
They hear a voice in every wind,
And snatch a fearful joy.     *40*

Gay hope is theirs by fancy fed,
Less pleasing when possessed;
The tear forgot as soon as shed,
The sunshine of the breast:
Theirs buxom health of rosy hue,
Wild wit, invention ever-new,
And lively cheer of vigour born;
The thoughtless day, the easy night,
The spirits pure, the slumbers light,
That fly th' approach of morn.     *50*

Alas, regardless of their doom,
The little victims play!
No sense have they of ills to come,
Nor care beyond to-day:
Yet see how all around 'em wait
The Ministers of human fate,
And black Misfortune's baleful train!
Ah, show them where in ambush stand
To seize their prey the murth'rous band
Ah, tell them, they are men!     *60*

These shall the fury Passions tear,
The vultures of the mind,
Disdainful Anger, pallid Fear,
And Shame that skulks behind;
Or pining Love shall waste their youth,
Or Jealousy with rankling tooth,
That inly gnaws the secret heart,
And Envy wan, and faded Care,
Grim-visaged comfortless Despair,
And Sorrow's piercing dart.     *70*

Ambition this shall tempt to rise,
Then whirl the wretch from high,
To bitter Scorn a sacrifice,
And grinning Infamy.
The stings of Falsehood those shall try
And hard Unkindness' altered eye,
That mocks the tear it forced to flow;
And keen Remorse with blood defiled,
And moody Madness laughing wild
Amid severest woe.     *80*

Lo, in the vale of years beneath
A grisly troop are seen,
The painful family of Death,
More hideous than their Queen:
This racks the joints, this fires the veins,
That every labouring sinew strains,
Those in the deeper vitals rage:
Lo, Poverty, to fill the band,
That numbs the soul with icy hand,
And slow-consuming Age.     *90*

To each his suff'rings: all are men,
Condemned alike to groan;
The tender for another's pain,
Th' unfeeling for his own.
Yet ah! why should they know their fate?
Since sorrow never comes too late,
And happiness too swiftly flies.
Thought would destroy their paradise.
No more; where ignorance is bliss,
'Tis folly to be wise.   (*1747*)     *100*

## Ode on the Death of a Favorite Cat, Drowned in a Tub of Gold Fishes

'Twas on a lofty vase's side,
Where China's gayest art had dyed
    The azure flowers, that blow;
Demurest of the tabby kind,
The pensive Selima reclined,
    Gazed on the lake below.

Her conscious tail her joy declared;
The fair round face, the snowy beard,
    The velvet of her paws,

Her coat, that with the tortoise vies,                        10
Her ears of jet, and emerald eyes,
   She saw; and purred applause.

Still had she gazed; but 'midst the tide
Two angel forms were seen to glide,
   The Genii of the stream:
Their scaly armor's Tyrian hue[1]
Through richest purple to the view
   Betrayed a golden gleam.

The hapless nymph with wonder saw:
A whisker first and then a claw,                              20
   With many an ardent wish,
She stretched in vain to reach the prize.
What female heart can gold despise?
   What cat's averse to fish?

Presumptuous maid! with looks intent
Again she stretched, again she bent,
   Nor knew the gulf between.
Malignant Fate sat by, and smiled;
The slippery verge her feet beguiled,
   She tumbled headlong in.                                   30

Eight times emerging from the flood
She mewed to every wat'ry god,
   Some speedy aid to send.
No dolphin came, no nereid[2] stirred:
Nor cruel Tom nor Susan heard.
   A favorite has no friend!

From hence, ye beauties, undeceived,
Know, one false step is ne'er retrieved,
   And be with caution bold.
Not all that tempts your wandering eyes                       40
And heedless hearts is lawful prize;
   Nor all that glisters, gold.   (*1747*)

# Elegy

## WRITTEN IN A COUNTRY CHURCHYARD

The curfew tolls the knell of parting day,
The lowing herd winds slowly o'er the lea,
The plowman homeward plods his weary way,
And leaves the world to darkness and to me.

Now fades the glimmering landscape on the sight,
And all the air a solemn stillness holds,
Save where the beetle wheels his droning flight,
And drowsy tinklings lull the distant folds;

---

[1] purple, the color of royal vestments            [2] sea nymph

Save that from yonder ivy-mantled tow'r
The moping owl does to the moon complain
Of such, as wand'ring near her secret bow'r,
Molest her ancient solitary reign.

Beneath those rugged elms, that yew-tree's shade,
Where heaves the turf in many a mould'ring heap,
Each in his narrow cell for ever laid,
The rude forefathers of the hamlet sleep.

The breezy call of incense-breathing morn,
The swallow twitt'ring from the straw-built shed,
The cock's shrill clarion, or the echoing horn,
No more shall rouse them from their lowly bed.

For them no more the blazing hearth shall burn,
Or busy housewife ply her evening care:
No children run to lisp their sire's return,
Or climb his knees the envied kiss to share.

Oft did the harvest to their sickle yield,
Their furrow oft the stubborn glebe[1] has broke;
How jocund did they drive their team afield!
How bowed the woods beneath their sturdy stroke!

Let not Ambition mock their useful toil,
Their homely joys, and destiny obscure;
Nor Grandeur hear with a disdainful smile,
The short and simple annals of the poor.

The boast of heraldry, the pomp of pow'r,
And all that beauty, all that wealth e'er gave
Awaits alike th' inevitable hour.
The paths of glory lead but to the grave.

Nor you, ye Proud, impute to these the fault,
If Mem'ry o'er their tomb no trophies raise,
Where through the long-drawn aisle and fretted vault
The pealing anthem swells the note of praise.

Can storied urn or animated bust
Back to its mansion call the fleeting breath?
Can Honour's voice provoke the silent dust,
Or Flatt'ry soothe the full cold ear of Death?

Perhaps in this neglected spot is laid
Some heart once pregnant with celestial fire;
Hands that the rod of empire might have swayed,
Or waked to ecstasy the living lyre.

But Knowledge to their eyes her ample page
Rich with the spoils of time did ne'er unroll:
Chill Penury repressed their noble rage,
And froze the genial current of the soul.

10

20

30

40

50

---
[1] sod

Full many a gem of purest ray serene,
The dark unfathomed caves of ocean bear:
Full many a flower is born to blush unseen,
And waste its sweetness on the desert air.

Some village Hampden,[2] that with dauntless breast
The little tyrant of his fields withstood;
Some mute inglorious Milton here may rest,
Some Cromwell guiltless of his country's blood.                    60

Th' applause of list'ning senates to command,
The threats of pain and ruin to despise,
To scatter plenty o'er a smiling land,
And read their hist'ry in a nation's eyes,

Their lot forbad: nor circumscribed alone
Their growing virtues, but their crimes confined;
Forbad to wade through slaughter to a throne,
And shut the gates of mercy on mankind,

The struggling pangs of conscious truth to hide,
To quench the blushes of ingenuous shame,                    70
Or heap the shrine of luxury and Pride
With incense kindled at the Muse's flame.

Far from the madding crowd's ignoble strife,
Their sober wishes never learned to stray;
Along the cool sequestered vale of life
They kept the noiseless tenor of their way.

Yet ev'n these bones from insult to protect
Some frail memorial still erected nigh,
With uncouth rhymes and shapeless sculpture decked,
Implores the passing tribute of a sigh.                    80

Their name, their years, spelt by th' unlettered muse,
The place of fame and elegy supply:
And many a holy text around she strews,
That teach the rustic moralist to die.

For who to dumb forgetfulness a prey,
This pleasing anxious being e'er resigned,
Left the warm precincts of the cheerful day,
Nor cast one longing ling'ring look behind?

On some fond breast the parting soul relies,
Some pious drops the closing eye requires;                    90
Ev'n from the tomb the voice of Nature cries,
Ev'n in our ashes live their wonted fires.

For thee, who mindful of th' unhonoured dead
Dost in these lines their artless tale relate;
If chance, by lonely contemplation led,
Some kindred spirit shall inquire thy fate,

[2] John Hampden (1594–1643) was a leader of the    of 1642–1649.
opposition to Charles I that led to the Civil War

Haply some hoary-headed swain may say,
"Oft have we seen him at the peep of dawn
Brushing with hasty steps the dews away
To meet the sun upon the upland lawn. 100

"There at the foot of yonder nodding beech
That wreathes its old fantastic roots so high,
His listless length at noontide would he stretch,
And pore upon the brook that babbles by.

"Hard by yon wood, now smiling as in scorn,
Mutt'ring his wayward fancies he would rove,
Now drooping, woeful wan, like one forlorn,
Or crazed with care, or crossed in hopeless love.

"One morn I missed him on the customed hill,
Along the heath and near his fav'rite tree; 110
Another came; nor yet beside the rill,
Nor up the lawn, nor at the wood was he;

"The next with dirges due in sad array
Slow through the church-way path we saw him borne.
Approach and read (for thou canst read) the lay,
Graved on the stone beneath yon agéd thorn."

### THE EPITAPH

*Here rests his head upon the lap of Earth*
*A Youth to Fortune and to Fame unknown.*
*Fair Science frowned not on his humble birth,*
*And Melancholy marked him for her own.* 120

*Large was his bounty, and his soul sincere,*
*Heav'n did a recompense as largely send:*
*He gave to Mis'ry all he had, a tear,*
*He gained from Heav'n ('twas all he wished) a friend.*

*No farther seek his merits to disclose,*
*Or draw his frailties from their dread abode,*
*(There they alike in trembling hope repose,)*
*The bosom of his Father and his God.* (1751)

# William Shakespeare to Mrs. Anne, Regular Servant to the Rev. Mr. Precentor of York

A moment's patience, gentle Mistress Anne,
  (But stint your clack for sweet St. Charity):
'Tis Willie begs, once a right proper man,
  Though now a book, and interleaved you see.
Much have I borne from cankered critic's spite,
  From fumbling baronets, and poets small,

Pert barristers, and parsons nothing bright:
　　But what awaits me now is worst of all.
'Tis true, our master's temper natural
　　Was fashioned fair in meek and dove-like guise;　　　　*10*
But may not honey's self be turned to gall
　　By residence, by marriage, and sore eyes?
If then he wreak on me his wicked will,
　　Steal to his closet at the hour of prayer;
And (when thou hear'st the organ piping shrill)
　　Grease his best pen, and all he scribbles, tear.
Better to bottom tarts and cheesecakes nice,
　　Better the roast meat from the fire to save,
　　Than thus be patched and cobbled in one's grave.　　　*20*
Better be twisted into caps for spice,
So York shall taste what Clouet never knew,
　　So from our works sublimer fumes shall rise;
While Nancy earns the praise to Shakespeare due,
　　For glorious puddings and immortal pies.　　(*1765*)

# WILLIAM COLLINS / 1721–1759

## Ode Written in the Beginning of the Year 1746

How sleep the brave[1] who sink to rest
By all their country's wishes blest!
When Spring, with dewy fingers cold,
Returns to deck their hallowed mold,
She there shall dress a sweeter sod
Than Fancy's feet have ever trod.

By fairy hands their knell is rung,
By forms unseen their dirge is sung;
There Honor comes, a pilgrim gray,
To bless the turf that wraps their clay,　　*10*
And Freedom shall awhile repair,
To dwell a weeping hermit there!

　　　　　　　　　　　　　　　　　(*1746*)

## Ode to Evening

If aught of oaten stop,[1] or pastoral song,
　May hope, chaste Eve, to sooth thy modest ear,
　　　Like thy own solemn springs,
　　　Thy springs, and dying gales,
　O nymph reserved, while now the bright-haired sun

---

[1] presumably the soldiers who fell in repelling the invasion of England by Scottish Jacobites under Bonnie Prince Charlie

[1] flute made of an oat straw

Sits in yon western tent, whose cloudy skirts,
    With brede² ethereal wove,
    O'erhang his wavy bed:
Now air is hushed, save where the weak-eycd bat,
With short shrill shriek flits by on leathern wing,        *10*
    Or where the beetle winds
    His small but sullen horn,
As oft he rises 'midst the twilight path,
Against the pilgrim born in heedless hum:
    Now teach me, maid composed,
    To breathe some softened strain,
Whose numbers stealing through thy dark'ning vale,
May not unseemly with its stillness suit,
    As musing slow, I hail
    They genial loved return!        *20*
For when thy folding star arising shows
His paly circlet, at his warning lamp
    The fragrant hours, and elves
    Who slept in flow'rs the day,
And many a nymph who wreaths her brows with sedge,
And sheds the fresh'ning dew, and lovelier still,
    The pensive pleasures sweet     ·
    Prepare thy shadowy car.
Then lead, calm vot'ress, where some sheety lake
Cheers the lone heath, or some time-hallowed pile,        *30*
    Or upland fallows gray
    Reflect its last cool gleam.
But when chill blust'ring winds, or driving rain,
Forbid my willing feet, be mine the hut,
    That from the mountain's side,
    Views wilds, and swelling floods,
And hamlets brown, and dim-discovered spires,
And hears their simple bell, and marks o'er all
    Thy dewy fingers draw
    The gradual dusky veil.        *40*
While Spring shall pour his show'rs, as oft he wont,
And bathe thy breathing tresses, meekest Eve!
    While Summer loves to sport
    Beneath thy ling'ring light;
While sallow Autumn fills thy lap with leaves;
Or Winter yelling through the troublous air,
    Affrights thy shrinking train,
    And rudely rends thy robes;
So long, sure-found beneath the sylvan shed,
Shall Fancy, Friendship, Science, rose-lipped Health,        *50*
    Thy gentlest influence own,
    And hymn thy fav'rite name!   (*1747*)

---

² embroidery

## Ode to Fear

### STROPHE

Thou, to whom the world unknown
With all its shadowy shapes is shown;
Who see'st appalled the unreal scene,
While Fancy lifts the veil between:
    Ah Fear! Ah frantic Fear!
    I see, I see thee near.
I know thy hurried step, thy haggard eye!
Like thee I start, like thee disordered fly,
For lo, what monsters in thy train appear!
Danger, whose limbs of giant mold                              10
What mortal eye can fixed behold?
Who stalks his round, an hideous form,
Howling amidst the midnight storm,
Or throws him on the ridgy steep
Of some loose hanging rock to sleep:
And with him thousand phantoms joined,
Who prompt to deeds accursed the mind:
And those, the fiends, who near allied,
O'er Nature's wounds and wrecks preside;
Whilst Vengeance, in the lurid air,                            20
Lifts her red arm, exposed and bare:
On whom that ravening brood of Fate,
Who lap the blood of Sorrow, wait;
Who, Fear, this ghastly train can see,
And look not madly wild, like thee?

### EPODE

In earliest Greece to thee with partial choice,
    The grief-full Muse[1] addressed her infant tongue;
The maids and matrons, on her awful voice,
    Silent and pale in wild amazement hung.

Yet he, the bard who first invoked thy name,[2]                30
    Disdained in Marathon its power to feel:
For not alone he nursed the poet's flame,
    But reached from virtue's hand the patriot's steel.

But who is he whom later garlands grace,[3]
    Who left a while o'er Hybla's[4] dews to rove,
With trembling eyes thy dreary steps to trace,
    Where thou and Furies shared the baleful grove?

Wrapped in thy cloudy veil, the incestuous queen
Sighed the sad call her son and husband heard,

---

[1] Melpomene, the Muse of Tragedy
[2] Aeschylus, the Greek tragedian, who was also a soldier in the Persian Wars
[3] Sophocles, another tragic playwright, who followed Aeschylus
[4] a city and mountain in Sicily

For he knows that God is his Saviour.

For there is nothing sweeter than his peace when at rest.

For there is nothing brisker than his life when in motion.

For he is of the Lord's poor, and so indeed is he called by benevolence
  perpetually—Poor Jeoffry! poor Jeoffry! the rat has bit thy throat.

For I bless the name of the Lord Jesus that Jeoffry is better.

For the divine spirit comes about his body to sustain it in complete cat.

For his tongue is exceeding pure so that it has in purity what it wants in
  music.

For he is docile and can learn certain things.                              50

For he can sit up with gravity, which is patience upon approbation.

For he can fetch and carry, which is patience in employment.

For he can jump over a stick, which is patience upon proof positive.

For he can spraggle upon waggle at the word of command.

For he can jump from an eminence into his master's bosom.

For he can catch the cork and toss it again.

For he is hated by the hypocrite and miser.

For the former is afraid of detection.

For the latter refuses the charge.

For he camels his back to bear the first notion of business.                60

For he is good to think on, if a man would express himself neatly.

For he made a great figure in Egypt for his signal services.

For he killed the Icneumon rat, very pernicious by land.

For his ears are so acute that they sting again.

For from this proceeds the passing quickness of his attention.

For by stroking of him I have found out electricity.

For I perceived God's light about him both wax and fire.

For the electrical fire is the spiritual substance which God sends from heaven
  to sustain the bodies both of man and beast.

For God has blessed him in the variety of his movements.

For, though he cannot fly, he is an excellent clamberer.                    70

For his motions upon the face of the earth are more than any other
  quadruped.

For he can tread to all the measures upon the music.

For he can swim for life.

For he can creep.   (*c. 1760*)

## An Elegy on That Glory of Her Sex, Mrs. Mary Blaize

Good people all, with one accord,
    Lament for Madam Blaize,
Who never wanted a good word—
    From those who spoke her praise.

The needy seldom passed her door,
    And always found her kind;
She freely lent to all the poor,—
    Who left a pledge behind.

She strove the neighbourhood to please,
    With manners wondrous winning,     10
And never followed wicked ways,—
    Unless when she was sinning.

At church, in silks and satins new,
    With hoop of monstrous size,
She never slumbered in her pew,—
    But when she shut her eyes.

Her love was sought, I do aver,
    By twenty beaus and more;
The king himself has followed her,—
    When she has walked before.     20

But now her wealth and finery fled,
    Her hangers-on cut short all;
The doctors found, when she was dead,—
    Her last disorder mortal.

Let us lament, in sorrow sore,
    For Kent Street well may say,
That had she lived a twelve-month more,
    She had not died today.   (1759)

## Song

When lovely woman stoops to folly,
    And finds too late that men betray,
What charm can sooth her melancholy,
    What art can wash her guilt away?

The only art her guilt to cover,
    To hide her shame from every eye,
To give repentance to her lover,
    And wring his bosom—is to die.
                                        (1766)

## An Elegy on the Death of a Mad Dog

Good people all, of every sort,
    Give ear unto my song;
And if you find it wondrous short,
    It cannot hold you long.

In Isling town there was a man,
    Of whom the world might say,
That still a godly race he ran,
    Whene'er he went to pray.

A kind and gentle heart he had,
    To comfort friends and foes;     10
The naked every day he clad,
    When he put on his clothes.

And in that town a dog was found,
    As many dogs there be,
Both mongrel, puppy, whelp and hound,
    And curs of low degree.

This dog and man at first were friends;
    But when a pique began,
The dog, to gain some private ends,
    Went mad and bit the man.     20

Around from all the neighboring streets,
    The wondering neighbors ran,
And swore the dog had lost his wits,
    To bite so good a man.

The wound it seemed both sore and sad,
    To every Christian eye;
And while they swore the dog was mad,
    They swore the man would die.

But soon a wonder came to light,
    That showed the rogues they lied,     30
The man recovered of the bite,
    The dog it was that died.   (1766)

## The Deserted Village

Sweet Auburn, loveliest village of the plain,
Where health and plenty cheered the labouring swain,
Where smiling spring its earliest visit paid,
And parting summer's lingering blooms delayed,
Dear lovely bowers of innocence and ease,
Seats of my youth, when every sport could please,
How often have I loitered o'er thy green,
Where humble happiness endeared each scene!
How often have I paused on every charm,
The sheltered cot, the cultivated farm,                          10
The never-failing brook, the busy mill,
The decent church that topped the neighbouring hill,
The hawthorn bush, with seats beneath the shade,
For talking age and whispering lovers made!
How often have I blessed the coming day,
When toil remitting lent its turn to play,
And all the village train, from labour free
Led up their sports beneath the spreading tree,
While many a pastime circled in the shade,
The young contending as the old surveyed;                        20
And many a gambol frolicked o'er the ground,
And sleights of art and feats of strength went round;
And still as each repeated pleasure tired,
Succeeding sports the mirthful band inspired;
The dancing pair that simply sought renown
By holding out to tire each other down;
The swain mistrustless of his smutted face,
While secret laughter tittered round the place;
The bashful virgin's side-long looks of love,
The matron's glance that would those looks reprove!              30
These were thy charms, sweet village; sports like these,
With sweet succession, taught even toil to please;
These round thy bowers their cheerful influence shed,
These were thy charms—But all these charms are fled.
  Sweet smiling village, loveliest of the lawn,
Thy sports are fled, and all thy charms withdrawn;
Amidst thy bowers the tyrant's hand is seen,
And desolation saddens all thy green:
One only master grasps the whole domain,
And half a tillage stints thy smiling plain;                     40
No more thy glassy brook reflects the day,
But choked with sedges, works its weedy way;
Along thy glades, a solitary guest,
The hollow-sounding bittern guards its nest;
Amidst thy desert walks the lapwing flies,
And tires their echoes with unvaried cries.

Sunk are thy bowers, in shapeless ruin all,
And the long grass o'ertops the mouldering wall;
And, trembling, shrinking from the spoiler's hand,
Far, far away, thy children leave the land.                              50
  Ill fares the land, to hastening ills a prey,
Where wealth accumulates, and men decay:
Princes and lords may flourish, or may fade;
A breath can make them, as a breath has made;
But a bold peasantry, their country's pride,
When once destroyed, can never be supplied.
  A time there was, ere England's griefs began,
When every rood of ground maintained its man;
For him light labour spread her wholesome store,
Just gave what life required, but gave no more:                          60
His best companions, innocence and health;
And his best riches, ignorance of wealth.
  But times are altered; trade's unfeeling train
Usurp the land and dispossess the swain;
Along the lawn, where scattered hamlets rose,
Unwieldy wealth, and cumbrous pomp repose;
And every want to opulence allied,
And every pang that folly pays to pride.
Those gentle hours that plenty bade to bloom,
Those calm desires that asked but little room,                          70
Those healthful sports that graced the peaceful scene,
Lived in each look, and brightened all the green;
These, far departing seek a kinder shore,
And rural mirth and manners are no more.
Sweet Auburn! parent of the blissful hour,
Thy glades forlorn confess the tyrant's power.
Here as I take my solitary rounds,
Amidst thy tangling walks, and ruined grounds,
And, many a year elapsed, return to view
Where once the cottage stood, the hawthorn grew,                        80
Remembrance wakes with all her busy train,
Swells at my breast, and turns the past to pain.
  In all my wanderings round this world of care,
In all my griefs—and God has given my share—
I still had hopes, my latest hours to crown,
Amidst these humble bowers to lay me down;
To husband out life's taper at the close,
And keep the flame from wasting by repose.
I still had hopes, for pride attends us still,
Amidst the swains to show my book-learned skill,                        90
Around my fire an evening group to draw,
And tell of all I felt, and all I saw;
And, as an hare whom hounds and horns pursue,
Pants to the place from whence at first she flew,
I still had hopes, my long vexations past,

Here to return—and die at home at last.
O blest retirement, friend to life's decline,
Retreats from care that never must be mine,
How happy he who crowns, in shades like these,
A youth of labour with an age of ease;       *100*
Who quits a world where strong temptations try,
And, since 'tis hard to combat, learns to fly!
For him no wretches, born to work and weep,
Explore the mine, or tempt the dangerous deep;
No surly porter stand in guilty state
To spurn imploring famine from the gate,
But on he moves to meet his latter end,
Angels around befriending virtue's friend;
Bends to the grave with unperceived decay,
While resignation gently slopes the way;       *110*
And, all his prospects brightening to the last,
His Heaven commences ere the world be past!
Sweet was the sound, when oft at evening's close,
Up yonder hill the village murmur rose;
There, as I passed with careless steps and slow,
The mingling notes came softened from below;
The swain responsive as the milk-maid sung,
The sober herd that lowed to meet their young,
The noisy geese that gabbled o'er the pool,
The playful children just let loose from school,       *120*
The watch-dog's voice that bayed the whispering wind,
And the loud laugh that spoke the vacant mind,
These all in sweet confusion sought the shade,
And filled each pause the nightingale had made.
But now the sounds of population fail,
No cheerful murmurs fluctuate in the gale,
No busy steps the grass-grown foot-way tread,
For all the bloomy flush of life is fled.
All but yon widowed, solitary thing
That feebly bends beside the plashy spring;       *130*
She, wretched matron, forced in age, for bread,
To strip the brook with mantling cresses spread,
To pick her wintry faggot from the thorn,
To seek her nightly shed, and weep till morn;
She only left of all the harmless train,
The sad historian of the pensive plain.
Near yonder copse, where once the garden smiled,
And still where many a garden-flower grows wild;
There, where a few torn shrubs the place disclose,
The village preacher's modest mansion rose.       *140*
A man he was, to all the country dear,
And passing rich with forty pounds a year;
Remote from towns he ran his godly race,
Nor e'er had changed, nor wished to change his place;

Unpractised he to fawn, or seek for power,
By doctrines fashioned to the varying hour;
Far other aims his heart had learned to prize,
More skilled to raise the wretched than to rise.
His house was known to all the vagrant train,
He chid their wanderings, but relieved their pain;                    *150*
The long-remembered beggar was his guest,
Whose beard descending swept his aged breast;
The ruined spendthrift, now no longer proud,
Claimed kindred there, and had his claims allowed;
The broken soldier, kindly bade to stay,
Sat by his fire, and talked the night away;
Wept o'er his wounds, or, tales of sorrow done,
Shouldered his crutch, and showed how fields were won.
Pleased with his guests, the good man learned to glow,
And quite forgot their vices in their woe;                    *160*
Careless their merits, or their faults to scan,
His pity gave ere charity began.
    Thus to relieve the wretched was his pride,
And even his failings leaned to Virtue's side;
But in his duty prompt at every call,
He watched and wept, he prayed and felt, for all.
And, as a bird each fond endearment tries,
To tempt its new-fledged offspring to the skies;
He tried each art, reproved each dull delay,
Allured to brighter worlds, and led the way.                    *170*
    Beside the bed where parting life was laid,
And sorrow, guilt, and pain, by turns, dismayed
The reverend champion stood. At his control,
Despair and anguish fled the struggling soul;
Comfort came down the trembling wretch to raise,
And his last faltering accents whispered praise.
    At church, with meek and unaffected grace,
His looks adorned the venerable place;
Truth from his lips prevailed with double sway,
And fools, who came to scoff, remained to pray.                    *180*
The service past, around the pious man,
With steady zeal, each honest rustic ran;
Even children followed, with endearing wile,
And plucked his gown, to share the good man's smile.
His ready smile a parent's warmth expressed,
Their welfare pleased him, and their cares distressed;
To them his heart, his love, his griefs were given,
But all his serious thoughts had rest in Heaven.
As some tall cliff that lifts its awful form,
Swells from the vale, and midway leaves the storm,                    *190*
Though round its breast the rolling clouds are spread,
Eternal sunshine settles on its head.
    Beside yon straggling fence that skirts the way,

With blossomed furze unprofitably gay,
There, in his noisy mansion, skilled to rule,
The village master taught his little school;
A man severe he was, and stern to view,
I knew him well, and every truant knew;
Well had the boding tremblers learned to trace
The day's disasters in his morning face; 200
Full well they laughed, with counterfeited glee,
At all his jokes, for many a joke had he:
Full well the busy whisper circling round,
Conveyed the dismal tidings when he frowned;
Yet he was kind, or if severe in aught,
The love he bore to learning was in fault;
The village all declared how much he knew;
'Twas certain he could write, and cipher too;
Lands he could measure, terms and tides presage,
And even the story ran that he could gauge. 210
In arguing too, the parson owned his skill,
For even though vanquished, he could argue still;
While words of learnéd length and thundering sound,
Amazed the gazing rustics ranged around;
And still they gazed, and still the wonder grew,
That one small head could carry all he knew.
　　But past is all his fame. The very spot
Where many a time he triumphed, is forgot.
Near yonder thorn, that lifts its head on high,
Where once the sign-post caught the passing eye, 220
Low lies that house where nut-brown draughts inspired,
Where grey-beard mirth and smiling toil retired,
Where village statesmen talked with looks profound,
And news much older than their ale went round.
Imagination fondly stoops to trace
The parlour splendours of that festive place;
The white-washed wall, the nicely sanded floor,
The varnished clock that clicked behind the door;
The chest contrived a double debt to pay,
A bed by night, a chest of drawers by day; 230
The pictures placed for ornament and use,
The twelve good rules,[1] the royal game of goose;
The hearth, except when winter chilled the day,
With aspen boughs, and flowers, and fennel gay,
While broken tea-cups, wisely kept for show,
Ranged o'er the chimney, glistened in a row.
　　Vain transitory splendours! Could not all
Reprieve the tottering mansion from its fall!
Obscure it sinks, nor shall it more impart
An hour's importance to the poor man's heart; 240

---

[1] rules of conduct supposed to have been composed by Charles I

Thither no more the peasant shall repair
To sweet oblivion of his daily care;
No more the farmer's news, the barber's tale,
No more the woodman's ballad shall prevail;
No more the smith his dusky brow shall clear,
Relax his ponderous strength, and lean to hear;
The host himself no longer shall be found
Careful to see the mantling bliss go round;
Nor the coy maid, half willing to be pressed,
Shall kiss the cup to pass it to the rest.                    250
  Yes! let the rich deride, the proud disdain,
These simple blessings of the lowly train;
To me more dear, congenial to my heart,
One native charm, than all the gloss of art;
Spontaneous joys, where Nature has its play,
The soul adopts, and owns their first-born sway;
Lightly they frolic o'er the vacant mind,
Unenvied, unmolested, unconfined.
But the long pomp, the midnight masquerade,
With all the freaks of wanton wealth arrayed,                260
In these, ere triflers half their wish to obtain,
The toiling pleasure sickens into pain;
And even while fashion's brightest arts decoy,
The heart distrusting asks, if this be joy.
  Ye friends to truth, ye statesmen, who survey
The rich man's joys increase, the poor's decay,
'Tis yours to judge, how wide the limits stand
Between a splendid and a happy land.
Proud swells the tide with loads of freighted ore,
And shouting Folly hails them from her shore;               270
Hoards even beyond the miser's wish abound,
And rich men flock from all the world around.
Yet count our gains. This wealth is but a name
That leaves our useful products still the same.
Not so the loss. The man of wealth and pride
Takes up a space that many poor supplied;
Space for his lake, his park's extended bounds,
Space for his horses, equipage, and hounds;
The robe that wraps his limbs in silken sloth,
Has robbed the neighbouring fields of half their growth;    280
His seat, where solitary sports are seen,
Indignant spurns the cottage from the green;
Around the world each needful product flies,
For all the luxuries the world supplies.
While thus the land, adorned for pleasure, all
In barren splendour feebly waits the fall.
  As some fair female unadorned and plain,
Secure to please while youth confirms her reign,
Slights every borrowed charm that dress supplies,

Nor shares with art the triumph of her eyes;                        290
But when those charms are past, for charms are frail,
When time advances, and when lovers fail,
She then shines forth, solicitous to bless,
In all the glaring impotence of dress.
Thus fares the land, by luxury betrayed;
In nature's simplest charms at first arrayed;
But verging to decline, its splendours rise,
Its vistas strike, its palaces surprise;
While, scourged by famine from the smiling land,
The mournful peasant leads his humble band;                         300
And while he sinks, without one arm to save,
The country blooms—a garden, and a grave.
 Where then, ah where, shall poverty reside,
To scape the pressure of contiguous pride?
If to some common's fenceless limits strayed,
He drives his flock to pick the scanty blade,
Those fenceless fields the sons of wealth divide,
And ev'n the bare-worn common is denied.
 If to the city sped—What waits him there?
To see profusion that he must not share;                            310
To see ten thousand baneful arts combined
To pamper luxury, and thin mankind;
To see those joys the sons of pleasure know,
Extorted from his fellow-creature's woe.
Here, while the courtier glitters in brocade,
There the pale artist plies the sickly trade;
Here, while the proud their long-drawn pomps display,
There the black gibbet glooms besides the way.
The dome where Pleasure holds her midnight reign,
Here, richly decked, admits the gorgeous train;                     320
Tumultuous grandeur crowds the blazing square,
The rattling chariots clash, the torches glare.
Sure scenes like these no troubles e'er annoy!
Sure these denote one universal joy!
Are these thy serious thoughts?—Ah, turn thine eyes
Where the poor houseless shivering female lies.
She once, perhaps, in village plenty blest,
Has wept at tales of innocence distressed;
Her modest looks the cottage might adorn,
Sweet as the primrose peeps beneath the thorn;                      330
Now lost to all; her friends, her virtue fled,
Near her betrayer's door she lays her head,
And, pinched with cold, and shrinking from the shower,
With heavy heart deplores that luckless hour
When idly first, ambitious of the town,
She left her wheel and robes of country brown.
 Do thine, sweet Auburn, thine, the loveliest train,
Do thy fair tribes participate her pain?

Even now, perhaps, by cold and hunger led,
At proud men's doors they ask a little bread!                          *340*
  Ah, no. To distant climes, a dreary scene,
Where half the convex world intrudes between,
Through torrid tracts with fainting steps they go,
Where wild Altama² murmurs to their woe.
Far different there from all that charmed before,
The various terrors of that horrid shore;
Those blazing suns that dart a downward ray,
And fiercely shed intolerable day;
Those matted woods where birds forget to sing,
But silent bats in drowsy clusters cling;                             *350*
Those poisonous fields with rank luxuriance crowned,
Where the dark scorpion gathers death around;
Where at each step the stranger fears to wake
The rattling terrors of the vengeful snake;
Where crouching tigers wait their hapless prey,
And savage men, more murderous still than they;
While oft in whirls the mad tornado flies,
Mingling the ravaged landscape with the skies.
Far different these from every former scene,
The cooling brook, the grassy vested green,                           *360*
The breezy covert of the warbling grove,
That only sheltered thefts of harmless love.
  Good Heaven! what sorrows gloomed that parting day,
That called them from their native walks away;
When the poor exiles, every pleasure past,
Hung round their bowers, and fondly looked their last,
And took a long farewell, and wished in vain
For seats like these beyond the western main;
And shuddering still to face the distant deep,
Returned and wept, and still returned to weep.                        *370*
The good old sire the first prepared to go
To new found worlds, and wept for others' woe.
But for himself, in conscious virtue brave,
He only wished for worlds beyond the grave.
His lovely daughter, lovelier in her tears,
The fond companion of his helpless years,
Silent went next, neglectful of her charms,
And left a lover's for a father's arms.
With louder plaints the mother spoke her woes,
And blessed the cot where every pleasure rose;                        *380*
And kissed her thoughtless babes with many a tear,
And clasped them close, in sorrow doubly dear;
Whilst her fond husband strove to lend relief
In all the silent manliness of grief.
  O luxury! thou cursed by Heaven's decree,

---

² the Altamaha River (Georgia)

How ill exchanged are things like these for thee!
How do thy potions, with insidious joy,
Diffuse their pleasures only to destroy!
Kingdoms, by thee, to sickly greatness grown,
Boast of a florid vigour not their own; 390
At every draught more large and large they grow,
A bloated mass of rank unwieldy woe;
Till sapped their strength, and every part unsound,
Down, down they sink, and spread a ruin round.
   Even now the devastation is begun,
And half the business of destruction done;
Even now, methinks, as pondering here I stand,
I see the rural virtues leave the land:
Down where yon anchoring vessel spreads the sail,
That idly waiting flaps with every gale, 400
Downward they move, a melancholy band,
Pass from the shore, and darken all the strand.
Contented toil, and hospitable care,
And kind connubial tenderness, are there;
And piety with wishes placed above,
And steady loyalty, and faithful love.
And thou, sweet Poetry, thou loveliest maid,
Still first to fly where sensual joys invade;
Unfit in these degenerate times of shame,
To catch the heart, or strike for honest fame; 410
Dear charming nymph, neglected and decried,
My shame in crowds, my solitary pride;
Thou source of all my bliss, and all my woe,
That found'st me poor at first, and keep'st me so;
Thou guide by which the nobler arts excel,
Thou nurse of every virtue, fare thee well!
Farewell, and O where'er thy voice be tried,
On Torno's[3] cliffs, or Pambamarca's[4] side,
Whether where equinoctial fervours glow,
Or winter wraps the polar world in snow, 420
Still let thy voice, prevailing over time,
Redress the rigours of the inclement clime;
Aid slighted truth with thy persuasive strain,
Teach erring man to spurn the rage of gain;
Teach him, that states of native strength possessed,
Though very poor, may still be very blest;
That trade's proud empire hastes to swift decay,
As ocean sweeps the laboured mole away;
While self-dependent power can time defy,
As rocks resist the billows and the sky. (*1770*) 430

---

[3] the Torne River (Sweden)      [4] mountain in South America

## The Three Pigeons

Let schoolmasters puzzle their brain,
　　With grammar, and nonsense, and learning;
Good liquor, I stoutly maintain,
　　Gives genius a better discerning.
Let them brag of their heathenish gods,
　　Their Lethes, their Styxes, and Stygians,[1]
Their Quis and their Quaes and their Quods,[2]
　　They're all but a parcel of pigeons.
　　　　*Toroddle, toroddle, toroll.*

When Methodist preachers come down,                                    10
　　A-preaching that drinking is sinful,
I'll wager the rascals a crown,
　　They always preach best with a skinful.
But when you come down with your pence,
　　For a slice of their scurvy religion,
I'll leave it to all men of sense,
　　But you, my good friend, are the pigeon.
　　　　*Toroddle, toroddle, toroll.*

Then come, put the jorum[3] about,
　　And let us be merry and clever,                                    20
Our hearts and our liquors are stout,
　　Here's the Three Jolly Pigeons for ever!
Let some cry up woodcock or hare,
　　Your bustards, your ducks, and your widgeons;
But of all the gay birds in the air,
　　Here's a health to the Three Jolly Pigeons!
　　　　*Toroddle, toroddle, toroll.*

# WILLIAM COWPER / 1731–1800

## Walking with God

*GENESIS 5:24*

Oh! for a closer walk with God,
　A calm and heav'nly frame;
A light to shine upon the road
　That leads me to the Lamb!

Where is the blessedness I knew
　When first I saw the Lord?
Where is the soul-refreshing view
　Of Jesus, and his word?

What peaceful hours I once enjoyed!
　How sweet their mem'ry still!                                    10
But they have left an aching void,
　The world can never fill.

---

[1] Lethe: the river of forgetfulness in Hades; Styx: the river in Hades across which Charon ferried the souls of the dead; Stygian: the adjective form of Styx

[2] a jumble of parodied Latin legal and learned terms

[3] a large bowl for wine or punch

Return, O holy Dove, return,
  Sweet messenger of rest;
I hate the sins that made thee mourn,
  And drove thee from my breast.

The dearest idol I have known,
  Whate'er that idol be;

Help me to tear it from thy throne,
  And worship only thee.     *20*

So shall my walk be close with God,
  Calm and serene my frame;
So purer light shall mark the road
  That leads me to the Lamb!  (*1779*)

## The Poplar Field

The poplars are felled; farewell to the shade,
And the whispering sound of the cool colonnade!
The winds play no longer and sing in the leaves,
Nor Ouse[1] on his bosom their image receives.

Twelve years have elapsed since I first took a view
Of my favourite field, and the bank where they grew;
And now in the grass behold they are laid,
And the tree is my seat that once lent me a shade!

The blackbird has fled to another retreat,
Where the hazels afford him a screen from the heat,     *10*
And the scene where his melody charmed me before
Resounds with his sweet flowing ditty no more.

My fugitive years are all hasting away,
And I must ere long lie as lowly as they,
With a turf on my breast, and a stone at my head,
Ere another such grove shall arise in its stead.

'Tis a sight to engage me, if any thing can,
To muse on the perishing pleasures of man;
Though his life be a dream, his enjoyments, I see,
Have a being less durable even than he.     *20*

## Lines Written Under the Influence of Delirium

Hatred and vengeance, my eternal
    portion,
Scarce can endure delay of execution,
Wait with impatient readiness to
    seize my
    Soul in a moment.

Damned below Judas; more abhorred
    than he was,
Who for a few pence sold his holy
    Master!

Twice-betrayed Jesus me, the last
    delinquent,
    Deems the profanest.

Man disavows, and Deity disowns me,
Hell might afford my miseries a
    shelter;     *10*
Therefore Hell keeps her ever-hungry
    mouths all
    Bolted against me.

---

[1] river flowing past Olney, the village where Cowper lived after 1763

Hard lot! encompassed with a thousand
    dangers;
Weary, faint, trembling with a thousand
    terrors,
I'm called, if vanquished, to receive a
    sentence
      Worse than Abiram's.[1]

*Him* the vindictive rod of angry justice
Sent quick and howling to the centre
    headlong;
*I*, fed with judgment, in a fleshy
    tomb, am
    Buried above ground.   *20*

## Sonnet to William Wilberforce, Esq.[1]

Thy country, Wilberforce, with just disdain,
Hears thee, by cruel men and impious called
Fanatic, for thy zeal to loose th' enthralled
From exile, public sale, and slavery's chain.
Friend of the poor, the wronged, the fetter-galled,
Fear not lest labour such as thine be vain.
Thou hast achieved a part; hast gained the ear
Of Britain's senate to thy glorious cause;
Hope smiles, joy springs, and though cold caution pause
And weave delay, the better hour is near        *10*
That shall remunerate thy toils severe
By peace for Afric, fenced with British laws.
Enjoy what thou hast won, esteem and love
From all the just on earth, and all the blest above.   *(1792)*

# PHILIP FRENEAU / 1752–1832

## To the Memory of the Brave Americans

### *UNDER GENERAL GREENE, IN SOUTH CAROLINA, WHO FELL IN THE ACTION OF SEPTEMBER 8, 1781*

At Eutaw Springs the valiant died;
    Their limbs with dust are covered o'er—
Weep on, ye springs, your tearful tide;
    How many heroes are no more!

If in this wreck or ruin, they
    Can yet be thought to claim a tear,
O smite your gentle breast, and say
    The friends of freedom slumber here!

---

[1] Abraham, called upon by God to sacrifice his beloved son Isaac

[1] William Wilberforce (1759–1833) led the struggle for the abolition of the slave trade and of slavery.

Thou, who shalt trace this bloody plain,
   If goodness rules thy generous breast,
Sigh for the wasted rural reign;
   Sigh for the shepherds, sunk to rest!     *10*

Stranger, their humble graves adorn;
   You too may fall, and ask a tear;
'Tis not the beauty of the morn
   That proves the evening shall be clear.—

They saw their injured country's woe;
   The flaming town, the wasted field;
Then rushed to meet the insulting foe;
   They took the spear—but left the shield.     *20*

Led by thy conquering genius, Greene,
   The Britons they compelled to fly;
None distant viewed the fatal plain,
   None grieved, in such a cause to die—

But, like the Parthian, famed of old,
   Who, flying, still their arrows threw,
These routed Britons, full as bold,
   Retreated, and retreating slew.

Now rest in peace, our patriot band;
   Though far from nature's limits thrown,     *30*
We trust they find a happier land,
   A brighter sunshine of their own.   (*1786*)

## The Wild Honey Suckle

Fair flower, that dost so comely grow,
Hid in this silent, dull retreat,
Untouched thy honied blossoms blow,
Unseen thy little branches greet:
   No roving foot shall crush thee here,
   No busy hand provoke a tear.

By Nature's self in white arrayed,
She bade thee shun the vulgar eye,
And planted here the guardian shade,
And sent soft waters murmuring by;     *10*
   Thus quietly thy summer goes,
   Thy days declining to repose.

Smit with those charms, that must decay,
I grieve to see your future doom;
They died—nor were those flowers more gay,
The flowers that did in Eden bloom;
   Unpitying frosts, and Autumn's power
   Shall leave no vestige of this flower.

From the morning suns and evening dews
At first thy little being came:             *20*
If nothing once, you nothing lose,
For when you die you are the same;
   The space between, is but an hour,
   The frail duration of a flower.   (*1788*)


## To Sir Toby

*A SUGAR PLANTER IN THE INTERIOR PARTS OF JAMAICA,*
*NEAR THE CITY OF SAN JAGO DE LA VEGA,*
*(SPANISH TOWN) 1784*

The motions of his spirit are black as night,
And his affections dark as Erebus.—SHAKESPEARE

   If there exists a hell—the case is clear—
Sir Toby's slaves enjoy that portion here:
Here are no blazing brimstone lakes, 'tis true;
But kindled rum too often burns as blue,
In which some fiend, whom nature must detest,
Steeps Toby's brand and marks poor Cudjoe's breast.
   Here whips on whips excite perpetual fears,
And mingled howlings vibrate on my ears:
Here nature's plagues abound, to fret and teaze,
Snakes, scorpions, despots, lizards, centipedes—     *10*
No art, no care escapes the busy lash;
All have their dues—and all are paid in cash—
The eternal driver keeps a steady eye
On a black herd, who would his vengeance fly,
But chained, imprisoned, on a burning soil,
For the mean avarice of a tyrant, toil!
The lengthy cart-whip guards this monster's reign—
And cracks, like pistols, from the fields of cane.
   Ye powers! who formed these wretched tribes, relate,
What had they done, to merit such a fate!     *20*
Why were they brought from Eboe's[1] sultry waste,
To see that plenty which they must not taste—
Food, which they cannot buy, and dare not steal;
Yams and potatoes—many a scanty meal!—
   One, with a gibbet wakes his Negro's fears,
One to the windmill nails him by the ears;
One keeps his slave in darkened dens, unfed,
One puts the wretch in pickle ere he's dead:
This, from a tree suspends him by the thumbs,
That, from his table grudges even the crumbs!     *30*

---

[1] an African tribal district in Nigeria

O'er yond' rough hills a tribe of females go,
Each with her gourd, her infant, and her hoe;
Scorched by a sun that has no mercy here,
Driven by a devil, whom men call overseer—
In chains, twelve wretches to their labours haste;
Twice twelve I saw, with iron collars graced!—
　Are such the fruits that spring from vast domains?
Is wealth, thus got, Sir Toby, worth your pains!—
Who would your wealth on terms, like these, possess,
Where all we see is pregnant with distress—　　　　40
Angola's natives scourged by ruffian hands,
And toil's hard product shipp'd to foreign lands.
　Talk not of blossoms and your endless spring;
What joy, what smile, can scenes of misery bring?—
Though Nature, here, has every blessing spread,
Poor is the labourer—and how meanly fed!—
　Here Stygian paintings light and shade renew,
Pictures of hell, that Virgil's pencil drew:
Here, surly Charons make their annual trip,
And ghosts arrive in every Guinea ship,　　　　　50
To find what beasts these western isles afford,
Plutonian scourges, and despotic lords:—
　Here, they, of stuff determined to be free,
Must climb the rude cliffs of the Liguanee;
Beyond the clouds, in skulking haste repair,
And hardly safe from brother traitors there.　*(1795)*

## On the Uniformity and Perfection of Nature

On one fixed point all nature moves,
Nor deviates from the track she loves;
Her system drawn from reason's source,
She scorns to change her wonted course.

Could she descend from that great plan
To work unusual things for man,
To suit the insect of an hour—
This would betray a want of power,

Unsettled in its first design
And erring, when it did combine　　　　　10
The parts that form the vast machine,
The figures sketched on nature's scene.

Perfections of the first great cause
Submit to no contracted laws,
But all-sufficient, all supreme,
Include no trivial views in them.

Who looks through nature with an eye
That would the scheme of heaven descry,
Observes her constant, still the same,
In all her laws, through all her frame.    *20*

No imperfection can be found
In all that is, above, around—
All nature made, in reason's sight,
Is order all and all is right.  (*1815*)

# GEORGE CRABBE / 1754–1832

*from* The Village

*from* BOOK I

    The village life, and every care that reigns
O'er youthful peasants and declining swains;
What labor yields, and what, that labor past,
Age, in its hour of languor, finds at last;
What from the real picture of the poor,
Demand a song—the Muse can give no more.
    Fled are those times when, in harmonious strains,
The rustic poet praised his native plains.
No shepherds now, in smooth altérnate verse,
Their country's beauty or their nymphs' rehearse;    *10*
Yet still for these we frame the tender strain,
Still in our lays fond Corydons complain,
And shepherds' boys their amorous pains reveal,
The only pains, alas! they never feel.
         .     .     .

    Lo! where the heath, with withering brake grown o'er,
Lends the light turf that warms the neighbouring poor;
From thence a length of burning sand appears,
Where the thin harvest waves its withered ears;
Rank weeds, that every art and care defy,
Reign o'er the land, and rob the blighted rye:
There thistles stretch their prickly arms afar,
And to the ragged infant threaten war;    *70*
There poppies, nodding, mock the hope of toil;
There the blue bugloss[1] paints the sterile soil;
Hardy and high, above the slender sheaf,
The slimy mallow waves her silky leaf;

---

[1] a coarse wild plant with dark blue flowers, which grows in open fields; pronounced béw-gloss

O'er the young shoot the charlock[2] throws a shade,
And clasping tares[3] cling round the sickly blade;
With mingled tints the rocky coasts abound,
And a sad splendor vainly shines around.
So looks the nymph whom wretched arts adorn,
Betrayed by man, then left for man to scorn;                80
Whose cheek in vain assumes the mimic rose,
While her sad eyes the troubled breast disclose;
Whose outward splendor is but folly's dress,
Exposing most, when most it gilds distress.
   Here joyless roam a wild amphibious race,
With sullen woe displayed in every face;
Who far from civil arts and social fly,
And scowl at strangers with suspicious eye.
   Here too the lawless merchant of the main
Draws from his plow the intoxicated swain;                90
Want only claimed the labor of the day,
But vice now steals his nightly rest away.
   Where are the swains, who, daily labor done,
With rural games played down the setting sun;
   Who struck with matchless force the bounding ball,
Or made the ponderous quoit obliquely fall;
While some huge Ajax, terrible and strong,
Engaged some artful stripling of the throng,
And fell beneath him, foiled, while far around
Hoarse triumph rose, and rocks returned the sound?                100
Where now are these?—Beneath yon cliff they stand,
To show the freighted pinnace where to land;
To load the ready steed with guilty haste;
To fly in terror o'er the pathless waste;
Or, when detected in their straggling course,
To foil their foes by cunning or by force;
Or, yielding part (which equal knaves demand),
To gain a lawless passport through the land.
Here, wandering long amid these frowning fields,
I sought the simple life that Nature yields;                110
Rapine and Wrong and Fear usurped her place,
And a bold, artful, surly, savage race;
Who, only skilled to take the finny tribe,
The yearly dinner, or septennial bribe,[4]
Wait on the shore, and, as the waves run high,
On the tossed vessel bend their eager eye,
Which to their coast directs its venturous way;
Theirs, or the ocean's, miserable prey.

          ·   ·   ·

   But these are scenes where Nature's niggard hand

---

[2] a wild mustard that is a troublesome weed in grain fields
[3] weeds

[4] in the Parliamentary elections, held at least every seven years

Gave a spare portion to the famished land;
Hers is the fault, if here mankind complain
Of fruitless toil and labor spent in vain.
But yet in other scenes, more fair in view,
Where Plenty smiles—alas! she smiles for few—
And those who taste not, yet behold her store,
Are as the slaves that dig the golden ore,
The wealth around them makes them doubly poor.
 Or will you deem them amply paid in health,    *140*
Labor's fair child, that languishes with wealth?
Go, then! and see them rising with the sun,
Through a long course of daily toil to run;
See them beneath the dog star's raging heat,
When the knees tremble and the temples beat;
Behold them, leaning on their scythes, look o'er
The labor past, and toils to come explore;
See them altérnate suns and showers engage,
And hoard up aches and anguish for their age;
Through fens and marshy moors their steps pursue,  *150*
When their warm pores imbibe the evening dew;
Then own that labor may as fatal be
To these thy slaves, as thine excess to thee.
 Amid this tribe too oft a manly pride
Strives in strong toil the fainting heart to hide;
There may you see the youth of slender frame
Contend, with weakness, weariness, and shame;
Yet, urged along, and proudly loath to yield,
He strives to join his fellows of the field;
Till long-contending nature droops at last,    *160*
Declining health rejects his poor repast,
His cheerless spouse the coming danger sees,
And mutual murmurs urge the slow disease.
 Yet grant them health, 'tis not for us to tell,
Though the head droops not, that the heart is well;
Or will you praise that homely, healthy fare,
Plenteous and plain, that happy peasants share?
Oh! trifle not with wants you cannot feel,
Nor mock the misery of a stinted meal,
Homely, not wholesome; plain, not plenteous; such  *170*
As you who praise would never deign to touch.
 Ye gentle souls, who dream of rural ease,
Whom the smooth stream and smoother sonnet please;
Go! if the peaceful cot your praises share,
Go, look within, and ask if peace be there:
If peace be his—that drooping weary sire,
Or theirs, that offspring round their feeble fire;
Or hers, that matron pale, whose trembling hand
Turns on the wretched hearth the expiring brand!

# The Romantic Period

## WILLIAM BLAKE / 1757–1827

### To the Evening Star

Thou fair-haired angel of the evening,
Now, while the sun rests on the mountains, light
Thy bright torch of love; thy radiant crown
Put on, and smile upon our evening bed!
Smile on our loves, and, while thou drawest the
Blue curtains of the sky, scatter thy silver dew
On every flower that shuts its sweet eyes
In timely sleep. Let thy west wind sleep on
The lake; speak silence with thy glimmering eyes,
And wash the dusk with silver. Soon, full soon,          10
Dost thou withdraw; then the wolf rages wide,
And the lion glares through the dun forest:
The fleeces of our flocks are covered with
Thy sacred dew: protect them with thine influence.   *(1783)*

### Mad Song

The wild winds sweep,
  And the night is a-cold;
Come hither, Sleep,
  And my griefs infold:
But lo! the morning peeps
  Over the eastern steeps,
And the rustling birds of dawn
The earth do scorn.

Lo! to the vault
  Of pavéd heaven,          10
With sorrow fraught
  My notes are driven:
They strike the ear of night,
  Make weep the eyes of day;
They make mad the roaring winds,
  And with tempests play.

Like a fiend in a cloud,
  With howling woe,
After night I do crowd,
  And with night will go;          20
I turn my back to the east,
From whence comforts have increased;
For light doth seize my brain
With frantic pain.   *(1783)*

### *Introduction to* Songs of Innocence

Piping down the valleys wild,
  Piping songs of pleasant glee,
On a cloud I saw a child,
  And he laughing said to me:

"Pipe a song about a Lamb!"
  So I piped with merry cheer.
"Piper, pipe that song again";
  So I piped: he wept to hear.

"Drop thy pipe, thy happy pipe;
  Sing thy songs of happy cheer!"          10
So I sung the same again,
  While he wept with joy to hear.

"Piper, sit thee down and write
  In a book that all may read."
So he vanished from my sight;
  And I plucked a hollow reed,

And I made a rural pen,
  And I stained the water clear,
And I wrote my happy songs
  Every child may joy to hear.    20
                  (1789)

## The Lamb

Little Lamb, who made thee?
  Dost thou know who made thee?
Gave thee life, and bid thee feed
By the stream and o'er the mead;

Gave thee clothing of delight,
Softest clothing, wooly, bright;
Gave thee such a tender voice,
Making all the vales rejoice?
  Little Lamb, who made thee?
  Dost thou know who made thee?    10

  Little Lamb, I'll tell thee,
  Little Lamb, I'll tell thee:
He is callèd by thy name,
For he calls himself a Lamb.
He is meek, and he is mild;
He became a little child.
I a child, and thou a lamb,
We are callèd by his name.
  Little Lamb, God bless thee!
  Little Lamb, God bless
    thee!  (1789)    20

## The Little Black Boy

My mother bore me in the southern wild,
And I am black, but O! my soul is white;
White as an angel is the English child,
But I am black, as if bereaved of light.

My mother taught me underneath a tree,
And sitting down before the heat of day,
She took me on her lap and kissèd me,
And pointing to the east, began to say:

"Look on the rising sun: there God does live,
And gives His light, and gives His heat away;    10
And flowers and trees and beasts and men receive
Comfort in morning, joy in the noonday.

"And we are put on earth a little space,
That we may learn to bear the beams of love;
And these black bodies and this sunburnt face
Is but a cloud, and like a shady grove.

"For when our souls have learned the heat to bear,
The cloud will vanish; we shall hear His voice,
Saying: 'Come out from the grove, my love and care,
And round my golden tent like lambs rejoice.'"    20

Thus did my mother say, and kissèd me;
And thus I say to little English boy:
When I from black and he from white cloud free,
And round the tent of God like lambs we joy,

I'll shade him from the heat, till he can bear
To lean in joy upon our Father's knee;
And then I'll stand and stroke his silver hair,
And be like him, and he will then love me.  (1789)

## The Chimney Sweeper

When my mother died I was very young,
And my father sold me while yet my tongue
Could scarcely cry "'weep! 'weep! 'weep! 'weep!"
So your chimneys I sweep, and in soot I sleep.

There's little Tom Dacre, who cried when his head,
That curled like a lamb's back, was shaved: so I said
"Hush, Tom! never mind it, for when your head's bare
You know that the soot cannot spoil your white hair."

And so he was quiet, and that very night,
As Tom was a-sleeping, he had such a sight!          10
That thousands of sweepers, Dick, Joe, Ned, and Jack,
Were all of them locked up in coffins of black.

And by came an Angel who had a bright key,
And he opened the coffins and set them all free;
Then down a green plain leaping, laughing, they run,
And wash in a river, and shine in the Sun.

Then naked and white, all their bags left behind,
They rise upon clouds and sport in the wind;
And the Angel told Tom, if he'd be a good boy,
He'd have God for his father, and never want joy.          20

And so Tom awoke; and we rose in the dark,
And got with our bags and our brushes to work.
Though the morning was cold, Tom was happy and warm;
So if all do their duty they need not fear harm.   (*1789*)

## The Divine Image

To Mercy, Pity, Peace, and Love
All pray in their distress;
And to these virtues of delight
Return their thankfulness.

For Mercy, Pity, Peace, and Love
Is God, our father dear,
And Mercy, Pity, Peace, and Love
Is Man, his child and care.

For Mercy has a human heart,
Pity a human face,
And Love, the human form divine,
And Peace, the human dress.

Then every man, of every clime,
That prays in his distress,
Prays to the human form divine,
Love, Mercy, Pity, Peace.

And all must love the human form,
In heathen, Turk, or Jew;
Where Mercy, Love, and Pity dwell
There God is dwelling too.   (*1789*)

## Holy Thursday (I)

'Twas on a Holy Thursday, their innocent faces clean,
The children walking two and two, in red and blue
                    and green,

Gray-headed beadles walked before, with wands as
        white as snow,
Till into the high dome of Paul's they like Thames'
        waters flow.

O what a multitude they seemed, these flowers of
        London town!
Seated in companies they sit with radiance all their own.
The hum of multitudes was there, but multitudes of
        lambs,
Thousands of little boys and girls raising their in-
        nocent hands.

Now like a mighty wind they raise to heaven the voice
        of song,
Or like harmonious thunderings the seats of Heaven
        among.                  *10*
Beneath them sit the agéd men, wise guardians of
        the poor;
Then cherish pity, lest you drive an angel from
        your door.  (*1789*)

## Holy Thursday (II)

Is this a holy thing to see
In a rich and fruitful land,
Babes reduced to misery,
Fed with cold and usurous hand?

Is that trembling cry a song?
Can it be a song of joy?
And so many children poor?
It is a land of poverty!

And their sun does never shine,
And their fields are bleak and bare,    *10*
And their ways are filled with thorns:
It is eternal winter there.

For where'er the sun does shine,
And where'er the rain does fall,
Babe can never hunger there,
Nor poverty the mind appall.  (*1794*)

## The Tyger

Tyger! Tyger! burning bright
In the forests of the night,
What immortal hand or eye
Could frame they fearful symmetry?

In what distant deeps or skies
Burnt the fire of thine eyes?
On what wings dare he aspire?
What the hand dare seize the fire?

And what shoulder, and what art,
Could twist the sinews of thy heart?    *10*
And when thy heart began to beat,
What dread hand? and what dread
    feet?

What the hammer? what the chain?
In what furnace was thy brain?
What the anvil? what dread grasp
Dare its deadly terrors clasp?

When the stars threw down their spears,
And watered heaven with their tears,
Did he smile his work to see?
Did he who made the Lamb make
    thee?             *20*

Tyger! Tyger! burning bright
In the forests of the night,
What immortal hand or eye,
Dare frame thy fearful symmetry?

                          (*1794*)

## The Clod and the Pebble

"Love seeketh not itself to please,
Nor for itself hath any care,
But for another gives its ease,
And builds a heaven in hell's despair."

So sung a little clod of clay,
Trodden with the cattle's feet,
But a pebble of the brook
Warbled out these metres meet:

"Love seeketh only self to please,
To bind another to its delight,                    10
Joys in another's loss of ease,
And builds a hell in heaven's
      despite." (*1794*)

## The Sick Rose

O rose, thou art sick!
The invisible worm
That flies in the night,
In the howling storm,

Has found out thy bed
Of crimson joy,
And his dark secret love
Does thy life destroy. (*1794*)

## London

I wander through each chartered street,
Near where the chartered Thames does
      flow,
And mark in every face I meet
Marks of weakness, marks of woe.

In every cry of every man,
In every infant's cry of fear,
In every voice, in every ban,
The mind-forged manacles I hear.

How the Chimney-sweeper's cry
Every black'ning church appalls;          10
And the hapless soldier's sigh
Runs in blood down palace walls.

But most through midnight streets I hear
How the youthful harlot's curse
Blasts the new-born infant's tear,
And blights with plagues the marriage
      hearse. (*1794*)

## A Poison Tree

I was angry with my friend:
I told my wrath, my wrath did end.
I was angry with my foe:
I told it not, my wrath did grow.

And I watered it in fears,
Night and morning with my tears;
And I sunnéd it with smiles,
And with soft deceitful wiles.

And it grew both day and night,
Till it bore an apple bright;                    10
And my foe beheld it shine,
And he knew that it was mine,

And into my garden stole
When the night had veiled the pole:
In the morning glad I see
My foe outstretched beneath the tree.
                                    (*1794*)

## The Garden of Love

I went to the Garden of Love,
And saw what I never had seen:
A Chapel was built in the midst,
Where I used to play on the green.

And the gates of this Chapel were shut,
And "Thou shalt not" writ over the door;
So I turned to the Garden of Love
That so many sweet flowers bore;

And I saw it was filled with graves,
And tombstones where flowers should
      be;                                        10
And priests in black gowns were walking
      their rounds,
And binding with briars my joys and
      desires. (*1794*)

## A Little Boy Lost

Naught loves another as itself
Nor venerates another so.
Nor is it possible to Thought
A greater than itself to know:

And Father, how can I love you,
Or any of my brothers more?
I love you like the little bird
That picks up crumbs around the door.

The Priest sat by and heard the child.
In trembling zeal he seized his hair:      10
He led him by his little coat:
And all admired the Priestly care.

And standing on the altar high,
Lo what a fiend is here! said he:
One who sets reason up for judge
Of our most holy Mystery.

The weeping child could not be heard,
The weeping parents wept in vain:
They stripped him to his little shirt,
And bound him in an iron chain.      20

And burned him in a holy place,
Where many had been burned before:
The weeping parents wept in vain.
Are such things done on Albion's
   shore?  (*1794*)


## Mock On, Mock On, Voltaire, Rousseau

Mock on, mock on, Voltaire,[1] Rousseau:[2]
Mock on, mock on: 'tis all in vain!
You throw the sand against the wind,
And the wind blows it back again.

And every sand becomes a gem
Reflected in the beams divine;
Blown back they blind the mocking
   eye,
But still in Israel's paths they shine.

The atoms of Democritus[3]
And Newton's[4] particles of light      10
Are sands upon the Red Sea shore,
Where Israel's tents do shine so bright.
                           (*1800?*)


## The Mental Traveler

I traveled through a land of men—
A land of men and women too—
And heard and saw such dreadful things,
As cold earth-wanderers never knew.

For there the babe is born in joy
That was begotten in dire woe,
Just as we reap in joy the fruit
Which we in bitter tears did sow.

And if the babe is born a boy,
He's given to a woman old,      10
Who nails him down upon a rock,
Catches his shrieks in cups of gold.

She binds iron thorns around his head;
She pierces both his hands and feet;
She cuts his heart out at his side
To make it feel both cold and heat.

Her fingers number every nerve,
Just as a miser counts his gold;
She lives upon his shrieks and cries,
And she grows young as he grows old.      20

Till he becomes a bleeding youth,
And she becomes a virgin bright.
Then he rends up his manacles
And binds her down for his delight.

He plants himself in all her nerves
Just as a husbandman his mould,
And she becomes his dwelling place
And garden fruitful seventy fold.

An agéd shadow soon he fades
Wandering round an earthly cot,      30
Full filled all with gems and gold
Which he by industry had got.

And these are the gems of the human soul,
The rubies and pearls of a lovesick eye,
The countless gold of the aching heart.
The martyrs groan and the lovers sigh.

---

[1] François Marie Arouet de Voltaire (1694–1778), French philosopher of the Enlightenment
[2] Jean Jacques Rousseau (1712–1778), Swiss-born rationalist philosopher
[3] Greek philosopher of the fifth century B.C., who postulated an infinite number of atoms in which resided the ultimate explanation of nature
[4] Sir Isaac Newton (1642–1727), English scientist whose particle theory of light was one more materialistic explanation of natural phenomena

They are his meat, they are his drink;
He feeds the beggar and the poor
And the wayfaring traveler,
For ever open is his door.                              40

His grief is their eternal joy;
They make the roofs and walls to ring,
Till from the fire on the hearth
A little female babe does spring.

And she is all of solid fire
And gems and gold, that none his hand
Dares stretch to touch her baby form
Or wrap her in his swaddling band.

But she comes to the man she loves;
If young or old or rich or poor,                        50
They soon drive out the agéd host,
A beggar at another's door.

He wanders weeping far away
Until some other take him in.
Oft blind and age-bent, sore distressed
Until he can a maiden win;

And to allay his freezing age
The poor man takes her in his arms.
The cottage fades before his sight,
The garden and its lovely charms.                       60

The guests are scattered through the land,
For the eye altering alters all.
The senses roll themselves in fear
And the flat earth becomes a ball.

The stars, sun, moon all shrink away;
A desert vast without a bound,
And nothing left to eat or drink;
And a dark desert all around.

The honey of her infant lips,
The bread and wine of her sweet smile,                  70
The wild game of her roving eye
Does him to infancy beguile.

For as he eats and drinks he grows
Younger and younger every day,
And on the desert wild they both
Wander in terror and dismay.

Like the wild stag she flees away;
Her fear plants many a thicket wild,
While he pursues her night and day
By various arts of love beguiled.                       80

By various arts of love and hate,
Till the wide desert planted o'er
With labyrinths of wayward love
Where roams the lion, wolf, and boar,

Till he becomes a wayward babe,
And she a weeping woman old.
Then many a lover wanders here,
The sun and stars are nearer rolled;

The trees bring forth sweet ecstasy
To all who in the desert roam,                          90
Till many a city there is built,
And many a pleasant shepherd's home.

But when they find the frowning babe
Terror strikes through the region wide;
They cry, "The babe, the babe is born,"
And fly away on every side.

For who dare touch the frowning form,
His arm is withered to its root;
Lions, boars, wolves all howling flee,
And every tree does shed its fruit.                     100

And none can touch that frowning form,
Except it be a woman old;
She nails him down upon the rock,
And all is done as I have told.   (*1800?*)

## Preface *to* Milton

And did those feet in ancient time
Walk upon England's mountains green?
And was the holy Lamb of God
On England's pleasant pastures seen?

And did the Countenance Divine
Shine forth upon our clouded hills?
And was Jerusalem builded here
Among these dark satanic mills?

Bring me my bow of burning gold:
Bring me my arrows of desire:                           10
Bring me my spear: O clouds unfold!
Bring me my chariot of fire.

I will not cease from mental fight,
Nor shall my sword sleep in my hand
Till we have built Jerusalem
In England's green and pleasant
  land.   (*1804*)

## To a Mouse

*ON TURNING HER UP IN HER NEST
WITH THE PLOUGH, NOVEMBER,
1785*

Wee, sleekit, cowrin, tim'rous beastie,
O, what a panic's in thy breastie!
Thou need na start awa sae hasty,
  Wi' bickering brattle![1]
I wad be laith to rin an' chase thee
  Wi' murd'ring pattle![2]

I'm truly sorry Man's dominion
Has broken Nature's social union,
An' justifies that ill opinion
  Which makes thee
    startle    10
At me, thy poor, earth-born companion,
  An' fellow-mortal!

I doubt na, whyles, but thou may
    thieve;
What then? poor beastie, thou maun live!
A daimen icker in a thrave[3]
  'S a sma' request.
I'll get a blessin wi' the lave,[4]
  And never miss't!

Thy wee bit housie, too, in ruin!  20
Its silly wa's the win's are strewin!
An' naething, now, to big[5] a new ane,
  O' foggage[6] green!
An' bleak December's winds ensuin,
  Baith snell[7] and keen!

Thou saw the fields laid bare an' waste,
An' weary Winter comin fast,
An' cozie here, beneath the blast,
  Thou thought to dwell,
Till crash! the cruel coulter past
  Out thro' they cell.  30

That wee bit heap o' leaves an' stibble,
Has cost thee mony a weary nibble!

Now thou's turned out, for a' thy trouble,
  But[8] house or hald,[9]
To thole[10] the Winter's sleety dribble,
  An' cranreuch[11] cauld!

But, Mousie, thou are no thy lane,[12]
In proving foresight may be vain:
The best-laid schemes o' Mice an' Men,
  Gang aft a-gley,[13]
An' lea'e us nought but grief and pain,
  For promised joy.

Still thou art blest, compared wi' me!
The present only toucheth thee;
But, Och! I backward cast my e'e,
  On prospects drear!
An' forward, tho' I canna see,
  I guess an' fear!  *(1786)*

## To a Louse, on Seeing One on a Lady's Bonnet at Church

Ha! where ye gaun, ye crowlan ferlie![1]
Your impudence protects you sairly:
I canna say but ye strunt rarely,
  Owre gawze and lace;
Tho' faith, I fear ye dine but sparely,
  On sic a place.

Ye ugly, creepan, blastet wonner,
Detested, shunn'd, by saunt an' sinner,
How daur ye set your fit upon her,
  Sae fine a Lady!  10
Gae somewhere else and seek your dinner,
  On some poor body.

Swith,[2] in some beggar's haffet[3]
    squattle;[4]
There ye may creep, and sprawl, and
    sprattle,[5]
Wi' ither kindred, jumping cattle,
  In shoals and nations;
Whare horn nor bane[6] ne'er daur
    unsettle,
  Your thick plantations.

---

[1] hurrying scramble  [2] a long-handled spade
[3] an occasional head of grain out of twenty-four
sheaves
[4] remainder  [5] build
[6] vegetation  [7] harsh  [8] without

[9] dwelling—redundant, but alliterative with *house*
[10] suffer  [11] hoarfrost  [12] not alone  [13] amiss
[1] wonder  [2] hurry  [3] lock of hair
[4] squat  [5] scramble
[6] (a comb of neither) horn nor bone

Now haud you there, ye're out o' sight,
Below the fatt'rels,[7] snug and tight,            20
Na faith ye yet! ye'll no be right,
        Till ye've got on it,
The vera tapmost, towrin height
        O' Miss's bonnet.

My sooth! right bauld ye set your nose
        out,
As plump an' gray as onie grozet:[8]
O for some rank, mercurial rozet,[9]
        Or fell, red smeddum,[10]
I'd gie you sic a hearty dose o't,
        Wad dress your
                droddum![11]                               30

I wad na been surpriz'd to spy
You on an auld wife's flainen toy;[12]
Or aiblins[13] some bit duddie[14] boy,
        On's wylecoat;[15]
But Miss's fine Lunardi, fye!
        How daur ye do't?

O Jenny dinna toss your head,
An' set your beauties a' abroad!
Ye little ken what curséd speed
        The blastie's makin!                           40
Thae winks and finger-ends, I dread,
        Are notice takin!

O wad some Pow'r the giftie gie us
To see oursels as others see us!
It wad frae monie a blunder free us
        An' foolish notion:
What airs in dress an' gait wad lea'e us,
        And ev'n Devotion!   (1786)

## Address to the Unco Guid, or the Rigidly Righteous

*My son, these maxims make a rule,*
    *And lump them ay thegither:*
*The rigid righteous is a fool,*
    *The rigid wise anither;*
*The cleanest corn that e'er was dight,[1]*
    *May hae some pyles o' caff[2] in;*

*So ne'er a fellow-creature slight*
    *For random fits o' daffin.[3]*
        *Solomon. Eccles., vii, 16.[4]*

O ye wha are sae guid yoursel,
    Sae pious and sae holy,
Ye've nought to do but mark and tell
    Your neibor's fauts and folly!
Whase life is like a weel-gaun mill,
    Supplied wi' store o' water;
The heapet happer's[5] ebbing still,
    And still the clap[6] plays clatter.

Hear me, ye venerable core,[7]
    As counsel for poor mortals,                    10
That frequent pass douce[8] Wisdom's
        door,
    For glaikit[9] Folly's portals;
I, for their thoughtless, careless sakes,
    Would here propone[10] defenses—
Their donsie[11] tricks, their black
        mistakes,
    Their failings and mischances.

Ye see your state wi' theirs compared,
    And shudder at the niffer;[12]
But cast a moment's fair regard—
    What maks the mighty differ?                    20
Discount what scant occasion gave,
    That purity ye pride in,
And (what's aft mair than a' the lave[13])
    Your better art o' hidin'.

Think, when your castigated pulse
    Gies now and then a wallop,
What ragings must his veins convulse,
    That still eternal gallop!
Wi' wind and tide fair i' your tail,
    Right on ye scud your seaway;                    30
But in the teeth o' baith to sail,
    It makes an unco[14] leeway.

See Social-life and Glee sit down,
    All joyous and unthinking,
Till, quite transmogrified, they're grown
    Debauchery and Drinking.

---

7 ends of ribbons      8 gooseberry      9 resin
10 powder      11 breeches
12 flannel headscarf      13 perhaps
14 tattered      15 undervest

1 winnowed      2 chaff      3 fooling
4 The Authorized King James Version puts it

this way: "Be not righteous over much; neither make thyself over wise: why shouldest thou destroy thyself?"
5 heaped hopper      6 clapper      7 company
8 sober      9 silly      10 proposed      11 perverse
12 barter      13 remainder      14 extreme

O would they stay to calculate
 Th' eternal consequences;
Or your more dread hell to state,
 Damnation of expenses!   40

Ye high, exalted, virtuous Dames,
 Tied up in godly laces,
Before ye gie poor Frailty names,
 Suppose a change o' cases;
A dear-loved lad, convenience snug,
 A treacherous inclination—
But, let me whisper i' your lug,[15]
 Ye're aiblins[16] nae temptation.

Then gently scan your brother man,
 Still gentler sister woman;  50
Though they may gang a kennin wrang,[17]
 To step aside is human.
One point must still be greatly dark,
 The moving Why they do it;
And just as lamely can ye mark
 How far perhaps they rue it.

Who made the heart, 'tis He alone
 Decidedly can try us;
He knows each chord, its various tone,
 Each spring its various bias.  60
Then at the balance let's be mute,
 We never can adjust it;
What's done we partly may compute,
 But know not what's resisted. (1787)


## Willie Brew'd a Peck o' Maut

O Willie brew'd a peck o' maut,
 And Rob and Allan cam to see;
Three blyther hearts, that lee-lang
  night,
 Ye wad na found in Christendie.

We are na fou',[1] we're no that fou,
 But just a drappie in our ee;
The cock may craw, the day may daw,
 And aye we'll taste the barley bree.

Here are we met, three merry boys,
 Three merry boys, I trow, are we; 10
And mony a night we've merry been,
 And mony mae we hope to be!

It is the moon, I ken her horn,
 That's blinkin' in the lift[2] sae hie;
She shines sae bright to wyle us hame,
 But, by my sooth! she'll wait a wee.

Wha first shall rise to gang awa,
 A cuckold, coward loun is he!
Wha first beside his chair shall fa',
 He is the King among us three!  20
          (1789)


## I Love My Jean

Of a' the airts[1] the wind can blaw,
 I dearly like the west,
For there the bony lassie lives,
 The lassie I lo'e best:
There's wild-woods grow, and rivers row,[2]
 And mony a hill between;
But day and night my fancy's flight
 Is ever wi' my Jean.

I see her in the dewy flowers,
 I see her sweet and fair;  10
I hear her in the tunefu' birds,
 I hear her charm the air:
There's not a bony flower, that springs
 By fountain, shaw,[3] or green,
There's not a bony bird that sings,
 But minds me o' my Jean. (1790)


## Afton Water

 Flow gently, sweet Afton, among thy green braes,[1]
 Flow gently, I'll sing thee a song in thy praise;
 My Mary's asleep by thy murmuring stream,
 Flow gently, sweet Afton, disturb not her dream.

---

[15] ear  [16] perhaps  [17] go wrong knowingly
[1] full  [2] sky

[1] ways  [2] roll  [3] thicket
[1] banks

Thou stock dove whose echo resounds through the glen,
Ye wild whistling blackbirds in yon thorny den,
Thou green-crested lapwing they screaming forbear,
I charge you disturb not my slumbering fair.

How lofty, sweet Afton, thy neighbouring hills,
Far marked with the courses of clear, winding rills;          10
There daily I wander as noon rises high,
My flocks and my Mary's sweet cot in my eye.

How pleasant thy banks and green valleys below,
Where wild in the woodlands the primroses blow;
There oft as mild evening weeps over the lea,
The sweet-scented birk[2] shades my Mary and me.

Thy crystal stream, Afton, how lovely it glides,
And winds by the cot where my Mary resides;
How wanton thy waters her snowy feet lave,
As gathering sweet flowerets she stems thy clear wave.        20

Flow gently, sweet Afton, among thy green braes,
Flow gently, sweet river, the theme of my lays;
My Mary's asleep by thy murmuring stream,
Flow gently, sweet Afton, disturb not her dream.   (*1792*)

## Scots Wha Hae

*ROBERT BRUCE'S ADDRESS TO
HIS ARMY, BEFORE THE
BATTLE OF BANNOCKBURN*

Scots, wha hae wi' Wallace bled,
Scots, wham Bruce has aften led,
Welcome to your gory bed,
    Or to victorie.

Now's the day, and now's the hour;
See the front o' battle lour!
See approach proud Edward's power—
    Chains and slaverie!

Wha will be a traitor knave?
Wha can fill a coward's grave?          10
Wha sae base as be a slave?
    Let him turn and flee!

Wha for Scotland's King and law
Freedom's sword will strongly draw,
Freeman stand, or freeman fa'?
    Let him follow me!

By oppression's woes and pains!
By your sons in servile chains!
We will drain our dearest veins,
    But they shall be free!          20

Lay the proud usurpers low!
Tyrants fall in every foe!
Liberty's in every blow!
    Let us do or die!   (*1793*)

## For A' That and A' That

Is there, for honest poverty,
    That hangs his head, and a' that;
The coward-slave, we pass him by,
    We dare be poor for a' that!
    For a' that, and a' that,
        Our toils obscure, and a' that,
    The rank is but the guinea's stamp,
        The man's the gowd[1] for a' that.

What though on hamely fare we dine,
    Wear hoddin[2] grey, and a' that;          10

----

[2] birch

[1] gold    [2] coarse woolen

Gie fools their silks, and knaves their
    wine,
A man's a man for a' that:
    For a' that, and a' that,
      Their tinsel show, and a' that;
    The honest man, though e'er sae
      poor,
      Is king o' men for a' that.

Ye see yon birkie,[3] ca'd a lord,
    Wha struts, and stares, and a' that;
Though hundreds worship at his word,
    He's but a coof[4] for a' that:      20
    For a' that, and a' that:
      His ribband, star, and a' that,
    The man of independent mind,
      He looks and laughs at a' that.

A prince can mak a belted knight,
    A marquis, duke, and a' that;
But an honest man's aboon his might,
    Guid faith, he maunna fa'[5] that!
    For a' that, and a' that,
      Their dignities, and a' that,     30
    The pith o' sense and pride o' worth,
      Are higher ranks than a' that.

Then let us pray that come it may,
    As come it will for a' that,
That sense and worth, o'er a' the earth,
    May bear the gree,[6] and a' that.
    For a' that, and a' that,
      It's comin' yet for a' that,
    That man to man, the warld o'er,
      Shall brothers be for a'
        that.  (1795)     40

## A Red, Red Rose

O, my luve is like a red red rose
    That's newly sprung in June:
O, my luve is like the melodie
    That's sweetly played in tune.

As fair art thou, my bonie lass,
    So deep in luve am I;
And I will luve thee still, my dear,
    Till a' the seas gang dry.

Till a' the seas gang dry, my dear,
    And the rocks melt wi' the sun;    10
And I will luve thee still, my dear,
    While the sands o' life shall run.

And fare thee weel, my only luve!
    And fare thee weel a while!
And I will come again, my luve,
    Tho' it were ten thousand mile.  (1796)

## O, Wert Thou in the Cauld Blast

O, wert thou in the cauld blast,
    On yonder lea, on yonder lea,
My plaidie to the angry airt,[1]
    I'd shelter thee, I'd shelter thee.
Or did misfortune's bitter storms
    Around thee blaw, around thee blaw,
Thy bield[2] should be my bosom,
    To share it a', to share it a'.

Or were I in the wildest waste,
    Sae black and bare, sae black and
      bare,    10
The desert were a paradise,
    If thou wert there, if thou wert there.
Or were I monarch o' the globe,
    Wi' thee to reign, wi' thee to reign,
The brightest jewel in my crown
    Wad be my queen, wad be my queen.
          (1796)

---

[3] fop    [4] fool    [5] must not claim
[6] win the reward

[1] direction    [2] shelter

## Written in Early Spring

I heard a thousand blended notes,
While in a grove I sate reclined,
In that sweet mood when pleasant thoughts
Bring sad thoughts to the mind.

To her fair works did Nature link
The human soul that through me ran;
And much it grieved my heart to think
What Man has made of Man.

Through primrose tufts, in that sweet bower,
The periwinkle trailed its wreaths;          10
And 'tis my faith that every flower
Enjoys the air it breathes.

The birds around me hopped and played,
Their thoughts I cannot measure,—
But the least motion which they made
It seemed a thrill of pleasure.

The budding twigs spread out their fan,
To catch the breezy air;
And I must think, do all I can,
That there was pleasure there.          20

If this belief from heaven be sent,
If such be Nature's holy plan,
Have I not reason to lament
What Man has made of Man?          (1798)

## Expostulation and Reply

"Why, William, on that old grey stone,
Thus for the length of half a day,
Why, William, sit you thus alone,
And dream your time away?

"Where are your books?—that light bequeathed
To beings else forlorn and blind!
Up! up! and drink the spirit breathed
From dead men to their kind.

"You look round on your Mother Earth
As if she for no purpose bore you;          10
As if you were her first-born birth,
And none had lived before you!"

One morning thus, by Esthwaite lake,
When life was sweet, I knew not why,
To me my good friend Matthew spake,
And thus I made reply:

"The eye—it cannot choose but see;
We cannot bid the ear be still;
Our bodies feel, where'er they be,
Against or with our will.          20

"Nor less I deem that there are Powers
Which of themselves our minds impress;
That we can feed this mind of ours
In a wise passiveness.

"Think you, 'mid all this mighty sum
Of things for ever speaking,
That nothing of itself will come,
But we must still be seeking?

"—Then ask not wherefore, here, alone,
Conversing as I may,          30
I sit upon this old grey stone,
And dream my time away."          (1798)

## Lines

### COMPOSED A FEW MILES ABOVE TINTERN ABBEY, ON REVISITING THE BANKS OF THE WYE DURING A TOUR. JULY 13, 1798

Five years have passed; five summers, with the length
Of five long winters! and again I hear
These waters, rolling from their mountain-springs

With a soft inland murmur.—Once again
Do I behold these steep and lofty cliffs,
That on a wild secluded scene impress
Thoughts of more deep seclusion; and connect
The landscape with the quiet of the sky.
The day is come when I again repose
Here, under this dark sycamore, and view                          10
These plots of cottage-ground, these orchard-tufts,
Which at this season, with their unripe fruits,
Are clad in one green hue, and lose themselves
'Mid groves and copses. Once again I see
These hedge-rows, hardly hedge-rows, little lines
Of sportive wood run wild: these pastoral farms,
Green to the very door; and wreaths of smoke
Sent up, in silence, from among the trees!
With some uncertain notice, as might seem
Of vagrant dwellers in the houseless woods,                       20
Or of some hermit's cave, where by his fire
The hermit sits alone.
                            These beauteous forms,
Through a long absence, have not been to me
As is a landscape to a blind man's eye:
But oft, in lonely rooms, and 'mid the din
Of towns and cities, I have owed to them
In hours of weariness, sensations sweet,
Felt in the blood, and felt along the heart;
And passing even into my purer mind,
With tranquil restoration:—feelings too                           30
Of unremembered pleasure: such, perhaps,
As have no slight or trivial influence
On that best portion of a good man's life,
His little, nameless, unremembered, acts
Of kindness and of love. Nor less, I trust,
To them I may have owed another gift,
Of aspect more sublime; that blessèd mood,
In which the burthen of the mystery,
In which the heavy and the weary weight
Of all this unintelligible world,                                 40
Is lightened:—that serene and blessèd mood,
In which the affections gently lead us on,—
Until, the breath of this corporeal frame
And even the motion of our human blood
Almost suspended, we are laid asleep
In body, and become a living soul:
While with an eye made quiet by the power
Of harmony, and the deep power of joy,
We see into the life of things.
                                      If this
Be but a vain belief, yet, oh! how oft—                           50

In darkness and amid the many shapes
Of joyless daylight; when the fretful stir
Unprofitable, and the fever of the world,
Have hung upon the beatings of my heart—
How oft, in spirit, have I turned to thee,
O sylvan Wye! thou wanderer through the woods,
How often has my spirit turned to thee!
   And now, with gleams of half-extinguished thought,
With many recognitions dim and faint,
And somewhat of a sad perplexity, 60
The picture of the mind revives again:
While here I stand, not only with the sense
Of present pleasure, but with pleasing thoughts
That in this moment there is life and food
For future years. And so I dare to hope,
Though changed, no doubt, from what I was when first
I came among these hills; when like a roe
I bounded o'er the mountains, by the sides
Of the deep rivers, and the lonely streams,
Wherever nature led: more like a man 70
Flying from something that he dreads, than one
Who sought the thing he loved. For nature then
(The coarser pleasures of my boyish days,
And their glad animal movements all gone by)
To me was all in all. I cannot paint
What then I was. The sounding cataract
Haunted me like a passion: the tall rock,
The mountain, and the deep and gloomy wood,
Their colors and their forms, were then to me
An appetite; a feeling and a love, 80
That had no need of a remoter charm,
By thought supplied, nor any interest
Unborrowed from the eye.—That time is past,
And all its aching joys are now no more,
And all its dizzy raptures. Not for this
Faint I, nor mourn nor murmur; other gifts
Have followed; for such loss, I would believe
Abundant recompense. For I have learned
To look on nature, not as in the hour
Of thoughtless youth; but hearing oftentimes 90
The still, sad music of humanity,
Nor harsh nor grating, though of ample power
To chasten and subdue. And I have felt
A presence that disturbs me with the joy
Of elevated thoughts; a sense sublime
Of something far more deeply interfused,
Whose dwelling is the light of setting suns,
And the round ocean and the living air,
And the blue sky, and in the mind of man;

A motion and a spirit, that impels                              *100*
All thinking things, all objects of all thought,
And rolls through all things. Therefore am I still
A lover of the meadows and the woods,
And mountains; and of all that we behold
From this green earth; of all the mighty world
Of eye, and ear,—both what they half create,
And what perceive; well pleased to recognise
In nature and the language of the sense,
The anchor of my purest thoughts, the nurse,
The guide, the guardian of my heart, and soul         *110*
Of all my moral being.
                        Nor perchance,
If I were not thus taught, should I the more
Suffer my genial spirits to decay:
For thou art with me here upon the banks
Of this fair river; thou my dearest friend,
My dear, dear friend; and in thy voice I catch
The language of my former heart, and read
My former pleasures in the shooting lights
Of thy wild eyes. Oh! yet a little while
May I behold in thee what I was once,                 *120*
My dear, dear Sister! and this prayer I make,
Knowing that Nature never did betray
The heart that loved her; 't is her privilege,
Through all the years of this our life, to lead
From joy to joy: for she can so inform
The mind that is within us, so impress
With quietness and beauty, and so feed
With lofty thoughts, that neither evil tongues,
Rash judgments, nor the sneers of selfish men,
Nor greetings where no kindness is, nor all           *130*
The dreary intercourse of daily life,
Shall e'er prevail against us, or disturb
Our cheerful faith, that all which we behold
Is full of blessings. Therefore let the moon
Shine on thee in thy solitary walk;
And let the misty mountain-winds be free
To blow against thee: and, in after years,
When these wild ecstasies shall be matured
Into a sober pleasure; when thy mind
Shall be a mansion for all lovely forms,              *140*
Thy memory be as a dwelling-place
For all sweet sounds and harmonies; oh! then,
If solitude, or fear, or pain, or grief,
Should be thy portion, with what healing thoughts
Of tender joy wilt thou remember me,
And these my exhortations! Nor, perchance—
If I should be where I no more can hear

Thy voice, nor catch from thy wild eyes these gleams
Of past existence—wilt thou then forget
That on the banks of this delightful stream         *150*
We stood together; and that I, so long
A worshipper of Nature, hither came
Unwearied in that service; rather say
With warmer love—oh! with far deeper zeal
Of holier love. Nor wilt thou then forget,
That after many wanderings, many years
Of absence, these steep woods and lofty cliffs,
And this green pastoral landscape, were to me
More dear, both for themselves and for thy sake!   *(1798)*

## Strange Fits of Passion Have I Known

Strange fits of passion have I known:
And I will dare to tell,
But in the lover's ear alone,
What once to me befell.

When she I loved looked every day
Fresh as a rose in June,
I to her cottage bent my way,
Beneath an evening-moon.

Upon the moon I fixed my eye,
All over the wide lea;         *10*
With quickening pace my horse drew
   nigh
Those paths so dear to me.

And now we reached the orchard-plot;
And, as we climbed the hill,
The sinking moon to Lucy's cot
Came near, and nearer still.

In one of those sweet dreams I slept,
Kind Nature's gentlest boon!
And all the while my eyes I kept
On the descending moon.         *20*

My horse moved on; hoof after hoof
He raised, and never stopped:
When down behind the cottage roof,
At once, the bright moon dropped.

What fond and wayward thoughts will
   slide
Into a lover's head!
"O mercy!" to myself I cried,
"If Lucy should be dead!"   *(1799)*

## She Dwelt Among the Untrodden Ways

She dwelt among the untrodden ways
   Beside the springs of Dove,
A maid whom there were none to praise,
   And very few to love.

A violet by a mossy stone
   Half-hidden from the eye!
—Fair as a star, when only one
   Is shining in the sky.

She lived unknown, and few could know
   When Lucy ceased to be;       *10*
But she is in her grave, and, oh,
   The difference to me!   *(1799)*

## I Travelled Among Unknown Men

I travelled among unknown men,
   In lands beyond the sea;
Nor, England! did I know till then
   What love I bore to thee.

'T is past, that melancholy dream!
   Nor will I quit thy shore
A second time; for still I seem
   To love thee more and more.

Among thy mountains did I feel
   The joy of my desire;       *10*
And she I cherished turned her wheel
   Beside an English fire.

Thy mornings showed, thy nights
  concealed
The bowers where Lucy played;
And thine too is the last green field
  That Lucy's eyes surveyed. (*1799*)

## Three Years She Grew in Sun and Shower

Three years she grew in sun and shower,
Then Nature said, "A lovelier flower
On earth was never sown;
This child I to myself will take;
She shall be mine, and I will make
A lady of my own.

"Myself will to my darling be
Both law and impulse: and with me
The girl, in rock and plain,
In earth and heaven, in glade and
  bower,                                    10
Shall feel an overseeing power
To kindle or restrain.

"She shall be sportive as the fawn
That wild with glee across the lawn,
Or up the mountain springs;
And hers shall be the breathing balm,
And hers the silence and the calm
Of mute insensate things.

"The floating clouds their state shall lend
To her; for her the willow bend;          20
Nor shall she fail to see
Even in the motions of the storm
Grace that shall mould the maiden's form
By silent sympathy.

"The stars of midnight shall be dear
To her; and she shall lean her ear
In many a secret place
Where rivulets dance their wayward
  round,
And beauty born of murmuring sound
Shall pass into her face.                  30

"And vital feelings of delight
Shall rear her form to stately height,
Her virgin bosom swell;
Such thoughts to Lucy I will give
While she and I together live
Here in this happy dell."

Thus Nature spake—The work was
  done—
How soon my Lucy's race was run!
She died, and left to me
This heath, this calm, and quiet scene;  40
The memory of what has been,
And never more will be. (*1799*)

## A Slumber Did My Spirit Seal

A slumber did my spirit seal;
  I had no human fears:
She seemed a thing that could not feel
  The touch of earthly years.

No motion has she now, no force;
  She neither hears nor sees;
Rolled round in earth's diurnal course,
  With rocks, and stones, and trees.
            (*1799*)

## Lucy Gray

Oft I had heard of Lucy Gray:
And when I crossed the wild,
I chanced to see at break of day
The solitary child.

No mate, no comrade Lucy knew;
She dwelt on a wide moor,
The sweetest thing that ever grew
Beside a human door!

You yet may spy the fawn at play,
The hare upon the green;                  10
But the sweet face of Lucy Gray
Will never more be seen.

"Tonight will be a stormy night—
You to the town must go;
And take a lantern, Child, to light
Your mother through the snow."

"That, Father! will I gladly do:
'Tis scarcely afternoon—
The minster-clock has just struck two,
And yonder is the moon!"                  20

At this the father raised his hook,
And snapped a faggot-band;
He plied his work;—and Lucy took
The lantern in her hand.

Not blither is the mountain roe:
With many a wanton stroke
Her feet disperse the powdery snow,
That rises up like smoke.

The storm came on before its time:
She wandered up and down;    30
And many a hill did Lucy climb:
But never reached the town.

The wretched parents all that night
Went shouting far and wide;
But there was neither sound nor sight
To serve them for a guide.

At day-break on a hill they stood
That overlooked the moor;
And thence they saw the bridge of wood
A furlong from their door.    40

They wept—and, turning homeward,
  cried
"In heaven we all shall meet!"
—When in the snow the mother spied
The print of Lucy's feet.

Then downwards from the steep hill's
  edge
They tracked the footmarks small;
And through the broken hawthorn
  hedge,
And by the long stone-wall:

And then an open field they crossed:
The marks were still the same;    50
They tracked them on, nor ever lost;
And to the bridge they came:

They followed from the snowy bank
Those footmarks, one by one,
Into the middle of the plank;
And further there were none!

—Yet some maintain that to this day
She is a living child;
That you may see sweet Lucy Gray
Upon the lonesome wild.    60

O'er rough and smooth she trips along,
And never looks behind;
And sings a solitary song
That whistles in the wind.   (*1799*)

## Michael

*A PASTORAL POEM*

If from the public way you turn your steps
Up the tumultuous brook of Green-head Ghyll,[1]
You will suppose that with an upright path
Your feet must struggle; in such bold ascent
The pastoral mountains front you, face to face.
But, courage! for around that boisterous brook
The mountains have all opened out themselves,
And made a hidden valley of their own.
No habitation can be seen; but they
Who journey thither find themselves alone    10
With a few sheep, with rocks and stones, and kites
That overhead are sailing in the sky.
It is in truth an utter solitude;
Nor should I have made mention of this Dell
But for one object which you might pass by,
Might see and notice not. Beside the brook
Appears a straggling heap of unhewn stones!
And to that simple object appertains
A story—unenriched with strange events,

---

[1] a narrow ravine with a rushing stream, in the Lake Country

Yet not unfit, I deem, for the fireside,                     *20*
Or for the summer shade. It was the first
Of those domestic tales that spake to me
Of Shepherds, dwellers in the valleys, men
Whom I already loved;—not verily
For their own sakes, but for the fields and hills
Where was their occupation and abode.
And hence this Tale, while I was yet a Boy
Careless of books, yet having felt the power
Of Nature, by the gentle agency
Of natural objects, led me on to feel                       *30*
For passions that were not my own, and think
(At random and imperfectly indeed)
On man, the heart of man, and human life.
Therefore, although it be a history
Homely and rude, I will relate the same
For the delight of a few natural hearts;
And, with yet fonder feeling, for the sake
Of youthful Poets, who among these hills
Will be my second self when I am gone.

Upon the forest-side in Grasmere Vale[2]                    *40*
There dwelt a Shepherd, Michael was his name;
An old man, stout of heart, and strong of limb.
His bodily frame had been from youth to age
Of an unusual strength: his mind was keen,
Intense, and frugal, apt for all affairs,
And in his shepherd's calling he was prompt
And watchful more than ordinary men.
Hence had he learned the meaning of all winds,
Of blasts of every tone; and oftentimes,
When others heeded not, he heard the South              *50*
Make subterraneous music, like the noise
Of bagpipers on distant Highland hills.
The Shepherd, at such warning, of his flock
Bethought him, and he to himself would say,
"The winds are now devising work for me!"
And, truly, at all times, the storm, that drives
The traveller to a shelter, summoned him
Up to the mountains: he had been alone
Amid the heart of many thousand mists,
That came to him, and left him, on the heights.         *60*
So lived he till his eightieth year was past.
And grossly that man errs, who should suppose
That the green valleys, and the streams and rocks,
Were things indifferent to the Shepherd's thoughts.
Fields, where with cheerful spirits he had breathed
The common air; hills, which with vigorous step

---

[2] site of Dove Cottage, Wordsworth's home in the Lake Country

He had so often climbed; which had impressed
So many incidents upon his mind
Of hardship, skill or courage, joy or fear;
Which, like a book, preserved the memory                    70
Of the dumb animals, whom he had saved,
Had fed or sheltered, linking to such acts
The certainty of honourable gain;
Those fields, those hills—what could they less? had
    laid
Strong hold on his affections, were to him
A pleasurable feeling of blind love,
The pleasure which there is in life itself.

His days had not been passed in singleness.
His Helpmate was a comely matron, old—
Though younger than himself full twenty years.              80
She was a woman of a stirring life,
Whose heart was in her house: two wheels she had
Of antique form, this large, for spinning wool;
That small, for flax; and, if one wheel had rest,
It was because the other was at work.
The Pair had but one inmate in their house,
An only Child, who had been born to them
When Michael, telling o'er his years, began
To deem that he was old,—in shepherd's phrase,
With one foot in the grave. This only Son,                  90
With two brave sheep-dogs tried in many a storm,
The one of an inestimable worth,
Made all their household. I may truly say,
That they were as a proverb in the vale
For endless industry. When day was gone,
And from their occupations out of doors
The Son and Father were come home, even then,
Their labour did not cease; unless when all
Turned to the cleanly supper-board, and there,
Each with a mess of pottage and skimmed milk,              100
Sat round the basket piled with oaten cakes,
And their plain home-made cheese. Yet when the meal
Was ended, Luke (for so the Son was named)
And his old Father both betook themselves
To such convenient work as might employ
Their hands by the fire-side; perhaps to card
Wool for the Housewife's spindle, or repair
Some injury done to sickle, flail, or scythe,
Or other implement of house or field.

Down from the ceiling, by the chimney's edge,             110
That in our ancient uncouth country style
With huge and black projection overbrowed
Large space beneath, as duly as the light

Of day grew dim the Housewife hung a lamp;
An aged utensil, which had performed
Service beyond all others of its kind.
Early at evening did it burn—and late,
Surviving comrade of uncounted hours,
Which, going by from year to year, had found,
And left, the couple neither gay perhaps                          *120*
Nor cheerful, yet with objects and with hopes,
Living a life of eager industry.
And now, when Luke had reached his eighteenth year,
There by the light of this old lamp they sate,
Father and Son, while far into the night
The Housewife plied her own peculiar work,
Making the cottage through the silent hours
Murmur as with the sound of summer flies.
This light was famous in its neighbourhood,
And was a public symbol of the life                              *. 130*
That thrifty Pair had lived. For, as it chanced,
Their cottage on a plot of rising ground
Stood single, with large prospect, north and south,
High into Easedale, up to Dunmail-Raise,[3]
And westward to the village near the lake;
And from this constant light, so regular,
And so far seen, the House itself, by all
Who dwelt within the limits of the vale,
Both old and young, was named THE EVENING STAR.

    Thus living on through such a length of years,               *140*
The Shepherd, if he loved himself, must needs
Have loved his Helpmate; but to Michael's heart
This son of his old age was yet more dear—
Less from instinctive tenderness, the same
Fond spirit that blindly works in the blood of all—
Than that a child, more than all other gifts
That earth can offer to declining man,
Brings hope with it, and forward-looking thoughts,
And stirrings of inquietude, when they
By tendency of nature needs must fail.                           *150*
Exceeding was the love he bare to him,
His heart and his heart's joy! For oftentimes
Old Michael, while he was a babe in arms,
Had done him female service, not alone
For pastime and delight, as is the use
Of fathers, but with patient mind enforced
To acts of tenderness; and he had rocked
His cradle, as with a woman's gentle hand.

    And in a later time, ere yet the Boy
Had put on boy's attire, did Michael love,                       *160*

---
[3] valley and pass near Grasmere

Albeit of a stern unbending mind,
To have the Young-one in his sight, when he
Wrought in the field, or on his shepherd's stool
Sate with a fettered sheep before him stretched
Under the large old oak, that near his door
Stood single, and, from matchless depth of shade,
Chosen for the Shearer's covert from the sun,
Thence in our rustic dialect was called
The CLIPPING TREE, a name which yet it bears.
There, while they two were sitting in the shade,                    *170*
With others round them, earnest all and blithe,
Would Michael exercise his heart with looks
Of fond correction and reproof bestowed
Upon the Child, if he disturbed the sheep
By catching at their legs, or with his shouts
Scared them, while they lay still beneath the shears.

And when by Heaven's good grace the boy grew up
A healthy Lad, and carried in his cheek
Two steady roses that were five years old;
Then Michael from a winter coppice cut                             *180*
With his own hand a sapling, which he hooped
With iron, making it throughout in all
Due requisites a perfect shepherd's staff,
And gave it to the Boy; wherewith equipt
He as a watchman oftentimes was placed
At gate or gap, to stem or turn the flock;
And, to his office prematurely called,
There stood the urchin, as you will divine,
Something between a hindrance and a help;
And for this cause not always, I believe,                          *190*
Receiving from his Father hire of praise;
Though nought was left undone which staff, or voice,
Or looks, or threatening gestures, could perform.

But soon as Luke, full ten years old, could stand
Against the mountain blasts; and to the heights,
Not fearing toil, nor length of weary ways,
He with his Father daily went, and they
Were as companions, why should I relate
That objects which the Shepherd loved before
Were dearer now? that from the Boy there came                      *200*
Feelings and emanations—things which were
Light to the sun and music to the wind;
And that the old Man's heart seemed born again?

Thus in his Father's sight the Boy grew up:
And now, when he had reached his eighteenth year,
He was his comfort and his daily hope.

While in this sort the simple household lived
From day to day, to Michael's ear there came

Distressful tidings. Long before the time
Of which I speak, the Shepherd had been bound                    210
In surety for his brother's son, a man
Of an industrious life, and ample means;
But unforeseen misfortunes suddenly
Had prest upon him; and old Michael now
Was summoned to discharge the forfeiture,
A grievous penalty, but little less
Than half his substance. This unlooked-for claim,
At the first hearing, for a moment took
More hope out of his life than he supposed
That any old man ever could have lost.                    220
As soon as he had armed himself with strength
To look his trouble in the face, it seemed
The Shepherd's sole resource to sell at once
A portion of his patrimonial fields.
Such was his first resolve; he thought again,
And his heart failed him. "Isabel," said he,
Two evenings after he had heard the news,
"I have been toiling more than seventy years,
And in the open sunshine of God's love
Have we all lived; yet, if these fields of ours                    230
Should pass into a stranger's hand, I think
That I could not lie quiet in my grave.
Our lot is a hard lot; the sun himself
Has scarcely been more diligent than I;
And I have lived to be a fool at last
To my own family. An evil man
That was, and made an evil choice, if he
Were false to us; and, if he were not false,
There are ten thousand to whom loss like this
Had been no sorrow. I forgive him;—but                    240
'Twere better to be dumb than to talk thus.
    "When I began, my purpose was to speak
Of remedies and of a cheerful hope.
Our Luke shall leave us, Isabel; the land
Shall not go from us, and it shall be free;
He shall possess it, free as is the wind
That passes over it. We have, thou know'st,
Another kinsman—he will be our friend
In this distress. He is a prosperous man,
Thriving in trade—and Luke to him shall go,                    250
And with his kinsman's help and his own thrift
He quickly will repair this loss, and then
He may return to us. If here he stay,
What can be done? Where every one is poor,
What can be gained?"
                    At this the old Man paused,
And Isabel sat silent, for her mind
Was busy, looking back into past times.

There's Richard Bateman, thought she to herself,
He was a parish-boy—at the church-door
They made a gathering for him, shillings, pence,                    260
And halfpennies, wherewith the neighbours bought
A basket, which they filled with pedlar's wares;
And, with this basket on his arm, the lad
Went up to London, found a master there,
Who, out of many, chose the trusty boy
To go and overlook his merchandise
Beyond the seas; where he grew wondrous rich,
And left estates and monies to the poor,
And, at his birth-place, built a chapel floored
With marble, which he sent from foreign lands.                     270
These thoughts, and may others of like sort,
Passed quickly through the mind of Isabel,
And her face brightened. The old Man was glad,
And thus resumed:—"Well, Isabel! this scheme
These two days has been meat and drink to me.
Far more than we have lost is left us yet.
We have enough—I wish indeed that I
Were younger;—but this hope is a good hope.
Make ready Luke's best garments, of the best
Buy for him more, and let us send him forth                        280
To-morrow, or the next day, or to-night:
If he *could* go, the Boy should go tonight."

Here Michael ceased, and to the fields went forth
With a light heart. The Housewife for five days
Was restless morn and night, and all day long
Wrought on with her best fingers to prepare
Things needful for the journey of her son.
But Isabel was glad when Sunday came
To stop her in her work: for, when she lay
By Michael's side, she through the last two nights                 290
Heard him, how he was troubled in his sleep;
And when they rose at morning she could see
That all his hopes were gone. That day at noon
She said to Luke, while they two by themselves
Were sitting at the door, "Thou must not go:
We have no other Child but thee to lose,
None to remember—do not go away,
For if thou leave thy Father he will die."
The Youth made answer with a jocund voice;
And Isabel, when she had told her fears,                           300
Recovered heart. That evening her best fare
Did she bring forth, and all together sat
Like happy people round a Christmas fire.

With daylight Isabel resumed her work;
And all the ensuing week the house appeared
As cheerful as a grove in Spring: at length

The expected letter from their kinsman came,
With kind assurances that he would do
His utmost for the welfare of the Boy;
To which, requests were added, that forthwith                        *310*
He might be sent to him. Ten times or more
The letter was read over; Isabel
Went forth to show it to the neighbours round;
Nor was there at that time on English land
A prouder heart than Luke's. When Isabel
Had to her house returned, the old Man said,
"He shall depart to-morrow." To this word
The Housewife answered, talking much of things
Which, if at such short notice he should go,
Would surely be forgotten, But at length                             *320*
She gave consent, and Michael was at ease.

   Near the tumultuous brook of Green-head Ghyll,
In that deep valley, Michael had designed
To build a Sheep-fold; and, before he heard
The tidings of his melancholy loss,
For this same purpose he had gathered up
A heap of stones, which by the streamlet's edge
Lay thrown together, ready for the work.
With Luke that evening thitherward he walked;
And soon as they had reached the place he stopped,                   *330*
And thus the old Man spake to him:—"My son,
Tomorrow thou wilt leave me: with full heart
I look upon thee, for thou art the same
That wert a promise to me ere thy birth,
And all thy life hast been my daily joy.
I will relate to thee some little part
Of our two histories; 'twill do thee good
When thou art from me, even if I should touch
On things thou canst not know of.—After thou
First camst into the world—as oft befalls                           *340*
To new-born infants—thou didst sleep away
Two days, and blessings from thy Father's tongue
Then fell upon thee. Day by day passed on,
And still I loved thee with increasing love.
Never to living ear came sweeter sounds
Than when I heard thee by our own fireside
First uttering, without words, a natural tune;
While thou, a feeding babe, didst in thy joy
Sing at thy Mother's breast. Month followed month,
And in the open fields my life was passed                           *350*
And on the mountains; else I think that thou
Hadst been brought up upon thy Father's knees.
But we were playmates, Luke: among these hills,
As well thou knowest, in us the old and young

Have played together, nor with me didst thou
Lack any pleasure which a boy can know."
Luke had a manly heart; but at these words
He sobbed aloud. The old Man grasped his hand,
And said, "Nay, do not take it so—I see
That these are things of which I need not speak.                    *360*
—Even to the utmost I have been to thee
A kind and a good Father: and herein
I but repay a gift which I myself
Received at others' hands; for, though now old
Beyond the common life of man, I still
Remember them who loved me in my youth.
Both of them sleep together: here they lived,
As all their Forefathers had done; and, when
At length their time was come, they were not loth
To give their bodies to the family mould.                          *370*
I wished that thou shouldst live the life they lived,
But 'tis a long time to look back, my Son,
And see so little gain from threescore years.
These fields were burthened when they came to me;
Till I was forty years of age, not more
Than half of my inheritance was mine.
I toiled and toiled; God blessed me in my work,
And till these three weeks past the land was free.
—It looks as if it never could endure
Another Master. Heaven forgive me, Luke,                           *380*
If I judge ill for thee, but it seems good
That thou shouldst go."
                                    At this the old Man paused;
Then, pointing to the stones near which they stood,
Thus, after a short silence, he resumed:
"This was a work for us; and now, my Son,
It is a work for me. But, lay one stone—
Here, lay it for me, Luke, with thine own hands.
Nay, Boy, be of good hope;—we both may live
To see a better day. At eighty-four
I still am strong and hale;—do thou thy part;                      *390*
I will do mine.—I will begin again
With many tasks that were resigned to thee:
Up to the heights, and in among the storms,
Will I without thee go again, and do
All works which I was wont to do alone,
Before I knew thy face.—Heaven bless thee, Boy!
Thy heart these two weeks has been beating fast
With many hopes; it should be so—yes—yes—
I knew that thou couldst never have a wish
To leave me, Luke: thou hast been bound to me                      *400*
Only by links of love: when thou art gone,
What will be left to us!—But I forget

My purposes. Lay now the corner-stone,
As I requested; and hereafter, Luke,
When thou art gone away, should evil men
Be thy companions, think of me, my Son,
And of this moment; hither turn thy thoughts,
And God will strengthen thee: amid all fear
And all temptation, Luke, I pray that thou
May'st bear in mind the life thy Fathers lived,                       410
Who, being innocent, did for that cause
Bestir them in good deeds. Now, fare thee well—
When thou return'st, thou in this place wilt see
A work which is not here: a covenant
'Twill be between us; but, whatever fate
Befall thee, I shall love thee to the last,
And bear thy memory with me to the grave."

     The Shepherd ended here; and Luke stooped down,
And, as his Father had requested, laid
The first stone of the Sheep-fold. At the sight                       420
The old Man's grief broke from him; to his heart
He pressed his Son, he kisséd him and wept;
And to the house together they returned.
—Hushed was that House in peace, or seeming peace
Ere the night fell:—with morrow's dawn the Boy
Began his journey, and, when he had reached
The public way, he put on a bold face;
And all the neighbours, as he passed their doors,
Came forth with wishes and with farewell prayers,
That followed him till he was out of sight.                           430

     A good report did from their Kinsman come,
Of Luke and his well-doing: and the Boy
Wrote loving letters, full of wondrous news,
Which, as the Housewife phrased it, were throughout
"The prettiest letters that were ever seen."
Both parents read them with rejoicing hearts.
So, many months passed on: and once again
The Shepherd went about his daily work
With confident and cheerful thoughts; and now
Sometimes when he could find a leisure hour                           440
He to that valley took his way, and there
Wrought at the Sheep-fold. Meantime Luke began
To slacken in his duty; and, at length,
He in the dissolute city gave himself
To evil courses: ignominy and shame
Fell on him, so that he was driven at last
To seek a hiding-place beyond the seas.

     There is a comfort in the strength of love;
'Twill make a thing endurable, which else
Would overset the brain, or break the heart:                          450

I have conversed with more than one who well
Remember the old Man, and what he was
Years after he had heard this heavy news.
His bodily frame had been from youth to age
Of an unusual strength. Among the rocks
He went, and still looked up to sun and cloud,
And listened to the wind; and, as before,
Performed all kinds of labour for his sheep,
And for the land, his small inheritance.
And to that hollow dell from time to time     460
Did he repair, to build the Fold of which
His flock had need. 'Tis not forgotten yet
The pity which was then in every heart
For the old Man—and 'tis believed by all
That many and many a day he thither went,
And never lifted up a single stone.
  There, by the Sheep-fold, sometimes was he seen
Sitting alone, or with his faithful Dog,
Then old, beside him, lying at his feet.
The length of full seven years, from time to time,     470
He at the building of this Sheep-fold wrought,
And left the work unfinished when he died.
Three years, or little more, did Isabel
Survive her Husband: at her death the estate
Was sold, and went into a stranger's hand.
The Cottage which was named THE EVENING STAR.
Is gone—the ploughshare has been through the ground
On which it stood; great changes have been wrought
In all the neighbourhood:—yet the oak is left
That grew beside their door; and the remains     480
Of the unfinished Sheep-fold may be seen
Beside the boisterous brook of Green-head Ghyll. (*1800*)

## My Heart Leaps Up When I Behold

My heart leaps up when I behold
 A rainbow in the sky:
So was it when my life began;
So is it now I am a man;
So be it when I shall grow old,
 Or let me die!
The Child is father of the Man;
And I could wish my days to be
Bound each to each by natural piety.

(*1802*)

## It Is a Beauteous Evening

It is a beauteous evening, calm and free,
The holy time is quiet as a nun
Breathless with adoration; the broad sun
Is sinking down in its tranquillity;

The gentleness of heaven broods o'er the sea:
Listen! the mighty being is awake,
And doth with his eternal motion make
A sound like thunder—everlastingly.
Dear child! dear girl! that walkest with me here,
If thou appear untouched by solemn thought,                    *10*
Thy nature is not therefore less divine:
Thou liest in Abraham's bosom all the year;
And worship'st at the temple's inner shrine,
God being with thee when we know it not.   (*1802*)

## With How Sad Steps

With how sad steps, O Moon, thou climb'st the sky,
"How silently, and with how wan a face!"
Where art thou? Thou so often seen on high
Running among the clouds a wood-nymph's race!
Unhappy nuns, whose common breath's a sigh
Which they would stifle, move at such a pace!
The northern wind, to call thee to the chase,
Must blow tonight his bugle horn. Had I
The power of Merlin,[1] Goddess! this should be:
And all the stars, fast as the clouds were riven,              *10*
Should sally forth, to keep thee company,
Hurrying and sparkling through the clear blue heaven;
But, Cynthia![2] should to thee the palm be given,
Queen both for beauty and for majesty.   (*1802*)

## Composed Upon Westminster Bridge

*SEPT. 3, 1802*

Earth has not anything to show more fair:
Dull would he be of soul who could pass by
A sight so touching in its majesty:
This city now doth, like a garment, wear
The beauty of the morning; silent, bare,
Ships, towers, domes, theatres, and temples lie
Open unto the fields, and to the sky;
All bright and glittering in the smokeless air.
Never did sun more beautifully steep
In his first splendour, valley, rock, or hill;                 *10*
Ne'er saw I, never felt, a calm so deep!
The river glideth at his own sweet will:
Dear God! the very houses seem asleep;
And all that mighty heart is lying still!   (*1802*)

---

[1] the magician of King Arthur's court, also known      [2] mythological personification of the moon
as a powerful musician

## Written in London, September, 1802

O Friend! I know not which way I must look
For comfort, being, as I am, oppressed,
To think that now our life is only dressed
For show; mean handy-work of craftsman, cook,
Or groom!—We must run glittering like a brook
In the open sunshine, or we are unblessed:
The wealthiest man among us is the best:
No grandeur now in nature or in book
Delights us. Rapine, avarice, expense,
This is idolatry; and these we adore:      *10*
Plain living and high thinking are no more:
The homely beauty of the good old cause
Is gone; our peace, our fearful innocence,
And pure religion breathing household laws.   *(1802)*


## London, 1802

Milton! thou should'st be living at this hour:
England hath need of thee: she is a fen
Of stagnant waters: altar, sword, and pen,
Fireside, the heroic wealth of hall and bower,
Have forfeited their ancient English dower
Of inward happiness. We are selfish men;
Oh! raise us up, return to us again;
And give us manners, virtue, freedom, power.
Thy soul was like a star, and dwelt apart:
Thou hadst a voice whose sound was like the sea:      *10*
Pure as the naked heavens, majestic, free,
So didst thou travel on life's common way,
In cheerful godliness; and yet thy heart
The lowliest duties on herself did lay.   *(1802)*


## The Solitary Reaper

Behold her, single in the field,
Yon solitary Highland Lass!
Reaping and singing by herself;
Stop here, or gently pass!
Alone she cuts and binds the grain,
And sings a melancholy strain;
O listen! for the vale profound
Is overflowing with the sound.

No nightingale did ever chaunt
More welcome notes to weary bands   *10*
Of travellers in some shady haunt,
Among Arabian sands:
A voice so thrilling ne'er was heard
In spring-time from the cuckoo-bird,
Breaking the silence of the seas
Among the farthest Hebrides.

Will no one tell me what she sings?—
Perhaps the plaintive numbers flow
For old, unhappy, far-off things,
And battles long ago:   *20*
Or is it some more humble lay,
Familiar matter of to-day?
Some natural sorrow, loss, or pain,
That has been, and may be again?

Whate'er the theme, the maiden sang
As if her song could have no ending;
I saw her singing at her work,
And o'er the sickle bending;—
I listened, motionless and still;
And, as I mounted up the hill,                    30
The music in my heart I bore,
Long after it was heard no more.   (*1803*)

## Stepping Westward

" *What, you are stepping westward?*"—
   " *Yea.*"
—'T would be a *wildish* destiny,
If we, who thus together roam
In a strange land, and far from home,
Were in this place the guests of Chance:
Yet who would stop, or fear to advance,
Though home or shelter he had none,

With such a sky to lead him on?
The dewy ground was dark and cold;
Behind, all gloomy to behold;                     10
And stepping westward seemed to be
A kind of *heavenly* destiny:
I liked the greeting; 't was a sound
Of something without place or bound;
And seemed to give me spiritual right
To travel through that region bright.

The voice was soft, and she who spake
Was walking by her native lake:
The salutation had to me
The very sound of courtesy:                        20
Its power was felt; and while my eye
Was fixed upon the glowing sky,
The echo of the voice enwrought
A human sweetness with the thought
Of travelling through the world that lay
Before me in my endless way.   (*1803*)

## Ode

### INTIMATIONS OF IMMORTALITY FROM RECOLLECTIONS OF EARLY CHILDHOOD

There was a time when meadow, grove, and stream,
The earth, and every common sight,
        To me did seem
        Apparelled in celestial light,
The glory and the freshness of a dream.
It is not now as it hath been of yore;—
        Turn wheresoe'er I may,
          By night or day,
The things which I have seen I now can see no more.

        The rainbow comes and goes,                      10
        And lovely is the rose,
        The moon doth with delight
Look round her when the heavens are bare,
        Waters on a starry night
        Are beautiful and fair;
        The sunshine is a glorious birth;
        But yet I know, where'er I go,
That there hath past away a glory from the earth.

Now, while the birds thus sing a joyous song,
        And while the young lambs bound                   20
        As to the tabor's sound,
To me alone there came a thought of grief:
A timely utterance gave that thought relief,
        And I again am strong:

The cataracts blow their trumpets from the steep;
No more shall grief of mine the season wrong;
I hear the echoes through the mountains throng,
The winds come to me from the fields of sleep,
    And all the earth is gay;
      Land and sea 30
    Give themselves up to jollity,
      And with the heart of May
    Doth every beast keep holiday;—
      Thou child of joy,
Shout round me, let me hear thy shouts, thou happy Shepherd-boy!

Ye blessèd creatures, I have heard the call
    Ye to each other make; I see
The heavens laugh with you in your jubilee;
    My heart is at your festival,
    My head hath its coronal, 40
The fulness of your bliss, I feel—I feel it all.
    Oh, evil day! if I were sullen
    While earth herself is adorning,
      This sweet May-morning,
    And the children are culling
      On every side,
    In a thousand valleys far and wide,
    Fresh flowers; while the sun shines warm,
And the babe leaps up on his mother's arm:—
    I hear, I hear, with joy I hear! 50
    —But there's a tree, of many, one,
A single field which I have looked upon,
Both of them speak of something that is gone:
    The pansy at my feet
    Doth the same tale repeat:
Whither is fled the visionary gleam?
Where is it now, the glory and the dream?

Our birth is but a sleep and a forgetting;
The soul that rises with us, our life's star,
    Hath had elsewhere its setting, 60
      And cometh from afar:
    Not in entire forgetfulness,
    And not in utter nakedness,
But trailing clouds of glory do we come
    From God, who is our home:
Heaven lies about us in our infancy!
Shades of the prison-house begin to close
    Upon the growing boy,
But he beholds the light, and whence it flows,
    He sees it in his joy; 70
The youth, who daily farther from the east
    Must travel, still is Nature's priest,
    And by the vision splendid

Is on his way attended;
At length the man perceives it die away,
And fade into the light of common day.

Earth fills her lap with pleasures of her own;
Yearnings she hath in her own natural kind,
And, even with something of a mother's mind,
    And no unworthy aim,                                    *80*
    The homely nurse doth all she can
To make her foster-child, her inmate man,
    Forget the glories he hath known,
And that imperial palace whence he came.

Behold the child among his new-born blisses,
A six years' darling of a pigmy size!
See, where 'mid work of his own hand he lies,
Fretted by sallies of his mother's kisses,
With light upon him from his father's eyes!
See, at his feet, some little plan or chart,                   *90*
Some fragment from his dream of human life,
Shaped by himself with newly-learnéd art;
    A wedding or a festival,
    A mourning or a funeral;
      And this hath now his heart,
    And unto this he frames his song:
      Then will he fit his tongue
To dialogues of business, love, or strife;
    But it will not be long
    Ere this be thrown aside,                           *100*
    And with new joy and pride
The little actor cons another part;
Filling from time to time his "humorous stage"
With all the persons, down to palsied Age,
That life brings with her in her equipage;
    As if his whole vocation
    Were endless imitation.

Thou, whose exterior semblance doth belie
    Thy soul's immensity;
Thou best philosopher, who yet dost keep                       *110*
Thy heritage, thou eye among the blind,
That, deaf and silent, read'st the eternal deep,
Haunted for ever by the eternal mind,—
    Mighty prophet! Seer blest!
    On whom those truths do rest,
Which we are toiling all our lives to find,
In darkness lost, the darkness of the grave;
Thou, over whom thy immortality
Broods like the day, a master o'er a slave,
A presence which is not to be put by:                          *120*
Thou little child, yet glorious in the might

Of heaven-born freedom on thy being's height,
Why with such earnest pains dost thou provoke
The years to bring the inevitable yoke,
Thus blindly with thy blessedness at strife?
Full soon thy soul shall have her earthly freight,
And custom lie upon thee with a weight,
Heavy as frost, and deep almost as life!

    O joy! that in our embers
    Is something that doth live,           130
    That nature yet remembers
    What was so fugitive!
The thought of our past years in me doth breed
Perpetual benediction: not indeed
For that which is most worthy to be blest—
Delight and liberty, the simple creed
Of childhood, whether busy or at rest,
With new-fledged hope still fluttering in his breast:—
    Not for these I raise
    The song of thanks and praise;       140
  But for those obstinate questionings
  Of sense and outward things,
  Fallings from us, vanishings;
  Blank misgivings of a creature
Moving about in worlds not realized,
High instincts before which our mortal nature
Did tremble like a guilty thing surprised:
    But for those first affections,
    Those shadowy recollections,
  Which, be they what they may,       150
Are yet the fountain light of all our day,
Are yet a master light of all our seeing;
  Uphold us, cherish, and have power to make
Our noisy years seem moments in the being
Of the eternal silence: truths that wake,
    To perish never;
Which neither listlessness, nor mad endeavour,
    Nor man nor boy,
Nor all that is at enmity with joy,
Can utterly abolish or destroy!       160
    Hence in a season of calm weather
    Though inland far we be,
Our souls have sight of that immortal sea
    Which brought us hither,
    Can in a moment travel thither,
And see the children sport upon the shore,
And hear the mighty waters rolling evermore.

Then sing, ye birds, sing, sing a joyous song!
    And let the young lambs bound

As to the tabor's sound!                                          *170*
We in thought will join your throng,
    Ye that pipe and ye that play,
    Ye that through your hearts today
    Feel the gladness of the May!
What though the radiance which was once so bright
Be now forever taken from my sight,
    Though nothing can bring back the hour
Of splendour in the grass, of glory in the flower;
    We will grieve not, rather find
    Strength in what remains behind;                          *180*
    In the primal sympathy
    Which having been must ever be;
    In the soothing thoughts that spring
    Out of human suffering;
    In the faith that looks through death,
In years that bring the philosophic mind.

And O, ye fountains, meadows, hills, and groves,
Forebode not any severing of our loves!
Yet in my heart of hearts I feel your might;
I only have relinquished one delight                              *190*
To live beneath your more habitual sway.
I love the brooks which down their channels fret,
Even more than when I tripped lightly as they;
The innocent brightness of a new-born day
    Is lovely yet;
The clouds that gather round the setting sun
Do take a sober colouring from an eye
That hath kept watch o'er man's mortality;
Another race hath been, and other palms are won.
Thanks to the human heart by which we live,                       *200*
Thanks to its tenderness, its joys, and fears,
To me the meanest flower that blows can give
Thoughts that do often lie too deep for tears.   (*1803*)

## I Wandered Lonely as a Cloud

I wandered lonely as a cloud
That floats on high o'er vales and hills,
When all at once I saw a crowd,
A host, of golden daffodils;
Beside the lake, beneath the trees,
Fluttering and dancing in the breeze.

Continuous as the stars that shine
And twinkle on the milky way,
They stretched in never-ending line
Along the margin of a bay:                            *10*
Ten thousand saw I at a glance,
Tossing their heads in sprightly dance.

The waves beside them danced; but they
Out-did the sparkling waves in glee:
A poet could not but be gay,
In such a jocund company:
I gazed—and gazed—but little thought
What wealth the show to me had brought:

For oft, when on my couch I lie,
In vacant or in pensive mood,                         *20*
They flash upon that inward eye
Which is the bliss of solitude;
And then my heart with pleasure fills,
And dances with the daffodils.   (*1804*)

## She Was a Phantom of Delight

She was a phantom of delight
When first she gleamed upon my sight;
A lovely apparition, sent
To be a moment's ornament;
Her eyes as stars of twilight fair;
Like twilight's, too, her dusky hair;
But all things else about her drawn
From May-time and the cheerful dawn;
A dancing shape, an image gay,
To haunt, to startle, and waylay.        10

I saw her upon nearer view,
A spirit, yet a woman too!
Her household motions light and free,
And steps of virgin-liberty;
A countenance in which did meet
Sweet records, promises as sweet;
A creature not too bright or good
For human nature's daily food;
For transient sorrows, simple wiles,
Praise, blame, love, kisses, tears, and
        smiles.        20

And now I see with eye serene
The very pulse of the machine;
A being breathing thoughtful breath,
A traveller between life and death;
The reason firm, the temperate will,
Endurance, foresight, strength, and skill;
A perfect woman, nobly planned,
To warn, to comfort, and command;
And yet a spirit still, and bright
With something of angelic light.        30

(1804)

## *from* The Prelude

### *from* BOOK I

Fair seed-time had my soul, and I grew up
Fostered alike by beauty and by fear:
Much favoured in my birth-place, and no less
In that belovéd Vale[1] to which erelong
We were transplanted; there were we let loose
For sports of wider range. Ere I had told
Ten birth-days, when among the mountain slopes
Frost, and the breath of frosty wind, had snapped
The last autumnal crocus, 't was my joy
With store of springes o'er my shoulder hung        10
To range the open heights where woodcocks run
Along the smooth green turf. Through half the night,
Scudding away from snare to snare, I plied
That anxious visitation;—moon and stars
Were shining o'er my head. I was alone,
And seemed to be a trouble to the peace
That dwelt among them. Sometimes it befell
In these night wanderings, that a strong desire
O'erpowered my better reason, and the bird
Which was the captive of another's toil        20
Became my prey; and when the deed was done
I heard among the solitary hills
Low breathings coming after me, and sounds
Of undistinguishable motion, steps
Almost as silent as the turf they trod.

[1] Esthwaite Vale, the region in which Wordsworth went to school

Nor less, when spring had warmed the cultured Vale,
Moved we as plunderers where the mother-bird
Had in high places built her lodge; though mean
Our object and inglorious, yet the end
Was not ignoble. Oh! when I have hung                          30
Above the raven's nest, by knots of grass
And half-inch fissures in the slippery rock
But ill sustained, and almost (so it seemed)
Suspended by the blast that blew amain,
Shouldering the naked crag, oh, at that time
While on the perilous ridge I hung alone,
With what strange utterance did the loud dry wind
Blow through my ear! the sky seemed not a sky
Of earth—and with what motion moved the clouds!

Dust as we are, the immortal spirit grows                      40
Like harmony in music; there is a dark
Inscrutable workmanship that reconciles
Discordant elements, makes them cling together
In one society. How strange, that all
The terrors, pains, and early miseries,
Regrets, vexations, lassitudes interfused
Within my mind, should e'er have borne a part,
And that a needful part, in making up
The calm existence that is mine when I
Am worthy of myself! Praise to the end!                        50
Thanks to the means which Nature deigned to employ;
Whether her fearless visitings, or those
That came with soft alarm, like hurtless light
Opening the peaceful clouds; or she would use
Severer interventions, ministry
More palpable, as best might suit her aim.

One summer evening (led by her) I found
A little boat tied to a willow tree
Within a rocky cove, its usual home.
Straight I unloosed her chain, and stepping in                 60
Pushed from the shore. It was an act of stealth
And troubled pleasure, nor without the voice
Of mountain-echoes did my boat move on;
Leaving behind her still, on either side,
Small circles glittering idly in the moon,
Until they melted all into one track
Of sparkling light. But now, like one who rows,
Proud of his skill, to reach a chosen point
With an unswerving line, I fixed my view
Upon the summit of a craggy ridge,                             70
The horizon's utmost boundary; far above
Was nothing but the stars and the grey sky.
She was an elfin pinnace; lustily

I dipped my oars into the silent lake,
And, as I rose upon the stroke, my boat
Went heaving through the water like a swan;
When, from behind that craggy steep till then
The horizon's bound, a huge peak, black and huge,
As if with voluntary power instinct,
Upreared its head. I struck and struck again,     *80*
And growing still in stature the grim shape
Towered up between me and the stars, and still,
For so it seemed, with purpose of its own
And measured motion like a living thing,
Strode after me. With trembling oars I turned,
And through the silent water stole my way
Back to the covert of the willow tree;
There in her mooring-place I left my bark,—
And through the meadows homeward went, in grave
And serious mood; but after I had seen     *90*
That spectacle, for many days, my brain
Worked with a dim and undetermined sense
Of unknown modes of being; o'er my thoughts
There hung a darkness, call it solitude
Or blank desertion. No familiar shapes
Remained, no pleasant images of trees,
Of sea or sky, no colours of green fields;
But huge and mighty forms, that do not live
Like living men, moved slowly through the mind
By day, and were a trouble to my dreams.     *100*

    Wisdom and Spirit of the universe!
Thou Soul that art the eternity of thought
That givest to forms and images a breath
And everlasting motion, not in vain
By day or star-light thus from my first dawn
Of childhood didst thou intertwine for me
The passions that build up our human soul;
Not with the mean and vulgar works of man,
But with high objects, with enduring things—
With life and nature—purifying thus     *110*
The elements of feeling and of thought,
And sanctifying, by such discipline,
Both pain and fear, until we recognise
A grandeur in the beatings of the heart.
Nor was this fellowship vouchsafed to me
With stinted kindness. In November days,
When vapours rolling down the valley made
A lonely scene more lonesome, among woods,
At noon and 'mid the calm of summer nights,
When, by the margin of the trembling lake,     *120*
Beneath the gloomy hills homeward I went

In solitude, such intercourse was mine;
Mine was it in the fields both day and night,
And by the waters, all the summer long.

    And in the frosty season, when the sun
Was set, and visible for many a mile
The cottage windows blazed through twilight gloom,
I heeded not their summons: happy time
It was indeed for all of us—for me
It was a time of rapture! Clear and loud                        130
The village clock tolled six,—I wheeled about,
Proud and exulting like an untired horse
That cares not for his home. All shod with steel,
We hissed along the polished ice in games
Confederate, imitative of the chase
And woodland pleasures,—the resounding horn,
The pack loud chiming, and the hunted hare.
So through the darkness and the cold we flew,
And not a voice was idle; with the din
Smitten, the precipices rang aloud;                            140
The leafless trees and every icy crag
Tinkled like iron; while far distant hills
Into the tumult sent an alien sound
Of melancholy not unnoticed, while the stars
Eastward were sparkling clear, and in the west
The orange sky of evening died away.
Not seldom from the uproar I retired
Into a silent bay, or sportively
Glanced sideway, leaving the tumultuous throng,
To cut across the reflex of a star                             150
That fled, and, flying still before me, gleamed
Upon the glassy plain; and oftentimes,
When we had given our bodies to the wind,
And all the shadowy banks on either side
Came sweeping through the darkness, spinning
    still
The rapid line of motion, then at once
Have I, reclining back upon my heels
Stopped short; yet still the solitary cliffs
Wheeled by me—even as if the earth had rolled
With visible motion her diurnal round!                         160
Behind me did they stretch in solemn train,
Feebler and feebler, and I stood and watched
Till all was tranquil as a dreamless sleep.

    Ye Presences of Nature in the sky
And on the earth! Ye Visions of the hills!
And Souls of lonely places! can I think
A vulgar hope was yours when ye employed
Such ministry, when ye, through many a year

Haunting me thus among my boyish sports,
On caves and trees, upon the woods and hills,                    *170*
Impressed, upon all forms, the characters
Of danger or desire; and thus did make
The surface of the universal earth,
With triumph and delight, with hope and fear,
Work like a sea?
              Not uselessly employed,
Might I pursue this theme through every change
Of exercise and play, to which the year
Did summon us in his delightful round.

We were a noisy crew; the sun in heaven
Beheld not vales more beautiful than ours;                       *180*
Nor saw a band in happiness and joy
Richer, or worthier of the ground they trod.
I could record with no reluctant voice
The woods of autumn, and their hazel bowers
With milk-white clusters hung; the rod and line,
True symbol of hope's foolishness, whose strong
And unreproved enchantment led us on
By rocks and pools shut out from every star,
All the green summer, to forlorn cascades
Among the windings hid of mountain brooks.                      *190*
—Unfading recollections! at this hour
The heart is almost mine with which I felt,
From some hill-top on sunny afternoons,
The paper kite high among fleecy clouds
Pull at her rein like an impetuous courser;
Or, from the meadows sent on gusty days,
Beheld her breast the wind, then suddenly
Dashed headlong, and rejected by the storm.

Ye lowly cottages wherein we dwelt,
A ministration of your own was yours;                           *200*
Can I forget you, being as you were
So beautiful among the pleasant fields
In which ye stood? or can I here forget
The plain and seemly countenance with which
Ye dealt out your plain comforts? Yet had ye
Delights and exultations of your own.
Eager and never weary we pursued
Our home-amusements by the warm peat-fire
At evening, when with pencil, and smooth slate
In square divisions parcelled out and all                       *210*
With crosses and with cyphers scribbled o'er,
We schemed and puzzled, head opposed to head
In strife too humble to be named in verse:
Or round the naked table, snow-white deal,
Cherry or maple, sate in close array,

And to the combat, Loo or Whist, led on
A thick-ribbed army; not, as in the world,
Neglected and ungratefully thrown by
Even for the very service they had wrought,
But husbanded through many a long campaign.                    *220*
Uncouth assemblage was it, where no few
Had changed their functions: some, plebeian cards
Which Fate, beyond the promise of their birth
Had dignified, and called to represent
The persons of departed potentates.
Oh, with what echoes on the board they fell!
Ironic diamonds,—clubs, hearts, diamonds, spades,
A congregation piteously akin!
Cheap matter offered they to boyish wit,
Those sooty knaves, precipitated down                          *230*
With scoffs and taunts, like Vulcan[2] out of heaven:
The paramount ace, a moon in her eclipse,
Queens gleaming through their splendour's last decay,
And monarchs surly at the wrongs sustained
By royal visages. Meanwhile abroad
Incessant rain was falling, or the frost
Raged bitterly, with keen and silent tooth;
And, interrupting oft that eager game,
From under Esthwaite's splitting fields of ice
The pent-up air, struggling to free itself,                    *240*
Gave out to meadow grounds and hills a loud
Protracted yelling, like the noise of wolves
Howling in troops along the Bothnic Main.[3]

   Nor, sedulous as I have been to trace
How Nature by extrinsic passion first
Peopled the mind with forms sublime or fair,
And made me love them, may I here omit
How other pleasures have been mine, and joys
Of subtler origin; how I have felt,
Not seldom even in that tempestuous time,                      *250*
Those hallowed and pure motions of the sense
Which seem, in their simplicity, to own
An intellectual charm; that calm delight
Which, if I err not, surely must belong
To those first-born affinities that fit
Our new existence to existing things,
And, in our dawn of being, constitute
The bond of union between life and joy.

   Yes, I remember when the changeful earth,
And twice five summers on my mind had stamped                  *260*
The faces of the moving year, even then

---

[2] god of fire and furnaces, cast out of heaven by        [3] Bothnia, region at the northern extremity of
Jupiter                                                     the Baltic Sea

I held unconscious intercourse with beauty
Old as creation, drinking in a pure
Organic pleasure from the silver wreaths
Of curling mist, or from the level plain
Of waters coloured by impending clouds.

    The sands of Westmoreland, the creeks and bays
Of Cumbria's[4] rocky limits, they can tell
How, when the Sea threw off his evening shade,
And to the shepherd's hut on distant hills                    *270*
Sent welcome notice of the rising moon,
How I have stood, to fancies such as these
A stranger, linking with the spectacle
No conscious memory of a kindred sight,
And bringing with me no peculiar sense
Of quietness or peace; yet have I stood,
Even while mine eye hath moved o'er many a league
Of shining water, gathering as it seemed,
Through every hair-breadth in that field of light,
New pleasure like a bee among the flowers.                    *280*

    Thus oft amid those fits of vulgar joy
Which, through all seasons, on a child's pursuits
Are prompt attendants, 'mid that giddy bliss
Which, like a tempest, works along the blood
And is forgotten; even then I felt
Gleams like the flashing of a shield;—the earth
And common face of Nature spake to me
Rememberable things; sometimes, 'tis true,
By chance collisions and quaint accidents
(Like those ill-sorted unions, work supposed                  *290*
Of evil-minded fairies), yet not vain
Nor profitless, if haply they impressed
Collateral objects and appearances,
Albeit lifeless then, and doomed to sleep
Until maturer seasons called them forth
To impregnate and to elevate the mind.
—And if the vulgar joy by its own weight
Wearied itself out of the memory,
The scenes which were a witness of that joy
Remained in their substantial lineaments                      *300*
Depicted on the brain, and to the eye
Were visible, a daily sight; and thus
By the impressive discipline of fear,
By pleasure and repeated happiness,
So frequently repeated, and by force
Of obscure feelings representative
Of things forgotten, these same scenes so bright,

---

4 Cumberland's

So beautiful, so majestic in themselves,
Though yet the day was distant, did become
Habitually dear, and all their forms                    *310*
And changeful colours by invisible links
Were fastened to the affections.   (*1805, 1850*)

## Nuns Fret Not

Nuns fret not at their convent's narrow room;
And hermits are contented with their cells;
And students with their pensive citadels;
Maids at the wheel, the weaver at his loom,
Sit blithe and happy; bees that soar for bloom,
High as the highest Peak of Furness-fells,
Will murmur by the hour in foxglove bells:
In truth the prison, unto which we doom
Ourselves, no prison is: and hence for me,
In sundry moods, 'twas pastime to be bound        *10*
Within the sonnet's scanty plot of ground;
Pleased if some souls (for such there needs must be)
Who have felt the weight of too much liberty,
Should find brief solace there, as I have found.   (*1806*)

## The World Is Too Much with Us

The world is too much with us; late and soon,
Getting and spending, we lay waste our powers:
Little we see in Nature that is ours;
We have given our hearts away, a sordid boon!
The sea that bares her bosom to the moon;
The winds that will be howling at all hours,
And are up-gathered now like sleeping flowers;
For this, for everything, we are out of tune;
It moves us not.—Great God! I'd rather be
A pagan suckled in a creed outworn;              *10*
So might I, standing on this pleasant lea,
Have glimpses that would make me less forlorn;
Have sight of Proteus rising from the sea;
Or hear old Triton blow his wreathéd horn.   (*1806*)

## Where Lies the Land

Where lies the Land to which yon Ship must go?
Fresh as a lark mounting at break of day,
Festively she puts forth in trim array;
Is she for tropic suns, or polar snow?
What boots the enquiry?—Neither friend nor foe
She cares for; let her travel where she may,

She finds familiar names, a beaten way
Ever before her, and a wind to blow.
Yet still I ask, what haven is her mark?
And, almost as it was when ships were rare,                   *10*
(From time to time, like Pilgrims, here and there
Crossing the waters) doubt, and something dark,
Of the old Sea some reverential fear,
Is with me at thy farewell, joyous Bark!  (*1807*)

## Surprised by Joy

Surprised by joy—impatient as the wind
I turned to share the transport—Oh! with whom
But Thee, deep buried in the silent tomb,
That spot which no vicissitude can find?
Love, faithful love, recalled thee to my mind—
But how could I forget thee? Through what power,
Even for the least division of an hour,
Have I been so beguiled as to be blind
To my most grievous loss?—That thought's return
Was the worst pang that sorrow ever bore,                    *10*
Save one, one only, when I stood forlorn,
Knowing my heart's best treasure was no more;
That neither present time, nor years unborn
Could to my sight that heavenly face restore.  (*1812?*)

## Mutability

From low to high doth dissolution climb,
And sink from high to low, along a scale
Of awful notes, whose concord shall not fail;
A musical but melancholy chime,
Which they can hear who meddle not with crime,
Nor avarice, nor over-anxious care.
Truth fails not; but her outward forms that bear
The longest date do melt like frosty rime
That in the morning whitened hill and plain
And is no more; drop like the tower sublime                  *10*
Of yesterday, which royally did wear
His crown of weeds, but could not even sustain
Some casual shout that broke the silent air,
Or the unimaginable touch of Time.  (*1821*)

## Scorn Not the Sonnet

Scorn not the sonnet; Critic, you have frowned,
Mindless of its just honours; with this key
Shakespeare unlocked his heart; the melody
Of this small lute gave ease to Petrarch's wound;

A thousand times this pipe did Tasso sound;
With it Camoëns soothed an exile's grief;
The sonnet glittered a gay myrtle leaf
Amid the cypress with which Dante crowned
His visionary brow: a glow-worm lamp,
It cheered mild Spenser, called from Faeryland      10
To struggle through dark ways; and when a damp
Fell round the path of Milton, in his hand
The thing became a trumpet; whence he blew
Soul-animating strains—alas, too few!   (*1827*)

## A Poet!—He Hath Put His Heart to School

A *poet!*—He hath put his heart to school,
Nor dares to move unpropped upon the staff
Which Art hath lodged within his hand—must laugh
By precept only, and shed tears by rule.
Thy Art be Nature; the live current quaff,
And let the groveller sip his stagnant pool,
In fear that else, when critics grave and cool
Have killed him, scorn should write his epitaph.
How does the meadow flower its bloom unfold?
Because the lovely little flower is free      10
Down to its root, and, in that freedom, bold;
And so the grandeur of the forest tree
Comes not by casting in a formal mould,
But from its *own* divine vitality.   (*1842*)

# SIR WALTER SCOTT / 1771–1832

## *from* Marmion

### LOCHINVAR

O, young Lochinvar is come out of the west,
Through all the wide border his steed was the best;
And save his good broadsword, he weapons had none,
He rode all unarmed, and he rode all alone.
So faithful in love, and so dauntless in war,
There never was knight like the young Lochinvar.

He staid not for brake,[1] and he stopped not for stone,
He swam the Eske river where ford there was none;
But, ere he alighted at Netherby gate,
The bride had consented, the gallant came late:     10
For a laggard in love, and a dastard in war,
Was to wed the fair Ellen of brave Lochinvar.

So boldly he entered the Netherby hall,
Among bride's-men, and kinsmen, and brothers, and all:
Then spoke the bride's father, his hand on his sword,
(For the poor craven bridegroom said never a word,)
"O come ye in peace here, or come ye in war,
Or to dance at our bridal, young Lord Lochinvar?"

"I long wooed your daughter, my suit you denied;
Love swells like the Solway, but ebbs like its tide;     20
And now am I come, with this lost love of mine,
To lead but one measure, drink one cup of wine.
There are maidens in Scotland, more lovely by far,
That would gladly be bride to the young Lochinvar."

The bride kissed the goblet; the knight took it up,
He quaffed off the wine, and he threw down the cup.
She looked down to blush, and she looked up to sigh,
With a smile on her lips, and a tear in her eye.
He took her soft hand, ere her mother could bar,—
"Now tread we a measure!" said young Lochinvar.     30

So stately his form, and so lovely her face,
That never a hall such a galliard[2] did grace:
While her mother did fret, and her father did fume,
And the bridegroom stood dangling his bonnet and plume;
And the bride-maidens whispered, "'Twere better by far
To have matched our fair cousin with young Lochinvar."

One touch to her hand, and one word in her ear,
When they reached the hall-door, and the charger stood near;
So light to the croupe the fair lady he swung,
So light to the saddle before her he sprung!     40
"She is won! we are gone, over bank, bush, and scaur;[3]
They'll have fleet steeds that follow," quoth young Lochinvar.
There was mounting 'mong Græmes of the Netherby clan;
Forsters, Fenwicks, and Musgraves, they rode and they ran:
There was racing and chasing, on Cannobie Lee,
But the lost bride of Netherby ne'er did they see.
So daring in love, and so dauntless in war,
Have ye e'er heard of gallant like young Lochinvar?

---

[1] thicket     [2] a lively dance     [3] outcrop of rock

## *from* The Lady of the Lake

### *HARP OF THE NORTH*

Harp of the North! that mouldering long hast hung
  On the witch-elm that shades Saint Fillan's spring,
And down the fitful breeze thy numbers flung,
  Till envious ivy did around thee cling,
  Muffling with verdant ringlet every string,—
    O minstrel harp, still must thine accents sleep?
Mid rustling leaves and fountains murmuring,
  Still must thy sweeter sounds their silence keep,
Nor bid a warrior smile, nor teach a maid to weep?

Not thus, in ancient days of Caledon,                                    10
  Was thy voice mute amid the festal crowd,
When lay of hopeless love, or glory won,
  Aroused the fearful, or subdued the proud.
At each according pause, was heard aloud
  Thine ardent symphony sublime and high!
Fair dames and crested chiefs attention bowed;
  For still the burden of thy minstrelsy
Was knighthood's dauntless deed and beauty's matchless eye.

O wake once more! how rude soe'er the hand
  That ventures o'er thy magic maze to stray;                      20
O wake once more! though scarce my skill command,
  Some feeble echoing of thine earlier lay:
Though harsh and faint, and soon to die away,
  And all unworthy of thy nobler strain,
Yet, if one heart throb higher at its sway,
  The wizard note has not been touched in vain.
Then silent be no more! Enchantress, wake again! (*1810*)

## *from* Rokeby

### *BRIGNALL BANKS*

O, Brignall banks are wild and fair,
  And Greta woods are green,
And you may gather garlands there
  Would grace a summer queen.
And as I rode by Dalton-hall,
  Beneath the turrets high,
A maiden on the castle wall
  Was singing merrily:—
"O Brignall banks are fresh and fair,
  And Greta woods are green;                                        10
I'd rather rove with Edmund there,
  Than reign our English queen."

"If, maiden, thou wouldst wend with me,
  To leave both tower and town,
Thou first must guess what life lead we,
  That dwell by dale and down.
And if thou canst that riddle read,
  As read full well you may,
Then to the greenwood shalt thou speed,
  As blithe as Queen of May."                                       20
Yet sung she, "Brignall banks are fair,
  And Greta woods are green;
I'd rather rove with Edmund there,
  Than reign our English queen.

"I read you, by your bugle-horn,
  And by your palfrey good,

I read you for a ranger sworn,
  To keep the king's greenwood."
"A ranger, lady, winds his horn,
  And 'tis at peep of light;      30
His blast is heard at merry morn,
  And mine at dead of night."
Yet sung she, "Brignall banks are fair,
  And Greta woods are gay;
I would I were with Edmund there,
  To reign his Queen of May!

"With burnished brand and musketoon,
  So gallantly you come,
I read you for a bold dragoon,
  That lists the tuck of drum."     40
"I list no more the tuck of drum,
  No more the trumpet hear;
But when the beetle sounds his hum,
  My comrades take the spear.
And O! though Brignall banks be fair,
  And Greta woods be gay,
Yet mickle[1] must the maiden dare,
  Would reign my Queen of May!

"Maiden! a nameless life I lead,
  A nameless death I'll die;     50
The fiend, whose lantern lights the mead,
  Were better mate than I!
And when I'm with my comrades met
  Beneath the greenwood bough,
What once we were we all forget,
  Nor think what we are now.
Yet Brignall banks are fresh and fair,
  And Greta woods are green,
And you may gather garlands there
  Would grace a summer
    queen."  (1813)     60

## Jock of Hazeldean

"Why weep ye by the tide, ladie?
  Why weep ye by the tide?
I'll wed ye to my youngest son,
  And ye sall be his bride:
And ye sall be his bride, ladie,
  Sae comely to be seen"—
But aye she loot the tears down fa'
  For Jock of Hazeldean.

"Now let this wilfu' grief be done,
  And dry that cheek so pale;     10
Young Frank is chief of Errington
  And lord of Langley-dale;
His step is first in peaceful ha',
  His sword in battle keen"—
But aye she loot the tears down fa'
  For Jock of Hazeldean.

"A chain of gold ye sall not lack,
  Nor braid to bind your hair,
Nor mettled hound, nor managed hawk,
  Nor palfrey fresh and fair;     20
And you, the foremost o' them a',
  Shall ride our forest queen"—
But aye she loot the tears down fa'
  For Jock of Hazeldean.

The kirk was decked at morning-tide,
  The tapers glimmered fair;
The priest and bridegroom wait the bride,
  And dame and knight are there.
They sought her baith by bower and ha';
  The ladie was not seen!     30
She's o'er the border and awa'
  Wi' Jock of Hazeldean.  (1816)

## from The Heart of Midlothian

### PROUD MAISIE

Proud Maisie is in the wood,
  Walking so early;
Sweet Robin sits on the bush,
  Singing so rarely.

"Tell me, thou bonny bird,
  When shall I marry me?"
"When six braw[1] gentlemen,
  Kirkward shall carry ye."

"Who makes the bridal bed,
  Birdie, say truly?"—     10
"The gray-headed sexton
  That delves the grave duly.

"The glow-worm o'er grave and stone
  Shall light thee steady;
The owl from the steeple sing,
  'Welcome, proud lady.'"  (1818)

---

[1] much

[1] fine

# SAMUEL TAYLOR COLERIDGE / 1772–1834

## This Lime-Tree Bower My Prison

### [ADDRESSED TO CHARLES LAMB, OF THE INDIA HOUSE, LONDON]

In the June of 1797 some long-expected friends[1] paid a visit to the author's cottage; and on the morning of their arrival, he met with an accident, which disabled him from walking during the whole time of their stay. One evening, when they had left him for a few hours, he composed the following lines in the garden-bower.

Well, they are gone, and here must I remain,
This lime-tree bower my prison! I have lost
Beauties and feelings, such as would have been
Most sweet to my remembrance even when age
Had dimmed mine eyes to blindness! They, meanwhile,
Friends, whom I never more may meet again,
On springy heath, along the hill-top edge,
Wander in gladness, and wind down perchance
To that still roaring dell, of which I told;
The roaring dell, o'erwooded, narrow, deep,        10
And only speckled by the mid-day sun;
Where its slim trunk the ash from rock to rock
Flings arching like a bridge;—that branchless ash,
Unsunned and damp, whose few poor yellow leaves
Ne'er tremble in the gale, yet tremble still,
Fanned by the water-fall! and there my friends
Behold the dark green file of long lank weeds,
That all at once (a most fantastic sight!)
Still nod and drip beneath the dripping edge
Of the blue clay-stone.

                    Now, my friends emerge        20
Beneath the wide wide Heaven—and view again
The many-steepled tract magnificent
Of hilly fields and meadows, and the sea,
With some fair bark, perhaps, whose sails light up
The slip of smooth clear blue betwixt two Isles
Of purple shadow! Yes! they wander on
In gladness all; but thou, methinks, most glad,
My gentle-hearted Charles! for thou hast pined
And hungered after Nature, many a year,
In the great City pent, winning thy way        30
With sad yet patient soul, through evil and pain
And strange calamity![2] Ah! slowly sink

---

[1] The friends were William and Dorothy Wordsworth, and Charles Lamb.
[2] Lamb worked all his adult life as a clerk at the East India House, pursuing his career as writer in off-hours, and caring for his sister Mary, who suffered occasional fits of insanity. During one of these spells she stabbed their mother fatally.

Behind the western ridge, thou glorious Sun!
Shine in the slant beams of the sinking orb,
Ye purple heath-flowers! richlier burn, ye clouds!
Live in the yellow light, ye distant groves!
And kindle, thou blue Ocean! So my friend
Struck with deep joy may stand, as I have stood,
Silent with swimming sense; yea, gazing round
On the wide landscape, gaze till all doth seem                    40
Less gross than bodily; and of such hues
As veil the Almighty Spirit, when yet he makes
Spirits perceive his presence.

               A delight
Comes sudden on my heart, and I am glad
As I myself were there! Nor in this bower,
This little lime-tree bower, have I not marked
Much that has soothed me. Pale beneath the blaze
Hung the transparent foliage; and I watched
Some broad and sunny leaf, and loved to see
The shadow of the leaf and stem above                             50
Dappling its sunshine! And that walnut-tree
Was richly tinged and a deep radiance lay
Full on the ancient ivy, which usurps
Those fronting elms, and now, with blackest mass
Makes their dark branches gleam a lighter hue
Through the late twilight; and though now the bat
Wheels silent by, and not a swallow twitters,
Yet still the solitary humble-bee
Sings in the bean-flower! Henceforth I shall know
That Nature ne'er deserts the wise and pure;                      60
No plot so narrow, be but Nature there,
No waste so vacant, but may well employ
Each faculty of sense, and keep the heart
Awake to Love and Beauty! and sometimes
'Tis well to be bereft of promised good,
That we may lift the soul, and contemplate
With lively joy the joys we cannot share.
My gentle-hearted Charles! when the last rook
Beats its straight path along the dusky air
Homewards, I blest it! deeming its black wing                     70
(Now a dim speck, now vanishing in light)
Had crossed the mighty Orb's dilated glory,
While thou stood'st gazing; or, when all was still,
Flew creeking o'er thy head, and had a charm
For thee, my gentle-hearted Charles, to whom
No sound is dissonant which tells of Life.  (*1797*)

# The Rime of the Ancient Mariner

### PART I

*An ancient Mariner
meeteth three Gallants
bidden to a wedding-
feast, and detaineth
one.*

It is an ancient Mariner,
And he stoppeth one of three.
"By thy long gray beard and glittering eye,
Now wherefore stopp'st thou me?

The Bridegroom's doors are opened wide,
And I am next of kin;
The guests are met, the feast is set:
May'st hear the merry din."

He holds him with his skinny hand,
"There was a ship," quoth he.                          *10*
"Hold off! unhand me, gray-beard loon!"
Eftsoons his hand dropt he.

*The Wedding-Guest
is spellbound by the
eye of the old sea-
faring man, and
constrained to hear
his tale.*

He holds him with his glittering eye—
The Wedding-Guest stood still,
And listens like a three years' child:
The Mariner hath his will.

The Wedding-Guest sat on a stone:
He cannot choose but hear;
And thus spake on that ancient man,
The bright-eyed Mariner.                               *20*

"The ship was cheered, the harbor cleared,
Merrily did we drop
Below the kirk, below the hill,
Below the lighthouse top.

*The Mariner tells how
the ship sailed south-
ward with a good wind
and fair weather, till
it reached the Line.*

The Sun came up upon the left,
Out of the sea came he!
And he shone bright, and on the right
Went down into the sea.

Higher and higher every day,
Till over the mast at noon—"                           *30*
The Wedding-Guest here beat his breast,
For he heard the loud bassoon.

*The Wedding-Guest
heareth the bridal
music; but the
Mariner continueth
his tale.*

The bride hath paced into the hall,
Red as a rose is she;
Nodding their heads before her goes
The merry minstrelsy.

The Wedding-Guest he beat his breast,
Yet he cannot choose but hear;
And thus spake on that ancient man,
The bright-eyed Mariner.                               *40*

<table>
<tr><td>The ship driven by a storm toward the south pole.</td><td>

"And now the storm-blast came, and he<br>
Was tyrannous and strong:<br>
He struck with his o'ertaking wings,<br>
And chased us south along.

With sloping masts and dipping prow,<br>
As who pursued with yell and blow<br>
Still treads the shadow of his foe,<br>
And forward bends his head,<br>
The ship drove fast, loud roared the blast,<br>
And southward aye we fled.       *50*

And now there came both mist and snow,<br>
And it grew wondrous cold:<br>
And ice, mast high, came floating by,<br>
As green as emerald.

</td></tr>
<tr><td>The land of ice, and of fearful sounds where no living thing was to be seen.</td><td>

And through the drifts the snowy clifts<br>
Did send a dismal sheen:<br>
Nor shapes of men nor beasts we ken—<br>
The ice was all between.

The ice was here, the ice was there,<br>
The ice was all around:       *60*<br>
It cracked and growled, and roared and howled,<br>
Like noises in a swound!

</td></tr>
<tr><td>Till a great sea-bird, called the Albatross, came through the snow-fog, and was received with great joy and hospitality.</td><td>

At length did cross an Albatross,<br>
Thorough the fog it came;<br>
As if it had been a Christian soul,<br>
We hailed it in God's name.

It ate the food it ne'er had eat,<br>
And round and round it flew.<br>
The ice did split with a thunder-fit;<br>
The helmsman steered us through!       *70*

</td></tr>
<tr><td>And lo! the Albatross proveth a bird of good omen, and followeth the ship as it returned northward through fog and floating ice.</td><td>

And a good south wind sprung up behind;<br>
The Albatross did follow,<br>
And every day, for food or play,<br>
Came to the mariners' hollo!

In mist or cloud, on mast or shroud,<br>
It perched for vespers nine;<br>
Whiles all the night, through fog-smoke white,<br>
Glimmered the white moon-shine."

</td></tr>
<tr><td>The ancient Mariner inhospitably killeth the pious bird of good omen.</td><td>

"God save thee, ancient Mariner!<br>
From the fiends, that plague thee thus!—       *80*<br>
Why look'st thou so?"—"With my crossbow<br>
I shot the Albatross."

</td></tr>
</table>

PART II

"The Sun now rose upon the right:
Out of the sea came he,
Still hid in mist, and on the left
Went down into the sea.

And the good south wind still blew behind
But no sweet bird did follow,
Nor any day for food or play
Came to the mariners' hollo!                                    *90*

*His shipmates cry out*
*against the ancient*
*Mariner, for killing the*
*bird of good luck.*

And I had done a hellish thing,
And it would work 'em woe:
For all averred, I had killed the bird
That made the breeze to blow.
'Ah wretch!' said they, 'the bird to slay,
That made the breeze to blow!'

*But when the fog*
*cleared off, they justify*
*the same, and thus*
*make themselves*
*accomplices in the*
*crime.*

Nor dim nor red, like God's own head,
The glorious Sun uprist:
Then all averred, I had killed the bird
That brought the fog and mist.                                 *100*
''Twas right,' said they, 'such birds to slay,
That bring the fog and mist.'

*The fair breeze*
*continues; the ship*
*enters the Pacific*
*Ocean, and sails*
*northward, even till it*
*reaches the Line. The*
*ship hath been suddenly*
*becalmed.*

The fair breeze blew, the white foam flew,
The furrow followed free;
We were the first that ever burst
Into that silent sea.

Down dropt the breeze, the sails dropt down,
'Twas sad as sad could be;
And we did speak only to break
The silence of the sea!                                        *110*

All in a hot and copper sky,
The bloody Sun, at noon,
Right up above the mast did stand,
No bigger than the Moon.

Day after day, day after day,
We stuck, nor breath nor motion;
As idle as a painted ship
Upon a painted ocean.

*And the Albatross*
*begins to be avenged.*

Water, water, everywhere,
And all the boards did shrink;                                 *120*
Water, water, everywhere
Nor any drop to drink.

The very deep did rot: O Christ!
That ever this should be!
Yea, slimy things did crawl with legs
Upon the slimy sea.

*A Spirit had followed them; one of the invisible inhabitants of this planet, neither departed souls nor angels; concerning whom the learned Jew, Josephus, and the Platonic Constantinopolitan, Michael Psellus, may be consulted. They are very numerous, and there is no climate or element without one or more.*

About, about, in reel and rout
The death-fires danced at night;
The water, like a witch's oils,
Burnt green, and blue, and white.                    130

And some in dreams assuréd were
Of the Spirit that plagued us so:
Nine fathom deep he had followed us
From the land of mist and snow.

And every tongue, through utter drought,
Was withered at the root;
We could not speak, no more than if
We had been choked with soot.

*The ship-mates, in their sore distress, would fain throw the whole guilt on the ancient Mariner: in sign whereof they hang the dead sea-bird round his neck.*

Ah! well a-day! what evil looks
Had I from old and young!                             140
Instead of the cross, the Albatross
About my neck was hung."

## PART III

*The ancient Mariner beholdeth a sign in the element afar off.*

"There passed a weary time. Each throat
Was parched, and glazed each eye.
A weary time! a weary time!
How glazed each weary eye,
When looking westward, I beheld
A something in the sky.

At first it seemed a little speck,
And then it seemed a mist;                            150
It moved and moved, and took at last
A certain shape, I wist.

A speck, a mist, a shape, I wist!
And still it neared and neared:
As if it dodged a water-sprite,
It plunged and tacked and veered.

*At its nearer approach, it seemeth him to be a ship; and at a dear ransom he freeth his speech from the bonds of thirst.*

With throats unslaked, with black lips baked,
We could nor laugh nor wail;
Through utter drought all dumb we stood!
I bit my arm, I sucked the blood,                     160
And cried, 'A sail! a sail!'

*A flash of joy;*

With throats unslaked, with black lips baked,
Agape they heard me call;
Gramercy! they for joy did grin,
And all at once their breath drew in,
As they were drinking all.

*And horror follows. For*
*can it be a ship that*
*comes onward without*
*wind or tide?*

'See! see! (I cried) she tacks no more!
Hither to work us weal;
Without a breeze, without a tide,
She steadies with upright keel!'                                    170

The western wave was all a-flame;
The day was well nigh done!
Almost upon the western wave
Rested the broad bright Sun;
When that strange shape drove suddenly
Betwixt us and the Sun.

*It seemeth him but the*
*skeleton of a ship:*

And straight the Sun was flecked with bars
(Heaven's Mother send us grace!)
As if through a dungeon-grate he peered
With broad and burning face.                                    180

Alas! (thought I, and my heart beat loud)
How fast she nears and nears!
Are those her sails that glance in the Sun,
Like restless gossameres?

*And its ribs are seen as*
*bars on the face of the*
*setting Sun. The*
*Spectre-Woman and*
*her Death-mate, and no*
*other on board the*
*skeleton-ship. Like*
*vessel, like crew!*

Are those her ribs through which the Sun
Did peer, as through a grate?
And is that Woman all her crew?
Is that a Death? and are there two?
Is Death that woman's mate?

Her lips were red, her looks were free,                                    190
Her locks were yellow as gold:
Her skin was a white leprosy,
The nightmare Life-in-Death was she,
Who thicks man's blood with cold.

*Death and Life-in-*
*Death have diced for*
*the ship's crew, and*
*she (the latter)*
*winneth the ancient*
*Mariner.*

The naked hulk alongside came,
And the twain were casting dice;
'The game is done! I've won! I've won!'
Quoth she and whistles thrice.

*No twilight within the*
*courts of the Sun.*

The Sun's rim dips; the stars rush out:
At one stride comes the dark;                                    200
With far-heard whisper, o'er the sea,
Off shot the spectre-bark.

*At the rising of the*
*Moon,*

We listened and looked sideways up!
Fear at my heart, as at a cup,
My life-blood seemed to sip!
The stars were dim, and thick the night,
The steersman's face by his lamp gleamed white;
From the sails the dew did drip—
Till clomb above the eastern bar
The hornéd Moon, with one bright star                                    210
Within the nether tip.

<table>
<tr><td>*One after another,*</td><td>One after one, by the star-dogged Moon,<br>Too quick for groan or sigh,<br>Each turned his face with a ghastly pang,<br>And cursed me with his eye.</td></tr>
</table>

*One after another,*

One after one, by the star-dogged Moon,
Too quick for groan or sigh,
Each turned his face with a ghastly pang,
And cursed me with his eye.

*His ship-mates drop
down dead.*

Four times fifty living men
(And I heard nor sigh nor groan)
With heavy thump, a lifeless lump,
They dropped down one by one.

*But Life-in-Death
begins her work on
the ancient Mariner.*

The souls did from their bodies fly—                220
They fled to bliss or woe!
And every soul, it passed me by,
Like the whizz of my cross-bow!"

### PART IV

*The Wedding-Guest
feareth that a Spirit
is talking to him;*

"I fear thee, ancient Mariner!
I fear thy skinny hand!
And thou art long, and lank, and brown,
As is the ribbed sea-sand.

*But the ancient
Mariner assureth him
of his bodily life, and
proceedeth to relate
his horrible penance.*

I fear thee and thy glittering eye,
And thy skinny hand, so brown."—
"Fear not, fear not, thou Wedding-Guest!                230
This body dropt not down.

Alone, alone, all, all alone,
Alone on a wide, wide sea!
And never a saint took pity on
My soul in agony.

*He despiseth the
creatures of the calm.*

The many men, so beautiful!
And they all dead did lie:
And a thousand thousand slimy things
Lived on; and so did I.

*And envieth that they
should live, and so
many lie dead.*

I looked upon the rotting sea,                240
And drew my eyes away;
I looked upon the rotting deck,
And there the dead men lay.

I looked to heaven, and tried to pray;
But or ever a prayer had gusht,
A wicked whisper came, and made
My heart as dry as dust.

I closed my lids, and kept them close,
And the balls like pulses beat;
For the sky and the sea, and the sea and the sky                250
Lay like a load on my weary eye,
And the dead were at my feet.

*But the curse liveth*
*for him in the eye of*
*the dead men.*

The cold sweat melted from their limbs,
Nor rot nor reek did they:
The look with which they looked on me
Had never passed away.

An orphan's curse would drag to hell
A spirit from on high;
But oh! more horrible than that
Is the curse in a dead man's eye!                              260
Seven days, seven nights, I saw that curse,
And yet I could not die.

*In his loneliness and*
*fixedness he yearneth*
*toward the journeying*
*Moon, and the stars*
*that still sojourn, yet*
*still move onward; and*
*everywhere the blue*
*sky belongs to them,*
*and is their appointed*
*rest, and their native*
*country and their own*
*natural homes, which*
*they enter unan-*
*nounced, as lords that*
*are certainly expected*
*and yet there is a silent*
*joy at their arrival.*

The moving Moon went up the sky,
And nowhere did abide:
Softly she was going up,
And a star or two beside—

Her beams bemocked the sultry main,
Like April hoar-frost spread;
But where the ship's huge shadow lay,
The charmèd water burnt alway                                 270
A still and awful red.

Beyond the shadow of the ship,
I watched the water-snakes:
They moved in tracks of shining white,
And when they reared, the elfish light
Fell off in hoary flakes.

*By the light of the*
*Moon he beholdeth*
*God's creatures of the*
*great calm.*

Within the shadow of the ship
I watched their rich attire:
Blue, glossy green, and velvet black,
They coiled and swam; and every track                        280
Was a flash of golden fire.

*Their beauty and their*
*happiness.*

O happy living things! no tongue
Their beauty might declare:
A spring of love gushed from my heart,
And I blessed them unaware:

*He blesseth them in*
*his heart.*

Sure my kind saint took pity on me,
And I blessed them unaware.

*The spell begins to*
*break.*

The selfsame moment I could pray;
And from my neck so free
The Albatross fell off, and sank                              290
Like lead into the sea."

PART V

"Oh, sleep! it is a gentle thing,
Beloved from pole to pole!
To Mary Queen the praise be given!
She sent the gentle sleep from Heaven,
That slid into my soul.

*By grace of the holy
Mother, the ancient
Mariner is refreshed
with rain.*

The silly[1] buckets on the deck,
That had so long remained,
I dreamt that they were filled with dew;
And when I awoke, it rained.                    *300*

My lips were wet, my throat was cold,
My garments all were dank;
Sure I had drunken in my dreams,
And still my body drank.

I moved, and could not feel my limbs;
I was so light—almost
I thought that I had died in sleep,
And was a blessèd ghost.

*He heareth sounds and
seeth strange sights
and commotions in the
sky and the element.*

And soon I heard a roaring wind:
It did not come anear;                          *310*
But with its sound it shook the sails,
That were so thin and sere.

The upper air burst into life!
And a hundred fire-flags sheen,
To and fro they were hurried about!
And to and fro, and in and out,
The wan stars danced between.

And the coming wind did roar more loud,
And the sails did sigh like sedge;
And the rain poured down from one black cloud;  *320*
The moon was at its edge.

The thick black cloud was cleft, and still
The Moon was at its side:
Like waters shot from some high crag,
The lightning fell with never a jag,
A river steep and wide.

The loud wind never reached the ship,
Yet now the ship moved on!
Beneath the lightning and the Moon
The dead men gave a groan.                      *330*

*The bodies of the
ship's crew are
inspired and the ship
moves on;*

They groaned, they stirred, they all uprose,
Nor spake, nor moved their eyes;
It had been strange, even in a dream,
To have seen those dead men rise.

The helmsman steered, the ship moved on;
Yet never a breeze up blew;
The mariners all 'gan work the ropes,
Where they were wont to do;
They raised their limbs like lifeless tools—
We were a ghastly crew.                         *340*

---

[1] empty

The body of my brother's son
Stood by me, knee to knee:
The body and I pulled at one rope
But he said nought to me."

*But not by the souls
of the men, nor by
daemons of earth or
middle air, but by a
blessed troop of
angelic spirits, sent
down by the invocation
of the guardian saint.*

"I fear thee, ancient Mariner!"
"Be calm, thou Wedding-Guest!
'Twas not those souls that fled in pain,
Which to their corses came again,
But a troop of spirits blest:

For when it dawned—they dropped their arms,                350
And clustered round the mast;
Sweet sounds rose slowly through their mouths,
And from their bodies passed.

Around, around, flew each sweet sound,
Then darted to the Sun;
Slowly the sounds came back again,
Now mixed, now one by one.

Sometimes a-dropping from the sky
I heard the sky-lark sing;
Sometimes all little birds that are,                        360
How they seemed to fill the sea and air
With their sweet jargoning!

And now 'twas like all instruments,
Now like a lonely flute;
And now it is an angel's song,
That makes the heavens be mute.

It ceased; yet still the sails made on
A pleasant noise till noon,
A noise like of a hidden brook
In the leafy month of June,                                 370
That to the sleeping woods all night
Singeth a quiet tune.

Till noon we quietly sailed on,
Yet never a breeze did breathe:
Slowly and smoothly went the ship
Moved onward from beneath.

*The lonesome Spirit
from the south pole
carries on the ship as
far as the Line, in
obedience to the
angelic troop, but still
requireth vengeance.*

Under the keel nine fathom deep,
From the land of mist and snow,
The Spirit slid: and it was he
That made the ship to go.                                   380
The sails at noon left off their tune,
And the ship stood still also.

The Sun, right up above the mast,
Had fixed her to the ocean:
But in a minute she 'gan stir,

With a short uneasy motion—
Backwards and forwards half her length
With a short uneasy motion.

Then like a pawing horse let go,
She made a sudden bound:                              390
It flung the blood into my head,
And I fell down in a swound.

*The Polar Spirit's*    How long in that same fit I lay,
*fellow-daemons, the*    I have not to declare;
*invisible inhabitants*    But ere my living life returned,
*of the element, take*    I heard and in my soul discerned
*part in his wrong; and*    Two voices in the air.
*two of them relate*
*one to the other, that*    'Is it he?' quoth one, 'Is this the man?
*penance long and*    By Him who died on cross,
*heavy for the ancient*    With his cruel bow he laid full low      400
*Mariner hath been*    The harmless Albatross.
*accorded to the Polar*
*Spirit, who returneth*    The Spirit who bideth by himself
*southward.*    In the land of mist and snow,
He loved the bird that loved the man
Who shot him with his bow.'

The other was a softer voice,
As soft as honey-dew:
Quoth he, 'The man hath penance done,
And penance more will do.'"

### PART VI

*First Voice*

"'But tell me, tell me! speak again,                  410
Thy soft response renewing—
What makes that ship drive on so fast?
What is the ocean doing?'

*Second Voice*

'Still as a slave before his lord,
The ocean hath no blast;
His great bright eye most silently
Up to the Moon is cast—

If he may know which way to go;
For she guides him smooth or grim.
See, brother, see! how graciously               420
She looketh down on him.'

*First Voice*

*The Mariner hath*    'But why drives on that ship so fast,
*been cast into a*    Without or wave or wind?'
*trance; for the angelic*
*power causeth the*    *Second Voice*
*vessel to drive north-*    'The air is cut away before,
*ward faster than*    And closes from behind.
*human life could*
*endure.*    Fly, brother, fly, more high, more high!
Or we shall be belated:

For slow and slow that ship will go,
When the Mariner's trance is abated.'

*The supernatural
motion is retarded;
the Mariner awakes,
and his penance
begins anew.*

I woke, and we were sailing on                              *430*
As in a gentle weather:
'Twas night, calm night, the Moon was high,
The dead men stood together.

All stood together on the deck,
For a charnel-dungeon fitter:
All fixed on me their stony eyes,
That in the Moon did glitter.

The pang, the curse, with which they died,
Had never passed away:
I could not draw my eyes from theirs,                       *440*
Nor turn them up to pray.

*The curse is finally
expiated.*

And now this spell was snapt: once more
I viewed the ocean green,
And looked far forth, yet little saw
Of what had else been seen—

Like one, that on a lonesome road
Doth walk in fear and dread,
And having once turned round walks on,
And turns no more his head;
Because he knows a frightful fiend                          *450*
Doth close behind him tread.

But soon there breathed a wind on me,
Nor sound nor motion made:
Its path was not upon the sea,
In ripple or in shade.

It raised my hair, it fanned my cheek
Like a meadow-gale of spring—
It mingled strangely with my fears,
Yet it felt like a welcoming.

Swiftly, swiftly flew the ship                              *460*
Yet she sailed softly too:
Sweetly, sweetly blew the breeze—
On me alone it blew.

*And the ancient
Mariner beholdeth
his native country.*

Oh! dream of joy! is this indeed
The light-house top I see?
Is this the hill? is this the kirk?
Is this mine own countree?

We drifted o'er the harbor-bar,
And I with sobs did pray—
O let me be awake, my God!                                  *470*
Or let me sleep alway.

The harbor-bay was clear as glass,
So smoothly it was strewn!
And on the bay the moonlight lay,
And the shadow of the Moon.

The rock shone bright, the kirk no less,
That stands above the rock:
The moonlight steeped in silentness
The steady weathercock.

And the bay was white with silent light          480
Till rising from the same,
Full many shapes, that shadows were,
In crimson colors came.

*The angelic spirits*    A little distance from the prow
*leave the dead bodies,*    Those crimson shadows were:
I turned my eyes upon the deck—
Oh, Christ, what saw I there!

*And appear in their*    Each corse lay flat, lifeless and flat,
*own forms of light.*    And, by the holy rood!
A man all light, a seraph-man,          490
On every corse there stood.

This seraph-band, each waved his hand;
It was a heavenly sight!
They stood as signals to the land
Each one a lovely light;

This seraph-band, each waved his hand,
No voice did they impart—
No voice; but oh! the silence sank
Like music on my heart.

But soon I heard the dash of oars,          500
I heard the Pilot's cheer;
My heard was turned perforce away,
And I saw a boat appear.

The Pilot and the Pilot's boy,
I heard them coming fast:
Dear Lord in Heaven! it was a joy
The dead men could not blast.

I saw a third—I heard his voice:
It is the Hermit good!
He singeth loudly his godly hymns          510
That he makes in the wood.
He'll shrieve my soul; he'll wash away
The Albatross's blood."

PART VII

*The Hermit of the*
*Wood.*

" This Hermit good lives in that wood
Which slopes down to the sea.
How loudly his sweet voice he rears!
He loves to talk with marineres
That come from a far countree.

He kneels at morn, and noon, and eve—
He hath a cushion plump:                                    520
It is the moss that wholly hides
The rotted old oak-stump.

The skiff-boat neared: I heard them talk,
'Why, this is strange, I trow!
Where are those lights so many and fair,
That signal made but now!'

*Approacheth the ship*
*with wonder.*

'Strange, by my faith!' the Hermit said—
'And they answered not our cheer!
The planks looked warped! and see those sails,
How thin they are and sere!                                 530
I never saw aught like to them,
Unless perchance it were

Brown skeletons of leaves that lag
My forest-brook along;
When the ivy-tod is heavy with snow,
And the owlet whoops to the wolf below,
That eats the she-wolf's young.'

'Dear Lord! it hath a fiendish look—
(The Pilot made reply)
I am a-feared'—'Push on, push on!'                          540
Said the Hermit cheerily.

The boat came closer to the ship,
But I nor spake nor stirred;
The boat came close beneath the ship,
And straight a sound was heard.

*The ship suddenly*
*sinketh.*

Under the water it rumbled on,
Still louder and more dread:
It reached the ship, it split the bay;
The ship went down like lead.

*The ancient Mariner*
*is saved in the Pilot's*
*boat.*

Stunned by that loud and dreadful sound,                    550
Which sky and ocean smote,
Like one that hath been seven days drowned
My body lay afloat;
But swift as dreams, myself I found
Within the Pilot's boat.

Upon the whirl, where sank the ship,
The boat spun round and round;

And all was still, save that the hill
Was telling of the sound.

I moved my lips—the Pilot shrieked 560
And fell down in a fit;
The holy Hermit raised his eyes,
And prayed where he did sit.

I took the oars: the Pilot's boy,
Who now doth crazy go,
Laughed loud and long, and all the while
His eyes went to and fro.
'Ha! ha!' quoth he, 'full plain I see,
The Devil knows how to row.'

And now, all in my own countree, 570
I stood on the firm land!
The Hermit stepped forth from the boat,
And scarcely he could stand.

*The ancient Mariner*
*earnestly entreateth*
*the Hermit to shrieve*
*him; and the penance*
*of life falls on him.*

'O shrieve me, shrieve me, holy man!'
The Hermit crossed his brow.
'Say quick,' quoth he, 'I bid thee say—
What manner of man art thou?'

Forthwith this frame of mine was wrenched
With a woful agony,
Which forced me to begin my tale; 580
And then it left me free.

*And ever and anon*
*throughout his future*
*life an agony*
*constraineth him to*
*travel from land to*
*land,*

Since then, at an uncertain hour,
That agony returns:
And till my ghastly tale is told,
This heart within me burns.

I pass, like night, from land to land;
I have strange power of speech;
That moment that his face I see,
I know the man that must hear me:
To him my tale I teach. 590

What loud uproar bursts from that door!
The wedding-guests are there:
But in the garden-bower the bride
And bride-maids singing are:
And hark the little vesper bell
Which biddeth me to prayer!

O Wedding-Guest! this soul hath been
Alone on a wide, wide sea;
So lonely 'twas, that God himself
Scarce seeméd there to be. 600

O sweeter than the marriage-feast,
'Tis sweeter far to me,
To walk together to the kirk
With a goodly company!—

To walk together to the kirk,
And all together pray,
While each to his great Father bends,
Old men, and babes, and loving friends,
And youths and maidens gay!

*And to teach, by his*
*own example, love*
*and reverence to all*
*things that God made*
*and loveth.*

Farewell, farewell! but this I tell                                   610
To thee, thou Wedding-Guest!
He prayeth well, who loveth well
Both man and bird and beast.

He prayeth best, who loveth best
All things both great and small;
For the dear God who loveth us,
He made and loveth all."

The Mariner, whose eye is bright,
Whose beard with age is hoar,
Is gone: and now the Wedding-Guest                                    620
Turned from the Bridegroom's door.

He went like one that hath been stunned,
And is of sense forlorn:
A sadder and a wiser man,
He rose the morrow morn.   (*1798*)


## Frost at Midnight

The frost performs its secret ministry,
Unhelped by any wind. The owlet's cry
Came loud—and hark, again! loud as before.
The inmates of my cottage, all at rest,
Have left me to that solitude, which suits
Abstruser musings: save that at my side
My cradled infant slumbers peacefully.
'Tis calm indeed! so calm, that it disturbs
And vexes meditation with its strange
And extreme silentness. Sea, hill, and wood,                          10
This populous village! Sea, and hill, and wood,
With all the numberless goings-on of life,
Inaudible as dreams! the thin blue flame
Lies on my low-burnt fire, and quivers not;
Only that film, which fluttered on the grate,
Still flutters there, the sole unquiet thing.
Methinks, its motion in this hush of nature

Gives it dim sympathies with me who live,
Making it a companionable form,
Whose puny flaps and freaks the idling Spirit                    *20*
By its own moods interprets, everywhere
Echo or mirror seeking of itself,
And makes a toy of Thought.

                     But O! how oft,
How oft, at school, with most believing mind,
Presageful, have I gazed upon the bars,
To watch that fluttering *stranger!* and as oft
With unclosed lids, already had I dreamt
Of my sweet birth-place, and the old church-tower,
Whose bells, the poor man's only music, rang
From morn to evening, all the hot Fair-day,                      *30*
So sweetly, that they stirred and haunted me
With a wild pleasure, falling on mine ear
Most like articulate sounds of things to come!
So gazed I, till the soothing things, I dreamt,
Lulled me to sleep, and sleep prolonged my dreams!
And so I brooded all the following morn,
Awed by the stern preceptor's face, mine eye
Fixed with mock study on my swimming book:
Save if the door half opened, and I snatched
A hasty glance, and still my heart leaped up,                    *40*
For still I hoped to see the *stranger's* face,
Townsman, or aunt, or sister more beloved,
My playmate when we both were clothed alike!

   Dear Babe, that sleepest cradled by my side,
Whose gentle breathing, heard in this deep calm,
Fill up the interspersèd vacancies
And momentary pauses of the thought!
My babe so beautiful! it thrills my heart
With tender gladness, thus to look at thee,
And think that thou shalt learn far other lore,                 *50*
And in far other scenes! For I was reared
In the great city, pent 'mid cloisters dim,
And saw nought lovely but the sky and stars.
But *thou,* my babe! shalt wander like a breeze
By lakes and sandy shores, beneath the crags
Of ancient mountain, and beneath the clouds,
Which image in their bulk both lakes and shores
And mountain crags: so shalt thou see and hear
The lovely shapes and sounds intelligible
Of that eternal language, which thy God                         *60*
Utters, who from eternity doth teach
Himself in all, and all things in himself.
Great universal Teacher! he shall mold
Thy spirit, and by giving make it ask.

Therefore all seasons shall be sweet to thee,
Whether the summer clothe the general earth
With greenness, or the redbreast sit and sing
Betwixt the tufts of snow on the bare branch
Of mossy apple-tree, while the nigh thatch
Smokes in the sun-thaw; whether the eavedrops fall          70
Heard only in the trances of the blast,
Or if the secret ministry of frost
Shall hang them up in silent icicles,
Quietly shining to the quiet Moon.    (*1798*)

## Kubla Khan

In Xanadu did Kubla Khan
A stately pleasure-dome decree:
Where Alph, the sacred river, ran
Through caverns measureless to man
  Down to a sunless sea.
So twice five miles of fertile ground
With walls and towers were girdled round:
And here were gardens bright with sinuous rills,
Where blossomed many an incense-bearing tree,
And here were forests ancient as the hills,          10
Enfolding sunny spots of greenery.

But oh! that deep romantic chasm which slanted
Down the green hill athwart a cedarn cover!
A savage place! as holy and enchanted
As e'er beneath a waning moon was haunted
By woman wailing for her demon-lover!
And from this chasm, with ceaseless turmoil seething,
As if this earth in fast thick pants were breathing,
A mighty fountain momently was forced,
Amid whose swift half-intermitted burst          20
Huge fragments vaulted like rebounding hail,
Or chaffy grain beneath the thresher's flail:
And 'mid these dancing rocks at once and ever
It flung up momently the sacred river.
Five miles meandering with a mazy motion
Through wood and dale the sacred river ran,
Then reached the caverns measureless to man,
And sank in tumult to a lifeless ocean:
And 'mid this tumult Kubla heard from far
Ancestral voices prophesying war!          30
    The shadow of the dome of pleasure
    Floated midway on the waves;
    Where was heard the mingled measure
    From the fountain and the caves.
It was a miracle of rare device,

A sunny pleasure-dome with caves of ice!
   A damsel with a dulcimer
   In a vision once I saw:
   It was an Abyssinian maid,
   And on her dulcimer she played,
   Singing of Mount Abora.
Could I revive within me
   Her symphony and song,
   To such a deep delight 'twould win me,
That with music loud and long,
I would build that dome in air,
That sunny dome! those caves of ice!
And all who heard should see them there,
And all should cry, Beware! Beware!
His flashing eyes, his floating hair!
Weave a circle round him thrice,
And close your eyes with holy dread,
For he on honey-dew hath fed,
And drunk the milk of Paradise.  (*1798*)

## Dejection: An Ode

*Late, late yestreen I saw the New Moon,*
*With the old Moon in her arms:*
*And I fear, I fear, my Master dear!*
*We shall have a deadly storm.*
        Ballad of Sir Patrick Spence.

### 1

Well! If the Bard was weather-wise, who made
   The grand old ballad of Sir Patrick Spence,
   This night, so tranquil now, will not go hence
Unroused by winds, that ply a busier trade
Than those which mould yon cloud in lazy flakes,
Or the dull sobbing draft, that moans and rakes
Upon the strings of this Æolian lute,
   Which better far were mute.
   For lo! the New-moon winter-bright!
   And overspread with phantom light,
   (With swimming phantom light o'erspread
   But rimmed and circled by a silver thread)
I see the old Moon in her lap, foretelling
   The coming-on of rain and squally blast.
And oh! that even now the gust were swelling,
   And the slant night-shower driving loud and fast!
Those sounds which oft have raised me, whilst they awed,
   And sent my soul abroad,
Might now perhaps their wonted impulse give,
Might startle this dull pain, and make it move and live!

2

A grief without a pang, void, dark, and drear,
  A stifled, drowsy, unimpassioned grief,
  Which finds no natural outlet, no relief,
        In word, or sigh, or tear—
O Lady! in this wan and heartless mood,
To other thoughts by yonder throstle woo'd,
  All this long eve, so balmy and serene,
Have I been gazing on the western sky,
  And its peculiar tint of yellow green:
And still I gaze—and with how blank an eye!                    30
And those thin clouds above, in flakes and bars,
That give away their motion to the stars;
Those stars, that glide behind them or between,
Now sparkling, now bedimmed, but always seen:
Yon crescent Moon, as fixed as if it grew
In its own cloudless, starless lake of blue;
I see them all so excellently fair,
I see, not feel, how beautiful they are!

3

    My genial spirits fail;
    And what can these avail
To lift the smothering weight from off my breast?
    It were a vain endeavour,
    Though I should gaze for ever
On that green light that lingers in the west:
I may not hope from outward forms to win
The passion and the life, whose fountains are within.

4

O Lady! we receive but what we give,
And in our life alone does Nature live:
Ours is her wedding garment, ours her shroud!
  And would we aught behold, of higher worth,                  50
Than that inanimate cold world allowed
To the poor loveless ever-anxious crowd,
    Ah! from the soul itself must issue forth
A light, a glory, a fair luminous cloud
    Enveloping the Earth—
And from the soul itself must there be sent
  A sweet and potent voice, of its own birth,
Of all sweet sounds the life and element!

5

O pure of heart! thou need'st not ask of me
What this strong music in the soul may be!                     60
What, and wherein it doth exist,
This light, this glory, this fair luminous mist,
This beautiful and beauty-making power.

Joy, virtuous Lady! Joy that ne'er was given,
Save to the pure, and in their purest hour,
Life, and Life's effluence, cloud at once and shower,
Joy, Lady! is the spirit and the power,
Which wedding Nature to us gives in dower
   A new Earth and new Heaven,
Undreamt of by the sensual and the proud—        *70*
Joy is the sweet voice, Joy the luminous cloud—
     We in ourselves rejoice!
And thence flows all that charms or ear or sight,
   All melodies the echoes of that voice,
All colours a suffusion from that light.

6

There was a time when, though my path was rough,
   This joy within me dallied with distress,
And all misfortunes were but as the stuff
   Whence Fancy made me dreams of happiness:
For hope grew round me, like the twining vine,       *80*
And fruits, and foliage, not my own, seemed mine.
But now afflictions bow me down to earth:
Nor care I that they rob me of my mirth;
   But oh! each visitation
Suspends what nature gave me at my birth,
   My shaping spirit of Imagination.
For not to think of what I needs must feel,
   But to be still and patient, all I can;
And haply by abstruse research to steal
   From my own nature all the natural man—      *90*
   This was my sole resource, my only plan:
Till that which suits a part infects the whole,
And now is almost grown the habit of my soul.

7

Hence, viper thoughts, that coil around my mind,
    Reality's dark dream!
I turn from you, and listen to the wind,
   Which long has raved unnoticed. What a scream
Of agony by torture lengthened out
That lute sent forth! Thou Wind, that rav'st without,
   Bare crag, or mountain-tairn,[1] or blasted tree,    *100*
Or pine-grove whither woodman never clomb,
Or lonely house, long held the witches' home,
   Methinks were fitter instruments for thee,
Mad Lutanist! who in this month of showers,
Of dark-brown gardens, and of peeping flowers,

---

[1] Tairn is a small lake, generally if not always applied to the lakes up in the mountains and which are the feeders of those in the valleys. This address to the Storm-wind will not appear extravagant to those who have heard it at night and in a mountainous country. [S.T.C.]

Mak'st Devils' yule, with worse than wintry song,
The blossoms, buds, and timorous leaves among.
  Thou Actor, perfect in all tragic sounds!
Thou mighty Poet, e'en to frenzy bold!
    What tell'st thou now about?                                          *110*
    'Tis of the rushing of an host in rout,
  With groans, of trampled men, with smarting wounds—
At once they groan with pain, and shudder with the cold!
But hush! there is a pause of deepest silence!
  And all that noise, as of a rushing crowd,
With groans, and tremulous shudderings—all is over—
  It tells another tale, with sounds less deep and loud!
    A tale of less affright,
    And tempered with delight,
As Otway's[2] self had framed the tender lay,—                           *120*
    'Tis of a little child
    Upon a lonesome wild,
Not far from home, but she hath lost her way:
And now moans low in bitter grief and fear,
And now screams loud, and hopes to make her mother hear.

### 8

'Tis midnight, but small thoughts have I of sleep:
Full seldom may my friend such vigils keep!
Visit her, gentle Sleep! with wings of healing,
  And may this storm be but a mountain-birth,
May all the stars hang bright above her dwelling,                        *130*
  Silent as though they watched the sleeping Earth!
    With light heart may she rise,
    Gay fancy, cheerful eyes,
  Joy lift her spirit, joy attune her voice;
To her may all things live, from pole to pole,
Their life the eddying of her living soul!
  O simple spirit, guided from above,
Deary Lady! friend devoutest of my choice,
Thus mayest thou ever, evermore rejoice.   (*1802*)

## Work Without Hope

*LINES COMPOSED 21st FEBRUARY 1825*

    All nature seems at work. Slugs leave their lair—
    The bees are stirring—birds are on the wing—
    And winter slumbering in the open air,
    Wears on his smiling face a dream of spring!
    And I the while, the sole unbusy thing,
    Nor honey make, nor pair, nor build, nor sing.

---

[2] Thomas Otway (1652–1685), English dramatist

Yet well I ken the banks where amaranths blow,
Have traced the fount whence streams of nectar flow.
Bloom, O ye amaranths! bloom for whom ye may,
For me ye bloom not! Glide, rich streams, away!          *10*
With lips unbrightened, wreathless brow, I stroll:
And would you learn the spells that drowse my soul?
Work without hope draws nectar in a sieve,
And hope without an object cannot live.   (*1825*)


# WALTER SAVAGE LANDOR / 1775–1864

## Rose Aylmer

Ah, what avails the sceptred race!
  Ah, what the form divine!
What every virtue, every grace!
  Rose Aylmer, all were thine.

Rose Aylmer, whom these wakeful eyes
  May weep, but never see,
A night of memories and of sighs
  I consecrate to thee.   (*1806*)

## To Corinth

Queen of the double sea,[1] beloved of him[2]
Who shakes the world's foundations, thou hast seen
Glory in all her beauty, all her forms;
Seen her walk back with Theseus when he left
The bones of Sciron bleaching to the wind,[3]
Above the ocean's roar and cormorant's flight,
So high that vastest billows from above
Show but like herbage waving in the mead;
Seen generations throng thy Isthmian games,[4]
And pass away; the beautiful, the brave,          *10*
And them who sang their praises. But, O Queen,
Audible still, and far beyond thy cliffs,
As when they first were uttered, are those words
Divine which praised the valiant and the just;
And tears have often stopped, upon that ridge
So perilous, him who brought before his eye
The Colchian babes. "Stay! spare him! save the last!
Medea![5] Is that blood? again! it drops
From my imploring hand upon my feet!
I will invoke the Eumenides[6] no more,          *20*

---

[1] Corinth is situated on an isthmus between the Gulf of Corinth and the Saronic Gulf.
[2] Julius Caesar, who rebuilt the city in 46 B.C.
[3] Theseus slew Sciron, who made a practice of kicking travelers into the sea from the Scironian Rock.
[4] athletic contests held at Corinth
[5] Medea of Colchis revenged herself for the desertion of her husband, Jason, by killing their two children.
[6] the avenging deities

I will forgive thee, bless thee, bend to thee
In all thy wishes, do but thou, Medea,
Tell me, one lives." "And shall I too deceive?"
Cries from the fiery car [7] an angry voice;
And swifter than two falling stars descend
Two breathless bodies; warm, soft, motionless,
As flowers in stillest noon before the sun,
They lie three paces from him: such they lie
As when he left them sleeping side by side,
A mother's arm round each, a mother's cheeks                    30
Between them, flushed with happiness and love.
He was more changed than they were, doomed to show
Thee and the stranger, how defaced and scarred
Grief hunts us down the precipice of years,
And whom the faithless prey upon the last.
    To give the inertest masses of our earth [8]
Her loveliest forms was thine, to fix the Gods
Within thy walls, and hang their tripods round
With fruits and foliage knowing not decay.
A nobler work remains: thy citadel                              40
Invites all Greece: o'er lands and floods remote
Many are the hearts that still beat high for thee:
Confide then in thy strength, and unappalled
Look down upon the plain, while yokemate kings
Run bellowing, where their herdsmen goad them on.
Instinct is sharp in them and terror true,
They smell the floor whereon their necks must lie.   (1831)

## Past Ruined Ilion Helen Lives

Past ruined Ilion Helen lives,
    Alcestis rises from the shades;
Verse calls them forth; 'tis verse that gives
    Immortal youth to mortal maids.

Soon shall Oblivion's deepening veil
    Hide all the peopled hills you see,
The gay, the proud, while lovers hail
    These many summers you and me.
                                        (1831)

## Dirce

Stand close around, ye Stygian set,
    With Dirce in one boat conveyed,
Or Charon,[1] seeing, may forget
    That he is old, and she a shade.
                                        (1831)

## To Robert Browning

There is delight in singing, though none hear
Beside the singer; and there is delight
In praising, though the praiser sit alone
And see the praised far off him, far above.

---

[7] Medea fled in a chariot drawn by winged dragons.

[8] The Corinthians were noted for their fine clay vases.

[1] Charon rowed the souls of the dead across the River Styx into the underworld.

Shakespeare is not our poet, but the world's;
Therefore on him no speech! and brief for thee,
Browning! Since Chaucer was alive and hale,
No man hath walked along our roads with step
So active, so inquiring an eye, or tongue
So varied in discourse. But warmer climes                    10
Give brighter plumage, stronger wing: the breeze
Of alpine heights thou playest with, borne on
Beyond Sorrento and Amalfi,[1] where
The siren[2] waits thee, singing song for song.   (*1846*)

## You Smiled, You Spoke, and I Believed

You smiled, you spoke, and I believed,
By every word and smile deceived.

Another man would hope no more;
Nor hope I what I hoped before:
But let not this last wish be vain;
Deceive, deceive me once again!   (*1846*)

## On the Hellenics

Come back, ye wandering Muses, come back home,
Ye seem to have forgotten where it lies:
Come, let us walk upon the silent sands
Of Simois,[1] where deep footmarks show long strides;
Thence we may mount, perhaps, to higher ground,
Where Aphrodite from Athene won
The golden apple, and from Here too,
And happy Ares[2] shouted far below.
  Or would ye rather choose the grassy vale
Where flows Anapos[3] through anemones,                       10
Hyacinths, and narcissuses, that bend
To show their rival beauty in the stream?
  Bring with you each her lyre, and each in turn
Temper a graver with a lighter song.   (*1847*)

---

[1] Italian cities. Browning removed to Italy shortly after his marriage in 1846.
[2] sea nymphs who charm voyagers by their song
[1] a river near Troy

[2] The Judgment of Paris, which awarded the prize for beauty to Aphrodite, led to the Trojan War; Ares, the god of war, therefore rejoices.
[3] river in western Greece

## LEIGH HUNT / 1784–1859

### To the Grasshopper and the Cricket

Green little vaulter in the sunny grass,
Catching your heart up at the feel of June,
Sole voice that's heard amidst the lazy noon,
When even the bees lag at the summoning brass;—
And you, warm little housekeeper, who class
With those who think the candles come too soon,
Loving the fire, and with your tricksome tune
Nick the glad silent moments as they pass;—
Oh, sweet and tiny cousins, that belong,
One to the fields, the other to the hearth,                    10
Both have your sunshine; both, though small, are strong
At your clear hearts; and both were sent on earth
To sing in thoughtful ears this natural song—
In doors and out,—summer and winter,—Mirth.   (1817)

### Rondeau

Jenny kissed me when we met,
  Jumping from the chair she sat in;
Time, you thief, who love to get
  Sweets into your list, put that in:

Say I'm weary, say I'm sad,
  Say that health and wealth have missed
  me,
Say I'm growing old, but add,
  Jenny kissed me.   (1838)

## GEORGE GORDON, LORD BYRON / 1788–1824

### When We Two Parted

When we two parted
  In silence and tears,
Half broken-hearted
  To sever for years,
Pale grew thy cheek and cold,
  Colder thy kiss;
Truly that hour foretold
  Sorrow to this.

The dew of the morning
  Sunk chill on my brow—        10
It felt like the warning
  Of what I feel now.

Thy vows are all broken,
  And light is thy fame:
I hear thy name spoken,
  And share in its shame.

They name thee before me,
  A knell to mine ear;
A shudder comes o'er me—
  Why wert thou so dear?         20
They know not I knew thee,
  Who knew thee too well:—
Long, long shall I rue thee,
  Too deeply to tell.

In secret we met—
  In silence I grieve,
That thy heart could forget,
  Thy spirit deceive.
If I should meet thee
  After long years,            30
How should I greet thee?—
  With silence and tears.   (1808?)


## She Walks in Beauty

She walks in Beauty, like the night
  Of cloudless climes and starry skies;
And all that's best of dark and bright
  Meet in her aspect and her eyes:
Thus mellowed to that tender light
  Which Heaven to gaudy day denies.

One shade the more, one ray the less,
  Had half impaired the nameless grace
Which waves in every raven tress,
  Or softly lightens o'er her face;    10
Where thoughts serenely sweet express,
  How pure, how dear their dwelling-
    place.

And on that cheek, and o'er that brow,
  So soft, so calm, yet eloquent,
The smiles that win, the tints that glow,
  But tell of days in goodness spent,
A mind at peace with all below,
  A heart whose love is innocent!
                            (1814)


## When Coldness Wraps This Suffering Clay

When coldness wraps this suffering clay,
  Ah! whither strays the immortal mind?
It cannot die, it cannot stay,
  But leaves its darkened dust behind.
Then, unembodied, doth it trace
  By steps each planet's heavenly way?
Or fill at once the realms of space,
  A thing of eyes, that all survey?

Eternal, boundless, undecayed,
  A thought unseen, but seeing all,    10
All, all in earth or skies displayed,
  Shall it survey, shall it recall:
Each fainter trace that memory holds
  So darkly of departed years,
In one broad glance the soul beholds,
  And all, that was, at once appears.

Before Creation peopled earth,
  Its eye shall roll through chaos back;
And where the furthest heaven had birth,
  The spirit trace its rising track.   20
And where the future mars or makes,
  Its glance dilate o'er all to be,
While sun is quenched or system breaks,
  Fixed in its own eternity.

Above or Love, Hope, Hate, or Fear,
  It lives all passionless and pure:
An age shall fleet like earthly year;
  Its years as moments shall endure.
Away, away, without a wing,
  O'er all, through all, its thought shall
    fly,                    30
A nameless and eternal thing,
  Forgetting what it was to die.   (1815)


## Stanzas for Music

There be none of Beauty's daughters
  With a magic like thee;
And like music on the waters
  Is thy sweet voice to me:
When, as if its sound were causing
  The charmèd ocean's pausing,
The waves lie still and gleaming,
  And the lulled winds seem dreaming:

And the midnight moon is weaving
  Her bright chain o'er the deep,    10
Whose breast is gently heaving
  As an infant's sleep:
So the spirit bows before thee,
  To listen and adore thee;
With a full but soft emotion
  Like the swell of Summer's ocean.
                            (1816)

## Stanzas to Augusta

Though the day of my destiny's over,
  And the star of my fate hath declined,
Thy soft heart refused to discover
  The faults which so many could find;
Though thy soul with my grief was
    acquainted,
  It shrunk not to share it with me,
And the love which my spirit hath
    painted
  It never hath found but in *thee*.

Then when nature around me is smiling,
The last smile which answers to mine,   *10*
I do not believe it beguiling,
  Because it reminds me of thine;
And when winds are at war with the
    ocean,
  As the breasts I believed in with me,
If their billows excite an emotion,
  It is that they bear me from *thee*.

Though the rock of my last hope is
    shivered,
  And its fragments are sunk in the wave,
Though I feel that my soul is delivered
  To pain—it shall not be its slave.   *20*
There is many a pang to pursue me:
  They may crush, but they shall not
    contemn;
They may torture, but shall not subdue
    me;
'Tis of *thee* that I think—not of them.

Though human, thou didst not deceive
    me,
  Though woman, thou didst not forsake,
Though loved, thou forborest to grieve
    me,
  Though slandered thou never couldst
    shake;
Though trusted, thou didst not disclaim
    me,
  Though parted, it was not to fly,   *30*
Though watchful, 'twas not to defame
    me,
  Nor, mute, that the world might belie.

Yet I blame not the world, nor despise it,
  Nor the war of the many with one;
If my soul was not fitted to prize it,
  'Twas folly not sooner to shun:
And if dearly that error hath cost me,
  And more than I once could foresee,
I have found that, whatever it lost me,
  It could not deprive me of *thee*.   *40*

From the wreck of the past, which hath
    perished,
  Thus much I at least may recall,
It hath taught me that what I most
    cherished
  Deserved to be dearest of all:
In the desert a fountain is springing,
  In the wide waste there still is a tree,
And a bird in the solitude singing,
  Which speaks to my spirit of *thee*.

                          *(1816)*

## Sonnet on Chillon

Eternal spirit of the chainless Mind!
Brightest in dungeons, Liberty! thou art,
For there thy habitation is the heart—
The heart which love of thee alone can bind;
And when thy sons to fetters are consigned—
To fetters, and the damp vault's dayless gloom,
Their country conquers with their martyrdom,
And Freedom's fame finds wings on every wind.
Chillon! thy prison is a holy place,
And thy sad floor an altar—for 'twas trod,   *10*

Until his very steps have left a trace
Worn, as if thy cold pavement were a sod,
By Bonnivard[1]—May none those marks efface!
For they appeal from tyranny to God.   (*1816*)

## Darkness

I had a dream, which was not all a dream.
The bright sun was extinguished, and the stars
Did wander darkling in the eternal space,
Rayless, and pathless, and the icy earth
Swung blind and blackening in the moonless air;
Morn came and went—and came, and brought no day,
And men forgot their passions in the dread
Of this their desolation; and all hearts
Were chilled into a selfish prayer for light:
And they did live by watchfires—and the thrones,                    *10*
The palaces of crownéd kings—the huts,
The habitations of all things which dwell,
Were burnt for beacons; cities were consumed,
And men were gathered round their blazing homes
To look once more into each other's face;
Happy were those who dwelt within the eye
Of the volcanoes, and their mountain-torch:
A fearful hope was all the world contained;
Forests were set on fire—but hour by hour
They fell and faded—and the crackling trunks                         *20*
Extinguished with a crash—and all was black.
The brows of men by the despairing light
Wore an unearthly aspect, as by fits
The flashes fell upon them; some lay down
And hid their eyes and wept; and some did rest
Their chins upon their clenchéd hands, and smiled;
And others hurried to and fro, and fed
Their funeral piles with fuel, and looked up
With mad disquietude on the dull sky,
The pall of a past world; and then again                            *30*
With curses cast them down upon the dust,
And gnashed their teeth and howled: the wild birds shrieked
And, terrified, did flutter on the ground,
And flap their useless wings; the wildest brutes
Came tame and tremulous; and vipers crawled
And twined themselves among the multitude,
Hissing, but stingless—they were slain for food.

---

[1] François Bonivard [*sic*], a Swiss cleric and political leader who was imprisoned by the Duke of Savoy in the Castle of Chillon on Lake Geneva, 1532–36, and who became a symbol of resistance to tyranny in popular ballads

And War, which for a moment was no more,
Did glut himself again:—a meal was bought
With blood, and each sate sullenly apart                        40
Gorging himself in gloom: no love was left;
All earth was but one thought—and that was death,
Immediate and inglorious; and the pang
Of famine fed upon all entrails—men
Died, and their bones were tombless as their flesh;
The meagre by the meagre were devoured,
Even dogs assailed their masters, all save one,
And he was faithful to a corse, and kept
The birds and beasts and famished men at bay,
Till hunger clung them, or the dropping dead                    50
Lured their lank jaws; himself sought out no food,
But with a piteous and perpetual moan,
And a quick desolate cry, licking the hand
Which answered not with a caress—he died.
The crowd was famished by degrees; but two
Of an enormous city did survive,
And they were enemies: they met beside
The dying embers of an altar-place
Where had been heaped a mass of holy things
For an unholy usage; they raked up,                             60
And shivering scraped with their cold skeleton hands
The feeble ashes, and their feeble breath
Blew for a little life, and made a flame
Which was a mockery; then they lifted up
Their eyes as it grew lighter, and beheld
Each other's aspects—saw, and shrieked, and died—
Even of their mutual hideousness they died,
Unknowing who he was upon whose brow
Famine had written Fiend. The world was void,
The populous and the powerful was a lump                       70
Seasonless, herbless, treeless, manless, lifeless,
A lump of death—a chaos of hard clay.
The rivers, lakes, and ocean all stood still,
And nothing stirred within their silent depths;
Ships sailorless lay rotting on the sea,
And their masts fell down piecemeal: as they dropped
They slept on the abyss without a surge—
The waves were dead; the tides were in their grave,
The Moon, their mistress, had expired before;
The winds were withered in the stagnant air,                   80
And the clouds perished; Darkness had no need
Of aid from them—She was the Universe. (*1816*)

# So We'll Go No More A-Roving

So we'll go no more a-roving
  So late into the night,
Though the heart be still as loving,
  And the moon be still as bright.

For the sword outwears its sheath,
  And the soul wears out the breast,
And the heart must pause to breathe,
  And Love itself have rest.

Though the night was made for loving,
  And the day returns too soon,           *10*
Yet we'll go no more a-roving
  By the light of the moon.   (*1817*)

## *from* Childe Harold's Pilgrimage

### *from* CANTO TWO

.   .   .

Fair Greece! sad relic of departed Worth!
Immortal, though no more; though fallen, great!
Who now shall lead thy scattered children forth,
And long accustomed bondage uncreate?
Not such thy sons who whilome did await,
The hopeless warriors of a willing doom,
In bleak Thermopylæ's[1] sepulchral strait—
Oh! who that gallant spirit shall resume,
Leap from Eurotas'[2] banks, and call thee from the tomb?

Spirit of Freedom! when on Phyle's brow           *10*
Thou sat'st with Thrasybulus[3] and his train,
Couldst thou forebode the dismal hour which now
Dims the green beauties of thine Attic plain?
Not thirty tyrants now enforce the chain,
But every carle[4] can lord it o'er thy land;
Nor rise thy sons, but idly rail in vain,
Trembling beneath the scourge of Turkish hand,[5]
From birth till death enslaved—in word, in deed, unmanned.

In all save form alone, how changed! and who
That marks the fire still sparkling in each eye,           *20*
Who but would deem their bosoms burned anew
With thy unquenchéd beam, lost Liberty!
And many dream withal the hour is nigh
That gives them back their fathers' heritage:
For foreign arms and aid they fondly sigh,
Nor solely dare encounter hostile rage,
Or tear their name defiled from Slavery's mournful page.

Hereditary Bondsmen! know ye not
*Who* would be free *themselves* must strike the blow?

---

[1] a pass at which the Greeks under Leonidas made a desperate resistance to the Persian invaders under Xerxes in 480 B.C.
[2] river on which Sparta stood
[3] Greek patriot who led the successful effort to overthrow the Thirty Tyrants and restore Athenian democracy in 403 B.C.
[4] a boor
[5] Greece was under Turkish dominion from the fifteenth century through the first quarter of the nineteenth century.

By their right arms the conquest must be wrought?            *30*
Will Gaul or Muscovite redress ye? No!
True—they may lay your proud despoilers low,
But not for you will Freedom's Altars flame.
Shades of the Helots![6] triumph o'er your foe!
Greece! change thy lords, thy state is still the same;
Thy glorious day is o'er, but not thine years of shame.

.    .    .

### *from* CANTO THREE

Stop!—for thy tread is on an Empire's dust!
An Earthquake's spoil is sepulchred below!
Is the spot marked with no colossal bust?
Nor column trophied for triumphal show?            *40*
None; but *the moral's truth* tells simpler so.
As the ground was before, thus let it be;—
How that red rain hath made the harvest grow!
And is this all the world has gained by thee,
Thou first and last of Fields! king-making Victory?

And Harold stands upon this place of skulls,
The grave of France, the deadly Waterloo!
How in an hour the Power which gave annuls
Its gifts, transferring fame as fleeting too!—
In "pride of place" here last the Eagle[7] flew,            *50*
Then tore with bloody talon the rent plain,
Pierced by the shaft of banded nations through;
Ambition's life and labours all were vain—
He wears the shattered links of the World's broken chain.[8]

Fit retribution! Gaul may champ the bit
And foam in fetters;—but is Earth more free?
Did nations combat to make *One* submit?
Or league to teach all Kings true Sovereignty?
What! shall reviving Thraldom again be
The patched-up Idol of enlightened days?            *60*
Shall we, who struck the Lion down, shall we
Pay the Wolf homage? proffering lowly gaze
And servile knees to Thrones? No! *prove* before ye praise!

If not, o'er one fallen Despot boast no more!
In vain fair cheeks were furrowed with hot tears
For Europe's flowers long rooted up before
The trampler of her vineyards; in vain, years
Of death, depopulation, bondage, fears,
Have all been borne, and broken by the accord
Of roused-up millions: all that most endears            *70*

---

6 the slave class of ancient Sparta
7 The eagle was the Napoleonic battle emblem;
thus Napoleon himself is designated. "Pride of
place" is a term from falconry, denoting the

highest point of flight.
8 Napoleon was, at the time Byron wrote Canto
Three, a prisoner on St. Helena.

Glory, is when the myrtle wreathes a Sword—
Such as Harmodius drew on Athens' tyrant Lord.[9]

There was a sound of revelry by night,
And Belgium's Capital had gathered then
Her Beauty and her Chivalry—and bright
The lamps shone o'er fair women and brave men;
A thousand hearts beat happily; and when
Music arose with its voluptuous swell,
Soft eyes looked love to eyes which spake again,
And all went merry as a marriage bell;                                      80
But hush! hark! a deep sound strikes like a rising knell!

Did ye not hear it?—No—t'was but the Wind,
Or the car rattling o'er the stony street;
On with the dance! let joy be unconfined;
No sleep till morn, when Youth and Pleasure meet
To chase the glowing Hours with flying feet—
But hark!—that heavy sound breaks in once more,
As if the clouds its echo would repeat;
And nearer—clearer—deadlier than before!
Arm! Arm! it is—it is—the cannon's opening roar!                           90

Within a windowed niche of that high hall
Sate Brunswick's fated Chieftain;[10] he did hear
That sound the first amidst the festival,
And caught its tone with Death's prophetic ear;
And when they smiled because he deemed it near,
His heart more truly knew that peal too well
Which stretched his father on a bloody bier,
And roused the vengeance blood alone could quell;
He rushed into the field, and, foremost fighting, fell.

Ah! then and there was hurrying to and fro—                               100
And gathering tears, and tremblings of distress,
And cheeks all pale, which but an hour ago
Blushed at the praise of their own loveliness—
And there were sudden partings, such as press
The life from out young hearts, and choking sighs
Which ne'er might be repeated; who could guess
If ever more should meet those mutual eyes,
Since upon night so sweet such awful morn could rise!

And there was mounting in hot haste—the steed,
The mustering squadron, and the clattering car,                           110
Went pouring forward with impetuous speed,
And swiftly forming in the ranks of war—
And the deep thunder peal on peal afar;

[9] Harmodius, who carried a sword garlanded with myrtle as part of his garb on a festival day, murdered the Athenian tyrant Hipparchus in 514 B.C. and, with his accomplice Aristogiton, became a symbol of patriotic resistance to tyranny.
[10] the Duke of Brunswick, who was killed at the engagement of Quatre Bras, opening the Battle of Waterloo

And near, the beat of the alarming drum
Roused up the soldier ere the Morning Star;
While thronged the citizens with terror dumb,
Or whispering, with white lips—"The foe! They come! they come!"

And wild and high the "Cameron's Gathering" rose!
The war-note of Lochiel, which Albyn's[11] hills
Have heard, and heard, too, have her Saxon foes:—                    *120*
How in the noon of night that pibroch[12] thrills,
Savage and shrill! But with the breath which fills
Their mountain pipe, so fill the mountaineers
With the fierce native daring which instils
The stirring memory of a thousand years,
And Evan's—Donald's[13]—fame rings in each clansman's ears!

And Ardennes[14] waves above them her green leaves,
Dewy with Nature's tear-drops, as they pass—
Grieving, if aught inanimate e'er grieves,
Over the unreturning brave,—alas!                                   *130*
Ere evening to be trodden like the grass
Which *now* beneath them, but *above* shall grow
In its next verdure, when this fiery mass
Of living Valour, rolling on the foe
And burning with high Hope, shall moulder cold and low.

Last noon beheld them full of lusty life:—
Last eve in Beauty's circle proudly gay;
The Midnight brought the signal-sound of strife,
The Morn the marshalling in arms,—the Day
Battle's magnificently-stern array!                                 *140*
The thunder-clouds close o'er it, which when rent
The earth is covered thick with other clay
Which her own clay shall cover, heaped and pent,
Rider and horse,—friend,—foe—in one red burial blent!

Their praise is hymned by loftier harps than mine;
Yet one I would select from that proud throng,
Partly because they blend me with his line,
And partly that I did his Sire some wrong,
And partly that bright names will hallow song;
And his was of the bravest, and when showered                       *150*
The death-bolts deadliest the thinned files along,
Even where the thickest of War's tempest lowered,
They reached no nobler breast than thine, young, gallant Howard!

There have been tears and breaking hearts for thee,
And mine were nothing, had I such to give;
But when I stood beneath the fresh green tree,

---

11 "Cameron's Gathering" was the battle song of          13 Sir Evan Cameron and his descendant Donald
the clan, whose chief was known as Lochiel.              were supporters of the Stuart cause.
Albyn: Scotland                                          14 a forest repeatedly famous as a battle site
12 bagpipe music, here martial in character

Which living waves where thou didst cease to live,
And saw around me the wide field revive
With fruits and fertile promise, and the Spring
Come forth her work of gladness to contrive,                          *160*
With all her reckless birds upon the wing,
I turned from all she brought to those she could not bring.

I turned to thee, to thousands, of whom each
And one as all a ghastly gap did make
In his own kind and kindred, whom to teach
Forgetfulness were mercy for their sake;
The Archangel's trump, not Glory's, must awake
Those whom they thirst for; though the sound of Fame
May for a moment soothe, it cannot slake
The fever of vain longing, and the name                               *170*
So honoured but assumes a stronger, bitterer claim.

They mourn, but smile at length—and, smiling, mourn:
The tree will wither long before it fall;
The hull drives on, though mast and sail be torn;
The roof-tree sinks, but moulders on the hall
In massy hoariness; the ruined wall
Stands when its wind-worn battlements are gone;
The bars survive the captive they enthral;
The day drags through though storms keep out the sun;
And thus the heart will break, yet brokenly live on:                  *180*

Even as a broken Mirror, which the glass
In every fragment multiplies—and makes
A thousand images of one that was
The same—and still the more, the more it breaks;
And thus the heart will do which not forsakes,
Living in shattered guise; and still, and cold,
And bloodless, with its sleepless sorrow aches,
Yet withers on till all without is old,
Showing no visible sign, for such things are untold.

There is a very life in our despair,                                  *190*
Vitality of poison,—a quick root
Which feeds these deadly branches; for it were
As nothing did we die; but Life will suit
Itself to Sorrow's most detested fruit,
Like to the apples on the Dead Sea's shore,[15]
All ashes to the taste: Did man compute
Existence by enjoyment, and count o'er
Such hours 'gainst years of life,—say, would he name threescore?

The Psalmist numbered out the years of man:
They are enough; and if thy tale be *true,*                           *200*

---

[15] Apples growing on the shore of Asphaltites were said to show an attractive outward appear- ance, but to be ashes within.

Thou, who didst grudge him even that fleeting span,
More than enough, thou fatal Waterloo!
Millions of tongues record thee, and anew
Their children's lips shall echo them, and say—
"Here, where the sword united nations drew,
Our countrymen were warring on that day!"
And this is much—and all—which will not pass away.

There sunk the greatest, nor the worst of men,[16]
Whose Spirit, antithetically mixed,
One moment of the mightiest, and again                          210
On little objects with like firmness fixed;
Extreme in all things! hadst thou been betwixt,
Thy throne had still been thine, or never been;
For Daring made thy rise as fall: thou seek'st
Even now to re-assume the imperial mien,
And shake again the world, the Thunderer of the scene!

Conqueror and Captive of the Earth art thou!
She trembles at thee still, and thy wild name
Was ne'er more bruited in men's minds than now
That thou art nothing, save the jest of Fame,                   220
Who wooed thee once, thy Vassal, and became
The flatterer of thy fierceness—till thou wert
A God unto thyself; nor less the same
To the astounded kingdoms all inert,
Who deemed thee for a time whate'er thou didst assert.

Oh, more or less than man—in high or low—
Battling with nations, flying from the field;
Now making monarchs' necks thy footstool, now
More than thy meanest soldier taught to yield;
An Empire thou couldst crush, command, rebuild,                 230
But govern not thy pettiest passion, nor,
However deeply in men's spirits skilled,
Look through thine own, nor curb the lust of War,
Nor learn that tempted Fate will leave the loftiest Star.

Yet well thy soul hath brooked the turning tide
With that untaught innate philosophy,
Which, be it Wisdom, Coldness, or deep Pride,
Is gall and wormwood to an enemy.
When the whole host of hatred stood hard by,
To watch and mock thee shrinking, thou hast smiled              240
With a sedate and all-enduring eye;—
When Fortune fled her spoiled and favourite child,
He stood unbowed beneath the ills upon him piled.

Sager than in thy fortunes; for in them
Ambition steeled thee on too far to show

---

[16] Napoleon

That just habitual scorn, which could contemn
Men and their thoughts; 'twas wise to feel, not so
To wear it ever on thy lip and brow,
And spurn the instruments thou wert to use
Till they were turned unto thine overthrow:                              *250*
'Tis but a worthless world to win or lose;
So hath it proved to thee, and all such lot who choose.

If, like a tower upon a headland rock,
Thou hadst been made to stand or fall alone,
Such scorn of man had helped to brave the shock;
But men's thoughts were the steps which paved thy throne,
*Their* admiration thy best weapon shone
The part of Philip's son [17] was thine—not then
(Unless aside thy Purple had been thrown)
Like stern Diogenes [18] to mock at men:                                 *260*
For sceptred Cynics Earth were far too wide a den.

But Quiet to quick bosoms is a Hell,
And *there* hath been thy bane; there is a fire
And motion of the Soul which will not dwell
In its own narrow being, but aspire
Beyond the fitting medium of desire;
And, but once kindled, quenchless evermore,
Preys upon high adventure, nor can tire
Of aught but rest; a fever at the core,
Fatal to him who bears, to all who ever bore.                           *270*

This makes the madmen who have made men mad
By their contagion; Conquerors and Kings,
Founders of sects and systems, to whom add
Sophists, Bards, Statesmen, all unquiet things
Which stir too strongly the soul's secret springs,
And are themselves the fools to those they fool;
Envied, yet how unenviable! what stings
Are theirs! One breast laid open were a school
Which would unteach Mankind the lust to shine or rule:

Their breath is agitation, and their life                               *280*
A storm whereon they ride, to sink at last,
And yet so nursed and bigoted to strife,
That should their days, surviving perils past,
Melt to calm twilight, they feel overcast
With sorrow and supineness, and so die;
Even as a flame unfed, which runs to waste
With its own flickering, or a sword laid by,
Which eats into itself, and rusts ingloriously.

---

[17] Alexander the Great (356–323 B.C.)
[18] the philosopher of Cynicism, whom Alexander admired

He who ascends to mountain tops, shall find
The loftiest peaks most wrapt in clouds and snow;                    *290*
He who surpasses or subdues mankind,
Must look down on the hate of those below.
Though high *above* the Sun of Glory glow,
And far *beneath* the Earth and Ocean spread,
*Round* him are icy rocks, and loudly blow
Contending tempests on his naked head,
And thus reward the toils which to those summits led.

. . .

### *from* CANTO FOUR

Oh! that the Desert were my dwelling-place,
With one fair Spirit for my minister,
That I might all forget the human race,                             *300*
And, hating no one, love but only her!
Ye elements!—in whose ennobling stir
I feel myself exalted—Can ye not
Accord me such a Being? Do I err
In deeming such inhabit many a spot?
Though with them to converse can rarely be our lot.

There is pleasure in the pathless woods,
There is a rapture on the lonely shore,
There is society, where none intrudes,
By the deep sea, and Music in its roar:                             *310*
I love not Man the less, but Nature more,
From these our interviews, in which I steal
From all I may be, or have been before,
To mingle with the Universe, and feel
What I can ne'er express—yet can not all conceal.

Roll on, thou deep and dark blue Ocean—roll!
Ten thousand fleets sweep over thee in vain;
Man marks the earth with ruin—his control
Stops with the shore;—upon the watery plain
The wrecks are all thy deed, nor doth remain                        *320*
A shadow of man's ravage, save his own,
When, for a moment, like a drop of rain,
He sinks into thy depths with bubbling groan—
Without a grave—unknelled, uncoffined, and unknown.

His steps are not upon thy paths,—thy fields
Are not a spoil for him,—thou dost arise
And shake him from thee; the vile strength he wields
For Earth's destruction thou dost all despise,
Spurning him from thy bosom to the skies—
And send'st him, shivering in thy playful spray                     *330*
And howling, to his Gods, where haply lies
His petty hope in some near port or bay,
And dashest him again to Earth:—there let him lay.

The armaments which thunderstrike the walls
Of rock-built cities, bidding nations quake,
And Monarchs tremble in their Capitals,
The oak Leviathans, whose huge ribs make
Their clay creator the vain title take
Of Lord of thee, and Arbiter of War—
These are thy toys, and, as the snowy flake,                         340
They melt into thy yeast of waves, which mar
Alike the Armada's pride, or spoils of Trafalgar.[19]

Thy shores are empires, changed in all save thee—
Assyria—Greece—Rome—Carthage—what are they?
Thy waters washed them power while they were free,
And many a tyrant since; their shores obey
The stranger, slave, or savage; their decay
Has dried up realms to deserts:—not so thou,
Unchangeable save to thy wild waves' play;
Time writes no wrinkle on thine azure brow—                          350
Such as Creation's dawn beheld, thou rollest now.

Thou glorious mirror, where the Almighty's form
Glasses itself in tempests; in all time,
Calm or convulsed—in breeze, or gale, or storm—
Icing the Pole, or in the torrid clime
Dark-heaving—boundless, endless, and sublime—
The image of Eternity—the throne
Of the Invisible; even from out thy slime
The monsters of the deep are made—each Zone
Obeys thee—thou goest forth, dread, fathomless, alone.              360

And I have loved thee, Ocean! and my joy
Of youthful sports was on thy breast to be
Borne, like thy bubbles, onward: from a boy
I wantoned with thy breakers—they to me
Were a delight; and if the freshening sea
Made them a terror—'twas a pleasing fear,
For I was as it were a Child of thee,
And trusted to thy billows far and near,
And laid my hand upon thy mane—as I do here.

My task is done—my song hath ceased—my theme                        370
Has died into an echo; it is fit
The spell should break of this protracted dream.
The torch shall be extinguished which hath lit
My midnight lamp—and what is writ, is writ,—
Would it were worthier! but I am not now
That which I have been—and my visions flit
Less palpably before me—and the glow
Which in my spirit dwelt is fluttering, faint, and low.

[19] Many of the ships in both the Spanish Armada    Trafalgar (1805), were lost in storms.
(1588) and the French fleet, defeated by Nelson at

Farewell! a word that must be, and hath been—
A sound which makes us linger;—yet—farewell!                    *380*
Ye! who have traced the Pilgrim to the scene
Which is his last—if in your memories dwell
A thought which once was his—if on ye swell
A single recollection—not in vain
He wore his sandal-shoon, and scallop-shell;[20]
Farewell! with *him* alone may rest the pain,
If such there were—with *you,* the Moral of his Strain.   *(1817)*


## *from* Don Juan

> "*Difficile est propriè communia dicere.*"
> —*Horace*

> "*Dost thou think, because thou art virtuous, there shall be no more cakes and ale?
> Yes, by Saint Anne, and ginger shall be hot i' the mouth, too!*"
> —*Shakespeare*, Twelfth Night, or What You Will.

### FRAGMENT

#### ON THE BACK OF THE POET'S MS. OF CANTO I

I would to heaven that I were so much clay,
    As I am blood, bone, marrow, passion, feeling—
Because at least the past were passed away—
    And for the future—(but I write this reeling,
Having got drunk exceedingly today,
    So that I seem to stand upon the ceiling)
I say—the future is a serious matter—
And so—for God's sake—hock and soda-water!

### DEDICATION

Bob Southey! You're a poet—Poet-laureate,
    And representative of all the race;
Although 'tis true that you turned out a Tory at
    Last,—yours has lately been a common case,
And now, my Epic Renegade! what are ye at?
    With all the Lakers,[1] in and out of place?
A nest of tuneful persons, to my eye
Like "four and twenty blackbirds in a pie;

"Which pie being opened they began to sing"
    (This old song and new simile holds good),                 *10*
"A dainty dish to set before the King,"
    Or Regent, who admires such kind of food;—

---

[20] Pilgrims traditionally wore sandals as emblems of travel by land, and a scallop-shell in the hat as an emblem of travel by sea.

[1] the "Lake Poets" associated with England's Lake District; primarily Wordsworth, Coleridge, and Southey

And Coleridge, too, has lately taken wing,
  But like a hawk encumbered with his hood,—
Explaining metaphysics to the nation—
I wish he would explain his Explanation.

You, Bob! are rather insolent, you know,
  At being disappointed in your wish
To supersede all warblers here below,
  And be the only blackbird in the dish;                          20
And then you overstrain yourself, or so,
  And tumble downward like the flying fish
Gasping on deck, because you soar too high, Bob,
And fall, for lack of moisture quite a-dry, Bob!

And Wordsworth, in a rather long "Excursion"
  (I think the quarto holds five hundred pages),
Has given a sample from the vasty version
  Of his new system to perplex the sages;
'Tis poetry—at least by his assertion,
  And may appear so when the dog-star rages—                     30
And he who understands it would be able
To add a story to the Tower of Babel.

You—Gentlemen! by dint of long seclusion
  From better company, have kept your own
At Keswick,[2] and, through still continued fusion
  Of one another's minds, at last have grown
To deem as a most logical conclusion,
  That Poesy has wreaths for you alone:
There is a narrowness in such a notion,
Which makes me wish you'd change your lakes for ocean.           40

I would not imitate the petty thought,
  Nor coin my self-love to so base a vice,
For all the glory your conversion brought,
  Since gold alone should not have been its price.
You have your salary: was't for that you wrought?
  And Wordsworth has his place in the Excise.
You're shabby fellows—true—but poets still,
And duly seated on the immortal hill.

Your bays may hide the baldness of your brows—
  Perhaps some virtuous blushes;—let them go—                    50
To you I envy neither fruit nor boughs—
  And for the fame you would engross below,
The field is universal, and allows
  Scope to all such as feel the inherent glow:
Scott, Rogers, Campbell, Moore, and Crabbe, will try
'Gainst you the question of posterity.

---

[2] Southey's place of residence in the Lake District

For me, who, wandering with pedestrian Muses,
   Contend not with you on the wingéd steed,
I wish your fate may yield ye, when she chooses,
   The fame you envy, and the skill you need;          *60*
And recollect a poet nothing loses
   In giving to his brethren their full meed
Of merit, and complaint of present days
Is not the certain path to future praise.

He that reserves his laurels for posterity
   (Who does not often claim the bright reversion)
Has generally no great crop to spare it, he
   Being only injured by his own assertion;
And although here and there some glorious rarity
   Arise like Titan from the sea's immersion,          *70*
The major part of such appellants go
To—God knows where—for no one else can know.

If, fallen in evil days on evil tongues,
   Milton appealed to the Avenger, Time,
If Time, the Avenger, execrates his wrongs,
   And makes the word "Miltonic" mean "*sublime*,"
*He* deigned not to belie his soul in songs,
   Nor turn his very talent to a crime;
*He* did not loathe the Sire to laud the Son,
But closed the tyrant-hater he begun.          *80*

Think'st thou, could he—the blind Old Man—arise,
   Like Samuel from the grave, to freeze once more
The blood of monarchs with his prophecies,
   Or be alive again—again all hoar
With time and trials, and those helpless eyes,
   And heartless daughters—worn—and pale—and poor;
Would *he* adore a sultan? *he* obey
The intellectual eunuch Castlereagh?[3]

Cold-blooded, smooth-faced, placid miscreant!
   Dabbling its sleek young hands in Erin's gore,          *90*
And thus for wider carnage taught to pant,
   Transferred to gorge upon a sister shore,
The vulgarest tool that Tyranny could want,
   With just enough of talent, and no more,
To lengthen fetters by another fixed,
And offer poison long already mixed.

An orator of such set trash of phrase
   Ineffably—legitimately vile,
That even its grossest flatterers dare not praise,
   Nor foes—all nations—condescend to smile;          *100*

[3] Robert Stewart, Viscount Castlereagh (1769–1822), Tory statesman and diplomat

Not even a sprightly blunder's spark can blaze
  From that Ixion grindstone's ceaseless toil,
That turns and turns to give the world a notion
  Of endless torments and perpetual motion.

A bungler even in its disgusting trade,
  And botching, patching, leaving still behind
Something of which its masters are afraid,
  States to be curbed, and thoughts to be confined,
Conspiracy or Congress to be made—
  Cobbling at manacles for all mankind— 110
A tinkering slave-maker, who mends old chains,
With God and man's abhorrence for its gains.

If we may judge of matter by the mind,
  Emasculated to the marrow *It*
Hath but two objects, how to serve, and bind,
  Deeming the chain it wears even men may fit,
Eutropius [4] of its many masters,—blind
  To worth as freedom, wisdom as to wit.
Fearless—because *no* feeling dwells in ice,
Its very courage stagnates to a vice. 120

Where shall I turn me not to *view* its bonds
  For I will never *feel* them;—Italy!
Thy late reviving Roman soul desponds
  Beneath the lie this State-thing breathed o'er thee—
Thy clanking chain, and Erin's yet green wounds,
  Have voices—tongues to cry aloud for me.
Europe has slaves, allies, kings, armies still,
And Southey lives to sing them very ill.

Meantime, Sir Laureate, I proceed to dedicate,
  In honest simple verse, this song to you. 130
And, if in flattering strains I do not predicate,
  'Tis that I still retain my "buff and blue"; [5]
My politics as yet are all to educate:
  Apostasy's so fashionable, too,
To keep *one* creed's a task grown quite Herculean:
Is it not so, my Tory, Ultra-Julian? [6]  (*1818*)

## Stanzas Written on the Road Between Florence and Pisa

Oh, talk not to me of a name great in story;
The days of our youth are the days of our glory:
And the myrtle and ivy of sweet two-and-twenty
Are worth all your laurels, though ever so plenty.

---

[4] a eunuch in the service of Arcadius, emperor of the Byzantine Empire, A.D. 395–408
[5] colors of the Whig party
[6] Southey's apostasy exceeds that of the Emperor Julian, "the Apostate."

What are garlands and crowns to the brow that is wrinkled?
'Tis but as a dead-flower with May-dew besprinkled.
Then away with all such from the head that is hoary!
What care I for the wreaths that can *only* give glory!

Oh FAME!—if I e'er took delight in thy praises,                    10
'Twas less for the sake of thy high-sounding phrases,
Than to see the bright eyes of the dear one discover,
She thought that I was not unworthy to love her.

*There* chiefly I sought thee, *there* only I found thee;
Her glance was the best of the rays that surround thee;
When it sparkled o'er aught that was bright in my story,
I knew it was love, and I felt it was glory.   (*1821*)


## On This Day I Complete My Thirty-Sixth Year

*MISSOLONGHI,*[1] *JAN. 22, 1824*

'Tis time this heart should be unmoved,
   Since others it hath ceased to move:
Yet, though I cannot be beloved,
   Still let me love!

My days are in the yellow leaf;
   The flowers and fruits of love are gone;
The worm, the canker, and the grief
   Are mine alone!

The fire that on my bosom preys
   Is lone as some volcanic isle;        10
No torch is kindled at its blaze—
   A funeral pile.

The hope, the fear, the jealous care,
   The exalted portion of the pain
And power of love, I cannot share,
   But wear the chain.

But 'tis not *thus*—and 'tis not *here*—
   Such thoughts should shake my soul,
     nor *now*,

Where glory decks the hero's bier,
   Or binds his brow.              20

The sword, the banner, and the field,
   Glory and Greece, around me see!
The Spartan, borne upon his shield,
   Was not more free.

Awake! (not Greece—she *is* awake!)
   Awake, my spirit! Think through *whom*
Thy life-blood tracks its parent lake,
   And then strike home!

Tread those reviving passions down,
   Unworthy manhood!—unto thee       30
Indifferent should the smile or frown
   Of beauty be.

If thou regrett'st thy youth, *why live?*
   The land of honourable death
Is here:—up to the field, and give
   Away thy breath!

Seek out—less often sought than found—
   A soldier's grave, for thee the best;
Then look around, and choose thy
     ground
   And take thy rest.   (*1824*)     40

---

[1] Byron volunteered to train troops for the Greeks in their war for independence from Turkey. He succumbed to fever at Missolonghi shortly after he wrote this poem.

# PERCY BYSSHE SHELLEY / 1792–1822

## Hymn to Intellectual Beauty

The awful shadow of some unseen Power
  Floats though unseen among us,—visiting
  This various world with as inconstant wing
As summer winds that creep from flower to flower,—
Like moonbeams that behind some piny mountain shower,
  It visits with inconstant glance
  Each human heart and countenance;
Like hues and harmonies of evening,—
  Like clouds in starlight widely spread,—
  Like memory of music fled,—          10
  Like aught that for its grace may be
Dear, and yet dearer for its mystery.

Spirit of Beauty, that dost consecrate
  With thine own hues all thou dost shine upon
  Of human thought or form,—where art thou gone?
Why dost thou pass away and leave our state,
This dim vast vale of tears, vacant and desolate?
  Ask why the sunlight not for ever
  Weaves rainbows o'er yon mountain-river,
Why aught should fail and fade that once is shown,    20
  Why fear and dream and death and birth
  Cast on the daylight of this earth
  Such gloom,—why man has such a scope
For love and hate, despondency and hope?

No voice from some sublimer world hath ever
  To sage or poet these responses given—
  Therefore the names of Demon, Ghost, and Heaven,
Remain the records of their vain endeavour,
Frail spells—whose uttered charm might not avail to sever,
  From all we hear and all we see,       30
  Doubt, chance, and mutability.
Thy light alone—like mist o'er mountains driven,
  Or music by the night-wind sent
  Through strings of some still instrument,
  Or moonlight on a midnight stream,
Gives grace and truth to life's unquiet dream.

Love, Hope, and Self-esteem, like clouds depart
  And come, for some uncertain moments lent.
  Man were immortal, and omnipotent,
Didst thou, unknown and awful as thou art,     40
Keep with thy glorious train firm state within his heart.
  Thou messenger of sympathies,

That wax and wane in lovers' eyes—
Thou—that to human thought art nourishment,
  Like darkness to a dying flame!
  Depart not as thy shadow came,
  Depart not—lest the grave should be,
Like life and fear, a dark reality.

While yet a boy I sought for ghosts, and sped
  Through many a listening chamber, cave and ruin,          50
  And starlight wood, with fearful steps pursuing
Hopes of high talk with the departed dead.
I called on poisonous names with which our youth is fed;
  I was not heard—I saw them not—
  When musing deeply on the lot
Of life, at that sweet time when winds are wooing
  All vital things that wake to bring
  News of birds and blossoming,—
  Sudden, thy shadow fell on me;
I shrieked, and clasped my hands in ecstasy!                60

I vowed that I would dedicate my powers
  To thee and thine—have I not kept the vow?
  With beating heart and streaming eyes, even now
I call the phantoms of a thousand hours
Each from his voiceless grave: they have in visioned bowers
  Of studious zeal or love's delight
  Outwatched with me the envious night—
They know that never joy illumed my brow
  Unlinked with hope that thou wouldst free
  This world from its dark slavery,                         70
  That thou—O awful Loveliness,
Wouldst give whate'er these words cannot express.

The day becomes more solemn and serene
  When noon is past—there is harmony
  In autumn, and a lustre in its sky,
Which through the summer is not heard or seen,
As if it could not be, as if it had not been!
  Thus let thy power, which like the truth
  Of nature on my passive youth
Descended, to my onward life supply                         80
  Its calm—to one who worships thee,
  And every form containing thee,
  Whom, Spirit fair, thy spells did bind
To fear himself, and love all human kind.   (*1816*)

## Ozymandias

              I met a traveller from an antique land
              Who said: Two vast and trunkless legs of stone
              Stand in the desert . . . Near them, on the sand,
              Half sunk, a shattered visage lies, whose frown,

And wrinkled lip, and sneer of cold command,
Tell that its sculptor well those passions read
Which yet survive, stamped on these lifeless things,
The hand that mocked them, and the heart that fed:
And on the pedestal these words appear:
"My name is Ozymandias, king of kings:                           *10*
Look on my works, ye Mighty, and despair!"
Nothing beside remains. Round the decay
Of that colossal wreck, boundless and bare
The lone and level sands stretch far away.   (*1817*)


## Stanzas Written in Dejection, Near Naples

The sun is warm, the sky is clear,
    The waves are dancing fast and bright,
Blue isles and snowy mountains wear
    The purple noon's transparent might,
    The breath of the moist earth is light,
        Around its unexpanded buds;
    Like many a voice of one delight,
The winds, the birds, the ocean floods,
The City's voice itself, is soft like Solitude's.

I see the Deep's untrampled floor                                    *10*
    With green and purple seaweeds strown;
I see the waves upon the shore,
    Like light dissolved in star-showers, thrown:
    I sit upon the sands alone,—
        The lightning of the noontide ocean
    Is flashing round me, and a tone
Arises from its measured motion,
How sweet! did any heart now share in my emotion.

Alas! I have nor hope nor health,
    Nor peace within nor calm around,                                *20*
Nor that content surpassing wealth
    The sage in meditation found,
    And walked with inward glory crowned—
        Nor fame, nor power, nor love, nor leisure.
    Others I see whom these surround—
Smiling they live, and call life pleasure,—
To me that cup has been dealt in another measure.

Yet now despair itself is mild,
    Even as the winds and waters are;
I could lie down like a tired child,                                 *30*
    And weep away the life of care
    Which I have borne and yet must bear,

Till death like sleep might steal on me,
     And I might feel in the warm air
My cheek grow cold, and hear the sea
Breathe o'er my dying brain its last monotony.

Some might lament that I were cold,
     As I, when this sweet day is gone,
Which my lost heart, too soon grown old,
     Insults with this untimely moan;                              40
     They might lament—for I am one
Whom men love not,—and yet regret,
     Unlike this day, which, when the sun
Shall on its stainless glory set,
Will linger, though enjoyed, like joy in memory yet.   *(1818)*

## Song to the Men of England

Men of England, wherefore plough
For the lords who lay ye low?
Wherefore weave with toil and care
The rich robes your tyrants wear?

Wherefore feed, and clothe, and save,
From the cradle to the grave,
Those ungrateful drones who would
Drain your sweat—nay, drink your blood?

Wherefore, Bees of England, forge
Many a weapon, chain, and scourge,         10
That these stingless drones may spoil
The forcéd produce of your toil?

Have ye leisure, comfort, calm,
Shelter, food, love's gentle balm?
Or what is it ye buy so dear
With your pain and with your fear?

The seed ye sow, another reaps;
The wealth ye find, another keeps;
The robes ye weave, another wears;
The arms ye forge, another bears.           20

Sow seed,—but let no tyrant reap;
Find wealth,—let no impostor heap;
Weave robes,—let not the idle wear;
Forge arms,—in your defence to bear.

Shrink to your cellars, holes, and cells;
In halls ye deck, another dwells.
Why shake the chains ye wrought? Ye see
The steel ye tempered glance on ye.

With plough and spade, and hoe and
       loom,
Trace your grave, and build your
       tomb,                                  30
And weave your winding-sheet, till fair
England be your sepulchre.   *(1819)*

## Sonnet: England in 1819

An old, mad, blind, despised, and dying king,[1]
Princes, the dregs of their dull race, who flow
Through public scorn—mud from a muddy spring,—
Rulers who neither see, nor feel, nor know,
But leech-like to their fainting country cling,
Till they drop, blind in blood, without a blow,—
A people starved and stabbed in the untilled field,[2]—
An army, which liberticide and prey

---

[1] George III
[2] The Peterloo Massacre in Manchester in 1819 resulted in the death of eleven people and the injuring of hundreds when volunteer cavalry units were ordered to disperse a crowd of upwards of 50,000 assembled at St. Peter's Field to hear an orator advocate parliamentary reform. The name "Peterloo" was formed by analogy to Waterloo, the site of the climactic battle of the Napoleonic Wars in 1815.

Makes as a two-edged sword to all who wield—
Golden and sanguine laws which tempt and slay;      *10*
Religion Christless, Godless—a book sealed;
A Senate,—Time's worst statute unrepealed,[3]—
Are graves, from which a glorious Phantom may
Burst, to illumine our tempestuous day.   (*1819*)

## Ode to the West Wind

### I

O wild West Wind, thou breath of Autumn's being,
Thou, from whose unseen presence the leaves dead
Are driven, like ghosts from an enchanter fleeing,

Yellow, and black, and pale, and hectic red,
Pestilence-stricken multitudes: O thou,
Who chariotest to their dark wintry bed

The wingéd seeds, where they lie cold and low,
Each like a corpse within its grave, until
Thine azure sister of the Spring shall blow

Her clarion o'er the dreaming earth, and fill      *10*
(Driving sweet buds like flocks to feed in air)
With living hues and odours plain and hill:

Wild Spirit, which art moving everywhere;
Destroyer and preserver; hear, oh hear!

### II

Thou on whose stream, mid the steep sky's commotion,
Loose clouds like earth's decaying leaves are shed,
Shook from the tangled boughs of Heaven and Ocean,

Angels of rain and lightning: there are spread
On the blue surface of thine aëry surge,
Like the bright hair uplifted from the head      *20*

Of some fierce Maenad,[1] even from the dim verge
Of the horizon to the zenith's height,
The locks of the approaching storm. Thou dirge

Of the dying year, to which this closing night
Will be the dome of a vast sepulchre,
Vaulted with all thy congregated might

Of vapours, from whose solid atmosphere
Black rain, and fire, and hail will burst: oh, hear!

---

[3] The Test Acts, a variety of laws excluding Catholics, Protestant Dissenters, and others from exercise of the full rights of citizenship, were adopted at various times from the seventeenth century onward and were repealed finally in 1828.

[1] a frenetic female worshipper of Dionysus, god of wine and fertility

### III

Thou who didst waken from his summer dreams
The blue Mediterranean, where he lay,                    *30*
Lulled by the coil of his crystálline streams,

Beside a pumice isle in Baiae's bay,[2]
And saw in sleep old palaces and towers
Quivering within the wave's intenser day,

All overgrown with azure moss and flowers
So·sweet, the sense faints picturing them! Thou
For whose path the Atlantic's level powers

Cleave themselves into chasms, while far below
The sea-blooms and the oozy woods which wear
The sapless foliage of the ocean, know                    *40*

Thy voice, and suddenly grow gray with fear,
And tremble and despoil themselves: oh, hear!

### IV

If I were a dead leaf thou mightest bear;
If I were a swift cloud to fly with thee;
A wave to pant beneath thy power, and share

The impulse of thy strength, only less free
Than thou, O uncontrollable! If even
I were as in my boyhood, and could be

The comrade of thy wanderings over Heaven,
As then, when to outstrip thy skiey speed                    *50*
Scarce seemed a vision; I would ne'er have striven

As thus with thee in prayer in my sore need.
O, lift me as a wave, a leaf, a cloud!
I fall upon the thorns of life! I bleed!

A heavy weight of hours has chained and bowed
One too like thee: tameless, and swift, and proud.

### V

Make my thy lyre, even as the forest is:
What if my leaves are falling like its own!
The tumult of thy mighty harmonies

Will take from both a deep, autumnal tone,                    *60*
Sweet though in sadness. Be thou, Spirit fierce,
My spirit! Be thou me, impetuous one!

Drive my dead thoughts over the universe
Like withered leaves to quicken a new birth!
And, by the incantation of this verse,

---

[2] on the west coast of Italy

Scatter, as from an unextinguished hearth
Ashes and sparks, my words among mankind!
Be through my lips to unawakened earth

The trumpet of a prophecy! O, Wind,
If Winter comes, can Spring be far behind?  *(1819)*  70

# Hymn of Apollo[1]

The sleepless Hours who watch me as I lie,
　　Curtained with star-inwoven tapestries
From the broad moonlight of the sky,
　　Fanning the busy dreams from my dim eyes,—
Waken me when their Mother, the gray Dawn,
Tells them that dreams and that the moon is gone.

Then I arise, and climbing Heaven's blue dome,
　　I walk over the mountains and the waves,
Leaving my robe upon the ocean foam;
　　My footsteps pave the clouds with fire; the caves  10
Are filled with my bright presence, and the air
Leaves the green earth to my embraces bare.

The sunbeams are my shafts, with which I kill
　　Deceit, that loves the night and fears the day;
All men who do or even imagine ill
　　Fly me, and from the glory of my ray
Good minds and open actions take new might,
Until diminished by the reign of Night.

I feed the clouds, the rainbows and the flowers,
　　With their æthereal colours; the moon's globe  20
And the pure stars in their eternal bowers
　　Are cinctured with my power as with a robe;
Whatever lamps on Earth or Heaven may shine
Are portions of one power, which is mine.

I stand at noon upon the peak of Heaven,
　　Then with unwilling steps I wander down
Into the clouds of the Atlantic even;
　　For grief that I depart they weep and frown:
What look is more delightful than the smile
With which I soothe them from the western isle?  30

I am the eye with which the Universe
　　Beholds itself and knows it is divine;
All harmony of instrument or verse,
　　All prophecy, all medicine is mine,
All light of art or nature;—to my song
Victory and praise in its own right belong.  *(1820)*

---

[1] the sun-god, identified with intellect, imagination, and the arts

# Hymn of Pan[1]

From the forests and highlands
  We come, we come;
From the river-girt islands,
  Where loud waves are dumb
    Listening to my sweet pipings.
The wind in the reeds and the rushes,
  The bees on the bells of thyme,
The birds on the myrtle bushes,
  The cicale above in the lime,
And the lizards below in the grass,    10
Were silent as ever old Tmolus was,[2]
    Listening to my sweet pipings.

Liquid Peneus was flowing,
  And all dark Tempe lay
In Pelion's shadow, outgrowing
  The light of the dying day,
    Speeded by my sweet pipings.
The Sileni, and Sylvans, and Fauns,[3]
  And the Nymphs of the woods and
    the waves,
To the edge of the moist river-lawns, 20
  And the brink of the dewy caves,
    And all that did then attend and follow,
Were silent with love, as you now,
    Apollo,
    With envy of my sweet pipings.

I sang of the dancing stars,
  I sang of the daedal Earth,
And of heaven—and the giant wars,
  And Love, and Death, and Birth,—
    And then I changed my pipings,—
Singing how down the vale of
    Maenalus    30
I pursued a maiden and clasped a reed.[4]
Gods and men, we are all deluded thus!

---

[1] Pan was a demigod associated with nature and with man's physical being.
[2] The god of Mount Tmolus was called on to judge the musical competition between Apollo and Pan.
[3] creatures associated with Pan
[4] When Pan pursued the nymph Syrinx, she was transformed into a reed, from which Pan fashioned his pipes.

---

[1] garments    [2] Greece
[3] river in Thessaly, flowing through the vale of Tempe
[4] a particularly beautiful valley in Thessaly
[5] the Cyclades, a circle of Aegean islands

It breaks in our bosom and then we
    bleed:
All wept, as I think both ye now would,
If envy or age had not frozen your blood,
    At the sorrow of my sweet pipings.
                    (1820)

# Chorus *from* Hellas

The world's great age begins anew,
  The golden years return,
The earth doth like a snake renew
  Her winter weeds[1] outworn:
Heaven smiles, and faiths and empires
    gleam,
Like wrecks of a dissolving dream.

A brighter Hellas[2] rears its mountains
  From waves serener far;
A new Peneus[3] rolls his fountains
  Against the morning star.    10
Where fairer Tempes[4] bloom, there sleep
Young Cyclads[5] on a sunnier deep.

A loftier Argo[6] cleaves the main,
  Fraught with a later prize;
Another Orpheus[7] sings again,
  And loves, and weeps, and dies.
A new Ulysses[8] leaves once more
Calypso[9] for his native shore.

Oh, write no more the tale of Troy,[10]
  If earth Death's scroll must be!    20
Nor mix with Laian rage[11] the joy
  Which dawns upon the free:
Although a subtler Sphinx[12] renew
Riddles of death Thebes never knew.

Another Athens shall arise,
  And to remoter time

---

[6] the ship Jason sailed in the quest for the Golden Fleece
[7] renowned poet and musician of myth
[8] hero of the Trojan War and famed wanderer on his ten years' voyage home
[9] nymph who tried to detain Ulysses when he was shipwrecked on her island during his homeward voyage
[10] the substance of *The Iliad*
[11] King Laius of Thebes was killed in a quarrel with his son, Oedipus, who did not recognize him
[12] a monster in Thebes, which posed a riddle to passersby and killed all who could not solve it

Bequeath, like sunset to the skies,
  The splendour of its prime;
And leave, if nought so bright may live,
All earth can take or Heaven can
    give.           30

Saturn and Love[13] their long repose
  Shall burst, more bright and good
Than all who fell,[14] than One who rose,[15]
  Than many unsubdued:[16]
Not gold, not blood, their altar dowers,
But votive tears and symbol flowers.

Oh, cease! must hate and death return?
  Cease! must men kill and die?
Cease! drain not to its dregs the urn
  Of bitter prophecy.
The world is weary of the past,    40
Oh, might it die or rest at last!   *(1821)*

## To Night

Swiftly walk over the western wave,
  Spirit of Night!
Out of the misty eastern cave,
Where, all the long and lone daylight,
Thou wovest dreams of joy and fear
Which make thee terrible and dear,—
  Swift be thy flight!

Wrap thy form in a mantle gray,
  Star-inwrought!
Blind with thine hair the eyes of
    Day;           10
Kiss her until she be wearied out:
Then wander o'er city and sea and land,
Touching all with thine opiate wand—
  Come, long-sought!

When I arose and saw the dawn,
  I sighed for thee;
When light rode high, and the dew was
    gone,
And noon lay heavy on flower and tree,
And the weary Day turned to his rest
Lingering like an unloved guest,    20
  I sighed for thee.

Thy brother Death came, and cried,
  'Wouldst thou me?'
Thy sweet child Sleep, the filmy-eyed,
Murmured like a noontide bee,
'Shall I nestle near thy side?
Wouldst thou me?'—And I replied,
  'No, not thee!'

Death will come when thou art dead,
  Soon, too soon—        30
Sleep will come when thou art fled;
Of neither would I ask the boon
I ask of thee, belovéd Night—
Swift be thine approaching flight,
  Come soon, soon!   *(1821)*

## To ——

Music, when soft voices die,
Vibrates in the memory—
Odours, when sweet violets sicken,
Live within the sense they quicken.

Rose leaves, when the rose is dead,
Are heaped for the belovéd's bed;
And so thy thoughts, when thou art gone,
Love itself shall slumber on.   *(1821)*

## To ——

One word is too often profaned
  For me to profane it,
One feeling too falsely disdained
  For thee to disdain it;
One hope is too like despair
  For prudence to smother,
And Pity from thee more dear
  Than that from another.

I can give not what men call love;
  But wilt thou accept not    10
The worship the heart lifts above
  And the Heavens reject not,—
The desire of the moth for the star,
  Of the night for the morrow,
The devotion to something afar
  From the sphere of our sorrow?
                    *(1821)*

---

[13] rulers in the Golden Age
[14] deposed pagan deities   [15] Christ
[16] surviving pagan gods

# Adonais[1]

*AN ELEGY ON THE DEATH OF JOHN KEATS*[2]

I weep for Adonais—he is dead!
O, weep for Adonais! though our tears
Thaw not the frost which binds so dear a head!
And thou, sad Hour, selected from all years
To mourn our loss, rouse thy obscure compeers,
And teach them thine own sorrow, say: "With me
Died Adonais; till the Future dares
Forget the Past, his fate and fame shall be
An echo and a light unto eternity!"

Where wert thou, mighty Mother, when he lay,                    10
When thy Son lay, pierced by the shaft which flies
In darkness? where was lorn Urania[3]
When Adonais died? With veiléd eyes,
'Mid listening Echoes, in her Paradise
She sate, while one, with soft enamoured breath,
Rekindled all the fading melodies,
With which, like flowers that mock the corse beneath,
He had adorned and hid the coming bulk of Death.

Oh, weep for Adonais—he is dead!
Wake, melancholy Mother, wake and weep!                         20
Yet wherefore? Quench within their burning bed
Thy fiery tears, and let thy loud heart keep
Like his, a mute and uncomplaining sleep;
For he is gone, where all things wise and fair
Descend;—oh, dream not that the amorous Deep
Will yet restore him to the vital air;
Death feeds on his mute voice, and laughs at our despair.

Most musical of mourners, weep again!
Lament anew, Urania!—He died,
Who was the Sire[4] of an immortal strain,                     30
Blind, old, and lonely, when his country's pride,
The priest, the slave, and the liberticide,
Trampled and mocked with many a loathéd rite
Of lust and blood; he went, unterrified,
Into the gulf of death; but his clear Sprite
Yet reigns o'er earth; the third[5] among the sons of light.

---

[1] Adonis was a noble mortal with whom Venus fell in love. She counseled him to hunt safe game only, but he refused to be timid. Adonis wounded a boar, which in its fury slew the youth.
[2] Shelley assumed that Keats's early death (actually from tuberculosis) was caused by an unfavorable review of his *Endymion* in the *Quarterly Review* three years earlier.

[3] Shelley identifies Urania with Venus, and addresses her as both an earth-mother figure and as the muse of lyric poetry.
[4] Milton, whose *Lycidas* Shelley identifies as the origin of the elegiac tradition in English poetry
[5] Milton followed Homer and Dante in the epic tradition.

Most musical of mourners, weep anew!
Not all to that bright station dared to climb;
And happier they their happiness who knew,
Whose tapers yet burn through that night of time          *40*
In which suns perished; others more sublime,
Struck by the envious wrath of man or god,
Have sunk, extinct in their refulgent prime;
And some yet live, treading the thorny road,
Which leads, through toil and hate, to Fame's serene abode.

But now, thy youngest, dearest one, has perished—
The nursling of thy widowhood, who grew,
Like a pale flower by some sad maiden cherished,
And fed with true-love tears, instead of dew,[6]
Most musical of mourners, weep anew!          *50*
Thy extreme hope, the loveliest and the last,
The bloom, whose petals nipped before they blew
Died on the promise of the fruit, is waste;
The broken lily lies—the storm is overpast.

To that high Capital,[7] where kingly Death
Keeps his pale court in beauty and decay,
He came; and bought, with price of purest breath,
A grave among the eternal.—Come away!
Haste, while the vault of blue Italian day
Is yet his fitting charnel-roof! while still          *60*
He lies, as if in dewy sleep he lay;
Awake him not! surely he takes his fill
Of deep and liquid rest, forgetful of all ill.

He will awake no more, oh, never more!—
Within the twilight chamber spreads apace
The shadow of white Death, and at the door
Invisible Corruption waits to trace
His extreme way to her dim dwelling-place;
The eternal Hunger sits, but pity and awe
Soothe her pale rage, nor dares she to deface          *70*
So fair a prey, till darkness, and the law
Of change, shall o'er his sleep the mortal curtain draw.

Oh, weep for Adonais!—The quick Dreams,
The passion-wingéd Ministers of thought,
Who were his flocks, whom near the living streams
Of his young spirit he fed, and whom he taught
The love which was its music, wander not—
Wander no more, from kindling brain to brain,
But droop there, whence they sprung; and mourn their lot
Round the cold heart, where, after their sweet pain,          *80*
They ne'er will gather strength, or find a home again.

---

[6] Keats's *Isabella* includes such an incident.          [7] Rome

And one with trembling hands clasps his cold head,
And fans him with her moonlight wings, and cries;
"Our love, our hope, our sorrow, is not dead;
See, on the silken fringe of his faint eyes,
Like dew upon a sleeping flower, there lies
A tear some Dream has loosened from his brain."
Lost Angel of a ruined Paradise!
She knew not 'twas her own; as with no stain
She faded, like a cloud which had outwept its rain.                90

One from a lucid urn of starry dew
Washed his light limbs as if embalming them;
Another clipped her profuse locks, and threw
The wreath upon him, like an anadem,[8]
Which frozen tears instead of pearls begem;
Another in her wilful grief would break
Her bow and wingéd reeds, as if to stem
A greater loss with one which was more weak;
And dull the barbéd fire against his frozen cheek.

Another Splendour on his mouth alit,                              100
That mouth, whence it was wont to draw the breath
Which gave it strength to pierce the guarded wit,
And pass into the panting heart beneath
With lightning and with music: the damp death
Quenched its caress upon his icy lips;
And, as a dying meteor stains a wreath
Of moonlight vapour, which the cold night clips,
It flushed through his pale limbs, and passed to its eclipse.

And others came . . . Desires and Adorations,
Wingéd Persuasions and veiled Destinies,                          110
Splendours, and Glooms, and glimmering Incarnations
Of hopes and fears, and twilight Phantasies;
And Sorrow, with her family of Sighs,
And Pleasure, blind with tears, led by the gleam
Of her own dying smile instead of eyes,
Came in slow pomp;—the moving pomp might seem
Like pageantry of mist on an autumnal stream.

All he had loved, and moulded into thought,
From shape, and hue, and odour, and sweet sound,
Lamented Adonais. Morning sought                                  120
Her eastern watch-tower, and her hair unbound,
Wet with the tears which should adorn the ground,
Dimmed the aëreal eyes that kindle day;
Afar the melancholy thunder moaned,
Pale Ocean in unquiet slumber lay,
And the wild Winds flew round, sobbing in their dismay.

---

[8] garland

Lost Echo[9] sits amid the voiceless mountains,
And feeds her grief with his remembered lay,
And will no more reply to winds or fountains,
Or amorous birds perched on the young green spray,                    *130*
Or herdsman's horn, or bell at closing day;
Since she can mimic not his lips, more dear
Than those for whose disdain she pined away
Into a shadow of all sounds:—a drear
Murmur, between their songs, is all the woodmen hear.

Grief made the young Spring wild, and she threw down
Her kindling buds, as if she Autumn were,
Or they dead leaves; since her delight is flown,
For whom should she have waked the sullen year?
To Phoebus was not Hyacinth[10] so dear                              *140*
Nor to himself Narcissus, as to both
Thou, Adonais: wan they stand and sere
Amid the faint companions of their youth,
With dew all turned to tears; odour, to sighing ruth.

Thy spirit's sister, the lorn nightingale
Mourns not her mate with such melodious pain;
Not so the eagle, who like thee could scale
Heaven, and could nourish in the sun's domain
Her mighty youth with morning, doth complain,
Soaring and screaming round her empty nest,                          *150*
As Albion[11] wails for thee: the curse of Cain
Light on his head who pierced thy innocent breast,
And scared the angel soul that was its earthly guest!

Ah, woe is me! Winter is come and gone,
But grief returns with the revolving year;
The airs and streams renew their joyous tone;
The ants, the bees, the swallows reappear;
Fresh leaves and flowers deck the dead Seasons' bier;
The amorous birds now pair in every brake,
And build their mossy homes in field and brere;                     *160*
And the green lizard, and the golden snake,
Like unimprisoned flames, out of their trance awake.

Through wood and stream and field and hill and Ocean,
A quickening life from the Earth's heart has burst
As it has ever done, with change and motion,
From the great morning of the world when first
God dawned on Chaos; in its stream immersed,
The lamps of Heaven flash with a softer light;
All baser things pant with life's sacred thirst;
Diffuse themselves; and spend in love's delight,                    *170*
The beauty and the joy of their renewéd might.

---

[9] Shunned by Narcissus, who loved his own reflection, Echo dwindled away until she was only a voice.

[10] Phoebus loved Hyacinthus, a lovely youth whom he accidentally killed.
[11] England

The leprous corpse, touched by this spirit tender,
Exhales itself in flowers of gentle breath;
Like incarnations of the stars, when splendour
Is changed to fragrance, they illumine death
And mock the merry worm that wakes beneath;
Nought we know, dies. Shall that alone which knows
Be as a sword consumed before the sheath
By sightless lightning?—the intense atom glows
A moment, then is quenched in a most cold repose.          *180*

Alas! that all we loved of him should be,
But for our grief, as if it had not been,
And grief itself be mortal! Woe is me!
Whence are we, and why are we? of what scene
The actors or spectators? Great and mean
Meet massed in death, who lends what life must borrow.
As long as skies are blue, and fields are green,
Evening must usher night, night urge the morrow,
Month follow month with woe, and year wake year to sorrow.

*He* will awake no more, oh, never more!                   *190*
"Wake thou," cried Misery, "childless, Mother, rise
Out of thy sleep, and slake, in thy heart's core,
A wound more fierce than his, with tears and sighs."
And all the Dreams that watched Urania's eyes,
And all the Echoes whom their sister's song
Had held in holy silence, cried: "Arise!"
Swift as a Thought by the snake Memory stung,
From her ambrosial rest the fading Splendour sprung.

She rose like an autumnal Night, that springs
Out of the East, and follows wild and drear                *200*
The golden Day, which, on eternal wings,
Even as a ghost abandoning a bier,
Had left the Earth a corpse. Sorrow and fear
So struck, so roused, so rapt Urania;
So saddened round her like an atmosphere
Of stormy mist; so swept her on her way
Even to the mournful place where Adonais lay.

Out of her secret Paradise she sped,
Through camps and cities rough with stone, and steel,
And human hearts, which to her aery tread                  *210*
Yielding not, wounded the invisible
Palms of her tender feet where'er they fell:
And barbéd tongues, and thoughts more sharp than they,
Rent the soft Form they never could repel,
Whose sacred blood, like the young tears of May,
Paved with eternal flowers that undeserving way.

In the death-chamber for a moment Death,
Shamed by the presence of that living Might,

Blushed to annihilation, and the breath
Revisited those lips, and Life's pale light                                    *220*
Flashed through those limbs, so late her dear delight.
"Leave me not wild and drear and comfortless,
As silent lightning leaves the starless night!
Leave me not!" cried Urania: her distress
Roused Death: Death rose and smiled, and met her vain caress.

"Stay yet awhile! speak to me once again;
Kiss me, so long but as a kiss may live;
And in my heartless breast and burning brain
That word, that kiss, shall all thoughts else survive,
With food of saddest memory kept alive,                                        *230*
Now thou art dead, as if it were a part
Of thee, my Adonais! I would give
All that I am to be as thou now art!
But I am chained to Time, and cannot thence depart!

"O gentle child, beautiful as thou wert,
Why didst thou leave the trodden paths of men
Too soon and with weak hands though mighty heart
Dare the unpastured dragon in his den?
Defenceless as thou wert, oh, where was then
Wisdom the mirrored shield,[12] or scorn the spear?                            *240*
Or hadst thou waited the full cycle, when
Thy spirit should have filled its crescent sphere,
The monsters of life's waste had fled from thee like deer.

"The herded wolves, bold only to pursue;
The obscene ravens, clamorous o'er the dead;
The vultures to the conqueror's banner true
Who feed where Desolation first has fed,
And whose wings rain contagion;—how they fled,
When, like Apollo, from his golden bow
The Pythian of the age[13] one arrow sped                                      *250*
And smiled!—The spoilers tempt no second blow,
They fawn on the proud feet that spurn them lying low.

"The sun comes forth, and many reptiles spawn;
He sets, and each ephemeral insect then
Is gathered into death without a dawn,
And the immortal stars awake again;
So is it in the world of living men:
A godlike mind soars forth, in its delight
Making earth bare and veiling heaven, and when
It sinks, the swarms that dimmed or shared its light                           *260*
Leave to its kindred lamps the spirit's awful night."

---

[12] Perseus avoided being turned to stone by the gaze of Medusa by using his shield as a mirror.
[13] Byron, who had attacked the critics in *English Bards and Scotch Reviewers*, as Apollo "the Pythian" had attacked the Python

Thus ceased she: and the mountain shepherds came,
Their garlands sere, their magic mantles rent;
The Pilgrim of Eternity,[14] whose fame
Over his living head like Heaven is bent,
An early but enduring monument,
Came, veiling all the lightnings of his song
In sorrow; from her wilds Ierne[15] sent
The sweetest lyrist[16] of her saddest wrong,
And Love taught Grief to fall like music from his tongue.                   270

Midst others of less note, came one frail Form,[17]
A phantom among men; companionless
As the last cloud of an expiring storm
Whose thunder is its knell; he, as I guess,
Had gazed on Nature's naked loveliness,
Actaeon-like,[18] and now he fled astray
With feeble steps o'er the world's wilderness,
And his own thoughts, along that rugged way,
Pursued, like raging hounds, their father and their prey.

A pardlike Spirit beautiful and swift—                                       280
A Love in desolation masked;—a Power
Girt round with weakness;—it can scarce uplift
The weight of the superincumbent hour;
It is a dying lamp, a falling shower,
A breaking billow;—even whilst we speak
Is it not broken? On the withering flower
The killing sun smiles brightly: on a cheek
The life can burn in blood, even while the heart may break.

His head was bound with pansies overblown,
And faded violets, white, and pied, and blue;                                290
And a light spear topped with a cypress cone,
Round whose rude shaft dark ivy-tresses[19] grew
Yet dripping with the forest's noonday dew,
Vibrated, as the ever-beating heart
Shook the weak hand that grasped it; of that crew
He came the last, neglected and apart;
A herd-abandoned deer struck by the hunter's dart.

All stood aloof, and at his partial moan
Smiled through their tears; well knew that gentle band
Who in another's fate now wept his own,                                      300
As in the accents of an unknown land
He sung new sorrow; sad Urania scanned
The Stranger's mien, and murmured: "Who art thou?"

---

14 Byron, here likened to Childe Harold
15 Ireland
16 Thomas Moore, contemporary Irish lyric poet
17 Shelley
18 Actaeon saw Diana bathing; as punishment he

was turned into a stag and was killed by his own
hounds.
19 In flower symbolism, pansies represent thought;
violets, modesty; cypress, mourning; and ivy,
fidelity.

He answered not, but with a sudden hand
Made bare his branded and ensanguined brow,
Which was like Cain's or Christ's[20]—oh! that it should be so!

What softer voice[21] is hushed over the dead?
Athwart what brow is that dark mantle thrown?
What form leans sadly o'er the white death-bed,
In mockery of monumental stone,                                310
The heavy heart heaving without a moan?
If it be He, who, gentlest of the wise,
Taught, soothed, loved, honoured the departed one,
Let me not vex, with inharmonious sighs,
The silence of that heart's accepted sacrifice.

Our Adonais has drunk poison—oh!
What deaf and viperous murderer could crown
Life's early cup with such a draught of woe?
The nameless worm[22] would now itself disown:
It felt, yet could escape, the magic tone                       320
Whose prelude held all envy, hate, and wrong,
But what was howling in one breast alone,
Silent with expectation of the song,
Whose master's hand is cold, whose silver lyre unstrung.

Live thou, whose infamy is not thy fame!
Live! fear no heavier chastisement from me,
Thou noteless blot on a remembered name!
But be thyself, and know thyself to be!
And ever at thy season be thou free
To spill the venom when thy fangs o'erflow;                     330
Remorse and Self-contempt shall cling to thee;
Hot Shame shall burn upon thy secret brow,
And like a beaten hound tremble thou shalt—as now.

Nor let us weep that our delight is fled
Far from these carrion kites that scream below;
He wakes or sleeps with the enduring dead;
Thou canst not soar where he is sitting now.—
Dust to the dust! but the pure spirit shall flow
Back to the burning fountain whence it came,
A portion of the Eternal, which must glow                       340
Through time and change, unquenchably the same,
Whilst thy cold embers choke the sordid hearth of shame.

Peace, peace! he is not dead, he doth not sleep—
He hath awakened from the dream of life—
'Tis we, who lost in stormy visions, keep
With phantoms an unprofitable strife,
And in mad trance, strike with our spirit's knife

---

[20] His brow bore a mark like that placed upon Cain for his sin, or like Christ's wounds from the Crown of Thorns.

[21] Leigh Hunt, contemporary poet, and a close friend of Keats

[22] the anonymous snake who reviewed *Endymion*

Invulnerable nothings.—*We* decay
Like corpses in a charnel; fear and grief
Convulse us and consume us day by day,                              *350*
And cold hopes swarm like worms within our living clay.

He has outsoared the shadow of our night;
Envy and calumny and hate and pain,
And that unrest which men miscall delight,
Can touch him not and torture not again;
From the contagion of the world's slow stain
He is secure, and now can never mourn
A heart grown cold, a head grown gray in vain;
Nor, when the spirit's self has ceased to burn,
With sparkless ashes load an unlamented urn.                        *360*

He lives, he wakes—'tis Death is dead, not he;
Mourn not for Adonais.—Thou young Dawn,
Turn all thy dew to splendour, for from thee
The spirit thou lamentest is not gone;
Ye caverns and ye forests, cease to moan!
Cease, ye faint flowers and fountains, and thou Air,
Which like a mourning veil thy scarf hadst thrown
O'er the abandoned Earth, now leave it bare
Even to the joyous stars which smile on its despair!

He is made one with Nature: there is heard                          *370*
His voice in all her music, from the moan
Of thunder, to the song of night's sweet bird;
He is a presence to be felt and known
In darkness and in light, from herb and stone,
Spreading itself where'er that Power may move
Which has withdrawn his being to its own;
Which wields the world with never-wearied love,
Sustains it from beneath, and kindles it above.

He is a portion of the loveliness
Which once he made more lovely: he doth bear                        *380*
His part, while the one Spirit's plastic stress
Sweeps through the dull dense world, compelling there,
All new successions to the forms they wear;
Torturing th' unwilling dross that checks its flight
To its own likeness, as each mass may bear;
And bursting in its beauty and its might
From trees and beasts and men into the Heaven's light.

The splendours of the firmament of time
May be eclipsed, but are extinguished not;
Like stars to their appointed height they climb,                   *390*
And death is a low mist which cannot blot
The brightness it may veil. When lofty thought
Lifts a young heart above its mortal lair,
And love and life contend in it, for what

Shall be its earthly doom, the dead live there
And more like winds of light on dark and stormy air.

The inheritors of unfulfilled renown
Rose from their thrones, built beyond mortal thought,
Far in the Unapparent. Chatterton [23]
Rose pale,—his solemn agony had not                          400
Yet faded from him; Sidney,[24] as he fought
And as he fell and as he lived and loved
Sublimely mild, a Spirit without spot,
Arose; and Lucan,[25] by his death approved:
Oblivion as they rose shrank like a thing reproved.

And many more, whose names on Earth are dark,
But whose transmitted effluence cannot die
So long as fire outlives the parent spark,
Rose, robed in dazzling immortality.
"Thou art become as one of us," they cry,                    410
"It was for thee yon kingless sphere has long
Swung blind in unascended majesty,
Silent alone amid an Heaven of Song.
Assume thy wingéd throne, thou Vesper of our throng!"

Who mourns for Adonais? Oh, come forth,
Fond wretch! and know thyself and him aright.
Clasp with thy panting soul the pendulous Earth;
As from a centre, dart thy spirit's light
Beyond all worlds, until its spacious might
Satiate the void circumference: then shrink                  420
Even to a point within our day and night;
And keep thy heart light lest it make thee sink
When hope has kindled hope, and lured thee to the brink.

Or go to Rome, which is the sepulchre,[26]
Oh, not of him, but of our joy: 'tis nought
That ages, empires, and religions there
Lie buried in the ravage they have wrought;
For such as he can lend,—they borrow not
Glory from those who made the world their prey;
And he is gathered to the kings of thought                   430
Who waged contention with their time's decay,
And of the past are all that cannot pass away.

Go thou to Rome,—at once the Paradise,
The grave, the city, and the wilderness;
And where its wrecks like shattered mountains rise,
And flowering weeds, and fragrant copses dress
The bones of Desolation's nakedness

[23] Thomas Chatterton (1752–1770), a poet who, like Sidney and Lucan, died young with "unfulfilled renown"
[24] Sir Philip Sidney (1554–1586)
[25] Marcus Annaeus Lucanus (39–65)
[26] Keats was buried in the Protestant Cemetery in Rome.

Pass, till the spirit of the spot shall lead
Thy footsteps to a slope of green access
Where, like an infant's smile, over the dead                                    *440*
A light of laughing flowers along the grass is spread;

And gray walls moulder round, on which dull Time
Feeds, like slow fire upon a hoary brand;
And one keen pyramid[27] with wedge sublime,
Pavilioning the dust of him who planned
This refuge for his memory, doth stand
Like flame transformed to marble; and beneath,
A field is spread, on which a newer band
Have pitched in Heaven's smile their camp of death,
Welcoming him we lose with scarce extinguished breath.                          *450*

Here pause: these graves are all too young as yet
To have outgrown the sorrow which consigned
Its charge to each; and if the seal is set,
Here, on one fountain of a mourning mind,
Break it not thou! too surely shalt thou find
Thine own well full, if thou returnest home,
Of tears and gall. From the world's bitter wind
Seek shelter in the shadow of the tomb.
What Adonais is, why fear we to become?

The One remains, the many change and pass;                                      *460*
Heaven's light forever shines, Earth's shadows fly;
Life, like a dome of many-coloured glass,
Stains the white radiance of Eternity,
Until Death tramples it to fragments.—Die,
If thou wouldst be with that which thou dost seek!
Follow where all is fled!—Rome's azure sky,
Flowers, ruins, statues, music, words, are weak
The glory they transfuse with fitting truth to speak.

Why linger, why turn back, why shrink, my Heart?
Thy hopes are gone before: from all things here                                 *470*
They have departed; thou shouldst now depart!
A light is passed from the revolving year,
And man, and woman; and what still is dear
Attracts to crush, repels to make thee wither.
The soft sky smiles,—the low wind whispers near:
'Tis Adonais calls! oh, hasten thither,
No more let Life divide what Death can join together.

That light whose smile kindles the Universe,
That Beauty in which all things work and move,
That Benediction which the eclipsing Curse                                      *480*
Of birth can quench not, that sustaining Love
Which through the web of being blindly wove

---

27 The cemetery is bordered on one side by the pyramidal tomb of a Roman statesman.

By man and beast and earth and air and sea,
Burns bright or dim, as each are mirrors of
The fire for which all thirst; now beams on me,
Consuming the last clouds of cold mortality.

The breath whose might I have invoked in song
Descends on me; my spirit's bark is driven,
Far from the shore, far from the trembling throng
Whose sails were never to the tempest given;        *490*
The massy earth and spheréd skies are riven!
I am borne darkly, fearfully, afar;
Whilst, burning through the inmost veil of Heaven,
The soul of Adonais, like a star,
Beacons from the abode where the Eternal are.   *(1821)*

## A Dirge

Rough wind, that moanest loud
  Grief too sad for song;
Wild wind, when sullen cloud
  Knells all the night long;
Sad storm, whose tears are vain,
Bare woods, whose branches strain,
Deep caves and dreary main,—
  Wail, for the world's wrong!   *(1822)*

## Lines: When the Lamp Is Shattered

When the lamp is shattered
The light in the dust lies dead—
  When the cloud is scattered
The rainbow's glory is shed.
  When the lute is broken,
Sweet tones are remembered not;
  When the lips have spoken,
Loved accents are soon forgot.

  As music and splendour
Survive not the lamp and the lute,        *10*
  The heart's echoes render
No song when the spirit is mute:—
  No song but sad dirges,
Like the wind through a ruined cell,
  Or the mournful surges
That ring the dead seaman's knell.

When hearts have once mingled
Love first leaves the well-built nest;
  The weak one is singled
To endure what it once possessed.        *20*
  O Love! who bewailest
The frailty of all things here,
  Why choose you the frailest
For your cradle, your home, and your
  bier?

  Its passions will rock thee
As the storms rock the ravens on high;
  Bright reason will mock thee,
Like the sun from a wintry sky.
  From thy nest every rafter
Will rot, and thine eagle home        *30*
  Leave thee naked to laughter,
When leaves fall and cold winds come.
                                    *(1822)*

# JOHN CLARE / 1793–1864

## Gypsies

The snow falls deep; the forest lies alone;
The boy goes hasty for his load of brakes,[1]
Then thinks upon the fire and hurries back;
The gypsy knocks his hands and tucks them up,
And seeks his squalid camp, half hid in snow,
Beneath the oak which breaks away the wind,
And bushes close in snow like hovel warm;
There tainted mutton wastes upon the coals,
And the half-wasted dog squats close and rubs,
Then feels the heat too strong, and goes aloof;                    10
He watches well, but none a bit can spare,
And vainly waits the morsel thrown away.
'Tis thus they live—a picture to the place,
A quiet, pilfering, unprotected race.  (*1837*)

## I Am

I am: yet what I am none cares or knows,
  My friends forsake me like a memory lost,
I am the self-consumer of my woes—
  They rise and vanish in oblivious host,
Like shadows in love's frenzied stifled throes—
And yet I am, and live—like vapors tossed

Into the nothingness of scorn and noise,
  Into the living sea of waking dreams,
Where there is neither sense of life or joys,
  But the vast shipwreck of my life's esteems;          10
And e'en the dearest, that I love the best,
Are strange—nay, rather stranger than the rest.

I long for scenes, where man hath never trod,
  A place where woman never smiled or wept—
There to abide with my Creator, God,
  And sleep as I in childhood sweetly slept,
Untroubling, and untroubled where I lie,
The grass below—above the vaulted sky.  (*1848*)

## The Swallow

Swift goes the sooty swallow o'er the heath,
Swifter than skims the cloud-rack of the skies;
As swiftly flies its shadow underneath,
And on his wing the twittering sunbeam lies,

---

[1] brush for firewood or kindling

436

As bright as water glitters in the eyes
Of those it passes; 'tis a pretty thing,
The ornament of meadows and clear skies:
With dingy breast and narrow pointed wing,
Its daily twittering is a song to Spring.   (*1873*)

## Secret Love

I hid my love when young till I
Couldn't bear the buzzing of a fly;
I hid my life to my despite
Till I could not bear to look at light:
I dare not gaze upon her face
But left her memory in each place;
Where'er I saw a wild flower lie
I kissed and bade my love good-bye.

I met her in the greenest dells,
Where dewdrops pearl the wood bluebells;                    10
The lost breeze kissed her bright blue eye,
The bee kissed and went singing by,
A sunbeam found a passage there,
A gold chain round her neck so fair;
As secret as the wild bee's song
She lay there all the summer long.

I hid my love in field and town
Till e'en the breeze would knock me down;
The bees seemed singing ballads o'er,
The fly's bass turned a lion's roar;                         20
And even silence found a tongue,
To haunt me all the summer long;
The riddle nature could not prove
Was nothing else but secret love.

# WILLIAM CULLEN BRYANT / 1794–1878

## Thanatopsis

To him who in the love of Nature holds
Communion with her visible forms, she speaks
A various language; for his gayer hours
She has a voice of gladness, and a smile
And eloquence of beauty, and she glides
Into his darker musings, with a mild

And healing sympathy, that steals away
Their sharpness, ere he is aware. When thoughts
Of the last bitter hour come like a blight
Over thy spirit, and sad images                                         *10*
Of the stern agony, and shroud, and pall,
And breathless darkness, and the narrow house,
Make thee to shudder, and grow sick at heart;—
Go forth, under the open sky, and list
To Nature's teachings, while from all around—
Earth and her waters, and the depths of air—
Comes a still voice—Yet a few days, and thee
The all-beholding sun shall see no more
In all his course; nor yet in the cold ground,
Where thy pale form was laid, with many tears,                          *20*
Nor in the embrace of ocean, shall exist
Thy image. Earth, that nourished thee, shall claim
Thy growth, to be resolved to earth again,
And, lost each human trace, surrendering up
Thine individual being, shalt thou go
To mix for ever with the elements,
To be a brother to the insensible rock
And to the sluggish clod, which the rude swain
Turns with his share, and treads upon. The oak
Shall send his roots abroad, and pierce thy mould.                      *30*

    Yet not to thine eternal resting-place
Shalt thou retire alone, nor couldst thou wish
Couch more magnificent. Thou shalt lie down
With patriarchs of the infant world—with kings,
The powerful of the earth—the wise, the good,
Fair forms, and hoary seers of ages past,
All in one mighty sepulchre. The hills
Rock-ribbed and ancient as the sun—the vales
Stretching in pensive quietness between;
The venerable woods—rivers that move                                    *40*
In majesty, and the complaining brooks
That make the meadows green; and, poured round all,
Old Ocean's gray and melancholy waste,—
Are but the solemn decorations all
Of the great tomb of man. The golden sun,
The planets, all the infinite host of heaven,
Are shining on the sad abodes of death,
Through the still lapse of ages. All that tread
The globe are but a handful to the tribes
That slumber in its bosom.—Take the wings                              *50*
Of morning, pierce the Barcan wilderness,
Or lose thyself in the continuous woods
Where rolls the Oregon, and hears no sound,
Save his own dashings—yet the dead are there:

And millions in those solitudes, since first
The flight of years began, have laid them down
In their last sleep—the dead reign there alone.
So shalt thou rest, and what if thou withdraw
In silence from the living, and no friend
Take note of thy departure? All that breathe                    60
Will share thy destiny. The gay will laugh
When thou art gone, the solemn brood of care
Plod on, and each one as before will chase
His favorite phantom; yet all these shall leave
Their mirth and their employments, and shall come,
And make their bed with thee. As the long train
Of ages glide away, the sons of men,
The youth in life's green spring, and he who goes
In the full strength of years, matron and maid,
The speechless babe, and the gray-headed man—                   70
Shall one by one be gathered to thy side,
By those, who in their turn shall follow them.

  So live, that when thy summons comes to join
The innumerable caravan, which moves
To that mysterious realm, where each shall take
His chamber in the silent halls of death,
Thou go not, like the quarry-slave at night,
Scourged to his dungeon, but, sustained and soothed
By an unfaltering trust, approach thy grave,
Like one who wraps the drapery of his couch                     80
About him, and lies down to pleasant dreams.   (*1811*)

## Inscription for the Entrance to a Wood

Stranger, if thou hast learned a truth which needs
No school of long experience, that the world
Is full of guilt and misery, and hast seen
Enough of all its sorrows crimes and cares
To tire thee of it, enter this wild wood
And view the haunts of Nature. The calm shade
Shall bring a kindred calm; and the sweet breeze,
That makes the green leaves dance, shall waft a balm
To thy sick heart. Thou wilt find nothing here
Of all that pained thee in the haunts of men                    10
And made thee loathe thy life. The primal curse
Fell, it is true, upon the unsinning earth,
But not in vengeance. God hath yoked to guilt
Her pale tormentor, misery. Hence these shades
Are still the abodes of gladness: the thick roof
Of green and stirring branches is alive
And musical with birds, that sing and sport
In wantonness of spirit; while below,

The squirrel, with raised paws and form erect,
Chirps merrily. Throngs of insects in the shade                    20
Try their thin wings and dance in the warm beam
That waked them into life. Even the green trees
Partake the deep contentment; as they bend
To the soft winds, the sun from the blue sky
Looks in and sheds a blessing on the scene.
Scarce less the cleft-born wild-flower seems to enjoy
Existence than the wingéd plunderer
That sucks its sweets. The mossy rocks themselves,
And the old ponderous trunks of prostrate trees
That lead from knoll to knoll a causey rude                        30
Or bridge the sunken brook, and their dark roots,
With all their earth upon them, twisting high,
Breathe the fixed tranquillity. The rivulet
Sends forth glad sounds, and, tripping o'er its bed
Of pebbly sands or leaping down the rocks,
Seems with continuous laughter to rejoice
In its own being. Softly tread the marge,
Lest from her midway perch thou scare the wren
That dips her bill in water. The cool wind,
That stirs the stream in play, shall come to thee,                 40
Like one that loves thee nor will let thee pass
Ungreeted, and shall give its light embrace.    (*1815*)


# JOHN KEATS / 1795–1821


## To One Who Has Been Long in City Pent

To one who has been long in city pent,
'Tis very sweet to look into the fair
And open face of heaven,—to breathe a prayer
Full in the smile of the blue firmament.
Who is more happy, when, with heart's content,
Fatigued he sinks into some pleasant lair
Of wavy grass, and reads a debonair
And gentle tale of love and languishment?
Returning home at evening, with an ear
Catching the notes of Philomel,[1]—an eye                          10
Watching the sailing cloudlet's bright career,
He mourns that day so soon has glided by
E'en like the passage of an angel's tear
That falls through the clear ether silently.    (*1816*)

---

[1] the nightingale

# On First Looking into Chapman's Homer[1]

Much have I travelled in the realms of gold,
And many goodly states and kingdoms seen:
Round many western islands have I been
Which bards in fealty to Apollo[2] hold.
Oft of one wide expanse had I been told
That deep-browed Homer ruled as his demesne;[3]
Yet did I never breathe its pure serene
Till I heard Chapman speak out loud and bold:
Then felt I like some watcher of the skies
When a new planet swims into his ken;                                10
Or like stout Cortez[4] when with eagle eyes
He stared at the Pacific—and all his men
Looked at each other with a wild surmise—
Silent, upon a peak in Darien.   (*1816*)

# On the Grasshopper and the Cricket

The poetry of earth is never dead:
When all the birds are faint with the hot sun,
And hide in cooling trees, a voice will run
From hedge to hedge about the new-mown mead;
That is the Grasshopper's—he takes the lead
In summer luxury,—he has never done
With his delights; for when tired out with fun
He rests at ease beneath some pleasant weed.
The poetry of earth is ceasing never:
On a lone winter evening, when the frost                             10
Has wrought a silence, from the stove there shrills
The Cricket's song, in warmth increasing ever,
And seems to one in drowsiness half lost,
The Grasshopper's among some grassy hills.   (*1816*)

# On Seeing the Elgin Marbles[1] for the First Time

My spirit is too weak; mortality
Weighs heavily on me like unwilling sleep,
And each imagined pinnacle and steep
Of godlike hardship tells me I must die
Like a sick eagle looking at the sky.

---

[1] George Chapman (c. 1559–1634) published translations of *The Iliad* (1611) and *The Odyssey* (1616).
[2] god of poetry    [3] estate
[4] Hernando Cortez (1485–1547), Spanish conqueror of Mexico. Actually it was Vasco Nuñez de Balboa (1475–1517) who first sighted the Pacific from a mountain in Darien, a region in eastern Panama.

[1] A large collection of sculptures from the Parthenon was taken to England by Lord Elgin, who sold it to the British Museum shortly before Keats wrote this sonnet.

Yet 'tis a gentle luxury to weep,
That I have not the cloudy winds to keep
Fresh for the opening of the morning's eye.
Such dim-conceivéd glories of the brain
Bring round the heart an indescribable feud;                    *10*
So do these wonders a most dizzy pain,
That mingles Grecian grandeur with the rude
Wasting of old Time—with a billowy main,
A sun, a shadow of a magnitude.   (*1817*)


## After Dark Vapours Have Oppressed Our Plains

After dark vapours have oppressed our plains
For a long dreary season, comes a day
Born of the gentle South, and clears away
From the sick heavens all unseemly stains.
The anxious month, relievéd of its pains,
Takes as a long-lost right the feel of May;
The eyelids with the passing coolness play
Like rose leaves with the drip of summer rains.
The calmest thoughts come round us; as of leaves
Budding—fruit ripening in stillness—autumn suns              *10*
Smiling at eve upon the quiet sheaves—
Sweet Sappho's cheek—a smiling infant's breath—
The gradual sand that through an hour-glass runs—
A woodland rivulet—a poet's death.   (*1817*)


## from Endymion, *Book I*

### CREDO, LINES 1–24

A thing of beauty is a joy forever:
Its loveliness increases; it will never
Pass into nothingness; but still will keep
A bower quiet for us, and a sleep
Full of sweet dreams, and health, and quiet breathing.
Therefore, on every morrow, are we wreathing
A flowery band to bind us to the earth,
Spite of despondence, of the inhuman dearth
Of noble natures, of the gloomy days,
Of all the unhealthy and o'er-darkened ways                    *10*
Made for our searching: yes, in spite of all,
Some shape of beauty moves away the pall
From our dark spirits. Such the sun, the moon,
Trees old, and young, sprouting a shady boon
For simple sheep; and such are daffodils
With the green world they live in; and clear rills
That for themselves a cooling covert make

'Gainst the hot season; the mid-forest brake,
Rich with a sprinkling of fair musk-rose blooms:
And such too is the grandeur of the dooms          20
We have imagined for the mighty dead;
All lovely tales that we have heard or read:
An endless fountain of immortal drink,
Pouring unto us from the heaven's brink.   (*1817*)

## Lines on the Mermaid Tavern[1]

Souls of Poets dead and gone,
What Elysium[2] have ye known,
Happy field or mossy cavern,
Choicer than the Mermaid Tavern?
Have ye tippled drink more fine
Than mine host's Canary wine?
Or are fruits of paradise
Sweeter than those dainty pies
Of venison? O generous food!
Dressed as though bold Robin Hood      10
Would, with his maid Marian,
Sup and bowse[3] from horn and can.

I have heard that on a day
Mine host's sign-board flew away,
Nobody knew whither, till
An astrologer's old quill
To a sheepskin gave the story,
Said he saw you in your glory,
Underneath a new old sign
Sipping beverage divine,                20
And pledging with contented smack
The Mermaid in the Zodiac.[4]

Souls of Poets dead and gone,
What Elysium have ye known,
Happy field or mossy cavern,
Choicer than the Mermaid Tavern?
                                   (*1818*)

## Ode

Bards of Passion and of Mirth,
Ye have left your souls on earth!
Have ye souls in heaven too,
Double-lived in regions new?

Yes, and those of heaven commune
With the spheres of sun and moon;
With the noise of fountains wond'rous,
And the parle of voices thund'rous;
With the whisper of heaven's trees
And one another, in soft ease          10
Seated on Elysian lawns
Browsed by none but Dian's fawns
Underneath large blue-bells tented,
Where the daisies are rose-scented,
And the rose herself has got
Perfume which on earth is not;
Where the nightingale doth sing
Not a senseless, trancéd thing,
But divine melodious truth;
Philosophic numbers smooth;            20
Tales and golden histories
Of heaven and its mysteries.

Thus ye live on high, and then
On the earth ye live again;
And the souls ye left behind you
Teach us, here, the way to find you,
Where your other souls are joying,
Never slumbered, never cloying.
Here, your earth-born souls still speak
To mortals, of their little week;      30
Of their sorrows and delights;
Of their passions and their spites;
Of their glory and their shame;
What does strengthen and what maim.
Thus ye teach us, every day,
Wisdom, though fled far away.

Bards of Passion and of Mirth,
Ye have left your souls on earth!
Ye have souls in heaven too,
Double-lived in regions new!   (*1819*)   40

---

[1] a favorite London gathering place of Elizabethan poets
[2] in classical mythology, the abode of the blessed either in the western regions of the earth or in the underworld
[3] carouse
[4] a ring of constellations lying along the sun's path

## When I Have Fears That I May Cease to Be

When I have fears that I may cease to be
Before my pen has gleaned my teeming brain,
Before high-piléd books, in charactery,
Hold like rich garners the full-ripened grain;
When I behold, upon the night's starred face,
Huge cloudy symbols of a high romance,
And think that I may never live to trace
Their shadows, with the magic hand of chance;
And when I feel, fair creature of an hour,
That I shall never look upon thee more,                    10
Never have relish in the faery power
Of unreflecting love;—then on the shore
Of the wide world I stand alone, and think
Till love and fame to nothingness do sink.   (*1818*)

## Bright Star! Would I Were Steadfast As Thou Art

Bright star! would I were steadfast as thou art—
Not in lone splendour hung aloft the night
And watching, with eternal lids apart,
Like Nature's patient, sleepless Eremite,[1]
The moving waters at their priestlike task
Of pure ablution round earth's human shores,
Or gazing on the new soft fallen mask
Of snow upon the mountains and the moors—
No—yet still steadfast, still unchangeable,
Pillowed upon my fair love's ripening breast,          10
To feel for ever its soft fall and swell,
Awake for ever in a sweet unrest,
Still, still to hear her tender-taken breath,
And so live ever—or else swoon to death.   (*1819*)

## On the Sonnet

If by dull rhymes our English must be chained,
And, like Andromeda,[1] the sonnet sweet
Fettered, in spite of painéd loveliness,
Let us find, if we must be constrained,
Sandals more interwoven and complete
To fit the naked foot of Poesy:
Let us inspect the lyre, and weigh the stress
Of every chord, and see what may be gained

---

[1] hermit; one who keeps a vigil

[1] chained to a rock to appease the sea nymphs, who had been angered by boasts of her superior beauty

By ear industrious, and attention meet;
Misers of sound and syllable, no less          *10*
Than Midas[2] of his coinage, let us be
Jealous of dead leaves in the bay wreath crown;
So, if we may not let the Muse be free,
She will be bound with garlands of her own.   *(1819)*

## Why Did I Laugh Tonight?

Why did I laugh tonight? No voice will tell:
No God, no Demon of severe response,
Deigns to reply from Heaven or from Hell.
Then to my human heart I turn at once.
Heart! Thou and I are here sad and alone;
I say, why did I laugh? O mortal pain!
O Darkness! Darkness! ever must I moan,
To question Heaven and Hell and Heart in vain.
Why did I laugh? I know this Being's lease,
My fancy to its utmost blisses spreads;      *10*
Yet would I on this very midnight cease,
And the world's gaudy ensigns see in shreds;
Verse, Fame, and Beauty are intense indeed,
But Death intenser—Death is Life's high meed.  *(1819)*

## The Eve of St. Agnes

St. Agnes' Eve—Ah, bitter chill it was!
The owl, for all his feathers, was a-cold;
The hare limped trembling through the frozen grass,
And silent was the flock in woolly fold:
Numb were the Beadsman's fingers, while he told
His rosary, and while his frosted breath,
Like pious incense from a censer old,
Seemed taking flight for Heaven, without a death,
Past the sweet Virgin's picture, while his prayer he saith.

His prayer he saith, this patient, holy man;      *10*
Then takes his lamp, and riseth from his knees,
And back returneth, meagre, barefoot, wan,
Along the chapel aisle by slow degrees:
The sculptured dead on each side seem to freeze,
Imprisoned in black, purgatorial rails:
Knights, ladies, praying in dumb orat'ries,
He passeth by; and his weak spirit fails
To think how they may ache in icy hoods and mails.

---

[2] King of Phrygia, famed for immense wealth

Northward he turneth through a little door,
And scarce three steps, ere music's golden tongue                    20
Flattered to tears this agéd man and poor;
But no   already had his deathbell rung:
The joys of all his life were said and sung.
His was harsh penance on St. Agnes' Eve:
Another way he went, and soon among
Rough ashes sat he for his soul's reprieve,
And all night kept awake, for sinners' sake to grieve.

That ancient Beadsman heard the prelude soft;
And so it chanced, for many a door was wide,
From hurry to and fro. Soon, up aloft,                               30
The silver, snarling trumpets 'gan to chide:
The level chambers, ready with their pride,
Were glowing to receive a thousand guests:
The carvéd angels, ever eager-eyed,
Stared, where upon their heads the cornice rests,
With hair blown back, and wings put crosswise on their breasts.

At length burst in the argent revelry,
With plume, tiara, and all rich array,
Numerous as shadows haunting faerily
The brain, new stuffed, in youth, with triumphs gay                  40
Of old romance. These let us wish away,
And turn, sole-thoughted, to one Lady there,
Whose heart had brooded, all that wintry day,
On love, and winged St. Agnes' saintly care,
As she had heard old dames full many times declare.

They told her how, upon St. Agnes' Eve,
Young virgins might have visions of delight,
And soft adorings from their loves receive
Upon the honeyed middle of the night,
If ceremonies due they did aright;                                   50
As, supperless to bed they must retire,
And couch supine their beauties, lily white;
Nor look behind, nor sideways, but require
Of Heaven with upward eyes for all that they desire.

Full of this whim was thoughtful Madeline:
The music, yearning like a God in pain,
She scarcely heard: her maiden eyes divine,
Fixed on the floor, saw many a sweeping train
Pass by—she heeded not at all: in vain
Came many a tiptoe, amorous cavalier,                                60
And back retired; not cooled by high disdain,
But she saw not: her heart was otherwhere:
She sighed for Agnes' dreams, the sweetest of the year.

She danced along with vague, regardless eyes,
Anxious her lips, her breathing quick and short:

The hallowed hour was near at hand: she sighs
Amid the timbrels, and the thronged resort
Of whisperers in anger, or in sport;
'Mid looks of love, defiance, hate, and scorn,
Hoodwinked with faery fancy; all amort,[1]    *70*
Save to St. Agnes and her lambs unshorn,
And all the bliss to be before tomorrow morn.

So, purposing each moment to retire,
She lingered still. Meantime, across the moors,
Had come young Porphyro, with heart on fire
For Madeline. Beside the portal doors,
Buttressed from moonlight, stands he, and implores
All saints to give him sight of Madeline,
But for one moment in the tedious hours,
That he might gaze and worship all unseen;    *80*
Perchance speak, kneel, touch, kiss—in sooth such things have been.

He ventures in: let no buzzed whisper tell:
All eyes be muffled, or a hundred swords
Will storm his heart, Love's fev'rous citadel:
For him, those chambers held barbarian hordes,
Hyena foemen, and hot-blooded lords,
Whose very dogs would execrations howl
Against his lineage: not one breast affords
Him any mercy, in that mansion foul,
Save one old beldame, weak in body and in soul.    *90*

Ah, happy chance! the agéd creature came,
Shuffling along with ivory-headed wand,
To where he stood, hid from the torch's flame,
Behind a broad hall-pillar, far beyond
The sound of merriment and chorus bland:
He startled her; but soon she knew his face,
And grasped his fingers in her palsied hand,
Saying, "Mercy, Porphyro! hie thee from this place:
They are all here to-night, the whole blood-thirsty race!

"Get hence! get hence! there's dwarfish Hildebrand;    *100*
He had a fever late, and in the fit
He curséd thee and thine, both house and land:
Then there's that old Lord Maurice, not a whit
More tame for his gray hairs—Alas me! flit!
Flit like a ghost away."—"Ah, Gossip dear,
We're safe enough; here in this arm chair sit,
And tell me how"—"Good saints! not here, not here;
Follow me, child, or else these stones will be thy bier."

He followed through a lowly archéd way,
Brushing the cobwebs with his lofty plume,    *110*

---

[1] lifeless

And as she muttered "Well-a—well-a-day!"
He found him in a little moonlight room,
Pale, latticed, chill, and silent as a tomb.
"Now tell me where is Madeline," said he,
"Oh tell me, Angela, by the holy loom
Which none but secret sisterhood may see,
When they St. Agnes' wool are weaving piously."

"St. Agnes! Ah! it is St. Agnes' Eve—
Yet men will murder upon holy days:
Thou must hold water in a witch's sieve,                         *120*
And be liege-lord of all the Elves and Fays,
To venture so: it fills me with amaze
To see thee, Porphyro!—St. Agnes' Eve!
God's help! my lady fair the conjuror plays
This very night: good angels her deceive!
But let me laugh awhile, I've mickle² time to grieve."

Feebly she laugheth in the languid moon
While Porphyro upon her face doth look,
Like puzzled urchin on an agéd crone
Who keepeth closed a wond'rous riddle-book,                      *130*
As spectacled she sits in chimney nook.
But soon his eyes grew brilliant, when she told
His lady's purpose; and he scarce could brook
Tears, at the thought of those enchantments cold,
And Madeline asleep in lap of legends old.

Sudden a thought came like a full-blown rose,
Flushing his brow, and in his painéd heart
Made purple riot: then doth he propose
A stratagem, that makes the beldame start:
"A cruel man and impious thou art:                               *140*
Sweet lady, let her pray, and sleep, and dream
Alone with her good angels, far apart
From wicked men like thee. Go, go!—I deem
Thou canst not surely be the same that thou didst seem."

"I will not harm her, by all saints I swear,"
Quoth Porphyro: "O may I ne'er find grace
When my weak voice shall whisper its last prayer,
If one of her soft ringlets I displace,
Or look with ruffian passion in her face:
Good Angela, believe me by these tears;                          *150*
Or I will, even in a moment's space,
Awake, with horrid shout, my foemen's ears,
And beard them, though they be more fanged than wolves and bears."

"Ah! why wilt thou affright a feeble soul?
A poor, weak, palsy-stricken, churchyard thing,

_____
² much

Whose passing-bell may ere the midnight toll;
Whose prayers for thee, each morn and evening,
Were never missed."—Thus plaining, doth she bring
A gentler speech from burning Porphyro;
So woful, and of such deep sorrowing,       *160*
That Angela gives promise she will do
Whatever he shall wish, betide her weal or woe.

Which was, to lead him, in close secrecy,
Even to Madeline's chamber, and there hide
Him in a closet, of such privacy
That he might see her beauty unespied,
And win perhaps that night a peerless bride,
While legioned faeries paced the coverlet,
And pale enchantment held her sleepy-eyed.
Never on such a night have lovers met,       *170*
Since Merlin paid his Demon all the monstrous debt.[3]

"It shall be as thou wishest," said the Dame:
"All cates[4] and dainties shall be storéd there
Quickly on this feast-night: by the tambour frame[5]
Her own lute thou wilt see: no time to spare,
For I am slow and feeble, and scarce dare
On such a catering trust my dizzy head.
Wait here, my child, with patience; kneel in prayer
The while: Ah! thou must needs the lady wed,
Or may I never leave my grave among the dead."       *180*

So saying she hobbled off with busy fear,
The lover's endless minutes slowly passed;
The dame returned, and whispered in his ear
To follow her; with agéd eyes aghast
From fright of dim espial. Safe at last,
Through many a dusky gallery, they gain
The maiden's chamber, silken, hushed, and chaste;
Where Porphyro took covert, pleased amain.
His poor guide hurried back with agues in her brain.

Her faltering hand upon the balustrade,       *190*
Old Angela was feeling for the stair,
When Madeline, St. Agnes' charméd maid,
Rose, like a missioned spirit, unaware:
With silver taper's light, and pious care,
She turned, and down the agéd gossip led
To a safe level matting. Now prepare,
Young Porphyro, for gazing on that bed;
She comes, she comes again, like ring-dove frayed[6] and fled.

---

[3] Merlin, the great enchanter in Arthurian legend, was engendered by a demon and ultimately enchanted by Vivian, thus paying the debt for his monstrous origin. A great storm raged over the land on the night following his enchantment.
[4] delicacies
[5] embroidery hoop resembling a drumhead
[6] frightened

Out went the taper as she hurried in;
Its little smoke, in pallid moonshine, died:                        *200*
She closed the door, she panted, all akin
To spirits of the air, and visions wide:
No uttered syllable, or, woe betide!
But to her heart, her heart was voluble,
Paining with eloquence her balmy side;
As though a tongueless nightingale should swell
Her throat in vain, and die, heart-stifled, in her dell.

A casement high and triple-arched there was,
All garlanded with carven imag'ries
Of fruits, and flowers, and bunches of knot-grass,                 *210*
And diamonded with panes of quaint device,
Innumerable of stains and splendid dyes,
As are the tiger-moth's deep-damasked wings;
And in the midst, 'mong thousand heraldries,
And twilight saints, and dim emblazonings,
A shielded scutcheon blushed with blood of queens and kings.

Full on this casement shone the wintry moon,
And threw warm gules [7] on Madeline's fair breast,
As down she knelt for heaven's grace and boon;
Rose-bloom fell on her hands, together prest,                      *220*
And on her silver cross soft amethyst,
And on her hair a glory, like a saint:
She seemed a splendid angel, newly drest,
Save wings, for heaven:—Porphyro grew faint:
She knelt, so pure a thing, so free from mortal taint.

Anon his heart revives: her vespers done,
Of all its wreathéd pearls her hair she frees;
Unclasps her warméd jewels one by one;
Loosens her fragrant bodice, by degrees
Her rich attire creeps rustling to her knees:                     *230*
Half-hidden like a mermaid in sea-weed,
Pensive awhile she dreams awake, and sees,
In fancy, fair St. Agnes in her bed,
But dares not look behind, or all the charm is fled.

Soon trembling in her soft and chilly nest,
In sort of wakeful swoon, perplexed she lay,
Until the poppied warmth of sleep oppressed
Her soothéd limbs, and soul fatigued away;
Flown, like a thought, until the morrow day;
Blissfully havened both from joy and pain;                        *240*
Clasped like a missal where swart Paynims [8] pray;
Blinded alike from sunshine and from rain,
As though a rose should shut, and be a bud again.

---

[7] red (in heraldic designs)                    [8] pagans, usually Moslems

Stolen to this paradise, and so entranced,
Porphyro gazed upon her empty dress,
And listened to her breathing, if it chanced
To wake into a slumberous tenderness;
Which when he heard, that minute did he bless,
And breathed himself: then from the closet crept,
Noiseless as fear in a wide wilderness,                                      250
And over the hushed carpet, silent stept,
And 'tween the curtains peeped, where lo!—how fast she slept.

Then by the bedside, where the faded moon
Made a dim, silver twilight, soft he set
A table, and, half anguished, threw thereon
A cloth of woven crimson, gold, and jet:—
O for some drowsy Morphean [9] amulet!
The boisterous, midnight, festive clarion,
The kettle-drum, and far-heard clarinet,
Affray his ears, though but in dying tone:—                                  260
The hall door shuts again, and all the noise is gone.

And still she slept an azure-lidded sleep,
In blanchéd linen, smooth, and lavendered,
While he from forth the closet brought a heap
Of candied apple, quince, and plum, and gourd;
With jellies soother than the creamy curd,
And lucent syrups, tinct with cinnamon;
Manna and dates, in argosy transferred
From Fez; and spicéd dainties, every one,
From silken Samarcand to cedared Lebanon.                                    270

These delicates he heaped with glowing hand
On golden dishes and in baskets bright
Of wreathéd silver: sumptuous they stand
In the retiréd quiet of the night,
Filling the chilly room with perfume light.—
"And now, my love, my seraph fair, awake!
Thou art my heaven, and I thine eremite: [10]
Open thine eyes for meek St. Agnes' sake,
Or I shall drowse beside thee, so my soul doth ache."

Thus whispering, his warm, unnervéd arm                                      280
Sank in her pillow. Shaded was her dream
By the dusk curtains:—'twas a midnight charm
Impossible to melt as icéd stream:
The lustrous salvers in the moonlight gleam;
Broad golden fringe upon the carpet lies:
It seemed he never, never could redeem
From such a steadfast spell his lady's eyes;
So mused awhile, entoiled in wooféd phantasies.

---

9 adjectival form of Morpheus                10 hermit; hence, servile worshipper

Awakening up, he took her hollow lute,—
Tumultuous,—and, in chords that tenderest be,                           *290*
He played an ancient ditty, long since mute,
In Provence called, "La belle dame sans mercy":
Close to her ear touching the melody;—
Wherewith disturbed, she uttered a soft moan:
He ceased—she panted quick—and suddenly
Her blue affrayéd eyes wide open shone:
Upon his knees he sank, pale as smooth-sculptured stone.

Her eyes were open, but she still beheld,
Now wide awake, the vision of her sleep:
There was a painful change, that nigh expelled                          *300*
The blisses of her dream so pure and deep;
At which fair Madeline began to weep,
And moan forth witless words with many a sigh;
While still her gaze on Porphyro would keep;
Who knelt, with joinéd hands and piteous eye,
Fearing to move or speak, she looked so dreamingly.

"Ah, Porphyro!" said she, "but even now
Thy voice was at sweet tremble in mine ear,
Made tuneable with every sweetest vow;
And those sad eyes were spiritual and clear:                            *310*
How changed thou art! how pallid, chill, and drear!
Give me that voice again, my Porphyro,
Those looks immortal, those complainings dear!
Oh leave me not in this eternal woe,
For if thou diest, my Love, I know not where to go."

Beyond a mortal man impassioned far
At these voluptuous accents, he arose,
Ethereal, flushed, and like a throbbing star
Seen mid the sapphire heaven's deep repose;
Into her dream he melted, as the rose                                   *320*
Blendeth its odour with the violet,—
Solution sweet: meantime the frost-wind blows
Like Love's alarum pattering the sharp sleet
Against the window-panes; St. Agnes' moon hath set.

'Tis dark: quick pattereth the flaw-blown sleet:
"This is no dream, my bride, my Madeline!"
'Tis dark: the icéd gusts still rave and beat:
"No dream, alas! alas! and woe is mine!
Porphyro will leave me here to fade and pine,—
Cruel! what traitor could thee hither bring?                            *330*
I curse not, for my heart is lost in thine,
Though thou forsakest a deceivéd thing;—
A dove forlorn and lost with sick unprunéd wing."

"My Madeline! sweet dreamer! lovely bride!
Say, may I be for ay thy vassal blest?

Thy beauty's shield, heart-shaped and vermeil[11] dyed?
Ah, silver shrine, here will I take my rest
After so many hours of toil and quest,
A famished pilgrim,—saved by miracle.
Though I have found, I will not rob thy nest                                  340
Saving of thy sweet self; if thou think'st well
To trust, fair Madeline, to no rude infidel.

"Hark! 'tis an elfin-storm from faery land,
Of haggard seeming, but a boon indeed:
Arise—arise! the morning is at hand;—
The bloated wassaillers will never heed:—
Let us away, my love, with happy speed;
There are no ears to hear, or eyes to see,—
Drowned all in Rhenish and the sleepy mead:
Awake! arise! my love, and fearless be,                                      350
For o'er the southern moors I have a home for thee."

She hurried at his words, beset with fears,
For there were sleeping dragons all around,
At glaring watch, perhaps, with ready spears—
Down the wide stairs a darkling way they found.—
In all the house was heard no human sound.
A chain-drooped lamp was flickering by each door;
The arras, rich with horseman, hawk, and hound,
Fluttered in the besieging wind's uproar;
And the long carpets rose along the gusty floor.                             360

They glide, like phantoms, into the wide hall;
Like phantoms, to the iron porch they glide;
Where lay the Porter, in uneasy sprawl,
With a huge empty flagon by his side:
The wakeful bloodhound rose, and shook his hide,
But his sagacious eye an inmate owns:
By one, and one, the bolts full easy slide:—
The chains lie silent on the footworn stones;—
The key turns, and the door upon its hinges groans.

And they are gone: aye, ages long ago                                        370
These lovers fled away into the storm.
That night the Baron dreamt of many a woe,
And all his warrior-guests, with shade and form
Of witch, and demon, and large coffin-worm
Were long be-nightmared. Angela the old
Died palsy-twitched, with meagre face deform;
The Beadsman, after thousand aves told,
For ay unsought for slept among his ashes cold.    (*1819*)

---

[11] vermilion

## La Belle Dame sans Merci

O what can ail thee, knight-at-arms,
    Alone and palely loitering?
The sedge has witherèd from the lake,
    And no birds sing.

O what can ail thee, knight-at-arms,
    So haggard and so woe-begone?
The squirrel's granary is full,
    And the harvest's done.

I see a lily on thy brow
    With anguish moist and fever
      dew,                10
And on thy cheek a fading rose
    Fast withereth too.

I met a lady in the meads,
    Full beautiful—a faery's child,
Her hair was long, her foot was light,
    And her eyes were wild.

I made a garland for her head,
    And bracelets too, and fragrant zone;
She looked at me as she did love,
    And made sweet moan.        20

I set her on my pacing steed,
    And nothing else saw all day long,
For sidelong would she bend, and sing
    A faery's song.

She found me roots of relish sweet,
    And honey wild, and manna dew,
And sure in language strange she said—
    "I love thee true."

She took me to her elfin grot,
    And there she wept, and sighed full
      sore.               30
And there I shut her wild wild eyes
    With kisses four.

And there she lullèd me asleep,
    And there I dreamed—Ah! woe betide!
The latest dream I ever dreamed
    On the cold hill side.

I saw pale kings and princes too,
    Pale warriors, death-pale were they all;
They cried—"La Belle Dame sans Merci
    Hath thee in thrall!"      40

I saw their starved lips in the gloam,
    With horrid warning gapéd wide,
And I awoke and found me here,
    On the cold hill's side.

And this is why I sojourn here,
    Alone and palely loitering,
Though the sedge is withered from the
      lake,
And no birds sing.    (1819)

## This Living Hand

This living hand, now warm and capable
Of earnest grasping, would, if it were cold
And in the icy silence of the tomb,
So haunt thy days and chill thy dreaming nights
That thou wouldst wish thine own heart dry of blood
So in my veins red life might stream again,
And thou be conscience-calmed—see here it is—
I hold it towards you.    (1819)

## Ode on a Grecian Urn

Thou still unravished bride of quietness,
    Thou foster-child of silence and slow time,
Sylvan historian, who canst thus express
    A flowery tale more sweetly than our rhyme:
What leaf-fringed legend haunts about thy shape

Of deities or mortals, or of both,
   In Tempe[1] or the dales of Arcady?[2]
What men or gods are these? What maidens loth?
   What mad pursuit? What struggle to escape?
     What pipes and timbrels? What wild ecstasy?     *10*

Heard melodies are sweet, but those unheard
   Are sweeter; therefore, ye soft pipes, play on;
Not to the sensual ear, but, more endeared,
   Pipe to the spirit ditties of no tone:
Fair youth, beneath the trees, thou canst not leave
   Thy song, nor ever can those trees be bare;
     Bold Lover, never, never canst thou kiss,
Though winning near the goal—yet, do not grieve;
   She cannot fade, though thou hast not thy bliss,
     For ever wilt thou love, and she be fair!     *20*

Ah, happy, happy boughs! that cannot shed
   Your leaves, nor ever bid the spring adieu;
And, happy melodist, unwearièd,
   For ever piping songs for ever new;
More happy love! more happy, happy love!
   For ever warm and still to be enjoyed,
     For ever panting, and for ever young;
All breathing human passion far above,
   That leaves a heart high-sorrowful and cloyed,
     A burning forehead, and a parching tongue.     *30*

Who are these coming to the sacrifice?
   To what green altar, O mysterious priest,
Lead'st thou that heifer lowing at the skies,
   And all her silken flanks with garlands dressed?
What little town by river or sea shore,
   Or mountain-built with peaceful citadel,
     Is emptied of this folk, this pious morn?
And, little town, thy streets for evermore
   Will silent be; and not a soul to tell
     Why thou art desolate, can e'er return.     *40*

O Attic[3] shape! Fair attitude! with brede[4]
   Of marble men and maidens overwrought,
With forest branches and the trodden weed;
   Thou, silent form, dost tease us out of thought
As doth eternity: Cold Pastoral!
   When old age shall this generation waste,
     Thou shalt remain, in midst of other woe
Than ours, a friend to man, to whom thou say'st,
   "Beauty is truth, truth beauty,"—that is all
     Ye know on earth, and all ye need to know.   *(1819)*   *50*

---

[1] valley in Thessaly, noted for natural beauty      usually the setting for pastoral poetry
[2] Arcadia, a region in Peloponnesus which is      [3] of Attica; hence, "classic"    [4] embroidery

## Ode on Melancholy

No, no, go not to Lethe,[1] neither twist
    Wolf's bane,[2] tight-rooted, for its poisonous wine;
Nor suffer thy pale forehead to be kissed
    By nightshade, ruby grape of Proserpine;[3]
Make not your rosary of yew berries,[4]
    Nor let the beetle, nor the death-moth be
        Your mournful Psyche,[5] nor the downy owl
A partner in your sorrow's mysteries;
    For shade to shade will come too drowsily,
        And drown the wakeful anguish of the soul.          10

But when the melancholy fit shall fall
    Sudden from heaven like a weeping cloud,
That fosters the droop-headed flowers all,
    And hides the green hill in an April shroud;
Then glut thy sorrow on a morning rose,
    Or on the rainbow of the salt sand-wave,
        Or on the wealth of globéd peonies;
Or if thy mistress some rich anger shows,
    Emprison her soft hand, and let her rave,
        And feed deep, deep upon her peerless eyes.         20

She dwells with Beauty—Beauty that must die;
    And Joy, whose hand is ever at his lips
Bidding adieu; and aching Pleasure nigh,
    Turning to poison while the bee-mouth sips:
Ay, in the very temple of delight
    Veiled Melancholy has her sovran shrine,
        Though seen of none save him whose strenuous tongue
Can burst Joy's grape against his palate fine;
    His soul shall taste the sadness of her might,
        And be among her cloudy trophies hung.   (1819)     30

## Ode to a Nightingale

My heart aches, and a drowsy numbness pains
    My sense, as though of hemlock[1] I had drunk,
Or emptied some dull opiate to the drains
    One minute past, and Lethe-wards[2] had sunk:
'Tis not through envy of thy happy lot,
    But being too happy in thine happiness,—
        That thou, light-wingéd Dryad[3] of the trees,
        In some melodious plot
Of beechen green, and shadows numberless,
        Singest of summer in full-throated ease.          10

---

[1] river of forgetfulness in Hades
[2] like nightshade, poisonous herb
[3] queen of the underworld
[4] Yew is associated with death and funerals.
[5] the soul

[1] a poisonous herb administered as a liquid
[2] toward Lethe, the river of forgetfulness in Hades
[3] wood nymph

O, for a draught of vintage! that hath been
  Cooled a long age in the deep-delvéd earth,
Tasting of Flora [4] and the country green,
  Dance, and Provençal [5] song, and sunburnt mirth!
O for a beaker full of the warm South,
  Full of the true, the blushful Hippocrene, [6]
    With beaded bubbles winking at the brim,
      And purple-stainéd mouth;
That I might drink, and leave the world unseen,
  And with thee fade away into the forest dim:       20

Fade far away, dissolve, and quite forget
  What thou among the leaves hast never known,
The weariness, the fever, and the fret
  Here, where men sit and hear each other groan;
Where palsy shakes a few, sad, last gray hairs,
  Where youth grows pale, and spectre-thin, and dies;
    Where but to think is to be full of sorrow
      And leaden-eyed despairs,
Where Beauty cannot keep her lustrous eyes,
  Or new Love pine at them beyond to-morrow.      30

Away! away! for I will fly to thee,
  Not charioted by Bacchus [7] and his pards, [8]
But on the viewless wings of Poesy,
  Though the dull brain perplexes and retards:
Already with thee! tender is the night,
  And haply the Queen-Moon is on her throne,
    Clustered around by all her starry Fays; [9]
      But here there is no light,
Save what from heaven is with the breezes blown
  Through verdurous glooms and winding mossy ways.    40

I cannot see what flowers are at my feet,
  Nor what soft incense hangs upon the boughs,
But, in embalméd darkness, guess each sweet
  Wherewith the seasonable month endows
The grass, the thicket, and the fruit-tree wild;
  White hawthorn, and the pastoral eglantine;
    Fast fading violets covered up in leaves;
      And mid-May's eldest child,
The coming musk-rose, full of dewy wine,
  The murmurous haunt of flies on summer eves.      50

Darkling I listen; and, for many a time
  I have been half in love with easeful Death,
Called him soft names in many a muséd rhyme,
  To take into the air my quiet breath;

---

[4] goddess of flowers; hence, flowers      [6] a fountain on Mt. Helicon, sacred to the Muses
[5] of Provence, a province of France noted for its    [7] god of wine   [8] leopards   [9] fairies
minstrelsy

Now more than ever seems it rich to die,
  To cease upon the midnight with no pain,
    While thou art pouring forth thy soul abroad
      In such an ecstasy!
  Still wouldst thou sing, and I have ears in vain—
    To thy high requiem become a sod.                         60

Thou wast not born for death, immortal Bird!
  No hungry generations tread thee down;
The voice I hear this passing night was heard
  In ancient days by emperor and clown: [10]
Perhaps the self-same song that found a path
  Through the sad heart of Ruth,[11] when, sick for home,
    She stood in tears amid the alien corn;
      The same that oft-times hath
Charmed magic casements, opening on the foam
    Of perilous seas, in faery lands forlorn.                70

Forlorn! the very word is like a bell
  To toll me back from thee to my sole self!
Adieu! the fancy cannot cheat so well
  As she is famed to do, deceiving elf.
Adieu! adieu! thy plaintive anthem fades
  Past the near meadows, over the still stream,
    Up the hill-side; and now 'tis buried deep
      In the next valley-glades:
Was it a vision, or a waking dream?
  Fled is that music:—Do I wake or sleep?   (*1819*)        80

## To Autumn

Season of mists and mellow fruitfulness,
  Close bosom-friend of the maturing sun;
Conspiring with him how to load and bless
  With fruit the vines that round the thatch-eves run;
To bend with apples the mossed cottage-trees,
  And fill all fruit with ripeness to the core;
    To swell the gourd, and plump the hazel shells
  With a sweet kernel; to set budding more,
And still more, later flowers for the bees,
Until they think warm days will never cease,                   10
    For Summer has o'er-brimmed their clammy cells.

Who hath not seen thee oft amid thy store?
  Sometimes whoever seeks abroad may find
Thee sitting careless on a granary floor,
  Thy hair soft-lifted by the winnowing wind;

---

[10] farm hand
[11] heroine of the Old Testament Book of Ruth, who went with her mother-in-law to an alien land

Or on a half-reaped furrow sound asleep,
    Drowsed with the fume of poppies, while thy hook
      Spares the next swath and all its twinéd flowers:
And sometimes like a gleaner thou dost keep
    Steady thy laden head across a brook;          20
    Or by a cider-press, with patient look,
      Thou watchest the last oozings hours by hours.

Where are the songs of Spring? Ay, where are they?
    Think not of them, thou hast thy music too,—
While barred clouds bloom the soft-dying day,
    And touch the stubble-plains with rosy hue;
Then in a wailful choir the small gnats mourn
    Among the river sallows[1] borne aloft
      Or sinking as the light wind lives or dies;
And full-grown lambs loud bleat from hilly bourn;[2]     30
    Hedge-crickets sing; and now with treble soft
    The red-breast whistles from a garden-croft;[3]
      And gathering swallows twitter in the skies.  *(1819)*

# THOMAS LOVELL BEDDOES / 1803–1849

## Dream of Dying

Shivering in fever, weak and parched to sand,
My ears, those entrances of word-dressed thoughts,
My pictured eyes, and my assuring touch,
Fell from me, and my body turned me forth
From its beloved abode: then I was dead;
And in my grave beside my corpse I sat,
In vain attempting to return: meantime
There came the untimely spectres of two babes,
And played in my abandoned body's ruins;
They went away; and, one by one, by snakes     10
My limbs were swallowed; and, at last, I sat
With only one, blue-eyed, curled round my ribs,
Eating the last remainder of my heart,
And hissing to himself. O sleep, thou fiend!
Thou blackness of the night! how sad and frightful
Are these thy dreams!  *(1823)*

---

[1] willows    [2] field    [3] enclosed garden

## Song

Old Adam, the carrion crow,
　The old crow of Cairo,
He sat in the shower, and let if flow
Under his tail and over his crest;
　And through every feather
　Leaked the wet weather;
And the bough swung under his nest;
For his beak it was heavy with marrow.
　Is that the wind dying? O no;
　It's only two devils, that blow                                10
Through a murderer's bones, to and fro,
　In the ghosts' moonshine.

Ho! Eve, my gray carrion wife,
　When we have supped on kings' marrow,
Where shall we drink and make merry our life?
Our nest it is queen Cleopatra's skull,
　'Tis cloven and cracked,
　And battered and hacked,
But with tears of blue eyes it is full:
Let us drink then, my raven of Cairo.                            20
　Is that the wind dying? O no;
　It's only two devils, that blow
Through a murderer's bones, to and fro,
　In the ghosts' moonshine.   (*1825–1828*)


## Lyrical Fragments II:
## Stanzas from the Ivory Gate[1]

The mighty thought of an old world
Fans, like a dragon's wing unfurled,
　The surface of my yearnings deep;
And solemn shadows then awake,
Like the fish-lizard in the lake,
　Troubling a planet's morning sleep.

My waking is a Titan's[2] dream,
Where a strange sun, long set, doth beam
　Through Montezuma's[3] cypress
　　bough:

Through the fern wilderness forlorn            10
Glisten the giants harts' great horn,
　And serpents vast with helméd brow.

The measureless from caverns rise
With steps of earthquake, thunderous
　　cries,
　And graze upon the lofty wood;
The palmy grove, through which doth
　　gleam
Such antediluvian ocean's steam,
　Haunts shadowy my domestic mood.
　　　　　　　　　　　　　　(*c. 1837*)

---

[1] In *The Odyssey* deceptive dreams come from
the Gate of Ivory, true dreams from the Gate
of Horn.
[2] The Titans were children of Uranus (heaven)
and Gaea (earth), a race of giants who stormed
heaven.
[3] Aztec ruler of Mexico at the time of the Spanish
Conquest

## The Phantom Wooer

A ghost, that loved a lady fair,
Ever in the starry air
   Of midnight at her pillow stood;
And, with a sweetness skies above
The luring words of human love,
   Her soul the phantom wooed.
Sweet and sweet is their poisoned note,
The little snakes of silver throat,
In mossy skulls that nest and lie,
Ever singing, "Die, oh! die."     *10*

Young soul put off your flesh, and come
With me into the quiet tomb,
   Our bed is lovely, dark, and sweet;
The earth will swing us as she goes,
Beneath our coverlid of snows,
   And the warm leaden sheet.
Dear and dear is their poisoned note,
The little snakes of silver throat,
In mossy skulls that nest and lie,
Ever singing "Die, oh! die."  *(1851)*   *20*

---

## RALPH WALDO EMERSON / 1803–1882

### The Rhodora[1]

#### *ON BEING ASKED, WHENCE IS THE FLOWER?*

In May, when sea-winds pierced our solitudes,
I found the fresh Rhodora in the woods,
Spreading its leafless blooms in a damp nook,
To please the desert and the sluggish brook.
The purple petals, fallen in the pool,
Made the black water with their beauty gay;
Here might the red-bird come his plumes to cool,
And court the flower that cheapens his array.
Rhodora! if the sages ask thee why
This charm is wasted on the earth and sky,    *10*
Tell them, dear, that if eyes were made for seeing,
Then Beauty is its own excuse for being:
Why thou wert there, O rival of the rose!
I never thought to ask, I never knew:
But, in my simple ignorance, suppose
The self-same Power that brought me there brought
   you.  *(1834)*

### Each and All

Little thinks, in the field, yon red-cloaked clown[1]
Of thee from the hill-top looking down;
The heifer that lows in the upland farm,
Far-heard, lows not thine ear to charm;

---

[1] a small shrub related to the rhododendron    [1] farm laborer

The sexton, tolling his bell at noon,
Deems not that great Napoleon
Stops his horse, and lists with delight,
Whilst his files sweep round yon Alpine height;
Nor knowest thou what argument
Thy life to thy neighbor's creed has lent.                          10
Are all needed by each one;
Nothing is fair or good alone.
I thought the sparrow's note from heaven,
Singing at dawn on the alder bough;
I brought him home, in his nest, at even;
He sings the song, but it cheers not now,
For I did not bring home the river and sky;
He sang to my ear,—they sang to my eye.
The delicate shells lay on the shore;
The bubbles of the latest wave                                      20
Fresh pearls to their enamel gave,
And the bellowing of the savage sea
Greeted their safe escape to me.
I wiped away the weeds and foam,
I fetched my sea-born treasures home;
But the poor, unsightly, noisome things
Had left their beauty on the shore
With the sun and the sand and the wild uproar.
The lover watched his graceful maid,
As 'mid the virgin train she strayed,                               30
Nor knew her beauty's best attire
Was woven still by the snow-white choir.
As last she came to his hermitage,
Like the bird from the woodlands to the cage;—
The gay enchantment was undone,
A gentle wife, but fairy none.
Then I said, "I covet truth;
Beauty is unripe childhood's cheat;
I leave it behind with the games of youth:"—
As I spoke, beneath my feet                                         40
The ground-pine curled its pretty wreath,
Running over the club-moss[2] burrs;
I inhaled the violet's breath;
Around me stood the oaks and firs;
Pine-cones and acorns lay on the ground;
Over me soared the eternal sky,
Full of light and of deity;
Again I saw, again I heard,
The rolling river, the morning bird;—
Beauty through my senses stole;                                     50
I yielded myself to the perfect whole.   (*1834*)

---

[2] low-growing, ground-cover plants

## The Snow-Storm

Announced by all the trumpets of the sky,
Arrives the snow, and, driving o'er the fields,
Seems nowhere to alight: the whited air
Hides hills and woods, the river, and the heaven,
And veils the farm-house at the garden's end.
The sled and traveler stopped, the courier's feet
Delayed, all friends shut out, the housemates sit
Around the radiant fireplace, enclosed
In a tumultuous privacy of storm.

Come see the north wind's masonry. 10
Out of an unseen quarry evermore
Furnished with tile, the fierce artificer
Curves his white bastions with projected roof
Round every windward stake, or tree, or door.
Speeding, the myriad-handed, his wild work
So fanciful, so savage, nought cares he
For number or proportion. Mockingly,
On coop or kennel he hangs Parian[1] wreaths;
A swan-like form invests the hidden thorn;
Fills up the farmer's lane from wall to wall, 20
Maugre[2] the farmer's sighs; and at the gate
A tapering turret overtops the work.
And when his hours are numbered, and the world
Is all his own, retiring, as he were not,
Leaves, when the sun appears, astonished Art
To mimic in slow structures, stone by stone,
Built in an age, the mad wind's night-work,
The frolic architecture of the snow. (*1835*)

## Nature

The rounded world is fair to see,
Nine times folded in mystery:
Though baffled seers cannot impart
The secret of its laboring heart,
Throb thine with Nature's throbbing
   breast,
And all is clear from east to west.
Spirit that lurks each form within
Beckons the spirit of its kin;
Self-kindled every atom glows
And hints the future which it
   owes.[1] (*1844*) 10

## Ode

*INSCRIBED TO W. H. CHANNING*

Though loathe to grieve
The evil time's sole patriot,
I cannot leave
My honied thought
For the priest's cant,
Or statesman's rant.

If I refuse
My study for their politique,
Which at the best is trick,
The angry Muse 10
Puts confusion in my brain.

---

[1] of Paros, one of the Cyclades islands in the Aegean noted for its beautiful marble

[2] despite

[1] owns

But who is he that prates
Of the culture of mankind,
Of better arts and life?
Go, blindworm, go,
Behold the famous States
Harrying Mexico
With rifle and with knife![1]

Or who, with accent bolder,
Dare praise the freedom-loving
    mountaineer?                                      20
I found by thee, O rushing Contoocook![2]
And in thy valleys, Agiochook![3]
The jackels of the negro-holder.

The God who made New Hampshire
Taunted the lofty land
With little men;—
Small bat and wren
House in the oak:—
If earth-fire cleave
The upheaved land, and bury the folk,   30
The southern crocodile would grieve.
Virtue palters; Right is hence;
Freedom praised, but hid;
Funeral eloquence
Rattles the coffin-lid.

What boots thy zeal,
O glowing friend,
That would indignant rend
The northland from the south?
Wherefore? to what good end?            40
Boston Bay and Bunker Hill
Would serve things still;
Things are of the snake.

The horseman serves the horse,
The neatherd serves the neat,
The merchant serves the purse,
The eater serves his meat;
'Tis the day of the chattel,
Web to weave, and corn to grind;
Things are in the saddle,                      50
And ride mankind.

There are two laws discrete,
Not reconciled,—
Law for man, and law for thing;
The last builds town and fleet,
But it runs wild,
And doth the man unking.

'Tis fit the forest fall,
The steep be graded,
The mountain tunneled,                      60
The sand shaded,
The orchard planted,
The glebe tilled,
The prairie granted,
The steamer built.

Let man serve law for man;
Live for friendship, live for love,
For truth's and harmony's behoof;
The state may follow how it can,
As Olympus[4] follows Jove.[5]              70

    Yet do not I implore
The wrinkled shopman to my sounding
    woods,
Nor bid the unwilling senator
Ask votes of thrushes in the solitudes.
Every one to his chosen work;—
Foolish hands may mix and mar;
Wise and sure the issues are.
Round they roll till dark is light,
Sex to sex, and even to odd;—
The over-god                                       80
Who marries Right to Might,
Who peoples, unpeoples,—
He who exterminates
Races by stronger races,
Black by white faces,—
Knows to bring honey
Out of the lion;[6]
Grafts gentlest scion
On pirate and Turk.

The Cossack eats Poland,                     90
Like stolen fruit;

---

[1] the Mexican War (1846–48), which Emerson, like many others, opposed as an effort to extend slave territory. Channing had urged Emerson to take an active part in opposition to the war.
[2] river in New Hampshire
[3] the White Mountains

[4] dwelling place of the god, Jove
[5] king of the gods
[6] Samson killed a lion and left it exposed; after a time bees had built honeycomb in the putrefying carcass (Judges 14:5–9).

Her last noble is ruined,
Her last poet mute:
Straight, into double band
The victors divide;

Half for freedom strike and stand;[7]—
The astonished Muse finds thousands at
her side.  (*1846*)

## Hamatreya

Bulkeley, Hunt, Willard, Hosmer, Meriam, Flint,
Possessed the land which rendered to their toil
Hay, corn, roots, hemp, flax, apples, wool and wood.
Each of these landlords walked amidst his farm,
Saying, "'Tis mine, my children's and my name's.
How sweet the west wind sounds in my own trees!
How graceful climb those shadows on my hill!
I fancy these pure waters and the flags
Know me, as does my dog: we sympathize;
And, I affirm, my actions smack of the soil."                    10

Where are these men? Asleep beneath their grounds:
And strangers, fond as they, their furrows plough.
Earth laughs in flowers, to see her boastful boys
Earth-proud, proud of the earth which is not theirs;
Who steer the plough, but cannot steer their feet
Clear of the grave.
They added ridge to valley, brook to pond,
And sighed for all that bounded their domain;
"This suits me for a pasture; that's my park;
We must have clay, lime, gravel, granite-ledge,                  20
And misty lowland, where to go for peat.
The land is well,—lies fairly to the south.
'T is good, when you have crossed the sea and back,
To find the sitfast acres where you left them."
Ah! the hot owner sees not Death, who adds
Him to his land, a lump of mould the more.
Hear what the Earth says:—

### EARTH-SONG

"Mine and yours;
Mine, not yours.
Earth endures;                                                   30
Stars abide—
Shine down in the old sea;
Old are the shores;
But where are old men?
I who have seen much,
Such have I never seen.

---

[7] After decades of Russian oppression, Polish patriots carried out an uprising in 1830.

"The lawyer's deed
Ran sure,
In tail,
To them, and to their heirs                              *40*
Who shall succeed,
Without fail,
Forevermore.

"Here is the land,
Shaggy with wood,
With its old valley,
Mound and flood.
But the heritors?—
Fled like the flood's foam.
The lawyer, and the laws,                                *50*
And the kingdom,
Clean swept herefrom.

"They called me theirs,
Who so controlled me;
Yet every one
Wished to stay, and is gone,
How am I theirs,
If they cannot hold me,
But I hold them?"

When I heard the Earth-song                              *60*
I was no longer brave;
My avarice cooled
Like lust in the chill of the grave.   *(1847)*

## Nature

A subtle chain of countless rings
The next unto the farthest brings;
The eye reads omens where it goes,
And speaks all languages the rose;
And, striving to be man, the worm
Mounts through all the spires of form.
                                       *(1849)*

## Days

Daughters of Time, the hypocritic Days,
Muffled and dumb like barefoot
    dervishes,[1]
And marching single in an endless file,
Bring diadems and fagots in their hands.
To each they offer gifts after his will,
Bread, kingdoms, stars, and sky that
    holds them all.
I, in my pleachéd[2] garden, watched the
    pomp,
Forgot my morning wishes, hastily
Took a few herbs and apples, and the
    Day
Turned and departed silent. I, too late, *10*
Under her solemn fillet[3] saw the scorn.
                                       *(1851)*

---

[1] Moslem mendicant friars          [2] trimmed and trained   [3] headband

## Pan

O what are heroes, prophets, men,
But pipes through which the breath of Pan doth blow
A momentary music. Being's tide
Swells hitherward, and myriads of forms
Live, robed with beauty, painted by the sun;
Their dust, pervaded by the nerves of God,
Throbs with an overmastering energy
Knowing and doing. Ebbs the tide, they lie
White hollow shells upon the desert shore,
But not the less the eternal wave rolls on          *10*
To animate new millions, and exhale
Races and planets, its enchanted foam.

## Terminus

It is time to be old,
To take in sail:—
The god of bounds,
Who sets to seas a shore,
Came to me in his fatal rounds,
And said: "No more!
No farther shoot
Thy broad ambitious branches, and thy
    root.
Fancy departs: no more invent;
Contract thy firmament          *10*
To compass of a tent.
There's not enough for this and that,
Make thy option which of two;
Economize the failing river,
Not the less revere the Giver,
Leave the many and hold the few.
Timely wise accept the terms,
Soften the fall with wary foot;
A little while

Still plan and smile,          *20*
And,—fault of novel germs,—
Mature the unfallen fruit.
Curse, if thou wilt, thy sires,
Bad husbands[1] of their fires,
Who, when they gave thee breath,
Failed to bequeath
The needful sinew stark as once,
The Baresark[2] marrow to thy bones,
But left a legacy of ebbing veins,
Inconstant heat and nerveless reins,—          *30*
Amid the Muses, left thee deaf and
    dumb,
Amid the gladiators, halt and numb."

As the bird trims her to the gale,
I trim myself to the storm of time,
I man the rudder, reef the sail,
Obey the voice at eve obeyed at prime:
"Lowly faithful, banish fear,
Right onward drive unharmed;
The port, well worth the cruise, is near,
And every wave is charmed."   (*1867*)  *40*

---

[1] conservers
[2] in Norse mythology, a warrior who in battle was seized by a madness that made him a formidable foe

## Mezzo Cammin[1]

Half of my life is gone, and I have let
The years slip from me and have not fulfilled
The aspiration of my youth, to build
Some tower of song with lofty parapet.
Not indolence, nor pleasure, nor the fret
Of restless passions that would not be stilled,
But sorrow,[2] and a care that almost killed,
Kept me from what I may accomplish yet;
Though, half-way up the hill, I see the Past
Lying beneath me with its sounds and sights,—     *10*
A city in the twilight dim and vast,
With smoking roofs, soft bells, and gleaming lights,—
And hear above me on the autumnal blast
The cataract of Death far thundering from the heights.   (*1842*)

## The Arsenal at Springfield

This is the Arsenal. From floor to ceiling,
  Like a huge organ, rise the burnished arms;
But from their silent pipes no anthem pealing
  Startles the villages with strange alarms.

Ah! what a sound will rise, how wild and dreary,
  When the death-angel touches those swift keys!
What loud lament and dismal Miserere
  Will mingle with their awful symphonies!

I hear even now the infinite fierce chorus,
  The cries of agony, the endless groan,     *10*
Which, through the ages that have gone before us,
  In long reverberations reach our own.

On helm and harness rings the Saxon hammer,
  Through Cimbric forest roars the Norseman's song,
And loud, amid the universal clamor,
  O'er distant deserts sounds the Tartar gong.

I hear the Florentine, who from his palace
  Wheels out his battle-bell with dreadful din,
And Aztec priests upon their teocallis
  Beat the wild war-drums made of serpent's skin;     *20*

The tumult of each sacked and burning village;
  The shout that every prayer for mercy drowns;

---

[1] the middle of the journey. Longfellow was thirty-five when he wrote this sonnet; he had lived half of the "three score years and ten" allotted in the Bible.

[2] Longfellow's first wife died in 1835.

The soldiers' revels in the midst of pillage;
    The wail of famine in beleaguered towns;

The bursting shell, the gateway wrenched asunder,
    The rattling musketry, the clashing blade;
And ever and anon, in tones of thunder
    The diapason of the cannonade.

Is it, O man, with such discordant noises,
    With such accurséd instruments as these,           *30*
Thou drownest Nature's sweet and kindly voices,
    And jarrest the celestial harmonies?

Were half the power that fills the world with terror,
    Were half the wealth bestowed on camps and courts,
Given to redeem the human mind from error,
    There were no need of arsenals or forts:

The warrior's name would be a name abhorréd!
    And every nation, that should lift again
Its hand against a brother, on its forehead
    Would wear forevermore the curse of Cain!           *40*

Down the dark future, through long generations,
    The echoing sounds grow fainter and then cease;
And like a bell, with solemn, sweet vibrations,
    I hear once more the voice of Christ say, "Peace!"

Peace! and no longer from its brazen portals
    The blast of War's great organ shakes the skies!
But beautiful as songs of the immortals,
    The holy melodies of love arise.   (*1846*)

## Sonnets on the Divina Commedia[1]

### I

Oft have I seen at some cathedral door
A laborer, pausing in the dust and heat,
Lay down his burden, and with reverent feet
Enter, and cross himself, and on the floor
Kneel to repeat his paternoster[2] o'er;
Far off the noises of the world retreat;
The loud vociferations of the street
Become an undistinguishable roar.
So, as I enter here from day to day,
And leave my burden at this minster[3] gate,           *10*
Kneeling in prayer, and not ashamed to pray,
The tumult of the time disconsolate

---

[1] Longfellow translated Dante's *Divine Comedy* in the 1860s.   [2] "Our Father": the Lord's Prayer   [3] church attached to a monastery

To inarticulate murmurs dies away,
While the eternal ages watch and wait.

II

How strange the sculptures that adorn these towers!
This crowd of statues, in whose folded sleeves
Birds build their nests; while canopied with leaves
Parvis[1] and portal bloom like trellised bowers,
And the vast minster seems a cross of flowers!
But fiends and dragons on the gargoyled eaves
Watch the dead Christ between the living thieves,
And, underneath, the traitor Judas lowers!
Ah! from what agonies of heart and brain,
What exultations trampling on despair,                                10
What tenderness, what tears, what hate of wrong,
What passionate outcry of a soul in pain,
Uprose this poem of the earth and air,
This medieval miracle of song!

III

I enter, and I see thee in the gloom
Of the long aisles, O poet saturnine!
And strive to make my steps keep pace with thine.
The air is filled with some unknown perfume;
The congregation of the dead make room
For thee to pass; the votive tapers shine;
Like rooks that haunt Ravenna's[1] groves of pine
The hovering echoes fly from tomb to tomb.
From the confessionals I hear arise
Rehearsals[2] of forgotten tragedies,                                 10
And lamentations from the crypts below;
And then a voice celestial that begins
With the pathetic words, "Although your sins
As scarlet be," and ends with "as the snow."[3]

IV

With snow-white veil and garments as of flame,
She[1] stands before thee, who so long ago
Filled thy young heart with passion and the woe
From which thy song and all its splendors came;
And while with stern rebuke she speaks thy name,
The ice about thy heart melts as the snow
On mountain heights, and in swift overflow
Comes gushing from thy lips in sobs of shame.
Thou makest full confession; and a gleam,
As of the dawn on some dark forest cast,                             10

---

[1] an enclosed square before the church
[1] Italian city where Dante spent his last years and
was buried
[2] retellings

[3] Isaiah, 1:18: "though your sins be as scarlet,
they shall be as white as snow."
[1] Beatrice, Dante's beloved

Seems on thy lifted forehead to increase;
Lethe[2] and Eunoë[3]—the remembered dream
And the forgotten sorrow—bring at last
That perfect pardon which is perfect peace.

### V

I lift mine eyes, and all the windows blaze
With forms of saints and holy men who died,
Here martyred and hereafter glorified;
And the great Rose[1] upon its leaves displays
Christ's triumph, and the angelic roundelays,
With splendor upon splendor multiplied;
And Beatrice again at Dante's side
No more rebukes, but smiles her words of praise.
And then the organ sounds, and unseen choirs
Sing the old Latin hymns of peace and love,                        *10*
And benedictions of the Holy Ghost;
And the melodious bells among the spires
O'er all the house-tops and through heaven above
Proclaim the elevation of the Host![2]

### VI

O star of morning and of liberty!
O bringer of the light, whose splendor shines
Above the darkness of the Apennines,[1]
Forerunner of the day that is to be!
The voices of the city and the sea,
The voices of the mountains and the pines,
Repeat thy song, till the familiar lines
Are footpaths for the thought of Italy!
Thy flame is blown abroad from all the heights,
Through all the nations, and a sound is heard,                      *10*
As of a mighty wind, and men devout,
Strangers of Rome,[2] and the new proselytes,
In their own language hear the wondrous word,
And many are amazed and many doubt.   (*1864–1867*)

## Killed at the Ford

He is dead, the beautiful youth,
The heart of honor, the tongue of truth,
He, the life and light of us all,
Whose voice was blithe as a bugle-call,

---

[2] the river of forgetfulness in the underworld
[3] the river of remembrance of the good

[1] Dante's climactic vision in "Paradiso" is of a rose whose petals are various personages in the Christian story. The rose symbolizes the all-encompassing unity and perfect harmony of God. Longfellow, continuing his conceit of viewing *The Divine Comedy* as a cathedral, refers also to the circular "rose" window of stained glass which is customarily located over the portal of a Gothic cathedral.

[2] the particle of bread held aloft in the hands of the celebrant during the Consecration of the Mass

[1] central spine of mountains that runs the length of Italy

[2] non-Catholics

Whom all eyes followed with one consent,
The cheer of whose laugh, and whose pleasant word,
Hushed all murmurs of discontent.

Only last night, as we rode along,
Down the dark of the mountain gap,
To visit the picket-guard at the ford,                              10
Little dreaming of any mishap,
He was humming the words of some old song:
"Two red roses he had on his cap
And another he bore at the point of his sword."

Sudden and swift a whistling ball
Came out of a wood, and the voice was still;
Something I heard in the darkness fall,
And for a moment my blood grew chill;
I spake in a whisper, as he who speaks
In a room where some one is lying dead;                             20
But he made no answer to what I said.

We lifted him up to his saddle again,
And through the mire and the mist and the rain
Carried him back to the silent camp,
And laid him as if asleep on his bed;
And I saw by the light of the surgeon's lamp
Two white roses upon his cheeks,
And one, just over his heart, blood-red!

And I saw in a vision how far and fleet
That fatal bullet went speeding forth,                              30
Till it reached a town in the distant North,
Till it reached a house in a sunny street,
Till it reached a heart that ceased to beat
Without a murmur, without a cry;
And a bell was tolled, in that far-off town,
For one who had passed from cross to crown,
And the neighbors wondered that she should die.   (*1867*)


## Milton

I pace the sounding sea-beach and behold
How the voluminous billows roll and run,
Upheaving and subsiding, while the sun
Shines through their sheeted emerald far unrolled,
And the ninth wave, slow gathering fold by fold
All its loose-flowing garments into one,
Plunges upon the shore, and floods the dun
Pale reach of sands, and changes them to gold.
So in majestic cadence rise and fall
The mighty undulations of thy song,                                 10

O sightless bard, England's Mæonides!
And ever and anon, high over all
Uplifted, a ninth wave superb and strong.
Floods all the soul with its melodious seas.  *(1875)*

## Keats

The young Endymion sleeps Endymion's sleep;
The shepherd-boy whose tale was left half told!
The solemn grove uplifts its shield of gold
To the red rising moon, and loud and deep
The nightingale is singing from the steep;
It is midsummer, but the air is cold;
Can it be death? Alas, beside the fold
A shepherd's pipe lies shattered near his sheep.
Lo! in the moonlight gleams a marble white,
On which I read: "Here lieth one whose name          *10*
Was writ in water." And was this the meed
Of his sweet singing? Rather let me write:
"The smoking flax before it burst to flame
Was quenched by death, and broken the bruised reed."  *(1875)*

## The Tide Rises, The Tide Falls

The tide rises, the tide falls,
The twilight darkens, the curlew calls;
Along the sea-sands damp and brown
The traveller hastens toward the town,
      And the tide rises, the tide falls.

Darkness settles on roofs and walls,
But the sea, the sea in the darkness calls,
The little waves, with their soft, white hands,
Efface the footprints in the sands,
      And the tide rises, the tide falls.          *10*

The morning breaks; the steeds in their stalls
Stamp and neigh, as the hostler calls;
The day returns, but nevermore
Returns the traveller to the shore,
      And the tide rises, the tide falls.  *(1880)*

## The Cross of Snow

In the long, sleepless watches of the night,
A gentle face—the face of one long dead—
Looks at me from the wall, where round its head
The night-lamp casts a halo of pale light.
Here in this room she died; and soul more white

Never through martyrdom of fire was led
To its repose; nor can in books be read
The legend of a life more benedight.
There is a mountain in the distant West
That, sun-defying, in its deep ravines                        10
Displays a cross of snow upon its side.
Such is the cross I wear upon my breast
These eighteen years, through all the changing scenes
And seasons, changeless since the day she died.   (*1886*)


## EDGAR ALLAN POE / 1809–1849

### A Dream Within a Dream

Take this kiss upon the brow!
And, in parting from you now,
Thus much let me avow—
You are not wrong, who deem
That my days have been a dream;
Yet if Hope has flown away
In a night, or in a day,
In a vision, or in none,
Is it therefore the less *gone*?
*All* that we see or seem                           10
Is but a dream within a dream.

I stand amid the roar
Of a surf-tormented shore,
And I hold within my hand
Grains of the golden sand—
How few! yet how they creep
Through my fingers to the deep,
While I weep—while I weep!
O God! can I not grasp
Them with a tighter clasp?                          20
O God! can I not save
*One* from the pitiless wave?
Is *all* that we see or seem
But a dream within a dream?   (*1827*)

### Romance

Romance, who loves to nod and sing,
With drowsy head and folded wing,
Among the green leaves as they shake
Far down within some shadowy lake,
To me a painted paroquet
Hath been—a most familiar bird—
Taught me my alphabet to say—
To lisp my very earliest word
While in the wild wood I did lie,
A child—with a most knowing eye.                    10

Of late, eternal Condor years
So shake the very Heaven on high
With tumult as they thunder by,
I have no time for idle cares
Through gazing on the unquiet sky.
And when an hour with calmer wings
Its down upon my spirit flings—
That little time with lyre and rhyme
To while away—forbidden things!
My heart would feel to be a crime                   20
Unless it trembled with the strings.
                                                (*1829*)

### Sonnet: To Science

Science! true daughter of Old Time thou art!
Who alterest all things with thy peering eyes.
Why preyest thou thus upon the poet's heart,
Vulture, whose wings are dull realities?

How should he love thee? or how deem thee wise,
Who wouldst not leave him in his wandering
To seek for treasure in the jewelled skies,
Albeit he soared with an undaunted wing?
Hast thou not dragged Diana[1] from her car?
And driven the Hamadryad[2] from the wood          10
To seek a shelter in some happier star?
Hast thou not torn the Naiad[3] from her flood,
The Elfin[4] from the green grass, and from me
The summer dream beneath the tamarind tree?[5]          (*1829*)

## The City in the Sea

Lo! Death has reared himself a throne
In a strange city lying alone
Far down within the dim West,
Where the good and the bad and the
    worst and the best
Have gone to their eternal rest.
There shrines and palaces and towers
(Time-eaten towers that tremble not!)
Resemble nothing that is ours.
Around, by lifting winds forgot,
Resignedly beneath the sky          10
The melancholy waters lie.

No rays from the holy heaven come
    down
On the long night-time of that town;
But light from out the lurid sea
Streams up the turrets silently—
Gleams up the pinnacles far and free—
Up domes—up spires—up kingly halls—
Up fanes—up Babylon-like walls—
Up shadowy long-forgotten bowers
Of sculptured ivy and stone flowers—          20
Up many and many a marvellous shrine
Whose wreathéd friezes intertwine
The viol, the violet, and the vine.
Resignedly beneath the sky
The melancholy waters lie.
So blend the turrets and shadows there
That all seem pendulous in air,
While from a proud tower in the town
Death looks gigantically down.

There open fanes and gaping graves          30
Yawn level with the luminous waves;
But not the riches there that lie
In each idol's diamond eye—
Not the gayly-jewelled dead
Tempt the waters from their bed;
For no ripples curl, alas!
Along that wilderness of glass—
No swellings tell that winds may be
Upon some far-off happier sea—
No heavings hint that winds have
    been          40
On seas less hideously serene.

But lo, a stir is in the air!
The wave—there is a movement there!
As if the towers had thrust aside,
In slightly sinking, the dull tide—
As if their tops had feebly given
A void within the filmy Heaven.
The waves have now a redder glow—
The hours are breathing faint and low—
And when, amid no earthly moans,          50
Down, down that town shall settle hence,
Hell, rising from a thousand thrones,
Shall do it reverence.          (*1831*)

## To Helen

Helen,[1] thy beauty is to me
    Like those Nicéan[2] barks of yore,
That gently, o'er a perfumed sea,
    The weary, way-worn wanderer bore
    To his own native shore.

---

[1] a fertility goddess later identified as a huntress
and as goddess of the moon
[2] a wood nymph          [3] a fresh-water nymph
[4] elf

[5] a tropical tree, here representing the exotic
[1] probably Helen of Troy
[2] pertaining to Nicea, a city in Asia Minor

On desperate seas long wont to roam,            Lo! in yon brilliant window-niche
   Thy hyacinth[3] hair, thy classic face,         How statue-like I see thee stand,
Thy Naiad airs[4] have brought me home            The agate lamp within thy hand!
   To the glory that was Greece                     Ah, Psyche,[5] from the regions which
And the grandeur that was Rome.    *10*            Are Holy Land!  (*1831*)


# OLIVER WENDELL HOLMES / 1809–1894


## The Ballad of the Oysterman

It was a tall young oysterman lived by the river-side,
His shop was just upon the bank, his boat was on the tide;
The daughter of a fisherman, that was so straight and slim,
Lived over on the other bank, right opposite to him.

It was the pensive oysterman that saw a lovely maid,
Upon a moonlight evening, a sitting in the shade:
He saw her wave her handkerchief, as much as if to say,
"I'm wide awake, young oysterman, and all the folks away."

Then up arose the oysterman, and to himself said he,
"I guess I'll leave the skiff at home, for fear that folks should see; *10*
I read it in the story-book, that, for to kiss his dear,
Leander swam the Hellespont,—and I will swim this here."

And he has leaped into the waves, and crossed the shining stream,
And he has clambered up the bank, all in the moonlight gleam;
Oh there were kisses sweet as dew, and words as soft as rain,—
But they have heard her father's step, and in he leaps again!

Out spoke the ancient fisherman,—"Oh, what was that, my
    daughter?"
"'Twas nothing but a pebble, sir, I threw into the water."
"And what is that, pray tell me, love, that paddles off so fast?"
"It's nothing but a porpoise, sir, that's been a-swimming past."  *20*

Out spoke the ancient fisherman,—"Now bring me my harpoon!
I'll get into my fishing boat, and fix the fellow soon."
Down fell that pretty innocent, as falls a snow-white lamb,
Her hair dropped round her pallid cheeks, like seaweed on a clam.

Alas for those two loving ones! she waked not from her swound,
And he was taken with the cramp, and in the waves was drowned;
But Fate has metamorphosed them, in pity of their woe,
And now they keep an oyster-shop for mermaids down below.  (*1830*)

---

[3] a classical epithet frequently applied to hair,    [4] the graceful manner of a fresh-water nymph
probably in reference to curliness                     [5] the soul

## The Chambered Nautilus[1]

This is the ship of pearl, which, poets feign,
　　Sails the unshadowed main,—
　　The venturous bark that flings
On the sweet summer wind its purpled wings
In gulfs enchanted, where the Siren[2] sings.
　　And coral reefs lie bare,
Where the cold sea-maids rise to sun their streaming hair.

Its webs of living gauze no more unfurl;
　　Wrecked is the ship of pearl!
　　And every chambered cell,                                              *10*
Where its dim dreaming life was wont to dwell,
As the frail tenant shaped his growing shell,
　　Before thee lies revealed,—
Its irised ceiling rent, its sunless crypt unsealed!

Year after year beheld the silent toil
　　That spread his lustrous coil;
　　Still, as the spiral grew,
He left the past year's dwelling for the new,
Stole with soft step its shining archway through,
　　Built up its idle door,                                                *20*
Stretched in his last-found home, and knew the old no more.

Thanks for the heavenly message brought by thee,
　　Child of the wandering sea,
　　Cast from her lap, forlorn!
From thy dead lips a clearer note is born
Than ever Triton[3] blew from wreathéd horn!
　　While on mine ear it rings,
Through the deep caves of thought I hear a voice that sings:—

Build thee more stately mansions, O my soul,
　　As the swift seasons roll!                                             *30*
　　Leave thy low-vaulted past!
Let each new temple, nobler than the last,
Shut thee from heaven with a dome more vast,
　　Till thou at length art free,
Leaving thine outgrown shell by life's unresting sea!   (*1858*)

---

[1] a shellfish which develops a spiral shell in which each year's growth is divided from earlier portions by a septum

[2] sea nymph whose song enthralled passing voyagers

[3] sea god who blew his horn to calm the waves

# JONES VERY / 1813–1880

## Yourself

'Tis to yourself I speak; you cannot know
Him whom I call in speaking such an one,
For thou beneath the earth lie buried low,
Which he alone as living walks upon;
Thou mayst at times have heard him speak to you,
And often wished perchance that you were he;
And I must ever wish that it were true,
For then thou couldst hold fellowship with me;
But now thou hear'st us talk as strangers, met
Above the room wherein thou liest abed;                  *10*
A word perhaps loud spoken thou mayst get,
Or hear our feet when heavily they tread;
But he who speaks, or him who's spoken to,
Must both remain as strangers still to you.   *(1839)*

## On the Completion of the Pacific Telegraph

Swift to the western bounds of this wide land,
Swifter than light, the Electric Message flies;
The continent is in a moment spanned,
And furthest West to furthest East replies.
While War asunder drives the nearest States,
And doth to them all intercourse deny,
Science new bonds of Union still creates,
And the most distant brings forever nigh!
I hail this omen for our Country's cause;
For it the stars do in their courses fight!                *10*
In vain men strive against the eternal laws
Of Peace, and Liberty, and social Right,
Rebel against the light, and hope to stay
The dawn on earth of Freedom's perfect day.   *(1886)*

## The Broken Bowl

The fountain flows, but where the bowl
    To catch from heaven the living stream
That ever shall refresh the soul,
    And make life's ills a passing dream?

'T is broken at the cistern, broke;
    Its waters spilled upon the ground;
The words of old the preacher spoke,
    I too their truth like him have found.

Prepare, prepare new vessels still,
 Though broken fragments round thee lie; 10
Thou must from hence thy pitcher fill,
 And often drink, or thou wilt die.

Behold the Rock, that smitten gave
 To Israel, on the burning sand,
Life in its cool, refreshing wave;
 'T will flow when smitten by thy hand.

Ho all that thirst! come, drink ye all!
 The fountain pours its waters free.
Come, heed the Saviour's earnest call;
 Come, every one who thirsts, to me.   *(1886)* 20

## The New World

The night that has no star lit up by God,
The day that round men shines who still are blind,
The earth their grave-turned feet for ages trod,
And sea swept over by His mighty wind,—
All these have passed away; the melting dream
That flitted o'er the sleepers' half-shut eye,
When touched by morning's golden-darting beam;
And he beholds around the earth and sky
What ever real stands; the rolling spheres,
And heaving billows of the boundless main, 10
That show, though time is past, no trace of years,
And earth restored he sees as his again,
The earth that fades not, and the heavens that stand,
Their strong foundations laid by God's right hand!   *(1886)*

## CHRISTOPHER PEARSE CRANCH / 1813–1892

### The Pines and the Sea

Beyond the low marsh-meadows and the beach,
Seen through the hoary trunks of windy pines,
The long blue level of the ocean shines.
The distant surf, with hoarse, complaining speech,
Out from its sandy barrier seems to reach;
And while the sun behind the woods declines,
The moaning sea with sighing boughs combines,
And waves and pines make answer, each to each.

O melancholy soul, whom far and near,
In life, faith, hope, the same sad undertone                          *10*
Pursues from thought to thought! thou needs must hear
An old refrain, too much, too long thine own:
'Tis thy mortality infects thine ear;
The mournful strain was in thyself alone.

## Enosis[1]

Thought is deeper than all speech,
  Feeling deeper than all thought:
Souls to souls can never teach
  What unto themselves was taught.

We are spirits clad in veils;
  Man by man was never seen;
All our deep communing fails
  To remove the shadowy screen.

Heart to heart was never known;
  Mind with mind did never meet;   *10*
We are columns left alone
  Of a temple once complete.

Like the stars that gem the sky,
  Far apart though seeming near,
In our light we scattered lie;
  All is thus but starlight here.

What is social company
  But a babbling summer stream:
What our wise philosophy
  But the glancing of a dream?   *20*

Only when the sun of love
  Melts the scattered stars of thought,
Only when we live above
  What the dim-eyed world hath taught,

Only when our souls are fed
  By the Fount which gave them birth,
And by inspiration led
  Which they never drew from earth,

We, like parted drops of rain,
  Swelling till they meet and run,   *30*
Shall be all absorbed again,
  Melting, flowing into one.

# HENRY DAVID THOREAU / 1817–1862

## Light-Winged Smoke, Icarian Bird

Light-winged Smoke, Icarian bird,
Melting thy pinions in thy upward flight,
Lark without song, and messenger of dawn,
Circling above the hamlets as thy nest;
Or else, departing dream, and shadowy form
Of midnight vision, gathering up thy skirts;
By night star-veiling, and by day
Darkening the light and blotting out the sun;
Go thou my incense upward from this hearth,
And ask the gods to pardon this clear flame.   (*1895*)   *10*

---

[1] union

## Lines

Though all the Fates should prove
    unkind,
Leave not your native land behind.
The ship, becalmed, at length stands still;
The steed must rest beneath the hill;
But swiftly still our fortunes pace
To find us out in every place.

The vessel, though her masts be firm,
Beneath her copper bears a worm;
Around the Cape,[1] across the Line,[2]
Till fields of ice her course confine;    *10*
It matters not how smooth the breeze,
How shallow or how deep the seas.

Whether she bears Manilla twine,
Or in her hold Madeira wine,
Or China teas, or Spanish hides,
In port or quarantine she rides;
Far from New England's blustering shore,
New England's worm her bulk shall bore,
And sink her in the Indian seas,—
Twine, wine, and hides, and China
    teas.    (*1895*)    *20*

## Woof of the Sun, Ethereal Gauze

Woof of the sun, ethereal gauze,
Woven of Nature's richest stuffs,
Visible heat, air-water, and dry sea,
Last conquest of the eye;
Toil of the day displayed, sun-dust,
Aerial surf upon the shores of earth,
Ethereal estuary, frith of light,
Breakers of air, billows of heat,
Fine summer spray on inland seas;
Bird of the sun, transparent-winged    *10*
Owlet of noon, soft-pinioned,
From heath or stubble rising without song;
Establish thy serenity o'er the fields.    (*1895*)

## HERMAN MELVILLE / 1819–1891

## The Portent

(*1859*)

Hanging from the beam,
    Slowly swaying (such the law),
Gaunt the shadow on your green,
    Shenandoah!
The cut is on the crown
    (Lo, John Brown),
And the stabs shall heal no more.

Hidden in the cap
    Is the anguish none can draw,
So your future veils its face,    *10*
    Shenandoah!
But the streaming beard is shown
    (Weird John Brown),
The meteor of the war.    (*1866*)

---

[1] Cape Horn    [2] the Equator

## Misgivings

*(1860)*

When ocean clouds over inland hills
   Sweep storming in late autumn brown,
And horror the sodden valley fills,
   And the spire falls crashing in the town,
I muse upon my country's ills—
   The tempest bursting from the waste of Time
On the world's fairest hope linked with man's foulest crime.

Nature's dark side is heeded now—
   (Ah! optimist-cheer disheartened flown)—
A child may read the moody brow          10
   Of yon black mountain lone.
With shouts the torrents down the gorges go,
And storms are formed behind the storm we feel:
The hemlock shakes in the rafter, the oak in the driving keel.   *(1866)*


## Shiloh

### A REQUIEM (APRIL, 1862)

Skimming lightly, wheeling still,
   The swallows fly low
Over the field in clouded days,
   The forest-field of Shiloh—
Over the field where April rain
Solaced the parched ones stretched in pain
Through the pause of night
That followed the Sunday fight
   Around the church of Shiloh—
The church so lone, the log-built one,      10
That echoed to many a parting groan
    And natural prayer
   Of dying foemen mingled there—
Foemen at morn, but friends at eve—
   Fame or country least their care:
(What like a bullet can undeceive!)
   But now they lie low,
While over them the swallows skim,
   And all is hushed at Shiloh.   *(1866)*


## The Maldive Shark

About the Shark, phlegmatical one,
Pale sot of the Maldive sea,
The sleek little pilot-fish, azure and slim,
How alert in attendance be.

From his saw-pit of mouth, from his charnel of maw
They have nothing of harm to dread,
But liquidly glide on his ghastly flank
Or before his Gorgonian head;
Or lurk in the port of serrated teeth
In white triple tiers of glittering gates,                              *10*
And there find a haven when peril's abroad,
An asylum in jaws of the Fates!
They are friends; and friendly they guide him to prey,
Yet never partake of the treat—
Eyes and brains to the dotard lethargic and dull,
Pale ravener of horrible meat.   (*1888*)


# WALT WHITMAN / 1819–1892


## Out of the Cradle Endlessly Rocking

Out of the cradle endlessly rocking,
Out of the mocking-bird's throat, the musical shuttle,
Out of the Ninth-month midnight,
Over the sterile sands and the fields beyond, where the
    child leaving his bed wandered alone, bareheaded,
    barefoot,
Down from the showered halo,
Up from the mystic play of shadows twining and twisting
    as if they were alive,
Out from the patches of briers and blackberries,
From the memories of the bird that chanted to me,
From your memories sad brother, from the fitful risings
    and fallings I heard,
From under that yellow half-moon late-risen and swollen
    as if with tears,                                                   *10*
From those beginning notes of yearning and love there in
    the mist,
From the thousand responses of my heart never to cease,
From the myriad thence-aroused words,
From the word stronger and more delicious than any,
From such as now they start the scene revisiting,
As a flock, twittering, rising, or overhead passing,
Borne hither, ere all eludes me, hurriedly,
A man, yet by these tears a little boy again,
Throwing myself on the sand, confronting the waves,

I, chanter of pains and joys, uniter of here and hereafter,                    20
Taking all hints to use them, but swiftly leaping beyond
    them,
A reminiscence sing.[1]

Once Paumanok,[2]
When the lilac-scent was in the air and Fifth-month
    grass was growing,
Up this seashore in some briers,
Two feathered guests from Alabama, two together,
And their nest, and four light-green eggs spotted with
    brown,
And every day the he-bird to and fro near at hand,
And every day the she-bird crouched on her nest, silent,
    with bright eyes,
And every day I, a curious boy, never too close, never
    disturbing them,                                                            30
Cautiously peering, absorbing, translating.

*Shine! shine! shine!*
*Pour down your warmth, great sun!*
*While we bask, we two together,*

*Two together!*
*Winds blow south, or winds blow north,*
*Day come white, or night come black,*
*Home, or rivers and mountains from home,*
*Singing all time, minding no time,*
*While we two keep together.*                                                   40

Till of a sudden,
May-be killed, unknown to her mate,
One forenoon the she-bird crouched not on the nest,
Nor returned that afternoon, nor the next,
Nor ever appeared again.

And thenceforward all summer in the sound of the sea,
And at night under the full of the moon in calmer
    weather,
Over the hoarse surging of the sea,
Or flitting from brier to brier by day,
I saw, I heard at intervals the remaining one, the he-bird,    50
The solitary guest from Alabama.

*Blow! blow! blow!*
*Blow up sea-winds along Paumanok's shore;*
*I wait and I wait till you blow my mate to me.*

Yes, when the stars glistened,
All night long on the prong of a moss-scalloped stake,
Down almost amid the slapping waves,
Sat the lone singer wonderful causing tears.

---

[1] Whitman echoes the epic formula of Virgil's    the man I sing."
*Aeneid* (as translated by John Dryden): "Arms and    [2] Long Island

He called on his mate,
He poured forth the meanings which I of all men know.          60

Yes my brother I know,
The rest might not, but I have treasured every note,
For more than once dimly down to the beach gliding,
Silent, avoiding the moonbeams, blending myself with the
    shadows,
Recalling now the obscure shapes, the echoes, the sounds
    and sights after their sorts,
The white arms out in the breakers tirelessly tossing,
I, with bare feet, a child, the wind wafting my hair,
Listened long and long.
Listened to keep, to sing, now translating the notes,
Following you my brother.                                      70

*Soothe! soothe! soothe!*
*Close on its wave soothes the wave behind,*
*And again another behind embracing and lapping, every*
    *one close,*
*But my love soothes not me, not me.*

*Low hangs the moon, it rose late,*
*It is lagging—O I think it is heavy with love, with love.*

*O madly the sea pushes upon the land,*
*With love, with love.*

*O night! do I not see my love fluttering out among the*
    *breakers?*
*What is that little black thing I see there in the white?*       80

*Loud! loud! loud!*
*Loud I call to you, my love!*
*High and clear I shoot my voice over the waves,*
*Surely you must know who is here, is here,*
*You must know who I am, my love.*

*Low-hanging moon!*
*What is that dusky spot in your brown yellow?*

*O it is the shape, the shape of my mate!*
*O moon do not keep her from me any longer.*

*Land! land! O land!*                                            90
*Whichever way I turn, O I think you could give me my*
    *mate back again if you only would,*
*For I am almost sure I see her dimly whichever way I*
    *look.*

*O rising stars!*
*Perhaps the one I want so much will rise, will rise with*
    *some of you.*

*O throat! O trembling throat!*
*Sound clearer through the atmosphere!*

*Pierce the woods, the earth,*
*Somewhere listening to catch you must be the one I want.*

*Shake out carols!*
*Solitary here, the night's carols!*                                    100
*Carols of lonesome love! death's carols!*
*Carols under that lagging, yellow, waning moon!*
*O under that moon where she droops down into the*
*    sea!*
*O reckless despairing carols.*

*But soft! sink low!*
*Soft! let me just murmur,*
*And do you wait a moment you husky-noised sea,*
*For somewhere I believe I heard my mate responding to*
*    me,*
*So faint, I must be still, be still to listen,*
*But not altogether still, for then she might not come*
*    immediately to me.*                                                110

*Hither my love!*
*Here I am! here!*
*With this just-sustained note I announce myself to you,*
*This gentle call is for you my love, for you.*

*Do not be decoyed elsewhere,*
*That is the whistle of the wind, it is not my voice,*
*That is the fluttering, the fluttering of the spray,*
*Those are the shadows of leaves.*

*O darkness! O in vain!*
*O I am very sick and sorrowful.*                                       120

*O brown halo in the sky near the moon, drooping upon the*
*    sea!*
*O troubled reflection in the sea!*
*O throat! O throbbing heart!*
*And I singing uselessly, uselessly all the night.*

*O pass! O happy life! O song of joy!*
*In the air, in the woods, over fields,*
*Loved! loved! loved! loved!*
*But my mate no more, no more with me!*
*We two together no more.*

The aria sinking,                                                       130
All else continuing, the stars shining,
The winds blowing, the notes of the birds continuous
    echoing,
With angry moans the fierce old mother incessantly
    moaning,
On the sands of Paumanok's shore gray and rustling,
The yellow half-moon enlarged, sagging down, drooping,
    the face of the sea almost touching,

The boy ecstatic, with his bare feet the waves, with his hair
    the atmosphere dallying,
The love in the heart long pent, now loose, now at last
    tumultuously bursting,
The aria's meaning, the ears, the soul, swiftly depositing,
The strange tears down the cheeks coursing,
The colloquy there, the trio, each uttering,                      *140*
The undertone, the savage old mother incessantly crying,
To the boy's soul's questions sullenly timing, some drowned
    secret hissing,
To the outsetting bard.

Demon or bird! (said the boy's soul,)
Is it indeed toward your mate you sing? or is it really to
    me?
For I, that was a child, my tongue's use sleeping, now I
    have heard you,
Now in a moment I know what I am for, I awake,
And already a thousand singers, a thousand songs, clearer,
    louder and more sorrowful than yours,
A thousand warbling echoes have started to life within
    me, never to die.

O you singer, solitary, singing by yourself, projecting me,        *150*
O solitary me listening, never more shall I cease per-
    petuating you,
Never more shall I escape, never more the reverberations,
Never more the cries of unsatisfied love be absent from
    me,
Never again leave me to be the peaceful child I was before
    what there in the night,
By the sea under the yellow and sagging moon,
The messenger there aroused, the fire, the sweet hell
    within,
The unknown want, the destiny of me.

O give me the clew! (it lurks in the night here somewhere,)
O if I am to have so much, let me have more!

A word then, (for I will conquer it,)                             *160*
The word final, superior to all,
Subtle, sent up—what is it?— I listen;
Are you whispering it, and have been all the time, you
    sea waves?
Is that it from your liquid rims and wet sands?

Whereto answering, the sea,
Delaying not, hurrying not,
Whispered me through the night, and very plainly before
    daybreak,
Lisped to me the low and delicious word death,
And again death, death, death, death,

Hissing melodious, neither like the bird nor like my
  aroused child's heart,                                                  170
But edging near as privately for me rustling at my feet,
Creeping thence steadily up to my ears and laving me
  softly all over.
Death, death, death, death, death.

Which I do not forget,
But fuse the song of my dusky demon and brother,

That he sang to me in the moonlight on Paumanok's gray
  beach,
With the thousand responsive songs at random,
My own songs awaked from that hour,
And with them the key, the word up from the waves,
The word of the sweetest song and all songs,                             180
That strong and delicious word which, creeping to my
  feet,
(Or like some old crone rocking the cradle, swathed in
  sweet garments, bending aside,)
The sea whispered me.    (*1859; 1881*)


## A Noiseless Patient Spider

A noiseless patient spider,
I marked where on a little promontory it stood isolated,
Marked how to explore the vacant vast surrounding,
It launched forth filament, filament, filament, out of itself,
Ever unreeling them, ever tirelessly speeding them.

And you O my soul where you stand,
Surrounded, detached, in measureless oceans of space,
Ceaselessly musing, venturing, throwing, seeking the
  spheres to connect them,
Till the bridge you will need be formed, till the ductile
  anchor hold,
Till the gossamer thread you fling catch somewhere, O my
  soul.    (*1863?*)                                                     10


## Cavalry Crossing a Ford

A line in long array where they wind betwixt green islands,
They take a serpentine course, their arms flash in the sun—
  hark to the musical clank,
Behold the silvery river, in it the splashing horses loitering
  stop to drink,
Behold the brown-faced men, each group, each person a
  picture, the negligent rest on the saddles,

Some emerge on the opposite bank, others are just
    entering the ford—while,
Scarlet and blue and snowy white,
The guidon flags flutter gayly in the wind.  (*1865*)

## A Sight in Camp in the Daybreak Gray and Dim

A sight in camp in the daybreak gray and dim,
As from my tent I emerge so early sleepless,
As slow I walk in the cool fresh air the path near by the
    hospital tent,
Three forms I see on stretchers lying, brought out there
    untended lying,
Over each the blanket spread, ample brownish woolen
    blanket,
Gray and heavy blanket, folding, covering all.

Curious I halt and silent stand,
Then with light fingers I from the face of the nearest the
    first just lift the blanket;
Who are you elderly man so gaunt and grim, with well-grayed
    hair, and flesh all sunken about thy eyes?
Who are you my dear comrade?          *10*

Then to the second I step—and who are you my child and
    darling?
Who are you sweet boy with cheeks yet blooming?

Then to the third—a face nor child nor old, very calm, as
    of beautiful yellow-white ivory;
Young man I think I know you—I think this face is the face
    of the dead Christ himself,
Dead and divine and brother of all, and here again he lies.  (*1865*)

## When Lilacs Last in the Dooryard Bloomed

### I

When lilacs last in the dooryard bloomed,
And the great star early drooped in the western sky in the night,
I mourned, and yet shall mourn with ever-returning spring.

Ever-returning spring, trinity sure to me you bring,
Lilac blooming perennial, and drooping star in the west,
And thought of him I love.

### 2

O powerful western fallen star!
O shades of night—O moody, tearful night!
O great star disappeared—O the black murk that hides the star!
O cruel hands that hold me powerless—O helpless soul of me!    *10*
O harsh surrounding cloud that will not free my soul.

3

In the dooryard fronting an old farm-house near the white-washed palings,
Stands the lilac-bush tall-growing with heart-shaped leaves of rich green,
With many a pointed blossom rising delicate, with the perfume strong I love,
With every leaf a miracle—and from this bush in the dooryard,
With delicate-colored blossoms and heart-shaped leaves of rich green,
A sprig with its flower I break.

4

In the swamp in secluded recesses,
A shy and hidden bird is warbling a song.
Solitary the thrush,                                                                      20
The hermit withdrawn to himself, avoiding the settlements,
Sings by himself a song.

Song of the bleeding throat,
Death's outlet song of life, (for well dear brother I know,
If thou wast not granted to sing thou would'st surely die.)

5

Over the breast of the spring, the land, amid cities,
Amid lanes and through old woods, where lately the violets peeped from
    the ground, spotting the gray debris,
Amid the grass in the fields each side of the lanes, passing the endless grass,
Passing the yellow-speared wheat, every grain from its shroud in the dark-
    brown fields uprisen,
Passing the apple-tree blows of white and pink in the orchards,                             30
Carrying a corpse to where it shall rest in the grave,
Night and day journeys a coffin.

6

Coffin that passes through lanes and streets,
Through day and night with the great cloud darkening the land,
With the pomp of the inlooped flags with the cities draped in black,
With the show of the States themselves as of crape-veiled women standing,
With processions long and winding and the flambeaus of the night,
With the countless torches lit, with the silent sea of faces and the unbared
    heads,
With the waiting depot, the arriving coffin, and the sombre faces,
With dirges through the night, with the thousand voices rising strong and
    solemn,                                                                               40
With all the mournful voices of the dirges poured around the coffin,
The dim-lit churches and the shuddering organs—where amid these you
    journey,
With the tolling tolling bells' perpetual clang,
Here, coffin that slowly passes,
I give you my sprig of lilac.

7

(Nor for you, for one alone,
Blossoms and branches green to coffins all I bring,

For fresh as the morning, thus would I chant a song for you O sane and
    sacred death.

All over bouquets of roses,
O death, I cover you over with roses and early lilies,        *50*
But mostly and now the lilac that blooms the first,
Copious I break, I break the sprigs from the bushes,
With loaded arms I come, pouring for you,
For you and the coffins all of you O death.)

### 8

O western orb sailing the heaven,
Now I know what you must have meant as a month since I walked,
As I walked in silence the transparent shadowy night,
As I saw you had something to tell as you bent to me night after night,
As you dropped from the sky low down as if to my side, (while the other
    stars all looked on,)
As we wandered together the solemn night, (for something I know not what
    kept me from sleep,)        *60*
As the night advanced, and I saw on the rim of the west how full you were of
    woe,
As I stood on the rising ground in the breeze in the cool transparent night,
As I watched where you passed and was lost in the netherward black of the
    night,
As my soul in its trouble dissatisfied sank, as where you sad orb,
Concluded, dropt in the night, and was gone.

### 9

Sing on there in the swamp,
O singer bashful and tender, I hear your notes, I hear your call,
I hear, I come presently, I understand you,
But a moment I linger, for the lustrous star has detained me,
The star my departing comrade holds and detains me.        *70*

### 10

O how shall I warble myself for the dead one there I loved?
And how shall I deck my song for the large sweet soul that has gone?
And what shall my perfume be for the grave of him I love?

Sea-winds blown from east and west,
Blown from the Eastern sea and blown from the Western sea, till there
    on the prairies meeting,
These and with these and the breath of my chant,
I'll perfume the grave of him I love.

### 11

O what shall I hang on the chamber walls?
And what shall the pictures be that I hang on the walls,
To adorn the burial-house of him I love?        *80*

Pictures of growing spring and farms and homes,
With the Fourth-month eve at sundown, and the gray smoke lucid and bright,

With floods of the yellow gold of the gorgeous, indolent, sinking sun, burning,
    expanding the air,
With the fresh sweet herbage under foot, and the pale green leaves of the
    trees prolific,
In the distance the flowing glaze, the breast of the river, with a wind-dapple
    here and there,
With ranging hills on the banks, with many a line against the sky, and
    shadows,
And the city at hand with dwellings so dense, and stacks of chimneys,
And all the scenes of life and the workshops, and the workmen homeward
    returning.

### 12

Lo, body and soul—this land,
My own Manhattan with spires, and the sparkling and hurrying tides, and
    the ships,                                                                    90
The varied and ample land, the South and the North in the light, Ohio's
    shores and flashing Missouri,
And ever the far-spreading prairies covered with grass and corn.

Lo, the most excellent sun so calm and haughty,
The violet and purple morn with just-felt breezes,
The gentle soft-born measureless light,
The miracle spreading bathing all, the fulfilled noon,
The coming eve delicious, the welcome night and the stars,
Over my cities shining all, enveloping man and land.

### 13

Sing on, sing on you gray-brown bird,
Sing from the swamps, the recesses, pour your chant from the bushes,            100
Limitless out of the dusk, out of the cedars and pines.

Sing on dearest brother, warble your reedy song,
Loud human song, with voice of uttermost woe.

O liquid and free and tender!
O wild and loose to my soul—O wondrous singer!
You only I hear—yet the star holds me, (but will soon depart,)
Yet the lilac with mastering odor holds me.

### 14

Now while I sat in the day and looked forth,
In the close of the day with its light and the fields of spring, and the farmers
    preparing their crops,
In the large unconscious scenery of my land with its lakes and forests,         110
In the heavenly aerial beauty, (after the perturbed winds and the storms,)
Under the arching heavens of the afternoon swift passing, and the voices
    of children and women,
The many-moving sea-tides, and I saw the ships how they sailed,
And the summer approaching with richness, and the fields all busy with labor,
And the infinite separate houses, how they all went on, each with its meals
    and minutia of daily usages,

And the streets how their throbbings throbbed, and the cities pent—lo, then
    and there,
Falling upon them all and among them all, enveloping me with the rest,
Appeared the cloud, appeared the long black trail,
And I knew death, its thought, and the sacred knowledge of death.

Then with the knowledge of death as walking one side of me,           *120*
And the thought of death close-walking the other side of me,
And I in the middle as with companions, and as holding the hands of
    companions,
I fled forth to the hiding receiving night that talks not,
Down to the shores of the water, the path by the swamp in the dimness,
To the solemn shadowy cedars and ghostly pines so still.

And the singer so shy to the rest received me,
The gray-brown bird I know received us comrades three,
And he sang the carol of death, and a verse for him I love.

From deep secluded recesses,
From the fragrant cedars and the ghostly pines so still,           *130*
Came the carol of the bird,

And the charm of the carol rapt me,
As I held as if by their hands my comrades in the night,
And the voice of my spirit tallied the song of the bird.

*Come lovely and soothing death,*
*Undulate round the world, serenely arriving, arriving,*
*In the day, in the night, to all, to each,*
*Sooner or later delicate death.*

*Praised be the fathomless universe,*
*For life and joy, and for objects and knowledge curious,*           *140*
*And for love, sweet love—but praise! praise! praise!*
*For the sure-enwinding arms of cool-enfolding death.*

*Dark mother always gliding near with soft feet,*
*Have none chanted for thee a chant of fullest welcome?*
*Then I chant it for thee, I glorify thee above all,*
*I bring thee a song that when thou must indeed come, come unfalteringly.*

*Approach strong deliveress,*
*When it is so, when thou hast taken them I joyously sing the dead,*
*Lost in thy loving floating ocean of thee,*
*Laved in the flood of thy bliss O death.*           *150*

*From me to thee glad serenades,*
*Dances for thee I propose saluting thee, adornments and feastings for thee,*
*And the sights of the open landscape and the high-spread sky are fitting,*
*And life and the fields, and the huge and thoughtful night.*

*The night in silence under many a star,*
*The ocean shore and the husky whispering wave whose voice I know,*
*And the soul turning to thee O vast and well-veiled death,*
*And the body gratefully nestling close to thee.*

*Over the tree-tops I float thee a song,*
*Over the rising and sinking waves, over the myriad fields and the prairies wide,* 160
*Over the dense-packed cities all and the teeming wharves and ways,*
*I float this carol with joy, with joy to thee O death.*

### 15

To the tally of my soul,
Loud and strong kept up the gray-brown bird,
With pure deliberate notes spreading filling the night.

Loud in the pines and cedars dim,
Clear in the freshness moist and the swamp-perfume,
And I with my comrades there in the night.

While my sight that was bound in my eyes unclosed,
As to long panoramas of visions.                                           *170*

And I saw askant the armies,
I saw as in noiseless dreams hundreds of battle-flags,
Borne through the smoke of the battles and pierced with missiles I saw them,
And carried hither and yon through the smoke, and torn and bloody,
And at last but a few shreds left on the staffs, (and all in silence,)
And the staffs all splintered and broken.

I saw battle-corpses, myriads of them,
And the white skeletons of young men, I saw them,
I saw the debris and debris of all the slain soldiers of the war,
But I saw they were not as was thought,                                    *180*
They themselves were fully at rest, they suffered not,
The living remained and suffered, the mother suffered,
And the wife and the child and the musing comrade suffered,
And the armies that remained suffered.

### 16

Passing the visions, passing the night,
Passing, unloosing the hold of my comrade's hands,
Passing the song of the hermit bird and the tallying song of my soul,
Victorious song, death's outlet song, yet varying ever-altering song,
As low and wailing, yet clear the notes, rising and falling, flooding the night,
Sadly sinking and fainting, as warning and warning, and yet again bursting
    with joy,                                                              *190*
Covering the earth and filling the spread of the heaven,
As that powerful psalm in the night I heard from recesses,
Passing, I leave thee lilac with heart-shaped leaves,
I leave thee there in the dooryard, blooming, returning with spring.

I cease from my song for thee,
From my gaze on thee in the west, fronting the west communing with thee,
O comrade lustrous with silver face in the night.

Yet each to keep and all, retrievements out of the night,
The song, the wondrous chant of the gray-brown bird,
And the tallying chant, the echo aroused in my soul,                       *200*
With lustrous and drooping star with the countenance full of woe,

With the holders holding my hand nearing the call of the bird,
Comrades mine and I in the midst, and their memory ever to keep, for the
    dead I loved so well,
For the sweetest, wisest soul of all my days and lands—and this for his dear
    sake,
Lilac and star and bird twined with the chant of my soul,
There in the fragrant pines and the cedars dusk and dim.  (*1865*)


## To a Locomotive in Winter

Thee for my recitative,
Thee in the driving storm even as now, the snow, the winter-day declining,
Thee in thy panoply, thy measured dual throbbing and thy beat convulsive,
Thy black cylindric body, golden brass and silvery steel,
Thy ponderous side-bars, parallel and connecting rods, gyrating, shuttling at
    thy sides,
Thy metrical, now swelling pant and roar, now tapering in the distance,
Thy great protruding head-light fixed in front,
Thy long, pale, floating vapor-pennants, tinged with delicate purple,
The dense and murky clouds out-belching from thy smoke-stack,
Thy knitted frame, thy springs and valves, the tremulous twinkle of thy
    wheels,                                                    10
Thy train of cars behind, obedient, merrily following,
Through gale or calm, now swift, now slack, yet steadily careering;
Type of the modern—emblem of motion and power—pulse of the continent,
For once come serve the Muse and merge in verse, even as here I see thee,
With storm and buffeting gusts of wind and falling snow,
By day thy warning ringing bell to sound its notes,
By night thy silent signal lamps to swing.

Fierce-throated beauty!
Roll though my chant with all thy lawless music, thy swinging lamps at night,
Thy madly-whistled laughter, echoing, rumbling like an earthquake,
    rousing all,                                                   20
Law of thyself complete thine own track firmly holding,
(No sweetness debonair of tearful harp or glib piano thine,)
Thy trills of shrieks by rocks and hills returned,
Launched o'er the prairies wide, across the lakes,
To the free skies unpent and glad and strong.  (*1876*)

# The Victorian Age

## JOHN HENRY, CARDINAL NEWMAN / 1801–1890

### The Pillar of the Cloud

Lead, Kindly Light, amid the encircling gloom,
    Lead Thou me on!
The night is dark, and I am far from home—
    Lead Thou me on!
Keep Thou my feet; I do not ask to see
The distant scene,—one step enough for me.

I was not ever thus, nor prayed that Thou
    Shouldst lead me on.
I loved to choose and see my path; but now
    Lead Thou me on!                      10
I loved the garish day, and, spite of fears,
Pride ruled my will: remember not past years.

So long Thy power hath blest me, sure it still
    Will lead me on,
O'er moor and fen, o'er crag and torrent, till
    The night is gone;
And with the morn those angel faces smile
Which I have loved long since, and lost awhile.    (*1833*)

## ELIZABETH BARRETT BROWNING / 1806–1861

### *from* Sonnets from the Portuguese

XXV

A heavy heart, Belovéd, have I borne
From year to year until I saw thy face,
And sorrow after sorrow took the place
Of all those natural joys as lightly worn
As the stringed pearls, each lifted in its turn
By a beating heart at dance-time. Hopes apace
Were changed to long despairs, till God's own grace
Could scarcely lift above the world forlorn
My heavy heart. Then *thou* didst bid me bring

And let it drop adown thy calmly great                    *10*
Deep being. Fast it sinketh, as a thing
Which its own nature doth precipitate,
While thine doth close above it, mediating
Betwixt the stars and the unaccomplished fate.

### XLIII

How do I love thee? Let me count the ways.
I love thee to the depth and breadth and height
My soul can reach, when feeling out of sight
For the ends of Being and ideal Grace.
I love thee to the level of every day's
Most quiet need, by sun and candlelight.
I love thee freely, as men strive for Right;
I love thee purely, as they turn from Praise;
I love thee with the passion put to use
In my old griefs, and with my childhood's faith.          *10*
I love thee with a love I seemed to lose
With my lost saints,—I love thee with the breath,
Smiles, tears, of all my life!—and, if God choose,
I shall but love thee better after death.

### XLIV

Belovéd, thou hast brought me many flowers
Plucked in the garden, all the summer through
And winter, and it seemed as if they grew
In this close room, nor missed the sun and showers.
So, in the like name of that love of ours,
Take back these thoughts which here unfolded too,
And which on warm and cold days I withdrew
From my heart's ground. Indeed, those beds and bowers
Be overgrown with bitter weeds and rue,
And wait thy weeding; yet here's eglantine,                *10*
Here's ivy!—take them, as I used to do
Thy flowers, and keep them where they shall not pine.
Instruct thine eyes to keep their colors true,
And tell thy soul their roots are left in mine.   (*1850*)

## A Musical Instrument

What was he doing, the great god Pan,
    Down in the reeds by the river?
Spreading ruin and scattering ban,
Splashing and paddling with hoofs of a goat,
And breaking the golden lilies afloat
    With the dragon-fly on the river?

He tore out a reed, the great god Pan,
    From the deep cool bed of the river.
The limpid water turbidly ran,

And the broken lilies a-dying lay,                                    *10*
And the dragon-fly had fled away,
   Ere he brought it out of the river.

High on the shore sate the great god Pan,
   While turbidly flowed the river,
And hacked and hewed as a great god can,
With his hard bleak steel at the patient reed,
Till there was not a sign of a leaf indeed
   To prove it fresh from the river.

He cut it short did the great god Pan,
   (How tall it stood in the river!)                        *20*
Then drew the pith like the heart of a man,
Steadily from the outside ring,
Then notched the poor dry empty thing
   In holes as he sate by the river.

'This is the way,' laughed the great god Pan,
   (Laughed while he sate by the river!)
'The only way since gods began
To make sweet music, they could succeed,'
Then dropping his mouth to a hole in the reed,
   He blew in power by the river.                             *30*

Sweet, sweet, sweet, O Pan,
   Piercing sweet by the river!
Blinding sweet, O great god Pan!
The sun on the hill forgot to die,
And the lilies revived, and the dragon-fly
Came back to dream on the river.

Yet half a beast is the great god Pan
   To laugh, as he sits by the river,
Making a poet out of a man.
The true gods sigh for the cost and the pain—                        *40*
For the reed that grows never more again
   As a reed with the reeds of the river.   (*1860*)

# EDWARD FITZGERALD / 1809–1883

## *from* The Rubáiyát of Omar Khayyám of Naishápúr[1]

### I–1

Awake! for Morning in the Bowl of Night
Has flung the Stone that puts the Stars to Flight:
   And Lo! the Hunter of the East has caught
The Sultán's Turret in a Noose of Light.

### I–2

Dreaming when Dawn's Left Hand was in the Sky,
I heard a Voice within the Tavern cry,
   "Awake, my Little Ones, and fill the Cup
"Before Life's Liquor in its Cup be dry."

### I–3

And, as the Cock crew, those who stood before
The Tavern shouted—"Open then the Door!
   "You know how little while we have to stay,
"And once departed, may return no more."          *10*

### I–4

Now the New Year[2] reviving old Desires,
The thoughtful Soul to Solitude retires,
   Where the *White Hand of Moses*[3] on the Bough
Puts out, and Jesus[3] from the Ground suspires.

### V–5

Iram[4] indeed is gone with all his Rose,
And Jamshyd's Sev'n-ringed Cup[5] where no one knows;
   But still a Ruby kindles in the Vine,
And many a Garden by the Water blows.         *20*

### V–6

And David's lips are lockt; but in divine
High-piping Péhlevi,[6] with "Wine! Wine! Wine!
   "Red Wine!"—the Nightingale cries to the Rose
That sallow cheek of hers t' incarnadine.

### V–7

Come, fill the Cup, and in the fire of Spring
Your Winter garment of Repentance fling:

---

[1] FitzGerald's poem is a free rendering of a Persian original written in *rubā 'ī* (quatrains rhyming *a a x a*) by Omar the Tentmaker (died c. 1123), a mathematician, astronomer, and poet from Naishápúr, a Persian town. The editor has selected stanzas from both the first and fifth editions, as indicated by the numbering of the quatrains.

[2] the opening of spring
[3] flowers named for minor prophets
[4] a royal garden now lost in the desert
[5] This legendary king had a cup symbolizing the seven heavens, seas, and planets.
[6] the ancient literary language of Persia, a version of Sanskrit

The Bird of Time has but a little way
To flutter—and the Bird is on the Wing.

v–8

Whether at Naishápúr or Babylon,
Whether the Cup with sweet or bitter run,                                    30
    The Wine of Life keeps oozing drop by drop,
The Leaves of Life keep falling one by one.

I–8

And look—a thousand Blossoms with the Day
Woke—and a thousand scattered into Clay:
    And this first Summer Month that brings the Rose
Shall take Jamshyd and Kaikobád[7] away.

v–10

Well, let it take them! What have we to do
With Kaikobád the Great, or Kaikhosrú?[8]
    Let Zál and Rustum[9] bluster as they will,
Or Hátim[10] call to Supper—heed not you.                                    40

v–11

With me along the strip of Herbage strown
That just divides the desert from the sown,
    Where name of Slave and Sultán is forgot—
And Peace to Mahmúd[11] on his golden Throne!

v–12

A Book of Verses underneath the Bough,
A Jug of Wine, a Loaf of Bread—and Thou
    Beside me singing in the Wilderness—
Oh, Wilderness were Paradise enow!

v–13

Some for the Glories of This World; and some
Sigh for the Prophet's[12] Paradise to come;                                    50
    Ah, take the Cash, and let the Credit go,
Nor heed the rumble of a distant Drum!

v–14

Look to the blowing Rose about us—"Lo
Laughing," she says, "into the world I blow,
    "At once the silken tassel of my Purse
"Tear, and its Treasure on the Garden throw."

v–15

And those who husbanded the Golden grain,
And those who flung it to the winds like Rain,
    Alike to no such aureate[13] Earth are turned
As, buried once, Men want dug up again.                                    60

---

7 first king of the Kaianian dynasty of Persia
8 a successor of Kaikobád
9 father and son who were heroes of Persian battle
10 a representative of Persian generosity

11 of Ghazni (971–1030), Moslem conqueror of India
12 Mohammed's        13 golden

### v–16

The Worldly Hope men set their Hearts upon
Turns Ashes—or it prospers; and anon,
   Like Snow upon the Desert's dusty Face,
Lighting a little hour or two—is gone.

### v–17

Think, in this battered Caravanserai [14]
Whose Portals are alternate Night and Day,
   How Sultán after Sultán with his Pomp
Abode his destined Hour, and went his way.

### v–18

They say the Lion and the Lizard keep
The courts where Jamshyd gloried and drank deep;        *70*
   And Bahrám, [15] that great Hunter—the Wild Ass
Stamps o'er his Head, but cannot break his Sleep.

### v–19

I sometimes think that never blows so red
The Rose as where some buried Caesar bled;
   That every Hyacinth the Garden wears
Dropt in her Lap from some once lovely Head.

### v–20

And this reviving Herb whose tender Green
Fledges the River-Lip on which we lean—
   Ah, lean upon it lightly! for who knows
From what once lovely Lip it springs unseen!        *80*

### ɪ–20

Ah, my Belovéd, fill the Cup that clears
*To-day* of past Regrets and future Fears—
   *To-morrow?*—Why, To-morrow I may be
Myself with Yesterday's Sev'n Thousand Years.

### v–22

For some we loved, the loveliest and the best
That from his Vintage rolling Time hath prest,
   Have drunk their Cup a Round or two before,
And one by one crept silently to rest.

### ɪ–22

And we, that now make merry in the Room
They left, and Summer dresses in new Bloom,        *90*
   Ourselves must we beneath the Couch of Earth
Descend, ourselves to make a Couch—for whom?

---

[14] inn for the accommodation of caravans
[15] a Persian ruler who died in a swamp while hunting the wild ass

### v–24

Ah, make the most of what we yet may spend,
Before we too into the Dust descend;
    Dust into Dust, and under Dust to lie,
Sans [16] Wine, sans Song, sans Singer, and—sans End!

### I–47

And if the Wine you drink, the Lip you press,
End in the Nothing all Things end in—Yes—
    Then fancy while Thou art, Thou art but what
Thou shalt be—Nothing—thou shalt not be less.                          *100*

### v–43

So when that Angel of the darker Drink
At last shall find you by the river-brink,
    And, offering his Cup, invite your Soul
Forth to your Lips to quaff—you shall not shrink.

### v–46

And fear not lest Existence closing your
Account, and mine, should know the like no more;
    The Eternal Sáki [17] from that Bowl has poured
Millions of Bubbles like us, and will pour.

### v–54

Waste not your Hour, nor in the vain pursuit
Of this and That endeavor and dispute;                                 *110*
    Better be jocund with the fruitful Grape
Than sadden after none, or bitter, Fruit.

### v–55

You know, my Friends, with what a brave Carouse
I made a Second Marriage in my house;
    Divorced old barren Reason from my Bed,
And took the Daughter of the Vine to Spouse.

### I–41

For "*Is*" and "*Is-not*" though *with* Rule and Line,
And "*Up-and-down*" *Without,* I could define,
    I yet in all I only cared to know
Was never deep in anything but—Wine.                                   *120*

### v–57

Ah, by my Computations, People say,
Reduce the Year to better reckoning? [18]—Nay,
    'Twas only striking from the Calendar
Unborn To-morrow and dead Yesterday.

---

[16] without     [17] wine bearer
[18] Omar was a member of a commission to adjust the calendar.

### i-42

And lately, by the Tavern Door agape,
Came stealing through the Dusk an Angel Shape
   Bearing a Vessel on his Shoulder; and
He bid me taste of it; and 'twas—the Grape!

### i-43

The Grape that can with Logic absolute
The Two-and-Seventy jarring Sects [19] confute:        *130*
   The subtle Alchemist that in a Trice
Life's leaden Metal into Gold transmute;

### i-44

The mighty Mahmúd, the victorious Lord,
That all the misbelieving and black Horde
   Of Fears and Sorrows that infest the Soul
Scatters and slays with his enchanted Sword.

### v-61

Why, be this Juice the growth of God, who dare
Blaspheme the twisted tendril as a Snare?
   A Blessing, we should use it, should we not?
And if a Curse—why, then, Who set it there?        *140*

### v-62

I must abjure the Balm of Life, I must,
Scared by some After-reckoning ta'en on trust,
   Or lured with Hope of some Diviner Drink,
To fill the Cup—when crumbled into Dust!

### v-63

Oh, threats of Hell and Hopes of Paradise!
One thing at least is certain—*This* Life flies;
   One thing is certain and the rest is Lies;
The Flower that once has blown for ever dies.

### v-64

Strange, is it not? that of the myriads who
Before us passed the door of Darkness through,        *150*
   Not one returns to tell us of the Road,
Which to discover we must travel too.

### v-65

The Revelations of Devout and Learned
Who rose before us, and as Prophets burned,
   Are all but Stories, which, awoke from Sleep
They told their comrades, and to Sleep returned.

### v-66

I sent my Soul through the Invisible,
Some letter of that After-life to spell:

---

[19] the number of religious sects assumed to exist in the world

And by and by my Soul returned to me,
And answered "I Myself am Heaven and Hell:"                    *160*

v–67

Heav'n but the Vision of fulfilled Desire,
And Hell the Shadow from a Soul on fire,
　　Cast on the Darkness into which Ourselves,
So late emerged from, shall so soon expire.

I–45

But leave the Wise to wrangle, and with me
The Quarrel of the Universe let be:
　　And, in some corner of the Hubbub coucht,
Make Game of that which makes as much of Thee.

I–46

For in and out, above, about, below,
'Tis nothing but a Magic Shadow-show,                          *170*
　　Played in a Box whose Candle is the Sun,
Round which we Phantom Figures come and go.

I–49

'Tis all a Chequer-board of Nights and Days
Where Destiny with Men for Pieces plays:
　　Hither and thither moves, and mates, and slays,
And one by one back in the Closet lays.

v–70

The Ball no question makes of Ayes and Noes,
But Here or There as strikes the Player goes;[20]
　　And He that tossed you down into the Field,
*He* knows about it all—*he* knows—*he* knows!              *180*

v–71

The Moving Finger writes; and, having writ,
Moves on: nor all your Piety nor Wit
　　Shall lure it back to cancel half a Line,
Nor all your Tears wash out a Word of it.

v–72

And that inverted Bowl they call the Sky,
Whereunder crawling cooped we live and die,
　　Lift not your hands to *It* for help—for It
As impotently moves as you or I.

I–53

With Earth's first Clay They did the Last Man's knead
And then of the Last Harvest sowed the Seed:                   *190*
　　Yea, the first Morning of Creation wrote
What the Last Dawn of Reckoning shall read.

---

[20] The game indicated is polo.

v–74

*Yesterday This* Day's Madness did prepare;
*To-morrow's* Silence, Triumph, or Despair:
  Drink! for you know not whence you came, nor why:
Drink! for you know not why you go nor where.

v–77

And this I know: whether the one True Light
Kindle to Love, or Wrath consume me quite,
  One Flash of It within the Tavern caught
Better than in the Temple lost outright.                    *200*

ɪ–57

Oh Thou, who didst with Pitfall and with Gin
Beset the Road I was to wander in,
  Thou wilt not with Predestination round
Enmesh me, and impute my Fall to Sin?

ɪ–58

Oh, Thou, who Man of baser Earth didst make,
And who with Eden didst devise the Snake;
  For all the Sin wherewith the Face of Man
Is blackened, Man's Forgiveness give—and take!

      .   .   .

v–82

As under cover of departing Day
Slunk hunger-stricken Ramazán [21] away,                    *210*
  Once more within the Potter's house alone
I stood, surrounded by the Shapes of Clay.

v–84

Said one among them—"Surely not in vain
"My substance of the common Earth was ta'en
  "And to this Figure moulded, to be broke,
"Or trampled back to shapeless Earth again."

v–85

Then said a Second—"Ne'er a peevish Boy
"Would break the Bowl from which he drank in joy;
  "And He that with his hand the Vessel made
"Will surely not in after Wrath destroy."                   *220*

v–86

After a momentary silence spake
Some Vessel of a more ungainly Make;
  "They sneer at me for leaning all awry:
"What! did the Hand then of the Potter shake?"

---

[21] the Moslem month of fasting

### v–87

Whereat some one of the loquacious Lot—
I think a Súfi [22] pipkin [23]—waxing hot—
    "All this of Pot and Potter   Tell me then,
"Who is the Potter, pray, and who the Pot?"

### v–88

"Why," said another, "Some there are who tell
"Of one who threatens he will toss to Hell                                    230
    "The luckless Pots he marred in making—Pish!
"He's a Good Fellow, and 'twill all be well."

### v–89

"Well," murmured one, "Let whoso make or buy,
"My Clay with long Oblivion is gone dry:
    "But fill me with the old familiar Juice,
"Methinks I might recover by and by."

### I–66

So while the Vessels one by one were speaking,
One spied the little Crescent [24] all were seeking:
    And then they jogged each other, "Brother! Brother!
"Hark to the Porter's Shoulder-knot a-creaking!"                                    240
                    .     .     .

### I–67

Ah, with the Grape my fading Life provide,
And wash my Body whence the Life has died,
    And in a Winding-sheet of Vine-leaf wrapt,
So bury me by some sweet Garden-side.

### I–68

That ev'n my buried Ashes such a Snare
Of Perfume shall fling up into the Air,
    As not a True Believer passing by
But shall be overtaken unaware.

### I–69

Indeed the Idols I have loved so long
Have done my Credit in Men's Eyes much wrong:                                    250
    Have drowned my Honour in a shallow Cup
And sold my Reputation for a Song.

### I–70

Indeed, indeed, Repentance oft before
I swore—but was I sober when I swore?
    And then and then came Spring, and Rose-in-hand
My thread-bare Penitence apieces tore.

---

[22] a Persian mystic    [23] a small earthen jar
[24] the new moon that indicates the end of Ramazán

v–95

And much as Wine has played the Infidel,
And robbed me of my Robe of Honour—Well,
   I wonder often what the Vintners buy       260
One half so precious as the stuff they sell.

v–96

Yet Ah, that Spring should vanish with the Rose!
That Youth's sweet-scented manuscript should close!
   The Nightingale that in the branches sang,
Ah whence, and whither flown again, who knows!

I–73

Ah Love! could thou and I with Fate conspire
To grasp this sorry Scheme of Things entire,
   Would not we shatter it to bits—and then
Remould it nearer to the Heart's Desire!

I–74

Ah, Moon of my Delight who know'st no wane,
The Moon of Heav'n is rising once again:      270
   How oft hereafter rising shall she look
Through this same Garden after me—in vain!

I–75

And when Thyself with shinging Foot shall pass
Among the Guests Star-scattered on the Grass,
   And in thy joyous Errand reach the Spot
Where I made one—turn down an empty Glass!

                  *Tamám shud*[25] *(1859; 1879)*

# ALFRED, LORD TENNYSON / 1809–1892

## Song

A spirit haunts the year's last hours
Dwelling amid these yellowing bowers:
   To himself he talks:
For at eventide, listening earnestly,
At his work you may hear him sob and
    sigh
   In the walks;
   Earthward he boweth the heavy
    stalks
Of the mouldering flowers:
   Heavily hangs the broad sunflower

Over its grave i' the earth so
   chilly;      10
Heavily hangs the hollyhock,
   Heavily hangs the tiger-lily.

The air is damp, and hushed, and close,
As a sick man's room when he takes
    repose
   An hour before death;
My very heart faints and my whole soul
   grieves
At the moist rich smell of the rotting
   leaves,

---

[25] It is finished.

And the breath
Of the fading edges of box beneath,
And the year's last rose.                    20
Heavily hangs the broad sunflower
   Over its grave i' the earth so chilly;
Heavily hangs the hollyhock,
   Heavily hangs the tiger-lily.   (1830)

## The Kraken[1]

Below the thunders of the upper deep;
Far, far beneath in the abysmal sea,
His ancient, dreamless, uninvaded sleep
The Kraken sleepeth: faintest sunlights
   flee
About his shadowy sides: above him
   swell
Huge sponges of millennial growth and
   height;
And far away into the sickly light,
From many a wondrous grot and secret
   cell
Unnumbered and enormous polypi
Winnow with giant arms the slumbering
   green.                                    10
There hath he lain for ages and will lie
Battening upon huge seaworms in his
   sleep,
Until the latter fire shall heat the deep;
Then once by man and angels to be seen,
In roaring he shall rise and on the surface
   die.   (1830)

## The Lotos-Eaters[1]

"Courage!" he said, and pointed toward the land,
"This mounting wave will roll us shoreward soon."
In the afternoon they came unto a land
In which it seeméd always afternoon.
All round the coast the languid air did swoon,
Breathing like one that hath a weary dream.
Full-faced above the valley stood the moon;
And, like a downward smoke, the slender stream
Along the cliff to fall and pause and fall did seem.

A land of streams! some, like a downward smoke,          10
Slow-dropping veils of thinnest lawn,[2] did go;
And some through wavering lights and shadows broke,
Rolling a slumbrous sheet of foam below.
They saw the gleaming river seaward flow
From the inner land; far off, three mountain-tops,
Three silent pinnacles of agéd snow,
Stood sunset-flushed; and dewed with showery drops,
Up-clomb the shadowy pine above the woven copse.

The charméd sunset lingered low adown
In the red West; through mountain cleft and dale          20
Was seen far inland, and the yellow down
Bordered with palm, and many a winding vale
And meadow, set with slender galingale;[3]

---

[1] a legendary sea creature of enormous bulk

[1] In his homeward wandering Ulysses encountered a race who fed on lotos, a fruit which induced languor.

[2] a filmy cloth     [3] a rushlike plant

A land where all things always seemed the same!
And round about the keel with faces pale,
Dark faces pale against that rosy flame,
The mild-eyed melancholy Lotos-eaters came.

Branches they bore of that enchanted stem,
Laden with flower and fruit, whereof they gave
To each, but whoso did receive of them                     30
And taste, to him the gushing of the wave
Far far away did seem to mourn and rave
On alien shores; and if his fellow spake,
His voice was thin, as voices from the grave;
And deep-asleep he seemed, yet all awake,

And music in his ears his beating heart did make.
They sat them down upon the yellow sand,
Between the sun and the moon upon the shore;
And sweet it was to dream of Fatherland,
Of child, and wife, and slave; but evermore                 40
Most weary seemed the sea, weary the oar,
Weary the wandering fields of barren foam.
Then some one said, "We will return no more;"
And all at once they sang, "Our island home
Is far beyond the wave; we will no longer roam."   (*1832*)

## St. Agnes' Eve[1]

Deep on the convent-roof the snows
  Are sparkling to the moon:
My breath to heaven like vapour goes:
  May my soul follow soon!
The shadows of the convent-towers
  Slant down the snowy sward,
Still creeping with the creeping hours
  That lead me to my Lord:
Make Thou my spirit pure and clear
  As are the frosty skies,                       10
Or this first snowdrop of the year
  That in my bosom lies.

As these white robes are soiled and dark
  To yonder shining ground;
As this pale taper's earthly spark,
  To yonder argent round;
So shows my soul before the Lamb,
  My spirit before Thee;

So in mine earthly house I am,
  To that I hope to be.                          20
Break up the heavens, O Lord! and far,
  Through all yon starlight keen,
Draw me, thy bride, a glittering star,
  In raiment white and clean.

He lifts me to the golden doors;
  The flashes come and go;
All heaven bursts her starry floors,
  And strows her lights below,
And deepens on and up! the gates
  Roll back, and far within                       30
For me the Heavenly Bridegroom waits,
  To make me pure of sin.
The sabbaths of Eternity,
  One sabbath deep and wide—
A light upon the shining sea—
  The Bridegroom with his bride!   (*1837*)

---

[1] According to legend, a maiden might, under certain conditions, have a glimpse of her destined spouse on the eve of St. Agnes' day, January 21.

Compare this poem with Keats's *The Eve of St. Agnes.*

# You Ask Me, Why, Though Ill at Ease

You ask me, why, though ill at ease,
    Within this region I subsist,
    Whose spirits falter in the mist,
And languish for the purple seas.

It is the land that freemen till,
    That sober-suited Freedom chose,
    The land, where girt with friends or
        foes
A man may speak the thing he will;

A land of settled government,
    A land of just and old renown,      10
    Where Freedom slowly broadens
        down
From precedent to precedent:

Where faction seldom gathers head,
    But by degrees to fullness wrought,
    The strength of some diffusive
        thought
Hath time and space to work and spread.

Should banded unions persecute
    Opinion, and induce a time
    When single thought is civil crime,
And individual freedom mute;          20

Though Power should make from land to
        land
    The name of Britain trebly great—
    Though every channel of the State
Should fill and choke with golden sand—

Yet waft me from the harbour-mouth,
    Wild wind! I seek a warmer sky,

And I will see before I die
The palms and temples of the South.
                                    (1842)

# Of Old Sat Freedom on the Heights

Of old sat Freedom on the heights,
    The thunders breaking at her feet:
Above her shook the starry lights:
    She heard the torrents meet.

There in her place she did rejoice,
    Self-gathered in her prophet-mind,
But fragments of her mighty voice
    Came rolling on the wind.

Then stepped she down through town
        and field
    To mingle with the human race,      10
And part by part to men revealed
    The fullness of her face—

Grave mother[1] of majestic works,
    From her isle-altar gazing down,
Who, God-like, grasps the triple forks,
    And, King-like wears the crown:

Her open eyes desire the truth.
    The wisdom of a thousand years
Is in them. May perpetual youth
    Keep dry their light from tears;     20

That her fair form may stand and shine,
    Make bright our days and light our
        dreams,
Turning to scorn with lips divine
    The falsehood of extremes!   (1842)

[1] Britannia, representing England, the "isle-altar" (l. 14), holds the trident ("triple forks") of Neptune to symbolize her dominion of the sea.

## Morte d'Arthur

So all day long the noise of battle rolled
Among the mountains by the winter sea;
Until King Arthur's table, man by man,
Had fallen in Lyonnesse[1] about their Lord,
King Arthur: then, because his wound was deep,
The bold Sir Bedivere uplifted him,
Sir Bedivere, the last of all his knights,
And bore him to a chapel nigh the field,
A broken chancel with a broken cross,
That stood on a dark strait of barren land.　　　　　*10*
On one side lay the Ocean, and on one
Lay a great water, and the moon was full.
　Then spake King Arthur to Sir Bedivere:
"The sequel of today unsolders all
The goodliest fellowship of famous knights
Whereof this world holds record. Such a sleep
They sleep—the men I loved, I think that we
Shall never more, at any future time,
Delight our souls with talk of knightly deeds,
Walking about the gardens and the halls　　　　　*20*
Of Camelot,[2] as in the days that were.
I perish by this people which I made,—
Though Merlin[3] sware that I should come again
To rule once more—but let what will be, be,
I am so deeply smitten through the helm
That without help I cannot last till morn.
Thou therefore take my brand[4] Excalibur,
Which was my pride: for thou rememberest how
In those old days, one summer noon, an arm
Rose up from out the bosom of the lake,　　　　　*30*
Clothed in white samite,[5] mystic, wonderful,
Holding the sword—and how I rowed across
And took it, and have worn it, like a king:
And, wheresoever I am sung or told
In aftertime, this also shall be known:
But now delay not: take Excalibur,
And fling him far into the middle mere:[6]
Watch what thou seëst, and lightly bring me word."
　To him replied the bold Sir Bedivere:
"It is not meet, Sir King, to leave thee thus,　　　　　*40*
Aidless, alone, and smitten through the helm.
A little thing may harm a wounded man.
Yet I thy hest will all perform at full,
Watch what I see, and lightly bring thee word."

---

[1] a country supposedly once located between Cornwall and the Scilly Isles, but now sunk into the sea; site of many Arthurian adventures
[2] King Arthur's legendary capitol city in Cornwall
[3] the magician of Arthur's court　[4] sword
[5] heavy silk　[6] the "great water" of l. 12

So saying, from the ruined shrine he stept
And in the moon athwart the place of tombs,
Where lay the mighty bones of ancient men,
Old knights, and over them the sea-wind sang
Shrill, chill, with flakes of foam. He, stepping down
By zig-zag paths, and juts of pointed rock,                          50
Came on the shining levels of the lake.
　　There drew he forth the brand Excalibur,
And o'er him, drawing it, the winter moon,
Brightening the skirts of a long cloud, ran forth
And sparkled keen with frost against the hilt:
For all the haft twinkled with diamond sparks,
Myriads of topaz-lights, and jacinth-work
Of subtlest jewellery. He gazed so long
That both his eyes were dazzled, as he stood,
This way and that dividing the swift mind,                           60
In act to throw: but at the last it seemed
Better to leave Excalibur concealed
There in the many-knotted waterflags,
That whistled stiff and dry about the marge.
So strode he back slow to the wounded King.
　　Then spake King Arthur to Sir Bedivere:
"Hast thou performed my mission which I gave?
What is it thou hast seen? or what hast heard?"
And answer made the bold Sir Bedivere:
"I heard the ripple washing in the reeds,                            70
And the wild water lapping on the crag."
　　To whom replied King Arthur, faint and pale:
"Thou hast betrayed thy nature and thy name,
Not rendering true answer, as beseemed
Thy fealty, nor like a noble knight:
For surer sign had followed, either hand,
Or voice, or else a motion of the mere.
This is a shameful thing for men to lie.
Yet now, I charge thee, quickly go again
As thou art lief⁷ and dear, and do the thing                        80
I bade thee, watch, and lightly bring me word."
　　Then went Sir Bedivere the second time
Across the ridge, and paced beside the mere,
Counting the dewy pebbles, fixed in thought;
But when he saw the wonder of the hilt,
How curiously and strangely chased,⁸ he smote
His palms together, and he cried aloud,
　　"And if indeed I cast the brand away,
Surely a precious thing, one worthy note,
Should thus be lost for ever from the earth,                        90
Which might have pleased the eyes of many men.

⁷ beloved　　⁸ engraved

What good should follow this, if this were done?
What harm, undone? deep harm to disobey,
Seeing obedience is the bond of rule.
Were it well to obey then, if a kind demand
An act unprofitable, against himself?
The King is sick, and knows not what he does.
What record, or what relic of my lord
Should be to aftertime, but empty breath
And rumours of a doubt? but were this kept,                          *100*
Stored in some treasure-house of mighty kings,
Some one might show it at a joust of arms,
Saying, 'King Arthur's sword, Excalibur,
Wrought by the lonely maiden of the Lake.
Nine years she wrought it, sitting in the deeps
Upon the hidden bases of the hills.'
So might some old man speak in the aftertime
To all the people, winning reverence.
But now much honour and much fame were lost."
    So spake he, clouded with his own conceit,[9]              *110*
And hid Excalibur the second time,
And so strode back slow to the wounded King.
    Then spoke King Arthur, breathing heavily:
"What is it thou hast seen? or what hast heard?"
    And answer made the bold Sir Bedivere:
"I heard the water lapping on the crag,
And the long ripple washing in the reeds,"
    To whom replied King Arthur, much in wrath:
"Ah, miserable and unkind, untrue,
Unknightly, traitor-hearted! Woe is me!                              *120*
Authority forgets a dying king,
Laid widowed of the power in his eye
That bowed the will. I see thee what thou art,
For thou, the latest-left of all my knights,
In whom should meet the offices of all,
Thou wouldst betray me for the precious hilt;
Either from lust of gold, or like a girl
Valuing the giddy pleasure of the eyes.
Yet, for a man may fail in duty twice,
And the third time may prosper, get thee hence:                      *130*
But, if thou spare to fling Excalibur,
I will arise and slay thee with my hands."
    Then quickly rose Sir Bedivere, and ran,
And, leaping down the ridges lightly, plunged
Among the bulrush-beds, and clutched the sword,
And strongly wheeled and threw it. The great brand
Made lightnings in the splendour of the moon,
And flashing round and round, and whirled in an arch,

---

[9] imaginings

Shot like a streamer of the northern morn,[10]
Seen where the moving isles of winter[11] shock                          *140*
By night, with noises of the northern sea.
So flashed and fell the brand Excalibur:
But ere he dipt the surface, rose an arm
Clothed in white samite, mystic, wonderful,
And caught him by the hilt, and brandished him
Three times, and drew him under in the mere.
And lightly went the other to the King.
    Then spoke King Arthur, drawing thicker breath:
"Now see I by thine eyes that this is done.
Speak out: what is it thou hast heard, or seen?"                         *150*
    And answer made the bold Sir Bedivere:
"Sir King, I closed mine eyelids, lest the gems
Should blind my purpose, for I never saw,
Nor shall see, here or elsewhere, till I die,
Not though I live three lives of mortal men,
So great a miracle as yonder hilt.
Then with both hands I flung him, wheeling him;
But when I looked again, behold an arm,
Clothed in white samite, mystic, wonderful,
That caught him by the hilt, and brandished him                          *160*
Three times, and drew him under in the mere."
    And answer made King Arthur, breathing hard:
"My end draws nigh; 'tis time that I were gone.
Make broad thy shoulders to receive my weight,
And bear me to the margin; yet I fear
My wound hath taken cold, and I shall die."
    So saying, from the pavement he half rose,
Slowly, with pain, reclining on his arm,
And looking wistfully with wide blue eyes
As in a picture. Him Sir Bedivere                                        *170*
Remorsefully regarded through his tears,
And would have spoken, but he found not words,
Then took with care, and kneeling on one knee,
O'er both his shoulders drew the languid hands,
And rising bore him through the place of tombs.
    But, as he walked, King Arthur panted hard,
Like one that feels a nightmare on his bed
When all the house is mute. So sighed the King,
Muttering and murmuring at his ear, "Quick, quick!
I fear it is too late, and I shall die."                                  *180*
But the other swiftly strode from ridge to ridge,
Clothed with his breath, and looking, as he walked,
Larger than human on the frozen hills.
He heard the deep behind him, and a cry
Before. His own thought drove him, like a goad.

---

[10] northern lights    [11] icebergs

Dry clashed his harness in the icy caves
And barren chasms, and all to left and right
The bare black cliff clanged round him, as he based
His feet on juts of slippery crag that rang
Sharp-smitten with the dint of arméd heels—          190
And on a sudden, lo! the level lake,
And the long glories of the winter moon.

   Then saw they how there hove a dusky barge,
Dark as a funeral scarf from stem to stern,
Beneath them; and descending they were ware
That all the decks were dense with stately forms
Black-stoled, black-hooded, like a dream—by these
Three Queens with crowns of gold—and from them rose
A cry that shivered to the tingling stars,
And, as it were one voice, an agony          200
Of lamentation, like a wind, that shrills
All night in a waste land, where no one comes,
Or hath come, since the makings of the world.
   Then murmured Arthur, "Place me in the barge,"
And to the barge they came. There those three Queens
Put forth their hands, and took the King, and wept.
But she, that rose the tallest of them all
And fairest, laid his head upon her lap,
And loosed the shattered casque,[12] and chafed his hands,
And called him by his name, complaining loud,          210
And dropping bitter tears against his brow
Striped with dark blood: for all his face was white
And colourless, and like the withered moon
Smote by the fresh beam of the springing east;
And all his greaves[13] and cuisses[14] dashed with drops
Of onset;[15] and the light and lustrous curls—
That made his forehead like a rising sun
High from the daïs-throne—were parched with dust;
Or, clotted into points and hanging loose,
Mixed with the knightly growth that fringed his lips.          220
So like a shattered column lay the King;
Not like that Arthur who, with lance in rest,
From spur to plume a star of tournament,
Shot through the lists of Camelot, and charged
Before the eyes of ladies and of kings.
   Then loudly cried the bold Sir Bedivere,
"Ah! my Lord Arthur, whither shall I go?
Where shall I hide my forehead and my eyes?
For now I see the true old times are dead,
When every morning brought a noble chance,          230
And every chance brought out a noble knight.

---

[12] helmet    [13] shin guards    [14] plates to protect the thighs    [15] blood, as from an attack

Such times have been not since the light that led
The holy Elders with the gift of myrrh.
But now the whole Round Table is dissolved
Which was an image of the mighty world;
And I, the last, go forth companionless,
And the days darken round me, and the years,
Among new men, strange faces, other minds."
    And slowly answered Arthur from the barge:
"The old order changeth, yielding place to new,       *240*
And God fulfils Himself in many ways,
Lest one good custom should corrupt the world.
Comfort thyself: what comfort is in me?
I have lived my life, and that which I have done
May He within Himself make pure! but thou,
If thou shouldst never see my face again,
Pray for my soul. More things are wrought by prayer
Than this world dreams of. Wherefore, let thy voice
Rise like a fountain for me night and day.
For what are men better than sheep or goats       *250*
That nourish a blind life within the brain,
If, knowing God, they lift not hands of prayer
Both for themselves and those who call them friend?
For so the whole round earth is every way
Bound by gold chains about the feet of God.
But now farewell. I am going a long way
With these thou seëst—if indeed I go—
(For all my mind is clouded with a doubt)
To the island-valley of Avilion;[16]
Where falls not hail, or rain, or any snow,       *260*
Nor ever wind blows loudly; but it lies
Deep-meadowed, happy, fair with orchard-lawns
And bowery hollows crowned with summer sea,
Where I will heal me of my grievous wound."
    So said he, and the barge with oar and sail
Moved from the brink, like some full-breasted swan
That, fluting a wild carol ere her death,
Ruffles her pure cold plume, and takes the flood
With swarthy webs. Long stood Sir Bedivere
Revolving many memories, till the hull       *270*
Looked one black dot against the verge of dawn,
And on the mere the wailing died away.    (*1842*)

## Ulysses[1]

It little profits that an idle king,
By this still hearth, among these barren crags,
Matched with an agéd wife,[2] I mete and dole

---

16 Avalon, the earthly paradise of heroes
1 Tennyson takes his theme from Dante, who, in *The Inferno*, depicts the hero of *The Odyssey* as restless and eager to continue the search for knowledge and virtue.
2 Penelope

Unequal laws unto a savage race,
That hoard, and sleep, and feed, and know not me.
I cannot rest from travel; I will drink
Life to the lees. All times I have enjoyed
Greatly, have suffered greatly, both with those
That loved me, and alone; on shore, and when
Through scudding drifts the rainy Hyades[3]
Vext the dim sea. I am become a name; 10
For always roaming with a hungry heart
Much have I seen and known,—cities of men
And manners, climates, councils, governments,
Myself not least, but honored of them all,—
And drunk delight of battle with my peers,
Far on the ringing plains of windy Troy.
I am a part of all that I have met;
Yet all experience is an arch wherethrough
Gleams that untravelled world whose margin fades 20
For ever and for ever when I move.
How dull it is to pause, to make an end,
To rust unburnished, not to shine in use!
As though to breathe were life! Life piled on life
Were all too little, and of one to me
Little remains; but every hour is saved
From that eternal silence, something more,
A bringer of new things; and vile it were
For some three suns to store and hoard myself,
And this gray spirit yearning in desire 30
To follow knowledge like a sinking star,
Beyond the utmost bound of human thought.
    This is my son, mine own Telemachus,
To whom I leave the sceptre and the isle,[4]
Well-loved of me, discerning to fulfill
This labor, by slow prudence to make mild
A rugged people, and through soft degrees
Subdue them to the useful and the good.
Most blameless is he, centred in the sphere
Of common duties, decent not to fail 40
In offices of tenderness, and pay
Meet adoration to my household gods,
When I am gone. He works his work, I mine.
    There lies the port; the vessel puffs her sail;
There gloom the dark, broad seas. My mariners,
Souls that have toiled, and wrought, and thought with me,—
That ever with a frolic welcome took
The thunder and the sunshine, and opposed
Free hearts, free foreheads,—you and I are old;
Old age hath yet his honor and his toil. 50
Death closes all; but something ere the end,

[3] a constellation whose rising at the same time as    [4] Ithaca
the sun was anciently believed to bring rain

Some work of noble note, may yet be done,
Not unbecoming men that strove with Gods.
The lights begin to twinkle from the rocks;
The long day wanes; the slow moon climbs; the deep
Moans round with many voices. Come, my friends.
'T is not too late to seek a newer world.
Push off, and sitting well in order smite
The sounding furrows; for my purpose holds
To sail beyond the sunset, and the baths                          60
Of all the western stars, until I die.
It may be that the gulfs will wash us down;
It may be we shall touch the Happy Isles,[5]
And see the great Achilles,[6] whom we knew.
Though much is taken, much abides; and though
We are not now that strength which in old days
Moved earth and heaven, that which we are, we are,—
One equal temper of heroic hearts,
Made weak by time and fate, but strong in will
To strive, to seek, to find, and not to yield.  (*1842*)       70

## Break, Break, Break

Break, break, break,
  On thy cold gray stones, O Sea!
And I would that my tongue could utter
  The thoughts that arise in me.

O well for the fisherman's boy,
  That he shouts with his sister at play!
O well for the sailor lad,
  That he sings in his boat on the bay!

And the stately ships go on
  To their haven under the hill;                                  10
But O for the touch of a vanished hand,
  And the sound of a voice that is still!

Break, break, break,
  At the foot of thy crags, O Sea!
But the tender grace of a day that is dead
  Will never come back to me.  (*1842*)

## *Songs from* The Princess

### SWEET AND LOW

Sweet and low, sweet and low,
  Wind of the western sea,
Low, low, breathe and blow,
  Wind of the western sea!
Over the rolling waters go,
Come from the dying moon, and blow,
  Blow him again to me;
While my little one, while my pretty one sleeps.

Sleep and rest, sleep and rest,
  Father will come to thee soon;                                  10

---

[5] the Islands of the Blessed in the western extremity
of the ocean

[6] the major hero of the Trojan War, in which he
was killed

Rest, rest, on mother's breast,
    Father will come to thee soon;
Father will come to his babe in the nest,
Silver sails all out of the west
    Under the silver moon;
Sleep, my little one, sleep, my pretty one, sleep.

## THE SPLENDOUR FALLS ON CASTLE WALLS

The splendour falls on castle walls
    And snowy summits old in story:
The long light shakes across the lakes,
    And the wild cataract leaps in glory.
Blow, bugle, blow, set the wild echoes flying,
Blow, bugle, answer, echoes, dying, dying, dying.

O hark, O hear; how thin and clear,
    And thinner, clearer, farther going!
O sweet and far from cliff and scar
    The horns of Elfland faintly blowing!                                        10
Blow, let us hear the purple glens replying:
Blow, bugle; answer, echoes, dying, dying, dying.

O love, they die in yon rich sky,
    They faint on hill or field or river:
Our echoes roll from soul to soul,
    And grow for ever and for ever.
Blow, bugle, blow, set the wild echoes flying,
And answer, echoes, answer, dying, dying, dying.

## NOW SLEEPS THE CRIMSON PETAL

Now sleeps the crimson petal, now the white;
Nor waves the cypress in the palace walk;
Nor winks the gold fin in the porphyry font.
The fire-fly wakens; waken thou with me.

Now droops the milk-white peacock like a ghost,
And like a ghost she glimmers on to me.

Now lies the Earth all Danaë[1] to the stars,
And all thy heart lies open unto me.

Now slides the silent meteor on, and leaves
A shining furrow, as thy thoughts in me.                                         10

Now folds the lily all her sweetness up,
And slips into the bosom of the lake.
So fold thyself, my dearest, thou, and slip
Into my bosom and be lost in me.   (*1850*)

---

[1] a princess of Greek mythology who was impregnated by Zeus disguised as a golden shower

## *from* In Memoriam A. H. H.[1]

### OBIIT MDCCCXXXIII

Strong Son of God, immortal Love,
   Whom we, that have not seen thy face,
   By faith, and faith alone, embrace,
Believing where we cannot prove;

Thine are these orbs of light and shade;
   Thou madest Life in man and brute;
   Thou madest Death; and lo, thy foot
Is on the skull which thou hast made.

Thou wilt not leave us in the dust:
   Thou madest man, he knows not
     why,                  *10*
   He thinks he was not made to die;
And thou hast made him: thou art just.

Thou seemest human and divine,
   The highest, holiest manhood, thou.
   Our wills are ours, we know not how;
Our wills are ours, to make them thine.

Our little systems have their day;
   They have their day and cease to be;
   They are but broken lights of thee,
And thou, O Lord, art more than
     they.               *20*

We have but faith: we cannot know,
   For knowledge is of things we see;
   And yet we trust it comes from thee,
A beam in darkness: let it grow.

Let knowledge grow from more to more;
   But more of reverence in us dwell;
   That mind and soul, according well,
May make one music as before,

But vaster. We are fools and slight;
   We mock thee when we do not fear;  *30*
   But help thy foolish ones to bear;
Help thy vain worlds to bear thy light.

Forgive what seemed my sin in me,
   What seemed my worth since I began;
   For merit lives from man to man,
And not from man, O Lord, to thee.

Forgive my grief for one removed,
   Thy creature, whom I found so fair.
   I trust he lives in thee, and there
I find him worthier to be loved.     *40*

Forgive these wild and wandering cries,
   Confusions of a wasted youth;
   Forgive them where they fail in truth,
And in thy wisdom make me wise.

                       *(1849)*

### I

I held it truth, with him[2] who sings
   To one clear harp in divers tones,
   That men may rise on stepping-stones
Of their dead selves to higher things.

But who shall so forecast the years
   And find in loss a gain to match?   *50*
   Or reach a hand through time to catch
The far-off interest of tears?

Let Love clasp Grief lest both be
     drowned,
   Let darkness keep her raven gloss.
   Ah, sweeter to be drunk with loss,
To dance with Death, to beat the ground,

Than that the victor Hours should scorn
   The long result of love, and boast,
   "Behold the man that loved and lost,
But all he was is overworn."     *60*

### II

Old yew, which graspest at the stones
   That name the underlying dead,
   Thy fibres net the dreamless head,
Thy roots are wrapt about the bones.

The seasons bring the flower again,
   And bring the firstling to the flock;
   And in the dusk of thee the clock
Beats out the little lives of men.

O, not for thee the glow, the bloom,
   Who changest not in any gale,    *70*
   Nor branding summer suns avail
To touch thy thousand years of gloom;

And gazing on thee, sullen tree,
   Sick for thy stubborn hardihood,

---

[1] Arthur Henry Hallam, Tennyson's intimate friend, who died in 1833 on a tour of the Continent
[2] Johann Wolfgang von Goethe (1749–1823), German poet and dramatist, whom Tennyson considered one of the foremost lyricists of his age

I seem to fail from out my blood
And grow incorporate into thee.

VI

One writes, that "other friends remain,"
   That "loss is common to the race"—
   And common is the commonplace,
And vacant chaff well meant for
     grain.              *80*

That loss is common would not make
   My own less bitter, rather more.
   Too common! Never morning wore
To evening, but some heart did break.

O father, wheresoe'er thou be,
   Who pledgest now thy gallant son,
   A shot, ere half thy draught be done,
Hath stilled the life that beat from thee.

O mother, praying God will save
   Thy sailor,—while thy head is
     bowed,            *90*
   His heavy-shotted hammock-shroud
Drops in his vast and wandering grave.

Ye know no more than I who wrought
   At that last hour to please him well;
   Who mused on all I had to tell,
And something written, something
     thought;

Expecting still his advent home;
   And ever met him on his way
   With wishes, thinking, "here today,"
Or "here tomorrow will he come."   *100*

O, somewhere, meek, unconscious dove,
   That sittest ranging golden hair;
   And glad to find thyself so fair,
Poor child, that waitest for thy love!

For now her father's chimney glows
   In expectation of a guest;
   And thinking "this will please him
     best,"
She takes a riband or a rose;

For he will see them on tonight;
   And with the thought her color
     burns;           *110*

And, having left the glass, she turns
Once more to set a ringlet right;

And, even when she turned, the curse
   Had fallen, and her future lord
   Was drowned in passing through the
     ford,
Or killed in falling from his horse.

O, what to her shall be the end?
   And what to me remains of good?
   To her perpetual maidenhood,
And unto me no second friend.   *120*

VII

Dark house, by which once more I stand
   Here in the long unlovely street,
   Doors, where my heart was used to beat
So quickly, waiting for a hand,

A hand that can be clasped no more—
   Behold me, for I cannot sleep,
   And like a guilty thing I creep
At earliest morning to the door.

He is not here; but far away
   The noise of life begins again,   *130*
   And ghastly through the drizzling rain
On the bald street breaks the blank day.

XI

Calm is the morn without a sound,
   Calm as to suit a calmer grief,
   And only through the faded leaf
The chestnut pattering to the ground;

Calm and deep peace on this high wold,[3]
   And on these dews that drench the
     furze,[4]
   And all the silvery gossamers[5]
That twinkle into green and gold;   *140*

Calm and still light on yon great plain
   That sweeps with all its autumn
     bowers,
   And crowded farms and lessening
     towers,
To mingle with the bounding main;

Calm and deep peace in this wide air,
   These leaves that redden to the fall,

---

[3] an upland plain
[4] an evergreen shrub of the pea family, common in waste places
[5] cobwebs

And in my heart, if calm at all,
If any calm, a calm despair;

Calm on the seas, and silver sleep,
    And waves that sway themselves in
        rest,                                                                     150
    And dead calm in that noble breast
Which heaves but with the heaving deep.

### XV

Tonight the winds begin to rise
    And roar from yonder dropping day;
    The last red leaf is whirled away,
The rooks are blown about the skies;

The forest cracked, the waters curled,
    The cattle huddled on the lea;
    And wildly dashed on tower and tree
The sunbeam strikes along the world: 160

And but for fancies, which aver
    That all thy motions gently pass
    Athwart a plane of molten glass,
I scarce could brook the strain and stir

That makes the barren branches loud;
    And but for fear it is not so,
    The wild unrest that lives in woe
Would dote and pore on yonder cloud

That rises upward always higher,
    And onward drags a laboring
        breast,                                                                  170
    And topples round the dreary west,
A looming bastion fringed with fire.

### XXI

I sing to him that rests below,
    And, since the grasses round me wave,
    I take the grasses of the grave,
And make them pipes whereon to blow.

The traveller hears me now and then,
    And sometimes harshly will he speak:
    "This fellow would make weakness
        weak,
And melt the waxen hearts of men."     180

Another answers: "Let him be,
    He loves to make parade of pain,
    That with his piping he may gain
The praise that comes to constancy."

------
6 a small finch common in Europe

A third is wroth: "Is this an hour
    For private sorrow's barren song,
    When more and more the people
        throng
The chairs and thrones of civil power?

"A time to sicken and to swoon,
    When Science reaches forth her
        arms                                                                     190
    To feel from world to world, and
        charms
Her secret from the latest moon?"

Behold, ye speak an idle thing;
    Ye never knew the sacred dust.
    I do but sing because I must,
And pipe but as the linnets 6 sing;

And one is glad; her note is gay,
    For now her little ones have ranged;
    And one is sad; her note is changed,
Because her brood is stolen away.      200

### XXVII

I envy not in any moods
    The captive void of noble rage,
    The linnet born within the cage,
That never knew the summer woods;

I envy not the beast that takes
    His license in the field of time,
    Unfettered by the sense of crime,
To whom a conscience never wakes;

Nor, what may count itself as blest,
    The heart that never plighted troth 210
    But stagnates in the weeks of sloth;
Nor any want-begotten rest.

I hold it true, whate'er befall;
    I feel it, when I sorrow most;
    'Tis better to have loved and lost
Than never to have loved at all.

### XXVIII

The time draws near the birth of Christ.
    The moon is hid, the night is still;
    The Christmas bells from hill to hill
Answer each other in the mist.         220

Four voices of four hamlets round,
    From far and near, on mead and moor,

Swell out and fail, as if a door
Were shut between me and the sound;

Each voice four changes on the wind,
   That now dilate, and now decrease,
   Peace and goodwill, goodwill and peace,
Peace and goodwill, to all mankind.

This year I slept and woke with pain,
   I almost wished no more to wake,   230
   And that my hold on life would break
Before I heard those bells again;

But they my troubled spirit rule,
   For they controlled me when a boy;
   They bring me sorrow touched with
      joy,
The merry, merry bells of Yule.

### XXXIV

My own dim life should teach me this,
   That life shall live for evermore,
   Else earth is darkness at the core,
And dust and ashes all that is;   240

This round of green, this orb of flame,
   Fantastic beauty; such as lurks
   In some wild poet, when he works
Without a conscience or an aim.

What then were God to such as I?
   'T were hardly worth my while to
      choose
   Of things all mortal, or to use
A little patience ere I die;

'T were best at once to sink to peace,
   Like birds the charming serpent
      draws,   250
   To drop head-foremost in the jaws
Of vacant darkness and to cease.

### XLV

The baby new to earth and sky,
   What time his tender palm is prest
   Against the circle of the breast,
Has never thought that "this is I";

But as he grows he gathers much,
   And learns the use of "I" and "me,"
   And finds "I am not what I see,
And other than the things I touch."   260

So rounds he to a separate mind
   From whence clear memory may begin,
   As through the frame that binds him in
His isolation grows defined.

This use may lie in blood and breath,
   Which else were fruitless of their due,
   Had man to learn himself anew
Beyond the second birth of death.

### XLVII

That each, who seems a separate whole,
   Should move his rounds, and fusing
      all   270
   The skirts of self again, should fall
Remerging in the general Soul,

Is faith as vague as all unsweet.
   Eternal form shall still divide
   The eternal soul from all beside;
And I shall know him when we meet;

And we shall sit at endless feast,
   Enjoying each the other's good.
   What vaster dream can hit the mood
Of Love on earth? He seeks at least   280

Upon the last and sharpest height,
   Before the spirits fade away,
   Some landing-place, to clasp and say,
"Farewell! We lose ourselves in light."

### LIV

O, yet we trust that somehow good
   Will be the final goal of ill,
   To pangs of nature, sins of will,
Defects of doubt, and taints of blood;

That nothing walks with aimless feet;
   That not one life shall be
      destroyed,   290
   Or cast as rubbish to the void,
When God hath made the pile complete;

That not a worm is cloven in vain;
   That not a moth with vain desire
   Is shrivelled in a fruitless fire,
Or but subserves another's gain.

Behold, we know not anything;
   I can but trust that good shall fall
   At last—far off—at last, to all,
And every winter change to spring.   300

So runs my dream; but what am I?
　　An infant crying in the night;
　　An infant crying for the light,
And with no language but a cry.

### LV

The wish, that of the living whole
　　No life may fail beyond the grave,
　　Derives it not from what we have
The likest God within the soul?

Are God and Nature then at strife,
　　That Nature lends such evil
　　　　dreams?                                    310
　　So careful of the type she seems,
So careless of the single life,

That I, considering everywhere
　　Her secret meaning in her deeds,
　　And finding that of fifty seeds
She often brings but one to bear,

I falter where I firmly trod,
　　And falling with my weight of cares
　　Upon the great world's altar-stairs
That slope through darkness up to
　　　　God,                                        320

I stretch lame hands of faith, and grope,
　　And gather dust and chaff, and call
　　To what I feel is Lord of all,
And faintly trust the larger hope.

### LVI

"So careful of the type?" but no
　　From scarpéd cliff and quarried stone
　　She cries, "A thousand types are gone;
I care for nothing, all shall go.

"Thou makest thine appeal to me:
　　I bring to life, I bring to death;              330
　　The spirit does but mean the breath:
I know no more," And he, shall he,

Man, her last work, who seemed so fair,
　　Such splendid purpose in his eyes,
　　Who rolled the psalm to wintry skies,
Who built him fanes of fruitless prayer,

Who trusted God was love indeed
　　And love Creation's final law—

Though Nature, red in tooth and claw
With ravine, shrieked against his
　　creed—                                          340

Who loved, who suffered countless ills,
　　Who battled for the True, the Just,
　　Be blown about the desert dust,
Or sealed within the iron hills?

No more? A monster then, a dream,
　　A discord. Dragons of the prime,
　　That tare[7] each other in their slime,
Were mellow music matched with him.

O life as futile, then, as frail!
　　O for thy voice to soothe and bless!           350
　　What hope of answer, or redress?
Behind the veil, behind the veil.

### LXXXII

I wage not any feud with Death
　　For changes wrought on form and face;
　　No lower life that earth's embrace
May breed with him can fright my faith.

Eternal process moving on,
　　From state to state the spirit walks;
　　And these are but the shattered stalks,
Or ruined chrysalis of one.                           360

Nor blame I Death, because he bare
　　The use of virtue out of earth;
　　I know transplanted human worth
Will bloom to profit, otherwhere.

For this alone on Death I wreak
　　The wrath that garners in my heart:
　　He put our lives so far apart
We cannot hear each other speak.

### XCVI

You say, but with no touch of scorn,
　　Sweet-hearted, you, whose light-blue
　　　　eyes                                        370
　　Are tender over drowning flies,
You tell me doubt is Devil-born.

I know not: one[8] indeed I knew
　　In many a subtle question versed,
　　Who touched a jarring lyre at first,
But ever strove to make it true;

_____
[7] archaic form of *tear*
[8] Hallam, who had written some verse expressive of doubt

Perplext in faith, but pure in deeds,
  At last he beat his music out.
  There lives more faith in honest doubt,
Believe me, than in half the creeds.    *380*

He fought his doubts and gathered
    strength,
  He would not make his judgment
    blind,
  He faced the spectres of the mind
And laid them; thus he came at length

To find a stronger faith his own,
  And Power was with him in the night,
  Which makes the darkness and the
    light,
And dwells not in the light alone,

But in the darkness and the cloud,
  As over Sinaï's peaks of old,    *390*
  While Israel made their gods of gold,
Although the trumpet blew so loud.⁹

### CVI

Ring out, wild bells, to the wild sky,
  The flying cloud, the frosty light:
  The year is dying in the night;
Ring out, wild bells, and let him die.

Ring out the old, ring in the new,
  Ring, happy bells, across the snow:
  The year is going, let him go;
Ring out the false, ring in the true.    *400*

Ring out the grief that saps the mind,
  For those that here we see no more;
  Ring out the feud of rich and poor,
Ring in redress to all mankind.

Ring out a slowly dying cause,
  And ancient forms of party strife;
  Ring in the nobler modes of life,
With sweeter manners, purer laws.

Ring out the want, the care, the sin,
  The faithless coldness of the times;    *410*
  Ring out, ring out my mournful
    rhymes,
But ring the fuller minstrel in.

Ring out false pride in place and blood,
  The civic slander and the spite;

Ring in the love of truth and right,
  Ring in the common love of good.

Ring out old shapes of foul disease;
  Ring out the narrowing lust of gold;
  Ring out the thousand wars of old,
Ring in the thousand years of
    peace.¹⁰    *420*

Ring in the valiant man and free,
  The larger heart, the kindlier hand;
  Ring out the darkness of the land,
Ring in the Christ that is to be.

### CXV

Now fades the last long streak of snow,
  Now burgeons every maze of quick
  About the flowering squares, and thick
By ashen roots the violets blow.

Now rings the woodland loud and long,
  The distance takes a lovelier hue,    *430*
  And drowned in yonder living blue
The lark becomes a sightless¹¹ song.

Now dance the lights on lawn and lea,
  The flocks are whiter down the vale,
  And milkier every milky sail
On winding stream or distant sea;

Where now the seamew¹² pipes, or dives
  In yonder greening gleam, and fly
  The happy birds, that change their sky
To build and brood, that live their
    lives    *440*

From land to land; and in my breast
  Spring wakens too, and my regret
  Becomes an April violet,
And buds and blossoms like the rest.

### CXVIII

Contemplate all this work of Time,
  The giant¹³ laboring in his youth;
  Nor dream of human love and truth,
As dying Nature's earth and lime;

But trust that those we call the dead
  Are breathers of an ampler day    *450*
  For ever nobler ends. They say,
The solid earth whereon we tread

---

9 Exodus 19 and 32
10 Revelation 20    11 invisible    12 sea gull

13 the titan Cronos, erroneously identified as the
god of time

In tracts of fluent heat began
  And grew to seeming-random forms,
  The seeming prey of cyclic storms,
Till at the last arose the man;

Who throve and branched from clime to
    clime,
  The herald of a higher race,
  And of himself in higher place,
If so he type this work of time     *460*

Within himself, from more to more;
  Or, crowned with attributes of woe
  Like glories, move his course, and show
That life is not as idle ore,

But iron dug from central gloom,
  And heated hot with burning fears,
  And dipt in baths of hissing tears,
And battered with the shocks of doom

To shape and use. Arise and fly
  The reeling Faun, the sensual feast; *470*
  Move upward, working out the beast,
And let the ape and tiger die.

### CXXIII

There rolls the deep where grew the tree.
  O earth, what changes hast thou seen!
  There where the long street roars hath
    been
The stillness of the central sea.

The hills are shadows, and they flow
  From form to form, and nothing
    stands;
  They melt like mist, the solid lands,
Like clouds they shape themselves and
    go.     *480*

But in my spirit will I dwell,
  And dream my dream, and hold it true;
  For though my lips may breathe adieu,
I cannot think the thing farewell.

### CXXVII

And all is well, though faith and form
  Be sundered in the night of fear;
  Well roars the storm to those that hear
A deeper voice across the storm,

Proclaiming social truth shall spread,
  And justice, even though thrice
    again     *490*
  The red fool-fury of the Seine [14]
Should pile her barricades with dead.

But ill for him that wears a crown,
  And him, the lazar, in his rags!
  They tremble, the sustaining crags;
The spires of ice are toppled down,

And molten up, and roar in flood;
  The fortress crashes from on high,
  The brute earth lightens to the sky,
And the great Æon sinks in blood,    *500*

And compassed by the fires of hell;
  While thou, dear spirit, happy star,
  O'erlook'st the tumult from afar,
And smilest, knowing all is well.

### CXXX

Thy voice is on the rolling air;
  I hear thee where the waters run;
  Thou standest in the rising sun,
And in the setting thou art fair.

What art thou then? I cannot guess;
  But though I seem in star and
    flower     *510*
  To feel thee some diffusive power,
I do not therefore love thee less.

My love involves the love before;
  My love is vaster passion now;
  Though mixed with God and Nature
    thou,
I seem to love thee more and more.

Far off thou art, but ever nigh;
  I have thee still, and I rejoice;
  I prosper, circled with thy voice;
I shall not lose thee though I die.    *520*

### CXXXI

O living will that shalt endure
  When all that seems shall suffer shock,
  Rise in the spiritual rock, [15]
Flow through our deeds and make them
    pure,

---

14 the Parisian revolt of either 1830 or 1848

15 Christ; I Corinthians 10:4

That we may lift from out of dust
   A voice as unto him that hears,
   A cry above the conquered years
To one that with us works, and trust,

With faith that comes of self-control,
   The truths that never can be proved 530
   Until we close with all we loved,
And all we flow from, soul in soul.

       ·    ·    ·

O true and tried, so well and long,
   Demand not thou a marriage lay;
   In that it is thy marriage day[16]
Is music more than any song.

Nor have I felt so much of bliss
   Since first he[17] told me that he loved
   A daughter of our house, nor proved
Since that dark day a day like this;   540

Though I since then have numbered o'er
   Some thrice three years; they went and
      came,
   Remade the blood and changed the
      frame,
And yet is love not less, but more;

No longer caring to embalm
   In dying songs a dead regret,
   But like a statue solid-set,
And moulded in colossal calm.

Regret is dead, but love is more
   Than in the summers that are
      flown      550
   For I myself with these have grown
To something greater than before;

Which makes appear the songs I made
   As echoes out of weaker times,
   As half but idle brawling rhymes,
The sport of random sun and shade.

But where is she, the bridal flower,
   That must be made a wife ere noon?
   She enters, glowing like the moon
Of Eden on its bridal bower.    560

On me she bends her blissful eyes
   And then on thee; they meet thy look
   And brighten like the star that shook
Betwixt the palms of Paradise.

O, when her life was yet in bud,
   He too foretold the perfect rose.
   For thee she grew, for thee she grows
For ever, and as fair as good.

And thou art worthy, full of power;
   As gentle; liberal-minded, great,   570
   Consistent; wearing all that weight
Of learning lightly like a flower.

But now set out: the noon is near,
   And I must give away the bride;
   She fears not, or with thee beside
And me behind her, will not fear.

For I that danced her on my knee,
   That watched her on her nurse's arm,
   That shielded all her life from harm,
At last must part with her to thee;   580

Now waiting to be made a wife,
   Her feet, my darling, on the dead;[18]
   Their pensive tablets round her head,
And the most living words of life

Breathed in her ear. The ring is on,
   The "Wilt thou?" answered, and again
   The "Wilt thou?" asked, till out of
      twain
Her sweet "I will" has made you one.

Now sign your names, which shall be
      read,
   Mute symbols of a joyful morn,   590
   By village eyes as yet unborn.
The names are signed, and overhead

Begins the clash and clang that tells
   The joy to every wandering breeze;
   The blind wall rocks, and on the trees
The dead leaf trembles to the bells.

O happy hour, and happier hours
   Await them. Many a merry face

---

[16] The epilogue celebrates the marriage of Tennyson's sister Cecilia to Professor Edmund Lushington.
[17] Hallam, who had been engaged to Tennyson's

sister Emily
[18] She walks over the vaults of those buried beneath the church floor.

Salutes them—maidens of the place,
That pelt us in the porch with
    flowers.                                              *600*

O happy hour, behold the bride
    With him to whom her hand I gave.
    They leave the porch, they pass the
    grave
That has today its sunny side.

Today the grave is bright for me,
    For them the light of life increased,
    Who stay to share the morning feast,
Who rest tonight beside the sea.

Let all my genial spirits advance
    To meet and greet a whiter sun;          *610*
    My drooping memory will not shun
The foaming grape of eastern France.

It circles round, and fancy plays,
    And hearts are warmed and faces
    bloom
    As drinking health to bride and groom
We wish them store of happy days,

Nor count me all to blame if I
    Conjecture of a stiller guest,
    Perchance, perchance, among the rest,
And, though in silence, wishing joy.     *620*

But they must go, the time draws on,
    And those white-favored horses wait;
    They rise, but linger; it is late;
Farewell, we kiss, and they are gone.

A shade falls on us like the dark
    From little cloudlets on the grass,
    But sweeps away as out we pass
To range the woods, to roam the park,

Discussing how their courtship grew,
    And talk of others that are wed,        *630*
    And how she looked, and what he said,
And back we come at fall of dew.

Again the feast, the speech, the glee,
    The shade of passing thought, the
    wealth
    Of words and wit, the double health,
The crowning cup, the three-times-
    three,[19]

And last the dance;—till I retire.
    Dumb is that tower which spake so
    loud,
    And high in heaven the streaming
    cloud,
And on the downs a rising fire:          *640*

And rise, O moon, from yonder down,
    Till over down and over dale
    All night the shining vapor sail
And pass the silent-lighted town,

The white-faced halls, the glancing rills,
    And catch at every mountain head,
    And o'er the friths[20] that branch and
    spread
Their sleeping silver through the hills;

And touch with shade the bridal doors,
    With tender gloom the roof, the
    wall;                                   *650*
    And breaking let the splendor fall
To spangle all the happy shores

By which they rest, and ocean sounds,
    And, star and system rolling past,
    A soul shall draw from out the vast
And strike his being into bounds,

And, moved through life of lower phase,
    Result in man, be born and think,
    And act and love, a closer link
Betwixt us and the crowning race         *660*

Of those that, eye to eye, shall look
    On knowledge; under whose command
    Is Earth and Earth's, and in their hand
Is Nature like an open book;

No longer half-akin to brute,
    For all we thought and loved and did,
    And hoped, and suffered, is but seed
Of what in them is flower and fruit;

Whereof the man that with me trod
    This planet was a noble type            *670*
    Appearing ere the times were ripe,
That friend of mine who lives in God,

That God, which ever lives and loves,
    One God, one law, one element,
    And one far-off divine event,
To which the whole creation moves.

                            *(1850)*

---

[19] a cheer    [20] estuaries

## The Eagle

He clasps the crag with crooked hands;
Close to the sun in lonely lands,
Ringed with the azure world he stands.

The wrinkled sea beneath him crawls;
He watches from his mountain walls,
And like a thunderbolt he falls.   *(1851)*

## Tithonus[1]

The woods decay, the woods decay and fall,
The vapors weep their burthen to the ground,
Man comes and tills the field and lies beneath,
And after many a summer dies the swan.
Me only cruel immortality
Consumes; I wither slowly in thine arms,
Here at the quiet limit of the world,
A white-haired shadow roaming like a dream
The ever-silent spaces of the East
Far-folded mists, and gleaming halls of morn.          10
   Alas! for this gray shadow, once a man—
So glorious in his beauty and thy choice,
Who madest him thy chosen, that he seemed
To his great heart none other than a God!
I asked thee, "Give me immortality."
Then didst thou grant mine asking with a smile,
Like wealthy men who care not how they give.
But thy strong Hours indignant worked their wills,
And beat me down and marred and wasted me,
And though they could not end me, left me maimed          20
To dwell in presence of immortal youth,
Immortal age beside immortal youth,
And all I was in ashes. Can thy love,
Thy beauty, make amends, though even now,
Close over us, the silver star, thy guide,
Shines in those tremulous eyes that fill with tears
To hear me? Let me go; take back thy gift.
Why should a man desire in any way
To vary from the kindly race of men,
Or pass beyond the goal of ordinance          30
Where all should pause, as is most meet for all!
   A soft air fans the cloud apart; there comes
A glimpse of that dark world where I was born.
Once more the old mysterious glimmer steals
From thy pure brows, and from thy shoulders pure,
And bosom beating with a heart renewed.
Thy cheek begins to redden through the gloom,
Thy sweet eyes brighten slowly close to mine,

---

[1] a prince in Greek mythology, loved by Aurora, goddess of the dawn, who secured for him the gift of eternal life, but not of eternal youth

Ere yet they blind the stars, and the wild team
Which love thee, yearning for thy yoke, arise                    40
And shake the darkness from their loosened manes,
And beat the twilight into flakes of fire.
    Lo! ever thus thou growest beautiful
In silence, then before thine answer given
Departest, and thy tears are on my cheek.
    Why wilt thou ever scare me with thy tears,
And make me tremble lest a saying learnt,
In days far-off, on that dark earth, be true?
"The Gods themselves cannot recall their gifts."
    Ay me! ay me! with what another heart               50
In days far-off, and with what other eyes
I used to watch—if I be he that watched—
The lucid outline forming round thee; saw
The dim curls kindle into sunny rings;
Changed with thy mystic change, and felt my blood
Glow with the glow that slowly crimsoned all
Thy presence and thy portals, while I lay,
Mouth, forehead, eyelids, growing dewy-warm
With kisses balmier than half-opening buds
Of April, and could hear the lips that kissed              60
Whispering I knew not what of wild and sweet,
Like that strange song I heard Apollo sing,
While Ilion[2] like a mist rose into towers.
    Yet hold me not for ever in thine East;
How can my nature longer mix with thine?
Coldly thy rosy shadows bathe me, cold
Are all thy lights, and cold my wrinkled feet
Upon thy glimmering thresholds, when the steam
Floats up from those dim fields about the homes
Of happy men that have the power to die,                   70
And grassy barrows of the happier dead.
Release me, and restore me to the ground.
Thou seest all things, thou wilt see my grave;
Thou wilt renew thy beauty morn by morn,
I earth in earth forget these empty courts,
And thee returning on thy silver wheels.    *(1860)*

## De Profundis: I

Out of the deep, my child, out of the deep,
Where all that was to be, in all that was,
Whirled for a million eons through the vast
Waste dawn of multitudinous-eddying light—
Out of the deep, my child, out of the deep,
Through all this changing world of changeless law,

---

2 Troy, whose walls were built by Apollo as he sang

And every phase of ever-heightening life,
And nine long months of antenatal gloom,
With this last moon, this crescent—her dark orb
Touched with earth's light—thou comest, darling boy;                10
Our own; a babe in lineament and limb
Perfect, and prophet of the perfect man;
Whose face and form are hers and mine in one,
Indissolubly married like our love;
Live, and be happy in thyself, and serve
This mortal race thy kin so well, that men
May bless thee as we bless thee, O young life
Breaking with laughter from the dark; and may
The fated channel where thy motion lives
Be prosperously shaped, and sway thy course                         20
Along the years of haste and random youth
Unshattered; then full-current through full man;
And last in kindly curves, with gentlest fall,
By quiet fields, a slowly-dying power,
To that last deep where we and thou are still.   (*1880*)

## Crossing the Bar[1]

Sunset and evening star,
   And one clear call for me!
And may there be no moaning of the bar,
   When I put out to sea,

But such a tide as moving seems asleep,
   Too full for sound and foam,
When that which drew from out the
     boundless deep
   Turns again home.

Twilight and evening bell,
   And after that the dark!                                 10
And may there be no sadness of farewell,
   When I embark;

For though from out our bourne[2] of
     Time and Place
   The flood may bear me far,
I hope to see my Pilot face to face
   When I have crost the bar.   (*1889*)

## ROBERT BROWNING / 1812–1889

## Porphyria's Lover

The rain set early in tonight,
   The sullen wind was soon awake,
It tore the elm-tops down for spite,
   And did its worst to vex the lake:
   I listened with heart fit to break.
When glided in Porphyria; straight

She shut the cold out and the storm,
And kneeled and made the cheerless grate
   Blaze up, and all the cottage warm;
   Which done, she rose, and from her
     form                                              10
Withdrew the dripping cloak and shawl,
   And laid her soiled gloves by, untied
Her hat and let the damp hair fall,

---

[1] sandbar partly enclosing a harbor    [2] realm

And, last, she sat down by my side
  And called me. When no voice replied,
She put my arm about her waist,
  And made her smooth white shoulder
    bare,
And all her yellow hair displaced,
  And, stooping, made my cheek lie
    there,
  And spread, o'er all, her yellow
    hair,               20
Murmuring how she loved me—she
  Too weak, for all her heart's endeavour,
To set its struggling passion free
  From pride, and vainer ties dissever,
And give herself to me for ever.
But passion sometimes would prevail,
  Nor could tonight's gay feast restrain
A sudden thought of one so pale
  For love of her, and all in vain:
So, she was come through wind and
    rain.              30
Be sure I looked up at her eyes
  Happy and proud; at last I knew
Porphyria worshipped me; surprise
  Made my heart swell, and still it grew
While I debated what to do.
That moment she was mine, mine, fair,
  Perfectly pure and good: I found
A thing to do, and all her hair
  In one long yellow string I wound
Three times her little throat around,  40
And strangled her. No pain felt she;
  I am quite sure she felt no pain.
As a shut bud that holds a bee,
  I warily oped her lids: again
Laughed the blue eyes without a stain.
And I untightened next the tress
  About her neck; her cheek once more
Blushed bright beneath my burning kiss:
  I propped her head up as before,
  Only, this time my shoulder bore  50
Her head, which droops upon it still:
  The smiling rosy little head,
So glad it has its utmost will,
  That all it scorned at once is fled,
  And I, its love, am gained instead!
Porphyria's love: she guessed not how
  Her darling one wish would be heard.

---

1 hail to thee

And thus we sit together now,
  And all night long we have not stirred,
And yet God has not said a
    word!  *(1836)*      60

## Soliloquy of the Spanish Cloister

Gr-r-r—there go, my heart's abhorrence!
  Water your damned flower-pots, do!
If hate killed men, Brother Lawrence,
  God's blood, would not mine kill you!
What? your myrtle-bush wants trimming?
  Oh, that rose has prior claims—
Needs its leaden vase filled brimming?
  Hell dry you up with its flames!

At the meal we sit together;
  *Salve tibi!*[1] I must hear    10
Wise talk of the kind of weather,
  Sort of season, time of year:
*Not a plenteous cork-crop: scarcely*
  *Dare we hope oak-galls, I doubt;*
*What's the Latin name for "parsley"?*
  What's the Greek name for Swine's
    Snout?

Whew! We'll have our platter burnished,
  Laid with care on our own shelf!
With a fire-new spoon we're furnished,
  And a goblet for ourself,    20
Rinsed like something sacrificial
  Ere 'tis fit to touch our chaps—
Marked with L for our initial!
  (He-he! There his lily snaps!)

*Saint,* forsooth! While brown Dolores
  Squats outside the Convent bank
With Sanchicha, telling stories,
  Steeping tresses in the tank,
Blue-black, lustrous, thick like horsehairs,
  —Can't I see his dead eye glow,  30
Bright as 'twere a Barbary corsair's?
  (That is, if he'd let it show!)

When he finishes refection,
  Knife and fork he never lays
Cross-wise, to my recollection,
  As do I, in Jesu's praise.

I the Trinity illustrate,
   Drinking watered orange-pulp—
In three sips the Arian[2] frustrate;
   While he drains his at one gulp!    40

Oh, those melons? If he's able
   We're to have a feast! so nice!
One goes to the Abbot's table,
   All of us get each a slice.
How go on your flowers? None double?
   Not one fruit-sort can you spy?
Strange!—And I, too, at such trouble,
   Keep them close-nipped on the sly!

There's a great text in Galatians,
   Once you trip on it, entails    50
Twenty-nine distinct damnations,
   One sure, if another fails:
If I trip him just a-dying,
   Sure of heaven as sure can be,
Spin him round and send him flying
   Off to hell, a Manichee?[3]

Or, my scrofulous French novel
   On grey paper with blunt type!
Simply glance at it, you grovel
   Hand and foot in Belial's gripe:    60
If I double down its pages
   At the woeful sixteenth print,
When he gathers his greengages,
   Ope a sieve and slip it in't?

Or, there's Satan!—one might venture
   Pledge one's soul to him, yet leave
Such a flaw in the indenture
   As he'd miss till, past retrieve,
Blasted lay that rose-acacia
   We're so proud of! *Hy, Zy,*
    *Hine. . . .*    70
'St, there's Vespers! *Plena gratiâ*
   *Ave, Virgo!*[4] Gr-r-r—you
    swine!  (*1842*)

## My Last Duchess

*FERRARA*

That's my last Duchess painted on the wall,
Looking as if she were alive; I call
That piece a wonder, now: Frà Pandolf's[1] hands
Worked busily a day, and there she stands.
Will't please you sit and look at her? I said
"Frà Pandolf" by design, for never read
Strangers like you that pictured countenance,
The depth and passion of its earnest glance,
But to myself they turned (since none puts by
The curtain I have drawn for you, but I)    10
And seemed as they would ask me, if they durst,
How such a glance came there; so, not the first
Are you to turn and ask thus. Sir, 'twas not
Her husband's presence only, called that spot
Of joy into the Duchess' cheek: perhaps
Frà Pandolf chanced to say "Her mantle laps
Over my Lady's wrist too much," or "Paint
Must never hope to reproduce the faint

---

2 one who accepts the doctrine of Arius (*c.* A.D. 260–336), which denies the trinitarian concept of the Deity
3 a believer in the heresy of Manes (*c.* A.D. 216– *c.* 276), which holds that good and evil are thor-oughly mingled, and which denies the primacy of God
4 Hail, Mary, full of grace
1 an imaginary artist, as is Claus of Innsbruck of line 56

Half-flush that dies along her throat'': such stuff
Was courtesy, she thought, and cause enough                    *20*
For calling up that spot of joy. She had
A heart—how shall I say?—too soon made glad,
Too easily impressed; she liked whate'er
She looked on, and her looks went everywhere.
Sir, 'twas all one! My favor at her breast,
The dropping of the daylight in the West.
The bough of cherries some officious fool
Broke in the orchard for her, the white mule
She rode with round the terrace—all and each
Would draw from her alike the approving speech,               *30*
Or blush, at least. She thanked men,—good; but thanked
Somehow—I know not how—as if she ranked
My gift of a nine-hundred-years-old name
With anybody's gift. Who'd stoop to blame
This sort of trifling? Even had you skill
In speech—(which I have not)—to make your will
Quite clear to such an one, and say, "Just this
Or that in you disgusts me; here you miss,
Or there exceed the mark"—and if she let
Herself be lessoned so, nor plainly set                      *40*
Her wits to yours, forsooth, and made excuse,
—E'en then would be some stooping, and I choose
Never to stoop. Oh, Sir, she smiled, no doubt,
Whene'er I passed her; but who passed without
Much the same smile? This grew; I gave commands;
Then all smiles stopped together. There she stands
As if alive. Will't please you rise? We'll meet
The company below, then. I repeat,
The Count your Master's known munificence
Is ample warrant that no just pretence                       *50*
Of mine for dowry will be disallowed;
Though his fair daughter's self, as I avowed
At starting, is my object. Nay, we'll go
Together down, Sir! Notice Neptune, though,
Taming a sea-horse, thought a rarity,
Which Claus of Innsbruck cast in bronze for me.   (*1842*)


## Meeting at Night

The grey sea and the long black land;
And the yellow half-moon large and low;
And the startled little waves that leap
In fiery ringlets from their sleep,
As I gain the cove with pushing prow,
And quench its speed i' the slushy sand.

Then a mile of warm sea-scented beach;
Three fields to cross till a farm appears;
A tap at the pane, the quick sharp scratch
And blue spurt of a lighted match,
And a voice less loud, through its joys and fears,
Than the two hearts beating each to each!   (*1845*)

10

## Parting at Morning

Round the cape of a sudden came the sea,
And the sun looked over the mountain's rim:
And straight was a path of gold for him,
And the need of a world of men for me.   (*1845*)

## Home-Thoughts, from Abroad

Oh, to be in England
Now that April's there,
And whoever wakes in England
Sees, some morning, unaware,
That the lowest boughs and the brushwood sheaf
Round the elm-tree bole are in tiny leaf,
While the chaffinch sings on the orchard bough
In England—now!

And after April, when May follows,
And the whitethroat builds, and all the swallows!
Hark, where my blossomed pear-tree in the hedge
Leans to the field and scatters on the clover
Blossoms and dewdrops—at the bent spray's edge—
That's the wise thrush; he sings each song twice over,
Lest you should think he never could recapture
The first fine careless rapture!
And though the fields look rough with hoary dew
All will be gay when noontide wakes anew
The buttercups, the little children's dower—
Far brighter than this gaudy melon-flower.   (*1845*)

10

20

## Home-Thoughts, from the Sea

Nobly, nobly Cape Saint Vincent to the north-west died away;
Sunset ran, one glorious blood-red, reeking into Cadiz Bay;
Bluish 'mid the burning water, full in face Trafalgar lay;
In the dimmest north-east distance, dawned Gibraltar grand and grey;
"Here and here did England help me: how can I help England?"—say,
Whoso turns as I, this evening, turn to God to praise and pray,
While Jove's planet rises yonder, silent over Africa.   (*1845*)

## The Bishop Orders His Tomb at Saint Praxed's Church

*(ROME, 15–.)*

Vanity, saith the preacher, vanity!
Draw round my bed: is Anselm keeping back?
Nephews—sons mine . . . ah God, I know not! Well—
She, men would have to be your mother once,
Old Gandolf envied me, so fair she was!
What's done is done, and she is dead beside,
Dead long ago, and I am Bishop since,
And as she died so must we die ourselves,
And thence ye may perceive the world's a dream.
Life, how and what is it? As here I lie                                     10
In this state-chamber, dying by degrees,
Hours and long hours in the dead night, I ask
"Do I live, am I dead?" Peace, peace seems all.
Saint Praxed's ever was the church for peace;
And so, about this tomb of mine. I fought
With tooth and nail to save my niche, ye know:
—Old Gandolf cozened me, despite my care;
Shrewd was that snatch from out the corner South
He graced his carrion with, God curse the same!
Yet still my niche is not so cramped but thence                            20
One sees the pulpit o' the epistle-side,[1]
And somewhat of the choir, those silent seats,
And up into the aery dome where live
The angels, and a sunbeam's sure to lurk:
And I shall fill my slab of basalt there,
And 'neath my tabernacle[2] take my rest,
With those nine columns round me, two and two,
The odd one at my feet where Anselm stands:
Peach-blossom marble all, the rare, the ripe
As fresh-poured red wine of a mighty pulse                                 30
—Old Gandolf with his paltry onion-stone,
Put me where I may look at him! True peach,
Rosy and flawless: how I earned the prize!
Draw close: that conflagration of my church
—What then? So much was saved if aught were missed!
My sons, ye would not be my death? Go dig
The white-grape vineyard where the oil-press stood,
Drop water gently till the surface sinks,
And if ye find . . . Ah, God I know not, I! . . .
Bedded in store of rotten figleaves soft,                                  40
And corded up in a tight olive-frail,[3]
Some lump, ah God, of lapis lazuli,

---

[1] the right side as one faces the altar. The epistle
is read from this side.

[2] the canopy which the Bishop imagines over his
tomb

[3] a basket of rushes

Big as a Jew's head cut off at the nape,
Blue as a vein o'er the Madonna's breast . . .
Sons, all have I bequeathed you, villas, all,
That brave Frascati villa with its bath,
So, let the blue lump poise between my knees,
Like God the Father's globe on both His hands
Ye worship in the Jesu Church so gay,
For Gandolf shall not choose but see and burst!                  50
Swift as a weaver's shuttle fleet our years:
Man goeth to the grave, and where is he?
Did I say basalt for my slab, sons? Black—
'Twas ever antique-black I meant! How else
Shall ye contrast my frieze to come beneath?
The bas-relief in bronze ye promised me,
Those Pans and Nymphs ye wot of, and perchance
Some tripod, thyrsus,[4] with a vase or so,
The Saviour at his sermon on the mount,
Saint Praxed in a glory, and one Pan                             60
Ready to twitch the Nymph's last garment off,
And Moses with the tables . . . but I know
Ye mark me not! What do they whisper thee,
Child of my bowels, Anselm? Ah, ye hope
To revel down my villas while I gasp
Bricked o'er with beggar's mouldy travertine
Which Gandolf from his tomb-top chuckles at!
Nay, boys, ye love me—all of jasper, then!
'Tis jasper ye stand pledged to, lest I grieve
My bath must needs be left behind, alas!                         70
One block, pure green as a pistachio-nut,
There's plenty jasper somewhere in the world—
And have I not Saint Praxed's ear to pray
Horses for ye, and brown Greek manuscripts,
And mistresses with great smooth marbly limbs?
—That's if ye carve my epitaph aright,
Choice Latin, picked phrase, Tully's[5] every word,
No gaudy ware like Gandolf's second line—
Tully, my masters? Ulpian[6] serves his need!
And then how I shall lie through centuries,                      80
And hear the blessèd mutter of the mass,
And see God made and eaten all day long,
And feel the steady candle-flame, and taste
Good strong thick stupefying incense-smoke!
For as I lie here, hours of the dead night,
Dying in state and by such slow degrees,
I fold my arms as if they clasped a crook,

---

4 a staff decorated with vine leaves and denoting
pagan revelry
5 Marcus Tullius Cicero (106–43 B.C.), noted for
the eloquence and purity of his Latin style

6 Domitius Ulpianus (c. A.D. 170–228), a prolific
writer whose works are known chiefly through
Justinian's *Digest*

And stretch my feet forth straight as stone can point
And let the bedclothes for a mortcloth drop
Into great laps and folds of sculptor's-work:                          90
And as yon tapers dwindle, and strange thoughts
Grow, with a certain humming in my ears,
About the life before I lived this life,
And this life too, popes, cardinals and priests,
Saint Praxed at his sermon on the mount,
Your tall pale mother with her talking eyes,
And new-found agate urns as fresh as day,
And marble's language, Latin pure, discreet,
—Aha, ELUCESCEBAT[7] quoth our friend?
No Tully, said I, Ulpian at the best!                                  100
Evil and brief hath been my pilgrimage.
All lapis, all, sons! Else I give the Pope
My villas: will ye ever eat my heart?
Ever your eyes were as a lizard's quick,
They glitter like your mother's for my soul,
Or ye would heighten my impoverished frieze,
Piece out its starved design, and fill my vase
With grapes, and add a vizor and a Term,[8]
And to the tripod ye would tie a lynx
That in his struggle throws the thyrsus down,                         110
To comfort me on my entablature
Whereon I am to lie till I must ask
"Do I live, am I dead?" There, leave me, there!
For ye have stabbed me with ingratitude
To death—ye wish it—God, ye wish it! Stone—
Gritstone, a-crumble! Clammy squares which sweat
As if the corpse they keep were oozing through—
And no more lapis to delight the world!
Well, go! I bless ye. Fewer tapers there,
But in a row: and, going, turn your backs                             120
—Ay, like departing altar-ministrants,
And leave me in my church, the church for peace,
That I may watch at leisure if he leers—
Old Gandolf, at me, from his onion-stone,
As still he envied me, so fair she was!   (*1845*)


## Up at a Villa—Down in the City

### (*AS DISTINGUISHED BY AN ITALIAN PERSON OF QUALITY*)

Had I but plenty of money, money enough and to spare,
The house for me, no doubt, were a house in the city-square;
Ah, such a life, such a life, as one leads at the window there!

---

[7] He was renowned; but the form of the word    [8] a commemorative bust on a pedestal
is that of decadent Latin.

Something to see by Bacchus, something to hear, at least!
There, the whole day long, one's life is a perfect feast;
While up at a villa one lives, I maintain it, no more than a beast.

Well now, look at our villa! stuck like the horn of a bull
Just on a mountain-edge as bare as the creature's skull,
Save a mere shag of a bush with hardly a leaf to pull!
—I scratch my own, sometimes, to see if the hair's turned wool.               *10*

But the city, oh the city—the square with the houses! Why?
They are stone-faced, white as a curd, there's something to take the eye!
Houses in four straight lines, not a single front awry;
You watch who crosses and gossips, who saunters, who hurries by;
Green blinds, as a matter of course, to draw when the sun gets high;
And the shops with fanciful signs which are painted properly.

What of a villa? Though winter be over in March by rights,
'Tis May perhaps ere the snow shall have withered well off the heights:
You've the brown ploughed land before, where the oxen steam and wheeze,
And the hills over-smoked behind by the faint gray olive-trees.                *20*

Is it better in May, I ask you? You've summer all at once;
In a day he leaps complete with a few strong April suns.
'Mid the sharp short emerald wheat, scarce risen three fingers well,
The wild tulip, at end of its tube, blows out its great red bell
Like a thin clear bubble of blood, for the children to pick and sell.

Is it ever hot in the square? There's a fountain to spout and splash!
In the shade it sings and springs; in the shine such foamblows flash
On the horses with curling fish-tails, that prance and paddle and pash
Round the lady atop in her conch—fifty gazers do not abash,
Though all that she wears is some weeds round her waist in a sort of sash.      *30*

All the year long at the villa, nothing to see though you linger,
Except yon cypress that points like death's lean lifted forefinger.
Some think fireflies pretty, when they mix i' the corn and mingle,
Or thrid the stinking hemp till the stalks of it seem a-tingle.
Late August or early September, the stunning cicala is shrill,
And the bees keep their tiresome whine round the resinous firs on the hill.
Enough of the seasons,—I spare you the months of the fever and chill.

Ere you open your eyes in the city, the blessed church-bells begin:
No sooner the bells leave off than the diligence rattles in:
You get the pick of the news, and it costs you never a pin.                    *40*
By and by there's the travelling doctor gives pills, lets blood, draws teeth;
Or the Pulcinello-trumpet breaks up the market beneath.
At the post-office such a scene-picture—the new play, piping hot!
And a notice how, only this morning, three liberal thieves were shot.
Above it behold the Archbishop's most fatherly of rebukes,
And beneath, with his crown and his lion, some little new law of the Duke's!
Or a sonnet with flowery marge, to the Reverend Don So-and-so,
Who is Dante, Boccaccio, Petrarca, Saint Jerome, and Cicero,

"And moreover," (the sonnet goes rhyming,) "the skirts of Saint Paul had
   reached,
Having preached us those six Lent-lectures more unctuous than ever he
   preached."                                                                          50
Noon strikes,—here sweeps the procession! our Lady borne smiling and smart
With a pink gauze gown all spangles, and seven swords stuck in her heart!
*Bang-whang-whang* goes the drum, *tootle-te-tootle* the fife;
No keeping one's haunches still: it's the greatest pleasure in life.

But bless you, it's dear—it's dear! fowls, wine, at double the rate.
They have clapped a new tax upon salt, and what oil pays passing the gate
It's a horror to think of. And so, the villa for me, not the city!
Beggars can scarcely be choosers: but still—ah, the pity, the pity!
Look, two and two go the priests, then the monks with cowls and sandals,
And the penitents dressed in white shirts, a-holding the yellow candles;        60
One, he carries a flag up straight, and another a cross with handles,
And the Duke's guard brings up the rear, for the better prevention of scandals:
*Bang-whang-whang* goes the drum, *tootle-te-tootle* the fife.
Oh, a day in the city-square, there is no such pleasure in life!   *(1855)*

## Memorabilia

Ah, did you once see Shelley plain,
   And did he stop and speak to you
And did you speak to him again?
   How strange it seems and new!

But you were living before that,
   And also you are living after;
And the memory I started at—
   My starting moves your laughter.

I crossed a moor, with a name of its own
   And a certain use in the world no
      doubt,                                                              10
Yet a hand's breadth of it shines alone
   'Mid the blank miles round about:

For there I picked up on the heather
   And there I put inside my breast
A moulted feather, an eagle-feather!
   Well, I forget the rest.   *(1855)*

## Andrea del Sarto[1]

### (*CALLED "THE FAULTLESS PAINTER"*)

But do not let us quarrel any more,
No, my Lucrezia; bear with me for once:
Sit down and all shall happen as you wish.
You turn your face, but does it bring your heart?
I'll work then for your friend's friend, never fear,
Treat his own subject after his own way,
Fix his own time, accept too his own price,
And shut the money into this small hand
When next it takes mine. Will it? tenderly?
Oh, I'll content him,—but to-morrow, Love!                                        10
I often am much wearier than you think,

---

[1] The speaker of the monologue is an actual painter (1486–1531).

This evening more than usual, and it seems
As if—forgive now—should you let me sit
Here by the window with your hand in mine
And look a half-hour forth on Fiesole,
Both of one mind, as married people use,
Quietly, quietly, the evening through,
I might get up to-morrow to my work
Cheerful and fresh as ever. Let us try.
To-morrow, how you shall be glad for this!                                      20
Your soft hand is a woman of itself,
And mine the man's bared breast she curls inside.
Don't count the time lost, either; you must serve
For each of the five pictures we require:
It saves a model. So! keep looking so—
My serpentining beauty, rounds on rounds!
—How could you ever prick those perfect ears,
Even to put the pearl there! oh, so sweet—
My face, my moon, my everybody's moon,
Which everybody looks on and calls his,                                         30
And, I suppose, is looked on by in turn,
While she looks—no one's: very dear, no less.
You smile? why, there's my picture ready made,
There's what we painters call our harmony!
A common greyness silvers everything,—
All in a twilight, you and I alike
—You, at the point of your first pride in me
(That's gone, you know),—but I, at every point;
My youth, my hope, my art, being all toned down
To yonder sober pleasant Fiesole.                                               40
There's the bell clinking from the chapel-top;
That length of convent-wall across the way
Holds the trees safer, huddled more inside;
The last monk leaves the garden; days decrease
And autumn grows, autumn in everything.
Eh? the whole seems to fall into a shape
As if I saw alike my work and self
And all that I was born to be and do.
A twilight-piece. Love, we are in God's hand.
How strange now, looks the life he makes us lead!                               50
So free we seem, so fettered fast we are!
I feel he laid the fetter: let it lie!
This chamber for example—turn your head—
All that's behind us! you don't understand
Nor care to understand about my art,
But you can hear at least when people speak;
And that cartoon, the second from the door
—It is the thing, Love! so such things should be—
Behold Madonna, I am bold to say.
I can do with my pencil what I know,                                            60

What I see, what at bottom of my heart
I wish for, if I ever wish so deep—
Do easily, too—when I say, perfectly,
I do not boast, perhaps: yourself are judge
Who listened to the Legate's talk last week,
And just as much they used to say in France.
At any rate 'tis easy, all of it!
No sketches first, no studies, that's long past—
I do what many dream of all their lives
—Dream? strive to do, and agonize to do,                        70
And fail in doing. I could count twenty such
On twice your fingers, and not leave this town,
Who strive—you don't know how the others strive
To paint a little thing like that you smeared
Carelessly passing with your robes afloat,—
Yet do much less, so much less, Someone says,
(I know his name, no matter) so much less!
Well, less is more, Lucrezia: I am judged.
There burns a truer light of God in them,
In their vexed, beating, stuffed and stopped-up brain,           80
Heart, or whate'er else, than goes on to prompt
This low-pulsed forthright craftsman's hand of mine.
Their works drop groundward, but themselves, I know,
Reach many a time a heaven that's shut to me,
Enter and take their place there sure enough,
Though they come back and cannot tell the world.
My works are nearer heaven, but I sit here.
The sudden blood of these men! at a word—
Praise them, it boils, or blame them, it boils too.
I, painting from myself and to myself,                          90
Know what I do, am unmoved by men's blame
Or their praise either. Somebody remarks
Morello's[2] outline there is wrongly traced,
His hue mistaken; what of that? or else,
Rightly traced and well ordered, what of that?
Speak as they please, what does the mountain care?
Ah, but a man's reach should exceed his grasp,
Or what's a heaven for? All is silver-grey
Placid and perfect with my art: the worse!
I know both what I want and what might gain,                     100
And yet how profitless to know, to sigh
"Had I been two, another and myself,
Our head would have o'erlooked the world!" No doubt.
Yonder's a work, now, of that famous youth,
The Urbinate[3] who died five years ago.
('Tis copied, George Vasari[4] sent it me.)

---

[2] a peak of the Appenines
[3] Raphael (1483–1520) was born at Urbino.

[4] Giorgio Vasari (1511–1574), architect, painter, and art historian

Well, I can fancy how he did it all,
Pouring his soul, with kings and popes to see,
Reaching, that heaven might so replenish him,
Above and through his art—for it gives way;                    *110*
That arm is wrongly put—and there again—
A fault to pardon in the drawing's lines,
Its body, so to speak: its soul is right,
He means right—that, a child may understand.
Still, what an arm! and I could alter it;
But all the play, the insight and the stretch—
Out of me, out of me! And wherefore out?
Had you enjoined them on me, given me soul,
We might have risen to Rafael, I and you!
Nay, Love, you did give all I asked, I think—              *120*
More than I merit, yes, by many times.
But had you—oh, with the same perfect brow,
And perfect eyes, and more than perfect mouth,
And the low voice my soul hears, as a bird
The fowler's pipe, and follows to the snare—
Had you, with these the same, but brought a mind!
Some women do so. Had the mouth there urged
"God and the glory! never care for gain.
The present by the future, what is that?
Live for fame, side by side with Agnolo![5]                *130*
Rafael is waiting: up to God all three!"
I might have done it for you. So it seems:
Perhaps not. All is as God overrules.
Beside, incentives come from the soul's self;
The rest avail not. Why do I need you?
What wife had Rafael, or has Agnolo?
In this world, who can do a thing, will not;
And who would do it, cannot, I perceive:
Yet the will's somewhat—somewhat, too, the power—
And thus we half-men struggle. At the end,                 *140*
God, I conclude, compensates, punishes.
'Tis safer for me, if the award be strict,
That I am something underrated here,
Poor this long while, despised, to speak the truth.
I dared not, do you know, leave home all day,
For fear of chancing on the Paris lords.
The best is when they pass and look aside;
But they speak sometimes; I must bear it all.
Well may they speak! That Francis,[6] that first time,
And that long festal year at Fontainebleau!              *150*
I surely then could sometimes leave the ground,
Put on the glory, Rafael's daily wear,

---

[5] Michelangelo (1475–1564)
[6] King Francis I of France, patron of Andrea at Fontainebleau

In that humane great monarch's golden look,—
One finger in his beard or twisted curl
Over his mouth's good mark that made the smile,
One arm about my shoulder, round my neck,
The jingle of his gold chain in my ear,
I painting proudly with his breath on me,
All his court round him, seeing with his eyes,
Such frank French eyes, and such a fire of souls                    160
Profuse, my hand kept plying by those hearts,—
And, best of all, this, this, this face beyond,
This in the background, waiting on my work,
To crown the issue with a last reward!
A good time was it not, my kingly days?
And had you not grown restless . . . but I know—
'Tis done and past; 'twas right, my instinct said;
Too live the life grew, golden and not grey,
And I'm the weak-eyed bat no sun should tempt
Out of the grange whose four walls make his world.                  170
How could it end in any other way?
You called me, and I came home to your heart.
The triumph was—to reach and stay there; since
I reached it ere the triumph, what is lost?
Let my hands frame your face in your hair's gold,
You beautiful Lucrezia that are mine!
"Rafael did this, Andrea painted that;
The Roman's is the better when you pray,
But still the other's Virgin was his wife—"
Men will excuse me. I am glad to judge                              180
Both pictures in your presence; clearer grows
My better fortune, I resolve to think.
For, do you know, Lucrezia, as God lives,
Said one day Agnolo, his very self,
To Rafael . . . I have known it all these years . . .
(When the young man was flaming out his thoughts
Upon a palace-wall for Rome to see,
Too lifted up in heart because of it)
"Friend, there's a certain sorry little scrub
Goes up and down our Florence, none cares how,                      190
Who, were he set to plan and execute
As you are, pricked on by your popes and kings,
Would bring the sweat into that brow of yours!"
To Rafael's!—and indeed the arm is wrong.
I hardly dare . . . yet, only you to see,
Give the chalk here—quick, thus the line should go!
Ay, but the soul! he's Rafael! rub it out!
Still, all I care for, if he spoke the truth,
(What he? why, who but Michel Agnolo?
Do you forget already words like those?)                            200
If really there was such a chance, so lost,—

Is, whether you're—not grateful—but more pleased.
Well, let me think so. And you smile indeed!
This hour has been an hour! Another smile?
If you would sit thus by me every night
I should work better, do you comprehend?
I mean that I should earn more, give you more.
See, it is settled dusk now; there's a star;
Morello's gone, the watch-lights show the wall,
The cue-owls speak the name we call them by.          210
Come from the window, love,—come in, at last,
Inside the melancholy little house
We built to be so gay with. God is just.
King Francis may forgive me: oft at nights
When I look up from painting, eyes tired out,
The walls become illumined, brick from brick
Distinct, instead of mortar, fierce bright gold,
That gold of his I did cement them with!
Let us but love each other. Must you go?
That Cousin here again? he waits outside?          220
Must see you—you, and not with me? Those loans?
More gaming debts to pay? you smiled for that?
Well, let smiles buy me! have you more to spend?
While hand and eye and something of a heart
Are left me, work's my ware, and what's it worth?
I'll pay my fancy. Only let me sit
The grey remainder of the evening out,
Idle, you call it, and muse perfectly
How I could paint, were I but back in France,
One picture, just one more—the Virgin's face,          230
Not yours this time! I want you at my side
To hear them—that is, Michel Agnolo—
Judge all I do and tell you of its worth.
Will you? To-morrow, satisfy your friend.
I take the subjects for his corridor,
Finish the portrait out of hand—there, there,
And throw him in another thing or two
If he demurs; the whole should prove enough
To pay for this same Cousin's freak. Beside,
What's better and what's all I care about,          240
Get you the thirteen scudi for the ruff!
Love, does that please you? Ah, but what does he,
The Cousin! what does he to please you more?

    I am grown peaceful as old age to-night.
I regret little, I would change still less.
Since there my past life lies, why alter it?
The very wrong to Francis!—it is true
I took his coin, was tempted and complied,
And built this house and sinned, and all is said.

My father and my mother died of want.                                    *250*
Well, had I riches of my own? you see
How one gets rich! Let each one bear his lot.
They were born poor, lived poor, and poor they died:
And I have laboured somewhat in my time
And not been paid profusely. Some good son
Paint my two hundred pictures—let him try!
No doubt, there's something strikes a balance. Yes,
You loved me quite enough, it seems to-night.
This must suffice me here. What would one have?
In heaven, perhaps, new chances, one more chance—        *260*
Four great walls in the New Jersualem,
Meted on each side by the angel's reed,
For Leonard,[7] Rafael, Agnolo and me
To cover—the three first without a wife,
While I have mine! So—still they overcome
Because there's still Lucrezia,—as I choose.

Again the Cousin's whistle! Go, my Love.   (*1855*)


# Prospice[1]

Fear death?—to feel the fog in my throat,
        The mist in my face,
When the snows begin, and the blasts denote
        I am nearing the place,
The power of the night, the press of the storm,
        The post of the foe;
Where he stands, the Arch Fear in a visible form,
        Yet the strong man must go:
For the journey is done and the summit attained,
        And the barriers fall,                                          *10*
Though a battle's to fight ere the guerdon be gained,
        The reward of it all.
I was ever a fighter, so—one fight more,
        The best and the last!
I would hate that death bandaged my eyes, and forbore,
        And bade me creep past.
No! let me taste the whole of it, fare like my peers,
        The heroes of old,
Bear the brunt, in a minute pay glad life's arrears
        Of pain, darkness, and cold.                                   *20*
For sudden the worst turns the best to the brave,
        The black minute's at end,
And the elements' rage, the fiend-voices that rave,
        Shall dwindle, shall blend,

---

[7] Leonardo da Vinci (1452–1519)          [1] look ahead; pronounced prŏs′pĭs

Shall change, shall become first a peace out of pain,
     Then a light, then thy breast,
O thou soul of my soul! I shall clasp thee again,
     And with God be the rest! *(1861)*


# EMILY BRONTË / 1818–1848

## Remembrance

Cold in the earth—and the deep snow piled above thee,
Far, far removed, cold in the dreary grave!
Have I forgot, my only Love, to love thee,
Severed at last by Time's all-severing wave?

Now, when alone, do my thoughts no longer hover
Over the mountains, on that northern shore,
Resting their wings where heath and fern-leaves cover
Thy noble heart for ever, ever more?

Cold in the earth—and fifteen wild Decembers,
From those brown hills, have melted into spring:                     10
Faithful, indeed, is the spirit that remembers
After such years of change and suffering!

Sweet Love of youth, forgive, if I forget thee,
While the world's tide is bearing me along;
Other desires and other hopes beset me,
Hopes which obscure, but cannot do thee wrong!

No later light has lightened up my heaven,
No second morn has ever shone for me;
All my life's bliss from thy dear life was given,
All my life's bliss is in the grave with thee.                       20

But, when the days of golden dreams had perished,
And even Despair was powerless to destroy;
Then did I learn how existence could be cherished,
Strengthened and fed without the aid of joy.

Then did I check the tears of useless passion—
Weaned my young soul from yearning after thine;
Sternly denied its burning wish to hasten
Down to that tomb already more than mine.

And, even yet, I dare not let it languish,
Dare not indulge in memory's rapturous pain;                         30
Once drinking deep of that divinest anguish,
How could I seek the empty world again? *(1845)*

## To Imagination

When weary with the long day's care,
  And earthly change from pain to pain,
And lost, and ready to despair,
  Thy kind voice calls me back again
Oh, my true friend! I am not lone,
While thou canst speak with such a tone!

So hopeless is the world without,
  The world within I doubly prize;
Thy world, where guile and hate and
    doubt
  And cold suspicion never rise;                    10
Where thou and I and Liberty
Have undisputed sovereignty.

What matters it, that all around
  Danger and guilt and darkness lie,
If but within our bosom's bound
  We hold a bright, untroubled sky,
Warm with ten thousand mingled rays
Of suns that know no winter days?

Reason, indeed, may oft complain
  For Nature's sad reality,                         20
And tell the suffering heart how vain
  Its cherished dreams must always be;
And Truth may rudely trample down
The flowers of Fancy, newly-blown:

But thou art ever there, to bring
  The hovering vision back, and breathe
New glories o'er the blighted spring,
  And call a lovelier Life from Death,
And whisper, with a voice divine,
Or real worlds, as bright as thine.                30

I trust not to thy phantom bliss,
  Yet, still, in evening's quiet hour,
With never-failing thankfulness,
  I welcome thee, Benignant Power,
Sure solacer of human cares,
And sweeter hope, when hope
    despairs!   (*1846*)

# ARTHUR HUGH CLOUGH / 1819–1861

## Say Not, the Struggle Nought Availeth

Say not, the struggle nought availeth,
  The labour and the wounds are vain,
The enemy faints not, nor faileth,
  And as things have been they remain.

If hopes were dupes, fears may be liars;
  It may be, in yon smoke concealed,
Your comrades chase e'en now the fliers,
  And, but for you, possess the field.

For while the tired waves, vainly breaking,
  Seem here no painful inch to gain,        10
Far back, through creeks and inlets
    making,
  Comes silent, flooding in, the main,

And not by eastern windows only,
  When daylight comes, comes in the
    light,
In front, the sun climbs slow, how slowly,
  But westward, look, the land is
    bright.   (*1849*)

## Where Lies the Land?

Where lies the land to which the ship would go?
Far, far ahead, is all her seamen know.
And where the land she travels from? Away,
Far, far behind, is all that they can say.

On sunny noons upon the deck's smooth face,
Linked arm in arm, how pleasant here to pace;
Or, o'er the stern reclining, watch below
The foaming wake far widening as we go.

On stormy nights when wild north-westers rave,
How proud a thing to fight with wind and wave!                    *10*
The dripping sailor on the reeling mast
Exults to bear, and scorns to wish it past.

Where lies the land to which the ship would go?
Far, far ahead, is all her seamen know.
And where the land she travels from? Away,
Far, far behind, is all that they can say.   *(1852)*

## The Latest Decalogue

Thou shalt have one God only; who
Would be at the expense of two?
No graven images may be
Worshipped, except the currency:
Swear not at all; for, for thy curse
Thine enemy is none the worse:
At church on Sunday to attend
Will serve to keep the world thy friend:
Honour thy parents; that is, all
From whom advancement may befall:   *10*
Thou shalt not kill; but need'st not strive
Officiously to keep alive:
Do not adultery commit;
Advantage rarely comes of it:
Thou shalt not steal; an empty feat,
When 'tis so lucrative to cheat:
Bear not false witness; let the lie
Have time on its own wings to fly:
Thou shalt not covet, but tradition
Approves all forms of
   competition.   *(1862)*     *20*

## All Is Well

Whate'er you dream with doubt
   possessed,
Keep, keep it snug within your breast,
And lay you down and take your rest;
Forget in sleep the doubt and pain,
And when you wake, to work again.
The wind it blows, the vessel goes,
And where and whither, no one knows.

'Twill all be well: no need of care;
Though how it will, and when, and where,
We cannot see, and can't declare.      *10*
In spite of dreams, in spite of thought,
'Tis not in vain, and not for naught,
The wind it blows, the ship it goes,
Though where and whither, no one
   knows.   *(1869)*

## MATTHEW ARNOLD / 1822–1888

### Written in Emerson's Essays

"O monstrous, dead, unprofitable world,
That thou canst hear, and hearing, hold thy way!
A voice oracular hath pealed today,
Today a hero's banner is unfurled;
Hast thou no lip for welcome?"—So I said.
Man after man, the world smiled and passed by;
A smile of wistful incredulity
As though one spake of life unto the dead—
Scornful, and strange, and sorrowful, and full
Of bitter knowledge. Yet the will is free;                    10
Strong is the soul, and wise, and beautiful;
The seeds of godlike power are in us still;
Gods are we, bards, saints, heroes, if we will!—
Dumb judges, answer, truth or mockery?    (*1849*)

### The Forsaken Merman

Come, dear children let us away;
Down and away below!
Now my brothers call from the bay,
Now the great winds shoreward blow,
Now the salt tides seaward flow;
Now the wild white horses play,
Champ and chafe and toss in the spray.
Children dear, let us away!
This way, this way!

Call her once before you go—                    10
Call once yet!
In a voice that she will know:
"Margaret! Margaret!"
Children's voices should be dear
(Call once more) to a mother's ear;
Children's voices, wild with pain—
Surely she will come again!
Call her once and come away;
This way, this way!
"Mother dear, we cannot stay!                    20
The wild white horses foam and fret."
Margaret! Margaret!

Come, dear children, come away down!
Call no more!
One last look at the white walled town,
And the little grey church on the windy
        shore;
Then come down!
She will not come though you call all
        day;
Come away, come away!

Children dear, was it yesterday                    30
We heard the sweet bells over the bay?
In the caverns where we lay,
Through the surf and through the swell,
The far-off sound of a silver bell?
Sand-strewn caverns, cool and deep,
Where the winds are all asleep;
Where the spent lights quiver and gleam,
Where the salt weed sways in the stream,
Where the sea-beasts, ranged all around,
Feed in the ooze of their pasture-
        ground:                    40
Where the sea-snakes coil and twine,
Dry their mail and bask in the brine;
Where great whales come sailing by,
Sail and sail, with unshut eye,
Round the world for ever and aye?
When did music come this way?
Children dear, was it yesterday?

Children dear, was it yesterday
(Call yet once) that she went away?

550

Once she sate with you and me,                    50
On a red gold throne in the heart of the
    sea,
And the youngest sate on her knee.
She combed its bright hair, and she
    tended it well,
When down swung the sound of a far-off
    bell
She sighed, she looked up through the
    clear green sea;
She said: "I must go, for my kinsfolk
    pray
In the little grey church on the shore
    to-day.
'Twill be Easter-time in the world—ah
    me!
And I lose my poor soul, Merman! here
    with thee."
I said: "Go up, dear heart, through the
    waves;                                          60
Say thy prayer, and come back to the
    kind sea-caves!"
She smiled, she went up through the
    surf in the bay.
Children dear, was it yesterday?

    Children dear, were we long alone?
"The sea grows stormy, the little ones
    moan;
Long prayers," I said, "in the world they
    say:
Come!" I said; and we rose through the
    surf in the bay.
We went up the beach, by the sandy
    down
Where the sea-stocks bloom, to the
    white-walled town;
Through the narrow paved streets, where
    all was still,                                   70
To the little grey church on the windy
    hill.
From the church came a murmur of folk
    at their prayers,
But we stood without in the cold blowing
    airs.
We climbed on the graves, on the
    stones worn with rains,
And we gazed up the aisle through the
    small leaded panes

She sate by the pillar; we saw her clear:
"Margaret, hist! come quick, we are here!
Dear heart," I said, "we are long alone;
The sea grows stormy, the little ones
    moan."
But, ah, she gave me never a look,        80
For her eyes were sealed to the holy book!
Loud prays the priest; shut stands the
    door.
Come away, children call no more!
Come away, come down, call no more!

    Down, down, down!
Down to the depths of the sea!
She sits at her wheel in the humming
    town,
Singing most joyfully.
Hark what she sings: "O joy, O joy,
For the humming street, and the child
    with its toy!                                   90
For the priest, and the bell, and the holy
    well;
For the wheel where I spun,
And the blessed light of the sun!"
And so she sings her fill,
Singing most joyfully,
Till the spindle drops from her hand,
And the whizzing wheel stands still.
She steals to the window, and looks at
    the sand,
And over the sand at the sea;
And her eyes are set in a stare;          100
And anon there breaks a sigh,
And anon there drops a tear,
From a sorrow-clouded eye,
And a heart sorrow-laden,
A long, long sigh;
For the cold strange eyes of a little
    Mermaiden
And the gleam of her golden hair.

    Come away, away children;
Come children come down!
The hoarse wind blows coldly;             110
Lights shine in the town.
She will start from her slumber
When gusts shake the door;
She will hear the winds howling,
Will hear the waves roar.
We shall see, while above us

The waves roar and whirl,
A ceiling of amber,
A pavement of pearl,
Singing: "Here came a mortal,          120
But faithless was she!
And alone dwell for ever
The kings of the sea."

But, children, at midnight,
When soft the winds blow,
When clear falls the moonlight,
When spring-tides are low;
When sweet airs come seaward
From heaths starred with broom,
And high rocks throw mildly          130
On the blanched sands a gloom;
Up the still, glistening beaches,
Up the creeks we will hie,
Over banks of bright seaweed
The ebb-tide leaves dry.
We will gaze, from the sand-hills,
At the white, sleeping town;
At the church on the hill-side—
And then come back down,
Singing: "There dwells a loved one,   140
But cruel is she!
She left lonely for ever
The kings of the sea."    (*1849*)

## To Marguerite

Yes! in the sea of life enisled,
With echoing straits between us thrown,
Dotting the shoreless watery wild,
We mortal millions live *alone*.
The islands feel the enclasping flow,
And then their endless bounds they know.

But when the moon their hollows lights,
And they are swept by balms of spring,
And in their glens, on starry nights
The nightingales divinely sing;          10
And lovely notes, from shore to shore,
Across the sounds and channels pour—

Oh! then a longing like despair
Is to their farthest caverns sent;
For surely once, they feel, we were
Parts of a single continent!
Now round us spreads the watery plain—
Oh might our marges meet again!

Who ordered, that their longing's fire
Should be, as soon as kindled,
    cooled?                              20
Who renders vain their deep desire?—
A God, a God their severance ruled!
And bade betwixt their shores to be
The unplumbed, salt, estranging sea.
                                    (*1852*)

## Philomela[1]

Hark, ah, the nightingale—
The tawny-throated!
Hark, from that moonlit cedar what a
    burst!
What triumph! hark!—what pain!
O wanderer from a Grecian shore,
Still, after many years, in distant lands,
Still nourishing in thy bewildered brain
That wild, unquenched, deep-sunken,
    old-world pain—
Say, will it never heal?
And can this fragrant lawn              10
With its cool trees, and night,
And the sweet, tranquil Thames,
And moonshine, and the dew,
To thy racked heart and brain
Afford no balm?

Dost thou tonight behold,
Here, through the moonlight on this
    English grass,
The unfriendly palace in the Thracian
    wild?
Dost thou again peruse
With hot cheeks and seared eyes        20

---

[1] King Tereus of Thrace married Philomela, but later raped her sister, Procne, and cut out her tongue. Procne wove a tapestry ("the too clear web"—l. 21) revealing the story and sent it to Philomela. The sisters killed Tereus' son Itylus and served the flesh to the king. When Tereus discovered the crime, he pursued the sisters, so that they called upon the gods for help, Philomela was transformed into the nightingale, Procne into the swallow, and Tereus into the hawk.

The too clear web, and thy dumb
    sister's shame?
Dost thou once more assay
Thy flight, and feel come over thee,
Poor fugitive, the feathery change
Once more, and once more seem to make
    resound
With love and hate, triumph and agony,
Lone Daulis,[2] and the high Cephissian
    vale?[3]
Listen, Eugenia[4]—
How thick the bursts come crowding
    through the leaves!
Again—thou hearest?            *30*
Eternal passion!
Eternal pain!   (*1853*)

# Requiescat[1]

Strew on her roses, roses,
    And never a spray of yew!
In quiet she reposes;
    Ah, would that I did too!

Her mirth the world required;
    She bathed it in smiles of glee.
But her heart was tired, tired,
    And now they let her be.

Her life was turning, turning,
    In mazes of heat and sound.      *10*
But for peace her soul was yearning,
    And now peace laps her round.

Her cabined, ample spirit,
    It fluttered and failed for breath.
Tonight it doth inherit
    The vasty hall of death.   (*1853*)

# The Scholar-Gipsy[1]

Go, for they call you, Shepherd, from the hill;
    Go, Shepherd, and untie the wattled cotes:
        No longer leave thy wistful flock unfed,
    Nor let thy bawling fellows rack their throats,
        Nor the cropped grasses shoot another head.
            But when the fields are still,
    And the tired men and dogs all gone to rest,
        And only the white sheep are sometimes seen
        Cross and recross the strips of moon-blanched green;
    Come, Shepherd, and again begin the quest.     *10*

Here, where the reaper was at work of late,
    In this high field's dark corner, where he leaves
        His coat, his basket, and his earthen cruse,
    And in the sun all morning binds the sheaves,

---

[2] site of the transformation
[3] valley in Phocis, home of Tereus
[4] imaginary listener

[1] May she rest.

[1] Arnold prefaced the poem with a condensed quotation from Joseph Glanvil, *Vanity of Dogmatizing*, 1661: "There was very lately a lad in the University of Oxford, who was by his poverty forced to leave his studies there; and at last to join himself to a company of vagabond gipsies. Among these extravagant people, by the insinuating subtilty of his carriage, he quickly got so much of their love and esteem as that they discovered to him their mystery. After he had been a pretty while exercised in the trade, there chanced to ride by a couple of scholars, who had formerly been of his acquaintance. They quickly spied out their old friend among the gipsies; and he gave them an account of the necessity which drove him to that kind of life, and told them that the people he went with were not such impostors as they were taken for, but that they had a traditional kind of learning among them, and could do wonders by the power of imagination, their fancy binding that of others: that himself had learned much of their art, and when he had compassed the whole secret, he intended, he said, to leave their company, and give the world an account of what he had learned."

Then here, at noon, comes back his stores to use;
    Here will I sit and wait,
While to my ear from uplands far away
The bleating of the folded flocks is borne,
With distant cries of reapers in the corn—
All the live murmur of a summer's day.          20

Screened in this nook o'er the high, half-reaped field,
And here till sundown, Shepherd, will I be.
Through the thick corn the scarlet poppies peep,
And round green roots and yellowing stalks I see
    Pale blue convolvulus in tendrils creep:
      And air-swept lindens yield
Their scent, and rustle down their perfumed showers
Of bloom on the bent grass where I am laid,
And bower me from the August sun with shade;
And the eye travels down to Oxford's towers:     30

And near me on the grass lies Glanvil's book—
Come, let me read the oft-read tale again:
The story of that Oxford scholar poor,
Of pregnant parts and quick inventive brain,
    Who, tired of knocking at Preferment's door,
      One summer morn forsook
His friends, and went to learn the Gipsy lore,
And roamed the world with that wild brotherhood,
And came, as most men deemed, to little good,
But came to Oxford and his friends no more.      40

But once, years after, in the country lanes,
Two scholars, whom at college erst he knew,
Met him, and of his way of life inquired.
Whereat he answered that the Gipsy crew,
    His mates, had arts to rule as they desired
      The workings of men's brains;
And they can bind them to what thoughts they will:
"And I," he said, "the secret of their art,
When fully learned, will to the world impart:
But it needs Heaven-sent moments for this skill!"    50

This said, he left them, and returned no more,
But rumours hung about the country-side,
That the lost Scholar long was seen to stray,
Seen by rare glimpses, pensive and tongue-tied,
    In hat of antique shape, and cloak of grey,
      The same the Gipsies wore.
Shepherds had met him on the Hurst[2] in spring;
At some lone alehouse in the Berkshire moors,
On the warm ingle-bench, the smock-frocked boors
Had found him seated at their entering,      60

---

[2] Cumner Hurst, a hill near Oxford

But, 'mid their drink and clatter, he would fly:
And I myself seem half to know thy looks,
   And put the shepherds, Wanderer, on thy trace;
And boys who in lone wheatfields scare the rooks
   I ask if thou hast passed their quiet place;
     Or in my boat I lie
Moored to the cool bank in the summer heats,
   'Mid wide grass meadows which the sunshine fills,
   And watch the warm green-muffled Cumner hills,
And wonder if thou haunt'st their shy retreats.     70

For most, I know, thou lov'st retiréd ground.
   Thee, at the ferry, Oxford riders blithe,
     Returning home on summer nights, have met
Crossing the stripling Thames at Bablock-hithe,
   Trailing in the cool stream thy fingers wet,
     As the slow punt swings round:
And leaning backwards in a pensive dream,
   And fostering in thy lap a heap of flowers
   Plucked in shy fields and distant Wychwood bowers,
And thine eyes resting on the moonlit stream:     80

And then they land, and thou art seen no more.
   Maidens who from the distant hamlets come
     To dance around the Fyfield elm in May,
Oft through the darkening fields have seen thee roam,
   Or cross a stile into the public way.
     Oft thou hast given them store
Of flowers—the frail-leafed, white anemone—
   Dark bluebells drenched with dews of summer eves,
   And purple orchises with spotted leaves—
But none has words she can report of thee.     90

And, above Godstow Bridge, when hay-time's here
   In June, and many a scythe in sunshine flames,
     Men who through those wide fields of breezy grass
Where black-winged swallows haunt the glittering Thames,
   To bathe in the abandoned lasher[3] pass,
     Have often passed thee near
Sitting upon the river bank o'ergrown:
   Marked thine outlandish garb, thy figure spare,
   Thy dark vague eyes, and soft abstracted air;
But, when they came from bathing, thou wert gone.     100

At some lone homestead in the Cumner hills,
   Where at her open door the housewife darns,
     Thou hast been seen, or hanging on a gate
To watch the threshers in the mossy barns.
     Children, who early range these slopes and late
       For cresses from the rills,

---

[3] the pool below a dam

Have known thee watching, all an April day,
  The spring pastures and the feeding kine,
  And marked thee, when the stars come out and shine,
Through the long dewy grass move slow away.      *110*

In autumn, on the skirts of Bagley Wood,
  Where most the Gipsies by the turf-edged way
  Pitch their smoked tents, and every bush you see
With scarlet patches tagged and shreds of gray,
  Above the forest-ground called Thessaly—
    The blackbird picking food
Sees thee, nor stops his meal, nor fears at all;
  So often has he known thee past him stray
  Rapt, twirling in thy hand a withered spray,
And waiting for the spark from Heaven to fall.      *120*

And once, in winter, on the causeway chill
  Where home through flooded fields foot-travellers go,
  Have I not passed thee on the wooden bridge
Wrapt in thy cloak and battling with the snow,
  Thy face towards Hinksey and its wintry ridge?
    And thou hast climbed the hill
And gained the white brow of the Cumner range:
  Turned once to watch, while thick the snowflakes fall,
  The line of festal light in Christ Church hall—
Then sought thy straw in some sequestered grange.      *130*

But what—I dream! Two hundred years are flown
  Since first thy story ran through Oxford halls,
  And the grave Glanvil did the tale inscribe
That thou wert wandered from the studious walls
  To learn strange arts, and join a Gipsy tribe:
    And thou from earth art gone
Long since, and in some quiet churchyard laid;
  Some country nook, where o'er thy unknown grave
  Tall grasses and white flowering nettles wave—
Under a dark red-fruited yew-tree's shade.      *140*

—No, no, thou hast not felt the lapse of hours.
  For what wears out the life of mortal men?
    'Tis that from change to change their being rolls:
'Tis that repeated shocks, again, again,
  Exhaust the energy of strongest souls,
    And numb the elastic powers.
Till having used our nerves with bliss and teen,[4]
  And tired upon a thousand schemes our wit,
  To the just-pausing Genius we remit
Our worn-out life, and are—what we have been.      *150*

---

[4] sorrow

Thou hast not lived, why shouldst thou perish, so?
   Thou hadst *one* aim, *one* business, *one* desire:
     Else wert thou long since numbered with the dead—
   Else hadst thou spent, like other men, thy fire.
     The generations of thy peers are fled,
       And we ourselves shall go;
   But thou possessed an immortal lot,
     And we imagine thee exempt from age
     And living as thou liv'st on Glanvil's page,
   Because thou hadst—what we, alas, have not!        *160*

For early didst thou leave the world, with powers
   Fresh, undiverted to the world without,
     Firm to their mark, not spent on other things;
   Free from the sick fatigue, the languid doubt,
     Which much to have tried, in much been battled, brings.
       O Life unlike to ours!
   Who fluctuate idly without term or scope,
     Of whom each strives, nor knows for what he strives,
     And each half lives a hundred different lives;
   Who wait like thee, but not, like thee, in hope.       *170*

Thou waitest for the spark from Heaven: and we,
   Vague half-believers of our casual creeds,
     Who never deeply felt, nor clearly willed,
   Whose insight never has borne fruit in deeds,
     Whose weak resolves never have been fulfilled;
       For whom each year we see
   Breeds new beginnings, disappointments new;
     Who hesitate and falter life away,
     And lose to-morrow the ground won to-day—
   Ah, do not we, Wanderer, await it too?       *180*

Yes, we await it, but it still delays,
   And then we suffer; and amongst us One,
     Who most has suffered, takes dejectedly
   His seat upon the intellectual throne;
     And all his store of sad experience he
       Lays bare of wretched days;
   Tells us his misery's birth and growth and signs,
     And how the dying spark of hope was fed,
     And how the breast was soothed, and how the head,
   And all his hourly varied anodynes.       *190*

This for our wisest: and we others pine,
   And wish the long unhappy dream would end,
     And waive all claim to bliss, and try to bear,
   With close-lipped Patience for our only friend,
     Sad Patience, too near neighbour to Despair:
       But none has hope like thine.

Thou through the fields and through the woods dost stray
   Roaming the country-side, a truant boy,
   Nursing thy project in unclouded joy,
And every doubt long blown by time away.          *200*

O born in days when wits were fresh and clear,
   And life ran gaily as the sparkling Thames;
   Before this strange disease of modern life,
With its sick hurry, its divided aims,
   Its heads o'ertaxed, its palsied hearts, was rife—
     Fly hence, our contact fear!
Still fly, plunge deeper in the bowering wood!
   Averse, as Dido did with gesture stern
   From her false friend's approach in Hades turn,
Wave us away, and keep thy solitude.          *210*

Still nursing the unconquerable hope,
   Still clutching the inviolable shade,
   With a free onward impulse brushing through,
By night, the silvered branches of the glade—
   Far on the forest-skirts, where none pursue,
     On some mild pastoral slope
Emerge, and resting on the moonlit pales,
   Freshen thy flowers, as in former years,
   With dew, or listen with enchanted ears,
From the dark dingles, to the nightingales!          *220*

But fly our paths, our feverish contact fly!
   For strong the infection of our mental strife,
   Which, though it gives no bliss, yet spoils for rest;
And we should win thee from thy own fair life,
   Like us distracted, and like us unblest.
     Soon, soon thy cheer would die,
Thy hopes grow timorous, and unfixed thy powers,
   And thy clear aims be cross and shifting made:
   And then thy glad perennial youth would fade,
Fade, and grow old at last, and die like ours.         *230*

Then fly our greetings, fly our speech and smiles!
   —As some grave Tyrian[5] trader, from the sea,
   Descried at sunrise an emerging prow
Lifting the cool-haired creepers stealthily,
   The fringes of a southward-facing brow
     Among the Ægean isles;
And saw the merry Grecian coaster come,
   Freighted with amber grapes, and Chian wine,
   Green bursting figs, and tunnies steeped in brine;
And knew the intruders on his ancient home,         *240*

---

[5] of Tyre, a trading city of the Phoenicians

The young light-hearted masters of the waves;
  And snatched his rudder, and shook out more sail,
    And day and night held on indignantly
O'er the blue Midland waters[6] with the gale,
  Betwixt the Syrtes[7] and soft Sicily,
    To where the Atlantic raves
Outside the Western Straits, and unbent sails
  There, where down cloudy cliffs, through sheets of foam,
  Shy traffickers, the dark Iberians come;
And on the beach undid his corded bales.   (*1853*)

## Dover Beach

The sea is calm to-night,
The tide is full, the moon lies fair
Upon the Straits;—on the French coast, the light
Gleams, and is gone; the cliffs of England stand,
Glimmering and vast, out in the tranquil bay.
Come to the window, sweet is the night air!
Only, from the long line of spray
Where the ebb meets the moon-blanched sand,
Listen! you hear the grating roar
Of pebbles which the waves suck back, and fling,         *10*
At their return, up the high strand,
Begin, and cease, and then again begin,
With tremulous cadence slow, and bring
The eternal note of sadness in.

  Sophocles[1] long ago
Heard it on the Ægean, and it brought
Into his mind the turbid ebb and flow
Of human misery; we
Find also in the sound a thought,
Hearing it by this distant northern sea.           *20*

The sea of faith
Was once, too, at the full, and round earth's shore
Lay like the folds of a bright girdle furled;
But now I only hear
Its melancholy, long, withdrawing roar,
Retreating to the breath
Of the night-wind down the vast edges drear
And naked shingles[2] of the world.

Ah, love, let us be true
To one another! for the world, which seems       *30*

---

6 Mediterranean Sea
7 two gulfs on the African coast across from Sicily
1 Greek tragedian (*c.* 496–*c.* 405 B.C.). In *Antigone*
he likens the curse of heaven to the ebb and flow of the sea.
2 beaches covered with coarse gravel

To lie before us like a land of dreams,
So various, so beautiful, so new,
Hath really neither joy, nor love, nor light,
Nor certitude, nor peace, nor help for pain;
And we are here as on a darkling plain
Swept with confused alarms of struggle and flight,
Where ignorant armies clash by night.   (*1867*)

## Rugby Chapel[1]

### *NOVEMBER 1857*

Coldly, sadly descends
The autumn-evening. The Field
Strewn with its dank yellow drifts
Of withered leaves, and the elms,
Fade into dimness apace,
Silent;—hardly a shout
From a few boys late at their play!
The lights come out in the street,
In the school-room windows;—but cold,
Solemn, unlighted, austere,                10
Through the gathering darkness, arise
The chapel-walls, in whose bound
Thou, my father! art laid.

There thou dost lie, in the gloom
Of the autumn evening. But ah!
That word, *gloom*, to my mind
Brings thee back, in the light
Of thy radiant vigor, again;
In the gloom of November we passed
Days not dark at thy side;                 20
Seasons impaired not the ray
Of thy buoyant cheerfulness clear.
Such thou wast! and I stand
In the autumn evening and think
Of bygone autumns with thee.

Fifteen years have gone round
Since thou arosest to tread,
In the summer-morning, the road
Of death, at a call unforeseen,
Sudden. For fifteen years,                 30
We who till then in thy shade
Rested as under the boughs
Of a mighty oak, have endured
Sunshine and rain as we might,

Bare, unshaded, alone,
Lacking the shelter of thee.

O strong soul, by what shore
Tarriest thou now? For that force,
Surely, has not been left vain!
Somewhere, surely, afar,                   40
In the sounding labor-house vast
Of being, is practised that strength,
Zealous, beneficent, firm!

Yes, in some far-shining sphere,
Conscious or not of the past,
Still thou performest the word
Of the Spirit in whom thou dost live—
Prompt, unwearied, as here!
Still thou upraisest with zeal
The humble good from the ground,           50
Sternly repressest the bad!
Still, like a trumpet, dost rouse
Those who with half-open eyes
Tread the border-land dim
Twixt vice and virtue; reviv'st,
Succorest!—this was thy work;
This was thy life upon earth.

What is the course of the life
Of mortal men on the earth?—
Most men eddy about                        60
Here and there—eat and drink,
Chatter and love and hate,
Gather and squander, are raised
Aloft, are hurled in the dust,
Striving blindly, achieving
Nothing; and then they die—
Perish;—and no one asks
Who or what they have been,
More than he asks what waves,
In the moonlit solitudes mild              70

[1] The poem commemorates Dr. Thomas Arnold, father of the poet, and for fourteen years the headmaster of Rugby School. On his death in 1842 he was buried in the school's chapel.

Of the midmost Ocean, have swelled,
Foamed for a moment, and gone.

And there are some, whom a thirst
Ardent, unquenchable, fires,
Not with the crowd to be spent,
Not without aim to go round
In an eddy of purposeless dust,
Effort unmeaning and vain,
Ah yes! some of us strive
Not without action to die          80
Fruitless, but something to snatch
From dull oblivion, nor all
Glut the devouring grave!
We, we have chosen our path—
Path to a clear-purposed goal,
Path of advance!—but it leads
A long, steep journey, through sunk
Gorges, o'er mountains in snow.
Cheerful, with friends, we set forth—
Then on the height, comes the storm.          90
Thunder crashes from rock
To rock, the cataracts reply,
Lightnings dazzle our eyes.
Roaring torrents have breached
The track, the stream-bed descends
In the place where the wayfarer once
Planted his footsteps—the spray
Boils o'er its borders! aloft
The unseen snow-beds dislodge
Their hanging ruin; alas,          100
Havoc is made in our train!
Friends who set forth at our side,
Falter, are lost in the storm.
We, we only are left!
With frowning foreheads, with lips
Sternly compressed, we strain on,
On—and at nightfall at last
Come to the end of our way,
To the lonely inn 'mid the rocks;
Where the gaunt and taciturn host          110
Stands on the threshold, the wind
Shaking his thin white hairs—
Holds his lantern to scan
Our storm-beat figures, and asks:
Whom in our party we bring?
Whom we have left in the snow?

Sadly we answer: We bring
Only ourselves! we lost

Sight of the rest in the storm.
Hardly ourselves we fought through,          120
Stripped, without friends, as we are.
Friends, companions, and train,
The avalanche swept from our side.

But thou would'st not *alone*
Be saved, my father! *alone*
Conquer and come to thy goal,
Leaving the rest in the wild.
We were weary and we
Fearful, and we in our march
Fain to drop down and to die.          130
Still thou turnedst, and still
Beckonedst the trembler, and still
Gavest the weary thy hand.

If, in the paths of the world,
Stones might have wounded thy feet,
Toil or dejection have tried
Thy spirit, of that we saw
Nothing—to us thou wast still
Cheerful, and helpful, and firm!
Therefore to thee it was given          140
Many to save with thyself;
And, at the end of thy day,
O faithful shepherd! to come,
Bringing thy sheep in thy hand.

And through thee I believe
In the noble and great who are gone;
Pure souls honored and blest
By former ages, who else—
Such, so soulless, so poor,
Is the race of men whom I see—          150
Seemed but a dream of the heart,
Seemed but a cry of desire.
Yes! I believe that there lived
Others like thee in the past,
Not like the men of the crowd
Who all round me today
Bluster or cringe, and make life
Hideous, and arid, and vile;
But souls tempered with fire,
Fervent, heroic, and good,          160
Helpers and friends of mankind.

Servants of God!—or sons
Shall I not call you? because
Not as servants ye knew
Your Father's innermost mind,

His, who unwillingly sees
One of his little ones lost—
Yours is the praise, if mankind
Hath not as yet in its march
Fainted, and fallen, and died!    170

See! In the rocks of the world
Marches the host of mankind,
A feeble, wavering line.
Where are they tending?—A God
Marshalled them, gave them their goal.
Ah, but the way is so long!
Years they have been in the wild!
Sore thirst plagues them, the rocks,
Rising all round, overawe;
Factions divide them, their host    180
Threatens to break, to dissolve.
—Ah, keep, keep them combined!
Else of the myriads who fill
That army, not one shall arrive;
Sole they shall stray; in the rocks
Stagger for ever in vain
Die one by one in the waste.

Then, in such hour of need
Of your fainting, dispirited race,
Ye, like angels, appear,    190
Radiant with ardor divine!
Beacons of hope, ye appear!
Languor is not in your heart,
Weakness is not in your word,
Weariness not on your brow.
Ye alight in our van! at your voice,
Panic, despair, flee away.
Ye move through the ranks, recall
The stragglers, refresh the outworn,
Praise, re-inspire the brave!    200
Order, courage, return;
Eyes rekindling, and prayers,
Follow your steps as ye go.
Ye fill up the gaps in our files,
Strengthen the wavering line,
Stablish, continue our march,
On, to the bound of the waste,
On, to the City of God.    (1867)

# COVENTRY PATMORE / 1823–1896

## The Toys

My little Son, who looked from
  thoughtful eyes
And moved and spoke in quiet grown-up
  wise,
Having my law the seventh time
  disobeyed,
I struck him, and dismissed
With hard words and unkissed,
—His Mother, who was patient, being
  dead.
Then, fearing lest his grief should hinder
  sleep,
I visited his bed,
But found him slumbering deep,
With darkened eyelids, and their lashes
  yet    10
From his late sobbing wet.

And I, with moan,
Kissing away his tears, left others of my
  own;
For, on a table drawn beside his head,
He had put, within his reach,
A box of counters and a red-veined stone,
A piece of glass abraded by the beach
And six or seven shells,
A bottle with bluebells,
And two French copper coins, ranged
  there with careful art,    20
To comfort his sad heart.
So when that night I prayed
To God, I wept, and said:
Ah, when at last we lie with trancéd
  breath,
Not vexing Thee in death,
And thou rememberest of what toys
We made our joys,

How weakly understood,
Thy great commanded good,
Then, fatherly not less                              30
Than I whom thou hast moulded from
    the clay,
Thou'lt leave Thy wrath, and say,
"I will be sorry for their childishness."
                                        (*1877*)

## Magna Est Veritas[1]

Here, in this little Bay,
Full of tumultuous life and great repose,
Where, twice a day,
The purposeless, glad ocean comes and
    goes,
Under high cliffs, and far from the huge
    town,
I sit me down.
For want of me the world's course will
    not fail:
When all its work is done, the lie shall
    rot;
The truth is great, and shall prevail,
When none cares whether it prevail or
    not.  (*1877*)                                  10

---

# DANTE GABRIEL ROSSETTI / 1828–1882

## The Blesséd Damozel

The blesséd damozel leaned out
    From the gold bar of Heaven;
Her eyes were deeper than the depth
    Of waters stilled at even;
She had three lilies in her hand,
    And the stars in her hair were seven.

Her robe, ungirt from clasp to hem,
    No wrought flowers did adorn,
But a white rose of Mary's gift,
    For service meetly worn;                        10
Her hair that lay along her back
    Was yellow like ripe corn.

Her seemed she scarce had been a day
    One of God's choristers;
The wonder was not yet quite gone
    From that still look of hers;
Albeit, to them she left, her day
    Had counted as ten years.

(To one, it is ten years of years.
    ... Yet now, and in this place,                 20
Surely she leaned o'er me—her hair
    Fell all about my face. ...
Nothing: the autumn-fall of leaves.
    The whole year sets apace.)

It was the rampart of God's house
    That she was standing on;
By God built over the sheer depth
    The which is Space begun;
So high, that looking downward thence
    She scare could see the sun.                    30

It lies in Heaven, across the flood
    Of ether, as a bridge.
Beneath, the tides of day and night
    With flame and darkness ridge
The void, as low as where this earth
    Spins like a fretful midge.

Around her, lovers, newly met
    'Mid deathless love's acclaims,
Spoke evermore among themselves
    Their heart-remembered names;                   40
And the souls mounting up to God
    Went by her like thin flames.

And still she bowed herself and stooped
    Out of the circling charm;
Until her bosom must have made
    The bar she leaned on warm,
And the lilies lay as if asleep
    Along her bended arm.

---

[1] The truth is great; compare l. 9.

From the fixed place of Heaven she saw
  Time like a pulse shake fierce       *50*
Through all the worlds. Her gaze still
    strove
Within the gulf to pierce
  Its path; and now she spoke as when
The stars sang in their spheres.

The sun was gone now; the curled moon
  Was like a little feather
Fluttering far down the gulf, and now
  She spoke through the still weather.
Her voice was like the voice the stars
  Had when they sang together.      *60*

(Ah sweet! Even now, in that bird's song
  Strove not her accents there,
Fain to be hearkened? When those bells
  Possessed the midday air,
Strove not her steps to reach my side
  Down all the echoing stair?)

"I wish that he were come to me,
  For he will come," she said.
"Have I not prayed in Heaven?—on
    earth,
Lord, Lord, has he not prayed?      *70*
Are not two prayers a perfect strength?
  And shall I feel afraid?

"When round his head the aureole clings,
  And he is clothed in white,
I'll take his hand and go with him
  To the deep wells of light;
As unto a stream we will step down,
  And bathe there in God's sight.

"We two will stand beside that shrine,
  Occult, withheld, untrod,      *80*
Whose lamps are stirred continually
  With prayer sent up to God;
And see our old prayers, granted, melt
  Each like a little cloud.

"We two will lie i' the shadow of
  That living mystic tree
Within whose secret growth the Dove[1]
  Is sometimes felt to be.
While every leaf that His plumes touch
  Saith His Name audibly.      *90*

"And I myself will teach to him,
  I myself, lying so,
The songs I sing here; which his voice
  Shall pause in, hushed and slow,
And find some knowledge at each pause,
  Or some new thing to know."

(Alas! we two, we two, thou say'st!
  Yea, one wast thou with me
That once of old. But shall God lift
  To endless unity      *100*
The soul whose likeness with thy soul
  Was but its love for thee?)

"We two," she said, "will seek the groves
  Where the lady Mary is,
With her five handmaidens, whose names
  Are five sweet symphonies,
Cecily, Gertrude, Magdalen,
  Margaret and Rosalys.[2]

"Circlewise sit they, with bound locks
  And foreheads garlanded;      *110*
Into the fine cloth white like flame
  Weaving the golden thread,
To fashion the birth-robes for them
  Who are just born, being dead.

"He shall fear, haply and be dumb.
  Then will I lay my cheek
To his, and tell about our love,
  Not once abashed or weak:
And the dear Mother will approve
  My pride, and let me speak.      *120*

"Herself shall bring us, hand in hand,
  To Him round whom all souls
Kneel, the clear-ranged unnumbered
    heads
Bowed with their aureoles:
  And angels meeting us shall sing
To their citherns and citoles.[3]

"There will I ask of Christ the Lord
  Thus much for him and me:—
Only to live as once on earth
  With Love, only to be,      *130*
As then awhile, for ever now
  Together, I and he."

---

[1] the Holy Ghost
[2] These are musical, rather than meaningful, names.

[3] strummed string instruments related to the guitar

She gazed and listened and then said,
　　Less sad of speech than mild,—
"All this is when he comes." She ceased.
　　The light thrilled towards her, filled
With angels in strong level flight.
　　Her eyes prayed, and she smiled.

(I saw her smile.) But soon their path
　　Was vague in distant spheres:　　　*140*
And then she cast her arms along
　　The golden barriers,
And laid her face between her hands,
　　And wept. (I heard her tears.)　*(1847)*

## Autumn Song

Know'st thou not at the fall of the leaf
How the heart feels a languid grief
　　Laid on it for a covering;
　　And how sleep seems a goodly thing
In Autumn at the fall of the leaf?

And how the swift beat of the brain
Falters because it is in vain,
　　In Autumn at the fall of the leaf
　　Knowest thou not? and how the chief
Of joys seems—not to suffer pain?　　*10*

Know'st thou not at the fall of the leaf
How the soul feels like a dried sheaf
　　Bound up at length for harvesting,
　　And how death seems a comely thing
In Autumn at the fall of the leaf?　*(1848)*

## The Sea-Limits

Consider the sea's listless chime:
　　Time's self it is, made audible,—
　　The murmur of the earth's own shell.
Secret continuance sublime
　　Is the sea's end: our sight may pass
　　No furlong further. Since time was,
This sound hath told the lapse of time.

No quiet, which is death's,—it hath
　　The mournfulness of ancient life,
　　Enduring always at dull strife.　　*10*
As the world's heart of rest and wrath,
　　Its painful pulse is in the sands.
　　Last utterly, the whole sky stands,
Grey and not known, along its path.

Listen alone beside the sea,
　　Listen alone among the woods;
　　Those voices of twin solitudes
Shall have one sound alike to thee:
　　Hark where the murmurs of thronged men
　　Surge and sink back and surge again,—　　*20*
Still the one voice of wave and tree.

Gather a shell from the strown beach
　　And listen at its lips: they sigh
　　The same desire and mystery,
The echo of the whole sea's speech.
　　And all mankind is thus at heart
　　Not anything but what thou art:
And Earth, Sea, Man, are all in each.
　　　　　　　　　　　　　　*(1849)*

## A Little While

A little while a little love
　　The hour yet bears for thee and me
　　Who have not drawn the veil to see
If still our heaven be lit above.
Thou merely, at the day's last sigh,
　　Hast felt thy soul prolong the tone;
And I have heard the night-wind cry
　　And deemed its speech mine own.

A little while a little love
　　The scattering autumn hoards for us　　*10*
　　Whose bower is not yet ruinous
Nor quite unleaved our songless grove.
Only across the shaken boughs
　　We hear the flood-tides seek the sea,
And deep in both our hearts they rouse
　　One wail for thee and me.

A little while a little love
　　May yet be ours who have not said
　　The word it makes our eyes afraid
To know that each is thinking of.　　*20*
Not yet the end: be our lips dumb
　　In smiles a little season yet:
I'll tell thee, when the end is come,
　　How we may best forget.　*(1859)*

*from* The House of Life

### THE SONNET

A sonnet is a moment's monument—
Memorial from the Soul's eternity
To one dead deathless hour. Look that it be,
Whether for lustral[1] rite or dire portent,
Of its own arduous fullness reverent.
Carve it in ivory or in ebony,
As Day or Night may rule; and let Time see
Its flowering crest impearled and orient.[2]
A sonnet is a coin; its face reveals
The Soul—its converse, to what Power 'tis due:—                10
Whether for tribute to the august appeals
Of Life, or dower in Love's high retinue,
It serve; or 'mid the dark wharf's cavernous breath,
In Charon's[3] palm it pay the toll to Death.   (*1881*)

### XIV. YOUTH'S SPRING-TRIBUTE

On this sweet bank your head thrice sweet and dear
I lay, and spread your hair on either side,
And see the newborn woodflowers bashful-eyed
Look through the golden tresses here and there.
On these debateable borders of the year
Spring's foot half falters; scarce she may yet know
The leafless blackthorn-blossom from the snow;
And through her bowers the wind's way still is clear.
But April's sun strikes down the glades today;
So shut your eyes upturned, and feel my kiss                10
Creep, as the Spring now thrills through every spray,
Up your warm throat to your warm lips: for this
Is even the hour of Love's sworn suitservice,
With whom cold hearts are counted castaway.   (*1881*)

### XIX. SILENT NOON

Your hands lie open in the long fresh grass,—
The finger-points look through like rosy blooms:
Your eyes smile peace. The pasture gleams and glooms
'Neath billowing skies that scatter and amass.
All round our nest, far as the eye can pass,
Are golden kingcup-fields with silver edge
Where the cow-parsley skirts the hawthorn-edge.
'Tis visible silence, still as the hour-glass.
Deep in the sun-searched growths the dragon-fly
Hangs like a blue thread loosened from the sky—                10
So this winged hour is dropt to us from above.
Oh! clasp we to our hearts, for deathless dower,

---

[1] purifying      [2] lustrous, as a pearl
[3] the boatman who ferried the shades of the dead across the river Styx into the underworld

This close-companioned inarticulate hour
When two-fold silence was the song of love.   (*1870*)

### LXIX. AUTUMN IDLENESS

This sunlight shames November where he grieves
In dead red leaves, and will not let him shun
The day, though bough with bough be overrun.
But with a blessing every glade receives
High salutation; while from hillock-eaves
The deer gaze calling, dappled white and dun,
As if, being foresters of old, the sun
Had marked them with the shade of forest-leaves.
Here dawn today unveiled her magic glass;
Here noon now gives the thirst and takes the dew;     *10*
Till eve bring rest when other good things pass.
And here the lost hours the lost hours renew
While I still lead my shadow o'er the grass,
Nor know, for longing, that which I should do.   (*1870*)

### LXXVIII. BODY'S BEAUTY

Of Adam's first wife, Lilith,[1] it is told
(The witch he loved before the gift of Eve,)
That, ere the snake's, her sweet tongue could deceive,
And her enchanted hair was the first gold.
And still she sits, young while the earth is old,
And, subtly of herself contemplative,
Draws men to watch the bright net she can weave,
Till heart and body and life are in its hold.
The rose and poppy are her flowers; for where
Is he not found, O Lilith, whom shed scent     *10*
And soft-shed kisses and soft sleep shall snare?
Lo! as that youth's eyes burned at thine, so went
Thy spell through him, and left his straight neck bent,
And round his heart one strangling golden hair.

### LXXXIII. BARREN SPRING

Once more the changed year's turning wheel returns:
And as a girl sails balanced in the wind,
And now before and now again behind
Stoops as it swoops, with cheek that laughs and burns,—
So spring comes merry towards me now, but earns
No answering smile from me, whose life is twined
With the dead boughs that winter still must bind,
And whom today the Spring no more concerns.
Behold, this crocus is a withering flame;
This snowdrop, snow; this apple-blossom's part     *10*
To breed the fruit that breeds the serpent's art.
Nay, for these Spring-flowers, turn thy face from them,
Nor gaze till on the year's last lily-stem
The white cup shrivels round the golden heart.   (*1870*)

---

[1] The figure appears in the Rabbinical literature and is related to older legends of female demons.

# GEORGE MEREDITH / 1828–1909

## *from* Modern Love

### I

By this he knew she wept with waking eyes:
That, at his hand's light quiver by her head,
The strange low sobs that shook their common bed,
Were called into her with a sharp surprise,
And strangled mute, like little gaping snakes,
Dreadfully venomous to him. She lay
Stone-still, and the long darkness flowed away
With muffled pulses. Then, as midnight makes
Her giant heart of Memory and Tears
Drink the pale drug of silence, and so beat          *10*
Sleep's heavy measure, they from head to feet
Were moveless, looking through their dead black years,
By vain regret scrawled over the blank wall.
Like sculptured effigies they might be seen
Upon their marriage-tomb, the sword between;[1]
Each wishing for the sword that severs all.

### II

It ended, and the morrow brought the task.
Her eyes were guilty gates, that let him in
By shutting all too zealous for their sin:
Each sucked a secret, and each wore a mask.
But, oh, the bitter taste her beauty had!
He sickened as at breath of poison-flowers:
A languid humour stole among the hours,
And if their smiles encountered, he went mad,
And raged deep inward, till the light was brown
Before his vision, and the world, forgot,          *10*
Looked wicked as some old dull murder-spot
A star with lurid beams, she seemed to crown
The pit of infamy: and then again
He fainted on his vengefulness, and strove
To ape the magnanimity of love,
And smote himself, a shuddering heap of pain.

### XVII

At dinner, she is hostess, I am host.
Went the feast ever cheerfuller? She keeps
The Topic over intellectual deeps
In buoyancy afloat. They see no ghost.
With sparkling surface-eyes we ply the ball:

[1] In the Middle Ages, a naked sword between lovers was presumed to ensure chaste behavior.

It is in truth a most contagious game:
*Hiding the skeleton,* shall be its name.
Such play as this the devils might appal!
But here's the greater wonder; in that we
Enamoured of an acting nought can tire,
Each other, like true hypocrites admire;
Warm-lighted looks, Love's ephemerioe,[1]
Shoot gaily o'er the dishes and the wine.
We waken envy of our happy lot.
Fast, sweet, and golden, shows the marriage-knot.
Dear guests, you now have seen Love's corpse-light[2] shine.

### XXII

What may the woman labor to confess?
There is about her mouth a nervous twitch.
'Tis something to be told, or hidden:—which?
I get a glimpse of hell in this mild guess.
She has desires of touch, as if to feel
That all the household things are things she knew.
She stops before the glass. What sight in view?
A face that seems the latest to reveal!
For she turns from it hastily, and tossed
Irresolute steals shadow-like to where
I stand: and wavering pale before me there,
Her tears fall still as oak-leaves after frost.
She will not speak. I will not ask. We are
League-sundered by the silent gulf between.
You burly lovers on the village green,
Yours is a lower, and a happier star!

### XXXIV

Madam would speak with me. So, now it comes:
The Deluge or else Fire! She's well; she thanks
My husbandship. Our chain on silence clanks.
Time leers between, above his twiddling thumbs.
Am I quite well? Most excellent in health!
The journals, too, I diligently peruse.
Vesuvius is expected to give news:
Niagara is no noisier. By stealth
Our eyes dart scrutinizing snakes. She's glad
I'm happy, says her quivering under-lip.
"And are not you?" "How can I be?" "Take ship!
For happiness is somewhere to be had."
"Nowhere for me!" Her voice is barely heard.
I am not melted, and make no pretense.
With commonplace I freeze her, tongue and sense.
Niagara or Vesuvius is deferred.

10

10

10

---

[1] ephemeridae; short-lived insects such as mayflies    [2] the phosphorescent glow from decaying matter

### XLIII

Mark where the pressing wind shoots javelin-like
Its skeleton shadow on the broad-backed wave!
Here is a fitting spot to dig Love's grave;
Here where the ponderous breakers plunge and strike,
And dart their hissing tongues high up the sand:
In hearing of the ocean, and in sight
Of those ribbed wind-streaks running into white.
If I the death of Love had deeply planned,
I never could have made it half so sure,
As by the unblest kisses which upbraid
The full-waked sense; or failing that, degrade!
'Tis morning: but no morning can restore
What we have forfeited. I see no sin:
The wrong is mixed. In tragic life, God wot,
No villain need be! Passions spin the plot:
We are betrayed by what is false within.

### L

Thus piteously Love closed what he begat:
The union of this ever-diverse pair!
These two were rapid falcons in a snare,
Condemned to do the flitting of the bat.
Lovers beneath the singing sky of May,
They wandered once; clear as the dew on flowers:
But they fed not on the advancing hours:
Their hearts held cravings for the buried day.
Then each applied to each that fatal knife,
Deep questioning, which probes to endless dole.
Ah, what a dusty answer gets the soul
When hot for certainties in this our life!—
In tragic hints here see what evermore,
Moves dark as yonder midnight ocean's force,
Thundering like ramping hosts of warrior horse,
To throw that faint thin line upon the shore!   (*1862*)

## Lucifer[1] in Starlight

On a starred night Prince Lucifer uprose.
Tired of his dark dominion swung the fiend
Above the rolling ball in cloud part screened,
Where sinners hugged their spectre of repose.
Poor prey to his hot fit of pride were those.
And now upon his western wing he leaned,
Now his huge bulk o'er Afric's sands careened,
Now the black planet shadowed Arctic snows.

---

[1] the archangel who rebelled against God and was hurled into hell

Soaring through wider zones that pricked his scars
With memory of the old revolt from Awe,                               10
He reached a middle height, and at the stars,
Which are the brain of heaven, he looked, and sank.
Around the ancient track marched, rank on rank,
The army of unalterable law.   (*1883*)


## EMILY DICKINSON / 1830–1886

### 76[1]

Exultation is the going
Of an inland soul to sea,
Past the houses—past the headlands—
Into deep Eternity—

Bred as we, among the mountains,
Can the sailor understand
The divine intoxication
Of the first league out from land?
                                       (*1859?*)


### 108

Surgeons must be very careful
When they take the knife!
Underneath their fine incisions
Stirs the Culprit—*Life*!   (*1859?*)


### 241

I like a look of Agony,
Because I know it's true—
Men do not sham Convulsion,
Nor simulate, a Throe—

The Eyes glaze once—and that is Death—
Impossible to feign
The Beads upon the Forehead
By homely Anguish strung.   (*1861?*)


### 258

There's a certain Slant of light,
Winter Afternoons—
That oppresses, like the Heft
Of Cathedral Tunes—

Heavenly Hurt, it gives us—
We can find no scar,
But internal difference,
Where the Meanings, are—

None may teach it—Any—
'Tis the Seal Despair—                                                10
An imperial affliction
Sent us of the Air—

When it comes, the Landscape listens—
Shadows—hold their breath—
When it goes, 'tis like the Distance
On the look of Death—   (*c. 1861*)


### 318

I'll tell you how the Sun rose—
A Ribbon at a time—
The Steeples swam in Amethyst—
The news, like Squirrels, ran—
The Hills untied their Bonnets—
The Bobolinks—begun—
Then I said softly to myself—
"That must have been the Sun"!

---

[1] The numbers and dates attached to Dickinson's poems are those supplied by Thomas H. Johnson (ed.), *The Complete Poems of Emily Dickinson* (Boston: Little, Brown, 1960).

But how he set—I know not—
There seemed a purple stile                                      10
That little Yellow boys and girls
Were climbing all the while—
Till when they reached the other side,
A Dominie in Gray—
Put gently up the evening Bars—
And led the flock away—    (*c. 1860*)

But—should the play
Prove piercing earnest—                                          10
Should the glee—glaze—
In Death's—stiff—stare—

Would not the fun
Look too expensive!
Would not the jest—
Have crawled too far!   (*c. 1862*)

### 328

A Bird came down the Walk—
He did not know I saw—
He bit an Angleworm in halves
And ate the fellow, raw,

And then he drank a Dew
From a convenient Grass—
And then hopped sidewise to the Wall
To let a Beetle pass—

He glanced with rapid eyes
That hurried all around—                                         10
They looked like frightened Beads, I
    thought—
He stirred his Velvet Head

Like one in danger, Cautious,
I offered him a Crumb
And he unrolled his feathers
And rowed him softer home—

Than Oars divide the Ocean,
Too silver for a seam—
Or Butterflies, off Banks of Noon
Leap, plashless as they
    swim.   (*1862*)                                            20

### 435

Much Madness is divinest Sense—
To a discerning Eye—
Much Sense—the starkest Madness—
'Tis the Majority
In this, as All, prevail—
Assent—and you are sane—
Demur—you're straightway dangerous—
And handled with a Chain—   (*c. 1862*)

### 449

I died for Beauty—but was scarce
Adjusted in the Tomb
When One who died for Truth, was lain
In an adjoining Room—

He questioned softly "Why I failed"?
"For Beauty", I replied—
"And I—for Truth—Themself are One—
We Brethren, are", He said—

And so, as Kinsmen, met a Night—
We talked between the Rooms—                                     10
Until the Moss had reached our lips—
And covered up—our names—   (*c. 1862*)

### 338

I know that He exists.
Somewhere—in Silence—
He has hid his rare life
From our gross eyes.

'Tis an instant's play.
'Tis a fond Ambush—
Just to make Bliss
Earn her own surprise!

### 465

I heard a Fly buzz—when I died—
The Stillness in the Room
Was like the Stillness in the Air—
Between the Heaves of Storm—

The Eyes around—had wrung them dry—
And Breaths were gathering firm
For that last Onset—when the King
Be witnessed—in the Room—

I willed my Keepsakes—Signed away
What portion of me be          10
Assignable—and then it was
There interposed a Fly—

With Blue—uncertain stumbling Buzz—
Between the light—and me—
And then the Windows failed—and then
I could not see to see—   (*c. 1862*)

**510**

It was not Death, for I stood up,
And all the Dead, lie down—
It was not Night, for all the Bells
Put out their Tongues, for Noon.

It was not Frost, for on my Flesh
I felt Siroccos—crawl—
Nor Fire—for just my Marble feet
Could keep a Chancel, cool—

And yet, it tasted, like them all,
The Figures I have seen          10
Set orderly, for Burial,
Reminded me, of mine—

As if my life were shaven,
And fitted to a frame,
And could not breathe without a key,
And 'twas like Midnight, some—

When everything that ticked—has
stopped—
And Space stares all around—
Or Grisly frosts—first Autumn morns,
Repeal the Beating Ground—          20

But, most, like Chaos—Stopless—cool—
Without a Chance, or Spar—
Or even a Report of Land—
To justify—Despair.   (*1862?*)

**712**

Because I could not stop for Death—
He kindly stopped for me—
The Carriage held but just Ourselves—
And Immortality.

We slowly drove—He knew not haste
And I had put away
My labor and my leisure too,
For His Civility—

We passed the School, where Children
strove
At Recess—in the Ring—          10
We passed the Fields of Gazing Grain—
We passed the Setting Sun—

Or rather—He passed Us—
The Dews drew quivering and chill—
For only Gossamer,[1] my Gown—
My Tippet[2]—only Tulle[3]—

We paused before a House that seemed
A Swelling of the Ground—
The Roof was scarcely visible—
The Cornice—in the Ground—          20

Since then—'tis Centuries—and yet
Feels shorter than the Day
I first surmised the Horses' Heads
Were toward Eternity—   (*c. 1863*)

**754**

My Life had stood—a Loaded Gun—
In Corners—till a Day
The Owner passed—identified—
And carried Me away—

And now We roam in Sovereign Woods—
And now We hunt the Doe—
And every time I speak for Him—
The Mountains straight reply—

And do I smile, such cordial light
Upon the Valley glow—          10
It is as a Vesuvian face
Had let its pleasure through—

And when at Night—Our good Day
done—
I guard My Master's Head—
'Tis better than the Eider-Duck's
Deep Pillow—to have shared—

---

[1] the filmiest of fabrics      [2] a scarf          [3] a thin netted fabric

To foe of His—I'm deadly foe—
None stir the second time—
On whom I lay a Yellow Eye—
Or an emphatic Thumb—                    20

Though I than He—may longer live
He longer must—than I—
For I have but the power to kill,
Without—the power to die—    *(1863?)*

## 861

Split the Lark—and you'll find the
    Music—
Bulb after Bulb, in Silver rolled—
Scantily dealt to the Summer Morning
Saved for your Ear when Lutes be old.

Loose the Flood—you shall find it
    patent—
Gush after Gush, reserved for you—
Scarlet Experiment! Sceptic Thomas!
Now, do you doubt that your Bird was
    true?  *(1864?)*

## 875

I stepped from Plank to Plank
A slow and cautious way
The Stars about my Head I felt
About my Feet the Sea.

I knew not but the next
Would be my final inch—
This gave me that precarious Gait
Some call Experience.  *(1864?)*

## 986

A narrow Fellow in the Grass
Occasionally rides—
You may have met Him—did you not
His notice sudden is—

The Grass divides as with a Comb—
A spotted shaft is seen—
And then it closes at your feet
And opens further on—

He likes a Boggy Acre
A Floor too cool for Corn—        10

Yet when a Boy, and Barefoot—
I more than once at Noon
Have passed, I thought, a Whip lash
Unbraiding in the Sun
When stooping to secure it
It wrinkled, and was gone—

Several of Nature's People
I know, and they know me—
I feel for them a transport
Of cordiality—                        20

But never met this Fellow
Attended, or alone
Without a tighter breathing
And Zero at the Bone—    *(c. 1865)*

## 1100

The last Night that She lived
It was a Common Night
Except the Dying—this to Us
Made Nature different

We noticed smallest things—
Things overlooked before
By this great light upon our Minds
Italicized—as 'twere.

As we went out and in
Between Her final Room        10
And Rooms where Those to be alive
Tomorrow were, a Blame

That Others could exist
While She must finish quite
A Jealousy for Her arose
So nearly infinite—

We waited while She passed—
It was a narrow time—
Too jostled were Our Souls to speak
At length the notice came.        20

She mentioned, and forgot—
Then lightly as a Reed
Bent to the Water, struggled scarce—
Consented, and was dead—

And We—We placed the Hair—
And drew the Head erect—
And then an awful leisure was
Belief to regulate—    *(c. 1866)*

1129

Tell all the Truth but tell it slant—
Success in Circuit lies
Too bright for our infirm Delight
The Truth's superb surprise

As Lightning to the Children eased
With explanation kind
The Truth must dazzle gradually
Or every man be blind—   (*1868?*)

1484

We shall find the Cube of the Rainbow.
Of that, there is no doubt.
But the Arc of a Lover's conjecture
Eludes the finding out.   (*1880?*)

1593

There came a Wind like a Bugle—
It quivered through the Grass
And a Green Chill upon the Heat
So ominous did pass
We barred the Windows and the Doors
As from an Emerald Ghost—
The Doom's electric Moccasin
That very instant passed—
On a strange Mob of panting Trees

And Fences fled away                    10
And Rivers where the Houses ran
Those looked that lived—that Day—
The Bell within the steeple wild
The flying tidings told—
How much can come
And much can go,
And yet abide the World!   (*c. 1883*)

1624

Apparently with no surprise
To any happy Flower
The Frost beheads it at its play—
In accidental power—
The blonde Assassin passes on—
The Sun proceeds unmoved
To measure off another Day
For an Approving God.   (*c. 1884*)

1732

My life closed twice before its close—
It yet remains to see
If Immortality unveil
A third event to me

So huge, so hopeless to conceive
As these that twice befell.
Parting is all we know of heaven,
And all we need of hell.

# CHRISTINA ROSSETTI / 1830–1894

## Song

When I am dead, my dearest,
  Sing no sad songs for me;
Plant thou no roses at my head,
  Nor shady cypress tree:
Be the green grass above me
  With showers and dewdrops wet;
And if thou wilt, remember,
  And if thou wilt, forget.

I shall not see the shadows,
  I shall not feel the rain;                10
I shall not hear the nightingale
  Sing on, as if in pain;
And dreaming through the twilight
  That doth not rise nor set,
Haply I may remember,
  And haply may forget.   (*1848*)

## Three Seasons

"A cup for hope!" she said,
In springtime ere the bloom was old;
The crimson wine was poor and cold
  By her mouth's richer red.

"A cup for love!" how low,
How soft the words; and all the while
Her blush was rippling with a smile
  Like summer after snow.

"A cup for memory!"
Cold cup that one must drain alone;     10
While autumn winds are up and moan
  Across the barren sea.

Hope, memory, love:
Hope for fair morn, and love for day,
And memory for the evening gray
  And solitary dove.   (*1853*)

## The Bourne

Underneath the growing grass,
  Underneath the living flowers,
  Deeper than the sound of showers:
  There we shall not count the hours
By the shadows as they pass.

Youth and health will be but vain,
  Beauty reckoned of no worth:
  There a very little girth
  Can hold round what once the earth
Seemed too narrow to
  contain.   (*1854*)                    10

## After Death

The curtains were half drawn, the floor was swept
And strewn with rushes, rosemary and may
Lay thick upon the bed on which I lay,
Where through the lattice ivy-shadows crept.
He leaned above me, thinking that I slept
And could not hear him; but I heard him say:
"Poor child, poor child": and as he turned away
Came a deep silence, and I knew he wept.
He did not touch the shroud, or raise the fold
That hid my face, or take my hand in his,      10
Or ruffle the smooth pillows for my head:
He did not love me living; but once dead
He pitied me; and very sweet it is
To know he still is warm though I am cold.   (*1849*)

## A Birthday

My heart is like a singing bird
  Whose nest is in a watered shoot;
My heart is like an apple-tree
  Whose boughs are bent with thickset
    fruit;
My heart is like a rainbow shell
  That paddles in a halcyon sea;
My heart is gladder than all these,
  Because my love is come to me.

Raise me a daïs of silk and down;
  Hang it with vair[1] and purple
    dyes;                               10
Carve it in doves and pomegranates,
  And peacocks with a hundred eyes;
Work it in gold and silver grapes,
  In leaves and silver fleur-de-lys;
Because the birthday of my life
  Is come, my love is come to
    me.   (*1857*)

---

[1] costly fur

# LEWIS CARROLL / 1832–1898

## *from* Through the Looking-Glass

### JABBERWOCKY

'Twas brillig,[1] and the slithy toves
    Did gyre and gimble in the wabe;
All mimsy were the borogoves,
    And the mome raths outgrabe.

"Beware the Jabberwock, my son!
    The jaws that bite, the claws that catch!
Beware the Jubjub bird, and shun
    The frumious Bandersnatch!"

He took his vorpal sword in hand;
    Long time the manxome foe he sought—         10
So rested he by the Tumtum tree,
    And stood awhile in thought.

And, as in uffish thought he stood,
    The Jabberwock, with eyes of flame,
Came whiffling through the tulgey wood,
    And burbled as it came!

One, two! One, two! And through and through
    The vorpal blade went snicker-snack!
He left it dead, and with its head
    He went galumphing back.         20

"And hast thou slain the Jabberwock?
    Come to my arms, my beamish boy!
O frabjous day! Callooh! Callay!"
    He chortled in his joy.

'Twas brillig, and the slithy toves
    Did gyre and gimble in the wabe;
All mimsy were the borogoves,
    And the mome raths outgrabe.   *(1855)*

[1] In *Through the Looking-Glass*, where "Jabberwocky" appears, Carroll offers the following explanations of some of the words in the poem:
  *brillig:* four o' clock in the afternoon, when you begin broiling things for dinner
  *slithy:* lithe and slimy; a "portmanteau word" which packs up two meanings into one word
  *toves:* something like badgers, something like lizards, something like corkscrews
  *gyre:* to go round and round like a gyroscope
  *gimble:* to make holes like a gimlet
  *wabe:* the grass plot around a sundial: it goes a long way before it, a long way behind it, and a long way beyond it on each side
  *mimsy:* flimsy and miserable
  *borogove:* a thin shabby-looking bird with its feathers sticking out all round, something like a live mop
  *mome:* perhaps short for "from home," meaning that they had lost their way
  *rath:* a sort of green pig
  *outgrabe:* past tense of "outgribe," something between to bellow and to whistle, with a kind of sneeze in the middle

*THE WHITE KNIGHT'S SONG*

I'll tell thee everything I can,
   There's little to relate.
I saw an agéd, agéd man,
   A-sitting on a gate.
"Who are you, agéd man?" I said.
   "And how is it you live?"
And his answer trickled through my head
   Like water through a sieve.

He said "I look for butterflies
   That sleep among the wheat:     10
I make them into mutton-pies,
   And sell them in the street.
I sell them unto men," he said.
   "Who sail on stormy seas;
And that's the way I get my bread—
   A trifle, if you please."

But I was thinking of a plan
   To dye one's whiskers green,
And always use so large a fan
   That they could not be seen.     20
So, having no reply to give
   To what the old man said,
I cried, "Come, tell me how you live!"
   And thumped him on the head.

His accents mild took up the tale;
   He said, "I go my ways,
And when I find a mountain-rill,
   I set it in a blaze;
And thence they make a stuff they call
   Rowland's Macassar Oil—     30
Yet twopence-halfpenny is all
   They give me for my toil."

But I was thinking of a way
   To feed oneself on batter,
And so go on from day to day
   Getting a little fatter.
I shook him well from side to side,
   Until his face was blue;
"Come, tell me how you live," I cried
   "And what it is you do!"     40

He said, "I hunt for haddocks' eyes
   Among the heather bright,
And work them into waistcoat-buttons
   In the silent night.
And these I do not sell for gold
   Or coin of silvery shine,
But for a copper halfpenny,
   And that will purchase nine.

"I sometimes dig for buttered rolls,
   Or set limed twigs for crabs;     50
I sometimes search the grassy knolls
   For wheels of hansom-cabs.
And that's the way" (he gave a wink)
   "By which I get my wealth—
And very gladly will I drink
   Your Honor's noble health."

I heard him then, for I had just
   Completed my design
To keep the Menai bridge from rust
   By boiling it in wine.     60
I thanked him much for telling me
   The way he got his wealth,
But chiefly for his wish that he
   Might drink my noble health.

And now, if e'er by chance I put
   My fingers into glue,
Or madly squeeze a right-hand foot
   Into a left-hand shoe,
Or if I drop upon my toe
   A very heavy weight,     70
I weep, for it reminds me so
   Of that old man I used to know—
Whose look was mild, whose speech was
   slow,
Whose hair was whiter than the snow,
Whose face was very like a crow,
With eyes, like cinders, all aglow,
Who seemed distracted with his woe.
Who rocked his body to and fro,
And muttered mumblingly and low,
As if his mouth were full of dough,     80
Who snorted like a buffalo—
That summer evening long ago
   A-sitting on a gate.   *(1856)*

# ALGERNON CHARLES SWINBURNE / 1837–1909

## Chorus from Atalanta[1] in Calydon

When the hounds of spring are on winter's traces,
　　The mother of months[2] in meadow or plain
Fills the shadows and windy places
　　With lisp of leaves and ripple of rain;
And the brown bright nightingale amorous
Is half assuaged for Itylus,[3]
For the Thracian ships and the foreign faces,
　　The tongueless vigil, and all the pain.

Come with bows bent and with emptying of quivers,
　　Maiden most perfect, lady of light,　　　　　　　　　　　　　　　　10
With a noise of winds and many rivers,
　　With a clamour of waters, and with might;
Bind on thy sandals, O thou most fleet,
Over the splendour and speed of thy feet;
For the faint east quickens, the wan west shivers,
　　Round the feet of the day and the feet of the night.

Where shall we find her, how shall we sing to her,
　　Fold our hands round her knees, and cling?
O that man's heart were as fire and could spring to her,
　　Fire, or the strength of the streams that spring!　　　　　　　　　20
For the stars and the winds are unto her
As raiment, as songs of the harp-player;
For the risen stars and the fallen cling to her,
　　And the southwest wind and the west wind sing.

For the winter's rains and ruins are over,
　　And all the season of snows and sins;
The days dividing lover and lover,
　　The light that loses, the night that wins;
And time remembered is grief forgotten,
And frosts are slain and flowers begotten,　　　　　　　　　　　　　30
And in green underwood and cover
　　Blossom by blossom the spring begins.

The full streams feed on flower of rushes,
　　Ripe grasses trammel a travelling foot,
The faint fresh flame of the young year flushes
　　From leaf to flower and flower to fruit;

---

[1] maiden noted in mythology for fleetness of foot and for taking part in the hunt for the boar that devastated Calydon
[2] Artemis, goddess of the moon
[3] Tereus, king of Thrace, cut his wife Procne's tongue out to keep her silent while he married her sister Philomela. The sisters retaliated by roasting the flesh of Itylus, son of Procne and Tereus, and serving it to the father. Subsequently Procne was transformed into the nightingale and Philomela into the swallow to rescue them from pursuit by Tereus. (Some accounts reverse in part the roles of Procne and Philomela.)

579

And fruit and leaf are as gold and fire,
And the oat[4] is heard above the lyre,
And the hooféd heel of a satyr[5] crushes
    The chestnut-husk at the chestnut-root.          40

And Pan[6] by noon and Bacchus[7] by night,
    Fleeter of foot than the fleet-foot kid,
Follows with dancing and fills with delight
    The Mænad and the Bassarid;[8]
And soft as lips that laugh and hide
The laughing leaves of the trees divide,
And screen from seeing and leave in sight
    The god pursuing, the maiden hid.

The ivy falls with the Bacchanal's hair
    Over her eyebrows hiding her eyes;               50
The wild vine slipping down leaves bare
    Her bright breast shortening into sighs;
The wild vine slips with the weight of its leaves,
But the berried ivy catches and cleaves
To the limbs that glitter, the feet that scare
    The wolf that follows, the fawn that flies.   (*1865*)


# Hymn to Proserpine[1]

## (AFTER THE PROCLAMATION IN ROME OF THE CHRISTIAN FAITH)[2]

*Vicisti, Galilæe*[3]

I have lived long enough, having seen one thing, that love hath an end;
Goddess and maiden and queen, be near me now and befriend.
Thou art more than the day or the morrow, the seasons that laugh or that
    weep;
For these give joy and sorrow; but thou, Proserpina, sleep.
Sweet is the treading of wine, and sweet the feet of the dove;
But a goodlier gift is thine than foam of the grapes or love.
Yea, is not even Apollo,[4] with hair and harpstring of gold,
A bitter God to follow, a beautiful God to behold?
I am sick of singing; the bays burn deep and chafe: I am fain
To rest a little from praise and grievous pleasure and pain.          10
For the Gods we know not of, who give us our daily breath,
We know they are cruel as love or life, and lovely as death.
O Gods dethroned and deceased, cast forth, wiped out in a day!

---

4 the oat-straw pipe of the shepherd
5 a demigod, part man and part goat, noted for lascivious behavior
6 Greek god of flocks and wild creatures
7 god of wine
8 female and male worshippers of Bacchus
1 Proserpina was the Roman name equivalent to the Greek Persephone. She was the wife of Pluto and hence the queen of the underworld.
2 By the Edict of Milan in A.D. 313, the Emperor Constantine recognized Christianity.
3 Thou hast conquered, Galilean (i.e., Christ).
4 god of the sun, light, music, and the arts generally

From your wrath is the world released, redeemed from your chains, men
   say.
New Gods are crowned in the city, their flowers have broken your rods;
They are merciful, clothed with pity, the young compassionate Gods.
But for me their new device is barren, the days are bare;
Things long past over suffice, and men forgotten that were.
Time and the Gods are at strife: ye dwell in the midst thereof,
Draining a little life from the barren breasts of love.           20
I say to you, cease, take rest; yea, I say to you all, be at peace,
Till the bitter milk of her breast and the barren bosom shall cease.
Wilt thou yet take all, Galilean? but these thou shalt not take,
The laurel, the palms and the pæan, the breasts of the nymphs in the brake;
Breasts more soft than a dove's, that tremble with tenderer breath;
And all the wings of the Loves, and all the joy before death;
All the feet of the hours that sound as a single lyre,
Dropped and deep in the flowers, with strings that flicker like fire.
More than these wilt thou give, things fairer than all these things?
Nay, for a little we live, and life hath mutable wings.          30
A little while and we die; shall life not thrive as it may?
For no man under the sky lives twice, outliving his day.
And grief is a grievous thing, and a man hath enough of his tears;
Why should he labour, and bring fresh grief to blacken his years?
Thou hast conquered, O pale Galilean; the world has grown grey from thy
   breath;
We have drunken of things Lethean,[5] and fed on the fullness of death.
Laurel is green for a season, and love is sweet for a day;
But love grows bitter with treason, and laurel outlives not May.
Sleep, shall we sleep after all? for the world is not sweet in the end;
For the old faiths loosen and fall, the new years ruin and rend.      40
Fate is a sea without shore, and the soul is a rock that abides;
But her ears are vexed with the roar and her face with the foam of the
   tides.
O lips that the live blood faints in, the leavings of racks and rods!
O ghastly glories of saints, dead limbs of gibbeted Gods!
Though all men abase them before you in spirit, and all knees bend,
I kneel not neither adore you, but standing, look to the end.
All delicate days and pleasant, all spirits and sorrows are cast
Far out with the foam of the present that sweeps to the surf of the past:
Where beyond the extreme sea-wall, and between the remote sea-gates,
Waste water washes, and tall ships founder, and deep death waits:    50
Where, mighty with deepening sides, clad about with the seas as with wings,
And impelled of invisible tides, and fulfilled of unspeakable things,
White-eyed and poisonous-finned, shark-toothed and serpentine-curled,
Rolls, under the whitening wind of the future, the wave of the world.
The depths stand naked in sunder behind it, the storms flee away;
In the hollow before it the thunder is taken and snared as a prey;
In its sides is the north-wind bound; and its salt is of all men's tears;

---

[5] inducing forgetfulness, as the waters of the river Lethe do

With light of ruin, and sound of changes, and pulse of years:
With travail of day after day, and with trouble of hour upon hour;
And bitter as blood is the spray; and the crests are as fangs that devour:      *60*
And its vapour and storm of its steam as the sighing of spirits to be;
And its noise as the noise in a dream; and its depth as the roots of the sea:
And the height of its heads as the height of the utmost stars of the air:
And the ends of the earth at the might thereof tremble, and time is made
    bare.
Will ye bridle the deep sea with reins, will ye chasten the high sea with rods?
Will ye take her to chain her with chains, who is older than all ye Gods?
All ye as a wind shall go by, as a fire shall ye pass and be past;
Ye are Gods, and behold ye shall die, and the waves be upon you at last.
In the darkness of time, in the deeps of the years, in the changes of things,
Ye shall sleep as a slain man sleeps, and the world shall forget you for kings.    *70*
Though the feet of thine high priests tread where thy lords and our
    forefathers trod,
Though these that were Gods are dead, and thou being dead art a God,
Though before thee the throned Cytherean[6] be fallen, and hidden her head,
Yet thy kingdom shall pass, Galilean, thy dead shall go down to thee dead.
Of the maiden thy mother men sing as a goddess with grace clad around;
Thou art throned where another was king; where another was queen she is
    crowned.
Yea, once we had sight of another: but now she is queen, say these.
Not as thine, not as thine was our mother, a blossom of flowering seas,
Clothed round with the world's desire as with raiment, and fair as the foam,
And fleeter than kindled fire, and a goddess, and mother of Rome.[7]      *80*
For thine came pale and a maiden, and sister to sorrow; but ours,
Her deep hair heavily laden with odour and colour of flowers,
White rose of the rose-white water, a silver splendour, a flame,
Bent down unto us that besought her, and earth grew sweet with her name.
For thine came weeping, a slave among slaves, and rejected; but she
Came flushed from the full-flushed wave, and imperial, her foot on the sea,
And the wonderful waters knew her, the winds and the viewless ways,
And the roses grew rosier, and bluer the sea-blue stream of the bays.
Ye are fallen, our lords, by what token? we wist that ye should not fall.
Ye were all so fair that are broken; and one more fair than ye all.      *90*
But I turn to her still, having seen she shall surely abide in the end;
Goddess and maiden and queen, be near me now and befriend.
O daughter of earth, of my mother, her crown and blossom of birth,
I am also, I also, thy brother; I go as I came unto earth.
In the night where thine eyes are as moons are in heaven, the night where
    thou art,
Where the silence is more than all tunes, where sleep overflows from the
    heart,
Where the poppies are sweet as the rose in our world, and the red rose is
    white,
And the wind falls faint as it blows with the fume of the flowers of the night,

---

[6] Venus     [7] Aphrodite

And the murmur of spirits that sleep in the shadow of Gods from afar
Grows dim in thine ears and deep as the deep dim soul of a star,                   *100*
In the sweet low light of thy face, under heavens untrod by the sun,
Let my soul with their souls find place, and forget what is done and
    undone.
Thou art more than the Gods who number the days of our temporal
    breath;
For these give labor and slumber; but thou, Proserpina, death.
Therefore now at thy feet I abide for a season in silence. I know
I shall die as my fathers died, and sleep as they sleep; even so.
For the glass of the years is brittle wherein we gaze for a span;
A little soul for a little bears up this corpse which is man.
So long I endure, no longer; and laugh not again, neither weep.
For there is no God found stronger than death; and death is a sleep.            *110*
                                              *(1866)*

## The Garden of Proserpine[1]

Here, where the world is quiet;
  Here, where all trouble seems
Dead winds' and spent waves' riot
  In doubtful dreams of dreams;
I watch the green field growing
For reaping folk and sowing,
For harvest-time and mowing,
  A sleepy world of streams.

I am tired of tears and laughter,
  And men that laugh and weep;          *10*
Of what may come hereafter
  For men that sow to reap:
I am weary of days and hours,
Blown buds of barren flowers,
Desires and dreams and powers
  And everything but sleep.

Here life has death for neighbour,
  And far from eye or ear
Wan waves and wet winds labour,
  Weak ships and spirits steer;          *20*
They drive adrift, and whither
They wot not who make thither;
But no such winds blow hither,
  And no such things grow here.

No growth of moor or coppice,
  No heather-flower or vine,
But bloomless buds of poppies,
  Green grapes of Proserpine,

Pale beds of blowing rushes,
Where no leaf blooms or blushes          *30*
Save this whereout she crushes
  For dead men deadly wine.

Pale, without name or number,
  In fruitless fields of corn,
They bow themselves and slumber
  All night till light is born;
And like a soul belated,
In hell and heaven unmated,
By cloud and mist abated
  Comes out of darkness morn.          *40*

Though one were strong as seven,
  He too with death shall dwell,
Nor wake with wings in heaven,
  Nor weep for pains in hell;
Though one were fair as roses,
His beauty clouds and closes;
And well though love reposes,
  In the end it is not well.

Pale, beyond porch and portal,
  Crowned with calm leaves, she
    stands          *50*
Who gathers all things mortal
  With cold immortal hands;
Her languid lips are sweeter
Than love's who fears to greet her,
To men that mix and meet her
  From many times and lands.

_____
[1] goddess who was queen of the underworld

She waits for each and other,
    She waits for all men born;
Forgets the earth her mother,
    The life of fruits and corn;                          60
And spring and seed and swallow
Take wing for her and follow
Where summer song rings hollow
    And flowers are put to scorn.

There go the loves that wither,
    The old loves with wearier wings;
And all dead years draw thither,
    And all disastrous things;
Dead dreams of days forsaken,
Blind buds that snows have shaken,            70
Wild leaves that winds have taken,
    Red strays of ruined springs.

We are not sure of sorrow,
    And joy was never sure;
Today will die tomorrow;
    Time stoops to no man's lure;

And love, grown faint and fretful,
With lips but half regretful
Sighs, and with eyes forgetful
    Weeps that no lives endure.                            80

From too much love of living,
    From hope and fear set free,
We thank with brief thanksgiving
    Whatever gods may be
That no life lives for ever;
That dead men rise up never;
That even the weariest river
    Winds somewhere safe to sea.

Then star nor sun shall waken,
    Nor any change of light:                               90
Nor sound of waters shaken,
    Nor any sound or sight:
Nor wintry leaves nor vernal,
Nor days nor things diurnal;
Only the sleep eternal
    In an eternal night.    *(1866)*

## A Ballad of Dreamland

I hid my heart in a nest of roses,
    Out of the sun's way, hidden apart;
In a softer bed than the soft white snow's is,
    Under the roses I hid my heart.
    Why would it sleep not? why should it start,
    When never a leaf of the rose-tree stirred?
    What made sleep flutter his wings and part?
Only the song of a secret bird.

Lie still, I said, for the wind's wing closes,
    And mild leaves muffle the keen sun's dart;
Lie still, for the wind on the warm sea dozes,            10
    And the wind is unquieter yet than thou art.
    Does a thought in thee still as a thorn's wound smart?
    Does the fang still fret thee of hope deferred?
    What bids the lids of thy sleep dispart?
Only the song of a secret bird.

The green land's name that a charm encloses,
    It never was writ in the traveller's chart,
And sweet on its trees as the fruit that grows is,
    It never was sold in the merchant's mart.             20
    The swallows of dreams through its dim fields dart,
    And sleep's are the tunes in its tree-tops heard;
    No hound's note wakens the wildwood hart,
Only the song of a secret bird.

ENVOI

In the world of dreams I have chosen my part,
To sleep for a season and hear no word
Of true love's truth or of light love's art,
Only the song of a secret bird.   (*1878*)


# GERARD MANLEY HOPKINS / 1844–1889

## Heaven-Haven

*A NUN TAKES THE VEIL*

I have desired to go
Where springs not fail,
To fields where flies no sharp and sided hail
And a few lilies blow.

And I have asked to be
Where no storms come,
Where the green swell is in the havens dumb,
And out of the swing of the sea.
(*1865*)


## The Habit of Perfection

Elected Silence, sing to me
And beat upon my whorlèd ear,
Pipe me to pastures still and be
The music that I care to hear.

Shape nothing, lips; be lovely-dumb:
It is the shut, the curfew sent
From there where all surrenders come
Which only makes you eloquent.

Be shellèd, eyes, with double dark
And find the uncreated light:                               10
This ruck and reel which you remark
Coils, keeps, and teases simple sight.

Palate, the hutch of tasty lust,
Desire not to be rinsed with wine:
The can must be so sweet, the crust
So fresh that come in fasts divine!

Nostrils, your careless breath that spend
Upon the stir and keep of pride,
What relish shall the censers send
Along the sanctuary side!                                   20

O feel-of-primrose hands, O feet
That want the yield of plushy sward,
But you shall walk the golden street
And you unhouse and house the Lord.

And, Poverty, be thou the bride
And now the marriage feast begun,
And lily-coloured clothes provide
Your spouse not laboured-at nor
spun.   (*1866*)


## God's Grandeur

The world is charged with the grandeur of God.
It will flame out, like shining from shook foil;
It gathers to a greatness, like the ooze of oil
Crushed. Why do men then now not reck his rod?
Generations have trod, have trod, have trod;
And all is seared with trade; bleared, smeared with toil;
And wears man's smudge and shares man's smell: the soil
Is bare now, nor can foot feel, being shod.

And for all this, nature is never spent;
There lives the dearest freshness deep down things;                    10
And though the last lights off the black West went
Oh, morning, at the brown brink eastward, springs
Because the Holy Ghost over the bent
World broods with warm breast and with ah! bright wings.   (*1877*)

## The Starlight Night

Look at the stars! look, look up at the skies!
  O look at all the fire-folk sitting in the air!
  The bright boroughs, the circle-citadels there!
Down in dim woods the diamond delves! the elves'-eyes!
The grey lawns cold where gold, where quickgold lies!
  Wind-beat whitebeam! airy abeles [1] set on a flare!
  Flake-doves sent floating forth at a farmyard scare!—
Ah well! it is all a purchase, all is a prize.
Buy then! bid then!—What?—Prayer, patience, alms, vows.
Look, look: a May-mess, like on orchard boughs!                        10
  Look! March-bloom, like on mealed-with-yellow sallows!
These are indeed the barn; withindoors house
The shocks. This piece-bright paling shuts the spouse
  Christ home, Christ and his mother and all his hallows.   (*1877*)

## Spring

Nothing is so beautiful as spring—
When weeds, in wheels, shoot long and lovely and lush;
Thrush's eggs look little low heavens, and thrush
Through the echoing timber does so rinse and wring
The ear, it strikes like lightnings to hear him sing;
The glassy peartree leaves and blooms, they brush
The descending blue; that blue is all in a rush
With richness; the racing lambs too have fair their fling.
What is all this juice and all this joy?
A strain of the earth's sweet being in the beginning                   10
In Eden garden.—Have, get, before it cloy,
Before it cloud, Christ, lord, and sour with sinning,
Innocent mind and Mayday in girl and boy,
Most, O maid's child, thy choice and worthy the winning.   (*1877*)

## The Windhover:

### TO CHRIST OUR LORD

I caught this morning morning's minion, king-
    dom of daylight's dauphin, dapple-dawn-drawn Falcon, in his riding
    Of the rolling level underneath him steady air, and striding

---

[1] white poplars

High there, how he rung upon the rein of a wimpling wing
In his ecstasy! then off, off forth on swing,
    As a skate's heel sweeps smooth on a bow-bend: the hurl and gliding
    Rebuffed the big wind. My heart in hiding
Stirred for a bird,—the achieve of, the mastery of the thing!

Brute beauty and valor and act, oh, air, pride, plume, here
    Buckle! AND the fire that breaks from thee then, a billion       *10*
Times told lovelier, more dangerous, O my chevalier!

    No wonder of it: sheér plód makes plow down sillion[1]
Shine, and blue-bleak embers, ah my dear,
    Fall, gall themselves, and gash gold-vermilion.   *(1877)*


## Pied Beauty

    Glory be to God for dappled things—
      For skies of couple-color as a brinded[1] cow;
        For rose-moles all in stipple[2] upon trout that swim;
    Fresh-firecoal chestnut-falls;[3] finches' wings;
      Landscape plotted and pieced—fold, fallow, and plow;
        And áll trádes, their gear and tackle and trim.

    All things counter, original, spare, strange;
      Whatever is fickle, freckled (who knows how?)
        With swift, slow; sweet, sour; adazzle, dim;
    He fathers-forth whose beauty is past change:       *10*
          Praise him.  *(1877)*


## Hurrahing in Harvest

    Summer ends now; now, barbarous in beauty, the stooks rise
    Around; up above, what wind-walks! what lovely behaviour
    Of silk-sack clouds! has wilder, wilful-wavier
    Meal-drift moulded ever and melted across skies?

    I walk, I lift up, I lift up heart, eyes,
    Down all that glory in the heavens to glean our Saviour;
    And, éyes, heárt, what looks, what lips yet gave you a
    Rapturous love's greeting of realer, of rounder replies?

    And the azurous hung hills are his world-wielding shoulder
    Majestic—as a stallion stalwart, very-violet-sweet!—      *10*
    These things, these things were here and but the beholder
    Wanting; which two when they once meet,
    The heart rears wings bold and bolder
    And hurls for him, O half hurls earth for him off under his feet.  *(1877)*

---

[1] the ridge between two furrows
[1] streaked or spotted

[2] shading with small dots
[3] fallen chestnuts as bright as coals of fire

## The Caged Skylark

As a dare-gale skylark scanted in a dull cage
Man's mounting spirit in his bone-house, mean house, dwells —
That bird beyond the remembering his free fells;
This in drudgery, day-labouring-out life's age.

Though aloft on turf or perch or poor low stage,
Both sing sometímes the sweetest, sweetest spells,
Yet both droop deadly sómetimes in their cells
Or wring their barriers in bursts of fear or rage.

Not that the sweet-fowl, song-fowl, needs no rest—
Why, hear him, hear him babble and drop down to his nest,     *10*
But his own nest, wild nest, no prison.

Man's spirit will be flesh-bound when found at best,
But uncumberèd: meadow-down is not distressed
For a rainbow footing it nor he for his bónes rísen.   (*1877*)


## Binsey Poplars

*FELLED 1879*

My aspens dear, whose airy cages quelled,
Quelled or quenched in leaves the leaping sun,
All felled, felled, are all felled;
   Of a fresh and following folded rank
        Not spared, not one
        That dandled a sandalled
     Shadow that swam or sank
On meadow and river and wind-wandering weed-winding bank.

   O if we but knew what we do
      When we delve or hew—                              *10*
   Hack and rack the growing green!
      Since country is so tender
   To touch, her being só slender,
   That, like this sleek and seeing ball
   But a prick will make no eye at all,
   Where we, even where we mean
       To mend her we end her,
     When we hew or delve:
After-comers cannot guess the beauty been.
   Ten or twelve, only ten or twelve                     *20*
      Strokes of havoc únselve
      The sweet especial scene,
     Rural scene, a rural scene,
     Sweet especial rural scene.   (*1879*)

## The Candle Indoors

Some candle clear burns somewhere I come by.
I muse at how its being puts blissful back
With yellowy moisture mild night's blear-all black,
Or to-fro tender trambeams truckle at the eye.

By that window what task what fingers ply,
I plod wondering, a-wanting, just for lack
Of answer the eagerer a-wanting Jessy or Jack
There / God to aggrándise, God to glorify.—

Come you indoors, come home; your fading fire
Mend first and vital candle in close heart's vault:                    *10*
You there are master, do your own desire;

What hinders? Are you beam-blind, yet to a fault
In a neighbour deft-handed? are you that liar
And, cast by conscience out, spendsavour salt?   (*1879*)

## Felix Randal

Felix Randal the farrier, O is he dead then? my duty all ended,
Who have watched his mould of man, big-boned and hardy-handsome
Pining, pining, till time when reason rambled in it and some
Fatal four disorders, fleshed there, all contended?

Sickness broke him. Impatient, he cursed at first, but mended
Being anointed and all; though a heavenlier heart began some
Months earlier, since I had our sweet reprieve and ransom
Tendered to him. Ah well, God rest him all road ever he offended!

This seeing the sick endears them to us, us too it endears.
My tongue had taught thee comfort, touch had quenched thy tears,     *10*
Thy tears that touched my heart, child, Felix, poor Felix Randal;

How far from then forethought of, all thy more boisterous years,
When thou at the random grim forge, powerful amidst peers,
Didst fettle for the great grey drayhorse his bright and battering sandal!

(*1880*)

## Spring and Fall:

### TO A YOUNG CHILD

Márgarét áre you gríeving
Over Goldengrove unleaving?
Leáves, líke the things of man, you
With your fresh thoughts care for, can
  you?
Áh! ás the heart grows older
It will come to such sights colder

By and by, nor spare a sigh
Though worlds of wanwood[1] leafmeal[2]
  lie;
And yet you *will* weep and know why.
Now no matter, child, the name:                *10*
Sórrow's spríngs áre the same.
Nor mouth had, no nor mind, expressed
What heart heard of, ghost[3] guessed:
It ís the blight man was born for,
It is Margaret you mourn for.   (*1880*)

[1] woods pale, as though bloodless
[2] dropped leaf by leaf; cf. piecemeal

[3] soul

# The Leaden Echo and the Golden Echo

## (*MAIDENS' SONG FROM ST. WINEFRED'S WELL*)

### THE LEADEN ECHO

How to kéep—is there ány any, is there none such, nowhere known some,
    bow or brooch or braid or brace, láce, latch or catch or key to keep
Back beauty, keep it, beauty, beauty, beauty, . . . from vanishing away?
Ó is there no frowning of these wrinkles, rankèd wrinkles deep,
Dówn? no waving off of these most mournful messengers, still messengers,
    sad and stealing messengers of grey?—
No there's none, there's none, O no there's none,
Nor can you long be, what you now are, called fair,
Do what you may do, what, do what you may,
And wisdom is early to despair:
Be beginning; since, no, nothing can be done
To keep at bay                                                                 *10*
Age and age's evils, hoar hair,
Ruck and wrinkle, drooping, dying, death's worst, winding sheets, tombs and
    worms and tumbling to decay;
So be beginning, be beginning to despair.
O there's none; no no no there's none:
Be beginning to despair, to despair,
Despair, despair, despair, despair.

### THE GOLDEN ECHO

      Spare!
There ís one, yes I have one (Hush there!),
Only not within seeing of the sun.
Not within the singeing of the strong sun,
Tall sun's tingeing, or treacherous the tainting of the earth's air,
Somewhere elsewhere there is ah well where! one,
Óne. Yes I cán tell such a key, I dó know such a place,
Where whatever's prizèd and passes of us, everything that's fresh and fast
    flying of us, seems to us sweet of us and swiftly away with, done away
    with, undone,
Undone, done with, soon done with, and yet dearly and dangerously sweet
Of us, the wimpled-water-dimpled, not-by-morning-matchèd face,                *10*
The flower of beauty, fleece of beauty, too too apt to, ah! to fleet,
Never fleets móre, fastened with the tenderest truth
To its own best being and its loveliness of youth: it is an everlastingness of,
    O it is an all youth!
Come then, your ways and airs and looks, locks, maidengear, gallantry and
    gaiety and grace,
Winning ways, airs innocent, maiden manners, sweet looks, loose locks, long
    locks, lovelocks, gaygear, going gallant, girlgrace—
Resign them, sign them, seal them, send them, motion them with breath,
And with sighs soaring, soaring síghs, deliver
Them; beauty-in-the-ghost, deliver it, early now, long before death

Give beauty back, beauty, beauty, beauty, back to God, beauty's self and
    beauty's giver.
See; not a hair is, not an eyelash, not the least lash lost; every hair     *20*
Is, hair of the head, numbered.
Nay, what we had lighthanded left in surly the mere mould
Will have waked and have waxed and have walked with the wind what while
    we slept,
This side, that side hurling a heavyheaded hundredfold
What while we, while we slumbered.
O then, weary then whý should we tread? O why are we so haggard at the
    heart, so care-coiled, care-killed, so fagged, so fashed, so cogged, so
    cumbered,
When the thing we freely fórfeit is kept with fonder a care,
Fonder a care kept than we could have kept it, kept
Far with fonder a care (and we, we should have lost it) finer, fonder
A care kept.—Where kept? do but tell us where kept, where.—     *30*
Yonder.—What high as that! We follow, now we follow.—
    Yonder, yes yonder, yonder,
Yonder.  *(1882)*

## (Carrion Comfort)

Not, I'll not, carrion comfort, Despair, not feast on thee;
Not untwist—slack they may be—these last strands of man
In me ór, most weary, cry *I can no more*. I can;
Can something, hope, wish day come, not choose not to be.

But ah, but O thou terrible, why wouldst thou rude on me
Thy wring-world right foot rock? lay a lionlimb against me? scan
With darksome devouring eyes my bruisèd bones? and fan,
O in turns of tempest, me heaped there; me frantic to avoid thee and flee?

Why? That my chaff might fly; my grain lie, sheer and clear.
Nay in all that toil, that coil, since (seems) I kissed the rod,     *10*
Hand rather, my heart lo! lapped strength, stole joy, would laugh, chéer.
Cheer whom though? The hero whose heaven-handling flung me, fóot tród
Me? or me that fought him? O which one? is it each one?
    That night, that year
Of now done darkness I wretch lay wrestling with (my God!) my God.  *(1885)*

## "I Wake and Feel the Fell of Dark"

    I wake and feel the fell of dark, not day.
    What hours, O what black hoürs we have spent
    This night! what sights you, heart, saw; ways you went!
    And more must, in yet longer light's delay.

    With witness I speak this. But where I say
    Hours I mean years, mean life. And my lament
    Is cries countless, cries like dead letters sent
    To dearest him that lives alas! away.

I am gall, I am heartburn. God's most deep decree
Bitter would have me taste: my taste was me;                          10
Bones built in me, flesh filled, blood brimmed the curse.

Selfyeast of spirit a dull dough sours, I see
The lost are like this, and their scourge to be
As I am mine, their sweating selves; but worse.   (1885)


## "Thou Art Indeed Just, Lord"

*Justus quidem tu es, Domine, si disputem tecum: verumtamen justa loquar ad te: Quare via
impiorum prosperatur? &c.*[1]

Thou art indeed just, Lord, if I contend
With thee; but, sir, so what I plead is just.
Why do sinners' ways prosper? and why must
Disappointment all I endeavour end?
Wert thou my enemy, O thou my friend,
How wouldst thou worse, I wonder, than thou dost
Defeat, thwart me? Oh, the sots and thralls of lust
Do in spare hours more thrive than I that spend,
Sir, life upon thy cause. See, banks and brakes
Now, leavèd how thick! lacèd they are again        10
With fretty chervil,[2] look, and fresh wind shakes
Them; birds build—but not I build; no, but strain,
Time's eunuch, and not breed one work that wakes.
Mine, O thou lord of life, send my roots rain.   (1889)


## WILLIAM ERNEST HENLEY / 1849–1903

### Where Forlorn Sunsets

Where forlorn sunsets flare and fade
On desolate sea and lonely sand,
Out of the silence and the shade
What is the voice of strange command
Calling you still, as friend calls friend
With love that cannot brook delay
To rise and follow the ways that wend
Over the hills and far away?

Hark in the city, street on street
A roaring reach of death and
life,                                     10
Of vortices that clash and fleet

And ruin in appointed strife,
Hark to it calling, calling clear,
Calling until you cannot stay
From dearer things than your own most
dear
Over the hills and far away?

Out of the sound of the ebb-and-flow,
Out of the sight of lamp and star,
It calls you where the good winds blow,
And the unchanging meadows
are:                                      20
From faded hopes and hopes agleam,
It calls you, calls you night and day
Beyond the dark into the dream
Over the hills and far away.   (1892)

[1] Jeremiah 12:1 in the Latin Vulgate Version,
translated in the first three lines

[2] cow parsnip, a wayside herb with finely divided
("fretty") leaves

## *from* In Hospital

### WAITING

A square, squat room (a cellar on promotion),
Drab to the soul, drab to the very daylight;
Plasters astray in unnatural-looking tinware;
Scissors and lint and apothecary's jars.

Here, on a bench skeleton would writhe from,
Angry and sore, I wait to be admitted;
Wait till my heart is lead upon my stomach,
While at their ease two dressers do their chores.

One has a probe—it feels to me a crowbar.
A small boy sniffs and shudders after bluestone.[1]           10
A poor old tramp explains his poor old ulcers.
Life is (I think) a blunder and a shame.   (*1874*)

## Invictus[1]

Out of the night that covers me,
  Black as the Pit from pole to pole,
I thank whatever gods may be
  For my unconquerable soul.

In the fell clutch of circumstance
  I have not winced nor cried aloud.
Under the bludgeonings of chance
  My head is bloody, but unbowed.

Beyond this place of wrath and tears
  Looms but the Horror of the shade,   10
And yet the menace of the years
  Finds, and shall find, me unafraid.

It matters not how strait the gate,
  How charged with punishments the
    scroll,
I am the master of my fate;
  I am the captain of my soul.   (*1875*)

## Madam Life's a Piece in Bloom

Madam Life's a piece in bloom
  Death goes dogging everywhere:
She's the tenant of the room,
  He's the ruffian on the stair.

You shall see her as a friend,
  You shall bilk him once or twice;
But he'll trap you in the end,
  And he'll stick you for her price.

With his kneebones at your chest,
  And his knuckles in your throat,   10
You would reason—plead—protest!
  Clutching at her petticoat;

But she's heard it all before,
  Well she knows you've had your fun,
Gingerly she gains the door,
  And your little job is done.   (*1877*)

## A Late Lark Twitters

A late lark twitters from the quiet skies;
And from the west,
Where the sun, his day's work ended,
Lingers as in content,
There falls on the old, grey city
An influence luminous and serene,
A shining peace.

---

[1] blue vitriol, administered to induce vomiting     [1] unvanquished

The smoke ascends
In a rosy-and-golden haze. The spires
Shine, and are changed. In the valley                    *10*
Shadows rise. The lark sings on. The sun,
Closing his benediction,
Sinks, and the darkening air
Thrills with a sense of the triumphing night—
Night with her train of stars
And her great gift of sleep.

So be my passing!
My task accomplished and the long day done,
My wages taken, and in my heart
Some late lark singing,                                  *20*
Let me be gathered to the quiet west,
The sundown splendid and serene,
Death.   (*1888*)


# ROBERT LOUIS STEVENSON / 1850–1894

## Requiem

Under the wide and starry sky
Dig the grave and let me lie:
Glad did I live and gladly die,
　　And I laid me down with a will.

This be the verse you grave for me:
*Here he lies where he longed to be;*
*Home is the sailor, home from sea,*
　　*And the hunter home from the*
　　　　*hill.*   (*1884*)


## The Land of Counterpane

When I was sick and lay a-bed,
I had two pillows at my head,
And all my toys beside me lay
To keep me happy all the day.

And sometimes for an hour or so
I watched my leaden soldiers go
With different uniforms and drills,
Among the bed-clothes, through the
　　hills;

And sometimes sent my ships in fleets
All up and down among the sheets;   *10*

Or brought my trees and houses out,
And planted cities all about.

I was the giant great and still
That sits upon the pillow-hill,
And sees before him, dale and plain,
The pleasant land of
　　counterpane.   (*1885*)


## The Land of Nod

From breakfast on through all the day
At home among my friends I stay,
But every night I go abroad
Afar into the Land of Nod.

All by myself I have to go,
With none to tell me what to do—
All alone beside the streams
And up the mountain-sides of dreams.

The strangest things are there for me,
Both things to eat and things to see   *10*
And many frightening sights abroad
Till morning in the Land of Nod.

Try as I like to find the way,
I never can get back by day,
Nor can remember plain and clear
The curious music that I hear.   (*1885*)

## Escape at Bedtime

The lights from the parlor and kitchen shone out
  Through the blinds and the windows and bars;
And high overhead and all moving about,
  There were thousands of millions of stars,
There ne'er were such thousands of leaves on a tree,
  Nor of people in church or the Park,
As the crowds of the stars that looked down upon me,
  And that glittered and winked in the dark.

The Dog, and the Plough, and the Hunter, and all,
  And the star of the sailor, and Mars,          *10*
These shone in the sky, and the pail by the wall
  Would be half full of water and stars.
They saw me at last, and they chased me with cries,
  And they soon had me packed into bed;
But the glory kept shining and bright in my eyes,
  And the stars going round in my head.  (*1885*)

## Skerryvore[1]

For love of lovely words, and for the sake
Of those, my kinsmen and my countrymen,
Who early and late in the windy ocean toiled
To plant a star for seamen, where was then
The surfy haunt of seals and cormorants:
I, on the lintel of this cot, inscribe
The name of a strong tower.  (*1887*)

## Skerryvore: The Parallel

Here all is sunny, and when the truant gull
Skims the green level of the lawn, his wing
Dispetals roses; here the house is framed
Of kneaded brick and the plumed mountain pine,
Such clay as artists fashion and such wood
As the tree-climbing urchin breaks. But there
Eternal granite hewn from the living isle
And dowelled with brute iron, rears a tower
That from its wet foundation to its crown
Of glittering glass, stands, in the sweep of winds,    *10*
Immovable, immortal, eminent.  (*1887*)

---

[1] the name of a lighthouse built by his uncle, which Stevenson applied to his house in Bournemouth

## My House

My house, I say. But hark to the sunny doves
That make my roof the arena of their loves,
That gyre about the gable all day long
And fill the chimneys with their murmurous song:
Our house, they say; and mine, the cat declares
And spread his golden fleece upon the chairs;
And mine the dog, and rises stiff with wrath
If any alien foot profane the path.
So, too, the buck that trimmed my terraces,
Our whilom gardener, called the garden his;                10
Who now, deposed, surveys my plain abode
And his late kingdom, only from the road.   (1887)


# FRANCIS THOMPSON / 1859–1907

## The Hound of Heaven

I fled Him, down the nights and down the days;
I fled Him, down the arches of the years;
I fled Him, down the labyrinthine ways
Of my own mind; and in the mist of tears
I hid from Him, and under running laughter.
          Up vistaed hopes, I sped;
          And shot, precipitated
Adown Titanic[1] glooms of chasméd fears,
From those strong Feet that followed, followed after.
          But with unhurrying chase,                         10
          And unperturbéd pace,
Deliberate speed, majestic instancy,
          They beat—and a Voice beat
          More instant than the Feet—
"All things betray thee, who betrayest Me."

          I pleaded, outlaw-wise,
By many a hearted casement, curtained red,
          Trellised with intertwining charities;
(For though I knew His love Who followéd,
          Yet was I sore adread                              20
Lest, having Him, I must have naught beside)
But, if one little casement parted wide,
          The gust of His approach would clash it to.
Fear wist not to evade as Love wist[2] to pursue.
Across the margent[3] of the world I fled,

---

[1] gigantic    [2] knew    [3] border

And troubled the gold gateways of the stars,
   Smiting for shelter on their clangéd bars;
      Fretted to dulcet jars
And silvern chatter the pale ports o' the moon.
I said to dawn: Be sudden—to eve: Be soon;     *30*
   With thy young skiey blossoms heap me over
      From this tremendous Lover!
Float thy vague veil about me, lest He see!
   I tempted all His servitors, but to find
My own betrayal in their constancy,
In faith to Him their fickleness to me,
   Their traitorous trueness, and their loyal deceit.
To all swift things for swiftness did I sue;
   Clung to the whistling mane of every wind.
      But whether they swept, smoothly fleet,     *40*
    The long savannahs[4] of the blue:
      Or whether, Thunder-driven,
    They clanged His chariot 'thwart a heaven,
Plashy with flying lightnings round the spurn o' their feet:—
   Fear wist not to evade as Love wist to pursue.
      Still with unhurrying chase,
      And unperturbéd pace,
    Deliberate speed, majestic instancy,
      Came on the following Feet,
      And a Voice above their beat—     *50*
   "Naught shelters thee, who wilt not shelter Me."

I sought no more that after which I strayed,
   In face of man or maid;
But still within the little children's eyes
   Seems something, something that replies,
*They* at least are for me, surely for me!
I turned me to them very wistfully;
But just as their young eyes grew sudden fair
   With dawning answers there,
Their angel plucked them from me by the hair.     *60*
"Come then, ye other children, Nature's—share
With me" (said I) "your delicate fellowship;
   Let me greet you lip to lip,
   Let me twine with you caresses,
      Wantoning
   With our Lady-Mother's vagrant tresses,
      Banqueting
   With her in her wind-walled palace,
   Underneath her azured daïs,
   Quaffing, as your taintless way is,     *70*
      From a chalice
Lucent-weeping out of the dayspring."

---

[4] grassy plains

So it was done:
*I* in their delicate fellowship was one—
Drew the bolt of Nature's secrecies.
    *I* knew all the swift importings
    On the wilful face of skies;
    I knew how the clouds arise
    Spuméd of the wild sea-snortings;
        All that's born or dies          *80*
  Rose and drooped with—made them shapers
Of mine own moods, or wailful or divine—
    With them joyed and was bereaven.
    I was heavy with the even,
    When she lit her glimmering tapers
    Round the day's dead sanctities.
    I laughed in the morning's eyes.
I triumphed and I saddened with all weather,
    Heaven and I wept together,
And its sweet tears were salt with mortal mine;     *90*
Against the red throb of its sunset-heart
    I laid my own to beat,
    And share commingling heat;
But not by that, by that, was eased my human smart.
In vain my tears were wet on Heaven's gray cheek,
For, ah! we know not what each other says,
    These things and I; in sound *I* speak—
*Their* sound is but their stir, they speak by silences.
Nature, poor stepdame, cannot slake my drouth;
    Let her, if she would owe me,        *100*
Drop yon blue bosom-veil of sky, and show me
    The breasts o' her tenderness:
Never did any milk of hers once bless
    My thirsting mouth.
    Nigh and nigh draws the chase,
    With unperturbéd pace,
  Deliberate speed, majestic instancy,
    And past those noiséd Feet
    A Voice comes yet more fleet!—
"Lo! naught contents thee, who content'st not Me."    *110*

Naked I wait Thy love's uplifted stroke.
My harness[5] piece by piece Thou hast hewn from me,
    And smitten me to my knee;
    I am defenceless utterly.
    I slept, methinks, and woke
And, slowly gazing, find me stripped in sleep.
In the rash lustihead of my young powers,
    I shook the pillaring hours

---

[5] armor

And pulled my life upon me;[6] grimed with smears,
I stand amid the dust o' the mounded years—
My mangled youth lies dead beneath the heap,
My days have crackled and gone up in smoke,
Have puffed and burst as sun-starts[7] on a stream.
     Yea, faileth now even dream
The dreamer, and the lute the lutanist;
Even the linked fantasies, in whose blossomy twist
I swung the earth a trinket at my wrist,
Are yielding; cords of all too weak account
For earth with heavy griefs so overplussed.
     Ah! is Thy love indeed
A weed, albeit an amaranthine[8] weed,
Suffering no flowers except its own to mount?
       Ah! must—
       Designer Infinite!—
Ah! must Thou char the wood ere Thou canst limn[9] with it?
My freshness spent its wavering shower i' the dust;
And now my heart is as a broken fount,
Wherein tear-drippings stagnate, spilt down ever
     From the dank thoughts that shiver
Upon the sighful branches of my mind.
     Such is; what is to be?
The pulp so bitter, how shall taste the rind?
I dimly guess what Time in mists confounds;
Yet ever and anon a trumpet sounds
From the hid battlements of Eternity;
Those shaken mists a space unsettle, then
Round the half-glimpséd turrets slowly wash again;
     But not ere him who summoneth
     I first have seen, enwound
With glooming robes purpureal, cypress-crowned;
His name I know, and what his trumpet saith.
Whether man's heart or life it be which yields
     Thee harvest, must Thy harvest fields
     Be dunged with rotten death?

     Now of that long pursuit
    Comes on at hand the bruit;[10]
That Voice is round me like a bursting sea;
    "And is thy earth so marred,
     Shattered in shard[11] on shard?
     Lo, all things fly thee, for thou fliest Me!
     Strange, piteous, futile thing!
Wherefore should any set thee love apart?
Seeing none but I make much of naught" (He said),

120

130

140

150

160

---

6 Samson destroyed himself along with his enemies when he pulled down the pillars supporting the temple of Dagon (Judges 16:29–30).
7 bubbles

8 The amaranth was a legendary immortal, ever-blooming flower.
9 sketch
10 noise   11 fragment of pottery

"And human love needs human meriting:
How hast thou merited—
Of all man's clotted clay, the dingiest clot?
Alack, thou knowest not
How little worthy of any love thou art!
Whom wilt thou find to love ignoble thee,
Save Me, save only Me?                                    170
All which I took from thee I did but take,
Not for thy harms,
But just that thou might'st seek it in My arms.
All which thy child's mistake
Fancies as lost, I have stored for thee at home:
Rise, clasp My hand, and come."

Halts by me that footfall:
Is my gloom, after all,
Shade of His hand, outstretched caressingly?
"Ah, fondest,[12] blindest, weakest!                      180
I am He Whom thou seekest!
Thou dravest love from thee, who dravest Me."   (*1893*)

## The Kingdom of God

*"IN NO STRANGE LAND"*

O world invisible, we view thee,
O world intangible, we touch thee,
O world unknowable, we know thee,
Inapprehensible, we clutch thee!

Does the fish soar to find the ocean,
The eagle plunge to find the air—
That we ask of the stars in motion
If they have rumour of thee there?

Not where the wheeling systems darken,
And our benumbed conceiving soars!—   10
The drifts of pinions, would we
    hearken,
Beats at our own clay-shuttered doors.

The angels keep their ancient places;—
Turn but a stone, and start a wing!
'Tis ye, 'tis your estrangéd faces,
That miss the many-splendoured thing.

But (when so sad thou canst not sadder)
Cry;—and upon thy so sore loss
Shall shine the traffic of Jacob's ladder
Pitched betwixt Heaven and Charing
    Cross.                                              20

Yea, in the night, my Soul, my daughter,
Cry,—clinging Heaven by the hems;
And lo, Christ walking on the water
Not of Gennesareth,[1] but Thames!
                                            (*1913*)

---

12 most foolish                          1 the Sea of Galilee

# The Modern Period

## THOMAS HARDY / 1840–1928

### Neutral Tones

We stood by a pond that winter day,
And the sun was white, as though
    chidden of God,
And a few leaves lay on the starving sod;
    —They had fallen from an ash, and
    were gray.

Your eyes on me were as eyes that rove
Over tedious riddles of years ago;
And some words played between us to
    and fro
    On which lost the more by our love.

The smile on your mouth was the deadest
    thing
Alive enough to have strength to die;    *10*
And a grin of bitterness swept thereby
Like an ominous bird a-wing. . . .

Since then, keen lessons that love deceives,
And wrings with wrong, have shaped to
    me
Your face, and the God-curst sun, and a
    tree,
    And a pond edge with grayish leaves.
                    (*1867*)

### Drummer Hodge

They throw in Drummer Hodge, to rest
    Uncoffined—just as found:
His landmark is a kopje-crest[1]
    That breaks the veldt around:
And foreign constellations west
    Each night above his mound.

Young Hodge the Drummer never
    knew—
    Fresh from his Wessex home—
The meaning of the broad Karoo,[2]
    The Bush, the dusty loam,    *10*
And why uprose to nightly view
    Strange stars amid the gloam.

Yet portion of that unknown plain
    Will Hodge forever be;
His homely Northern breast and brain
    Grow to some Southern tree,
And strange-eyed constellations reign
    His stars eternally.   (*1902*)

### The Darkling Thrush

*DECEMBER 31, 1900*

I leant upon a coppice[1] gate
    When Frost was spectre-gray,
And Winter's dregs made desolate
    The weakening eye of day.
The tangled bine-stems[2] scored the sky
    Like strings of broken lyres,
And all mankind that haunted nigh
    Had sought their household fires.

The land's sharp features seemed to be
    The Century's corpse outleant,   *10*
His crypt the cloudy canopy,
    The wind his death-lament.
The ancient pulse of germ and birth
    Was shrunken hard and dry,
And every spirit upon earth
    Seemed fervorless as I.

---

[1] hillock (pron. kôp′ĭ)
[2] a dry plateau in South Africa

[1] a small thicket
[2] the wirelike shoots of a climbing plant

At once a voice arose among
    The bleak twigs overhead
In a full-hearted evensong
    Of joy illimited;      20
An agéd thrush, frail, gaunt, and small,
    In blast-beruffled plume,
Had chosen thus to fling his soul
    Upon the growing gloom.

So little cause for carolings
    Of such ecstatic sound
Was written on terrestrial things
    Afar or nigh around,
That I could think there trembled through
    His happy good-night air      30
Some blessed Hope, whereof he knew
    And I was unaware.    *(1902)*

## The Man He Killed

    "Had he and I but met
      By some old ancient inn,
We should have sat us down to wet
      Right many a nipperkin![1]

    "But ranged as infantry,
      And staring face to face,
I shot at him as he at me,
      And killed him in his place.

    "I shot him dead because—
      Because he was my foe,      10
Just so: my foe of course he was;
      That's clear enough; although

    "He thought he'd 'list, perhaps,
      Offhand like—just as I—
Was out of work—had sold his traps—
      No other reason why.

    "Yes; quaint and curious war is!
      You shoot a fellow down
You'd treat if met where any bar is,
      Or help to half-a-
        crown."    *(1902)*      20

## The Woman in the Rye

"Why do you stand in the dripping rye,
Cold-lipped, unconscious, wet to the
    knee,

---

[1] a half-pint glass for beer or ale

When there are firesides near?" said I.
"I told him I wished him dead," said
    she.

"Yea, cried it in my haste to one
Whom I had loved, whom I well loved
    still;
And die he did. And I hate the sun,
And stand here lonely, aching, chill;

"Stand waiting, waiting under skies
That blow reproach, the while I see      10
The rooks sheer off to where he lies
Wrapt in a peace withheld from me!"

## Shut Out That Moon

Close up the casement, draw the blind,
    Shut out that stealing moon,
She wears too much the guise she wore
    Before our lutes were strewn
With years-deep dust, and names we
      read
    On a white stone were hewn.

Step not out on the dew-dashed lawn
    To view the Lady's Chair,
Immense Orion's glittering form,
    The Less and Greater Bear:      10
Stay in; to such sights we were drawn
    When faded ones were fair.

Brush not the bough for midnight scents
    That come forth lingeringly,
And wake the same sweet sentiments
    They breathed to you and me
When living seemed a laugh, and love
    All it was said to be.

Within the common lamp-lit room
    Prison my eyes and thought;      20
Let dingy details crudely loom,
    Mechanic speech be wrought:
Too fragrant was Life's early bloom,
    Too tart the fruit it brought!    *(1904)*

## The Year's Awakening

How do you know that the pilgrim track
Along the belting zodiac
Swept by the sun in his seeming rounds
Is traced by now to the Fishes' bounds

And into the Ram, when weeks of cloud
Have wrapt the sky in a clammy shroud,
And never as yet a tinct of spring
Has shown in the Earth's apparelling;
    O vespering bird, how do you know,
        How do you know?     10

How do you know, deep underground,
Hid in your bed from sight and sound,

Without a turn in temperature,
With weather life can scarce endure,
That light has won a fraction's strength,
And day put on some moments' length,
Whereof in merest rote will come,
Weeks hence, mild airs that do not numb,
    O crocus root, how do you know,
        How do you know?   *(1910)*  *20*

## The Convergence of the Twain

### (*LINES ON THE LOSS OF THE* TITANIC)[1]

    In a solitude of the sea
    Deep from human vanity,
And the Pride of Life that planned her, stilly couches she.

    Steel chambers, late the pyres
    Of her salamandrine fires,[2]
Cold currents thrid,[3] and turn to rhythmic tidal lyres.

    Over the mirrors meant
    To glass the opulent
The sea-worm crawls—grotesque, slimed, dumb, indifferent.

    Jewels in joy designed          *10*
    To ravish the sensuous mind
Lie lightless, all their sparkles bleared and black and blind.

    Dim moon-eyed fishes near
    Gaze at the gilded gear
And query: "What does this vaingloriousness down here?" . . .

    Well: while was fashioning
    This creature of cleaving wing,
The Immanent Will that stirs and urges everything

    Prepared a sinister mate
    For her—so gaily great—         *20*
A Shape of Ice, for the time far and dissociate.

    And as the smart ship grew
    In stature, grace, and hue,
In shadowy silent distance grew the Iceberg too.

    Alien they seemed to be:
    No mortal eye could see
The intimate welding of their later history,

---

[1] the "unsinkable" luxury liner that collided with an iceberg on her maiden voyage and sank, taking with her many leaders of high society

[2] such a fire as the legendary salamander might live in

[3] thread

Or sign that they were bent
By paths coincident
On being anon twin halves of one august event,    *30*

Till the Spinner of the Years
Said "Now!" And each one hears,
And consummation comes, and jars two hemispheres.    *(1912)*

## "I Found Her Out There"

I found her out there
On a slope few see,
That falls westwardly
To the salt-edged air,
Where the ocean breaks
On the purple strand,
And the hurricane shakes
The solid land.

I brought her here,
And have laid her to rest    *10*
In a noiseless nest
No sea beats near.
She will never be stirred
In her loamy cell
By the waves long heard
And loved so well.

So she does not sleep
By those haunted heights
The Atlantic smites
And the blind gales sweep,    *20*
Whence she often would gaze
At Dundagel's famed head,
While the dipping blaze
Dyed her face fire-red;

And would sigh at the tale
Of sunk Lyonnesse,
As a wind-tugged tress
Flapped her cheek like a flail;
Or listen at whiles
With a thought-bound brow    *30*
To the murmuring miles
She is far from now.

Yet her shade, maybe,
Will creep underground
Till it catch the sound
Of that western sea

As it swells and sobs
Where she once domiciled,
And joy in its throbs
With the heart of a child.    *(1914)*    *40*

## Ah, Are You Digging on My Grave?

"Ah, are you digging on my grave
   My loved one?—planting rue?"
      —"No: yesterday he went to wed
      One of the brightest wealth has bred.
      'It cannot hurt her now,' he said,
         'That I should not be true.'"

"Then who is digging on my grave?
   My nearest, dearest kin?"
      —"Ah, no: they sit and think, 'What
         use!
      What good will planting flowers
         produce?    *10*
      No tendance of her mound can loose
      Her spirit from Death's gin.'"

"But someone digs upon my grave?
   My enemy?—prodding sly?"
      —"Nay: when she heard you had
         passed the Gate
      That shuts on all flesh soon or late,
      She thought you no more worth her
         hate,
      She cares not where you lie."

"Then, who is digging on my grave?
   Say—since I have not guessed!"    *20*
      —"O it is I, my mistress dear,
      Your little dog, who still lives near,
      And much I hope my movements here
         Have not disturbed your rest?"

"Ah, yes! *You* dig upon my grave. . . .
  Why flashed it not on me
That one true heart was left behind!
What feeling do we ever find
To equal among human kind
  A dog's fidelity!"                                    30

  "*Mistress, I dug upon your grave*
    *To bury a bone, in case*
  *I should be hungry near this spot*
  *When passing on my daily trot.*
  *I am sorry, but I quite forgot*
    *It was your resting-place.*"  (*1914*)

## Channel Firing

That night your great guns, unawares,
Shook all our coffins as we lay,
And broke the chancel window squares,
We thought it was the Judgment-day

And sat upright. While drearisome
Arose the howl of wakened hounds:
The mouse let fall the altar-crumb,
The worms drew back into the mounds,

The glebe cow drooled. Till God called,
  "No;
It's gunnery practice out at sea            10
Just as before you went below;
The world is as it used to be:

"All nations striving strong to make
Red war yet redder. Mad as hatters
They do no more for Christés sake
Than you who are helpless in such
  matters.

"That this is not the judgment-hour
For some of them's a blesséd thing,
For if it were they'd have to scour
Hell's floor for so much
  threatening . . .                          20

"Ha, ha. It will be warmer when
I blow the trumpet (if indeed
I ever do; for you are men,
And rest eternal sorely need)."

So down we lay again. "I wonder,
Will the world ever saner be,"
Said one, "than when He sent us under
In our indifferent century!"

And many a skeleton shook his head.
"Instead of preaching forty years,"       30
My neighbor Parson Thirdly said,
"I wish I had stuck to pipes and beer."

Again the guns disturbed the hour,
Roaring their readiness to avenge,
As far inland as Stourton Tower,[1]
And Camelot,[2] and starlit Stonehenge.[3]
                                           (*1914*)

## In Time of "The Breaking of Nations"

(*JEREMIAH 51:02*)

Only a man harrowing clods
  In a slow silent walk
With an old horse that stumbles and
    nods
  Half asleep as they stalk.

Only thin smoke without flame
  From the heaps of couch-grass;
Yet this will go onward the same
  Though Dynasties pass.

Yonder a maid and her wight
  Come whispering by:                       10
War's annals will fade into night
  Ere their story die.  (*1915*)

## Near Lanivet, 1872

There was a stunted handpost just on the crest,
  Only a few feet high:
She was tired, and we stopped in the twilight-time for her rest,
  At the crossways close thereby.

---

[1] memorial to King Alfred
[2] legendary capital of King Arthur
[3] ancient temple of massive upright stones on Salisbury Plain

She leant back, being so weary, against its stem,
　　And laid her arms on its own,
Each open palm stretched out to each end of them,
　　Her sad face sideways thrown.

Her white-clothed form at this dim-lit cease of day
　　Made her look as one crucified                                                    10
In my gaze at her from the midst of the dusty way,
　　And hurriedly "Don't," I cried.

I do not think she heard. Loosing thence she said,
　　As she stepped forth ready to go,
"I am rested now.—Something strange came into my head;
　　I wish I had not leant so!"

And wordless we moved onward down from the hill
　　In the west cloud's murked obscure,
And looking back we could see the handpost still
　　In the solitude of the moor.                                                    20

"It struck her too," I thought, for as if afraid
　　She heavily breathed as we trailed;
Till she said, "I did not think how 'twould look in the shade,
　　When I leant there like one nailed."

I, lightly: "There's nothing in it. For *you*, anyhow!"
　　—"O I know there is not," said she . . .
"Yet I wonder . . . If no one is bodily crucified now,
　　In spirit one may be!"

And we dragged on and on, while we seemed to see
　　In the running of Time's far glass                                            30
Her crucified, as she had wondered if she might be
　　Some day.—Alas, alas!  (*1917*)

## During Wind and Rain

They sing their dearest songs—
He, she, all of them—yea,
Treble and tenor and bass,
　　And one to play;
With the candles mooning each
　　face. . . .
　　Ah, no; the years O!
How the sick leaves reel down in throngs!

They clear the creeping moss—
Elders and juniors—aye,
Making the pathways neat          10
　　And the garden gay;
And they build a shady seat. . . .
　　Ah, no; the years, the years;
See, the white storm-birds wing across!

They are blithely breakfasting all—
Men and maidens—yea,
Under the summer tree,
　　With a glimpse of the bay,
While pet fowl come to the knee. . . .
　　Ah, no; the years O!                          20
And the rotten rose is ript from the wall.

They change to a high new house,
He, she, all of them—aye,
Clocks and carpets and chairs
　　On the lawn all day,
And brightest things that are
　　theirs. . . .
　　Ah, no; the years, the years;
Down their carved names the rain-drop
　　ploughs.  (*1917*)

## Snow in the Suburbs

Every branch big with it,
Bent every twig with it;
Every fork like a white web-foot;
Every street and pavement mute:
Some flakes have lost their way, and grope back upward, when
Meeting those meandering down they turn and descend again.
The palings are glued together like a wall,
And there is no waft of wind with the fleecy fall.

A sparrow enters the tree,
Whereon immediately                                          10
A snow-lump thrice his own slight size
Descends on him and showers his head and eyes,
And overturns him,
And near inurns him,
And lights on a nether twig, when its brush
Starts off a volley of other lodging lumps with a rush.

The steps are a blanched slope,
Up which, with feeble hope,
A black cat comes, wide-eyed and thin;
And we take him in.  (*1925*)                                 20

## ROBERT BRIDGES / 1844–1930

## Elegy

The wood is bare: a river-mist is steeping
The trees that winter's chill of life bereaves:
Only their stiffened boughs break silence, weeping
Over their fallen leaves;

That lie upon the dank earth brown and rotten,
Miry and matted in the soaking wet:
Forgotten with the spring, that is forgotten
By them that can forget.

Yet it was here we walked when ferns were springing,
And through the mossy bank shot bud and blade:—             10
Here found in summer, when the birds were singing,
A green and pleasant shade.

'Twas here we loved in sunnier days and greener;
And now, in this disconsolate decay,
I come to see her where I most have seen her,
And touch the happier day.

For on this path, at every turn and corner,
   The fancy of her figure on me falls:
Yet walks she with the slow step of a mourner,
     Nor hears my voice that calls.       20

So through my heart there winds a track of feeling,
   A path of memory, that is all her own:
Whereto her phantom beauty ever stealing
     Haunts the sad spot alone.

About her steps the trunks are bare, the branches
   Drip heavy tears upon her downcast head;
And bleed from unseen wounds that no sun stanches,
     For the year's sun is dead.

And dead leaves wrap the fruits that summer planted:
   And birds that love the South have taken wing.       30
The wanderer, loitering o'er the scene enchanted,
     Weeps, and despairs of spring.    (*1873*)

## London Snow

When men were all asleep the snow came flying,
In large white flakes falling on the city brown,
Stealthily and perpetually settling and loosely lying,
   Hushing the latest traffic of the drowsy town;
Deadening, muffling, stifling its murmurs failing;
Lazily and incessantly floating down and down:
   Silently sifting and veiling road, roof and railing;
Hiding difference, making unevenness even,
Into angles and crevices softly drifting and sailing.
   All night it fell, and when full inches seven       10
It lay in the depth of its uncompacted lightness,
The clouds blew off from a high and frosty heaven;
   And all woke earlier for the unaccustomed brightness
Of the winter dawning, the strange unheavenly glare:
The eye marvelled—marvelled at the dazzling whiteness;
   The ear hearkened to the stillness of the solemn air;
No sound of wheel rumbling nor of foot falling,
And the busy morning cries came thin and spare.
   Then boys I heard, as they went to school, calling,
They gathered up the crystal manna to freeze       20
Their tongues with tasting, their hands with snowballing;
   Or rioted in a drift, plunging up to the knees;
Or peering up from under the white-mossed wonder,
"O look at the trees!" they cried, "O look at the trees!"
   With lessened load a few carts creak and blunder,
Following along the white deserted way,
A country company long dispersed asunder:

When now already the sun, in pale display
Standing by Paul's high dome, spread forth below
His sparkling beams, and awoke the stir of the day.                    *30*
For now doors open, and war is waged with the snow;
And trains of somber men, past tale of number,
Tread long brown paths, as toward their toil they go:
But even for them awhile no cares encumber
Their minds diverted; the daily word is unspoken,
The daily thoughts of labour and sorrow slumber
At the sight of the beauty that greets them, for the charm they have broken.

(*1880*)

## Awake, My Heart

Awake, my heart, to be loved, awake,
    awake!
The darkness silvers away, the morn
    doth break,
It leaps in the sky: unrisen lustres slake
The o'ertaken moon. Awake, O heart,
    awake!

She too that loveth awaketh and hopes
    for thee;
Her eyes already have sped the shades
    that flee,
Already they watch the path thy feet
    shall take:
Awake, O heart, to be loved, awake,
    awake!

And if thou tarry from her,—if this
    could be,—
She cometh herself, O heart, to be loved,
    to thee;                                                          *10*
For thee would unashamed herself
    forsake:
Awake to be loved, my heart, awake,
    awake!

Awake, the land is scattered with light,
    and see,
Uncanopied sleep is flying from field
    and tree:
And blossoming boughs of April in
    laughter shake;
Awake, O heart, to be loved, awake,
    awake!

Lo all things wake and tarry and look
    for thee:
She looketh and saith, "O sun, now
    bring him to me.
Come more adored, O adored, for his
    coming's sake,
And awake my heart to be loved:
    awake, awake!" (*1890*)            *20*

## So Sweet Love Seemed
## That April Morn

So sweet love seemed that April morn,
When first we kissed beside the thorn,
So strangely sweet, it was not strange
We thought that love could never change.

But I can tell—let truth be told—
That love will change in growing old;
Though day by day is nought to see,
So delicate his motions be.

And in the end 'twill come to pass
Quite to forget what once he was,            *10*
Nor even in fancy to recall
The pleasure that was all in all.

His little spring, that sweet we found,
So deep in summer floods is drowned,
I wonder, bathed in joy complete,
How love so young could be so sweet.

(*1893*)

## Nightingales

Beautiful must be the mountains whence ye come,
And bright in the fruitful valleys the streams, wherefrom
   Ye learn your song:
Where are those starry woods? O might I wander there,
Among the flowers, which in that heavenly air
   Bloom the year long!

Nay, barren are those mountains and spent the streams:
Our song is the voice of desire, that haunts our dreams,
   A throe of the heart,
Whose pining visions dim, forbidden hopes profound,          10
No dying cadence nor long sigh can sound,
   For all our art.

Alone, aloud in the raptured ear of men
We pour our dark nocturnal secret; and then,
   As night is withdrawn
From these sweet-springing meads and bursting boughs of May,
Dream, while the innumerable choir of day
   Welcome the dawn.   (*1893*)

## Eros

Why hast thou nothing in thy face?
Thou idol of the human race,
Thou tyrant of the human heart,
The flower of lovely youth that art;
Yea, and that standest in thy youth
An image of eternal Truth,
With thy exuberant flesh so fair,
That only Pheidias[1] might compare,
Ere from his chaste marmoreal form
Time had decayed the colours warm;          10
Like to his gods in thy proud dress,
Thy starry sheen of nakedness.

Surely thy body is thy mind,
For in thy face is nought to find,
Only thy soft unchristened smile,
That shadows neither love nor guile,
But shameless will and power immense,
In secret sensuous innocence.

O king of joy, what is thy thought?
I dream thou knowest it is nought,          20
And wouldst in darkness come, but thou
Makest the light where'er thou go.
Ah yet no victim of thy grace,
None who e'er longed for thy embrace,
Hath cared to look upon thy face.

                (*1899*)

[1] Phidias, the greatest of the ancient Greek sculptors

# A. E. HOUSMAN / 1859–1936

## Loveliest of Trees

Loveliest of trees, the cherry now
Is hung with bloom along the bough,
And stands about the woodland ride,
Wearing white for Eastertide.

Now, of my threescore years and ten,
Twenty will not come again,
And take from seventy springs a score,
It only leaves me fifty more.

And since to look at things in bloom
Fifty springs are little room,                    10
About the woodlands I will go
To see the cherry hung with snow.    (*1896*)

## When I Was
## One-and-Twenty

When I was one-and-twenty
  I heard a wise man say,
"Give crowns and pounds and guineas
  But not your heart away;
Give pearls away and rubies
  But keep your fancy free."
But I was one-and-twenty,
  No use to talk to me.

When I was one-and-twenty
  I heard him say again,                    10
"The heart out of the bosom
  Was never given in vain;
'Tis paid with sighs a plenty
  And sold for endless rue."
And I am two-and-twenty,
  And oh, 'tis true, 'tis true.    (*1896*)

## On the Idle Hill of Summer

On the idle hill of summer,
  Sleepy with the flow of streams,
Far I hear the steady drummer
  Drumming like a noise in dreams.

Far and near and low and louder
  On the roads of earth go by,
Dear to friends and food for powder,
  Soldiers marching, all to die.

East and west on fields forgotten
  Bleach the bones of comrades slain,    10
Lovely lads and dead and rotten;
  None that go return again.

Far the calling bugles hollo,
  High the screaming fife replies,
Gay the files of scarlet follow:
  Woman bore me, I will rise.    (*1896*)

## On Wenlock Edge

On Wenlock Edge[1] the wood's in
    trouble;
His forest fleece the Wrekin[2] heaves;
The gale, it plies the saplings double,
And thick on Severn[3] snow the leaves.

'Twould blow like this through holt[4]
    and hangar[5]
When Uricon[6] the city stood:
'Tis the old wind in the old anger,
But then it threshed another wood.

Then, 'twas before my time, the Roman
At yonder heaving hill would stare:    10
The blood that warms an English yeoman,
The thoughts that hurt him, they were
    there.

There, like the wind through woods in
    riot,
Through him the gale of life blew high;
The tree of man was never quiet:
Then 'twas the Roman, now 'tis I.

The gale, it plies the saplings double,
It blows so hard, 'twill soon be gone:
Today the Roman and his trouble
Are ashes under Uricon.    (*1896*)    20

---

[1] a long ridge in Shropshire    [2] a hill
[3] river flowing through Shropshire for a part of
its course

[4] woods    [5] shelter, such as a shed
[6] Roman fortress town

## To an Athlete Dying Young

The time you won your town the race
We chaired you through the market-
   place;
Man and boy stood cheering by,
And home we brought you shoulder-high.

To-day, the road all runners come,
Shoulder-high we bring you home,
And set you at your threshold down,
Townsman of a stiller town.

Smart lad, to slip betimes away
From fields where glory does not stay,    *10*
And early though the laurel grows
It withers quicker than the rose.

Eyes the shady night has shut
Cannot see the record cut,
And silence sounds no worse than cheers
After earth has stopped the ears.

Now you will not swell the rout
Of lads that wore their honors out,
Runners whom renown outran
And the name died before the man.    *20*

So set, before its echoes fade,
The fleet foot on the sill of shade,
And hold to the low lintel up
The still-defended challenge-cup.

And round that early-laurelled head
Will flock to gaze the strengthless dead,
And find unwithered on its curls
The garland briefer than a girl's.    *(1896)*

## Is My Team Ploughing. . .?''

"Is my team ploughing,
   That I was used to drive
And hear the harness jingle
   When I was man alive?"

Ay, the horses trample,
   The harness jingles now;
No change though you lie under
   The land you used to plough.

"Is football playing
   Along the river shore,    *10*

With lads to chase the leather,
   Now I stand up no more?"

Ay, the ball is flying,
   The lads play heart and soul;
The goal stands up, the keeper
   Stands up to keep the goal.

"Is my girl happy,
   That I thought hard to leave,
And has she tired of weeping
   As she lies down at eve?"    *20*

Ay, she lies down lightly,
   She lies not down to weep:
Your girls is well contented.
   Be still, my lad, and sleep.

"Is my friend hearty,
   Now I am thin and pine,
And has he found to sleep in
   A better bed than mine?"

Yes, lad, I lie easy,
   I lie as lads would choose;    *30*
I cheer a dead man's sweetheart—
   Never ask me whose.    *(1896)*

## ''Terence, This is Stupid Stuff''

"Terence, this is stupid stuff:
You eat your victuals fast enough;
There can't be much amiss, 'tis clear,
To see the rate you drink your beer.
But oh, good Lord, the verse you make,
It gives a chap the belly-ache.
The cow, the old cow, she is dead;
It sleeps well, the hornéd head:
We poor lads, 'tis our turn now
To hear such tunes as killed the cow.    *10*
Pretty friendship 'tis to rhyme
Your friends to death before their time
Moping melancholy mad:
Come, pipe a tune to dance to, lad."

Why, if 'tis dancing you would be,
There's brisker pipes than poetry.
Say, for what were hop-yards meant,
Or why was Burton built on Trent?[1]

---

[1] city in Staffordshire noted for breweries

Oh, many a peer of England brews
Livelier liquor than the Muse,     20
And malt does more than Milton can
To justify God's ways to man.[2]
Ale, man, ale's the stuff to drink
For fellows whom it hurts to think:
Look into the pewter pot
To see the world as the world's not.
And faith, 'tis pleasant till 'tis past:
The mischief is that 'twill not last.
Oh, I have been to Ludlow[3] fair
And left my necktie God knows
     where,     30
And carried half-way home, or near,
Pints and quarts of Ludlow beer:
Then the world seemed none so bad,
And I myself a sterling lad;
And down in movely muck I've lain,
Happy till I woke again.
Then I saw the morning sky:
Heigho, the tale was all a lie;
The world, it was the old world yet,
I was I, my things were wet,     40
And nothing now remained to do
But begin the game anew.

    Therefore, since the world has still
Much good, but much less good than ill,
And while the sun and moon endure
Luck's a chance, but trouble's sure,
I'd face it as a wise man would,

And train for ill and not for good.
'Tis true, the stuff I bring for sale
Is not so brisk a brew as ale:     50
Out of a stem that scored the hand
I wrung it in a weary land.
But take it: if the smack is sour,
The better for the embittered hour;
It should do good to heart and head
When your soul is in my soul's stead;
And I will friend you, if I may,
In the dark and cloudy day.

    There was a king[4] reigned in the East:
There, when kings will sit to feast,     60
They get their fill before they think
With poisoned meat and poisoned drink.
He gathered all that springs to birth
From the many-venomed earth;
First a little, thence to more,
He sampled all her killing store;
And easy, smiling, seasoned sound,
Sate the king when healths went round.
They put arsenic in his meat
And stared aghast to watch him eat;     70
They poured strychnine in his cup
And shook to see him drink it up:
They shook, they stared as white's their
     shirt:
Them it was their poison hurt.
—I tell the tale that I heard told.
Mithridates, he died old.    (*1896*)

## Eight O'Clock

     He stood, and heard the steeple
       Sprinkle the quarters on the morning town.
    One, two, three, four, to market-place and people
       It tossed them down.

     Strapped, noosed, nighing his hour,
       He stood and counted them and cursed his luck;
    And then the clock collected in the tower
       Its strength, and struck.    (*1922*)

---

[2] Milton's avowed purpose in *Paradise Lost*
[3] town in the south of Shropshire
[4] Mithridates VI, King of Pontus (*c.* 133 B.C.–63

B.C.), was the subject of the legend Housman summarizes here.

## Revolution

West and away the wheels of darkness roll,
    Day's beamy banner up the east is borne,
Specters and fears, the nightmare and her foal,
    Drown in the golden deluge of the morn.

But over sea and continent from sight
    Safe to the Indies has the earth conveyed
The vast and moon-eclipsing cone of night,
    Her towering foolscap of eternal shade.

See, in mid heaven the sun is mounted; hark,
    The belfries tingle to the noonday chime.                            10
'Tis silent, and the subterranean dark
    Has crossed the nadir, and begins to climb.   (*1922*)

## The Chestnut Casts His Flambeaux

The chestnut casts his flambeaux, and the flowers
    Stream from the hawthorn on the wind away,
The doors clap to, the pane is blind with showers.
    Pass me the can, lad; there's an end of May.

There's one spoilt spring to scant our mortal lot,
    One season ruined of our little store.
May will be fine next year as like as not:
    Oh ay, but then we shall be twenty-four.

We for a certainty are not the first
    Have sat in taverns while the tempest hurled                         10
Their hopeful plans to emptiness, and cursed
    Whatever brute and blackguard made the world.

It is in truth iniquity on high
    To cheat our sentenced souls of aught they crave,
And mar the merriment as you and I
    Fare on our long fool's-errand to the grave.

Iniquity it is; but pass the can.
    My lad, no pair of kings our mothers bore;
Our only portion is the estate of man:
    We want the moon, but we shall get no more.                          20

If here to-day the cloud of thunder lours
    To-morrow it will hie on far behests;
The flesh will grieve on other bones than ours
    Soon, and the soul will mourn in other breasts.

The troubles of our proud and angry dust
    Are from eternity, and shall not fail.
Bear them we can, and if we can we must.
    Shoulder the sky, my lad, and drink your ale.   (*1922*)

## The Laws of God, The Laws of Man

The laws of God, the laws of man,
He may keep that will and can;
Not I: let God and man decree
Laws for themselves and not for me;
And if my ways are not as theirs
Let them mind their own affairs.
Their deed I judge and much condemn,
Yet when did I make laws for them?
Please yourselves, say I, and they
Need only look the other way.          10
But no, they will not; they must still
Wrest their neighbour to their will,
And make me dance as they desire
With jail and gallows and hell-fire.
And how am I to face the odds
Of man's bedevilment and God's?
I, a stranger and afraid
In a world I never made.
They will be master, right or wrong;
Though both are foolish, both are
   strong          20
And since, my soul, we cannot fly
To Saturn nor to Mercury,
Keep we must, if keep we can,
These foreign laws of God and man.
                              (*1922*)

## Easter Hymn

If in that Syrian garden, ages slain,
You sleep, and know not you are dead in vain,
Nor even in dreams behold how dark and bright
Ascends in smoke and fire by day and night
The hate you died to quench and could but fan,
Sleep well and see no morning, son of man.

But if, the grave rent and the stone rolled by,
At the right hand of majesty on high
You sit, and sitting so remember yet
Your tears, your agony and bloody sweat,          10
Your cross and passion and the life you gave,
Bow hither out of heaven and see and save.   (*1936*)

# RUDYARD KIPLING / 1865–1936

## Danny Deever

"What are the bugles blowin' for?" said Files-on-Parade.
"To turn you out, to turn you out," the Color-Sergeant said.
"What makes you look so white, so white?" said Files-on-Parade.
"I'm dreadin' what I've got to watch," the Color-Sergeant said.
   For they're hanging' Danny Deever, you can 'ear the Dead March play,
   The regiment's in 'ollow square—they're hangin' him today;
   They've taken of his buttons off an' cut his stripes away,
   An' they're hangin' Danny Deever in the mornin'.

"What makes the rear-rank breathe so 'ard?" said Files-on-Parade.
"It's bitter cold, it's bitter cold," the Color-Sergeant said.      *10*
"What makes that front-rank man fall down?" says Files-on-Parade.
"A touch of sun, a touch of sun," the Color-Sergeant said.
> They are hangin' Danny Deever, they are marchin' of 'im round.
> They 'ave 'alted Danny Deever by 'is coffin on the ground;
> An 'e'll swing in 'arf a minute for a sneakin', shootin' hound—
> O they're hanging' Danny Deever in the mornin'!

"'Is cot was right-'and cot to mine," said Files-on-Parade.
"'E's sleepin' out an' far tonight," the Color-Sergeant said.
"I've drunk 'is beer a score o' times," said Files-on-Parade.
"'E's drinkin' bitter beer alone," the Color-Sergeant said.      *20*
> They are hangin' Danny Deever, you must mark 'im to 'is place,
> For 'e shot a comrade sleepin'—you must look 'im in the face;
> Nine 'undred of 'is county an' the regiment's disgrace,
> While they're hangin' Danny Deever in the mornin.'

"What's that so black agin the sun?" said Files-on-Parade.
"It's Danny fightin' 'ard for life," the Color-Sergeant said.
"What's that that whimpers over'ead?" said Files-on-Parade.
"It's Danny's soul that's passin' now," the Color-Sergeant said.
> For they're done with Danny Deever, you can 'ear the quickstep play,
> The regiment's in column, an' they're marchin' us away;      *30*
> Ho! the young recruits are shakin', an' they'll want their beer today,
> After hangin' Danny Deever in the mornin'.    (*1890*)

## L'Envoi

> When Earth's last picture is painted, and the tubes are twisted and dried,
> When the oldest colours have faded, and the youngest critic has died,
> We shall rest, and, faith, we shall need it—lie down for an æon or two,
> Till the Master of All Good Workmen shall set us to work anew!
>
> And those that were good shall be happy: they shall sit in a golden chair;
> They shall splash at a ten-league canvas with brushes of comet's hair;
> They shall find real saints to draw from—Magdalene, Peter, and Paul;
> They shall work for an age at a sitting and never be tired at all!
>
> And only the Master shall praise us, and only the Master shall blame;
> And no one shall work for money, and no one shall work for fame;      *10*
> But each for the joy of the working, and each, in his separate star,
> Shall draw the Thing as he sees It for the God of Things as They are!    (*1892*)

## Recessional

> God of our fathers, known of old,      The tumult and the shouting dies;
>    Lord of our far-flung battle-line,      The captains and the kings depart:
> Beneath whose awful Hand we hold      Still stands Thine ancient sacrifice,
>    Dominion over palm and pine—      An humble and a contrite heart.      *10*
> Lord God of Hosts, be with us yet,      Lord God of Hosts, be with us yet,
> Lest we forget—lest we forget!      Lest we forget—lest we forget!

Far-called, our navies melt away;
  On dune and headland sinks the fire:
Lo, all our pomp of yesterday
  Is one with Nineveh and Tyre!
Judge of the Nations, spare us yet,
Lest we forget—lest we forget!

If, drunk with sight of power, we loose
  Wild tongues that have not Thee in
    awe,                  20
Such boastings as the Gentiles use,

  Or lesser breeds without the Law—
Lord God of Hosts, be with us yet,
  Lest we forget—lest we forget!

For heathen heart that puts her trust
  In reeking tube and iron shard,
All valiant dust that builds on dust,
  And guarding, calls not Thee to guard,
For frantic boast and foolish word—
  They mercy on Thy people,
    Lord!   (*1897*)         30

## Cold Iron

*"Gold is for the mistress—silver for the maid—*
*Copper for the craftsman cunning at his trade."*
"Good!" said the Baron, sitting in his hall,
"But Iron—Cold Iron—is master of them all."

So he made rebellion 'gainst the King his liege,
Camped before his citadel and summoned it to siege.
"Nay!" said the cannoneer on the castle wall,
"But Iron—Cold Iron—shall be master of you all!"

Woe for the Baron and his knights so strong,
When the cruel cannon-balls laid 'em all along;       10
He was taken prisoner, he was cast in thrall,
And Iron—Cold Iron—was master of it all!

Yet his King spake kindly (ah, how kind a Lord!)
"What if I release thee now and give thee back thy sword?"
"Nay!" said the Baron, "mock not at my fall,
For Iron—Cold Iron—is master of them all."

*"Tears are for the craven, prayers are for the clown—*
*Halters for the silly neck that cannot keep a crown."*
"As my loss is grievous, so my hope is small,
For Iron—Cold Iron—must be master of men all!"     20

Yet his King made answer (few such Kings there be!)
"Here is Bread and here is Wine—sit and sup with me.
Eat and drink in Mary's Name, the whiles I do recall
How Iron—Cold Iron—can be master of men all!"

He took the Wine and blessed it. He blessed and brake the Bread.
With His own Hands He served Them, and presently He said:
"See! These Hands they pierced with nails, outside My city wall,
Show Iron—Cold Iron—to be master of men all.

"Wounds are for the desperate, blows are for the strong.
Balm and oil for weary hearts all cut and bruised with wrong.   30
I forgive thy treason—I redeem thy fall—
For Iron—Cold Iron—must be master of men all!"

"*Crowns are for the valiant—scepters for the bold!*
*Thrones and powers for mighty men who dare to take and hold!*"
"Nay!" said the Baron, kneeling in his hall,
"But Iron—Cold Iron—is master of men all!
Iron out of Calvary is master of men all!"   (*1909*)

## Jobson's Amen

"Blesséd be the English and all their ways and works.
Curséd be the Infidels, Hereticks, and Turks!"
"Amen," quo' Jobson, "but where I used to lie
Was neither Candle, Bell nor Book to curse my brethren by.

"But a palm-tree in full bearing, bowing down, bowing down,
To a surf that drove unsparing at the brown, walled town—
Conches in a temple, oil-lamps in a dome—
And a low moon out of Africa said: 'This way home!'"

"Blesséd be the English and all that they profess.
Curséd be the Savages that prance in nakedness!"                    10
"Amen," quo' Jobson, "but where I used to lie
Was neither shirt nor pantaloons to catch my brethren by:

"But a well-wheel slowly creaking, going round, going round,
By a water-channel leaking over drowned, warm ground—
Parrots very busy in the trellised pepper-vine—
And a high sun over Asia shouting: 'Rise and shine!'"

"Blesséd be the English and everything they own.
Curséd be the Infidels that bow to wood and stone!"
"Amen," quo' Jobson, "but where I used to lie
Was neither pew nor Gospelleer to save my brethren by:              20

"But a desert stretched and stricken, left and right, left and right,
Where the piled mirages thicken under white-hot light—
A skull beneath a sand-hill and a viper coiled inside—
And a red wind out of Libya roaring: 'Run and hide!'"

"Blesséd be the English and all they make or do.
Curséd be the Hereticks who doubt that this is true!"
"Amen," quo' Jobson, "but where I mean to die
Is neither rule nor calliper to judge the matter by:

"But Himalaya heavenward-heading, sheer and vast, sheer and vast,
In a million summits bedding on the last world's past—              30
A certain sacred mountain where the scented cedars climb,
And—the feet of my Belovéd hurrying back through Time!"   (*1917*)

## The Way Through the Woods

They shut the road through the woods
Seventy years ago.
Weather and rain have undone it again,
And now you would never know

There was once a road through the woods
Before they planted the trees.
It is underneath the coppice and heath
And the thin anemones.
Only the keeper sees
That, where the ring-dove broods,                                    *10*
And the badgers roll at ease,
There was once a road through the woods.
Yet, if you enter the woods
Of a summer evening late,
When the night-air cools on the trout-ringed pools
Where the otter whistles his mate,
(They fear not men in the woods,
Because they see so few.)
You will hear the beat of a horse's feet,
And the swish of a skirt in the dew,                                 *20*
Steadily cantering through
The misty solitudes,
As though they perfectly knew
The old lost road through the woods. . . .
But there is no road through the woods.

# WILLIAM BUTLER YEATS / 1865–1939

## To the Rose Upon the Rood of Time

*Red Rose, proud Rose, sad Rose of all my days!*
*Come near me, while I sing the ancient ways:*
*Cuchulain battling with the bitter tide;*
*The Druid, grey, wood-nurtured, quiet-eyed,*
*Who cast round Fergus dreams, and ruin untold;*
*And thine own sadness, whereof stars, grown old*
*In dancing silver-sandalled on the sea,*
*Sing in their high and lonely melody.*
*Come near, that no more blinded by man's fate,*
*I find under the boughs of love and hate,*                         *10*
*In all poor foolish things that live a day,*
*Eternal beauty wandering on her way.*

*Come near, come near, come near—Ah, leave me still*
*A little space for the rose-breath to fill!*
*Lest I no more hear common things that crave;*
*The weak worm hiding down in its small cave,*
*The field-mouse running by me in the grass,*
*And heavy mortal hopes that toil and pass;*
*But seek alone to hear the strange things said*
*By God to the bright hearts of those long dead,*                    20
*And learn to chaunt a tongue men do not know.*
*Come near; I would, before my time to go,*
*Sing of old Eire and the ancient ways:*
*Red Rose, proud Rose, sad Rose of all my days*   *(1893)*


## The Lake Isle of Innisfree

I will arise and go now, and go to Innisfree,
And a small cabin build there, of clay and wattles made:
Nine bean-rows will I have there, a hive for the honey bee,
And live alone in the bee-loud glade.

And I shall have some peace there, for peace comes dropping slow,
Dropping from the veils of the morning to where the cricket sings;
There midnight's all a glimmer, and noon a purple glow,
And evening full of the linnet's wings.

I will arise and go now, for always night and day
I hear lake water lapping with low sounds by the shore;                  10
While I stand on the roadway, or on the pavements grey,
I hear it in the deep heart's core.   *(1893)*


## The Lover Tells of the Rose in His Heart

All things uncomely and broken, all things worn out and old,
The cry of a child by the roadway, the creak of a lumbering cart,
The heavy steps of the ploughman, splashing the wintry mould,
Are wronging your image that blossoms a rose in the deeps of my
    heart.

The wrong of unshapely things is a wrong too great to be told;
I hunger to build them anew and sit on a green knoll apart,
With the earth and the sky and the water, remade, like a casket of
    gold
For my dreams of your image that blossoms a rose in the deeps of
    my heart.   *(1899)*

# The Song of Wandering Aengus

I went out to the hazel wood,
Because a fire was in my head,
And cut and peeled a hazel wand,
And hooked a berry to a thread;
And when white moths were on the wing,
And moth-like stars were flickering out,
I dropped the berry in a stream
And caught a little silver trout.

When I had laid it on the floor
I went to blow the fire aflame,                    10
But something rustled on the floor,
And some one called me by my name:
It had become a glimmering girl
With apple blossom in her hair
Who called me by my name and ran
And faded through the brightening air.

Though I am old with wandering
Through hollow lands and hilly lands,
I will find out where she has gone,
And kiss her lips and take her hands;        20
And walk among long dappled grass,
And pluck till time and times are done
The silver apples of the moon,
The golden apples of the sun.   (1899)

## I

# To a Child Dancing in the Wind

Dance there upon the shore;
What need have you to care
For wind or water's roar?
And tumble out your hair
That the salt drops have wet;
Being young you have not known
The fool's triumph, nor yet
Love lost as soon as won,
Nor the best labourer dead
And all the sheaves to bind.                    10
What need have you to dread
The monstrous crying of wind?

## II

# Two Years Later

Has no one said those daring
Kind eyes should be more learned?
Or warned you how despairing
The moths are when they are burned?
I could have warned you; but you are young,
So we speak a different tongue.

O you will take whatever's offered
And dream that all the world's a friend.
Suffer as your mother suffered,
Be as broken in the end.                    10
But I am old and you are young,
And I speak a barbarous tongue.   (1914)

# The Wild Swans at Coole[1]

The trees are in their autumn beauty,
The woodland paths are dry,
Under the October twilight the water
Mirrors a still sky;
Upon the brimming water among the stones
Are nine-and-fifty swans.

The nineteenth autumn has come upon me
Since I first made my count;
I saw, before I had well finished,
All suddenly mount                    10
And scatter wheeling in great broken rings
Upon their clamorous wings.

I have looked upon those brilliant creatures,
And now my heart is sore.
All's changed since I, hearing at twilight,
The first time on this shore,
The bell-beat of their wings above my head,
Trod with a lighter tread.

---

[1] Coole Park in Galway was the estate of Lady Augusta Gregory. Yeats spent a number of summers as her guest.

Unwearied still, lover by lover,
They paddle in the cold                                    20
Companionable streams or climb the air;
Their hearts have not grown old;
Passion or conquest, wander where they
    will,
Attend upon them still.

But now they drift on the still water,
Mysterious, beautiful;
Among what rushes will they build,
By what lake's edge or pool
Delight men's eyes when I awake some
    day
To find they have flown
    away?  (*1916*)                                        30

## An Irish Airman Foresees His Death

I know that I shall meet my fate
Somewhere among the clouds above;
Those that I fight I do not hate,
Those that I guard I do not love;
My country is Kiltartan Cross,
My countrymen Kiltartan's poor,
No likely end could bring them loss
Or leave them happier than before.
Nor law, nor duty bade me fight,
Nor public men, nor cheering crowds,  10
A lonely impulse of delight
Drove to this tumult in the clouds;
I balanced all, brought all to mind,
The years to come seemed waste of
    breath,
A waste of breath the years behind
In balance with this life, this death.

                                            (*1919*)

## Easter 1916

I have met them at close of day
Coming with vivid faces
From counter or desk among grey
Eighteenth-century houses.
I have passed with a nod of the head
Or polite meaningless words,
Or have lingered awhile and said
Polite meaningless words,

And thought before I had done
Of a mocking tale or a gibe                                10
To please a companion
Around the fire at the club,
Being certain that they and I
But lived where motley is worn:
All changed, changed utterly:
A terrible beauty is born.

That woman's days were spent
In ignorant good-will,
Her nights in argument
Until her voice grew shrill.                                20
What voice more sweet than hers
When, young and beautiful,
She rode to harriers?
This man had kept a school
And rode our wingéd horse;
This other his helper and friend
Was coming into his force;
He might have won fame in the end,
So sensitive his nature seemed,
So daring and sweet his thought.                           30
This other man I had dreamed
A drunken, vainglorious lout.
He had done most bitter wrong
To some who are near my heart,
Yet I number him in the song;
He, too, has resigned his part
In the casual comedy;
He, too, has been changed in his turn,
Transformed utterly:
A terrible beauty is born.                                  40

Hearts with one purpose alone
Through summer and winter seem
Enchanted to a stone
To trouble the living stream.
The horse that comes from the road,
The rider, the birds that range
From cloud to tumbling cloud,
Minute by minute they change;
A shadow of cloud on the stream
Changes minute by minute;                                  50
A horse-hoof slides on the brim,
And a horse plashes within it;
The long-legged moor-hens dive,
And hens to moor-cocks call;
Minute by minute they live:
The stone's in the midst of all.

Too long a sacrifice
Can make a stone of the heart.
O when may it suffice?
That is Heaven's part, our part          60
To murmur name upon name,
As a mother names her child
When sleep at last has come
On limbs that had run wild.
What is it but nightfall?
No, no, not night but death;
Was it needless death after all?
For England may keep faith
For all that is done and said.
We know their dream; enough          70
To know they dreamed and are dead;
And what if excess of love
Bewildered them till they died?
I write it out in a verse—
MacDonagh and MacBride
And Connolly and Pearse
Now and in time to be,
Wherever green is worn,
Are changed, changed utterly:
A terrible beauty is born.   *(1921)*          80

## The Second Coming

Turning and turning in the widening
     gyre[1]
The falcon cannot hear the falconer;
Things fall apart; the centre cannot hold;

Mere anarchy is loosed upon the world,
The blood-dimmed tide is loosed, and
     everywhere
The ceremony of innocence is drowned;
The best lack all conviction, while the
     worst
Are full of passionate intensity.

Surely some revelation is at hand;
Surely the Second Coming is at hand.   10
The Second Coming! Hardly are those
     words out
When a vast image out of *Spiritus
     Mundi*[2]
Troubles my sight: somewhere in sands
     of the desert
A shape with lion body and the head of
     a man,
A gaze blank and pitiless as the sun,
Is moving its slow thighs, while all about
     it
Reel shadows of the indignant desert
     birds.
The darkness drops again; but now I
     know
That twenty centuries of stony sleep
Were vexed to nightmare by a rocking
     cradle,                               20
And what rough beast, its hour come
     round at last,
Slouches towards Bethlehem to be born?
                                      *(1921)*

## Sailing to Byzantium[1]

That is no country for old men. The young
In one another's arms, birds in the trees
—Those dying generations—at their song,
The salmon-falls, the mackerel-crowded seas,
Fish, flesh, or fowl, commend all summer long
Whatever is begotten, born, and dies.
Caught in that sensual music all neglect
Monuments of unageing intellect.

---

[1] a centrifugal motion which Yeats associates with the conclusion of a cycle of history
[2] the soul of the world, a reservoir of the racial memory

[1] for Yeats, a symbol of the integrity of life perfected by art, and "out of nature"—i.e., the realm of "the artifice of eternity"

An agéd man is but a paltry thing,
A tattered coat upon a stick, unless                                    10
Soul clap its hands and sing, and louder sing
For every tatter in its mortal dress,
Nor is there singing school but studying
Monuments of its own magnificence;
And therefore I have sailed the seas and come
To the holy city of Byzantium.

O sages standing in God's holy fire
As in the gold mosaic of a wall,
Come from the holy fire, perne in a gyre,[2]
And be the singing-masters of my soul.                                    20
Consume my heart away; sick with desire
And fastened to a dying animal
It knows not what it is; and gather me
Into the artifice of eternity.

Once out of nature I shall never take
My bodily form from any natural thing,
But such a form as Grecian goldsmiths make
Of hammered gold and gold enamelling
To keep a drowsy Emperor awake;
Or set upon a golden bough to sing                                    30
To lords and ladies of Byzantium
Of what is past, or passing, or to come.   (*1928*)

# Two Songs from a Play

### I

I saw a staring virgin stand
Where holy Dionysus[1] died,
And tear the heart out of his side,
And lay the heart upon her hand
And bear that beating heart away;
And then did all the Muses sing
Of Magnus Annus at the spring,[2]
As though God's death were but a play.

Another Troy must rise and set,
Another lineage feed the crow,                                    10
Another Argo's[3] painted prow
Drive to a flashier bauble yet.
The Roman Empire stood appalled:
It dropped the reigns of peace and war
When that fierce virgin and her Star
Out of the fabulous darkness called.

### II

In pity for man's darkening thought
He walked that room and issued thence
In Galilean turbulence;
The Babylonian starlight brought                                    20
A fabulous, formless darkness in;
Odor of blood when Christ was slain
Made all Platonic tolerance vain
And vain all Doric discipline.

Everything that man esteems
Endures a moment or a day.
Love's pleasure drives his love away,
The painter's brush consumes his dreams;
The herald's cry, the soldier's tread
Exhaust his glory and his might:                                    30
Whatever flames upon the night
Man's own resinous heart has fed.   (*1928*)

---

[2] turn about in a helical path—a motion identified
in Yeats's work with the whirling of fate
[1] Greek fertility god

[2] the beginning of a new cycle of history
[3] Jason's vessel in his quest of the Golden Fleece

# Fragments

### I

Locke sank into a swoon;
The Garden died;
God took the spinning-jenny
Out of his side.

### II

Where got I that truth?
Out of a medium's mouth,
Out of nothing it came,
Out of the forest loam,
Out of dark night where lay
The crowns of Nineveh.        (*1928*)        10

## Leda[1] and the Swan

A sudden blow: the great wings beating still
Above the staggering girl, her thighs caressed
By the dark web, her nape caught in his bill,
He holds her helpless breast upon his breast.

How can those terrified vague fingers push
The feathered glory from her loosening thighs?
And how can body, laid in that white rush,
But feel the strange heart beating where it lies?

A shudder in the loins engenders there
The broken wall, the burning roof and tower                     10
And Agamemnon dead.
                                    Being so caught up,
So mastered by the brute blood of the air,
Did she put on his knowledge with his power
Before the indifferent beak could let her drop?        (*1928*)

## Among School Children

I walk through the long schoolroom questioning;
A kind old nun in a white hood replies;
The children learn to cipher and to sing,
To study reading-books and history,
To cut and sew, be neat in everything
In the best modern way—the children's eyes
In momentary wonder stare upon
A sixty-year-old smiling public man.

I dream of a Ledæan[1] body, bent
Above a sinking fire, a tale that she                           10
Told of a harsh reproof, or trivial event
That changed some childish day to tragedy—
Told, and it seemed that our two natures blent
Into a sphere from youthful sympathy,
Or else, to alter Plato's parable,[2]
Into the yolk and white of the one shell.

---

[1] Ravished by Zeus in the form of a swan, she gave birth to Helen of Troy and to Clytemnestra, who murdered her husband Agamemnon, after his return from the Trojan War.

[1] pertaining to Leda, a mortal of Greek mythology, who is represented in art as gracefully beautiful

[2] Plato suggested that man and woman are the separated halves of a single spherical whole.

And thinking of that fit of grief or rage
I look upon one child or t'other there
And wonder if she stood so at that age—
For even daughters of the swan can share                    20
Something of every paddler's heritage—
And had that color upon cheek or hair,
And thereupon my heart is driven wild:
She stands before me as a living child.

Her present image floats into the mind—
Did Quattrocento[3] finger fashion it
Hollow of cheek as though it drank the wind
And took a mess of shadows for its meat?
And I though never of Ledæan kind
Had pretty plumage once—enough of that,                    30
Better to smile on all that smile, and show
There is a comfortable kind of old scarecrow.

What youthful mother, a shape upon her lap
Honey of generation had betrayed,
And that must sleep, shriek, struggle to escape
As recollection or the drug decide,
Would think her son, did she but see that shape
With sixty or more winters on its head,
A compensation for the pang of his birth,
Or the uncertainty of his setting forth?                    40

Plato thought nature but a spume that plays
Upon a ghostly paradigm of things;[4]
Solider Aristotle played the taws
Upon the bottom of a king of kings;[5]
World-famous golden-thighed Pythagoras[6]
Fingered upon a fiddle-stick or strings
What a star sang and careless Muses heard:
Old clothes upon old sticks to scare a bird.

Both nuns and mothers worship images,
But those the candles light are not as those          50
That animate a mother's reveries,
But keep a marble or a bronze repose.
And yet they too break hearts—O Presences
That passion, piety or affection knows,
And that all heavenly glory symbolize—
O self-born mockers of man's enterprise;

---

[3] of the fifteenth century, especially as applied to Italian art
[4] Plato's philosophical idealism cast doubt upon the actuality of matter.
[5] Aristotle, as tutor to Alexander the Great, had occasion to whip his pupil.

[6] Greek philosopher of the sixth century B.C., who applied arithmetic to the study of music, developed the theory of the music of the spheres, and was worshipped by his disciples as a god with a golden thigh

Labor is blossoming or dancing where
The body is not bruised to pleasure soul,
Nor beauty born out of its own despair,
Nor blear-eyed wisdom out of midnight oil.     *60*
O chestnut-tree, great-rooted blossomer,
Are you the leaf, the blossom or the bole?
O body swayed to music, O brightening glance,
How can we know the dancer from the dance?    *(1928)*

## Coole Park, 1929

I meditate upon a swallow's flight,
Upon an agéd woman and her house,
A sycamore and lime-tree lost in night
Although that western cloud is luminous,
Great works constructed there in nature's spite
For scholars and for poets after us,
Thoughts long knitted into a single thought,
A dance-like glory that those walls begot.

There Hyde before he had beaten into prose
That noble blade the Muses buckled on,     *10*
There one that ruffled in a manly pose
For all his timid heart, there that slow man,
That meditative man, John Synge, and those
Impetuous men, Shawe-Taylor and Hugh Lane,
Found pride established in humility,
A scene well set and excellent company.

They came like swallows and like swallows went,
And yet a woman's powerful character
Could keep a swallow to its first intent;
And half a dozen in formation there,     *20*
That seemed to whirl upon a compass-point,
Found certainty upon the dreaming air,
The intellectual sweetness of those lines
That cut through time or cross it withershins.

Here, traveller, scholar, poet, take your stand
When all those rooms and passages are gone,
When nettles wave upon a shapeless mound
And saplings root among the broken stone,
And dedicate—eyes bent upon the ground,
Back turned upon the brightness of the sun     *30*
And all the sensuality of the shade—
A moment's memory to that laurelled head.    *(1933)*

# Byzantium[1]

The unpurged images of day recede;
The Emperor's drunken soldiery are
    abed;
Night resonance recedes, night-walkers'
    song
After great cathedral gong;
A starlit or a moonlit dome disdains
All that man is,
All mere complexities,
The fury and the mire of human veins.

Before me floats an image, man or shade,
Shade more than man, more image than a
    shade;           10
For Hades' bobbin[2] bound in mummy-
    cloth
May unwind the winding path;
A mouth that has no moisture and no
    breath
Breathless mouths may summon;
I hail the superhuman;
I call it death-in-life and life-in-death.

Miracle, bird or golden handiwork,
More miracle than bird or handiwork,
Planted on the star-lit golden bough,
Can like the cocks of Hades crow,    20
Or, by the moon embittered, scorn aloud
In glory of changeless metal
Common bird or petal
And all complexities of mire or blood.

At midnight on the Emperor's pavement
    flit
Flames that no faggot feeds, nor steel
    has lit,
Nor storm disturbs, flames begotten of
    flame,
Where blood-begotten spirits come
And all complexities of fury leave,
Dying into a dance,    30
An agony of trance,
An agony of flame that cannot singe a
    sleeve.

Astraddle on the dolphin's[3] mire and
    blood,

Spirit after spirit! The smithies break the
    flood,
The golden smithies of the Emperor!
Marbles of the dancing floor
Break bitter furies of complexity,
Those images that yet
Fresh images beget,
That dolphin-torn, that gong-tormented
    sea.  *(1933)*        40

# Crazy Jane Talks with the Bishop

I met the Bishop on the road
And much said he and I.
"Those breasts are flat and fallen now,
Those veins must soon be dry;
Live in a heavenly mansion,
Not in some foul sty."

"Fair and foul are near of kin,
And fair needs foul," I cried.
"My friends are gone, but that's a truth
Nor grave nor bed denied,    10
Learned in bodily lowliness
And in the heart's pride.

"A woman can be proud and stiff
When on love intent;
But Love has pitched his mansion in
The place of excrement;
For nothing can be sole or whole
That has not been rent."   *(1933)*

# Lapis Lazuli

*(FOR HARRY CLIFTON)*

I have heard that hysterical women say
They are sick of the palette and fiddle-
    bow,
Of poets that are always gay,
For everybody knows or else should know
That if nothing drastic is done

---

[1] See note to "Sailing to Byzantium."
[2] the spool from which man's destiny unwinds

[3] In ancient mythology, souls were translated
from one state to another astride a dolphin.

Aeroplane and Zeppelin will come out,
Pitch like King Billy[1] bomb-balls in
Until the town lie beaten flat.

All perform their tragic play,
There struts Hamlet, there is Lear,    10
That's Ophelia, that Cordelia;
Yet they, should the last scene be there,
The great stage curtain about to drop,
If worthy their prominent part in the
    play,
Do not break up their lines to weep.
They know that Hamlet and Lear are gay;
Gaiety transfiguring all that dread.
All men have aimed at, found and lost;
Black out; Heaven blazing into the head:
Tragedy wrought to its uttermost.    20
Though Hamlet rambles and Lear rages,
And all the drop-scenes drop at once
Upon a hundred thousand stages,
It cannot grow by an inch or an ounce.

On their own feet they came, or on
    shipboard,
Camel-back, horse-back, ass-back, mule-
    back,
Old civilizations put to the sword.
Then they and their wisdom went to rack:
No handiwork of Callimachus,[2]
Who handled marble as if it were
    bronze,    30

Made draperies that seemed to rise
When sea-wind swept the corner, stands:
His long lamp-chimney shaped like the
    stem
Of a slender palm, stood but a day;
All things fall and are built again,
And those that build them again are gay.

Two Chinamen,[3] behind them a third,
Are carved in lapis lazuli,
Over them flies a long-legged bird,
A symbol of longevity;    40
The third, doubtless a serving-man,
Carries a musical instrument.

Every discoloration of the stone,
Every accidental crack or dent,
Seems a water-course or an avalanche,
Or lofty slope where it still snows
Though doubtless plum or cherry-branch
Sweetens the little half-way house
Those Chinamen climb towards, and I
Delight to imagine them seated there;    50
There, on the mountain and the sky,
On all the tragic scene they stare.
One asks for mournful melodies;
Accomplished fingers begin to play.
Their eyes mid many wrinkles, their eyes,
Their ancient, glittering eyes, are gay.

(1936)

## Why Should Not Old Men Be Mad?

Why should not old men be mad?
Some have known a likely lad
That had a sound fly-fisher's wrist
Turn to a drunken journalist;
A girl that knew all Dante once
Live to bear children to a dunce;
A Helen of social welfare dream,
Climb on a wagonette to scream.
Some think it a matter of course that chance
Should starve good men and bad advance,    10

[1] William III, then of Orange, who bombed Irish
towns in 1690 in a war against the deposed King
James II
[2] Greek sculptor of the fifth century B.C., who
reverted to a pure Ionic style
[3] Here and in the lines following, Yeats describes
a lapis lazuli carving sent him by a friend.

That if their neighbours figured plain,
As though upon a lighted screen,
No single story would they find
Of an unbroken happy mind,
A finish worthy of the start.
Young men know nothing of this sort,
Observant old men know it well;
And when they know what old books tell,
And that no better can be had,
Know why an old man should be mad.   (*1939*)                    20

## The Circus Animals' Desertion

### I

I sought a theme and sought for it in vain,
I sought it daily for six weeks or so.
Maybe at last, being but a broken man,
I must be satisfied with my heart, although
Winter and summer till old age began
My circus animals were all on show,
Those stilted boys, that burnished chariot,
Lion and woman and the Lord knows what.

### II

What can I but enumerate old themes?
First that sea-rider Oisin led by the nose                       10
Through three enchanted islands, allegorical dreams,
Vain gaiety, vain battle, vain repose,
Themes of the embittered heart, or so it seems,
That might adorn old songs or courtly shows;
But what cared I that set him on to ride,
I, starved for the bosom of his faery bride?

And then a counter-truth filled out its play,
*The Countess Cathleen* was the name I gave it;
She, pity-crazed, had given her soul away,
But masterful Heaven had intervened to save it.                 20
I thought my dear must her own soul destroy,
So did fanaticism and hate enslave it,
And this brought forth a dream and soon enough
This dream itself had all my thought and love.

And when the Fool and Blind Man stole the bread
Cuchulain fought the ungovernable sea;
Heart-mysteries there, and yet when all is said
It was the dream itself enchanted me:
Character isolated by a deed
To engross the present and dominate memory.                     30
Players and painted stage took all my love,
And not those things that they were emblems of.

III

Those masterful images because complete
Grew in pure mind, but out of what began?
A mound of refuse or the sweepings of a street,
Old kettles, old bottles, and a broken can,
Old iron, old bones, old rags, that raving slut
Who keeps the till. Now that my ladder's gone,
I must lie down where all the ladders start,
In the foul rag-and-bone shop of the heart.   (*1939*)          *40*

# EDWIN ARLINGTON ROBINSON / 1869–1935

## Sonnet

Oh for a poet—for a beacon bright
To rift this changeless glimmer of dead gray;
To spirit back the Muses, long astray,
And flush Parnassus with a newer light;
To put these little sonnet-men to flight
Who fashion, in a shrewd mechanic way,
Songs without souls, that flicker for a day,
To vanish in irrevocable night.
What does it mean, this barren age of ours?
Here are the men, the women, and the flowers,          *10*
The seasons, and the sunset, as before.
What does it mean? Shall there not one arise
To wrench one banner from the western skies,
And mark it with his name forevermore?   (*c. 1895*)

## Luke Havergal

Go to the western gate, Luke Havergal,
There where the vines cling crimson on the wall,
And in the twilight wait for what will come.
The leaves will whisper there of her, and some,
Like flying words, will strike you as they fall;
But go, and if you listen she will call.
Go to the western gate, Luke Havergal—
Luke Havergal.

No, there is not a dawn in eastern skies
To rift the fiery night that's in your eyes;          *10*
But there, where western glooms are gathering,
The dark will end the dark, if anything:

God slays Himself with every leaf that flies,
And hell is more than half of paradise.
No, there is not a dawn in eastern skies—
In eastern skies.

Out of a grave I come to tell you this,
Out of a grave I come to quench the kiss
That flames upon your forehead with a glow
That blinds you to the way that you must go.　　　　　　20
Yes, there is yet one way to where she is,
Bitter, but one that faith may never miss.
Out of a grave I come to tell you this—
To tell you this.

There is the western gate, Luke Havergal,
There are the crimson leaves upon the wall.
Go, for the winds are tearing them away,—
Nor think to riddle the dead words they say,
Nor any more to feel them as they fall;
But go, and if you trust her she will call.　　　　　　30
There is the western gate, Luke Havergal—
Luke Havergal.　(*1896*)

## Credo

I cannot find my way: there is no star
In all the shrouded heavens anywhere;
And there is not a whisper in the air
Of any living voice but one so far
That I can hear it only as a bar
Of lost, imperial music, played when fair
And angel fingers wove, and unaware,
Dead leaves to garlands where no roses are.
No, there is not a glimmer, nor a call,
For one that welcomes, welcomes when he fears,　　　10
The black and awful chaos of the night;
For through it all—above, beyond it all—
I know the far-sent message of the years,
I feel the coming glory of the Light.　(*1896*)

## Richard Cory

Whenever Richard Cory went down town,
We people on the pavement looked at him:
He was a gentleman from sole to crown,
Clean favored, and imperially slim.

And he was always quietly arrayed,
And he was always human when he talked;
But still he fluttered pulses when he said,
"Good-morning," and he glittered when he walked.

And he was rich—yes, richer than a king—
And admirably schooled in every grace: *10*
In fine, we thought that he was everything
To make us wish that we were in his place.

So on we worked, and waited for the light,
And went without the meat, and cursed the bread;
And Richard Cory, one calm summer night,
Went home and put a bullet through his head.   *(1897)*

## Octaves

### XVIII

Like a white wall whereon forever breaks
Unsatisfied the tumult of green seas,
Man's unconjectured godliness rebukes
With its imperial silence the lost waves
Of insufficient grief. This mortal surge
That beats against us now is nothing else
Than plangent ignorance. Truth neither shakes
Nor wavers; but the world shakes, and we shriek.

### XX

The prophet of dead words defeats himself:
Whoever would acknowledge and include
The foregleam and the glory of the real,
Must work with something else than pen and ink
And painful preparation: he must work
With unseen implements that have no names,
And he must win withal, to do that work,
Good fortitude, clean wisdom, and strong skill.

### XXIII

Here by the windy docks I stand alone,
But yet companioned. There the vessel goes,
And there my friend goes with it; but the wake
That melts and ebbs between that friend and me
Love's earnest is of Life's all-purposeful
And all-triumphant sailing, when the ships
Of Wisdom loose their fretful chains and swing
Forever from the crumbled wharves of Time. (*c. 1897*)

## How Annandale Went Out

"They called it Annandale—and I was there
To flourish, to find words, and to attend:
Liar, physician, hypocrite, and friend,
I watched him; and the sight was not so fair
As one or two that I had seen elsewhere:

An apparatus not for me to mend—
A wreck, with hell between him and the end,
Remained of Annandale; and I was there.
I knew the ruin as I knew the man;
So put the two together, if you can,                               *10*
Remembering the worst you know of me.
Now view yourself as I was, on the spot—
With a slight kind of engine. Do you see?
Like this . . . . You wouldn't hang me? I thought not."   (*1910*)

## For a Dead Lady

No more with overflowing light
Shall fill the eyes that now are faded,
Nor shall another's fringe with night
Their woman-hidden world as they did.
No more shall quiver down the days
The flowing wonder of her ways,
Whereof no language may requite
The shifting and the many-shaded.

The grace, divine, definitive,
Clings only as a faint forestalling;                               *10*
The laugh that love could not forgive
Is hushed, and answers to no calling;
The forehead and the little ears
Have gone where Saturn keeps the years;
The breast where roses could not live
Has done with rising and with falling.

The beauty, shattered by the laws
That have creation in their keeping,
No longer trembles at applause,
Or over children that are sleeping;                                *20*
And we who delve in beauty's lore
Know all that we have known before
Of what inexorable cause
Makes Time so vicious in his reaping.   (*1910*)

## Eros Turannos[1]

She fears him, and will always ask
 What fated her to choose him;
She meets in his engaging mask
 All reasons to refuse him;
But what she meets and what she fears
Are less than are the downward years,
Drawn slowly to the foamless weirs
 Of age, were she to lose him.

Between a blurred sagacity
 That once had power to sound him,   *10*
And Love, that will not let him be
 The Judas that she found him,
Her pride assuages her almost,
As if it were alone the cost.
He sees that he will not be lost,
 And waits and looks around him.

---

[1] tyrannic love

A sense of ocean and old trees
  Envelops and allures him;
Tradition, touching all he sees,
  Beguiles and reassures him;      20
And all her doubts of what he says
Are dimmed with what she knows of
  days—
Till even prejudice delays
  And fades, and she secures him.

The falling leaf inaugurates
  The reign of her confusion;
The pounding wave reverberates
  The dirge of her illusion;
And home, where passion lived and died,
Becomes a place where she can hide,   30
While all the town and harbor-side
  Vibrate with her seclusion.

We tell you, tapping on our brows,
  The story as it should be,
As if the story of a house
  Were told, or ever could be;
We'll have no kindly veil between
Her visions and those we have seen,—
As if we guessed what hers have been,
  Or what they are or would be.     40

Meanwhile we do no harm; for they
  That with a god have striven,
Not hearing much of what we say,
  Take what the god has given;
Though like waves breaking it may be,
Or like a changed familiar tree,
Or like a stairway to the sea
  Where down the blind are driven.
                     *(1916)*

## The Dark Hills

Dark hills at evening in the west,
Where sunset hovers like a sound
Of golden horns that sang to rest
Old bones of warriors under ground,

Far now from all the bannered ways
Where flash the legions of the sun,
You fade—as if the last of days
Were fading, and all wars were done.
                     *(1920)*

## Mr. Flood's Party

Old Eben Flood, climbing alone one
  night
Over the hill between the town below
And the forsaken upland hermitage
That held as much as he should ever
  know
On earth again of home, paused warily.
The road was his with not a native near;
And Eben, having leisure, said aloud,
For no man else in Tilbury Town[1] to
  hear:

"Well, Mr. Flood, we have the harvest
  moon
Again, and we may not have many
  more;                  10
The bird is on the wing, the poet says,
And you and I have said it here before.
Drink to the bird." He raised up to the
  light
The jug that he had gone so far to fill,
And answered huskily: "Well, Mr. Flood,
Since you propose it, I believe I will."

Alone, as if enduring to the end
A valiant armor of scarred hopes outworn,
He stood there in the middle of the road
Like Roland's[2] ghost winding a silent
  horn.                 20
Below him, in the town among the trees,
Where friends of other days had honored
  him,
A phantom salutation of the dead
Rang thinly till old Eben's eyes were dim.

Then, as a mother lays her sleeping child
Down tenderly, fearing it may awake,
He set the jug down slowly at his feet
With trembling care, knowing that most
  things break;
And only when assured that on firm earth
It stood, as the uncertain lives of
  men                   30
Assuredly did not, he paced away,
And with his hand extended paused
  again:

---

[1] the fictional site of several of Robinson's poems
[2] hero of the medieval French *Song of Roland*, who blew three mighty blasts on his horn to summon aid for his rearguard, who were ambushed at Roncevalles as they covered Charlemagne's retreat from Spain

"Well, Mr. Flood, we have not met like
    this
In a long time; and many a change has
    come
To both of us, I fear, since last it was
We had a drop together. Welcome
    home!"
Convivially returning with himself,
Again he raised the jug up to the light;
And with an acquiescent quaver said:
"Well, Mr. Flood, if you insist, I
    might.                                              40

"Only a very little, Mr. Flood—
For auld lang syne. No more, sir; that
    will do."
So, for the time, apparently it did,
And Eben evidently thought so too;
For soon amid the silver loneliness

Of night he lifted up his voice and sang,
Secure, with only two moons listening,
Until the whole harmonious landscape
    rang—

"For auld lang syne." The weary throat
    gave out,
The last word wavered; and the song
    being done,                                        50
He raised again the jug regretfully
And shook his head, and was again alone.
There was not much that was ahead of
    him,
And there was nothing in the town
    below—
Where strangers would have shut the
    many doors
That many friends had opened long ago.
                                              (1921)

## Karma[1]

Christmas was in the air and all was well
With him, but for a few confusing flaws
In divers of God's images. Because
A friend of his would neither buy nor sell,
Was he to answer for the axe that fell?
He pondered; and the reason for it was,
Partly, a slowly freezing Santa Claus
Upon the corner, with his beard and bell.
Acknowledging an improvident surprise,
He magnified a fancy that he wished                10
The friend whom he had wrecked were here again.
Not sure of that, he found a compromise;
And from the fulness of his heart he fished
A dime for Jesus who had died for men.   (1925)

## The Sheaves

Where long the shadows of the wind had rolled,
Green wheat was yielding to the change assigned;
And as by some vast magic undivined
The world was turning slowly into gold.
Like nothing that was ever bought or sold
It waited there, the body and the mind;
And with a mighty meaning of a kind
That tells the more the more it is not told.

---

[1] in Hinduism and Buddhism, the ethical consequence of one's acts

So in a land where all days are not fair,
Fair days went on till on another day                            *10*
A thousand golden sheaves were lying there,
Shining and still, but not for long to stay—
As if a thousand girls with golden hair
Might rise from where they slept and go away.   (*1925*)


# RALPH HODGSON / 1871–1962

## Eve

Eve, with her basket, was
Deep in the bells and grass,
Wading in bells and grass
Up to her knees.
Picking a dish of sweet
Berries and plums to eat,
Down in the bells and grass
Under the trees.

Mute as a mouse in a
Corner the cobra lay,                                            *10*
Curled round a bough of the
Cinnamon tall. . . .
Now to get even and
Humble proud heaven and
Now was the moment or
Never at all.

"Eva!" Each syllable
Light as a flower fell,
"Eva!" he whispered the
Wondering maid,                                                  *20*
Soft as a bubble sung
Out of a linnet's lung,
Soft and most silverly
"Eva!" he said.

Picture that orchard sprite;
Eve, with her body white,
Supple and smooth to her
Slim finger tips;
Wondering, listening,
Listening, wondering,                                            *30*
Eve with a berry
Half-way to her lips.

Oh, had our simple Eve
Seen through the make-believe!
Had she but known the
Pretender he was!
Out of the boughs he came,
Whispering still her name,
Tumbling in twenty rings
Into the grass.                                                  *40*

Here was the strangest pair
In the world anywhere,
Eve in the bells and grass
Kneeling, and he
Telling his story low. . . .
Singing birds saw them go
Down the dark path to
The Blasphemous Tree.

Oh, what a clatter when
Titmouse and Jenny Wren                                          *50*
Saw him successful and
Taking his leave!
How the birds rated him,
How they all hated him!
How they all pitied
Poor motherless Eve!

Picture her crying
Outside in the lane,
Eve, with no dish of sweet
Berries and plums to eat,                                        *60*
Haunting the gate of the
Orchard in vain. . . .
Picture the lewd delight
Under the hill tonight—
"Eva!" the toast goes round,
"Eva!" again.   (*1913*)

## The Bells of Heaven

'Twould ring the bells of Heaven    Knelt down with angry prayers
The wildest peal for years,          For tamed and shabby tigers
If Parson lost his senses            And dancing dogs and bears,
And people came to theirs,           And wretched, blind pit ponies,
And he and they together             And little hunted hares.   *(1917)*        10

# PAUL LAURENCE DUNBAR / 1872–1906

## Sympathy

I know what the caged bird feels, alas!
    When the sun is bright on the upland slopes;
When the wind stirs soft through the springing grass,
And the river flows like a stream of glass;
    When the first bird sings and the first bud opes,
And the faint perfume from its chalice steals—
I know what the caged bird feels!

I know why the caged bird beats his wing
    Till its blood is red on the cruel bars;
For he must fly back to his perch and cling                    10
When he fain would be on the bough a-swing;
    And a pain still throbs in the old, old scars
And they pulse again with a keener sting—
I know why he beats his wing!

I know why the caged bird sings, ah me,
    When his wing is bruised and his bosom sore,—
When he beats his bars and would be free;
It is not a carol of joy or glee,
    But a prayer that he sends from his heart's deep core,
But a plea, that upward to Heaven, he flings—                  20
I know why the caged bird sings!

## A Negro Love Song

Seen my lady home las' night,          Hyeahd de win' blow thoo de pine,
    Jump back, honey, jump back.            Jump back, honey, jump back.        10
Hel' huh han' an' sque'z it tight,     Mockin'-bird was singing' fine,
    Jump back, honey, jump back.            Jump back, honey, jump back.
Hyeahd huh sigh a little sigh,         An' my hea't was beatin' so,
Seen a light gleam f'om huh eye,       When I reached my lady's do',
An' a smile go flittin' by—            Dat I could n't ba' to go—
    Jump back, honey, jump back.            Jump back, honey, jump back.

Put my ahm aroun' huh wais',
  Jump back, honey, jump back.
Raised huh lips an' took a tase,
  Jump back, honey, jump back.    20

Love me, honey, love me true?
Love me well ez I love you?
An' she answe'd, "'Cose I do"—
  Jump back, honey, jump back.

## When Malindy Sings

G'way an' quit dat noise, Miss Lucy—
  Put dat music book away;
What's de use to keep on tryin'?
  Ef you practise twell you're gray,
You cain't sta't no notes a-flyin'
  Lak de ones dat rants and rings
F'om de kitchen to de big woods
  When Malindy sings.

You ain't got de nachel o'gans
  Fu' to make de soun' come right,    *10*
You ain't got de tu'ns an' twistin's
  Fu' to make it sweet an' light.
Tell you one thing now, Miss Lucy,
  An' I 'm tellin' you fu' true,
When hit comes to raal right singin',
  'T ain't no easy thing to do.

Easy 'nough fu' folks to hollah,
  Lookin' at de lines an' dots,
When dey ain't no one kin sence it,
  An' de chune comes in, in spots;    *20*
But fu' real melojous music,
  Dat jes' strikes yo' hea't and clings,
Jes' you stan' an' listen wif me
  When Malindy sings.

Ain't you nevah hyeahd Malindy?
  Blesséd soul, tek up de cross!
Look hyeah, ain't you jokin', honey?
  Well, you don't know whut you los'.
Y' ought to hyeah dat gal a-wa'blin',
  Robins, la'ks, an' all dem things.    *30*
Heish dey moufs an' hides dey faces
  When Malindy sings.

Fiddlin' man jes' stop his fiddlin'.
  Lay his fiddle on de she'f;
Mockin'-bird quit tryin' to whistle,
  'Cause he jes' so shamed hisse'f.
Folks a-playin' on de banjo
  Drap dey fingahs on de strings—
Bless yo' soul—fu'gits to move em,
  When Malindy sings.    *40*

She jes' spreads huh mouf and hollahs,
  "Come to Jesus," twell you hyeah
Sinnahs' tremblin' steps and voices
  Timid-lak a-drawin' neah;
Den she tu'ns to "Rock of Ages,"
  Simply to de cross she clings;
An' you fin' yo' teahs a-drappin'
  When Malindy sings.

Who dat says dat humble praises
  Wif de Master nevah counts?                                50
Heish yo' mouf, I hyeah dat music,
  Ez hit rises up an' mounts—
Floatin' by de hills an' valleys,
  Way above dis buryin' sod,
Ez hit makes its way in glory
  To de very gates of God!

Oh, hit 's sweetah dan de music
  Of an edicated band;
An hit 's dearah dan de battle's
  Song o' triumph in de lan'.                                60
It seems holier dan evenin'
  When de solemn chu'ch bell rings,
Ez I sit an' ca'mly listen
  While Malindy sings.

Towsah, stop dat ba'kin', hyeah me!
  Mandy, mek dat chile keep still;
Don't you hyeah de echoes callin'
  F'om de valley to de hill?
Let me listen, I can hyeah it,
  Th'oo de bresh of angels' wings,                           70
Sof' an' sweet, "Swing Low, Sweet Chariot,"
  Ez Malindy sings.

## Harriet Beecher Stowe

She told the story, and the whole world wept
At wrongs and cruelties it had not known
But for this fearless woman's voice alone.
She spoke to consciences that long had slept:
Her message, Freedom's clear reveille, swept
From heedless hovel to complacent throne.
Command and prophecy were in the tone
And from its sheath the sword of justice leapt.
Around two peoples swelled a fiery wave,
But both came forth transfigured from the flame.           10
Blest be the hand that dared be strong to save,
And blest be she who in our weakness came—
Prophet and priestess! At one stroke she gave
A race to freedom and herself to fame.

# WALTER DE LA MARE / 1873–1956

## Shadow

Even the beauty of the rose doth cast,
When its bright, fervid noon is past,
A still and lengthening shadow in the dust
    Till darkness come
    And take its strange dream home.

The transient bubbles of the water paint
'Neath their frail arch a shadow faint;
The golden nimbus of the windowed saint,
    Till shine the stars,
    Casts pale and trembling bars.          *10*

The loveliest thing earth hath, a shadow hath,
A dark and livelong hint of death,
Haunting it ever till its last faint breath . . .
    Who, then, may tell
    The beauty of heaven's shadowless asphodel?    *(1906)*

## The Listeners

"Is there anybody there?" said the Traveller,
    Knocking on the moonlit door;
And his horse in the silence champed the grasses
    Of the forest's ferny floor:
And a bird flew up out of the turret,
    Above the Traveller's head:
And he smote upon the door again a second time;
    "Is there anybody there?" he said.
But no one descended to the Traveller;
    No head from the leaf-fringed sill          *10*
Leaned over and looked into his grey eyes,
    Where he stood perplexed and still.
But only a host of phantom listeners
    That dwelt in the lone house then
Stood listening in the quiet of the moonlight
    To that voice from the world of men:
Stood thronging the faint moonbeams on the dark stair,
    That goes down to the empty hall,
Hearkening in an air stirred and shaken
    By the lonely Traveller's call.          *20*
And he felt in his heart their strangeness,
    Their stillness answering his cry,
While his horse moved, cropping the dark turf,
    'Neath the starred and leafy sky;

For he suddenly smote on the door, even
   Louder, and lifted his head:—
"Tell them I came, and no one answered,
   That I kept my word," he said.
Never the least stir made the listeners,
   Though every word he spake                30
Fell echoing through the shadowiness of the still house
   From the one man left awake:
Ay, they heard his foot upon the stirrup,
   And the sound of iron on stone,
And how the silence surged softly backward,
   When the plunging hoofs were gone.   (*1912*)


## Silver

     Slowly, silently, now the moon
     Walks the night in her silver shoon;
     This way, and that, she peers, and sees
     Silver fruit upon silver trees;
     One by one the casements catch
     Her beams beneath the silvery thatch;
     Crouched in his kennel, like a log,
     With paws of silver sleeps the dog;
     From their shadowy cote the white breasts peep
     Of doves in a silver-feathered sleep;      10
     A harvest mouse goes scampering by,
     With silver claws, and silver eye;
     And moveless fish in the water gleam,
     By silver reeds in a silver stream.   (*1913*)


## The Song of Shadows

Sweep thy faint strings, Musician,
   With thy long lean hand;
Downward the starry tapers burn,
   Sinks soft the waning sand;
The old hound whimpers couched in
     sleep.
   The embers smolder low;
Across the walls the shadows
     Come, and go

Sweep softly thy strings, Musician,
   The minutes mount to hours;     10
Frost on the windless casement weaves
   A labyrinth of flowers;
Ghosts linger in the darkening air,
   Hearken at the open door;
Music hath called them, dreaming,
     Home once more.   (*1913*)


## The Dreamer

O thou who giving helm and sword,
   Gav'st to the rusting rain,
And starry dark's all tender dews
   To blunt and stain:

Out of the battle I am sped,
   Unharmed, yet stricken sore;
A living shape amid whispering shades
   On Lethe's shore.

No trophy in my hands I bring,
   To this sad, sighing stream,     10
The neighings and the trumps and cries
   Were but a dream.

Traitor to life, of life betrayed
   O, of thy mercy deep,
A dream my all, the all I ask
   Is sleep.   (*1918*)

## The Last Chapter

I am living more alone now than I did;
This life tends inward, as the body ages;
And what is left of its strange book to read
Quickens in interest with the last few pages.

Problems abound. Its authorship? A sequel?
Its hero-villain, whose ways so little mend?
The plot? still dark. The style? a shade unequal.
And what of the dénouement? And, the end?

No, no, have done! Lay the thumbed thing aside;
Forget its horrors, folly, incitements, lies;  10
In silence and in solitude abide,
And con what yet may bless your inward eyes.

Pace, still, for pace with you, companion goes,
Though now, through dulled and inattentive ear,
No more—as when a child's—your sick heart knows
His infinite energy and beauty near.

His, too, a World, though viewless save in glimpse;
He, too, a book of imagery bears;
And, as your halting foot beside him limps,
Mark you whose badge and livery he wears.   (*1938*)  20

## The Song of Finis

At the edge of All the Ages
  A Knight sate on his steed,
His armor red and thin with rust,
  His soul from sorrow freed;
And he lifted up his visor
  From a face of skin and bone,
And his horse turned head and whinnied
  As the twain stood there alone.

No Bird above that steep of time
  Sang of a livelong quest;  10
No wind breathed,
    Rest:
"Lone for an end!" cried Knight to
    steed,
  Loosed an eager rein—
Charged with his challenge into Space:
  And quiet did quiet remain.

## Peace

Night is o'er England, and the winds are still;
Jasmine and honeysuckle steep the air;
Softly the stars that are all Europe's fill
Her heaven-wide dark with radiancy fair;
That shadowed moon now waxing in the west
Stirs not a rumour in her tranquil seas;
Mysterious sleep has lulled her heart to rest,
Deep even as theirs beneath her churchyard trees.
Secure, serene; dumb now the night-hawk's threat;
The guns' low thunder drumming o'er the tide;  10
The anguish pulsing in her stricken side . . . .
All is at peace. Ah, never, heart, forget
For this her youngest, best, and bravest died,
These bright dews once were mixed with bloody sweat.

# ROBERT FROST / 1874–1963

## A Line-Storm Song

The line-storm clouds fly tattered and swift.
  The road is forlorn all day,
Where a myriad snowy quartz-stones lift,
  And the hoofprints vanish away.
The roadside flowers, too wet for the bee,
  Expend their bloom in vain.
Come over the hills and far with me,
  And be my love in the rain.

The birds have less to say for themselves
  In the wood-world's torn despair              10
Than now these numberless years the elves,
  Although they are no less there:
All song of the woods is crushed like some
  Wild, easily shattered rose.
Come, be my love in the wet woods, come,
  Where the boughs rain when it blows.

There is the gale to urge behind
  And bruit our singing down,
And the shallow waters aflutter with wind
  From which to gather your gown.               20
What matter if we go clear to the west,
  And come not through dry-shod?
For wilding brooch, shall wet your breast
  The rain-fresh goldenrod.

Oh, never this whelming east wind swells
  But it seems like the sea's return
To the ancient lands where it left the shells
  Before the age of the fern;
And it seems like the time when, after doubt,
  Our love came back amain.                     30
Oh, come forth into the storm and rout
  And be my love in the rain.   (*1907*)

## Mending Wall

Something there is that doesn't love a wall,
That sends the frozen-ground-swell under it
And spills the upper boulders in the sun,
And makes gaps even two can pass abreast.
The work of hunters is another thing:
I have come after them and made repair
Where they have left not one stone on a stone,

But they would have the rabbit out of hiding,
To please the yelping dogs. The gaps I mean,
No one has seen them made or heard them made,      10
But at spring mending-time we find them there.
I let my neighbor know beyond the hill;
And on a day we meet to walk the line
And set the wall between us once again.
We keep the wall between us as we go.
To each the boulders that have fallen to each.
And some are loaves and some so nearly balls
We have to use a spell to make them balance:
"Stay where you are until our backs are turned!"
We wear our fingers rough with handling them.      20
Oh, just another kind of outdoor game,
One on a side. It comes to little more:
There where it is we do not need the wall:
He is all pine and I am apple orchard.
My apple trees will never get across
And eat the cones under his pines, I tell him.
He only says, "Good fences make good neighbors."
Spring is the mischief in me, and I wonder
If I could put a notion in his head:
"*Why* do they make good neighbors? Isn't it      30
Where there are cows? But here there are no cows.
Before I built a wall I'd ask to know
What I was walling in or walling out,
And to whom I was like to give offense.
Something there is that doesn't love a wall,
That wants it down." I could say "Elves" to him,
But it's not elves exactly, and I'd rather
He said it for himself. I see him there,
Bringing a stone grasped firmly by the top
In each hand, like an old-stone savage armed.      40
He moves in darkness as it seems to me,
Not of woods only and the shade of trees.
He will not go behind his father's saying,
And he likes having thought of it so well
He says again, "Good fences make good neighbors."      (*1914*)

## The Black Cottage

We chanced in passing by that afternoon
To catch it in a sort of special picture
Among tar-banded ancient cherry trees,
Set well back from the road in rank lodged grass,
The little cottage we were speaking of,
A front with just a door between two windows,
Fresh painted by the shower a velvet black.

We paused, the minister and I, to look.
He made as if to hold it at arm's length
Or put the leaves aside that framed it in.                    10
"Pretty," he said. "Come in. No one will care."
The path was a vague parting in the grass
That led us to a weathered windowsill.
We pressed our faces to the pane. "You see," he said,
"Everything's as she left it when she died.
Her sons won't sell the house or the things in it.
They say they mean to come and summer here
Where they were boys. They haven't come this year.
They live so far away—one is out West—
It will be hard for them to keep their word.               20
Anyway they won't have the place disturbed."
A buttoned haircloth lounge spread scrolling arms
Under a crayon portrait on the wall,
Done sadly from an old daguerreotype.
"That was the father as he went to war.
She always, when she talked about the war,
Sooner or later came and leaned, half knelt,
Against the lounge beside it, though I doubt
If such unlifelike lines kept power to stir
Anything in her after all the years.                        30
He fell at Gettysburg or Fredericksburg,
I ought to know—it makes a difference which:
Fredericksburg wasn't Gettysburg, of course.
But what I'm getting to is how forsaken
A little cottage this has always seemed;
Since she went, more than ever, but before—
I don't mean altogether by the lives
That had gone out of it, the father first,
Then the two sons, till she was left alone.
(Nothing could draw her after those two sons.             40
She valued the considerate neglect
She had at some cost taught them after years.)
I mean by the world's having passed it by—
As we almost got by this afternoon.
It always seems to me a sort of mark
To measure how far fifty years have brought us.
Why not sit down if you are in no haste?
These doorsteps seldom have a visitor.
The warping boards pull out their own old nails
With none to tread and put them in their place.            50
She had her own idea of things, the old lady.
And she liked talk. She had seen Garrison
And Whittier, and had her story of them.
One wasn't long in learning that she thought,
Whatever else the Civil War was for,
It wasn't just to keep the States together,

Nor just to free the slaves, though it did both.
She wouldn't have believed those ends enough
To have given outright for them all she gave.
Her giving somehow touched the principle
That all men are created free and equal.
And to hear her quaint phrases—so removed
From the world's view today of all those things.
That's a hard mystery of Jefferson's.
What did he mean? Of course the easy way
Is to decide it simply isn't true.
It may not be. I heard a fellow say so.
But never mind, the Welshman got it planted
Where it will trouble us a thousand years.
Each age will have to reconsider it.
You couldn't tell her what the West was saying,
And what the South, to her serene belief.
She had some art of hearing and yet not
Hearing the latter wisdom of the world.
White was the only race she ever knew.
Black she had scarcely seen, and yellow never.
But how could they be made so very unlike
By the same hand working in the same stuff?
She had supposed the war decided that.
What are you going to do with such a person?
Strange how such innocence gets its own way.
I shouldn't be surprised if in this world
It were the force that would at last prevail.
Do you know but for her there was a time
When, to please younger members of the church,
Or rather say non-members in the church,
Whom we all have to think of nowadays,
I would have changed the Creed a very little?
Not that she ever had to ask me not to;
It never got so far as that; but the bare thought
Of her old tremulous bonnet in the pew,
And of her half asleep, was too much for me.
Why, I might wake her up and startle her.
It was the words 'descended into Hades'
That seemed too pagan to our liberal youth.
You know they suffered from a general onslaught.
And well, if they weren't true why keep right on
Saying them like the heathen? We could drop them.
Only—there was the bonnet in the pew.
Such a phrase couldn't have meant much to her.
But suppose she had missed it from the Creed,
As a child misses the unsaid Good-night
And falls asleep with heartache—how should *I* feel?
I'm just as glad she made me keep hands off,
For, dear me, why abandon a belief

60

70

80

90

100

Merely because it ceases to be true.
Cling to it long enough, and not a doubt
It will turn true again, for so it goes.
Most of the change we think we see in life
Is due to truths being in and out of favor.                    *110*
As I sit here, and oftentimes, I wish
I could be monarch of a desert land
I could devote and dedicate forever
To the truths we keep coming back and back to.
So desert it would have to be, so walled
By mountain ranges half in summer snow,
No one would covet it or think it worth
The pains of conquering to force change on.
Scattered oases where men dwelt, but mostly
Sand dunes held loosely in tamarisk                            *120*
Blown over and over themselves in idleness.
Sand grains should sugar in the natal dew
The babe born to the desert, the sandstorm
Retard mid-waste my cowering caravans—

"There are bees in this wall." He struck the clapboards,
Fierce heads looked out; small bodies pivoted.
We rose to go. Sunset blazed on the windows.    *(1914)*


## The Wood-Pile

Out walking in the frozen swamp one gray day,
I paused and said, "I will turn back from here.
No, I will go on farther—and we shall see."
The hard snow held me, save where now and then
One foot went through. The view was all in lines
Straight up and down of tall slim trees
Too much alike to mark or name a place by
So as to say for certain I was here
Or somewhere else: I was just far from home.
A small bird flew before me. He was careful        *10*
To put a tree between us when he lighted,
And say no word to tell me who he was
Who was so foolish as to think what *he* thought.
He thought that I was after him for a feather—
The white one in his tail; like one who takes
Everything said as personal to himself.
One flight out sideways would have undeceived him.
And then there was a pile of wood for which
I forgot him and let his little fear
Carry him off the way I might have gone,            *20*
Without so much as wishing him good-night.
He went behind it to make his last stand.

It was a cord of maple, cut and split
And piled—and measured, four by four by eight.
And not another like it could I see.
No runner tracks in this year's snow looped near it.
And it was older sure than this year's cutting,
Or even last year's or the year's before.
The wood was gray and the bark warping off it
And the pile somewhat sunken. Clematis          *30*
Had wound strings round and round it like a bundle.
What held it, though, on one side was a tree
Still growing, and on one a stake and prop,
These latter about to fall. I thought that only
Someone who lived in turning to fresh tasks
Could so forget his handiwork on which
He spent himself, the labor of his ax,
And leave it there far from a useful fireplace
To warm the frozen swamp as best it could
With the slow smokeless burning of decay.  *(1914)*          *40*

## The Road Not Taken

Two roads diverged in a yellow wood,
And sorry I could not travel both
And be one traveler, long I stood
And looked down one as far as I could
To where it bent in the undergrowth;

Then took the other, as just as fair,
And having perhaps the better claim,
Because it was grassy and wanted wear;
Though as for that, the passing there
Had worn them really about the same,          *10*

And both that morning equally lay
In leaves no step had trodden black.
Oh, I kept the first for another day!
Yet knowing how way leads on to way,
I doubted if I should ever come back.

I shall be telling this with a sigh
Somewhere ages and ages hence:
Two roads diverged in a wood, and I—
I took the one less traveled by,
And that has made all the difference.  *(1915)*          *20*

## Birches

When I see birches bend to left and right
Across the lines of straighter darker trees,
I like to think some boy's been swinging them.

But swinging doesn't bend them down to stay
As ice storms do. Often you must have seen them
Loaded with ice a sunny winter morning
After a rain. They click upon themselves
As the breeze rises, and turn many-colored
As the stir cracks and crazes their enamel.
Soon the sun's warmth makes them shed crystal shells          10
Shattering and avalanching on the snow crust—
Such heaps of broken glass to sweep away
You'd think the inner dome of heaven had fallen.
They are dragged to the withered bracken by the load,
And they seem not to break; though once they are bowed
So low for long, they never right themselves:
You may see their trunks arching in the woods
Years afterwards, trailing their leaves on the ground
Like girls on hands and knees that throw their hair
Before them over their heads to dry in the sun.              20
But I was going to say when Truth broke in
With all her matter of fact about the ice storm,
I should prefer to have some boy bend them
As he went out and in to fetch the cows—
Some boy too far from town to learn baseball,
Whose only play was what he found himself,
Summer or winter, and could play alone.

One by one he subdued his father's trees
By riding them down over and over again
Until he took the stiffness out of them,                     30
And not one but hung limp, not one was left
For him to conquer. He learned all there was
To learn about not launching out too soon
And so not carrying the tree away
Clear to the ground. He always kept his poise
To the top branches, climbing carefully
With the same pains you use to fill a cup
Up to the brim, and even above the brim.
Then he flung outward, feet first, with a swish,
Kicking his way down through the air to the ground.          40
So was I once myself a swinger of birches.
And so I dream of going back to be.
It's when I'm weary of considerations,
And life is too much like a pathless wood
Where your face burns and tickles with the cobwebs
Broken across it, and one eye is weeping
From a twig's having lashed across it open.
I'd like to get away from earth awhile
And then come back to it and begin over.
May no fate willfully misunderstand me                       50
And half grant what I wish and snatch me away

Not to return. Earth's the right place for love:
I don't know where it's likely to go better.
I'd like to go by climbing a birch tree,
And climb black branches up a snow-white trunk
*Toward* heaven, till the tree could bear no more,
But dipped its top and set me down again
That would be good both going and coming back.
One could do worse than be a swinger of birches.  (*1915*)

## "Out, Out—"

The buzz saw snarled and rattled in the yard
And made dust and dropped stove-length sticks of wood,
Sweet-scented stuff when the breeze drew across it.
And from there those that lifted eyes could count
Five mountain ranges one behind the other
Under the sunset far into Vermont.
And the saw snarled and rattled, snarled and rattled,
As it ran light, or had to bear a load.
And nothing happened: day was all but done.
Call it a day, I wish they might have said                         10
To please the boy by giving him the half hour
That a boy counts so much when saved from work.
His sister stood beside them in her apron
To tell them "Supper." At the word, the saw,
As if to prove saws knew what supper meant,
Leaped out at the boy's hand, or seemed to leap—
He must have given the hand. However it was,
Neither refused the meeting. But the hand!
The boy's first outcry was a rueful laugh,
As he swung toward them holding up the hand,                       20
Half in appeal, but half as if to keep
The life from spilling. Then the boy saw all—
Since he was old enough to know, big boy
Doing a man's work, though a child at heart—
He saw all spoiled. "Don't let him cut my hand off—
The doctor, when he comes. Don't let him, sister!"
So. But the hand was gone already.
The doctor put him in the dark of ether.
He lay and puffed his lips out with his breath.
And then—the watcher at his pulse took fright.                     30
No one believed. They listened at his heart.
Little—less—nothing!—and that ended it.
No more to build on there. And they, since they
Were not the one dead, turned to their affairs.  (*1916*)

## Fire and Ice

Some say the world will end in fire,
Some say in ice.
From what I've tasted of desire
I hold with those who favor fire.
But if it had to perish twice,
I think I know enough of hate
To say that for destruction ice
Is also great
And would suffice.   (*1923*)

## Nothing Gold Can Stay

Nature's first green is gold,
Her hardest hue to hold.
Her early leaf's a flower;
But only so an hour.
Then leaf subsides to leaf.
So Eden sank to grief,
So dawn goes down to day.
Nothing gold can stay.   (*1923*)

## Stopping by Woods on a Snowy Evening

Whose woods these are I think I know.
His house is in the village, though;
He will not see me stopping here
To watch his woods fill up with snow.

My little horse must think it queer
To stop without a farmhouse near
Between the woods and frozen lake
The darkest evening of the year.

He gives his harness bells a shake
To ask if there is some mistake.                                      *10*
The only other sound's the sweep
Of easy wind and downy flake.

The woods are lovely, dark, and deep,
But I have promises to keep,
And miles to go before I sleep,
And miles to go before I sleep.   (*1923*)

## Two Look at Two

Love and forgetting might have carried them
A little further up the mountainside
With night so near, but not much further up.
They must have halted soon in any case
With thoughts of the path back, how rough it was
With rock and washout, and unsafe in darkness;
When they were halted by a tumbled wall
With barbed-wire binding. They stood facing this,
Spending what onward impulse they still had
In one last look the way they must not go,                           *10*
On up the failing path, where, if a stone
Or earthslide moved at night, it moved itself;

No footstep moved it. "This is all," they sighed,
"Good-night to woods." But not so; there was more.
A doe from round a spruce stood looking at them
Across the wall, as near the wall as they.
She saw them in their field, they her in hers.
The difficulty of seeing what stood still,
Like some up-ended boulder split in two,
Was in her clouded eyes: they saw no fear there.                    20
She seemed to think that, two thus, they were safe.
Then, as if they were something that, though strange,
She could not trouble her mind with too long,
She sighed and passed unscared along the wall.
"*This,* then, is all. What more is there to ask?"
But no, not yet. A snort to bid them wait.
A buck from round the spruce stood looking at them
Across the wall, as near the wall as they.
This was an antlered buck of lusty nostril,
Not the same doe come back into her place.                         30
He viewed them quizzically with jerks of head,
As if to ask, "Why don't you make some motion?
Or give some sign of life? Because you can't.
I doubt if you're as living as you look."
Thus till he had them almost feeling dared
To stretch a proffering hand—and a spell-breaking.
Then he too passed unscared along the wall.
Two had seen two, whichever side you spoke from.
"This *must* be all." It was all. Still they stood,
A great wave from it going over them,                              40
As if the earth in one unlooked-for favor
Had made them certain earth returned their love.    (*1923*)


## A Soldier

He is that fallen lance that lies as hurled,
That lies unlifted now, come dew, come rust,
But still lies pointed as it plowed the dust.
If we who sight along it round the world,
See nothing worthy to have been its mark,
It is because like men we look too near,
Forgetting that as fitted to the sphere,
Our missiles always make too short an arc.
They fall, they rip the grass, they intersect
The curve of earth, and striking, break their own;                 10
They make us cringe for metal-point on stone.
But this we know, the obstacle that checked
And tripped the body, shot the spirit on
Further than target ever showed or shone.    (*1927*)

## Once by the Pacific

The shattered water made a misty din.
Great waves looked over others coming in,
And thought of doing something to the shore
That water never did to land before.
The clouds were low and hairy in the skies,
Like locks blown forward in the gleam of eyes.
You could not tell, and yet it looked as if
The shore was lucky in being backed by cliff,
The cliff in being backed by continent;
It looked as if a night of dark intent                              10
Was coming, and not only a night, an age.
Someone had better be prepared for rage.
There would be more than ocean-water broken
Before God's last *Put out the Light* was spoken.   (*1928*)

## Desert Places

Snow falling and night falling fast, oh, fast
In a field I looked into going past,
And the ground almost covered smooth in snow,
But a few weeds and stubble showing last.

The woods around it have it—it is theirs.
All animals are smothered in their lairs.
I am too absent-spirited to count;
The loneliness includes me unawares.

And lonely as it is, that loneliness
Will be more lonely ere it will be less—                           10
A blanker whiteness of benighted snow
With no expression, nothing to express.

They cannot scare me with their empty spaces
Between stars—on stars where no human race is.
I have it in me so much nearer home
To scare myself with my own desert places.   (*1934*)

## A Drumlin Woodchuck

One thing has a shelving bank,
Another a rotting plank,
To give it cozier skies
And make up for its lack of size.

My own strategic retreat
Is where two rocks almost meet,
And still more secure and snug,
A two-door burrow I dug.

With those in mind at my back
I can sit forth exposed to attack,                                 10
As one who shrewdly pretends
That he and the world are friends.

All we who prefer to live
Have a little whistle we give,
And flash, at the least alarm
We dive down under the farm.

We allow some time for guile
And don't come out for a while,
Either to eat or drink.
We take occasion to think.                    20

And if after the hunt goes past
And the double-barreled blast
(Like war and pestilence
And the loss of common sense),

If I can with confidence say
That still for another day,
Or even another year,
I will be there for you, my dear,

It will be because, though small
As measured against the All,                    30
I have been so instinctively thorough
About my crevice and burrow.    (*1936*)

## Design

I found a dimpled spider, fat and white,
On a white heal-all, holding up a moth
Like a white piece of rigid satin cloth—
Assorted characters of death and blight
Mixed ready to begin the morning right,
Like the ingredients of a witches' broth—
A snow-drop spider, a flower like a froth,
And dead wings carried like a paper kite.

What had that flower to do with being white,
The wayside blue and innocent heal-all?                    10
What brought the kindred spider to that height,
Then steered the white moth thither in the night?
What but design of darkness to appall?—
If design govern in a thing so small.    (*1936*)

## The Draft Horse

With a lantern that wouldn't burn
In too frail a buggy we drove
Behind too heavy a horse
Through a pitch-dark limitless grove.

And a man came out of the trees
And took our horse by the head
And reaching back to his ribs
Deliberately stabbed him dead.

The ponderous beast went down
With a crack of a broken shaft.                    10
And the night drew through the trees
In one long invidious draft.

The most unquestioning pair
That ever accepted fate
And the least disposed to ascribe
Any more than we had to to hate,

We assumed that the man himself
Or someone he had to obey
Wanted us to get down
And walk the rest of the way.    (*1936*)                    20

## The Silken Tent

She is as in a field a silken tent
At midday when a sunny summer breeze
Has dried the dew and all its ropes relent,
So that in guys it gently sways at ease,
And its supporting central cedar pole,
That is its pinnacle to heavenward
And signifies the sureness of the soul,
Seems to owe naught to any single cord,
But strictly held by none, is loosely bound
By countless silken ties of love and thought          *10*
To everything on earth the compass round,
And only by one's going slightly taut
In the capriciousness of summer air
Is of the slightest bondage made aware.   (*1942*)

## Directive

Back out of all this now too much for us,
Back in a time made simple by the loss
Of detail, burned, dissolved, and broken off
Like graveyard marble sculpture in the weather,
There is a house that is no more a house
Upon a farm that is no more a farm
And in a town that is no more a town.
The road there, if you'll let a guide direct you
Who only has at heart your getting lost,
May seem as if it should have been a quarry—         *10*
Great monolithic knees the former town
Long since gave up pretense of keeping covered.
And there's a story in a book about it:
Besides the wear of iron wagon wheels
The ledges show lines ruled southeast-northwest,
The chisel work of an enormous Glacier
That braced his feet against the Arctic Pole.
You must not mind a certain coolness from him
Still said to haunt this side of Panther Mountain.
Nor need you mind the serial ordeal                  *20*
Of being watched from forty cellar holes
As if by eye pairs out of forty firkins.
As for the woods' excitement over you
That sends light rustle rushes to their leaves,
Charge that to upstart inexperience.
Where were they all not twenty years ago?
They think too much of having shaded out
A few old pecker-fretted apple trees.
Make yourself up a cheering song of how
Someone's road home from work this once was,       *30*

Who may be just ahead of you on foot
Or creaking with a buggy load of grain.
The height of the adventure is the height
Of country where two village cultures faded
Into each other. Both of them are lost.
And if you're lost enough to find yourself
By now, pull in your ladder road behind you
And put a sign up CLOSED to all but me.
Then make yourself at home. The only field
Now left's no bigger than a harness gall.                          40
First there's the children's house of make-believe,
Some shattered dishes underneath a pine,
The playthings in the playhouse of the children.
Weep for what little things could make them glad.
Then for the house that is no more a house,
But only a belilaced cellar hole,
Now slowly closing like a dent in dough.
This was no playhouse but a house in earnest.
Your destination and your destiny's
A brook that was the water of the house,                          50
Cold as a spring as yet so near its source,
Too lofty and original to rage.
(We know the valley streams that when aroused
Will leave their tatters hung on barb and thorn.)
I have kept hidden in the instep arch
Of an old cedar at the waterside
A broken drinking goblet like the Grail
Under a spell so the wrong ones can't find it,
So can't get saved, as Saint Mark says they mustn't.
(I stole the goblet from the children's playhouse.)                60
Here are your waters and your watering place.
Drink and be whole again beyond confusion.   (*1946*)

## Come In

As I came to the edge of the woods,
Thrush music—hark!
Now if it was dusk outside,
Inside it was dark.

Too dark in the woods for a bird
By sleight of wing
To better its perch for the night,
Though it still could sing.

The last of the light of the sun
That had died in the west            10

Still lived for one song more
In a thrush's breast.

Far in the pillared dark
Thrush music went—
Almost like a call to come in
To the dark and lament.

But no, I was out for stars:
I would not come in.
I meant not even if asked,
And I hadn't been.   (*1942*)            20

# EDWARD THOMAS / 1878–1917

## Lights Out

I have come to the borders of sleep,
The unfathomable deep
Forest where all must lose
Their way, however straight,
Or winding, soon or late;
They cannot choose.

Many a road and track
That, since the dawn's first crack,
Up to the forest brink,
Deceived the travelers,                    10
Suddenly now blurs,
And in they sink.

Here love ends,
Despair, ambition ends;
All pleasure and all trouble,
Although most sweet or bitter,
Here ends in sleep that is sweeter
Than tasks most noble.

There is not any book
Or face of dearest look                    20
That I would not turn from now
To go into the unknown
I must enter, and leave, alone,
I know not how.

The tall forest towers;
Its cloudy foliage lowers
Ahead, shelf above shelf;
Its silence I hear and obey
That I may lose my way
And myself.   (1917)                        30

## Cock-Crow

Out of the wood of thoughts that grows by night
To be cut down by the sharp ax of light,—
Out of the night, two cocks together crow,
Cleaving the darkness with a silver blow:

And bright before my eyes twin trumpeters stand,
Heralds of splendor, one at either hand,
Each facing each as in a coat of arms:—
The milkers lace their boots up at the farms.

## The Gallows

There was a weasel lived in the sun
With all his family,
Till a keeper shot him with his gun
And hung him upon a tree,
Where he swings in the wind and rain,
In the sun and in the snow,
Without pleasure, without pain,
On the dead oak tree bough.

There was a crow who was no sleeper,
But a thief and a murderer                    10
Till a very late hour; and this keeper

Made him one of the things that were,
To hang and flap in rain and wind,
In the sun and in the snow.
There are no more sins to be sinned
On the dead oak tree bough.

There was a magpie, too,
Had a long tongue and a long tail;
He could both talk and do—
But what did that avail?                                              20
He, too, flaps in the wind and rain
Alongside weasel and crow,
Without pleasure, without pain,
On the dead oak tree bough.

And many other beasts
And birds, skin, bone, and feather,
Have been taken from their feasts
And hung up there together,
To swing and have endless leisure
In the sun and in the snow,                                          30
Without pain, without pleasure,
On the dead oak tree bough.    *(1917)*

## Out in the Dark

Out in the dark over the snow
The fallow fawns invisible go
With the fallow doe;
And the winds blow
Fast as the stars are slow.

Stealthily the dark haunts round
And, when a lamp goes, without sound
At a swifter bound
Than the swiftest hound,
Arrives, and all else is drowned;                                    10

And I and star and wind and deer,
Are in the dark together,—near,
Yet far,—and fear
Drums on my ear
In that sage company drear.

How weak and little is the light,
All the universe of sight,
Love and delight,
Before the might,
If you love it not, of night.                                        20

# JOHN MASEFIELD / 1878–1967

## Sea-Fever

I must go down to the seas again, to the lonely sea and the sky,
And all I ask is a tall ship and a star to steer her by,
And the wheel's kick and the wind's song and the white sail's shaking,
And a grey mist on the sea's face and a grey dawn breaking.

I must go down to the seas again, for the call of the running tide
Is a wild call and a clear call that may not be denied;
And all I ask is a windy day with the white clouds flying,
And the flung spray and the blown spume, and the sea-gulls crying.

I must go down to the seas again to the vagrant gypsy life,
To the gull's way and the whale's way where the wind's like a whetted knife;    *10*
And all I ask is a merry yarn from a laughing fellow-rover,
And quiet sleep and a sweet dream when the long trick's over.  (*1902*)

## Cargoes

Quinquireme[1] of Nineveh[2] from distant Ophir[3]
Rowing home to haven in sunny Palestine,
With a cargo of ivory,
And apes and peacocks,
Sandalwood, cedarwood, and sweet white wine.

Stately Spanish galleon coming from the Isthmus,
Dipping through the Tropics by the palm-green shores,
With a cargo of diamonds,
Emeralds, amethysts,
Topazes, and cinnamon, and gold moidores.[4]    *10*

Dirty British coaster with a salt-caked smoke-stack
Butting through the Channel in the mad March days,
With a cargo of Tyne coal,
Road-rail, pig-lead,
Firewood, iron-ware, and cheap tin trays.  (*1910*)

## Sonnet

Is there a great green commonwealth of Thought
Which ranks the yearly pageant, and decides
How Summer's royal progress shall be wrought,
By secret stir which in each plant abides?
Does rocking daffodil consent that she,

---

[1] a galley with five banks of oars
[2] ancient capital of Assyria

[3] ancient source of fine gold
[4] a Portuguese gold coin

The snowdrop of wet winters, shall be first?
Does spotted cowslip with the grass agree
To hold her pride before the rattle burst?
And in the hedge what quick agreement goes,
When hawthorn blossoms redden to decay,                    *10*
That Summer's pride shall come, the Summer's rose.
Before the flower be on the bramble spray?
Or is it, as with us, unresting strife,
And each consent a lucky gasp for life?    (*1916*)


## The Lemmings

Once in a hundred years the Lemmings come
Westward, in search of food, over the snow,
Westward, until the salt sea drowns them dumb,
Westward, till all are drowned, those Lemmings go.
Once, it is thought, there was a westward land
(Now drowned) where there was food for those starved things,
And memory of the place has burnt its brand
In the little brains of all the Lemming Kings.
Perhaps, long since, there was a land beyond
Westward from death, some city, some calm place,          *10*
Where one could taste God's quiet and be fond
With the little beauty of a human face;
But now the land is drowned, yet still we press
Westward, in search, to death, to nothingness.   (*1920*)


## CARL SANDBURG / 1878–1967

## Fog

The fog comes
on little cat feet.

It sits looking
over harbor and city
on silent haunches
and then moves on.   (*1916*)

## Nocturne in a Deserted Brickyard

Stuff of the moon
Runs on the lapping sand
Out to the longest shadows.
Under the curving willows,
And round the creep of the wave line,
Fluxions of yellow and dusk on the
    waters
Make a wide dreaming pansy of an old
    pond in the night.

## Chicago

Hog Butcher for the World,
Tool Maker, Stacker of Wheat,
Player with Railroads and the Nation's Freight Handler;
Stormy, husky, brawling,
City of the Big Shoulders:

They tell me you are wicked and I believe them, for I have seen your painted
women under the gas lamps luring the farm boys.
And they tell me you are crooked and I answer: Yes, it is true I have seen the
gunman kill and go free to kill again.
And they tell me you are brutal and my reply is: On the faces of women and
children I have seen the marks of wanton hunger.
And having answered so I turn once more to those who sneer at this my city, and
I give them back the sneer and say to them:
Come and show me another city with lifted head singing so proud to be alive and
coarse and strong and cunning.
Flinging magnetic curses amid the toil of piling job on job, here is a tall bold
slugger set vivid against the little soft cities;
Fierce as a dog with tongue lapping for action, cunning as a savage pitted against
the wilderness,
Bareheaded,
Shoveling,
Wrecking,
Planning,
Building, breaking, rebuilding,
Under the smoke, dust all over his mouth, laughing with white teeth,
Under the terrible burden of destiny laughing as a young man laughs,
Laughing even as an ignorant fighter laughs who has never lost a battle,
Bragging and laughing that under his wrist is the pulse, and under his ribs the
heart of the people,
Laughing!
Laughing the stormy, husky, brawling laughter of Youth, half-naked, sweating,
proud to be Hog Butcher, Tool Maker, Stacker of Wheat, Player with Rail-
roads and Freight Handler to the Nation.    (*1916*)


## Broken-Face Gargoyles

All I can give you is broken-face gargoyles.
It is too early to sing and dance at funerals,
Though I can whisper to you I am looking for an undertaker humming a lullaby
and throwing his feet in a swift and mystic buck-and-wing, now you see it
and now you don't.

Fish to swim a pool in your garden flashing a speckled silver,
A basket of wine-saps filling your room with flame-dark for your eyes and the tang
of valley orchards for your nose,

Such a beautiful pail of fish, such a beautiful peck of apples, I cannot bring you
   now.
It is too early and I am not footloose yet.

I shall come in the night when I come with a hammer and saw.
I shall come near your window, where you look out when your eyes open in the
   morning,
And there I shall slam together bird-houses and bird-baths for wing-loose wrens
   and hummers to live in, birds with yellow wing tips to blur and buzz soft
   all summer,           *10*

So I shall make little fool homes with doors, always open doors for all and each
   to run away when they want to,
I shall come just like that even though now it is early and I am not yet footloose,
Even though I am still looking for an undertaker with a raw, wind-bitten face and
   a dance in his feet.
I make a date with you (put it down) for six o'clock in the evening a thousand
   years from now.

All I can give you now is broken-face gargoyles.
All I can give you now is a double gorilla head with two fish mouths and four
   eagle eyes hooked on a street wall, spouting water and looking two ways
   to the ends of the street for the new people, the young strangers, coming,
   coming, always coming.

      It is early.
      I shall yet be footloose.   (*1920*)

## Jazz Fantasia

Drum on your drums, batter on your banjos, sob on the long cool winding saxo-
   phones. Go to it, O jazzmen.

Sling your knuckles on the bottoms of the happy tin pans, let your trombones
   ooze, and go husha-husha-hush with the slippery sandpaper.

Moan like an autumn wind high in the lonesome treetops, moan soft like you
   wanted somebody terrible, cry like a racing car slipping away from a motor-
   cycle-cop, bang-bang! you jazzmen, bang altogether drums, traps, banjos,
   horns, tin cans—make two people fight on the top of a stairway and scratch
   each other's eyes in a clinch tumbling down the stairs.

Can the rough stuff... Now a Mississippi steamboat pushes up the night river
   with a hoo-hoo-hoo-oo ... and the green lanterns calling to the high soft
   stars ... a red moon rides on the humps of the low river hills.... Go to
   it, O jazzmen.

# VACHEL LINDSAY / 1879–1931

## General William Booth[1] Enters into Heaven

*(TO BE SUNG TO THE TUNE OF "THE BLOOD OF THE LAMB"
WITH INDICATED INSTRUMENTS.)*

### I

    *(Bass drum beaten loudly.)*
Booth led boldly with his big bass drum—
(Are you washed in the blood of the Lamb?)
The Saints smiled gravely and they said: "He's come."
(Are you washed in the blood of the Lamb?)
Walking lepers followed, rank on rank,
Lurching bravos from the ditches dank,
Drabs from the alleyways and drug fiends pale—
Minds still passion-ridden, soul-powers frail:—
Vermin-eaten saints with moldy breath,
Unwashed legions with the ways of Death—         10
(Are you washed in the blood of the Lamb?)

    *(Banjos.)*
Every slum had sent its half-a-score
The round world over. (Booth had groaned for more.)
Every banner that the wide world flies
Bloomed with glory and transcendent dyes.
Big-voiced lasses made their banjos bang;
Tranced, fanatical they shrieked and sang:—
"Are you washed in the blood of the Lamb?"
Hallelujah! It was queer to see
Bull-necked convicts with that land make free.        20
Loons with trumpets blowed a blare, blare, blare
On, on upward thro' the golden air!
(Are you washed in the blood of the Lamb?)

### II

    *(Bass drum slower and softer).*
Booth died blind and still by faith he trod,
Eyes still dazzled by the ways of God.
Booth led boldly, and he looked the chief,
Eagle countenance in sharp relief,
Beard a-flying, air of high command
Unabated in that holy land.

    *(Sweet flute music.)*
Jesus came from out the court-house door,        30
Stretched his hands above the passing poor.
Booth saw not, but led his queer ones there
Round and round the mighty court-house square.

---

[1] founder of the Salvation Army (1829–1912)

Then, in an instant all that blear review
Marched on spotless, clad in raiment new.
The lame were straightened, withered limbs uncurled
And blind eyes opened on a new, sweet world.

(*Bass drum louder.*)
Drabs and vixens in a flash made whole!
Gone was the weasel-head, the snout, the jowl!
Sages and sibyls now, and athletes clean,                    40
Rulers of empires, and of forests green!

(*Grand chorus of all instruments. Tambourines to the foreground.*)
The hosts were sandalled, and their wings were fire!
(Are you washed in the blood of the Lamb?)
But their noise played havoc with the angel-choir.
(Are you washed in the blood of the Lamb?)
Oh, shout Salvation! It was good to see
Kings and Princes by the Lamb set free.
The banjos rattled and the tambourines
Jing-jing-jingled in the hands of Queens.

(*Reverently sung, no instruments.*)
And when Booth halted by the curb for prayer          50
He saw his Master thro' the flag-filled air.
Christ came gently with a robe and crown
For Booth the soldier, while the throng knelt down.
He saw King Jesus. They were face to face,
And he knelt a-weeping in that holy place.
Are you washed in the blood of the Lamb? (*1913*)

## The Mouse That Gnawed the Oak-Tree Down

The mouse that gnawed the oak-tree
     down
Began his task in early life.
He kept so busy with his teeth
He had no time to take a wife.

He gnawed and gnawed through sun
     and rain
When the ambitious fit was on,
Then rested in the sawdust till
A month of idleness had gone.

He did not move about to hunt
The coteries of mousie-men.                    10

He was a snail-paced, stupid thing
Until he cared to gnaw again.

The mouse that gnawed the oak-tree
     down,
When that tough foe was at his feet—
Found in the stump no angel-cake
Nor buttered bread, nor cheese nor
     meat—

The forest-roof let in the sky.
"This light is worth the work," said he.
"I'll make this ancient swamp more
     light."
And started on another tree. (*1914*)    20

## When the Mississippi Flowed in Indiana

*INSCRIBED TO BRUCE
CAMPBELL, WHO READ "TOM
SAWYER" WITH ME IN THE OLD
HOUSE*

Beneath Time's roaring cannon
Many walls fall down.
But though the guns break every stone,
Level every town:—
Within our Grandma's old front hall
Some wonders flourish yet:—
The Pavement of Verona,
Where stands young Juliet;
The roof of Blue-beard's palace,
And Kubla Khan's wild ground;                 10
The cave of young Aladdin,
Where the jewel-flowers were found;
And the garden of old Sparta
Where little Helen played;
The grotto of Miranda
That Prospero arrayed;

And the cave, by the Mississippi,
Where Becky Thatcher strayed.

On that Indiana stairway
Gleams Cinderella's shoe.                      20
Upon that mighty mountainside
Walks Snow-white in the dew.
Upon that grassy hillside
Trips shining Nicolette:—
That stairway of remembrance
Time's cannon will not get—
That chattering slope of glory
Our little cousins made,
That hill by the Mississippi
Where Becky Thatcher strayed.                  30

Spring beauties on that cliffside,
Love in the air,
While the soul's deep Mississippi
Sweeps on, forever fair.
And he who enters in the cave,
Nothing shall make afraid,
The cave by the Mississippi
Where Tom and Becky strayed.    *(1920)*

## WALLACE STEVENS / 1879–1955

## A High-Toned Old Christian Woman

Poetry is the supreme fiction, madame.
Take the moral law and make a nave of it
And from the nave build haunted heaven. Thus,
The conscience is converted into palms,
Like windy citherns hankering for hymns.
We agree in principle. That's clear. But take
The opposing law and make a peristyle,
And from the peristyle project a masque
Beyond the planets. Thus, our bawdiness,
Unpurged by epitaph, indulged at last,                 10
Is equally converted into palms,
Squiggling like saxophones. And palm for palm,
Madame, we are where we began. Allow,
Therefore, that in the planetary scene
Your disaffected flagellants, well-stuffed,

Smacking their muzzy bellies in parade,
Proud of such novelties of the sublime,
Such tink and tank and tunk-a-tunk-tunk,
May, merely may, madame, whip from themselves
A jovial hullabaloo among the spheres. 20
This will make widows wince. But fictive things
Wink as they will. Wink most when widows wince. (*1923*)

## The Emperor of Ice-Cream

Call the roller of big cigars,
The muscular one, and bid him whip
In kitchen cups concupiscent curds.
Let the wenches dawdle in such dress
As they are used to wear, and let the boys
Bring flowers in last month's newspapers.
Let be be finale of seem.
The only emperor is the emperor of ice-cream.

Take from the dresser of deal,
Lacking the three glass knobs, that sheet 10
On which she embroidered fantails once
And spread it so as to cover her face.
If her horny feet protrude, they come
To show how cold she is, and dumb.
Let the lamp affix its beam.
The only emperor is the emperor of ice-cream. (*1923*)

## Anecdote of the Jar

I placed a jar in Tennessee,
And round it was, upon a hill.
It made the slovenly wilderness
Surround that hill.

The wilderness rose up to it,
And sprawled around, no longer wild.
The jar was round upon the ground
And tall and of a port in air.

It took dominion everywhere.
The jar was gray and bare. 10
It did not give of bird or bush,
Like nothing else in Tennessee. (*1923*)

## The Idea of Order at Key West

She sang beyond the genius of the sea.
The water never formed to mind or voice,
Like a body wholly body, fluttering
Its empty sleeves; and yet its mimic motion
Made constant cry, caused constantly a cry,
That was not ours although we understood,
Inhuman, of the veritable ocean.

The sea was not a mask. No more was she.
The song and water were not medleyed sound
Even if what she sang was what she heard,                    *10*
Since what she sang was uttered word by word.
It may be that in all her phrases stirred
The grinding water and the gasping wind;
But it was she and not the sea we heard.

For she was the maker of the song she sang.
The ever-hooded, tragic-gestured sea
Was merely a place by which she walked to sing.
Whose spirit is this? we said, because we knew
It was the spirit that we sought and knew
That we should ask this often as she sang.                    *20*

If it was only the dark voice of the sea
That rose, or even colored by many waves;
If it was only the outer voice of sky
And cloud, of the sunken coral water-walled,
However clear, it would have been deep air,
The heaving speech of air, a summer sound
Repeated in a summer without end
And sound alone. But it was more than that,
More even than her voice, and ours, among
The meaningless plungings of water and the wind,            *30*
Theatrical distances, bronze shadows heaped
On high horizons, mountainous atmospheres
Of sky and sea.
                        It was her voice that made
The sky acutest at its vanishing.
She measured to the hour its solitude.
She was the single artificer of the world
In which she sang. And when she sang, the sea,
Whatever self it had, became the self
That was her song, for she was the maker. Then we,
As we beheld her striding there alone,                       *40*
Knew that there never was a world for her
Except the one she sang and, singing, made.

Ramon Fernandez,[1] tell me, if you know,
Why, when the singing ended and we turned
Toward the town, tell why the glassy lights,
The lights in the fishing boats at anchor there,
As the night descended, tilting in the air,
Mastered the night and portioned out the sea,
Fixing emblazoned zones and fiery poles,
Arranging, deepening, enchanting night.                      *50*

---

[1] French esthetician (1894–1944)

Oh! Blésséd rage for order, pale Ramon,
The maker's rage to order words of the sea,
Words of the fragrant portals, dimly-starred,
And of ourselves and of our origins,
In ghostlier demarcations, keener sounds.  (*1935*)

## The Sense of the Sleight-of-Hand Man

One's grand flights, one's Sunday baths,
One's tootings at the weddings of the soul
Occur as they occur. So bluish clouds
Occurred above the empty house and the leaves
Of the rhododendrons rattled their gold,
As if someone lived there. Such floods of white
Came bursting from the clouds. So the wind
Threw its contorted strength around the sky.

Could you have said the bluejay suddenly
Would swoop to earth? It is a wheel, the rays                    *10*
Around the sun. The wheel survives the myths.
The fire eye in the clouds survives the gods.
To think of a dove with an eye of grenadine
And pines that are cornets, so it occurs,
And a little island full of geese and stars:
It may be that the ignorant man, alone,
Has any chance to mate his life with life
That is the sensual, pearly spouse, the life
That is fluent in even the wintriest bronze.  (*1942*)

## Of Hartford in a Purple Light

A long time you have been making the trip
From Havre to Hartford, Master Soleil,
Bringing the lights of Norway and all that.

A long time the ocean has come with you,
Shaking the water off, like a poodle,
That splatters incessant thousands of drops,

Each drop a petty tricolor. For this,
The aunts in Pasadena, remembering,
Abhor the plaster of the western horses,

Souvenirs of museums. But, Master, there are          *10*
Lights maculine and lights feminine.
What is this purple, this parasol,

This stage-light of the Opera?
It is like a region full of intonings.
It is Hartford seen in a purple light.

A moment ago, light masculine,
Working, with big hands, on the town,
Arranged its heroic attitudes.

But now as in an amour of women
Purple sets purple round. Look, Master,                    *20*
See the river, the railroad, the cathedral . . .

When male light fell on the naked back
Of the town, the river, the railroad were clear.
Now, every muscle slops away.

Hi! Whisk it, poodle, flick the spray
Of the ocean, ever-freshening,
On the irised hunks, the stone bouquet.   (*1942*)


## Of Modern Poetry

The poem of the mind in the act of finding
What will suffice. It has not always had
To find: the scene was set; it repeated what
Was in the script.
                        Then the theatre was changed
To something else. Its past was a souvenir.
It has to be living, to learn the speech of the place.
It has to face the men of the time and to meet
The women of the time. It has to think about war
And it has to find what will suffice. It has
To construct a new stage. It has to be on that stage    *10*
And, like an insatiable actor, slowly and
With meditation, speak words that in the ear,
In the delicatest ear of the mind, repeat,
Exactly, that which it wants to hear, at the sound
Of which, an invisible audience listens,
Not to the play, but to itself, expressed
In an emotion as of two people, as of two
Emotions becoming one. The actor is
A metaphysician in the dark, twanging
An instrument, twanging a wiry string that gives        *20*
Sounds passing through sudden rightnesses, wholly
Containing the mind, below which it cannot descend,
Beyond which it has no will to rise.
                                    It must
Be the finding of a satisfaction, and may
Be of a man skating, a woman dancing, a woman
Combing. The poem of the act of the mind.   (*1942*)

## Bouquet of Roses in Sunlight

Say that it is a crude effect, black reds,
Pink yellows, orange whites, too much as they are
To be anything else in the sunlight of the room,

Too much as they are to be changed by metaphor,
Too actual, things that in being real
Make any imaginings of them lesser things.

And yet this effect is a consequence of the way
We feel and, therefore, is not real, except
In our sense of it, our sense of the fertilest red,

Of yellow as first color and of white,                                    10
In which the sense lies still, as a man lies,
Enormous, in a completing of his truth.

Our sense of these things changes and they change,
Not as in metaphor, but in our sense
Of them. So sense exceeds all metaphor.

It exceeds the heavy changes of the light.
It is like a flow of meanings with no speech
And of as many meanings as of men.

We are two that use these roses as we are,
In seeing them. This is what makes them seem             20
So far beyond the rhetorician's touch.   (*1950*)


## WILLIAM CARLOS WILLIAMS / 1883–1963

### Dawn

Ecstatic bird songs pound
the hollow vastness of the sky
with metallic clinkings—
beating color up into it
at a far edge,—beating it, beating it
with rising, triumphant ardor,—
stirring it into warmth,

quickening in it a spreading change,—
bursting wildly against it as
dividing the horizon, a heavy sun         10
lifts himself—is lifted—
bit by bit above the edge
of things,—runs free at last
out into the open—! lumbering
glorified in full release upward—
                              songs cease.


### The Yachts

contend in a sea which the land partly encloses
shielding them from the too heavy blows
of an ungoverned ocean which when it chooses

tortures the biggest hulls, the best man knows
to pit against its beating, and sinks them pitilessly.
Mothlike in mists, scintillant in the minute

brilliance of cloudless days, with broad bellying sails
they glide to the wind tossing green water
from their sharp prows while over them the crew crawls

ant-like, solicitously grooming them, releasing,                    10
making fast as they turn, lean far over and having
caught the wind again, side by side, head for the mark.

In a well guarded arena of open water surrounded by
lesser and greater craft which, sycophant, lumbering
and flittering follow them, they appear youthful, rare

as the light of a happy eye, live with the grace
of all that in the mind is feckless, free and
naturally to be desired. Now the sea which holds them

is moody, lapping their glossy sides, as if feeling
for some slightest flaw but fails completely.                       20
Today no race. Then the wind comes again. The yachts

move, jockeying for a start, the signal is set and they
are off. Now the waves strike at them but they are too
well made, they slip through, though they take in canvas.

Arms with hands grasping seek to clutch at the prows.
Bodies thrown recklessly in the way are cut aside.
It is a sea of faces about them in agony, in despair

until the horror of the race dawns staggering the mind,
the whole sea become an entanglement of watery bodies
lost to the world bearing what they cannot hold. Broken,          30

beaten, desolate, reaching from the dead to be taken up
they cry out, failing, failing! their cries rising
in waves still as the skillful yachts pass over.   (*1935*)

## The Dance

In Breughel's great picture, The Kermess,
the dancers go round, they go round and
around, the squeal and the blare and the
tweedle of bagpipes, a bugle and fiddles
tipping their bellies (round as the thick-
sided glasses whose wash they impound)
their hips and their bellies off balance
to turn them. Kicking and rolling about
the Fair Grounds, swinging their butts, those
shanks must be sound to bear up under such            10
rollicking measures, prance as they dance
in Breughel's great picture, The Kermess.   (*1944*)

## The Semblables

The red brick monastery in
the suburbs over against the dust-
hung acreage of the unfinished
and all but subterranean

munitions plant: those high
brick walls behind which at Easter
the little orphans and bastards
in white gowns sing their Latin

responses to the hoary ritual
while frankincense and myrrh                10
round out the dark chapel making
an enclosed sphere of it

of which they are the worm:
that cell outside the city beside
the polluted stream and dump
heap, uncomplaining, and the field

of upended stones with a photo
under glass fastened here and there
to one of them near the deeply
carved name to distinguish it:             20

that trinity of slate gables
the unembellished windows piling

up, the chapel with its round
window between the dormitories

peaked by the bronze belfry
peaked in turn by the cross,
verdegris—faces all silent
that miracle that has burst sexless

from between the carrot rows.
Leafless white birches, their           30
empty tendrils swaying in
the all but no breeze guard

behind the spiked monastery fence
the sacred statuary. But ranks
of brilliant car-tops row on row
give back in all his glory the

late November sun and hushed
attend, before that tumbled
ground, those sightless walls
and shovelled entrances where no        40

one but a lonesome cop swinging
his club gives sign, that agony
within where the wrapt machines
are praying . . .   (*1946*)

## *from* Paterson: Book I

### PREFACE

"Rigor of beauty is the quest. But how will
you find beauty when it is locked in the mind
past all remonstrance?"

To make a start,
out of particulars
and make them general, rolling
up the sum, by defective means—
Sniffing the trees,
just another dog
among a lot of dogs. What
else is there? And to do?
The rest have run out—
after the rabbits.                        10
Only the lame stands—on
three legs. Scratch front and back.
Deceive and eat. Dig
a musty bone

For the beginning is assuredly
the end—since we know nothing, pure
and simple, beyond
our own complexities.

                Yet there is
no return: rolling up out of chaos,       20
a nine months' wonder, the city
the man, an identity—it can't be
otherwise—an
interpenetration, both ways. Rolling
up! obverse, reverse;
the drunk the sober; the illustrious
the gross; one. In ignorance
a certain knowledge and knowledge,
undispersed, its own undoing.

                (The multiple seed,      30
packed tight with detail, soured,
is lost in the flux and the mind,
distracted, floats off in the same
scum)

Rolling up, rolling up heavy with
numbers.

        It is the ignorant sun
rising in the slot of
hollow suns risen, so that never in this
world will a man live well in his body    *40*
save dying—and not know himself
dying; yet that is
the design. Renews himself
thereby, in addition and subtraction,
walking up and down.

        and the craft,
subverted by thought, rolling up, let
him beware lest he turn to no more than
the writing of stale poems . . .

Minds like beds always made up,
        (more stony than a shore) *50*
unwilling or unable.

        Rolling in, top up,
under, thrust and recoil, a great clatter:
lifted as air, boated, multicolored, a
wash of seas—
from mathematics to particulars—

        divided as the dew,
floating mists, to be rained down and
regathered into a river that flows
and encircles:        *60*

        shells and animalcules
generally and so to man,

        to Paterson.   *(1946)*

# D. H. LAWRENCE / 1885–1930

## Lightning

    I felt the lurch and halt of her heart
      Next my breast, where my own heart was beating;
    And I laughed to feel it plunge and bound,
    And strange in my blood-swept ears was the sound
      Of the words I kept repeating,
    Repeating with tightened arms, and the hot blood's blind-fold art.

    Her breath flew warm against my neck,
      Warm as a flame in the close night air;
    And the sense of her clinging flesh was sweet
    Where her arms and my neck's blood-surge could meet.   *10*
      Holding her thus, did I care
    That the black night hid her from me, blotted out every speck?

    I leaned me forward to find her lips,
      And claim her utterly in a kiss,
    When the lightning flew across her face,
    And I saw her for the flaring space
      Of a second, afraid of the clips
    Of my arms, inert with dread, wilted in fear of my kiss.

    A moment, like a wavering spark,
      Her face lay there before my breast,   *20*
    Pale love lost in a snow of fear,

And guarded by a glittering tear,
   And lips apart with dumb cries;
A moment, and she was taken again in the merciful dark.

I heard the thunder, and felt the rain,
   And my arm fell loose, and I was dumb.
Almost I hated her, she was so good,
Hated myself, and the place, and my blood,
   Which burned with rage, as I bade her come
Home, away home, ere the lightning floated forth again.   *(1913)*   30

## Gloire de Dijon

When she rises in the morning
I linger to watch her;
Spreads the bath-cloth underneath the window
And the sunbeams catch her
Glistening white on the shoulders,
While down her sides the mellow
Golden shadow glows as
She stoops to the sponge, and the swung breasts
Sway like full-blown yellow
Gloire de Dijon roses.                                          10

She drips herself with water, and the shoulders
Glisten as silver, they crumple up
Like wet and falling roses, and I listen
For the sluicing of their rain-dishevelled petals.
In the window full of sunlight
Concentrates her golden shadow
Fold on fold, until it glows as
Mellow as the glory roses.   *(Icking, 1917)*

## Piano

Softly, in the dusk, a woman is singing to me;
Taking me back down the vista of years, till I see
A child sitting under the piano, in the boom of the tingling strings
And pressing the small, poised feet of a mother who smiles as she sings.

In spite of myself, the insidious mastery of song
Betrays me back, till the heart of me weeps to belong
To the old Sunday evenings at home, with winter outside
And hymns in the cozy parlour, the tinkling piano our guide.

So now it is vain for the singer to burst into clamour
With the great black piano appassionato. The glamour          10
Of childish days is upon me, my manhood is cast
Down in the flood of remembrance, I weep like a child for the past.

                                                         *(1918)*

## Snake

A snake came to my water-trough
On a hot, hot day, and I in pyjamas for the heat,
To drink there.

In the deep, strange-scented shade of the great dark carob tree
I came down the steps with my pitcher
And must wait, must stand and wait, for there he was at the trough before
    me.

He reached down from a fissure in the earth-wall in the gloom
And trailed his yellow-brown slackness soft-bellied down, over the edge of
    the stone trough
And rested his throat upon the stone bottom,
And where the water had dripped from the tap, in a small clearness,                    10
He sipped with his straight mouth,
Softly drank through his straight gums, into his slack long body,
Silently.

Someone was before me at my water-trough,
And I, like a second comer, waiting.

He lifted his head from his drinking, as cattle do,
And looked at me vaguely, as drinking cattle do,
And flickered his two-forked tongue from his lips, and mused a moment,
And stooped and drank a little more,
Being earth-brown, earth-golden from the burning bowels of the earth          20
On the day of Sicilian July, with Etna smoking.

The voice of my education said to me
He must be killed,
For in Sicily the black, black snakes are innocent, the gold are venomous.
And voices in me said, If you were a man
You would take a stick and break him now, and finish him off.

But must I confess how I liked him,
How glad I was he had come like a guest in quiet, to drink at my
    water-trough
And depart peaceful, pacified, and thankless,
Into the burning bowels of this earth?                                                30

Was it cowardice, that I dared not kill him?
Was it perversity, that I longed to talk to him?
Was it humility, to feel so honoured?
I felt so honoured.

And yet those voices:
*If you were not afraid, you would kill him!*

And truly I was afraid, I was most afraid,
But even so, honoured still more
That he should seek my hospitality
From out the dark door of the secret earth.                                           40

He drank enough
And lifted his head, dreamily, as one who has drunken,
And flickered his tongue like a forked night on the air, so black,
Seeming to lick his lips,
And looked around like a god, unseeing, into the air,
And slowly turned his head,
And slowly, very slowly, as if thrice adream,
Proceeded to draw his slow length curving round
And climb again the broken bank of my wall-face.

And as he put his head into that dreadful hole,                                    50
And as he slowly drew up, snake-easing his shoulders, and entered farther,
A sort of horror, a sort of protest again his withdrawing into that horrid
    black hole,
Deliberately going into the blackness, and slowly drawing himself after,
Overcame me now his back was turned.

I looked around, I put down my pitcher,
I picked up a clumsy log
And threw it at the water-trough with a clatter.

I think I did not hit him,
But suddenly that part of him that was left behind convulsed in undignified
    haste,
Writhed like lightning, and was gone                                               60
Into the black hole, the earth-lipped fissure in the wall-front,
At which, in the intense still noon, I stared with fascination.

And immediately I regretted it.
I thought how paltry, how vulgar, what a mean act!
I despised myself and the voices of my accursed human education.

And I thought of the albatross,
And I wished he would come back, my snake.

For he seemed to me again like a king,
Like a king in exile, uncrowned in the underworld,
Now due to be crowned again.                                                       70

And so, I missed my chance with one of the lords
Of life.
And I have something to expiate;
A pettiness.   *(1923)*


## Brooding Grief

> A yellow leaf, from the darkness
> Hops like a frog before me;
> Why should I start and stand still?

I was watching the woman that bore me
Stretched in the brindled darkness
Of the sick-room, rigid with will
To die: and the quick leaf tore me
Back to this rainy swill
Of leaves and lamps and the city street mingled before me.  (*1925*)

## When the Ripe Fruit Falls

When the ripe fruit falls
its sweetness distils and trickles away into the veins of the earth.

When fulfilled people die
the essential oil of their experience enters
the veins of living space, and adds a glisten
to the atom, to the body of immortal chaos.

For space is alive
and it stirs like a swan
whose feathers glisten
silky with oil of distilled experience.  (*1929*)                    10

## Bavarian Gentians

Not every man has gentians in his house
In soft September, at slow, sad Michaelmas.

Bavarian gentians, tall and dark, but dark
Darkening the day-time torch-like with the smoking blueness of Pluto's
    gloom
Ribbed hellish flowers erect, with their blaze of darkness spread blue
Blown into points, by the heavy white draught of the day.

Torch-flowers of the blue-smoking darkness, Pluto's dark blue haze
Black lamps from the halls of Dis, smoking dark blue
Giving off darkness, blue darkness, upon Demeter's yellow-pale day
Reach me a gentian, give me a torch!                                 10
Let me guide myself with the blue, forked torch of a flower
Down the darker and darker stairs, where blue is darkened on blueness
Down the way Persephone goes, just now, in first-frosted September
To the sightless realm where darkness is married to dark
And Persephone herself is but a voice, as a bride
A gloom invisible enfolded in the deeper dark
Of the arms of Pluto as he ravishes her once again
And pierces her once more with his passion of the utter dark.

Among the splendour of black-blue torches, shedding fathomless darkness
    on the nuptials.

Give me a flower on a tall stem, and three dark flames,                20
For I will go to the wedding, and be wedding-guest
At the marriage of the living dark.  (*1932*)

## City-Life

When I am in a great city, I know that I despair.
I know there is no hope for us, death waits, it is useless to care.
For oh the poor people, that are flesh of my flesh,
I, that am flesh of their flesh,
when I see the iron hooked into their faces
their poor, their fearful faces
I scream in my soul, for I know I cannot
take the iron hooks out of their faces, that make them so drawn,
nor cut the invisible wires of steel that pull them
back and forth, to work,                                                    *10*
back and forth to work,
like fearful and corpse-like fishes hooked and being played
by some malignant fisherman on an unseen shore
where he does not choose to land them yet, hooked fishes of the factory world.

*(1932)*

## Shadows

And if tonight my soul may find her peace
in sleep, and sink in good oblivion
and in the morning wake like a new-opened flower
then I have been dipped again in God, and new-created.
And if, as weeks go round, in the dark of the moon
my spirit darkens and goes out, and soft strange gloom
pervades my movements and my thoughts and words
then I shall know that I am walking still
with God, we are close together now the moon's in shadow.

And if, as autumn deepens and darkens                                        *10*
I feel the pain of falling leaves, and stems that break in storms
and trouble and dissolution and distress
and then the softness of deep shadows folding, folding
around my soul and spirit, around my lips
so sweet, like a swoon, or more like the drowse of a low, sad song
singing darker than the nightingale, on, on to the solstice
and the silence of short days, the silence of the year, the shadow,
then I shall know that my life is moving still
with the dark earth, and drenched
with the deep oblivion of earth's lapse and renewal.                        *20*

And if, in the changing phases of man's life
I fall in sickness and in misery
my wrists seem broken and my heart seems dead
and strength is gone, and my life
is only the leavings of a life:
and still, among it all, snatches of lovely oblivion, and snatches of renewal
odd, wintry flowers upon the withered stem, yet new, strange flowers
such as my life has not brought forth before, new blossoms of me—

then I must know that still
I am in the hands of the unknown God,                              *30*
he is breaking me down to his own oblivion
to send me forth on a new morning, a new man.   (*1932*)


# EZRA POUND / 1885–1972


## A Virginal

No, no! Go from me. I have left her lately.
I will not spoil my sheath with lesser brightness,
For my surrounding air hath a new lightness;
Slight are her arms, yet they have bound me straitly
And left me cloaked as with a gauze of æther;
As with sweet leaves: as with a subtle clearness.
Oh, I have picked up magic in her nearness
To sheathe me half in half the things that sheathe her.
No, no! Go from me. I have still the flavor,
Soft as spring wind that's come from birchen bowers.     *10*
Green come the shoots, aye April in the branches,
As winter's wound with her sleight hand she staunches,
Hath of the trees a likeness of the savor:
As white their bark, so white this lady's hours.   (*1912*)


## Portrait d'une Femme

Your mind and you are our Sargasso Sea,[1]
London has swept about you this score years
And bright ships left you this or that in fee:
Ideas, old gossip, oddments of all things,
Strange spars of knowledge and dimmed wares of price.
Great minds have sought you—lacking someone else.
You have been second always. Tragical?
No. You preferred it to the usual thing:
One dull man, dulling and uxorious,
One average mind—with one thought less each year.       *10*
Oh, you are patient, I have seen you sit
Hours, where something might have floated up.
And now you pay one. Yes, you richly pay.
You are a person of some interest, one comes to you
And takes strange gain away:
Trophies fished up; some curious suggestion;
Fact that leads nowhere; and a tale or two,

---

[1] an area of relatively quiet water in the Atlantic, full of seaweed and once believed to be a graveyard of ships

Pregnant with mandrakes, or with something else
That might prove useful and yet never proves,
That never fits a corner or shows use,                    20
Or finds its hour upon the loom of days:
The tarnished, gaudy, wonderful old work;
Idols and ambergris and rare inlays,
These are your riches, your great store; and yet
For all this sea-hoard of deciduous things,
Strange woods half sodden, and new brighter stuff;
In the slow float of differing light and deep,
No! there is nothing! In the whole and all,
Nothing that's quite your own.
                        Yet this is you.                    30


## In a Station of the Metro

The apparition of these faces in the crowd;
Petals on a wet, black bough.   (*1916*)


*from* Hugh Selwyn Mauberley

(*LIFE AND CONTACTS*)

*Vocat Æstus in Umbram*[1]—*Nemesianus Ec.
IV*
*E. P. Ode pour l'Election de son Sepulchre*[2]

I

For three years, out of key with his time,
He strove to resuscitate the dead art
Of poetry; to maintain "the sublime"[3]
In the old sense. Wrong from the start—

No, hardly, but seeing he had been born
In a half savage country, out of date;
Bent resolutely on wringing lilies from the
    acorn;
Capaneus;[4] trout for factitious bait;

"Ἴδμεν γάρ τοι πάνθ, ὅσ᾽ ἐνὶ Τροίῃ[5]
Caught in the unstopped ear;                    10
Giving the rocks small lee-way
The chopped sea held him, therefore,
    that year.

His true Penelope was Flaubert,[6]
He fished by obstinate isles;
Observed the elegance of Circe's[7] hair
Rather than the mottoes on sun-dials.

Unaffected by "the march of events,"
He passed from men's memory in *l'an
    trentiesme
De son eage;*[8] the case presents
No adjunct to the Muses' diadem.                    20

II

The age demanded an image
Of its accelerated grimace,

---

[1] Summer calls us into the shade.
[2] Ode for the Choice of His Tomb
[3] a reference to Longinus, *On the Sublime*, a
famous Greek treatise on aesthetics
[4] one of the seven warriors of legend who fought
against Thebes
[5] For we know all that is in Troy.
[6] Penelope was the wife to whom Ulysses was
returning through his ten-years' voyage after
the Trojan War. Gustave Flaubert (1821–1880),
French realistic novelist
[7] witch-enchantress who tried to lure Ulysses
to his destruction
[8] in the thirtieth year of his life; paraphrase of
a line from François Villon, *The Grand Testa-
ment*, implying devotion to the poetic life

Something for the modern stage,
Not, at any rate, an Attic[9] grace;

Not, not certainly, the obscure reveries
Of the inward gaze;
Better mendacities
Than the classics in paraphrase!

The "age demanded" chiefly a mould in
   plaster,
Made with no loss of time,        30
A prose kinema, not, not assuredly,
   alabaster
Or the "sculpture" of rhyme.

### III

The tea-rose tea-gown, etc.
Supplants the mousseline of Cos,[10]
The pianola "replaces"
Sappho's barbitos.[11]

Christ follows Dionysus,[12]
Phallic and ambrosial
Made way for macerations;
Caliban casts out Ariel.[13]       40

All things are a flowing,
Sage Heracleitus says;[14]
But a tawdry cheapness
Shall outlast our days.

Even the Christian beauty
Defects—after Samothrace;[15]
We see τὸ χαλὸν[16]
Decreed in the market place.

Faun's flesh is not to us,
Nor the saint's vision.       50
We have the press for wafer;
Franchise for circumcision.

All men, in law, are equals.
Free of Pisistratus,[17]
We choose a knave or an eunuch
To rule over us.

O bright Apollo,[18]
τίν' ἄνδρα, τίν'ἥρωα, τίνα θεὸν,[19]
What god, man or hero
Shall I place a tin wreath upon!     60

### IV

These fought in any case,
and some believing,
          pro domo,[20] in any
case . . .

Some quick to arm,
some for adventure,
some from fear of weakness,
some from fear of censure,
some for love of slaughter, in imagination,
learning later . . .
some in fear, learning love of
   slaughter;       70

Died some, pro patria,
     non "dulce" non "et decor"[21] . . .
walked eye-deep in hell
believing in old men's lies, then
   unbelieving
came home, home to a lie,
home to many deceits,
home to old lies and new infamy;
usury age-old and age-thick
and liars in public places.

Daring as never before, wastage as never
   before      80
Young blood and high blood,
fair cheeks, and fine bodies;

fortitude as never before,

frankness as never before,
disillusions as never told in the old days,
hysterias, trench confessions,
laughter out of dead bellies.

---

[9] simple, pure, elegant
[10] a cloth like muslin from one of the Dodecanese Islands
[11] Sappho, Greek poetess of the sixth century B.C.; barbitos, lyrelike instruments
[12] Greek god of vegetation and wine
[13] In *The Tempest* Caliban is an evil demon and Ariel is a benevolent sprite.
[14] Greek philosopher who flourished about 500 B.C.

[15] ancient city on an Aegan island of the same name
[16] the beautiful
[17] Athenian tyrant who died in 527 B.C.
[18] god of light, purity, and the arts
[19] what man, what hero, what god
[20] for home
[21] Dulce et decorum est pro patria mori—Horace. (It is sweet and proper to die for one's country.)

v

There died a myriad,
And of the best, among them,
For an old bitch gone in the teeth, 90
For a botched civilization,

Charm, smiling at the good mouth,
Quick eyes gone under earth's lid,

For two gross of broken statues,
For a few thousand battered books.

(*1920*)

## Ancient Music

Winter is icumen in,
Lhude sing Goddamm,
Raineth drop and staineth slop,
And how the wind doth ramm!
    Sing: Goddamm.
Skiddeth bus and sloppeth us,
An ague hath my ham.
Freezeth river, turneth liver,
    Damn you, sing: Goddamm.
Goddamm, Goddamm, 'tis why I am, Goddamm,      *10*
    So 'gainst the winter's balm.
Sing goddamm, damm, sing Goddamm,
Sing goddamm, sing goddamm, DAMM.

## EDWIN MUIR / 1887–1959

## The Mythical Journey

First in the North. The black sea-tangle beaches,
Brine-bitter stillness, tablet strewn morass,
Tall women against the sky with heads covered,
The witch's house below the black-toothed mountain,
Wave-echo in the roofless chapel,
The twice-dead castle on the swamp-green mound,
Darkness at noon-day, wheel of fire at midnight,
The level sun and the wild shooting shadows.

How long ago? Then sailing up to summer
Over the edge of the world. Black hill of water,     *10*
Rivers of running gold. The sun! The sun!
Then the free summer isles.
But the ship hastened on and brought him to
The towering walls of life and the great kingdom.

Where long he wandered seeking that which sought him
Through all the little hills and shallow valleys

Of the green world. One whose form and features,
Race and speech he knew not, shapeless, tongueless,
Known to him only by the impotent heart,
And whether at all on earth the place of meeting,                    20
Beyond all knowledge. Only the little hills,
Head-high, and the winding valleys,
Winding, returning, until there grew a pattern,
And it was held. And there stood each in his station
With the hills between them. And that was the meaning.

   Though sometimes through the wavering light and shadow
He thought he saw it a moment as he watched
The red deer walking by the riverside
At evening, when the bells were ringing,
And the bright stream leapt silent from the mountain                 30
High in the sunset. But as he looked, nothing
Was there but lights and shadows.

   And then the vision
Of the conclusion without fulfilment.
The plain like glass, and in the crystal grave
That which he had sought, that which had sought him
Glittering in death. And all the dead scattered
Like fallen stars, clustered like leaves hanging
From the sad boughs of the mountainous tree of Adam
Planted far down in Eden. And on the hills                           40
The gods reclined and conversed with each other
From summit to summit.

                          Conclusion
Without fulfilment. Thence the dream rose upward,
The living dream sprung from the dying vision,
Overarching all. Beneath its branches
He builds in faith and doubt his shaking house.  *(1937)*


## The Horses

Barely a twelvemonth after
The seven days war that put the world to sleep,
Late in the evening the strange horses came.
By then we had made our covenant with silence,
But in the first few days it was so still
We listened to our breathing and were afraid.
On the second day
The radios failed; we turned the knobs; no answer.
On the third day a warship passed us, heading north,
Dead bodies piled on the deck. On the sixth day                      10
A plane plunged over us into the sea. Thereafter

Nothing. The radios dumb;
And still they stand in corners of our kitchens,
And stand, perhaps, turned on, in a million rooms
All over the world. But now if they should speak,
If on a sudden they should speak again,
If on the stroke of noon a voice should speak,
We would not listen, we would not let it bring
That old bad world that swallowed its children quick
At one great gulp. We would not have it again.                              20
Sometimes we think of the nations lying asleep,
Curled blindly in impenetrable sorrow,
And then the thought confounds us with its strangeness.

The tractors lie about our fields; at evening
They look like dank sea-monsters couched and waiting.
We leave them where they are and let them rust:
"They'll moulder away and be like other loam."
We make our oxen drag our rusty ploughs,
Long laid aside. We have gone back
Far past our fathers' land.
                            And then, that evening                            30
Late in the summer the strange horses came.
We heard a distant tapping on the road,
A deepening drumming; it stopped, went on again
And at the corner changed to hollow thunder.
We saw the heads
Like a wild wave charging and were afraid.
We had sold our horses in our fathers' time
To buy new tractors. Now they were strange to us
As fabulous steeds set on an ancient shield
Or illustrations in a book of knights.                                       40
We did not dare go near them. Yet they waited,
Stubborn and shy, as if they had been sent
By an old command to find our whereabouts
And that long-lost archaic companionship.
In the first moment we had never a thought
That they were creatures to be owned and used.
Among them were some half-a-dozen colts
Dropped in some wilderness of the broken world,
Yet new as if they had come from their own Eden.
Since then they have pulled our ploughs and borne our loads,                 50
But that free servitude still can pierce our hearts.
Our life is changed; their coming our beginning.  (*1952*)

# ROBINSON JEFFERS / 1887–1962

## To the Stone-Cutters

Stone-cutters fighting time with marble, you fore-defeated
Challengers of oblivion
Eat cynical earnings, knowing rock splits, records fall down,
The square-limbed Roman letters
Scale in the thaws, wear in the rain. The poet as well
Builds his monument mockingly;
For man will be blotted out, the blithe earth die, the brave sun
Die blind and blacken to the heart:
Yet stones have stood for a thousand years, and pained thoughts found
The honey of peace in old poems.  (*c. 1922*)                    10

## Shine, Perishing Republic

While this America settles in the mould of its vulgarity, heavily thickening to
    empire,
And protest, only a bubble in the molten mass, pops and sighs out, and the mass
    hardens,
I sadly smiling remember that the flower fades to make fruit, the fruit rots to
    make earth.
Out of the mother; and through the spring exultances, ripeness and decadence;
    and home to the mother.
You making haste haste on decay: not blameworthy; life is good, be it stubbornly
    long or suddenly
A mortal splendor: meteors are not needed less than mountains: shine, perishing
    republic.
But for my children, I would have them keep their distance from the thickening
    center; corruption
Never has been compulsory, when the cities lie at the monster's feet there are left
    the mountains.
And boys, be in nothing so moderate as in love of man, a clever servant, in-
    sufferable master.
There is the trap that catches noblest spirits, that caught—they say,—God, when
    he walked on earth.  (*1925*)                    10

## Apology for Bad Dreams

### I

In the purple light, heavy with redwood, the slopes drop seaward,
Headlong convexities of forest, drawn in together to the steep ravine. Below, on
    the sea-cliff,

A lonely clearing; a little field of corn by the streamside; a roof under spared
    trees. Then the ocean
Like a great stone someone has cut to a sharp edge and polished to shining. Beyond
    it, the fountain
And furnace of incredible light flowing up from the sunk sun. In the little clearing
    a woman
Is punishing a horse; she had tied the halter to a sapling at the edge of the wood,
    but when the great whip
Clung to the flanks the creature kicked so hard she feared he would snap the
    halter; she called from the house
The young man her son; who fetched a chain tie-rope, they working together
Noosed the small rusty links round the horse's tongue
And tied him by the swollen tongue to the tree.                                                    *10*
Seen from this height they are shrunk to insect size,
Out of all human relation. You cannot distinguish
The blood dripping from where the chain is fastened,
The beast shuddering; but the thrust neck and the legs
Far apart. You can see the whip fall on the flanks. . . .
The gesture of the arm. You cannot see the face of the woman.
The enormous light beats up out of the west across the cloud-bars of the trade-
    wind. The ocean
Darkens, the high clouds brighten, the hills darken together. Unbridled and
    unbelievable beauty
Covers the evening world . . . not covers, grows apparent out of it, as Venus down
    there grows out
From the lit sky. What said the prophet? "I create good; and I create evil: I am
    the Lord."                                                                                                   *20*

II

This coast crying out for tragedy like all beautiful places,
(The quiet ones ask for quieter suffering; but here the granite cliff the gaunt
    cypresses' crown
Demands what victim? The dykes of red lava and black what Titan? The hills
    like pointed flames
Beyond Soberanes,[1] the terrible peaks of the bare hills under the sun, what
    immolation?)
This coast crying out for tragedy like all beautiful places: and like the passionate
    spirit of humanity
Pain for its bread: God's, many victims', the painful deaths, the horrible disfigure-
    ments: I said in my heart,
"Better invent than suffer: imagine victims
Lest your own flesh be chosen the agonist, or you
Martyr some creature to the beauty of the place." And I said,
"Burn sacrifices once a year to magic                                                              *30*
Horror away from the house, this little house here
You have built over the ocean with your own hands
Beside the standing boulders: for what are we,

---

[1] This and other place names mentioned refer to the California coastal region around Jeffers' home at
Point Sur.

The beast that walks upright, with speaking lips
And little hair, to think we should always be fed,
Sheltered, intact, and self-controlled? We sooner more liable
Than the other animals. Pain and terror, the insanities of desire; not accidents
    but essential,
And crowd up from the core." I imagined victims for those wolves, I made them
    phantoms to follow.
They have hunted the phantoms and missed the house. It is not good to forget
    over what gulfs the spirit
Of the beauty of humanity, the petal of a lost flower blown seaward by the night-
    wind, floats to its quietness.                                                            40

### III

Boulders blunted like an old bear's teeth break up from the headland; below
    them
All the soil is thick with shells, the tide-rock feasts of a dead people.
Here the granite flanks are scarred with ancient fire, the ghosts of the tribe
Crouch in the nights beside the ghost of a fire, they try to remember the sun-
    light,
Light has died out of their skies. These have paid something for the future
Luck of the country, while we living keep old griefs in memory: though God's
Envy is not a likely fountain of ruin, to forget evils calls down
Sudden reminders from the cloud: remembered deaths be our redeemers;
Imagined victims our salvation; white as the half moon at midnight
Someone flamelike passed me, saying, "I am Tamar Cauldwell,[2] I have my
    desire,"                                                                                    50
Then the voice of the sea returned, when she had gone by, the stars to their
    towers.
. . . Beautiful country, burn again, Point Pinos down to the Sur Rivers
Burn as before with bitter wonders, land and ocean and the Carmel water.

### IV

He brays humanity in a mortar to bring the savor
From the bruised root: a man having bad dreams, who invents victims, is only
    the ape of that God.
He washes it out with tears and many waters, calcines it with fire in the red
    crucible,
Deforms it, makes it horrible to itself: the spirit flies out and stands naked, he
    sees the spirit.
He takes it in the naked ecstasy; it breaks in his hand, the atom is broken, the
    power that massed it
Cries to the power that moves the stars, "I have come home to myself, behold
    me.
I bruised myself in the flint mortar and burnt me                                           60
In the red shell, I tortured myself, I flew forth,
Stood naked of myself and broke me in fragments,
And here am I moving the stars that are me."

---

[2] protagonist of Jeffers' long narrative poem, *Tamar*

I have seen these ways of God: I know of no reason
For fire and change and torture and the old returnings.
He being sufficient might be still. I think they admit no reason; they are the ways
of my love.
Unmeasured power, incredible passion, enormous craft; no thought apparent
but burns darkly
Smothered with its own smoke in the human brain-vault: no thought outside:
a certain measure in phenomena:
The fountains of the boiling stars, the flowers on the forehand, the ever-returning
roses of dawn. (*1926*)


## Hurt Hawks

### I

The broken pillar of the wing jags from the clotted shoulder,
The wing trails like a banner in defeat,
No more to use the sky forever but live with famine
And pain a few days: cat nor coyote
Will shorten the week of waiting for death, there is game without talons.
He stands under the oak-bush and waits
The lame feet of salvation; at night he remembers freedom
And flies in a dream, the dawns ruin it.
He is strong and pain is worse to the strong, incapacity is worse.
The curs of the day come and torment him                                    10
At distance, no one but death the redeemer will humble that head,
The intrepid readiness, the terrible eyes.
The wild God of the world is sometimes merciful to those
That ask mercy, not often to the arrogant.
You do not know him, you communal people, or you have forgotten him;
Intemperate and savage, the hawk remembers him;
Beautiful and wild, the hawks, and men that are dying, remember him.

### II

I'd sooner, except the penalties, kill a man than a hawk, but the great redtail
Had nothing left but unable misery
From the bone too shattered for mending, the wing that trailed under his talons
when he moved.                                                               20
We had fed him six weeks, I gave him freedom,
He wandered over the foreland hill and returned in the evening, asking for
death,
Not like a begger, still eyed with the old
Implacable arrogance. I gave him the lead gift in the twilight. What fell was
relaxed,
Owl-downy, soft feminine feathers; but what
Soared: the fierce rush: the night-herons by the flooded river cried fear at its
rising
Before it was quite unsheathed from reality. (*1928*)

## Ocean

The gray whales are going south: I see their fountains
Rise from black sea: great dark bulks of hot blood
Plowing the deep cold sea to their trysting-place
Off Mexican California, where water is warm, and love
Finds massive joy: from the flukes to the blowhole the whole giant
Flames like a star. In February storm the ocean
Is black and rainbowed; the high spouts of white spray
Rise and fall over in the wind.There is no April in the ocean;
How do these creatures know that spring is at hand?
    They remember their ancestors
That crawled on earth: the little fellows like otters, who took to sea          10
And have grown great. Go out to the ocean, little ones,
You will grow great or die.
                And there the small trout
Flicker in the streams that tumble from the coast mountain,
Little quick flames of life: but from time to time
One of them goes mad, wanting room and freedom; he slips between the rock
    jaws
And takes to sea, where from time immemorial
The long sharks wait. If he lives he becomes a steelhead,
A rainbow trout grown beyond nature in the ocean. Go out to the great ocean,
Grow great or die.
            O ambitious children,
It would be wiser no doubt to rest in the brook          20
And remain little. But if the devil drives
I hope you will scull far out to the wide ocean and find your fortune, and beware
    of teeth.
It is not important. There are deeps you will never reach and peaks you will never
    explore,
Where the great squids and kraken lie in the gates, in the awful twilight
The whip-armed hungers; and mile under mile below,
Deep under deep, on the deep floor, in the darkness
Under the weight of the world: like lighted galleons the ghost-fish,
With phosphorescent portholes along their flanks,
Sail over and eat each other: the condition of life,
To eat each other: but in the slime below          30
Prodigious worms as great and as slow as glaciers burrow in the sediment,
Mindless and blind, huge tubes of muddy flesh
Sucking not meat but carrion, drippings and offal
From the upper sea. They move a yard in a year,
Where there are no years, no sun, no seasons, darkness and slime;
They spend nothing on action, all on gross flesh.
                    O ambitious ones,
Will you grow great, or die? It hardly matters; the words are comparative;
Greatness is but less little; and death's changed life. (*1954*)

## But I Am Growing Old and Indolent

I have been warned. It is more than thirty years since I wrote—
Thinking of the narrative poems I made, which always
Ended in blood and pain, though beautiful enough—my pain, my blood,
They were my creatures—I understood, and wrote to myself:
"Make sacrifices once a year to magic
Horror away from the house"—for that hangs imminent
Over all men and all houses—"This little house here
You have built over the ocean with your own hands
Beside the standing sea-boulders . . ." So I listened
To my Demon warning me that evil would come                              *10*
If my work ceased, if I did not make sacrifice
Of storied and imagined lives, Tamar and Cawdor
And Thurso's wife—"imagined victims be our redeemers"—
At that time I was sure of my fates and felt
My poems guarding the house, well-made watchdogs
Ready to bite.
                But time sucks out the juice,
A man grows old and indolent.  *(1963)*

# MARIANNE MOORE / 1887–1972

## Poetry

I, too, dislike it: there are things that are important beyond all this fiddle.
  Reading it, however, with a perfect contempt for it, one discovers in
  it after all, a place for the genuine.
     Hands that can grasp, eyes
       that can dilate, hair that can rise
         if it must, these things are important not because a

high-sounding interpretation can be put upon them but because they are
  useful. When they become so derivative as to become unintelligible,
  the same thing may be said for all of us, that we
     do not admire what                                                    *10*
       we cannot understand: the bat
         holding on upside down or in quest of something to

eat, elephants pushing, a wild horse taking a roll, a tireless wolf under
  a tree, the immovable critic twitching his skin like a horse that feels a flea,
      the base-
  ball fan, the statistician—
     nor is it valid
       to discriminate against "business documents and

school-books";[1] all these phenomena are important. One must make a
    distinction
  however: when dragged into prominence by half poets, the result is not
    poetry,
nor till the poets among us can be                                                    20
  "literalists of
  the imagination"[2]—above
    insolence and triviality and can present

for inspection, "imaginary gardens with real toads in them," shall we have
  it. In the meantime, if you demand on the one hand,
  the raw material of poetry in
    all its rawness and
    that which is on the other hand
      genuine, you are interested in poetry.   (1921)


## To a Steam Roller

    The illustration
  is nothing to you without the application.
    You lack half wit. You crush all the particles down
      into close conformity, and then walk back and forth on them.

    Sparkling chips of rock
  are crushed down to the level of the parent block.
    Were not "impersonal judgment in aesthetic
      matters, a metaphysical impossibility," you

    might fairly achieve
  it. As for butterflies, I can hardly conceive                                 10
    of one's attending upon you, but to question
      the congruence of the complement is vain, if it exists.   (1924)


## The Steeple-Jack

    Dürer[1] would have seen a reason for living
    in a town like this, with eight stranded whales
  to look at; with the sweet sea air coming into your house
  on a fine day, from water etched
    with waves as formal as the scales
  on a fish.

    One by one, in two's, in three's, the seagulls keep
    flying back and forth over the town clock,
    or sailing around the lighthouse without moving their wings—

---

[1] a quotation from Tolstoi, who had written,
". . . poetry is everything with the exception of
business documents and school-books"
[2] a quotation from Yeats, who characterizes Blake

as a "too literal realist of the imagination"
[1] Albrecht Dürer (1471–1528), German artist in
oils, woodcuts, and etchings, noted for meticulous
detail

rising steadily with a slight
    quiver of the body—or flock
mewing where

a sea the purple of the peacock's neck is
    paled to greenish azure as Dürer changed
the pine green of the Tyrol to peacock blue and guinea
grey. You can see a twenty-five-
    pound lobster and fishnets arranged
to dry. The

whirlwind fife-and-drum of the storm bends the salt
    marsh grass, disturbs stars in the sky and the
star on the steeple; it is a privilege to see so
much confusion.

            A steeple-jack in red, has let
    a rope down as a spider spins a thread;
he might be part of a novel, but on the sidewalk a
sign says C. J. Poole, Steeple-Jack,
    in black and white; and one in red
and white says

Danger. The church portico has four fluted
    columns, each a single piece of stone, made
modester by white-wash. This would be a fit haven for
waifs, children, animals, prisoners,
    and presidents who have repaid
sin-driven

senators by not thinking about them. One
    sees a school-house, a post-office in a
store, fish-houses, hen-houses, a three-masted schooner on
the stocks. The hero, the student,
    the steeple-jack, each in his way,
is at home.

It scarcely could be dangerous to be living
    in a town like this, of simple people
who have a steeple-jack placing danger-signs by the
        church
when he is gilding the solid-
    pointed star, which on a steeple
stands for hope.   (*1935*)


## Bird-Witted

           With innocent wide penguin eyes, three
              large fledgling mockingbirds below
           the pussy-willow tree,
              stand in a row,

wings touching, feebly solemn,
till they see
    their no longer larger
    mother bringing
something which will partially
feed one of them.                                                    *10*

Toward the high-keyed intermittent squeak
   of broken carriage springs, made by
the three similar, meek-
    coated bird's-eye
freckled forms she comes; and when
from the beak
    of one, the still living
    beetle has dropped
out, she picks it up and puts
it in again.                                                         *20*

Standing in the shade till they have dressed
   their thickly filamented, pale
pussy-willow-surfaced
   coats, they spread tail
and wings, showing one by one,
the modest
    white stripe lengthwise on the
    tail and crosswise
underneath the wing, and the
accordion                                                            *30*

is closed again. What delightful note
   with rapid unexpected flute
sounds leaping from the throat
   of the astute
grown bird, comes back to one from
the remote
    unenergetic sun-
    lit air before
the brood was here? How harsh
the bird's voice has become.                                         *40*

A piebald cat observing them,
   is slowly creeping toward the trim
trio on the tree stem.
   Unused to him
the three make room—uneasy
new problem.
    A dangling foot that missed
    its grasp, is raised
and finds the twig on which it
planned to perch. The                                                *50*

parent darting down, nerved by what chills
    the blood, and by hope rewarded—
of toil—since nothing fills
    squeaking unfed
mouths, wages deadly combat,
and half kills
    with bayonet beak and
    cruel wings, the
intellectual cautious-
ly creeping cat.  (*1941*)

60

# T. S. ELIOT / 1888–1965

## The Love Song of J. Alfred Prufrock

*S'io credesse che mia risposta fosse
A persona che mai tornasse al mondo,
Questa fiamma staria senza piu scosse.
Ma perciocche giammai di questo fondo
Non torno vivo alcun, s'i'odo il vero,
Senza tema d'infamia ti rispondo.*[1]

Let us go then, you and I,
When the evening is spread out against the sky
Like a patient etherised upon a table;
Let us go, through certain half-deserted streets,
The muttering retreats
Of restless nights in one-night cheap hotels
And sawdust restaurants with oyster-shells:
Streets that follow like a tedious argument
Of insidious intent
To lead you to an overwhelming question . . .
Oh, do not ask, "What is it?"
Let us go and make our visit.

In the room the women come and go
Talking of Michelangelo.

The yellow fog that rubs its back upon the window-panes,
The yellow smoke that rubs its muzzle on the window-panes
Licked its tongue into the corners of the evening,
Lingered upon the pools that stand in drains,
Let fall upon its back the soot that falls from chimneys,

10

---

[1] Dante, *Inferno*, XXVII, ll. 61–66: "If I thought that my answer were directed to anyone who could ever return to the world, this flame would quiver no longer; but because, as I hear, no one ever returns alive from this depth, I reply to you without fear of infamy."

Slipped by the terrace, made a sudden leap,                                    20
And seeing that it was a soft October night,
Curled once about the house, and fell asleep.

And indeed there will be time
For the yellow smoke that slides along the street
Rubbing its back upon the window-panes;
There will be time, there will be time
To prepare a face to meet the faces that you meet;
There will be time to murder and create,
And time for all the works and days of hands
That lift and drop a question on your plate;                                    30
Time for you and time for me,
And time yet for a hundred indecisions,
And for a hundred visions and revisions,
Before the taking of a toast and tea.

In the room the women come and go
Talking of Michelangelo.

And indeed there will be time
To wonder, "Do I dare?" and, "Do I dare?"
Time to turn back and descend the stair,
With a bald spot in the middle of my hair—                                     40
(They will say: "How his hair is growing thin!")
My morning coat, my collar mounting firmly to the chin,
My necktie rich and modest, but asserted by a simple pin—
(They will say: "But how his arms and legs are thin!")
Do I dare
Disturb the universe?
In a minute there is time
For decisions and revisions which a minute will reverse.

For I have known them all already, known them all—
Have known the evenings, mornings, afternoons,                                 50
I have measured out my life with coffee spoons;
I know the voices dying with a dying fall
Beneath the music from a farther room.
     So how should I presume?

And I have known the eyes already, known them all—
The eyes that fix you in a formulated phrase,
And when I am formulated, sprawling on a pin,
When I am pinned and wriggling on the wall,
Then how should I begin
To spit out all the butt-ends of my days and ways?                            60
     And how should I presume?

And I have known the arms already, known them all—
Arms that are braceleted and white and bare
(But in the lamplight, downed with light brown hair!)
Is it perfume from a dress

That makes me so digress?
Arms that lie along a table, or wrap about a shawl.
   And should I then presume?
   And how should I begin?

                                        .    .    .

Shall I say, I have gone at dusk through narrow streets                          70
And watched the smoke that rises from the pipes
Of lonely men in shirt-sleeves, leaning out of windows?...

I should have been a pair of ragged claws
Scuttling across the floors of silent seas.

                                        .    .    .

And the afternoon, the evening, sleep so peacefully!
Smoothed by long fingers,
Asleep . . . tired . . . or it malingers,
Stretched on the floor, here beside you and me.
Should I, after tea and cakes and ices,
Have the strength to force the moment to its crisis?                             80
But though I have wept and fasted, wept and prayed,
Though I have seen my head (grown slightly bald) brought in upon a platter,[2]
I am no prophet—and here's no great matter;
I have seen the moment of my greatness flicker,
And I have seen the eternal Footman hold my coat, and snicker,
And in short, I was afraid.

And would it have been worth it, after all,
After the cups, the marmalade, the tea,
Among the porcelain, among some talk of you and me,
Would it have been worth while,                                                  90
To have bitten off the matter with a smile,
To have squeezed the universe into a ball
To roll it toward some overwhelming question,
To say: "I am Lazarus,[3] come from the dead,
Come back to tell you all, I shall tell you all"—
If one, settling a pillow by her head,
   Should say: "That is not what I meant at all;
   That is not it, at all."

And would it have been worth it, after all,
Would it have been worth while,                                                 100
After the sunsets and the dooryards and the sprinkled streets,
After the novels, after the teacups, after the skirts that trail along the floor—
And this, and so much more?—
It is impossible to say just what I mean!
But as if a magic lantern threw the nerves in patterns on a screen:
Would it have been worth while
If one, settling a pillow or throwing off a shawl,
And turning toward the window, should say:

---

[2] John the Baptist was beheaded at the insistence of Salome, to whom his head was delivered on a platter. See Matthew 14:3–11 or Mark 6:16–28.

[3] One of the miracles of Jesus was the raising of Lazarus from the dead after he had lain in the grave four days. See John 11:1–44.

"That is not it at all,
That is not what I meant, at all."                                      *110*

No! I am not Prince Hamlet, nor was meant to be;
Am an attendant lord, one that will do
To swell a progress, start a scene or two,
Advise the prince; no doubt, an easy tool,
Deferential, glad to be of use,
Politic, cautious, and meticulous;
Full of high sentence,[4] but a bit obtuse;
At times, indeed, almost ridiculous—
Almost, at times, the Fool.

I grow old . . . I grow old . . .                                       *120*
I shall wear the bottoms of my trousers rolled.

Shall I part my hair behind? Do I dare to eat a peach?
I shall wear white flannel trousers, and walk upon the beach.
I have heard the mermaids singing, each to each.

I do not think that they will sing to me.

I have seen them riding seaward on the waves
Combing the white hair of the waves blown back
When the wind blows the water white and black.

We have lingered in the chambers of the sea
By sea-girls wreathed with seaweed red and brown                        *130*
Till human voices wake us, and we drown.   *(1917)*


## Preludes

### I

The winter evening settles down
With smell of steaks in passageways.
Six o'clock.
The burnt-out ends of smoky days.
And now a gusty shower wraps
The grimy scraps
Of withered leaves about your feet
And newspapers from vacant lots;
The showers beat
On broken blinds and chimney-pots,                                      *10*
And at the corner of the street
A lonely cab-horse steams and stamps.
And then the lighting of the lamps.

---

[4] *sententia,* wise sayings

## II

The morning comes to consciousness
Of faint stale smells of beer
From the sawdust-trampled street
With all its muddy feet that press
To early coffee-stands.
With the other masquerades
That time resumes,                                              20
One thinks of all the hands
That are raising dingy shades
In a thousand furnished rooms.

## III

You tossed a blanket from the bed,
You lay upon your back, and waited;
You dozed, and watched the night revealing
The thousand sordid images
Of which your soul was constituted;
They flickered against the ceiling.
And when all the world came back                               30
And the light crept up between the shutters
And you heard the sparrows in the gutters,
You had such a vision of the street
As the street hardly understands;
Sitting along the bed's edge, where
You curled the papers from your hair,
Or clasped the yellow soles of feet
In the palms of both soiled hands.

## IV

His soul stretched tight across the skies
That fade behind a city block,                                 40
Or trampled by insistent feet
At four and five and six o'clock;
And short square fingers stuffing pipes,
And evening newspapers, and eyes
Assured of certain certainties,
The conscience of a blackened street
Impatient to assume the world.

I am moved by fancies that are curled
Around these images, and cling:
The notion of some infinitely gentle                           50
Infinitely suffering thing.

Wipe your hand across your mouth, and laugh;
The worlds revolve like ancient women
Gathering fuel in vacant lots.   (*1917*)

## Journey of the Magi

"A cold coming we had of it,
Just the worst time of the year
For a journey, and such a long journey:
The ways deep and the weather sharp,
The very dead of winter."
And the camels galled, sore-footed, refractory,
Lying down in the melting snow.
There were times we regretted
The summer palaces on slopes, the terraces,
And the silken girls bringing sherbet.                                    10
Then the camel men cursing and grumbling
And running away, and wanting their liquor and women,
And the night-fires going out, and the lack of shelters,
And the cities hostile and the towns unfriendly
And the villages dirty and charging high prices:
A hard time we had of it.
At the end we preferred to travel all night,
Sleeping in snatches,
With the voices singing in our ears, saying
That this was all folly.                                    20

Then at dawn we came down to a temperate valley,
Wet, below the snow line, smelling of vegetation;
With a running stream and a water-mill beating the darkness,
And three trees on the low sky,
And an old white horse galloped away in the meadow.
Then we came to a tavern with vine-leaves over the lintel,
Six hands at an open door dicing for pieces of silver,
And feet kicking the empty wine-skins.
But there was no information, and so we continued
And arrived at evening, not a moment too soon                                    30
Finding the place; it was (you may say) satisfactory.

All this was a long time ago, I remember,
And I would do it again, but set down
This set down
This: were we led all that way for
Birth or Death? There was a Birth, certainly,
We had evidence and no doubt. I had seen birth and death,
But had thought they were different; this Birth was
Hard and bitter agony for us, like Death, our death.
We returned to our places, these Kingdoms,                                    40
But no longer at ease here, in the old dispensation,
With an alien people clutching their gods.
I should be glad of another death.   (*1927*)

# Burnt Norton

τοῦ λόγου δ'ἐόντος ξυνοῦ ζώουσιν οἱ πολλοί
ὡς ἰδίαν ἔχοντες φρόνησιν.
                                    *I. p. 77. Fr. 2*
ὁδὸς ἄνω κάτω μία καὶ ὡυτή.
                                    *I. p. 89. Fr. 60*
Diels: *Die Fragmente der Vorsokratiker* (Herakleitos).

I

Time present and time past
Are both perhaps present in time future,
And time future contained in time past.
If all time is eternally present
All time is unredeemable.
What might have been is an abstraction
Remaining a perpetual possibility
Only in a world of speculation.
What might have been and what has been
Point to one end, which is always present.                10
Footfalls echo in the memory
Down the passage which we did not take
Towards the door we never opened
Into the rose-garden. My words echo
Thus, in your mind.
                    But to what purpose
Disturbing the dust on a bowl of rose-leaves
I do not know.
                    Other echoes
Inhabit the garden. Shall we follow?
Quick, said the bird, find them, find them,
Round the corner. Through the first gate,
Into our first world, shall we follow                     20
The deception of the thrush? Into our first world.
There they were, dignified, invisible,
Moving without pressure, over the dead leaves,
In the autumn heat, through the vibrant air,
And the bird called, in response to
The unheard music hidden in the shrubbery,
And the unseen eyebeam crossed, for the roses
Had the look of flowers that are looked at.
There they were as our guests, accepted and accepting.    30
So we moved, and they, in a formal pattern,
Along the empty alley, into the box circle,
To look down into the drained pool.
Dry the pool, dry concrete, brown edged,
And the pool was filled with water out of sunlight,
And the lotos rose, quietly, quietly,
The surface glittered out of heart of light,

And they were behind us, reflected in the pool.
Then a cloud passed, and the pool was empty.
Go, said the bird, for the leaves were full of children,                    *40*
Hidden excitedly, containing laughter.
Go, go, go, said the bird: human kind
Cannot bear very much reality.
Time past and time future
What might have been and what has been
Point to one end, which is always present.

II

Garlic and sapphires in the mud
Clot the bedded axle-tree.
The trilling wire in the blood
Sings below inveterate scars                    *50*
And reconciles forgotten wars.
The dance along the artery
The circulation of the lymph
Are figured in the drift of stars
Ascend to summer in the tree
We move above the moving tree
In light upon the figured leaf
And hear upon the sodden floor
Below, the boarhound and the boar
Pursue their pattern as before                    *60*
But reconciled among the stars.

At the still point of the turning world. Neither flesh nor fleshless;
Neither from nor towards; at the still point, there the dance is,
But neither arrest nor movement. And do not call it fixity,
Where past and future are gathered. Neither movement from nor towards,
Neither ascent nor decline. Except for the point, the still point,
There would be no dance, and there is only the dance.
I can only say, *there* we have been: but I cannot say where.
And I cannot say, how long, for that is to place it in time.

The inner freedom from the practical desire,                    *70*
The release from action and suffering, release from the inner
And the outer compulsion, yet surrounded
By a grace of sense, a white light still and moving,
*Erhebung*[1] without motion, concentration
Without elimination, both a new world
And the old made explicit, understood
In the completion of its partial ecstasy,
The resolution of its partial horror.
Yet the enchainment of past and future
Woven in the weakness of the changing body,                    *80*
Protects mankind from heaven and damnation

---

[1] elevation

Which flesh cannot endure.

                 Time past and time future
Allow but a little consciousness.
To be conscious is not to be in time
But only in time can the moment in the rose-garden,
The moment in the arbour where the rain beat,
The moment in the draughty church at smokefall
Be remembered; involved with past and future.
Only through time time is conquered.

III

Here is a place of disaffection                        *90*
Time before and time after
In a dim light: neither daylight
Investing form with lucid stillness
Turning shadow into transient beauty
With slow rotation suggesting permanence
Nor darkness to purify the soul
Emptying the sensual with deprivation
Cleansing affection from the temporal.
Neither plenitude nor vacancy. Only a flicker
Over the strained time-ridden faces                  *100*
Distracted from distraction by distraction
Filled with fancies and empty of meaning
Tumid apathy with no concentration
Men and bits of paper, whirled by the cold wind
That blows before and after time,
Wind in and out of unwholesome lungs
Time before and time after.
Eructation of unhealthy souls
Into the faded air, the torpid
Driven on the wind that sweeps the gloomy hills of London,     *110*
Hampstead and Clerkenwell, Campden and Putney,
Highgate, Primrose and Ludgate.[2] Not here
Not here the darkness, in this twittering world.

    Descend lower, descend only
Into the world of perpetual solitude,
World not world, but that which is not world.
Internal darkness, deprivation
And destitution of all property,
Desiccation of the world of sense,
Evacuation of the world of fancy,                   *120*
Inoperancy of the world of spirit;
This is the one way, and the other
Is the same, not in movement
But abstention from movement; while the world moves
In appetency, on its metalled ways
Of time past and time future.

---

[2] regions of London

IV

Time and the bell have buried the day,
The black cloud carries the sun away.
Will the sunflower turn to us, will the clematis
Stray down, bend to us; tendril and spray                     130
Clutch and cling?
Chill
Fingers of yew be curled
Down on us? After the kingfisher's wing
Has answered light to light, and is silent, the light is still
At the still point of the turning world.

V

Words move, music moves
Only in time; but that which is only living
Can only die. Words, after speech, reach
Into the silence. Only by the form, the pattern,            140
Can words or music reach
The stillness, as a Chinese jar still
Moves perpetually in its stillness.
Not the stillness of the violin, while the note lasts,
Not that only, but the co-existence,
Or say that the end precedes the beginning,
And the end and the beginning were always there
Before the beginning and after the end.
And all is always now. Words strain,
Crack and sometimes break, under the burden,               150
Under the tension, slip, slide, perish,
Decay with imprecision, will not stay in place,
Will not stay still. Shrieking voices
Scolding, mocking, or merely chattering,
Always assail them. The Word in the desert
Is most attacked by voices of temptation,
The crying shadow in the funeral dance,
The loud lament of the disconsolate chimera.

    The detail of the pattern is movement,
As in the figure of the ten stairs.                         160
Desire itself is movement
Not in itself desirable;
Love is itself unmoving,
Only the cause and end of movement,
Timeless, and undesiring
Except in the aspect of time
Caught in the form of limitation
Between un-being and being.
Sudden in a shaft of sunlight
Even while the dust moves                                    170
There rises the hidden laughter

Of children in the foliage
Quick now, here, now, always—
Ridiculous the waste sad time
Stretching before and after.   (*1935*)


## Macavity: The Mystery Cat

Macavity's a Mystery Cat: he's called the Hidden Paw—
For he's the master criminal who can defy the Law.
He's the bafflement of Scotland Yard, the Flying Squad's despair:
For when they reach the scene of crime—*Macavity's not there!*

Macavity, Macavity, there's no one like Macavity,
He's broken every human law, he breaks the law of gravity.
His powers of levitation would make a fakir stare,
And when you reach the scene of crime—*Macavity's not there!*
You may seek him in the basement, you may look up in the air—
But I tell you once and once again, *Macavity's not there!*                    10

Macavity's a ginger cat, he's very tall and thin;
You would know him if you saw him, for his eyes are sunken in.
His brow is deeply lined with thought, his head is highly domed;
His coat is dusty from neglect, his whiskers are uncombed.
He sways his head from side to side, with movements like a snake;
And when you think he's half asleep, he's always wide awake.

Macavity, Macavity, there's no one like Macavity,
For he's a fiend in feline shape, a monster of depravity.
You may meet him in a by-street, you may see him in the square—
But when a crime's discovered, then *Macavity's not there!*                     20

He's outwardly respectable. (They say he cheats at cards.)
And his footprints are not found in any file of Scotland Yard's.
And when the larder's looted, or the jewel-case is rifled,
Or when the milk is missing, or another Peke's been stifled,
Or the greenhouse glass is broken, and the trellis past repair—
Ay, there's the wonder of the thing! *Macavity's not there!*

And when the Foreign Office find a Treaty's gone astray,
Or the Admiralty lose some plans and drawings by the way,
There may be a scrap of paper in the hall or on the stair—
But it's useless to investigate—*Macavity's not there!*                        30
And when the loss has been disclosed, the Secret Service say:
"It *must* have been Macavity!"—but he's a mile away.
You'll be sure to find him resting, or a-licking of his thumbs,
Or engaged in doing complicated long division sums.

Macavity, Macavity, there's no one like Macavity,
There never was a Cat of such deceitfulness and suavity.
He always has an alibi, and one or two to spare:
At whatever time the deed took place—MACAVITY WASN'T THERE!

And they say that all the Cats whose wicked deeds are widely known
(I might mention Mungojerrie, I might mention Griddlebone)                    40
Are nothing more than agents for the Cat who all the time
Just controls their operations: the Napoleon of Crime! (*1939*)


## JOHN CROWE RANSOM / 1888–

### Bells for Whiteside's Daughter

There was such speed in her little body,
And such lightness in her footfall,
It is no wonder her brown study
Astonishes us all.

Her wars were bruited in our high
    window.
We looked among orchard trees and
    beyond,
Where she took arms against her shadow,
Or harried unto the pond

The lazy geese, like a snow cloud
Dripping their snow on the green
    grass,                                                    10
Tricking and stopping, sleepy and proud,
Who cried in goose, Alas,

For the tireless heart within the little
Lady with rod that made them rise
From their noon apple-dreams and scuttle
Goose-fashion under the skies!

But now go the bells, and we are ready,
In one house we are sternly stopped
To say we are vexed at her brown study,
Lying so primly propped. (*1924*)            20


### Philomela

Procne, Philomela, and Itylus,[1]
Your names are liquid, your improbable tale
Is recited in the classic numbers of the nightingale.
Ah, but our numbers are not felicitous,
It goes not liquidly for us.

Perched on a Roman ilex,[2] and duly apostrophized,
The nightingale descanted unto Ovid;[3]
She has even appeared to the Teutons, the swilled and gravid;
At Fontainbleau it may be the bird was gallicized;
Never was she baptized.                                              10

To England came Philomela with her pain,
Fleeing the hawk her husband; querulous ghost,
She wanders when he sits heavy on his roost,
Utters herself in the original again,
The untranslatable refrain.

---

[1] See notes to Matthew Arnold's "Philomela."
[2] holly tree

[3] Roman author of *Metamorphoses*, a major source of ancient myth

Not to these shores she came! this other Thrace,
Environ barbarous to the royal Attic;
How could her delicate dirge run democractic,
Delivered in a cloudless boundless public place
To an inordinate race? 20

I pernoctated[4] with the Oxford students once,
And in the quadrangles, in the cloisters, on the Cher,[5]
Precociously knocked at antique doors ajar,
Fatuously touched the hems of the hierophants,
Sick of my dissonance.

I went out to Bagley Wood,[6] I climbed the hill;
Even the moon had slanted off in a twinkling,
I heard the sepulchral owl and a few bells tinkling,
There was no more villainous day to unfulfil,
The diuturnity was still. 30

Up from the darkest wood where Philomela sat,
Her fairy numbers issued. What then ailed me?
My ears are called capacious but they failed me,
Her classics registered a little flat!
I rose, and venomously spat.

Philomela, Philomela, lover of song,
I am in despair if we may make us worthy,
A bantering breed sophistical and swarthy;
Unto more beautiful, persistently more young,
Thy fabulous provinces belong.  (*1924*) 40

## Prelude to an Evening

Do not enforce the tired wolf
Dragging his infected wound homeward
To sit tonight with the warm children
Naming the pretty kings of France.

The images of the invaded mind
Being as monsters in the dreams
Of your most brief enchanted headful,
Suppose a miracle of confusion:

That dreamed and undreamt become each other
And mix the night and day of your mind; 10
And it does not matter your twice crying
From mouth unbeautied against the pillow

---

[4] spent the night     [5] a river near Oxford
[6] an area near Oxford, frequented by students on

outings. See Arnold's "Scholar-Gipsy," lines 111
and following.

To avert the gun of the swarthy soldier,
For cry, cock-crow, or the iron bell
Can crack the sleep-sense of outrage,
Annihilate phantoms who were nothing.
But now, by our perverse supposal,
There is a drift of fog on your mornings;
You in your peignoir, dainty at your orange-cup,
Feel poising round the sunny room                      20

Invisible evil, deprived and bold.
All day the clock will metronome
Your gallant fear; the needles clicking,
The heels detonating the stair's cavern.

Freshening the water in the blue bowls
For the buckberries with not all your love,
You shall be listening for the low wind,
The warning sibilance of pines.

You like a waning moon, and I accusing
Our too banded Eumenides,[1]                            30
You shall make Noes but wanderingly,
Smoothing the heads of the hungry children.   (*1945*)


# CONRAD AIKEN / 1889–1973


## Music I Heard with You

Music I heard with you was more than music,
And bread I broke with you was more than bread;
Now that I am without you, all is desolate;
All that was once so beautiful is dead.

Your hands once touched this table and this silver,
And I have seen your fingers hold this glass.
These things do not remember you, belovéd,
And yet your touch upon them will not pass.

For it was in my heart you moved among them,
And blessed them with your hands and with your eyes;   10
And in my heart they will remember always,—
They knew you once, O beautiful and wise.

---

[1] in Greek mythology, the Avenging Deities

# The Room

Through that window—all else being extinct
Except itself and me—I saw the struggle
Of darkness against darkness. Within the room
It turned and turned, dived downward. Then I saw
How order might—if chaos wished—become:
And saw the darkness crush upon itself,
Contracting powerfully; it was as if
It killed itself, slowly: and with much pain.
Pain. The scene was pain, and nothing but pain.
What else, when chaos draws all forces inward          10
To shape a single leaf? . . .
               For the leaf came
Alone and shining in the empty room;
After a while the twig shot downward from it;
And from the twig a bough; and then the trunk,
Massive and coarse; and last the one black root.
The black root cracked the walls. Boughs burst the window:
The great tree took possession.
               Tree of trees!
Remember (when time comes) how chaos died
To shape the shining leaf. Then turn, have courage,
Wrap arms and roots together, be convulsed          20
With grief, and bring back chaos out of shape.
I will be watching then as I watch now.
I will praise darkness now, but then the leaf.   (*1925*)

# At a Concert of Music

Be still, while the music rises about us: the deep enchantment
   Towers, like a forest of singing leaves and birds,
Built for an instant by the heart's troubled beating,
   Beyond all power of words.

And while you are silent, listening, I escape you,
   And I run, by a secret path, through that bright wood
To another time, forgotten, and another woman,
   And another mood.

Then, too, the music's pure algebra of enchantment
   Wrought all about us a bird-voice-haunted grove.          10
Then, too, I escaped, as now, to an earlier moment
   And a brighter love.

Alas! Can I never have peace in the shining instant?
   The hard bright crystal of being, in time and space?
Must I always touch, in the moment, a remembered moment,
   A remembered face?

Absolve me: I would adore you, had I the secret,
    With all this music's power, for yourself alone:
I would try to answer, in the world's chaotic symphony,
    Your one clear tone:                                              20

But alas, alas, being everything you are nothing;
    The history of all my life is in your face;
And all I can grasp is an earlier, more haunted moment,
    And a happier place.


## North Infinity Street

The alarm clocks tick in a thousand furnished rooms,
tick and are wound for a thousand separate dooms;
all down both sides of North Infinity Street
you hear that contrapuntal pawnshop beat.

Hall bedrooms, attic rooms, where the gas-ring sings,
rooms in the basement where the loud doorbell rings;
carpeted or bare, by the rail at the head of the stair,
the curtains drawn, a mirror, a bed, and a chair,

in midnight darkness, when the last footfall creaks,
in northeast rain, when the broken window leaks,                     10
at dawn, to the sound of dishes, the kitchen steam,
at dusk, when the muted radio croons a dream,

there, amid combs and the waiting shoes and socks,
and the bathrobes hung in closets, tick the clocks:
on the chest of drawers, on the table beside the bed,
facing the pillow, facing the recumbent head:

yes, from here to forever, from here to never,
one long sidereal curve of ticking fever,
all down both sides of North Infinity Street
you hear that contrapuntal pawnshop beat.   (*1942*)                 20


## CLAUDE McKAY / 1890–1948

### The Harlem Dancer

Applauding youths laughed with young prostitutes
And watched her perfect, half-clothed body sway;
Her voice was like the sound of blended flutes
Blown by black players upon a picnic day.
She sang and danced on gracefully and calm,

The light gauze hanging loose about her
    form;
To me she seemed a proudly-swaying
    palm
Grown lovelier for passing through a
    storm.
Upon her swarthy neck black shiny
    curls
Luxuriant fell; and tossing coins in
    praise,          10
The wine-flushed, bold-eyed boys, and
    even the girls,
Devoured her shape with eager,
    passionate gaze;
But looking at her falsely-smiling face,
I knew her self was not in that strange
    place.  (*1917*)

## America

Although she feeds me bread of bitterness,
And sinks into my throat her tiger's tooth,
Stealing my breath of life, I will confess
I love this cultured hell that tests my
    youth!
Her vigor flows like tides into my blood,
Giving me strength erect against her
    hate.
Her bigness sweeps my being like a flood,
Yet as a rebel fronts a king in state,
I stand within her walls with not a shred
Of terror, malice, not a word of jeer.   *10*
Darkly I gaze into the days ahead,
And see her might and granite wonders
    there,
Beneath the touch of Time's unerring
    hand,
Like priceless treasures sinking in the
    sand.  (*1920*)

## The Tropics in New York

Bananas ripe and green, and ginger-root,
    Cocoa in pods and alligator pears,
And tangerines and mangoes and grape
    fruit,
    Fit for the highest prize at parish fairs,

Set in the window, bringing memories
    Of fruit-trees laden by low-singing rills,
And dewy dawns, and mystical blue skies
    In benediction over nun-like hills.

My eyes grew dim, and I could no more
    gaze;
    A wave of longing through my body
    swept,          *10*
And hungry for the old, familiar ways,
    I turned aside and bowed my head and
    wept.  (*1920*)

## Flame-Heart

So much I have forgotten in ten years,
So much in ten brief years! I have forgot
What time the purple apples come to
    juice,
And what month brings the shy
    forget-me-not.
I have forgot the special, startling season
Of the pimento's flowering and fruiting;
What time of year the ground doves
    brown the fields
And fill the noonday with their curious
    fluting.
I have forgotten much, but still
    remember
The poinsettia's red, blood-red, in warm
    December.          *10*

I still recall the honey-fever grass,
But cannot recollect the high days when
We rooted them out of the ping-wing
    path
To stop the mad bees in the rabbit pen.
I often try to think in what sweet month
The languid painted ladies used to
    dapple
The yellow by-road mazing from the
    main,
Sweet with the golden threads of the
    rose-apple.
I have forgotten—strange—but quite
    remember
The poinsettia's red, blood-red, in warm
    December.          *20*

What weeks, what months, what time
    of the mild year
We cheated school to have our fling at
    tops?
What days our wine-thrilled bodies
    pulsed with joy
Feasting upon blackberries in the copse?
Oh some I know! I have embalmed the
    days,

Even the sacred moments when we
    played,
All innocent of passion, uncorrupt,
At noon and evening in the flame-heart's
    shade.
We were so happy, happy, I remember,
Beneath the poinsettia's red in warm
    December.   *(1920)*                              30


# EDNA ST. VINCENT MILLAY / 1892–1950


## God's World

          O World, I cannot hold thee close enough!
            Thy winds, thy wide grey skies!
            Thy mists, that roll and rise!
          Thy woods, this autumn day, that ache and sag
          And all but cry with color! That gaunt crag
          To crush! To lift the lean of that black bluff!
          World, World, I cannot get thee close enough!

          Long have I known a glory in it all,
            But never knew I this;
            Here such a passion is                        10
          As stretcheth me apart,—Lord, I do fear
          Thou'st made the world too beautiful this year;
          My soul is all but out of me,—let fall
          No burning leaf; prithee, let no bird call.   *(1917)*


## Wild Swans

          I looked in my heart while the wild swans went over.
          And what did I see I had not seen before?
          Only a question less or a question more;
          Nothing to match the flight of wild birds flying.
          Tiresome heart, forever living and dying,
          House without air, I leave you and lock your door.
          Wild swans, come over the town, come over
          The town again, trailing your legs and crying!   *(1921)*

# I Know I Am But Summer to Your Heart

I know I am but summer to your heart,
And not the full four seasons of the year;
And you must welcome from another part
Such noble moods as are not mine, my dear.
No gracious weight of golden fruits to sell
Have I, nor any wise and wintry thing;
And I have loved you all too long and well
To carry still the high sweet breast of Spring.
Wherefore I say: O love, as summer goes,
I must be gone, steal forth with silent drums,                    10
That you may hail anew the bird and rose
When I come back to you, as summer comes.
Else will you seek, at some not distant time,
Even your summer in another clime.   (*1923*)

# Euclid Alone Has Looked On Beauty Bare

Euclid alone has looked on Beauty bare.
Let all who prate of Beauty hold their peace,
And lay them prone upon the earth and cease
To ponder on themselves, the while they stare
At nothing, intricately drawn nowhere
In shapes of shifting lineage; let geese
Gabble and hiss, but heroes seek release
From dusty bondage into luminous air.
O blinding hour, O holy, terrible day,
When first the shaft into his vision shone                        10
Of light anatomized! Euclid alone
Has looked on Beauty bare. Fortunate they
Who, though once only and then but far away,
Have heard her massive sandal set on stone.   (*1923*)

# Love Is Not All

Love is not all; it is not meat nor drink
Nor slumber nor a roof against the rain,
Nor yet a floating spar to men that sink
And rise and sink and rise and sink again;
Love can not fill the thickened lung with breath,
Nor clean the blood, nor set the factured bone;
Yet many a man is making friends with death
Even as I speak, for lack of love alone.
It well may be that in a difficult hour,
Pinned down by pain and moaning for release,                      10
Or nagged by want past resolution's power,

I might be driven to sell your love for peace,
Or trade the memory of this night for food.
It well may be. I do not think I would.   *(1931)*


## ARCHIBALD MACLEISH / 1892–

### Ars Poetica

A poem should be palpable and mute
As a globed fruit,

Dumb
As old medallions to the thumb,

Silent as the sleeve-worn stone
Of casement ledges where the moss has grown—

A poem should be wordless
As the flight of birds.

A poem should be motionless in time
As the moon climbs,                                                          *10*

Leaving, as the moon releases
Twig by twig the night-entangled trees,

Leaving, as the moon behind the winter leaves,
Memory by memory the mind—

A poem should be motionless in time
As the moon climbs

A poem should be equal to:
Not true

For all the history of grief
An empty doorway and a maple leaf                                            *20*

For love
The leaning grasses and the two lights above the sea—

A poem should not mean
But be   *(1926)*


### The End of the World

Quite unexpectedly as Vasserot
The armless ambidextrian was lighting
A match between his great and second toe
And Ralph the lion was engaged in biting

The neck of Madame Sossman while the drum
Pointed, and Teeny was about to cough
In waltz-time swinging Jocko by the thumb—
Quite unexpectedly the top blew off:
And there, there overhead, there, there, hung over
Those thousands of white faces, those dazed eyes,        *10*
There in the starless dark the poise, the hover,
There with vast wings across the canceled skies,
There in the sudden blackness the black pall
Of nothing, nothing, nothing—nothing at all.   *(1926)*

## American Letter: For Gerald Murphy

The wind is east but the hot weather continues,
Blue and no clouds, the sound of the leaves thin,
Dry like the rustling of paper, scored across
With the slate-shrill screech of the locusts.
                              The tossing of
Pines is the low sound. In the wind's running
The wild carrots smell of the burning sun.
Why should I think of the dolphins at Capo di Mele?[1]
Why should I see in my mind the taut sail
And the hill over St.-Tropez[2] and your hand on the tiller?
Why should my heart be troubled with palms still?     *10*
I am neither a sold boy nor a Chinese official
Sent to sicken in Pa for some Lo-Yang[3] dish.
This is my own land, my sky, my mountain:
This—not the humming pines and the surf and the sound
At the Ferme Blanche, nor Port Cros[4] in the dusk and the harbor
Floating the motionless ship and the sea-drowned star.
I am neither Po Chü-i[5] nor another after
Far from home, in a strange land, daft
For the talk of his own sort and the taste of his lettuces.
This land is my native land. And yet             *20*
I am sick for home for the red roofs and the olives,
And the foreign words and the smell of the sea fall.
How can a wise man have two countries?
How can a man have the earth and the wind and want
A land far off, alien, smelling of palm-trees
And the yellow gorse[6] at noon in the long calms?

It is a strange thing—to be an American.
Neither an old house it is with the air
Tasting of hung herbs and the sun returning
Year after year to the same door and the churn         *30*

---

[1] a cape on the Mediterranean coast of Italy      [5] Chinese lyric poet (772–846)
[2] resort on the French Riviera      [6] common European shrub
[3] Chinese towns    [4] French towns

Making the same sound in the cool of the kitchen
Mother to son's wife, and the place to sit
Marked in the dusk by the worn stone at the wellhead—
That—nor the eyes like each other's eyes and the skull
Shaped to the same fault and the hands' sameness.
Neither a place it is nor a blood name.
America is West and the wind blowing
America is a great word and the snow,
A way, a white bird, the rain falling,
A shining thing in the mind and the gulls' call.          *40*
America is neither a land nor a people,
A word's shape it is, a wind's sweep—
America is alone: many together,
Many of one mouth, of one breath,
Dressed as one—and none brothers among them:
Only the taught speech and the aped tongue.
America is alone and the gulls calling.
It is a strange thing to be an American.
It is strange to live on the high world in the stare
Of the naked sun and the stars as our bones live.          *50*
Men in the old lands housed by their rivers.
They built their towns in the vales in the earth's shelter.
We first inhabit the world. We dwell
On the half earth, on the open curve of a continent.
Sea is divided from sea by the day-fall. The dawn
Rides the low east with us many hours;
First are the capes, then are the shorelands, now
The blue Appalachians faint at the day rise;
The willows shudder with light on the long Ohio:
The Lakes scatter the low sun: the prairies          *60*
Slide out of dark: in the eddy of clean air
The smoke goes up from the high plains of Wyoming:
The steep Sierras arise: the struck foam
Flames at the wind's heel on the far Pacific.
Already the noon leans to the eastern cliff:
The elms darken the door and the dust-heavy lilacs.

It is strange to sleep in the bare stars and to die
On an open land where few bury before us:
(From the new earth the dead return no more.)
It is strange to be born of no race and no people.          *70*
In the old lands they are many together. They keep
The wise past and the words spoken in common.
They remember the dead with their hands, their mouths dumb.
They answer each other with two words in their meeting.
They live together in small things. They eat
The same dish, their drink is the same and their proverbs.
Their youth is like. They are like in their ways of love.
They are many men. There are always others beside them.

Here it is one man and another and wide
On the darkening hills the faint smoke of the houses. 80
Here it is one man and the wind in the boughs.

Therefore our hearts are sick for the south water.
The smell of the gorse comes back to our night thought.
We are sick at heart for the red roofs and the olives;
We are sick at heart for the voice and the foot fall . . .

Therefore we will not go though the sea call us.

This, this is our land, this is our people,
This that is neither a land nor a race. We must reap
The wind here in the grass for our soul's harvest:
Here we must eat our salt or our bones starve. 90
Here we must live or live only as shadows.
This is our race, we that have none, that have had
Neither the old walls nor the voices around us,
This is our land, this is our ancient ground—
The raw earth, the mixed bloods and the strangers,
The different eyes, the wind, and the heart's change.
These we will not leave though the old call us.
This is our country-earth, our blood, our kind.
Here we will live our years till the earth blind us—
The wind blows from the east. The leaves fall. 100
Far off in the pines a jay rises.
The wind smells of haze and the wild ripe apples.

I think of the masts at Cette[7] and the sweet rain.   (*1929*)

## WILFRED OWEN / 1893–1918

## Strange Meeting

It seemed that out of battle I escaped
Down some profound dull tunnel, long since scooped
Through granites which titanic wars had groined.
Yet also there encumbered sleepers groaned,
Too fast in thought or death to be bestirred.
Then, as I probed them, one sprang up, and stared
With piteous recognition in fixed eyes,
Lifting distressful hands as if to bless.
And by his smile I knew that sullen hall,
By his dead smile I knew we stood in Hell. 10
With a thousand pains that vision's face was grained;

---

[7] Sète, French seaport on the Mediterranean

Yet no blood reached there from the upper ground,
And no guns thumped, or down the flues made moan.
"Strange friend," I said, "here is no cause to mourn."
"None," said the other, "save the undone years,
The hopelessness. Whatever hope is yours,
Was my life also; I went hunting wild
After the wildest beauty in the world,
Which lies not calm in eyes, or braided hair,
But mocks the steady running of the hour,                          20
And if it grieves, grieves richlier than here.
For by my glee might many men have laughed,
And of my weeping something had been left,
Which must die now. I mean the truth untold,
The pity of war, the pity war distilled.
Now men will go content with what we spoiled,
Or, discontent, boil bloody and be spilled.
They will be swift with swiftness of the tigress,
None will break ranks, though nations trek from progress.
Courage was mine, and I had mystery,                               30
Wisdom was mine, and I had mastery;
To miss the march of this retreating world
Into vain citadels that are not walled.
Then, when much blood had clogged their chariot wheels
I would go up and wash them from sweet wells,
Even with truths that lie too deep for taint.
I would have poured my spirit without stint
But not through wounds; not on the cess of war.
Foreheads of men have bled where no wounds were.
I am the enemy you killed, my friend.                              40
I knew you in this dark; for so you frowned
Yesterday, through me as you jabbed and killed.
I parried, but my hands were loath and cold.
Let us sleep now. . . ."   (*1918*)


## Arms and the Boy

Let the boy try along this bayonet-blade
How cold steel is, and keen with hunger of blood;
Blue with all malice, like a madman's flash;
And thinly drawn with famishing for flesh.

Lend him to stroke these blind, blunt bullet-heads
Which long to nuzzle in the hearts of lads,
Or give him cartridges of fine zinc teeth,
Sharp with the sharpness of grief and death.

For his teeth seem for laughing round an apple.
There lurk no claws behind his fingers supple;                     10
And God will grow no talons at his heels,
Nor antlers through the thickness of his curls.   (*1920*)

## Dulce et Decorum Est

Bent double, like old beggars under sacks,
Knock-kneed, coughing like hags, we cursed through sludge,
Till on the haunting flares we turned our backs
And towards our distant rest began to trudge.
Men marched asleep. Many had lost their boots
But limped on, blood-shod. All went lame; all blind;
Drunk with fatigue; deaf even to the hoots
Of tired, outstripped Five-Nines that dropped behind.

Gas! Gas! Quick, boys!—An ecstasy of fumbling,
Fitting the clumsy helmets just in time;                                    10
But someone still was yelling out and stumbling
And flound'ring like a man in fire or lime...
Dim, through the misty panes and thick green light,
As under a green sea, I saw him drowning.

In all my dreams before my helpless sight,
He plunges at me, guttering, choking, drowning.

If in some smothering dreams you too could pace
Behind the wagon that we flung him in,
And watch the white eyes writhing in his face,
His hanging face, like a devil's sick of sin;                                20
If you could hear, at every jolt, the blood
Come gargling from the froth-corrupted lungs,
Obscene as cancer, bitter as the cud
Of vile, incurable sores on innocent tongues,—
My friend, you would not tell with such high zest
To children ardent for some desperate glory,
The old Lie: Dulce et decorum est
Pro patria mori.   (*1920*)

## E. E. CUMMINGS / 1894–1962

## who's most afraid of death? thou

who's most afraid of death? thou
                              art of him
utterly afraid, i love of thee
(beloved) this

             and truly i would be
near when his scythe takes crisply the whim
of thy smoothness.   and mark the fainting
murdered petals.   with the caving stem.

But of all most would i be one of them

round the hurt heart which do so frailly cling . . . .)                    *10*
i who am but imperfect in my fear

Or with thy mind against my mind, to hear
nearing our hearts' irrevocable play—
through the mysterious high futile day

an enormous stride
                                    (and drawing thy mouth toward

my mouth, steer our lost bodies carefully downward)   *(1925)*


## next to of course god america i

"next to of course god america i
love you land of the pilgrims' and so forth oh
say can you see by the dawn's early my
country 'tis of centuries come and go
and are no more what of it we should worry
in every language even deafanddumb
thy sons acclaim your glorious name by gorry
by jingo by gee by gosh by gum
why talk of beauty what could be more beaut-
iful than these heroic happy dead                          *10*
who rushed like lions to the roaring slaughter
they did not stop to think they died instead
then shall the voice of liberty be mute?"

He spoke.    And drank rapidly a glass of water   *(1926)*


## somewhere i have never travelled

somewhere i have never travelled,gladly beyond
any experience,your eyes have their silence:
in your most frail gesture are things which enclose me,
or which i cannot touch because they are too near

your slightest look easily will unclose me
though i have closed myself as fingers,
you open always petal by petal myself as Spring opens
(touching skilfully,mysteriously)her first rose

or if your wish be to close me,i and
my life will shut very beautifully,suddenly,                    *10*
as when the heart of this flower imagines
the snow carefully everywhere descending;

nothing which we are to perceive in this world equals
the power of your intense fragility:whose texture
compels me with the colour of its countries,
rendering death and forever with each breathing

(i do not know what it is about you that closes
and opens;only something in me understands
the voice of your eyes is deeper than all roses)
nobody,not even the rain,has such small hands    *(1931)*    20


r-p-o-p-h-e-s-s-a-g-r

                        r-p-o-p-h-e-s-s-a-g-r
                 who
    a)s w(e loo)k
    upnowgath
           PPEGORHRASS
                    eringint(o-
  aThe):l
      eA
      !p:
S                                           a        *10*
            (r
  rIvInG                .gRrEaPsPhOs)
                          to
  rea(be)rran(com)gi(e)ngly
  ,grasshopper;    *(1935)*


## anyone lived in a pretty how town

anyone lived in a pretty how town
(with up so floating many bells down)
spring summer autumn winter
he sang his didn't he danced his did

Women and men(both little and small)
cared for anyone not at all
they sowed their isn't they reaped their
  same
sun moon stars rain.

children guessed(but only a few
and down they forgot as up they grew   *10*
autumn winter spring summer)
that noone loved him more by more

when by now and tree by leaf
she laughed his joy she cried his grief
bird by snow and stir by still
anone's any was all to her

someones married their everyones
laughed their cryings and did their dance
(sleep wake hope and then)they
said their nevers they slept their dream   *20*

stars rain sun moon
(and only the snow can begin to explain
how children are apt to forget to remember
with up so floating many bells down)

one day anyone died i guess
(and noone stooped to kiss his face)
busy folk buried them side by side
little by little and was by was

all by all and deep by deep
and more by more they dream their sleep   *30*
noone and anyone earth by april
wish by spirit and if by yes.

Women and men(both dong and ding)
summer autumn winter spring
reaped their sowing and went their came
sun moon stars rain    *(1940)*

## a peopleshaped toomany-ness far too

a peopleshaped toomany-ness far too

and will it tell us who we are and will
it tell us why we dream and will it tell
us how we drink crawl eat walk die fly do?

a notalive undead too-nearishness

and shall we cry and shall we laugh and shall
entirely our doom steer his great small
wish into upward deepness of less fear
much than more climbing hope meets most despair?

all knowing's having and have is(you guess)                10
perhaps the very unkindest way to kill
each of those creatures called one's self so we'll

not have(but i imagine that yes is
the only living thing)and we'll make yes   (*1940*)


## pity this busy monster,manunkind

pity this busy monster,manunkind,

not. Progress is a comfortable disease:
your victim(death and life safely beyond)

plays with the bigness of his littleness
—electrons deify one razorblade
into a mountainrange;lenses extend

unwish through curving wherewhen till unwish
returns on its unself.
                                        A world of made
is not a world of born—pity poor flesh                     10

and trees,poor stars and stones,but never this
fine specimen of hypermagical

ultraomnipotence. We doctors know

a hopeless case if—listen:there's a hell
of a good universe next door;let's go   (*1944*)


## all ignorance toboggans into know

all ignorance toboggans into know
and trudges up to ignorance again:
but winter's not forever,even snow
melts;and if spring should spoil the game,what then?

all history's a winter sport or three:
but were it five,i'd still insist that all
history is too small for even me;
for me and you,exceedingly too small.

Swoop(shrill collective myth)into thy grave
merely to toil the scale to shrillerness                          *10*
per every madge and mabel dick and dave
—tomorrow is our permanent address

and there they'll scarcely find us(if they do,
we'll move away still further:into now   (*1944*)


## when faces called flowers float out of the ground

when faces called flowers float out of the ground
and breathing is wishing and wishing is having—
but keeping is downward and doubting and never
—it's april(yes,april;my darling)it's spring!
yes the pretty birds frolic as spry as can fly
yes the little fish gambol as glad as can be
(yes the mountains are dancing together)

when every leaf opens without any sound
and wishing is having and having is giving—
but keeping is doting and nothing and nonsense                   *10*
—alive;we're alive,dear:it's(kiss me now)spring!
now the pretty birds hover so she and so he
now the little fish quiver so you and so i
(now the mountains are dancing,the mountains)

when more than was lost has been found has been found
and having is giving and giving is living—
but keeping is darkness and winter and cringing
—it's spring(all our night becomes day)o,it's spring!
all the pretty birds dive to the heart of the sky
all the little fish climb through the mind of the sea            *20*
(all the mountains are dancing;are dancing)   (*1950*)


## JEAN TOOMER / 1894–1967


## Song of the Son

Pour O pour that parting soul in song,
O pour it in the sawdust glow of night,
Into the velvet pine-smoke air to-night,
And let the valley carry it along.
And let the valley carry it along.

O land and soil, red soil and sweet-gum tree,
So scant of grass, so profligate of pines,
Now just before an epoch's sun declines
Thy son, in time, I have returned to thee,
Thy son, I have in time returned to thee.                              *10*

In time, for though the sun is setting on
A song-lit race of slaves, it has not set;
Though late, O soil, it is not too late yet
To catch thy plaintive soul, leaving, soon gone,
Leaving, to catch thy plaintive soul soon gone.

O Negro slaves, dark purple ripened plums,
Squeezed, and bursting in the pine-wood air,
Passing, before they stripped the old tree bare
One plum was saved for me, one seed becomes

An everlasting song, a singing tree,                                   *20*
Caroling softly souls of slavery,
What they were, and what they are to me,
Caroling softly souls of slavery.   (*1923*)

## Evening Song

Full moon rising on the waters of my heart,
Lakes and moon and fires,
Cloine tires,
Holding her lips apart.

Promises of slumber leaving shore to charm the moon,
Miracle made vesper-keeps,
Cloine sleeps,
And I'll be sleeping soon.

Cloine, curled like the sleepy waters where the moon-waves start,
Radiant, resplendently she gleams,                                     *10*
Cloine dreams,
Lips pressed against my heart.   (*1923*)

## Georgia Dusk

The sky, lazily disdaining to pursue
    The setting sun, too indolent to hold
    A lengthened tournament for flashing gold,
Passively darkens for night's barbecue,

A feast of moon and men and barking hounds,
    An orgy for some genius of the South
    With blood-hot eyes and cane-lipped scented mouth,
Surprised in making folk-songs from soul sounds.

The sawmill blows its whistle, buzz-saws stop,
   And silence breaks the bud of knoll and hill,      *10*
   Soft settling pollen where plowed lands fulfill
Their early promise of a bumper crop.

Smoke from the pyramidal sawdust pile
   Curls up, blue ghosts of trees, tarrying low
   Where only chips and stumps are left to show
The solid proof of former domicile.

Meanwhile, the men, with vestiges of pomp,
   Race memories of king and caravan,
   High-priests, an ostrich, and a juju-man,
Go singing through the footpaths of the swamp.      *20*

Their voices rise . . the pine trees are guitars,
   Strumming, pine-needles fall like sheets of rain . .
   Their voices rise . . the chorus of the cane
Is caroling a vesper to the stars. .

O singers, resinous and soft your songs
   Above the sacred whisper of the pines,
   Give virgin lips to cornfield concubines,
Bring dreams of Christ to dusky cane-lipped throngs.   (*1923*)

# ROBERT GRAVES / 1895–

## Escape

(*August 6, 1916—Officer previously reported died of wounds, now reported wounded: Graves, Captain R., Royal Welch Fusiliers.*)

   . . . But I *was* dead, an hour or more.
I woke when I'd already passed the door
That Cerberus[1] guards, and half-way down the road
To Lethe,[2] as an old Greek signpost showed.
Above me, on my stretcher swinging by,
I saw new stars in the subterrene sky:
A Cross, a Rose in bloom, a Cage with bars,
And a barbed Arrow feathered in fine stars.
I felt the vapours of forgetfulness
Float in my nostrils. Oh, may Heaven bless      *10*
Dear Lady Proserpine,[3] who saw me wake,
And, stooping over me, for Henna's[4] sake
Cleared my poor buzzing head and sent me back

---

[1] the three-headed dog that guarded the gate of the underworld in Greek mythology
[2] the river of forgetfulness in the underworld
[3] queen of the underworld
[4] the Sicilian village near the meadow of flowers from which Pluto captured Proserpine

Breathless, with leaping heart along the track.
After me roared and clattered angry hosts
Of demons, heroes, and policeman-ghosts.
"Life! life! I can't be dead! I won't be dead!
Damned if I'll die for anyone!" I said. . . .

Cerberus stands and grins above me now,
Wearing three heads—lion, and lynx, and sow.          *20*
"Quick, a revolver! But my Webley's [5] gone,
Stolen! . . . No bombs . . . no knife. . . . The crowd swarms on,
Bellows, hurls stones. . . . Not even a honeyed sop . . .
Nothing. . . . Good Cerberus! . . . Good dog! . . . but stop!
Stay! . . . A great luminous thought . . . I do believe
There's still some morphia that I bought on leave."
Then swiftly Cerberus' wide mouths I cram
With army biscuit smeared with ration jam;
And sleep lurks in the luscious plum and apple.
He crunches, swallows, stiffens, seems to grapple      *30*
With the all-powerful poppy . . . then a snore,
A crash; the beast blocks up the corridor
With monstrous hairy carcase, red and dun—
Too late! for I've sped through.
            O Life! O Sun!   (*1916*)

## Lost Love

His eyes are quickened so with grief,
He can watch a grass or leaf
Every instant grow; he can
Clearly through a flint wall see,
Or watch the startled spirit flee
From the throat of a dead man.
  Across two counties he can hear
And catch your words before you speak.
The woodlouse or the maggot's weak
Clamour rings in his sad ear,          *10*
And noise so slight it would surpass
Credence—drinking sound of grass,

Worm talk, clashing jaws of moth
Chumbling holes in cloth;
The groan of ants who undertake
Gigantic loads for honour's sake
(Their sinews creak, their breath comes
    thin);
Whir of spiders when they spin,
And minute whispering, mumbling, sighs
Of idle grubs and flies.          *20*
  This man is quickened so with grief,
He wanders god-like or like thief
Inside and out, below, above,
Without relief seeking lost love.   (*1923*)

## The Blue-fly

Five summer days, five summer nights,
The ignorant, loutish, giddy blue-fly
Hung without motion on the cling peach,
Humming occasionally: "O my love, my fair one!"
    As in the *Canticles*.[1]

---

[5] British service pistol          [1] in the King James Version, The Song of Solomon

Magnified one thousand times, the insect
Looks farcically human; laugh if you will!
Bald head, stage-fairy wings, blear eyes,
A caved-in chest, hairy black mandibles,
      Long spindly thighs.      *10*

The crime was detected on the sixth day.
What then could be said or done? By anyone?
It would have been vindictive, mean and what-not
To swat that fly for being a blue-fly,
      For debauch of a peach.

Is it fair, either, to bring a microscope
To bear on the case, even in search of truth?
Nature, doubtless, has some compelling cause
To glut the carriers of her epidemics—
      Nor did the peach complain.   (*1953*)     *20*


# HART CRANE / 1899–1932


## Repose of Rivers

The willows carried a slow sound,
A sarabande the wind mowed on the mead.
I could never remember
That seething, steady leveling of the marshes
Till age had brought me to the sea.

Flags, weeds. And remembrance of steep alcoves
Where cypresses shared the noon's
Tyranny; they drew me into hades almost.
And mammoth turtles climbing sulphur dreams
Yielded, while sun-silt rippled them     *20*
Asunder . . .

How much I would have bartered! the black gorge
And all the singular nestings in the hills
Where beavers learn stitch and tooth.
The pond I entered once and quickly fled—
I remember now its singing willow rim.

And finally, in that memory all things nurse;
After the city that I finally passed
With scalding unguents spread and smoking darts
The monsoon cut across the delta     *20*
At gulf gates . . . There, beyond the dykes

I heard wind flaking sapphire, like this summer,
And willows could not hold more steady sound.   (*1926*)


## *from* For the Marriage of Faustus and Helen

### III

Capped arbiter of beauty in this street
That narrows darkly into motor dawn,—
You, here beside me, delicate ambassador
Of intricate slain numbers that arise
In whispers, naked of steel;

                        religious gunman!
Who faithfully, yourself, will fall too soon,
And in other ways than as the wind settles
On the sixteen thrifty bridges of the city:
Let us unbind our throats of fear and pity.

                We even,
Who drove speediest destruction                                    10
In corymbulous formations of mechanics,—
Who hurried the hill breezes, spouting malice
Plangent over meadows, and looked down
On rifts of torn and empty houses
Like old women with teeth unjubilant
That waited faintly, briefly and in vain:

We know, eternal gunman, our flesh remembers
The tensile boughs, the nimble blue plateaus,
The mounted, yielding cities of the air!
That saddled sky that shook down vertical                          20
Repeated play of fire—no hypogeum
Of wave or rock was good against one hour.

We did not ask for that, but have survived,
And will persist to speak again before
All stubble streets that have not curved
To memory, or known the ominous lifted arm
That lowers down the arc of Helen's brow
To saturate with blessing and dismay.

A goose, tobacco and cologne—
Three-winged and gold-shod prophecies of heaven,                   30
The lavish heart shall always have to leaven
And spread with bells and voices, and atone
The abating shadows of our conscript dust.

Anchises' navel, dripping of the sea,—
The hands Erasmus dipped in gleaming tides,
Gathered the voltage of blown blood and vine;
Delve upward for the new and scattered wine,
O brother-thief of time, that we recall.

Laugh out the meager penance of their days
Who dare not share with us the breath released,        *40*
The substance drilled and spent beyond repair
For golden, or the shadow of gold hair.

Distinctly praise the years, whose volatile
Blamed bleeding hands extend and thresh the height
The imagination spans beyond despair,
Outpacing bargain, vocable and prayer.   (*1926*)

## At Melville's Tomb

Often beneath the wave, wide from this ledge
The dice of drowned men's bones he saw bequeath
An embassy. Their numbers as he watched,
Beat on the dusty shore and were obscured.

And wrecks passed without sound of bells,
The calyx of death's bounty giving back
A scattered chapter, livid hieroglyph,
The portent wound in corridors of shells.

Then in the circuit calm of one vast coil,
Its lashings charmed and malice reconciled,        *10*
Frosted eyes there were that lifted altars;
And silent answers crept across the stars.

Compass, quadrant and sextant contrive
No farther tides . . . High in the azure steeps
Monody shall not wake the mariner.
This fabulous shadow only the sea keeps.   (*1926*)

## *from* Voyages

### II

And yet this great wink of eternity,
Of rimless floods, unfettered leewardings,
Samite sheeted and processioned where
Her undinal vast belly moonward bends,
Laughing the wrapt inflections of our love;

Take this Sea, whose diapason knells
On scrolls of silver snowy sentences,
The sceptred terror of whose sessions rends
As her demeanors motion well or ill,
All but the pieties of lovers' hands.        *10*

And onward, as bells off San Salvador
Salute the crocus lustres of the stars,
In these poinsettia meadows of her tides,—
Adagios of islands, O my Prodigal,
Complete the dark confessions her veins spell.

Mark how her turning shoulders wind the hours,
And hasten while her penniless rich palms
Pass superscription of bent foam and wave,—
Hasten, while they are true,—sleep, death, desire,
Close round one instant in one floating flower.                    20

Bind us in time, O Seasons clear, and awe.
O minstrel galleons of Carib fire,
Bequeath us to no earthly shore until
Is answered in the vortex of our grave
The seal's wide spindrift gaze toward paradise.

IV

Whose counted smile of hours and days, suppose
I know as spectrum of the sea and pledge
Vastly now parting gulf on gulf of wings
Whose circles bridge, I know, (from palms to the severe
Chilled albatross's white immutability)
No stream of greater love advancing now
Than, singing, this mortality alone
Through clay aflow immortally to you.

All fragrance irrefragibly, and claim
Madly meeting logically in this hour                               10
And region that is ours to wreathe again,
Portending eyes and lips and making told
The chancel port and portion of our June—

Shall they not stem and close in our own steps
Bright staves of flowers and quills to-day as I
Must first be lost in fatal tides to tell?
In signature of the incarnate word
The harbor shoulders to resign in mingling
Mutual blood, transpiring as foreknown
And widening noon within your breast for gathering                 20
All bright insinuations that my years have caught
For islands where must lead inviolably
Blue latitudes and levels of your eyes,—

In this expectant, still exclaim receive
The secret oar and petals of all love.    (*1926*)


## To Brooklyn Bridge

How many dawns, chill from his rippling rest
The seagull's wings shall dip and pivot him,
Shedding white rings of tumult, building high
Over the chained bay waters Liberty—

Then, with inviolate curve, forsake our eyes
As apparitional as sails that cross
Some page of figures to be filed away;
—Till elevators drop us from our day . . .

I think of cinemas, panoramic sleights
With multitudes bent toward some flashing scene          10
Never disclosed, but hastened to again,
Foretold to other eyes on the same screen;

And Thee, across the harbor, silver-paced
As though the sun took step of thee, yet left
Some motion ever unspent in thy stride,—
Implicitly thy freedom staying thee!

Out of some subway scuttle, cell or loft
A bedlamite speeds to thy parapets,
Tilting there momently, shrill shirt ballooning,
A jest falls from the speechless caravan.                20

Down Wall, from girder into street noon leaks,
A rip-tooth of the sky's acetylene;
All afternoon the cloud-flown derricks turn . . .
Thy cables breathe the North Atlantic still.

And obscure as that heaven of the Jews,
Thy guerdon[1] . . . Accolade thou dost bestow
Of anonymity time cannot raise:
Vibrant reprieve and pardon thou dost show.

O harp and altar, of the fury fused,
(How could mere toil align thy choiring strings!)        30
Terrific threshold of the prophet's pledge,
Prayer of pariah,[2] and the lover's cry,—

Again the traffic lights that skim thy swift
Unfractioned idiom, immaculate sigh of stars,
Beading thy path—condense eternity:
And we have seen night lifted in thine arms.

Under thy shadow by the piers I waited;
Only in darkness is thy shadow clear.
The City's fiery parcels all undone,
Already snow submerges an iron year . . .                40

O Sleepless as the river under thee,
Vaulting the sea, the prairies' dreaming sod,
Unto us lowliest sometime sweep, descend
And of the curveship lend a myth to God.   (*1930*)

---

[1] reward     [2] outcast

## The Broken Tower

The bell-rope that gathers God at dawn
Dispatches me as though I dropped down the knell
Of a spent day—to wander the cathedral lawn
From pit to crucifix, feet chill on steps from hell.

Have you not heard, have you not seen that corps
Of shadows in the tower, whose shoulders sway
Antiphonal carillons launched before
The stars are caught and hived in the sun's ray?

The bells, I say, the bells break down their tower;
And swing I know not where. Their tongues engrave          10
Membrane through marrow, my long-scattered score
Of broken intervals. . . . And I, their sexton slave!

Oval encyclicals in canyons heaping
The impasse high with choir. Banked voices slain!
Pagodas, campaniles with reveilles outleaping—
O terraced echoes prostrate on the plain! . . .

And so it was I entered the broken world
To trace the visionary company of love, its voice
An instant in the wind (I know not whither hurled)
But not for long to hold each desperate choice.           20

My word I poured. But was it cognate, scored
Of that tribunal monarch of the air
Whose thigh embronzes earth, strikes crystal Word
In wounds pledged once to hope—cleft to despair?

The steep encroachments of my blood left me
No answer (could blood hold such a lofty tower
As flings the question true?)—or is it she
Whose sweet mortality stirs latent power?—

And through whose pulse I hear, counting the strokes
My veins recall and add, revived and sure                 30
The angelus of wars my chest evokes:
What I hold healed, original now, and pure . . .

And builds, within, a tower that is not stone
(Not stone can jacket heaven)—but slip
Of pebbles—visible wings of silence sown
In azure circles, widening as they dip

The matrix of the heart, lift down the eye
That shrines the quiet lake and swells a tower . . .
The commodious, tall decorum of that sky
Unseals her earth, and lifts love in its shower.   (*1933*)      40

# ALLEN TATE / 1899–

## Ode to the Confederate Dead

Row after row with strict impunity
The headstones yield their names to the element,
The wind whirrs without recollection;
In the riven troughs the splayed leaves
Pile up, of nature the casual sacrament
To the seasonal eternity of death;
Then driven by the fierce scrutiny
Of heaven to their election in the vast breath,
They sough the rumor of mortality.

Autumn is desolation in the plot                                     10
Of a thousand acres where these memories grow
From the inexhaustible bodies that are not
Dead, but feed the grass row after rich row.
Think of the autumns that have come and gone!—
Ambitious November with the humors of the year,
With a particular zeal for every slab,
Staining the uncomfortable angels that rot
On the slabs, a wing chipped here, an arm there:
The brute curiosity of an angel's stare
Turns you, like them, to stone,                                      20
Transforms the heaving air
Till plunged to a heavier world below
You shift your sea-space blindly
Heaving, turning like the blind crab.

  Dazed by the wind, only the wind
  The leaves flying, plunge

You know who have waited by the wall
The twilight certainty of an animal,
Those midnight restitutions of the blood
You know—the immitigable pines, the smoky frieze                     30
Of the sky, the sudden call: you know the rage,
The cold pool left by the mounting flood,
Of muted Zeno and Parmenides.[1]
You who have waited for the angry resolution
Of those desires that should be yours tomorrow,
You know the unimportant shrift of death
And praise the vision
And praise the arrogant circumstance
Of those who fall
Rank upon rank, hurried beyond decision—                             40
Here by the sagging gate, stopped by the wall.

---

[1] presocratic philosophers who maintained that the universe is immutable

Seeing, seeing only the leaves
Flying, plunge and expire

Turn your eyes to the immoderate past,
Turn to the inscrutable infantry rising
Demons out of the earth—they will not last.
Stonewall,[2] Stonewall, and the sunken fields of hemp,
Shiloh, Antietam, Malvern Hill, Bull Run.[3]
Lost in that orient of the thick-and-fast
You will curse the setting sun.                                          *50*

Cursing only the leaves crying
Like an old mán in a storm

You hear the shout, the crazy hemlocks point
With troubled fingers to the silence which
Smothers you, a mummy, in time.

The hound bitch
Toothless and dying, in a musty cellar
Hears the wind only.

Now that the salt of their blood
Stiffens the saltier oblivion of the sea,
Seals the malignant purity of the flood,
What shall we who count our days and bow                                 *60*
Our heads with a commemorial woe
In the ribboned coats of grim felicity,
What shall we say of the bones, unclean,
Whose verdurous anonymity will grow?
The ragged arms, the ragged heads and eyes
Lost in these acres of the insane green?
The gray lean spiders come, they come and go;
In a tangle of willows without light
The singular screech-owl's tight
Invisible lyric seeds the mind                                           *70*
With the furious murmur of their chivalry.

We shall say only the leaves
Flying, plunge and expire

We shall say only the leaves whispering
In the improbable mist of nightfall
That flies on multiple wing;
Night is the beginning and the end
And in between the ends of distraction
Waits mute speculation, the patient curse
That stones the eyes, or like the jaguar leaps                           *80*
For his own image in a jungle pool, his victim.

---

[2] "Stonewall" Jackson, Confederate general        [3] notable battles of the Civil War
killed at Chancellorsville

What shall we say who have knowledge
Carried to the heart? Shall we take the act
To the grave? Shall we, more hopeful, set up the grave
In the house? The ravenous grave?

                                        Leave now
The shut gate and the decomposing wall:
The gentle serpent, green in the mulberry bush,
Riots with his tongue through the hush—
Sentinel of the grave who counts us all!   (*1928*)                    90


## The Subway

Dark accurate plunger down the successive knell
Of arch on arch, where ogives burst a red
Reverberance of hail upon the dead
Thunder like an exploding crucible!
Harshly articulate, musical steel shell
Of angry worship, hurled religiously
Upon your business of humility
Into the iron forestries of hell:

Till broken in the shift of quieter
Dense altitudes tangential of your steel,                              10
I am become geometries, and glut
Expansions like a blind astronomer
Dazed, while the worldless heavens bulge and reel
In the cold revery of an idiot.   (*1928*)


## The Wolves

There are wolves in the next room waiting
With heads bent low, thrust out, breathing
At nothing in the dark; between them and me
A white door patched with light from the hall
Where it seems never (so still is the house)
A man has walked from the front door to the stair.
It has all been forever. Beasts claw the floor.
I have brooded on angels and archfiends
But no man has ever sat where the next room's
Crowded with wolves, and for the honor of man                          10
I affirm that never have I before. Now while
I have looked for the evening star at a cold window
And whistled when Arcturus spilt his light,
I've heard the wolves scuffle, and said: So this
Is man; so—what better conclusion is there—
The day will not follow night, and the heart
Of man has a little dignity, but less patience

Than a wolf's and a duller sense that cannot
Smell its own mortality. (This and other
Meditations will be suited to other times                    20
After dog silence howls his epitaph).
Now remember courage, go to the door,
Open it and see whether coiled on the bed
Or cringing by the wall, a savage beast
Maybe with golden hair, with deep eyes
Like a bearded spider on a sunlit floor
Will snarl—and man can never be alone.   (*1932*)


# LANGSTON HUGHES / 1902–1967


## *from* Montage of a Dream Deferred

NOTE: In terms of current Afro-American popular music and the sources from which
it has progressed—jazz, ragtime, swing, blues, boogie-woogie, and be-bop—this poem
on contemporary Harlem, like be-bop, is marked by conflicting changes, sudden nuances,
sharp and impudent interjections, broken rhythms, and passages sometimes in the
manner of the jam session, sometimes the popular song, punctuated by the riffs, runs,
breaks, and disc-tortions of the music of a community in transition.

                                                              L.H.


### BOOGIE SEGUE TO BOP

#### DREAM BOOGIE

Good morning daddy!
Ain't you heard
The boogie-woogie rumble
Of a dream deferred?

Listen closely:
You'll hear their feet
Beating out and beating out a—

    You think
    It's a happy beat?

Listen to it closely:                                        10
Ain't you heard
something underneath
like a—

    What did I say?

Sure,
I'm happy!
Take it away!

Hey, pop!
Re-bop!
Mop

Y-e-a-h!

.    .    .

CHILDREN'S RHYMES

When I was a chile we used to play,
"One—two—buckle my shoe!"
and things like that. But now, Lord,
listen at them little varmints!

    By what sends
    the white kids
    I ain't sent:
    I know I can't
    be President.

There is two thousand children                                          10
in this block, I do believe!

    What don't bug
    them white kids
    sure bugs me:
    We knows everybody
    ain't free!

Some of these young ones is cert'ly bad—
One batted a hard ball right through my window
and my gold fish et the glass.

    What's written down                                  20
    for white folks

    ain't for us a-tall:
    "Liberty and Justice—
    Huh—For All."

    Oop-pop-a-da!
    Skee! Daddle-de-do!
    Be-bop!

    Salt'peanuts!

De-dop!

.    .    .

BUDDY

That kid's my buddy,
still and yet
I don't see him much.
He works downtown for Twelve a week.

Has to give his mother Ten—
she says he can have
the other Two
to pay his carfare, buy a suit,
coat, shoes,
anything he wants out of it.                                        *10*

### JUKE BOX LOVE SONG

I could take the Harlem night
and wrap around you
Take the neon lights and make a crown,
Take the Lenox Avenue busses,
Taxis, subways,
And for your love song tone their rumble down.
Take Harlem's heartbeat,
Make a drumbeat,
Put it on a record, let it whirl,
And while we listen to it play,                                    *10*
Dance with you till day—
Dance with you, my sweet brown Harlem girl.

·   ·   ·

### WONDER

Early blue evening.
Lights ain't come on yet.
          Looky yonder!
They come on now!

### EASY BOOGIE

Down in the bass
That steady beat
Walking walking walking
Like marching feet.

Down in the bass
That easy roll,
Rolling like I like it
In my soul.

          Riffs, smears, breaks.

Hey, Lawdy, Mama!                                                  *10*
Do you hear what I said?
Easy like I rock it
In my bed!

## DIG AND BE DUG

### MOVIES

The Roosevelt, Renaissance, Gem, Alhambra:
Harlem laughing in all the wrong places

at the crocodile tears
of crocodile art
that you know
in your heart
is crocodile:

(Hollywood
laughs at me,
black—
so I laugh
back.)

10

.  .  .

WHAT? SO SOON!

I believe my old lady's
pregnant again!

Fate must have
some kind of trickeration
to populate the
cullud nation!

COMMENT AGAINST LAMP POST

You call it fate?

.  .  .

MOTTO

I play it cool
and dig all jive
That's the reason
I stay alive.
My motto,
As I live and learn,
      is:
Dig and Be Dug
In Return.

.  .  .

ADVICE

Folks, I'm telling you,
birthing is hard
and dying is mean—
so get yourself
a little loving
in between.

GREEN MEMORY

A wonderful time—the War:
when money rolled in
and blood rolled out.

> But blood
> was far away
> from here—

Money was near.

. . .

*EARLY BRIGHT*

. . .

### MELLOW

Into the laps
of black celebrities
white girls fall
like pale plums from a tree
beyond a high tension wall
wired for killing
which makes it
more thrilling.

### LIVE AND LET LIVE

Maybe it ain't right—
but the people of the night
will give even
a snake
a break.

. . .

*VICE VERSA TO BACH*

### THEME FOR ENGLISH B

The instructor said,

> Go home and write
> a page tonight.
> And let that page come out of you—
> Then, it will be true.

I wonder if it's that simple?
I am twenty-two, colored, born in Winston-Salem.
I went to school there, then Durham, then here
to this college on the hill above Harlem.
I am the only colored student in my class.                    10
The steps from the hill lead down into Harlem,
through a park, then I cross St. Nicholas,
Eighth Avenue, Seventh, and I come to the Y,
the Harlem Branch Y, where I take the elevator
up to my room, sit down, and write this page:

It's not easy to know what is true for you or me
at twenty-two, my age. But I guess I'm what
I feel and see and hear. Harlem, I hear you:
hear you, hear me—we two—you, me talk on this page.
(I hear New York, too.) Me—who?                    20

Well, I like to eat, sleep, drink, and be in love.
I like to work, read, learn, and understand life.
I like a pipe for a Christmas present,
or records—Bessie, bop, or Bach.

I guess being colored doesn't make me not like
the same things other folks like who are other races.
So will my page be colored that I write?
Being me, it will not be white.
But it will be
a part of you, instructor.                                         *30*
You are white—
yet a part of me, as I am a part of you.
That's American.
Sometimes perhaps you don't want to be a part of me.
Nor do I often want to be a part of you.
But we are, that's true!
As I learn from you,
I guess you learn from me—
although you're older—and white—
and somewhat more free.                                            *40*

This is my page for English B.

### COLLEGE FORMAL: RENAISSANCE CASINO

Golden girl
in a golden gown
in a melody night
in Harlem town
lad tall and brown
tall and wise
college boy smart
eyes in eyes
the music wraps
them both around                                                   *10*
in mellow magic
of dancing sound
till they're the heart
of the whole big town
gold and brown

## DREAM DEFERRED

### TESTIMONIAL

If I just had a piano
if I just had a organ,
if I just had a drum,
how I could praise my Lord!

But I don't need no piano,
    neither organ
    nor drum
for to praise my Lord!

### PASSING

On sunny summer Sunday afternoons in Harlem
when the air is one interminable ball game
and grandma cannot get her gospel hymns
from the Saints of God in Christ
on account of the Dodgers on the radio,
on sunny Sunday afternoons
when the kids look all new
and far too clean to stay that way,
and Harlem has its
washed-and-ironed-and-cleaned-best out,                                    *10*
the ones who've crossed the line
to live downtown
miss you,
Harlem of the bitter dream,
since their dream has
come true.

                    .    .    .

### BLUES AT DAWN

I don't dare start thinking in the morning
I don't dare start thinking in the morning.
    If I thought thoughts in bed,
    Them thoughts would bust my head—
So I don't dare start thinking in the morning.
I don't dare remember in the morning.
Don't dare remember in the morning.
    If I recall the day before,
    I wouldn't get up no more—
So I don't dare remember in the morning.                                    *10*

                    .    .    .

### ARGUMENT

White is right,
Yellow mellow,
Black, get back!

    Do you believe that, Jack?

Sure do!

    Then you're a dope
    for which there ain't no hope.
    Black is fine!
    And, God knows,
    It's mine!                                                              *10*

LIKEWISE

The Jews:
    Groceries
    Suits
    Fruit
    Watches
    Diamond rings
    THE DAILY NEWS
Jews sell me things.
Yom Kippur, no!
Shops all over Harlem                                              10
close up tight that night.

Some folks blame high prices on the Jews.
(Some folks blame too much on Jews.)
But in Harlem they don't answer back,
Just maybe shrug their shoulders,
"What's the use?"

    What's the use
    In Harlem?
    What's the use?
    What's the Harlem                                        20
    use in Harlem
    what's the lick?
    Hey!
    Baba-re-bop!
    Mop.
    On a be-bop kick!

Sometimes I think
Jews must have heard
the music of a
dream deferred.                                                   30

LENOX AVENUE MURAL

HARLEM

What happens to a dream deferred?

    Does it dry up
    like a raisin in the sun?
    Or fester like a sore—
    And then run?
    Does it stink like rotten meat?
    Or crust and sugar over—
    like a syrupy sweet?

Maybe it just sags
like a heavy load.                                        *10*

Or does it explode?

   .   .   .

### ISLAND

Between two rivers,
North of the park,
like darker rivers
The streets are dark.

Black and white,
Gold and brown—
Chocolate-custard
Pie of a town.

Dream within a dream
Our dream deferred.                                       *10*

Good morning, daddy!

Ain't you heard?   (*1951*)

## OGDEN NASH / 1902–

## The Octopus

Tell me, O Octopus, I begs,
Is those things arms, or is they legs?
I marvel at thee, Octopus;
If I were thou, I'd call me Us.   (*1942*)

## Kindly Unhitch That Star, Buddy

I hardly suppose I know anybody who wouldn't rather be a success than a failure,
Just as I suppose every piece of crabgrass in the garden would much rather be an
    azalea,
And in celestial circles all the run-of-the-mill angels would rather be archangels
    or at least cherubim and seraphim,
And in the legal world all the little process-servers hope to grow up into great
    big bailiffim and sheriffim.
Indeed, everybody wants to be a wow,
But not everybody knows exactly how.
Some people think they will eventually wear diamonds instead of rhinestones
Only by everlastingly keeping their noses to their ghrinestones,
And other people think they will be able to put in more time at Palm Beach and
    the Ritz

By not paying too much attention to attendance at the office but rather in being
    brilliant by starts and fits.       *10*
Some people after a full day's work sit up all night getting a college education
    by correspondence,
While others seem to think they'll get just as far by devoting their evenings to
    the study of the difference in temperament between brunettance and
    blondance.
In short, the world is filled with people trying to achieve success,
And half of them think they'll get it by saying No and half of them by saying
    Yes,
And if all the ones who say No said Yes, and vice versa, such is the fate of
    humanity that ninety-nine per cent of them still wouldn't be any better off
    than they were before,
Which perhaps is just as well because if everybody was a success nobody could
    be contemptuous of anybody else and everybody would start in all over
    again trying to be a bigger success than everybody else so they would have
    somebody to be contemptuous of and so on forevermore,
Because when people start hitching their wagons to a star,
That's the way they are.  *(1945)*

## Listen . . .

There is a knocking in the skull,
An endless silent shout
Of something beating on a wall,
And crying, Let me out.

That solitary prisoner
Will never hear reply,
No comrade in eternity
Can hear the frantic cry.

No heart can share the terror
That haunts his monstrous dark;    *10*
The light that filters through the chinks
No other eye can mark.

When flesh is linked with eager flesh,
And words run warm and full,
I think that he is loneliest then,
The captive in the skull.

Caught in a mesh of living veins,
In cell of padded bone,
He loneliest is when he pretends
That he is not alone.    *20*

We'd free the incarcerate race of man
That such a doom endures
Could only you unlock my skull,
Or I creep into yours.  *(1945)*

## Song of the Open Road

I think that I shall never see
A billboard lovely as a tree.
Indeed, unless the billboards fall
I'll never see a tree at all.   (*1945*)

## The Hamster

There is not much about the hamster
To stimulate the epigramster.
The essence of his simple story,
He populates the laboratory.
Then leaves his offspring in the lurch,
Martyrs to medical research.
Was he as bright as people am,
New York would be New Hamsterdam.   (*1952*)

## COUNTEE CULLEN / 1903–1946

## Yet Do I Marvel

I doubt not God is good, well-meaning, kind,
And did He stoop to quibble could tell why
The little buried mole continues blind,
Why flesh that mirrors Him must some day die,
Make plain the reason tortured Tantalus
Is baited by the fickle fruit, declare
If merely brute caprice dooms Sisyphus[1]
To struggle up a never-ending stair.
Inscrutable His ways are, and immune
To catechism by a mind too strewn                                    10
With petty cares to slightly understand
What awful brain compels His awful hand.
Yet do I marvel at this curious thing:
To make a poet black, and bid him sing!   (*1925*)

---

[1] corrupt king of Corinth punished in Hades by having to push uphill a huge stone which rolled down again each time it reached the top (*Odyssey*, XI, 593–600)

# Four Epitaphs

## 1  FOR MY GRANDMOTHER

This lovely flower fell to seed;
Work gently sun and rain;
She held it as her dying creed
That she would grow again.

## 2  FOR JOHN KEATS, APOSTLE OF BEAUTY

Not writ in water nor in mist,
Sweet lyric throat, thy name.
Thy singing lips that cold death kissed
Have seared his own with flame.

## 3  FOR PAUL LAURENCE DUNBAR

Born of the sorrowful of heart
Mirth was a crown upon his head;
Pride kept his twisted lips apart
In jest, to hide a heart that bled.

## 4  FOR A LADY I KNOW

She even thinks that up in heaven
    Her class lies late and snores,
While poor black cherubs rise at seven
    To do celestial chores.   (*1925*)

# Scottsboro,[1] Too, Is Worth Its Song

## (*A POEM TO AMERICAN POETS*)

I said:
Now will the poets sing,—
Their cries go thundering
Like blood and tears
Into the nation's ears,
Like lightning dart
Into the nation's heart.
Against the disease and death and all things fell,
And war,
Their strophes rise and swell                                    10
To jar
The foe smug in his citadel.

---

[1] Nine Negro boys were tried in Scottsboro, Alabama, in 1931 on charges of raping two white girls. Eight of the nine were convicted. Liberals and radicals contended that racial prejudice had produced the decision. The Supreme Court ordered a retrial. One of the girls acknowledged that she had lied, but one man was sentenced to death. A second review by the Supreme Court produced another retrial resulting in four convictions and the dismissal of charges against five of the defendants.

Remembering their sharp and pretty
Tunes for Sacco and Vanzetti,[2]
I said:
Here too's a cause divinely spun
For those whose eyes are on the sun,
Here in epitome

Is all disgrace
And epic wrong,                                                                20
Like wine to brace
The minstrel heart, and blare it into song.

Surely, I said,
Now will the poets sing.
    But they have raised no cry.
    I wonder why.   (*1935*)

# C. DAY LEWIS / 1904–1972

## Let Us Now Praise Famous Men

Let us now praise famous men,
Not your earth-shakers, not the dynamiters,
But who in the Home Counties[1] or the Khyber,[2]
Trimming their nails to meet an ill wind,
Facing the Adversary with a clean collar,
Justified the system.
Admire the venerable pile that bred them,
Bones are its foundations,
The pinnacles are stone abstractions,
Whose halls are whispering-galleries designed                 10
To echo voices of the past, dead tongues.
White hopes of England here
Are taught to rule by learning to obey,
Bend over before vested interests,
Kiss the rod, salute the quarter-deck;
Here is no savage discipline
Of peregrine swooping, of fire destroying,
But a civil code; no capital offender

But the cool cad, the man who goes too far.
Ours the curriculum                                          20
Neither of building birds nor wasteful waters,
Bound in book not violent in vein:
Here we inoculate with dead ideas
Against blood-epidemics, against
The infection of faith and the excess of life.
Our methods are up to date; we teach
Through head and not by heart,
Language with gramophones and sex with charts,
Prophecy by deduction, prayer by numbers.
For honors see prospectus: those who leave us          30
Will get a post and pity the poor;
Their eyes glaze at strangeness;
They are never embarrassed, have a word for everything,
Living on credit, dying when the heart stops;
Will wear black armlets and stand a moment in silence
For the passing of an era, at their own funeral.   (1933)


## Come, Live with Me and Be My Love

Come, live with me and be my love,
And we will all the pleasures prove
Of peace and plenty, bed and board,
That chance employment may afford.

I'll handle dainties on the docks
And thou shalt read of summer frocks:
At evening by the sour canals
We'll hope to hear some madrigals.

Care on thy maiden brow shall put
A wreath of wrinkles, and thy foot          10
Be shod with pain: not silken dress
But toil shall tire thy loveliness.

Hunger shall make thy modest zone
And cheat fond death of all but bone—
If these delights thy mind may move,
Then live with me and be my love.

(1935)


## Newsreel

Enter the dream-house, brothers and sisters, leaving
Your debts asleep, your history at the door:
This is the home for heroes, and this loving
Darkness a fur you can afford.

Fish in their tank electrically heated
Nose with envy the glass wall: for them
Clerk, spy, nurse, killer, prince, the great and the defeated,
Move in a mute day-dream.

Bathed in this common source, you gape incurious
At what your active hours have willed—          10
Sleep-walking on that silver wall, the furious
Sick shapes and pregnant fancies of your world.

There is the mayor opening the oyster season:
A society wedding: the autumn hats look swell:
An old crocks' race, and a politician
In fishing-waders to prove that all is well.

Oh, look at the warplanes! Screaming hysteric treble
In the long power-dive, like gannets they fall steep.
But what are they to trouble—
These silver shadows to trouble your watery, womb-deep sleep?     *20*

See the big guns, rising, groping, erected
To plant death in your world's soft womb.
Fire-bud, smoke-blossom, iron seed projected—
Are these exotics? They will grow nearer home:

Grow nearer home—and out of the dream-house stumbling
One night into a strangling air and the flung
Rags of children and thunder of stone niagaras tumbling,
You'll know you slept too long.   *(1935)*


## RICHARD EBERHART / 1904–

### The Groundhog

In June, amid the golden fields,
I saw a groundhog lying dead.
Dead lay he; my senses shook,
And mind outshot our naked frailty.
There lowly in the vigorous summer
His form began its senseless change,
And made my senses waver dim
Seeing nature ferocious in him.
Inspecting close his maggots' might
And seething cauldron of his being,     *10*
Half with loathing, half with a strange
    love,
I poked him with an angry stick.
The fever rose, became a flame
And Vigor circumscribed the skies,
Immense energy in the sun,
And through my frame a sunless trembling.
My stick had done nor good nor harm.
Then stood I silent in the day
Watching the object, as before;

And kept my reverence for knowledge   *20*
Trying for control, to be still,
To quell the passion of the blood;
Until I had bent down on my knees
Praying for joy in the sight of decay.
And so I left: and I returned
In Autumn strict of eye, to see
The sap gone out of the groundhog,
But the bony sodden hulk remained.
But the year had lost its meaning,
And in intellectual chains     *30*
I lost both love and loathing,
Mured[1] up in the wall of wisdom.
Another summer took the fields again
Massive and burning, full of life,
But when I chanced upon the spot
There was only a little hair left,
And bones bleaching in the sunlight
Beautiful as architecture;
I watched them like a geometer,
And cut a walking stick from a birch.   *40*
It has been three years, now.

---

[1] walled

There is no sign of the groundhog.
I stood there in the whirling summer,
My hand capped a withered heart,
And thought of China and of Greece,

Of Alexander[2] in his tent;
Of Montaigne[3] in his tower,
Of Saint Theresa[4] in her wild lament.

(*1936*)

## The Fury of Aerial Bombardment

You would think the fury of aerial bombardment
Would rouse God to relent; the infinite spaces
Are still silent. He looks on shock-pried faces.
History, even, does not know what is meant.

You would feel that after so many centuries
God would give man to repent; yet he can kill
As Cain could, but with multitudinous will,
No farther advanced than in his ancient furies.

Was man made stupid to see his own stupidity?
Is God by definition indifferent, beyond us all?      *10*
Is the eternal truth man's fighting soul
Wherein the Beast ravens in its own avidity?

Of Van Wettering I speak, and Averill,
Names on a list, whose faces I do not recall
But they are gone to early death, who late in school
Distinguished the belt feed lever from the belt holding pawl.[1]      (*1944*)

# JOHN BETJEMAN / 1906–

## The Arrest of Oscar Wilde at the Cadogan Hotel

He sipped at a weak hock and seltzer
As he gazed at the London skies
Through the Nottingham lace of the curtains
Or was it his bees-winged[1] eyes?

To the right and before him Pont Street
Did tower in her new built red,
As hard as the morning gaslight
That shone on his unmade bed,

---

[2] the Great; Macedonian conqueror, 356 B.C.–323 B.C.
[3] Michel de Montaigne (1533–1592), French essayist, used a tower set apart from his house as a study.

[4] Spanish mystic (1515–1582), noted for particularly intense visions
[1] parts of a machine gun
[1] filmy

"I want some more hock in my seltzer,
    And Robbie,[2] please give me your hand—                          *10*
Is this the end or beginning?
    How can I understand?

"So you've brought me the latest *Yellow Book:*[3]
    And Buchan[4] has got in it now:
Approval of what is approved of
    Is as false as a well-kept vow.

"More hock, Robbie—where is the seltzer?
    Dear boy, pull again at the bell!
They are all little better than *cretins,*
    Though this *is* the Cadogan Hotel.                              *20*

"One astrakhan coat is at Willis's—
    Another one's at the Savoy:
Do fetch my morocco portmanteau,
    And bring them on later, dear boy."

A thump, and a murmur of voices—
    ("Oh why must they make such a din?")
As the door of the bedroom swung open
    And TWO PLAIN CLOTHES POLICEMEN came in:

"Mr. Woilde, we 'ave come for tew take yew
    Where felons and criminals dwell:[5]                             *30*
We must ask yew tew leave with us quoietly
    For this *is* the Cadogan Hotel."

He rose, and he put down *The Yellow Book.*
    He staggered—and, terrible-eyed,
He brushed past the palms on the staircase
    And was helped to a hansom outside.   (*1937*)


## In Westminster Abbey

Let me take this other glove off
    As the *vox humana*[1] swells,
And the beauteous fields of Eden
    Bask beneath the Abbey bells.
Here, where England's statesmen lie,
Listen to a lady's cry.

Gracious Lord, oh bomb the Germans.
    Spare their women for Thy Sake,
And if that is not too easy
    We will pardon Thy Mistake.                                      *10*

But, gracious Lord, whate'er shall be,
Don't let anyone bomb me.

Keep our Empire undismembered
    Guide our Forces by Thy Hand,
Gallant blacks from far Jamaica,
    Honduras and Togoland;
Protect them Lord in all their fights,
And, even more, protect the whites.

Think of what our Nation stands for,
    Books from Boots'[2] and country
    lanes,                                                           *20*

---

[2] Wilde's companion, Robert Ross
[3] an avant-garde quarterly published briefly in the 1890s
[4] a writer who later became famous for his entertaining novels
[5] In 1895 Wilde was convicted of homosexual practices and sentenced to two years at hard labor.
[1] an organ stop intended to imitate the human voice
[2] an English chain of chemist's shops (i.e., drug stores) that include lending libraries

Free speech, free passes, class distinction
  Democracy and proper drains.
Lord, put beneath Thy special care
One-eighty-nine Cadogan Square.[3]

Although dear Lord I am a sinner,
  I have done no major crime;
Now I'll come to Evening Service
  Whensoever I have time.
So, Lord, reserve for me a crown,
And do not let my shares go down.    *30*
I will labour for Thy Kingdom,

Help our lads to win the war,
Send white feathers to the cowards,
  Join the Women's Army Corps,
Then wash the Steps around Thy Throne
In the Eternal Safety Zone.

Now I feel a little better,
  What a treat to hear Thy Word,
Where the bones of leading statesmen,
  Have so often been interred.    *40*
And now, dear Lord, I cannot wait
Because I have a luncheon date.   *(1940)*

## The Cottage Hospital

At the end of a long-walled garden
  in a red provincial town,
A brick path led to a mulberry—
  scanty grass at its feet.
I lay under blackening branches
  where the mulberry leaves hung down
Sheltering ruby fruit globes
  from a Sunday-tea-time heat.
Apple and plum espaliers
  basked upon bricks of brown;   *10*
The air was swimming with insects,
  and children played in the street.

Out of this bright intentness
  into the mulberry shade
*Musca domestica* (housefly)
  swung from the August light
Slap into slithery rigging
  by the waiting spider made

Which spun the lithe elastic
  till the fly was shrouded tight.   *20*
Down came the hairy talons
  and horrible poison blade
And none of the garden noticed
  that fizzing, hopeless fight.

Say in what Cottage Hospital
  whose pale green walls resound
With the tap upon polished parquet
  of inflexible nurses' feet
Shall I myself be lying
  when they range the screens around?  *30*
And say shall I groan in dying,
  as I twist the sweaty sheet?
Or gasp for breath uncrying,
  as I feel my senses drown'd
While the air is swimming with insects
  and children play in the street?  *(1954)*

## The Licorice Fields at Pontefract

In the licorice fields at Pontefract
  My love and I did meet
And many a burdened licorice bush
  Was blooming round our feet;
Red hair she had and golden skin,
Her sulky lips were shaped for sin,
Her sturdy legs were flannel-slack'd,
The strongest legs in Pontefract.

---

[3] a moderately fashionable address

The light and dangling licorice flowers
 Gave off the sweetest smells;                                    *10*
From various black Victorian towers
 The Sunday evening bells
Came pealing over dales and hills
And tanneries and silent mills
And lowly streets where country stops
And little shuttered corner shops.

She cast her blazing eyes on me
 And plucked a licorice leaf;
I was her captive slave and she
 My red-haired robber chief.                                    *20*
Oh love! for love I could not speak,
It left me winded, wilting, weak
And held in brown arms strong and bare
And wound with flaming ropes of hair.   (*1954*)


# WILLIAM EMPSON / 1906–


## Legal Fiction

Law makes long spokes of the short stakes of men.
Your well fenced out real estate of mind
No high flat of the nomad citizen
Looks over, or train leaves behind.

Your rights extend under and above your claim
Without bound; you own land in Heaven and Hell;
Your part of earth's surface and mass the same,
Of all cosmos' volume, and all stars as well.

Your rights reach down where all owners meet, in Hell's
Pointed exclusive conclave, at earth's centre                    *10*
(Your spun farm's root still on that axis dwells);
And up, through galaxies, a growing sector.

You are nomad yet; the lighthouse beam you own
Flashes, like Lucifer,[1] through the firmament.
Earth's axis varies; your dark central cone
Wavers, a candle's shadow, at the end.   (*1935*)

---

[1] Lucifer (light-bringer) is identified with the planet Venus and with Satan fallen from Heaven.

## Villanelle

It is the pain, it is the pain, endures.
Your chemic beauty burned my muscles through.
Poise of my hands reminded me of yours.

What later purge from this deep toxin cures?
What kindness now could the old salve renew?
It is the pain, it is the pain, endures.

The infection slept (custom or change inures)
And when pain's secondary phase was due
Poise of my hands reminded me of yours.

How safe I felt, whom memory assures,                          *10*
Rich that your grace safely by heart I knew.
It is the pain, it is the pain, endures.

My stare drank deep beauty that still allures.
My heart pumps yet the poison draught of you.
Poise of my hands reminded me of yours.

You are still kind whom the same shape immures.
Kind and beyond adieu. We miss our cue.
It is the pain, it is the pain, endures.
Poise of my hands reminded me of yours.   *(1935)*


## This Last Pain

This last pain for the damned the Fathers found:
"They knew the bliss with which they were not crowned."
      Such, but on earth, let me foretell,
      Is all, of heaven or of hell.

Man, as the prying housemaid of the soul,
May know her happiness by eye to hole:
      He's safe; the key is lost; he knows
      Door will not open, nor hole close.

"What is conceivable can happen too,"
Said Wittgenstein,[1] who had not dreamt of you;          *10*
      But wisely; if we worked it long
      We should forget where it was wrong.

Those thorns are crowns which, woven into knots,
Crackle under and soon boil fool's pots;
      And no man's watching, wise and long,
      Would ever stare them into song.

---

[1] Ludwig J. J. Wittgenstein (1889–1951), Austrian-born English philosopher, noted for his assertion that language cannot symbolize real facts

Thorns burn to a consistent ash, like man;
A splendid cleanser for the frying-pan:
    And those who leap from pan to fire
    Should this brave opposite admire.        20

All those large dreams by which men long live well
Are magic-lanterned on the smoke of hell;
    This then is real, I have implied,
    A painted, small, transparent slide.

These the inventive can hand-paint at leisure,
Or most emporia would stock our measure;
    And feasting in their dappled shade
    We should forget how they were made.

Feign then what's by a decent tact believed
And act that state is only so conceived,        30
    And build an edifice of form
    For house where phantoms may keep warm.

Imagine, then, by miracle, with me,
(Ambiguous gifts, as what gods give must be)
    What could not possibly be there,
    And learn a style from a despair.   (*1935*)

## The World's End

    "Fly with me then to all's and the world's end
    And plumb for safety down the gaps of stars;
    Let the last gulf or topless cliff befriend,
    What tyrant there our variance debars?"

    Alas, how hope for freedom, no bars bind;
    Space is like earth, rounded, a padded cell;
    Plumb the stars' depth, your lead bumps you behind;
    Blind Satan's voice rattled the whole of Hell.

    On cushioned air what is such metal worth
    To pierce to the gulf that lies so snugly curled?    10
    Each tangent plain touches one top of earth,
    Each point in one direction ends the world.

    Apple of knowledge and forgetful mere
    From Tantalus too differential bend.
    The shadow clings. The world's end is here.
    This place's curvature precludes its end.   (*1935*)

## Missing Dates

    Slowly the poison the whole blood stream fills.
    It is not the effort nor the failure tires.
    The waste remains, the waste remains and kills.

It is not your system or clear sight that mills
Down small to the consequence a life requires;
Slowly the poison the whole blood stream fills.

They bled an old dog dry yet the exchange rills
Of young dog blood gave but a month's desires;
The waste remains, the waste remains and kills.

It is the Chinese tombs and the slag hills                                    10
Usurp the soil, and not the soil retires.
Slowly the poison the whole blood stream fills.

Not to have fire is to be a skin that shrills.
The complete fire is death. From partial fires
The waste remains, the waste remains and kills.

It is the poems you have lost, the ills
From missing dates, at which the heart expires.
Slowly the poison the whole blood stream fills.
The waste remains, the waste remains and kills.    (*1940*)

# LOUIS MACNEICE / 1907–1964

## Birmingham

Smoke from the train-gulf hid by hoardings[1] blunders upward, the brakes of cars
Pipe as the policeman pivoting round raises his flat hand, bars
With his figure of a monolith Pharaoh the queue of fidgety machines
(Chromium dogs on the bonnet,[2] faces behind the triplex screens),
Behind him the streets run away between the proud glass of shops,
Cubical scent-bottles artificial legs arctic foxes and electric mops,
But beyond this center the slumward vista thins like a diagram:
There, unvisited, are Vulcan's[3] forges who doesn't care a tinker's damn.
Splayed outwards through the suburbs houses, houses for rest
Seducingly rigged by the builder, half-timbered houses with lips pressed     10
So tightly and eyes staring at the traffic through bleary haws[4]
And only a six-inch grip of the racing earth in their concrete claws;
In these houses men as in a dream pursue the Platonic Forms[5]
With wireless and cairn terriers[6] and gadgets approximating to the fickle norms
And endeavor to find God and score one over the neighbor
By climbing tentatively upward on jerry-built beauty and sweated labor.
The lunch hour: the shops empty, shopgirls' faces relax
Diaphanous as green glass, empty as old almanacs

---

[1] billboards     [2] hood                        [5] ideal prototypes in the mind of God
[3] Roman god of fire and metalwork                [6] a small Scottie; a house dog
[4] hawthorn bushes

As incoherent with ticketed gewgaws tiered behind their heads
As the Burne-Jones[7] windows in St. Philip's broken by crawling leads;       20
Insipid color, patches of emotion, Saturday thrills
(This theatre is sprayed with "June")—the gutter take our old playbills,
Next week-end it is likely in the heart's funfair we shall pull
Strong enough on the handle to get back our money; or at any rate it is possible.
On shining lines the trams like vast sarcophagi move
Into the sky, plum after sunset, merging to duck's egg, barred with mauve
Zeppelin clouds, and Pentecost-like the cars' headlights bud
Out from sideroads and the traffic signals, crème de menthe or bull's blood,
Tell one to stop, the engine gently breathing, or to go on
To where like black pipes of organs in the frayed and fading zone       30
Of the West the factory chimneys on sullen sentry will all night wait
To call, in the harsh morning, sleep-stupid faces through the daily gate.   (*1933*)

## Museums

Museums offer us, running from among the buses,
A centrally heated refuge, parquet floors and sarcophaguses,
Into whose tall fake porches we hurry without a sound
Like a bettle under a brick that lies, useless, on the ground.
Warmed and cajoled by the silence the cowed cypher revives,
Mirrors himself in the cases of pots, paces himself by marble lives,
Makes believe it was he that was the glory that was Rome,
Soft on his cheek the nimbus of other people's martyrdom,
And then returns to the street, his mind an arena where sprawls
Any number of consumptive Keatses and dying Gauls.   (*1933; 1935*)   10

## Bagpipe Music

It's no go the merrygoround, it's no go the rickshaw,
All we want is a limousine and a ticket for the peepshow.
Their knickers[1] are made of crêpe-de-chine, their shoes are made of python,
Their halls are lined with tiger rugs and their walls with heads of bison.

John MacDonald found a corpse, put it under the sofa,
Waited till it came to life and hit it with a poker,
Sold its eyes for souvenirs, sold its blood for whiskey,
Kept its bones for dumb-bells to use when he was fifty.

It's no go the Yogi-Man, it's no go Blavatsky,[2]
All we want is a bank balance and a bit of skirt in a taxi.       10

Annie MacDougall went to milk, caught her foot in the heather,
Woke to hear a dance record playing of Old Vienna.
It's no go your maindenheads, it's no go your culture,
All we want is a Dunlop tyre and the devil mend the puncture.

---

[7] pre-Raphaelite painter and worker in stained glass
[1] panties
[2] Madame Blavatsky, born Helena Petrovna Hahn (1831–1891), Russian-born founder of the Theosophical Society, who claimed psychic powers

The Laird o' Phelps spent Hogmannay[3] declaring he was sober;
Counted his feet to prove the fact and found he had one foot over.
Mrs. Carmichael had her fifth, looked at the job with repulsion,
Said to the midwife "Take it away; I'm through with overproduction."

It's no go the gossip column, it's no go the Céilidh,[4]
All we want is a mother's help and a sugar-stick for the baby.          20

Willie Murray cut his thumb, couldn't count the damage,
Took the hide of an Ayrshire cow and used it for a bandage.
His brother caught three hundred cran[5] when the seas were lavish,
Threw the bleeders back in the sea and went upon the parish.

It's no go the Herring Board,[6] it's no go the Bible,
All we want is a packet of fags when our hands are idle.

It's no go the picture palace, it's no go the stadium,
It's no go the country cot with a pot of pink geraniums.
It's no go the Government grants, it's no go the elections,
Sit on your arse for fifty years and hang your hat on a pension.        30

It's no go my honey love, it's no go my poppet;[7]
Work your hands from day to day, the winds will blow the profit.
The glass is falling hour by hour, the glass will fall for ever,
But if you break the bloody glass you won't hold up the weather.   (*1938*)

## Explorations

The whale butting through scarps of moving marble,
The tapeworm probing the intestinal darkness,
The swallows drawn collectively to their magnet,
      These are our prototypes and yet,
Though we may envy them still, they are merely patterns
      To wonder at—and forget.

For the ocean-carver, cumbrous but unencumbered,
Who tired of land looked for his freedom and frolic in water,
Though he succeeded, has failed; it is only instinct
      That plots his graph and he,                                     10
Though appearing to us a free and a happy monster, is merely
      An appanage of the sea.

And the colourless blind worm, triumphantly self-degraded,
Who serves as an image to men of the worst adjustment—
Oxymoron of parasitical glory—
      Cannot even be cursed,
Lacking the only pride of his way of life, not knowing
      That he has chosen the worst.

So even that legion of birds who appear so gladly
Purposeful, with air in their bones, enfranchised               20

---

[3] New Year's Eve    [4] Scottish songfest          Scottish trade
[5] about a quarter of a million herring      [7] doll
[6] a government agency designed to help a failing

Citizens of the sky and never at odds with
    The season or out of line,
Can be no model to us; their imputed purpose
    Is a foregone design—

And ours is not. For we are unique, a conscious
Hoping and therefore despairing creature, the final
Anomaly of the world, we can learn no method
    From whales or birds or worms;
Our end is our own to be won by our own endeavour
    And held on our own terms.   (*1944*)                    30

# W. H. AUDEN / 1907–1973

## Song: "O Where Are You Going?"

"O where are you going?" said reader to rider,
    "That valley is fatal when furnaces burn,
Yonder's the midden whose odours will madden,
    That gap is the grave where the tall return."

"O do you imagine," said fearer to farer,
    "That dusk will delay on your path to the pass,
Your diligent looking discover the lacking
    Your footsteps feel from granite to grass?"

"O what was that bird," said horror to hearer,
    "Did you see that shape in the twisted trees?                    10
Behind you swiftly the figure comes softly,
    The spot on your skin is a shocking disease."

"Out of this house"—said rider to reader,
    "Yours never will"—said farer to fearer,
"They're looking for you"—said hearer to horror,
    As he left them there, as he left them there.   (*1932*)

## The Wanderer

Doom is dark and deeper than any sea-dingle.
    Upon what man it fall
In spring, day-wishing flowers appearing,
Avalanche sliding, white snow from rock-face,
    That he should leave his house,
No cloud-soft hand can hold him, restraint by women;
    But ever that man goes
Through place-keepers, through forest trees,

A stranger to strangers over undried sea,
Houses for fishes, suffocating water,                              *10*
Or lonely on fell as chat,
By pot-holed becks
A bird stone-haunting, an unquiet bird.

There head falls forward, fatigued at evening,
And dreams of home,
Waving from window, spread of welcome,
Kissing of wife under single sheet;
But waking sees
Bird-flocks nameless to him, through doorway voices
Of new men making another love.                                   *20*
Save him from hostile capture,
From sudden tiger's leap at corner;
Protect his house,
His anxious house where days are counted
From thunderbolt protect,
From gradual ruin spreading like a stain;
Converting number from vague to certain,
Bring joy, bring day of his returning,
Lucky with day approaching, with leaning dawn.   (*1934*)


# In Memory of W. B. Yeats

(*d. Jan. 1939*)

## I

He disappeared in the dead of winter:
The brooks were frozen, the airports almost deserted,
And snow disfigured the public statues;
The mercury sank in the mouth of the dying day.
What instruments we have agree
The day of his death was a dark cold day.

Far from his illness
The wolves ran on through the evergreen forests,
The peasant river was untempted by the fashionable quays;
By mourning tongues                                               *10*
The death of the poet was kept from his poems.

But for him it was his last afternoon as himself,
An afternoon of nurses and rumours;
The provinces of his body revolted,
The squares of his mind were empty,
Silence invaded the suburbs,
The current of his feeling failed; he became his admirers.

Now he is scattered among a hundred cities
And wholly given over to unfamiliar affections,
To find his happiness in another kind of wood                     *20*

And be punished under a foreign code of conscience.
The words of a dead man
Are modified in the guts of the living.
But in the importance and noise of to-morrow
When the brokers are roaring like beasts on the floor of the Bourse,
And the poor have the sufferings to which they are fairly accustomed,
And each in the cell of himself is almost convinced of his freedom,
A few thousand will think of this day
As one thinks of a day when one did something slightly unusual.
What instruments we have agree                                        *30*
The day of his death was a dark cold day.

## II

You were silly like us; your gift survived it all:
The parish of rich women, physical decay,
Yourself. Mad Ireland hurt you into poetry.
Now Ireland has her madness and her weather still,
For poetry makes nothing happen: it survives
In the valley of its making where executives
Would never want to tamper, flows on south
From ranches of isolation and the busy griefs,
Raw towns that we believe and die in; it survives,              *40*
A way of happening, a mouth.

## III

Earth, receive an honoured guest:
William Yeats is laid to rest.
Let the Irish vessel lie
Emptied of its poetry.

In the nightmare of the dark
All the dogs of Europe bark,
And the living nations wait,
Each sequested in its hate;

Intellectual disgrace                                                 *50*
Stares from every human face,
And the seas of pity lie
Locked and frozen in each eye.

Follow, poet, follow right
To the bottom of the night,
With your unconstraining voice
Still persuade us to rejoice;

With the farming of a verse
Make a vineyard of the curse,
Sing of human unsuccess                                               *60*
In a rapture of distress;

In the deserts of the heart
Let the healing fountain start,
In the prison of his days
Teach the free man how to praise.   (*1939*)

## Musée des Beaux Arts

About suffering they were never wrong,
The Old Masters: how well they understood
Its human position; how it takes place
While someone else is eating or opening a window or just walking dully along;
How, when the agéd are reverently, passionately waiting
For the miraculous birth, there always must be
Children who did not specially want it to happen, skating
On a pond at the edge of the wood:
They never forget
That even the dreadful martyrdom must run its course      *10*
Anyhow in a corner, some untidy spot
Where the dogs go on with their doggy life and the torturer's horse
Scratches its innocent behind on a tree.

In Brueghel's[1] *Icarus*, for instance: how everything turns away
Quite leisurely from the disaster; the ploughman may
Have heard the splash, the forsaken cry,
But for him it was not an important failure; the sun shone
As it had to on the white legs disappearing into the green
Water; and the expensive delicate ship that must have seen
Something amazing, a boy falling out of the sky,      *20*
Had somewhere to get to and sailed calmly on.   (*1940*)

## The Shield of Achilles

    She looked over his shoulder
      For vines and olive trees,
    Marble well-governed cities
      And ships upon untamed seas,
    But there on the shining metal
      His hands had put instead
    An artificial wilderness
      And a sky like lead.

A plain without a feature, bare and brown,
    No blade of grass, no sign of neighbourhood,      *10*
Nothing to eat and nowhere to sit down,
    Yet, congregated on its blankness, stood
    An unintelligible multitude,
A million eyes, a million boots in line,
Without expression, waiting for a sign.

Out of the air a voice without a face
    Proved by statistics that some cause was just
In tones as dry and level as the place:
    No one was cheered and nothing was discussed;

---

[1] Pieter Brueghel, Flemish painter, *c.* 1520–1569. Icarus and his father, Dædalus, fashioned wings and attached them to their shoulders with wax. Icarus flew too close to the sun; he fell from the sky when the sun melted the wax.

Column by column in a cloud of dust                               *20*
They marched away enduring a belief
Whose logic brought them, somewhere else, to grief.

    She looked over his shoulder
      For ritual pieties,
    White flower-garlanded heifers,
      Libation and sacrifice,
    But there on the shining metal
      Where the altar should have been,
    She saw by his flickering forge-light
      Quite another scene.                               *30*

Barbed wire enclosed an arbitrary spot
  Where bored officials lounged (one cracked a joke)
And sentries sweated for the day was hot:
  A crowd of ordinary decent folk
  Watched from without and neither moved nor spoke
As three pale figures were led forth and bound
To three posts driven upright in the ground.
The mass and majesty of this world, all
  That carries weight and always weighs the same
Lay in the hands of others; they were small                        *40*
  And could not hope for help and no help came:
  What their foes liked to do was done, their shame
Was all the worst could wish; they lost their pride
And died as men before their bodies died.

    She looked over his shoulder
      For athletes at their games,
    Men and women in a dance
      Moving their sweet limbs
    Quick, quick, to music,
      But there on the shining shield              *50*
    His hands had set no dancing-floor
      But a weed-choked field.

A ragged urchin, aimless and alone,
  Loitered about that vacancy, a bird
Flew up to safety from his well-aimed stone:
  That girls are raped, that two boys knife a third,
  Were axioms to him, who'd never heard
Of any world where promises were kept,
Or one could weep because another wept.

    The thin-lipped armourer,                         *60*
      Hephaestos hobbled away,
    Thetis of the shining breasts
      Cried out in dismay
    At what the god had wrought
      To please her son, the strong
    Iron-hearted man-slaying Achilles
      Who would not live long.   *(1955)*

# THEODORE ROETHKE / 1908–1963

## Moss-Gathering

To loosen with all ten fingers held wide and limber
And lift up a patch, dark-green, the kind for lining cemetery baskets,
Thick and cushiony, like an old-fashioned door-mat,
The crumbling small hollow sticks on the underside mixed with roots,
And wintergreen berries and leaves still stuck to the top,—
That was moss-gathering.

But something always went out of me when I dug loose those carpets
Of green, or plunged to my elbows in the spongy yellowish moss of the marshes:
And afterwards I always felt mean, jogging back over the logging road,
As if I had broken the natural order of things in that swampland;     *10*
Disturbed some rhythm, old and of vast importance,
By pulling off flesh from the living planet;
As if I had committed, against the whole scheme of life, a desecration.   (*1948*)

## Dolor

I have known the inexorable sadness of pencils,
Neat in their boxes, dolor of pad and paper-weight,
All the misery of manila folders and mucilage,
Desolation in immaculate public places,
Lonely reception room, lavatory, switchboard,
The unalterable pathos of basin and pitcher,
Ritual of multigraph, paper-clip, comma,
Endless duplication of lives and objects.
And I have seen dust from the walls of institutions,
Finer than flour, alive, more dangerous than silica,     *10*
Sift, almost invisible, through long afternoons of tedium,
Dripping a fine film on nails and delicate eyebrows,
Glazing the pale hair, the duplicate gray standard faces.   (*1948*)

## My Papa's Waltz

The whiskey on your breath
Could make a small boy dizzy;
But I held on like death:
Such waltzing was not easy.

We romped until the pans
Slid from the kitchen shelf;
My mother's countenance
Could not unfrown itself.

The hand that held my wrist
Was battered on one knuckle;     *10*
At every step I missed
My right ear scraped a buckle.

You beat time on my head
With a palm caked hard by dirt,
Then waltzed me off to bed
Still clinging to your shirt.   (*1948*)

## Elegy for Jane

### (*MY STUDENT, THROWN BY A HORSE*)

I remember the neckcurls, limp and damp as tendrils,
And her quick look, a sidelong pickerel smile;
And how, once startled into talk, the light syllables leaped for her,
And she balanced in the delight of her thought,
A wren, happy, tail into the wind,
Her song trembling the twigs and small branches.
The shade sang with her;
The leaves, their whispers turned to kissing;
And the mould sang in the bleached valleys under the rose.

Oh, when she was sad, she cast herself down into such a pure depth,     10
Even a father could not find her;
Scraping her cheek against straw;
Stirring the clearest water.

My sparrow, you are not here,
Waiting like a fern, making a spiny shadow.
The sides of wet stones cannot console me,
Nor the moss, wound with the last light.

If only I could nudge you from this sleep,
My maimed darling, my skittery pigeon.
Over this damp grave I speak the words of my love:     20
I, with no rights in this matter,
Neither father nor lover.   (*1953*)

## I Knew a Woman

I knew a woman, lovely in her bones,
When small birds sighed, she would sigh back at them;
Ah, when she moved, she moved more ways than one:
The shapes a bright container can contain!
Of her choice virtues only gods should speak,
Or English poets who grew up on Greek
(I'd have them sing in chorus, cheek to cheek).

How well her wishes went! She stroked my chin,
She taught me Turn, and Counter-turn, and Stand;
She taught me Touch, that undulant white skin;     10
I nibbled meekly from her proffered hand;
She was the sickle; I, poor I, the rake,
Coming behind her for her pretty sake
(But what prodigious mowing we did make).

Love likes a gander, and adores a goose:
Her full lips pursed, the errant note to seize;
She played it quick, she played it light and loose;
My eyes, they dazzled at her flowing knees;
Her several parts could keep a pure repose,

Or one hip quiver with a mobile nose                                    *20*
(She moved in circles, and those circles moved).

Let seed be grass, and grass turn into hay:
I'm martyr to a motion not my own;
What's freedom for? To know eternity.
I swear she cast a shadow white as stone.
But who would count eternity in days?
These old bones live to learn her wanton ways:
(I measure time by how a body sways).   (*1958*)

## In a Dark Time

In a dark time, the eye begins to see,
I meet my shadow in the deepening shade;
I hear my echo in the echoing wood—
A lord of nature weeping to a tree.
I live between the heron and the wren,
Beasts of the hill and serpents of the den.

What's madness but nobility of soul
At odds with circumstance? The day's on fire!
I know the purity of pure despair,
My shadow pinned against a sweating wall.[1]                            *10*
That place among the rocks—is it a cave,
Or winding path? The edge is what I have.

A steady storm of correspondences![2]
A night flowing with birds, a ragged moon,
And in broad day the midnight come again!
A man goes far to find out what he is—
Death of the self in a long, tearless night,
All natural shapes blazing unnatural light.

Dark, dark my light, and darker my desire.
My soul, like some heat-maddened summer fly,                            *20*
Keeps buzzing at the sill. Which I is *I?*
A fallen man, I climb out of my fear.
The mind enters itself, and God the mind,
And one is One, free in the tearing wind.   (*1964*)

## The Far Field

### 1

I dream of journeys repeatedly:
Of flying like a bat deep into a narrowing tunnel,
Of driving alone, without luggage, out a long peninsula,
The road lined with snow-laden second growth,

[1] Plato's Myth of the Cave compares man's limited knowledge of reality to that of a person so bound that he can see only his own shadow cast on a cave wall by a fire behind him.

[2] The transcendental doctrine of correspondences, essentially Platonic in origin, holds that earthly actualities are imperfect reflections of perfect divine ideas.

A fine dry snow ticking the windshield,
Alternate snow and sleet, no on-coming traffic,
And no lights behind, in the blurred side-mirror,
The road changing from glazed tarface to a rubble of stone,
Ending at last in a hopeless sand-rut,
Where the car stalls,                                                    10
Churning in a snowdrift
Until the headlights darken.

2

At the field's end, in the corner missed by the mower,
Where the turf drops off into a grass-hidden culvert,
Haunt of the cat-bird, nesting-place of the field-mouse,
Not too far away from the ever-changing flower-dump,
Among the tin cans, tires, rusted pipes, broken machinery,—
One learned of the eternal;
And in the shrunken face of a dead rat, eaten by rain and ground-beetles
(I found it lying among the rubble of an old coal bin)                    20
And the tom-cat, caught near the pheasant-run,
Its entrails strewn over the half-grown flowers,
Blasted to death by the night watchman.

I suffered for birds, for young rabbits caught in the mower,
My grief was not excessive.
For to come upon warblers in early May
Was to forget time and death:
How they filled the oriole's elm, a twittering restless cloud, all one morning,
And I watched and watched till my eyes blurred from the bird shapes,—
Cape May, Blackburnian, Cerulean[1]—                                     30
Moving, elusive as fish, fearless,
Hanging, bunched like young fruit, bending the end branches,
Still for a moment,
Then pitching away in half-flight,
Lighter than finches,
While the wrens bickered and sang in the half-green hedgerows,
And the flicker drummed from his dead tree in the chicken-yard.

—Or to lie naked in sand,
In the silted shallows of a slow river,
Fingering a shell,                                                       40
Thinking:
Once I was something like this, mindless,
Or perhaps with another mind, less peculiar;
Or to sink down to the hips in a mossy quagmire;
Or, with skinny knees, to sit astride a wet log,
Believing:
I'll return again,
As a snake or a raucous bird,
Or, with luck, as a lion.

---

[1] several varieties of warbler

I learned not to fear infinity, 50
The far field, the windy cliffs of forever,
The dying of time in the white light of tomorrow,
The wheel turning away from itself,
The sprawl of the wave,
The on-coming water.

### 3

The river turns on itself,
The tree retreats into its own shadow.
I feel a weightless change, a moving forward
As of water quickening before a narrowing channel
When banks converge, and the wide river whitens; 60
Or when two rivers combine, the blue glacial torrent
And the yellowish-green from the mountainy upland,—
At first a swift rippling between rocks,
Then a long running over flat stones
Before descending to the alluvial plain,
To the clay banks, and the wild grapes hanging from the elmtrees.
The slightly trembling water
Dropping a fine yellow silt where the sun stays;
And the crabs bask near the edge,
The weedy edge, alive with small snakes and bloodsuckers— 70
I have come to a still, but not a deep center,
A point outside the glittering current;
My eyes stare at the bottom of a river,
At the irregular stones, iridescent sandgrains,
My mind moves in more than one place,
In a country half-land, half-water.

I am renewed by death, thought of my death,
The dry scent of a dying garden in September,
The wind fanning the ash of a low fire.
What I love is near at hand, 80
Always, in earth and air.

### 4

The lost self changes,
Turning toward the sea,
A sea-shape turning around—
An old man with his feet before the fire,
In robes of green, in garments of adieu.

A man faced with his own immensity
Wakes all the waves, all their loose wandering fire.
The murmur of the absolute, the why
Of being born fails on his naked ears. 90
His spirit moves like monumental wind
That gentles on a sunny blue plateau.
He is the end of things, the final man.

All finite things reveal infinitude:
The mountain with its singular bright shade
Like the blue shine on freshly frozen snow,
The after-light upon ice-burdened pines;
Odor of basswood on a mountain-slope,
A scent beloved of bees;
Silence of water above a sunken tree:                          *100*
The pure serene of memory in one man—
A ripple widening from a single stone
Winding around the waters of the world.   *(1964)*


# STEPHEN SPENDER / 1909–


## The Express

After the first powerful plain manifesto
The black statement of pistons, without more fuss
But gliding like a queen, she leaves the station.
Without bowing and with restrained unconcern
She passes the houses which humbly crowd outside,
The gasworks and at last the heavy page
Of death, printed by gravestones in the cemetery.
Beyond the town there lies the open country
Where, gathering speed, she acquires mystery,
The luminous self-possession of ships on ocean.        *10*
It is now she begins to sing—at first quite low
Then loud, and at last with a jazzy madness—
The song of her whistle screaming at curves,
Of deafening tunnels, brakes, innumerable bolts.
And always light, aerial, underneath
Goes the elate meter of her wheels.
Steaming through metal landscape on her lines
She plunges new eras of wild happiness
Where speed throws up strange shapes, broad curves
And parallels clean like the steel of guns.            *20*
At last, further than Edinburgh or Rome,
Beyond the crest of the world, she reaches night
Where only a low streamline brightness
Of phosphorus on the tossing hills is white.
Ah, like a comet through flames she moves entranced
Wrapt in her music no bird song, no, nor bough
Breaking with honey buds, shall ever equal.   *(1933)*

## I Think Continually of Those

I think continually of those who were truly great.
Who, from the womb, remembered the soul's history
Through corridors of light where the hours are suns,
Endless and singing. Whose lovely ambition
Was that their lips, still touched with fire,
Should tell of the spirit clothed from head to foot in song.
And who hoarded from the spring branches
The desires falling across their bodies like blossoms.

What is precious is never to forget
The essential delight of the blood drawn from ageless springs    10
Breaking through rocks in worlds before our earth.
Never to deny its pleasure in the morning simple light
Nor its grave evening demand for love.
Never to allow gradually the traffic to smother
With noise and fog the flowering of the spirit.

Near the snow, near the sun, in the highest fields,
See how these names are fêted by the waving grass
And by the streamers of white cloud
And whispers of wind in the listening sky.
The names of those who in their lives fought for life,    20
Who wore at their hearts the fire's centre.
Born of the sun, they travelled a short while toward the sun
And left the vivid air signed with their honour.  (*1933*)


## Not Palaces, an Era's Crown

Not palaces, an era's crown
Where the mind dwells, intrigues, rests;
Architectural gold-leaved flower
From people ordered like a single mind,
I build. This only what I tell:
It is too late for rare accumulation,
For family pride, for beauty's filtered dusts;
I say, stamping the words with emphasis,
Drink from here energy and only energy,
As from the electric charge of a battery,    10
To will this Time's change
Eye, gazelle, delicate wanderer,
Drinker of horizon's fluid line;
Ear that suspends on a chord
The spirit drinking timelessness;
Touch, love, all senses;
Leave your gardens, your singing feasts,
Your dreams of suns circling before our sun,
Of heaven after our world.

Instead, watch images of flashing brass                          20
That strike the outward sense, the polished will
Flag of our purpose which the wind engraves.
No spirit seek here rest. But this: No one
Shall hunger: Man shall spend equally.
Our goal which we compel: Man shall be man.
      That programme of the antique Satan
Bristling with guns on the indented page,
With battleship towering from hilly waves:
For what? Drive of a ruining purpose
Destroying all but its age-long exploiters.                      30
Our programme like this, but opposite,
Death to the killers, bringing light to life.   (*1933*)

## Judas Iscariot

The eyes of twenty centuries
Pursue me along corridors to where
I am painted at their ends on many walls.
    Ever-revolving futures recognize
This red hair and red beard, where I am seated
Within the dark cave of the feast of light.
    Out of my heart-shaped shadow I stretch my hand
Across the white table into the dish
But not to dip the bread. It is as though
The cloth on each side of one dove-bright face                   10
Spread dazzling wings on which the apostles ride
Uplifting them into the vision
Where their eyes watch themselves enthroned.
    My russet hand across the dish
Plucks enviously against one feather
    —But still the rushing wings spurn me below!

    Saint Sebastian [1] of wickedness
I stand: all eyes legitimate arrows piercing through
The darkness of my wickedness. They recognize
My halo hammered from thirty silver pieces                       20
And the hemp rope around my neck
Soft as that spirit's hanging arms
When on my cheek he answered with the kiss
Which cuts for ever—
                My strange stigmata,
All love and hate, all fire and ice!

    But who betrayed whom? O you,
Whose light gaze forms the azure corridor
Through which those other pouring eyes
Arrow into me—answer! Who

---

[1] Saint Sebastian is usually pictured as pierced by numerous arrows shot by archers who attempted to kill him on Diocletian's orders. Sebastian lived about 250 years later than Judas.

Betrayed whom? Who had foreseen 30
All, from the first? Who read
In his mind's light from the first day
That the kingdom of heaven on earth must always
Reiterate the garden of Eden,
And each day's revolution be betrayed
Within man's heart each day?
                    Who wrapped
The whispering serpent round the tree
And hung between the leaves the glittering purse
And trapped the fangs with God-appointed poison?
Who knew 40
I must betray the truth, and made the lie
Betray its truth in me?

      Those hypocrite eyes which aimed at you
Now aim at me. And yet, beyond this world
We are alone, eternal opposites,
Each turning on his pole of truth, your pole
Invisible light, and mine
Becoming what man is. We stare
Across two thousand years, and heaven, and hell,
Into each other's gaze. 50

## An Elementary School Classroom in a Slum

Far far from gusty waves, these children's faces.
Like rootless weeds the torn hair round their paleness.
The tall girl with her weighed-down head. The paper-
seeming boy with rat's eyes. The stunted unlucky heir
Of twisted bones, reciting a father's gnarled disease,
His lesson from his desk. At back of the dim class,
One unnoted, sweet and young: his eyes live in a dream
Of squirrels' game, in tree room, other than this.

On sour cream walls, donations. Shakespeare's head
Cloudless at dawn, civilized dome riding all cities. 10
Belled, flowery, Tyrolese valley. Open-handed map
Awarding the world its world. And yet, for these
Children, these windows, not this world, are world,
Where all their future's painted with a fog,
A narrow street sealed in with a lead sky,
Far far from rivers, capes, and stars of words.

Surely Shakespeare is wicked, the map a bad example
With ships and sun and love tempting them to steal—
For lives that slyly turn in their cramped holes
From fog to endless night? On their slag heap, these children 20
Wear skins peeped through by bones and spectacles of steel
With mended glass, like bottle bits on stones.

All of their time and space are foggy slum
So blot their maps with slums as big as doom.

Unless, governor, teacher, inspector, visitor,
This map becomes their window and these windows
That open on their lives like crouching tombs
Break, O break open, till they break the town
And show the children to the fields and all their world
Azure on their sands, to let their tongues                    *30*
Run naked into books, the white and green leaves open
The history theirs whose language is the sun.   (*1939*)


# CHARLES OLSON / 1910–1970

## The Kingfishers

1

What does not change / is the will to change

He woke, fully clothed, in his bed. He
remembered only one thing, the birds, how
when he came in, he had gone around the rooms
and got them back in their cage, the green one first,
she with the bad leg, and then the blue,
the one they had hoped was a male

Otherwise? Yes, Fernand, who had talked
                    lispingly of Albers & Angkor Vat.[1]
He had left the party without a word.
                    How he got up, got into his coat,
I do not know. When I saw him, he was
                    at the door, but it did not matter,
he was already sliding along the wall of the night, losing himself
in some crack of the ruins. That it should have
                    been he who said, "The Kingfishers!

who cares
for their feathers
now?"

His last words had been, "The pool is slime." Suddenly everyone,    *20*
ceasing their talk, sat in a row around him, watched
they did not so much hear, or pay attention, they
wondered, looked at each other, smirked, but listened,
he repeated and repeated, could not go beyond his thought
"The pool   the kingfishers' feathers were wealth   why
did the export stop?"

---

[1] ruin of an ancient temple in Cambodia

It was then he left
I thought of the E on the stone, and of what Mao said
la lumière"
                    but the kingfisher                                                    *30*
de l'aurore"
                    but the kingfisher flew west
est devant nous!" [2]
                    he got the color of his breast
                    from the heat of the setting sun!

The features are, the feebleness of the feet
                    (syndactylism [3] of the 3rd & 4th digit)
the bill, serrated, sometimes a pronounced beak, the wings
where the color is, short and round, the tail
inconspicuous.                                                                            *40*

But not these things were the factors. Not the birds.
The legends are
legends. Dead, hung up indoors, the kingfisher
will not indicate a favoring wind,
or avert the thunderbolt. Nor, by its nesting,
still the waters, with the new year, for seven days.
It is true, it does nest with the opening
                                    year, but not on the waters.
It nests at the end of a tunnel bored by itself in a bank. There,
six or eight white and translucent eggs are laid, on fishbones     *50*
not on bare clay, on bones thrown up in pellets by the birds.

                    On these rejectamenta
(as they accumulate they form a cup-shaped
                                    structure) the young are born.
And, as they are fed and grown, this
                    nest of excrement and decayed fish becomes
                    a dripping, fetid mass
          Mao concluded:
                    nous devons
                              nous lever                                                  *60*
                                        et agir! [4]

                              3

When the attentions change / the jungle
leaps in
                    even the stones are split
                              they rive

Or,
enter
that other conqueror we more naturally recognize
he so resembles ourselves

---

[2] The light of the dawn is before us.                    [4] We must rise and act. (Cf. line 148.)
[3] fusion of the toes

But the E                                                              70
cut so rudely on that oldest stone
sounded otherwise,
was differently heard

as, in another time, were treasures used:

(and, later, much later, a fine ear thought
a scarlet coat)

      "of green feathers   feet, beaks and eyes
      of gold

      "animals likewise,
      resembling snails                                    80

      "a large wheel, gold,
                  with figures of unknown four-foots,
      and worked with tufts of leaves, weight
      3800 ounces

      "last, two birds, of thread and featherwork, the quills
      gold, the feet
      gold, the two birds perched on two reeds
      gold, the  reeds arising from two embroidered mounds,
      one yellow, the other
      white.                                               90

           "And from each reed hung
           seven feathered tassels."

In this instance, the priests
(in dark cotton robes, and dirty,
their dishevelled hair matted with blood, and flowing wildly
over their shoulders)
rush in among the people, calling on them
to protect their gods

And all now is war
where so lately there was peace,                                       100
and the sweet brotherhood, the use
of tilled fields.

                4

Not one death but many,
not accumulation but change, the feed-back proves,
                              the feed-back is
the law

      Into the same river no man steps twice
      When fire dies air dies
      No one remains, nor is, one

Around an appearance, one common model, we grow up    *110*
many. Else how is it,
if we remain the same,
we take pleasure now
in what we did not take pleasure before? love
contrary objects? admire and / or find fault? use
other words, feel other passions, have
nor figure, appearance, disposition, tissue
the same?

      To be in different states without a change
      is not a possibility    *120*

We can be precise. The factors are
in the animal and / or the machine the factors are
communication and / or control, both involve
the message. And what is the message? The message is
a discrete or continuous sequence of measurable
                  events distributed in time

is the birth of air, is
the birth of water, is
a state between
the origin and    *130*
the end, between
birth and the beginning of
another fetid nest

is change, presents
no more than itself

And the too strong grasping of it,
when it is pressed together and condensed,
loses it

This very thing you are

             II

      They buried their dead in a sitting posture    *140*
      serpent   cane   razor   ray of the sun

      And she sprinkled water on the head of the child, crying
      "Cioa-coatl! Cioa-coatl!"
      with her face to the west

      Where the bones are found, in each personal heap
      with what each enjoyed, there is always
      the Mongolian louse

The light is in the east. Yes. And we must rise, act. Yet
in the west, despite the apparent darkness (the whiteness
which covers all), if you look, if you can bear, if you can,    *150*
                 long enough

as long as it was necessary for him, my guide
to look into the yellow of that longest-lasting rose
so you must, and, in that whiteness, into that face,
                     with what candor, look

and, considering the dryness of the place
    the long absence of an adequate race

        (of the two who first came, each a conquistador,
                          one healed, the other
      tore the eastern idols down, toppled                160
      the temple walls, which, says the excuser
      were black from human gore)

hear
hear, where the dry blood talks
    where the old appetite walks

                  la piu saporita et migliore
                  che si possa truovar al mondo [5]

where it hides, look
in the eye how it runs
in the flesh / chalk                                170

        but under these petals
        in the emptiness
        regard the light, contemplate
        the flower

whence it arose

        with what violence benevolence is bought
        what cost in gesture justice brings
        what wrongs domestic rights involve
        what stalks
        this silence                            180

what pudor [6] pejorocracy [7] affronts
how awe, night-rest and neighborhood can rot
what breeds where dirtiness is law
what crawls
below

                        III

I am no Greek, hath not th'advantage.
And of course, no Roman:
he can take no risk that matters
the risk of beauty least of all.

---

[5] the most savory and best which may be found in
the world
[6] modesty

[7] apparently a coinage meaning rule by that which
tends to worsen

But I have my kin, if for no other reason than                                    *190*
(as he said, next of kin) I commit myself, and,
given my freedom, I'd be a cad
if I didn't. Which is most true.

It works out this way, despite the disadvantage.
I offer, in explanation, a quote:
si j'ai du goût, ce n'est guères
que pour la terre et les pierres [8]

Despite the discrepancy (an ocean   courage   age)
this is also true: if I have any taste
it is only because I have interested myself                                        *200*
in what was slain in the sun

    I pose you your question:

shall you uncover honey / where maggots are?

    I hunt among stones

# ELIZABETH BISHOP / 1911–

## The Man-Moth[1]

        Here, above,
cracks in the buildings are filled with battered moonlight.
The whole shadow of Man is only as big as his hat.
It lies at his feet like a circle for a doll to stand on,
and he makes an inverted pin, the point magnetized to the moon.
He does not see the moon; he observes only her vast properties,
feeling the queer light on his hands, neither warm nor cold,
of a temperature impossible to record in thermometers.

        But when the Man-Moth
pays his rare, although occasional, visits to the surface,                          *10*
the moon looks rather different to him. He emerges
from an opening under the edge of one of the sidewalks
and nervously begins to scale the faces of the buildings.
He thinks the moon is a small hole at the top of the sky,
proving the sky quite useless for protection.
He trembles, but must investigate as high as he can climb.

---

[8] If I have any taste, it is for hardly anything but earth and stones.      suggested by a newspaper misprint for "mammoth."

[1] Bishop notes that the title and subject were

                    Up the façades,
his shadow dragging like a photographers' cloth behind him,
he climbs fearfully, thinking that this time he will manage
to push his small head through that round clean opening                    20
and be forced through, as from a tube, in black scrolls on the light.
(Man, standing below him, has no such illusions.)
But what the Man-Moth fears most he must do, although
he fails, of course, and falls back scared but quite unhurt.

                    Then he returns
to the pale subways of cement he calls his home. He flits,
he flutters, and cannot get aboard the silent trains
fast enough to suit him. The doors close swiftly.
The Man-Moth always seats himself facing the wrong way
and the train starts at once at its full, terrible speed,                    30
without a shift in gears or a gradation of any sort.
He cannot tell the rate at which he travels backwards.

                    Each night he must
be carried through artificial tunnels and dream recurrent dreams.
Just as the ties recur beneath his train, these underlie
his rushing brain. He does not dare look out the window,
for the third rail, the unbroken draught of poison,
runs there beside him. He regards it as a disease
he has inherited the susceptibility to. He has to keep
his hands in his pockets, as others must wear mufflers.                    40

                    If you catch him,
hold up a flashlight to his eye. It's all dark pupil,
an entire night itself, whose haired horizon tightens
as he stares back, and closes up the eye. Then from the lids
one tear, his only possession, like the bee's sting, slips.
Slyly he palms it, and if you're not paying attention
he'll swallow it. However, if you watch, he'll hand it over,
cool as from underground springs and pure enough to drink.   (1948)


## At the Fishhouses

                Although it is a cold evening,
                down by one of the fishhouses
                an old man sits netting,
                his net, in the gloaming almost invisible,
                a dark purple-brown,
                and his shuttle worn and polished.
                The air smells so strong of codfish
                it makes one's nose run and one's eyes water.
                The five fishhouses have steeply peaked roofs
                and narrow, cleated gangplanks slant up                    10
                to storerooms in the gables

for the wheelbarrows to be pushed up and down on.
All is silver: the heavy surface of the sea,
swelling slowly as if considering spilling over,
is opaque, but the silver of the benches,
the lobster pots, and masts, scattered
among the wild jagged rocks,
is of an apparent translucence
like the small old buildings with an emerald moss
growing on their shoreward walls.                                               20
The big fish tubs are completely lined
with layers of beautiful herring scales
and the wheelbarrows are similarly plastered
with creamy iridescent coats of mail,
with small iridescent flies crawling on them.
Up on the little slope behind the houses,
set in the sparse bright sprinkle of grass,
is an ancient wooden capstan,
cracked, with two long bleached handles
and some melancholy stains, like dried blood,                                   30
where the ironwork has rusted.

The old man accepts a Lucky Strike.
He was a friend of my grandfather.
We talk of the decline in the population
and of codfish and herring
while he waits for a herring boat to come in.
There are sequins on his vest and on his thumb.
He has scraped the scales, the principal beauty,
from unnumbered fish with that black old knife,
the blade of which is almost worn away.                                         40

Down at the water's edge, at the place
where they haul up the boats, up the long ramp
descending into the water, thin silver
tree trunks are laid horizontally
across the gray stones, down and down
at intervals of four or five feet.

Cold dark deep and absolutely clear,
element bearable to no mortal,
to fish and to seals . . . One seal particularly
I have seen here evening after evening.                                         50
He was curious about me. He was interested in music;
like me a believer in total immersion,
so I used to sing him Baptist hymns.
I also sang "A Mighty Fortress Is Our God."
He stood up in the water and regarded me
steadily, moving his head a little.
Then he would disappear, then suddenly emerge
almost in the same spot, with a sort of shrug

as if it were against his better judgment.
Cold dark deep and absolutely clear,                                60
the clear gray icy water . . . Back, behind us,
the dignified tall firs begin.
Bluish, associating with their shadows,
a million Christmas trees stand
waiting for Christmas. The water seems suspended
above the rounded gray and blue-gray stones.
I have seen it over and over, the same sea, the same,
slightly, indifferently swinging above the stones,
icily free above the stones,
above the stones and then the world.                                70
If you should dip your hand in,
your wrist would ache immediately,
your bones would begin to ache and your hand would burn
as if the water were a transmutation of fire
that feeds on stones and burns with a dark-gray flame.
If you tasted it, it would first taste bitter,
then briny, then surely burn your tongue.
It is like what we imagine knowledge to be:
dark, salt, clear, moving, utterly free,
drawn from the cold hard mouth                                      80
of the world, derived from the rocky breasts
forever, flowing and drawn, and since
our knowledge is historical, flowing, and flown.

## Sandpiper

The roaring alongside he takes for granted,
and that every so often the world is bound to shake.
He runs, he runs to the south, finical, awkward,
in a state of controlled panic, a student of Blake.

The beach hisses like fat. On his left, a sheet
of interrupting water comes and goes
and glazes over his dark and brittle feet.
He runs, he runs straight through it, watching his toes.

—Watching, rather, the spaces of sand between them,
where (no detail too small) the Atlantic drains             10
rapidly backwards and downwards. As he runs,
he stares at the dragging grains.

The world is a mist. And then the world is
minute and vast and clear. The tide
is higher or lower. He couldn't tell you which.
His beak is focussed; he is preoccupied,

looking for something, something, something.
Poor bird, he is obsessed!
The millions of grains are black, white, tan, and gray,
mixed with quartz grains, rose and amethyst.                            *20*

# DELMORE SCHWARTZ / 1913–1966

## In the Naked Bed, in Plato's Cave

In the naked bed, in Plato's cave,[1]
Reflected headlights slowly slid the wall,
Carpenters hammered under the shaded window,
Wind troubled the window curtains all night long,
A fleet of trucks strained uphill, grinding,
Their freights covered, as usual.
The ceiling lightened again, the slanting diagram
Slid slowly forth.
                Hearing the milkman's chop,
His striving up the stair, the bottle's chink,
I rose from bed, lit a cigarette,                                              *10*
And walked to the window. The stony street
Displayed the stillness in which buildings stand,
The street-lamp's vigil and the horse's patience.
The winter sky's pure capital
Turned me back to bed with exhausted eyes.

Strangeness grew in the motionless air. The loose
Film grayed. Shaking wagons, hooves' waterfalls,
Sounded far off, increasing, louder and nearer.
A car coughed, starting. Morning, softly
Melting the air, lifted the half-covered chair                             *20*
From underseas, kindled the looking-glass,
Distinguished the dresser and the white wall.
The bird tentatively, whistled, called,
Bubbled and whistled, so! Perplexed, still wet
With sleep, affectionate, hungry and cold. So, so,
O son of man, the ignorant night, the travail
Of early morning, the mystery of beginning
Again and again,
             while Time is unforgiven.   (*1938*)

---

[1] In his myth of the cave, Plato illustrated the illusory character of the material world by picturing men as bound in a cave so that their only reality is the shadows cast on the wall by a fire behind them.

## For the One Who Would Take Man's Life in His Hands

Tiger Christ unsheathed his sword,
Threw it down, became a lamb.
Swift spat upon the species, but
Took two women to his heart.
Samson who was strong as death
Paid his strength to kiss a slut.
Othello that stiff warrior
Was broken by a woman's heart.
Troy burned for a sea-tax, also for
Possession of a charming whore.                  10
What do all examples show?
What must the finished murderer know?

You cannot sit on bayonets,
Nor can you eat among the dead.

When all are killed, you are alone,
A vacuum comes where hate has fed.
Murder's fruit is silent stone,
The gun increases poverty.
With what do these examples shine?
The soldier turned to girls and wine.          20
Love is the tact of every good,
The only warmth, the only peace.

"What have I said?" asked Socrates,
"Affirmed extremes, cried yes and no,
Taken all parts, denied myself,
Praised the caress, extolled the blow,
Soldier and lover quite deranged
Until their motions are exchanged.
—What do all examples show?
What can any actor know?                          30
The contradiction in every act,
The infinite task of the human heart."

## ROBERT HAYDEN / 1913–

## Middle Passage

I

*Jesús, Estrella, Esperanza, Mercy:*[1]

Sails flashing to the wind like weapons,
sharks following the moans the fever and the dying;
horror the corposant[2] and compass rose.

Middle Passage:
            voyage through death
                        to life upon these shores.

"10 April 1800—
Blacks rebellious. Crew uneasy. Our linguist says
their moaning is a prayer for death,                        10
ours and their own. Some try to starve themselves.
Lost three this morning leaped with crazy laughter
to the waiting sharks, sang as they went under."

*Desire, Adventure, Tartar, Ann:*

Standing to America, bring home
black gold, black ivory, black seed.

---

[1] This line and line 14 list "miserably misnamed" slave ships. See also lines 95–97.
[2] a ball of light caused by discharge of static electricity on spars or mastheads during thunder storms at sea

> *Deep in the festering hold thy father lies,*
> *of his bones New England pews are made,*
> *those are altar lights that were his eyes.*[3]

Jesus   Saviour   Pilot   Me                                        20
Over   Life's   Tempestuous   Sea

We pray that Thou wilt grant, O Lord,
safe passage to our vessels bringing
heathen souls unto Thy chastening.

Jesus   Saviour

"8 bells. I cannot sleep, for I am sick
with fear, but writing eases fear a little
since still my eyes can see these words take shape
upon the page & so I write, as one
would turn to exorcism. 4 days scudding,                            30
but now the sea is calm again. Misfortune
follows in our wake like sharks (our grinning
tutelary gods). Which one of us
has killed an albatross? A plague among
our blacks—Ophthalmia: blindness—& we
have jettisoned the blind to no avail.
It spreads, the terrifying sickness spreads.
Its claws have scratched sight from the Capt.'s eyes
& there is blindness in the fo'c'sle
& we must sail 3 weeks before we come                               40
to port."

> *What port awaits us, Davy Jones'*[4]
> *or home? I've heard of slavers drifting, drifting,*
> *playthings of wind and storm and chance, their crews*
> *gone blind, the jungle hatred*
> *crawling up on deck.*

Thou   Who   Walked   On   Galilee

"Deponent further sayeth *The Bella J*
left the Guinea Coast
with cargo of five hundred blacks and odd                          50
for the barracoons of Florida:

"That there was hardly room 'tween-decks for half
the sweltering cattle stowed spoon-fashion there;
that some went mad of thirst and tore their flesh
and sucked the blood:

"That Crew and Captain lusted with the comeliest
of the savage girls kept naked in the cabins;
that there was one they called The Guinea Rose
and they cast lots and fought to lie with her:

---

[3] Cf. Shakespeare, "Full Fathom Five" from    [4] "Davy Jones' Locker"—the bottom of the sea
*The Tempest*, p. 132. See also lines 108–110.

"That when the Bo's'n piped all hands, the flames                    60
spreading from starboard already were beyond
control, the negroes howling and their chains
entangled with the flames:

"That the burning blacks could not be reached,
that the Crew abandoned ship,
leaving their shrieking negresses behind,
that the Captain perished drunken with the wenches:

"Futher Deponent sayeth not."

Pilot   Oh   Pilot   Me

II

Aye, lad, and I have seen those factories,                           70
Gambia, Rio Pongo, Calabar;[5]
have watched the artful mongos baiting traps
of war wherein the victor and the vanquished

Were caught as prizes for our barracoons.
Have seen the nigger kings whose vanity
and greed turned wild black hides of Fellatah,
Mandingo, Ibo, Kru[6] to gold for us.

And there was one—King Anthracite we named him—
fetish face beneath French parasols
of brass and orange velvet, impudent mouth                           80
whose cups were carven skulls of enemies:

He'd honor us with drum and feast and conjo
and palm-oil-glistening wenches deft in love,
and for tin crowns that shone with paste,
red calico and German-silver trinkets

Would have the drums talk war and send
his warriors to burn the sleeping villages
and kill the sick and old and lead the young
in coffles to our factories.

Twenty years a trader, twenty years,                                 90
for there was wealth aplenty to be harvested
from those black fields, and I'd be trading still
but for the fevers melting down my bones.

III

Shuttles in the rocking loom of history,
the dark ships move, the dark ships move,
their bright ironical names
like jests of kindness on a murderer's mouth;
plough through thrashing glister toward
fata morgana's[7] lucent melting shore,

---

[5] African place names     [6] African tribes     [7] a mirage

weave toward New World littorals that are 100
mirage and myth and actual shore.

Voyage through death,
                                voyage whose chartings are unlove.

A charnel stench, effluvium of living death
spreads outward from the hold,
where the living and the dead, the horribly dying,
lie interlocked, lie foul with blood and excrement.

> *Deep in the festering hold thy father lies,*
> *the corpse of mercy rots with him,*
> *rats eat love's rotten gelid eyes.* 110

> *But, oh, the living look at you*
> *with human eyes whose suffering accuses you,*
> *whose hatred reaches through the swill of dark*
> *to strike you like a leper's claw.*

> *You cannot stare that hatred down*
> *or chain the fear that stalks the watches*
> *and breathes on you its fetid scorching breath;*
> *cannot kill the deep human wish,*
> *the timeless will.*

"But for the storm that flung up barriers 120
of wind and wave, *The Amistad,* señores,
would have reached the port of Príncipe in two,
three days at most; but for the storm we should
have been prepared for what befell.
Swift as the puma's leap it came. There was
that interval of moonless calm filled only
with the water's and the rigging's usual sounds,
then sudden movement, blows and snarling cries
and they had fallen on us with machete
and marlinspike. It was as though the very 130
air, the night itself were striking us.
Exhausted by the rigors of the storm,
we were no match for them. Our men went down
before the murderous Africans. Our loyal
Celestino ran from below with gun
and lantern and I saw, before the cane-
knife's wounding flash, Cinquez,
that surly brute who calls himself a prince,
directing, urging on the ghastly work.
He hacked the poor mulatto down, and then 140
he turned on me. The decks were slippery
when daylight finally came. It sickens me
to think of what I saw, of how these apes
threw overboard the butchered bodies of
our men, true Christians all, like so much jetsam.

Enough, enough. The rest is quickly told:
Cinquez was forced to spare the two of us
you see to steer the ship to Africa,
and we like phantoms doomed to rove the sea
voyaged east by day and west by night,                                150
deceiving them, hoping for rescue,
prisoners on our own vessel, till
at length we drifted to the shores of this
your land, America, where we were freed
from our unspeakable misery. Now we
demand, good sirs, the extradition of
Cinquez and his accomplices to La
Havana. And it distresses us to know
there are so many here who seem inclined
to justify the mutiny of these blacks.                                160
We find it paradoxical indeed
that you whose wealth, whose tree of liberty
are rooted in the labor of your slaves
should suffer the august John Quincy Adams [8]
to speak with so much passion of the right
of chattel slaves to kill their lawful masters
and with his Roman rhetoric weave a hero's
garland for Cinquez. I tell you that
we are determined to return to Cuba
with our slaves and there see justice done. Cinquez—       170
or let us say 'the Prince'—Cinquez shall die."

The deep immortal human wish,
the timeless will:

Cinquez its deathless primaveral image,
life that transfigures many lives.

Voyage through death
                    to life upon these shores.   (*1966*)


# KARL SHAPIRO / 1913–

## Auto Wreck

Its quick soft silver bell beating, beating,
And down the dark one ruby flare
Pulsing out red light like an artery,
The ambulance at top speed floating
    down
Past beacons and illuminated clocks
Wings in a heavy curve, dips down,

And brakes speed, entering the crowd.
The doors leap open, emptying light;
Stretchers are laid out, the mangled lifted
And stowed into the little hospital.          10
Then the bell, breaking the hush, tolls
    once,
And the ambulance with its terrible cargo
Rocking, slightly rocking, moves away,
As the doors, an afterthought, are closed.

---

[8] During his years as a member of the House of Representatives after his Presidency, Adams was a leader of the opposition to the extension of slavery.

We are deranged, walking among the cops
Who sweep glass and are large and
  composed.
One is still making notes under the light.
One with a bucket douches ponds of
  blood
Into the street and gutter.
One hangs lanterns on the wrecks that
  cling,                                          20
Empty husks of locusts, to iron poles.
Our throats were tight as tourniquets,
Our feet were bound with splints, but
  now,
Like convalescents intimate and gauche,
We speak through sickly smiles and warn
With the stubborn saw of common sense,
The grim joke and the banal resolution.
The traffic moves around with care,
But we remain, touching a wound
That opens to our richest horror.         30
Already old, the question Who shall die?
Becomes unspoken Who is innocent?
For death in war is done by hands;
Suicide has cause and stillbirth, logic;
And cancer, simple as a flower, blooms.
But this invites the occult mind,
Cancels our physics with a sneer,
And spatters all we knew of denouement
Across the expedient and wicked stones.
                                         (1942)


# Scyros[1]

### SNUFFLE AND SNIFF AND HANDKERCHIEF

The doctor punched my vein
  The captain called me Cain
Upon my belly sat the sow of fear
  With coins on either eye
  The President came by
And whispered to the braid what none
    could hear

  High over where the storm
  Stood steadfast cruciform

The golden eagle sank in wounded wheels
  White Negroes laughing still           10
  Crept fiercely on Brazil
Turning the navies upward on their keels

  Now one by one the trees
  Stripped to their naked knees
To dance upon the heads of shrunken
    dead
  The roof of England fell
  Great Paris tolled her bell
And China staunched her milk and wept
    for bread

  No island singly lay
  But lost its name that day            20
The Ainu[2] dived across the plunging
    sands
  From dawn to dawn to dawn
  King George's birds came on
Strafing the tulips from his children's
    hands

  Thus in the classic sea
  South-east from Thessaly
The dynamited mermen washed ashore
  And tritons dressed in steel
  Trolled heads with rod and reel
And dredged potatoes from the Aegean
    floor                               30

  Hot is the sky and green
  Where Germans have been seen
The moon leaks metal on the Atlantic
    fields
  Pink boys in birthday shrouds
  Loop lightly through the clouds
Or coast the peaks of Finland on their
    shields

  That prophet year by year
  Lay still but could not hear
Where scholars tapped to find his new
    remains
  Gog and Magog[3] ate pork            40
  In vertical New York
And war began next Wednesday on the
    Danes   (1942)

---

[1] a rocky island in the Aegan off the coast of
Thessaly
[2] a member of the indigenous tribes of Japan

[3] mentioned in Ezekiel and Revelations as powers
opposed to God, which shall appear before the
Last Judgment

## Drug Store

*I do remember an apothecary,*
*And hereabouts 'a dwells*[1]

It baffles the foreigner like an idiom,
And he is right to adopt it as a form
Less serious than the living-room or bar;
    For it disestablishes the cafe,
Is a collective, and on basic country.

Not that it praises hygiene and corrupts
The ice-cream parlor and the
    tobacconist's
Is it a center; but that the attractive
    symbols
        Watch over puberty and leer
Like rubber bottles waiting for
    sick-use.                                    10

Youth comes to jingle nickles and crack
wise;

The baseball scores are his, the magazines
Devoted to lust, the jazz, the Coca-Cola,
        The lending-library of love's latest.
He is the customer; he is heroized.

And every nook and cranny of the flesh
Is spoken to by packages with wiles.
"Buy me, buy me," they whimper and
    cajole;
        The hectic range of lipstick pouts,
Revealing the wicked and the simple
    mouth.                                        20

With scarcely any evasion in their eye
They smoke, undress their girls, exact a
    stance;
But only for a moment. The clock goes
    round;
        Crude fellowships are made and
        lost;
They slump in booths like rags, not even
drunk.  *(1942)*

## The Progress of Faust

He was born in Deutschland, as you would suspect,
And graduated in magic from Cracow
In Fifteen Five. His portraits show a brow
Heightened by science. The eye is indirect,
As of bent light upon a crooked soul,
And that he bargained with the prince of Shame
For pleasures intellectually foul
Is known by every court that lists his name.

His frequent disappearances are put down
To visits in the regions of the dammed                    10
And to the periodic deaths he shammed,
But, unregenerate and in Doctor's gown,
He would turn up to lecture at the fair
And do a minor miracle for a fee.
Many a life he whispered up the stair
To teach the black art of anatomy.

He was as deaf to angels as an oak
When, in the fall of Fifteen Ninety-four,
He went to London and crashed through the floor
In mock damnation of the play-going folk.[1]            20
Weekending with the scientific crowd,
He met Sir Francis Bacon and helped draft

---

[1] *Romeo and Juliet*, V, i, 37–38

[1] in Christopher Marlowe's play, *Doctor Faustus*

"Colours of Good and Evil" and read aloud
An obscene sermon at which no one laughed.

He toured the Continent for a hundred years
And subsidized among the peasantry
The puppet play, his tragic history;
With a white glove he boxed the devil's ears
And with a black his own. Tired of this,
He published penny poems about his sins,                     *30*
In which he placed the heavy emphasis
On the white glove which, for a penny, wins.

Some time before the hemorrhage of the Kings
Of France, he turned respectable and taught;
Quite suddenly everything that he had thought
Seemed to grow scholars' beards and angels' wings.
It was the Overthrow. On Reason's throne
He sat with the fair Phrygian[2] on his knees
And called all universities his own,
As plausible a figure as you please.                         *40*

Then back to Germany as the sages' sage
To preach comparative science to the young
Who came from every land in a great throng
And knew they heard the master of the age.
When for a secret formula he paid
The Devil another fragment of his soul,
His scholars wept, and several even prayed
That Satan would restore him to them whole.

Backwardly tolerant, Faustus was expelled
From the Third Reich in Nineteen Thirty-nine.              *50*
His exit caused the breaching of the Rhine,
Except for which the frontier might have held.
Five years unknown to enemy and friend
He hid, appearing on the sixth to pose
In an American desert at war's end
Where, at his back, a dome of atoms rose.


## The Sickness of Adam

In the beginning, at every step, he turned
As if by instinct to the East to praise
The nature of things. Now every path was learned
He lost the lifted, almost flower-like gaze

Of a temple dancer. He began to walk
Slowly, like one accustomed to be alone.
He found himself lost in the field of talk;
Thinking became a garden of its own.

---

[2] Helen of Troy, whose love was part of Faust's bargain with Mephistopheles

In it were new things: words he had never said,
Beasts he had never seen and knew were not                                      10
In the true garden, terrors, and tears shed
Under a tree by him, for some new thought.

And the first anger. Once he flung a staff
At softly coupling sheep and struck the ram.
It broke away. And God heard Adam laugh
And for his laughter made the creature lame.

And wanderlust. He stood upon the Wall
To search the unfinished countries lying wide
And waste, where not a living thing could crawl,
And yet he would descend, as if to hide.                                        20

His thought drew down the guardian at the gate,
To whom man said, "What danger am I in?"
And the angel, hurt in spirit, seemed to hate
The wingless thing that worried after sin,

For it said nothing but marvelously unfurled
Its wings and arched them shimmering overhead,
Which must have been the signal from the world
That the first season of our life was dead.

Adam fell down with labor in his bones,
And God approached him in the cool of day                                       30
And said, "This sickness in your skeleton
Is longing. I will remove it from your clay."

He said also, "I made you strike the sheep."
It began to rain and God sat down beside
The sinking man. When he was fast asleep
He wet his right hand deep in Adam's side

And drew the graceful rib out of his breast.
Far off, the latent streams began to flow
And birds flew out of Paradise to nest
On earth. Sadly the angel watched them go.   (*1953*)                           40


# DYLAN THOMAS / 1914–1953


## The Force That Through the Green Fuse Drives the Flower

The force that through the green fuse drives the flower
Drives my green age; that blasts the roots of trees
Is my destroyer.
And I am dumb to tell the crooked rose
My youth is bent by the same wintry fever.

The force that drives the water through the rocks
Drives my red blood; that dries the mouthing streams
Turns mine to wax.
And I am dumb to mouth unto my veins
How at the mountain spring the same mouth sucks.                    *10*

The hand that whirls the water in the pool
Stirs the quicksand; that ropes the blowing wind
Hauls my shroud sail.
And I am dumb to tell the hanging man
How of my clay is made the hangman's lime.

The lips of time leech to the fountain head;
Love drips and gathers, but the fallen blood
Shall calm her sores.
And I am dumb to tell a weather's wind
How time has ticked a heaven round the stars.                     *20*

And I am dumb to tell the lover's tomb
How at my sheet goes the same crooked worm.   (*1934*)

## And Death Shall Have No Dominion

And death shall have no dominion.
Dead men naked they shall be one
With the man in the wind and the west moon;
When their bones are picked clean and the clean bones gone,
They shall have stars at elbow and foot;
Though they go mad they shall be sane,
Though they sink through the sea they shall rise again;
Though lovers be lost love shall not;
And death shall have no dominion.

And death shall have no dominion.                                 *10*
Under the windings of the sea
They lying long shall not die windily;
Twisting on racks when sinews give way,
Strapped to a wheel, yet they shall not break;
Faith in their hands shall snap in two,
And the unicorn evils run them through;
Split all ends up they shan't crack;
And death shall have no dominion.

And death shall have no dominion.
No more may gulls cry at their ears                               *20*
Or waves break loud on the seashores;
Where blew a flower may a flower no more
Lift its head to the blows of the rain;
Though they be mad and dead as nails,
Heads of the characters hammer through daisies;
Break in the sun till the sun breaks down,
And death shall have no dominion.   (*1936*)

## When All My Five and Country Senses See

When all my five and country senses see,
The fingers will forget green thumbs and mark
How, through the halfmoon's vegetable eye,
Husk of young stars and handfull zodiac,
Love in the frost is pared and wintered by,
The whispering ears will watch love drummed away
Down breeze and shell to a discordant beach,
And, lashed to syllables, the lynx tongue cry
That her fond wounds are mended bitterly.
My nostrils see her breath burn like a bush.                    *10*

My one and noble heart has witnesses
In all love's countries, that will grope awake;
And when blind sleep drops on the spying senses,
The heart is sensual, though five eyes break.

## In My Craft or Sullen Art

In my craft or sullen art
Exercised in the still night
When only the moon rages
And the lovers lie abed
With all their griefs in their arms,
I labour by singing light
Not for ambition or bread
Or the strut and trade of charms
On the ivory stages
But for the common wages                                        *10*
Of their most secret heart.

Not for the proud man apart
From the raging moon I write
On these spindrift pages
Nor for the towering dead
With their nightingales and psalms
But for the lovers, their arms
Round the griefs of the ages,
Who pay no praise or wages
Nor heed my craft or art.   *(1945)*                            *20*

## Fern Hill

Now as I was young and easy under the apple boughs
About the lilting house and happy as the grass was green,
    The night above the dingle starry,
        Time let me hail and climb
    Golden in the heydays of his eyes,
And honoured among wagons I was prince of the apple towns
And once below a time I lordly had the trees and leaves
        Trail with daisies and barley
    Down the rivers of the windfall light.

And as I was green and carefree, famous among the barns       *10*
About the happy yard and singing as the farm was home,
    In the sun that is young once only,
        Time let me play and be
    Golden in the mercy of his means,

And green and golden I was huntsman and herdsman, the calves
Sang to my horn, the foxes on the hills barked clear and cold,
    And the sabbath rang slowly
      In the pebbles of the holy streams.

All the sun long it was running, it was lovely, the hay
Fields high as the house, the tunes from the chimneys, it was air    20
    And playing, lovely and watery
      And fire green as grass.
    And nightly under the simple stars
As I rode to sleep the owls were bearing the farm away,
All the moon long I heard, blessed among stables, the night-jars
    Flying with the ricks, and the horses
      Flashing into the dark.

And then to awake, and the farm, like a wanderer white
With the dew, come back, the cock on his shoulder: it was all
    Shining, it was Adam and maiden,    30
      The sky gathered again
    And the sun grew round that very day.
So it must have been after the birth of the simple light
In the first, spinning place, the spellbound horses walking warm
    Out of the whinnying green stable
      On to the fields of praise.

And honoured among foxes and pheasants by the gay house
Under the new made clouds and happy as the heart was long,
    In the sun born over and over,
      I ran my heedless ways,    40
    My wishes raced through the house high hay
And nothing I cared, at my sky blue trades, that time allows
In all his tuneful turning so few and such morning songs
    Before the children green and golden
      Follow him out of grace,

Nothing I cared, in the lamb white days, that time would take me
Up to the swallow thronged loft by the shadow of my hand,
    In the moon that is always rising,
      Nor that riding to sleep
    I should hear him fly with the high fields    50
And wake to the farm forever fled from the childless land.
Oh as I was young and easy in the mercy of his means,
    Time held me green and dying
    Though I sang in my chains like the sea.

# In Country Sleep

### I

Never and never, my girl riding far and near
In the land of the hearthstone tales, and spelled asleep,
    Fear or believe that the wolf in a sheepwhite hood

Loping and bleating roughly and blithely shall leap,
                           My dear, my dear,
Out of a lair in the flocked leaves in the dew dipped year
To eat your heart in the house in the rosy wood.

Sleep, good, for ever, slow and deep, spelled rare and wise,
My girl ranging the night in the rose and shire
Of the hobnail tales: no gooseherd or swine will turn
Into a homestall king or hamlet of fire
                        And prince of ice       *10*
To court the honeyed heart from your side before sunrise
In a spinney of ringed boys and ganders, spike and burn,

Nor the innocent lie in the rooting dingle wooed
And staved, and riven among plumes my rider weep.
From the broomed witch's spume you are shielded by fern
And flower of country sleep and the greenwood keep.
                      Lie fast and soothed,
Safe be and smooth from the bellows of the rushy brood.
Never, my girl, until tolled to sleep by the stern

Bell believe or fear that the rustic shade or spell
Shall harrow and snow the blood while you ride wide and
    near,                                   *20*
For who unmanningly haunts the mountain ravened eaves
Or skulks in the dell moon but moonshine echoing clear
                      From the starred well?
A hill touches an angel! Out of a saint's cell
The nightbird lauds through nunneries and domes of leaves

Her robin breasted tree, three Marys in the rays.
*Sanctum sanctorum* the animal eye of the wood
In the rain telling its beads, and the gravest ghost
The owl at its knelling. Fox and holt kneel before blood.
                      Now the tales praise
The star rise at pasture and nightlong the fables graze
On the lord's-table of the bowing grass. Fear most       *30*

For ever of all not the wolf in his baaing hood
Nor the tusked prince, in the ruttish farm, at the rind
And mire of love, but the Thief as meek as the dew.
The country is holy: O bide in that country kind,
                      Know the green good,
Under the prayer wheeling moon in the rosy wood
Be shielded by chant and flower and gay may you
Lie in grace. Sleep spelled at rest in the lowly house
In the squirrel nimble grove, under linen and thatch
And star: held and blessed, though you scour the high four
Winds, from the dousing shade and the roarer at the latch,
                      Cool in your vows.       *40*
Yet out of the beaked, web dark and the pouncing boughs
Be you sure the Thief will seek a way sly and sure

And sly as snow and meek as dew blown to the thorn,
This night and each vast night until the stern bell talks
In the tower and tolls to sleep over the stalls
Of the hearthstone tales my own, lost love; and the soul
      walks
                                          The waters shorn.
This night and each night since the falling star you were born,
Ever and ever he finds a way, as the snow falls,

As the rain falls, hail on the fleece, as the vale mist rides
Through the haygold stalls, as the dew falls on the wind-            50
Milled dust of the apple tree and the pounded islands
Of the morning leaves, as the star falls, as the winged
                                          Apple seed glides,
And falls, and flowers in the yawning wound at our sides,
As the world falls, silent as the cyclone of silence.

                              II

Night and the reindeer on the clouds above the haycocks
And the wings of the great roc ribboned for the fair!
The leaping saga of prayer! And high, there, on the hare-
                        Heeled winds the rooks
Cawing from their black bethels soaring, the holy books
Of birds! Among the cocks like fire the red fox

Burning! Night and the vein of birds in the winged, sloe
      wrist                                                          60
Of the wood! Pastoral beat of blood through the laced
      leaves!
The stream from the priest black wristed spinney and sleeves
                              Of thistling frost
Of the nightingale's din and tale! The upgiven ghost
Of the dingle torn to singing and the surpliced

Hill of cypresses! The din and tale in the skimmed
Yard of the buttermilk rain on the pail! The sermon
Of blood! The bird loud vein! The saga from mermen
                              To seraphim
Leaping! The gospel rooks! All tell, this night, of him
Who comes as red as the fox and sly as the heeled wind.
Illumination of music! the lulled black-backed                      70
Gull, on the wave with sand in its eyes! And the foal moves
Through the shaken greensward lake, silent, on moonshod
      hooves,
                              In the winds' wakes.
Music of elements, that a miracle makes!
Earth, air, water, fire, singing into the white act,

The haygold haired, my love asleep, and the rift blue
Eyed, in the haloed house, in her rareness and hilly

High riding, held and blessed and true, and so stilly
                                        Lying the sky
Might cross its planets, the bell weep, night gather her eyes,
The Thief fall on the dead like the willy nilly dew,

Only for the turning of the earth in her holy                          80
Heart! Slyly, slowly, hearing the wound in her side go
Round the sun, he comes to my love like the designed snow,
                                        And truly he
Flows to the strand of flowers like the dew's ruly sea,
And surely he sails like the ship shape clouds. Oh he
Comes designed to my love to steal not her tide raking
Wound, nor her riding high, nor her eyes, nor kindled hair,
But her faith that each vast night and the saga of prayer
                                        He comes to take
Her faith that this last night for his unsacred sake
He comes to leave her in the lawless sun awaking

Naked and forsaken to grieve he will not come.                         90
Ever and ever by all your vows believe and fear
My dear this night he comes and night without end my dear
                                        Since you were born:
And you shall wake, from country sleep, this dawn and each
     first dawn,
Your faith as deathless as the outcry of the ruled sun.


# RANDALL JARRELL / 1914–1965


## 90 North

At home, in my flannel gown, like a bear to its floe,
I clambered to bed; up the globe's impossible sides
I sailed all night—till at last, with my black beard,
My furs and my dogs, I stood at the northern pole.

There in the childish night my companions lay frozen,
The stiff furs knocked at my starveling throat,
And I gave my great sigh—the flakes came huddling;
Were they really my end? In the darkness I turned to my rest.

Here, the flag snaps in the glare and silence
Of the unbroken ice. And I stand here,                                 10
The dogs bark, my beard is black, and I stare
At the North Pole. And now what? Why, go back.

Turn as I please, my step is to the south.
The world—my world spins on this final point

Of cold and wretchedness: all lines, all winds
End in this whirlpool I at last discover.

And it is meaningless. In the child's bed
After the night's voyage, in that warm world
Where people work and suffer till the death
That crowns the pain—in that Cloud-Cuckoo-Land          20

I reached my North and it had meaning.
Here at the actual pole of my existence,
Where all that I have done is meaningless,
Where I die or live by accident alone—

Where, living or dying, I am still alone;
Here where North, the night, the berg of death
Crowd to me out of the ignorant darkness
I see at last that all the knowledge

I wrung from the darkness—that the darkness flung me—
Is worthless as ignorance: nothing comes from nothing,          30
The darkness from the darkness. Pain comes from the darkness,
And we call it wisdom. It is pain.  (*1942*)


## The Death of the Ball Turret Gunner

From my mother's sleep I fell into the State,
And I hunched in its belly till my wet fur froze.
Six miles from earth, loosed from its dream of life,
I woke to black flak and the nightmare fighters.
When I died they washed me out of the turret with a hose.  (*1945*)


## Eighth Air Force

If, in an odd angle of the hutment,
A puppy laps the water from a can
Of flowers, and the drunk sergeant shaving
Whistles *O Paradiso!*[1]—shall I say that man
Is not as men have said: a wolf to man?

The other murderers troop in yawning;
Three of them play Pitch,[2] one sleeps, and one
Lies counting missions, lies there sweating
Till even his heart beats: One; One; One.
*O murderers!* . . . Still, this is how it's done:          10

This is a war. . . . But since these play, before they die,
Like puppies with their puppy; since, a man,
I did as these have done, but did not die—
I will content the people as I can
And give up these to them: Behold the man![3]

---

[1] popular aria from Meyerbeer's *L'Africaine*     [2] a card game     [3] See John 19:5.

I have suffered, in a dream, because of him,
Many things; for this last saviour, man,
I have lied as I lie now. But what is lying?
Men wash their hands, in blood, as best they can:
I find no fault in this just man.   (*1948*)                    20


## The Woman at the Washington Zoo

The saris go by me from the embassies.

Cloth from the moon. Cloth from another planet.
They look back at the leopard like the leopard.

And I. . . .
            this print of mine, that has kept its color
Alive through so many cleanings; this dull null
Navy I wear to work, and wear from work, and so
To my bed, so to my grave, with no
Complaints, no comment: neither from my chief,
The Deputy Chief Assistant, nor his chief—
Only I complain. . . . this serviceable                        10
Body that no sunlight dyes, no hand suffuses
But, dome-shadowed, withering among columns,
Wavy beneath fountains—small, far-off, shining
In the eyes of animals, these beings trapped
As I am trapped but not, themselves, the trap,
Aging, but without knowledge of their age,
Kept safe here, knowing not of death, for death—
Oh, bars of my own body, open, open!

The world goes by my cage and never sees me.
And there come not to me, as come to these,                    20
The wild beasts, sparrows pecking the llamas' grain,
Pigeons settling on the bears' bread, buzzards
Tearing the meat the flies have clouded. . . .
                              Vulture,
When you come for the white rat that the foxes left,
Take off the red helmet of your head, the black
Wings that have shadowed me, and step to me as man:
The wild brother at whose feet the white wolves fawn,
To whose hand of power the great lioness
Stalks, purring . . . .
                  You know what I was,
You see what I am: change me, change me!   (*1960*)           30

# JOHN BERRYMAN / 1914–1972

## *from* The Dream Songs

### 14

Life, friends, is boring. We must not say so.
After all, the sky flashes, the great sea yearns,
we ourselves flash and yearn,
and moreover my mother told me as a boy
(repeatingly) 'Ever to confess you're bored
means you have no

Inner Resources.' I conclude now I have no
inner resources, because I am heavy bored.
Peoples bore me,
literatures bores me, especially great literature,       *10*
Henry bores me, with his plights & gripes
as bad as achilles,

who loves people and valiant art, which bores me.
And the tranquil hills, & gin, look like a drag
and somehow a dog
has taken itself & its tail considerably away
into mountains or sea or sky, leaving
behind: me, wag.

### 40

I'm scared a lonely. Never see my son,
easy be not to see anyone,
combers out to sea
know they're goin somewhere but not me.
Got a little poison, got a little gun,
I'm scared a lonely.

I'm scared a only one thing, which is me,
from othering I don't take nothin, see,
for any hound dog's sake.
But this is where I livin, where I rake       *10*
my leaves and cop my promise, this' where we
    cry oursel's awake.

Wishin was dyin but I gotta make
it all this way to that bed on these feet
where peoples said to meet.
Maybe but even if I see my son
forever never, get back on the take,
free, black & forty-one.

## 167

*HENRY'S MAIL*

His mail is brimming with Foundation reports
and with the late inaction of the Courts
in his case, and his insurance firms
are rich with info enigmatic and
stuff stranger still from his main Bank is here to hand,
the Washington Post is all about germs,

and he and she want this and that—Christ God,
it's growing hard to get up in the morning
particularly since our postal service—
I hear Togo's is better: Couldn't we prod                    *10*
that Cabinet jerk say into resembling
London or Paris

almost a hundred years ago

or the town in Okie-land when I was young—
three and four deliveries a day!—
now gives me, toward noon, ONE.
And I dote on my mail: I need its bung:
and the postman may indeed follow the moon and the sun
but believe me he follows not Henry.

## 171

Go, ill-sped book, and whisper to her or
storm out the message for her only ear
that she is beautiful.
Mention sunsets, be not silent of her eyes
and mouth and other prospects, praise her size,
say her figure is full.

Say her small figure is heavenly & full,
so as stunned Henry yatters like a fool
& maketh little sense.
Say she is soft in speech, stately in walking,              *10*
modest at gatherings, and in every thing
declare her excellence.

Forget not, when the rest is wholly done
and all her splendours opened one by one
to add that she likes Henry,
for reasons unknown, and fate has bound them fast
one to another in linkages that last
and that are fair to see.

260

Tides of dreadful creation rocked lonely Henry
isolated in the midst of his family
as solitary as his dog.
In another world he'll have more to say of this,—
concepts came forward & were greeted with a kiss
in the passionate fog.

Lucid his project lay, beyond. Can he?
Loose to the world lay unimaginable Henry,
loose to the world,
taut with his vision as it has to be,                    *10*
open & closed sings on his mystery
furled & unfurled.

Flags lift, strange chords lift to a climax. Henry
is past. Returning from his travail, he
can't think of what to say.
The house's all about him, so is his family.
Tame doors swing upon his mystery
until another day.

342

Fan-mail from foreign countries, is that fame?
Imitations & parodies in your own,
translations?
Most of the relevant prizes, your private name
splashed on page one, with a photograph alone
or you with your lovely wife?

Interviews on television & radio
on various continents, can that be fame?
Henry could not find out.
Before he left the ship at Cobh he was photographed,    *10*
I don't know how they knew he was coming
He said as little as possible.

They wanted to know whether        his sources of inspiration
might now be Irish: I cried out 'of course'
& waved him off with my fountain pen.
The tender left the liner & headed for shore.
Cobh (pronounced Khōve) approached, our luggage was ready,
and anonymously we went into Customs.

A lone letter from a young man: that is fame.

382

At Henry's bier let some thing fall out well:
enter there none who somewhat has to sell,
the music ancient & gradual,

the voices solemn but the grief subdued,
no hairy jokes but everybody's mood
subdued, subdued,

until the Dancer comes, in a short short dress
hair black & long & loose, dark dark glasses,
uptilted face,
pallor & strangeness, the music changes                     *10*
to 'Give!' & 'Ow!' and how! the music changes,
she kicks a backward limb

on tiptoe, pirouettes, & she is free
to the knocking music, sails, dips, & suddenly
returns to the terrible gay
occasion hopeless & mad, she weaves, it's hell,
she flings to her head a leg, bobs, all is well,
she dances Henry away.


# HENRY REED / 1914–


## Chard Whitlow

### (MR. ELIOT'S SUNDAY EVENING POSTSCRIPT)

As we get older we do not get any younger.
Seasons return, and today I am fifty-five,
And this time last year I was fifty-four,
And this time next year I shall be sixty-two.
And I cannot say I should like (to speak for myself)
To see my time over again—if you can call it time:
Fidgeting uneasily under a draughty stair,
Or counting sleepless nights in the crowded Tube.[1]

There are certain precautions—though none of them very reliable—
Against the blast from bombs and the flying splinter,                  *10*
But not against the blast from heaven, *vento dei venti*,[2]
The wind within a wind unable to speak for wind;
And the frigid burnings of purgatory will not be touched
By any emollient.
                    I think you will find this put,
Better than I could ever hope to express it,
In the words of Kharma:[3] "It is, we believe,
Idle to hope that the simple stirrup-pump
Will extinguish hell."

---

[1] subway
[2] *ventus:* wind, spirit, or flatulence; *deus:* god
[3] in Hinduism and Bhuddism, the ethical consequence of one's acts

                    Oh, listeners,
And you especially who have turned off the wireless,
And sit in Stoke or Basingstoke listening appreciatively to the silence,          20
(Which is also the silence of hell) pray not for your selves but your souls.
And pray for me also under the draughty stair.
As we get older we do not get any younger.

And pray for Kharma under the holy mountain.   *(1947)*


## Lessons of the War: Naming of Parts

*(TO ALAN MICHELL)*

> *Vixi duellis nuper idoneus*
> *Et militavi non sine gloria*[1]

Today we have naming of parts. Yesterday,
We had daily cleaning. And tomorrow morning,
We shall have what to do after firing. But today,
Today we have naming of parts. Japonica
Glistens like coral in all of the neighbouring gardens,
     And today we have naming of parts.

This is the lower sling swivel. And this
Is the upper sling swivel, whose use you will see,
When you are given your slings. And this is the piling swivel,
Which in your case you have not got. The branches                                 10
Hold in the gardens their silent, eloquent gestures,
     Which in our case we have not got.

This is the safety-catch, which is always released
With an easy flick of the thumb. And please do not let me
See anyone using his finger. You can do it quite easy
If you have any strength in your thumb. The blossoms
Are fragile and motionless, never letting anyone see
     Any of them using their finger.

And this you can see is the bolt. The purpose of this
Is to open the breech, as you see. We can slide it                                20
Rapidly backwards and forwards: we call this
Easing the spring. And rapidly backwards and forwards
The early bees are assaulting and fumbling the flowers:
     They call it easing the Spring.

They call it easing the Spring: it is perfectly easy
If you have any strength in your thumb: like the bolt,
And the breech, and the cocking-piece, and the point of balance,
Which in our case we have not got; and the almond-blossom
Silent in all of the gardens and the bees going backwards and forwards,
     For today we have naming of parts.   *(1947)*                               30

---

[1] I have lived of late in a manner suitable to the wars, and have followed the military life not without
glory.

# WILLIAM STAFFORD / 1914–

## West of Your City

West of your city into the fern
sympathy, sympathy rolls the train
all through the night on a lateral line
where the shape of game fish tapers down
from a reach where cougar paws touch water.

Corn that the starving Indians held
all through moons of cold for seed
and then they lost in stony ground
the gods told them to plant it in—
west of your city that corn still lies.          *10*

Cocked in that land tactile as leaves
wild things wait crouched in those valleys
west of your city outside your lives
in the ultimate wind, the whole land's wave.
Come west and see; touch these leaves.   (*1960*)

## The Well Rising

The well rising without sound,
the spring on a hillside,
the plowshare brimming through deep ground
everywhere in the field—

The sharp swallows in their swerve
flaring and hesitating
hunting for the final curve
coming closer and closer—

The swallow heart from wing beat to wing beat
counseling decision, decision:          *10*
thunderous examples. I place my feet
with care in such a world.   (*1960*)

## Traveling Through the Dark

Traveling through the dark I found a deer
dead on the edge of the Wilson River road.
It is usually best to roll them into the canyon:
that road is narrow; to swerve might make more dead.

By glow of the tail-light I stumbled back of the car
and stood by the heap, a doe, a recent killing;
she had stiffened already, almost cold.
I dragged her off: she was large in the belly.

My fingers touching her side brought me the reason—
her side was warm; her fawn lay there waiting,                              *10*
alive, still, never to be born.
Beside that mountain road I hesitated.

The car aimed ahead its lowered parking lights;
under the hood purred the steady engine.
I stood in the glare of the warm exhaust turning red;
around our group I could hear the wilderness listen.

I thought hard for us all—my only swerving—,
then pushed her over the edge into the river.   (*1960*)


## Lake Chelan

They call it regional, this relevance—
the deepest place we have: in this pool forms
the model of our land, a lonely one,
responsive to the wind. Everything we own
has brought us here: from here we speak.

The sun stalks among these peaks to sight
the lake down aisles, long like a gun;
a ferryboat, lost by a century, toots
for trappers, the pelt of the mountains
rinsed in the sun and that sound.                                          *10*

Suppose a person far off to whom this lake
occurs: told a problem, he might hear a word
so dark he drowns an instant, and stands dumb
for the centuries of his country and the suave
hills beyond the stranger's sight.

Is this man dumb, then, for whom Chelan lives
in the wilderness? On the street you've seen
someone like a trapper's child pause,
and fill his eyes with some irrelevant flood—
a tide stops him, delayed in his job.                                      *20*

Permissive as a beach, he turns inland,
harks like a fire, glances through the dark
like an animal drinking, and arrives along that line
a lake has found far back in the hills
where what comes finds a brim gravity exactly requires.   (*1962*)

# GWENDOLYN BROOKS / 1917–

## The Mother

Abortions will not let you forget.
You remember the children you got that you did not get,
The damp small pulps with a little or with no hair,
The singers and workers that never handled the air.
You will never neglect or beat
Them, or silence or buy with a sweet.
You will never wind up the sucking-thumb
Or scuttle off ghosts that come.
You will never leave them, controlling your luscious sigh,
Return for a snack of them, with gobbling mother-eye.                    10

I have heard in the voices of the wind the voices of my
    dim killed children.
I have contracted. I have eased
My dim dears at the breasts they could never suck.
I have said, Sweets, if I sinned, if I seized
Your luck
And your lives from your unfinished reach,
If I stole your births and your names,
Your straight baby tears and your games,
Your stilted or lovely loves, your tumults, your marriages,
    aches, and your deaths,
If I poisoned the beginnings of your breaths,                           20
Believe that even in my deliberateness I was not deliberate.
Though why should I whine,
Whine that the crime was other than mine?—
Since anyhow you are dead.
Or rather, or instead,
You were never made.

But that too, I am afraid,
Is faulty: oh, what shall I say, how is the truth to be said?
You were born, you had body, you died.
It is just that you never giggled or planned or cried.                  30

Believe me, I loved you all.
Believe me, I knew you, though faintly, and I loved, I loved you
All.

## We Real Cool

*THE POOL PLAYERS.*
*SEVEN AT THE GOLDEN SHOVEL*

We real cool. We
Left school. We

808

Lurk late. We
Strike straight. We

Sing sin. We
Thin gin. We

Jazz June. We
Die soon.   (*1960*)


## Two Dedications

### I  THE CHICAGO PICASSO

August 15, 1967

" *Mayor Daley tugged a white ribbon, loosing the blue percale wrap. A hearty cheer went up
as the covering slipped off the big steel sculpture that looks at once like a bird and a woman.*"
—Chicago *Sun-Times*

(*Seiji Ozawa leads the Symphony.
The Mayor smiles.
And 50,000 See.*)

Does man love Art? Man visits Art, but squirms.
Art hungers. Art urges voyages—
and it is easier to stay at home,
the nice beer ready.
   In commonrooms
we belch, or sniff, or scratch.
Are raw.

But we must cook ourselves and style ourselves for Art, who
is a requiring courtesan.
We squirm.
We do not hug the Mona Lisa.
We
may touch or tolerate
an astounding fountain, or a horse-and-rider.
At most, another Lion.

Observe the tall cold of a Flower
which is as innocent and as guilty,
as meaningful and as meaningless as any
other flower in the western field.

10

### II  THE WALL

August 27, 1967

For Edward Christmas

" *The side wall of a typical slum building on the corner of 43rd and Langley became a mural
communicating black dignity. . . .*"

—*Ebony*

A drumdrumdrum.
Humbly we come.
South of success and east of gloss and glass are
sandals;
flowercloth;
grave hoops of wood or gold, pendant
from black ears, brown ears, reddish-brown
and ivory ears;

black boy-men.
Black                                                                        10
boy-men on roofs fist out "Black Power!" Val,
a little black stampede
in African
images of brass and flowerswirl,
fists out "Black Power!"—tightens pretty eyes,
leans back on mothercountry and is tract,
is treatise through her perfect and tight teeth.

Women in wool hair chant their poetry.
Phil Cohran gives us messages and music
made of developed bone and polished and honed cult.            20
It is the Hour of tribe and of vibration,
the day-long Hour. It is the Hour
of ringing, rouse, of ferment-festival.

On Forty-third and Langley
black furnaces resent ancient
legislatures
of ploy and scruple and practical gelatin.
They keep the fever in,
fondle the fever.

All                                                                          30
worship the Wall.

I mount the rattling wood. Walter
says, "She is good." Says, "She
our Sister is." In front of me
hundreds of faces, red-brown, brown, black, ivory,
yield me hot trust, their yea and their Announcement
that they are ready to rile the high-flung ground.
Behind me, Paint.
Heroes.
No child has defiled                                                        40
the Heroes of this Wall this serious Appointment
this still Wing
this Scald this Flute this heavy Light this Hinge.

An emphasis is paroled.
The old decapitations are revised,
the dispossessions beakless.

And we sing.   (*1968*)

ROBERT LOWELL / 1917–

## Children of Light

Our fathers wrung their bread from stocks and stones
And fenced their gardens with the Redman's bones;
Embarking from the Nether Land of Holland,
Pilgrims unhouseled by Geneva's night,
They planted here the Serpent's seeds of light;
And here the pivoting searchlights probe to shock
The riotous glass houses built on rock,
And candles gutter by an empty altar,
And light is where the landless blood of Cain
Is burning, burning the unburied grain.   (*1944*)

## Mary Winslow

Her Irish maids could never spoon out mush
Or orange-juice enough; the body cools
And smiles as a sick child
Who adds up figures, and a hush
Grips at the poised relations sipping sherry
And tracking up the carpets of her four
Room kingdom. On the rigid Charles,[1] in snow,
Charon,[2] the Lubber, clambers from his wherry,
And stops her hideous baby-squawks and yells,
Wit's clownish afterthought. Nothing will go                    *10*
Again. Even the gelded picador
Baiting the twinned runt bulls
With walrus horns before the Spanish Belles
Is veiled with all the childish bibelots.

Mary Winslow is dead. Out on the Charles
The shells hold water and their oarblades drag,
Littered with captivated ducks, and now
The bell-rope in King's Chapel Tower unsnarls
And bells the bestial cow
From Boston Common; she is dead. But stop,                     *20*
Neighbor, these pillows prop
Her that her terrified and child's cold eyes
Glass what they're not: our Copley[3] ancestress,
Grandiloquent, square-jowled and worldly-wise,
A Cleopatra in her housewife's dress;
Nothing will go again. The bells cry: "Come,
Come home," the babbling Chapel belfry cries:
"Come, Mary Winslow, come; I bell thee home."   (*1946*)

[1] river separating Boston and Cambridge, Mass.
[2] boatman who ferried dead souls across the River Styx into Hades
[3] as painted by John Singleton Copley (1737–1815), American portraitist

811

## Mr. Edwards and the Spider[1]

I saw the spiders marching through the air,
Swimming from tree to tree that mildewed day
   In latter August when the hay
   Came creaking to the barn. But where
      The wind is westerly,
   Where gnarled November makes the spiders fly
   Into the apparitions of the sky,
   They purpose nothing but their ease and die
Urgently beating east to sunrise and the sea;
What are we in the hands of the great God?                    10
It was in vain you set up thorn and briar
   In battle array against the fire
   And treason crackling in your blood;
      For the wild thorns grow tame
   And will do nothing to oppose the flame;
   Your lacerations tell the losing game
   You play against a sickness past your cure.
How will the hands be strong? How will the heart endure?

A very little thing, a little worm,
Or hourglass-blazoned spider, it is said,                    20
   Can kill a tiger. Will the dead
   Hold up his mirror and affirm
      To the four winds the smell
   And flash of his authority? It's well
   If God who holds you to the pit of hell,
   Much as one holds a spider,[2] will destroy,
Baffle and dissipate your soul. As a small boy

On Windsor Marsh, I saw the spider die
When thrown into the bowels of fierce fire:
   There's no long struggle, no desire                    30
   To get up on its feet and fly—
      It stretches out its feet
   And dies. This is the sinner's last retreat;
   Yes, and no strength exerted on the heat
   Then sinews the abolished will, when sick
And full of burning, it will whistle on a brick.

But who can plumb the sinking of that soul?
Josiah Hawley, picture yourself cast
   Into a brick-kiln where the blast
   Fans your quick vitals to a coal—                    40
      If measured by a glass,

---

[1] Jonathan Edwards (1703–1758), greatest of the New England Puritan divines, at the age of twelve wrote an essay on flying spiders.
[2] In his famous sermon, "Sinners in the Hands of an Angry God," Edwards said, "The God that holds you over the pit of hell, much as one holds a spider . . . abhors you, and is dreadfully provoked."

How long would it seem burning! Let their pass
A minute, ten, ten trillion, but the blaze
Is infinite, eternal; this is death,
To die and know it. This is the Black Widow, death.   (*1946*)


## The Quaker Graveyard in Nantucket

### (*FOR WARREN WINSLOW, DEAD AT SEA*)

*Let man have dominion over the fishes of the sea and the fowls of the air and the beasts
and the whole earth, and every creeping creature that moveth upon the earth.*

I

A brackish reach of shoal off Madaket,—
The sea was still breaking violently and night
Had steamed into our North Atlantic Fleet,
When the drowned sailor clutched the drag-net. Light
Flashed from his matted head and marble feet,
He grappled at the net
With the coiled, hurdling muscles of his thighs:
The corpse was bloodless, a botch of reds and whites,
Its open, staring eyes
Were lustreless dead-lights                                           *10*
Or cabin-windows on a stranded hulk
Heavy with sand. We weight the body, close
Its eyes and heave it seaward whence it came,
Where the heel-headed dogfish barks its nose
On Ahab's[1] void and forehead; and the name
Is blocked in yellow chalk.
Sailors, who pitch this portent at the sea
Where dreadnaughts shall confess
Its hell-bent deity,
When you are powerless                                                *20*
To sand-bag this Atlantic bulwark, faced
By the earth-shaker, green, unwearied, chaste
In his steel scales: ask for no Orphean lute[2]
To pluck life back. The guns of the steeled fleet
Recoil and then repeat
The hoarse salute.

II

Whenever winds are moving and their breath
Heaves at the roped-in bulwarks of this pier,
The terns and sea-gulls tremble at your death
In these home waters. Sailor, can you hear                            *30*
The Pequod's sea wings, beating landward, fall
Headlong and break on our Atlantic wall

---

[1] captain of the *Pequod* in Melville's *Moby Dick*      consent to recover his wife from the underworld.
[2] Orpheus charmed Pluto with his music and won

Off 'Sconset, where the yawing S-boats splash
The bellbuoy, with ballooning spinnakers,
As the entangled, screeching mainsheet clears
The blocks: off Madaket, where lubbers lash
The heavy surf and throw their long lead squids
For blue-fish? Sea-gulls blink their heavy lids
Seaward. The winds' wings beat upon the stones,
Cousin, and scream for you and the claws rush                    40
At the sea's throat and wring it in the slush
Of this old Quaker graveyard where the bones
Cry out in the long night for the hurt beast
Bobbing by Ahab's whaleboats in the East.

### III

All you recovered from Poseidon[3] died
With you, my cousin, and the harrowed brine
Is fruitless on the blue beard of the god,
Stretching beyond us to the castles in Spain,
Nantucket's westward haven. To Cape Cod
Guns, cradled on the tide,                                       50
Blast the eelgrass about a waterclock
Of bilge and backwash, roil the salt and sand
Lashing earth's scaffold, rock
Our warships in the hand
Of the great God, where time's contrition blues
Whatever it was these Quaker sailors lost
In the mad scramble of their lives. They died
When time was open-eyed,
Wooden and childish; only bones abide
There, in the nowhere, where their boats were tossed            60
Sky-high, where mariners had fabled news
Of IS, the whited monster. What it cost
Them is their secret. In the sperm-whale's slick
I see the Quakers drown and hear their cry:
"If God himself had not been on our side,
If God himself had not been on our side,
When the Atlantic rose against us, why,
Then it had swallowed us up quick."

### IV

This is the end of the whaleroad and the whale
Who spewed Nantucket bones on the thrashed swell                70
And stirred the troubled waters to whirlpools
To send the Pequod packing off to hell:
This is the end of them, three-quarters fools,
Snatching at straws to sail
Seaward and seaward on the turntail whale,
Spouting out blood and water as it rolls,

---

[3] god of the sea

Sick as a dog to these Atlantic shoals:
*Clamavimus,*[4] O depths. Let the sea-gulls wail
For water, for the deep where the high tide
Mutters to its hurt self, mutters and ebbs.       *80*
Waves wallow in their wash, go out and out,
Leave only the death-rattle of the crabs,
The beach increasing, its enormous snout
Sucking the ocean's side.
This is the end of running on the waves;
We are poured out like water. Who will dance
The mast-lashed master of Leviathans
Up from this field of Quakers in their unstoned graves?

V

When the whale's viscera go and the roll
Of its corruption overruns this world       *90*
Beyond tree-swept Nantucket and Wood's Hole
And Martha's Vineyard,[5] Sailor, will your sword
Whistle and fall and sink into the fat?
In the great ash-pit of Jehoshaphat[6]
The bones cry for the blood of the white whale,
The fat flukes arch and whack about its ears,
The death-lance churns into the sanctuary, tears
The gun-blue swingle, heaving like a flail,
And hacks the coiling life out: it works and drags
And rips the sperm-whale's midriff into rags,       *100*
Gobbets of blubber spill to wind and weather,
Sailor, and gulls go round the stoven timbers
Where the morning stars sing out together
And thunder shakes the white surf and dismembers
The red flag hammered in the mast-head. Hide,
Our steel, Jonas Messias,[7] in Thy side.

VI

OUR LADY OF WALSINGHAM[8]

There once the penitents took off their shoes
And then walked barefoot the remaining mile;
And the small trees, a stream and hedgerows file
Slowly along the munching English lane,       *110*
Like cows to the old shrine, until you lose
Track of your dragging pain.
The stream flows down under the druid tree,
Shiloah's whirlpools gurgle and make glad
The castle of God. Sailor, you were glad
And whistled Sion by that stream. But see:

---

4 We have cried out.
5 Wood's Hole is on Cape Cod near Nantucket Island. Martha's Vineyard is another island in the vicinity; like Nantucket it was a great nineteenth-century whaling port.

6 where God will judge the heathen
7 Like Christ, Jonah rose after three days of entombment—in the belly of the whale.
8 The passage describes a shrine in Norfolk.

Our Lady, too small for her canopy,
Sits near the altar. There's no comeliness
At all or charm in that expressionless
Face with its heavy eyelids. As before,                                    *120*
This face, for centuries a memory,
*Non est species, neque decor,*
Expressionless, expresses God: it goes
Past castled Sion. She knows what God knows,
Not Calvary's Cross nor crib at Bethlehem
Now, and the world shall come to Walsingham.

### VII

The empty winds are creaking and the oak
Splatters and splatters on the cenotaph,
The boughs are trembling and a gaff
Bobs on the untimely stroke                                                *130*
Of the greased wash exploding on a shoal-bell
In the old mouth of the Atlantic. It's well;
Atlantic, you are fouled with the blue sailors,
Sea-monsters, upward angel, downward fish:
Unmarried and corroding, spare of flesh
Mart once of supercilious, winged clippers,
Atlantic, where your bell-trap guts its spoil
You could cut the brackish winds with a knife
Here in Nantucket, and cast up the time
When the Lord God formed man from the sea's slime            *140*
And breathed into his face the breath of life,
And blue-lunged combers lumbered to the kill.
The Lord survives the rainbow of His will.   *(1946)*

## After the Surprising Conversions[1]

*September twenty-second,* Sir: today
I answer. In the latter part of May,
Hard on our Lord's Ascension, it began
To be more sensible. A gentleman
Of more than common understanding, strict
In morals, pious in behavior, kicked
Against our goad. A man of some renown,
An useful, honored person in the town,
He came of melancholy parents; prone
To secret spells, for years they kept alone—                              *10*
His uncle, I believe, was killed of it:
Good people, but of too much or little wit.
I preached one Sabbath on a text from Kings;

---

[1] The poem reflects events of the Great Awakening, a religious revival in Massachusetts, beginning in 1734. Lowell draws on accounts and correspondence of Jonathan Edwards, one of the clergymen chiefly involved in the Awakening.

He showed concernment for his soul. Some things
In his experience were hopeful. He
Would sit and watch the wind knocking a tree
And praise this countryside our Lord has made.
Once when a poor man's heifer died, he laid
A shilling on the doorsill; though a thirst
For loving shook him like a snake, he durst                    20
Not entertain much hope of his estate
In heaven. Once we saw him sitting late
Behind his attic window by a light
That guttered on his Bible; through that night
He meditated terror, and he seemed
Beyond advice or reason, for he dreamed
That he was called to trumpet Judgment Day
To Concord. In the latter part of May
He cut his throat. And though the coroner
Judged him delirious,[2] soon a noisome stir                   30
Palsied our village. At Jehovah's nod
Satan seemed more let loose amongst us: God
Abandoned us to Satan, and he pressed
Us hard, until we thought we could not rest
Till we had done with life. Content was gone.
All the good work was quashed. We were undone.
The breath of God had carried out a planned
And sensible withdrawal from this land;
The multitude, once unconcerned with doubt,
One neither callous, curious nor devout,                       40
Jumped at broad noon, as though some peddler groaned
At it in its familiar twang: "My friend,
Cut your own throat. Cut your own throat. Now! Now!"
September twenty-second, Sir, the bough
Cracks with the unpicked apples, and at dawn
The small-mouth bass breaks water, gorged with spawn.   (*1946*)


## Dunbarton

My grandfather found
his grandchild's fogbound solitudes
sweeter than human society.

When Uncle Devereux died,
Daddy was still on sea-duty in the Pacific;
it seemed spontaneous and proper
for Mr. MacDonald, the farmer,
Karl, the chauffeur, and even my grandmother
to say, "your father." They meant my grandfather.
He was my father. I was his son.                               10

---

[2] Edwards's uncle, Joseph Hawley, committed suicide in this way in 1735.

On our yearly autumn get-aways from Boston
to the family graveyard in Dunbarton,[1]
he took the wheel himself—
like an admiral at the helm.
Freed from Karl and chuckling over the gas he was saving,
he let his motor roller-coaster
out of control down each hill.
We stopped at the *Priscilla* in Nashua
for brownies and root-beer,
and later "pumped ship" together in the Indian Summer . . .          20

At the graveyard, a sauve Venetian Christ
gave a sheepdog's nursing patience
to Grandfather's Aunt Lottie,
his mother, the stone but not the bones
of his father, Francis.
Failing as when Francis Winslow could count
them on his fingers,
the clump of virgin pine still stretched patchy ostrich necks
over the disused millpond's fragrantly woodstained water,
a reddish blur,                                                      30
like the ever-blackening wine-dark coat
in our portrait of Edward Winslow
once sheriff for George the Second,
the sire of bankrupt Tories.

Grandfather and I
raked leaves from our dead forebears,
defied the dank weather
with "dragon" bonfires.

Our helper, Mr. Burroughs,
had stood with Sherman at Shiloh—                                   40
his thermos of shockless coffee
was milk and grounds;
his illegal home-made claret
was as sugary as grape jelly
in a tumbler capped with paraffin.

I borrowed Grandfather's cane
carved with the names and altitudes
of Norwegian mountains he had scaled—
more a weapon than a crutch.
I lanced it in the fauve[2] ooze for newts.                         50
In a tobacco tin after capture, the umber yellow mature newts
lost their leopard spots,
lay grounded as numb
as scrolls of candied grapefruit peel.
I saw myself as a young newt,

---

[1] in New Hampshire          [2] fawn-colored

neurasthenic, scarlet
and wild in the wild coffee-colored water.

In the mornings I cuddled like a paramour
in my grandfather's bed,
while he scouted about the chattering greenwood stove.   *(1959)*   60

## Skunk Hour

*(FOR ELIZABETH BISHOP)*

Nautilus Island's hermit
heiress still lives through winter in her Spartan cottage;
her sheep still graze above the sea.
Her son's a bishop. Her farmer
is first selectman in our village;
she's in her dotage.

Thirsting for
the hierarchic privacy
of Queen Victoria's century,
she buys up all                                            10
the eyesores facing her shore,
and lets them fall.

The season's ill—
we've lost our summer millionaire,
who seemed to leap from an L. L. Bean[1]
catalogue. His nine-knot yawl
was auctioned off to lobstermen.
A red fox stain covers Blue Hill.

And now our fairy
decorator brightens his shop for fall;                     20
his fishnet's filled with orange cork,
orange, his cobbler's bench and awl;
there is no money in his work,
he'd rather marry.

One dark night,
my Tudor Ford climbed the hill's skull;
I watched for love-cars. Lights turned down,
they lay together, hull to hull,
where the graveyard shelves on the town. . . .
My mind's not right.                                       30

A car radio bleats,
"Love, O careless Love. . . ." I hear
my ill-spirit sob in each blood cell,
as if my hand were at its throat. . . .
I myself am hell;
nobody's here—

---

[1] a Maine supplier of outdoor equipment and clothing

only skunks, that search
in the moonlight for a bite to eat.
They march on their soles up Main Street:
white stripes, moonstruck eyes' red fire                           40
under the chalk-dry and spar spire
of the Trinitarian Church.

I stand on top
of our back steps and breathe the rich air—
a mother skunk with her column of kittens swills the garbage pail.
She jabs her wedge-head in a cup
of sour cream, drops her ostrich tail,
and will not scare.   *(1959)*


## The Public Garden

Burnished, burned-out, still burning as the year
you lead me to our stamping ground.
The city and its cruising cars surround
the Public Garden. All's alive—
the children crowding home from school at five,
punting a football in the bricky air,
the sailors and their pick-ups under trees
with Latin labels. And the jaded flock
of swanboats paddles to its dock.
The park is drying.                                               10
Dead leaves thicken to a ball
inside the basin of a fountain, where
the heads of four stone lions stare
and suck on empty fawcets. Night
deepens. From the arched bridge, we see
the shedding park-bound mallards, how they keep
circling and diving in the lanternlight,
searching for something hidden in the muck.
And now the moon, earth's friend, that cared so much
for us, and cared so little, comes again—                         20
always a stranger! As we walk,
It lies like chalk
over the waters. Everything's aground.
Remember summer? Bubbles filled
the fountain, and we splashed. We drowned
in Eden, while Jehovah's grass-green lyre
was rustling all about us in the leaves
that gurgled by us, turning upside down . . .
The fountain's falling waters flash around
the garden. Nothing catches fire.   *(1964)*                      30

# LAWRENCE FERLINGHETTI / 1919–

## In Goya's Greatest Scenes

In Goya's greatest scenes[1] we seem to see
                          the people of the world
     exactly at the moment when
       they first attained the title of
                  "suffering humanity"
    They writhe upon the page
           in a veritable rage
               of adversity
   Heaped up
         groaning with babies and bayonets           10
                 under cement skies
     in an abstract landscape of blasted trees
      bent statues bats' wings and beaks
         slippery gibbets
      cadavers and carnivorous cocks
     and all the final hollering monsters
      of the
            "imagination of disaster"
     they are so bloody real
            it is as if they really still existed     20

   And they do

      Only the landscape is changed

 They still are ranged along the roads
    plagued by legionaires
             false windmills and demented roosters

  They are the same people
        only further from home
  on freeways fifty lanes wide
       on a concrete continent
           spaced with bland billboards     30
    illustrating imbecile illusions of happiness

   The scene shows fewer tumbrils
       but more maimed citizens
            in painted cars
   and they have strange license plates
   and engines
       that devour America

---

[1] *The Disasters of War* (1810–1820) was a series
of etchings by Francisco José de Goya (1746–
1828), a Spanish satiric artist.

821

# Dog

The dog trots freely in the street
and sees reality
and the things he sees
are bigger than himself
and the things he sees
and his reality
Drunks in doorways
Moons on trees
The dog trots freely thru the street
and the things he sees                                                    10
are smaller than himself
Fish on newsprint
Ants in holes
Chickens in Chinatown windows
their heads a block away
The dog trots freely in the street
and the things he smells
smell something like himself
The dog trots freely in the street
past puddles and babies                                                  20
cats and cigars
poolrooms and policemen
He doesn't hate cops
He merely has no use for them
and he goes past them
and past the dead cows hung up whole
in front of the San Francisco Meat Market
He would rather eat a tender cow
than a tough policeman
though either might do                                                   30
And he goes past the Romeo Ravioli Factory
and past Coit's Tower
and past Congressman Doyle
He's afraid of Coit's Tower
but he's not afraid of Congressman Doyle
although what he hears is very discouraging
very depressing
very absurd
to a sad young dog like himself
to a serious dog like himself                                            40
But he has his own free world to live in
His own fleas to eat
He will not be muzzled
Congressman Doyle is just another
fire hydrant
to him
The dog trots freely in the street

and has his own dog's life to live
and to think about
and to reflect upon                                                                              *50*
touching and tasting and testing everything
investigating everything
without benefit of perjury
a real realist
with a real tale to tell
and a real tail to tell it with
a real live
                barking
                                democratic dog
engaged in real                                                                                   *60*
                        free enterprise
with something to say
                        about ontology
something to say
                about reality
                                and how to see it
                                        and how to hear it
with his head coked sideways
                                at streetcorners
as if he is just about to have                                                                    *70*
                                his picture taken
                                        for Victor Records
                listening for
                        His Master's Voice
        and looking
                        like a living questionmark
                                into the
                                great gramaphone
                                of puzzling existence
with its wondrous hollow horn                                                                     *80*
                which always seems
                just about to spout forth
                                some Victorious answer
                                to everything   (*1958*)


# HOWARD NEMEROV / 1920—

## Truth

            Around, above my bed, the pitch-dark fly
            Buzzed in the darkness still in my mind's eye
            His blue sound made the image of my thought
            An image that his resonance had brought
            Out of a common midden of the sun—

A garbage pit, and pile where glittering tin
Cans turned the ragged edges of their eyes
In a mean blindness on mine, where the loud flies
Would blur the summer afternoons out back
Beyond our house. Sleepy, insomniac, black                       *10*
Remainder of a dream, what house? and when?
Listening now, I knew never again
That wingéd image as in amber kept
Might come, summoned from darkness where it slept
The common sleep of all such sunken things
By the fly's loud buzzing and his dreaming wings.

I listened in an angry wakefulness;
The fly was bitter. Between dream and guess
About a foundered world, about a wrong
The mind refused, I waited long, long,                           *20*
And then that humming of the garbage heap
I drew beneath the surface of my sleep
Until I saw the helmet of the king
Of Nineveh,[1] pale gold and glittering
On the king's brow, yet sleeping knew that I
But thought the deepening blue thought of the fly.

## The Goose Fish

On the long shore, lit by the moon
To show them properly alone,
Two lovers suddenly embraced
So that their shadows were as one.
The ordinary night was graced
For them by the swift tide of blood
That silently they took at flood,
And for a little time they prized
       Themselves emparadised.

Then, as if shaken by stage-fright        *10*
Beneath the hard moon's bony light,
They stood together on the sand
Embarrassed in each other's sight
But still conspiring hand in hand,
Until they saw, there underfoot,
As though the world had found them out,
The goose fish turning up, though dead,
       His hugely grinning head.

There in the china light he lay,
Most ancient and corrupt and grey.        *20*
They hesitated at his smile,
Wondering what it seemed to say

To lovers who a little while
Before had thought to understand,
By violence upon the sand,
The only way that could be known
       To make a world their own.

It was a wide and moony grin
Together peaceful and obscene;
They knew not what he would express,      *30*
So finished a comedian
He might mean failure or success,
But took it for an emblem of
Their sudden, new and guilty love
To be observed by, when they kissed,
       That rigid optimist.

So he became their patriarch,
Dreadfully mild in the half-dark.
His throat that the sand seemed to choke,
His picket teeth, these left their mark   *40*
But never did explain the joke
That so amused him, lying there
While the moon went down to disappear
Along the still and tilted track
       That bears the zodiac.   (*1955*)

---

[1] ruined city on the Tigris River, ancient capital of the Assyrian Empire, in what is now Iraq

## The Town Dump

> *"The art of our necessities is strange*
> *That can make vile things precious."*

A mile out in the marshes, under a sky
Which seems to be always going away
In a hurry, on that Venetian land threaded
With hidden canals, you will find the city
Which seconds ours (so cemeteries, too,
Reflect a town from hillsides out of town),
Where Being most Becomingly ends up
Becoming some more. From cardboard tenements,
Windowed with cellophane, or simply tenting
In paper bags, the angry mackerel eyes                                          *10*
Glare at you out of stove-in, sunken heads
Far from the sea; the lobster, also, lifts
An empty claw in his most minatory
Of gestures; oyster, crab, and mussel shells
Lie here in heaps, savage as money hurled
Away at the gate of hell. If you want results,
These are results.
              Objects of value or virtue,
However, are also to be picked up here,
Though rarely, lying with bones and rotten meat,
Eggshells and mouldy bread, banana peels                                        *20*
No one will skid on, apple cores that caused
Neither the fall of man nor a theory
Of gravitation. People do throw out
The family pearls by accident, sometimes,
Not often; I've known dealers in antiques
To prowl this place by night, with flashlights, on
The off-chance of somebody's having left
Derelict chairs which will turn out to be
By Hepplewhite, a perfect set of six
Going to show, I guess, that in any sty                                         *30*
Someone's heaven may open and shower down
Riches responsive to the right dream; though
It is a small chance, certainly, that sends
The ghostly dealer, heavy with fly-netting
Over his head, across these hills in darkness,
Stumbling in cut-glass goblets, lacquered cups,
And other products of his dreamy midden
Pencilled with light and guarded by the flies.

For there are flies, of course. A dynamo
Composed, by thousands, of our ancient black                                    *40*
Retainers, hums here day and night, steady
As someone telling beads, the hum becoming
A high whine at any disturbance; then,

Settled again, they shine under the sun
Like oil-drops, or are invisible as night,
By night.
            All this continually smoulders,
Crackles, and smokes with mostly invisible fires
Which, working deep, rarely flash out and flare,
And never finish. Nothing finishes;
The flies, feeling the heat, keep on the move.        *50*

Among the flies, the purifying fires,
The hunters by night, acquainted with the art
Of our necessities, and the new deposits
That each day wastes with treasure, you may say
There should be ratios. You may sum up
The results, if you want results. But I will add
That wild birds, drawn to the carrion and flies,
Assemble in some numbers here, their wings
Shining with light, their flight enviably free,
Their music marvelous, though sad, and strange.  *(1958)*   *60*

# RICHARD WILBUR / 1921–

## Still, Citizen Sparrow

Still, citizen sparrow, this vulture which you call
Unnatural, let him but lumber again to air
Over the rotten office, let him bear
The carrion ballast up, and at the tall

Tip of the sky lie cruising. Then you'll see
That no more beautiful bird is in heaven's height,
No wider more placid wings, no watchfuller flight;
He shoulders nature there, the frightfully free,

The naked-headed one. Pardon him, you
Who dart in the orchard aisles, for it is he        *10*
Devours death, mocks mutability,
Has heart to make an end, keeps nature new.

Thinking of Noah, childheart, try to forget
How for so many bedlam hours his saw
Soured the song of birds with its wheezy gnaw,
And the slam of his hammer all the day beset

The people's ears. Forget that he could bear
To see the towns like coral under the keel,
And the fields so dismal deep. Try rather to feel
How high and weary it was, on the waters where    *20*

He rocked his only world, and everyone's.
Forgive the hero, you who would have died
Gladly with all you knew; he rode that tide
To Ararat;[1] all men are Noah's sons.  (*1950*)


## The Pardon

My dog lay dead five days without a grave
In the thick of summer, hid in a clump of pine
And a jungle of grass and honeysuckle-vine.
I who had loved him while he kept alive

Went only close enough to where he was
To sniff the heavy honeysuckle-smell
Twined with another odor heavier still
And hear the flies' intolerable buzz.

Well, I was ten and very much afraid.
In my kind world the dead were out of range          10
And I could not forgive the sad or strange
In beast or man. My father took the spade

And buried him. Last night I saw the grass
Slowly divide (it was the same scene
But now it glowed a fierce and mortal green)
And saw the dog emerging. I confess

I felt afraid again, but still he came
In the carnal sun, clothed in a hymn of flies,
And death was breeding in his lively eyes.
I started in to cry and call his name,                20

Asking forgiveness of his tongueless head.
. . . I dreamt the past was never past redeeming:
But whether this was false or honest dreaming
I beg death's pardon now. And mourn the dead.  (*1950*)


## Mind

Mind in the purest play is like some bat
That beats about in caverns all alone,
Contriving by a kind of senseless wit
Not to conclude against a wall of stone.

It has no need to falter or explore;
Darkly it knows what obstacles are there,
And so may weave and flitter, dip and soar
In perfect courses through the blackest air.

---

[1] mountain on which the Ark was grounded when the flood receded

And has this simile a like perfection?
The mind is like a bat. Precisely. Save                          *10*
That in the very happiest intellection
A graceful error may correct the cave.   *(1956)*


## The Beautiful Changes

One wading a Fall meadow finds on all sides
The Queen Anne's Lace[1] lying like lilies
On water; it glides
So from the walker, it turns
Dry grass to a lake, as the slightest shade of you
Valleys my mind in fabulous blue Lucernes.[2]

The beautiful changes as a forest is changed
By a chameleon's tuning his skin to it;
As a mantis, arranged
On a green leaf, grows                                           *10*
Into it, makes the leaf leafier, and proves
Any greenness is deeper than anyone knows.

Your hands hold roses always in a way that says
They are not only yours; the beautiful changes
In such kind ways,
Wishing ever to sunder
Things and things' selves for a second finding, to lose
For a moment all that it touches back to wonder.   *(1947)*


## Lamarck[1] Elaborated

*"THE ENVIRONMENT CREATES THE ORGAN."*

The Greeks were wrong who said our eyes have rays;
Not from these sockets or these sparkling poles
Comes the illumination of our days.
It was the sun that bored these two blue holes.

It was the song of doves begot the ear
And not the ear that first conceived of sound:
That organ bloomed in vibrant atmosphere,
As music conjured Ilium[2] from the ground.

[1] a common field weed with flat circular clusters of small white flowers
[2] Lake Lucerne, in Switzerland
[1] Chevalier de Lamarck (1744–1829), French naturalist best known for his pre-Darwinian evolutionary theory, which includes the dis-credited principle paraphrased in Wilbur's epigraph
[2] According to one version of the legend, Apollo built the walls of Troy (Ilium) to the accompaniment of his lyre.

The yielding water, the repugnant stone,
The poisoned berry and the flaring rose                    *10*
Attired in sense the tactless finger-bone
And set the taste-buds and inspired the nose.

Out of our vivid ambiance came unsought
All sense but that most formidably dim.
The shell of balance[3] rolls in seas of thought.
It was the mind that taught the head to swim.

Newtonian numbers set to cosmic lyres[4]
Whelmed us in whirling worlds we could not know,
And by the imagined floods of our desires
The voice of Sirens[5] gave us vertigo.   *(1956)*        *20*


## Advice to a Prophet

When you come, as you soon must, to the streets of our city,
Mad-eyed from stating the obvious,
Not proclaiming our fall but begging us
In God's name to have self-pity,

Spare us all word of the weapons, their force and range,
The long numbers that rocket the mind;
Our slow, unreckoning hearts will be left behind,
Unable to fear what is too strange.

Nor shall you scare us with talk of the death of the race.
How should we dream of this place without us?—           *10*
The sun mere fire, the leaves untroubled about us,
A stone look on the stone's face?

Speak of the world's own change. Though we cannot conceive
Of an undreamt thing, we know to our cost
How the dreamt cloud crumbles, the vines are blackened by frost,
How the view alters. We could believe,

If you told us so, that the white-tailed deer will slip
Into perfect shade, grown perfectly shy,
The lark avoid the reaches of our eye,
The jack-pine lose its knuckled grip                        *20*

On the cold ledge, and every torrent burn
As Xanthus[1] once, its gliding trout
Stunned in a twinkling. What should we be without
The dolphin's arc, the dove's return,

---

[3] the inner ear, which provides the sense of balance
[4] Sir Isaac Newton, English scientist (1642–1727), made major contributions to mathematics and celestial mechanics.
[5] sea nymphs whose singing lured mariners to their destruction

[1] The river Xanthus assaulted Achilles to defend Troy against him, but the goddess Hera rescued the Achaian hero by having her son Hephaestus blast the river with fire. (*Iliad*, XXI)

These things in which we have seen ourselves and spoken?
Ask us, prophet, how we shall call
Our natures forth when that live tongue is all
Dispelled, that glass obscured or broken

In which we have said the rose of our love and the clean
Horse of our courage, in which beheld                                      *30*
The singing locust of the soul unshelled,
And all we mean or wish to mean.

Ask us, ask us whether with the worldless rose
Our hearts shall fail us; come demanding
Whether there shall be lofty or long standing
When the bronze annals of the oak-tree close.   (*1959*)


# PHILIP LARKIN / 1922–

## Church Going

Once I am sure there's nothing going on
I step inside, letting the door thud shut.
Another church: matting, seats, and stone,
And little books; sprawlings of flowers, cut
For Sunday, brownish now; some brass and stuff
Up at the holy end; the small neat organ;
And a tense, musty, unignorable silence,
Brewed God knows how long. Hatless, I take off
My cycle-clips in awkward reverence,

Move forward, run my hand around the font.                                 *10*
From where I stand, the roof looks almost new—
Cleaned, or restored? Someone would know: I don't.
Mounting the lectern, I peruse a few
Hectoring large-scale verses, and pronounce
"Here endeth" much more loudly than I'd meant.
The echoes snigger briefly. Back at the door
I sign the book, donate an Irish sixpence,
Reflect the place was not worth stopping for.

Yet stop I did: in fact I often do,
And always end much at a loss like this,                                    *20*
Wondering what to look for; wondering, too,
When churches fall completely out of use
What we shall turn them into, if we shall keep
A few cathedrals chronically on show,
Their parchment, plate and pyx in locked cases,
And let the rest rent-free to rain and sheep.
Shall we avoid them as unlucky places?

Or, after dark, will dubious women come
To make their children touch a particular stone;
Pick simples for a cancer; or on some                         30
Advised night see walking a dead one?
Power of some sort or other will go on
In games, in riddles, seemingly at random;
But superstition, like belief, must die,
And what remains when disbelief has gone?
Grass, weedy pavement, brambles, buttress, sky,

A shape less recognisable each week,
A purpose more obscure. I wonder who
Will be the last, the very last, to seek
This place for what it was; one of the crew                   40
That tap and jot and know what rood-lofts were?
Some ruin-bibber, randy for antique,
Or Christmas-addict, counting on a whiff
Of gown-and-bands and organ-pipes and myrrh?
Or will he be my representative,

Bored, uninformed, knowing the ghostly silt
Dispersed, yet tending to this cross of ground
Through suburb scrub because it held unspilt
So long and equably what since is found
Only in separation—marriage, and birth,                      50
And death, and thoughts of these—for whom was built
This special shell? For, though I've no idea
What this accoutred frowsty barn is worth,
It pleases me to stand in silence here;

A serious house on serious earth it is,
In whose blent air all our compulsions meet,
Are recognised, and robed as destinies.
And that much never can be obsolete,
Since someone will forever be surprising
A hunger in himself to be more serious,                       60
And gravitating with it to this ground,
Which, he once heard, was proper to grow wise in,
If only that so many dead lie round.   (*1955*)

## Poetry of Departures

Sometimes you hear, fifth-hand,
As epitaph:
*He chucked up everthing*
*And just cleared off,*
And always the voice will sound
Certain you approve
This audacious, purifying,
Elemental move.

And they are right, I think.
We all hate home                                              10
And having to be there:
I detest my room,
Its specially-chosen junk,
The good books, the good bed,
And my life, in perfect order:
So to hear it said

He walked out on the whole crowd
Leaves me flushed and stirred,
Like *Then she undid her dress*
Or *Take that you bastard;*                    20
Surely I can, if he did?
And that helps me stay
Sober and industrious.
But I'd go today,

Yes, swagger the nut-strewn roads,
Crouch in the fo'c'sle
Stubbly with goodness, if
It weren't so artificial,
Such a deliberate step backwards
To create an object:                           30
Books; china; a life
Reprehensibly perfect.   (*1955*)


## No Road

Since we agreed to let the road between us
Fall to disuse,
And bricked our gates up, planted trees to screen us,
And turned all time's eroding agents loose,
Silence, and space, and strangers—our neglect
Has not had much effect.
Leaves drift unswept, perhaps; grass creeps unmown;
No other change.
So clear it stands, so little overgrown,
Walking that way tonight would not seem strange,      10
And still would be allowed. A little longer,
And time will be the stronger,
Drafting a world where no such road will run
From you to me;
To watch that world come up like a cold sun,
Rewarding others, is my liberty.
Not to prevent it is my will's fulfilment.
Willing it, my ailment.   (*1955*)


## Next, Please

Always too eager for the future, we
Pick up bad habits of expectancy.
Something is always approaching; every day
*Till then* we say,

Watching from a bluff the tiny, clear,
Sparkling armada of promises draw near.
How slow they are! And how much time they waste,
Refusing to make haste!

Yet still they leave us holding wretched stalks
Of disappointment, for, though nothing balks
Each big approach, leaning with brasswork prinked,       10
Each rope distinct,

Flagged, and the figurehead with golden tits
Arching our way, it never anchors; it's
No sooner present than it turns to past.
Right to the last

We think each one will heave to and unload
All good into our lives, all we are owed
For waiting so devoutly and so long.
But we are wrong:                                              20

Only one ship is seeking us, a black-
Sailed unfamiliar, towing at her back
A huge and birdless silence. In her wake
No waters breed or break.   (*1955*)


# JAMES DICKEY / 1923–


## In the Mountain Tent

I am hearing the shape of the rain
Take the shape of the tent and believe it,
Laying down all around where I lie
A profound, unspeakable law.
I obey, and am free-falling slowly

Through the thought-out leaves of the wood
Into the minds of animals.
I am there in the shining of water
Like dark, like light, out of Heaven.

I am there like the dead, or the beast
Itself, which thinks of a poem—                                10
Green, plausible, living, and holy—
And cannot speak, but hears,
Called forth from the waiting of things,

A vast, proper, reinforced crying
With the sifted, harmonious pause,
The sustained intake of all breath
Before the first word of the Bible.

At midnight water dawns
Upon the held skulls of the foxes
And weasels and tousled hares
On the eastern side of the mountain.
Their light is the image I make                                20

As I wait as if recently killed,
Receptive, fragile, half-smiling,
My brow watermarked with the mark
On the wing of a moth

And the tent taking shape on my body
Like ill-fitting, Heavenly clothes.
From holes in the ground comes my voice
In the God-silenced tongue of the beasts.
"I shall rise from the dead," I am saying.   (*1961*)


## The Heaven of Animals

Here they are. The soft eyes open.
If they have lived in a wood
It is a wood.
If they have lived on plains
It is grass rolling
Under their feet forever.

Having no souls, they have come,
Anyway, beyond their knowing.
Their instincts wholly bloom
And they rise.                                           10
The soft eyes open

To match them, the landscape flowers,
Outdoing, desperately
Outdoing what is required:
The richest wood,
The deepest field.

For some of these,
It could not be the place
It is, without blood.
These hunt, as they have done,                          20
But with teeth and claws grown perfect.

More deadly than they can believe.
They stalk more silently,
And crouch on the limbs of trees,
And their descent
Upon the bright backs of their prey

May take years
In a sovereign floating of joy.
And those that are hunted
Know this as their life,                                 30
Their reward: to walk

Under such trees in full knowledge
Of what is in glory above them,
And to feel no fear,
But acceptance, compliance.
Fulfilling themselves without pain

At the cycle's center,
They tremble, they walk
Under the tree,
They fall, they are torn,
They rise, they walk again.  *(1961)*  40

## The Beholders

Far away under us, they are mowing on the green steps
Of the valley, taking long, unending swings
Among the ripe wheat.
It is something about them growing,
Growing smaller, that makes us look up and see
That what has come over them is a storm.

It is a blue-black storm the shape of this valley,
And includes, perhaps, in its darkness,
Three men in the air
Taking long, limber swings, cutting water.  10
Swaths start to fall and, on earth,
The men come closer together as they mow.

Now in the last stand of wheat they bend.
From above, we watch over them like gods,
Our chins on our hands,
Our great eyes staring, our throats dry
And aching to cry down on their heads
Some curse or blessing,

Some word we have never known, but we feel
That when the right time arrives, and more stillness,  20
Lightning will leap
From our mouths in reasonless justice
As they arc their scythes more slowly, taking care
Not to look up.

As darkness increases there comes
A dancing into each of their swings,
A dancing like men in a cloud.
We two are coming together
Also, along the wall.
No lightning yet falls from us  30

Where their long hooks catch on the last of the sun
And the color of the wheat passes upward,
Drawn off like standing water
Into the cloud, turning green;
The field becomes whiter and darker,
And fire in us gathers and gathers

Not to call down death to touch brightly
The only metal for miles
In the hands of judged, innocent men,
But for our use only, who in the first sheaves of rain                    40
Sit thunderstruck, having now the power to speak
With deadly intent of love.   (*1962*)


# ALAN DUGAN / 1923–


## Love Song: I and Thou

Nothing is plumb, level or square:
  the studs are bowed, the joists
are shaky by nature, no piece fits
  any other piece without a gap
or pinch, and bent nails
  dance all over the surfacing
like maggots. By Christ
  I am no carpenter. I built
the roof for myself, the walls
  for myself, the floors                                               10
for myself, and got
  hung up in it myself. I
danced with a purple thumb
  at this house-warming, drunk
with my prime whiskey: rage.
  Oh I spat rage's nails
into the frame-up of my work:
  it held. It settled plumb,
level, solid, square and true
  for that great moment. Then                                          20
it screamed and went on through,
  skewing as wrong the other way.
God damned it. This is hell,
  but I planned it, I sawed it
I nailed it, and I
  will live in it until it kills me.

I can nail my left palm
　　　　to the left-hand cross-piece but
I can't do everything myself.
　　　　I need a hand to nail the right,                          *30*
　　　　a help, a love, a you, a wife.   (*1961*)


## Funeral Oration for a Mouse

　　　　This, Lord, was an anxious brother and
a living diagram of fear: full of health himself,
　　　　he brought diseases like a gift
to give his hosts. Masked in a cat's moustache
　　　　but sounding like a bird, he was a ghost
　　　　of lesser noises and a kitchen pest
for whom some ladies stand on chairs. So,
Lord, accept our felt though minor guilt
　　　　for an ignoble foe and ancient sin:
　　　　　the murder of a guest                                    *10*
who shared our board: just once he ate
　　　　too slowly, dying in our trap
from necessary hunger and a broken back.

Humors of love aside, the mousetrap was our own
　　　　opinion of the mouse, but for the mouse
　　　　it was the tree of knowledge with
　　　　its consequential fruit, the true cross
and the gate of hell. Even to approach
　　　　it makes him like or better than
its maker: his courage as a spoiler never once            *20*
impressed us, but to go out cautiously at night,
　　　　into the dining room;—what bravery, what
　　　　hunger! Younger by far, in dying he
was older than us all: his mobile tail and nose
　　　　spasmed in the pinch of our annoyance. Why,
then, at that snapping sound, did we, victorious,
　　　　begin to laugh without delight?

　　　　Our stomachs, deep in an analysis
　　　　of their own stolen baits
(and asking, "Lord, Host, to whom are we the pests?"),   *30*
　　　　contracted and demanded a retreat
from our machine and its effect of death,
　　　　as if the mouse's fingers, skinnier
than hairpins and as breakable as cheese,
　　　　could grasp our grasping lives, and in
their drowning movement pull us under too,
into the common death beyond the mousetrap.   (*1961*)

## The Life and Death of the Cantata System

When the Lord was a man of war and sailed out
through the sky at night with all the stars
of all the constellations as his riding lights,
those beneath his oceanic, personal ascendancy
ascended in fated systems. The massed shouts
of the chorus sailed a regular sea of violins
as Galleons of the Line!, with hulls of bassos,
decks of baritones and altos, ornate in poop
and prow in rigging up the masts of soloists
which bore aloft, in turn, soprano mainsails,          10
top-gallants of the children's chorus, and
pennants of castrati streaming on the heights!
The Great Armada sang "Invincible!" to the deep,
but when the time came for a change in craft
the Lord's storms wrecked the vessels of the Lord
and the voices poured out on the air still singing.
The Empirical English conquered in the shallows. He
withdrew his stars to favor those made by machines.   *(1963)*

## Sailing to Jerusalem

On coming up on deck Palm Sunday morning, oh
we saw the seas the dancy little tourist ship
climbed up and down all night in cabin dreams.
They came along in ridges an horizon wide!
and ran away astern to the Americas we left,
to break on headlands and be called "the surf."
After services below, the pilgrims to the east
carried their processed palm fronds up on deck
and some of them went overboard from children's hands.
So, Christ: there were the palm leaves on the water   10
as the first fruits of the ocean's promised land.
They promise pilgrims resurrection out at sea,
though sea-sick fasters in their bunks below
cry out for harbor, order, and stability.
This is the place for it! The sky is high
with it, the water deep, the air its union: spray!
We all walk the water just below the decks
too, helplessly dancing to the world's variety
like your Jerusalem, Byzantium, and Rome.   *(1967)*

# ANTHONY HECHT / 1923–

## The Vow

In the third month, a sudden flow of blood,
The mirth of tabrets ceaseth, and the joy
Also of the harp. The frail image of God
Lay spilled and formless. Neither girl nor boy,
But yet blood of my blood, nearly my child.
      All that long day
Her pale face turned to the window's mild
      Featureless grey.

And for some nights she whimpered as she dreamed
The dead thing spoke, saying: "Do not recall           10
Pleasure at my conception. I am redeemed
From pain and sorrow. Mourn rather for all
Who breathlessly issue from the bone gates,
      The gates of horn,
For truly it is best of all the fates
      Not to be born.

"Mother, a child lay gasping for bare breath
On Christmas Eve when Santa Claus had set
Death in the stocking, and the lights of death
Flamed in the tree. O, if you can, forget           20
You were the child, turn to my father's lips
      Against the time
When his cold hand puts forth its fingertips
      Of jointed lime."

Doctors of Science, what is man that he
Should hope to come to a good end? *The best
Is not to have been born.* And could it be
That Jewish diligence and Irish jest
The consent of flesh and a midwinter storm
      Had reconciled,           30
Was yet too bold a mixture to inform
      A simple child?

Even as gold is tried, Gentile and Jew.
If that ghost was a girl's, I swear to it:
Your mother shall be far more blessed than you.
And if a boy's, I swear: The flames are lit
That shall refine us; they shall not destroy
      A living hair.
Your younger brothers shall confirm in joy
      This that I swear. *(1957)*         40

## The Dover Bitch

*A CRITICISM OF LIFE*

FOR ANDREWS WANNING

So there stood Matthew Arnold and this girl
With the cliffs of England crumbling away behind them,
And he said to her, "Try to be true to me,
And I'll do the same for you, for things are bad
All over, etc., etc."
Well now, I knew this girl. It's true she had read
Sophocles in a fairly good translation
And caught that bitter allusion to the sea,
But all the time he was talking she had in mind
The notion of what his whiskers would feel like                10
On the back of her neck. She told me later on
That after a while she got to looking out
At the lights across the channel, and really felt sad,
Thinking of all the wine and enormous beds
And blandishments in French and the perfumes.
And then she got really angry. To have been brought
All the way down from London, and then be addressed
As sort of a mournful cosmic last resort
Is really tough on a girl, and she was pretty.
Anyway, she watched him pace the room                          20
And finger his watch-chain and seem to sweat a bit,
And then she said one or two unprintable things.
But you mustn't judge her by that. What I mean to say is,
She's really all right. I still see her once in a while
And she always treats me right. We have a drink
And I give her a good time, and perhaps it's a year
Before I see her again, but there she is,
Running to fat, but dependable as they come,
And sometimes I bring her a bottle of *Nuit d'Amour.*   (*1960*)


# DENISE LEVERTOV / 1923–


## The Novel

A wind is blowing. The book being written
shifts, halts, pages
yellow and white drawing apart
and inching together in
new tries. A single white half-sheet
skims out under the door.

And cramped in their not yet
halfwritten leaves, a man and a woman
grimace in pain. Their cat
yawning its animal secret,                                          10
stirs in the monstrous limbo of erasure.
They live (when they live) in fear

of blinding, of burning, of choking under a
mushroom cloud in the year of the roach.
And they want (like us) the eternity
of today, they want this fear to be
struck out at once by a thick black
magic marker, everywhere, every page,

the whole sheets of it crushed, crackling,
and tossed in the fire                                              20
  and when they were fine ashes
  the stove would cool and be cleaned
  and a jar of flowers would be put to stand
  on top of the stove in the spring light.

Meanwhile from page to page they
buy things, acquiring the look of a
full life; they argue, make silence bitter,
play journeys, move house, implant
despair in each other
and then in the nick of time                                        30

they save one another with tears,
remorse, tenderness—
hooked on those wonder-drugs.
Yet they do have
—don't they—like us—
their days of grace, they

halt, stretch, a vision
breaks in on the cramped grimace,
inscape of transformation.
Something sundered begins to knit.                                  40
By scene, by sentence, something is rendered
back into life, back to the gods. (*1964*)


# Advent 1966

Because in Vietnam the vision of a Burning Babe[1]
is multiplied, multiplied,
      the flesh on fire
not Christ's, as Southwell saw it, prefiguring
the Passion upon the Eve of Christmas,

---

[1] See Robert Southwell, "The Burning Babe," page 124.

but wholly human and repeated, repeated,
infant after infant, their names forgotten,
their sex unknown in the ashes,
set alight, flaming but not vanishing,
not vanishing as his vision but lingering,                          10

cinders upon the earth or living on
moaning and stinking in hospitals three abed;

because of this my strong sight,
my clear caressive sight, my poet's sight I was given
that it might stir me to song,
is blurred.
              There is a cataract filming over
my inner eyes. Or else a monstrous insect
has entered my head, and looks out
from my sockets with multiple vision,                               20

seeing not the unique Holy Infant
burning sublimely, an imagination of redemption,
furnace in which souls are wrought into new life,
but, as off a beltline, more senseless figures aflame.

And this insect (who is not there—
it is my own eyes do my seeing, the insect
is not there, what I see is there)
will not permit me to look elsewhere,

or if I look, to see except dulled and unfocused
the delicate, firm, whole flesh of the still unburned.             30


# LOUIS SIMPSON / 1923–

## The Inner Part

When they had won the war
And for the first time in history
Americans were the most important people—

When the leading citizens no longer lived in their shirt sleeves,
And their wives did not scratch in public;
Just when they'd stopped saying "Gosh!"—

When their daughters seemed as sensitive
As the tip of a fly rod,
And their sons were as smooth as a V-8 engine—

Priests, examining the entrails of birds,           *10*
Found the heart misplaced, and seeds
As black as death, emitting a strange odor.

# Simplicity

Climbing the staircase
step by step, feeling my way . . .
I seem to have some trouble with my vision.
The stairs are littered with paper,
eggshells, and other garbage.
Then she comes to the door.
Without eye-shadow or lipstick,
with her hair tied in a bun,
in a white dress, she seems ethereal.

"Peter," she says, "how nice!           *10*
I thought that you were Albert,
but he hardly ever comes."
She says, "I hope you like my dress.
It's simple. I made it myself.
Nowadays everyone's wearing simple things.
The thing is to be sincere,
and then, when you're tired of something,
you just throw it away."

I'll spare you the description
of all her simple objects:           *20*
the bed pushed in one corner;
the naked bulb that hangs
on a wire down from the ceiling
that is stamped out of metal
in squares, each square containing
a pattern of leaves and flowers;
the window with no blinds, admitting
daylight, and the wall
where a stream of yellow ice hangs down
in waves.           *30*
          She is saying
"I have sat in this room
all day. There is a time
when you just stare at the wall
all day, and nothing moves.
I can't go on like this any longer,
counting the cracks in the wall,
doting on my buttons."

I seem to be disconnected
from the voice that is speaking           *40*
and the sound of the voice that answers.

Things seem to be moving into a vacuum.
I put my head in my hands
and try to concentrate.
But the light shines through my hands,

and then (how shall I put it
exactly?) it's as though she begins
giving off vibrations,
waves of resentment, an aura
of hate you could cut with a knife. . . .      50
Squirming, looking over her shoulder. . . .
Her whole body seems
to shrink, and she speaks in hisses:

"They want to remove my personality.
They're giving me psychotherapy
and *ikebana*, the art of flower-arrangement.
Some day, I suppose, I'll be cured,
and then I'll go and live in the suburbs,
doting on dogs and small children."

I go down the stairs, feeling my way      60
step by step. When I come out,
the light on the snow is blinding.
My shoes crunch on ice and my head
goes floating along, and a voice
from a high, barred window cries
"Write me a poem!"

## My Father in the Night Commanding No

My father in the night commanding No
Has work to do. Smoke issues from his lips;
    He reads in silence.
The frogs are croaking and the streetlamps glow.

And then my mother winds the gramophone;
The Bride of Lammermoor begins to shriek—
    Or reads a story
About a prince, a castle, and a dragon.

The moon is glittering above the hill.
I stand before the gateposts of the King—      10
    So runs the story—
Of Thule, at midnight when the mice are still.

And I have been in Thule! It has come true—
The journey and the danger of the world,
    All that there is
To bear and to enjoy, endure and do.

Landscapes, seascapes . . . where have I been led?
The names of cities—Paris, Venice, Rome—
  Held out their arms.
A feathered god, seductive, went ahead. 20

Here is my house. Under a red rose tree
A child is swinging; another gravely plays.
  They are not surprised
That I am here; they were expecting me.

And yet my father sits and reads in silence,
My mother sheds a tear, the moon is still,
  And the dark wind
Is murmuring that nothing ever happens.

Beyond his jurisdiction as I move
Do I not prove him wrong? And yet, it's true 30
  *They* will not change
There, on the stage of terror and of love.

The actors in that playhouse always sit
In fixed positions—father, mother, child
  With painted eyes.
How sad it is to be a little puppet!

Their heads are wooden. And you once pretended
To understand them! Shake them as you will,
  They cannot speak.
Do what you will, the comedy is ended. 40

Father, why did you work? Why did you weep,
Mother? Was the story so important?
  "*Listen!*" the wind
Said to the children, and they fell asleep.


## Walt Whitman at Bear Mountain

" . . . life which does not give the preference to
any other life, of any previous period, which
therefore prefers its own existence . . . "
                                    ORTEGA Y GASSET

Neither on horseback nor seated,
But like himself, squarely on two feet,
The poet of death and lilacs
Loafs by the footpath. Even the bronze looks alive
Where it is folded like cloth. And he seems friendly.

"Where is the Mississippi panorama
And the girl who played the piano?
Where are you, Walt?
The Open Road goes to the used-car lot.

"Where is the nation you promised?                                    10
These houses built of wood sustain
Colossal snows,
And the light above the street is sick to death.

"As for the people—see how they neglect you!
Only a poet pauses to read the inscription."
"I am here," he answered.
"It seems you have found me out.
Yet, did I not warn you that it was Myself
I advertised? Were my words not sufficiently plain?

"I gave no prescriptions,                                             20
And those who have taken my moods for prophecies
Mistake the matter."
Then, vastly amused—"Why do you reproach me?
I freely confess I am wholly disreputable.
Yet I am happy, because you have found me out."

A crocodile in wrinkled metal loafing . . .

Then all the realtors,
Pickpockets, salesmen, and the actors performing
Official scenarios,
Turned a deaf ear, for they had contracted                           30
American dreams.

But the man who keeps a store on a lonely road,
And the housewife who knows she's dumb,
And the earth, are relieved.

All that grave weight of America
Cancelled! Like Greece and Rome.
The future in ruins!
The castles, the prisons, the cathedrals
Unbuilding, and roses
Blossoming from the stones that are not there. . . .                 40

The clouds are lifting from the high Sierras,
The Bay mists clearing.
And the angel in the gate, the flowering plum,
Dances like Italy, imagining red.


# ALLEN GINSBERG / 1926–

## A Supermarket in California

What thoughts I have of you tonight, Walt Whitman, for I walked down
the sidestreets under the trees with a headache self-conscious looking at the full
moon.

In my hungry fatigue, and shopping for images, I went into the neon fruit supermarket, dreaming of your enumerations!

What peaches and what penumbras! Whole families shopping at night! Aisles full of husbands! Wives in the avocados, babies in the tomatoes!—and you, Garcia Lorca, what were you doing down by the watermelons?

I saw you, Walt Whitman, childless, lonely old grubber, poking among the meats in the refrigerator and eyeing the grocery boys.

I heard you asking questions of each: Who killed the pork chops? What price bananas? Are you my Angel?

I wandered in and out of the brilliant stacks of cans following you, and followed in my imagination by the store detective.

We strode down the open corridors together in our solitary fancy tasting artichokes, possessing every frozen delicacy, and never passing the cashier.

Where are we going, Walt Whitman? The doors close in an hour. Which way does your beard point tonight?

(I touch your book and dream of our odyssey in the supermarket and feel absurd.)

Will we walk all night through solitary streets? The trees add shade to shade, lights out in the houses, we'll both be lonely.                                    10

Will we stroll dreaming of the lost America of love past blue automobiles in driveways, home to our silent cottage?

Ah, dear father, graybeard, lonely old courage-teacher, what America did you have when Charon quit poling his ferry and you got out on a smoking bank and stood watching the boat disappear on the black waters of Lethe?   *(1956)*


## My Sad Self

*TO FRANK O'HARA*[1]

Sometimes when my eyes are red
I go up on top of the RCA Building
    and gaze at my world, Manhattan—
        my buildings, streets I've done feats in,
        lofts, beds, coldwater flats
    —on Fifth Ave below which I also bear in mind,
        its ant cars, little yellow taxis, men
        walking the size of specks of wool—
Panorama of the bridges, sunrise over Brooklyn machine,
        sun go down over New Jersey where I was born        10
        & Paterson where I played with ants—
    my later loves on 15th Street,
        my greater loves of Lower East Side,
        my once fabulous amours in the Bronx
                faraway—

[1] a poet contemporary with Ginsberg

paths crossing in these hidden streets,
my history summed up, my absences
and ecstasies in Harlem—
—sun shining down on all I own
in one eyeblink to the horizon                                    20
in my last eternity—
matter is water.

Sad,
I take the elevator and go
down, pondering,
and walk on the pavements staring into all man's
plateglass, faces,
questioning after who loves,
and stop, bemused
in front of an automobile shopwindow          30
standing lost in calm thought,
traffic moving up & down 5th Avenue blocks
behind me
waiting for a moment when. . . .
Time to go home & cook supper & listen to
the romantic war news on the radio

. . . all movement stops
& I walk in the timeless sadness of existence,
tenderness flowing thru the buildings,
my finger tips touching reality's face,                           40
my own face streaked with tears in the mirror
of some window—at dusk—
where I have no desire—
for bonbons—or to own the dresses or Japanese
lampshades of intellection—

Confused by the spectacle around me,
Man struggling up the street
with packages, newspapers,
ties, beautiful suits
toward his desire                                                 50
Man, woman, streaming over the pavements
red lights clocking hurried watches &
movements at the curb—

And all these streets leading
so crosswise, honking, lengthily,
by avenues
stalked by high buildings or crusted into slums
thru such halting traffic
screaming cars and engines
so painfully to this                                              60

countryside, this graveyard
this stillness
on deathbed or mountain
once seen
never regained or desired
in the mind to come
where all Manhattan that I've seen must disappear.   (*1963*)

# W. D. SNODGRASS / 1926–

## The Campus on the Hill

Up the reputable walks of old established trees
They stalk, children of the *nouveaux riches*: chimes
Of the tall Clock Tower drench their heads in blessing:
"I don't wanna play at your house;
I don't like you any more."
My house stands opposite, on the other hill,
Among meadows, with the orchard fences down and falling;
Deer come almost to the door.
You cannot see it, even in this clearest norning.
White birds hang in the air between                                     10
Over the garbage landfill and those homes thereto adjacent,
Hovering slowly, turning, settling down
Like the flakes sifting imperceptibly onto the little town
In a waterball of glass.
And yet, this morning, beyond this quiet scene,
The floating birds, the backyards of the poor,
Beyond the shopping plaza, the dead canal, the hillside lying
        tilted in the air,
Tomorrow has broken out today:
Riot in Algeria, in Cyprus, in Alabama;
Aged in wrong, the empires are declining,                               20
And China gathers, soundlessly, like evidence.
What shall I say to the young on such a morning?—
Mind is the one salvation?—also grammar?—
No; my little ones lean not toward revolt. They
Are the Whites, the vaguely furiously driven, who resist
Their souls with such passivity
As would make Quakers swear. All day, dear Lord, all day
They wear their godhead lightly.
They look out from their hill and say,
To themselves, "We have nowhere to go but down:                        30

The great destination is to stay."
Surely the nations will be reasonable;
They look at the world—don't they?—the world's way?
The clock just now has nothing more to say.  (*1959*)


## Returned to Frisco, 1946

We shouldered like pigs along the rail to try
And catch that first gray outline of the shore
Of our first life. A plane hung in the sky
From which a girl's voice sang: ". . . you're home once more."

For that one moment, we were dulled and shaken
By fear. What could still catch us by surprise?
We had known all along we would be taken
By hawkers, known what authoritative lies

Would plan us as our old lives had been planned.
We had stood years and, then, scrambled like rabbits                    *10*
Up hostile beaches; why should we fear this land
Intent on luxuries and its old habits?

A seagull shrieked for garbage. The Bay Bridge,
Busy with noontime traffic, rose ahead.
We would have liberty, the privilege
Of lingering over steak and white, soft bread

Served by women, free to get drunk or fight,
Free, if we chose, to blow in our back pay
On smart girls or trinkets, free to prowl all night
Down streets giddy with lights, to sleep all day,                       *20*

Pay our own way and make our own selections;
Free to choose just what they meant we should;
To turn back finally to our old affections,
The ties that lasted and which must be good.

Off the port side, through haze, we could discern
Alcatraz, lavender with flowers. Barred,
The Golden Gate, fading away astern,
Stood like the closed gate of your own backyard.  (*1959*)


## *from* Heart's Needle

### 5

Winter again and it is snowing;
Although you are still three,
You are already growing
Strange to me.

You chatter about new playmates, sing
Strange songs; you do not know
*Hey ding-a-ding-a-ding*
Or where I go

Or when I sang for bedtime, *Fox*                                        *10*
*Went out on a chilly night,*
Before I went for walks
And did not write;

You never mind the squalls and storms
That are renewed long since;
Outside, the thick snow swarms
Into my prints

And swirls out by warehouses, sealed,
Dark cowbarns, huddled, still,
Beyond to the blank field,
The fox's hill                                        20

Where he backtracks and sees the paw,
Gnawed off, he cannot feel;
Conceded to the jaw
Of toothed, blue steel.   (*1959*)

                    7

Here in the scuffled dust
    is our ground of play.

I lift you on your swing and must
    shove you away,
see you return again,
    drive you off again, then

stand quiet till you come.
    You, though you climb
higher, farther from me, longer,
    will fall back to me stronger.                     10
Bad penny, pendulum,
    you keep my constant time

to bob in blue July
    where fat goldfinches fly
over the glittering, fecund
    reach of our growing lands.
Once more now, this second,
    I hold you in my hands.

## Lying Awake

This moth caught in the room tonight
Squirmed up, sniper-style, between
The rusty edges of the screen;
Then, long as the room stayed light,

Lay here, content, in some cornerhole.
Now that we've settled into bed
Though, he can't sleep. Overhead,
He throws himself at the blank wall.

Each night hordes of these flutterers haunt
And climb my study windowpane;                         10
Fired by reflection, their insane
Eyes gleam; they know what they want.

How do the petulant things survive?
Out in the fields they have a place
And proper work, furthering the race;
Why this blind fanatical drive

Indoors? Why rush at every spark,
Cigar, headlamp, or railway warning
To break off your wings and starve by morning?
And what could a moth fear in the dark                  20

Compared with what you meet inside?
Still, he rams the fluorescent face
Of the clock, thinks that's another place
Of light and families, where he'll hide.

We ought to trap him in a jar,
Or come, like the white-coats, with a net
And turn him out toward living. Yet
We don't; we take things as they are.    (*1960*)

## Mementos, 1

Sorting out letters and piles of my old
    Cancelled checks, old clippings, and yellow note cards
That meant something once, I happened to find
    Your picture. *That* picture. I stopped there cold,
Like a man raking piles of dead leaves in his yard
    Who has turned up a severed hand.

Yet, that first second, I was glad: you stand
    Just as you stood—shy, delicate, slender,
In the long gown of green lace netting and daisies
    That you wore to our first dance. The sight of you stunned    10
Us all. Our needs seemed simpler, then;
    And our ideals came easy.

Then through the war and those two long years
    Overseas, the Japanese dead in their shacks
Among dishes, dolls, and lost shoes—I carried
    This glimpse of you, there, to choke down my fear,
Prove it had been, that it might come back.
    That was before we got married.

—Before we drained out one another's force
    With lies, self-denial, unspoken regret                    20
And the sick eyes that blame; before the divorce
    And the treachery. Say it: before we met.
Still, I put back your picture. Someday, in due course,
    I will find that it's still there.    (*1960*)

## The Men's Room in the College Chapel

Here, in the most Unchristian basement
of this "fortress for the Christian mind,"
they close these four gray walls, shut out shame,
and scribble of sex and excrement,
draw bestial pictures and sign their names—
the old, lewd defiance of mankind.

The subversive human in his cell—
burn his vile books, stamp out his credo,
lock him away where no light falls,
and no live word can go back to tell                             10
where he's entombed like Monte Cristo—
yet, he'll carve his platform in the walls.

In need, men have painted the deep caves
to summon their animal, dark gods:
even the reviled, early Christians
prayed in catacombs to outlawed Good,
laid their honored dead and carved out graves
with pious mottos of resistance.

This is the last cave, where the soul
turns in its corner like a beast                                    *20*
nursing its wounds, where it contemplates
vengeance, how it shall gather to full
strength, what lost cause shall it vindicate,
returning, masterless and twisted.    (*1960*)


# W. S. MERWIN / 1927–

## One-Eye

('*IN THE COUNTRY OF THE BLIND THE ONE-EYED MAN IS KING.*')

On that vacant day
After kicking and moseying here and there
For some time, he lifted that carpet-corner
    His one eye-lid, and the dyed light
Leapt at him from all sides like dogs. Also hues
That he had never heard of, in that place
    Were bleeding and playing.

    Even so, it was
Only at the grazing of light fingers
Over his face, unannounced, and then his                            *10*
    Sight of many mat eyes, paired white
Irises like dried peas looking, that it dawned
On him: his sidelong idlings had found
    The country of the blind.

    Whose swarming digits
Knew him at once: their king, come to them
Out of a saying. And chanting an anthem
    Unto his one eye, to the dry
Accompaniment that their leaping fingers made
Flicking round him like locusts in a cloud,                         *20*
    They took him home with them.

    Their shapely city
Shines like a suit. On a plain chair he was set
In a cloak of hands, and crowned, to intricate
    Music. They sent him their softest

Daughters, clad only in scent and their own
Vast ears, meantime making different noises
        In each ante-chamber.

        They can be wakened
Sometimes by a feather falling on the next                               *30*
Floor, and they keep time by the water-clocks'
        Dropping even when they sleep. Once
He would expound to them all, from his only
Light, day breaking, the sky spiked and the
        Earth amuck with color.

        And they would listen,
Amazed at his royalty, gaping like
Sockets, and would agree, agree, blank
        As pearls. At the beginning.
Alone in brightness, soon he spoke of it                                 *40*
In sleep only: 'Look, look', he would call out
        In the dark only.

        Now in summer gaudy
With birds he says nothing; of their thefts, often
Beheld, and their beauties, now for a long time
        Nothing. Nothing, day after day,
To see the black thumb as big as a valley
Over their heads descending silently
        Out of a quiet sky.   (*1958*)


## Noah's Raven

Why should I have returned?
My knowledge would not fit into theirs.
I found untouched the desert of the unknown,
Big enough for my feet. It is my home.
It is always beyond them. The future
Splits the present with the echo of my voice.
Hoarse with fulfilment, I never made promises.   (*1963*)


# JAMES WRIGHT / 1927–


## A Presentation of Two Birds to My Son

Chicken. How shall I tell you what it is,
And why it does not float with tanagers?
Its ecstasy is dead, it does not care.
Its children huddle underneath its wings,

And altogether lounge against the shack,
Warm in the slick tarpaulin, smug and soft.

You must not fumble in your mind
The genuine ecstasy of climbing birds
With that dull fowl.
When your grandfather held it by the feet          *10*
And laid the skinny neck across
The ragged chopping block,
The flop of wings, the jerk of the red comb
Were a dumb agony,
Stupid and meaningless. It was no joy
To leave the body beaten underfoot;
Life was a flick of corn, a steady roost.
Chicken. The sound is plain.

Look up and see the swift above the trees.
How shall I tell you why he always veers          *20*
And banks around the shaken sleeve of air,
Away from ground? He hardly flies on brains;
Pockets of air impale his hollow bones.
He leans against the rainfall or the sun.

You must not mix this pair of birds
Together in your mind before you know
That both are clods.
What makes the chimney swift approach the sky
Is ecstasy, a kind of fire
That beats the bones apart                         *30*
And lets the fragile feathers close with air.
Flight too is agony,
Stupid and meaningless. Why should it be joy
To leave the body beaten underfoot,
To mold the limbs against the wind, and join
Those clean dark glides of Dionysian birds?
The flight is deeper than your father, boy.

## A Song for the Middle of the Night

By way of explaining to my son the following
curse by Eustace Deschamps: "Happy is he
who has no children; for babies bring nothing
but crying and stench."

Now first of all he means the night
    You beat the crib and cried
And brought me spinning out of bed
    To powder your backside.

I rolled your buttocks over
    And I could not complain:
Legs up, la la, legs down, la la,
    Back to sleep again.

Now second of all he means the day
    You dabbled out of doors          *10*
And dragged a dead cat Billy-be-damned
    Across the kitchen floors.
I rolled your buttocks over
    And made you sing for pain:
Legs up, la la, legs down, la la,
    Back to sleep again.

But third of all my father once
  Laid me across his knee
And solved the trouble when he beat
  The yowling out of me.          20
He rocked me on his shoulder
  When razor straps were vain:
Legs up, la la, legs down, la la,
  Back to sleep again.

So roll upon your belly, boy,
  And bother being cursed.
You turn the household upside down,
  But you are not the first.
Deschamps the poet blubbered too,
  For all his fool disdain:        30
Legs up, la la, legs down, la la,
  Back to sleep again.


## Two Hangovers

### NUMBER ONE

I slouch in bed.
Beyond the streaked trees of my window,
All groves are bare.
Locusts and poplars changed to unmarried women
Sorting slate from anthracite
Between railroad ties:
The yellow-bearded winter of the depression
Is still alive somewhere, an old man
Counting his collection of bottle caps
In a tarpaper shack under the cold trees        10
Of my grave.

I still feel half drunk,
And all those old women beyond my window
Are hunching toward the graveyard.

Drunk, mumbling Hungarian,
The sun staggers in,
And his big stupid face pitches
Into the stove.
For two hours I have been dreaming
Of green butterflies searching for diamonds        20
In coal seams;
And children chasing each other for a game
Through the hills of fresh graves.
But the sun has come home drunk from the sea,
And a sparrow outside
Sings of the Hanna Coal Co. and the dead moon.
The filaments of cold light bulbs tremble
In music like delicate birds.
Ah, turn it off.

### NUMBER TWO: I TRY TO WAKEN AND GREET THE WORLD ONCE AGAIN

In a pine tree,
A few yards away from my window sill,
A brilliant blue jay is springing up and down, up and down.

On a branch.
I laugh, as I see him abandon himself
To entire delight, for he knows as well as I do
That the branch will not break.

## A Blessing

Just off the highway to Rochester, Minnesota,
Twilight bounds softly forth on the grass.
And the eyes of those two Indian ponies
Darken with kindness.
They have come gladly out of the willows
To welcome my friend and me.
We step over the barbed wire into the pasture
Where they have been grazing all day, alone.
They ripple tensely, they can hardly contain their happiness
That we have come.                                            10
They bow shyly as wet swans. They love each other.
There is no loneliness like theirs.
At home once more,
They begin munching the young tufts of spring in the darkness.
I would like to hold the slenderer one in my arms,
For she has walked over to me
And nuzzled my left hand.
She is black and white,
Her mane falls wild on her forehead,
And the light breeze moves me to caress her long ear          20
That is delicate as the skin over a girl's wrist.
Suddenly I realize
That if I stepped out of my body I would break
Into blossom.   (*1961*)

## The Jewel

There is this cave
In the air behind my body
That nobody is going to touch:
A cloister, a silence

Closing around a blossom of fire.
When I stand upright in the wind,
My bones turn to dark emeralds.

## Youth

Strange bird,
His song remains secret.
He worked too hard to read books.
He never heard how Sherwood Anderson
Got out of it, and fled to Chicago, furious to free himself
From his hatred of factories.

My father toiled fifty years
At Hazel-Atlas Glass,
Caught among girders that smash the kneecaps
Of dumb honyaks.                                                          10
Did he shudder with hatred in the cold shadow of grease?
Maybe. But my brother and I do know
He came home as quiet as the evening.

He will be getting dark, soon,
And loom through new snow.
I know his ghost will drift home
To the Ohio River, and sit down, alone,
Whittling a root.
He will say nothing.
The waters flow past, older, younger                                      20
Than he is, or I am.  (*1964*)


# ANNE SEXTON / 1928–1974


## Ringing the Bells

And this is the way they ring
the bells in Bedlam
and this is the bell-lady
who comes each Tuesday morning
to give us a music lesson
and because the attendants make you go
and because we mind by instinct,
like bees caught in the wrong hive,
we are the circle of the crazy ladies
who sit in the lounge of the mental house                                 10
and smile at the smiling woman
who passes us each a bell,
who points at my hand
that holds my bell, E flat,
and this is the gray dress next to me
who grumbles as if it were special
to be old, to be old,
and this is the small hunched squirrel girl
on the other side of me
who picks at the hairs over her lip,                                      20
who picks at the hairs over her lip all day,
and this is how the bells really sound,
as untroubled and clean

as a workable kitchen,
and this is always my bell responding
to my hand that responds to the lady
who points at me, E flat;
and although we are no better for it,
they tell you to go. And you do.   (*1960*)


## You, Doctor Martin

You, Doctor Martin, walk
from breakfast to madness. Late August,
I speed through the antiseptic tunnel
where the moving dead still talk
of pushing their bones against the thrust
of cure. And I am queen of this summer hotel
or the laughing bee on a stalk

of death. We stand in broken
lines and wait while they unlock
the door and count us at the frozen gates                              10
of dinner. The shibboleth is spoken
and we move to gravy in our smock
of smiles. We chew in rows, our plates
scratch and whine like chalk

in school. There are no knives
for cutting your throat. I make
moccasins all morning. At first my hands
kept empty, unraveled for the lives
they used to work. Now I learn to take
them back, each angry finger that demands                             20
I mend what another will break

tomorrow. Of course, I love you;
you lean above the plastic sky,
god of our block, prince of all the foxes.
The breaking crowns are new
that Jack wore. Your third eye
moves among us and lights the separate boxes
where we sleep or cry.

What large children we are
here. All over I grow most tall                                       30
in the best ward. Your business is people,
you call at the madhouse, an oracular
eye in our nest. Out in the hall
the intercom pages you. You twist in the pull
of the foxy children who fall

like floods of life in frost.
And we are magic talking to itself,
noisy and alone. I am queen of all my sins
forgotten. Am I still lost?
Once I was beautiful. Now I am myself,                              40
counting this row and that row of moccasins
waiting on the silent shelf.   (1960)


## Some Foreign Letters

I knew you forever and you were always old,
soft white lady of my heart. Surely you would scold
me for sitting up late, reading your letters,
as if these foreign postmarks were meant for me.
You posted them first in London, wearing furs
and a new dress in the winter of eighteen-ninety.
I read how London is dull on Lord Mayor's Day,[1]
where you guided past groups of robbers, the sad holes
of Whitechapel,[2] clutching your pocketbook, on the way
to Jack the Ripper[3] dissecting his famous bones.                 10
This Wednesday in Berlin, you say, you will
go to a bazaar at Bismarck's[4] house. And I
see you as a young girl in a good world still,
writing three generations before mine. I try
to reach into your page and breathe it back . . .
but life is a trick, life is a kitten in a sack.

This is the sack of time your death vacates.
How distant you are on your nickel-plated skates
in the skating park in Berlin, gliding past
me with your Count, while a military band                          20
plays a Strauss waltz. I loved you last,
a pleated old lady with a crooked hand.
Once you read Lohengrin and every goose
hung high while you practiced castle life
in Hanover. Tonight your letters reduce
history to a guess. The Count had a wife.
You were the old maid aunt who lived with us.
Tonight I read how the winter howled around
the towers of Schloss Schwöbber, how the tedious
language grew in your jaw, how you loved the sound                 30
of the music of the rats tapping on the stone
floors. When you were mine you wore an earphone.

This is Wednesday, May 9th, near Lucerne,
Switzerland, sixty-nine years ago. I learn

---

[1] November 9, a day of pageantry marking the inauguration of the Lord Mayor
[2] a poverty-stricken district of London
[3] perpetrator of a series of brutal murders in London in 1888
[4] Prussian statesman (1815–1898), chancellor of the German empire

your first climb up Mount San Salvatore;
this is the rocky path, the hole in your shoes,
the yankee girl, the iron interior
of her sweet body. You let the Count choose
your next climb. You went together, armed
with alpine stocks, with ham sandwiches                    40
and seltzer wasser. You were not alarmed
by the thick woods of briars and bushes,
nor the rugged cliff, nor the first vertigo
up over Lake Lucerne. The Count sweated
with his coat off as you waded through top snow.
He held your hand and kissed you. You rattled
down on the train to catch a steamboat for home;
or other postmarks: Paris, Verona, Rome.

This is Italy. You learn its mother tongue.
I read how you walked on the Palatine⁵ among              50
the ruins of the palaces of the Caesars;
alone in the Roman autumn, alone since July.
When you were mine they wrapped you out of here
with your best hat over your face. I cried
because I was seventeen. I am older now.
I read how your student ticket admitted you
into the private chapel of the Vatican and how
you cheered with the others, as we used to do
on the Fourth of July. One Wednesday in November
you watched a balloon, painted like a silver ball,      60
float up over the Forum, up over the lost emperors,
to shiver its little modern cage in an occasional
breeze. You worked your New England conscience out
beside artisans, chestnut vendors and the devout.

Tonight I will learn to love you twice;
learn your first days, your mid-Victorian face.
Tonight I will speak up and interrupt
your letters, warning you that wars are coming,
that the Count will die, that you will accept
your America back to live like a prim thing              70
on the farm in Maine, I tell you, you will come
here, to the suburbs of Boston, to see the blue-nose
world go drunk each night, to see the handsome
children jitterbug, to feel your left ear close
one Friday at Symphony. And I tell you,
you will tip your boot feet out of that hall,
rocking from its sour sound, out onto
the crowded street, letting your spectacles fall
and your hair net tangle as you stop passers-by
to mumble your guilty love while your ears die.  (*1960*)    80

---

⁵ one of the seven hills of Rome

## The Monster

I left my room at last, I walked
The streets of that decaying town,
I took the turn I had renounced
Where the carved cherub crumbled down.

Eager as to a granted wish
I hurried to the cul de sac.
Forestalled by whom? Before the house
I saw an unmoved waiting back.

How had she never vainly mentioned
This lover, too, unsatisfied?          10
Did she dismiss one every night?
I walked up slowly to his side.

Those eyes glazed like her windowpane,
That wide mouth ugly with despair,
Those arms held tight against the haunches,
Poised, but heavily staying there:

At once I knew him, gloating over
A grief defined and realized,
And living only for its sake.
It was myself I recognized.          20

I could not watch her window now,
Standing before this man of mine,
The constant one I had created
Lest the pure feeling should decline.

What if I were within the house,
Happier than the fact had been
—Would he, then, still be gazing here,
The man who never can get in?

Or would I, leaving at the dawn
A suppler love than he could guess,          30
Find him awake on my small bed,
Demanding still some bitterness?

## Vox Humana

Being without quality
I appear to you at first
as an unkempt smudge, a blur,
an indefinite haze, mere-
ly pricking the eyes, almost
nothing. Yet you perceive me.

I have been always most close
when you had least resistance,
falling asleep, or in bars;
during the unscheduled hours,                                   *10*
though strangely without substance,
I hang, there and ominous.

Aha, sooner or later
you will have to name me, and,
as you name, I shall focus,
I shall become more precise.
O Master (for you command
in naming me, you prefer)!

I was, for Alexander,
the certain victory; I                                          *20*
was hemlock for Socrates;
and, in the dry night, Brutus
waking before Philippi
stopped me, crying out "Caesar!"

Or if you call me the blur
that in fact I am, you shall
yourself remain blurred, hanging
Like smoke indoors. For you bring,
to what you define now, all
there is, ever, of future.                                      *30*

## ADRIENNE RICH / 1929–

### The Knight

A knight rides into the noon,
and his helmet points to the sun,
and a thousand splintered suns
are the gaiety of his mail.
The soles of his feet glitter
and his palms flash in reply,
and under his crackling banner
he rides like a ship in sail.

A knight rides into the noon,
and only his eye is living,                     *10*
a lump of bitter jelly

set in a metal mask,
betraying rags and tatters
that cling to the flesh beneath
and wear his nerves to ribbons
under the radiant casque.

Who will unhorse this rider
and free him from between
the walls of iron, the emblems
crushing his chest with their weight?     *20*
Will they defeat him gently,
or leave him hurled on the green,
his rags and wounds still hidden
under the great breastplate?

## The Trees

The trees inside are moving out into the forest,
the forest that was empty all these days
where no bird could sit
no insect hide
no sun bury its feet in shadow
the forest that was empty all these nights
will be full of trees by morning.

All night the roots work
to disengage themselves from the cracks
in the veranda floor.                                                    10
The leaves strain toward the glass
small twigs stiff with exertion
long-cramped boughs shuffling under the roof
like newly discharged patients
half-dazed, moving
to the clinic doors.

I sit inside, doors open to the veranda
writing long letters
in which I scarcely mention the departure
of the forest from the house.                                           20
The night is fresh, the whole moon shines
in a sky still open
the smell of leaves and lichen
still reaches like a voice into the rooms.
My head is full of whispers
which tomorrow will be silent.

Listen. The glass is breaking.
The trees are stumbling forward
into the night. Winds rush to meet them.
The moon is broken like a mirror,                                       30
its pieces flash now in the crown
of the tallest oak.

## Two Songs

### 1

Sex, as they harshly call it,
I fell into this morning
at ten o'clock, a drizzling hour
of traffic and wet newspapers.
I thought of him who yesterday
clearly didn't
turn me to a hot field
ready for plowing,
and longing for that young man

pierced me to the roots                                                 10
bathing every vein, etc.
All day he appears to me
touchingly desirable,
a prize one could wreck one's peace for.
I'd call it love if love
didn't take so many years
but lust too is a jewel
a sweet flower and what
pure happiness to know
all our high-toned questions                                           20
breed in a lively animal.

2
That "old last act"!
And yet sometimes
all seems post coitum triste[1]
and I a mere bystander.
Somebody else is going off,
getting shot to the moon.
Or, a moon-race!
Split seconds after
my opposite number lands

I make it—                                    10
we lie fainting together
at a crater-edge
heavy as mercury in our moonsuits
till he speaks—
in a different language
yet one I've picked up
through cultural exchanges . . .
we murmur the first moonwords:
*Spasibo*.[2] *Thanks. O.K.*

# TED HUGHES / 1930–

## The Jaguar

The apes yawn and adore their fleas in the sun.
The parrots shriek as if they were on fire, or strut
Like cheap tarts to attract the stroller with the nut.
Fatigued with indolence, tiger and lion

Lie still as the sun. The boa-constrictor's coil
Is a fossil. Cage after cage seems empty, or
Stinks of sleepers from the breathing straw.
It might be painted on a nursery wall.

But who runs like the rest past these arrives
At a cage where the crowd stands, stares, mesmerized,          10
As a child at a dream, at a jaguar hurrying enraged
Through prison darkness after the drills of his eyes

On a short fierce fuse. Not in boredom—
The eye satisfied to be blind in fire,
By the bang of blood in the brain deaf the ear—
He spins from the bars, but there's no cage to him

More than to the visionary his cell:
His stride is wildernesses of freedom:
The world rolls under the long thrust of his heel.
Over the cage floor the horizons come.   (*1957*)          20

## Hawk Roosting

I sit in the top of the wood, my eyes closed.
Inaction, no falsifying dream
Between my hooked head and hooked feet:
Or in sleep rehearse perfect kills and eat.

---

[1] sad after coitus    [2] Thank you. (Russian)

The convenience of the high trees!
The air's buoyancy and the sun's ray
Are of advantage to me;
And the earth's face upward for my inspection.

My feet are locked upon the rough bark.
It took the whole of Creation                                    10
To produce my foot, my each feather:
Now I hold Creation in my foot

Or fly up, and revolve it all slowly—
I kill where I please because it is all mine.
There is no sophistry in my body:
My manners are tearing off heads—

The allotment of death.
For the one path of my flight is direct
Through the bones of the living.
No arguments assert my right:                                    20

The sun is behind me.
Nothing has changed since I began.
My eye has permitted no change.
I am going to keep things like this.  (*1960*)


# GARY SNYDER / 1930–

## Milton by Firelight

### PIUTE CREEK, AUGUST 1955

"O hell, what do mine eyes
             with grief behold?"[1]
Working with an old
Singlejack miner, who can sense
The vein and cleavage
In the very guts of rock, can
Blast granite, build
Switchbacks that last for years
Under the beat of snow, thaw, mule-hooves.
What use, Milton, a silly story                                  10
Of our lost general parents,
             eaters of fruit?

---

[1] *Paradise Lost*, Bk. IV, line 358. Satan thus ex-
claims when he first beholds Adam and Eve in
Paradise and begins to plot their fall.

The Indian, the chainsaw boy,
And a string of six mules
Came riding down to camp
Hungry for tomatoes and green apples.
Sleeping in saddle-blankets
Under a bright night-sky
Han River slantwise by morning.
Jays squall                                                    20
Coffee boils

In ten thousand years the Sierras
Will be dry and dead, home of the scorpion.
Ice-scratched slabs and bent trees.
No paradise, no fall,
Only the weathering land
The wheeling sky,
Man, with his Satan
Scouring the chaos of the mind.
Oh Hell!                                                       30

Fire down
Too dark to read, miles from a road
The bell-mare clangs in the meadow
That packed dirt for a fill-in
Scrambling through loose rocks
On an old trail
All of a summer's day.   (*1959*)

## Above Pate Valley

We finished clearing the last
Section of trail by noon,
High on the ridge-side
Two thousand feet above the creek—
Reached the pass, went on
Beyond the white pine groves,
Granite shoulders, to a small
Green meadow watered by the snow,
Edged with Aspen—sun
Straight high and blazing                                      10
But the air was cool.
Ate a cold fried trout in the
Trembling shadows. I spied
A glitter, and found a flake
Black volcanic glass—obsidian—
By a flower. Hands and knees
Pushing the Bear grass, thousands
Of arrowhead leavings over a
Hundred yards. Not one good
Head, just razor flakes                                        20

On a hill snowed all but summer,
A land of fat summer deer,
They came to camp. On their
Own trails. I followed my own
Trail here. Picked up the cold-drill,
Pick, singlejack, and sack
of dynamite.
Ten thousand years.   (*1965*)

## Running Water Music

under the trees
under the clouds
by the river
on the beach,

"sea roads."
whales      great sea-path beasts—
                 salt;   cold
                 water;   smoky fire.
steam, cereal,
                 stone, wood boards.        10

bone awl, pelts,                                 sat on a rock in the sun,
    bamboo pins and spoons.          watched the old pine
unglazed bowl.                                   wave
a band around the hair.                          over blinding fine white
    *beyond wounds.*                          river sand.   *(1970)*          20


# SYLVIA PLATH / 1932–1963


## Morning Song

Love set you going like a fat gold watch.
The midwife slapped your footsoles, and your bald cry
Took its place among the elements.

Our voices echo, magnifying your arrival. New statue.
In a drafty museum, your nakedness
Shadows our safety. We stand round blankly as walls.

I'm no more your mother
Than the cloud that distils a mirror to reflect its own slow
Effacement at the wind's hand.

All night your moth-breath                                            10
Flickers among the flat pink roses. I wake to listen:
A far sea moves in my ear.

One cry, and I stumble from bed, cow-heavy and floral
In my Victorian nightgown.
Your mouth opens clean as a cat's. The window square

Whitens and swallows its dull stars. And now you try
Your handful of notes;
The clear vowels rise like balloons.   *(1962)*


## Lady Lazarus

I have done it again.
One year in every ten
I manage it—

A sort of walking miracle, my skin
Bright as a Nazi lampshade,
My right foot

A paperweight,
My face a featureless, fine
Jew linen.

Peel off the napkin                                                      *10*
O my enemy.
Do I terrify?—

The nose, the eye pits, the full set of teeth?
The sour breath
Will vanish in a day.

Soon, soon the flesh
The grave cave ate will be
At home on me

And I a smiling woman.
I am only thirty.                                                        *20*
And like the cat I have nine times to die.

This is Number Three.
What a trash
To annihilate each decade.

What a million filaments.
The peanut-crunching crowd
Shoves in to see

Them unwrap me hand and foot—
The big strip tease.
Gentleman, ladies,                                                      *30*

These are my hands,
My knees.
I may be skin and bone,

Nevertheless, I am the same, identical woman.
The first time it happened I was ten.
It was an accident.

The second time I meant
To last it out and not come back at all.
I rocked shut

As a seashell.                                                          *40*
They had to call and call
And pick the worms off me like sticky pearls.

Dying
Is an art, like everything else.
I do it exceptionally well.

I do it so it feels like hell.
I do it so it feels real.
I guess you could say I've a call.

It's easy enough to do it in a cell.
It's easy enough to do it and stay put.                                 *50*
It's the theatrical

Comeback in broad day
To the same place, the same face, the same brute
Amused shout:

"A miracle!"
That knocks me out.
There is a charge

For the eyeing of my scars, there is a charge
For the hearing of my heart—
It really goes.                                                                60

And there is a charge, a very large charge,
For a word or a touch
Or a bit of blood

Or a piece of my hair or my clothes.
So, so, Herr Doktor.
So, Herr Enemy.

I am your opus,
I am your valuable,
The pure gold baby

That melts to a shriek.                                                        70
I turn and burn.
Do not think I underestimate your great concern.

Ash, ash—
You poke and stir.
Flesh, bone, there is nothing there—

A cake of soap,
A wedding ring,
A gold filling.

Herr God, Herr Lucifer,
Beware                                                                          80
Beware.

Out of the ash
I rise with my red hair
And I eat men like air.   (*1962*)


# Tulips

The tulips are too excitable, it is winter here.
Look how white everything is, how quiet, how snowed-in.
I am learning peacefulness, lying by myself quietly
As the light lies on these white walls, this bed, these hands.
I am nobody; I have nothing to do with explosions.
I have given my name and my day-clothes up to the nurses
And my history to the anaesthetist and my body to surgeons.

They have propped my head between the pillow and the sheet-cuff
Like an eye between two white lids that will not shut.
Stupid pupil, it has to take everything in.                                    *10*
The nurses pass and pass, they are no trouble,
They pass the way gulls pass inland in their white caps,
Doing things with their hands, one just the same as another,
So it is impossible to tell how many there are.

My body is a pebble to them, they tend it as water
Tends to the pebbles it must run over, smoothing them gently.
They bring me numbness in their bright needles, they bring me sleep.
Now I have lost myself I am sick of baggage—
My patent leather overnight case like a black pillbox,
My husband and child smiling out of the family photo;                          *20*
Their smiles catch onto my skin, little smiling hooks.

I have let things slip, a thirty-year-old cargo boat
Stubbornly hanging on to my name and address.
They have swabbed me clear of my loving associations.
Scared and bare on the green plastic-pillowed trolley
I watched my tea-set, my bureaus of linen, my books
Sink out of sight, and the water went over my head.
I am a nun now, I have never been so pure.

I didn't want any flowers, I only wanted
To lie with my hands turned up and be utterly empty.                           *30*
How free it is, you have no idea how free—
The peacefulness is so big it dazes you,
And it asks nothing, a name tag, a few trinkets.
It is what the dead close on, finally; I imagine them
Shutting their mouths on it, like a Communion tablet.

The tulips are too red in the first place, they hurt me.
Even through the gift paper I could hear them breathe
Lightly, through their white swaddlings, like an awful baby.
Their redness talks to my wound, it corresponds.
They are subtle: they seem to float, though they weigh me down,          *40*
Upsetting me with their sudden tongues and their colour,
A dozen red lead sinkers round my neck.

Nobody watched me before, now I am watched.
The tulips turn to me, and the window behind me
Where once a day the light slowly widens and slowly thins,
And I see myself, flat, ridiculous, a cut-paper shadow
Between the eye of the sun and the eyes of the tulips,
And I have no face, I have wanted to efface myself.
The vivid tulips eat my oxygen.

Before they came the air was calm enough,                                      *50*
Coming and going, breath by breath, without any fuss.
Then the tulips filled it up like a loud noise.
Now the air snags and eddies round them the way a river

Snags and eddies round a sunken rust-red engine.
They concentrate my attention, that was happy
Playing and resting without committing itself.

The walls, also, seem to be warming themselves.
The tulips should be behind bars like dangerous animals;
They are opening like the mouth of some great African cat,
And I am aware of my heart: it opens and closes                    60
Its bowl of red blooms out of sheer love of me.
The water I taste is warm and salt, like the sea,
And comes from a country far away as health.   (1962)


## Little Fugue

The yew's black fingers wag;
Cold clouds go over.
So the deaf and dumb
Signal the blind, and are ignored.

I like black statements.
The featurelessness of that cloud, now!
White as an eye all over!
The eye of the blind pianist

At my table on the ship.
He felt for his food.                                              10
His fingers had the noses of weasels.
I couldn't stop looking.

He could hear Beethoven:
Black yew, white cloud,
The horrific complications.
Finger-traps—a tumult of keys.

Empty and silly as plates,
So the blind smile.
I envy the big noises,
The yew hedge of the Grosse Fuge.[1]                               20

Deafness is something else.
Such a dark funnel, my father!
I see your voice
Black and leafy, as in my childhood,

A yew hedge of orders,
Gothic and barbarous, pure German.
Dead men cry from it.
I am guilty of nothing.

---
[1] Beethoven's Opus 133 for string quartet

The yew my Christ, then.
Is it not as tortured? 30
And you, during the Great War
In the California delicatessen

Lopping the sausages!
They colour my sleep,
Red, mottled, like cut necks.
There was a silence!

Great silence of another order.
I was seven, I knew nothing.
The world occurred.
You had one leg, and a Prussian mind. 40

Now similar clouds
Are spreading their vacuous sheets.
Do you say nothing?
I am lame in the memory.

I remember a blue eye,
A briefcase of tangerines.
This was a man, then!
Death opened, like a black tree, blackly.

I survive the while,
Arranging my morning. 50
These are my fingers, this my baby.
The clouds are a marriage dress, of that pallor.   (*1962*)

## Edge

The woman is perfected.
Her dead

Body wears the smile of accomplishment,
The illusion of a Greek necessity

Flows in the scrolls of her toga,
Her bare

Feet seem to be saying:
We have come so far, it is over.

Each dead child coiled, a white serpent,
One at each little 10

Pitcher of milk, now empty.
She has folded

Them back into her body as petals
Of a rose close when the garden

Stiffens and odours bleed
From the sweet, deep throats of the night flower.

The moon has nothing to be sad about,
Staring from her hood of bone.

She is used to this sort of thing.
Her blacks crackle and drag.   (*1962*)                    20


# IMAMU AMIRI BARAKA (LeRoi Jones)/ 1934–

## Preface to a Twenty Volume Suicide Note

FOR KELLIE JONES, BORN 16 MAY 1959

Lately, I've become accustomed to the way
The ground opens up and envelopes me
Each time I go out to walk the dog.
Or the broad edged silly music the wind
Makes when I run for a bus . . .

Things have come to that.

And now, each night I count the stars,
And each night I get the same number.
And when they will not come to be counted,
I count the holes they leave.                    10

Nobody sings anymore.

And then last night, I tiptoed up
To my daughter's room and heard her
Talking to someone, and when I opened
The door, there was no one there . . .
Only she on her knees, peeking into

Her own clasped hands.


## An Agony. As Now

I am inside someone
who hates me. I look
out from his eyes. Smell
what fouled tunes come in
to his breath. Love his
wretched women.

Slits in the metal, for sun. Where
my eyes sit turning, at the cool air
the glance of light, or hard flesh
rubbed against me, a woman, a man,                    10
without shadow, or voice, or meaning.

This is the enclosure (flesh,
where innocence is a weapon. An
abstraction. Touch. (Not mine.
Or yours, if you are the soul I had
and abandoned when I was blind and had
my enemies carry me as a dead man
(if he is beautiful, or pitied.

It can be pain. (As now, as all his
flesh hurts me.) It can be that. Or                    20
pain. As when she ran from me into
that forest.
          Or pain, the mind
silver spiraled whirled against the
sun, higher than even old men thought
God would be. Or pain. And the other. The
*yes.* (Inside his books, his fingers. They
are withered yellow flowers and were never
beautiful.) The yes. You will, lost soul, say
'beauty.' Beauty, practiced, as the tree. The
slow river. A white sun in its wet sentences.          30

Or, the cold men in their gale. Ecstasy. Flesh
or soul. The yes. (Their robes blown. Their bowls
empty. They chant at my heels, not at yours.)
    Flesh
or soul, as corrupt. Where the answer moves
    too quickly.
Where the God is a self, after all.)

Cold air blown through narrow blind eyes.
    Flesh,
white hot metal. Glows as the day with its sun.
It is a human love, I live inside. A bony skeleton     40
you recognize as words or simple feeling.

But it has no feeling. As the metal, is hot, it is
    not,
given to love.

It burns the thing
inside it. And that thing
screams.

## A Poem for Black Hearts

For Malcolm's eyes, when they broke
the face of some dumb white man, For
Malcolm's hands raised to bless us

all black and strong in his image
of ourselves, For Malcolm's words
fire darts, the victor's tireless
thrusts, words hung above the world
change as it may, he said it, and
for this he was killed, for saying,
and feeling, and being/ change, all                                              *10*
collected hot in his heart, For Malcolm's
heart, raising us above our filthy cities,
for his stride, and his beat, and his address
to the grey monsters of the world, For Malcolm's
pleas for your dignity, black men, for your life,
black men, for the filling of your minds
with righteousness, For all of him dead and
gone and vanished from us, and all of him which
clings to our speech black god of our time.
For all of him, and all of yourself, look up,                                    *20*
black man, quit stuttering and shuffling, look up,
black man, quit whining and stooping, for all of him,
For Great Malcolm a prince of the earth, let nothing in us rest
until we avenge ourselves for his death, stupid animals
that killed him, let us never breathe a pure breath if
we fail, and white men call us faggots till the end of
the earth.


leroy

I wanted to know my mother when she sat
looking sad across the campus in the late 20's
into the future of the soul, there were black angels
straining above her head, carrying life from our ancestors,
and knowledge, and the strong nigger feeling. She sat
(in that photo in the yearbook I showed Vashti) getting into
new blues, from the old ones, the trips and passions
showered on her by her own. Hypnotizing me, from so far
ago, from that vantage of knowledge passed on to her passed on
to me and all the other black people of our time.                                *10*
When I die, the consciousness I carry I will to
black people. May they pick me apart and take the
useful parts, the sweet meat of my feelings. And leave
the bitter bullshit rotten white parts
alone.

# LAURENCE LIEBERMAN / 1935–

## The Crayon World

In the crayon world there are waves
in the sky.
The fish of the sea
may climb the air like swallows,
and roost all day in clouds mistaken for giant

sea-kelp. Birds of the air
may nap
under stone-gray waters.
The smoke of a house can race
back in through the window in a direct circular arc                    *10*

from the usual chimney, though the air
be quiet
and lazy as bears
in winter. Crayon people
don't wear any clothes. Their colors keep them warm.

A brown sleeve may be worn,
and the amber
jacket discarded.
My pockets were filled with gold
rings and tears. I forget where I left my clothes.                    *20*

My neighbor and I shake hands.
Our fingers
all fit together
and become invisibly sealed.
We don't even try to let go. We go for a walk,
and leave them behind in the yard.
When we return,
the hands have grown
roots and branches. Butterflies
nestle in the leaves. We are puzzled. We do not know                    *30*

who watered them, but smile because
they didn't even
have to be planted.
Sometimes the colors of our hair
and skin mix freely with the air. I love to grow

vines through my arms. A few
sand-grains
in my ear may become
a desert. But I am asleep
in the grass that I wear on my back like a carpet. My heart                    *40*

is a fountain. When I breathe deep,
it is just
like taking a drink.
The knees that I lean on may melt,
and the bones turn to mosses. But my eyes go right on
                                    singing.   (*1962*)

## Sand and Snow

Let's take a trip somewhere, we say,
before we crack up. Someplace
with hills, bridges, trees, country,
space. The beach down here covers
practically everything,
except the water which covers
it. That time we buried each
other in the sand (a child
helped me finish my legs) our heads
konked, lightly, our only parts ex-                                    10
posed, juxtaposed. We saw light,
but our eyes were black with boredom
of mock-burial—we closed them,
imagining the helicopter
overhead fancied it spotted
two loose bowling balls on the beach,
just touching, mouths for thumb-sockets,
solid granite inside. A roving
smart-aleck kid kicked up sand
in our faces and finished                                             20
the job of burial. I was
afraid to breathe for a minute,
but that wasn't it. Sand covered
our toes, our necks, our eyes, our
whispering souls. Any more
we'd inhale through nostrils was (*is*)
superfluous. We miss the snow.
Our daughter has never seen
any. In her two years. We had
better hurry. She must taste snow.                                    30
No child of ours will live three winters
a stranger to its crystalline
Godmother, like a favorite
Great aunt *we* grew up with. We
tested her pulse, the happiness
nerves. Had she really survived
(with all her parts intact—a spec-
imen of health) some twenty-four
months, minus a rosy-cheeked,
numb-fingered, muffler-necked, long-red-                              40

flanneled heritage of sleds
and ice skates, snowmen, igloos
(sand-castles are for sea urchins),
snowball fights (pillow fights suit
slugabeds), and ice hockey
with a puck that blackens eyes,
shins, ankles, but sweeps on ice-silk
wings to the goal? So we sped her
off to the mountains for her first
snow. We couldn't be sure where it 50
started on the long ascent
to the peak. A few scattered balls
of cotton, streaks of fallen
tinsel, a dozen or so lost
scraps of laundry (unironed shirts, sheets,
white socks), heaped in a corner
of brush, propped on a tree stump,
or loose quilts spread on the soft
shoulder. Sun-glint caught in the crys-
tals . . . and we knew what we felt was ice- 60
life kicking. She registered
proper awe, surprise. At length,
when she tasted her first snow-crumbs
("This ice-cream sure tastes funny")
we knew whose treat it was. It was
our own haggard bone-dry nosing-
backward selves we coddled—we, lost
snow-people, steeped in a luke-
warm monotony of tropics. (*1968*)

## Homage to Austin Warren

### I. AT THE BOOK SALE: A MEMORY

A leatherette relic smelling of musk and camphor falls
Open in my cup of hands to a zany overmarked
Page: there is
No mistaking the scrawled marginalia of Austin Warren
Crowding the print off the page,

Demanding, insisting, bickering in a kingly true lover's
Tiff over word flesh-and-blood, I am swept
Back into the aura of that raspy
Voice   slow-gurgling   weighted down by tonnage
Of learnéd reference 10

Warren's voice—unmistakably no one else's—blazing into
memory

As I pore over the remarks in a worried
Black script, penned in that familiar, crabbed, near
Illegible hand (whether difficult

From nerves, illumination, or sheer weight of mind

On edge I was never to know)   I recall
I'd chewed for hours like a dog on a pant leg
At obscure marks on themes, some words
Beginning with odd caps placed wrongly   for emphasis
Which one my grade?   Somewhere   I                                    20

Guessed   in that barbwire alphabet   the clue to my future

### 2. IN FRONTROOM CHAPEL

The summer I first winged words   sent them flying   arrows
Effortlessly zinging   feathered into being . . .
In the apartment upstairs,   I could not seem to open
My eyes wide enough to take
In the foreignness of frontroom chapel   breath-

Drugging incense smoke-curling up from the altar
The crucifixion   between wooden frames
Wire-hung on a bent hook   imperceptibly awry   the wine-
Maroon walls   papered unbrokenly   tier                               30
Upon tier   with oilskin of bookbacks   outspreading
From floor to ceiling
                                who was it   who I
Kneeling at his feet   not in prayer   shakily   who
He   leafing pages of type-
Script   his high forehead scrunching at wrongnesses
Everywhere met   all efforts
To conceal the badness of words his eyes scanned
Failed
Who we   his one voice speaking                                        40
For two the sound coming or seeming to come from one point
Above and from another inside my head

Falling out of the room upper air
As out of a cloud

Our bodies   our lives in the present are strange
To us   of all the beings to whose lips he lifted my hands
His selves were the least known   a breath

From Shakespeare's nostrils warmed
My fingertips   there was room for Donne and me to share
Intimacies in Warren's one                                            50
Skin of his poems   sentences of Henry James
He spoke inflated the unused ear of my mind like a third lung air
Found in my second wind of hearing a better place

To stream   I took one step   from hearing to breathing one
Step   the trained ear flowering into voice
Shaking loose   my own voice   a blossom   opening   (*1973*)

# Index of Authors, Titles, and Literary Terms